Managing Financial Institutions

Fifth Edition

Mona J. Gardner
Illinois Wesleyan University

Dixie L. Mills
Illinois State University

Elizabeth S. Cooperman
University of Colorado at Denver

THOMSON

SOUTH-WESTERN

Australia · Canada · Mexico · Singapore · Spain · United Kingdom · United States

THOMSON

SOUTH-WESTERN

Managing Financial Institutions, 5e

Mona J. Gardner, Dixie L. Mills, and Elizabeth S. Cooperman

VP/Editorial Director:
Jack W. Calhoun

VP/Editor-in-Chief:
Dave Shaut

Executive Editor:
Michael R. Reynolds

Sr. Developmental Editor:
Elizabeth R. Thomson

Marketing Manager:
Heather MacMaster

Production Editor:
Emily S. Gross

Sr. Manufacturing Coordinator:
Sandee Milewski

Technology Project Editor:
John Barans

Internal and Cover Designer:
Chris Miller

Production House:
Lachina Publishing Services

Cover Images:
© Getty Images

Printer:
West Group
Eagan, MN

For permission to use material from this text or product, submit a request online at http://www.thomsonrights.com.
Any additional questions about permissions can be submitted by email to thomsonrights@thomson.com.

For more information contact South-Western,
5191 Natorp Boulevard,
Mason, Ohio, 45040.
Or you can visit our Internet site at:
http://www.swlearning.com

Dedication:

To our students—past, present, and future.
Gardner and Mills

To dear family and friends, and especially
to Bob, my precious muse; Gail, my favorite
twin; and my wonderful mother-in-law,
Ann Fox.
Cooperman

Contents in Brief

Contents

Preface

Previous editions of this book appearing in 1988, 1991, 1994, and 2000 were written during periods of dramatic change for the financial services industry and financial system in the United States. Prior to the deregulatory period of the 1980s, regulatory policy and management practice for financial institutions for decades had been influenced by the Great Depression and World War II, events that most Baby Boomers, generation Xers, echo-boomers, and beyond never knew. With the deregulation of interest rates and volatility of financial markets during the 1980s, banks, as the dominant financial institution in the United States, faced a great challenge in managing interest rate risk. Hence, the previous editions' subtitle, "An Asset/Liability Approach" reflected the dependence of banks and other depository institutions on net interest income (interest revenues less interest expenses) for profits.

Over the latter 1980s and through the 1990s, financial services firms and especially commercial banks experienced tremendous changes and challenges. With greater competition from nonbank institutions and increased expenditures for new technology, larger banks realized that they could no longer depend solely on net interest income to cover rising operating expenses. Sources of noninterest revenue or fee income became more and more important. Reflecting the reality of a very competitive marketplace, regulators began offering more liberal interpretations to product restrictions previously imposed under the Glass–Stegall Act of 1933, and liberalization occurred both geographically with the Riegle-Neal Interstate Banking and Branching Efficiency Act of 1994 and by product line with the Gramm-Leach-Bliley Financial Services Modernization Act of 1999. Today, financial institutions can operate nationwide, with insurance, investment, and banking services provided under the same umbrella. Securitization—packaging and selling loans as securities to investors—has also become an important source of noninterest income and has transformed the way financial service institutions operate. Technology has changed the way financial services are delivered, making it easier to manage huge enterprises. Now there are mega-financial services institutions, such as Citigroup, Inc., with more than $1 trillion in assets, managing billions of dollars globally. With consolidation, technological changes, and globalization have come greater scandals in the financial services industry, greater need for risk management due to increased operational risk, and greater corporate governance difficulties.

Our new edition covers dramatic changes and other recent major events, including innovations that have come about because of technological advances such as structured financing, Internet banking, and the role of financial institutions in E-commerce. We have also added greater coverage of financial institutions as risk-takers including strategic considerations and other financial innovations, such as credit derivatives, catastrophic insurance futures, and project financing. The Basel II Accord and the development of a two-pronged banking system with different capital regulations for very large international banks and community banks is also discussed, as is the growing trend for financial institutions to be diversified originators and sellers of loans, transferring risk to the capital markets and investors. The growth and management of mutual funds, trading scandals, and regulatory reforms are also examined, along with ethical considerations for financial institution managers.

We attempt to capture the major forces that are changing the financial landscape for financial institutions. However, with constant changes in financial markets and institutions, we continue to believe in our opening comment in the preface to the first edition, "Perhaps the only task more challenging than managing financial institutions today is writing for students who will manage them tomorrow." In this text we provide Websites and other sources of information and references for students to be able to find information on new issues and regulations affecting financial institution managers in the spirit of "continuous learning." We hope also that the text will bring "real world" issues to life for students including challenges that financial institution managers face to meet often conflicting goals to satisfy stockholders, meet regulations, and serve customers, employees, and the community well. Reputation is an essential asset for financial institutions, so ethical considerations should be a key concern for financial institution managers.

Although much new information has been added, the fifth edition has been streamlined from twenty-seven chapters in 1994 to twenty-two chapters in 2000 to nineteen chapters today. Despite this streamlining, the text still provides the depth that students need to have a comparative advantage as potential financial and nonfinancial institution managers. All chapters have been carefully updated to incorporate new research and political and economic events, as well as technological and financial innovations.

For a book this length, it would be impossible to list all the changes since the last edition. The following are among the most important, however:

- Excellent Internet exercises at the end of each chapter by Ronnie Phillips at Colorado State University have been extended by the Authors in the new edition for students to gain Internet skills and become familiar with special resources available for financial institutions.

- Learning Objectives at the beginning of each chapter and Concept Questions throughout help students understand key concepts in each chapter. End-of-chapter Questions, Problems, and Case Studies have been updated as well.

- Recommended cases from the Darden School, Harvard Business School, and Richard Ivey School of Business listed at the end of chapters and in more detail in the *Instructor's Manual* will help students apply concepts from the text.

- A discussion of ethical considerations, corporate governance, and proposed SEC regulations for securities firms and mutual funds provides more complete information on special management issues for these firms.

- Updated chapters on depository and nondepository institutions include new issues facing each institution.

- A thorough discussion of UBPRs includes step-by-step instructions for students in how to download reports from the Internet. Also, we provide a detailed overview of other Web sources for financial institution information and research in each chapter.

- We have written a new chapter on financial institution risk and risk management considerations.

- We have written a new chapter on changes with technology, including securitization, structured financing, Internet banking, and the role of financial institutions in E-commerce.

- We have included a discussion of Basel II and its implications for depository institutions and changes in thinking about the role of capital and capital management for these institutions.

- A chapter appendix provides an overview of credit risk models including the KMV Model, and updated sources for students interested in examining credit risk models in greater depth.

The early parts of the book continue to provide a theoretical framework that transcends the changes in the institutional environment that we now routinely expect. At the same time, we hope to give students a sense of the dynamic nature of financial markets and institutions and the challenges faced by those who choose a career in institutions management. Also, as in other editions, latter portions of the book cover specific management problems in specific types of institutions. The book continues to be written for upper-level undergraduate and master's students, and all readers will benefit considerably from an introductory course in corporate finance. In many cases, introductory material in typical courses on money and banking or money and capital markets is useful, but not essential.

Organization and Use of the Book

Managing Financial Institutions is divided into five parts. Part I (Chapters 1 to 3) explores the environment in which financial institutions operate, including the changes financial institutions face today, the role of financial institutions as risk-taking intermediaries, and the impact of regulation, technology, and financial innovation. Part II (Chapters 4 to 7) provides background and a performance analysis of depository institutions, including coverage of credit unions and savings institutions, capital management and the Basel I and II requirements, and changes with technology, including securitization, structured financing, Internet banking, and E-commerce. Part III (Chapters 8 to 12) covers interest rate risk management, including theories of exchange rates, the theory of interest rates and interest rate measurement and immunization using duration, and interest rate and foreign exchange rate risk management and hedging with derivatives. Part IV (Chapters 13 to 15) covers managing credit risk, liquidity, and liability management focusing on depository institutions, including an overview of new risk models and a sample bank credit analysis. Part V (Chapters 16 to 19) examines different aspects of management for nondepository institutions, including insurance companies, investment banks, securities firms, and venture capitalists; mutual fund and pension fund management, securities firms; and finance companies, mortgage banks, and diversified services firms, along with merger and international management issues.

Special Features

We believe this edition has several features that continue to distinguish it from others currently available. First, the book has a consistent framework emphasizing the necessity for financial institution managers to innovate and to react creatively to a constantly changing regulatory, technological, and global financial environment. Second, the book provides the depth that students need to have a competitive advantage in its historical overview of different types of financial institutions, including a discussion of Kane's regulatory dialectic that has occurred in the United States. The book also covers the history of recent events. As George Santayana, the Spanish-born American educator, philosopher, and poet, once said, "Those who forget the past are condemned to repeat it." Third, the book is thorough, providing students with the edge they need in a competitive financial environment. The thorough coverage of interest rates and tools for managing interest rate risk, for instance, provides a good foundation for appreciating the specific management problems that financial institutions face.

As in the previous editions, given the dynamic nature of the material, we put special effort into identifying issues for which significant change is possible in the next decade. Our approach is to outline clearly as many facets of these issues as possible, so that students understand the nature and history of current controversies. When change occurs, instructors should have a relatively smooth time incorporating the specific course of action taken by regulators or by Congress.

Users have told us that their students find the book interesting and well organized. The opening quotations and vignettes, almost all of which have been completely revised with each edition, often inject a humorous or interesting note to catch students' attention. In addition, we have tried throughout to provide useful and interesting examples of the application of many management tools. Students should enjoy the new Internet exercises provided at the end of each chapter. Also, students will discover many useful Website links throughout the book. In addition, case study suggestions at the end of most chapters and in more detail in the *Instructor's Manual* provide instructors with excellent cases to which students have responded favorably in previous financial institution management classes. We have also tried to attain a relatively challenging level for many of the end-of-chapter problems to help students develop analytical skills.

Ancillary Materials

The *Instructor's Manual,* complete with answers to end-of-chapter Questions and Problems, is available in print and on the book's Website at *http://gardner.swlearning.com.* A completely revised *Test Bank* will also be available in print and on the book's Website. The *Lecture Presentation Software* in PowerPoint will be available online.

Acknowledgments

This edition has benefited immeasurably from the comments of the users of the first three editions and the reviewers of the revised manuscript. Although we may not have completely satisfied all of them in this edition, we have considered every suggestion seriously and carefully. We extend special appreciation to the following people for comments, suggestions, and help for this edition:

Timothy Craft, Wichita State University

Kenneth N. Daniels, Virginia Commonwealth University

Frederick H. Duncan, Winthrop University

Rich Fortin, University of Michigan–Flint

Owen Gregory, University of Illinois, Chicago

Mahfuzul Haque, Indiana State University

James E. McNulty, Florida Atlantic University

Seyed Mehdian, University of Michigan–Flint

David T. Nelson, Bentley College

William E. O'Connell, College of William & Mary

Dennis Reher, Northern Illinois University

Martha Soleau, University of Michigan

Suresh Srivastava, University of Alaska–Anchorage

Dr. William Welch, Florida International University

Users or readers who provided complete or partial reviews of previous editions and made suggestions that continue to shape the text in important ways include:

Bruce Bagamery, Central Washington University

Sheldon Balbirer, University of North Carolina–Greensboro

Elijah Brewer, III, Federal Reserve Bank of Chicago

Omer Carey, University of Alaska–Anchorage

M. Carry Collins, University of Tennessee

Tony Cherin, San Diego State University

Arthur T. Cox, University of Northern Iowa

Gary Dokes, San Diego State University

David Durst, University of Akron

John W. Ellis, Colorado State University

David Ely, San Diego State University

Harvey Faram, Northern Arizona University

Deborah Ford, University of Baltimore

James R. Gale, Michigan Technological University

Phil Glasgo, Xavier University

Erika Gilbert, Illinois State University

James Gilkeson, Central Florida University

George Hachey, Bentley College

John H. Hand, Auburn University

Sylvia Hudgins, Old Dominion University

Jack Hayden, Eastern Montana University

Muhammad Husan, Kent State University

Jerry Johnson, University of South Dakota

Keith Johnson, University of Connecticut

Han Bin Kang, Illinois State University

Dan Kaufman, Wright State University

Richard Klein, Clemson University

Gary Koppenhaver, Iowa State University

William Kracaw, Pennsylvania State University

Rick LeCompte, Wichita State University

C. F. Lee, Rutgers University

John Lewis, Stephen F. Austin University

Pamela Lowry, Illinois Wesleyan University

Inayat U. Mangla, Western Michigan University

Robert L. Mills, Jr., Western Southern Life Insurance

Jeff Moore, Texas Christian University

Theresa Morgan, Illinois State University

Louis Mougoue, Loyola University–New Orleans

Prasad Naisetty, Indian University

Joe Newman, Northern Illinois University

James Nielsen, Oregon State University

Carl Nielson, Wichita State University

Phillip R. Perry, State University of New York–Buffalo

Ronnie Phillips, Colorado State University

Nanda Rangan, Southern Illinois University

Alan Reichert, Cleveland State University

John Rozycki, Pennsylvania State University

William Sartoris, Indiana University

William Scott, Illinois State University

Michael Seeborg, Illinois Wesleyan University

Alan Severns, University of Detroit

Todd M. Shank, University of Portland

John Simms, University of North Carolina–Greensboro

Mike Spivey, Clemson University

Roger Stover, Iowa State University

Maurice Tse, Michigan State University

Edward Waller, University of Houston, Clear Lake

Ronald Watson, Custodial Trust Company

Walter Woerheide, Rochester Institute of Technology

Harold Wolfe, University of Texas at Austin

Students who were particularly helpful in the development of various editions include Bala Balakumar, Rhonda Jenkins, Kristen McGavin Anthony (Allstate Insurance Company), Sergio Murer (Prudential Mortgage), Diane M. Hustad (Del E. Webb Corporation), Thomas Smith (Continental Illinois National Bank), Kevin Stoelting (United Parcel Service), Michael J. Wright (Arthur Andersen and Company), Michelle Woodham, and Lisa Wurm. Gardner and Mills appreciate the moral support they received from Robert Jefferson, Illinois State University, and from colleagues at Illinois State University and Illinois Wesleyan University. Cooperman appreciates the moral support she received from Robert Cooperman, whose cheer got her through the difficulties of this project; from dear family who also carried her through including Ann and Al Fox; Roz, Phil, Steven, and Michelle Lerner; Jeff and Lori Cooperman; Rae and Jerry Blumberg; Ann and Albert, Terrell, Alby, Caroline, and Lizzie Singleton; and Gail, Mike, Oakleigh and Roscoe, and Yuko Welply; Edward B. and Margaret Ann Singleton; and Mary and John McMurray; and from friends extraordinaire including Eleanor Swanson and Bud Fogerty; Charles Register; Patty Moran; Sinan and Fatma Cebenoyan; Susan Baillet and Herman Asarnow; Liz and Dave Ingram; Laura Clifton; Randi Briscoe; Dave Bailey; Joel, Paula, and Lillian Mazzoline; and from Rene Gash, Sueann Ambron, Dean, JC Bosch, Executive Associate Dean, and Ken Bettenhausen, Associate Dean at The Business School, University of Colorado at Denver for their cheer and support, and other wonderful colleagues at the University of Colorado–Denver. Cooperman also thanks Yash Gupta for his moral support in an earlier edition, and Virginia Berkeley, President of Colorado Business Bank in Denver (CBB) and other colleagues at CBB for taking her into the real world in her externship with the bank. We also thank wonderful professors, Joe Sinkey and Jim Verbrugge, who made an English major love finance as well.

Finally, we thank the professional staff at South-Western/Thomson Publishing for this edition. We are particularly grateful to Elizabeth Thomson, Senior Developmental Editor; Emily Gross, Production Editor; Mike Reynolds, Executive Editor; Chris Miller, Designer; and Sheila McGill at Lachina Publishing Services, who are remarkable. A special thanks also to the copyeditor, Kathleen Deselle; proofreader, Amy Mayfield; and indexer, Leoni McVey. The book continues to benefit from the previous work of Ronnie Phillips, Edward Waller, Yvette Bendeck, Terry House, Charlie Watson, Colby Alexander, Burl Sloan, Eddie Dawson, Mike Roche, Liz Widdicombe, Ann Heath, Carla Houx, Betsy Webster, Dan Coran, Karen Vertovec, Karen Shaw, Jeanne Calabrese, Wendy Kemp, Judy Lary, Alan Wendt, and Karen Schenkenfelder, who held various editorial assignments for the first four editions. The inevitable errors, however regrettable, are our own.

Mona J. Gardner
Dixie L. Mills
Bloomington, Illinois

Elizabeth S. Cooperman
Denver, Colorado
June 2004

The Environment of Financial Institutions Management

I

Changing Times for Financial Institutions

"Mergers or not, laws or not, technology has changed banking forever."

MARTIN MAYER, Banking Analyst; quotation from Barron's, April 20, 1998, p. 20.

"The rapidly cascading mutual fund scandals have brought unwelcome attention to 11 major firms that manage about $1 trillion. For an industry that only six months ago was bragging that 'We've never had a major scandal,' it's been an astonishingly rapid comeuppance."

JOHN C. BOGLE, "Not-So-Mutual Funds," The Wall Street Journal, November 14, 2003, A12.

A s suggested by the opening quotations, managers of financial institutions are wrestling with dramatic changes today, with many changes happening as the result of the technological revolution. Martin Mayer in the *Barron's* article cited in the opening quotes points out that technology has allowed huge banks to operate nationwide, allowing an increased span of control for bank executives and giving the banking industry greater economies of scale, with new customers adding "virtually no cost at all." He points out also that immense databases allow different types of financial institutions to enter each other's market areas and cross-sell products. With declining profits from traditional activities, financial institutions have sought new ways of doing business, gaining synergies, and increasing fee income. Technology also increases global competition, since information systems based on high-speed computers support sales of financial products to customers throughout the world.[1]

Learning Objectives

After completing this chapter, you will be able to:

1 Understand how the economic environment, technology, and globalization have changed the financial management strategies and challenges of financial institutions over time.

2 Identify the different types of financial institutions and the economic functions and intermediary services that they provide.

3 Understand the basic components of depository institution profitability and asset/liability management including concepts of the net interest margin, the burden, and provision for loan losses.

4 Consider the social and ethical concerns that financial institution managers face in the twenty-first century.

5 Understand the balancing act that financial managers of financial institutions face in terms of differences in objectives for stakeholders in financial institutions.

The last two decades have brought about remarkable changes and greater freedom for financial institutions. The Riegle-Neal Interstate Banking and Branching Efficiency Act in 1994 removed remaining interstate banking restrictions for banks in the United States, allowing banks to have branches and to merge with other banks across the nation. The Gramm-Leach-Bliley (Financial Modernization) Act of 1999 allowed greater product diversification for financial institutions by allowing investment, insurance, and banking services to be offered by the same firm, and acquisitions across these different types of financial institutions. Large commercial banks, in particular, have responded to increased competition in traditional lending markets by becoming diversified financial services firms, from both a geographical and a product perspective.

A classic example is the case history of Fleet Bank in New Hampshire. During Fleet's transformation, Fleet encountered difficulties its founders could never have anticipated in 1791—the year George Washington gave his farewell address. As banks received greater geographical and product freedoms in the 1980s, Fleet acquired Norstar Bancorp of New York in 1988. It diversified with a discount brokerage unit in the mid-1980s. Later in the 1990s it acquired Shawmut Bank in Massachusetts in 1995, among other acquisitions, including an investment bank, Robertson Stevens. Eventually, in 1999, it merged with Bank Boston Corporation, becoming FleetBoston. In 2004, FleetBoston itself was acquired by Bank of America. Fleet had to abide by numerous regulatory restrictions over this time period. To acquire Norstar, for instance, Fleet had to divest its holdings in neighboring Connecticut, since a patchwork of state laws for regional branching existed at that time. To acquire Shawmut in 1995, Fleet had to increase its low-income lending to meet increasingly stringent Community Reinvestment Act regulations.

Juggling its new product mix was not always easy. Fleet's discount brokerage and its international loan portfolio suffered large losses with the stock market crash and international loan crisis in 1987. Later in the early 1990s, Fleet suffered large commercial real estate losses, and tangled with regulators over its financial reporting practices. Fleet also suffered large losses on its investment bank and venture capital operations during the dot.com collapse in the early 2000s, resulting in the closure of its investment bank. In the early 2000s, the managers of FleetBoston decided to refocus strategically on traditional lending. Taking a retail focus, FleetBoston installed customer greeters in its branches and removed many fees to attract consumers. It also enacted a strategy of cross-selling mutual funds, credit cards, online banking, and brokerage services through its discount brokerage, Quick and Reilly.

---

1 Martin Mayer. "Apples Meet Oranges." *Barron's* (April 20, 1998), 20, 22.

FleetBoston strengthened its money management division as well to take advantage of affluent customers in New England. It engaged in charitable giving practices and achieved high regard by offering affordable housing projects and lending in low-income communities. With the merger with Bank of America, analysts hope these practices will continue. However, FleetBoston had another bump in the road, prior to this merger, with a $59.4 million settlement with the SEC for charges of trading abuses by its NYSE trading unit in March of 2004.[2]

Although not all financial institutions have adopted such aggressive strategies, all face similar challenges and opportunities. Some, like FleetBoston and Bank of America, have generally had profitable operations; others, such as Bank of New England in the early 1990s and Superior Bank in the early 2000s, have faltered or failed. The success or failure of a financial services firm is often traced to how well its managers understand the new financial environment and whether they respond by adopting financial management techniques. This book addresses financial management issues for financial institutions in the early twenty-first century.

This introductory chapter provides a macro view of the setting for financial institutions, discussing the ongoing changes for financial institutions, differences between financial and nonfinancial institutions, and the major financial institutions and the economic services that they provide.

What Do Financial Institutions Do?

Many observers think of financial institutions as "money specialists." Until recently, people paid little attention to the fact that financial institutions have their own financial management problems. Instead, the common belief was that financial institutions solve the financial management problems of others—not a surprising thought because most individuals initiate relationships with several financial institutions from early ages. A typical consumer might have

- a checking account at a local bank,
- a credit card issued by a bank headquartered in another state,
- a home mortgage from an area savings and loan association,
- an automobile loan from the credit union at work,
- a life insurance policy from an insurer with offices in fifty states,
- automobile and homeowner's insurance from a different firm,
- savings for retirement entrusted to a mutual fund, and
- an account with the regional office of a national brokerage company.

As Martin Mayer observes, "To an extent previously unknown in history, the American household is itself today a financial intermediary, owing big-time for mortgages and credit cards, owning big-time in mutual funds, stocks, certificates of deposit, insurance policies, asset-backed securities. Households are targets for the inventors of financial products, developing new ways to borrow and ways to invest. Some of these inventors are bankers, some are brokers, and some are insurers."[3] Times are changing for financial institutions. Financial institutions are changing, as well, with progressively more diversified financial institutions offering an expanding variety of services.

Changing Times for Financial Institutions

So many financial institutions operate today in the United States and around the world and people have grown so accustomed to them that their existence, functions, and continued operations are often taken

2 Geoffrey Smith. "Fleet's Ship Comes In." *Business Week* (November 9, 1992), 104; Peter Truell. "Fleet Taking Another Fork in Road to Bank Expansion." *New York Times* (September 18, 1997), C4; Rose Kerber. "Fleet Financial Faces a Choice: Buy or Be Bought?" *The Wall Street Journal* (December 2, 1997), B4; Rose Kerber, "Amid Banks' Merger Frenzy, Fleet Goes on the Prowl." *The Wall Street Journal* (May 4, 1998), B4. Leslie Miller. "Fleet-Bank Boston Merger May Presage New National Institution." *The Denver Post* (March 16, 1999), 5C; Carrick Mollenkamp and John Hechinger. "Bank of America Bets on Consumer." *The Wall Street Journal* (October 28, 2003), A1; "New England Unnerved by Fleet Deal." *The Wall Street Journal* (October 28, 2003), A13; and "Fleet-Boston Expects to Pay U.S. $59 Million." *New York Times,* March 8, 2004, C5.

3 Mayer, "Apples Meet Oranges," 22.

for granted. Trillions of dollars worth of checks and other payments are cleared and reconciled every day throughout the world, allowing economies to run smoothly and individuals to buy food, pay rent or mortgage, pay tuition, and save for the future. Yet, financial crises in recent years provide reminders of the importance of financial institutions, such as the U.S. savings and loan crisis of 1988 to 1991, the Asian financial crisis during 1997 to 1999, and the Latin American currency crisis of 1998 to 1999. As the financial crises remind us, this was not always the case. In the early 1930s, in the wake of a great depression, widespread concern about the safety and soundness of financial institutions provoked state and federal legislatures in the United States to enact laws to assure the public that financial institutions were sound and viable.

Laws limited the activities of most financial institutions for several decades, making their financial management not a terribly complex process. Managers engaged in specific, legally permissible activities, charging prices with legally mandated maximums, and incurring legally determined costs. Regulators set prices and costs that ensured that financial institutions could operate profitably, and relatively few failed.

A Different View in the 1970s and 1980s: Inflation, Technological Change, and Deregulation

As time passed and memories of the 1930s faded, the perceived need for regulation of financial institutions diminished. Also, as interest rates rose in the 1970s to compensate for rising inflation, depositors became dissatisfied with the low rates paid by financial institutions and withdrew their funds in search of higher returns elsewhere. Banks and savings institutions could not respond because laws of the 1930s limited the rates they could offer. Rapid developments in technology and innovation brought about new products and new competition for banks, such as money market funds offered by securities firms that allowed customers check-writing privileges and higher interest rates, removing the previous dominance that banks had in check-writing.

Beginning in 1978, Congress reacted and loosened or removed many restrictions on banks and savings institutions. This period of deregulation coincided with, and was encouraged by, rapid developments in technology and innovation in the products of financial institutions. Although virtually all financial institutions are still regulated, regulations are less restrictive than in previous decades.

During deregulation, the U.S. economy experienced significant changes, such as population migration to the South and West and a decline in the fortunes of basic manufacturing, agricultural, and energy-related industries. These fundamental changes resulted in the movement of money from one region to another and from some industries to others. Because financial institutions are "money specialists," they were definitely affected. As a result of these combined forces, the complexity of managing a financial institution dramatically increased. Technology expanded competition and allowed new financial innovations. An example is securitization of loans, repackaging pools of mortgages for sale as securities by specialized financial institutions. Technology and deregulation also provided opportunities for corporations to directly issue their own bonds, resulting in banks losing business with large Fortune 500 companies, their best borrowers, and leaving them to focus more on medium-sized and small businesses. With lower profits resulting from interest rate problems, increased competition, and overcapacity in their industries, banks and savings institutions increased loans to ever-riskier customers to make up for lost profits. The regional U.S. recessions left many banks in failure in the late 1980s and early 1990s. U.S. savings institutions experienced severe losses, as well, necessitating a massive government bailout. Hundreds of savings institutions were closed or merged in the late 1980s and early 1990s. Management excess and abuse often contributed to failures, resulting in public outrage and demand for new approaches to regulation and supervision to protect customers and taxpayers from unacceptable risks.

The 1990s: Globalization, Mergers, Re-regulation, and then Deregulation

In the early 1990s, the United States suffered a severe credit crunch, and new regulations were put in place providing greater supervision of depository institutions, mandating that regulators close weak institutions. The period 1989 to 1993 was a time of significant re-regulation for U.S. depository institutions. The globalization of financial markets, reflected in unprecedented competition from Japanese and European financial institutions, forced Congress and U.S. regulators to recognize the need for international policy coordination including the Basel I (or Basle) Accord in 1987, which mandated uniform risk-based capital requirements for international banks and was also phased in for all U.S. banks by 1993. Examinations for the Community Reinvestment Act (CRA) also became more rigorous, and institutions were required to disclose their CRA examination, which could range from outstanding to substantial noncompliance. Since 1992, lenders have also been required to analyze their lending on a detailed geographical basis. Institutions failing to demonstrate community reinvestment can face denial or be required to make amends before receiving permission to branch, merge, or acquire another institution.

The period 1994 to 1999, however, marked a time of significant deregulation for U.S. financial services firms, as Congress and regulators recognized that legislation preventing interstate branching and forbidding investment banks, commercial banks, and insurance companies to operate together no longer reflected economic realities. With international competition and the need for financial institutions to be larger to compete, thousands of mergers occurred in the 1980s and 1990s, continuing on into the 2000s. With greater size, large banks and savings institutions took advantage of new technology that allowed greater economies of scale and cross-selling opportunities. Competition squeezed profits from traditional sources, creating the need for other sources of profits. Large banks merged with other types of financial institutions, as illustrated by FleetBoston. Congress passed the Riegle-Neal Interstate Banking and Branching Efficiency Act in 1994, which allowed interstate branching across the United States to be phased in by mid-1997. The merger of NationsBank with Bank of America created a U.S. bank with branches on each coast. With mergers, there has also been concern about whether large, out-of-state, interstate banks would continue to serve their communities. Regulators helped to ensure continued community service of merged banks by allowing consumer groups to make comments before mergers would be approved.

Globalization and the development of a common currency in Europe brought opportunities for U.S. financial institutions to profit from providing advice as consultants, selling products to customers abroad, and international trading activities. Technology increased the use and trading of derivatives—futures, options, and swaps (financial contracts with payment streams based on the future price changes of underlying securities). These instruments now provide hedging benefits for financial institutions, but they also expand opportunities for risky speculation. A number of financial scandals and huge trading losses on derivatives rocked securities firms in the 1990s. For example, a single rogue trader, Nick Leeson, accumulated losses trading futures on the Japanese Nikkei stock market index totaling more than $1 billion in 1995. This resulted in the failure of Barings, a formerly prestigious British investment firm that had been in business for centuries.

With globalization and technological changes, regulations passed in the 1930s that prevented commercial banks, investment firms, and insurance companies from operating together were obsolete. International banks in other countries were allowed to provide commercial banking and investment banking services to customers, making it difficult for U.S. banks to compete worldwide. With technology, financial institutions could develop loopholes to circumvent these laws. In 1999, the Gramm-Leach-Bliley (Financial Services Modernization) Act was passed, which allowed firms in these different businesses to operate together as one firm. This act was passed after years of debate in response to regulatory challenges, including the merger of a huge bank, Citicorp, and a giant insurance/investment/finance company, Travelers Group, in 1998 to create Citigroup. Mergers between different financial institutions have created opportunities for synergies and cross-selling of products, allowing diversification and new sources of revenues.

Operational Risk and Security Concerns: New Regulations in the 2000s

However, such mergers also increase operational risk management problems for institutions. Cultural problems arose between conservative cultures of commercial banks and the more "gun-slinging" environments of securities firms. Risk and culture management have become important aspects of management practices for financial institutions that managers have attempted to address. With the new Basel II Capital Accord, proposed to take place for large international banks by year-end 2006, operational risk has key importance, with capital required to be held for this risk, as well as credit and other risks. The early 2000s entailed numerous financial accounting scandals that regulators have attempted to deal with as well, discussed in more detail later in this chapter. Financial institutions have also had to deal more with global and security problems following the attacks of September 11, 2001, on the

New York World Trade Center, which resulted in devastation for many financial firms located in the Center. Cantor Fitzgerald, a leading securities firm specializing in the development of electronic marketplaces, for instance, lost 658 of its employees. Similarly, financial institutions have had to develop emergency disaster plans to ensure that financial systems can continue to operate in the event of such a disaster and to employ greater surveillance and security in their operations to prevent such a disaster. U.S. banks were also asked to serve as watchdogs for suspicious activities under acts passed by Congress including the Bank Secrecy Act of 1996 and Patriot Act of 2003. International banking organizations have had to be watchdogs as well, with greater security and surveillance concerns. With technology, larger financial institutions with subsidiaries across the world can be managed more easily. However, with greater complexity and distance, there are also new corporate governance problems, with greater opportunity for operational problems and fraud.

Looking Ahead in the Twenty-first Century: Niches, New Opportunities, Global Joint Ventures

Looking into the early twenty-first century, financial institutions in the United States and across the world have or are attempting to find their niches. Large financial institutions are deciding strategically whether they want to become international financial conglomerates, such as the Citicorp/Travelers Group. Alternatively, other financial institutions have focused on national, regional, or industry-specialist niches. Similarly, smaller community banks have either merged or found their own niches by emphasizing personalized service and by gaining customers who feel overlooked by very large institutions. With new technology, business and retail customers have often come to expect new services. Wachovia Corporation, a large North Carolina bank that recently merged with First Union Bank *(http://www.wachovia.com/corp_inst)*, for instance, offers online cash management services, bill paying on the Internet, and other home banking services for consumers, along with asset management, benefits and retirement services, capital market services, cash management and deposits services, insurance, international banking services, online banking services, trust services for businesses, as well as traditional deposit-taking, lending, and financing services. Large financial institutions have invested in expensive new technology in the last two decades to be able to offer these services. This technology increases the fixed costs of financial institutions, creating incentives for mergers to spread costs over more customers.

Financial institutions have also found more global partnerships. New opportunities were created with the new European Monetary Union (EMU) and the adoption of the Euro as a common currency in 1999, with the phasing out of former currencies by July 1, 2002. The European countries involved include more than 290 million inhabitants (greater than the U.S. population), accounting for about 19 percent of world trade and world gross domestic product. The Euro zone government bond market of over $1.9 trillion is also almost as big as the U.S. Treasury market. Europeans, with traditionally high savings rates, had found fewer investment opportunities than in the United States, previously limiting their abilities to invest in a wide variety of mutual funds or to take out home mortgages. Hence, with the unification of Europe, many U.S. investment banks, such as Morgan Stanley, Goldman Sachs, and Merrill Lynch, as well as mutual funds and other financial services firms shifted workers to Europe. Technology now helps financial services firms offer products to international customers. Many banks have established joint ventures with European banks. In November 2003, for instance, the Treasury Service Division of Wachovia Corporation joined with the Cash Management Division of BNP Paribas, a large French investment bank, to combine their networks to offer a range of international cash management services to corporate customers. The combination provided a network of more than 4,500 financial centers (2,400 from Wachovia and 2,100 from BNP Paribas) in Europe and the United States for corporate clients of both banks *(http://www.bnparibas.com)*. Other European banks have acquired U.S. financial institutions, such as UBS, a large Swiss bank's acquisition of U.S. securities firm Paine Webber. Worldwide expansion has become global as well, with international financial firms doing business in the United States, Europe, Latin America, and Asia. Governments in many countries such as China have also initiated economic reforms, including opening up markets to foreign financial services firms, to support development of increasingly efficient and competitive financial markets. International investment banks have specialized in providing advice and help for emerging countries with reforms, such as bank privatizations, and financing needs as well.

1 Imagine an economy, such as that of the United States, with no financial institutions. What would it be like?

2 Why is the safety and soundness of a financial system important, and why does it tend to take on greater importance in periods of financial distress?

3 How has technology changed the way financial institutions operate? Give some examples of how your bank uses technology.

4 How have forces including globalization and technology led to deregulation for financial institutions in the United States in the last decade? Give an example of the effect of each force on the way financial institutions operate.

Change Isn't Easy for Consumers, Either: A Problem of Ethics

Evidence suggests that the public may not be altogether comfortable with or accustomed to the new financial environment. Consumers have been very uneasy about financial institution megamergers. For instance, a consumer group expressed concern about the Citicorp–Travelers Group merger, fearing misuse of customers' personal data and erosion of personal privacy. Large lawsuits have targeted brokerage and insurance firms, claiming misrepresentation of products and unethical selling behavior. In response to these concerns, legislation was passed including provisions of the Financial Modernization Act of 1999 to limit the ability of financial companies to share personal financial information with certain nonaffiliates including service providers hired by the financial company, joint marketing companies, and other third parties. Financial companies must inform customers of their information-sharing practices and give them the opportunity to opt out. Other protections are provided by individual agencies that regulate the particular type of financial company that can be contracted (see *http://www.fdic.gov/consumers/privacy/privacychoices/index.html*).

Financial institutions felt a strong backlash from consumers' and taxpayers' reaction to huge government bailouts to resolve insolvencies at hundreds of federally insured savings institutions in the United States in the early 1990s. Few industries in financial difficulty endure the media attention accorded financial institutions, and indeed, few businesses seem as fragile. In the late 1990s, the crisis of financial institutions in Thailand, Indonesia, South Korea, and Japan contributed to serious economic problems for these countries. The Thai government, for instance, closed fifty-six of fifty-eight failing finance companies in December 1997. The causes of the financial crisis, including excessive speculation and poor underwriting of risky commercial real estate loans by financial institutions, were similar to those of the U.S. thrift crisis. The Asian banking crisis led to a plunge in the value of regional currencies and a huge bailout program by the International Monetary Fund. These events and current events including the restructuring of the Japanese banks and Chinese banks, which suffered large loan losses in the early 2000s, emphasize the importance of financial management in financial institutions as a topic of study.

It is appropriate to begin this study with some basic definitions. The next section discusses the difference between the financial assets that financial institutions handle and physical assets, such as plant and equipment. It also provides an overview of the differences between the balance sheets of financial versus nonfinancial firms.

Financial versus Real Assets and Financial versus Nonfinancial Firms

Financial institutions deal with financial assets, assets that promise future payments from financial contracts, such as securities and loans. These institutions also deliver services, relying on their reputations to attract customers for relationships often based on trust. Similarly, a nonfinancial business expects future benefits in the form of cash from sales of its tangible and service products, as well as from owning a recognizable trademark or slogan (like Nike's Just Do It) or a patent on a production process.

Because so many things are assets, it is convenient to divide them into two major subsets: **real assets** and **financial assets.** Real, tangible assets are those expected to provide benefits based on their fundamental qualities. A person's home transfers benefits commensurate with the quality of its construction, its location, and its size. A corporation's main computer provides benefits based on its speed, the size of its memory, the ease of its use, and the frequency with which it needs repair. A financial asset, in contrast, is a contract that offers a promise of payment in the future from the party that issued the contract.

Most business firms—steelmakers, automobile manufacturers, restaurants, and department stores—acquire and use real assets in ways that make the value of future benefits received greater than the cost of obtaining them. Cash to acquire assets may come from lenders or creditors with legal expectations for repayment from the firm's use of real assets. Cash may also come from those who take an ownership (or equity) interest in the firm, hoping for (but with no legal promise of) shares in the excess of asset benefits over costs. Regardless of the sources of its funds, however, the firm has issued obligations that become the financial assets of others. Funds generated by issuing financial obligations are then used to acquire real assets.

Like other businesses, a financial institution acquires and uses assets so that the value of their benefits exceeds their costs. The key difference between financial institutions and other firms is that most of the assets that financial institutions hold are financial assets. Financial institutions use funds from their own creditors and owners to acquire financial claims against others. They may lend funds to individuals, businesses, and governments or they may purchase ownership shares in other businesses. The future benefits that financial institutions expect to receive thus depend on the performance of the parties whose financial liabilities they purchase. The main distinction between financial institutions and other firms is not so much in how they raise funds, because all businesses issue financial liabilities to do so, but in what they do with these funds.

To illustrate the difference between a nonfinancial and financial firm, see the respective assets on simplified balance sheets for a manufacturing firm and a bank in Table 1.1.

Notice that over 82 percent of assets for Manny's Manufacturing are real, physical assets (inventory and net plant and equipment). In contrast, only 3 percent of a typical bank's assets are real, physical assets (its building and equipment). The manufacturing firm has higher operating leverage, with high fixed costs associated with its fixed assets. The bank has lower operating leverage, since it has a low percentage of fixed assets; it has a more labor-intensive operation. However, 96 percent of the bank's assets are financial assets, securities and loans, which are claims for future cash flows. Thus, the bank's profits depend on financial contracts promising future cash flows from other parties. A loan will provide

table 1.1   COMPARISON OF BALANCE SHEETS AND OPERATIONS FOR A BANK VERSUS A MANUFACTURING FIRM

MANNY'S MANUFACTURING FIRM		THE MANNY BANK	
Assets ($million)		**Assets ($million)**	
Cash	$10 (0.50%)	Cash	$ 20 (1.00%)
Accounts receivable	350 (17.41%)	Securities	724 (36.00%)
Inventory	650 (32.34%)	Loans	1,206 (60.00%)
Net plant and equipment	1,000 (49.75%)	Building/equipment	60 (3.00%)
Total assets	2,010 (100.00%)	Total assets	$2,010 (100.00%)
Liabilities and Equity ($million)		**Liabilities and Equity ($million)**	
Accounts payable	$ 10	Transaction deposits	$ 600
Notes payable	500	Savings deposits	800
Total current liabilities	510	Certificates of deposit	249
Long-term bonds	500	Total deposits	1,649
Total debt	1,010 (50.00%)	Other borrowing	200
Common stock	200	Total debt	1,849 (92.00%)
Retained earnings	800	Common stock	61
Total equity	1,000 (50.00%)	Retained earnings	100
Total liabilities and equity	$2,010 (100.00%)	Total equity	$ 161 (8.00%)
		Total liabilities and equity	$2,010 (100.00%)

future benefits only if the bank's customer continues to pay interest. The bank depends on the loan customer's performance to benefit from the financial asset.

This concept of financial assets implies that one party's financial asset is another party's **financial liability**—that is, the other party has an obligation (often a legal one) to provide future benefits to the owner of the financial asset. For instance, a customer with a savings account at the bank has a financial asset, which is a financial liability of the bank to pay interest on the balance in the savings account.

To illustrate this concept, look at the liabilities for Manny's Manufacturing and The Manny Bank. Their liabilities and equity accounts differ in important ways: The liabilities of the manufacturing firm, current and long-term debt, represent financial claims that are financial assets of suppliers for accounts payable, banks for notes payable, and investors for long-term bonds. Liabilities for the bank are deposit accounts and other borrowings. The Manny Bank has issued financial contracts for these deposits, promising to pay given interest payments. Unlike the liabilities of Manny's Manufacturing, which have definite maturities for repayment, the deposit liabilities at The Manny Bank can be withdrawn (repayment demanded on the spot) at any time. This creates liquidity problems for the bank that the manufacturer does not experience.

Notice that the manufacturing firm is financed with about 50 percent equity and 50 percent debt. The Manny Bank has much higher financial leverage with about 92 percent debt and 8 percent equity, typical proportions for financial institutions. Thus, the bank has much higher interest expenses than the manufacturing firm (i.e., higher financial leverage). By having such a low fraction of equity financing, financial institutions have greater risk of a fall in the value of their assets, wiping out the value of equity. For instance, The Manny Bank would be technically bankrupt if it suffered loan losses of $161 million (about 13 percent of its loans).

Banks and savings institutions can use higher financial leverage than other firms, because most of their deposits (liabilities) are federally insured. This protection gives confidence to depositors in the banks' conditions and future repayment of liabilities, so they do not demand higher premiums for their funds. If a manufacturing firm had such a high debt ratio, it would experience a horrendous cost of funds, because lenders would demand a much higher risk premium for the bankruptcy risk they would incur. Also, since financial institutions have lower operating leverage, entailing lower fixed costs, they can afford higher financial leverage, which entails higher interest expenses. The Manny Bank, in essence, makes its profits from the spread between the interest rate it receives on its financial assets and the interest rate it pays on its financial liabilities. Manny's Manufacturing, in contrast, makes profits from the spread between the cost of producing and selling a physical product.

Managing the Spread, Burden, and Loan Loss Provisions

Because financial institutions interact in the financial markets by issuing financial liabilities and purchasing financial assets, one critical element of their management is managing the **spread,** the dollar difference between the interest earned on assets and the interest cost of liabilities, or **net interest income (NII)**. This spread, often expressed as a percentage of total assets or more specifically as a percentage of earning assets (assets that earn interest revenue), is called the **net interest margin (NIM):**

$$\text{Net Interest Income (or Spread) (NII)} = \text{\$ Interest Revenue} - \text{\$ Interest Expense} \qquad [1.1]$$

$$\text{Net Interest Margin (NIM)} = \text{Net Interest Spread / Earning Assets} \qquad [1.2]$$

A high NIM value may allow the institution to offset the noninterest expenses (cost of labor, check-clearing operations, etc.) of the services it provides. Most institutions charge fees for these services, but unless the fees are competitive, investors may find more economical options such as switching to other institutions or engaging in direct investment. When institutions experience negative spreads for extended periods, and interest costs actually exceed interest earned on assets, few can make up the difference with other sources of income, unless they have made strategic moves into other types of businesses that provide fee income or other sources of noninterest revenues, such as fees on deposits, brokerage fees, mutual fund management fees, trust and investment management fees, fees from check processing or bill-paying businesses, among many others.

Given the importance of the NIM, the profits of many financial institutions change with changes in relative rates of return on assets and liabilities. Many banks and savings and loans, for instance, gener-

1   Since a financial asset represents the future, what type of risk does a financial asset have?

2   If you have a deposit account with a bank, whose financial asset is it and whose financial liability?

3   Why do banks and savings institutions have so much more debt (financial leverage) than nonfinancial firms?

4   How do banks and savings institutions make their traditional operating profits? Give an example of how interest rate changes could have a positive or negative effect on their profits.

ally have greater fixed rate assets (loans) and variable-rate liabilities (deposits and short-term borrowing). If interest rates rise, they must cope with a larger rise in the rates on their liabilities than on their assets, resulting in a decline in their NIMs. Alternatively, such institutions benefit when interest rates fall, with rates on liabilities falling more than the rates on assets, resulting in rising NIMs, such as in much of the 1990s. With predominantly financial assets, managing a financial institution's NIM is an important part of financial management, known as asset/liability management. Asset/liability management involves managing a financial institution's interest rate risk to maximize its NIM and reduce the volatility (risk) of large fluctuations in the NIM.

Increasing competition dramatically reduced NIMs for banks and savings and loans, particularly, in the last two decades. To widen diminished margins, many have focused on reducing their noninterest expenses and increasing noninterest revenues. The difference between noninterest expenses and noninterest revenues is commonly referred to as an institution's *burden*, often stated as a percentage of total assets.

$$\text{Burden} = \text{Noninterest Expenses} - \text{Noninterest Revenues} \qquad [1.3]$$

$$\text{Burden \%} = \text{Burden} / \text{Total Assets} \qquad [1.4]$$

The burden has become very important in managing a financial institution's profitability, particularly for diversified financial services firms. Noninterest revenues generated help to cover high noninterest expenses.

With loans often a larger percentage of a financial institution's assets, another very important component of many financial institutions' profitability is the provision for loan losses (PLL), which is the expense that financial institution managers make for expected loan losses. This expense is also allocated to the balance sheet by adding it each year to a contra account, the bank's allowance for loan losses, which is deducted from gross loans to create net loans, a more accurate measure of a firm's actual loan holdings (net of expected losses). Putting the three components together, traditional operating earnings before taxes, capital gains and losses, and extraordinary items, for a bank or savings institution include the NII, Burden, and PLL:

$$\text{Operating Earnings Before Taxes} = \text{NII} - \text{Burden} - \text{PLL} \qquad [1.5]$$

These are three important components for managing a bank's traditional profits. Although this section has focused on traditional operating earnings for banking institutions, most financial institutions have to be concerned about losses in market value with interest rate changes as well. Chapter 2 discusses interest rate risk in more detail.

Financial Institutions: What Are They?

Although all financial institutions have predominantly financial assets and low percentages of fixed assets, they specialize in varying types of financial assets and services. The major types are depositories, finance companies, contractual intermediaries, investment companies, and securities firms. The chapters to follow explore similarities and differences in detail. Table 1.2 introduces the specific institutions that are the focus of this textbook.

table **1.2** PERCENTAGE DISTRIBUTION OF FINANCIAL ASSETS OF FINANCIAL INSTITUTIONS

An increasingly competitive financial environment is evident. The percentage of total financial assets held by commercial banks and life insurers fell from 1950 to 1990, rising again in 2000. The total share held by thrift institutions peaked in 1980, then sharply fell. Investment companies' (mutual and money market funds) share of financial assets has increased markedly since 1980.

	YEAR						
Institution	1950	1960	1970	1980	1990	2000	2003
Commercial Banks	56.88%	41.88%	40.38%	38.57%	33.11%	36.98%	36.63%
Thrifts	13.23	18.22	19.70	20.65	13.47	8.04	7.78
Credit Unions	0.34	1.02	1.40	1.80	2.15	2.81	3.11
Finance Companies	3.13	4.49	5.00	5.27	7.73	6.53	5.73
Life Insurers	21.55	19.44	15.67	12.08	13.54	14.36	15.25
Property/Liability Insurers	N/A	4.89	3.89	4.54	5.08	3.76	3.67
Private Pension Funds	2.39	6.19	8.74	12.22	11.52	4.92	4.48
Investment Companies	1.11	2.76	3.96	3.68	10.80	18.65	19.80
Securities Firms	1.36	1.09	1.27	1.19	2.60	3.95	3.55
Total Percent	100.00	100.00	100.00	100.00	100.00	100.00	100.00
Total Assets (billions)	$296.94	$615.10	$1,281.73	$3,842.20	$10,095.80	$13,537.40	$15,913.20
GSEs, Federally Related Mortgage Pools, and Asset-Backed Securities (not included in Total Assets above)				N/A	N/A	$5,884.40	$7,939.00

Notes: N/A = Not available. Figures for commercial bank assets exclude bank personal trusts and estates managed (2003: $186.4 billion). Figures for investment company assets include money market securities, mutual funds, and REITs. Figures for private pension funds do not include state and government funds (2003: $820.6 billion).

Source: *"Flow of Funds: Financial Assets & Liabilities."* Federal Reserve Bulletin, 1964–2003 (October 2003).

Depository Institutions

Depository institutions are financial institutions that take deposits and make loans. They control the largest proportion of financial assets. This category includes commercial banks, savings institutions (savings banks and savings and loan associations), and credit unions. Their primary financial liabilities are deposits.

In 2003, U.S. **commercial banks** held financial assets of over $7.9 trillion. Commercial banks have long served the corporate community as a primary source of short-term and intermediate-term loans, and for years, regulatory restrictions made them the only depositories allowed to offer checking accounts payable on demand. The Fleet Financial Group's activities discussed earlier indicate that such a description is hardly adequate in the current era. Banks have rapidly expanded their services and markets, and many offer diversified sets of products. They have recently encountered considerable competition in their traditional area of specialization—lending—as is apparent from the decline in banks' share of total financial institution assets from about 56.9 percent in 1950 to 33.1 percent in 1990 and then a rise again to 36.6 percent in 2003. They have also lost deposits, as former depositors have turned to direct market investment securities and money market and mutual funds for higher yields.

In addition to competition from other financial institutions, banks and savings institutions face competition, as well as support, from government-sponsored and private enterprises dealing with mortgage financing and loan securitizations. GSEs and private enterprises held over $7.9 trillion in assets in 2003. Within the banking industry, increasingly aggressive competition has arisen in domestic and foreign markets. To compete in global markets, a number of very large banks have merged in the United States and abroad to create megabanks.[4] As regulators relaxed restrictions to match market

---

4 John Tagliabue. "Two of the Big 3 Swiss Banks to Join to Seek Global Heft." *New York Times* (December 9, 1997), C8; "Are Mega Banks—Once Unimaginable, Now Inevitable—Better . . . for Customers, the Nation's Economy, or Even for Banks?" *Business Week* (April 27, 1998), 32–37; and Joshua Cooper Ramo. "The Big Bank Theory and What It Says about the Future of Money." *Time* (April 27, 1998), 47–57.

realities, large banks acquired and continue to acquire other types of financial firms. With narrow profit margins and widespread overcapacity in the industry, banks underwent considerable restructuring and consolidation in the 1980s and 1990s that continues in the 2000s. Between 1990 and the second quarter of 2003, as reported by FDIC historical trends *(http://www2.fdic.gov/hsob/index.asp),* there were 6,245 commercial bank mergers and 1,218 savings institution mergers occurring in the United States. The number of commercial banks fell from 12,343 in 1990 to 7,833 in 2003, and the number of savings institutions fell from 2,815 in 1990 to 1,434 in 2003. Despite the decline in banks' share of financial assets and the number of banks, their activities have expanded in other ways. Banks have packaged loans, selling them as securities to investors, provided conditional guarantees for firms, and served as dealers for instruments to hedge interest rate risk. Consequently, off-balance-sheet activities of banks (activities that generate fee income not included as balance sheet assets) have expanded exponentially. These activities provide banks with fee income, reducing their reliance on traditional banking activities. Just one segment of bank off-balance-sheet items in 2003 totaled over $61.4 trillion *(http://www.occ.treas.gov/ftp/deriv/dq103.pdf).* The percentage of total asset figures are also somewhat deceptive, since many banks operate as financial services firms with investment company, securities firms, finance company, and insurance company operations, as well.

Thrift institutions include **savings and loan associations (S&Ls)** and **savings banks** often jointly referred to as **savings institutions.** They traditionally rely on savings deposits as sources of funds, although they can now offer checkable deposits. S&Ls, the largest of the thrifts by total asset size, have expanded beyond their traditional role as suppliers of home mortgage loans since economic changes and congressional action gave them the power to do so. This expansion met with mixed success, and S&Ls faced greater asset restrictions in the 1990s, as discussed in more depth in a later chapter. Savings banks resemble S&Ls, but they have more diversified asset bases. Table 1.2 indicates that thrifts' share of total financial assets peaked in 1980 and then began declining. Between 1980 and 2003, the percentage of financial assets held by thrifts fell from 20.65 percent in 1980 to only 7.8 percent in 2003. The number of thrifts dropped, as well, with hundreds of closures and mergers following the thrift crisis of the late 1980s.

Many very large thrifts emerged from the crisis operating with nonthrift subsidiaries, much like large commercial banks. With a series of acquisitions, for instance, Washington Mutual (often known as WaMu, *http://www.wamu.com*) in Seattle laid the ground for a coast-to-coast network. Consequently, WaMu, with more than $286 billion in total assets, became the second largest home lender in the United States in 2003, with about 12 percent of the market, next only to the large San Francisco–based commercial bank, Wells Fargo.[5] Small, profitable thrifts have also developed local community banking niches. Analysts have observed alliances among small commercial banks and institutions traditionally classified as thrifts. These developments have resulted in a new category of community depositories, consisting of thrifts and banks with less than $1 billion in assets, emphasizing **community banking.**

Credit unions (CUs) are distinguished by offering their services only to members, who must share some "common bond" representing the basis for forming the union. Another important difference between CUs and other financial institutions is their status as not-for-profit organizations, which exempts CUs from taxation. Often they run on volunteer labor. Thus, their managerial objectives and resulting strategies may differ somewhat from those of other depositories. With banks raising their fees for consumer accounts to cover increasing costs and declining margins, many U.S. consumers moved accounts to credit unions in the 1990s and early 2000s. On the other hand, with credit unions crediting deposits to the wrong accounts and committing other lapses, members of less professionally managed credit unions also have fled to the more capable banks. CUs are subject to a common bond requirement and cannot make commercial loans. In recent years, many large credit unions have aggressively stretched common bond boundaries, becoming more like banks by offering credit cards and other investment services and extending their common bond to a greater population of customers. This extension and CUs' tax-exempt status has been controversial among their for-profit competitors. As shown in Table 1.2, although CUs' share of financial assets is relatively small, 3.11 percent in 2003, it grew dramatically over the last two decades from only 1.80 percent in 1980.

---

5 Joseph T. Hallinan. "As Banks Elbow for Consumers, Washington Mutual Thrives." *The Wall Street Journal* (November 6, 2003), A1, A10.

Finance Companies

Similar to depositories in terms of loans dominating the financial assets that they hold, **finance companies** specialize in loans to businesses and consumers. Their financial liabilities are quite different from those of depositories, however. They acquire most of their funds by selling commercial paper and bonds and by borrowing from their rivals, commercial banks. Finance companies had a 5.73 percent share of financial institution assets in 2003. The twenty largest finance companies command about a 71 percent share of total industry loans (called *receivables*). This dominance reflects the activities of some very large finance companies, often owned by manufacturing firms, such as General Motors Acceptance Corporation (GMAC). Finance companies have benefited from financing by increased securitization (packaging and selling loans as securities to investors). This practice gives finance companies increased liquidity (cash) to make new loans, removes previous loans from their balance sheets, and provides fee income for originating and continuing to service these loans.[6]

Contractual Intermediaries

A third category of institutions consists of **insurance companies** (both life insurers and property/liability insurers) and **pension funds,** which together are considered **contractual savings institutions,** because they operate under formal agreements with policyholders or pensioners who entrust their funds to these firms. The insurance industry has sold risk protection to the public for hundreds of years. Life insurers, because they make long-term commitments to customers, traditionally hold asset portfolios structured quite differently from those of property/liability insurers, which offer shorter-term policies such as automobile and home coverage. U.S. life insurers, like commercial banks and thrifts, underwent a period of restructuring and consolidation in the late 1980s and 1990s. A number of insurance firms, like many S&Ls and banks, took on risky investments in the 1980s and paid the price in the 1990s, with many failures. Massive layoffs accompanied restructuring of the firms, reducing costs to boost profitability. Until 1990, life insurers were the second-largest category of financial institutions in the United States. After 1990, however, investment companies moved into second place. As shown in Table 1.2, in 2003, life insurance companies held about a 15.25 percent share of financial institution assets, and property/casualty insurers held 3.67 percent.

Pension funds generally are designed to collect funds from employers and sometimes employees and to repay those funds, along with investment returns, after employees have retired or become disabled. The most widely known retirement fund is the U.S. government's social security program, but the category includes many other public and private funds. Currently, the U.S. social security system is projected to turn to a deficit, as the nation's largest demographic group, the Baby Boomers, begin and continue to retire. Congress has been devising plans to revise the current system, but many Baby Boomers planning for retirement do not think they will be able to rely on social security funds, increasing their need for investments in private pension funds. Table 1.2 includes only the assets of private pension funds. The percentage of financial assets held in 2003 seems small at 4.48 percent. This figure is somewhat deceptive, however, since the pension fund assets managed by banks, investment companies (including mutual funds), and insurance companies are excluded. Many pension plans have changed from being defined as benefit managed (by employers) to produce a given retirement benefit to defined contribution, where money is given to employees for retirement that they must manage themselves by investing contributions in mutual funds of their choice. In 2003, private and government pension funds held over $1.3 trillion in financial assets.

Investment Companies

Investment companies include mutual funds, money market funds, and REITs (real estate investment trusts). In 2003, investment companies had the second largest share of financial assets for the institutions listed in Table 1.2, with 19.8 percent, rising from a mere 3.68 percent in 1980. Investment companies provide a means through which small savers can pool funds to invest in a variety of financial instruments. The resulting economies of scale offer investors the benefits of professional portfolio

---

6 "Survey of Finance Companies, 1996." *Federal Reserve Bulletin* (July 1997), 543–556.

management, reduced transactions costs, and the reduced risk exposure within large, diversified portfolios. The best-known and largest types of investment companies are **mutual funds.** In the early 1980s, **money market mutual funds** dominated the industry. By providing easy access to funds and market rates of return, they achieved an enviable rate of growth. By the 1990s, the popularity of stock and bond funds increased, as well, despite rather pronounced swings in the financial markets. The lowest short-term interest rates in fifty years caused investors to flee money market funds in pursuit of higher returns. With the booming stock market in the mid- to late 1990s, equity funds and mixed funds—with both stock and bond investments—grew incredibly from $500 billion to $4.308 trillion from 1992 to 2000. With the dot.com bust and downturn in the stock market in the early 2000s, net assets in equity and hybrid funds fell to $2.995 trillion in 2002. Mutual fund assets peaked in 2001 at $6.975 trillion, falling to $6.392 trillion in 2002. In 2003, a trading scandal resulted in some turmoil for some mutual funds, discussed later in this chapter.[7]

Securities Firms

Securities firms assist customers with purchasing and selling stocks, bonds, and other financial assets. Securities firms generally act as issuers, traders, and brokers and, hence, are not in the business of holding assets, so have a much lower percentage of total financial assets, as shown in Table 1.2, 3.55 percent in 2003. The industry is often subdivided according to two major activities, investment banking and brokerage. **Investment bankers** assist in the creation and issuance of new securities, and **brokers** assist in transfers of ownership of previously issued securities. The second category includes both **full-service brokers** and **discount brokers.** Full-service brokers advise clients in addition to arranging securities purchases and sales; discount brokers execute trades but give no advice. Many securities firms engage in both investment banking and brokerage activities. After the October 1987 stock market crash, securities firms went through a major restructuring and consolidation phase. In 1997, a number of securities firms merged with other types of financial institutions. These deals include Salomon Brothers' merger with the Travelers Group, Alex Brown's merger with Bankers Trust, and Montgomery Securities' merger with NationsBank, among many others. With the Financial Modernization Act of 1999 allowing banks, investment firms, and insurance firms to operate together as financial services firms, a number of mergers occurred between investment firms, insurance firms, and banks in the 2000s. As previously mentioned, UBS, a large Swiss bank, purchased Paine Webber, a prominent investment bank and securities firm. However, with the decline in the stock market in the late 1990s and early 2000s, a number of large banks, such as FleetBoston, actually sold their previous investment bank purchases, refocusing on more traditional banking activities. With the stock market rising in late 2003, analysts again predicted greater merger activity. Securities firms have very cyclical performance, often with very large returns to investors during bull markets but low returns during bear markets, although diversified securities firms are often successful in stabilizing earnings, by relying on less cyclical activities, during downturns.

Government-Sponsored Enterprises, Other Federally Related Mortgage Pools, and Asset-Backed Securities

At the bottom of Table 1.2 for 2000 and 2003, not included in the total financial assets, are figures for Government-Sponsored Enterprises (GSEs), Other Federally Related Mortgage Pools, and Asset-Backed Securities. In 2000, these assets were $5.8 trillion, and by 2003 almost $8 trillion. These assets represent pools of securitized assets in the secondary mortgage market, where mortgages are sold and securitized (i.e., mortgages are pooled and packaged into securities, with a return based on the mortgage rates of the pool for investors). This provides liquidity for commercial banks, thrifts, and other issuers, who by selling or securitizing their loans have funds available to make new ones. Hence, the activities of banks, thrifts, and mortgage banks in making loans are understated by their earlier percentages of total financial assets. One government agency, the Government National Mortgage Association (GNMA; called Ginnie Mae), and two government-sponsored agencies, the Federal National

---

Mortgage Association (FNMA; called Fannie Mae) and the Federal Home Loan Mortgage Corporation (called Freddie Mac), act as intermediaries for these securitizations. The goal of the GSEs is to increase the availability of mortgage loan funding and, hence, more affordable housing in the United States. Ginnie Mae, in contrast to the other two GSEs, does not originate or purchase loans but facilitates and handles securitizations for depository institutions by providing a government guarantee for GNMA-issued mortgage securities. Fannie Mae and Freddie Mac also have automated loan origination systems on the Internet that prequalify borrowers who are then directed to prequalified lenders. This allows smaller banks, thrifts, and mortgage banks to compete with larger financial institutions. Only Ginnie Mae continues as a government-owned corporation, while Fannie Mae and Freddie Mac are publicly owned. However, Fannie Mae and Freddie Mac continue to have quasi-government sponsorship with their securities exempt from state and local taxes and a $2.25 billion line of credit from the Treasury Department. It is also implicitly understood that the government will not allow them to fail, given the large disruption this would have on mortgage markets. This quasi-government status allows Fannie and Freddie to borrow at close to risk-free rates, an advantage over competitors. Thus, large banks and thrifts with securitization operations, such as Washington Mutual Corporation, have challenged this advantage. To provide a feeling for just how large these securitization operations are: Ginnie Mae in 2003 reported 400 active mortgage-backed securities (MBS) issuers that administered over 400,000 mortgage pools, encompassing about 7.5 million single and multifamily loans. The Community Bankers Association also reported that in 2003 about 60 percent of community banks used the automated underwriting systems, up from 52 percent in 2002, and 38 percent in 2000.[8]

Balance Sheets Reveal Industry Differences

Differences in financial industry competitors are reflected in their asset and liability structures. Although comparisons are made in greater detail in later chapters, Figure 1.1 identifies major distinctions among three types of firms—commercial banks, life insurance companies, and mutual funds.

Panel A shows the types of assets held in 2003 by the three largest types of financial institutions, banks, investment companies (mutual funds), and life insurance companies. On average, 57 percent of commercial bank assets are net loans to individuals and businesses and other financial institutions. This excludes off-balance-sheet securitized loans, so it understates actual bank loan underwriting activity. Of the three types of institutions shown, banks alone hold a significant quantity of cash (in 2003, averaging 6 percent of assets), since they need greater liquidity and, hence, cash for reserve requirements and for depositor withdrawals. Banks are not permitted generally to invest in equity securities and are only permitted to invest in high-quality (investment-grade) corporate bonds and government securities (20 percent in 2003). Life insurance companies with long-term liabilities do not hold large amounts of cash. They take premiums paid for policies and use the funds to invest in corporate and government bonds (58 percent of assets), equity securities (23 percent), mortgages and real estate (8

Concept Questions

1 What are the key characteristics of depository institutions, finance companies, contractual institutions, investment companies, and securities firms?

2 What is the difference between a bank, thrift, and a credit union?

3 Who are the three GSEs, and what do they do?

4 What are the respective primary assets and liabilities of a bank, a life insurance company, and a mutual fund company?

5 Compare the maturity matches of assets and liabilities for the three financial institutions (bank, life insurance company, and mutual fund). Given this comparison, which of the three has the greatest maturity mismatch and, hence, interest rate risk?

---

8 Information from Websites for Ginnie Mae *(http://www.ginniemae.gov)*, Fannie Mae *(http://www.fanniemae.com)*, and Freddie Mac *(http://www.freddiemac.com)*; and "Why Big Lenders Are So Frightened by Fannie and Freddie." *The Wall Street Journal* (April 5, 2001), A1, A10.

figure **1.1**   ASSETS AND LIABILITIES OF SELECTED FINANCIAL INSTITUTIONS

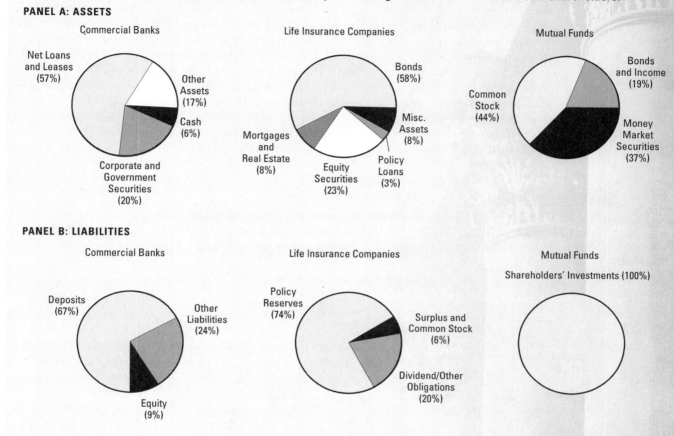

Commercial banks' asset portfolios are dominated by loans and their liabilities by deposits. In contrast, life insurers invest heavily in government and corporate securities, and their major liabilities are obligations to policyholders. Mutual funds also invest in corporate and government securities, but the major claims against them are from their own shareholders.

PANEL A: ASSETS

Commercial Banks

Net Loans and Leases (57%)
Other Assets (17%)
Cash (6%)
Corporate and Government Securities (20%)

Life Insurance Companies

Bonds (58%)
Misc. Assets (8%)
Policy Loans (3%)
Equity Securities (23%)
Mortgages and Real Estate (8%)

Mutual Funds

Bonds and Income (19%)
Money Market Securities (37%)
Common Stock (44%)

PANEL B: LIABILITIES

Commercial Banks

Deposits (67%)
Other Liabilities (24%)
Equity (9%)

Life Insurance Companies

Policy Reserves (74%)
Surplus and Common Stock (6%)
Dividend/Other Obligations (20%)

Mutual Funds

Shareholders' Investments (100%)

Sources: Prepared by the Authors with data from Mutual Fund Fact Book, *43rd ed. (Washington, DC: Investment Company Institute, 2003, http://www.ici.org); Life Insurance Fact Book 2003 (Washington, DC: American Council of Life Insurance, 2003, http://www.acli.com); and FDIC Statistics on Banking, 2nd Quarter 2003 (Washington, DC: Federal Deposit Insurance Corporation, 2003, http://www2.fdic.gov).*

percent), policy loans (3 percent), and miscellaneous assets (8 percent). The assets of the mutual fund industry in 2003 included 44 percent in common stock, 19 percent in bonds and other types of income-producing securities, and 37 percent in money market (short-term, liquid) securities.

Differences are also evident in the liability structures of the three types of institutions, shown in Panel B of Figure 1.1. Deposits constitute a majority of the funds of commercial banks (averaging 67 percent in 2003). In contrast, obligations to policyholders are the major liabilities of life insurers with policy reserves (74 percent in 2003). Mutual funds are quite different, because they issue virtually no debt obligations and derive all their funds from shareholders' investments. The shareholders of banks and insurers (equity), in contrast, provide only small proportions of funds. Commercial banks and life insurance companies have high financial leverage, with banks having an equity-to-assets ratio of about 9 percent and 6 percent for life insurance companies, in 2003.

The Economic Functions of Financial Institutions

The previous section gave a brief overview of the major types of financial institutions. To understand why financial institutions exist and the economic services that they provide, it is important to understand the different ways in which funds are transferred within an economy between businesses, government, and households (economic entities) that need to borrow funds (borrowers) and those that have surplus funds to lend (investors).

In a very simple economy without financial institutions, transactions between different borrowers and lenders are difficult to arrange. Borrowers and savers incur significant search and information costs trying to find each other. Transactions between borrowers and savers may also be limited, because few financial contracts involve only two parties. Similarly, risks are great, since individual entities have little or no knowledge of each other and little ability to monitor each other's actions. Also, the transactions costs may be so high that small entities may be unwilling to supply funds. Investors also have little ability to diversify their risk, due to the high cost of many financial contracts.

Figure 1.2, Panel B shows such direct transactions between lenders and borrowers.

Financial institutions help to reduce transactions, search, monitoring, and information costs. They provide risk management services and allow investors to diversify their risk and hold portfolios of financial assets by creating ways of indirect financing. Financial institutions also play important roles in an efficient payment system between entities and in managing pure risk (insurance).

figure **1.2** INTERMEDIATION AND DIRECT FINANCIAL INVESTMENT

Direct financial investment occurs when lenders supply funds to ultimate borrowers, with the assistance of brokers or investment bankers. Indirect financial investment supplies funds to financial institutions, which issue secondary securities in return. Intermediation occurs when institutions transform secondary securities into primary securities through their own direct investments.

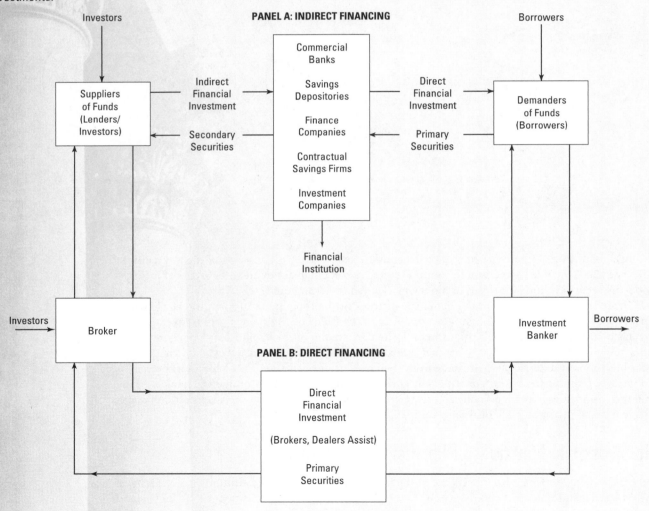

Panel A of Figure 1.2 shows the role of financial institutions as intermediaries between borrowers and lenders. This is explained in more detail in the following section.

Financial Institutions and the Transfer of Funds

The term **primary (direct) security** refers to direct financial claims against individuals, governments, and nonfinancial firms. Secondary securities are the financial liabilities of financial institutions—that is, claims against them. For example, in Figure 1.1, the asset holdings of banks, insurers, and mutual funds are primary securities—direct claims by these institutions against other parties. In contrast, the institutions' liabilities—deposits, policyholder obligations, and mutual fund shares—are **secondary (indirect) securities** or **claims against financial institutions.** A simple economy without any financial institutions would accommodate only direct financial claims or financial contracts. In effect, a borrower gives an investor a financial contract or direct financial claim or security that promises a stake in the borrower's company (i.e., shares of stock) or future payments returning the amount invested plus interest (i.e., a bond or some other sort of IOU). Figure 1.2 illustrates the general difference between financial and nonfinancial firms and the origin of primary and secondary securities. Investors (suppliers of funds) buy financial assets, either primary or secondary securities, because they have cash not needed for the immediate purchase of consumption goods or real assets. Rather than storing excess cash in a piggy bank, more investors wish to earn interest by purchasing a financial asset. For every financial asset, there is an offsetting financial liability issued by a party (demander of funds) who needs more cash and who is willing to pay interest to obtain it. Financial assets and liabilities are the means through which excess funds are transferred in the economic system at rates of return (or costs) anticipated in advance by the lender (or borrower). Investors face risk when they purchase assets, in terms of potential variation in returns to the investor. Accordingly, they will not lend unless the *expected return* is high enough to compensate for risk.

As an economy develops, markets emerge for trading direct securities. Some function as auction markets, where trading is carried out in one physical location, as occurs on the New York Stock Exchange. Others function as over-the-counter markets, where trading is carried out by distant contacts, perhaps over the phone and computer, as on the National Association of Security Dealers Automated Quotation (NASDAQ) system. Loans made directly with borrowers are another example of a primary or direct security, where a direct contract is made between a borrower and a bank or other individual lender. Table 1.3 provides examples of primary securities in the first column. The financial assets owned by banks, insurance companies, and mutual funds, such as loans, bonds, and common stock, are all direct securities, where the lenders give funds to the borrowers, and the lenders receive financial contracts guaranteeing repayment of funds plus interest or shares of ownership in the borrower companies. Again, this type of direct financing is shown in Panel B of Figure 1.2. Investors lend funds in return for a direct or primary security.

In contrast, **secondary (indirect) securities** are financial liabilities of financial institutions—that is, claims against financial institutions. In Table 1.3, financial institutions' liabilities—deposits, policyholder reserve obligations, and mutual fund shares—are secondary securities or claims against financial institutions. In effect, financial institutions created secondary securities that offer advantages over primary securities or direct financial claims. Panel A of Figure 1.2 shows this type of indirect financing.

table **1.3**   EXAMPLES OF PRIMARY AND SECONDARY SECURITIES

Primary Securities	Secondary Securities
Commercial Loans	Savings Deposits
Mortgage Loans	Transaction Deposits
Consumer Loans	Certificates of Deposit
Government Bonds	Insurance Policyholders Reserves
Corporate Bonds	Mutual Fund Shares
Corporate Common Stock	Pension Fund Reserves

With indirect financing, an investor with excess funds purchases a secondary security, such as a life insurance policy or a savings account, allowing the financial institution to determine the ultimate recipient of the funds. For instance, a life insurer may invest the premium payments of its policyholders in corporate bonds, or a CU may invest the savings of some of its members in home improvement loans to other members. The policyholder or the saver engages in **indirect financial investment,** receiving a claim on the financial institution, while the institution holds a direct claim on the corporation or the homeowner. The institution has thus transformed a secondary security into a primary security. This transformation is called **intermediation.**

Not all fund transfers involving financial institutions occur through intermediation. Sometimes an institution arranges or assists in the transfer of funds between parties without issuing its own financial liabilities in the process. When a financial institution acts in this limited capacity, it becomes a broker or a dealer. Dealers differ from brokers by actually owning and making a market for different types of securities. The role of **brokers and dealers** is illustrated in Figure 1.2, Panel B. As noted earlier, securities brokers and investment bankers seldom issue secondary securities themselves but rather assist in transfers of funds from lenders to borrowers. Many financial institutions act as both intermediaries and brokers and dealers from time to time.

Why Intermediaries? Reduced Transactions and Information Costs

In creating indirect investment possibilities through intermediation, and in acting as brokers and dealers, financial institutions provide important benefits that are unavailable with direct investment. Most of these benefits can be categorized as reductions in the costs of transactions, information, or both.[9] Because the return expected from a financial asset is reduced by the costs of acquiring the asset, an institution can create demand for its services if its costs are less than those incurred through direct financial investment. Conversely, institutions issuing financial liabilities want to minimize their transactions costs. Most costs reduced by intermediation or brokerage fall into five major categories. These categories or benefits of financial intermediation are discussed in greater deal in the following sections.

Information and Search Costs

Financial institutions provide ways to identify entities with excess funds and those needing funds, eliminating the need for individual lenders and borrowers to find one another. Investment bankers of securities firms, for instance, maintain lists of institutional investors and other wealthy individual investors who would like to invest in new firms that can provide good returns on their money. In this sense, investment bankers facilitate direct financial investment. Banks attract deposits from small investors as secondary securities guaranteeing given interest rate returns; they transform these deposits into loans, helping corporations to gather funds indirectly from numerous small investors. In turn, borrowers know that banks reduce their search costs for funds. By having economies of scale in collecting information and often specializing in particular industries, financial institutions reduce transaction costs of investors and borrowers. Financial analysts of investment firms also specialize in different industries and provide research advice to investors.

Portfolio Selection and Denomination Costs

Investors may wish to invest in financial assets in different dollar amounts, with different maturities, or with different risk levels from the financial liabilities borrowers wish to issue. Financial institutions issue secondary securities in forms attractive to lenders and then repackage the funds they obtain in forms attractive to borrowers. Again, a good illustration is a bank, which gathers small deposits and packages them into larger loans for individual borrowers. Hence, financial institutions offer a more favorable denomination for small investors, who if they invested directly in Treasury bills (T-bills), for instance, would have to have a minimum of $10,000 to purchase one T-bill. A mutual fund allows small

---

9 Parts of the following discussion are based on the analyses of Benston and Smith (1976); Diamond (1984); Berlin (1987); Williamson (1987); Haubrich (1989); Gorton and Pennacchi (1990); O'Hara (1990); and Seward (1990). For a recent theoretical article, see Gary Gorton and Andrew Winton. *Financial Intermediation.* NBER Working Paper, 2003, No. W8928 (SSRN network, *http://ssrn.com*).

investors to invest in a diversified portfolio, reducing the risk that they would incur if they held their savings only in one security. Mutual funds also provide diversification at much lower selection or transactions costs, by buying and selling large quantities of investments, than the investors would incur if they picked and paid brokerage costs to create individual securities portfolios.

Monitoring Costs

When two parties agree to a transfer of funds, whether through direct or indirect investment, the arrangement is usually formalized by a **financial contract.** A typical contract specifies the terms of a funds transfer—for example, its maturity and the interest rate at which it will occur. The contract also outlines provisions to protect both borrower and lender, such as the lender's recourse in case the borrower absconds with the funds.

Finance theorists have noted that financial contracts are often characterized by **asymmetric information;** that is, the contracting parties are not equally and fully informed about each other. In particular, borrowers often know more about their own financial situations and their abilities to honor contracts than do lenders. Information asymmetry in turn gives rise to **monitoring costs**—ongoing expenses incurred by investors to gather information so they can intervene if borrowers' financial situations change.

Financial institutions provide economies of scale in monitoring by employing appraisers, financial analysts, and other specialists to investigate large numbers of claims on a full-time basis. For this reason, many lenders can reduce their monitoring costs by investing through financial intermediaries instead of purchasing primary securities. In recent years, some experts have concluded that the reduction of monitoring costs is the most important reason for the existence of financial intermediaries. Financial institutions are also experts at due diligence, investigating and finding information about companies, such as investment bankers taking privately held firms public. With this expertise, many financial institutions, such as investment bankers and securities firms, are expert in providing advice on pricing.

Risk Management Costs

Many investors want to hold varied financial assets to reduce the risk inherent in a single claim against a party who may fail to meet its obligations. The investor can avoid that risk by holding shares in a mutual fund, that is, in secondary securities of a financial institution that holds a diversified portfolio. Although the investor must still monitor the financial institution, its diversified portfolio reduces the probability that the institution will suffer serious setbacks, since all its investments probably will not simultaneously fail. Some secondary securities, such as bank deposits, offer low risk exposure, because they are insured against institutional failure.

Other specialized financial institutions also take on risk management services. Insurance companies pool premiums from thousands of individuals and businesses as secondary securities (policyholder reserves), which they invest in securities that provide income and capital gains to fund payouts to individuals and businesses in the event of property damage, theft, loss of life, or other contingencies. In this way, insurance companies reduce risk for individuals and businesses. By pooling premiums of large numbers of customers, insurance companies can provide risk management services at a much lower cost than if individuals and businesses had to save the funds themselves to meet such possible contingencies. As another example of risk management, banks provide letters of credit that guarantee payment by other parties. This activity facilitates trade transactions between different parties (such as importing and exporting), since the risk associated with the default of either party is eliminated. Similarly, large investment banks and commercial banks provide instruments that can protect businesses and other financial institutions against interest rate and foreign exchange risk. The cash flows of these derivatives—swaps, forward contracts, caps, and floors, as explained in Chapters 11 and 12—are based on future price movements of underlying securities.

Maturity Intermediation and Liquidity

Often borrowers want to repay funds over long time horizons. An example is a business buying plant and equipment intended to generate returns for many years, from which the business will pay off debt incurred to purchase the assets. However, investors (particularly small savers) may want or need their money back quickly and may not be willing to lend funds for lengthy periods. Banks accept small amounts from numerous small investors as deposits (secondary securities) and transform them into longer-term loans (primary securities), in the process providing maturity intermediation services. Short-term funds are transferred into longer-term loans.

Depository institutions also provide liquidity and security to small investors as well as small to large businesses, who can write checks or withdraw funds from deposit accounts at any time at little more than the cost of writing a check or using a debit card, credit card, or transferring fund electronically, so they do not have to carry around large sums of cash. If particularly small investors had invested in long-term bonds, instead, when they needed liquidity, they would have to sell the bonds, incurring losses if rates had risen over the period, as well as brokerage fees. Financial institutions, particularly banks, are important in the flow of savings to productive investments by businesses, increasing the wealth of an economy. They also provide important support for an efficient payment system. These services increase the liquidity of the economy, leaving greater funds available for investment in productive assets.

Other specialized financial institutions, including private pensions, mutual funds, and insurance companies, also carry out maturity intermediation services. They allow small investors to save for long-term goals, such as retirement, by investing savings in diversified portfolios. Financial institutions also provide long-term financial planning advice, reducing planning and search costs by investors. With demographic data indicating a rising average age for the U.S. population and those of many other countries as the result of the baby boom after World War II, this role has become increasingly important, generating an increasing share of revenues for financial institutions. Hence, mutual funds and other investment companies have boomed.

Other Government Policy-Related Services

Many financial institutions, especially depository institutions, are state or federally chartered to serve their communities and, hence, are subject to significant government regulations and can have their charter taken away if they do not abide by these regulations. Hence, financial institutions are special and many were created to provide for economic needs for communities and specific sectors of the economy. During financial crises, investment bankers and commercial banks historically have often been called in to help stabilize the financial markets or banking system. Particular types of financial institutions were chartered for particular social purposes. For instance, both savings and loans and the GSEs were chartered to provide a more effective home mortgage market. Depository institutions also are important institutions for the efficiency of the payments systems, as well as having a special role in the transmission of monetary policy. They also have been asked to serve a policing role in apprehending criminals involved in schemes to defraud the U.S. government, including money laundering and check kiting schemes, as well as to notice suspicious behavior under the Bank Secrecy and Patriot acts mentioned earlier in the chapter.

The Changing Role of Financial Institutions in the Technological Age

With the development of technology and the Internet, information has become more accessible to firms and individuals, reducing the role of financial intermediaries as monitors and information

---

Concept Questions

1 Explain the difference between a direct security between investors and borrowers and an indirect security created by a financial institution.

2 Explain the benefits that a financial institution provides by issuing indirect securities including (1) search costs, (2) portfolio selection costs, (3) monitoring costs, (4) risk management costs, and (5) maturity intermediation costs.

3 What other special services do financial institutions provide?

4 Explain in your own words how costs to a society in terms of facilitating the transfer of funds are reduced by having financial intermediaries.

providers. For instance, technology allows large, creditworthy corporations to issue commercial paper and bonds around the world. As pointed out by Roy Smith in *The Global Bankers:*

> *Technology has made several things possible in international financial markets that would not have been otherwise: the ability to settle and deliver large numbers of transactions involving different instruments, currencies, and locations; the ability to keep track of more numerous and more complex trading positions than anyone ever imagined only a few years ago . . . and the ability to transmit large volumes of market and competitive data internationally at comparatively low cost. (Smith, 1990, p. 6)*

With technology, loans have been pooled and packaged into securities sold to investors. The remarkable boom in mortgage and credit card securities has transformed depository institutions and finance companies into more transaction-oriented institutions, reducing their monitoring (relationship-oriented) function. Technology also helps investors to find information about companies by accessing their Web pages. Internet services of discount brokers allow these securities firms to provide low-cost trading mechanisms, since they generally provide little or no investment advice, to support buying and selling securities. The role of financial intermediaries in having an information monopoly no longer exists. Firms with rich internal information sources such as AT&T and Sears have created their own credit cards using their immense collections of customer data. Later, these credit card divisions were sold to financial institutions. Software companies like Microsoft and Intuit have developed services that provide direct market access for financial transactions, such as bill paying, reducing the need for financial intermediaries for such transactions.[10]

Technology is reducing the role of financial intermediaries in the payments mechanism, as well. MasterCard, for instance, has invested millions in the development of an electronic (E-cash) system known as Mondex. The system's smart cards have tiny microchips embedded that store personalized electronic data that will allow consumers remote access to their funds at any time, anywhere. Hence, as pointed out by David Shaw, an investment banker, increasingly new technology implies greater change, and "The whole financial industry will likely be turned upside down, with shrinkage in some areas and perhaps some outright failures among those firms that are unable to use technology effectively." As noted by a recent Federal Reserve Bank of Kansas City study, the ATM (automated teller machine) and debit card industry has undergone significant change. Point-of-sale debit card transactions (where funds are automatically taken from an individual's bank account, similar to smart cards) have grown in the United States, while annual transactions per ATM have gone down. Nonbank ATM networks have also gone up, suggesting greater involvement of nonbanks in the payment process, which could be a risk issue for the banking system, since nonbanks are subject to far less supervision.[11]

Other roles of financial institutions have taken on growing importance, however. With changing demographics and Baby Boomers approaching retirement, financial institutions' role in maturity intermediation has increased. Mutual funds have grown at a staggering rate as investors save for retirement. Financial institutions have taken advantage of technological advances to create information databases that allow them to enhance financial planning services for customers and to develop new products to help customers save for retirement or meet other needs. Financial management needs for firms, such as working capital management, are also being offered by banks and securities firms through the benefits of technology. Banks and securities firms provide services that help businesses speed up cash collections and manage cash disbursements. They also provide automated clearinghouse (ACH) services that allow direct disbursement of payments to the accounts of employees within minutes, saving companies mailing and other accounting and transactions costs. In addition, with technology allowing large volumes of detailed information to be kept, loans can be packaged and transformed into securities. In turn, large banks, mortgage banks, and thrift institutions can earn fee revenues associated with securitizations. For instance, in the first month of 2004, the Federal Reserve Board data releases showed the securitization of about $410.2 billion in mortgage-backed securities and $169.1 billion in consumer loan securities by U.S. banks, with $126.5 billion as that month's gains on off-balance-sheet items (*http://www.federalreserve.gov/releases/*).

---

10 Ramo, "Big Bank Theory," 47–57.

11 Ramo, "Big Bank Theory," 47–57; and Hayashi, Sullivan, and Weiner (2003).

Financial institutions have entered new advisory roles, providing help and advice to small and medium-sized businesses for fee income. Many banks and securities firms advertise their services as small business partners. PC banking (allowing customers to initiate wire transfers of funds, move funds to different accounts, and pay bills electronically) has become very popular. A recent *New York Times* article (November 23, 2003, Personal Business, p. 8), citing a report by eMarketer, noted that the number of American households banking online more than doubled in three years to $27.8 million and is projected to be $36.3 million in 2005. Financial institutions also have improved their risk management services for business customers, as discussed earlier. The nature of financial institutions, the economic services they provide, and management techniques to meet new challenges and opportunities are constantly evolving. Technology provides opportunities for financial institutions to develop new, innovative products, and it also sharpens competition from the direct markets and nonfinancial firms.

New Risks with Technology

Expanding use of technology by financial institutions has increased the risks associated with technological failures. Technology can provide potential computer nightmares, such as the widely touted Y2K problem, due to some computer systems' inability to recognize dates after 1999 that fortunately was resolved, albeit with considerable expense for many large banks, without serious difficulty. Given the very technical nature of bank operations clearing millions of checks a day, technological risk associated with operations is a significant risk, necessitating serious planning and back-up systems. Spreading use of electronic payment systems also brings a danger of illegal use, fraud, overdrafts, or other errors. Regulators now require banks to set up risk management systems for electronic fund transfers and disaster management plans in the event of technological breakdowns. Access to accounts through home banking services on the Internet also entails considerable opportunities for fraud, viruses, and embezzlement. In light of these risks, as noted earlier, Basel II proposes new capital requirements for large international banks for the risks in their operations, whereby for the first time banks must hold separate, identifiable regulatory capital for operational risk and will face supervisory scrutiny for risk management in this area.[12]

Societal Concerns with Change and Banking for the Unbanked

In the midst of the dramatic changes for financial institutions and the bewildering array of new services for millions of customers, millions of poor citizens voice additional concerns. Those who cannot meet minimum bank balances or fee requirements are, in essence, unbanked. With banks growing in size, concern has increased that the unbanked will be ignored. Congress passed legislation in the late 1990s asking banks to provide services for the unbanked, including creating policies for direct deposits of U.S. government checks. This system saves millions of dollars in government mailing costs and prevents thefts of checks, but it also creates a significant, unreimbursed cost to financial institutions that must provide free banking services. Given that a banking relationship is often necessary to build a credit relationship and, hence, build wealth, there have been renewed societal concerns over how financial institutions can tap the unbanked market to help reduce poverty. The FDIC recently held a conference on this topic, with congressional panels discussing the benefits of providing a better financial education and services to all U.S. citizens. It is worth noting that the FDIC provides links to help consumers become more aware of financial services and protections on their Website at *http://www.fdic.gov/consumers*.

One type of financial institution that is often overlooked, pawnshops, has doubled since the mid-1980s, extending more than $9 billion in credit each year. Pawnshops cash checks for fees and offer cash loans for collateral at rates ranging from 24 percent to 240 percent. Pawnshops cater to poor customers not served by other financial institutions. Because of the great risk of default for these transactions, charges are very high to customers with little wealth; many who fail to repay their loans see their collateral sold. Some high-class pawnshops have also arisen, such as Lloyd's Funds International, a financial and management consulting firm for high-worth individuals, which has an online Website, noted

---

12 "Are Mega Banks—Once Unimaginable, Now Inevitable?" 32–37; Ramo, "Big Bank Theory," 47–57; "Basel Committee on Banking Supervision, Consultative Document: Overview of the New Basel Accord," Bank for International Settlements, April 2003; Carol Alexander, ed. *Operational Risk: Regulation, Analysis, and Management.* Upper Saddle River, NJ: FT Prentice Hall, Professional Finance Series, 2003, 4.

as "the world's largest pawnshop," which provides loans on pledges of diamonds, jewelry, rare coins, art collections, and other expensive goods.[13]

As part of banks' special charter to serve their communities, the Community Reinvestment Act (CRA) requires them to provide some low-income financing. Regulators can reject merger and branch applications or require banks to increase low-income lending before applications will be approved. Although many banks have embraced the CRA as a way to serve the community and also enhance their reputations, many have also argued that other types of financial institutions, such as finance companies, credit unions, and other financial institutions, should have similar requirements to provide a level competitive playing field.

New Accounting and Ethical Concerns: Scandals for Financial Institutions in the Early 2000s

Ethics is defined in Merriam Webster's Collegiate Encyclopedia (2000, p. 546) as "the branch of philosophy that inquires into the ultimate values and standards by which human actions can be judged right or wrong." Different ethical theories disagree on whether an action is right or wrong based only on its consequences or regardless of the consequences. In the theory of finance, it is often argued that maximizing shareholders' wealth is the objective of financial management. From this perspective, it is often stated, and is often implicitly thought, that unethical actions implicitly will not maximize shareholders' wealth. Ultimately, unethical actions catch up with firms. Since financial and accounting firms are institutions built on public confidence in their integrity, any unethical behavior by their managers can result in their demise. This was clear in the early 2000s when accounting scandals were rampant. Unfortunately, employees, debtholders, customers, and suppliers that did not engage in unethical behavior are punished as well as the individuals or managers that did engage in unethical behavior. One example is the case of a "rogue trader" that caused the failure of Barings, as mentioned earlier in the chapter. In the earlier 2000s a number of ethical problems and scandals occurred for financial institutions including: (1) the Enron scandal; (2) spinning by investment bankers: (3) accounting scandals by GSEs and mutual funds scandals briefly discussed below.

The Role of Financial Institutions in the Enron Scandal

In 2002 and 2003, accounting scandals dominated headlines, starting with the collapse of Enron, a large energy trading corporation. Enron's demise resulted in thousands of employees losing about $1 billion in pension savings. Several Wall Street banks and investment banks received $20 million each in fees in 2000 to help engineer controversial off-balance-sheet partnerships that removed billions of dollars of problem assets off Enron's balance sheets. Taking advantage of tax and accounting loopholes, these partnerships hid Enron's serious problems from auditors, analysts, and regulators. While some large banks engineered the complex, off-balance-sheet deals, the other large banks and investment banks put up big loans to finance the off-balance-sheet partnerships, with loan payments creatively transferred back to Enron to be booked as revenues. Congressional hearings also found that some investment bankers were promised future bond underwriting business in return for investing in the controversial off-balance-sheet partnerships. Enron was accused of threatening banks, including Chase, Credit Suisse, and Bank of America, that they would be discontinued as bankers or investment bankers for Enron if they didn't invest in the partnership. Technically, the parties involved may have felt that they were maximizing the wealth of their shareholders by generating fee income for the deals and also by maintaining Enron as a lucrative customer. From any ethical theoretical perspective, however, the bankers violated ethical standards by contributing to fraudulent behavior that ultimately led to Enron's demise and large losses and censures for their banks. Fraudulent behavior led to the demise of other firms in the early 2000s including Parmalet SpA, a large Italian dairy conglomerate that also was associated with large banks. In the case of Parmalet, a former Bank of America Corporation executive in

---

13 John P. Caskey. *Fringe Banking: Check-Cashing Outlets, Pawnshops, and the Poor.* New York: Russell Sage Foundation, 1994, xiv, 165.

Italy, for instance, confessed to misappropriating $27 million in a kickback scheme. Also, a central part of the fraud at Parmalet involved a multibillion dollar bank account that the company falsely claimed to hold on its financial statements.[14]

Conflicts of Interest for Analysts and Sales Teams at Investment Banks

Other conflicts of interest occurred in the 2000s with what is often referred to as "spinning," where desired shares of initial public offerings (IPOs) are given out as favors to investment bankers' "best" customers. Additional scandals occurred for investment banks in terms of the relationships between stock analysts and sales teams at investment banks, with pressure placed on the analysts to put a positive spin on stocks that the investment bank was selling. In May 2002, the U.S. Securities and Exchange Commission (SEC) approved rules forcing stock analysts to reveal more about their ties to companies they research. In July 2002, the **Sarbanes-Oxley Act,** discussed in more detail in Chapter 3, also set up rules to make analysts and accounting firms more independent. A number of investment banks were fined, including Merrill Lynch, the top U.S. investment bank, which agreed to pay $100 million to settle charges that its analysts endorsed stocks of companies being sold by its investment banking businesses that they had cited to be worthless stocks in private. In a joint settlement with the SEC, Eliot Spritzer, as prosecutor on behalf of New York security regulators, forced the investment banking industry to agree to pay fines of $1.4 billion and to change their practices.[15]

Accounting Errors for Quasi-GSEs and Mutual Funds Late-Day Trading Scandals

In 2003, scandals occurred for the two quasi-GSEs, Freddie Mac and Fannie Mae, with misstatements of their earnings, associated with their mortgage operations, including for Fannie Mae the use of billions of dollars in derivatives (complex financial instruments used to manage interest rate risk). This led as well to congressional hearings and greater oversight for the agencies. Also, mutual funds scandals occurred in the last quarter of 2003, associated with improper aftermarket trading where traders pocketed fees from after-hours trading to profit the fund corporation. Such rapid, market-timing trading is viewed as harmful to long-term fund investors by making fund managers buy and sell stocks quickly to keep up with flows of funds that, in turn, increases fund expenses. In essence, long-term investors' funds are used to reap profits for the mutual fund company.

Even well-reputed securities firms such as Charles Schwab, the discount brokerage that prides itself on its low costs for investors, uncovered some evidence of a practice called late-day trading for two funds for wealthy investors with outside professional (hedge fund) investors contracted to do trading. Normally, trades for mutual funds cannot be processed after 4 p.m., when the closing value of the fund is posted. Late-day trading is a practice that provides the opportunity for "privileged clients," such as institutional investors, to purchase fund shares after the market's close (and the posting closing valuation of funds) and thus make profits by benefiting from events after the close of trading that will likely move the market the following day. Although some practices technically aren't illegal under SEC regulations, if not prohibited in a fund's prospectus, by diluting earnings of long-term fund shareholders, it runs against a fund's fiduciary duty and, hence, is unethical.

As John C. Bogle, the founder and former CEO of Vanguard—a shareholder-controlled mutual fund—notes in the chapter opening quote, this scandal "brought unwelcome attention to 11 major firms that manage about $1 trillion." The attorney general of New York, Eliot Spitzer, brought "blue sky" law security-fraud charges against funds for these practices. The SEC and Congress also held investigations, filed lawsuits against funds involved in opportunistic trading, and developed new rules to curtail these practices. The scandals reduced the confidence of mutual fund customers in involved funds. For some funds, the scandals also hurt their reputations and business. Investors in Janus Capi-

---

14 See Financial Times (FT.com), *http://specials.ft.com/enron,* including Joshua Chaffin and Stephen Fidler. "Enron in Depth: CSFB Team Played Key Role in Enron Partnerships." *Financial Times* (February 28, 2002), 20:44 GMT (FT.com); Andrew Hill. "JP Morgan Headed to Trial over Enron Losses." *Financial Times* (March 6, 2002), 09:10 GMT (FT.com); Joshua Chaffin. "Enron Investigation and Hearings: Brokers Promised Business If Scheme Supported." *Financial Times* (March 15, 2002), 12:34 GMT (FT.com); Joshua Chaffin and Stephen Fidler. "Enron Investigations and Hearings: Enron's Alchemy Turns to Lead for Bankers." *Financial Times* (March 15, 2002), 12:34 GMT (FT.com); Thor Valdmanis. "Rules in the Works to Curb Conflicts." *USA Today* (September 26, 2002), *USA.Today.Com;* and "Ex-Parmalat Banker Admits Stealing $27 Million," *The Wall Street Journal,* February 27, 2004, A3.

15 Ibid.

tal Group, Inc., a prominent Denver-based fund, for instance, withdrew more than $1 billion from funds in the first two weeks of November. Investors in Putnam Investments, the initial firm charged in the mutual fund trading scandal, withdrew $14 billion as well. Two funds, PBHC (known as Pilgrim) Funds in Pennsylvania and Putnam Funds in Boston, attempted to assuage angry investors by ousting their executives and making changes to reduce the likelihood of opportunistic trading practices occurring again. Putnam set up new corporate governance practices to strengthen the independence of fund directors, improve compliance policies, and place restrictions on employee trading. Mr. Pilgrim, who ran the Growth Fund, a hedge fund for wealthy investors, agreed to repay the fund the money he had made from trades. Other funds including Janus followed suit in refunding funds to customers as well. Congress proposed new legislation at the end of 2003 to allow the SEC to develop rules to eliminate such abusive trading practices in the mutual fund industry. The SEC proposed a number of rules, to prevent these and other abuses as well [see *http://www.sec.gov/rules/proposed.shtml*) and the Investment Company Institute for updates on these rulings (*http://www.ici.org/issues*)], discussed in more detail in Chapter 18.[16]

The Role of Corporate Governance Problems and Ownership Form in the Scandals

With the large number of scandals that occurred in the early years of the twenty-first century, a number of analysts have blamed problems on weaknesses in corporate governance for publicly traded firms. For instance, Janus had just become a publicly traded company about a year earlier, spinning off from a parent firm, Stilwell Financial. Analysts have argued that this created a conflict of interest between stockholders in Janus, as a publicly traded company, and Janus's customers, the shareholders of mutual funds, with pressure placed on Janus to serve its public stockholders. John C. Bogle, the founder of Vanguard, which, in contrast, is owned by its mutual fund investors, argues that the mutual fund scandal brings out the problem of the conflict of interest between mutual fund investors and suppliers of services, the investment management, share distribution, and administration of funds, which controls the funds directors and all fees and activities. This organizational form will be discussed later in Chapter 18.[17]

A number of critics have also argued that the Enron scandal and the associated scandals for banks and investment banks in the early 2000s were related to corporate governance problems, associated with stock-based compensation and options. In effect, executive compensation including options that were determined by the performance of the firm's stock price gave strong incentives for managers to inflate their firm's stock price by hiding losses through creative accounting practices. Accordingly, the SEC and accounting regulators have tried to develop regulations that would reduce these incentives, including requiring expensing the value of options given to executives to discourage these practices and requiring greater independence of boards of directors to monitor managers. As the use of stock options in incentive packages continues to be debated, major financial institutions such as UBS, one of the largest international banks in the world, announced in late 2003 that it would dramatically reduce the number of stock options it awards.

The following section discusses agency theory and conflicts associated with corporate governance issues that can lead to unethical behavior or fraud, as discussed previously, that arise for financial institutions.

Financial Institution Management: Who Sets Objectives?

In the theory of corporate finance, the objective of financial managers should be to maximize the wealth of the owners of the firm, that is, stockholders. As mentioned earlier, this should imply managing to make a firm a desirable place to work, doing an excellent job to gain an excellent reputation, acting

---

16 John Hechinger and James Bandler. "Putnam Settles with SEC, Questions Remain." *The Wall Street Journal* (November 14, 2003), C1, C9; Ian McDonald and Tom Lauricella. "Timing Scandal Fells Pilgrim Baxter Founders." *The Wall Street Journal* (November 14, 2003), C1, C13; John C. Bogle. "Not-So-Mutual Funds." *The Wall Street Journal* (November 14, 2003), A12; Gretchen Morgenson. "2 Mutual Funds Move to Assure Angry Investors." *New York Times* (November 14, 2003), A1, C5; David Armstrong and John Hechinger. "Janus Capital Investors Withdraw More than $1 Billion from Funds." *The Wall Street Journal* (November 14, 2003), C9; Floyd Norris. "Manager Prospered as Investors Suffered." *New York Times* (November 14, 2003), C1; Landon Thomas, Jr. "Schwab Discloses Suspect Trades as Rift in Fund Inquiry Widens." *New York Times* (November 15, 2003), A1, B2; and "House May Soon Vote on Mutual-Fund Bill." *The Wall Street Journal.* (November 13, 2003), C13.

17 John C. Bogle, "Not-So-Mutual Funds," A12; and Allison Linn. "Torn Between Two Masters: Janus Walks Thin Line to Please Shareholders, Fund Investors." *Rocky Mountain News* (November 15, 2003), C1, C7.

with integrity, and treating customers well. In practice, as noted, sometimes financial managers misinterpret this objective in attempts to boost stock prices in the short run with unethical practices, while destroying the value of the firm in the long run. Financial institution managers have stakeholders in addition to stockholders that they must satisfy. For instance, if a bank does not satisfy regulatory requirements, their charter can be revoked. Because financial institution management involves managing the institution in accordance with its objectives, managers require a clear understanding of those objectives and the responsibility for setting them. Identifying objectives is somewhat more complex for financial institutions than for other businesses. To understand this complexity, begin by considering alternative theories for setting managerial objectives. Under a **normative approach,** based on classical theory, managers of nonfinancial firms operating in competitive product markets will act in the interests of owners (stockholders), ignoring their own personal risk/return preferences. Otherwise, unhappy owners will oust these managers. Under this theory, financing decisions are regarded as less important than decisions involving investments in real assets. The classical theory of the firm focuses on how managers *should* act, and thus it is considered a **normative theory** of decision making.[18] This approach states a clear criterion for managerial decision making: If a decision provides net benefits to owners, it should be made; otherwise, it should not. In finance theory, we often refer to the goal of the financial manager to maximize the owners' (stockholders) wealth. This goal goes along with the classical theory that leaves no doubt that the institution's owners are the ones to set objectives for asset/liability management.

In contrast, **positive theories** of managerial behavior focus on explaining how decisions are actually made by business managers rather than on prescribing how they *should* be made. When owners also manage their firms, the way managers should behave with respect to owners matches the way they do behave. But if owners and managers are different people, managers' risk/return preferences may differ from those of owners. Under these circumstances, what do managers do? Positive theories of managerial objectives attempt to explain the behavior of managers arising from the separation of ownership and control.

Agency Theory

Agency theory, a positive view of managerial decision making, suggests that managers are no different from other individuals: If left unmonitored, they will pursue their personal risk/return preferences. Thus, owners may incur costs in making sure that *their* preferences are recognized. Agency theory examines the relationships between nonowner-managers (**agents**) and owners (**principals**) and the contracts arising as a result. (These agent/principal agreements are yet another form of financial contracting, leading to associated monitoring costs.) At one extreme, an agent/principal contract could be structured so that every action of the agent would be prescribed and closely monitored, leaving the manager no discretion. Such a contract would be very costly for the principal to enforce. At the other extreme, the owner could take a "hands off" approach, leaving all matters to the manager's judgment. Although monitoring costs would be nil under such a contract, the potential losses to owners could be considerable if managers exclusively pursued their own interests. Normally, therefore, terms of agent/principal contracts fall between these extremes. Any reductions in benefits to owners stemming from contracts governing the separation of ownership and control are known as **agency costs.**[19]

In practice, agency costs can take many different forms, such as legal expenses to draw up contracts that limit managers' salaries and expense accounts and the resources managers spend on annual reports convincing owners that decisions consider their wishes; both are examples of explicit monitoring costs. Agency costs arising from managers' unmonitored actions may be more difficult to measure. One example is the potential benefits lost when a manager lends to a friend's business at a rate lower than might be strictly justified by the risk of the loan.

A firm may incur a special type of agency cost when managers are not closely monitored; this **managerial expense preference** is the tendency for some managers to enhance the benefits they receive

---

18 The classical theory of managerial objectives is developed in Fisher (1930). Extensions of Fisher's work are provided in Hirschleifer (1958, 1965).

19 Formal development of agency theory is attributed to Jensen and Meckling (1976). Jensen and Meckling, however, were not the first to recognize potential inadequacies in the classical theory of firm behavior when owners and managers are different people.

from their institutions by hiring larger staffs than necessary, furnishing offices lavishly, or enjoying large travel and expense accounts.[20] Financial institutions face even greater chances than nonfinancial firms for potential abuse by managers and other employees in the form of fraud and embezzlement. All types of agency costs reduce owners' welfare and would not be incurred if owners managed their companies. Examples of expense preference behavior are widespread. In particular, managers of a number of savings and loans in the 1980s made purchases that approached looting their institutions. David Paul, the CEO of Centrust Savings in Miami, Florida, for instance, bought expensive, rare art worth $29 million with bank funds, also spending $1.4 million for a corporate jet, $7 million for a yacht, $43,000 for limousines, while paying himself $15 million a year in salary and bonuses.

Many experts argue that the agency relationship is so important today that a discussion of managerial objectives is realistic only if it includes agent/principal contracts. Thus, attention must focus on ways to minimize agency costs. Under this positive theory, managers make decisions according to criteria based on whether they receive net benefits from the proposed actions. If they do, they will undertake the actions; otherwise, they will not. Owners must therefore structure contracts that align managers' rewards with their own to keep their costs lower than the costs they would incur by letting managers operate unchecked. Agency theory implies that managers set asset/liability objectives and that owners protect their interests by setting appropriate constraints. Given the environment that an institution operates in, it may have smaller or greater agency problems. For instance, a larger, more complex firm may have greater opportunities for managers to act in their own versus the firm's interests, creating a greater agency problem. Agency costs to reduce this problem include the costs to design performance contracts, such as managerial stock ownership, performance bonuses, or managerial stock options to attempt to align managers' interests with those of stockholders. However, as noted previously, sometimes these contracts may have unintended adverse consequences if they promote selfish behavior of managers to maximize their own wealth at the expense of the firm's long-run integrity. Financial institutions are thought to be subject to greater agency problems than nonfinancial firms, since managers engage in confidential transactions, such as making loans, which stockholders cannot easily monitor. This is often noted as greater **information asymmetries** between managers and owners. Financial institutions' managerial objectives are also more complex with a number of different stakeholders involved. The following section discusses these stakeholders.

Managerial Objectives in Financial Institutions

Although the classical theory has been applied to managerial decision making in financial institutions, one can argue that it is inadequate on both theoretical and empirical grounds.[21]

Customer Needs Affect Objectives

Because financial institutions provide liquidity to customers when issuing secondary securities such as demand deposits, the problems of financial institutions differ from those of nonfinancial firms, which face no need to honor financial liabilities on demand. Therefore, the need to provide customers with the benefits of intermediation must be considered in establishing managerial objectives for financial institutions. In addition, asset and liability decisions must be made simultaneously in financial institutions, but the classical theory of nonfinancial firms does not assume joint consideration of investment and financing decisions.[22] Just as mutual funds found out with the scandals in 2003, customers (mutual fund investors) can quickly withdraw their funds. Since federally chartered banks and savings institutions are federally insured and institutions are chartered to serve the needs of the community, consumers have a significant role, and hundreds of regulations are devoted to consumer protection, as well as great efforts to improve the financial education of consumer customers.

---

20 The theory of managerial expense preference was developed by Williamson (1963).

21 An example is Towey (1974).

22 See Sealey (1983).

Ownership Structure Affects Objectives

The ownership structures of many financial institutions also differ from those of nonfinancial firms. Instead of being owned by stockholders (people who have risked funds to start a business and who are entitled to residual profits that the firm generates), many financial institutions are mutually owned. The **mutual form of organization** is particularly prevalent among insurance companies, savings banks, and savings and loans, although many have converted in recent years to stockholder-owned organizations. So-called *owners* of mutual institutions are not owners in the classical sense, because they are not entitled to personal claims on residual profits. Therefore, the classical theory—based on the idea that those who risk funds are entitled to establish the objectives of the enterprise—may not be directly relevant to mutual organizations. From this perspective, it is often thought that managers of mutual firms, with less monitoring by diffuse owners (depositors) may engage in expense preference or other behavior to maximize their own utility versus depositor-owners (i.e., increased agency costs between managers and owners).[23] Alternatively, other financial economists argue that stockholders prefer greater risk-taking to maximize their unlimited claims on the residual value of the firm after debtholders are paid. Hence manager-owners of stock firms may take on greater risk than mutual firms. Still others argue that at low levels of ownership, entrenched managers may take on great risk by having enough control to protect against their ouster. However, at high levels of ownership managers will be more likely to engage in value-maximizing behavior to protect their wealth.[24] Empirical research finds mixed results, but a recent study finds by Sfiridis and Daniels (2004) examining stock and mutual thrifts suggests greater expense preference behavior by mutuals. Other studies generally suggest greater risk-taking by stock versus mutual firms and by manager-owners of stock firms, although this risk-taking appears to be value enhancing at higher ownership levels.[25]

Regulation Affects Objectives

Furthermore, even if owners were to manage their own financial institutions, they would experience agency relationships. These situations would arise from another agent/principal relationship between financial institutions and government representatives. This agency relationship is quite strong for some financial firms, such as commercial banks, which for many years have been expected to assist in carrying out the federal government's fiscal and monetary policies.

Virtually all financial institutions encounter agency relationships with the government, because most are involved in carrying out public policies such as the distribution of credit to disadvantaged borrowers. Also, because governments provide insurance for many financial institutions, they regularly employ examiners to monitor activities and ensure that managerial decisions do not unduly strain government insurance funds. In some instances, government agencies may actually remove managers from their positions for improper performance of their roles.[26] As observed in the recent mutual fund scandals, the agency relationships between regulators, managers, and stockholders will continue.

A Balancing Act

How, then, are asset/liability management objectives set? The perspective in this book reflects a model recognizing that owners, regulators, and managers themselves all influence managerial behavior. The

---

23 See Edwards (1977); Hannan and Mavinga (1980).

24 For summaries of these arguments, see Esty (1997) and Gorton and Rosen (1995).

25 See Mester (1989). Summaries of this research can be found in Snider (1994); Cebenoyan, Cooperman, and Register (1999); Hubbard and Palia (1994); and Federal Reserve Bank of New York Economic Policy Review, Special Issue: *Corporate Governance: What Do We Know, and What Is Different About Banks?* Vol. 9, No. 1. (April 2003). Also see Sfiridis and Daniels (2004); Mester (1993); Cebenoyan, Cooperman, Register, and Hudgins (1993); Esty (1997); Cordell, MacDonald, and Wohar (1993); and Cole and Eisenbeis (1996). Early research is reviewed in Woerheide(1984).

26 For instance, during the savings and loan crisis of the mid to late 1980s, regulators often put technically insolvent thrifts into conservatorship and replaced managers with regulatory-selected new managers. An example is the removal of Charles Knapp as CEO of Financial Corporation of America, a giant California thrift, in 1984, replacing him with their own CEO selection, William Popejoy.

model was developed specifically for banking firms, but its insight holds for other financial institutions, as well. As the author expresses it:

> *The banking firm is a complex organization. As a financial intermediary, it performs both a brokerage and a risk transformation function. As a business, it must yield a return to its owners. As a regulated enterprise, it must operate within the bounds specified by the supervisory agencies.*[27]

In most institutions, an individual manager or a management team is responsible for balancing the risk/return preferences of all parties. Most managers may personally wish to maximize performance, including maximizing the NIM and minimizing the burden and PLL, because their salaries and expense accounts come from funds remaining after interest and other expense obligations are paid. However, they also recognize that institutions must provide liquidity to customers, a requirement that may prohibit a risky plan to maximize spread. Owners whose risk/return preferences differ from those of managers may further restrict managers' actions by imposing constraints such as salary or expense limitations or by structuring incentive plans, such as stock options, that may reward managers for minimizing noninterest costs.

Finally, public policy expressed in government regulation also influences managers, and ultimate NIM and profit targets differ from those that would result in the absence of an institution/government relationship. Thus, from a manager's point of view, the objective of asset/liability management is to maximize the institution's profits, subject to the constraints imposed by owners, regulators, and the intermediation function. These constraints result in the pursuit of a profit target and a risk level that differs from the specific preferences of any single individual or group but that considers the priorities of all parties.

From the perspective of financial management theory, the goal of the firm is to maximize shareholder's wealth or the stock price of the firm. In recent years, with scandals, such as Enron, Tyco, Parmalat, among others, resulting in the collapse of firms to the loss of not only stockholders, but debtholders, employees, suppliers, communities, and other parties, regulators, legislators, and academics have struggled with this objective as a solitary objective for managers. This has been particularly the case with hidden accounting information affecting stock market efficiency, such as the case of Enron. With depository institutions' special charters to serve the needs of their communities, the concept of a single objective may be too one-dimensional. Financial managers have been struggling with agency problems and how to encourage ethical behavior in the best interests of the firm, community, regulators, consumers, and other parties that are affected by important decisions made by financial institution managers. Financial institution managers must balance different objectives including those of stockholders, regulators, customers, and employee needs, among others.

Economic Value Added (EVA) as a Goal for Risk-Profitability Management

Given concerns by financial institutions for managing the long-run value for financial institutions, economic value added (EVA) has been widely used by large, publicly traded financial institutions as well as nonfinancial institutions as an overall risk management and profitability measure for the continuing prosperity of a firm. EVA looks at the profitability of a firm after its stockholders or other long-term debtholders and other investors are paid. EVA provides an overall dollar measure of a firm's profit after the cost of the capital employed for all activities is subtracted:

$$\text{EVA} = \text{NOPAT} - (\text{Financial Capital Employed} \times \text{Average Cost of Capital}) \qquad [1.6]$$

NOPAT is the bank's operating profits before any costs paid to long-term investors (and excluding any accounting conventions that misrepresent cash flows). The long-term financial capital (long-term equity and debt capital) supplied for operations times the cost of capital (asarate) is subtracted from NOPAT to get EVA. For a nonfinancial institution, NOPAT typically is earnings before taxes $\times (1 - t)$,

---

27 See O'Hara (1983). For a discussion of the origin of the agency relationship between governments and commercial banks, see Shull (1984).

where t is the firm's marginal tax rate, thus, excluding all interest expenses. However, for a financial institution, short-term interest expenses are a normal part of the financial institution's operations, so NOPAT would typically include short-term interest expenses. So, taking Equation 1.5 for operating earnings for a depository institution and multiplying by $(1 - t)$:

$$\text{NOPAT} = \text{Operating Earnings Before Taxes } (1 - t) = (\text{NII} - \text{Burden} - \text{PLL})(1 - t) \qquad [1.7]$$

For instance, suppose that in 2003 The Manny Bank in Table 1.1 had an average interest rate of 8 percent on its $1,930 million of loans and securities and an average interest rate of 3 percent on its deposits and other short-term borrowings that total $1,849 million. Hence, The Manny Bank has a net interest spread of $ 98.93 million:

$$\text{NII} = \text{Interest Revenue} - \text{Interest Expense} = (\$1,930 \text{ mil.} \times 0.08) - (\$1,849 \times 0.03) = \$98.93 \text{ million}$$

Suppose The Manny Bank also has noninterest expenses of $0.5 million and noninterest revenues of $0.2 million, so its burden (noninterest expenses − noninterest revenues) equals a burden of $0.3 million. It also has a provision for loan losses of $0.1 million and a marginal tax rate of 30 percent. Hence, solving for The Manny Bank's NOPAT using Equation 1.7:

$$\text{NOPAT} = (\text{NII} - \text{Burden} - \text{PLL})(1 - t) = (\$98.93 \text{ mil.} - \$0.3 \text{ mil.} - \$0.1 \text{ mil.})(1 - 0.30)$$
$$= \$68.971 \text{ million}$$

As noted on The Manny Bank's balance sheet on Table 1.1, Manny does not have any long-term debt or preferred stock as capital. It does, however, have equity capital financing including both common stock and retained earnings of $161 million. Suppose the required return for the equity capital is 15 percent. Solving for economic value added (EVA) using Equation 1.6:

$$\text{EVA} = \text{NOPAT} - (\text{Financial Capital Employed} \times \text{Average Cost of Capital})$$
$$= \$68.971 \text{ mil.} - (\$161 \text{ mil.} \times 0.15) = \$68.971 \text{ mil.} - \$24.15 \text{ mil.} = \$ 44.821 \text{ million}$$

Hence, the economic value added for The Manny Bank in 2003 was $44.821 million. This shows a healthy trend. If EVA for The Manny Bank was negative, this would indicate serious problems for the bank. EVA implies that bank managers must generate sufficient revenues to cover both operating expenses and the returns demanded by investors based on the capital allocated for the banks' activities. EVA ensures that managers realize their obligations to stockholders as well as to long-term debt-holders. It also provides a formal mechanism by which to quantify the bank's overall risk structure in terms of the amount of capital allocated and its cost. In addition to providing an overall measure of economic value created by a firm's operations, EVA can be used for individual decisions, such as determining whether different types of bank operations are profitable. It can also be used to allocate equity capital based on the risk of these activities discussed in more detail in later chapters.[28]

Concept Questions

1 Give examples of how technology has changed the role of financial institutions.

2 What type of new risks do financial institutions encounter with technology?

3 Who are the stakeholders, and what are the financial management objectives for financial institutions?

4 Give an example of a corporate governance problem that could lead to a greater likelihood of a financial scandal for a financial institution.

5 How is economic value added (EVA) estimated for a financial institution? What advantages does EVA have as a goal for an organization over other simple performance measures?

28 See Dennis G. Uyemura, Charles C. Kantor, and Justin M. Pettit. "EVA for Banks: Value Creation, Risk Management, and Profitability Measurement." *Bank of America Journal of Applied Corporate Finance*, 9 (Summer 1996), 94–113. They point out that EVA provides advantages by being a "top down process," whereby managers can have risk and return metrics for each of the major lines of business and the drivers that are key to sustaining a high EVA.

Summary

Financial institutions are a unique set of business firms whose assets and liabilities, regulatory restrictions, and economic functions establish them as an important subject of study. Interest in techniques for financial management of these institutions has grown with the vast quantity of assets they control, changes introduced by deregulation in the 1970s and 1980s, and the challenges posed by globalization and the information technologies of the 1990s and 2000s.

Firms classified as financial institutions hold portfolios primarily composed of financial assets, in contrast to the real asset holdings of nonfinancial firms. Institutions are designed to offer intermediary or brokerage services to assist savers in allocating their funds. The services provided by financial institutions reduce transactions and information costs, including search, portfolio selection, monitoring, risk management, and liquidity and maturity intermediation costs to investors. With dramatic changes in information technology, search, information, and monitoring costs have fallen, reducing the monopoly that financial institutions previously held in these areas. These changes have caused some disintermediation (reduction in the use of financial institutions) for these services and increased the number of direct market relationships between many borrowers and lenders. Other roles have increased, however, including risk management for corporate customers and maturity intermediation for consumers, especially through retirement and financial planning. The transaction role of financial institutions has increased with technology, allowing loans to be packaged and traded as securities. Information technology helps financial institutions to assess customer needs and develop and offer a wider array of financial services to satisfy these needs. Corporate governance and operational risk considerations have become more important in the current decade, with a large number of scandals for financial institutions in the early part of the twenty-first century.

Plan of the Book

Part I examines the environment of financial management of financial institutions. Topics include important concepts, regulations, and trends that a financial institution manager needs to recognize and cope with in the changing environment of the twenty-first century. Chapter 2 provides an overview of the role of financial institutions as risk-takers and strategic considerations. Chapter 3 profiles the regulatory environment, with an appendix on the operations of the Federal Reserve System and international policy coordination.

Part II provides an understanding of the financial statements of depository institutions, which can be applied to other types of financial institutions, as well. Chapter 4 presents performance and risk analysis for depository institutions. Chapter 5 studies credit unions and thrifts and compares the performance of the three types of depository institutions. Chapter 6 covers capital management, and Chapter 7 examines changes with technology including securitization, structured finance, Internet banking, and the role of financial institutions in E-commerce.

Part III examines interest rate risk measurement in Chapters 8 to 10 and hedging with derivatives in Chapters 11 and 12.

Part IV provides an overview of special problems facing depository institutions including credit risk management in Chapter 13, liquidity and securities portfolio management in Chapter 14, and deposit and liability management in Chapter 15.

Part V examines other types of financial institutions and their trends, financial analysis, and particular management problems. Chapter 16 examines insurance companies, Chapter 17 investment banks, retail securities firms, and venture capital firms, Chapter 18 mutual fund and pension funds, and Chapter 19 finance companies, financial holding companies, merger considerations, and some international management issues.

Questions

1. What are your favorite and least favorite financial institutions that you do business with? List all the financial institutions that you have relationships with. How did you choose these institutions?
2. Why do you think so many financial institution mergers occurred in the last two decades? Why are consumers concerned about these mergers?
3. Give an example of a real physical asset and a financial asset. How do they differ? What types of assets and liabilities do financial institutions have compared with most businesses? Why do financial companies have such higher financial leverage than nonfinancial firms?
4. Give a specific of each of the following types of financial institutions: (a) depository institutions, (b) finance companies, (c) contractual intermediaries, (d) investment companies (mutual funds), and securities firms. Which institutions hold the most closely matched maturities of their assets and liabilities?

5. Why are insurance companies and pension fund companies called contractual institutions? What type of liabilities and assets do they have? How do contractual institutions have a better maturity match of assets and liabilities than depository institutions?

6. Give some examples of services that financial institutions provide as financial intermediaries. How does this make an economy more efficient rather than only having direct versus indirect financial intermediation?

7. What services do securities provide? What services do investment companies provide? How do their services benefit investors?

8. Financial agreements typically require financial contracts characterized by information asymmetry. What is information asymmetry? How might an agreement such as an automobile or mortgage loan involve asymmetric information? How does asymmetric information affect the risk position of the investor (lender)?

9. What are a depository institution's NIM, burden, and PLL? Explain how each of these factors is important in producing profits for a depository institution. Why has the burden become more important in recent years?

10. How does the separation of ownership and management complicate the theory of the firm? Give an example of expense preference behavior on the part of a manager. Do you think stockownership or performance-based compensation increases or reduces risky managerial behavior? Explain why or why not. With recent financial scandals, give an example where a financial manager acted in his or her own interests instead of those of other stakeholders.

11. Give an example of a monitoring cost for managers in a large commercial bank. What is the trade-off between monitoring costs incurred by owners and the degree of discretion allowed to managers?

12. Find an article on a poorly performing financial firm and one with good performance. What factors led to the difference in performance?

13. In addition to owners, what important groups influence the asset/liability management objectives pursued by financial institutions? Give an example of a situation in which the objectives of regulators and those of owners might conflict.

14. Discuss the societal concerns with banking for the unbanked. What does the Community Reinvestment Act require of banks? What are pawnshops, and why have they grown?

15. Do you think maximizing stockholders' wealth is the appropriate goal for a bank? Explain why or why not. What other objectives might a bank have? What is economic value added and how is it used?

Selected References

Benston, George J., and Clifford W. Smith, Jr. "A Transactions Cost Approach to the Theory of Financial Intermediation." *Journal of Finance* 31 (May 1976), 215–231.

Berlin, Mitchell. "Bank Loans and Marketable Securities: How Do Financial Contracts Control Borrowing Firms?" *Business Review*, Federal Reserve Bank of Philadelphia (July/August 1987), 9–18.

Cebenoyan, A. Sinan, Elizabeth S. Cooperman, and Charles A. Register. "Ownership Structure, Charter Value and Risk-Taking Behavior for Thrifts." *Financial Management*, Vol. 28, No. 1 (Spring 1999), 43–60.

Cebenoyan, A. Sinan, Elizabeth S. Cooperman, Charles A. Register, and Sylvia C. Hudgins. "The Relative Efficiency of Stock versus Mutual S&Ls: A Stochastic Cost Frontier Approach." *Journal of Financial Services Research* (1993). 151–170.

Cole, Rebel A., and Robert A. Eisenbeis. "The Role of Principal–Agent Conflicts in the 1980s Thrift Crisis." Federal Reserve Board, Finance and Economics Discussion Series, Division of Research and Statistics Division of Monetary Affairs, Working Paper 95–27, 1996.

Cordell, L. R., G. D. MacDonald, and M. E. Wohar. "Corporate Ownership and the Thrift Crisis." Research Report No. 93-01, Office of Thrift Supervision Research Report, January 1993.

Diamond, Douglas W. "Financial Intermediation and Delegated Monitoring." *Review of Economic Studies* 51 (July 1984), 393–414.

Edwards, Franklin R. "Managerial Objectives in Regulated Industries: Expense-Preference Behavior in Banking." *Journal of Political Economy* 85 (February 1977), 147–162.

Esty, Benjamin C. "A Case Study of Organization Form and Risk Shifting in the Savings & Loan Industry." *Journal of Financial Economics* (April 1997), 57–76.

Fisher, Irving. *The Theory of Interest.* New York: Macmillan, 1930.

Gorton, Gary, and George Pennacchi. "Financial Intermediaries and Liquidity Creation." *Journal of Finance* 45 (March 1990), 49–71.

Gorton, Gary, and Richard Rosen. "Corporate Control, Portfolio Choice, and the Decline of Banking." *Journal of Finance* 50 (December 1995), 1377–1420.

Gup, Benton E. *Bank Fraud: Exposing the Hidden Threat to Financial Institutions.* Rolling Meadows, IL: Bankers Publishing, 1990.

Hannan, Timothy H., and Ferdinand Mavinga. "Expense Preference and Managerial Control: The Case of the Banking Firm." *The Bell Journal of Economics* 11 (Autumn 1980), 671–682.

Haubrich, Joseph G. "Financial Intermediation: Delegated Monitoring and Long-Term Relationships." *Journal of Banking and Finance* 13 (March 1989), 9–20.

Hayashi, Fumiko, Richard Sullivan, and Stuart E. Weiner. *A Guide to the ATM and Debit Card Industry.* Kansas City, Missouri: Payment System Research Department, Federal Reserve Bank of Kansas City, 2003.

Hirschleifer, Jack. "On the Theory of Optimal Investment Decision." *Journal of Political Economy* 67 (August 1958), 329–352.

———. "Investment Decision under Uncertainty: Choice Theoretic Approaches." *Quarterly Journal of Economics* 79 (November 1965), 509–536.

Hubbard, R. Glenn, and Darius Palia. "Executive Pay and Performance: Evidence from the U.S. Banking Industry," NBER Working Paper, No. 4704, April 1994.

Jensen, Michael C., and William H. Meckling. "Theory of the Firm: Managerial Behavior, Agency Costs, and Ownership Structure." *Journal of Financial Economics* 3 (1976), 305–360.

Mester, Loretta. "Efficiency in the Savings and Loan Industry." *Journal of Banking and Finance* 17 (April 1993).

Mester, Loretta J. "Owners versus Managers: Who Controls the Bank?" *Business Review,* Federal Reserve Bank of Philadelphia (May/June 1989), 13–22.

O'Hara, Maureen. "Financial Contracts and International Lending." *Journal of Banking and Finance* 14 (1990), 11–31.

Ramo, Joshua Cooper, "The Big Bank Theory and What It Says about the Future of Money." *Time,* April 27, 1998, pp. 47–57.

Sealey, C. W. "Valuation, Capital Structure, and Shareholder Unanimity for Depository Financial Intermediaries." *Journal of Finance* 38 (June 1983), 857–871.

Seward, James K. "Corporate Financial Policy and the Theory of Financial Intermediation." *Journal of Finance* 45 (June 1990), 351–377.

Shull, Bernard. "The Separation of Banking and Commerce: An Historical Perspective." *Proceedings of a Conference on Bank Structure and Competition.* Chicago: Federal Reserve Bank of Chicago, 1984, 63–78.

Smith, Roy C. *The Global Bankers.* New York: Truman Talley Books/Plume, 1990.

Snider, Helen K. "CEO Pay and Firm Performance: Theory vs. Practice." *Financial Markets, Institutions, and Instruments,* Vol. 3, No. 5 (December 1994), New York University Salomon Center, Cambridge, MA: Blackwell Publishers.

Sfiridis, James M., and Kenneth N. Daniels. "The Relative Cost Efficiency of Stock versus Mutual Thrifts: A Bayesian Approach." *The Financial Review,* Vol. 39, No. 1 (February 2004), 153–178.

Towey, Richard E. "Money Creation and the Theory of the Banking Firm." *Journal of Finance* 29 (March 1974), 57–72.

Williamson, Oliver. "Managerial Discretion and Business Behavior." *American Economic Review* 53 (December 1963), 1032–1067.

Williamson, Stephen D. "Recent Developments in Modeling Financial Intermediation." *Quarterly Review,* Federal Reserve Bank of Minneapolis (Summer 1987), 19–29.

Woerheide, Walter J. *The Savings and Loan Industry: Current Problems and Possible Solutions.* Westport, CT: Quorum Books, 1984.

internet *exercise*

SHORT INVESTIGATIVE PAPER EXERCISE USING INFORMATION FROM THE INTERNET

Look up the Enron scandal on the Web (search at *http://www.google.com*). Look, particularly, at FT.com (the *Financial Times, http://www.ft.com,* has free access to good articles on Enron). Write a short paper on financial institutions involved in the scandal and give your opinion of these institutions as agents or victims in the scandal.

OTHER USEFUL SITES FOR FINANCIAL INSTITUTION DATA

Federal Financial Institutions Examination Council

http://www.ffiec.gov

Federal Deposit Insurance Corporation

http://www.fdic.gov

Board of Governors of the Federal Reserve System

http://www.federalreserve.gov

Office of the Comptroller of the Currency

http://www.occ.treas.gov/

Office of Thrift Supervision

http://www.ots.treas.gov

National Credit Union Administration

http://www.ncua.gov/

Securities and Exchange Commission

http://www.sec.gov

Ginnie Mae

http://www.ginniemae.gov

Fannie Mae

http://www.fanniemae.com

Freddie Mac

http://www.freddiemac.com

2

Financial Institutions as Risk-Takers—Strategic Considerations

"The business of banking involves taking and managing risks . . . changes in banking and financial markets have increased the complexity of banking risks. And the position of banks in modern economies has made the management of banking risks ever more important to financial stability and economic growth."

"Capital Standards for Banks: The Evolving Basel Accord." Federal Reserve Bulletin, *Vol. 89, No. 9, September 2003, 1 (adopted from testimony presented by Federal Reserve Board Vice Chairman Roger W. Ferguson, Jr., to House and Senate Committees on Banking and Financial Services, June 18–19, 2003).*

I n recent years, the role of financial institutions as risk intermediaries has come into greater play in discussions of their role in an economy, as noted in the chapter opening quotes. In turn, serving as risk-taking intermediaries, financial institutions need to strategically manage their own risks. As discussed in Chapter 1, financial institutions provide a number of different economic functions, and many of these roles result in a transferring of risk to financial institutions. For instance, banks take on roles of managing credit and liquidity and maturity intermediation risks, as well as managing operations and technology, which entail their own particular operational risks. As noted in the chapter opening quotes, taking on risks is part of the business of all types of financial services firms, and financial institutions lose millions of dollars each year because of poor risk management. This chapter focuses on an overview of the different types of risk that financial institutions face and introduces strategic management choices. Risks need to be considered in a portfolio framework to ensure that:

1. An adequate return is generated for the amount of risk taken on;
2. Adequate capital is kept to protect for losses;

After completing this chapter, you will be able to:

1 Understand risks of financial institution operations.
2 See how risks can be viewed and measured from a portfolio and strategic framework.
3 Explain diversification strategies of some banks to reduce earnings volatility.
4 Understand different aspects of managing major risks including credit risk, interest rate risk, liquidity risk, operational risk, and off-balance-sheet risks.
5 Understand ratios used to measure different types of risk in financial analysis.

3. The financial institution is not taking on overall excessive risk; and
4. Overall risk is diversified where possible.

The amount of risk that an institution takes on also depends on the goals and tolerance for risk for the owners and other relevant stakeholders of an institution. More detailed coverage of types of risk management for different types of financial institutions follows in particular chapters throughout the text.

Defining Risk

As noted by Christopher Marshall in a recent professional text, *Measuring and Managing Operational Risks in Financial Institutions,* "Risk can be broadly defined as the potential for events or ongoing trends to cause future losses or fluctuations in future income." He notes that the risks faced by most financial services institutions include market, credit, strategic, and operational risks, where: (1) credit risks "are fluctuations in net income or net asset values that result from a particular type of external event—the default of a counterparty, supplier, or borrower;" (2) strategic risks are "long-term environmental changes that can affect how a business adds value to its stakeholders;" and (3) operational risk is "the potential for any disruption in the firm's operational processes."[1] Within these broad categories are numerous other types of risk discussed in the following sections. Generally, risk is defined in finance theory as uncertainty that creates variability or volatility in returns, with two major types of risk, **firm-specific risk,** which involves uncertainty associated with operations for specific firms, and **systematic risk,** uncertainty affecting the whole economy and market. Financial services firms face both types of risk, and as engines of the economy, they are particularly affected by systemic factors, such as Federal Reserve Board policies, economic conditions, interest rate movements, and other factors that affect the entire economy.

The Risk/Return Positioning of Banks and Other Financial Institutions

Major principles in the theory of finance are **risk and return** and **portfolio theory.** Investors should be adequately compensated for the risks that they take on. Also, under portfolio theory, unsystematic risk can be reduced by diversification. Hence, the correlations between different investments should be examined. With diversification, the volatility of a portfolio's return falls, and investors will get the

1 See Marshall (2000), 23–25.

highest expected level of return for any given level of risk. Similarly, financial institutions need to establish portfolio strategies to maximize the returns to owners and minimize risk. Financial institutions strategically determine which group of risks they will take on. For instance, if a bank has low credit risk, it can take on more capital risk (hold a lower equity-to-assets ratios) than a bank with greater credit risk. Since many financial institutions also have public policy goals and many are heavily regulated, they also need to conform to regulations, including regulations for risk-based capital ratios that entail holding greater capital to cover potential losses on more risky assets.

With a growing number of new financial instruments and innovations with different risk/reward characteristics, regulators have been concerned about institutions' capacity to take on greater risk and the need for internal monitoring systems and for an understanding of their risk management capabilities. Similarly, new capital requirements for very large international banks under Basel II require this.[2]

Different Types of Risks in the Nature of Financial Institution Operations

Most financial institutions have a great degree of financial risk in their normal operations including **high financial leverage** (low equity-to-asset ratios) and, hence, **capital risk** (the risk of not being able to cover losses against equity and becoming insolvent), discussed further in Chapter 6. Also, the majority of their financial assets are financial. For many financial institutions, these financial assets also generally tend to be long-term or intermediate-term assets that are financed by short-term debt. Hence, by the nature of their operations they have significant **credit risk** (the risk of default on financial assets), **reinvestment/refinancing interest rate risk** (the risk of rates on interest revenues and interest expenses not moving together), and **market risk** (a risk of a fall in the value of financial assets and the market value of equity) with unfavorable interest rate or equity market changes. Other risks are also part of their normal operations including **liquidity risk,** the risk of not being able to meet upcoming obligations, particularly for depository institutions, with potential deposit withdrawals.

Financial institutions typically have **high financial leverage** but **low operating leverage** (a low percentage of fixed assets to total assets and, hence, fixed capital operating expenses). With large investments in technology, operating leverage has increased for some institutions, as has the need to spread costs over a large volume of transactions to cover these costs. The **technology risk** and other **operational risk** are also significant. For instance, depository institutions that clear billions of checks each day in their role in the payments system or carry on large online banking operations face significant technology and operational risk every day. Similarly, securities firms operating back-office security clearing operations with millions of dollars of security transactions cleared each day face significant operational risk. Given the nature of financial institution operations, there is serious **fraud and criminal risk** as well, which has grown greater with the advent of Internet transactions, offering new innovations for criminals. With globalization, large financial institutions operating in many different countries, or servicing customers that do, face additional risks including **foreign exchange risk** (the risk of loss on foreign exchange transactions), **country or sovereign risk** (the risk of expropriation), and **cultural risks,** the risk of violating cultural norms or mores.

Ethical or reputational and regulatory risks exist as well, such as in the Enron scandal, where large financial institutions assisted corporations to hide their liabilities in complex off-balance-sheet schemes. In addition to the U.S. Securities and Exchange Commission's (SEC) prosecution for violations and having to pay large fines, many financial institutions seriously damaged their reputations. Since financial institutions differentiate themselves by their reputations, such damage can lead to loss of consumer confidence, large financial losses, and even a firm's demise.

Similarly, mutual fund companies that engaged in illegal after-market trading in addition to SEC prosecution lost the confidence of investors, who withdrew millions of dollars. With the passage of the **Sarbanes-Oxley Act (SOA)** in 2002, mentioned in Chapter 1, there has been greater concern by corporations about **regulatory risks.** Under SOA, CEOs and CFOs of publicly traded firms must certify financial statements and are responsible for adequate internal control and independence of auditing committees, among other requirements. These include conflict of interest rules for research analysts and more timely disclosure of material changes in financial conditions for investment bankers underwriting issues. In a recent survey by PricewaterhouseCoopers, chief executives of global corporations

---

2　See "Capital Standards for Banks: The Evolving Basel Accord." *Federal Reserve Bulletin*, Vol. 89, No. 9 (September 2003), 1 (adopted from testimony presented by Federal Reserve Board Vice Chairman Roger W. Ferguson, Jr., to House and Senate Committees on Banking and Financial Services, June 18–19, 2003).

listed the risks that posed a serious threat to the growth of their businesses as first **regulation risk,** followed by **exchange rate risk, risk of terrorism, reputation risk, and corporate governance.**[3]

The many different types of risks may seem overwhelming, but financial services firms generally choose among risks based on their goals and strategic focus and attempt to mitigate the risks that they do have. As part of a financial institution's mission statement and financial objectives, a firm decides "who we are," and what type of customers it will serve and the types of risks it will undertake.

Risks should also be managed in a portfolio context. Many financial institutions have diversified into new areas including activities to increase noninterest revenues that are off-balance-sheet, such as issuing letters of credit that guarantee bond or other security issues. Such activities create another type of risk, **off-balance-sheet risks.** Most off-balance-sheet risks are **contingent risks,** risks that don't usually—but could possibly—occur, given an event. For instance, if a bank issues a **letter of credit** backing the obligation of a corporate borrower, it will only have to make good on its guarantee (contingent claim) in the event of a default by the corporation.

Diversification into Less Correlated Activities: An Illustration

Thinking of risks from a portfolio context, diversification into activities that are not correlated with other financial institution activities can reduce the overall volatility of a financial institution's earnings, such as new enterprises that produce fee income (noninterest revenue). For instance, National City Corporation (NCC), the largest Ohio-based holding company, with 1,100 branches in Illinois, Indiana, Kentucky, Michigan, Ohio, and Pennsylvania, decided to engage in a fee-income strategy in 1980 that would offset the volatility associated with its traditional banking and also offer cross-selling opportunities. From 1980 to 1990, NCC doubled its percentage of fee income as a percentage of revenues, from 20 percent to 40 percent. The firm gained stability, reducing its risk in terms of lower earnings volatility. NCC's strategic plan diversified into three primary fee-income areas: (1) an item processing division, (2) a trust operation, and (3) a mortgage-servicing division. The first, National City Processing, had the largest growth in fee income, handling about 70 percent of the receivables for the airline industry (payments from customers to travel agents and airlines). It also provided merchant bank-card services; retail lockbox processing; and check guarantee, verification, and collection services. In 2004, NCC's activities included an even more diverse portfolio of traditional lending, investment banking, asset management, trust services, lending, and leasing.[4]

Basel II and the Regulatory Need for Risk Measurement and Risk Management Techniques

Recognizing that risks need to be managed as a portfolio, financial institutions have improved their risk measurement and management techniques, have developed internal risk management capabilities, and continue to do so, although as noted in the opening quote, many financial institutions still have not implemented operational risk programs. The Basel Committee on Banking Supervision (BCBS) for the Bank of International Settlements (BIS), consisting of regulators of central banks from major countries, regulates large international banks, setting international capital regulations (regulations for equity and other capital requirements) known as the Basel Accord (for Basel, Switzerland). The BCBS has recently proposed the **New Basel Capital Accord,** or **Basel II,** to help reduce international banking risk and create a level playing field with uniform capital standards. Basel II's goals are to (1) **improve risk measurement and management;** (2) **link, to the extent possible, the amount of required capital to the amount of risk taken;** (3) **further focus the supervisor-bank dialogue on the measurement and management of risk and the connection between risk and capital;** and (4) **increase the transparency of bank risk-taking** to the customers and counterparties that ultimately fund—and hence share—these risk positions. Basel II (discussed in more detail in Chapter 6) creates a requirement for greater risk assessment by very large international banks for not only managing credit risk but also for managing operational risks.[5]

---

3 See Floyd Norris. "Too Much Regulation? Corporate Bosses Sing the Sarbanes-Oxley Blues." *New York Times* (January 23, 2004), C1.

4 See William R. Robertson. "The Fee-Income Phenomenon." *Bank Management* 70 (July/August 1994), 13–18; National City Corporation (NCC) Website *(http://www.nationalcity.com)*; and the report on NCC on Hoover's Online *(http://www.hoovers.com)*.

5 See *http://www.bis.org.*

1 Think of a financial institution that you use frequently. What types of risk as discussed in the preceding sections does that institution have to manage?

2 Which types of risks are securities firms, insurance firms, banks, mutual funds, and savings institutions more likely to have?

3 What is Basel II? What is the Sarbanes-Oxley Act? Why would corporations be concerned about regulatory risk?

4 Why are diversification and a portfolio framework for risk-taking strategies and risk measurement important?

Financial Holding Companies as a Means for Diversification

The **Financial Services Modernization Act of 1999,** discussed in more detail in Chapter 3, allows new **financial holding companies (FHCs)** in the United States to combine investment banking and securities activities, insurance, and commercial banking activities under a single umbrella. With the variety of activities, some financial services firms have hoped to achieve considerable diversification. At the same time, U.S. regulators have also been concerned about an increase in the risk of financial services firms entering into new nonbank activities and greater difficulties in supervising and monitoring the risk of these huge FHCs.

The following sections provide an overview of major risks and their management issues for financial institutions. Later chapters discuss different aspects of managing these risks in more depth.

Credit Risk

Credit risk management is one of the most important aspects of management for financial institutions, particularly for banks and other depository institutions. Banks in their intermediary role take on the credit risk that savers would otherwise experience; a necessary risk inherent in banking. Similarly, increasingly risky loans should pay progressively higher loan rates to compensate for this risk. If a bank has a loan portfolio composed of risky loans, but it earns lower rates than its peers, the bank is not properly pricing its loans. Financial assets, as promises to be repaid in the future, have the risk that this promise will not be kept. In addition to the risk of default, there is the risk of a change in the credit ratings given by credit agencies on the bonds that financial institutions hold, which results in a fall in the bonds' value.

As credit intermediaries, financial institutions are experts in collecting information evaluating the risk of borrowers and determining whether borrowers are creditworthy and in monitoring their borrowers to ensure that there are no problems with later repayment. Often borrower relationships help facilitate this monitoring, with community banks (less than $1 billion in assets) having lower loan loss rates on average than larger institutions, holding other factors constant, as shown in Panel A of Figure 2.1. Lenders are also experts in classifying loans as excellent, good, average, or substandard or other types of categories. They price loans to include risk premiums to compensate for a loan's future risk of default, require collateral as a secondary source of repayment, set restrictive covenants to prevent a borrower from taking on additional risk, and structure loans to facilitate the repayment of the loan. Many lenders specialize in lending to particular industries, since screening, monitoring, and structuring requires expertise in understanding an industry and the specific economic and competitive conditions that borrowers in each industry face. This specialization increases lenders' ability to originate and monitor specialized types of loans but also limits their ability to diversify their overall loan portfolio. Similarly, regional lenders often can perform better loan underwriting by knowing the industries and customers in their region better. However, regional recessions often occur, putting these lenders at greater risk. Figure 2.1, Panel B shows the percentage of nonpaying, **noncurrent assets** and **other real estate owned (repossessed collateral) to assets** for different regions in 2003. **Noncurrent assets** are financial assets not current on payments and **other real estate owned (OREO)** includes property taken (as previous collateral) for unpaid loans, listed at market value. Problem banks have large OREO accounts. The percentage of noncurrent assets and OREO is very different across regions, reflecting different regional conditions.

figure **2.1** LOAN QUALITY RATIOS OVER TIME AND BY GEOGRAPHICAL REGIONS

PANEL A: QUARTERLY NET CHARGE-OFF RATES BY ASSET SIZE, 1993–2003

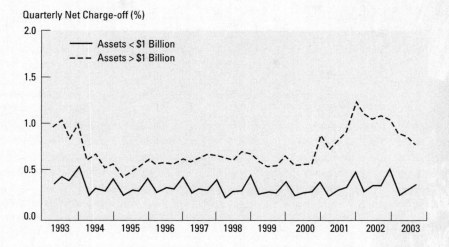

PANEL B: CONDITION RATIOS BY GEOGRAPHICAL REGIONS, NONCURRENT ASSETS PLUS OTHER REAL ESTATE OWNED TO ASSETS, SEPTEMBER 30, 2003

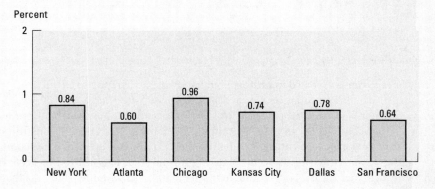

Source: FDIC Quarterly Banking Profile, QBP Graph Book, *January 1, 2004* (http://www2.fdic.gov/qbp/grgraph.asp).

Risk of Different Types of Loans

Loans and securities that are longer-term generally have greater default risk. Some types of loans have more credit risk than others. Accordingly, more risky loans entail different terms and protections. For instance, commercial real estate loans entail greater risk, since repayment may depend on the success of the construction being completed and on occupancy rates once such an enterprise as a shopping mall or apartment building is completed. Hence, these loans are structured to reduce a bank's risk by including up-front fees, surety bonds to ensure completion, and a commitment for another long-term lender, such as an insurance company to take over the loan once the construction is completed. Table 2.1 shows different net charge-offs (loan losses less any recoveries) for different types of loans over time for different types of lenders. Credit card consumer loan lenders had the highest net charge-off percentages, with a high of 6.07 percent in 2002. Home mortgage loans generally have steady payments on average and entail lower net charge-offs. During recessions loan losses rise, and during expansions loan losses generally decline. For instance, during the recessionary years of 1990 and 1991, the net charge-off percentage for commercial loan lenders peaked at 1.21 percent compared with only half a percent in 2003.

table **2.1** NET CHARGE-OFFS AS A PERCENTAGE OF AVERAGE LOANS AND LEASES BY ASSET CONCENTRATION GROUP

(Years to Date for the First Three Quarters [End of September] Each Year)

Year	International Banks	Agricultural Banks	Credit Card Lenders	Commercial Lenders	Mortgage Lenders	Consumer Lenders
2003	1.53	0.24	5.17	0.52	0.19	1.42
2002	1.78	0.28	6.07	0.87	0.16	1.12
2001	0.83	0.30	4.02	0.61	0.15	1.18
2000	0.44	0.18	3.68	0.40	0.12	0.20
1999	0.55	0.20	3.87	0.37	0.12	0.51
1998	0.80	0.20	4.41	0.33	0.18	0.86
1997	0.23	0.18	4.78	0.34	0.21	0.73
1996	0.33	0.22	4.08	0.31	0.28	0.70
1995	0.33	0.14	3.10	0.33	0.27	0.50
1994	0.83	0.12	3.05	0.41	0.44	0.43
1993	1.14	0.17	3.84	0.71	0.55	0.53
1992	1.88	0.32	4.80	0.88	0.48	0.80
1991	2.47	0.32	4.81	1.21	0.48	0.80
1990	2.38	0.34	3.82	1.04	0.39	0.73

Source: FDIC Quarterly Banking Profile, QBP Graph Book, *January 1, 2004* (http://www2.fdic.gov/qbp/grgraph.asp).

Credit Risk Ratios

Typical credit risk measures reported in **uniform bank performance reports (UBPR),** found on the Federal Financial Institutions Examination Council's (FFIEC) Website *(http://www.ffiec.gov)* discussed in more detail in Chapter 4, include the percentage of net losses and also how well banks provision against net losses (much like a bad debt reserve for a nonfinancial company). Depository institution managers take a **provision against expected future loan losses** as an expense on their income statements. As discussed in Chapter 1, this provision is accumulated in a total **loan loss allowance** account (deducted from gross loans to get net loans). **Nonaccrual loans** are loans with past due payments that are not currently accruing interest. Typical credit risk ratios for a depository institution include the following:

Net Loans and Leases to Total Assets

Net Charge-offs to Total Loans and Leases

Loan Loss Provision to Average Total Loans

Loan Loss Allowance to Nonaccrual Loans

Earnings Coverage to Net Loss

Net Loss to Average Loans and Leases

Noncurrent Assets plus OREO to Assets

Loan Loss Allowance to Total Loans

Loan Loss Allowance to Net Loss

Growth Rate in Loans and Leases

Financial analysis using these and other financial ratios will be discussed in Chapter 4. The *"to"* implies division, for example, Net Loans and Leases is divided by Total Assets, Net Charge-offs is divided by Total Loans and Leases, and so on. **The higher the net losses or net charge-offs or noncurrent assets and OREO, the more risk a financial institution has. The higher the loan loss provision and loan loss allowance to assets, and the higher the earnings to net losses (net income / net loss), the larger the protection that a bank has to cover future losses.** Larger growth rates in loans and leases and the larger percentage of loans held to assets also indicate greater credit risk. Thus, higher ratios for provisions for loan losses and loan loss allowances to total loans would be expected for that financial institution. The composition of loans (percent of each type of loan) also reveals the degree of a financial institution's risk, since commercial real estate loans, commercial loans, consumer loans, and home mortgage loans typically have more or less risk of loan losses in that order.

Banks generally classify loans into categories based on their quality per credit analysis including high quality AAA loans to very risky unrated loans. Classifications are often made using letters or corresponding high to low numbers, such as ratings of 1 to 10. Often for large publicly traded borrowers, loan quality is mapped with corresponding bond credit ratings by rating agencies.

Credit Review Process, Conflicts of Interest, and Lender Compensation

The credit review process is an important way for lenders to learn from previous mistakes and provides checks and balances to ensure that bank lending policies are abided by and lending decisions aren't clouded by relationships between loan officers and borrowers. Proper compensation for loan officers is also critical to reduce lending risks. In the late 1980s and early 1990s, many banks gave lenders bonuses for the number and size of loans they made. After loans were made, a separate division was in charge of monitoring and working out problem loans. Hence, lenders did not find out about their mistakes and were encouraged to make loans regardless of their quality. With huge loan losses incurred by many banks using these policies, financial institutions abandoned bonus policies based on the volume of loans. They implemented new policies that compensated lenders on the quality of their loans as well. Lenders were also encouraged to continue to contact borrowers whose loans they underwrote. Some institutions mandated that lenders be part of the credit review and monitoring process and help with workout arrangements if necessary for the loans they made that went bad.

Credit Models and Credit Derivatives

Credit scoring and credit models to measure an institution's overall credit risk have been developed and more widely used in recent years. Credit scoring models use statistical models to provide a score for a borrower, putting the borrower in a category of risk based on financial ratios or other information. Credit risk models, such as the **KMV Credit Monitor Model** to monitor an institution's overall exposure to credit risk are also discussed in more detail in Chapter 13. **Credit derivatives,** tools that transfer credit risk from one party to another, have also been developed to help institutions hedge against credit risk and are discussed in Chapter 12.[6]

Credit Culture

As noted by Caouette, Altman, and Narayanan (1998) in discussing the management of credit risk, from a strategic perspective, senior managers need to "establish a comfort zone for risk taking" that everyone in an organization understands and will keep to, including the amount of losses it will tolerate. In some cases they note in some businesses, such as trading activities, for instance, " [b]usinesses can learn to be comfortable—and profitable—with levels of risk that may seem high to outsiders."[7] Hence, executives of financial institutions must decide on the risk/return profile that should pervade throughout their organization. Banks and insurance firms have often had a conservative credit culture, while investment banks have had an aggressive risk-taking culture, although this depends on the particular firm. With mergers of banks and insurance firms, there have been cultural clashes and ultimately divestments, such as FleetBoston's closure of its securities firm, Robertson Stevens, and General Electric Financial Services' divestment of its security subsidiary, Kidder Peabody.

Caouette, Altman, and Narayanan (1998) note that credit cultures often begin with very rigorous screening and hiring processes, a formal mentoring system, and rewards for open discussion and communication. They point out as an example Banc One, a super-regional bank holding company that encompassed a strong community culture that encouraged and rewarded employees to reveal problems right away. Banc One tried to limit large loan exposures to individual companies and industries to avoid what they note as "event risk." When exposures became more than a certain size, loans or portions of loans would be sold or syndicated to other larger banks.[8]

Diversification of Credit Risk in Loan Portfolios

Diversification in lending is also a key to reducing the credit risk of an institution's portfolio of loans, since certain regions or industries may be particularly hard hit by recessions. In the early 1990s, for

---

6 Smithson (2003); and Glantz (2002) for more detailed discussion of these models and credit derivatives.

7 See Caouette, Altman, and Narayanan (1998), Chapter 2, "Credit Culture," 23–29.

8 Ibid.

Concept Questions

1. Why is credit risk a critical risk for depository institutions? Which types of lenders (shown in Table 2.1) have the most credit risk? Why does credit risk increase during recessions?

2. Why do community banks (with less than $1 billion in assets) on average tend to have lower credit risk ratios than larger banks (with greater than $1 billion in assets)?

3. Summarize the basic types of credit risk ratios. Why would banks with a larger percentage of loans and higher loan growth rates have greater credit risk? Why would banks with larger percentage of loans be expected to have higher loan loss provision or loan loss allowance to total loan ratios?

4. Why is it important for lenders and others not involved in making a loan to be part of the credit review process? Why is the type of compensation a lender receives important?

5. Why is diversification of a bank's credit risk portfolio important? Are bank's able to diversify their regional or industry-specific credit risk exposure? Explain why or why not.

instance, a large number of loan defaults and both bank and insurance firm failures were associated with commercial real estate loans in New England, with a plunge in commercial real estate prices. Similarly, in the early 2000s, the sudden drop in the technology sector resulted in loan losses in that sector. For banks with diversified loan portfolios, problems were less severe. For niche or regional banks, diversification may be more difficult. However, syndications and loan sales (where financial institutions pass on part or all of their loans to other financial institutions to reduce their total risk exposure or sell and buy loans from other financial institutions to achieve better geographical or industrywide diversification) provide opportunities for diversification. Securitization, mentioned in Chapter 1, is another method of diversification, where loans are pooled together as a portfolio and taken off-balance-sheet and turned into pass-through securities, where investors receive a share of the interest and principal payments on the loans.

For capital requirements, in the past regulators have not considered the diversification or correlation of different types of loans in a bank's portfolios. Under the proposed Basel II (discussed in more detail in Chapter 6), however, for very large U.S. international banks, regulators will allow an advanced internal ratings-based (A-IRB) capital requirement that allows capital to be held based on credit risk disclosures for five distinct portfolio exposures including corporate, equities, retail mortgages, retail nonmortgage with revolving exposures, and other nonmortgage retail. Hence, for very large banks, regulatory considerations are evolving toward looking at portfolio risk exposures at least within different lines of activities.

Interest Rate and Market Risk

Reinvestment and Market Risk

In addition to credit risk, by holding financial assets and liabilities of different maturities, financial institutions are subject to considerable interest rate risk and market risk. These, the measurement of interest rate risk, and ways to reduce or hedge this risk will be discussed in greater detail in later chapters. As an overview, basically, there are two types of interest rate risk: (1) what is often called **reinvestment risk or refinancing risk,** the risk of rates falling and having to reinvest maturing cash flows from securities or loans at a lower interest rate; and (2) **price or market value risk,** the risk of rates rising and having a loss in value for fixed rate loans or securities that an investor holds.

Hence, both falling and rising interest rates have their risks, depending on the nature of a financial institution's balance sheet and operations. For instance, most depository institutions benefit from falling interest rates and lower interest expense, but they are also hurt when long-term borrowers refinance their loans, such as home mortgages, at significantly lower rates when rates fall dramatically, therefore reducing interest revenues on assets, which is refinancing or **prepayment risk.** Similarly, when mutual fund or insurance fund managers invest new incoming funds in fixed-income securities, they risk falling rates, which is the **reinvestment risk** of having to invest securities at lower rates, producing lower interest revenues. On the other hand, with rates rising, the value of fixed rate bonds in a mutual fund or insurance fund's portfolio will fall, resulting in losses if these bonds must be sold prior to maturity, which is **price or market value risk.**

Interest Rate Risk for Depository Institutions

Repricing or Funding Gaps

For financial institutions, the overall effect of an interest rate change in their **net interest spread (interest revenues − interest expenses)** and **net interest margins (NIMs;** net interest spread/interest-earning assets), or sometimes for simplicity (net interest spread/total assets), depends on the composition of assets and liabilities on their balance sheets. The effect of relative changes in rates on interest revenue (IR) and interest expense (IE) and, hence, an institution's NIM, depend on the composition or mix of a bank's assets and liabilities and the interest sensitivity of these to a change in rates. If a bank holds matched fixed rate assets and liabilities, IR and IE, then its NIM will change very little. However, if its assets or liabilities are repricable (rate-sensitive) their rates will change with a change in rates. **Repricable (rate-sensitive) assets** include short-term and maturing securities and loans along with variable rate loans. **Repricable (rate-sensitive) liabilities** include short-term deposits and other maturing liabilities. The relationship between repricable assets and liabilities for any given time period is called a bank's **repricing or funding gap:**

$$\text{Repricing or Funding Gap} = \text{Repricable Assets} - \text{Repricable Liabilities} \qquad [2.1]$$

A larger gap (negative or positive) indicates increasing interest rate risk (volatility in NIM) with a change in interest rates.

To illustrate the effect of a bank's funding gap on its net interest income (NII), suppose you are a stockholder in Bank Negative, which has a large negative funding gap (repricable liabilities > repricable assets), as shown in the following simple balance sheet. For simplicity, we'll assume that Bank Negative has only one asset (ten-year fixed rate loans) and one liability (one-year deposits):

Bank Negative Balance Sheet ($ Million)

Assets		Liabilities and Equity	
10-year fixed rate loans		1-year deposits (9% rate)	$ 80
(10% rate)	$100	Equity	$ 20
Total Assets	$100	Total Liabilities & Equity	$100

Bank Negative has fixed rate assets of $100 million financed with $80 million of one-year deposits and $20 million in equity. Thus, for a one-year period, Bank Negative has **a negative repricing gap** (repricable assets less than repricable liabilities) of $0 million − $80 million = −$80 million. To calculate the net interest spread (NII) for the bank, simply take the loans times their rate as interest revenue (IR) less the deposits times their rate as interest expense (IE), as follows:

$$\text{NII} = \text{IR} - \text{IE} = \text{Loan Rate} \times \text{Loans} - \text{Deposit Rate} \times \text{Deposits}$$

$$= (0.10)(\$100 \text{ mil.}) - (0.09)(\$80 \text{ mil.}) = \$2.8 \text{ million}$$

If short-term interest rates rise 1 percent, however, the bank will be disappointed next year when the interest rate on short-term deposits rises to 10 percent, while the loan rate for the fixed rate loans stays the same, resulting in a lower NII by $0.8 million:

$$\text{NII} = (0.10)(\$100 \text{ mil.}) - (0.10)(\$80 \text{ mil.}) = \$2 \text{ million}$$

The expected change in NII with a change in rates can be calculated using the bank's repricing gap as:

$$\text{Expected Change in NII} = \text{Repricing Gap} \times \text{Change in Rates} \qquad [2.2]$$

$$\text{Expected Change in NII} = -\$80 \text{ mil.} \times (0.01) = -\$0.8 \text{ million}$$

Alternatively, if short-term rates fall by 100 basis points (1 percent; 1 basis point = 0.01%), the bank will be happy. The deposit rate will fall to 8 percent, reducing interest expense by $0.8 million, while interest revenue remains the same, resulting in a rise in NII from $2.8 million to $3.6 million or a rise by $0.8 million, as follows:

$$\text{Expected Change in NII} = -\$80 \text{ mil.} \times (-0.01) = +\$0.8 \text{ million}$$

Although depository institutions by the nature of their operations (taking in short-term deposits to finance longer-term loans) generally have negative funding gaps, they can also experience positive repricing gaps. For instance, a bank may sell most of its long-term loans and only keep short-term loans and may seek long-term time deposits or other forms of long-term debt for financing. For example, consider the situation of Bank Positive, as shown below, which has one-year consumer loans as assets financed by ten-year long-term deposits as liabilities and, hence, a positive repricing gap (RSA > RSL):

Bank Positive Balance Sheet ($ Million)

Assets		Liabilities and Equity	
1-year consumer loans		10-year long-term certificates of deposits	
(Rate 10%)	$100	(Rate 9%)	$ 80
Total Assets	$100	Equity	20
		Total Liabilities & Equity	$100

Bank Positive has a one-year positive repricing gap (RSA − RSL) of $100 million − $0 million = $100 million. It uses long-term deposits to finance short-term consumer loans. With such rate-sensitive assets, if rates rise 100 basis points, or 1 percent, interest revenues will rise, but interest expenses will not, resulting in a higher NII. The expected change in NII for Bank Positive will be

$$\text{Change in NII} = \text{Gap} \times \text{Change in Rate} = \$100 \text{ mil.} \times 0.01 = \$1 \text{ million.}$$

On the other hand, if rates fall 100 basis points (1 percent), interest revenues will fall by $1 million, while interest expense will stay the same, and NII will fall instead by $1 million:

$$\text{Change in NII} = \$100 \text{ mil.} \times (-.01) = -\$1 \text{ million.}$$

A bank's repricing gap determines whether NII will remain stable, fall, or rise when interest rates rise. Bank Positive and Bank Negative illustrate exaggerated cases, since real banks have a more complex mix of rate-sensitive assets and rate-sensitive liabilities. Also, rates on different types of assets and different types of liabilities may change by different amounts. Yet, the same principles hold, and a repricing gap measure is a good indicator of interest rate risk for a depository institution's NII.

A negative repricing gap puts a bank at risk if interest rates rise. A positive repricing gap puts a bank at risk if interest rates fall. A larger gap corresponds to larger risk of an unhappy fall in net interest income if rates move in the unfortunate direction. However, if rates move in the favorable direction, banks will experience rising net interest income. As the gap approaches zero, banks gain a more stable NIM but at times at a cost of lower potential profits.

Figure 2.2 shows trends in NIM from 1992 to 2003 for all U.S. banks. **Interest expense to assets** (often referred to as the **average cost of funding assets**) fell dramatically in 2002 by 1.26 percent, or 126 basis points (from 3.10 percent in 2001 to 1.84 percent in 2002), but interest revenue to assets (often referred to as the **average yield on assets**) fell by a similar amount, resulting in a stable NIM. In 2003, however, the average yield on assets fell less than the average cost of funds, resulting in a small rise of 14 basis points in the NIM. Although 14 basis points sounds like a small rise, with billions of dollars of loans held by banks, it resulted in a large increase in profits for banks in 2002. As shown in Figure 2.3, Quarterly NIMs changed with changing interest rates during 1999 to 2003 for both large and small banks.

Concept Questions

1 What is the difference between refinancing (repricing) risk and market (price) risk?

2 What is a funding gap, and how does it measure a financial institution's repricing risk?

3 What risk does a financial institution have if it has a negative repricing (funding) gap? A positive repricing gap?

4 Given an institution's funding gap, how can you estimate its expected change in net interest income with a given expected change in interest rates?

5 What type of interest rate risk does the repricing gap as an interest rate risk measure not include?

figure **2.2** TRENDS IN INTEREST REVENUES, INTEREST EXPENSES, AND NIM FOR ALL U.S. BANKS, 1992 TO 2003

PANEL A: GRAPH OF INTEREST REVENUES, INTEREST EXPENSES, AND NET INTEREST MARGIN OVER TIME

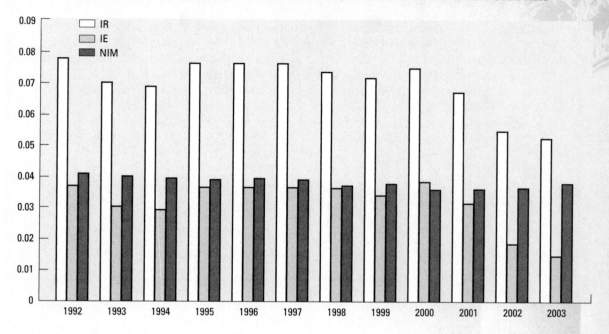

PANEL B: PERCENTAGE RATES FOR INTEREST REVENUE TO ASSETS, INTEREST EXPENSE TO ASSETS, AND NET INTEREST MARGIN, 1992 TO 2003

	IR	IE	NIM
1992	7.74	3.67	4.07
1993	7.00	3.00	4.00
1994	6.85	2.93	3.92
1995	7.52	3.67	3.85
1996	7.56	3.61	3.95
1997	7.57	3.67	3.90
1998	7.31	3.61	3.70
1999	7.13	3.39	3.74
2000	7.40	3.86	3.54
2001	6.66	3.10	3.56
2002	5.44	1.84	3.60
2003	5.18	1.44	3.74

Sources: Data used to create figures by Authors compiled from FDIC Quarterly Bank Profile and Historical Statistics on Banking at http://www2.fdic.gov/hsob *and for 2003 at* http://www2.fdic.gov/qbp/2003sep/cb4.html, *as confirmed in* Sheshunoff Bank and S&L Quarterly, *1993, 1997, and 2002 issues, Sheshunoff Information Services, Inc., Austin, Texas.*

The repricing gap as a risk measure is often expressed as a percentage of **assets (rate-sensitive assets − rate-sensitive liabilities) to assets,** and is often given for different periods, such as within three months or within one year, with larger ratios indicating greater interest rate risk. Volatility in NIM is also an indicator of greater interest rate risk. Larger holdings of long-term fixed rate loans or securities is another indicator. The funding gap measures reinvestment/refinancing risk for financial institutions. A better overall interest rate risk measure, an institution's duration gap (discussed in Chapter 10), takes into consideration market risk as well.

figure **2.3** QUARTERLY NET INTEREST MARGINS, ANNUALIZED, 1999–2003

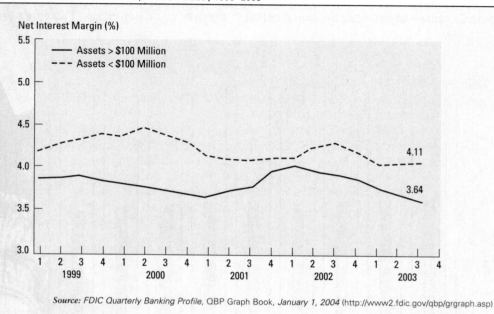

Source: FDIC Quarterly Banking Profile, QBP Graph Book, *January 1, 2004* (http://www2.fdic.gov/qbp/grgraph.asp).

Liquidity Risk

Many financial institutions provide liquidity intermediation services, particularly depository institutions. This activity encourages saving and, hence, increases the funds available to borrowers for productive uses within an economy. Thus, liquidity risk is an inherent risk in banking. However, other financial institutions face this risk to a certain degree as well, including insurance firms, mutual funds, and securities firms. To manage liquidity risk, depository institutions can hold short-term assets to meet liquidity needs or use liability management techniques, borrowing short-term funds as needed. The cost of holding short-term assets is lower interest revenue, while the cost of borrowing short-term funds is a possible rise in interest rates, increasing the depository institution's cost of funds. Such borrowing, so-called **purchased funds (or volatile funds),** are also very interest rate sensitive, and deposits may leave the institution at any time or not be renewed if bad news about a depository institution appears. Depository institution short-term liabilities are often classified into categories of **core (insured)** and **noncore (uninsured) liabilities or purchased funds.**

To measure the liquidity risk of a depository institution, analysis must consider the composition of both assets and liabilities, as well as the ability of depository institutions to engage in short-term borrowing using market liquidity measures, and off-balance-sheet commitments that will necessitate liquidity, such as promises to make future loans **(loan commitments).** Financial ratios often used to measure liquidity risk include:

Net Loans and Leases to Assets	Net Loans and Leases to Deposits
Core Deposits to Total Assets	Noncore Deposits to Total Assets
Short-Term Securities to Assets	Short-Term Securities to Volatile Liabilities
Percentage of Outstanding Loan Commitments	
Equity Capital to Assets	Market Value of Equity to Book Value of Equity
Ratings on Commercial Paper or Other Short-Term Securities	

As a depository institution becomes more loaned up (higher net loans to assets or to deposits), its liquidity diminishes. It cannot quickly sell or securitize loans to raise its liquidity (although large banks with loan sales or securitization subsidiaries may generate liquidity on a continuous basis). Also, as loans make up a rising percentage of a bank's assets, securities make up a falling percentage.

Since cash and due is generally held to meet reserve requirements, it is not often treated as a liquidity measure. However, the **ratio of short-term securities (one-year or shorter maturities) to assets** is

1 Why do depository institutions have the greatest liquidity risk?

2 What are core deposits? What are noncore (purchased or volatile) liabilities? Explain why noncore liabilities entail greater liquidity risk.

3 What are three basic types of ratios to measure liquidity risk for a depository institution? Why are asset and liability and off-balance-sheet ratios included as risk measures?

4 Why is the percentage of unused loan commitments an important indicator of future liquidity needs?

5 Why are capital ratios and short-term debt ratings important indicators of liquidity?

frequently used as a measure of short-term liquidity available on the asset side. On the liability side, the type of deposits a bank holds determines expected future liquidity needs. Core deposits (insured deposits less than $100,000) tend to be stable liabilities that are not interest rate sensitive. As a bank's ratio of **core deposits to assets** rises, its liquidity risk diminishes, since insured depositors do not change banks frequently. The opposite is true of **noncore deposits to assets,** since these balances are interest rate sensitive and may leave at any time. Frequently, the ratio of short-term securities to noncore or purchased (volatile) liabilities is also used as a relative measure of liquidity, with a rising ratio indicating greater liquidity. Off-balance-sheet items affect a bank's future liquidity needs as well. For instance, **unused loan commitments** (promises by banks for fees to make future customer loans) are likely to be drawn down in the future, so the **percentage of unused commitments** is a measure of these future needs for funds for promised loans to customers.

Other measures that are related to the ability to carry on liability management are more related to the marketability of a bank's short-term securities. Institutional investors (money market mutual funds, pension funds, insurance funds, among others) are often not allowed to purchase short-term liabilities or make short-term loans to financial institutions or other short-term borrowers, unless they have high ratings on their securities and high capital ratios, as a cushion against future losses. Hence, capital ratios and ratings on securities, such as commercial paper, are also indicators of the ability to borrow and, hence, liquidity of a financial institution. Other liquidity management considerations are discussed in more detail in Chapter 14.

Operational Risk

Despite the fact that often 80 percent or more of the activities in a financial institution are operational, frequently referred to as the *heart of a bank,* very little attention has been given to a depository institution's operational risk until recently. Technological innovations and the greater use of technology by financial institutions in recent decades increased this type of risk. As noted under the new Basel II Accord, which emphasizes capital requirements and greater controls for operational risk, operational, defined broadly to include technological risk as well, is "the risk of direct or indirect loss resulting from inadequate or failed internal processes, people, and systems or from external events."

Others have defined this risk even more broadly. Marshall (2001), in an excellent book on operational risks in financial institutions, notes that "[j]ust as managers, salespeople, and traders initiate transactions that cause market and credit risks for the firm, operations managers take actions that produce operational risks." With a rise in merger and acquisition activity for financial services firms in the past two decades, many large banks have suffered great difficulty trying to integrate diverse technological systems, often at times alienating customers in the process. Similarly, integrating operational practices and cultures has increased operational risks.[9]

A number of recent events have brought out the importance of managing operational risks from the perspective of the corporate governance of people, such as mutual fund traders carrying on illegal after-market trading activities, huge hidden trading losses by rogue traders of securities firms, and conflicts

---

9 See Glantz (2003), 1; and Marshall (2000), 23–25.

of interest with some securities firms pressuring research analysts to praise firms that a securities firm is underwriting, which is now illegal under Sarbanes-Oxley. A U.S. subsidiary of Allied Irish Banks alone lost about $750 million in 2002 due to fraudulent trading. Technology has also increased operational risks with hackers sometimes successfully embezzling funds by entering a bank's computer system or contaminating a financial institution's system with viruses. Electronic transfer of funds (ETFS) also contains technology and fraud risks, and special procedures and safeguard policies must be created and implemented to reduce this risk. Similarly, automatic payments through automated clearinghouses (ACHs), where funds such as payrolls are transferred from one bank account to another for payments to others, entail technology risk. Fraud, theft, terrorism, identify fraud, along with other risks associated with operations are often included. Marshall (2001, p. 27) provides examples of operational risks where financial services firms lost millions of dollars in the last decade, including unauthorized bond trading due to poor management controls, fraud and forgery, noncompliance of pension funds, poor lending control, check fraud, misrepresentation, and inadequate control of futures trading, totalling about $47 billion in losses.[10]

Regulatory Reasons for Managing Operating Risk

Given the previous illustrations, operational risk is clearly important for financial services firms who need to protect themselves from huge losses, as well as losses to their reputations. In addition, regulators have put increasing importance on financial services firms' management of operational risk, including under the Basel II proposal, higher capital requirements for the risk of operations for large international banks. Under the proposal, large international banks that have better internal management controls and measurements for operational risk will not have to hold as much capital against future operational losses as those that don't. Basel II has three pillars, including: (1) separate additional regulatory capital required for operational risk, (2) additional supervisory scrutiny of operational risk management including the capital charge the firm has taken for operational risk, and (3) the technique used to calculate operational risk. The Committee found a single approach for measuring operational risk to be too simplistic, given the variety of lines of business that international banks engage in. Consequently, the proposal allows alternative approaches including: (1) a **basic indicator** (at the time of this writing 15 percent of gross income); (2) a **standardized approach,** seeking different weights (termed betas) for operational risk for different predefined lines of business based on their relative risk; and (3) an **advanced measurement approach (AMA)** allowing credible internal measurement approaches by different financial institutions if they are verified and acceptable for supervisory purposes. For the very large international banks in the United States. (estimated to be about ten to twenty) for which Basel II will apply, U.S. regulators will require the third AMA to calculate a capital risk charge, discussed more in Chapter 6.[11]

Industry Initiatives for Managing Operational Risk

As noted by Marshall (2001, p. 35), industry groups for financial services firms have also promoted guidelines for good operations practice including the 1993 report by the G30 (Group of Thirty), an elite group of global investment banks. This report focused on good practices in operational management of derivatives for dealers and end users, with many of the guidelines becoming "de facto" industry standards. Examples of such de factor industry standards include separating front office and back office operations, having an independent risk management team to report to senior management, periodic and effective audits, quality information systems, and risk integration across the firm. The report also argued for "precisely defined risk management policies covering the scope and authorization of trading, acceptable control, product valuation and risk management approaches, and the critical importance of adequate disclosure and active senior management involvement." Thus, as Marshall points out, this document "set the tone for securities dealing and processing as a whole."[12]

---

10 See Marshall (2000), 27.

11 Basel Committee on Banking Supervision, Consultative Document on Operational Risk, Bank of International Settlements *(http://www.bis.org)*; and Ralph Nash. "The Three Pillars of Operational Risk," Chapter 1, in Alexander (2003).

12 See Marshall (2000), 23–25, 35.

What Does Operational Risk Management Entail?

Although detailed coverage of operational risk management is beyond the scope of this text, excellent books have recently come out that help managers to understand the elements of operational risk management, including Alexander (2003) and, as mentioned earlier, Marshall (2001). Marshall (2001, p. 29) notes that operational risk management should attempt to integrate financial and nonfinancial risks including: (1) the traditional use of financial risk management, such as insurance, hedging, and other methods to reduce one-time losses that could occur with one-time unexpected losses; (2) more systemic risk that might occur throughout a firm on a continuing basis; and (3) the response of management to different risks. Risks must be identified and measured, and procedures set up to mitigate operational risks, as well as holding adequate capital against potential losses. Marshall provides examples of the different disciplines in a financial services firm that provide operational risk management including financial risk managers, total quality managers, insurance managers, audit and internal control, operations management, and facilities management and contingency planning. Hence, operational risk management is not just a finance function but a function across an entire financial services firm.

Foreign Exchange and Other International Risk

With globalization increasingly larger numbers of financial institutions have been engaged in international transactions and investments. International risk for financial as well as nonfinancial firms includes several different types, such as: (1) **transaction risk,** the risk of a loss with changes in foreign exchange rates for international transactions; (2) **translation risk,** the risk of a loss in the value of a firm's equity with assets denominated in one currency and liabilities in another; (3) **country or sovereign risk,** the risk of a government declaring nonpayment of debt owed to a financial institution from another country or other conditions where debt contracted in another country will not be repaid; and (5) **economic risk,** the risk of having operations in another country that suffers severe economic problems.

Foreign Exchange (FX) Risk: An Illustration

An example of transaction and translation risk is shown in the following table for Bank European, which operates in Europe with loans to an international U.S. company denominated in U.S. dollars and financed by long-term deposits denominated in U.S. dollars:

Bank European

Loans: 100 million U.S. dollars (10% rate)	Deposits: 90 million Euros (6% rate)
	Equity: 10 million Euros
Total Assets: 100 million (equivalent in Euros)	Total Liabilities & Equity: 100 million Euros

Suppose when the loans were made, the exchange rate between U.S. dollars and the Euro was $1.00 = 1 Euro. Thus, at this time, assets (loans) in U.S. dollars were worth 100 million Euros and deposits financing the loans were 100 million Euros. When the loan is made, Bank European expects an interest rate spread in Euros of 100 mil. (.10) − 90 mil. (.06) equal to 4.6 million Euros. The U.S. borrower will pay Bank European interest on loans in U.S. dollars, which Bank European will exchange back into Euros for its operations in Europe. Bank European is taking on both **transaction risk** (the risk of a loss in the expected return on the loan) and **translation risk** (the risk of the value of the firm's assets falling below the value of its liabilities, and, hence, a fall in the value of its equity) if the value of the U.S. dollar falls relative to the Euro.

Concept Questions

1 How do operational risks differ from other bank risks? How would you define operational risk?

2 Why have financial services firms and their regulators become more concerned about operational risk in recent decades?

3 What do the three pillars of Basel II for operational risk include? What are three ways the proposal allows operational risk to be measured?

Suppose indeed, as in early 2004, the value of the U.S. dollar falls relative to the Euro to $1.00 = 0.80 Euros. With the fall in the value of the loans denominated in U.S. dollars to 80 percent of their previous value in Euros, the balance sheet valued in Euros is now:

Loans: 80 million equivalent Euros (10% rate)	Deposits: 90 million Euros (6% rate)
Total Assets: 80 million (equivalent in Euros)	Equity: −10 million Euros
	Total Liabilities & Equity: 80 million Euros

Bank European has experienced translation risk losses in the value of equity with the market value of equity in Euros equal to Total Assets in Euros less Total Liabilities in Euros becoming − 10 million in Euros.

Bank European has also experienced transaction risk losses with the interest spread in Euros falling to (80 million Euros Equivalent for Loans × .10) less (90 million Euros for Deposits × 0.06), which equals 2.6 million Euros (2 million less than the 4.6 million Euros expected).

Transaction and translation foreign exchange risk resulted in severe financial crises for financial institutions in different countries in the past. An example is the 1997 and 1998 Asian currency crisis. Financial institutions in a number of countries in Asia, including Indonesia, Malaysia, and Thailand, had liabilities denominated in U.S. dollars (borrowing from the United States and other countries) that were used to finance loans denominated in home currencies, which in turn were used to finance businesses in their own countries. When the value of domestic Asian currencies fell dramatically against the U.S. dollar, the interest expense to pay back liabilities in U.S. dollars soared, while the value of interest revenue on loans denominated in their domestic currencies plunged. This led to inadequate interest revenues to cover interest expenses, resulting in large losses and ultimately failure for hundreds of financial institutions. The crises of these financial institutions contributed to further instability, deposit runs, and lack of confidence in the currency of many other countries as well. Contrast the 1997 and 1998 Asian currency crisis, in which financial institutions did not hedge their foreign exchange risk, with a similar currency crisis in Latin America. Many Brazilian financial institutions were well insulated from a devaluation of their currency to the dollar by protecting (hedging) against foreign exchange rate risk. Many large international banks had considerable Latin American investor exposure at this time as well, including $47.6 billion for U.S. banks, and globally the United States, Germany, Spain, France, the United Kingdom, The Netherlands, and Japan had a $76.29 billion exposure to Brazil and $283 billion in Latin America overall.[13]

Other International Risks

Other risks associated with international operations of financial services firms include terrorism, differences in payment mechanisms and legal systems for recourse for losses, and reputation risk, associated with employees not understanding the culture or mores in different countries.

Country risk or sovereign risk includes any political, economic, social, cultural, or legal circumstances in the home country of the borrower that could prevent the timely fulfillment of debt obligations or profitable operations. The uncertainty can arise from many sources, such as social unrest; dependence on one export, which can lead to unrest if prices for that product fall; civil or international wars; economic decline; or a change in political ideology. An additional problem occurs when a country's economic condition weakens and a foreign borrower's government prohibits a currency exchange for repayments of debts, often called **transfer risk.** Economic risk entails the risk when a financial institution initiates operations in another country that suffers economic problems that in turn creates profitability for a financial institution. For instance, international financial institutions operating in Brazil in 1998 during its currency crisis and later economic downturn suffered economic losses. Even cultural attitudes toward indebtedness can affect borrowers' timely repayments of obligations.[14] In short, country risk includes any source of uncertainty specific to international rather than domestic lending or investing.

---

13 Bank for International Settlements, as cited in Matt Murray and Pamela Druckerman. "Big Banks Cool to Major Role in Brazil Bailout." *The Wall Street Journal* (October 13, 1998), A16; and Pamela Druckerman and Jonathan Friedland. "Global Stock Funds Shun Brazilian Shares." *The Wall Street Journal* (January 22, 1999), A9.

14 An interesting example of country risk occurred in 1986 after the price of crude oil fell dramatically, and some wealthy borrowers with significant indebtedness to U.S. banks in Saudi Arabia invoked the doctrine of *sharia*, which holds that payment of interest is an unethical practice. Although the conflict in doctrine had been avoided when loans were made by borrowers asking that "administrative fees" be used instead of interest payments, later when oil prices fell, some borrowers justified not making payments, based on fees also being considered as unethical (Bill Powell. "The Sheiks Rediscover Religion." *Newsweek* [May 12, 1986], 62–63).

As financial institutions have merged internationally, other cultural conflicts have often occurred associated with more aggressive U.S. Wall Street behavior involving a "me-centered, take no prisoners" approach versus more group-oriented or consensual cultures. A good example is when U.S. executives were hired to invigorate Deutsche Bank's (DB) investment bank subsidiary in London, Deutsche Morgan Grenfell (DMG). While DB's culture was one of gradual integration and building of an institution, the Wall Street executives wanted things done right away, leading to great infighting that tore apart DMG. However, DB continued its investment banking activities in the United States by purchasing Bankers Trust in 1998, which owns Alex Brown, a super-regional investment bank in Baltimore, but with a more conservative culture than the typical Wall Street firm. Many firms as they enter new cultures gain advantages by hiring professionals that have lived in or know and understand that culture. With globalization, financial institution managers need to be very aware of cultural differences, which often require different approaches to entering new international markets. Only through sensitive, cross-cultural awareness can international operations become successful.[15]

Moving Toward Comprehensive Risk Management

As banks enter new product areas that generate noninterest revenue, banks and regulators have been concerned about developing comprehensive new approaches to risk management. The value at risk (VAR) approach has become widely accepted by practitioners and regulators. In August 1996, U.S. Bank Regulatory Agencies adopted a market risk amendment (MRA) voted on by international regulators to the 1988 Basel Capital Accord. This MRA became effective in January 1998. It requires that banks with significant trading activity set aside capital to cover market risk exposure based on a bank's own value at risk estimates. However, many critics point out that while VAR is a useful tool, it needs to be implemented with caution as a measure for bank risk. Banks need to have a risk management program that encompasses broader efforts to control risk, including developing appropriate incentives and internal controls within a financial institution.[16]

What Is VAR?

Essentially, VAR asks "how much could the value of a bank's portfolio decline over a given period of time with a given probability?" That is, how much money might the bank lose in a specified length of time? For example, a bank might want to know, based on a 99 percent probability using historical data on interest rate changes, what the expected loss would be on its bond portfolio on a given day or in a given week.[17] Similarly, if the bank does foreign exchange trading or has a portfolio denominated in a foreign currency, it might want to estimate its expected loss on its foreign exchange portfolio based on historical variation in currency rates. Hence, the bank needs to

1. Designate a given time period to examine, such as a day or a few days;
2. Designate a given probability of loss, based on a given statistical distribution, such as the normal distribution; and
3. Obtain historical data on the volatility of interest rates, foreign exchange rates, or stock price movements, and so on, to calculate expected price changes for the bank's investments or trading activities in these areas.

Concept Questions

1 Give an example of transaction and translation risk for a financial services firm.

2 Why is it extremely risky for a financial institution to have assets in one currency and liabilities in another?

3 Give a recent example where a financial services firm experienced country risk. Why is it important to have managers in international subsidiaries aware of the subtleties of different cultures?

---

15 See Michael R. Sesit and Anita Raghavan. "Kultureshock: Deutsche Bank Hit Many Costly Snags in Its American Foray." *The Wall Street Journal* (May 4, 1998), A1, A10. For an excellent book on international banking, see Smith and Walter (2003). See also Smith and Walter (2003) for a discussion of cultural risks in banking.

16 See *http://www.bis.org* and Chorafas (1998).

17 Sources for the following sections on VAR models include Simons (1996), Culp, Miller, Neves (1998); Venkataraman (1997); and Saunders (1997).

The RiskMetrics Model

One of the most extensively used VAR techniques is RiskMetrics, developed by JPMorgan in 1994 that later merged with Chase Bank to become JPMorganChase. In 1998, with client demand greater than the resources available to the internal risk management division at JPMorgan, the RiskMetrics Group was spun off as a separate company that provides "financial analytics and wealth management solutions to hundreds of financial institutions, corporations, and central banks worldwide." The VAR technique estimates the market risk of fixed income securities, foreign exchange, and equities based on a huge volume of historical data.[18] Under this model, Daily Earnings at Risk (DEAR) is defined as the dollar value of a particular position (bonds, stock, foreign exchange) times the potential adverse change in that value on a daily basis. Generally, a distribution of price movements (e.g., the normal distribution) is used, and potential adverse changes are calculated based on the historical standard deviation in prices at a 99 percent or 95 percent confidence level. Historical simulations and the correlations between different types of assets that reduce a bank's total portfolio sensitivity are also incorporated to calculate the total risk for all the bank's positions. For instance, taking the dollar value of each of the bank's positions times the expected price volatility on a daily basis in that market, a bank might be expected to lose $50,000 on its fixed income portfolio, $30,000 on foreign exchange positions, and $100,000 on its equity positions on a daily basis. Its total DEAR is the sum of these, $180,000. However, if price movements for each of the positions are negatively correlated (move in opposition to each other), the DEAR for the entire bank portfolio will be lower, since the opposite movements in prices will reduce the expected earnings at risk. Consequently, adjusting for negative correlations, the DEAR for the entire portfolio may be $150,000 instead.[19] An example using VAR for mutual fund management can be found in Chapter 18.

Limitations of VAR

Although VAR techniques have been widely accepted and used, in recent years analysts have criticized these models for being deemed a *panacea* rather than being considered what they are, one useful tool. Limitations are that VAR models focus on a single point in a distribution of potential profits and losses versus looking at an entire distribution. Models also do not include information on how risks would be managed in extreme market crises, since data is based on normal situations. VAR is not very useful for long-term bank assets and liabilities that are infrequently traded, such as deposits and loans. Other methods may be more useful for depository institutions and other financial institutions such as insurance companies, which also have long-term assets. The RiskMetrics Group has developed a number of other risk models including models for managing credit risk changes, CreditMetrics, discussed in Chapter 13.[20]

A well-known bank consultant, Edward Furash, chairman of Furash & Co., argues that banks must develop a comprehensive risk management system to ensure that they can take and be paid for greater risk without suffering more losses than competitors that take less risk. As he states:

> The goal of a comprehensive risk management system is to apply a bank's risk-taking capacity profitably. To this end, senior management must aggregate and quantify its risk management resources—its "risk budget" so to speak—in order to allocate these resources to areas of greatest potential.[21]

Unfortunately, most banks have a fragmented risk assessment system that evaluates and manages risk within each line of business at a line management level. Few banks have a formal, comprehensive, institution-wide risk assessment system to optimize and prioritize a bank's resources for risk management.

In contrast to the more commonly used, conventional, fragmented systems at banks that come from the bottom up, as mentioned in Chapter 1, economic value added (EVA) provides a way of integrating

---

18 For a discussion of other types of distributions and estimation techniques that might be used, see Venkataraman (1997).

19 See the RiskMetrics Group Website at *http://www.riskmetrics.com/aboutus.html.* For a detailed description of JPMorgan's RiskMetrics, see Saunders (1997) and Saunders and Cornett (2003). As Saunders points out, JPMorgan's RiskMetrics calculated DEAR in three areas: fixed income, foreign exchange, and equities. The Bank for International Settlements' Bank Committee on Banking Supervision proposed a bank trading risk model discussed in detail in Saunders (1997).

20 See Saunders (1997) and Saunders and Cornett (2003) for a detailed mathematical example for calculating the portfolio DEAR for a bank that incorporates the correlation between different bank positions.

21 See Furash (1995). Also see John P. Drzik. "CFO Survey: Moving Towards Comprehensive Risk Management." *Bank Management* (May/June 1995), 38–39; and Daniel J. Kreps. "Risk-Based Strategic Planning." *The Bankers Magazine* (March/April 1994), 52–54.

risk and return analyses for a bank and provides an overall top-down system. EVA can be also used for objective goal setting for incentive compensation plans. Under such plans officers are rewarded for the economic value added that they provide to providers of capital incorporating the cost of risk capital needed for different ventures.

Models exist based on EVA or risk adjusted return on capital (RAROC), where a risk premium is added in pricing loans and securities to cover the cost of holding additional equity capital for activities that have greater risk based on expected losses. RAROC is discussed in more detail in Chapter 6. In brief, RAROC quantifies the dollar profitability or dollar return on a bank's different activities (including commercial lending, securities trading, and other investment activities) based on their risk by providing a charge for the capital required to support each activity. Thus, bank managers are involved in all aspects of risk management including "identification, quantification, and pricing." Banks, in turn, can use these models as strategic decision tools to evaluate business decisions, such as whether to enter or exit a given product line. Other more sophisticated models may be more effective in dealing with risks that are more complex. Innovative uses of technology can also improve banks' monitoring of different types of risk.[22]

Risk assessment modeling techniques also vary. They range from simple scenario analysis (best, average, worse case scenarios) to more sophisticated historic (back simulation) models using previous historical data to even more sophisticated Monte Carlo simulations using a random variable generator or Bayesian estimations that utilize objective and subjective data. Many consulting firms have developed in recent years to help financial services firms manage their overall risk, credit risk, and operational risk.[23]

A Brief Thought on Strategic Considerations

Given that financial services firms are in the business of taking risks, financial institution managers need to look at the overall risks that the institution is facing from a strategic perspective to ensure that based on the strategic objectives of the institution, overall risk is within these objectives and that risk management practices are in place to manage and mitigate when possible potential risks and maximize the economic value of the firm. A firm's mission statement typically tells "who we are." From that statement financial objectives can be determined including profitability, growth, risk, and risk management objectives, along with capital objectives based on the risk that a firm's overall risk. Risks need to be balanced in this context. If a firm has considerable credit risk, for instance, it may want to mitigate other risks, so that the overall risk profile fits its objectives and does not give the institution excessive overall risk.

With strategic planning, the firm then needs to look at the overall picture including what is often called a "SWOT" analysis including its strengths, weaknesses, opportunities, and threats. Action plans can then be initiated with goals and timetables. Different firms by the nature of their types have different inherent risks. For instance, a firm that evolves around fee-based activities, such as brokerage and back office processing activities may have greater operational risk. Another firm that concentrates on commercial lending in a particular high-risk industry entails greater credit risk. A savings institution with a large concentration of fixed-rate home mortgage loans has great interest rate risk. Hence, management and choice of risks often goes along with the type of firm and strategic choices that managers make. Given these choices, risk management practices and strategies can be developed to strategically manage the risks an institution faces, including looking at the correlations between risks, diversification and, hence, the overall systematic risk of the financial institution.

Concept Questions

1 Why is comprehensive risk management important for financial services firms?

2 What is value at risk (VAR)? How is it used to measure risk in a portfolio context?

3 What are the limitations of VAR?

---

22 Simons (1996) and Culp, Miller, and Neves (1998) point out alternative measures for risk that may be more useful to corporations and financial institutions, including cash flow volatility, RAROC (discussed in more detail later in the text), and a shortfall technique to estimate the probability that the value of assets will fall below that of liabilities and require a contribution by the plan sponsor for a pension plan. Also, see Uyemura, Kantor, and Pettit (1996), 103. They provide detailed examples of how a bank can implement the EVA financial system for different types of activities.

23 See Saunders and Cornett (2003), Chapter 10, for a discussion of these alternatives and other methods, Saunders and Allen (2002), Caouette, Altman, and Narayanan (1998), and Smithson (2003).

Summary

Financial services firms are in the business of risk transformation, taking on the risk of their customers. Property/liability insurance firms, for instance, take on the risk of loss for their customers by taking premiums and investing them wisely to pool risks for emergencies. Similarly, depository institutions take on liquidity, maturity intermediation, and credit management services for customers, among others. With predominantly financial assets and liabilities, which are promises to pay in the future, they have a number of different risks that nonfinancial institutions don't face. Accordingly, financial services firms need to manage their own risks in a portfolio framework and choose among risks from a strategic perspective. They also need to include a risk premium in their pricing of riskier activities to ensure that they have sufficient capital against future losses. Recently, with large operational losses and regulatory pressures, financial services firms have tried to develop internal risk management measures, policies, and models to manage their risks. Many firms have diversified into noninterest, fee-income generating activities to reduce the overall volatility of their earnings. Financial holding companies are now allowed to provide an umbrella for financial services firms to engage in varied activities including investment firms, banks, and insurance firms under the same umbrella.

Perhaps the most important risk that financial services firms face is credit risk. Risk measures for this risk include not only the percentage of nonpaying loans or loan losses but also the provisions that are taken to provide capital against future losses and the firm's earnings coverage of losses. Financial institutions engaged in lending activities need to develop a good credit review process, so lenders can learn from mistakes and avoid conflicts of interest. Lender compensation also needs to be tied to the quality versus just the volume of loans, and a credit culture of informal openness needs to be maintained. Diversification policies for lending help to reduce risk, although specialized lenders may not have this luxury. Other techniques, including credit derivatives, loan sales, and securitization can help a firm to diversify or reduce lending risk.

A second major risk that financial institutions face, particularly depository institutions, is interest rate risk. Interest rate risk includes reinvestment/refinancing risk, the risk of having to invest repricable or maturing assets in instruments with lower rates, and price/market risk, the risk of capital losses on fixed rate assets if interest rates fall. A financial institution's repricing/funding gap provides a measure of a firm's reinvestment/refinancing risk and can give an indication of the expected change in its interest spread with a change in interest rates. A positive repricing gap indicates risk of a lower interest spread if interest rates fall; while a negative repricing gap indicates risk of a lower interest spread if interest rates rise.

A third major risk is liquidity risk, which applies to many different types of financial services firms but is greater for depository institutions where customers can make instant withdrawals. This risk is managed from the asset side by holding short-term securities that can be sold quickly for liquidity and from the liability side by borrowing short-term funds, particularly for large banks.

A fourth major risk is operational risk, which is a broad risk for all the other risks in financial services operations, particularly associated with trading activities, payment services, fraud, and technological risks. With large operational losses for financial services firms in recent years and regulatory pressures to control this risk, operational risk has been in the limelight, and new models and risk management techniques to manage this risk have been developed.

With globalization and financial services firms setting up subsidiaries and merging with other firms in different countries, international risk management has also been of increasing concern. Foreign currency crises in recent years were exacerbated by financial institutions' poor management of foreign currency risk, where financial assets were financed domestically by borrowing in another currency. Other international risks including country risk have also become increasingly important to manage, including sensitive, cross-cultural awareness of cultural differences. Also, in recent years, new comprehensive approaches have been developed to manage risk including a firm's overall risk.

Questions

1. Why should a financial institution's risks be viewed in a portfolio framework? How is risk defined?
2. What does finance theory say about risk and return? Why does diversification reduce portfolio risk?
3. Think about a financial institution that you deal with, such as a bank, insurance firm, or securities firm. What type of risks does that institution face? Does that institution have a choice in the risks that it takes on?

4. What is Basel II? Do you think having to hold additional equity capital for operational risks is a good idea?

5. Why do corporations in light of Sarbanes-Oxley fear regulatory risk?

6. Why do different types of loans have more credit risk than others? Rank consumer loans, commercial real estate loans, home mortgage loans, and commercial loans according to their risk from high to low. Why are the riskier loans more risky?

7. Define reinvestment and market risk. When would a financial services firm face reinvestment risk? Market risk? Provide examples.

8. What risk does a financial institution face if it has a positive funding gap? Negative repricing (funding) gap? What type of institution is likely to have a positive repricing gap?

9. What is liquidity risk? Why are both asset measures and liability measures used to measure liquidity risk?

10. What is involved in operational risk management? Give examples of different aspects of operational risk for a securities firm, a bank, and an insurance firm.

11. Why are regulators particularly concerned about operational risk? What industry initiatives have been taken in the securities industry?

12. What is the difference between transaction risk, translation risk, and country risk in discussing the international risk of a financial institution? How has globalization increased these risks?

13. Why is comprehensive risk management important for a financial services firm? What, generally, is VAR? What is Daily Earnings at Risk? What is RAROC?

14. From a strategic perspective, why should financial institution managers think about their portfolio of risks rather than looking at risks in isolation?

Problems

1. The Texas Independence Bank has the following balance sheet:

Assets

Fixed rate loans (9.5%, 30 yrs.)	$50 mil.	Rate 9.5%
Total Assets	**$50 mil.**	

Liabilities and Equity

Demand deposits (< 1 yr.)	$12 mil.	Rate 0.0%
Fed funds purchased (< 1 yr.)	30 mil.	Rate 7.0%
Equity	8 mil.	
Total Claims	**$50 mil.**	

a. What is the bank's one-year funding gap? What risk does the bank have? What is the bank's expected net interest income?

b. Using the bank's funding gap, determine the expected change in net interest income if rates rise 1 percent and if rates fall 1 percent.

2. The Paris Extravaganza Bank has the following balance sheet:

Assets:	300,000 U.S. Dollars (8% rate)
Liabilities:	270,000 Euros (5% rate)
Equity:	30,000 Euros
Total Liabs. & Equity:	300,000 Euros

a. If 1 Euro is equal to 1 U.S. dollar, what interest spread does the bank expect on its loans?

b. If the U.S. dollar falls and is only worth 0.80 Euros, what is the new interest spread? How much did the institution lose? What type of foreign exchange rate risk does this reflect?

c. With the same scenario as part b, what is the new value of the bank's assets in Euros? Given that the value of equity equals the value of assets less the value of liabilities, what is the new value of equity? How much did the value of equity decrease by? What type of foreign exchange risk does this reflect?

d. How could the Paris Extravaganza Bank structure its balance sheet to reduce its foreign exchange risk?

Selected References

Alexander, Carol, ed. *Operational Risk: Regulation, Analysis and Management.* London: Pearson Education Limited (FT Prentice Hall Professional Books), 2003.

Caouette, John B., Edward I. Altman, and Paul Narayanan. *Managing Credit Risk: The Next Great Financial Challenge.* New York: John Wiley & Sons, 1998.

Chorafas, Dimitris N. *The Market Risk Amendment: Understanding the Marking-to-Model and Value-At-Risk.* Burr Ridge, IL: McGraw-Hill Irwin, 1998.

Culp, Christopher L., Merton H. Miller, and Andrea M. P. Neves. "Value at Risk: Uses and Abuses." *Bank of America Journal of Applied Corporate Finance* 10 (Winter 1998), 26–38.

Furash, Edward E. "Risk Challenges and Opportunities." *Bank Management* (May/June 1995), 35–38.

Glantz, Morton. *Managing Bank Risk: An Introduction to Broad-Base Credit Engineering.* San Diego, CA: Academic Press, 2003.

Marshall, Christopher. *Measuring and Managing Operational Risks in Financial Institutions: Tools, Techniques and Other Resources.* New York: Wiley Finance (John Wiley & Sons), 2001.

Saunders, Anthony. *Financial Institutions Management: A Modern Perspective,* 2nd ed. Chicago: Irwin, 1997.

Saunders, Anthony, and Linda Allen. *Credit Risk Measurement: New Approaches to Value at Risk and Other Paradigms,* 2nd ed. New York: Wiley Finance (John Wiley & Sons), 2002.

Saunders, Anthony, and Marcia Millon Cornett. *Financial Institutions Management: A Risk Management Approach,* 4th ed., Burr Ridge, IL: McGraw-Hill Irwin, 2003.

Simons, Katerina. "Value at Risk—New Approaches to Risk Management." *New England Economic Review* (Federal Reserve Bank of Boston) (September/October 1996), 3–13.

Smith, Roy C., and Ingo Walter. *Global Banking,* 2nd ed. New York: Oxford Finance (Oxford University Press), 2003.

Smithson, Charles W. *Credit Portfolio Management.* New York: Wiley Finance (John Wiley & Sons), 2003.

Uyemura, Dennis G., Charles C. Kantor, and Justin M. Pettit. "EVA for Banks: Value Creation, Risk Management, and Profitability Measurement." *Bank of America Journal of Applied Corporate Finance* 9 (Summer 1996), 94–113.

Venkataraman, Subu. "Value at Risk for a Mixture of Normal Distributions: The Use of Quasi-Bayesian Estimation Techniques." *Economic Perspective* (Federal Reserve Bank of Chicago) (March/April 1997), 2–13.

internet *exercise*

1 Look up the Bank of International Settlements (BIS) on the Internet at *http://www.bis.org*. What is its purpose? Use the menu to find a summary of the new Basel Accord, Basel II, and see what other information this site provides for researchers and banks interested in managing risk.

2 Look up the RiskMetrics Group on the Internet at *http://www.riskmetrics.com*. Click on Technical Documents under Research. Also, look under market risk, credit risk, and wealth. Give a summary of the consulting activities for the RiskMetrics Group.

Regulation, Technology, and Financial Innovation

3

"The Transformation of the U.S. Banking Industry: What a Long, Strange Trip It's Been"

ALLEN N. BERGER, ANIL K. KASHYAP, AND JOSEPH M. SCALISE, Title from Brookings Papers on Economic Activity 2 (1995).

"The increasingly competitive and dynamic environment of banking puts severe strains on the viability and effectiveness of regulation."

ARNOUD W. A. BOOT, SILVA DEZELAN, AND TODD T. MILBOURN, "Regulatory Distortions in a Competitive Financial Services Industry," Journal of Financial Services Research, Vol. 17, No. 1, 2000, p. 159.

As the chapter's opening quotations suggest, banks and other financial institutions have undergone a significant transformation over the last two decades. In the United States, much of the change has resulted from liberalization of bank regulations in the 1980s and a movement by both regulators and financial institutions to reinterpret regulations to meet market realities in the 1990s. This has led to further deregulation to reflect the realities of globalization and technological change that have made many regulations no longer relevant. In the early twenty-first century, with numerous financial scandals have come new regulations. Hence, financial managers need to be aware of frequently changing regulations.

An example of constantly changing regulations includes the Fed's liberalization of the types of activities it permitted subsidiaries of large bank holding companies under its jurisdiction in the 1980s to late 1990s, including investment banking and mutual fund activities. In 1997, the Office of the Comptroller of the Currency also created a new system for national banks to establish or expand operating subsidiaries to market new products, allowing small and mid-sized banks to underwrite municipal revenue bonds and market other types of securities and insurance services. Earlier in 1997, the Federal Reserve (the Fed) also expanded the percentage of revenues to 25 percent for bank holding company subsidiaries engaging in securities and other non-bank-related activities (known as *Section 20 subsidiaries*). This liberalization reflected the reality of a new marketplace, where banks faced increased competition from nonbank financial services firms that could offer banking-type services as well as a variety of products that banks at this time could not.

Eventually, the actions of financial managers forced Congress to remove regulations preventing banks from engaging in securities and insurance activities under the Glass–Steagall Act of 1933. Sanford Weill of Travelers Group and John Reed of Citicorp challenged this regulation by proposing the merger of Travelers Group, a large insurance securities firm and diversified finance company, with Citicorp in 1998. After decades of debate, Congress repealed Glass–Steagall, and on November 12, 1999, the Financial Services Modernization (Gramm-Leach-Bliley [GLB]) Act was passed, removing these restrictions. The GLB created a new financial holding company (FHC) that allowed securities firms, banks, insurance companies, and other financial services firms to operate under the same umbrella and thus engage and cross-sell affiliate products, with the Federal Reserve Board as a chief regulator.

In addition to product deregulation, banks underwent geographic regulation in the later 1990s. This also reflected a needed change with a shifting environment where technology allowed financial services to operate nationwide. State regulatory changes had allowed regional branching pacts, which permitted banks in particular regions to expand into other states. Under the McFadden Act of 1927, however, banks could not follow their customers nationwide. Even with regional pacts, banks had to have separate holding companies, creating inefficiencies. In 1994, Congress passed the Riegle–Neal Interstate Banking and Branching Efficiency Act, which allowed banks to branch across the United States for the first time in seventy years.

Deregulation has occurred in the area of international finance, as well. In December 1997, the World Trade Organization (WTO) passed a sweeping accord among WTO members to deregulate the global financial services industry. Under this pact, more than ninety nations opened their banking, insurance, and securities industries to foreign competition, which analysts suggest promotes innovative and efficient management for financial services firms in those countries.[1]

---

1 New Door Opens for Banks to Enter Securities Markets." *New York Times* (December 12, 1997), C2. See also Edmund L. Andrews. "Accord Is Reached to Lower Barriers in Global Finance." *New York Times* (December 13, 1997), A1; and Brian A. Johnson. "Financial Accord Will Benefit a Superbreed of Firms." *The Wall Street Journal* (December 16, 1997), A22. For a summary of recent changes, also see *The Financial Services Fact Book 2004* (Insurance Information Institute and The Financial Services Roundtable, *http://www.financialservicesfacts.org*).

The pages that follow explore the traditional regulatory structure and recent developments. A discussion like this one is never complete, because more changes are always on the horizon. Given the great importance of financial institutions to the economy, new legislation is introduced on a continual basis in Congress. In 2003, more than thirty different bills relating to financial institution regulation were introduced. The possibility of continued change means that managers can never take a given set of regulations for granted, and they must anticipate necessary efforts to develop strategies in a fluid environment. Successful financial managers need to understand not only existing regulations but also the regulatory process.

Why Regulate?

Governments regulate financial institutions for several reasons, including ensuring stability in the financial marketplace by maintaining safety and soundness, protecting consumers, preventing fraud and misrepresentation in sales of financial products, promoting efficiency in the operations of financial institutions and markets, providing efficiency and liquidity in the payments system, and promoting social policies, such as enhancing the welfare of underprivileged groups.

Many of the U.S. regulations to promote stability were passed in the 1930s following the Great Depression, during which thousands of banks failed. Depository institutions have been particularly closely regulated, since they play such an important role in maintaining the liquidity of the payment system. With the development of money market and mutual funds with check-writing privileges, electronic fund transfers, Internet bill-paying services, and credit cards offered by nonbank firms, other nonregulated institutions have taken on an important role, as well, but without such heavy regulation. With their comparatively heavy regulatory burden, depository institutions at times have had difficulty competing. Over time, some regulations have become very costly and inefficient burdens, particularly for depository institutions. Recognizing this fact, both depository institutions and regulators have devised loopholes to keep up with changes in the reality of the marketplace. Many of these loopholes have created suboptimal situations, however. Eventually, Congress eliminates or changes regulations to match economic reality.

Overview: The Changing Emphasis of Financial Institution Regulations

Edward Kane, a renowned professor of finance, introduced the concept of a regulatory dialectic to capture the impact of regulatory restrictions on managerial decisions. Under this concept, if regulations are no longer relevant, managers of financial institutions find loopholes to escape regulations. Although new regulations to patch up loopholes may be passed in reaction to managers' actions, eventually, if regulations become obsolete due to environmental and technological changes, onerous regulations are removed through deregulation. At times, regulators even create the loopholes themselves in terms of practicing a type of regulatory realism by relaxing regulations that are no longer relevant for financial institutions. Table 3.1 provides a chronological summary of major federal legislation affecting financial institutions, focusing particularly on depository institutions. This list may look intimidating, but think of regulations in terms of Kane's regulatory dialectic of regulations. It will be helpful to remember key legislation highlighted in the table as we discuss attempts to avoid regulation, re-regulation, and finally deregulation in more detail later in the chapter.[2]

Relationships between financial institutions and government regulators precede even the National Currency and Banking Acts of 1863 and 1864, but the Federal Reserve Act of 1913 set the stage for comprehensive regulation of the U.S. banking system. Legislators and government agencies usually articulate justifications for regulations when they are introduced, but experts believe that unannounced motivations often influence the regulators' decisions. Although financial institution regulations have eventually served other purposes, from the 1930s to 1980, their stated intent was to maintain stability in the nation's financial system. Later, however, their intent changed as discussed in the following sections for different time periods.

---

2 The concept of the regulatory dialectic was introduced in Kane (1977) and further developed in readings from (1981), (1986), (1989a), and (1996). (Selected references are listed in full at the end of this chapter.)

table **3.1**   MAJOR FINANCIAL LEGISLATION IN THE UNITED STATES

Year	Law	Key Provisions
I. Legislation before 1930 Setting up Bank Regulators and Branching Restrictions		
1863	**National Currency Act**	Established the Office of the Comptroller of the Currency (OCC)
		Set limits on the asset choices of banks
		Issued national bank notes
		Established system of reserve requirements
1864	**National Banking Act**	Authorized granting federal bank charters
		Originated the dual system of banking
1913	**Federal Reserve Act**	Established the system of Federal Reserve banks with several duties:
		Serve as lenders of last resort
		Promote elastic money supply
		Maintain a nationwide payment system
		Tighten bank supervision
1919	**Edge Act**	Permitted subsidiaries of banks to conduct international banking outside their home territories
1927	**McFadden–Pepper Act**	Gave states authority over branching laws
		Prohibited interstate branching without the state agreement
II. Legislation in the 1930s for Safety and Soundness and Regulating Thrifts after the Depression		
1932	**FHLB Act**	Established the Federal Home Loan Bank System as a lender of last resort to S&Ls
1933	**Home Owners' Loan Act**	Authorized granting federal charters for S&Ls
		Established the Federal Home Loan Bank Board
1934	**National Housing Act**	Established the Federal Savings and Loan Insurance Corporation
1934	**National Credit Union Act**	Established the Federal Credit Union Regulator (later renamed the National Credit Union Administration)
1933	**Glass–Steagall Act (Banking Act of 1933)**	Regulation Q set interest rate ceilings on deposits
		Limited banking activities to banks
		Established the Federal Deposit Insurance Corporation
1935	**Banking Act of 1935**	Elaborated the autonomy and power of the Federal Reserve Board
		Gave the OCC discretion in granting national bank charters
1933	**Securities Act of 1933**	Mandated registration of new securities–issues
		Required disclosure of truthful financial information on issuers
1934	**Securities Exchange Act**	Established the Securities and Exchange Commission
III. Legislation in the 1940s for Securities Firms and Insurance Companies		
1940	**Investment Company Act**	Required disclosure of financial statements and investments held
		Mandated articulation of objectives by investment companies
		Determined shareholders' rights
1940	**Investment Advisers Act**	Required individuals or firms selling investment advice to register with the Securities and Exchange Commission
1945	**McCarran–Ferguson Act**	Established the right of the federal government to regulate insurance companies if states fail to do so adequately
		Exempted insurers from certain antitrust laws

table **3.1**   MAJOR FINANCIAL LEGISLATION IN THE UNITED STATES (CONTINUED)

Year	Law	Key Provisions
IV. Legislation in the 1950s to 1970s for Patching up Regulatory Loopholes		
1956	**Bank Holding Company Act**	Gave the Federal Reserve control over multibank holding companies
1956	**Douglas Amendment to the Act**	Prohibited MBHCs[a] from acquiring out-of-state banks
		Identified factors in evaluating BHC acquisitions
1959	**Spence Act**	Forbade S&Ls from having multiple S&L holding companies
1966	**Interest Rate Adjustment Act**	Extended Regulation Q to thrifts
1968	**S&L Holding Company Act**	Allowed unitary holding companies meeting the IRS "thriftness test" to engage through non-FSLIC subsidiaries in any activity
1970	**Amendments to National Credit Union Act**	Established the National Credit Union Share Insurance Fund
1970	**Amendments to the BHC Act**	Gave the Fed authority over one-bank holding companies
		Limited acquisitions to businesses "closely related" to banking
V. Legislation in the Late 1960s and 1970s, Primarily for Consumer Protection		
1968	**Consumer Credit Protection Act**	Required disclosure of lending terms to consumers
1970	**Securities Investor Protection Act**	Established the securities investor protection corporation to promote investor confidence in the securities industry
1974	**Equal Credit Opportunity Act**	Prohibited discrimination in granting of credit
1974	**Employee Retirement Income Security Act (ERISA)**	Assigned fiduciary responsibility for pension fund managers
		Set standards for vesting of benefits and full funding of pension funds
		Established the Pension Benefit Guaranty Corporation
1975	**Securities Acts Amendments**	Mandated the development of a national securities market
1977	**Community Reinvestment Act**	Required depository institutions to consider the needs of all economic groups in their communities in granting credit
VI. Legislation in the Late 1970s and Early 1980s Regulating Foreign Banks/Deregulation		
1978	**International Banking Act**	Imposed requirements for insurance premiums and branching restrictions on foreign banks operating in the United States
1980	**Depository Institution Deregulation and Monetary Control Act of 1980**	Phased out Regulation Q by 1986
		Revised reserve requirements for depository institutions
		Extended federal insurance to $100,000 account balances
		Expanded asset powers for thrifts
		Preempted state usury ceilings
1982	**Garn–St. Germain Depository Institutions Act**	Gave emergency powers of regulators for failed thrifts
		Authorized net worth certificates to provide capital to thrifts
		Broadened asset/liability powers for thrifts
		Allowed MMDAs[b]

table 3.1 MAJOR FINANCIAL LEGISLATION IN THE UNITED STATES (CONTINUED)

Year	Law	Key Provisions
VII. Legislation in the Late 1980s and 1990s for Regulatory Stringency and Geographic Deregulation		
1987	Competitive Equality Banking Act	Declared a moratorium on nonbanks and nonbank activities
		Recapitalized the FSLIC
		Stated the full faith and credit of federal insurance
		Allowed forbearance in closure of weak institutions
		Extended net worth certificates
		Expedited check clearing by depositories
1989	Financial Institutions Reform, Recovery, and Enforcement Act	Improved supervision/regulation of thrifts
		Established a new insurance fund; FDIC-SAIF, for thrifts
		Created the Resolution Trust Corporation
		Permitted BHCs to acquire healthy thrifts
		Stiffened penalties for fraud
		Imposed product restrictions for thrifts
1991	Federal Deposit Insurance Corporation Improvement Act	Mandated specific examination schedules, tripwire, and prompt corrective action system
		Recapitalized the FDIC
		Set risk-based insurance premiums
		Increased penalties for manager/director fraud
		Imposed the same limits on activities of state-chartered banks as for national banks
		Encouraged institutional involvement in communities
		Called for a review of regulator's minimum capital requirements
		Strengthened the Fed's authority over foreign banks in the United States
1992	OTS Policy Change	Allowed interstate branching for federally chartered thrifts
1994	Riegle–Neal Interstate Banking and Branching Efficiency Act	Allowed interstate branching as of June 1, 1994, requiring states to opt in or out by 1997, with many states opting in earlier
1996	Special Provision of the Small Business Jobs Protection Act	The special treatment of thrift bad debt reserves was removed, eliminating advantages of the qualified thrift lender test and removing impediments to thrift charter changes to banks and, hence, bank/thrift mergers
1996	Economic Growth and Regulatory Paperwork Reduction Act	Required federal financial regulatory agencies to review their regulations at least once every ten years and to categorize regulations by type and request comments on which regulations are outdated, unnecessary, or unduly burdensome to pursue legislative changes to reduce regulatory burden
1999	Financial Services Modernization (Gramm-Leach-Bliley [GLB]) Act	Removed restrictions of Glass–Steagall allowing investment, insurance, and banking activities to be offered by a financial holding company (FHC)
2002	Sarbanes-Oxley Act	Required CEOs and CFOs of publicly traded firms to certify financial statements and be responsible for adequate internal controls and independence of auditing committees
		Reinforced securities and insider loan laws
		Conflict of interest rules for research analysts who recommend equities in research reports; more timely disclosure of material changes in financial condition or operations of an issuer
2006	Basel II Accord Proposed Implementation	Changes risk-based capital requirements for very large international banks to include capital charges for operational risk and allow internal risk-based models to be used for credit and operational risk charges

[a]MBHC = multiple bank holding companies.

[b]MMDA = money market deposit account.

The 1930s: Safety and Soundness

The core of modern financial regulation was drafted in the aftermath of the financial crisis of the 1930s. Laws and regulations centered on prohibiting excessive competition among financial institutions, which legislators viewed as a source of unacceptable risk. With the failure of thousands of banks and unemployment affecting millions of people during the Depression, lawmakers blamed abusive practices of banks and their securities arms for the economic problems, in effect making a scapegoat of banks. Hearings highlighted tales of banks foisting bad investments on the public, lending on overly easy terms to securities affiliates and purchasing poorly performing stocks for trust funds underwritten by securities affiliates. Some critics argue that securities abuses contributed minimally to bank failures, while others argue that legislation at this time restored confidence in banks and securities firms. The **Banking Act of 1933,** widely known as the **Glass–Steagall (G–S) Act,** attempted to restore confidence by:[3]

1. Establishing ceilings on deposit rates that banks could charge (in Regulation Q) and prohibiting payment of interest on demand deposit accounts by businesses. This act prevented banks from competing on deposit rates, discouraging them from taking on risky assets with high returns to cover high rate obligations.

2. Forcing banks to divest securities, investment banking, and insurance activities, allowing banks to engage only in banking-related services to avoid conflicts of interest and using bank funds to foster speculation. Such product restrictions on banks are frequently referred to as Glass–Steagall restrictions.

3. Reinforcing geographic restrictions of the McFadden Act of 1927, forbidding banks from branching across state lines, and making banks subject to state branching laws. The intent of the McFadden Act was to prevent formation of undesirably large and powerful banks.

4. Establishing the Federal Deposit Insurance Corporation (FDIC) to insure the balances of deposit accounts up to a specified limit. The FDIC was created to instill confidence in the banking system after massive bank failures and deposit runs in the 1930s.

Savings and loans (S&Ls) received geographic, product, and rate restrictions along with deposit insurance protection under the **Federal Home Loan Act of 1932,** the **National Housing Act of 1934,** and the **Interest Rate Adjustment Act of 1966.** Credit Unions came under increasing regulation under the **National Credit Union Act of 1924,** and later amendments in 1970 established a deposit insurance fund. Through these regulations, depository institutions were more strictly regulated than other financial institutions, a difference justified by their importance to the U.S. economy and its payments system.

Regulations restricting nondepository institutions were already in place in the 1930s, and additional ones were added in the following decades. Of particular importance were the **Securities Act of 1933** and the **Securities Exchange Act of 1934,** placing federal restrictions on brokers and investment bankers. These laws were followed by the **Investment Company Act of 1940,** bringing the practices of investment companies under federal control.

The 1960s to the 1980s: Other Intentions?

In the years after the Great Depression, the economic environment changed but regulations did not. Limitations continued to inhibit formation of new financial institutions, entry of existing institutions into distant markets, and development of new products, to name a few activities. Kane has argued that the implicit thrust of regulations eventually sought to limit competition, *not* for safety reasons, but to benefit selected market participants, such as small or weak institutions, that would suffer in a fiercely competitive environment. Restrictions of chartering, product creation, and interstate branching illustrate such intentions to keep other institutions outside the markets of some depository institutions. Exit restrictions, such as refusal to allow troubled depository institutions to fail, are other examples.

---

3 In fact, Congress passed two Glass–Steagall acts. The first in 1932 specified a bookkeeping provision allowing the Treasury to balance its account. The Banking Act of 1933, commonly known as the Glass–Steagall Act, contains a provision creating a wall between the banking and securities businesses. However, the act also provided groundwork that allowed the Federal Reserve to let banks into the securities business in a limited way. See Michael Schroeder. "It's Alive: Why Glass–Steagall, Reviled for Decades, Just Won't Go Away." *The Wall Street Journal* (April 10, 1998), A1, A6.

Kane has more recently suggested that regulators and legislators may delay revelations of serious and costly problems in the institutions they regulate to hide defects in existing regulations. In this way, they reduce their own embarrassment and may avoid removal from office.[4]

The Early 1980s: Deregulation to Help Banks and Savings Institutions Compete

In the 1980s, many savings and loans were severely undercapitalized and suffered from large losses by having long-term, fixed rate mortgages that paid lower rates than their cost of funds. Also, as discussed later in more detail, depositors left banks to get higher rates from the direct financial markets or new cash management accounts offered by securities firms. To provide greater liability flexibility for S&Ls and banks, Congress passed two important legislative acts: the **Depository Institutions Deregulation and Monetary Control Act of 1980** and the **Garn–St. Germain Depository Institutions Act of 1982.** These acts allowed banks and savings institutions to offer new types of deposits including money market accounts and nonmortgage loans and adjustable-rate mortgages.

The Late 1980s and Early 1990s: Backlash Toward Safety and Soundness

In 1989 and 1991, new legislation again emphasized safety and soundness, including the **Financial Institutions Reform, Recovery, and Enforcement Act of 1989,** following the U.S. thrift savings and loan crisis, and the **Federal Deposit Insurance Corporation Improvement Act (FDICIA) of 1991,** as a response to failures by hundreds of banks and savings institutions in the late 1980s. These acts restricted the activities that thrifts, in particular, could engage in, and set up greater controls for safety and soundness and greater assessment of the internal control structures and procedures for an institution's compliance with regulations. However, other legislation liberalized and removed many of the previous restrictions of the Banking Act of 1933, shifting regulatory emphasis toward the efficiency of the banking system and market realities.

The Mid-1990s: A Move Toward Efficiency: Removal of Geographical and Product Restrictions

In contrast to the re-regulation of the early 1990s, the later 1990s were characterized by deregulation with the elimination of geographical branching restrictions for banks under the **McFadden Act of 1927** and product restrictions previously imposed under the **Glass–Steagall Act of 1933.** The passage of the **Riegle–Neal Interstate Banking and Branching Efficiency Act (IBBEA) in 1994,** which was fully implemented by 1997, allowed free interstate branching for U.S. banks, and the **Financial Services Modernization (Gramm-Leach-Bliley [GLB]) Act in 1999** allowed banks, securities, insurance, and other types of financial services to be under a financial holding company (FHC) umbrella.

The Early 2000s: Response to Fraud and Ethical Problems

In the early 2000s, a number of ethical scandals including accounting fraud and deception, supported by investment advisers, led to the collapse of several large corporations. Other financial institutions were more directly involved in scandals, including illegal after-hour trading scandals by mutual fund companies, accounting scandals for government-sponsored enterprises, predatory lending by large banks, and conflicts of interest for investment banks in their trading, advising, and research activities. Congress and regulatory agencies imposed additional regulations and guidelines for financial institutions to try to curb unethical and fraudulent practices including the passage of the **Sarbanes-Oxley Act (SOA) in 2002.** Under SOA, financial institutions are required to perform greater due diligence, ensure the veracity of their financial statements, and provide greater oversight with audit committees. Also, bans were placed on loans to directors and officers, and other corporate governance rules were put into place. Penalties for violations of securities laws were also strengthened. Risk-based control structures were emphasized to control operational risks and avoid conflicts of interest. In 2003, congressional hearings were held on mutual fund regulations and proposals to prevent after-hours trading for mutual funds, and the SEC set up new rules to prevent abuses. The Office of Comptroller of the Currency

---

4 See Kane (1989a), 129–135; Also, see Edward J. Kane. "Ethical Foundations of Financial Regulation." *Journal of Financial Services Research,* Vol. 12 (August 1), 51–74; and "Technological and Regulatory Forces in the Developing Fusion of Financial Services Competition." *Journal of Finance,* Vol. 5, No. 4 (1984), 879–981. For a discussion on the changing philosophy of regulations, see Cargill and Garcia (1985), West (1982), and Carron (1982).

(OCC) also passed more stringent antipredatory lending rules in January 2004 for national banks, following consumer lawsuits after consumers were encouraged to take on risky subprime loans by a few subsidiaries of some large banks.[5]

Regulation of Depository Institutions

Regulations for depository institutions affect almost every aspect of their operations. The complexity of the regulatory process extends beyond the quantity of regulations. There are many rules and regulators.

Who Are the Regulators?

The federal regulatory structure is so complex that one institution may be answerable to four or five different agencies. In the sections that follow, we examine this labyrinthine structure more closely. A bank holding company and its banks may be subject to the Federal Reserve, the Office of the Comptroller of the Currency, the Federal Deposit Insurance Corporation, and state regulators, creating a web of regulators, as discussed in the following sections.

Commercial Banks

Banks may operate under charters granted at the federal or state level. Those in the first group are **national banks,** and those in the second are **state banks.** Many regulations for national banks are made and enforced by the **Office of the Comptroller of the Currency (OCC).**

The comptroller's office was created in the **National Currency Act of 1863** and given additional powers in the **National Banking Act of 1864.** Together, these laws established standards a bank had to meet before receiving a national charter. They also promoted the development of a uniform, nationwide currency by authorizing only banks with federal charters to issue national bank notes. Although public confidence in the notes encouraged many state-chartered banks to switch to federal charters, other state banks remained viable by popularizing checking accounts and encouraging customers to accept checks as an alternative to currency for the payment of bills. The current **dual banking system,** in which both state and federal governments issue bank charters, is traced to this period.

The **Federal Reserve System (the Fed)** supervises federally chartered institutions, which must be members of the system; state-chartered banks may voluntarily choose Fed membership. The Fed was created by the **Federal Reserve Act of 1913** to ensure the benefits of both a flexible payments system and a lender of last resort for troubled banks. The Fed's role in setting monetary policy and providing leadership in the international financial markets is so important that we discuss it in detail in Appendix 3A.

State-chartered banks also must comply with the regulations of banking authorities in the state. All banks are eligible to purchase deposit insurance from the **Bank Insurance Fund (BIF)** of the **Federal Deposit Insurance Corporation (FDIC);** the FDIC was created by the Glass–Steagall Act in 1933. Fed member banks must be insured by the FDIC. If a bank purchases insurance, it must comply with rules set by the FDIC.

Because the **three major federal banking regulators—the Comptroller, the Fed, and the FDIC—** arose at different times to serve different purposes, they are independent of one another. In addition to the three federal banking regulators, states have their own set of regulations that banks operating within their borders must abide by. The different regulators are not always legally required to coordinate their actions, and conflicts and even competition arise among them, creating an additional dimension to the regulatory dialectic. An example of recent conflicts between regulators is the stripping of state regulators' authority over national banks by the OCC in January 2004, which generally upset state regulators. Under the OCC's new rules, national banks are only accountable for state zoning, environmental, and criminal statues, while state-chartered banks would be accountable for all state-imposed regulations. The OCC also imposed tighter antipredatory lending regulations for national banks.[6]

---

5 See Bruce Treff and Paul Kirwan. "Implications of Sarbanes-Oxley on the Investment Company Industry." *The Investment Lawyer,* Vol. 10, No. 7 (January 2003), 21; "U.S. Senator Jim Bunning (R-KY) Holds Hearings on Mutual Fund Regulation." *Political/Congressional Transcript Wire,* November 18, 2003, FDCH e-media.

6 See Aldo Svaldi. "Feds End State Regulation of National Banks." *The Denver Post* (January 8, 2004), 1C, 8C; and Jathon Sapsford. "Critics Cry Foul Over New Rules on Bank Review." *The Wall Street Journal* (January 8, 2004), C1, C7.

Thrifts

Like commercial banks, thrifts may operate under either state or federal charters. In 1989, the Financial Institutions Reform, Recovery, and Enforcement Act (FIRREA), one of the major acts to be discussed in a later section of this chapter, mandated a major restructuring of the federal regulatory and insurance functions for the thrift industry, the most notable of which was the abolition of the **Federal Home Loan Bank Board (FHLBB)** and the **Federal Savings and Loan Insurance Corporation (FSLIC).** These agencies, created in the **Federal Home Loan Bank Act of 1932** and the **National Housing Act of 1934,** had comprised the federal chartering, regulatory, and insurance authority for thrifts for more than fifty years. The Federal Home Loan Bank still exists as a lending organization providing liquidity for over 8,000 thrift, bank, and credit union members.

FIRREA replaced them with an even more complex supervisory structure. The regulatory authority for federally chartered thrifts now rests with the **Office of Thrift Supervision (OTS),** which was established within the Treasury department but operates independently of the Secretary of the Treasury. Federal deposit insurance for thrifts is now provided by a newly created **Savings Association Insurance Fund (SAIF),** a subsidiary of the FDIC. The Federal Reserve Board continues to set reserve requirements on deposits held by thrift institutions. Over the last decade, legislation has been proposed to combine BIF and SAIF and remove the thrift charter; however, these proposals have failed to pass, yet continue to be debated.[7]

Credit Unions

Credit unions (CUs) also operate under a dual chartering system. The major federal credit union regulator is the **National Credit Union Administration (NCUA).** CUs may purchase deposit insurance from state funds or from the **National Credit Union Share Insurance Fund (NCUSIF),** established by 1970 amendments to the National Credit Union Act. The Federal Reserve Board enforces reserve requirements on deposits. The NCUA not only charters credit unions but also oversees the NCUA and all federally insured credit unions, including state-chartered credit unions that have federal share insurance and the **Central Liquidity Facility (CLF),** which makes loans to credit unions needing liquidity. The CLF has the power to borrow funds from the Federal Financing Bank, a government agency assisting agency financing needs. Credit unions can have national or state charters, and although not-for-profit and not taxed, they are subject to many of the same regulations as other depository institutions in terms of safety and soundness and protection of the payments system and other consumer regulations, such as truth in lending. Credit unions are restricted by law to a group with a common bond, and federal CUs need not pay taxes on profits retained to increase their net worth. The common bond requirement for membership in a CU—usually a tie formed as a result of occupational, religious, or social affiliations—is related to the cooperative motivation that theoretically underlies the formation of mutual financial institutions. In recent years, credit unions extended this common bond, leading to lawsuits by banking groups. Although the Supreme Court ruled in 1998 that credit union regulators had overstepped their bounds with such an extension, Congress responded with legislation allowing this extension in 1998 for credit unions with fewer than 3,000 people and permitting larger CUs to apply for exceptions. Recently, banking organizations have again sought to curb credit union expansion.

What Is Regulated?

Table 3.2 provides a summary, prepared by the Federal Reserve Bank of New York, of regulated management areas and the agencies responsible for monitoring institutions' behavior in each area. That compilation provides convincing evidence of extensive restrictions within a complex structure. For example, the table identifies twelve categories of control ranging from initial entry into an industry (chartering and licensing) to customer relationships (consumer protection).[8]

Table 3.2 identifies the agencies with which a single institution interacts. Consider, for example, a state-chartered S&L, in Row F of the table. Five state or federal authorities (the OTS, the state, the Fed,

---

7 See "Financial Restructuring: Highlights of Treasury's 1997 Legislative Proposal on Financial Modernization." *Banking Policy Report* (June 16, 1997), 7–9; and Bill Summary and Status 2003–2004 for a more recent proposal for such a merger *(http://thomas.loc.gov).*

8 Discussion of the details of these regulations is reserved for later chapters on individual management activities.

the FHLB, and the FDIC) either set the rules for its operations, enforce the rules, or do both. For instance, a state savings institution gets its charter from a state agency, but both state authorities and the OTS control its ability to branch or acquire other institutions. Its regional Federal Home Loan (FHL) Bank serves as a source of liquidity and provides funds for housing finance under terms established by FIRREA. Both the state and the OTS may conduct periodic examinations of the institution's financial condition and operations. The Federal Reserve Board determines savings institutions' reserve requirements on deposits, and these deposits may be insured by the FDIC (through its SAIF division) or by a nonfederal insurance fund. If insured by SAIF, the thrift is subject to additional regulations that the FDIC may choose to impose at any time to preserve the insurance fund's financial health. At the beginning of 2003, for 9,354 FDIC-insured banks and savings institutions, 57.2 percent had the FDIC as their chief regulator, 22.2 percent the OCC, 10.2 percent the Fed, and 10.4 percent the OTS (see *http://www2.fdic.gov/sdi/sob*).

Examination Process

The previous example highlights a major function of depository institution regulators: examining the financial condition and operations of the firms they supervise. At the federal level, the **Federal Financial Institutions Examination Council (FFIEC)** coordinates procedures for assuring compliance with a variety of regulations. The FFIEC consists of representatives from the Board of Governors of the Fed, the FDIC, the OTS, the NCUA, and the OCC. It controls requirements for financial reporting and disclosures that institutions must make to regulators, negotiates sharing of information between state and federal agencies, and even provides training programs for examiners of the member agencies. The FFIEC serves as a formal interagency body that is empowered to prescribe uniform principles, standards, and report forms for the federal examination of financial institutions across the different regulatory agencies and to make recommendations to promote uniformity in the supervision of financial institutions. It also provides public information by posting downloadable uniform bank performance reports (UBPR) on the Internet for any institution *(http://www.ffiec.gov/)*.

Examinations performed by the regulators consist of onsite visits by agency personnel, who audit the policies and procedures used to grant loans, purchase and sell securities, process deposits, manage cash, and keep financial records. Typically, from one to four examiners remain at an institution for a month or more. The frequency of examinations varies with the existing condition of a depository.

The **FDICIA of 1991** increased the examination frequency for many financial institutions. Federal bank regulators must examine all insured institutions with assets of $100 million or more at least once annually. Smaller institutions that are adequately capitalized and have superior examination ratings must be examined at least every eighteen months. Troubled or inadequately capitalized firms are subject to more frequent examinations. Frequent onsite examinations are intended to identify emerging problems for sound institutions and to help solve lingering problems of troubled firms.

Since 1993, regulators have used a set of so-called **tripwires** to identify unsafe or unsound banking practices. These tripwires establish minimum standards for virtually every area under management's influence or control. Four federal regulatory agencies—the Fed, the FDIC, the Comptroller of the Currency, and the NCUA—use a uniform rating system known by the acronym **CAMELS.** This system assigns 1 to 5 (best to worst) ratings to the institution's **C**apital, **A**ssets, **M**anagement, **E**arnings, **L**iquidity, and **S**ensitivity to market risks, including its interest rate, price, and foreign exchange exposure. The CAMEL system has been in effect since 1978; however, the last component, **S,** or **sensitivity to market risk,** was added in 1997. The NCUSIF also uses a CAMELS rating system, similar to the FDIC for credit union examinations.

CAMELS factors are viewed together, so the acceptability of one factor depends on the quality of the others. For instance, the acceptability of a bank's capital ratio may depend on the quality of its assets and its interest rate risk. Judgments of capital adequacy are based not only on meeting capital requirements but also on the composition of the bank's assets and liabilities as well as off-balance-sheet items. Judgments of asset quality are based on the risk of the bank's assets and their classification as good, substandard, doubtful, or losses. To evaluate management ability, examiners consider not only the quality of the bank's management, but the quality of its board of directors, as well. Evaluations of earnings are based on the earnings trends and levels relative to those of the institution's peers. Liquidity scores reflect credit conditions, volatility of deposits, loan commitments and other contingent claims, liquid assets, and ability to borrow funds quickly in case of need. For market rate risk, banks must demonstrate what

table 3.2 DEPOSITORY INSTITUTIONS AND THEIR REGULATORS

The regulatory structure for depository institutions is based on a dual banking system, in which both state and federal governments issue charters. A single institution may be supervised by state officials and by several federal regulators, depending on the activities in which it is engaged.

	Chartering and Licensing	Branching	Mergers and Acquisitions[a]
A. National banks	OCC	OCC	Fed and OCC
B. State member banks	State	Fed/State	Fed/State
C. Insured state nonmember	State	FDIC/State	FDIC/State
D. Noninsured state banks	State	State	State
E. Savings banks			
Federal	OTS	OTS	FDIC/OTS
State	State	FDIC/State	FDIC/State
F. Savings and Loans			
Federal	OTS	OTS	FDIC/OTS
State	State	FDIC	
G. Credit unions			
Federal	NCUAB	None	NCUA Board
State	State	State	State/NCUA Board

a For mergers and acquisitions, regulators' involvement varies depending on characteristics of merged or acquired firms.

Source: Adapted from Federal Reserve Bank of New York, "Depository Institutions and Their Regulators," 1988; updated by the Authors.

will happen to earnings with changes in interest rates and other factors affecting market exposure. The CAMELS system was revised in 1996 to give banks separate ratings for each of the five categories, as well. The new system is based on regulators' perception that banks need all the help they can get in a current global competitive environment, which entails greater perils, as well as opportunities, than ever before. Regulators have also added a risk management element to each of the CAMELS components.[9]

CAMELS ratings are not publicly available in order to protect banks from potential deposit runs. However, a number of private agencies, such as Sheshunoff in Austin, Texas, provide similar ratings, leaving out the management and market risk components. These agencies also sell software that allows banks and thrifts to perform computer simulations to estimate market risks. Methods to estimate market risk exposure are discussed later in the text.

The OTS has a separate, very similar system known as **MACRO.** Its composite ratings provide one basis for determining how often examiners arrive and even whether regulators can restrict institutions from activities available to safer depositories. Other examiners, such as state regulators, may operate on different schedules.

Does This Regulatory Structure Make Sense?

Few disagree that regulatory agencies duplicate the efforts of others. Efforts have been made as far back as the Hoover Administration to analyze the system and recommend reforms. In 1974, Arthur Burns, then chairman of the Board of Governors of the Federal Reserve, called the bank regulatory system "a jurisdictional tangle that boggles the mind." Some studies have advocated consolidating supervisory power in a single agency, whereas others have warned against giving any single organization too much power, arguing that competition between regulators provides cross checks that promote safety. The Bush Task Force on Deregulation of Financial Services recommended to Congress in 1984 that the agencies be reorganized along functional lines, giving one agency the authority over federal deposit

9 "CAMEL Is Evolving into CAMELS." *Banking Policy Report* (November 4, 1996), 3.

Reserve Requirements	Access to the Discount Window	Deposit Insurance	Supervision/ Examination	CONSUMER PROTECTION	
				Rulemaking	Enforcement
Fed	Fed	FDIC (BIF)	OCC	Fed	OCC
Fed	Fed	FDIC (BIF)	Fed/State	Fed/State	Fed/State
Fed	Fed	FDIC (BIF)	FDIC/State	Fed/State	FDIC/State
Fed	Fed	None/State	State	Fed/State	State/FTC
Fed	Fed	FDIC (SAIF)	OTS/FDIC	Fed/OTS	OTS
		(BIF)/State	FDIC/State	Fed/OTS/State	FDIC/OTS/State
Fed	Fed/FHLB	FDIC (SAIF)	OTS/FDIC	Fed/OTS	OTS
		or State	FDIC/State	Fed/OTS/State	FDIC/OTS/State
Fed	Fed/CLF	NCUSIF	NCUA Board	Fed/State	NCUA Board
		or State	State		State

insurance, another authority over examination and supervision, and so forth. As with earlier reports, however, Congress delayed action on the proposals. However, in recent years efforts have been made to streamline regulations and overlap between regulators.[10]

Regulation of Finance Companies

In contrast to depositories, the sources and uses of funds of finance companies are not heavily regulated at the federal level. These institutions raise funds in the debt markets rather than from deposits and do not have to meet Federal Reserve requirements or other asset restrictions. Some experts believe

Concept Questions

1 What trends in regulations have occurred during different time periods?

2 Why do banks have so many different regulators? What is the chief regulatory job of the Office of the Comptroller of the Currency (OCC), the Fed, and the FDIC, in terms of who they supervise?

3 How many regulators do thrifts have? Credit unions? Who are they?

4 How are examinations by regulators coordinated? What does the acronym CAMELS stand for, and how are these ratings determined?

---

10 Joseph B. Treaster. "Financial Services Consolidate, but Regulation Is Still Fragmented." *New York Times* (January 2, 1998), D1, D5. For earlier discussions of these issues, see Johnson (1984) and Gilbert (1984). The Economic Growth and Regulatory Paperwork Reduction Act of 1996 modified financial institution regulations, attempting to streamline regulations including those for the mortgage lending process, along with reducing record keeping requirements that increase the burden and the cost of credit under the Fair Credit Reporting Act. Details on regulations can be found with links to bills on the FDIC's Website: *http://www.fdic.gov/regulations/laws/important/index.html.*

that finance companies' recent success in competition against commercial banks is the result of technological and financial innovations, such as securitization, that have aided them in raising funds.[11]

Licensing Restrictions

Finance companies must seek permission from state authorities to open new offices. They enjoy more freedom than banks or thrifts to expand across state lines, however, because no federal restriction limits their interstate operations. Most states evaluate requests to open new offices by applying the "convenience and advantage" rule, which holds that expansion should occur only if the community would benefit. As a result, individual states or communities may limit competition.[12]

Consumer Protection Legislation

Finance companies face other regulations, as well. An extensive body of consumer protection legislation has accumulated since 1968 and affects the managerial decisions of finance companies and other consumer lenders. In the finance company industry, the Federal Trade Commission monitors compliance with consumer protection laws such as the **Consumer Credit Protection (Truth-in-Lending) Act of 1968** and **Equal Credit Opportunity Act of 1974.**

Federal regulations have focused on equality in the availability of credit and on the completeness, accuracy, and uniformity of information disclosed to potential borrowers. State regulations concentrate on the rates of interest that finance companies charge. In recent years, attention has focused on state **usury ceilings,** which are legal limitations on lending rates. When market interest rates rise significantly above the usury ceilings, as they did in the early 1980s, lenders experience severe problems, and the amount of available credit is restricted. In 1980, federal law removed usury ceilings from residential mortgage loans unless states overrode the action by 1983; most states did not. Many states increased or removed usury ceilings on personal loans after market interest rates rose to historic highs in 1980 and 1981.

Regulation of Insurance Companies

Life insurers and property/liability insurers operate within a regulatory system that falls somewhere in between those of depository institutions and finance companies. The **McCarran–Ferguson Act of 1945** gave the federal government the right to regulate insurance companies.[13] Congress agreed, however, that the federal government would not exercise the right to impose regulations if states adequately established and enforced standards for the industry. Although the legal basis for federal regulation of insurers continues, for all practical purposes, insurers operate under the oversight of state agencies. Some critics complain that state insurance commissions are often too closely tied to the industry, often consisting of ex-insurance executives whose oversight too often becomes overlooking. Insurance commissioners in each state wield considerable power individually and exert influence collectively through the **National Association of Insurance Commissioners (NAIC).** NAIC has no legal power but substantial political clout. States also organize life insurance guaranty funds to guard against problems due

---

Concept Questions

1 How are finance companies regulated? Why is this regulation more lenient than that for depository institutions?

2 Why is consumer protection regulation particularly important for finance companies?

---

11 Gorton and Pennacchi (1992).

12 Although the absence of a federal chartering agency removes a regulatory layer, it also means that a firm lacks any recourse if it is denied a state charter. The competitive effect of this and other state restrictions is explored more fully in Selden (1981).

13 Before 1945, the insurance regulatory structure was based on the ruling of the Supreme Court in *Paul v. Virginia* [75 U.S. 168, 8 Wall 168, 19 L ED 357 (1869)]. Under this ruling, insurance was not deemed to be interstate commerce and was therefore not subject to federal regulation. Thus, no federal regulatory structure existed before the McCarran–Ferguson Act was passed. More details on the McCarran–Ferguson Act can be found in "Open Season on an Old Law." *Journal of American Insurance* 63 (Quarter 1, 1987), 8–12.

to failure of insurers. In effect, solvent insurance companies in the state contribute to compensate the policyholders of the failed insurer in that state.

Recent increases in the cost of property/liability insurance have renewed calls for federal regulation of that industry or, at a minimum, for tighter regulation at the state level. The McCarran–Ferguson Act recognized that insurers often pool data on the frequency and causes of their customers' accidents, natural disasters, fires, and so forth to establish statistical databases that help them price insurance policies. Yet federal antitrust laws prohibit data sharing by competitors in most industries on the grounds that it can lead to collusion and price fixing. Thus, McCarran–Ferguson specifically exempts insurers from federal antitrust laws, unless firms can be shown to be engaged in "boycott, coercion, or intimidation" as a result of data sharing.

State regulators are supposed to ensure that these prohibited activities do not occur, but in the late 1980s, some critics complained of lax oversight of the insurance industry. By November 1988, charges of unfair pricing in the property/liability segment of the industry were widespread in some states. In California, voters decided that they paid too much for automobile insurance and passed **Proposition 103.** This referendum mandated a substantial reduction in the prices of some insurance policies issued in that state. The success of Proposition 103 encouraged other consumer advocates to challenge the antitrust exemptions of McCarran–Ferguson and to advocate the law's repeal, substituting instead direct federal regulation of the industry. Responding to criticisms of laxity and inadequate expertise among state regulators, the NAIC developed an accrediting system for state insurance regulators, but criticisms continue to arise at times. (See Chapter 16 for recent legislation.)

Licensing and Solvency Requirements

Regulatory structure aside, the scope and focus of regulations for insurers resemble those for depository institutions in many ways. For example, strict standards designed to protect the solvency of insurers are applied in granting company licenses. After entry is granted, annual financial statements are closely scrutinized, and insurers are subject to frequent examinations. Finally, analogous to deposit insurance agencies, insolvency guarantee funds are established in all states to protect policyholders in case insurers go bankrupt.

Rate Regulation

Insurance regulators devote considerable time to overseeing rates. Generally, regulators agree that rates charged by insurers, when combined with income from investments, must be sufficient to cover the firms' potential liabilities. At the same time, insurers must not charge excessive or unfairly discriminatory rates. Although insurers must differentiate between high-risk and low-risk customers and set charges according to risk, regulations attempt to prevent rate discrimination not justified by differing levels of risk. The approach that state legislators and insurance commissioners take toward achieving ideal rates differs from state to state and varies according to the category of insurer.

Generally, regulators do not directly control the policy premiums that life insurers may charge, but most states impose standards designed to guarantee sufficient reserves to cover future claims. Thus, the regulations establish floors for policy rates, because insurers must set rates high enough to generate the required reserves. For property/liability insurers, state regulations deal more extensively with policy rates. Most states require property/liability insurers to obtain the approval of regulators before increasing policy rates.[14]

Product Regulation

Just as depository institutions have operated under asset and deposit restrictions for many years, insurers must comply with limitations on the types of policies they can offer. In many states, insurers must seek the approval of the insurance commissioners before they can sell new products. The close scrutiny is intended to protect customers against unfair policy provisions and to protect the insurance firms from commitments that may undermine financial stability.

---

14 For an exhaustive review of the effect of rate regulations on property/liability firms, see Harrington (1984).

Asset Structure

Insurers' investments are also regulated. State insurance codes specify permissible categories and quality grades of assets. Many states restrict the percentage of firms' total assets that may be invested in specific types of securities, such as common stock. Despite these restrictions, the industry attracted attention in the early 1990s when several large insurers with extensive junk bond and commercial real estate holdings failed, leaving policyholders stranded. Since that time some state regulation passed stronger product restrictions. These events strengthened congressional interest in federal regulation of insurers.

Insurance Regulatory Modernization Action Plan

In response to mandates for modernization, in March of 2000, the National Association of Insurance Commissioners (NAIC) pledged to unify state regulatory processes to improve marketplace efficiencies and protect the needs of insurance consumers in the twenty-first century. The NAIC had a number of goals in mind:

1. **Consumer Protection:** Provide an open process with access to information and consumers' view to protect consumers.

2. **Market Regulation:** Use market analysis to assess the quality of every insurer's conduct in the marketplace, provide uniformity, and foster interstate collaboration to create a common set of standards for a uniform market regulatory oversight program that will include all states.

3. **Speed-to-Market for Insurance Products:** Promote interstate collaboration and filing operational efficiency reforms, whereby state insurance commissioners will improve the timeliness and quality of the reviews given to filings of insurance products and their corresponding advertising and rating systems.

4. **Producer Licensing:** Streamline forms and processes with the long-term goal of implementing a uniform, electronic licensing system for individuals and business entities that sell, solicit, or negotiate insurance.

5. **Insurance Company Licensing:** Make licensing as uniform as appropriate to support a competitive insurance market.

6. **Solvency Regulation:** More fully coordinate regulatory efforts of state insurance regulators to share information proactively, maximize technological tools, and realize efficiencies in the conduct of solvency monitoring.

7. **Change in Insurance Company Control:** Streamline the process for approval of mergers and other changes of control.[15]

Regulation of Pension Funds

Pension funds operate under contractual savings agreements that obligate them to pay retirement benefits to workers. The pension plans of private corporations are subject to the **Employee Retirement Income Security Act,** passed by Congress in 1974 and more commonly known as **ERISA.**

Concept Questions

1 Do you think state insurance agencies should have greater control over insurance regulation versus federal agencies? Why or why not?

2 Why was Proposition 103 passed, and what effect did it have on the public's access to insurance?

3 What are the different areas that must be regulated for insurance companies? Why are these areas particularly important to regulate?

4 Why is the NAIC's insurance modernization proposal important for the insurance industry?

---

15 See NAIC Website *(http://www.naic.org)* for updates on NAIC legislation; "Gramm-Leach-Bliley Act: The Statement of Intent—Delivering on a Promise"; "NAIC Testifies on Recent Steps in Modernizing State Insurance Regulation," October 22, 2003 *(http://www.assureusa.org/index.htm)*; "Nation's Top Insurance Regulators Support Interstate Compact," NAIC News Release: National Association of Insurance Commissioners *(http://www.naic.org/pressroom/releases/)*; NAIC, "A Reinforced Commitment: Insurance Regulatory Modernization Action Plan," 2003, National Association of Insurance Commissioners.

Investment Management

ERISA covers almost all areas of pension fund management. Two provisions set standards for vested benefits to plan participants and for funding a plan so that assets equal accrued liabilities. Vested benefits are those to which employees are entitled even if they leave their firms before retirement. ERISA requires early vesting of benefits and ensures that most employees are 100 percent vested after fifteen years of service.

ERISA also sets standards for employer contributions in relation to a fund's investment income and benefit liabilities. Generally, ERISA attempts to ensure that an employer works toward maintaining pension assets equal to the fund's obligations. Pension fund managers have **fiduciary responsibility** for investments of assets. Fiduciary responsibility is the obligation to act in the best interests of clients under a "prudent man" rule (i.e., acting as a prudent person would behave in managing his or her own investments). Fund managers are required to act solely in the interests of the fund's beneficiaries.

Pension Insurance

Another ERISA provision, also designed to protect the financial interests of fund members, established an insurance fund to guarantee that benefits are paid to eligible members even if a pension plan defaults on its obligations. This insurance is provided by a federal agency called the **Pension Benefit Guaranty Corporation (PBGC)** and is funded by assessments on employers according to the numbers of employees their plan covers and the risk of the funds' assets. To ensure the continuing financial stability of pension funds, the law imposes requirements for extensive and frequent reporting and disclosure. As explained later in the text, federal pension insurance has been plagued by many of the same difficulties as federal deposit insurance, evoking considerable concern among regulators and retirees, whose future incomes may be in jeopardy.

Regulation of Investment Companies and Mutual Funds

Investment companies act as portfolio managers for those to whom they sell ownership shares. Because investment company shares are sold publicly and because many of their assets are publicly traded, investment companies must comply with federal securities laws. Federal and state laws also define the obligations of fund managers to shareholders.

Federal Securities Laws

The issuance of ownership shares by investment companies and the frequency and accuracy of their financial reports are monitored by the **Securities and Exchange Commission (SEC),** under authority granted by the **Securities Act of 1933** and the **Securities Exchange Act of 1934.** Many provisions affecting investment companies also apply to other firms that issue securities for sale to the public. Some provisions address investment companies specifically, however, to ensure regular and truthful disclosures to current and potential shareholders.

The Securities Act of 1933 focused on new securities issues, requiring firms to provide full and accurate information about their financial positions and about new securities they offered. The Securities Exchange Act of 1934 established the SEC as the chief regulator of the securities markets and required regular disclosure of financial information by firms with publicly traded securities.

Securities laws are rooted in the belief that access to information is the best guarantor of the public interest. Depository institution legislation, in contrast, has produced elaborate regulatory systems for gathering information, much of it unavailable to the public. The securities and investment company

Concept Questions

1 What is ERISA? What requirements does ERISA impose on corporate pension plans?

2 What is the Pension Benefit Guaranty Corporation (PBGC), and what protection does it provide?

industries operate within strong systems of self-regulation monitored by trade organizations, whereas depository trade organizations resemble political action groups, seeking to preserve existing laws or to promote new legislation.

Regulations on Sources and Uses of Funds

The Investment Company Act of 1940 and subsequent amendments, and the **Investment Advisers Act** of the same year, are the foundations for specific regulations governing investment companies. These laws identify the responsibilities of investment advisers and fund managers. For example, they can make only limited use of financial leverage. Also, mutual fund managers must obtain shareholder approval of changes in investment objectives, so shareholders are guaranteed at least some control over their risk exposure and return potential.

The Investment Company Act also imposed diversification requirements to protect shareholders against the risk of total loss. An investment company may invest no more than 5 percent of its assets in securities issued by any one firm, and it may hold no more than 10 percent of the outstanding voting shares of a company. These restrictions apply to 75 percent of an investment company's portfolio; the remaining 25 percent is exempted from such restrictions to encourage investment in small businesses.

Another influence on managers is the exemption of investment company income from federal taxes if it distributes at least 90 percent of net capital gain income and 97 percent of dividend and interest income to shareholders. Taxes on such gains are paid only by individual shareholders, and no taxes are assessed on fund income, an approach to taxation known as the **conduit theory.** Finally, the federal regulatory and tax codes are supplemented by state codes placing additional responsibilities on fund managers.

In contrast to savings at depository institutions, pension funds, or insurance firms, people entrust funds to investment companies without any guarantee of recovery in case of fund failure. Regulation seeks instead to ensure availability of truthful information. If investors choose the wrong investment companies, however, no federal or state insurance will mitigate their losses.

Recent Proposals to Curb Mutual Fund After-Hour Trading Abuse

With the mutual fund scandals in 2003 including illegal after-hour trading by many funds for the benefit of managers versus the long-term interests of mutual fund investors, Congress held hearings on proposals for new mutual fund regulations to limit such practice and to give greater independence to boards of directors of mutual funds to provide better corporate governance. The SEC set up a regulatory blueprint for adopting new regulations to improve the transparency of fund operations and curtail abusive trading practices. Several congressional bills were also introduced in 2003 including: (1) S1971 to improve transparency relating to the fees and costs that mutual fund investors incur and to improve corporate governance of mutual funds; (2) S1958 to prevent the practice of late trading by mutual funds and for other purposes; and (3) S1822 to require disclosure of financial relationships between brokers and mutual fund companies and of certain brokerage commissions paid by mutual fund companies. These proposed bills are in addition to new, stronger SEC regulations for mutual funds that the SEC released on January 14, 2004, including new investment company governance requirements, new investment adviser codes of ethics requirements, and new confirmation and point-of-sale disclosure requirements, discussed in more detail in Chapter 17.[16]

Regulation of Securities Firms

Like investment companies, securities firms are subject to SEC scrutiny under the Securities Exchange Act and its amendments. The act established maximum levels of indebtedness for securities dealers and gave the Fed the authority to set **margin requirements** governing the proportions of loans by securities firms to customers for securities purchases and the proportions customers must pay in cash. In addition, securities firms are prohibited from using inside information about firms to profit at the expense of the public. Firms selling investment advice to clients are subject to the Investment Advisers

---

16 See Investment Company Institute Website *(http://www.ici.org/issues),* "Investigation of Mutual Fund Practices," in 2003, and links to legislation on *http://thomas.loc.gov,* which gives legislative summaries; and SEC Website *(http://www.sec.gov/news/press/2004-5.htm),* "SEC Proposes New Investment Company Governance Requirements, New Investment Adviser Codes of Ethics Requirements, and New Confirmation and Point of Sale Disclosure Requirements," January 14, 2004.

Act of 1940, which seeks to prevent fraudulent practices. The scope of a firm's operations determines additional constraints to which it is subject. For example, members of the New York Stock Exchange must conform to the self-regulating rules of the exchange. The **National Association of Securities Dealers (NASD)** is a self-regulating body that sets standards for all brokers and dealers interacting with the public.

The industry operates under congressional objectives for a national securities market articulated in the **Securities Acts Amendments of 1975.** This legislation directed the SEC to promote a fully competitive trading system under which investors nationwide have equal and instantaneous access to information. The policy sought to eliminate historical practices concentrating trades in a few locations, such as New York City. Despite progress toward this goal, it has not yet been fully achieved.

Before 1970, the daily volume of transactions processed by securities firms remained relatively small, and manual processing could accommodate all facets of each transaction, including the physical transfers of securities between buyers and sellers. As in other financial industries, however, investment activity quickened as memories of the Great Depression faded. In 1968 and 1969, several securities firms failed under the burden, and customers' securities were discovered missing. To promote public confidence in the industry, Congress passed the **Securities Investor Protection Act in 1970,** mandating the creation of the **Securities Investor Protection Corporation (SIPC).** The SIPC is an industry-funded organization providing reimbursement to customers of securities firms if they lose securities or cash balances due to failure of affiliated firms. The SIPC, however, does not insure against market losses. Although initiated by Congress, the federal government does not guarantee the SIPC's promises to investors, and it has no legal regulatory powers. Instead, it is a visible symbol of the industry's obligation to self-regulation.

Whether securities firms will continue to enjoy the relative freedom that many depository institutions seek is an important question. The last half of the 1980s brought many assaults on the industry's image for integrity. Between 1985 and 1991, several major scandals, led by disclosures discrediting junk bond king Michael Milken, rocked the industry. Charges focused on the practice of **insider trading**—transactions in which corporate managers, directors, or their securities advisors illegally profit from private information affecting the value of a firm's securities. Some observers blamed self-interested computerized trading by securities firms for the stock market crash of October 1987. In 1991, Salomon Brothers, a major securities firm, admitted to manipulating activities in the Treasury securities market for its own benefit.

Incidents such as these evoked cries for stepped-up government regulation. Congress responded to some of the criticisms with the passage of the **Insider Trading and Securities Fraud Enforcement Act of 1988,** more commonly known as the **Insider Trading Act.** The legislation established deterrents to the practice by strengthening penalties for violators and requiring firms to develop formal policies to prevent abuses. The act also increased federal agencies' ability to enforce regulations. The Salomon Brothers scandal resulted in rule changes in the Treasury securities market.

Despite the recognized need to increase scrutiny of securities activities, global market forces have increased competition from foreign firms and caused many experts to warn against shackling the industry with additional, costly regulatory taxes. Furthermore, as discussed earlier, technological change cannot be regulated away, and attempts to prevent securities firms from using today's computerized trading strategies are likely to lead only to different, unregulated strategies tomorrow.

Securities firms were particularly affected by the passage by Congress of the **Sarbanes-Oxley Act (SOA) of 2002,** which affects all publicly traded firms as well, but particularly securities firms. Chief financial officers and chief executive officers must provide internal controls to reduce risk and sign off on the reliability of financial statements to reduce the likelihood of accounting fraud and deception. Under SOA, securities firms had to set up internal controls to avoid fraud and conflicts of interest for research analysts and the marketing and underwriting areas of the investment bank. In particular, greater control mechanisms needed to be created for potential risks that could result in securities law violations and increased due diligence for underwriting activities. The SEC was also ordered and adopted rules to separate research analysts from the asset management and investment units of financial institutions.[17]

---

17 See "The Bottom Line on Sarbanes-Oxley." *Long Island Business News,* Vol. 49, No. 2 (September 27, 2002), 1A; "Summary of Sarbanes Oxley Act of 2002," AICPA Website *(http://www.aicpa.org/info/sarbanes_oxley_summary.htm);* Treff and Kirwan. "Implications of Sarbanes-Oxley," 2; Andrew J. Felo and Steven A. Solieri. "New Laws, New Challenges: Implications of Sarbanes-Oxley." *Strategic Finance,* Vol. 84, No. 4 (February 2003), 31; "Sarbanes-Oxley Act." *Mondaq Business Briefing* (April 11, 2003), NA; and Sarbanes-Oxley Act of 2002, Conference Report, July 24, 2002.

Concept Questions

1. What agency is the chief regulator of investment and securities firms?

2. What does the Securities Investor Protection Corporation do?

3. What acts were passed to prevent insider trading? Why is it important for public confidence in the financial markets to ensure against insider trading?

4. What has the SEC and Congress done to try to prevent mutual fund abuses?

5. What does the Investment Company Act require of investment companies?

6. How does the Sarbanes-Oxley Act particularly affect securities firms?

The Regulatory Dialectic: A Conceptual Framework for Regulation, Innovation, and Reform

A simple list of regulations and regulatory agencies governing U.S. financial institutions and particularly the banking industry cannot capture the impact of the restrictions on managerial decisions. The complex relationship between regulators and regulated institutions is best described as an interactive exchange. Only through an exploration of the interaction can historical developments and potential changes be viewed in proper perspective.

The word **dialectic** refers to changes occurring through a process of action and reaction by opposing forces. In his classic presentation, the philosopher Hegel described the dialectic process as (1) an initial set of arguments or rules (the **thesis**), (2) a conflicting set of arguments or responses (the **antithesis**), and (3) a change or modification (the **synthesis**) resulting from an exchange or interaction between the opposing forces. The idea that regulation of financial institutions is a dialectic—a series of cyclical interactions between opposing political and economic forces—as noted earlier, was introduced by Professor Edward Kane.[18] Kane's model of a **regulatory dialectic** has since been widely adopted as an insightful characterization of regulatory developments that are continuing today. The relationship between regulators and regulated institutions has been described as a cat-and-mouse game. According to Kane, operating rules that benefit a protected class provide a strong incentive for other regulated institutions to find loopholes. The desire to compete may eventually make regulatory avoidance an end in itself that consumes institutions' energy and resources rather than simply a means to achieving competitive freedom. One of management's goals becomes circumvention of restrictions (**antithesis**) in an effort to capture a portion of a market otherwise denied. Regulators look unfavorably on this "avoidance" behavior, and if institutions are too successful in circumventing the rules, regulations will be revised to remove loopholes (**a new thesis**). The revisions inspire further avoidance efforts, and the cycle begins anew, until eventually a **synthesis** occurs with the removal of obsolete regulations.

Several forces make regulations obsolete including: (1) **financial innovation,** new financial products and processes that lower costs or serve customers better that can avoid regulations that may be costly or impose regulatory taxes on institutions. Many of the financial products and asset/liability management tools discussed in later chapters (such as negotiable certificates of deposit, zero-coupon securities, securitization of loans, and financial futures) were introduced as financial innovations and have been "successful, significant" innovations. (2) **Technology and economic conditions** also drive the antithesis of the regulatory dialectic. As institutions search for financial innovations that do not violate existing regulations, changes in technology and the economy enhance opportunities for institutions to innovate and cause customers to demand new products. (3) **Globalization of financial markets** also makes regulations obsolete and avoidance of regulations easier.

The Regulatory Dialectic Illustrated

Many examples illustrate the cat-and-mouse game of financial innovation to avoid regulation. In 1863, the National Currency Act attempted to create a national currency for the Union during the Civil War

---

18 See Kane (1977, 1981, 1986, 1989a, 1996) . . . (Selected references are listed in full at the end of the chapter). Also see Henry Wallich. "A Broad View of Deregulation." Unpublished paper presented at the Conference on Pacific Basis Financial Reform, Federal Reserve Bank of San Francisco, December 1984, 3.

by allowing only federally chartered banks to issue bank notes. Rather than eliminating state-chartered banks, however, it resulted in the creation of check-writing accounts by those banks, which continue to operate alongside federally chartered banks today, creating a dual regulatory system. Another good example comes from institutions' activities to avoid restrictions on sources of funds and interest rates paid on deposits. In the 1960s, large commercial banks developed new kinds of deposits and tapped foreign markets to avoid **Regulation Q ceilings** on domestic deposit interest rates, creating innovations including Eurodollar certificates of deposits (CDs), dollar CDs in foreign branches of banks that were not technically under Reg Q. Small institutions found a loophole by offering gifts, such as silverware or toasters, to supplement low interest payments. As regulators observed the success that institutions achieved by raising funds through these unconventional methods, they imposed regulations on new innovations, but large banks responded by issuing nondeposit securities that were sufficiently different to avoid regulations. In playing this game, regulator and regulated institution alike expended considerable resources, but the activity spawned several successful financial innovations that are widely used today. Other regulations resulted in more expensive, suboptimal avoidance mechanisms, such as the creation of bank holding companies to circumvent branching restrictions discussed later in this chapter.[19]

As noted by Kane, eventually a synthesis occurs. With Reg Q, the regulatory synthesis (resolution) was the passage of the Depository Institutions Deregulation and Monetary Control Act (DIDMCA) in 1981, which phased out deposit rate ceilings by 1986, eliminating all but the restriction of no interest on business demand deposits under Reg Q. Figure 3.1 illustrates the regulatory dialectic resulting in the gradual elimination of Regulation Q, with the exception of not paying interest on demand deposits, which remains as a restriction. The following section describes this process along with other regulatory changes from a dialectic perspective.

The Regulatory Dialectic and Major Regulatory Changes from 1980 to 2000

Regulation of financial institutions is a dynamic process. Forces for change arise in part from the objectives of managers and owners of regulated institutions, but market forces also drive change. After a period of delay and analysis, regulations are adjusted. As long as any regulatory restrictions remain— and they certainly will—the dialectic continues. Synthesis in the regulatory dialectic is only a temporary equilibrium, because legal revisions immediately provoke new avoidance behavior. One cycle's synthesis is the next cycle's thesis. Regulatory changes have been introduced rapidly in the United

figure 3.1   DIAGRAM OF THE REGULATORY DIALECTIC

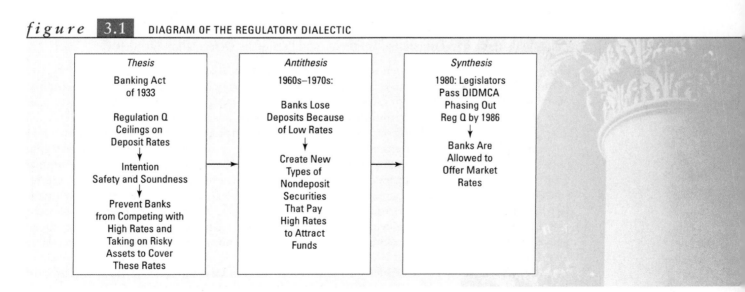

Thesis	Antithesis	Synthesis
Banking Act of 1933	1960s–1970s:	1980: Legislators Pass DIDMCA Phasing Out Reg Q by 1986
Regulation Q Ceilings on Deposit Rates ↓	Banks Lose Deposits Because of Low Rates ↓	↓
Intention Safety and Soundness ↓	Create New Types of Nondeposit Securities That Pay High Rates to Attract Funds	Banks Are Allowed to Offer Market Rates
Prevent Banks from Competing with High Rates and Taking on Risky Assets to Cover These Rates		

19 Summary discussions of the economic costs of avoidance behavior are available in the Federal Reserve Bank of Chicago's discussion of DIDMCA and in Gilbert (1986). Discussions of financial innovations can be found in Flood (1992), Finnerty (1988), Miller (1986), Van Horne (1985), and Silber (1983). The Miller article is the source for the definition of a "successful, significant" innovation.

1 Explain what a dialectic is, and give an example of a regulatory dialectic.

2 How do regulations lead to financial innovations? Give an example.

States. The reactions of financial institutions to new laws and continuing problems led to further regulatory dialectics embodied in additional laws passed in the late 1980s and 1990s. There are seven laws culminating this period of regulatory synthesis:

1. DIDMCA of 1980, mentioned earlier
2. Garn–St. Germain Depository Institutions Act of 1982 (G–St. G)
3. Competitive Equality Banking Act of 1987 (CEBA)
4. Financial Institutions Reform, Recovery, and Enforcement Act of 1989 (FIRREA)
5. Federal Deposit Insurance Corporation Improvement Act of 1991 (FDICIA)
6. Riegle–Neal Interstate Banking and Branching Efficiency Act of 1994 (IBBEA)
7. The Financial Services Modernization (Gramm-Leach-Bliley [GLB]) Act in 1999

These and remaining regulations from a prior era are today's thesis. The following sections discuss the regulatory dialectic that led to these regulations and the major provisions of the regulations. The first five regulations from 1980 to 1991 will be discussed as one dialectic, followed by discussions of organizational form and the two most recent major regulations for the depository institution industry as a second dialectic.

The Dialectic of Reform for Thrifts and Banks in the 1980s and Early 1990s

Kane's regulatory dialectic can be used as a conceptual model to understand the forces that led to the five major regulations from 1980 to 1991 in the previous list including DIDMCA of 1980, G–St. G of 1982, CEBA of 1987, FIRREA of 1989, and FDICA of 1991. All of these regulations reflect reactions to crises for depository institutions during the 1980s and early 1990s including aspects of both deregulation, to give banks and thrifts greater liability and asset powers to compete with nonbanks, and re-regulation, recapitalization of insurance funds and a clean-up of failed institutions following the U.S. thrift crisis and large number of U.S. bank failures in the late 1980s and early 1990s.

Conditions Leading to Loopholes (Antithesis) and Eventually Deregulation (Synthesis)

Banks and savings institutions were stuck with rigid regulations under Reg Q's rate ceilings in the late 1970s to the early 1980s in terms of being prevented from offering market interest rates to depositors. Although this ceiling kept deposit rates low, customers could get higher rates from new money market accounts offered by brokerage firms or by directly investing in Treasury bills or other direct securities. Consequently, banks and thrifts lost deposits to other intermediaries (**cross-intermediation**) or to direct financial markets (**disintermediation**). Large depository institutions responded by developing nondeposit investment-type funding (**liability management**) that, however, was more expensive than insured deposits. Small depositories offered implicit interest to customers by providing gifts or greater convenience. These strategies increased noninterest costs for depositories. At the same time, thrifts faced great interest rate risk with rising interest and noninterest expenses. Yet, their revenues were fixed with interest revenue based on previously set low rates on long-term fixed rate mortgages. At this time adjustable-rate mortgages were only allowed in a few states. Thus, thrifts in particular suffered large losses and deteriorating capital.

Several forces led to a need for deregulation including **nonbank competition,** with securities firms and diversified firms such as Merrill Lynch and Sears able to offer new types of financial services nationwide, creating protests by bankers for a level playing field; **declining Fed membership,** with nonmembers not subject to the same kinds of reserve requirements as Fed members, creating an inequitable system; and with **technological innovations,** creating new successful innovations by financial institutions that would allow them to escape current regulations. These technological innovations are summarized in Table 3.3. Over time, technology created new capabilities for institutions and also new customer demands for new services including cash management and electronic banking, which banks were not allowed to offer at this time. Nonbanks were able to develop and compete more easily as information providers. Thus, an antithesis was driven by economic and technological changes, as well as by the attitudes of regulators and the regulated institutions. In the face of advancing technology, regulations began to seem like antiquated relics. Regulators also reevaluated the harmful effects lack of competition had on safety and soundness of depository institutions.

The Synthesis in the Early 1980s

With these dramatic competitive, environmental, and technological changes, Congress realized that depository institutions needed greater product freedom on both the liability side and the asset side: liability flexibility to offer market interest rates on deposits, and asset flexibility for thrifts to offer limited amounts of other types of consumer and commercial loans and to offer adjustable-rate mortgages to reduce their interest rate risk. This led to the passage of the **DIDMCA in 1980** and **G–St. G in 1982.**

DIDMCA

The provisions of DIDMCA are listed in Table 3.4. DIDMCA incorporated two major components, as its name revealed: **deregulation of depository institutions** and **improved monetary control.** The deregulation provisions encouraged competition among depositories while improving financial services for small savers by phasing out Reg Q. The provisions (1) **allowed depository institutions to offer interest-paying checking accounts for consumers,** called NOW accounts; (2) **provided a higher deposit insurance coverage, up to $100,000** per account holder; (3) **provided greater asset powers for savings institutions** including commercial paper, investment company shares, education loans, and, to a limited extent, consumer loans; (4) **allowed thrifts to offer credit card and trust services** and **savings banks to make limited percentages of commercial loans and to accept demand deposits in conjunction with corporate loan relationships;** and (5) **removed state usury ceilings** (state rate ceilings on loans) to allow depository institutions to offer market rates. States could reinstate ceilings after April 1, 1983. The monetary control provisions improved the effectiveness of the Fed's responses to changing economic conditions and equalized the monetary policy burden among depositories by requiring **the same reserve requirements for all depository institutions.**

Garn–St. Germain

Despite DIDMCA, thrifts' profitability continued to decline at an alarming rate. In 1981, the FHLBB authorized thrifts to offer adjustable-rate mortgages, hoping the industry could then earn interest revenues above interest expenses. However, this measure came too late, and thrifts with rising interest expenses and fixed rate assets were suffering large losses. Also, disintermediation continued, since depository institutions were not allowed to offer money market funds (MMFs) that provided higher rates for depositors. Regulators also found that geographical constraints limited their responses to troubled institutions. The FSLIC had begun to increase its reliance on forced mergers for failing thrifts with stronger institutions, thus avoiding immediate payments to insured depositors; the difficulty of finding merger partners located near large, troubled institutions forced consideration of interstate mergers.

To address continuing problems and to rescue thrifts, Congress passed the Garn–St. Germain Act, which became law in October 1982. G–St. G provided for additional deregulatory steps including: (1) allowing **depository institutions to offer money market deposit accounts (MMDAs), phasing out Reg Q restrictions by 1983, with the exception of business demand deposits that were not allowed to pay interest;** (2) allowing **federal savings and loans to make commercial loans up to 10 percent of total assets by 1984, and they could invest increased percentages of their assets in consumer loans (from 20 percent to 30 percent of total assets)** and invest in securities issued by state and local governments; (3) thrifts were allowed to have **adjustable-rate mortgages** and to enforce due-on-sale provisions in mortgage loan contracts; (4) **thrifts were permitted to convert from state to federal charters, and vice versa,** to switch between S&L and savings bank charters, and **to convert from mutual to stock ownership;** and (5) the FDIC and the FSLIC were given broad powers to assist troubled banks and thrifts

table **3.3** TIMING AND CONTEXT OF SELECTED FINANCIAL INNOVATIONS

Regulatory avoidance is often manifest in financial innovations devised by the regulated. In turn, financial innovations are encouraged by technological and economic change, as seen from the increase in the number of financial innovations in the past twenty years.

Decade	Financial Innovation	Technological Innovation	Economic/Political Environment
1930s			Stock market crash
			Bank holiday, Great Depression
Major Laws and Policies: Thesis of Dialectic Instituted			
1940s			World War II begins
			World War II ends
			Fed controls interest rates
			Baby Boom
1950s		Television	Fed/Treasury "Accord:" Controls lifted on rates
			Cold war/ Korean war
1960s	Eurodollar deposits	Mainframe computers	Vietnam war escalates
	Bank credit cards		
	Fed funds market		
	Negotiable CDs		
1970s	Financial futures	Handheld financial	Gold standard abandoned
	Automated teller machines	calculators	Exchange rates float
	Money market mutual funds		Vietnam war ends
	Adjustable-rate mortgages		Oil embargo
	Negotiable order of withdrawal		Double-digit inflation
	(NOW) accounts		Change in Federal Reserve
	Discount brokerage accounts		System's open market policies
	Options, junk bonds		
1980s	Interest rate swaps	Microcomputers	Double-digit inflation ends
	Zero-coupon bonds	Fax machines	Stock market crash
	24-hour securities trading		Collapse of commercial real estate market
	Program trading		
	Universal/variable life insurance		
	Off-balance-sheet guarantees		
	Securitization		
1990s	Global futures trading	Internet	Corporate downsizing
	Bank mutual funds/annuities	Low-cost computers	Early 1990s: low interest rates (recession)
	Home banking and Internet	Increasing accessibility	Bilateral free-trade agreements and NAFTA
	securities trading	of technology	International accord: deregulation of
	Mergers among diverse		financial services firms
	financial firms		Tax law changes (new types of IRAs)
	Cash management & payment services		Demographics: aging Baby Boomers
	Consulting services for small firms		and demand for retirement products
Late 1990s	E-futures trading	Broadband: faster	Movement of jobs overseas for service
to 2000s	New types of credit	Internet services	functions that can be handled on the
	Derivatives	New firewalls for protection	Internet or by phone
	24-hour banking		Deregulation allowing banking, securities,
	Educational savings accounts		and insurance products to be cross-sold
	Noninterest gifts for opening		Low interest rates; economic cycles
	accounts and other services		including recession in 2001 and following
	Investment and insurance services		beginning of an expansion, but job losses

table   **3.4**   PROVISIONS OF THE DEPOSITORY INSTITUTIONS DEREGULATION AND MONETARY CONTROL ACT OF 1980

DIDMCA brought about the most sweeping changes in financial regulation since the 1930s. Its main effects were to deregulate deposit accounts, to extend the same reserve requirements to all depositories, to broaden the asset choices of thrifts, and to increase deposit insurance coverage.

Title I: Monetary Control Act of 1980

Phased in reserve requirements on transactions accounts at all depository institutions; authorized the Fed to impose supplemental interest-bearing reserve requirements if necessary; extended discount window borrowing privileges and other Fed services to any depository institution issuing transactions accounts or nonpersonal time deposits; mandated the development of a fee structure for Fed services

Title II: Depository Institutions Deregulation Act of 1980

Provided for the orderly phase-out and ultimate elimination of interest rate ceilings on deposit accounts

Title III: Consumer Checking Account Equity Act of 1980

Authorized interest-bearing transactions accounts at all depositories; increased federal deposit insurance coverage from $40,000 to $100,000 per account

Title IV: Expanded Powers for Thrifts

Allowed federally chartered S&Ls to invest in consumer and other loans, commercial paper, corporate bonds, and mutual funds; authorized federal thrifts to issue credit cards; increased powers for savings banks, including demand deposit accounts to commercial loan customers

Title V: Preemption of State Interest Rate Ceilings

Eliminated state usury ceilings on residential mortgage loans; tied ceilings rates on business and agricultural loans of $25,000 or more to the Fed discount rate; gave states until April 1, 1983, to reinstate usury ceilings on these loan categories; overrode state laws imposing ceilings on deposit interest rates

Title VI: Truth-in-Lending Simplification

Revised the Truth-in-Lending Act to help creditors comply with disclosure requirements; gave consumers additional rights in case of false disclosure

Title VII: Amendments to the National Banking Laws

Miscellaneous provisions on national banks and bank holding companies

Title VIII: Financial Regulation Simplification Act of 1980

Required regulators to limit regulations to those "for which a need has been established" and to minimize compliance costs

Title IX: Foreign Control of U.S. Financial Institutions

Imposed a moratorium until July 1, 1980, on foreign takeovers of U.S. financial institutions

including providing **net worth certificates, regulatory capital that could count for meeting capital requirements that was intended to be paid back eventually** to keep thrifts from failing. **Interstate and inter-industry mergers** were also allowed if other partners could not be found for failing institutions. Table 3.5 lists the provisions of the G–St. G Act of 1982.

The U.S. Thrift and Banking Crises in the Late 1980s and Early 1990s: Re-regulation with CEBA in 1987, FIRREA in 1989, and FDICIA in 1991

By 1987, hundreds of thrifts were technically insolvent when evaluated under generally accepted accounting principles (GAAP), but they continued operating, propped up by net worth certificates and other regulatory gimmicks allowed by DIDMCA's new regulatory accounting practices (RAP) provisions. The General Accounting Office (GAO) declared that the FSLIC was technically insolvent, with insufficient reserves to protect insured S&L depositors. As early as 1985, the FSLIC could not afford to close or arrange mergers for a number of very large thrifts, placing them instead in a consignment program, in which other thrifts or handpicked executives took over their management. Many insolvent thrifts were allowed to continue to operate to protect dwindling deposit insurance funds. These "zombie" S&Ls, as Kane calls them, attempted to gamble their way back to solvency in the mid-1980s by taking on great risks including overly rapid growth. This growth was funded by attracting large deposits insured up to

---

| *table* **3.5** | PROVISIONS OF THE GARN–ST GERMAIN DEPOSITORY INSTITUTIONS ACT OF 1982 |

Passage of G–St. G was hastened by an earnings crisis in the thrift industry. The law provided for interstate acquisitions and other measures to aid regulators of failing institutions. It further deregulated thrifts' asset portfolios and expanded the types of accounts depositories could offer.

Title I: The Deposit Insurance Flexibility Act

Gave the FDIC, FSLIC, and NCUSIF expanded options to handle failing institutions; established a priority system for emergency acquisitions of insolvent depositories, permitting interstate, inter-industry acquisitions as a last resort

Title II: The Net Worth Certificate Act

Permitted the FSLIC and FDIC to issue net worth certificates to provide capital assistance to qualifying S&Ls and savings banks

Title III: The Thrift Institution Restructuring Act

Broadened investment powers for federally chartered thrifts, allowing commercial loans up to 10 percent of total assets by 1984; increased the permissible percentage of consumer loans from 20 percent to 30 percent of total assets; authorized the creation of an account directly competitive with MMMFs (later named the MMDA) for all depositories; overrode state laws preventing the enforcement of due-on-sale clauses in mortgages; permitted S&Ls to offer demand deposits to commercial loan customers; increased chartering flexibility for thrifts

Title IV: Provisions Relating to National and Member Banks

Increased the amount that could be loaned to a single borrower; exempted small institutions from reserve requirements

Title V: Credit Union Amendments

Streamlined the regulatory process for federal CUs; expanded CUs' real estate lending powers; increased their authority to invest in government securities

Title VI: Amendment to the Bank Holding Company Act

Prohibited BHCs from selling or underwriting insurance

Title VII: Miscellaneous

Authorized the issuance of NOW accounts and share drafts to state and local governments

Title VIII: The Alternative Mortgage Transaction Act of 1982

Permitted state-chartered institutions to offer the same types of adjustable-rate mortgages authorized for federally chartered institutions, unless overridden by new state laws within three years

---

$100,000 (jumbo deposits), often sold by brokers (brokered) from depositors across the country. In liberally regulated states, such as California and Texas, state-chartered thrifts were allowed to take on very risky investments forbidden to other S&Ls. Some thrift managers made bad—even fraudulent—investment decisions that drove their institutions into insolvency as loans soured in the late 1980s.

These types of activities depleted privately insured savings funds. Private funds in Ohio and Maryland failed in 1985, and many depositors waited several years before receiving their deposits. Kane pointed out that the mishandling of these crises provided a wake-up call to the public concerning the poor condition of the FSLIC, resulting in a general loss of public confidence and a silent stream of deposit withdrawals from thrifts. The average rates that thrifts paid to keep deposits rose relative to bank rates at this time, particularly in states suffering economic distress, and thrifts suffered net deposit withdrawals. By 1987, about 15 percent of the industry had suffered overwhelming losses, straining the FSLIC's resources and creating a national crisis. The banking industry was not immune to the problems. In particular, the banking sector suffered severe strains in the middle to late 1980s. Many institutions failed and others reported record losses on commercial real estate and other risky loans. Most serious were the effects of economic problems in Texas, which led to the failure or near-failure of almost all the largest banks in that state, including First Republic and M Corp. To protect the deposit insurance funds from bankruptcy and to resolve these crises, CEBA, FIRREA, and FDICIA were passed.

The Competitive Equality Banking Act (CEBA) of 1987

CEBA, enacted in August 1987, placed a moratorium on nonbank activities, recapitalized the FSLIC, extended the net worth certificate program for five years, and made permanent provisions for the G–St. G emergency acquisition powers. It also placed the "full faith" of the U.S. government behind deposit insurance funds to stem deposit withdrawals from healthy thrifts. The provisions of CEBA are summarized in Table 3.6 and include: (1) **recapitalization and reorganization of the FSLIC to rebuild confidence and slow deposit withdrawals;** (2) **a moratorium on regulatory loopholes** including a prohibition against bank regulators approving nonbank banks and state regulators allowing banks and thrifts

table   **3.6**   PROVISIONS OF THE COMPETITIVE EQUALITY BANKING ACT OF 1987

CEBA was a short-run fix for several issues facing the financial system. It authorized additional funds to assist the FSLIC with the continuing thrift crisis, but the problem was much larger than the law recognized. CEBA also prohibited the spread of nonbank banks and temporarily postponed action on further expansion of banking powers.

Title I: Financial Institutions Competitive Equality Act

Expanded the definition of *bank* to include any institution insured by the FDIC (which did not apply to 168 nonbank banks in existence on March 5, 1987); permitted nonbank banks to acquire failing savings institutions; clarified regulations applying to thrift holding companies

Title II: Moratorium on Certain Nonbanking Activities

Prohibited federal bank regulators from approving new securities, real estate, or insurance activities until March 1, 1988, beginning retroactively on March 5, 1987; brought state-chartered banks that were not members of the Fed under G–St. G with regard to affiliations with securities firms; limited the securities activities of thrifts until March 1, 1988, unless those activities were in place before March 5, 1987

Title III: FSLIC Recapitalization Act

Authorized the FHL Bank system to borrow up to $10.825 billion, collateralized by zero-coupon Treasury securities, to assist the FSLIC; permitted assessment of FSLIC institutions to service the authorized debt; phased out the special assessment of FSLIC-insured institutions in effect since 1985; specified circumstances under which "exit fees" could be charged to institutions departing the FSLIC; established an FSLIC oversight committee

Title IV: Thrift Industry Recovery Act

Required regulators to forbear in closing troubled savings institutions during the period in which FSLIC recapitalization occurred, provided an institution's problem could be attributed to economic conditions; required uniform, generally accepted accounting standards for commercial banks and savings institutions by 1993

Title V: Financial Institutions Emergency Acquisitions Act

Extended the net worth certificate program for five years; made G–St. G emergency acquisition powers permanent; equalized emergency acquisition rules for commercial banks and savings institutions

Title VI: Expedited Funds Availability Act

By September 1, 1990, required depositories to make funds from local deposits available to customers within one business day

Title VII: Credit Union Amendments

Provided the NCUA with additional powers to tighten regulation of CUs

Title VIII: Loan Loss Amortization

Instituted special provisions for banks in agricultural areas, permitting them to write off selected loan losses over an extended period

Title IX: Full Faith and Credit of Federally Insured Depository Institutions

Reaffirmed Congress's intent to provide federal insurance for all qualifying depositors up to the legal limit

Title X: Government Checks

Required depository institutions to cash government checks for customers

Title XI: Interests to Certain Depositors

Ordered the FDIC to pay a specific rate of interest to depositors of a New York bank it had previously closed

Title XII: Miscellaneous Provisions

Mandated a study of junk bonds; required lenders to designate and disclose a cap on adjustable-rate loans

to engage in nonbank activities; (3) **limited relief from closure for insolvent institutions, technically allowing thrifts to continue to operate in economically troubled areas;** (4) **other technical consumer-oriented provisions, such as expediting check clearing times and requiring depository** institutions to cash government checks for customers, among others.

Antithesis: Re-Regulation—New Regulatory Stringency under FIRREA of 1989 and FDICIA of 1991

By December 1988, the FSLIC had fallen into such a desperate situation that the FHLBB was accused of virtually giving away thrifts to wealthy investors, who stood to make millions on the deals. The regulators launched a massive new program to find buyers for troubled thrifts, requiring that the acquirers inject cash into the institutions in exchange for long-term government assistance and substantial tax breaks. In February 1989, thrift bailout legislation was passed.[20]

Antithesis: FIRREA—Thrift Bailout Legislation

On August 9, 1989, Congress enacted the **Financial Institutions Reform, Recovery, and Enforcement Act (FIRREA),** introducing policies of regulatory stringency in reaction to the thrift crisis. The provisions of FIRREA are summarized in Table 3.7. FIRREA tightened supervision and regulatory standards for thrifts, making them equivalent to those for banks. Also, the act imposed new restrictions on the types of assets that thrifts could hold, turning back the "regulatory clock" to a time preceding DIDMCA. Congress's intent clearly was to punish the thrift industry and the FHLBB for the insolvency of the FSLIC. At the same time, legislators chose to ignore their own role in ducking the crisis throughout the mid-1980s and failed to address what many view as the root cause of depository institutions' difficulties: a generous deposit-insurance system not tied to the risk of insured institutions.

FIRREA contained a number of basic provisions: (1) **A regulatory reorganization** created the Office of Thrift Supervision (OTS) to regulate thrifts, and divided the FDIC into SAIF, the Savings Association Insurance Fund, and BIF, the Bank Insurance Fund. The twelve district FHL banks were put under a new regime, the Federal Housing Finance Board (FHFB), to provide loans to thrifts in their regions to develop and administer programs for affordable housing and community-oriented lending; (2) The **Resolution Funding Corporation (REFCORP) and Resolution Trust Corporation (RTC) were created to raise funds and manage the disposition of insolvent thrifts, including salvaging or liquidating assets of nearly 250 insolvent thrifts that the FDIC had acquired since 1989, plus any subsequent insolvencies;** (3) **Product restrictions were once again imposed, whereby** thrifts had to divest junk bond investments and focus on home mortgage lending. State-chartered thrifts were prohibited from engaging in activities barred to federally chartered thrifts. The act revised the **qualified thrift lender test (QTL),** so that in order to gain tax advantages, thrifts had to hold 70 percent (later reduced to 65 percent) of assets in mortgage-related products, reducing their ability to diversify holdings; (4) **New capital requirements for thrifts equivalent to those for banks** were phased in, along with uniform accounting rules. Regulators were given the power to halt risky practices in thrift institutions before the activities completely depleted the institutions' capital, and penalties for managers and directors who committed fraud increased. Thrifts that could not meet new capital requirements were mandated to be closed or merged with other institutions; (5) **Inter-industry, interstate mergers of healthy thrifts** allowed commercial banks to acquire healthy thrifts across state lines.[21]

20 See White (1991); Kane (1989b); Barth (1991); Brumbaugh (1988); Benston (1985); Brock (1980); Cargill and Garcia (1985); Carron (1982); and Cooperman, Lee, and Wolfe (1992) for reviews of the Ohio and Maryland S&L Crises and U.S. Thrift Crisis and regulatory responses and regulations.

21 FIRREA created a complex new regulatory structure. The Office of Thrift Supervision was created within the Treasury department, joining the OCC to regulate, supervise, and examine thrifts and thrift holding companies. The OTS also assumed extensive authority over the FHL bank system. Deposit insurance for savings institutions shifted to SAIF, as part of the FDIC, eliminating the FHLBB and FSLIC altogether. The OCC, Fed, OTS, and FHLBB all had supervisory relations with the RTC Oversight Board, and the FDIC, OTS, and RTC Oversight Board exercised powers over the RTC, making a very complicated structure. The QTL test at the time divided home mortgage-related assets by portfolio assets (total assets less basically noninvestment assets). The IRS tax advantage for QTL lenders was removed in 1996. FIRREA also added more stringent product restrictions. Thrifts had to dispose of junk bonds by 1994, and commercial real estate loans were restricted to four times a thrift's capital. Direct real estate investments could be made only through a separately capitalized subsidiary, and real estate loans had to meet loan-to-value limits. State S&Ls had to abide by the restrictions as federal thrifts, including a maximum of 3 percent of assets in services companies (see Cole and McKenzie [1994]; Cebenoyan, Cooperman, Register, and Hudgins [1998]).

table **3.7**   PROVISIONS OF THE FINANCIAL INSTITUTIONS REFORM, RECOVERY, AND ENFORCEMENT ACT OF 1989

FIRREA was passed in response to the financial crisis of the FSLIC. The law abolished existing federal thrift regulators, created a new supervisory structure, and transferred thrift deposit insurance to the FDIC. The law was viewed as a punitive strike at the thrift industry and a shortsighted attempt that failed to address more fundamental questions.

Title I: Purposes

Summarized congressional intentions to strengthen the thrift industry through improved supervision and stricter regulatory standards, to place the FDIC on sound financial footing, and to promote a safe and stable system of affordable housing finance

Title II: Federal Deposit Insurance Corporation

Designated the FDIC (with its BIF and SAIF divisions) as the sole federal deposit insurer for banks and thrifts; restricted thrifts' junk bond and real estate investments; gave FDIC increased authority over state-chartered thrifts

Title III: Savings Associations

Created the OTS under the Treasury department as the principal thrift regulator; required thrift institutions to adhere to capital standards "no less stringent" than those of national banks; increased enforcement powers of FDIC and OTS over insolvent or potentially insolvent institutions; mandated uniform accounting rules for banks and thrifts; increased the percentage of mortgage assets thrifts must hold to avoid stricter regulations

Title IV: Transfer of Functions, Personnel, and Property

Abolished the FSLIC and FHLBB and transferred their regulatory functions to other agencies

Title V: Financing for Thrift Resolution

Created the Resolution Trust Corporation, the Resolution Funding Corporation, and the Oversight Board to dispose of insolvent thrifts

Title VI: Thrift Acquisition Enhancement Provisions

Permitted BHCs to acquire healthy thrifts

Title VII: Federal Home Loan Bank System Reforms

Created the Federal Housing Finance Board to oversee the twelve district FHL banks; required the FHL banks to promote affordable housing and community investment programs; removed all thrift supervisory authority from the FHL banks

Title VIII: Bank Conservation Act Amendments

Clarified procedures related to bank conservatorships

Title IX: Regulatory Enforcement Authority

Stiffened penalties for depository institution managers and directors who commit fraudulent acts

Title X: Studies of Federal Deposit Insurance, Banking Services, and the Safety and Soundness
of Government-Sponsored Enterprises

Mandated studies on federal deposit insurance, cost and availability of retail banking services, and capital adequacy of government-sponsored organizations

Title XI: Real Estate Appraisal Reform Amendments

Required regulators to develop and enforce minimum standards for property appraisals

Title XII: Miscellaneous Provisions

Addressed community reinvestment, CUs, consumer protection, and other matters

Title XIII: Participation by State Housing Finance Authorities and Nonprofit Entities

Permitted state agencies to buy mortgage-related assets from the Resolution Trust Corporation or FDIC

Title XIV: Tax Provisions

Lowered tax benefits to acquirers of failed or failing thrifts

Deja Vu All over Again: Antithesis—FDICIA

FIRREA had failed to address comprehensively the systemic flaws in federal deposit insurance. A recession beginning in the summer of 1990 accelerated banks' losses from already shaky commercial real estate loans. Drowning in a sea of bad loans and pressured by regulators applying progressively more stringent policies in reaction to the huge S&L bailout, some institutions tightened credit standards, resulting in widely publicized fears of a **"credit crunch"** that would withhold funds from even creditworthy borrowers. Although many experts were skeptical that a crunch really existed, plummeting consumer confidence dried up loan demand by "good" borrowers in virtually every region. In this uncertain environment, nearly 300 commercial banks failed in 1990 and 1991, and the cost of handling the failures eroded BIF's available funds from $15 billion to almost nothing. With a host of new bank closures predicted through 1993, forecasters estimated that BIF would soon be insolvent without new sources of cash.[22] Meanwhile, the RTC surprised no one when it determined by the fall of 1990 that the funding initially provided in FIRREA was far less than it would need to dispose of the assets of the many failed and failing S&Ls for which it was responsible. The GAO estimated in April 1990 that these costs would be greater than $500 billion.

The funding crises at BIF and the RTC served as catalysts for the next step in the regulatory dialectic, the passage of FDICIA, whose provisions are summarized in Table 3.8, emphasizing safety and soundness and regulatory improvement. The provisions included: (1) **recapitalization of the FDIC;** (2) **a universal examination schedule** requiring exams for all depositories every twelve or eighteen months, depending on their size and condition and creating a tripwire system that examiners must use to determine their ratings of particular management areas; (3) **prompt corrective action (PCA) by regulators, requiring regulators** to classify institutions by combining their CAMEL or MACRO ratings

---

table **3.8**   PROVISIONS OF THE FEDERAL DEPOSIT INSURANCE CORPORATION IMPROVEMENT ACT OF 1991

FDICIA was passed amidst growing concern about the financial condition of the FDIC and the problems left unattended in FIRREA. The new law imposed risk-adjusted deposit insurance premiums and detailed rules of conduct on both regulators and depositories to prevent any reoccurrence of the crises of the 1980s.

Title I: Safety and Soundness

Increased the borrowing authority of the FDIC; established minimum level for the FDIC's reserves; mandated specific examination schedules for depositories and created tripwire system for detecting problem institutions; strengthened financial reporting rules for insured firms, including use of generally accepted accounting principles, market valuation of assets and liabilities, and complete analysis of contingent obligations; required regulators to take prompt corrective action against unsound firms; insisted that regulators resolve institution failures in the least costly manner

Title II: Regulatory Improvement (Foreign Banks and Consumer Protection)

Strengthened the Fed's authority over expansion or termination of foreign banking operations in the United States; required foreign banks accepting small deposits in the United States to obtain federal deposit insurance; reduced deposit insurance premiums to institutions offering low-cost checking accounts to consumers; encouraged institutions' involvement in "distressed" communities; imposed uniform disclosure of deposit account rates and fee schedules

Title III: Regulatory Improvement (Deposit Insurance)

Limited institutions' ability to take excessive risks in attracting new deposits; mandated risk-based federal deposit insurance premiums, effective no later than January 1, 1994; unless federal regulators approve, restricted the activities of state-chartered banks to those permitted to federally chartered banks; required periodic review of regulators' minimum capital standards

Title IV: Miscellaneous Provisions

Revised technical policies relating to interbank funds transfers, rights to financial privacy, the QTL test for thrifts, discount window borrowing, and real estate appraisal

Title V: Depository Institution Conversions

Changed rules under which merged institutions obtain federal deposit insurance

---

22 See Robert M. Garsson. "2d Thrift Bill Takes Shape, But Congress is Reluctant." *American Banker* (January 22, 1990), 1–17; Robert M. Garsson. "Bailout to Cost $325 Billion GAO Reports." *American Banker* (April 9, 1990), 2; and Robert A. Eisenbeis and Larry D. Wall. "Reforming Deposit Insurance and FDICIA." *Economic Review* (Federal Reserve Bank of Atlanta)(1st Quarter 2002), 1–16.

Concept Questions

1   What were the economic and competitive conditions facing banks and savings and loans in the early 1980s?

2   What response (antithesis) did depository institutions make to Reg Q in reaction to these conditions?

3   What did DIDMCA of 1980 do to help depository institutions?

4   What did Garn–St. Germain add (as a synthesis) to help depository institutions with their problems?

5   What crisis did the thrift industry face in the late 1980s? How did insolvent thrifts attempt to regain solvency?

6   What did CEBA do to try to help relieve the thrift crisis?

7   What were the primary provisions for FIRREA and FDICIA?

8   Explain how the provisions of FIRREA and FDICIA instituted a type of re-regulation for banks and thrifts.

and their capital-to-assets ratios and mandating the closure of severely undercapitalized institutions; (4) **increased supervision of foreign banks operating in the United States;** (5) **directives to reduce risk to the deposit insurance system** prohibiting insurance institutions from paying excessive interest rates or engaging in risky and aggressive efforts to attract new deposits, practices that many believe contributed to the thrift debacle. Also, in a major departure from historical practice, Congress required regulators to develop **a system of risk-based deposit insurance.** This system, which became effective January 1994, will be discussed later in the text; (6) **product extensions and restrictions** in which the FDICIA increased the percentage of consumer loans to assets for thrifts to 35 percent. The QTL test was reduced to 65 percent holdings of mortgage-related assets, and the definition of mortgage-related assets was broadened. Banks' hard-won permission to underwrite insurance in several states was rolled back, however, with selected exceptions; and (7) **a few provisions were included for consumer protection.** Under a **truth-in-savings** provision, depository institutions must inform borrowers of their credit costs on a comparable basis to facilitate "shopping" for credit. The law provided special benefits to institutions that offer inexpensive deposit accounts for low-income customers and encouraged lending to households and businesses in communities experiencing economic distress.

The Regulatory Dialectic and the Evolution of Financial Holding Companies

The preceding sections gave examples of the regulatory dialectic in the 1980s to early 1990s. In the mid- and late 1990s, revolutionary changes occurred for depository institutions through IBBEA of 1994 and GLB of 1999. To understand these changes and the regulatory dialectic associated with them, it's first important to understand organizational forms of financial institutions and how organizational forms were developed to circumvent geographical and product regulations, resulting eventually in synthesis with these acts and the creation of a new financial services holding company in 1999.

Equity as Ownership, and Ownership Forms for Financial Institutions

Webster's Tenth New Collegiate Dictionary defines equity as "a risk interest or ownership right in property." Individuals with equity in a business may be sole owners, as in a proprietorship, with full personal liability for any debt obligations of the business; they may share ownership and legal liability with others, as in a partnership; they may have ownership interest but no personal responsibility for the firm's debt obligations (limited liability), as in a corporation, whether a regular corporation or a Subchapter S corporation (S-corp), where owners are taxed against their personal income but have limited liability. The "ownership right" part of Webster's definition means that those with equity in a business are entitled to all residuals, or profits remaining after the debt of the organization is serviced, generally as dividends or capital gains. The "risk interest" part of Webster's definition means that a business may generate no residuals at all. Because of such potential variability, holders of equity are subject to considerable risk. Yet their willingness to invest allows the very existence of a business. Not surprisingly, then, much of finance theory is devoted to understanding and improving the risk/expected return relationship for equity holders of firms. Financial institutions also have different ownership forms that provide different advantages and disadvantages from tax, liability, and other perspectives. These include the following forms.

(1) Privately Owned Firms: Many smaller to medium-sized institutions are privately held and owned. For instance, some small community banks are privately owned by families or a few investors. Under a proprietorship or partnership, the bank's earnings are taxed as private income of the investors. Because of liability issues, most banks do not take this ownership form.

(2) Stock-Owned Firms (C Corporations; often called C-corps): Financial institutions frequently are incorporated, which allows shareholders limited liability, a protection that helps institutions to raise funds by selling new shares or tapping the commercial paper and bond markets. The primary disadvantage of the corporate form of ownership is double taxation of earnings, once when recognized by the corporation and again when paid as dividends to owners. Stockholders buy shares in a firm at a given par value (such as $1 a share) plus a surplus market value. Stockholders' equity interests, however, also include shares in a company's retained earnings or undivided profits, amounts not paid out as dividends but reinvested in the firm. Thus, equity for shareholder firms includes the common stock accounts as well as retained earnings, often called undivided profits for financial institutions.

(3) Subchapter S Firms (S Corporations; often called S-corps): These firms are incorporated but are given special tax treatment, being taxed against the personal income statements of owners but also having limited liability. Subchapter S firms are also subject to a number of special restrictions but do not have the reporting requirements that C-corps do. Most privately held small community banks are Subchapter S corporations, to allow limited liability, subject to a number of restrictions including a maximum of seventy-five shareholders, with tax treatment of income at the owners' personal tax rates.

New tax laws that lowered the top individual tax rate to 35 percent versus a total combined top corporate and individual federal tax rate of 44.75 percent provided a strong motivation for tax savings as an S-corp versus a C-corp form. Consequently, as noted in a 2003 study by Grant Thornton, a prominent consulting firm that specializes in banks, 2,009 (21.6 percent) of the 9,314 FDIC-insured banks and savings institutions are S corporations, mostly smaller, closely held community banks (representing only 3 percent of all FDIC-insured assets). Eight banks and seven stock thrifts with more than $1 billion in total assets also converted, with the largest S-corp thrift ($9.1 billion in assets) operating in Oklahoma. The largest percentage of S-corps operate in the southwestern United States (35.9 percent of banks and 18.6 percent of stock-thrifts in that region).[23]

(4) Limited Liability Companies (LLCs): On February 13, 2003, the Federal Deposit Insurance Corporation (FDIC) published a final rule that allowed state banks chartered as limited liability companies (LLCs) to apply for deposit insurance. Limited liability companies, chartered in most states, have the same advantages as S-corps of taxation against personal income and limited liability, avoiding the double taxation of a corporation and higher corporate tax rates. LLCs also have additional advantages in terms of being able to have more than seventy-five owners and more than one class of shares. They also do not have to have annual meetings of members, require less paperwork, and have fewer restrictions relative to corporations. Federal tax laws at the time of this writing did not permit pass-through treatment for LLCs that are state-chartered banks; however, pass-through treatment was allowed for state taxes. Community banks that chose to convert may also have hoped for a federal law change. The FDIC rule requires LLC-structured banks to satisfy four traditional attributes of a C corporation including centralized management, limited liability, free transferability of ownership, and perpetual succession.[24]

(5) Mutual Firms—Not All Ownership Is Equity: Many financial institutions are mutually organized, including many savings institutions and insurance companies. Depositors of mutual savings institutions or policyholders of mutual insurance companies are the "owners" of the mutual financial institutions. Their initial deposits or premium payments provide the funds for the institutions to begin

---

23 See Grant Thornton Website *(http://www.grantthornton.com)*, "Number of Financial Institutions Making S Corporation Conversion on the Rise."

24 LLC owners, rather than being called shareholders, are designated as members. There are some disadvantages from a tax perspective, however, for LLCs versus corporations including required social security and Medicare taxes on the profits of an LLC over and above a member's salary, and self-employment taxes on salaries and profits, which corporations do not have to pay. Also, owners of LLCs must immediately recognize profits, while corporations do not have to distribute profits to shareholders as dividends. Benefits received for member-employees of an LLC must be treated as taxable income, similar to stockholder-employees that own more than 2 percent of an S corporation, among other differences. See "FDIC Agrees to Insure State Banks Chartered as LLCs," by Alaina Gimbert, Assistant Council, Financial Update, First Quarter 2003, Federal Reserve Bank of Atlanta *(http://www.frbatlanta.org)*; and FDIC Federal Register Citations, 12CRF, Part 303, "Insurance of State Banks Chartered as Limited Liability Corporations, Final Rule" *(http://www.fdic.gov/regulations/laws/federal)*, and LLCs Library *(http://www.legalzoom.com/law_library/LLCs/introduction.html)*.

operations. Profits earned from investing these funds are returned to owner–customers as interest on deposits or refunds on past premiums. Unlike shareholder-owned businesses, in which an owner may sell shares to realize capital gains, however, profits not distributed to owner–members of a mutual fund are available for use only by the institution itself. Net income that is retained is subject to corporate taxes in the year earned, but profits distributed to policyholders or depositors of mutual firms are taxable as personal income. Hundreds of mutual financial institutions (primarily thrifts) have converted to stock ownership in recent years in order to issue stock to finance growth and to compete with other financial institutions. Also, mutual holding companies have been formed by mutual insurance companies and thrifts that allow the creation of a stock subsidiary to issue shares to raise funds for the company for growth and expansion, discussed in Chapter 5.

Because mutual firms are limited otherwise in raising capital only from retained earnings, many have converted to stock ownership in recent years. In 1992, for instance, there were 109 mutual life insurance companies (5.6 percent of life insurance companies), but by 2002 this number fell by about 24 percent to 83. However, most mutual life insurance companies are very large, so they held $1.8 trillion (about 12.4 percent) of life insurance in force in 2002. For thrift institutions regulated by the Office of Thrift Supervision (OTS), hundreds of conversions from mutual to stock organizations occurred after 1978. In 1978, about 82 percent of savings institutions were mutual organizations compared with only about 46 percent in 2003. Regulatory policy encouraged conversions to help undercapitalized thrifts raise capital, and many thrifts converted as well to facilitate mergers with banks and other thrifts in the later 1980s and 1990s.[25]

(6) Not-for-Profit Organizations: Credit unions (CUs) are organized as not-for-profits. Not-for-profit organizations provide goods and services at below-market or no cost to specific groups of beneficiaries. The organizations may distribute income they earn in excess of expenses to the beneficiary groups in the form of increased services or reduced costs, such as reduced loan interest rates or increased deposit rates. They may also provide refunds for previous payments or retain the income to provide a cushion against potential losses. No one holds any claim to residuals. Because not-for-profit organizations are presumed to serve charitable purposes, they do not pay taxes, even if they retain excess income. In recent years, independent banking groups have challenged CUs' tax exemption, arguing that large CUs operate similarly to community banks.

(7) Franchising and Chain Banks: Less common than other forms of organizations, these institutions were widely used as loopholes for branching regulations in the past. Under a franchise agreement, an independent financial institution leases the right to use the name and marketing programs of a larger umbrella organization. The initial application of franchising for a financial institution is attributed to a former company, First Interstate Bancorp, which leased its name and promotional strategies to independent banks around the country beginning in 1982. A franchised bank is not be a member of a holding company but uses a company's name. Franchisees enter such relationships to obtain the benefits of association, such as wide-ranging marketing and other managerial talents, while still retaining operational independence. Thrifts, such as First Nationwide, also participated in franchising by offering management support systems. Later, with the name changed to U.S. Banking Alliance, the thrift extended network membership opportunities to community banks.[26]

Chain banking is an arrangement that allows several banks to operate under one umbrella organization. Chain banking occurs when one investor owns 5 percent of the voting stock in one or more individual banks and holds a managerial post in each bank or when an individual or group owns at least 10 percent of the voting shares of two or more banks. In a few instances, individuals have formed chain-banking organizations with common ownership shares in two or more one-bank holding companies. Because of the relatively informal structure of chain banking, it allows a single investor or group to control a substantial amount of banking assets, while the banks remain independent units and are not subject to multiple reporting requirements or other regulations that govern bank holding companies.[27]

---

25 See Office of Thrift Supervision *2003 Fact Book*, which can be downloaded from the OTS Website. Also see American Council of Life Insurers, *Life Insurers Fact Book, 2003*, Washington, D.C., which can also be downloaded from their Website.

26 See Eickhoff (1985) and Carner (1986–1987).

27 For more information on chain banks, see Federal Reserve Bank of Kansas (1983), 9–11; and Cyrnak (1986).

1 What advantages and disadvantages would a privately held bank have by being a Subchapter S corporation, LLC, or C corporation?

2 Why have community banks converted to S-corps so rapidly?

3 What is a mutual organization? Why have many mutual firms, thrifts, and life insurance companies converted to stock organizations?

4 What advantages and disadvantages do credit unions have as nonprofit organizations?

5 What are franchising and chain banks?

More Complex Organizational Forms: Holding Companies

Shareholder-owned institutions also can take advantage of another organizational arrangement called the holding company. Holding companies are businesses formed to acquire the stock of other companies to control their operations. They make up the dominant proportion of U.S. financial organizations. Holding companies can be quite complex structures, consisting of many subsidiary holding companies as well. Holding companies own a controlling interest in the stock of one or several banks or nonbank subsidiaries, subject to regulatory approval. Bank holding companies (BHCs) are subject to special regulatory treatment with the Fed as their chief regulator. Under the Gramm-Leach-Bliley (GLB) Act of 1999, a new form of holding company, the financial holding company, was also inaugurated.

Growth of Bank Holding Companies and the Regulatory Dialectic

Interestingly, BHCs became popular initially as an innovation to avoid regulations, as part of the antithesis of the regulatory dialectic by providing loopholes to circumvent product restrictions. As shown in Figure 3.2, prior to GLB of 1999, there were two types of bank holding companies: multibank holding companies and one-bank holding companies. Multibank holding companies (MBHCs) have a holding company structure with a number of different bank subsidiaries. One-bank holding companies (OBHCs) have a holding company structure with one bank as a subsidiary and several nonbank subsidiaries, such as a data processing subsidiary, a finance company subsidiary, and a securities firm subsidiary.

A Regulatory Dialectic: Multibank Holding Companies and Geographic Diversification

Banks formed MBHCs initially to circumvent state branching restrictions under the **McFadden Act of 1927.** The McFadden Act gave authority over branching regulations to state regulators. Consequently, farming states and other states that feared big banks adopted regulations for unit banking, allowing no branches, or limited branching, allowing branching in contiguous counties or regions within a state. By creating a holding company with several affiliate banks operating in different parts of a state or across state lines, a MBHC could create de facto subsidiary branches. MBHCs could also circumvent intrastate and interstate branching restrictions by establishing separate interstate bank subsidiaries.

Within the regulatory dialectic, regulators initially closed the loophole that MBHCs opened for interstate banking by passing Section 3(d) of the **BHC Act of 1956, known as the Douglas Amendment,** which previously prohibited banks from acquiring banks in other states unless allowed by state law. With greater competition from nonbanks such as securities firms, which could operate nationwide, over time state branching regulations were liberalized. **Regional interstate banking pacts** arose in the 1980s, whereby state regulators allowed MBHCs to expand their holding companies into other states in the same region on a reciprocal basis. A Supreme Court ruling in 1996 confirmed the legality of these regional pacts. With the regional pacts, generally banks had to be MBHCs with separate subsidiaries in each state. This structure was very expensive, since separate banks required separate boards of directors and other organizational structures, a costly form of de facto interstate and intrastate branching. Many

figure **3.2** STRUCTURE OF BANK HOLDING COMPANIES

Note: Large banks combine numerous holding companies. Citicorp includes both multibank and one-bank holding companies. The Directory of Corporate Affiliates (found in the reference sections of most libraries) provides detailed listings.

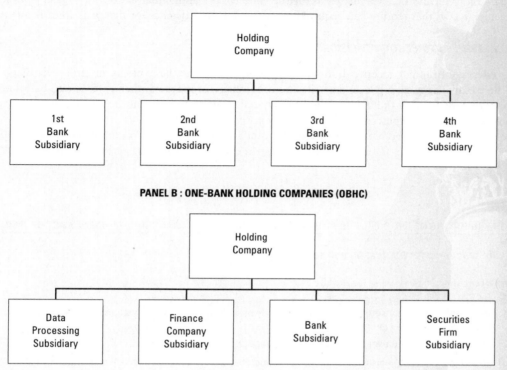

of these large, regional MBHCs rapidly made acquisitions and became known as super-regionals. By the early 1990s, almost all states had regional branching pacts and many had complete interstate branching networks, and federal thrifts were allowed interstate branching privileges as well. States also liberalized their intrastate branching restrictions. By 1992, unit banking (as a synthesis) was eliminated in all states, and only a couple of states continue to limit the areas within which banks may branch.

The Full Synthesis: The Riegle–Neal Interstate Branching and Efficiency Act (IBBEA) of 1994

After years of bank lobbying, in 1994 the **Riegle–Neal Interstate Branching and Efficiency Act (IBBEA)** was passed. Though required to be phased in by 1997, most states opted in earlier, and a synthesis in the branching regulatory dialectic was created. Interstate branching for banks became a reality, and MBHCs with interstate operations could convert costly subsidiaries into interstate branches. MBHCs could also make acquisitions across the country. For instance, NationsBank acquired Barnett Banks in Florida in 1997 and merged with Bank of America in 1998, creating a coast-to-coast company with operations in twenty-four states, and then it acquired Fleet in 2004, expanding operations to New England as well. Other large bank holding companies prefer to concentrate on particular regions. Commerce Bancorp, Inc., in New Jersey, for example, although one of the nation's largest fifty bank holding companies, continues to focus on New York, New Jersey, Pennsylvania, and Delaware. Once the MBHC form was no longer needed, banks operating in different states experienced dramatic savings, since separate holding companies in different states could be consolidated and converted into branches. Other banks have kept separate subsidiaries in different states for decentralization and marketing purposes.[28]

The major provisions of IBBEA, shown in Table 3.9, brought about interstate branching in the U.S. for the first time in seventy years. In addition to permitting adequately capitalized and managed BHCs to acquire banks in any state one year after enactment, banks could consolidate their affiliated interstate banks into branch offices via merger as early as June 1, 1997. Individual states could opt in prior to that time. State laws that required an acquired company to be in existence for five years were also retained.

Community Protection Provisions

To reflect continuing concerns about concentration of power in large banks and to prevent large out-of-state banks from taking local deposits and using them for loans in other states, a number of protections were included in the IBBEA. The Fed may not approve an interstate acquisition if a BHC would control more than 10 percent of the insured deposits in the United States or 30 percent of deposits in the state of the acquired bank. States may also establish their own caps on these percentages, and they may set their own rules for acquisitions of banks in existence for limited periods. Acquiring banks and

---

table **3.9** MAJOR PROVISIONS OF THE RIEGLE–NEAL INTERSTATE BANKING AND BRANCHING EFFICIENCY ACT OF 1994

IBBEA brought about interstate branching for the first time in seventy years.

Title I: Interstate Banking and Branching

1. Permitted adequately capitalized and managed BHCs to acquire banks in any state one year after enactment. They could consolidate their affiliated interstate banks into branch offices via merger as early as June 1, 1997, except in states that outlawed interstate branching by that time. Individual states could opt in prior to this time.

2. Banks headquartered in states opting out of the legislation could not engage in interstate mergers.

3. Regulatory agencies of states opting into the legislation could set up cooperative agreements to supervise multistate depository institutions.

4. Preserved state laws that required an acquired company to be in existence for five years or less.

5. Prohibited the Fed from approving an interstate acquisition if the BHC would control more than 10 percent of the insured deposits in the United States or 30 percent of those in the home state of the acquired bank.

6. Allowed states to establish their own caps on the percentages of deposits in the home states of acquired banks.

7. Required acquiring banks and branch offices to meet state community reinvestment laws. Branch offices taking deposits across state lines must create adequate volumes of loans (equal to half or more of the statewide average loan/deposit ratio) to support local communities. Written evaluations of an interstate bank's overall CRA performance in each state where it has branches must be prepared for state agencies.

8. Allowed federally insured banks to branch de novo into a state where they have no offices, if permitted by state law. States can tax branches as if they were full-service banks.

9. Subjected foreign-based banks to the same branching rules and to the same CRA reviews.

10. Subjected national banks to state laws in the areas of community support, consumer protection, fair lending, and interstate branching.

11. Required federal banking agencies to consult with community organizations before closing branch offices owned by interstate BHCs if the branches are located in low- or moderate-income areas.

Sources: J. Mark Leggett, Richard M. Whiting, and Julie L. Williams (Eds.). Interstate Banking under the Riegle–Neal Interstate Banking and Branching Efficiency Act of 1994. *Englewood Cliffs, NJ: Prentice-Hall Law & Business, 1994. See also Peter S. Rose. "The 1994 Interstate Banking Law and Its Implications for the Structure of U.S. Banking," in* Banking across State Lines: Public and Private Consequences. *Westport, CT: Quorum Books, 1997, Chapter 3.*

---

28 See Jith Jayaratne and Philip E. Strahan. "The Benefits of Branching Deregulation." *Regulation,* Vol. 22, No. 1 (1999) for an excellent discussion of the benefits of branch deregulation that provides dates for the removal of restrictions on geographic expansion in Table 1. The last unit banking state to remove its branching restrictions was Colorado in 1992. As of 1994, only Georgia, Iowa, and Kentucky retained some intrastate branching restrictions.

1 What is the difference between a one-bank holding company and a multibank holding company?

2 How did MBHCs as an innovation provide an antithesis to the thesis of branching regulations? How did regulators react to this loophole?

3 What type of interstate branching regulations did thrifts have in contrast to banks in 1991?

4 What are the major provisions of IBBEA including community protection provisions?

branch offices must also comply with **Community Reinvestment Act (CRA) laws.** CRA was enacted in 1977 to encourage federally insured depository institutions to help meet the credit needs of all of their local communities, including low-to-moderate income neighborhoods, consistent with safe and sound banking practices. In 1996, regulators revised CRA to emphasize an institution's actual performance in meeting the convenience and credit needs of its local communities through expanded direct and indirect lending and investments. Under IBBEA, branch offices across state lines taking deposits must create adequate volumes of loans, defined as one-half or more of the statewide average loan-to-deposit ratio, to support local communities. Merging banks are also scrutinized for their commitments to local communities. Often, they must make concessions to community leaders to allow mergers to reach completion. For example, Citicorp and Travelers Group announced that they would give $115 billion in loans to low- and moderate-income individuals as part of their proposed $70 billion merger.[29]

A Second Regulatory Dialectic: One-Bank Holding Companies and Product Expansion

A similar regulatory dialectic was associated with product restrictions for banks. Under the Glass–Steagall Act of 1933, banks, securities firms, and insurance companies were not allowed to operate together. To avoid this regulation (an antithesis), bank managers created OBHCs with nonbank subsidiaries that technically were not part of the bank. Again, regulators attempted to patch up this loophole by imposing new restrictions on OBHCs under the **Bank Holding Company (BHC) Act of 1956** and later amendments. These acts permitted OBHCs to acquire businesses "closely related to banking" as designated by the Fed and were subject to a number of different regulations tied to corporate separateness.

Continually over the 1980s and 1990s, banks faced great competition from investment companies, insurance firms, and securities firms that could engage in banklike activities, while banks could not engage in insurance and investment activities. Other types of financial institutions including finance companies and insurance companies formed holding companies that could operate under fewer restrictions than BHCs. In addition, S&Ls could form unitary holding companies (one savings and loan with nonbank subsidiaries) and under the **SLHC Act of 1968** engage in almost any type of activity, with much greater freedom than bank holding companies. The thrift unitary holding company served as a type of loophole to the Glass–Steagall Act as well, with many insurance companies and nonbank companies seeking unitary thrift charters, allowing them to engage in diverse activities and also to engage in banking through a thrift. For instance, in 1997, about forty to fifty diversified unitary thrift holding companies engaged to some degree in activities impermissible to BHCs including American Mutual Life Insurance Co., B.A.T. Industries, Prudential Insurance Company, Hawaiian Electric Industries, and United Services Automobile Association (USAA). In addition, since the 1950s, savings and loans with federal charters had been permitted to form **thrift service corporations (SCs)** to conduct diversified lines of business. An SC is formed when one or more associations purchase the stock in affiliated stockholder-owned organizations. Prior to FIRREA, service corporations in some states could invest almost any amount in any activity. FIRREA patched up this loophole by requiring state and federal charters to have the same limits, limiting SCs to no more than 3 percent of a thrift's total assets and limiting activities.

---

29 See Albert V. De Leon. "Community Reinvestment: The Future of CRA." *Banking Policy Report,* Vol. 16, No. 6 (March 17, 1997), 10–13. See also Robert D. Hershey, Jr. "2 Banks, One Goal: Cast Long Shadows." *New York Times* (November 15, 1997), B1; "First Union is Paying $17.1 Billion to Acquire Corestates." *New York Times* (November 19, 1997), A1, C4; and "Communities to Receive $115 Billion Citigroup Says." *New York Times* (May 5, 1998), C10.

Another loophole to get around the Glass–Steagall Act product restrictions (as well as geographical restrictions), was the creation of nonbank consumer banks by MBHCs such as Citicorp, as well as other industrial companies. By acquiring banks and divesting them of commercial loans, these so called "**consumer banks**" were no longer technically a bank, so could engage in diverse activities and be operated in different states. This loophole was eventually closed under the **Competitive Equality Banking Act (CEBA) of 1987** by redefining a bank as any institution insured by the FDIC, although a number of operating consumer banks were grandfathered at this time.

Partial Synthesis: Relaxation of Glass–Steagall Restrictions in the 1980s and Mid-1990s

In the mid-1980s to mid-1990s, with greater competition for banks from nonbanks, regulators also came to realize that Glass–Steagall restrictions from the 1930s were out of date. Hence, regulators became much more lenient over time in their interpretation of activities allowable for subsidiaries of BHCs. Under the Fed's Reg Y, the Fed could allow BHCs to form or acquire nonbank subsidiaries closely related to banking. Also, under Sections 16 and 20 of Glass–Steagall, commercial banks could underwrite government securities and act as government securities dealers. Under Section 20, many functions were allowed, such as brokerage activities in special Section 20 subsidiaries, as long as they were not the primary source of revenue of an affiliate. By 1997, **Section 20 subsidiaries** were limited by a Fed-determined maximum amount of 25 percent of a subsidiary's overall revenues. As early as 1987, member banks could underwrite, distribute, and trade securities, including municipal revenue bonds, commercial paper, and mortgage-backed securities, and by 1989 corporate bonds, and by 1990 corporate equity through a well-capitalized security affiliate. Hence, a large number of U.S. BHCs including Citicorp and JPMorgan used Section 20 subsidiaries to play major roles in securities markets. In the 1980s, the Fed and the OCC also allowed BHC subsidiaries to offer low-cost brokerage services and mutual funds, with, as pointed out by Kaufman (1995), over 90 percent of banks offering money markets predominantly but also many offering other types of mutual funds by 1992.

In 1997, the Fed phased out previous firewalls that prevented associations with securities affiliates by passing eight additional liberal operating standards for Section 20. These standards allowed some interactions with the bank, putting new internal controls in place including: (1) capital, (2) internal controls, (3) independent directors for subsidiaries, (4) customer disclosure, (5) credit for clearing purposes only, (6) restrictions on funding of securities purchases to Section 20 affiliates, (7) quarterly reporting requirements, and (8) prohibitions from advertising an association with a Section 20 affiliate. The Fed also streamlined procedures for nonbank acquisitions and the types of activities it permitted for subsidiaries of BHCs including acquisitions of investment banking and securities firm subsidiaries. In 1997, the OCC set up a Part 5 rule as well for national banks, known as the **Operating Subsidiary (Op-Sub) Rule,** allowing national banks to apply for approval to conduct new activities through operating subsidiaries rather than having to operate a Section 20 subsidiary. Many states also liberalized regulations for insurance and other activities. A landmark ruling occurred in 1995, when the Supreme Court ruled in favor of the legality of national banks to sell annuities in *NationsBank v. Variable Annuity Life Company (VALIC)*. The courts also upheld the rights of national banks and most state-chartered banks to allow subsidiaries to sell insurance in small towns of less than 5,000, and, in 1996, the Supreme Court in *Barnett Bank v. U.S.* allowed banks to sell insurance nationwide. In 1997, the OCC also supported the insurance agency activities (acting as a broker versus underwriting insurance through subsidiaries of affiliate national banks).[30]

Virtual Financial Institutions as Loopholes

In addition to loopholes banks found by acquiring thrifts for interstate expansion, some financial institutions were granted **electronic thrift or bank charters** to circumvent both geographical and product restrictions. In August 1997, the OCC granted its first national e-bank charter to CompuBank in Houston, Texas, which served a payments system function, making no loans, and holding only government

---

30 See Michael C. Conover. "Section 20 Subsidiary May Still Be Viable Option for Some Banks." *Bank Policy Report* (May 20, 1996), 19; and Benston and Kaufman (1997).

securities as assets. In 1997, the OTS granted electronic thrift charters to Security First Network, an Atlanta-based Internet bank, and to a cyberthrift unit of Principal Mutual Life Insurance Company. Thousands of financial institutions also posted Web pages allowing investors to apply for loans, do home banking and bill paying, order electronic funds transfers, and perform other banking activities. Virtual services allow financial institutions to develop nationwide relationships and garner deposits electronically or by mail, thus circumventing branching legislation.

Complete Synthesis: The Financial Services Modernization (Gramm-Leach-Bliley) Act of 1999

In 1999, after two decades of debate and in response to the proposed merger of Citicorp and Travelers Corporation, the synthesis of the regulatory dialectic for product restrictions arrived when Congress passed the **Financial Services Modernization (Gramm-Leach-Bliley [GLB]) Act.** GLB allows banks, insurance companies, and securities firms to affiliate with and sell each other's products and operate under the new financial holding company (FHC) umbrella. Table 3.10 lists the major provisions of the GLB Act. Basically, the restrictions on banks affiliating with securities in the Glass–Steagall Act were lifted and a new "financial holding company" was created under Section 4 of the Bank Holding Company Act. National banks were also allowed greater flexibility to engage in new product activities through operating subsidiaries. FHCs are described next.

New Financial Holding Companies (FHCs)

New FHCs can engage in a statutorily provided list of financial activities that includes insurance and securities underwriting and agency activities, merchant banking and insurance company portfolio investment activities, and complementary financial activities. Nonfinancial activities of firms with at least 85 percent of their activities in financial activities are grandfathered for at least ten years, with a possible five-year extension. To form an FHC, a firm must have well-capitalized and well-managed insured depository institution subsidiaries, as well as a satisfactory rating on its most recent CRA exam. Also, if an affiliate of an FHC has less than a satisfactory rating on its most recent CRA exam, federal bank regulators may not approve any additional new activities or acquisitions under the authority granted by the act. While the Fed is the primary regulatory agency of FHCs, state regulators will continue to regulate insurance activities of an FHC, subject to a standard that no state may discriminate against persons affiliated with a bank. No FDIC assistance can be given to nonbank affiliates. If an FHC falls out of compliance, such as having bank subsidiaries that are not well capitalized or managed, the Fed has considerable discretion to limit the activities of the FHC, and if compliance is not reached within 180 days, the Fed can require divestiture of the bank subsidiary. Similarly, if the FHC banks do not satisfy the CRA standard, the FHC may not be allowed to engage in additional activities.

National Bank Operating Subsidiaries

In addition, well-capitalized and well-managed national banks are allowed to engage in new financial activities in a financial subsidiary (i.e., an operating subsidiary), except for insurance underwriting, merchant banking, insurance company portfolio investments, and real estate development and investment, as long as the aggregate assets of all financial subsidiaries are not greater than 45 percent of the parent bank's assets or $50 billion, whichever is less. National banks are also allowed to underwrite municipal revenue bonds.

Hence, banks of all sizes had a choice of entering new product areas through an FHC or a financial subsidiary of a state or national bank. The FHC is regulated primarily by the Fed and must be well capitalized and well managed and have a CRA exam rating of satisfactory or better, while a financial subsidiary of a national bank is regulated primarily by the OCC, with activities more limited.

New Subordinated Debt Provision for the Largest 100 Banks

Under GLB, the top 100 banks are required to have an issue of outstanding subordinated debt to provide market discipline, and merchant banking activities may be approved as a permissible activity beginning five years after the date of enactment of the act.

table **3.10**   MAJOR PROVISIONS OF THE GRAMM-LEACH-BLILEY (FINANCIAL SERVICES MODERNIZATION) ACT OF 1999

Title I: Facilitating Affiliation among Banks, Securities Firms, and Insurance Companies

- Repeals restrictions on banks affiliating with securities firms contained in Sections 20 and 32 of the Glass–Steagall Act and creates a new "financial holding company" that can engage in a statutorily provided list of financial activities, including insurance and securities underwriting and agency activities, merchant banking and insurance company portfolio investment activities, and activities "complementary" to financial services. The nonfinancial activities of firms predominantly engaged in financial activities (at least 85 percent financial) are grandfathered for at least ten years, with a possibility for a five-year extension.

- The Federal Reserve may not permit a company to form a financial holding company if any of its insured depository institution subsidiaries are not well capitalized and well managed, or did not receive at least a satisfactory rating in their most recent CRA exam, and if any insured depository institution or insured depository institution affiliate of a financial holding company receives less than a satisfactory rating in its most recent CRA exam, the appropriate federal banking agency may not approve any additional new activities or acquisitions under the authorities granted under the Act.

- Provides for state regulation of insurance, subject to a standard that no state may discriminate against persons affiliated with a bank.

- Provides that bank holding companies organized as a mutual holding company will be regulated on terms comparable to other bank holding companies and lifts some restrictions governing nonbank banks.

- Provides for a study of the use of subordinated debt to protect the financial system and deposit funds from "too big to fail" institutions and a study on the effect of financial modernization on the accessibility of small business and farm loans. Also, the top 100 BHCs are mandated to an issue of subordinated debt.

- Streamlines bank holding company supervision by clarifying the regulatory roles of the Federal Reserve as the umbrella holding company supervisor, and the state and other federal financial regulators, which "functionally" regulate various affiliates, and provides for federal bank regulators to prescribe prudential safeguards for bank organizations engaging in new financial activities.

- Prohibits FDIC assistance to affiliates and subsidiaries of banks and thrifts and provides for federal bank regulators to prescribe prudential safeguards for bank organizations engaging in new financial activities.

- Allows well-capitalized and well-managed national banks to engage in new financial activities in an operating financial subsidiary, except for insurance underwriting, merchant banking, insurance company portfolio investments, real estate development, and real estate investment, so long as the aggregate assets of all financial subsidiaries do not exceed 45 percent of the parent bank's assets, or $50 billion, whichever is less. Merchant banking activities may be approved as a permissible activity beginning five years after the date of enactment of GLB. National banks are allowed to underwrite municipal revenue bonds.

- Ensures that appropriate antitrust review is conducted for new financial combinations allowed under GLB.

- Provides for national treatment for foreign banks wanting to engage in the new financial activities authorized under GLB.

Title II: Functional Regulation

- Amends the federal securities laws to incorporate functional regulation of bank securities activities.

- The broad exemptions banks have from broker-dealer regulation would be replaced by more limited exemptions designed to permit banks to continue their current activities and to develop new products.

- Provides for limited exemptions from broker-dealer registration for transactions in the following areas: trust, safekeeping, custodian, shareholder and employee benefit plans, sweep accounts, private placements (under certain conditions), and third-party networking arrangements to offer brokerage services to bank customers, among others.

- Allows banks to continue to be active participants in the derivatives business for all credit and equity swaps (other than equity swaps to retail customers).

- Provides for a "jump ball" rulemaking and resolution process between the SEC and the Federal Reserve regarding new hybrid products.

- Amends the Investment Company Act to address potential conflicts of interest in the mutual fund business and amendments to the Investment Advisers Act to require banks that advise mutual funds to register as investment advisers.

Title III: Insurance

- Provides for the functional regulation of insurance activities.

- Establishes which insurance products banks and bank subsidiaries may provide as principal.

- Prohibits national banks not currently engaged in underwriting or sale of title insurance from commencing that activity. However, sales activities by banks are permitted in states that specifically authorize such sales for state banks, but only on the same condition. National bank subsidiaries are permitted to sell all types of insurance including title insurance. Affiliates may underwrite or sell all types of insurance including title insurance.

- Allows multistate insurance agency licensing.

- Provides for interagency consultation and confidential sharing of information between the Federal Reserve Board and state insurance regulators.

Title IV: Unitary Savings and Loan Holding Companies

- De novo unitary thrift holding company applications received by the Office of Thrift Supervision after May 4, 1999, shall not be approved, and existing unitary thrift holding companies may only be sold to financial companies.

table   **3.10**   MAJOR PROVISIONS OF THE GRAMM-LEACH-BLILEY (FINANCIAL SERVICES MODERNIZATION) ACT OF 1999 (CONT.)

Title V: Privacy

- Requires clear disclosure by all financial institutions of their privacy policy regarding the sharing of nonpublic personal information with both affiliates and third parties.

- Requires a notice to consumers and an opportunity to "opt-out" of sharing nonpublic personal information with nonaffiliated third parties subject to certain limited exceptions.

- Assigns authority for enforcing the subtitle's provisions to the Federal Trade Commission and the Federal Banking agencies, the National Credit Union Administration, and the Securities and Exchange Commission, according to their respective jurisdictions, and provides for enforcement of the subtitle by the states.

Title VI: Federal Home Loan Bank System Modernization

- Banks with less than $500 million in assets may use long-term advances for loans to small businesses, small firms, and small agricultural businesses. Stock purchase requirements are equalized for banks and thrifts, and voluntary membership for federal savings associations takes effect six months after enactment. Governance and funding formulas were changed with governance of the Federal Home Loan Banks decentralized from the Federal Housing Finance Board to the individual Federal Home Loan Banks.

Title VII: Other Provisions

- Requires ATM operators who impose a fee for use of an ATM by a noncustomer to post a notice on the machine with the amount of the fee. Requires a notice when ATM cards are issued that surcharges may be imposed by other parties when transactions are initiated from ATMs not operated by the card issuer.

- Requires full public disclosure of CRA agreements and requires each bank and nonbank party to a CRA agreement to make a public report each year on how the money and other resources involved in the agreement were used.

Source: Senate Banking Committee Press Release, "News from the Senate Banking Committee," Senator Phil Gramm, Chairman, Wednesday, November 17, 1999 (http://banking.senate.gov/conf/).

Abolishment of Unitary S&L Charters

Other provisions included no longer chartering unitary savings and loan holding companies and allowing existing unitary savings and loan holding companies to be sold only to financial companies.

Privacy Provisions

Additional provisions included privacy provisions that protect customers from the sale of private information or misuse of information by financial institutions and offer remedies for violations. Furthermore, bank holding company supervision is streamlined by clarifying the regulatory roles of the Fed as the umbrella company supervisor and state and other federal financial regulators, which regulate various affiliates on a functional basis.

Number of FHCs in 2003

As of December 19, 2003, the Federal Reserve Board listed approximately 641 bank holding companies that had effectively elected to be FHCs. The ten financial holding companies with securities subsidiaries as include Citigroup, JPMorgan Chase & Co., Bank of America Corporation, Wells Fargo & Company, Wachovia Corporation, and Bank One Corporation. Most mergers among banks, securities firms, and insurance firms occurred among major players, with banks purchasing specialized securities firms and insurance agencies, predominantly. Interestingly, Citigroup spun off its Travelers' property/casualty insurance unit in March of 2002. The U.S. House of Representatives Banking Committee was also renamed the Financial Services Committee in 2001, reflecting the new financial services firm environment. An excellent example of BHCs taking advantage of both IBBEA and GLB is the merger of JPMorgan Chase and Bank One in 2004. With JPMorgan Chase involved prominently in investment banking activities and Bank One in retail consumer lending, this merger exemplifies the diversification abilities of GLB. At the same time, given the merger's large geographical reach across the country, such a merger would not have taken place without IBBEA.[31]

---

31 See the Financial Services Modernization Act, Gramm-Leach-Bliley, Summary of Provisions, Senate Banking Committee, *(http://www.senate.gov/~banking/conf/grmleach.htm)*; "The Gramm-Leach-Bliley Financial Services Modernization Act," presentation by Dr. Douglas V. Austin, Austin Financial Services, Inc., Midwest Finance Association Meeting, 2000. A listing of approved FHCs can be found on the Federal Reserve Board Website *(http://www.federalreserve.gov)*. See "J.P. Morgan Chase to Buy Bank One." *The Wall Street Journal* (January 15, 2004), A1, A10.

1 How did one-bank holding companies serve as an antithesis (loophole) to Glass–Steagall restrictions?

2 How were unitary thrift holding companies and consumer banks used as loopholes to escape Glass–Steagall?

3 What types of relaxations to Glass–Steagall regulations occurred in the 1980s and mid-1990s?

4 As a synthesis, the GLB Act was passed in 1999; what were its major provisions? What are two ways under GLB for a bank to engage in securities and insurance activities? What are their advantages and disadvantages?

The Regulatory Dialectic and Regulatory Concerns Continue

Continuing regulatory concerns include measuring risks associated with technology, as discussed in the first two chapters, and ethical concerns about fraud, corporate governance, off-balance-sheet exposure, globalization of financial markets, compliance with new and old U.S. congressional acts to prevent terrorism, money laundering, and other criminal activities. Under the **Bank Secrecy Act, as amended by the USA Patriot Act,** passed in September 2002, provisions were passed for financial institutions to establish formal anti-money laundering programs. Although the act primarily concerns depository institutions, other financial institutions including securities firms and insurance firms can be covered as well under different proposals. Under this act, five rules require financial institutions to report suspicious activity, abide by anti-money laundering program requirements, adhere to prohibitions on maintaining accounts to foreign shell banks, and provide information sharing between the government and the financial community. In addition, other regulations require financial institutions to have back-up disaster plans to ensure the safety of financial records and allow the payments system to continue. For banks in foreign countries, safeguards also have to be put into place against terrorism or other criminal activity. With the new FHCs, risk management of huge financial companies has become even more challenging, given their size and diverse operations, as discussed in the previous chapter. For instance, Citigroup, the largest U.S. FHC, had $1.097 trillion in assets as of March 2003, while the average-sized FHC had $11.1 billion. FHCs accounted for 19 percent of all U.S. financial sector assets according to the Financial Market Center. With the passage of **Sarbanes-Oxley of 2002,** greater concern has also been given to corporate governance issues and the independence and financial competence of boards of directors to ensure transparency and proper governance to ward off operating risks. The Basel Committee on Banking Supervision, which set standards for international banks' new proposed **Basel II,** mentioned in Chapter 2 (and which will be discussed in greater detail in Chapter 6 on capital), has been particularly concerned with internal models to control operating risks and adjusting capital requirements and with corporate governance and market discipline. With the great importance of financial institutions to the payments mechanism and the economy, these are only a few of many concerns that will constantly evolve with new innovations and new regulatory dialectics.[32]

New Views on Regulation: A Greater Role for Market Discipline?

As noted earlier in the chapter, views on regulation are constantly changing. With the **New Subordinated Debt Provision for the Largest 100 Banks under the GLB of 1999,** emphasis was placed on market discipline for the largest banks and financial holding companies, whereby uninsured public debtholders and bond-rating agencies provide monitoring of banks and indicators of problems. Also, a study was mandated for the greater use of subordinated debt as a market disciplinary device for financial institutions. Similarly, the Basel Committee on Bank Supervision identifies market discipline as one

---

32 See Christine M. Cumming and Beverly J. Hirtle. "The Challenges of Risk Management in Diversified Financial Companies." *Economic Policy Review* (Federal Reserve Bank of New York) 7 (March 2001), 1–17; and Thomas Baxter, Jr. "Governing the Financial or Bank Holding Company: How Legal Infrastructure Can Facilitate Consolidated Risk Management." Federal Reserve Bank of New York, *Current Issues in Economics and Finance,* Vol. 9, No. 3, (March 2003), 1–7. See Richard J. Herring. "The Basel 2 Approach to Bank Operations Risk: Regulators on the Wrong Track." *Journal of Risk Finance,* Vol. 4, No. 4 (Fall 2002), 42; "Financial Holding Companies." *Financial Service Facts,* Insurance Information Institute, 2003 *(http://financialservicefacts.org/financial);* GT Alert: USA Patriot Act—Proposed Regulations Affecting Insurance Companies (see also Alerts for Other Financial Institutions, 2003), by Alan B. Horn, Carl A. Fornaris, Ileana Gomez, and Greenberg Traurig, GT Alert, Greenberg Traurig, LLP, September 2002 *(http://www.gtlaw.com/pub/alerts/index.htm)* and 2003; and "Treasury Announces Final and Proposed Rules under USA Patriot Act." U.S. Treasury, *http://www.treasury.gov/press/releases,* September 18, 2002.

of three pillars on which effective regulatory oversight will be based. With deposit insurance, there is always an underlying concern about a moral hazard problem from the perspective of depositors having no incentive to monitor the risk-taking of their banks. Regulators are expected to provide the monitoring, but with FHCs with assets in or close to the trillions engaged in numerous types of activities, it's difficult for regulators to monitor all activities. For instance, the largest FHC in the United States, Citigroup, Inc., is very difficult to completely monitor with $1.097 trillion in assets and subsidiaries of different types operating in 100 countries and territories and numerous different types of activities based on an organizational structure divided into five groups: Citigroup Global Consumer Group, the Global Corporate and Investment Banking Group, Citigroup Global Investment Management, Citigroup International, and Smith Barney, a global private wealth management and equity research group (see *http://www.citigroup.com*). Hence, research is being conducted on the effectiveness of market discipline for U.S. financial institutions in terms of whether market information provides timely and accurate warnings and has an effect on the financial decisions of firms. Recent research has also questioned whether regulations introduce distortions, associated with credit crunches in the early 1990s, for instance, or prevent a level playing field in environments that are competitive and dynamic, making regulations difficult to be effective. Similarly, points have been made that regulations may provide too much protection, which leads to a weakening of market discipline, calling into question whether regulations and market discipline are complements or substitutes as financial institutions continue to evolve and change.[33]

Summary

Financial institutions have historically operated under tight regulation, although specific rules evolve as part of the regulatory dialectic. According to this concept, regulators articulate a set of regulations and the rationale for them (thesis); regulated firms respond by attempting to avoid regulations (antithesis); and eventually, a new set of regulations emerges (synthesis) as a result of these actions. In the course of the dialectic, financial innovation and technical and economic change powerfully influence the outcome. The dialectic has been especially evident in recent years.

Depository institutions have received the most attention from regulators. Over the years, a dual regulatory structure with state and federal oversight has emerged. Despite repeated expressions of concern about overlapping authority, Congress has not enacted many proposals to simplify the bureaucracy. Nondepository institutions are also regulated, but to a lesser extent. Most regulations governing finance companies are established at the state level and are less complex than those for depositories. Insurance companies are also governed by state regulators, which impose substantial regulation. Pension funds, investment companies, and securities firms are regulated by major federal statutes and by state laws. Depository institutions often feel that they struggle under an overly heavy regulatory burden.

Two of the most important regulatory reforms in the early 1980s were DIDMCA and G–St. G. These laws removed some restrictions on depositories' asset choices and on their sources of funds; they also increased similarity in the regulation of banks, thrifts, and credit unions. Regulators also received additional flexibility to handle failing institutions.

Almost immediately, however, forces for additional change were at work, spurred by the crisis in the thrift industry. In 1987, CEBA was passed, but it proved to be "too little, too late" to rescue the ailing FSLIC and served only to postpone

---

33 See Arnoud W. A. Boot, Silva Dezelan, and Todd T. Milbourn. "Regulatory Distortions in a Competitive Financial Services Industry." *Journal of Financial Services Research*, Vol. 17, No. 1 (2000), 159–168; Mark J. Flannery and Stanislava Nikolova. "Market Discipline of U.S. Financial Firms: Recent Evidence and Research Issues," forthcoming in William C. Hunter, George G. Kaufman, Claudio Borio, and Kostas Tsatsaronis (eds.), *Market Discipline Across Countries and Industries*, Cambridge: MIT Press, 2004; D. O. Cook, A. Hogan, and R. L. Kieschnick. "The Effects of Regulatory Oversight on Internal and External Mechanisms to Change Corporate Control." *Journal of Banking and Finance*, forthcoming, 2004; J. D. Wagster. "The Basle Accord of 1988 and the International Credit Crunch of 1989–1992." *Journal of Financial Services Research* 15 (March 1999), 123–143; R. Bliss and M. Flannery. "Market Discipline in Governance of U.S. Bank Holding Companies: Monitoring vs. Influencing." In *Prudential Supervision: What Works and What Doesn't*, ed. by F. Mishkin. NBER, University of Chicago Press, 2001; A. Berger. "Market Discipline in Banking." Proceedings of a Conference on Bank Structure and Competition, Federal Reserve Bank of Chicago, 1991, 419–437; Douglas D. Evanoff and Larry D. Wall. "Subordinated Debt and Bank Capital Reform." Working Paper, Federal Reserve Bank of Chicago, 2000; Federal Reserve Bank of New York, *Economic Policy Review, Special Issues: Corporate Governance: What Do We Know, and What is Different About Banks?* Vol. 9, No. 1 (April 2003).

more drastic action until 1989. FIRREA, passed in 1989, was a punitive law that did little to solve the systemic problems of deposit insurance and failed to address the question of appropriate bank powers. In 1991, FDICIA attempted to reform the deposit insurance system, reined in risk-taking behavior of depository institution managers, and required regulators to step up their aggressiveness in enforcing restrictions. Congress once again avoided important decisions on bank powers and regulatory restructuring. In 1997, banks experienced major changes in their geographical reach with the implementation of interstate branching under IBBEA, which allowed them to establish interstate branches for the first time in seventy years. In 1999, another revolutionary change occurred with the passage of the Financial Services Modernization (GLB) Act, which, for the first time since 1933, allows banking, investment, and insurance firms to operate under the same umbrella through new

financial holding companies. Concerns abound about fraud, corporate governance, off-balance-sheet exposure, globalization of financial markets, compliance with new and old U.S. congressional acts to prevent terrorism, money laundering, and other criminal activities. The Bank Secrecy Act, as amended by the USA Patriot Act, passed in September 2002, provides for financial institutions to establish formal anti-money laundering programs.

Current issues include better ways of measuring and controlling the risks taken by financial institutions, particularly huge financial holding companies; the impact of securitization and contingent liabilities; reform of the regulatory structure; regulation of institutions with international operations; and renewed emphasis on ethical behavior. Technology has offered financial institutions new opportunities, but also new competitors. Only one thing is certain: Change is an inevitable constant.

Questions

1. Explain in your own words the meaning of the term *regulatory dialectic*. Describe the three stages of the dialectic, and provide a historical example of each. Using current financial news or other publications, identify a recent regulatory decision and explain the reaction of financial institutions to it. Why do financial institutions seek to avoid regulations? How does the regulatory burden of banks compare with those of other institutions?

2. How is the process of financial innovation linked to regulation and the regulatory dialectic? How are developments in the economic/political/technological environment related to innovation? Based on emerging technology, economic conditions, and forecasts for the next decade, do you predict numerous or few financial innovations? Explain. Look on the Internet for a particular bank, insurance company, or securities firm. Does the institution maintain a Web page and offer services over the Internet?

3. The 1980s brought significant progress to ease the regulatory burden of financial institutions. Give an example of a regulatory restriction that hindered depository institutions' responses to changes in economic or technological developments in the 1980s. Discuss the rationale for revising regulations, many of which had their origins in the post-Depression years.

4. Explain how DIDMCA and G–St. G changed asset and liability management for depository institutions. How did this change reduce the risk of depository institutions? How did it increase the risk?

5. Explain the events and conditions that led to the creation of the Garn–St. Germain Act and CEBA. How did the deterioration in the financial condition of the thrift

industry and the FSLIC contribute to rapid congressional action? Briefly summarize the powers these acts gave to regulators to assist troubled institutions. In retrospect, were these provisions appropriate courses of action? Why or why not?

6. Do you agree with Professor Kane's opinion that the goals and objectives of legislators and financial institution regulators changed in the 1960s and 1970s from safety and soundness to limiting competition? Why or why not? How would you characterize the intent of legislators and regulators as demonstrated in FIRREA and FDICIA?

7. What developments, beginning almost immediately after FIRREA, prompted the passage of FDICIA? Do you believe that FDICIA was an adequate response? Why or why not? Explain FDICIA's prompt corrective action (PCA) provision. Why did Congress see a need for such a measure?

8. Choose two of the areas of continuing regulatory concern discussed in the last part of the chapter. Which one of these issues do you think will precipitate the next major congressional action? Using current publications, find a reference to or discussion of these issues by a legislator, a regulator, or a practitioner.

9. What explanations can you offer for the long-standing tradition of concentrating insurance regulation at the state rather than at the federal level? Do you believe other industries, such as banks, pension funds, or investment companies, could be effectively regulated only by the states?

10. Explain the impact of the McCarran–Ferguson Act on insurance pricing and the application of antitrust legislation to insurers. How did California's Proposition 103

present a challenge to the spirit of the McCarran–Ferguson law?

11. Briefly discuss the safeguards for employees included in the Employee Retirement Income Security Act (ERISA). What is the role of the Pension Benefit Guaranty Corporation (PBGC)?

12. Provide several examples of the types of regulations imposed on investment companies to control the risk exposure of shareholders.

13. In the 1970s and 1980s, Congress created regulatory safeguards to supplement the self-regulation already in place in the securities industry. What motivated these laws, and how did they restrict the activities of securities firms? What is insider trading, and what was its importance in the 1980s?

14. In the late 1980s and early 1990s, two prominent securities firms—Drexel Burnham Lambert and Salomon Brothers—were involved in financial scandals. Find a newspaper or journal article analyzing a recent example of unethical behavior within a financial institution. Do you anticipate a need for further legislation affecting the securities industry? Why or why not?

15. What are CAMELS and MACRO ratings? How are they used in evaluating depository institutions? Explain how FDICIA's tripwires strengthen examiners' authority.

16. Regulations are the rules under which financial institutions may operate, while supervision determines enforcement of those rules. Do you attribute the deposit insurance crisis primarily to shortcomings in regulations or supervision? How much did a mismatch in asset/liability maturities contribute to the crisis? Explain.

17. The later 1990s marked revolutionary new regulations with the advent of interstate branching in the United States and the freedom of banks, securities firms, and insurance firms to operate together under the same umbrella financial holding company. Do you agree or disagree that these were good trends? Why do you think it took so long for these regulations to pass?

18. How were one-bank holding companies and multibank holding companies used as loopholes (antithesis) in the regulatory dialectic? How did these loopholes create greater costs for banks in unit branching states? How did IBBEA and GLB help to reduce these costs?

19. What are some new regulatory concerns? How can market discipline be used to complement regulatory discipline?

Selected References

Barth, James R. *The Great Savings and Loan Debacle.* Washington, DC: American Enterprise Institute, 1991.

Benston, George J. *On Analysis of the Causes of Savings and Loan Association Failures.* Salomon Brothers Center for the Study of Financial Institutions Monograph Series (1985–4/5), Graduate School of Business, New York University.

Benston, George J., and George G. Kaufman. "Commercial Banking and Securities Activities: A Survey of the Risks and Returns." In *The Financial Services Revolution: Understanding the Changing Roles of Banks, Mutual Funds, and Insurance Companies,* ed. by Clifford E. Kirsch. Burr Ridge, IL: Irwin Professional, 1997, 3–28.

Berger, Allen N., Anil K. Kashyap, and Joseph M. Scalise. "The Transformation of the U.S. Banking Industry: What a Long, Strange Trip It's Been." *Brookings Papers on Economic Activity* 2 (1995), 55–218.

Broaddus, Alfred. "Financial Innovation in the United States— Background, Current Status, and Prospects." *Economic Review* (Federal Reserve Bank of Richmond) 71 (January/February 1985), 2–22.

Brock, Bronwyn. "Regulatory Changes Bring New Challenges to S&Ls, Other Depository Institutions." *Voice* (Federal Reserve Bank of Dallas) (September 1980), 5–9.

Brumbaugh, R. Dan, Jr. *Thrifts under Siege.* Cambridge, MA: Ballinger, 1988.

Cargill, Thomas F., and Gillian Garcia. *Financial Reform in the 1980s.* Stanford, CA: Hoover Institution Press, 1985.

Carner, William J. "An Analysis of Franchising in Retail Banking." *Journal of Retail Banking* 8 (Winter 1986–1987), 57–66.

Carron, Andrew S. *The Plight of the Thrift Institutions.* Washington, DC: Brookings Institution, 1982.

Cebenoyan, A. Sinan, Elizabeth S. Cooperman, Charles A. Register, and Sylvia C. Hudgins. "Cost Inefficiency and the Holding of Nontraditional Assets by Solvent Stock Thrifts." *Journal of Real Estate Economics* 26 (November 1998), 695–718.

Cole, Rebel A., and Joseph A. McKenzie. "Thrift Asset-Class Returns and the Efficient Diversification of Thrift Institution Portfolios." *Journal of Real Estate Economics* 22 (1994), 95–116.

Cooperman, Elizabeth S., Winson B. Lee, and Glenn A. Wolfe. "The Ohio Savings and Loan Crisis and Contagion for Retail CDs." *Journal of Finance* 3 (July 1992), 919–941.

Cyrnak, Anthony W. "Chain Banks and Competition: The Effectiveness of Federal Reserve Policy Since 1977." *Economic Review* (Federal Reserve Bank of San Francisco) (Spring 1986), 5–15.

Eickhoff, Gerald. "Going Interstate by Franchises or Networks." *Economic Review* (Federal Reserve Bank of Atlanta) 70 (January 1985), 32–35.

Federal Reserve Bank of Kansas. "Report on Chain Banking Organizations in Kansas, Nebraska, and Oklahoma." *Banking Studies* 1 (1983).

Finnerty, John D. "Financial Engineering in Corporate Finance: An Overview." *Financial Management* 17 (Winter 1988), 14–33.

Flood, Mark D. "Two Faces of Financial Innovations." *Review* (Federal Reserve Bank of St. Louis) 74 (September/October 1992), 3–17.

Garcia, Gillian, et al. "The Garn–St. Germain Depository Institutions Act of 1982." *Economic Perspectives* (Federal Reserve Bank of Chicago) 7 (March/April 1983), 2–31.

Gilbert, Gary G. "An Analysis of the Bush Task Group Recommendations for Regulatory Reform." *Issues in Bank Regulation* 7 (Spring 1984), 11–16.

Gilbert, R. Alton. "Requiem for Regulation Q: What It Did and Why It Passed Away." *Review* (Federal Reserve Bank of St. Louis) 68 (February 1986), 22–37.

————. "Implications of Annual Examinations for the Bank Insurance Fund." *Economic Review* (Federal Reserve Bank of St. Louis) 75 (January/February 1993), 35–52.

Goodman, Laurie S. "The Interface between Technology and Regulation in Banking." In *Technology and the Regulation of Financial Markets,* ed. by Anthony Saunders and Lawrence J. White. Lexington, MA: D. C. Heath, 1986, 181–186.

Gorton, Gary, and George Pennacchi. "Nonbanks and the Future of Banking." *Proceedings of a Conference on Bank Structure and Competition.* Chicago: Federal Reserve Bank of Chicago, 1992.

Greenspan, Alan. "An Overview of Financial Restructuring." In *The Financial Services Industry in the Year 2000.* Chicago: Federal Reserve Bank of Chicago, 1988, 3–9.

Harrington, Scott. "The Impact of Rate Regulation on Prices and Underwriting Results in the Property-Liability Insurance Industry: A Survey." *Journal of Risk and Insurance* 51 (December 1984), 577–623.

Johnson, Verle B. "Reorganization?" *Weekly Letter,* Federal Reserve Bank of San Francisco, March 2, 1984.

Kane, Edward J. "Good Intentions and Unintended Evil: The Case against Selective Credit Allocation." *Journal of Money, Credit, and Banking* 9 (February 1977), 55–69.

————. "Accelerating Inflation, Technological Innovation, and the Decreasing Effectiveness of Banking Regulation." *Journal of Finance* 36 (May 1981), 355–367.

————. "Technology and the Regulation of Financial Markets." In *Technology and the Regulation of Financial Markets,* ed. by Anthony Saunders and Lawrence J. White. Lexington, MA: D. C. Heath, 1986, 187–193.

————. "Changing Incentives Facing Financial-Services Regulators." *Journal of Financial Services Research* 2 (1989a), 265–274.

————. *The S&L Insurance Mess: How Did It Happen?* Washington, DC: Urban Institute Press, 1989b.

————. "De Jure Interstate Banking: Why Only Now?" *Journal of Money, Credit, and Banking* 28 (May 1996), 141–161.

Kaufman, George G. *The U.S. Financial System: Money, Markets, and Institutions,* 6th ed. Englewood Cliffs, NJ: Prentice Hall, 1995.

Miller, Merton H. "Financial Innovation: The Last Twenty Years and the Next." *Journal of Financial and Quantitative Analysis* 21 (December 1986), 459–471.

Myers, Forest, and Catharine Lemieux. "Three Decades of Banking." *Annual Banking Studies* (Federal Reserve Bank of Kansas City) (1991), 1–27.

Neuberger, Jonathon. "FIRREA and Deposit Insurance Reform." *Weekly Letter,* Federal Reserve Bank of San Francisco, December 1, 1989.

O'Keefe, John. "The Scheduling and Reliability of Bank Examinations: The Effect of FDICIA." Working Paper, Division of Research and Statistics, Federal Deposit Insurance Corporation, 1996.

Rhoades, Stephen A., and Donald T. Savage. "Controlling Nationwide Concentration under Interstate Banking." *Issues in Bank Regulation* 9 (Autumn 1985), 34–40.

Selden, Richard T. "Consumer-Oriented Intermediaries." In *Financial Institutions and Markets,* 2nd ed., ed. by Murray E. Polakoff and Thomas A. Durkin. Boston: Houghton Mifflin, 1981, 207–212.

Shull, Bernard. "Economic Efficiency, Public Regulation, and Financial Reform: Depository Institutions." In *Financial Institutions and Markets,* 2nd ed., ed. by Murray E. Polakoff and Thomas A. Durkin. Boston: Houghton Mifflin, 1981, 671–702.

Silber, William. "The Process of Financial Innovation." *American Economic Review* 73 (May 1983), 89–95.

Spong, Kenneth. *Banking Regulation: Its Purposes, Implementation, and Effects.* Kansas City: Federal Reserve Bank of Kansas City, 2002.

Treff, Bruce and Paul Kirwan. "Implications of Sarbanes-Oxley on the Investment Company Industry." *The Investment Lawyer,* Vol. 10, No. 7 (January 2003): 2, 21.

Van Horne, James C. "Of Financial Innovations and Excesses." *Journal of Finance* 40 (July 1985), 621–631.

West, Robert Craig. "The Depository Institutions Deregulation Act of 1980: A Historical Perspective." *Economic Review* (Federal Reserve Bank of Kansas City) 67 (February 1982), 3–13.

White, Lawrence J. *The S&L Debacle.* New York: Oxford University Press, 1991.

internet *exercise*

HOW DO I FIND INFORMATION ON INDIVIDUAL BANKS?

The Federal Deposit Insurance Corporation (FDIC) maintains an Institution Directory that provides a great deal of information about institutions covered by federal deposit insurance. This class includes virtually all U.S. financial institutions. Given the maze of banking regulatory agencies, confusion can sometimes cloud questions about the primary federal regulators for individual banks.

To find information on a particular institution:

1   Go to the FDIC Institution Website Directory at *http://www2.fdic.gov/idasp/index.asp*.

2   From the FDIC Institution Directory, you will be able to find a bank holding company or institution.

3   Select Find Institutions and click on it.

4   The screen will switch to a "Find an Institution" form. You just need to type in the name, city, and state of your institution. For a test, try typing in Wells Fargo, San Francisco, California. Then click on Find. You may be given several choices for Wells Fargo; click on the Cert link for the largest in San Francisco.

5   A new screen will display information for you to choose from including:

Current List of Offices	Bank Holding Company Ownership and Affiliates
Compare to Peer Group(s)	Organization Hierarchy from the Federal Reserve System
FFIEC Call/TFR Report	FFIEC Interagency CRA ratings
FFIEC Uniform Bank Performance Report (UBPR)	OCC CRA ratings
FDIC/OTS Summary of Deposits	California Regional Economic Conditions

Find out all about Wells Fargo and then try looking up your institution. The Uniform Bank Performance Report (UBPR) will be discussed in Chapter 4, but basically it gives all the financial statements for your bank, as do the call reports. The CRA ratings for the bank, economic conditions, organizational hierarchy, holding company structure, list of offices, and peer group comparison are all provided.

OTHER USEFUL SITES FOR FINANCIAL INSTITUTIONS DATA:

U.S. Senate Committee on Banking, Housing, and Urban Affairs

http://www.senate.gov/~banking/

U.S. House Committee on Financial Services

http://www.house.gov/banking/

Index for FDIC List of Major Banking Regulations

http://www.fdic.gov/regulations/laws/index.html

SEC Press Releases

http://www.sec.gov/news/press.shtml

FDIC Website

http://www.fdic.gov

Federal Reserve Board Website

http://www.federalreserve.gov

Federal Financial Institutions Examination Council

http://www.ffiec.gov

Office of the Comptroller of the Currency

http://www.occ.treas.gov

From the search engine at http://www.google.com, you can also type in any regulatory agency or bank and find links to their Websites.

The Federal Reserve System and International Policy Coordination

"America's financial markets are in many respects the wonder of the world for their efficiency and dynamism. But they are also constrained by numerous obsolete regulatory policies, and their very dynamism makes them a tempting target for new political impositions. The stakes for the U.S. economy are considerable."

CHARLES W. CALOMIRIS

Paul M. Montrone, Professor of Finance and Economics, Columbia University Graduate School of Business (1997). Quote from his book, The Postmodern Bank Safety Net: Lessons from Developed and Developing Economies. *Washington, DC: American Enterprise Institute, 1997.*

Fed officials are routine targets for public criticism such as favoring certain segments of society or political interest groups over others. Similarly, the quote by Professor Charles Calomiris praises but at the same time questions many of the regulations in U.S. markets, including many imposed by the Fed. Professional "Fed watchers" attempt to divine the future direction of interest rates—and thus the best management strategies for financial institutions—from even the most seemingly inconsequential remarks by the chairman.

Why does such an august institution play such a controversial yet influential role? This appendix answers that question by exploring the Fed's actions beyond the supervisory and regulatory functions discussed in Chapter 3. In particular, the appendix focuses on the Fed's role as a lender of last resort, guardian of the nation's payments system and financial stability, architect of monetary policy, and major participant in the international regulatory scene. Rapid technological and economic changes in the last decade have raised the Fed's profile in the financial environment, and its importance will undoubtedly increase as globalization of financial markets progresses.[1]

Why the Fed?

Although the nation has entered its third century, the Fed was created by a law signed by President Woodrow Wilson on December 23, 1913. For most of the country's history, it operated without such an organization.[2] Yet few financial institution managers envision a future without the Fed. Clearly, the financial system before 1913 suffered from inadequacies that the Fed has addressed with success, if not to everyone's complete satisfaction. Even economists at the St. Louis, Minneapolis, Cleveland, and Richmond Federal Reserve banks continue to question assumptions of defects in the system prior to the Fed, however, and whether it has made the right policy choices. The Fed's important economic role is regularly subjected to scrutiny.

A Brief History of the Days before the Fed

Historians identify the most important recurring and inter-related financial problems plaguing the nation before the Fed as (1) an unsatisfactory currency, (2) a deficient payments system for transferring funds from one party to another, and (3) periodic panics that led to widespread bank failures.[3]

Resolving each of these problems was an important objective to the framers of the Federal Reserve Act.

The Money Supply Problem

As noted in Chapter 3, the National Currency Act of 1863 and the National Banking Act of 1864 attempted to solve problems created by lack of a uniform currency by authorizing the formation of federally chartered banks that could issue national bank notes. To encourage public confidence and promote their acceptance as legal tender for transactions, national bank notes had to be collateralized by U.S. government securities. In the decades to follow, the U.S. Treasury also issued a fixed quantity of paper money backed by gold and silver reserves.

Although this system clearly improved confidence in paper money, promoted growth in the number and size of financial transactions, and encouraged interstate commerce, problems remained. The number of Treasury notes outstanding was tied directly to gold and silver reserves, and the number of national bank notes was tied to the volume of Treasury securities outstanding. These conditions made for an *inelastic* currency, the volume of which could not change spontaneously as the economy changed.

The Payments Problem

The Fed was designed to resolve additional difficulties related to a lack of confidence in the nation's payments system. Transactions depend on people's confidence that money they exchange has value and that they can rely on financial institutions to transfer funds efficiently, honestly, and reasonably quickly between parties. Without a strong authority to enforce minimum performance levels, some banks did not keep enough reserves to cover customers' withdrawals, and others failed to provide effective, fairly priced methods of clearing checks.

The "Panic" Problem

Variability of economic cycles was compounded by unsettling questions about the value of currency, its quantity, and the reliability of funds transfers, leading to periodic financial panics. At these times, banks failed when they were unable to meet demands for withdrawals. The failures of some banks created drains on others, causing them to fail, as well.

The Bank of England helped to prevent this problem in its homeland by acting as a **lender of last resort**—a central bank that could and would supply liquidity to other banks in emergencies. Because Americans distrusted centralized authority and resisted emulating Great Britain, however, no such institution operated in the United States. Thus, the banking system went through periods of severe contraction. A particularly drastic panic in 1907 caused political leaders to conclude that opposition to a central bank was no longer in the nation's best interests. They took six years more, how-ever, to devise the political solutions necessary to create the Federal Reserve System.

Organization of the Federal Reserve System

The law authorizing the Fed was an artful compromise. Advocates of a strong central bank wanted an institution with sweeping authority to supervise the money supply and the payments system; others feared that such a bank would support large institutions located in urban areas and ignore the needs of small, rural ones. The cornerstone of this compromise was the creation of not one but twelve Federal Reserve banks overseeing more than twenty additional branches located throughout the nation, as indicated in Figure 3A.1. Private-sector banks choosing to become members of the Fed contributed funds to begin district banks' operations. All national banks were required to be members, but state-chartered institutions could voluntarily join. A seven-member Board of Governors, located in Washington, DC, was charged with coordinating the activities of the district banks. Board members were required to represent diverse geographic regions.

In the early days, the regional banks had considerably more authority than they have today. They could set the rates at which they would lend to banks in their districts (the **discount rate**) without consulting the board; now, board approval is required. The district banks were also originally envisioned as the primary sources of influence on the nation's money supply. Events subsequently demonstrated defects in this approach, and today monetary policy is centralized in a single committee dominated by the seven Federal Reserve Board members. As a result, the district banks and their branches play a less important policy role than originally envisioned (although they actively assist in funds transfers). The Fed has gradually moved away from the original intent that it be the world's only *de*centralized central bank.

The Fed as a Financial Institution

The Fed is a critical policy-making entity and a regulator of others, but it is also a financial institution. It holds primarily financial assets, on which it earns interest revenues. An examination of a recent consolidated balance sheet from the Fed, shown in Table 3A.1, is a useful way to understand its primary functions today and their relative importance to financial institution management.

Assets of the Federal Reserve System

Clearly the Fed's largest asset is its holdings in U.S. Treasury and federal agency securities. Almost as an afterthought, the Federal Reserve Act gave the Fed the power to own and trade these assets. The inclusion of that power is fortuitous indeed, because the trading of government securities—called **open market operations**—is the single most important tool in the

figure **3A.1** FEDERAL RESERVE BANKS AND BRANCHES

The dispersion of district banks and branches around the country reflects a political compromise by the Fed's organizers, who recognized the need for a central banking system but feared concentration of financial power. The numbers and corresponding letters assigned to a district appear on Federal Reserve notes issued in that district.

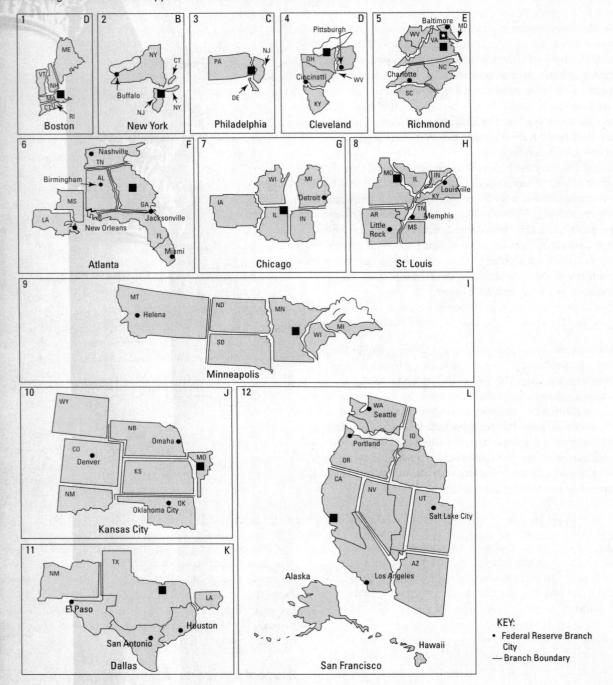

KEY:
• Federal Reserve Branch City
— Branch Boundary

Source: Federal Reserve Bulletin, *July 1993, A79.*

table 3A.1 TYPICAL BALANCE SHEET OF THE FEDERAL RESERVE SYSTEM ($ BILLION)

The Fed's balance sheet reflects its important responsibilities. Particularly notable are its securities portfolio, the vehicle through which it conducts open market operations; Federal Reserve notes, which serve as the nation's currency; and deposits of depository institutions, which are the reserves of the nation's banking system.

			Percentage of Total
Assets			
Gold certificates and coin		$ 14.227	1.94%
Loans to depository institutions	$ 0.040		
Secs. purchased under agreements to resell	39.500		
Federal agency securities	0.010		
Treasury securities	$629.406		
Total loans and securities		668.956	91.23
Items in the process of collection		11.498	1.57
Other assets and bank premises		$ 38.567	5.26
Total assets		$733.249	100.00%
Liabilities and Net Worth			
Federal Reserve notes, net		$654.273	89.23%
Secs. Sold under agreements to repurchase		21.091	2.87%
Deposits of depository institutions	22.541		
Other deposits	5.713		
Total deposits		28.254	3.85
Other liabilities		12.870	1.76
Total Liabilities		716.488	97.71
Capital		16.761	2.29
Total liabilities and capital		$733.249	100.00%

Source: Prepared by the Authors with data from the Board of Governors of the Federal Reserve System, 89th Annual Report *(Washington, DC: Board of Governors of the Federal Reserve System, 2002), Statement of Condition of the Federal Reserve Banks, December 31, 2002,* http://www.federalreserve.gov/boarddocs/rptcongress/annual02.

Fed's monetary policy activities, as discussed in more detail in subsequent sections.

Other asset accounts are much less significant on the balance sheet, arising as the Fed carries out important responsibilities. For example, the Fed occasionally buys and sells gold, often to assist the Treasury in international transactions. The Federal Reserve Banks do not physically store precious metals, so the "gold certificates and coin" account represents the Fed's claim on bullion stored in federal depositories, such as that at the U.S. Army installation at Fort Knox, Kentucky. The "loans to depository institutions" account symbolizes another major Fed activity—its role as lender of last resort.

As noted, the Fed is also responsible for promoting an effective and efficient payments system. The "items in the process of collection" account is the dollar amount of uncleared checks in process at the time the balance sheet was prepared. Although the volume on any one day is a relatively small proportion of Fed assets, as shown in Table 3A.1, a staggering volume of fund transfers pass through the Federal Reserve banks annually—running well into the trillions of dollars. The "other assets" account primarily represents physical facilities.

Liabilities and Capital of the Federal Reserve System

The largest liabilities of the Fed by far are Federal Reserve notes in circulation—the paper money Americans exchange daily in millions of transactions. The 1913 Federal Reserve Act called for replacing national bank notes with Federal Reserve notes. Originally, the Fed's notes had to be backed partially by gold and partially by other assets (not including government securities), a system that retained limitations on the total volume of currency that could be issued. Gradually, the asset categories allowed as backing for Federal Reserve notes were broadened. Today, the Fed recognizes many forms of money besides currency and is not bound by a particular formula in determining the amount of its notes outstanding as a proportion of total media of exchange. Each district bank issues paper money. (Figure 3A.1 shows the letter of the alphabet that appears on currency issued in a district.) Worn notes must be retired from circulation frequently, and currency production costs are among the Fed's largest expenses.

The account "deposits of depository institutions" reflects two of the Fed's main functions—regulator and architect of monetary policy. As mentioned in the Chapter 3 text, the Depository Institutions Deregulation and Monetary Control Act of 1980 (DIDMCA) authorized the Fed to establish universal reserve requirements for all depositories. These reserves appear as deposits of depository institutions on the Fed's balance sheet and serve both as assurances of sufficient liquidity for individual institutions to meet normal operating needs and also as targets for the Fed's monetary policy activities. Reserves are discussed in more detail later in the appendix.

"Other liabilities" comprise a collection of relatively small Fed obligations, including accounts payable that arise in the normal course of business. The "capital" account represents the contributions of member institutions, on which they earn a flat 6 percent dividend, plus a relatively small accumulated surplus. As a financial institution, the Fed has been quite profitable in recent years. In 1991, for example, it earned a net income of over $21 billion. After paying a 6 percent dividend to member banks and retaining a small sum, the Fed turned over more than $20 billion to the Treasury. It considered this payment to the Treasury as a form of interest on its outstanding Federal Reserve notes.[4]

The Fed as Guardian of the Payments System

Even in the 1990s, centuries-old methods of fund transfers persist; most Americans use both currency and checks to execute transactions. They never wonder whether a dollar bill received in Denver will be the equivalent of 100 cents in Boston the next day, nor do they worry about whether a utility company's bank will accept a check written on a local bank account at face value (assuming the account contains enough funds to honor the check). This confidence was not always so widespread, and the Fed has been instrumental in eliminating skepticism, and even panic, about predictable functioning of the payments system.

The Federal Reserve Act charged the Fed with improving the check-clearing process, especially between distant points. As a first step, member banks were required to clear checks drawn on other banks at face value, a practice by no means universal before 1913. Among other major improvements was the development in 1918 of **Fedwire,** through which member banks could transfer funds among themselves by telegraph, free of charge. Today, many types of electronic fund transfers occur, and the Fed led the way in their devel-

opment, although checks and wire transfers (no longer free) are still common payment tools. In as early as 1991, for example, the Fed cleared almost 19 billion paper checks, handled more than 66 million wire transfers, and electronically processed more than 1 billion commercial transfers.

Privately owned and operated fund transfer systems operate alongside the Fed's system, providing interesting (and not altogether friendly) competition among regulators and regulated institutions. Prior to 1980, the Fed had a monopoly role in the payments system, which many economists criticized. DIDMCA allowed private institutions to compete with the Fed by offering clearing services. Also, acknowledging banks' allegations of unfair competition, the Fed announced in 1990 that it would begin to reduce—but certainly not eliminate—its involvement in fund transfers and to allow the private sector to earn more of the rewards (while bearing more risk). Today, the Fed is rapidly losing its monopoly in the payments system, and many economists note improved competitiveness and cost efficiency as a result.[5]

Daylight Overdrafts

Current banking practices give rise to **daylight overdrafts,** which some experts believe pose a growing risk to the payments system. Daylight overdrafts arise when depository institutions overdraw their reserve deposit accounts at the Fed while making transfers through Fedwire during the course of a business day. Although the Fed has yet to lose money as a result, the volume of overdrafts is so large (averaging $112 billion daily in 1987) that the Fed now requires institutions to set internal policy limits on their overdrafts. Since 1991, it has required collateral for certain types of overdrafts. The Fed limits the dollar volume of overdrafts it will process for institutions, especially those under financial stress. In April 1994, the Fed began charging institutions when daylight overdrafts occur in their reserve and clearing accounts.[6]

Privately owned payments systems, such as Clearing House Interbank Payments System (**CHIPS**) in New York City, are also exposed to losses from members' daylight overdrafts. CHIPS members, about 130 important domestic and foreign banks, routinely exchange large volumes of funds and securities among themselves. Although the Fed would absorb a loss should a bank fail while overdrawn in its clearing balances, CHIPS members would have to bear the losses themselves in case of the failure of an overdrawn user of CHIPS. To limit this risk, the Fed requires that institutions include both CHIPS and Fedwire transactions in establishing their policy limits on daylight overdrafts.

The Fed's Role in Maintaining Financial Stability in Times of Crisis, Such as 9/11

As the guardian of the payments system, in recent decades the Fed has also taken on a significant role in maintaining financial stability in response to sudden shocks that threaten financial stability including the stock market crash of 1987, the dot.com stock market crash in early 2000, the Russian bond default in 1998, the Long-Term Capital Management crisis, and particularly during the 9/11 attacks in 2001. The Fed has ensured the stability of the payments system, as well as financial markets. For instance, the 9/11 attacks on the World Trade Center resulted in damage to the physical clearing process for payments for large dollar electronic transfers. In response, the Fed lent massive amounts of funds to banks and other lenders, so large payments could be made and a surge in loan demand could be met. With the air transportation shut down for three days after the crisis, the Fed had to implement extraordinary efforts to ensure that payment services including electronic funds transfers, check clearing, and currency processing were able to continue. To ensure orderly functioning of the economy and financial markets, the Fed also injected massive liquidity through both discount window loans and open market operations of about $100 billion a day for the three days following the attacks. Interest rates were also lowered over the following three weeks by 100 basis points to ensure market and economic stability. The Fed also set up swap lines with several foreign central banks to allow time for foreign banks with U.S. operations and their customers to deal with disruptions. Fees and penalties on daylight and overnight overdrafts were suspended to help banks that had difficulties managing reserve positions. Up to about ten days after the attacks, daylight overdrafts by depository institutions were about 30 percent higher than normal, with daylight overdrafts peaking at $150 billion, more than 60 percent higher than normal. Rules on securities lending were also temporarily suspended to ensure extra collateral was available to the markets. The Fed also worked with the SEC, Department of the Treasury, market participants, and other stakeholders to help reopen the financial markets by September 17. Hence, the Fed provided essential help in ensuring stability and efficient functioning of financial markets. In this crisis, the Fed used its roles as the guardian of the payments mechanism, supervisor of banks and bank holding companies, monetary policy maker, and as lender of last resort. Some observers note that having all of these roles in one agency worked well in preventing a financial crisis.[7]

The Fed as Lender of Last Resort

The Fed's first test as a lender of last resort came more than fifteen years after its founding, when the 1929 stock market crash and the Great Depression resulted in a series of bank failures. Many borrowers defaulted on bank loans, and depositors responded to the economic uncertainty by attempting to withdraw their deposits in cash. To obtain cash to meet depositors' demands, banks were forced to dump large quantities of their government securities holdings into the financial markets at "fire sale" prices, further

weakening their financial positions. Despite its mandate to support member banks needing cash, the Fed was slow to react to the crisis. Economic historians, although not in complete agreement, attribute the Fed's disappointing performance to inadequate tools, a lack of understanding of the economic system's needs, or both.[8] By 1933, nearly 9,000 banks had failed, almost half those in existence in 1929.

As noted in Chapter 3, experts now view much Depression-era legislation as outmoded and even based on erroneous interpretations of the events of the time. At least one legislative response to the Depression, however, established procedures that remain the foundation of some of the Fed's current activities. The Banking Act of 1935 made permanent several changes in Fed procedures that had been introduced as temporary measures in 1932 and 1933. Notably, the act widened the Fed's latitude in deciding what collateral to accept from banks wishing to borrow at the discount window (not a physical location but merely a set of procedures through which financial institutions can borrow from the Fed). The policies governing the Fed's discount window lending are stipulated in Regulation A. In general, the Fed can lend only on very safe collateral, such as Treasury securities provided by banks, but at times of great distress, this policy allows other types of collateral.

The Fed's actions in recent financial market crises have been almost universally praised. For example, in the aftermath of the 1987 stock market crash, the Fed received high marks for its responsiveness. By standing ready to buy unlimited quantities of government securities from banks that needed cash, and by clearly and frequently communicating its intention to do so, the Fed maintained liquidity in the financial system. Not one bank failure was attributed to the crash. Similarly, as previously discussed, the Fed did an excellent job in maintaining financial market stability after the attacks of 9/11. Subsequent analysis has led experts to conclude that the Fed successfully balanced its monetary policy objectives with its actions as lender of last resort.

However, some economists see moral hazard problems in the Fed's role as lender of last resort. Very large banks, knowing that the Fed waits to bail them out, may take on risks that they would otherwise avoid. As Charles Calomiris notes, "Thus, many [economists] came to view the safety net—previously lauded as a risk reducer—as the single most important destabilizing influence in the financial system." Economists have also expressed concern over the types of institutions that are allowed to borrow from the Fed.[9]

Whom Should a Lender of Last Resort Protect?

Today, questions surrounding the role of a lender of last resort are receiving renewed attention, primarily because of the thrift crisis and the failure of several large banks in the 1980s. Classical resort theory on the matter holds that the lender of last resort should (1) protect the *aggregate* money supply, not the safety of individual institutions; (2) lend only to well-managed institutions with temporary cash needs; (3) allow poorly managed institutions to fail; (4) require good collateral for all loans; and (5) announce these conditions well in advance of a crisis so that market participants know what to expect.[10] The Fed departed from these principles in 1974 in responding to Franklin National Bank, a large New York institution whose impending failure the Fed attempted to "manage" to avoid hurting other large banks. This limited action fortunately averted the collapse of other large banks, and Franklin National was merged with a large European bank shortly thereafter without losses to the Fed. Similar lending by the Fed helped to avert a banking crisis in the collapse of Continental Illinois National Bank ten years later.

Observers note, however, that the Fed and other regulators have kept hundreds of failing thrift institutions afloat since the early 1980s, departing drastically from the principles of safe lending. Concern escalated in April 1989, when the Fed lent $70 million to a bankrupt but still operating thrift institution that had *no* collateral, because its parent company had previously transferred all its good assets to other subsidiaries before declaring bankruptcy. With no apparent prospects for repayment, the Fed faced continuing withdrawals by the thrift's customers as their confidence deteriorated. During the same period, the Fed agreed to make similar loans to at least eight other thrifts. Most experts criticize discount window lending under these conditions as outside the intent of lender-of-last-resort legislation; however, the S&L crisis did not result in a loss of confidence in the safety of the federal deposit insurance system or break down the operation of the payments system. In the Federal Deposit Insurance Corporation Improvement Act (FDICIA), Congress attempted to curtail such practices by prohibiting the Fed from extending discount window loans to institutions in poor financial condition with no prospects of recovery. In the 1990s, conditions improved for banks and savings institutions, so this provision of FDICIA has not been stringently tested. Calomiris and others wonder whether loans will be withheld when political motives push regulators toward extending them.[11]

The Fed as Architect of Monetary Policy

Perhaps the Fed's single most important responsibility, and the one for which it most often receives criticism, is the conduct of monetary policy. **Monetary policy** encompasses the Fed's attempts to influence both the money supply and the level of interest rates. This section of the appendix identifies the goals of monetary policy, the primary methods by which the Fed attempts to achieve those goals, and the main effects of monetary policy on financial institution management.

Goals of Monetary Policy

Controlling the money supply is not an end in itself. Instead, most economists see a relationship between money and other important economic variables such as interest rates (and through them the supply and demand for credit), inflation, employment, national income, and currency exchange rates. Thus, the ultimate goal of monetary policy is to promote a healthy economy with low inflation, satisfactory growth in output, full employment, and an acceptable balance of trade. The importance of particular goals may change, as when Congress mandated special emphasis on jobs in the Full Employment and Balanced Growth Act of 1978. This act required the Fed to report to Congress semi-annually on the impact of its policies on the unemployment rate and other economic measures. Also the goals of monetary policy sometimes conflict; for example, a booming economy with a low jobless rate may lead to inflation and high interest rates. Nonetheless, the goals listed earlier are generally accepted.

First Things First: What Is Money?

Successful monetary policy cannot be conducted unless the Fed can define and measure money. Economists agree that "money" as an abstract concept is something accepted as a medium of exchange that holds its value. In a modern financial system, this definition can apply to a wide variety of financial instruments. For example, currency and balances in checking accounts, money market accounts, and even savings accounts can all pay for transactions. Recognizing this range, the Fed has defined several categories of money (called the **monetary aggregates**) as targets of its monetary policy operations. Recent definitions of main categories are summarized in Table 3A.2. The most fundamental type of money, the **monetary base,** consists of currency and reserves of depository institutions held within the Fed. Closely related is the narrowest monetary aggregate, M1, which adds checking account balances to the monetary base. M2 adds balances in other relatively liquid, interest-bearing accounts, and M3 is yet a broader measure.[12]

Economists also attempt to measure **money multipliers,** or relationships between the monetary base and the monetary aggregates, determined by the complex interactions of reserve requirements and public and institutional preferences for holding money. Recent research indicates, for example, that the multiplier between the monetary base and M2 during the period 1980 to 1988 ranged between 10 and 12; that is, for every $1 change in the monetary base, a $10 to $12 change in M2 would have been expected.[13] Unfortunately for the smooth conduct of monetary policy, money multipliers change as a result of economic changes and financial and technical innovations, magnifying the uncertainty of the policy-making process.

Policy makers must make a difficult decision about which measure of money to target to achieve ultimate monetary policy goals. A desirable target should be clearly related to important economic variables *and* an effect the Fed can influence directly without undesirable economic side effects. Economists debate the question vigorously without achieving

table **3A.2**   COMPONENTS OF THE MONETARY BASE AND MONETARY AGGREGATES

In today's sophisticated financial markets, many assets qualify as money, because they have lasting value and can be used to make transactions. The narrowest definition is the monetary base, but several broader monetary aggregates also exist. Deciding which definition is best for monetary policy purposes is a difficult choice.

Monetary Base

Currency in circulation (Federal Reserve notes, coins, U.S. Treasury certificates)

Reserve *deposits* of financial institutions

Other deposits and vault cash greater than reserves

Aggregate Measures of the Money Supply

M1

Cash held by the public

Traveler's checks of nonbank issuers

Demand deposits at commercial banks

Other checkable deposits (OCDs) consisting of negotiable order of withdrawal (NOW) accounts at depository institutions, credit union share draft accounts, and demand deposits at thrift institutions and automatic transfer service (ATS) accounts at depository institutions

M2

M1 plus:

Savings (including money market deposit accounts [MMDAs])

Small-denomination time deposits (time deposits including retail repurchase agreements [RPs]—in amounts less than $100,000)

Balances in retail money market mutual funds (excluding individual retirement accounts [IRAs] and Keogh balances at depository institutions and money market funds)

M3

M2 plus:

Large-denomination time deposits in amounts of $100,000 or more

Balances in institutional money funds

Repurchase Agreement (RP) liabilities (overnight and term) issued by all depository institutions

Eurodollars (overnight and term) held by U.S. residents at foreign branches of U.S. banks worldwide and at all banking offices in the United Kingdom and Canada. Excludes amounts held by depository institutions, the U.S. government, money market funds, and foreign banks and official institutions.

Source: Federal Reserve Bulletin *89 (August 2003), A4; and* Federal Reserve Statistical Release, H.6: Money Stock Measures, January 15, 2004 *(http://www.federalreserve.gov/releases/h6/Current/). Seasonal adjustments are also made for each measure, described in more detail in the preceding sources.*

consensus. For example, many experts believe that M2 shows the most stable relationship with ultimate policy variables, although that relationship is far from certain.[14] However, the monetary base is the most easily controlled measure of money, and its changes should, through the multiplier effect, result in changes in M2. Some argue, however, that manipulation of the monetary base could have undesirable effects on interest rates. Deregulation, increasing globalization, and shocks to the economic system—such as the stock market crash of 1987 and the 1989 culmination of the crisis in the thrift industry—further confuse the relationship between measures of money and monetary policy goals, fueling a continuing debate over appropriate targets.

Innovations continue to change the nature of money, such as new home-finance software that lets consumers pay bills directly on bank Websites, Internet banking and debit cards that have become more widely used (discussed more in Chapter 7), electronic cash services, and systems to send money in coded E-mail messages instead of checks. Such constant change further complicates efforts to define and control money.

Money or Interest Rate Targets?

In another important issue for monetary policy, some economists argue that the Fed can achieve ultimate economic goals most effectively not by focusing directly on money, however defined, but rather by establishing interest rate targets and managing the monetary aggregates to achieve the desired rates. According to this belief, interest rates at desirable levels will lead to acceptable levels of economic growth, inflation, employment, and trade. In this view, the level of any particular monetary aggregate is important only insofar as it increases or decreases interest rates beyond target levels.[15]

In recent years, the Fed itself has seemed to vacillate over the choice between monetary aggregates and interest rates as its true policy targets. Although public statements by Fed officials consistently have stressed monetary aggregates, Fed watchers universally believe that during the 1970s, monetary policy was really directed at maintaining interest rate levels by controlling the **federal funds rate,** the interest rate that depository institutions charge on the excess reserves they lend to one another. In October 1979, however, with inflation rising precipitously, the Fed took an abrupt turn toward focusing on monetary aggregates regardless of the effect on interest rates. In October 1983, the Fed switched back to target both monetary aggregates and interest rates. Statements in the early 1990s by Fed Chairman Alan Greenspan suggest that interest rates are once again the primary monetary policy target.

The perception of Fed ambivalence about the best targets arises from the political as well as economic pressures that influence its monetary policy. For example, many politicians, including presidents, focus on interest rates as highly visible symbols of the economy's performance. Thus, a monetary policy that targets monetary aggregates exclusively is unlikely to please prominent politicians if it leads, for example, to high mortgage rates. Similarly, inflation disturbs politicians, so a policy that targets interest rates but leads to inflationary monetary growth will also fail to win friends. Although the Fed is nominally independent of politics, the president appoints the members of the board, and the Fed chairman must report regularly to Congress. Thus, many expert Fed watchers believe that the political climate influences monetary policy as much as does economic theory. Further complicating monetary policy is the Fed's regulatory role. Some observers believe the Fed may delay or forgo certain monetary policy actions if these actions would adversely affect institutions it regulates.[16]

Tools of Monetary Policy

Regardless of the economic and political difficulties, Fed officials must reach decisions about monetary policy; then they must put policy directives in motion. The current structure for implementing monetary policy has its roots in post-Depression legislation. The Banking Act of 1935 made a permanent fixture of the **Federal Open Market Committee (FOMC),** although similar groups had operated since the early 1920s. The FOMC is the body through which all important monetary policy decisions are made. It consists of the seven members of the Board of Governors along with the presidents of five district Federal Reserve banks.[17] Besides deciding the appropriate targets of monetary policy activities, since the 1970s the FOMC has identified specific quantitative objectives, such as the rate of growth in the monetary aggregates. Finally, it considers how to apply its major policy tools—buying and selling government securities in the financial markets (open market operations).

In addition to open market operations, the Fed can pursue its desired monetary policy by changing reserve requirements for depository institutions and changing the discount rate. Although some disagree, most experts believe that these tools are relatively insignificant in monetary policy (even though they are important for other reasons).[18] Increasing or decreasing the amount of required reserves would instantaneously affect the money supply, but perhaps at the cost of a quite drastic expansion or contraction. Thus, changes in reserve requirements are seldom used to influence the money supply. A recent exception was the Fed's 1992 decision to lower, from 12 to 10 percent, the maximum proportion of selected deposits institutions must hold as reserves.

The Fed could also attempt to increase (or decrease) the level of reserves available to the banking system by lowering (or raising) the discount rate. Such a policy would influence the level of borrowing by depository institutions, as occurred many times during the recession of the early 1990s. Yet the Fed cannot force institutions to borrow, nor, as lender of last resort, can it easily refuse qualifying loan applications even if they conflict with monetary policy objectives. Thus, the subsequent discussion focuses exclusively on open market operations.

How Open Market Operations Influence the Money Supply and Interest Rates

The effect of open market operations was discovered accidentally in the early days of the Fed, as individual district banks purchased and sold government securities to increase their incomes. These activities immediately affected the monetary base. When district banks accepted payment for the securities they sold, reserve accounts of purchasers were debited, decreasing total reserves in the banking system and the money supply; when the Fed purchased securities, the payments effectively injected reserves into the system, raising the money supply. A simplified example illustrates these effects in Figure 3A.2. When the Fed sells securities to a commercial bank, as shown in Panel A of Figure 3A.2, the bank pays, and its reserves—and thus the monetary base and monetary aggregates—decrease. The decline in the money supply causes an increase in interest rates. When the Fed purchases securities in open market operations (Panel B), the opposite occurs: Bank reserves and the money supply grow, while interest rates decline.

Officials soon recognized that they should manage sales and purchases of government securities by Federal Reserve banks to avoid unplanned contractions or expansions of the

figure **3A.2**   EFFECTS OF OPEN MARKET OPERATIONS ON BANK RESERVES

A sale of securities by the Fed decreases the level of reserves and thus the monetary base. A Fed purchase of securities has the opposite effect.

PANEL A: OPEN MARKET SALE OF SECURITIES TO A COMMERCIAL BANK

Fed		Bank A	
− Securities Sold	− Reserve Deposits of Bank A	− Reserves on Deposit at Fed	
		+ Securities Purchased from Fed	

PANEL B: OPEN MARKET PURCHASE OF SECURITIES FROM A COMMERCIAL BANK

Fed		Bank A	
+ Securities Purchased	+ Reserve Deposits of Bank A	+ Reserves on Deposit at Fed	
		− Securities Sold to Fed	

monetary base and, thus, other monetary aggregates. Eventually, the authority to manage open market purchases and sales was vested in the FOMC, which implements the entire system's plans through a trading desk at the Federal Reserve Bank of New York. In between FOMC meetings, members of the board staff and at least one member of the FOMC talk daily with representatives of the trading desk.[19]

The FOMC meets several times a year to review progress toward annual targets and to provide short-run direction to the trading desk. To avoid undue interference from politicians and overreaction from the financial markets, the FOMC doesn't immediately release minutes of its meetings. This delay does not stop Fed watchers from speculating about changes in monetary policy and from attempting to divine the "true" motivations for the current activities of the New York trading desk.

Monetary Policy: A Summary

Theoretical relationships among monetary policy goals, targets, and tools are summarized in Figure 3A.3, which was designed by economists at the Federal Reserve Bank of Dallas. The three policy tools are shown on the left. Actions resulting from the tools are directed at some type of target, either the monetary base or a broader monetary aggregate, as the figure illustrates. The figure assumes that monetary policy focuses on a measure of money, but the Fed may substitute an interest rate target. Finally, the supply of money resulting from these activities interacts with the demand for money, ideally in a way that supports ultimate policy goals.

Unfortunately, a straight path in theory becomes a winding road in practice, and along the way, the Fed sometimes catches financial institution managers by surprise, as illustrated in the next section.

Monetary Policy and Asset/Liability Management

To understand how monetary policy affects financial institutions, recall that asset/liability management involves managing the spread (the difference between interest earned on assets and the interest cost of liabilities) as well as the associated risk (variability). Thus, anything that affects the level and variability of interest rates has a direct effect on asset/liability management.

Figure 3A.4 diagrams the process by which monetary policy actions affect a large financial institution's asset/liability policies. Specific lending, investment, and liability management policies are established only after reviewing the institution's current and projected financial position (balance sheet analysis) and forecasting interest rates (based on a forecast of monetary policy decisions). Unexpected changes in monetary policy, or a monetary policy that produces unexpected changes in interest rates, can be hazardous to a financial institution's health.

The Classic Example: October 1979

The effect of monetary policy on financial institutions shows up clearly in the Fed's change in October 1979 from a policy that concentrated primarily on interest rates to one that

f i g u r e 3A.3 RELATIONSHIPS AMONG MONETARY POLICY GOALS, TOOLS, AND TARGETS

The path from tools of monetary policy through intermediate monetary or interest rate targets to ultimate policy goals seems direct in theory, but it is difficult to find in practice.

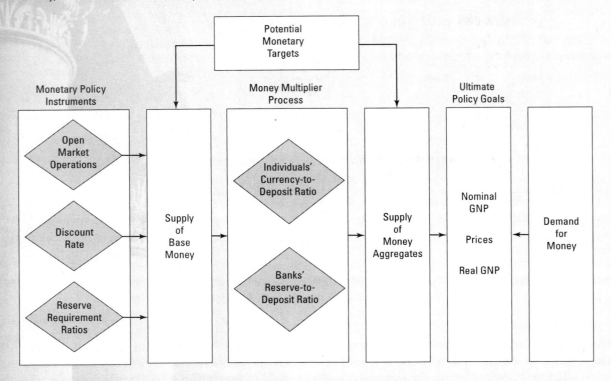

Source: Adapted from W. Michael Cox and Harvey Rosenblum. "Money and Inflation in a Deregulated Financial Environment: An Overview." Economic Review (Federal Reserve Bank of Dallas) (May 1989), 2.

f i g u r e 3A.4 EFFECTS OF MONETARY POLICY ON ASSET/LIABILITY MANAGEMENT

Monetary policy affects a financial institution's asset/liability management through the interest rate forecasts that managers use to plan loan, investment, and liability management activities.

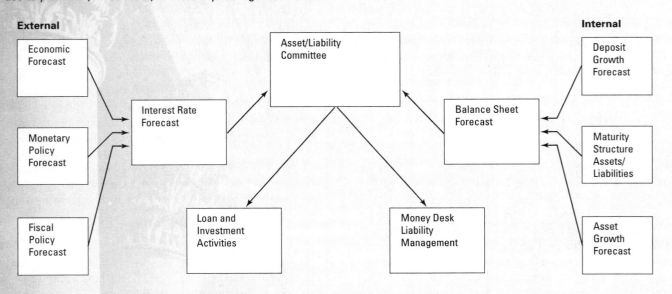

Source: Paul Meek. U.S. Monetary Policy and Financial Markets. New York: Federal Reserve Bank of New York, 1982, 42.

attempted to control inflation, regardless of the effect on interest rates. Under the policy in effect before October, the Fed had specified a relatively narrow range for the federal funds rate, then directed the trading desk to buy and sell securities in the financial markets to keep the rate within the target range. In September 1979, for example, the target range for the federal funds rate was 11.25 to 11.75 percent.[20] Relatively low interest rate volatility accompanied rates that were to seem rather modest, although they were climbing at the time of the change.

By October, the FOMC saw undesirably rapid monetary growth under the existing policy, resulting in unacceptable inflation. The trading desk was instructed to focus on targets for the monetary aggregates, reducing limits on control of the federal funds rate. Although targets for the funds rate remained in effect, they were much wider than those under the previous policy. For example, by December 1980, the FOMC's federal funds rate target range was between 15 and 20 percent.

Figure 3A.5 traces the trend in selected short-term interest rates before and after October 1979. Many financial insti-

tution managers reacted with astonishment to the level and volatility of rates after the monetary policy change. Eventually, banks' best customers had to pay interest rates of $21^{1}/_{2}$ percent if they wanted loans, and mortgage rates also reached historical highs. Business activity virtually ground to a halt, resulting in an economic recession. But inflation was licked, and the Fed Chairman Paul Volcker declined to apologize.

The 1979 change sparked an unprecedented wave of attention to interest rate risk management tools—attention that persists today and is the basis for much of the rest of this book. Financial institution managers are well-advised to continue their concern with risk management; recent research shows that potential risk-reduction benefits available to depositories (and especially to thrifts) after the passage of DIDMCA in 1980 were more than offset by the increase in interest rate volatility from the Fed's 1979 monetary policy change.[21] The policy change also sparked an unprecedented wave of "Fed-bashing" that persisted for several years. One cartoon, widely circulated in late 1981, showed the Federal Reserve Board in medical attire, operating on a patient (the U.S. economy) and using high interest

figure **3A.5**   SHORT-TERM INTEREST RATES BEFORE AND AFTER A CHANGE IN MONETARY POLICY

Before October 1979, the Fed's monetary policy targeted interest rates, but for several years afterward, monetary policy focused on the monetary aggregates, allowing freer movement in interest rates. Dramatic change in the level and volatility of interest rates greatly increased financial institution managers' concern for interest rate risk management.

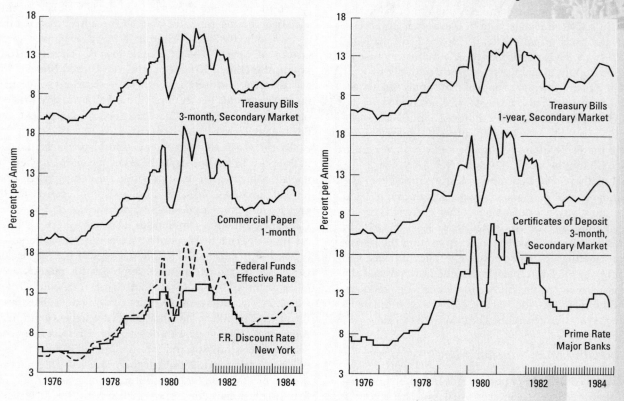

Source: Board of Governors of the Federal Reserve System. Federal Reserve Chart Book (November 1984), 72.

rates as the surgical tool. The caption read, "Congratulations, Doctor! It was a good operation on inflation . . . too bad the patient died."

Fortunately, reports of the patient's death were premature, and by 1982, Fed watchers had noted narrowing in the FOMC's target ranges for the federal funds rate. For example, in December 1988, the FOMC announced a target range between 7 percent and 11 percent, but results showed much smaller actual variations in the rate. Financial institution managers have learned, however, that they can never again afford to ignore monetary policy effects.

The Fed and International Policy Coordination

The Fed is not a strictly domestic institution; its actions affect, and are affected by, the larger world. This international dimension further complicates the Fed's attempts to conduct monetary policy and to regulate financial institutions operating in the United States.

The Gold Standard

International responsibilities are not new for the Fed. From its inception, it was charged with managing U.S. adherence to the **gold standard.** For decades before the formation of the Fed, the United States and several other countries had agreed to honor gold as the definitive standard of value and to maintain a fixed exchange rate between their currencies based on the price of gold. After 1913, the Fed's mandate required it to tie the expansion of the U.S. monetary base to the nation's supply of gold. As the world's supply of gold changed and as this country's share of that supply fluctuated, the U.S. money supply also changed, without regard for the effects on domestic economic conditions. Some economic historians, in fact, cite overriding loyalty to the gold standard to explain the Fed's failure to provide sufficient reserves to illiquid U.S. banks between 1929 and 1933.

Events of the Great Depression clearly showed that the gold standard was no longer workable, although fixed exchange rates between dollars and other currencies, based in part on gold reserves, continued from 1945 to 1971. In 1971, President Richard M. Nixon set in motion the transition to a "floating" system of exchange rates unrelated to gold in any way.[22] That transition did not, however, end the Fed's international responsibilities in the exchange markets. More and more, in fact, the Fed is required to coordinate its policies with those of central banks around the world.[23]

International Coordination and Monetary Policy

Any discussion of monetary policy leads inevitably to a discussion of the Fed in the international financial markets. Recall that one goal of monetary policy is to promote a satisfactory trade balance between the United States and other nations. To accomplish this goal, the Fed must be concerned about rates of exchange between U.S. dollars and the currencies of other countries. How does monetary policy affect exchange rates?

A full discussion of exchange rate determination is deferred until a later chapter, but basic principles are useful at this point. Under a floating exchange rate system, familiar supply–demand relationships apply in the currency markets. Increased demand for U.S. dollars (which results from high U.S. interest rates compared with those in other countries) pushes up the value of the dollar as investors seek to take advantage of high returns on dollar-denominated financial assets. When the value of the dollar rises, goods that U.S. firms hope to export become more expensive for purchasers in Japan, Europe, and other countries. Thus, U.S. exports may drop, causing an unfavorable change in the trade balance between the United States and other nations. The imbalance in trade may worsen if the Fed takes monetary policy actions that cause interest rates to increase even more for different reasons—say, because of concern about inflation at home.

G-5 and G-7 Agreements

Conflicts between these two *domestic* goals—keeping inflation down and promoting a favorable export climate—are not the only ones the Fed faces as it takes monetary policy actions. In 1985, the United States and four other major industrialized nations—called the *Group of Five* (G-5)—agreed to coordinate efforts to keep the U.S. dollar within a specified trading range relative to the currencies of other countries; in 1987, the Group of Five was expanded to the **Group of Seven (G-7; Canada, France, German, Italy, Japan, the United Kingdom, and the United States).** The actual range, a closely guarded secret by the G-7 governments, represents perceptions of the best collective interests of the nations. Experts believe that policy makers set a very flexible target rather than a narrow one.

To carry out the agreement, central banks in the G-7 nations buy or sell dollars in the exchange markets whenever its value threatens to break outside the range. When open market purchases and sales of dollars fail to reverse what the group considers an undesirable trend, the non-U.S. G-7 central banks sometimes attempt to increase or decrease interest rates in their own countries to counteract differentials between U.S. and non-U.S. interest rates. If the Fed decides to change its monetary policy approach for reasons unrelated to the G-7 agreement, that change can conflict with simultaneous actions of the other central banks, frustrating the process of policy coordination. Fed watchers continually monitor the Fed to determine whether it resolves any conflict between domestic and international objectives in favor of one or the other. Although the process of international policy coordination has not continued long enough to draw firm conclusions, many observers believe the Fed has favored domestic policy needs. The same statement seems to be true of central bankers in the other G-7 nations.[24] In a recent

Economic Trends by the Federal Reserve Bank of Cleveland (November 2003), central banks had not moved in concert lately, as shown in Figure 3A.6. While the Bank of Japan followed an easy policy in October of 2003, the Federal Reserve and the European Central Bank maintained a steady policy, and the Bank of England tightened its policy. In early 2004, financial analysts noted a lack of recent coordination among countries. For instance, on March 8, 2004, the financial press noted an expected fall in the U.S. dollar, with the European Central Bank signaling no shift toward interest rate cuts in its policy that would help strengthen the dollar. At this time many countries were concerned about the very cheap dollar that made exports in other countries more expensive. In an opposite direction, the U.S. and others have put pressure on authorities in several countries in Asia, particularly China, to stop intervening to hold the value of their currencies below the U.S. dollar. Although authorities in Beijing stated that they planned to make the yuan fully convertible (versus a pegged currency against the dollar), in 2003 and 2004, their first goal was given as maintaining a stable currency. Panel B shows the anticipated portion of the policy rate changes, computed by comparing the average change in the one-month riskless rate in a country before a change in policy target to the following day. Since 2001, as shown in the figure, about 60 percent of the change in policy rate was anticipated in the United States and Euro area, and about 50 percent in the United Kingdom.[25]

Policy Coordination within the European Community and the European Central Bank and the Eurosystem

Perhaps the strongest impetus for U.S. regulators to participate in international policy coordination came from the decision by the twelve member countries of the **European Community (EC)** to remove all internal barriers among themselves to trade, travel, and employment after December 31, 1992. The EC's Second Banking Directive of 1989 outlined uniform regulations for financial institutions. Member countries agreed on permissible banking powers, including securities but not insurance activities, and established the principle that an institution, once it is authorized by its home country to operate as a bank, may operate as a bank anywhere in the EC without formal approval from other host governments. The rules also include a **national treatment** policy, under which a financial institution from a non-EC country will be granted full competitive powers within the EC as long as EC banks are allowed to operate in the other country on an equal footing with that nation's domestic institutions. Hence, countries need not establish identical regulations; as long as EC banks are not at a competitive disadvantage when operating in another country, its banks will not be at a disadvantage in European markets.

Perhaps the most dramatic financial development accompanying European integration in 1992 was the decision by EC nations to consider abandoning separate currencies and forming a **European Monetary Union (EMU)** with a common currency, the **European Currency Unit (ECU or Euro)**. This agreement is known as the **Maastricht Accord** (for the city in The Netherlands in which it was signed). The European Union officially launched the Euro on January 1, 1999. Exchange rates were set for the currencies of the eleven nations initially joining the monetary union, including Austria, Belgium, Finland, France, Germany, Ireland, Italy, Luxembourg, The Netherlands, Portugal, and Spain, while Greece joined in 2001. By July 1, 2002, Euro notes and coins were in circulation, and the national currencies of the participating nations were fully abolished. Monetary policy governing the ECU is the responsibility of the European Central Bank. Since that time other nations have joined; the EMU is discussed in Chapter 8. The **Eurosystem** comprises the European Central Bank at its center as well as the national central banks of the countries participating in the monetary union. Although the decisions regarding monetary policy are made centrally by the Eurosystem's Governing Council, the open market operations, minimum reserve system, and management of facilities are performed in a decentralized way by the individual country's central banks. Total system assets of the Eurosystem as of December 2000 were about 836,000 million Euros, with about one-third devoted to lending to the financial sector in the form of repurchase operations. The Euro and Eurosystem will be discussed in greater detail in Chapters 8 and 11.[26]

International Coordination for Very Large International Banks

With concerns about safety and soundness and fair competition across large international banks, the **Basel Committee on Banking Supervision** (under the auspices of the **Bank for International Settlements [BIS]** in Basel, Switzerland) implemented the **Basel (or Basle) Accord,** setting risk-based capital requirements for international banks. What as come to be known as **Basel I** was adopted in more than 100 countries in 1993. In 2001, a second Basel Accord, **Basel II** (often called the "New Basel Capital Accord") has been proposed for implementation in 2006. The proposed Basel II includes capital to be held for operational risk, discussed in more detail in other chapters. Basel II contains three pillars that are meant to be reinforcing including Pillar 1 for capital requirements for market, credit, and operational risks; Pillar 2 for regulatory review and supervision; and Pillar 3 for greater transparency for risk exposure. Market discipline and corporate governance factors are also emphasized (see *http://www.bis.org* for details and summaries on the latest proposals).

Other differences in competition and safety and soundness may be more difficult to reconcile. For example, most foreign governments do not offer deposit insurance. Although some economists see no real need for it, most observers agree that the U.S. system will probably continue.

figure **3A.6**

BANK OF ENGLAND, EUROPEAN CENTRAL BANK, FEDERAL RESERVE, AND BANK OF JAPAN POLICY RATE CHANGES, THIRD QUARTER, 2001 TO 2003

Panel A shows Central Bank target ranges for monetary policy targets. Both the United States and Japan have considered greater transparency in relaying policy intentions. Panel B shows percentage of anticipated changes.

PANEL A: MONETARY POLICY TARGETS

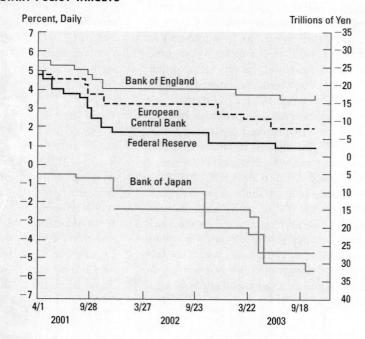

PANEL B: ANTICIPATED PORTION OF POLICY RATE CHANGES SINCE 2001

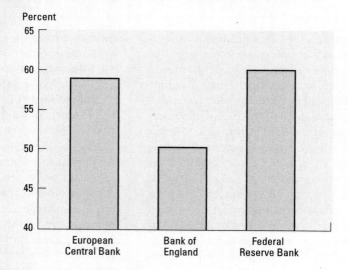

Source: Michele Lachman and Deborah Ring (Eds.). Economic Trends (Federal Reserve Bank of Cleveland) (November 2003), 18 (http://www.clevelandfed.org/research/ET2003/1103/trends.pdf).

Still other experts warn of the danger of relying on international policy coordination and regulation as a substitute for market-determined solutions to economic problems. Thus, the Fed's challenge is to promote competitive equality with other countries while maintaining free markets and preserving the unique features of the U.S. system. Regulation and economic policy in the international arena are certain to play a major role in the regulatory dialectic of the future.

Summary

Although many regulators oversee financial institutions, the Fed exerts the most pervasive influence. As the central bank of the United States, the Fed is charged with issuing currency, maintaining an efficient payments system, serving as a lender of last resort to institutions with liquidity problems, and developing and executing monetary policy that promotes the nation's economic well-being. The Fed must also coordinate its regulatory and monetary activities with those of central banks around the world. As might be expected, given the evolution and globalization in financial markets, each of these tasks has become increasingly complex in recent years.

In administering the payments system, the Fed finds that more and more funds are transferred by electronic means, and the daylight overdrafts of large banks pose new risks. Increasing numbers of depositories have borrowed from the Fed's discount window, raising questions about its proper role as a lender of last resort. Yet monetary policy poses perhaps the stiffest challenges for the Fed. Monetary policy decisions are made by members of the FOMC, who meet periodically to plan the Fed's purchases and sales of government securities. Unfortunately for the FOMC, innovations have introduced new difficulties in defining "money," and tenuous relationships link different measures of money and desirable economic outcomes. The growth of electronic and Internet-transmitted payments is changing the nature of money. The Fed and its critics debate whether the money supply ought to be targeted directly or whether interest rates are the appropriate targets for monetary policy. Through their effects on interest rates, monetary policy decisions have a substantial impact on financial institutions' asset/liability management decisions.

An issue of growing importance is the Fed's need to coordinate monetary policy and regulatory initiatives with those of central banks in other countries. Recent currency exchange agreements between the United States and other G-7 nations have affected the value of the U.S. dollar and the way in which monetary policy is conducted and interpreted. With the birth of the Euro on January 1, 1999, the new European Central Bank also has considerable power. The degree to which U.S. regulations are more or less restrictive than those abroad determines the competitiveness of U.S. institutions and markets. Although central banks have made strides toward greater policy coordination since the late 1980s, the U.S. financial system continues to be less integrated than those of other major powers. This fact is sure to influence the Fed's behavior, and thus the management of financial institutions, in the twenty-first century.

Questions

1. Congress created the Federal Reserve System in 1913 to solve several persistent economic problems, two of which were inadequate control over the money supply and uncertainties in the payments system. Explain briefly the nature of these problems, and describe how the powers of the Fed were designed to solve them.
2. The Fed is sometimes called a *decentralized* central bank. Explain how this term describes the structure of the Fed. What political and economic forces provided the motivation for this structure? Has the balance of power shifted toward or away from the Board of Governors since the system was created? Explain.
3. What is a Federal Reserve note? Do you have any? To what extent is the quantity of Federal Reserve notes issued today tied to the amount of gold or other assets held by the Fed? Does the current system reflect an elastic or an inelastic currency? Why?
4. Suppose the Fed hired you as a consultant to evaluate the safety and stability of the payments system. How would you describe the characteristics of an ideal

system? What are daylight overdrafts, and what risks to the payments system do they present? What incentives and disincentives motivate institutions to use daylight overdrafts?

5. An important activity of the Federal Reserve is serving as the lender of last resort for member banks. What is the meaning of this term, and how does this Fed power contribute to the stability of the banking system? Ideally, under what circumstances should the Fed lend money to an institution that is experiencing liquidity difficulties? In your opinion, was the Fed's support of problem thrifts in the late 1980s consistent with the theoretical objectives of a lender of last resort? Why or why not?

6. One of the Fed's important functions is to implement monetary policy. What principles guide the long-term objectives of monetary policy? Is the Fed always free to set its own targets for the level of economic activity and growth? Provide an example to support your answer.

7. The discount window and the discount rate are important tools for implementation of monetary policy and the Fed's role as lender of last resort. Explain how the discount window functions. How may management of the discount rate create conflicts between monetary policy goals and obligations as a lender of last resort?

8. Should the Fed be required to publish verbatim transcripts of its deliberations on open market operations? If so, what are the benefits? If not, what are the potential dangers of such public disclosure?

9. Economists have never agreed on a single definition of money. Develop your own general definition of money and its purpose. What monetary aggregate best matches your definition? Is the monetary base a better match for your definition? Why or why not?

10. Suppose that you must develop a procedure for controlling the money supply. Your salary and benefits depend on your success in keeping money within a target range. Would you prefer to use as your definition the monetary base or M2? Why? Now suppose instead that your future depends on your success in controlling inflation and the rate of growth in GNP. Under these circumstances, which definition of money would you choose to watch most closely, and why?

11. The FOMC has just voted unanimously to sell $100 million in government securities to dealers, who in turn will sell them to First National Bank. Explain how this transaction will affect (1) the total assets of First National Bank, (2) the assets and liabilities of the Fed,

and (3) the monetary base. What is the role of money multipliers in determining the potential effect on M2?

12. In addition to open market operations, the Fed has two other monetary policy tools. Describe these tools, and explain why some experts view them as less effective than the work of the FOMC. How does the Fed's obligation to protect the safety and soundness of the financial system complicate the use of these second and third monetary policy tools?

13. In October 1979, the Fed made an important change in monetary policy procedures by switching its focus from the money supply to interest rates as the principal policy target. Explain the subsequent effects on interest rates and the rate of inflation. What has been the lasting effect on financial management techniques in financial institutions? Why?

14. Survey current periodicals and newspapers for a recent report on the Fed's monetary policy decisions. What is the author's evaluation of the effectiveness of recent Fed decisions? What policy tools are mentioned? In the author's opinion, what intermediate target (i.e., money supply or interest rates) currently guides Fed policy decisions? How have innovations such as securitization, electronic banking, and cyberbanking affected the Fed's control of the money supply?

15. For several decades prior to 1971, the rate of exchange between the currencies of many countries was related to the value of gold. Is the floating system introduced in 1971 related in any way to gold? If not, what factors influence currency exchange rates? How do the activities of the G-7 countries reduce variability in exchange rates?

16. Some of the G-7 countries have complained about a lack of coordination in recent years. Look in the financial press, such as *The Wall Street Journal* in the markets section. What is happening with exchange rate movements for the Euro, British Pound, Yen, and Yuan? Do central bank policies and rate changes appear to be coordinated? Why has there been less coordination in recent years?

17. Explain the term *globalization*. Describe at least two recent developments contributing to globalization. Provide an example that indicates how globalization has increased the need for international coordination of the regulations under which financial institutions operate.

18. Explain the impact of a unified single European market on sales of financial services in Europe. Why does a single European market pressure U.S. regulators to modify long-standing laws and policies?

Selected References

Adamantopoulous, Constantinos G. "A Single Market for Financial Services in 1992." *Journal of Business and Society* 2 (Spring 1989). 49–59.

Aharony, Joseph, Anthony Saunders, and Itzhak Swary. "The Effects of DIDMCA on Bank Stockholders' Returns and Risk." *Journal of Banking and Finance* 12 (September 1988). 317–331.

Baer, Herb L., and Douglas D. Evanoff. "Payments System Risk in Financial Markets that Never Sleep." *Economic Perspectives* (Federal Reserve Bank of Chicago) 14 (November/December 1990). 2–15.

Belton, Terrence M., et al. "Daylight Overdrafts and Payments System Risk." *Federal Reserve Bulletin* 73 (November 1987). 839–852.

Bennett, Thomas, and Craig S. Hakkio. "Europe 1992: Implications for U.S. Firms." *Economic Review* (Federal Reserve Bank of Kansas City) 74 (April 1989). 3–17.

Board of Governors of the Federal Reserve System. *78th Annual Report.* Washington, DC: Federal Reserve System, 1991.

Bohne, Edward G. "Is There Consistency in Monetary Policy?" *Business Review* (Federal Reserve Bank of Philadelphia) (July/August 1987), 3–8.

Bordo, Michael D. "The Lender of Last Resort: Alternative Views and Historical Experience." *Economic Review* (Federal Reserve Bank of Richmond) 76 (January/February 1990), 18–29.

Boucher, Janice L. "Europe 1992: A Closer Look." *Economic Review* (Federal Reserve Bank of Atlanta) 76 (July/August 1991), 23–38.

Cargill, Thomas. *Central Bank Independence and Regulatory Responsibilities: The Bank of Japan and the Federal Reserve.* New York: Salomon Brothers Center for the Study of Financial Institutions, 1989.

Carlson, John B. "The Indicator P-Star: Just What Does It Indicate?" *Economic Commentary* (Federal Reserve Bank of Cleveland) (September 15, 1989).

Carré, Hervé, and Karen Johnson. "Progress toward a European Monetary Union." *Federal Reserve Bulletin* 77 (October 1991), 769–783.

Chriszt, Michael J. "European Monetary Union: How Close Is It?" *Economic Review* (Federal Reserve Bank of Atlanta) 76 (September/October 1991), 21–27.

Cox, W. Michael, and Harvey Rosenblum. "Money and Inflation in a Deregulated Financial Environment: An Overview." *Economic Review* (Federal Reserve Bank of Dallas) (May 1989), 1–19.

Crabbe, Leland. "The International Gold Standard and U.S. Monetary Policy from World War I to the New Deal." *Federal Reserve Bulletin* 75 (June 1989), 423–440.

Feldberg, Chester B. "Competitive Equality and Supervisory Convenience." *Economic Perspectives* (Federal Reserve Bank of Chicago) 14 (May/June 1990), 30–32.

Friedman, Milton, and Anna J. Schwartz. *A Monetary History of the United States, 1867–1960.* Princeton, NJ: Princeton University Press, 1963.

Garfinkel, Michelle R. "The FOMC in 1988: Uncertainty's Effects on Monetary Policy." *Review* (Federal Reserve Bank of St. Louis) 71 (March/April 1989), 16–33.

Gilbert, R. Alton. "Operating Procedures for Conducting Monetary Policy." *Review* (Federal Reserve Bank of St. Louis) 67 (February 1985), 13–21.

———. "Payments System Risk: What Is It and What Will Happen if We Try to Reduce It?" *Review* (Federal Reserve Bank of St. Louis) 71 (January/February 1989): 3–17.

Hayes, Alfred E. "The International Monetary System—Retrospect and Prospect." *Quarterly Review* (Federal Reserve Bank of New York) (Special 75th anniversary issue 1989), 29–34.

Humphrey, Thomas M. "Lender of Last Resort: The Concept in History." *Economic Review* (Federal Reserve Bank of Richmond) 75 (March/April 1989), 8–16.

———. "Precursors of the P-Star Model." *Economic Review* (Federal Reserve Bank of Richmond) 75 (July/August 1989), 3–9.

Juncker, George R., and Bruce J. Summers. "A Primer on the Settlement of Payments in the United States." *Federal Reserve Bulletin* 77 (November 1991), 847–858.

Kane, Edward J. "Selecting Monetary Targets in a Changing Financial Environment." In *Monetary Policy Issues in the 1980s.* Kansas City: Federal Reserve Bank of Kansas City, 1982, 181–206.

Kasman, Bruce. "A Comparison of Monetary Policy Operating Procedures in Six Industrial Countries." *Quarterly Review* (Federal Reserve Bank of New York) 17 (Summer 1992), 5–24.

Key, Sidney J. "Mutual Recognition: Integration of the Financial Sector in the European Community." *Federal Reserve Bulletin* 75 (September 1989), 591–609.

Kindleberger, Charles P. *Manias, Panics, and Crashes: A History of Financial Crises,* rev. ed. New York: Basic Books, 1989.

Meek, Paul. *U.S. Monetary Policy and Financial Markets.* New York: Federal Reserve Bank of New York, 1982.

Meulendyke, Ann-Marie. "A Review of Federal Reserve Policy Targets and Operating Guides in Recent Decades." *Quarterly Review* (Federal Reserve Bank of New York) 13 (Autumn 1988), 6–17.

———. "Reserve Requirements and the Discount Window in Recent Decades." *Quarterly Review* (Federal Reserve Bank of New York) 17 (Autumn 1992), 25–43.

Motley, Brian, and Herbert Runyon. "Interest Rates and the Fed." *Weekly Letter* (Federal Reserve Bank of San Francisco) (February 20, 1981).

Osborne, Dale K. "What Is Money Today?" *Economic Review* (Federal Reserve Bank of Dallas) (January 1985), 1–15.

Parthemos, James. "The Federal Reserve Act of 1913 in the Stream of U.S. Monetary History." *Economic Review* (Federal Reserve Bank of Richmond) 74 (July/August 1988), 19–28.

———. "The Origins of the Fed." *Cross Sections* (Federal Reserve Bank of Richmond) 5 (Fall 1988), 9–11.

Roberds, William. "What Hath the Fed Wrought? Interest Rate Smoothing in Theory and Practice." *Economic Review* (Federal Reserve Bank of Atlanta) 77 (January/February 1992), 12–24.

Robinson, Kenneth J. "Banking Difficulties and Discount Window Operations: Is Monetary Policy Affected?" *Financial Industry Studies* (Federal Reserve Bank of Dallas) (August 1992), 15–23.

Schwartz, Anna J. "The Misuse of the Fed's Discount Window." *Economic Review* (Federal Reserve Bank of St. Louis) 74 (September/October 1992), 58–69.

Sellon, Gordon H., Jr. "The Instruments of Monetary Policy." *Economic Review* (Federal Reserve Bank of Kansas City) (May 1984), 3–20.

————. "Restructuring the Financial System: Summary of the Bank's 1987 Symposium." *Economic Review* (Federal Reserve Bank of Kansas City) 73 (January 1988), 17–28.

Smith, Stephen D., and Larry D. Wall. "Financial Panics, Bank Failures, and the Role of Regulatory Policy." *Economic Review* (Federal Reserve Bank of Atlanta) 77 (January/February 1992), 1–11.

Spong, Kenneth. *Banking Regulation: Its Purpose, Implementation, and Effects.* Kansas City: Federal Reserve Bank of Kansas City, 2002.

Sproul, Allan. "Reflections of a Central Banker." *Quarterly Review* (Federal Reserve Bank of New York) (Special 75th anniversary issue 1989), 21–28.

Stevens, E. J. "Comparing Central Banks' Rulebooks." *Economic Review* (Federal Reserve Bank of Cleveland) 28 (Third Quarter 1992), 2–15.

Summers, Bruce J. "Clearing and Payments Systems: The Role of the Central Bank." *Federal Reserve Bulletin* 77 (February 1991), 81–91.

Todd, Walker F. "Lessons of the Past and Prospects for the Future in Lender of Last Resort Theory." In *Proceedings of a Conference on Bank Structure and Competition.* Chicago: Federal Reserve Bank of Chicago, 1988, 533–560.

Wallich, Henry C. "The Role of Operating Guides in U.S. Monetary Policy." *Federal Reserve Bulletin* 65 (September 1979), 679–691.

Walter, John R. "Monetary Aggregates: A User's Guide." *Economic Review* (Federal Reserve Bank of Richmond) 75 (January/February 1989), 20–28.

Weatherstone, Dennis. "A U.S. Perspective on Europe 1992." In *New York's Financial Markets: The Challenges of Globalization,* ed. by Thierry Noyelle. Boulder, CO: Westview Press, 1989, 115–118.

Weiner, Stuart E. "The Changing Role of Reserve Requirements in Monetary Policy." *Economic Review* (Federal Reserve Bank of Kansas City) 77 (Fourth Quarter 1992), 45–63.

Wenninger, John, and John Partlan. "Small Time Deposits and the Recent Weakness in M2." *Quarterly Review* (Federal Reserve Bank of New York) 17 (Spring 1992), 21–35.

Wheelock, David C. "The Fed's Failure to Act as Lender of Last Resort during the Great Depression, 1929–1933." In *Proceedings of a Conference on Bank Structure and Competition.* Chicago: Federal Reserve Bank of Chicago, 1989, 154–176.

Wormuth, Diana. "Europe Gets Ready for a New Era." *Best's Review* (Property/Casualty Edition) 90 (November 1989), 22–28.

Notes

[1] Alan Murray and Tom Herman. "Why the Fed's Efforts to Forestall Inflation Have Thus Far Failed." *The Wall Street Journal* (March 29, 1989), A1, A8; Claudia Cummins. "House Panel Scrutinizing Minutes of Fed's District Bank Meetings." *American Banker* (November 3, 1992), 2; and Bart Fraust. "Fed's Secrecy Comes under More Scrutiny." *American Banker* (July 26, 1993), 1, 16.

[2] Forerunners of the Fed included the First and Second National Banks of the United States; the charter for the latter expired in 1836. Although intended to perform functions similar to those of the Bank of England, which many credited for financial stability in Great Britain, these two institutions were widely distrusted by many Americans, who feared concentration of financial power in a central bank.

[3] This discussion draws on the views of James Parthemos, as expressed in "The Origins of the Fed" (1988) and "The Federal Reserve Act of 1913" (1988); it also reflects the influence of Spong (1990) and Kindleberger (1989). (References are listed in full at the end of the appendix.)

[4] See Board of Governors (1991), 256–261.

[5] See Board of Governors (1991), 227–229; and Jeanne Lida. "Fed Planning to Privatize Funds–Transfer Operations." *American Banker* (May 3, 1990), 1, 3.

[6] For further discussion of payments system risks, see Gilbert (1989); Belton et al. (1987); Summers (1991); Juncker and Summers (1991); Baer and Evanoff (1990); and *Fed Wire,* Federal Reserve Bank of Chicago (February 1993).

[7] William Poole. "The Fed's Role in Maintaining Financial Stability." President, Federal Reserve Bank of St. Louis, Presentation, April 24, 2003, University of Central Arkansas in Conway *(http://stlouisfed.org/news/speeches.html#2003);* "The Federal Reserve Board: Remarks by Vice Chairman Roger W. Ferguson, Jr." at Vanderbilt University, Nashville, Tennessee, February 5, 2003 *(http://www.federalreserve.gov/boarddocs/speeches/2003);* "Federal Reserve Bank of Chicago: Remarks by Michael H. Moskow, President and CEO, Federal Reserve Bank of Chicago," Federal Reserve Bank of Chicago Economic Forum, Ft. Wayne, Indiana, November 28, 2001*(http://www.chicagofed.org/news_and_conferences/ speeches/speech_index.cfm);* "Federal Reserve Bank of San Francisco FRBSF Economic Letter: Remarks by Robert T. Parry, President and CEO of the Federal Reserve Bank of San Francisco," delivered on November 19, 2001, at the 24th Annual Real Estate and Economics Symposium, U.C. Berkeley's Fischer Center for Real Estate and Urban Economics.

[8] See, for example, Friedman and Schwartz (1963), Todd (1988), Wheelock (1989), and Bordo (1990).

[9] See Charles W. Calomiris. *The Postmodern Bank Safety Net: Lessons from Developed and Developing Countries.* Washington, DC: American Enterprise Institute, 1997, 8. Also see Robinson (1992); and Alan Murray. "Fed's New Chairman Wins a Lot of Praise on Handling the Crash." *The Wall Street Journal* (November 25, 1987), 1, 7. The Fed was also praised

for its handling of a crisis in the commercial paper market in 1970. For an account of its actions, see Evelyn Hurley. "The Commercial Paper Market." *Federal Reserve Bulletin* 63 (June 1977), 525–536. For a discussion of the Fed's role as lender of last resort and systemic risk issues, see George G. Kaufman. *Research in Financial Services, Banking, Financial Markets, and Systemic Risk,* Vol. 7 (Greenwich, CT: JAI Press, 1995).

[10] A history of lender-of-last-resort theory is found in Humphrey (March/April 1989).

[11] Paulette Thomas. "Fed, Fulfilling Pledge, Advances Funds to Lincoln S&L as Lender of Last Resort." *The Wall Street Journal* (April 25, 1989), A2; Smith and Wall (1992); and Schwartz (1992).

[12] Definitions of money have received intense scrutiny in recent years. See, for example, Walter (1989), Osborne (1985), and Wenninger and Partlan (1992).

[13] See Cox and Rosenblum (1989). Derivation and complete analysis of money multipliers are not within the scope of this text. A representative discussion is found in Frederic S. Mishkin. *The Economics of Money, Banking, and Financial Markets.* Glenview, IL: Scott, Foresman, 1989.

[14] As an example, P-star (P*), a predictor of the relationship between the current level of M2 and future inflation, became a widely watched indicator of the success of monetary policy in controlling inflation. For more details, see Humphrey (July/August 1989) and Carlson (1989).

[15] These arguments are summarized in Motley and Runyon (1981), Bohne (1987), and Roberds (1992).

[16] See Cargill (1989), and Kane (1982).

[17] The early history of open market operations is described in Sproul (1989). Other accounts of monetary policy before the 1970s can be found in Wallich (1979) and Crabbe (1989). In recent years, the district presidents have become more outspoken and influential members of the FOMC. See Alan Murray. "Fed Banks' Presidents Hold Private Positions But Major Public Role." *The Wall Street Journal* (August 1, 1991), A1, A7.

[18] For arguments in defense of reserve requirements and the discount rate as effective tools of monetary policy, see Meulendyke (1992), Weiner (1992), and Sellon (1984).

[19] Detailed discussions of the process that translates policy targets into open market actions are found in Meek (1982), Gilbert (1985), Meulendyke (1988), and Garfinkel (1989).

[20] FOMC targets are reported in minutes of committee meetings and appear in press reports and several Fed publications.

[21] See Aharony, Saunders, and Swary (1988).

[22] See Crabbe (1989); for more information on exchange rates from World War II to the 1970s, see Hayes (1989).

[23] Kasman (1992) finds similarities in monetary policy procedures of central banks in six countries. Stevens (1992) compares rules and regulations in four countries.

[24] See, for example, Alan Murray and Walter S. Mossberg. "Raising Discount Rate, Fed Puts Inflation War ahead of Dollar Policy." *The Wall Street Journal* (August 10, 1988), 1, 8; Alan Murray and Michael R. Sesit. "As Dollar Marches On, Central Banks Prepare Big New Intervention." *The Wall Street Journal* (May 19, 1989), A1–A2; David Wessel and Terence Roth. "As Central Banks Go Their Own Ways, Global Tensions Rise." *The Wall Street Journal* (August 3, 1992), A1, A9; Clay Chandler. "Japan's Central Banker Begins to Win Praise for Saving Its 'Soul.'" *The Wall Street Journal* (June 15, 1993), A1, A5; and Michael Sesit, Glenn Whitney, and Terence Roth. "German Stance on Rates Sends ERM to Brink." *The Wall Street Journal* (July 30, 1993), C1, C13; A recent study by economists at the Federal Reserve did not find a significant change in the correlation of growth rates among the G-7 countries, despite the view that economic integration has markedly increased in terms of globalization of financial markets (see Brian M. Doyle and Jon Faust. "An Investigation of Co-movements among the Growth Rates of the G-7 Countries." *Federal Reserve Bulletin* [October 2002], 427–437). The group of 10 actually includes eleven countries and one territory, including the G-7 nations (United States, Canada, France, Great Britain, Japan, Germany, and Italy), plus Belgium, The Netherlands, Sweden, Switzerland, and the Grand Duchy of Luxembourg.

[25] See Tom Barkley. "Dollar's Decline Is Now Expected to Start Again." *The Wall Street Journal* (March 8, 2004) C6; and Dow Jones Newswires. "In Bet on Yuan, Chinese Bring Dollars Home." *The Wall Street Journal* (March 8, 2004) A14; and *Economic Trends* by the Federal Reserve Bank of Cleveland (November 2003), *http://www.clevelandfed.org/research/ET2003/1103/trends.pdf*.

[26] Carl W. Walsh. "EMU and the ECB." *Weekly Letter*. (Federal Reserve Bank of San Francisco) (June 5, 1992); Chriszt (1991); and Carré and Johnson (1991). Also see, "EMU Is Born Amid Battle over Central Bank." *The Wall Street Journal* (May 4, 1998), A17–A18; and Paul Mentre. "The Case for the Euro." In *A Single European Currency?* ed. by Jeffrey Gedmin. Washington, DC: American Enterprise Institute, 1997, 22–28. See also Jeffrey Gedmin (Ed.). *A Single European Currency?* Washington, DC: American Enterprise Institute, 1997; and Nicholas Bray. "Economic Climate Looks Good for Launch of New Currency." *The Wall Street Journal* (May 4, 1998), A17–A18; Christopher Rhoads. "Euro Expected to Spur European Bank Shakeout." *The Wall Street Journal* (May 4, 1998), A17. For more information on the EC 1992 agreement, see "Survey of World Banking"; Boucher (1991); Feldberg (1990); Weatherstone (1989); Wormuth (1989); Bennett and Hakkio (1989); Adamantopoulous (1989); and Key (1989). For recent studies of Central Bank Operations in different countries, see Federal Reserve Bank of Kansas City *Economic Review*, Vol, 87, No. 4 (Fourth Quarter 2002), *Special Issue on Central Bank Perspectives on Stabilization Policy;* and Federal Reserve Bank of Boston New England *Economic Review* (Second Quarter 2002), *Special Issue on Central Banking in Other Industrialized Countries*.

Overview and Performance Analysis of Depository Institutions

4 Depository Institution Performance and Risk Analysis

"Any business, large or small, can be described as a system of financial relationships and cash flows which are activated by management decisions."

ERICH A. HELFERT, Techniques of Financial Analysis: A Guide to Value Creation, *10th ed. New York: McGraw-Hill Higher Education, 2000, p. 1.*

"By the time financial statements are sent to the shareholders, they are a stewardship document, not the relevant current information about the company."

J. MICHAEL COOK, Chairman, Deloitte and Touche (1991).

B ecause financial firms buy, sell, and invest in money, they are more subject to fraud and accounting difficulties than other firms. Accounting for depository institutions is often more complex than accounting for nonfinancial firms and includes abiding by regulatory restrictions. As Michael Cook, chairman of a prominent accounting firm, suggests in the opening quote, financial statements reflect historic, not current operations. Financial assets and liabilities are ultimately promises of future payments. Hence, financial institutions are subject to greater market risk for changes in the values of assets and liabilities and equity. Historically, book value accounting has been used for most assets and liabilities versus market accounting. Critics have argued that market value accounting should be used, so investors can obtain more valuable information. In 1992, for instance, Sun Trust Bank of Atlanta reported a book value for its stock holdings in Coca Cola as $110,000, while the current market value of the bank's Coke stock was actually over $1 billion. Similarly, in 1992 Roosevelt Financial Group of St. Louis, a believer in market value accounting, voluntarily reported a 9 percent drop in the market value of the company's equity to unhappy investors, who otherwise would have been unaware of this drop.[1]

Financial statements may fail to reveal all an investor needs to know about a financial institution, but they do provide clues about how well the institution has been doing, as well as signaling risks and trends. Because financial reports are influenced by the accounting rules that managers are permitted to

Learning Objectives

After completing this chapter, you will be able to:

1 Read uniform bank performance reports and know how to get them online.

2 Understand different types of assets and liabilities for banks.

3 Explain the typical components of a bank's income statement and the key components of profits.

4 Use income relationships to forecast target net interest margins.

5 Understand the DuPont system for ratio analysis.

6 Understand typical off-balance-sheet items for banks and the growing importance of noninterest revenues.

7 Understand common ratios used for performance and risk analysis in banks.

use, experienced observers carefully look at many dimensions and sources of information before drawing conclusions. Management decisions influence the future performance of depository institutions, and managerial strategies are revealed in financial statements. This chapter presents the details of financial statements and financial performance analysis for depository institutions, focusing on commercial banks, as the most complex financial institution. Chapter 5 discusses credit unions and thrifts in expanded detail, followed by capital management in Chapter 6, and changes with technology including securitization, Internet banking, and the role of other financial institutions in E-commerce in Chapter 7.

Why Is Financial Analysis for Financial Services Firms Important?

With the passage of Sarbanes-Oxley in 2002, chief executive officers (CEOs) and chief financial officers (CFOs) of publicly traded firms must certify financial statements and are responsible for adequate internal controls and independence of auditing committees. The directors for boards are also expected to be financially astute. Hence, managers must verify the accuracy of financial information and are liable for errors made by others within their organizations. Clearly, being able to understand and analyze financial statements is of key importance. For financial institutions, financial statements are quite different than those of other nonfinancial firms, with many untypical items that you may not be familiar with. With so many unusual items and less transparency (for instance of the quality of loans), managers need to understand the subtleties of bank financial statements. Also, elements of a bank's strategy can be revealed along with its strengths and weaknesses for strategic planning purposes. Different types of banks focusing on different types of lending have distinct financial characteristics that analysts need to be aware of, and by comparing financial statements of peer banks, erroneous conclusions can be avoided.

---

1 Ford S. Worthy. "The Battle of the Bean Counters." *Fortune* (June 1, 1992), 117–126

Sources of Industry Information

To make a careful performance analysis, an analyst needs information on trends and/or comparative benchmarks for similar-size peers. In addition to published annual reports, a number of sources of financial information for depository institutions are discussed in the following sections. Depository institutions have to report data to regulators routinely, so a number of different regulatory sources for data are available.

Federal Financial Institutions Examination Council (FFIEC) Website

Figure 4.1 shows the home page for the FFIEC Website *(http://www.ffiec.gov)*, which has links to financial information on depository institutions. The FFIEC is a formal interagency that prescribes uniform principles, standards, and report forms for the federal examination of financial institutions by the

figure 4.1 FFIEC WEBSITE LINKS: GETTING UBPRS AND FINANCIAL PERFORMANCE (REGULATORY CALL) REPORTS

PANEL A: FFIEC HOME PAGE, *HTTP://WWW.FFIEC.GOV/*

FFIEC | Federal Financial Institutions Examination Council

Site Index | Search | Disclaimer | Privacy Policy

What's New
About the FFIEC
Press Releases
Reports
Reporting Forms
Handbooks & Catalogues
Enforcement Actions and Orders
On-line Information Systems

Other FFIEC Sites
Examiner Education Office
Appraisal Subcommittee
HMDA
CRA
Financial Institution Call Report Data

Welcome to the
Federal Financial Institutions Examination Council's (FFIEC) Web site.

The Council is a formal interagency body empowered to prescribe uniform principles, standards, and report forms for the federal examination of financial institutions by the Board of Governors of the Federal Reserve System (FRB), the Federal Deposit Insurance Corporation (FDIC), the National Credit Union Administration (NCUA), the Office of the Comptroller of the Currency (OCC), and the Office of Thrift Supervision (OTS) and to make recommendations to promote uniformity in the supervision of financial institutions.

Quick Links

* – Uniform Bank Performance Report (UBPR)
  – Bank Holding Company Performance Report (BHCPR)
* – FDIC Institution Directory
  – Economic Growth and Regulatory Paperwork Reduction Act of 1996 (EGRPRA)
  – Geocoding/Mapping System
  – Rate Spread Calculator
  – Census Report System
* – National Information Center
  – Information Technology Examination Handbook InfoBase

-HOME-

Note: Many of the documents available on-line are in Adobe Portable Document Format (PDF). Please visit our PDF help page for more information.

Maintained by the FFIEC. All suggestions regarding this site may be forwarded via e-mail to ffiec-suggest@frb.gov.
Last update: **02/11/2004 4:52 PM**

figure **4.1** FFIEC WEBSITE LINKS: GETTING UBPRS AND FINANCIAL PERFORMANCE (REGULATORY CALL) REPORTS (CONTINUED)

PANEL B: QUICK LINKS

Uniform Bank Performance Reports (UBPRs)

1. Click Quick Link: "Uniform Bank Performance Report (UBPR)."

2. New menu: Click "Search for a Uniform Bank Performance Report."

3. Enter Institution Name, City (optional), State, or FDIC Certificate Number (can find from FDIC Institution Directory).

4. Click "Find."

5. Click on the name of the institution that you want. (More than one may be displayed, so choose the one for the state you wish to examine. You may want to go to the FDIC Institution Directory discussed below first to find the correct institution.)

6. The institution's UBPR will open. At the top of the screen, choose "PRINT" or "EXPORT" (download as a text file).

FDIC Institution Directory (Also at *http://www3.fdic.gov/idasp/main.asp*)

1. Click Quick Link: "FDIC Institution Directory." Click "Find Institution" and then type in Name, State; click "Find."

2. The institution's name and FDIC number will be displayed; click and you can also find additional information on the firm.

National Information Center (NIC) of the Federal Reserve System (Also at *http://www.ffiec.gov/nic*)

1. Click Quick Link: "National Information Center."

2. On menu: Click "Financial & Performance Reports."

3. A new menu gives you downward arrows for choosing the type of institution you want. Click on Holding Company, Bank, Savings Institution, or Credit Union, and the year of the report and the type of report. If you want the consolidated (full) report of condition and income, it is the last item. Click "Submit."

4. New menu: Type in Name, City (sometimes optional), and/or State of Bank; click "Submit."

5. You will be directed to display (which you can print) or download the PDF report file (requires Adobe Acrobat Reader, which can be downloaded for free from the site).

Note: Site formats often change. If changes have occurred, follow the site's menu instructions.

Source: Federal Financial Institutions Examination Council Website, http://www.ffiec.gov.

Board of Governors of the Federal Reserve System (or Federal Reserve Board, FRB), the Federal Deposit Insurance Corporation (FDIC), the National Credit Union Administration (NCUA), the Office of the Comptroller of the Currency (OCC), and the Office of Thrift Supervision (OTS). Quick Links include links to (1) the Uniform Bank Performance Reports, which are excellent, detailed reports for banks and savings institutions; (2) the FDIC Institution Directory (also at *http://www3.fdic.gov/idasp/main.asp*), which provides a convenient online way to find and compare banks with peer banks; and (3) the National Information Center (NIC) (also at *http://www.ffiec.gov/nic*), which provides regulatory call reports with financial data for banks, savings institutions, and credit unions. As shown on Figure 4.1, other useful links and information are provided as well. These and some other links and data sources are described in more detail next.

Uniform Bank Performance Reports (UBPRs)

The FFIEC provides uniform bank performance reports that can be easily downloaded and printed out on its Website at *http://www.ffiec.gov*. The FFIEC also makes recommendations to promote uniformity in the supervision of financial institutions. Figure 4.1 outlines the steps for accessing the UBPRs. Just follow the instructions on each menu after you click the Quick Link for UBPR. UBPRs can be printed or individual sections can be exported (saved to a text file). In addition to financial statements, UBPRs contain details on the composition of assets, liabilities, and risk characteristics; comparisons for peer banks (banks of similar size); and information on state peer banks (at the end of the report). A menu on the UBPR link also allows you to download the UBPR User's Guide, including Section III, which gives definitions of UBPR items. Sample data from the UBPRs for financial performance and risk analysis of banks will be discussed in detail throughout this chapter.

National Information Center (NIC) Call Reports

The NIC requires depository institutions to file financial performance (call) reports with regulators, which are also available on the Web at *http://www.ffiec.gov/nic*. These financial reports follow a uniform format for simple (sometimes aggregated) balance sheet and income statements. Thus, they are not quite as informative as UBPRs but are timely and available for credit unions as well. As noted in Figure 4.1, the NIC home of the Federal Reserve System is a Quick Link on the FFIEC Website (*http://www.ffiec.gov*). This Website can also be found using a search engine (such as *http://www.google.com* or another search engine [enter search words "NIC Home" or "NIC-Federal Reserve System"]), if you are in a hurry and forget the Web address. Financial performance (call) reports are presented as PDF files (Adobe Acrobat Reader can be downloaded from the site) that can be saved or printed. While UBPRs focus on banks and savings institutions, the NIC call reports include credit unions as well. The NIC home page has lots of other information, displaying a number of choices to click on as follows:

Institution Search	Institution History	Organization Hierarchy
Financial & Performance Reports	Top 50 BHCs/Banks	FAQ
FFIEC Home		

The **Institution Search** allows you to search for a bank and, if it continues to exist, find general information about it. The **Institution History** allows you to search for "Who a Bank Took Over?" or "Who Took Over a Bank?" It provides the entire acquisition history of a bank or savings institution. The **Organization Hierarchy** choice allows you to see all the subsidiaries in a holding company. The **Financial & Performance Reports** has information from the call reports for credit unions, banks, and thrifts. The **Top 50 BHCs** link shows a list of the largest BHCs in the United States and lets you click on any to find their financial information.

FDIC Bank Data & Statistics Website

The FDIC Website (*http://www.fdic.gov*) contains lots of excellent information, with a large menu of information and data. From the main Website, a menu labeled "Quick Links by User" leads you to information for bankers, consumers, analysts, investors, and the press. Click "Analysts" and you'll be given menu choices for Trends & Statistics, Deposit Insurance, Resources & Publications, Laws & Regulations, and Industry Analysis. Under Trends & Statistics, you'll have a list of choices that provide excellent historical information for the banking and saving institution industries. The FDIC Outlook, FDIC Quarterly Banking Profile, FDIC Banking Review, and FDIC State Profiles provide current and historical trends. There is also a link for the Uniform Bank Performance Reports here as well. If you click on "Statistics on Banking," you can obtain industry average financial statements for the bank and savings institutions industries in the United States for particular years, as well as state average information.

National Credit Union Administration Website

The National Credit Union Administration Website (*http://www.ncua.gov*) provides lots of information and publications as well with an index of information available. The NCUA is an alternative to the NIC Website for finding a credit union and getting call report data, among other information. Look at the menu on their index: *http://www.ncua.gov/indexdata.html*.

Other Federal Reserve Bank Websites

Individual Federal Reserve Banks also have their own Websites with lots of data, research, and information. An index for the twelve Federal Reserve Banks can be found at *http://www.federalreserve.gov/FRAddress.htm*. This site lists the addresses and phone numbers for each of the twelve federal reserve banks and has direct links to each bank's Website (for instance, just click "Boston" on the site, and you'll be taken to the Federal Reserve Bank of Boston's Website). Each site provides economic research/working papers, economic data, publications on banking, and other excellent information that's generally all free. The Federal Reserve Bank of Chicago, in particular, allows downloads of bank and mergers and acquisitions data. Each Website provides excellent information on banking and economics, focusing as well on their particular regions. The Office of the Comptroller of the Currency *(http://www.occ.treas .gov)* and Office of Thrift Supervision *(http://www.ots.treas.gov)* also have informative Websites with data and research and public and supervisory information for, respectively, national banks and thrifts.

Bank Rating Services

There are also a number of private bank and savings institutions rating services that have books and other information that can be privately purchased. The FDIC never releases its supervisory CAMELS (capital, asset quality, management quality, earnings, liquidity, and market sensitivity) ratings on safety and soundness of banks and savings institutions to the public. Private bank rating services sell books and other materials giving ratings and at times detailed financial data. The FDIC Website *(http://www .fdic.gov)* in 2003 provided an alphabetical list of these services, including the following:

1. **BauerFinancial, Inc.,** in Coral Gables, Florida: (800) 388-6686 or *http://www.bauerfinancial.com/*
2. **IDC Financial Publishing** in Hartland, Wisconsin: (800) 525-5457 or *http://www.idcfp.com*
3. **LACE Financial Corp.** in Frederick, Maryland: (301) 662-1011 or *http://www.lacefinancial.com/*
4. **Sheshunoff Information Services** in Austin, Texas: (800) 456-2340 or *http://www.sheshunoff.com/*
5. **Veribanc, Inc.,** in Woonsocket, Rhode Island: (800) 837-4226 or *http://www.veribanc.com*
6. **Weiss Ratings, Inc.,** in Palm Beach Gardens, Florida: (800) 289-9222 or *http://www.weissratings.com*

Changes may occur in the list with frequent Website changes, so a search on the Web can help identify any changes. The FDIC provided a disclaimer that the list is not an endorsement or confirmation of FDIC information provided by these companies. Many of these services are widely used by banks, such as Sheshunoff Information Services, which also provides software and other products.

Other Sources of Financial Information

Most large, publicly traded banks and savings institutions post their annual reports on their own Websites. Click on "Investors Relations" to find the bank's annual report and sections of annual reports often in PDF (Adobe) or other downloadable format. Also, online services such as Yahoo! SEC filings (Yahoo! Finance at *http://finance.yahoo.com/*) will provide stock market information and links to financial statements and other information. The SEC Website *(http://www.sec.gov)* has a link to its Edgar database, which also provides copies of online filings *(http://www.sec.gov/edgar.shtml)*, and a number of private organizations have organized this database in an easier-to-use format for a charge. Federal agency Annual Reports to Congress can be found on links at *http://www.usdoj.gov*. The United States Department of Justice Website is also helpful for general information on trends in the credit union, savings institutions, and banking industries, including the semiannual and annual reports of the National Credit Union Association. News reports, annual reports, and other information can be found by using a search engine, such as *http://www.google.com*, and typing in the name of the financial institution that you're interested in.

Enforcement Actions and Orders

For information on Enforcement Actions that regulators have placed on particular institutions, see the link on the FFIEC Website *(http://www.ffiec.gov)* or go directly to *http://www.ffiec.gov/enforcement.htm.*

Concept Questions

1 What are the best Websites for financial information on depository institutions?

2 What is the FFIEC? What is a UBPR, and how can you get one?

3 Name a few bank rating services. Why don't regulators give out CAMELS ratings, while bank rating services try to provide ratings comparable to CAMELS?

4 What is another Website to find financial performance reports for a credit union?

This site provides links for enforcement actions and orders against institutions or their affiliated parties by their respective regulator including the Board of Governors of the Federal Reserve System (FRB), the Federal Deposit Insurance Corporation (FDIC), the National Credit Union Administration (NCUA), the Office of the Comptroller of the Currency (OCC), and the Office of Thrift Supervision (OTS).

Overview of Commercial Bank Financial Statements

The Elements of Traditional Operating Profit for Depository Institutions

Commercial banks facilitate the flow of funds in an economy by accepting funds from depositors and providing them to borrowers. In effect, banks buy funds from depositors at low, insured rates and sell funds at higher rates to borrowers. As discussed in Chapters 1 and 2, a bank's net interest margin (NIM) is a measure of the profitability of its traditional lending activities. Accordingly, traditional operating profits for banks are generally calculated as the **net interest income (NII)** (interest revenue less interest expense) **less the provision for loan losses (PLL)** (expense deducted for expected loan losses) **less the net operating expenses (Burden)** (noninterest expense less noninterest revenue):

$$\text{Traditional Operating Profit} = NII - PLL - \text{Burden} \tag{4.1}$$

Overview of Types of Assets and Liabilities Held by All FDIC-Insured Banks on Average

Financial assets generate interest revenue. Figure 4.2, Panel A shows the financial assets held on average for all U.S. commercial banks. At year-end of 2003, commercial bank assets were $7.6 trillion. **Net loans** clearly dominate bank holdings relative to total assets (about **57 percent**), followed by securities (about **23 percent**), which includes **securities used for pledging** (large government deposits often are required to be held in Treasury securities or other safe securities). **Trading account assets (about 5.5 percent) are also securities** that large banks (having assets greater than $1 billion) hold for trading activities for customers and on their own account. During recessions when loan demand falls, the security portfolio grows, providing countercyclical income. Securities are also a source of stored liquidity. Another small, but important item, is **cash and due (only 5.1 percent of assets).** This includes **vault cash,** deposits held at Federal Reserve banks and other financial institutions, and **cash in the process of collection (CIPC).** Vault cash covers deposit withdrawals. Deposits at Federal Reserve banks are used to meet the largest portion of a bank's reserve requirements, so are not really very liquid assets. Small banks often hold deposits at other financial institutions (**compensating balances**) as payments for check-clearing, advisory, and other services provided by these **correspondent banks.** CIPC includes checks written against other financial institutions but not yet cleared. Since cash and due funds generally do not earn interest, or for interest-bearing deposits earn low interest, banks try to minimize these holdings within safe limits on liquidity.

Banks have low operating leverage, with a very small **percentage of fixed assets (1.16 percent),** including **bank premises, fixed assets, and other real estate owned (OREO),** which includes assets that were repossessed as collateral for bad loans. **All other assets on average were only about 7.59 percent** of banks' assets in 2003.

Panel B of Figure 4.2 shows sources of bank financing: deposits, other borrowings, and equity. Banks have high financial leverage with **total liabilities financing about 91 percent of total assets** in 2003. Deposits remain the major financing source (**about 66 percent of total assets**). Other short-term liabilities as shown in Figure 4.2, Panel B include types of **borrowed funds and trading liabilities (12.60 percent)** and **federal funds purchased and repurchase agreements (7.50 percent),** short-term borrowings. Longer-term liabilities include **subordinated debt (1.31 percent), generally bonds issued** by large banks. As subordinated debt, it is paid off after deposits and other debt in the event of default. As noted in Chapter 3, under the Financial Services Modernization Act of 1999, the largest 100 Bank Holding Companies were required to issue subordinated debt, to initiate greater market discipline for these firms. **All other liabilities are only 3.69 percent** of total asset financing in 2003. **Equity capital** to total asset financing was only **9.12 percent.**

figure   **4.2**   AVERAGE ASSETS AND LIABILITIES FOR FDIC-INSURED BANKS IN 2003

PANEL A: ASSETS ON AVERAGE FOR FDIC-INSURED BANKS

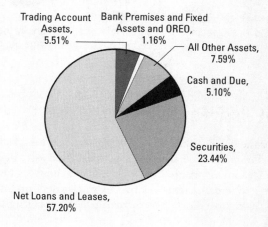

PANEL B: LIABILITIES ON AVERAGE FOR FDIC-INSURED BANKS

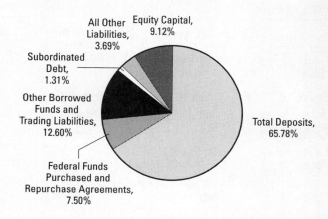

Source: FDIC Statistics on Banking 2003, http://www2.fdic.gov.

Trends in Balance Sheet Composition: 1950 to 2003

The composition of bank balance sheets has changed remarkably over time. In 1950, banks had very conservative balance sheets with only 32 percent of assets invested in loans and the majority held as cash and securities. Financing was cheap, since deposits financed over 90 percent of bank assets. By 1996, deposit financing had fallen to a low of 70 percent of assets, which fell again to about 66 percent in 2003. Banks lost deposits to the direct financial markets and to other financial institutions, especially money market funds and other mutual funds. Consequently, banks have had to rely on more expensive, nondeposit funds, increasing their interest expenses. To compensate for the rise in interest expenses, banks increased interest revenues by more aggressive asset utilization, taking on more loans that offered higher interest rates. Banks increased their percentage of loans from 48 percent in 1964 to about 60 percent in 1996. In 2003, this figure was slightly lower, 57 percent on average. As FDICIA raised capital requirements in 1991, the average bank's equity-to-asset ratio rose in the 1990s. In the early 1990s, the average equity to assets was only about 6 percent. In 1997, the average was 8 percent, and in 2003, this rose to 9.12 percent, much higher than the required regulatory equity capital to assets requirement (discussed in Chapter 6).

1 How do banks make their operating profits, that is, what are the key elements?

2 What are the largest three types of assets held by banks? Why has the ratio of loans to assets risen over the years?

3 What are the largest three types of liabilities held by banks? Why has the ratio of deposits to assets risen over the years?

4 Explain what is meant by the statement that banks have low operating leverage but high financial leverage.

Details on FDIC-Insured Bank Balance Sheets

Table 4.1 summarizes the balance sheets for FDIC-insured commercial banks using third-quarter 2003 figures. The table is a common size balance sheet (where each asset item is a percentage of total assets). Common size financial statements are useful for financial analysis by helping to spot changes in balance sheet or income statement items relative to total assets or total revenues. Balance sheets are ordered with the most liquid (shortest-term maturities) appearing first and longer-term maturities

table **4.1** COMMON SIZE BALANCE SHEETS FOR FDIC-INSURED COMMERCIAL BANKS, SEPTEMBER 30, 2003 (PERCENTAGES OF TOTAL ASSETS FOR EACH CATEGORY)

	Commercial Banks	Banks with Assets of Less Than $100 Million	Banks with Assets of $100 Million to $1 Billion	Banks with Assets of $1 Billion or More
Assets				
Cash and due	5.1%	6.0%	4.5%	5.2%
Investment securities	18.6	24.4	23.2	17.8
Fed funds sold and repurchase agreements	4.8	5.1	3.3	5.0
Assets held in trading accounts	5.5	0.0	0.1	6.5
Gross loans	68.2	61.0	65.0	57.1
Allowance for loan losses	1.0	0.9	1.0	1.0
Net loans and leases	67.2	60.1	64.0	56.1
Bank premises and fixed assets	1.1	1.8	1.8	1.0
Other real estate owned	0.1	0.2	0.1	0.1
Intangible assets	1.9	0.3	0.6	2.1
All other assets	5.7	2.2	2.5	6.3
Total assets	**100.0%**	**100.0%**	**100.0%**	**100.0%**
Total assets $	*$7.474 trillion*	*$204.149 billion*	*$907.812 billion*	*$6.362 trillion*
Total Liabilities and Equity Capital				
Total deposits	65.8%	84.1%	81.3%	63.0%
Fed funds purchased and repurchase agreements	7.5	0.8	2.5	8.4
Trading and other liabilities	3.6	0.0	0.0	4.2
Other borrowed money	9.0	3.1	5.4	9.7
Subordinated debentures & notes	1.3	0.0	0.1	1.5
All other liabilities	3.7	0.7	0.9	4.2
Total liabilities	90.9%	88.8%	90.1%	91.1%
Perpetual preferred stock	0.1	0.0	0.0	0.1
Common stock	0.4	1.6	0.9	0.3
Surplus	4.6	4.5	3.8	4.7
Undivided profits	4.1	5.2	5.2	3.9
Total equity capital	**9.1%**	**11.3%**	**9.9%**	**8.9%**
Total liabilities and equity	**100.0%**	**100.0%**	**100.0%**	**100.0%**

appearing last for both assets and liabilities. Note, generally, as the maturity of an asset or liability rises, entailing greater maturity and default risk, it has a higher interest rate (i.e., risk premium). Hence, generally short-term assets or liabilities pay lower rates, and longer-term assets or liabilities pay higher rates (holding other factors constant).

Table 4.1 also shows differences for very small banks (assets of less than $100 million), medium-size banks (assets of $100 million to $1 billion), and large banks (assets of $1 billion or more). Community banks are often defined as banks with assets of less than $1 billion. Since the largest banks have greater access to the financial markets, they can hold smaller percentages of securities than smaller banks and still meet future liquidity needs.

Different Types of Bank Assets

Since many types of bank assets are unusual, it's helpful to look at individual types. Table 4.1 provides a common size balance sheet for the U.S. banking industry and lists the major types of assets, including cash and due, investment securities, Fed funds sold and repurchase agreements, assets in trading accounts, different types of loans, and other assets discussed next.

Cash and due are held for reserve requirements and to meet upcoming liquidity demands, such as expected deposit withdrawals. Since they must be used for reserve requirements and expected transaction demands, they are not really liquid assets (i.e., they are not available for other liquidity demands, such as unexpected withdrawals or loan demands).

Investment securities of banks provide additional income, as well as longer-term storage for liquidity. Regulators require banks to hold securities with low default risk. Banks can hold unlimited amounts of U.S. Treasury and federal agency securities, including mortgage-backed securities issued by government agencies. They also can hold unlimited amounts of general obligation municipal securities (those guaranteed by the general funds of the issuers) as well as limited amounts of investment grade (BBB/Baa ratings or better) corporate bonds and municipal revenue bonds (those guaranteed by the revenues for the projects they finance). Banks must classify investment securities as **"held to maturity"** (held at book values) or **"available for sale"** (held at market values). As shown in Figure 4.3, about 93 percent of total securities held by commercial banks in 2003 were held at market value and thus available for sale for liquidity and other purposes.

Fed funds sold and reverse repurchase agreements (repos) are very short-term investments for liquidity purposes. Their maturities are tailor-made ranging from overnight to a year. Fed funds are excess reserves that banks hold with the Fed (greater than reserve requirements) that are traded at market rates between financial institutions in the Federal Funds Market. Banks that need extra reserves purchase Fed Funds (a liability), while banks that have extra reserves sell Fed Funds (Fed funds sold), an asset. **Fed funds sold shown here** are assets of the lending bank, and **Fed funds purchased (shown under liabilities)** are liabilities of the borrowing bank. The Fed Funds rate is a key indicator of liquidity

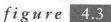 **4.3**   COMMERCIAL BANK TOTAL SECURITIES,* SEPTEMBER 30, 2003

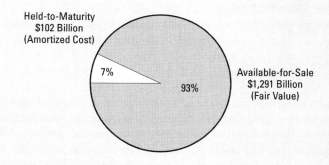

Held-to-Maturity
$102 Billion
(Amortized Cost)

7%

93%

Available-for-Sale
$1,291 Billion
(Fair Value)

*Excludes trading account assets

Source: *FDIC Quarterly Banking Profile, Graph Book, September 30, 2003,* http://www2.fdic.gov.

in bank markets. A high Fed Funds rate indicates scarce liquidity for the banking system. Repurchase agreements (repos) are short-term sales of Treasury bills or other liquid securities that are to be repurchased at a higher price on a negotiated maturity date by the borrower. As assets, reverse repurchase agreements are funds lent to other banks. As liabilities, they are funds borrowed from other banks. Large banks tend to be net purchasers of Fed Funds and borrowers for repurchase agreements (net liabilities), while small banks tend to be lenders (net assets).

Assets held in trading accounts are securities, primarily Treasury or municipal securities that are traded by large banks (those with greater than $1 billion in assets). Large banks often serve as government security dealers and/or municipal security underwriters, bearing any market risk for these issues. They make profits by selling securities for higher prices than they pay for the assets. Trading securities must appear on a bank's balance sheet at market value, with any market value losses or gains reflected in income.

To reduce their interest rate risk, banks generally prefer to avoid securities with maturities greater than ten years. Banks cannot own stock except shares they acquire as loan collateral or stock they hold in Federal Reserve banks. If a bank has uninsured government deposits as a liability, these **"pledged" deposits** must be held in low-risk securities; the funds cannot be invested in loans. Thus, if a bank has a lot of pledged deposits, it may not be very liquid, since pledge securities cannot be sold. Loans appear on the balance sheet as **Gross loans and leases,** the total book value of loans and leases the bank has made. Following this category, **Allowance for loan losses** records an offsetting account to cover expected loan losses. [Note the provision for loan losses is added to this allowance each year and the net loan charge-offs (loan charge-offs less recoveries) is subtracted each year.] **Net loans and leases** is gross loans less this allowance.[2]

Different Types of Loans

In the third quarter of 2003, FDIC statistics on all commercial banks reported the following average percentages for different types of loans as a percentage of total assets:

Gross Loans and Leases	58.25%	Real Estate Loans	30.41%	Commercial Loans	11.76%
Loans to Individuals	09.36%	Other Loans and Leases	06.11%	Farm Loans	0.62%

Hence, although commercial banks generally make commercial loans, they are actually supermarkets with lots of different loans and have moved heavily into real estate loans. Different types of lenders specialize in different types of loans, which has an effect on their funding base. For instance, lenders

---

Concept Questions

1 Why is cash and due really not a liquid asset for a bank?

2 What is the difference between a held to maturity and available for sale investment security?

3 What is the difference between Fed funds sold and Fed funds repurchased? Between Repurchase agreements and Reverse repurchase agreements?

4 What are Assets held in trading accounts? Pledged deposits? Allowances for loan losses? OREO?

5 What was the largest type of loan held by commercial banks in 2003?

---

2 Although bank managers subjectively determine the provision for loan losses for accounting purposes, regulators may ask for larger provisions. Tax laws determine the maximum amount of reserves that can be deducted from taxable income, which can differ from that reported for accounting purposes. Since 1997, the IRS has required banks with larger than $500 million in assets to employ a direct charge-off method based on their actual net losses as incurred during a current reporting period. Prior to 1997, large banks could opt for a more flexible method of calculating reserves based on their average ratios of net charge-offs to total loans for the previous six years. (Now, only banks with less than $500 million in assets or with problem loans equal to 75 percent or more of their capital can employ this method.) As discussed by Koch (1995, Chapter 23), banks often took the maximum provision for loan loss (PLL) for tax purposes and a lower provision for accounting purposes. This practice gave them excess tax savings equal to the excess of PLL on tax documents over that on accounting statements times their marginal tax rates. This excess represented the residual amount of retained earnings that would appear on tax documents if the two PLLs had been the same and was allocated to a special deferred tax reserve account.

specializing in commercial loans often have large amounts of business demand deposits, while lenders specializing in consumer loans have larger percentages of retail deposits. As noted in Chapter 2, the risk of different types of loans varies in terms of net charge-offs with commercial real estate loans and consumer loans often having higher charge-off (loan loss) rates. In terms of interest rate risk, real estate loans as often fixed rate, longer-term maturity loans have greater interest rate risk. **Commercial loans** generally are intermediate term (a few months to five or more years to maturity). A bank can not lend more than 15 percent of its equity capital or 25 percent if a loan is collateralized by risk-free securities to one borrower. Thus, often syndicates with other banks are used for large loans. **Consumer loans** (loans to individuals) are predominantly credit card loans and related plans (3.81 percent of assets) and other loans to individuals (5.55 percent) for car, education, and home improvement expenses, among others. Consumer loans are generally very short term (few months to three years). **Real Estate loans** are secured by real property and generally have long-term maturities and, hence, greater interest rate, market value, and prepayment risk, as discussed in Chapter 2. Banks often sell or securitize loans (package loans into portfolios that are sold as pass-through securities to investors) to reduce this risk. **Other loans** include loans of non-Fed Funds to other financial institutions; loans to brokers, dealers, and individuals for securities purchases; loans to not-for-profit organizations; agricultural loans; and loans to governments, among others.

    Other assets include bank premises and fixed assets, other real estate owned, intangible assets, and other items that are not significant enough to merit their own categories. **Bank premises and equipment** encompasses the depreciated value of bank buildings and equipment. **Other real estate owned** (OREO) includes property taken as collateral for unpaid loans, listed at market value. Problem banks carry large OREO accounts. Intangible assets include goodwill associated with bank mergers and acquisitions.

Bank Liabilities and Equity Capital

The lower panel of Table 4.1 shows the sources of financing for assets. Banks had high financial leverage (a large percentage of debt financing). As noted earlier in Figure 4.3, in the third quarter of 2003, the percentage of total asset financing was **about 91 percent debt and 9 percent equity financing.** Of this debt, **deposits continue to be the majority of financing (about 66 percent of total assets).** Comparing different size banks, community banks (with less than $1 billion in assets) have a much greater reliance on deposit financing (81 to 84 percent of total assets) compared with 63 percent for banks with assets greater than $1 billion. Deposits are predominantly interest-bearing deposits (52.82 percent of total assets in 2003).

    In 2003, deposits held in domestic offices included (with percentage of total assets):

- Transaction deposits   9.29% (demand deposits, 6.84%)
- Nontransaction deposits   47.22% including:

Money market deposit accounts (MMDAs)	21.73%
Other savings deposits (excluding MMDAs)	8.43%
Time deposits of less than $100,000	8.91%
Time deposits of $100,000 or more	8.15%

Deposits are eligible for federal deposit insurance up to $100,000 per account. Transaction deposits can pay interest, except for business demand deposits, which still are not allowed to pay interest (although many congressional bills have been proposed to remove this restriction).

    There are many different types of checking accounts, generally with higher rates and lower service charges for higher minimum amounts deposited including **Negotiable order of withdrawal (NOW) accounts.** Banks may limit the number of checks that can be written each month, particularly for **Money market deposit accounts (MMDAs),** which pay higher interest rates. **Nontransaction deposits include passbook savings accounts and time deposits.** Passbook savings accounts let savers withdraw funds but not write checks. They have lost some popularity in recent decades. **Time deposits** are often called certificates of deposit (CDs) and set fixed maturity dates. Banks often impose prepayment penalties equal to stated numbers of interest payments for early withdrawals. Relatively small CDs (those for less than $100,000) are often called retail CDs, while larger time deposits are called jumbo CDs. Deposit insurance covers the balances of NOW accounts, MMDAs, savings, and retail CDs (less than $100,000). These accounts are often called **core (insured) deposits,** since they tend to be stable and less interest

1 What was the average percentage of debt financing by banks in 2003? Equity financing?

2 What are core deposits? Noncore financing?

3 What are some types of core deposits? Noncore financing?

4 What are undivided profits? Contingency reserves?

rate sensitive than others. Banks had **48.4 percent of domestic deposits in core (insured, retail deposits)** in 2003. They also held 2.26 percent in IRAs and Keogh plan (retirement) accounts and 3.76% as brokered deposits. Banks also held about 9.26% deposits in foreign offices.

Negotiable jumbo CDs of large, well-known banks typically have denominations of $1 million and trade in a well-established secondary market. Securities firms often broker jumbo CDs for large banks, allowing their customers to buy securities with high rates, called brokered CDs. Brokered deposits were of concern during the savings and loan crisis of the late 1980s, so regulators now require that banks be well capitalized to actively engage in brokered deposits. Banks hold uninsured deposits and other borrowings, often called purchased funds, volatile liabilities, or hot funds. The list includes jumbo CDs, uninsured CDs greater than $100,000, and other types of borrowing that are very sensitive to interest rate changes. These volatile liabilities may leave a bank at any time if higher rates are offered elsewhere or bad news appears.

Below deposits, the liabilities section of a bank's balance sheet lists **Fed funds purchased (FFP), short-term borrowings of Fed funds from other financial institutions, and repurchase agreements (repos), short-term borrowings, often overnight, more often engaged in by large banks as liability managers. Other borrowed money is also used for liability management** and includes **commercial paper,** which matures in 270 days or less, and other short-term securities issued by large, well-known banks. By issuing such short-term securities, banks avoid the lengthy SEC registration process. This category also includes **Eurodollar CDs,** which are large dollar deposits held in foreign subsidiaries of U.S. banks. Also, **banker's acceptances** are short-term securities that represent firm IOUs to a bank as payments for foreign trade that are sold at a discount prior to maturity. **Negotiable CDs** are large denomination (wholesale) time deposits with a minimum maturity of seven days. For large banks, these short-term securities have brokers and dealers who carry them and are very marketable. They have large denominations, generally $100,000 or larger, and are often purchased by institutional investors.

The balance sheet category **Subordinated notes and debentures** includes all notes and bonds issued with maturities greater than one year that give claims subordinated to those of depositors. Subordinated debentures and perpetual preferred stock represent rather long-term capital for a bank, which regulatory agencies allow as secondary capital for regulatory capital requirements (as discussed in more detail in Chapter 6). **Other liabilities** include taxes and dividends payable, acceptances, and trade credit outstanding, among other miscellaneous items that do not fit in other categories.

Stockholder's equity, which is quite small relative to debt for a bank, includes **Common stock** reported at par value, **Surplus** (the amount paid over a legal par value), and **Undivided profits.** Undivided profits, similar to retained earnings, are earnings retained in excess of the common stock surplus account. Equity accounts also often include **other equity or contingency reserves.** This amount reflects reserves against losses on securities or other contingencies. Very small (assets of less than $100,000) banks generally have higher equity capital ratios (in 2003, on average, 11.3 percent versus 8.9 percent for banks with assets greater than $1 billion, as shown in Table 4.1). Since larger banks tend to be more diversified and have greater external sources of financing, they are thought to need a lower equity-to-asset cushion than community banks.

Details on FDIC-Insured Bank Income Statements

Table 4.2 shows a detailed income statement as a common statement (also as a percentage of total assets) for insured banks for 2003. Notice that total interest income (same as total interest revenue) and total interest expense, as the largest components of traditional bank operating earnings are presented first. Interest revenues and interest expenses go together, followed by net interest income, provision for loan losses, and noninterest revenue and noninterest expenses.

Revenues

Interest Revenue

A bank's income statement provides details for the source of interest revenues by asset type. Typically, a bank income statement reports tax equivalent revenues. Hence, any interest revenues for securities that are not subject to federal taxes, such as municipal securities, are adjusted by dividing by $(1 - t)$, where t is the bank's marginal tax rate to present **tax equivalent revenues.** Interest revenue as a percentage of total assets was 4.59 percent, with the majority of revenues (3.60 percent of revenues to total assets) from loan and lease financing.

table 4.2   COMMON SIZE STATEMENT (PERCENTAGE OF TOTAL ASSETS) REPORT OF INCOME OF ALL FDIC-INSURED COMMERCIAL BANKS, SEPTEMBER 30, 2003

	Total Commercial Banks	Banks with Assets of Less Than $100 Million	Banks with Assets of $100 Million to $1 Billion	Banks with Assets of $1 Billion or More
Percentage of Average Assets				
Total interest income (revenues)	**4.59%**	**5.46%**	**5.44%**	**4.45%**
Loans and lease financing	3.60	4.42	4.48	3.44
Balances at depository institutions	0.04	0.04	0.02	0.03
Investment securities	0.73	0.92	0.87	0.73
Assets held in trading accounts	0.11	0.00	0.00	0.14
Fed funds sold	0.07	0.06	0.04	0.07
Other interest income	0.04	0.02	0.03	0.04
Total Interest expenses	**1.34%**	**1.66%**	**1.61%**	**1.29%**
Domestic & foreign office deposits	0.89	1.52	1.37	0.79
Fed funds purchased	0.12	0.01	0.03	0.13
Trading liabilities & other borrowed money	0.27	0.13	0.21	0.30
Subordinated notes and debentures	0.06	0.00	0.00	0.07
Net interest income (NII)	**3.25%**	**3.80%**	**3.83%**	**3.16%**
Provisions for loan losses (PLL)	**0.48%**	**0.26%**	**0.31%**	**0.51%**
Total noninterest revenues (NIR)	**2.52%**	**1.09%**	**1.64%**	**2.69%**
Fiduciary activities	0.28	0.07	0.19	0.30
Service charges on deposit accounts	0.43	0.43	0.43	0.43
Trading account gains and fees	0.17	0.00	0.00	0.20
Additional noninterest income	1.64	0.59	1.02	1.76
Total noninterest expense (NIE)	**3.32%**	**3.43%**	**3.44%**	**3.30%**
Salaries and employee benefits	1.47	1.77	1.68	1.43
Premises and equipment	0.42	0.44	0.43	0.42
All other noninterest expense	1.43	1.22	1.33	1.45
Burden (NIE − NIR)	**0.80%**	**2.34%**	**1.80%**	**0.61%**
Pretax net operating income (NII − PLL − Burden)	**1.97%**	**1.20%**	**1.72%**	**2.04%**
Securities gain (losses)	0.10%	0.04%	0.05%	0.10%
Operating income + Security gains	**2.07%**	**1.24%**	**1.77%**	**2.14%**
Applicable income taxes	0.68%	0.28%	0.49%	0.72%
Income before extraordinary items	**1.39%**	**0.96%**	**1.28%**	**1.42%**
Net extraordinary gains	0.00%	0.00%	0.00%	0.00%
Net income	**1.39%**	**0.96%**	**1.28%**	**1.42%**

Source: FDIC Quarterly Banking Profile, Third Quarter, 2003, http://www2.fdic.gov/qbp.

Noninterest Revenue

Large banks generate greater proportions of noninterest revenue than smaller banks. In 2003, noninterest revenue for banks with assets greater than $1 billion was 2.69 percent of total assets compared with only 1.09 percent for the smallest banks. As shown in Figure 4.4, the percentage of noninterest revenue (income) rose dramatically to 44.8 percent for large banks with greater than $1 billion in assets, and 28.6 percent for community banks by 2003. Figure 4.5 shows the composition of commercial banks' noninterest income. Service charges are primary sources of noninterest revenues for smaller banks, representing about 12 percent of total noninterest income for all banks. Trading gains and fees (trades made by large banks for customers or their own accounts) were 6.8 percent of total bank noninterest revenue. Other sources of noninterest income include investment banking and brokerage fees (5.2 percent); fiduciary income for trusts and other services (11.2 percent); insurance commissions and fees (18 percent); net servicing fees (6.9 percent), where loans are sold or securitized and banks continue to service loans; net gains on asset sales (8.8 percent); and net securitization income, fees when banks transform loan portfolios into pass-through investment securities (11.5 percent).

The remaining noninterest income (about 31 percent) includes fees from numerous other bank activities including bill paying services, item processing, personal financial planning services, working capital management for nonfinancial firms, small firm consulting advice, managing and processing retirement funds, mutual fund fees, and correspondent banking, among others. Correspondent banks offer services for smaller banks for fees including check clearing, wire transfer, securities transfer and clearance and safekeeping, federal funds trading, loan participation, and investment advisory services. Among these services, check-clearing and data-processing services for smaller banks have been particularly profitable. Large banks engage in diverse off-balance-sheet activities that produce significant fee income as well, discussed in Appendix 4A.

Expenses

Interest and Noninterest Expenses In past years, interest expenses dominated banks' expenses; however, noninterest expenses are a larger percentage of total assets today. In 2003, interest expenses were 1.34 percent of assets, while noninterest expenses were 3.32 percent. Banks' major interest expense is interest paid on deposits, followed by other borrowed money and Fed Funds purchased and repurchase agreements. The largest noninterest expense relative to total assets is salaries and benefits. All other expenses, the next largest expense, include utilities and deposit insurance premiums along with

figure **4.4** NONINTEREST INCOME AS A PERCENTAGE OF NET OPERATING REVENUE,* 1995 TO 2003

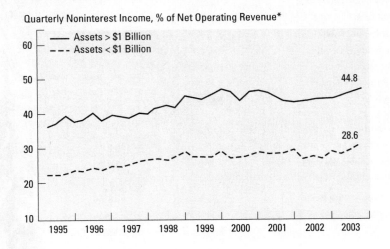

Quarterly Noninterest Income, % of Net Operating Revenue*

*Net operating revenue equals net interest income plus total noninterest income.

Source: *FDIC Quarterly Banking Profile, Graph Book, September 30, 2003,* http://www2.fdic.gov.

4.5 COMPOSITION OF COMMERCIAL BANKS' NONINTEREST INCOME, SEPTEMBER 30, 2003

figure

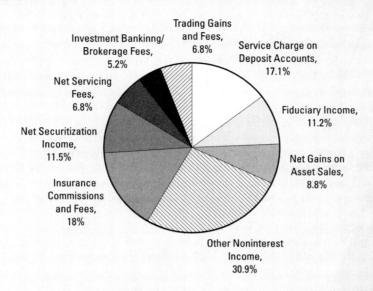

Source: FDIC Quarterly Banking Profile, Graph Book, September 30, 2003, http://www2.fdic.gov.

other operating expenses. Premises and equipment expenses follow, including rent and depreciation of premises and machinery. Banks have improved their efficiency in the past decade to reduce large non-interest expenses.

Net Income

This income statement shows both amounts and percentages of total revenues, making it a common size statement. The percentage next to net income at the bottom of the statement in Table 4.2 is the average bank return on assets (ROA), since this is a common income statement, divided by total assets. Pretax net operating income (net interest income less the provision for loan losses less the burden) is often used to calculate a pretax operating ROA that accurately reflects a bank's ordinary operations before one-time gains and losses on securities and extraordinary items. In 2003, the average bank's pre-tax **operating ROA** was 1.97 percent.

Gains (Losses) on Securities and Net Extraordinary Items

Security gains (or losses) come about when a bank sells securities from its investment portfolio at a higher or lower price than its book values for those assets. Losses and gains on security sales are taxed as ordinary income for banks. Extraordinary items are losses or gains on one-time items, such as a bank selling and leasing back its buildings or expenses for settling a lawsuit. Since these items do not recur, they are placed at the bottom of the income statement, although they can represent significant amounts. In 2003, you'll notice at the bottom of Table 4.2 that the security gain was 0.10 percent of assets, and net extraordinary gains were 0 percent on average, so the average net income to assets (ROA) (after deducting taxes) was 1.39 percent. Note differences across different size banks, with the largest banks (> 1 bil.) at this time having the highest average ROA of 1.42 percent versus 0.96 percent for very small banks.

Looking More Closely at Bank Profits

As noted in Chapter 1, and based on the common size balance sheets and income statements (as a percentage of total assets) just reviewed, the sources of a bank's operating net income (NI) excluding extraordinary items and security gains/losses equals:

$$NI = (NII - PLL - \text{Burden})(1 - t) \qquad [4.2]$$

where **NII** is net interest income (interest revenues less interest expenses); **PLL** is provision for loan losses; **Burden** is noninterest expenses less noninterest revenues; and **t** is a bank's marginal tax rate.

Stating these items as a fraction of assets, this becomes the equation for operating ROA:

$$ROA = (NIM - PLL\% - Burden\%)(1 - t) \qquad [4.3]$$

Equation 4.3 shows that a bank's profits depend on how well it manages its NIM, provision for loan losses, and burden. By looking at each of the three items, you can determine why operating ROA rose or fell and where the bank needs to improve its management. A historical example follows.

Effect on ROA of NIM, Provision for Loan Losses, and Burden

Table 4.3 shows trends in NIMs, Burden%, PLL%, and Operating ROA for all commercial banks on average from 1997 to 2003, providing a way to analyze trends in Operating ROA, as follows.

Example 1: Analysis for 1997 to 1998—Why did Pretax Operating ROA Fall?

Looking at Operating ROA shown on Table 4.3, which is equal to the NIM less PLL% less the Burden%, you'll notice a significant decline from 1997 to 1998 from 2.02 percent to 1.85 percent. This is a fall of 0.17 percent or −17 basis points (1 b.p. equals 0.01 percent). Although this seems like a small decline, since the banks average operating ROA is quite small, it is actually a very large decline of 8.42 percent (0.17 / 2.02 = 0.0842). Why did this decline in operating ROA occur? The key culprits are the NIM, PLL%, and Burden%.

Looking first at NIM, there was a significant decline of 0.20 percent or 20 basis points in NIM, resulting from interest revenue to assets (IR%) falling 26 basis points (0.26 percent) and interest expense to assets (IE%) falling only 6 basis points (0.06 percent). The provision for loan losses to assets (PLL%) rose only 1 basis point (0.01 percent). The Burden% fell slightly by just 4 basis points (0.04 percent). Hence, the lower NIM was responsible for the lower pretax operating ROA. The larger fall in interest revenue than interest expenses to assets resulted in the lower NIM and lower pretax operating ROA. In turn, this resulted in a lower after-tax ROA and ROE in 1998.

table **4.3**   TRENDS IN NET INTEREST MARGIN, BURDEN, AND ROA, 1997 TO 2003

	PERCENTAGE OF AVERAGE ASSETS						
	1997	**1998**	**1999**	**2000**	**2001**	**2002**	**2003**
Interest income (tax adjusted)	7.57	7.31	7.13	7.40	6.66	5.44	4.57
Interest expense	3.67	3.61	3.39	3.86	3.10	1.84	1.30
Net interest margin (NIM)	**3.90**	**3.70**	**3.74**	**3.54**	**3.56**	**3.60**	**3.27**
Provision for loan losses (PLL)	**0.42**	**0.43**	**0.40**	**0.49**	**0.68**	**0.70**	**0.47**
NIM after PLL	3.48	3.27	3.34	3.05	2.88	2.90	2.80
Noninterest expense	3.70	3.83	3.87	3.65	3.60	3.46	3.35
Noninterest income	2.24	2.41	2.70	2.55	2.52	2.51	2.54
Burden	**1.46**	**1.42**	**1.17**	**1.10**	**1.08**	**0.95**	**0.81**
Operating ROA[a] **(NIM − PLL − Burden)**	**2.02**	**1.85**	**2.17**	**1.95**	**1.80**	**1.95**	**1.99**
Security gain/losses & extr. items & taxes	0.72	0.62	0.81	0.73	0.58	0.60	0.59
ROA after taxes, sec. gains & adj.	**1.30%**	**1.23%**	**1.36%**	**1.22%**	**1.22%**	**1.35%**	**1.40%**
Equity multiplier (Assets / Equity)	**11.89**	**11.60**	**11.67**	**11.65**	**11.18**	**10.86**	**10.99**
Return on equity (ROE)	**15.46%**	**14.27%**	**15.87%**	**14.21%**	**13.64%**	**14.66%**	**15.39%**

a *Adjustments include security gains/losses and any gains/losses on extraordinary items.*

Sources: Sheshunoff Bank and S&L Quarterly, *1997, 2002 issue, Sheshunoff Information Services, Inc., Austin, Texas; and Third Quarter 2003 Quarterly Banking Profile,*
FDIC, http://www2.fdic.gov/qbp.

Example 2: 1998 to 1999—Why did Pretax Operating ROA Rise?

You'll notice, in contrast, that pretax Operating ROA rose dramatically from 1.85 percent in 1998 to 2.17 percent in 1999, a rise of 32 basis points (0.32 percent). This represents a growth rate in operating ROA of over 17 percent (0.32 / 1.85 = 0.173). What caused this happy result?

Looking at the NIM, there was very little change, only a 4 basis point (0.04 percent) rise. Similarly, the PLL% fell only slightly by 3 basis points (0.03 percent). However, the Burden% fell by a large 25 basis points (0.25 percent) from 1.42 percent to 1.17 percent (a 17.6 percent [0.25/1.42] decline). What happened? Noninterest expense rose 4 basis points, so was not responsible. The significant fall in the Burden% was the result of a nice rise in noninterest revenue to assets from 2.41 percent to 2.70 percent (a rise of 29 basis points, or 0.29 percent, which is a growth rate of 12 percent [0.29/2.41]). Hence, the rise in noninterest income was responsible for the large fall in the Burden% and rise in the pretax operating ROA.

For the after-tax ROA, a rise in security gains and extraordinary items, from 0.62 percent to 0.81 percent, also contributed to the total rise in ROA from 1.23 percent to 1.36 percent and rise in the ROE in 1999.

Other Trends in NIMs, PLL, and Burden over Time

Looking at trends in NIMs over time, you can get a hint of the banking industry's interest rate risk. A stable NIM indicates less risk, while a volatile NIM signals significant interest rate risk. For the banking industry as a whole, the NIM bounced around quite a bit between 1997 and 2003, suggesting volatility in interest rates over this period. The NIM had a range of 36 basis points with a decline from 3.90 in 1997 to 3.54 in 2000. From 2000 to 2003, the NIM fell 27 basis points from 3.54 in 2000 to 3.27 in 2003. Interest rates appeared to fall from 1997 to 1999, rise in 2000, and fall again from 2001 to 2003. Figure 4.6 shows the trends in interest revenue and interest expense to total assets from 1992 to 2003. Note the large drop in rates from 2000 to 2003. The industry average NIM benefited during the period of falling interest rates in the early 2000s, with interest expenses to assets falling more than interest revenue to assets. This suggests that on average banks held a net negative repricing gap in the early 2000s. Relative to these dramatic changes, the NIM is fairly stable, suggesting on average good interest rate risk management.

Figure 4.7 graphs these trends for the burden and its components. The burden fell significantly from 1992 to 2003, with the rise in the NIR% and stable NIE%. As shown in Table 4.3, the average burden

figure **4.6**   TRENDS IN INTEREST REVENUE, INTEREST EXPENSE, AND NIM AS % OF TOTAL ASSETS, 1992 TO 2003

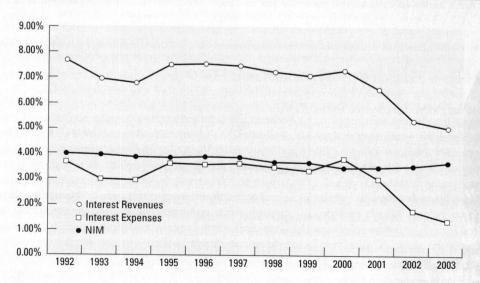

Sources: Graph compiled by Authors using average U.S. commercial bank interest revenue, interest expense data from the FDIC Quarterly Banking Profile, 2003, at http://www2.fdic.gov/qbp and this data presented for earlier years in the Sheshunoff Bank and S&L Quarterly data, 1993, 1997, 2002.

figure **4.7** TRENDS IN NONINTEREST EXPENSE, NONINTEREST REVENUE, AND BURDEN AS % OF TOTAL ASSETS, 1992 TO 2003

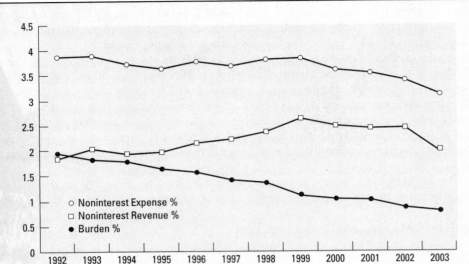

Sources: Graphs compiled by Authors using noninterest expense and noninterest revenue data for average U.S Commercial Banks from the FDIC Quarterly Banking Profile, 2003, at http://www2.fdic.gov/qbp *and this data presented for earlier years in the* Sheshunoff Bank and S&L Quarterly *data, 1993, 1997, 2002.*

to assets for the banking industry ranged 57 basis points (1.46 in 1997 to 0.81 in 2003). Noninterest revenue to assets (NIR%) rose dramatically from 2.24 in 1997 to 2.54 in 2003. Noninterest expense to assets (NIE%) also fell from 3.87 in 1999 to 3.46 in 2002, but fell again to 3.35 in 2003. These trends in Figure 4.7 and Table 4.3 illustrate the growing importance of noninterest revenue for banks. With the NIM about equal to the NIE%, without the significant rise in the NIR% each year, the operating ROA would have been negative. Of course, on the other hand, to produce noninterest revenues, large banks also must often incur higher noninterest (labor, technology, etc.) expenses

In Table 4.3, the provision for loan losses to assets ranged 28 basis points, from 0.40 in 1999 to 0.70 in 2002. With the dot.com collapse and downturn in the telecommunications industry in 2001 to 2002, many large banks lending to this industry had problem loans and thus increased their provision for loans. In 2003, with the economy improving, on average bank managers reduced their provision for loan losses back to 0.47.

Using Income Relationships to Forecast Target NIMs

Forecasting NIM Based on a Target ROA

The income statement relationships in Equation 4.3 can help managers to find the NIM a bank must achieve to meet a target ROA. The process begins with the operating ROA equation:

$$ROA = (NIM - PLL\% - Burden\%)(1 - t)$$

Hence, pretax operating ROA = ROA / (1−t). Substituting then to solve for pretax operating ROA:

$$ROA / (1 - t) = NIM - PLL\% - Burden\%$$

Solving for the Target NIM needed to provide a given pretax ROA:

$$\text{Target } NIM = [ROA / (1 - t)] + PLL\% + Burden\% \qquad [4.4]$$

Example: Suppose you are a manager for Bank Star National Bank, which has set a target for ROA of 1.24 percent. The company has a marginal tax rate of 30 percent, a PLL percentage of 0.30 percent, and a burden percentage of 1.5 percent. What NIM must the company achieve to make its target ROA? Using Equation 4.4, Bank Star's target NIM is

$$\text{Target } NIM = [1.24\% / (1 - 0.30)] + 0.30\% + 1.5\% = 3.57\%$$

What ratio of interest revenue to assets would Bank Star have to average to reach this NIM goal, if its interest expenses amount to 3.61 percent of assets? To answer the question, solve for IR% using (**NIM = IR% − IE%**):

$$IR\% = \text{Target } NIM + IE\% = 3.57\% + 3.61\% = 7.18\% \qquad [4.5]$$

Bank Star would have to earn an average of 7.18 percent on its assets to meet its NIM goal.

Forecasting NIM Based on a Forecast of ROE

This analysis can be extended to find goals that will produce a desired target Return on Equity (ROE). Recall from financial management theory, the DuPont relationship that ROE is a function of the ROA and a firm's financial leverage, proxied by its equity multiplier (EM), equal to (Assets / Equity), (i.e., the reciprocal of [Equity / Assets]), that is:

$$ROE = ROA \times EM, \text{ or} \qquad [4.6]$$

$$\text{Net Income / Equity } (ROE) = [\text{Net Income / Assets } (ROA)] \times [\text{Asset / Equity } (EM)]$$

Solving for ROA, given an ROE, ROA is equal to (ROE/EM), and pretax ROA is equal to (pretax ROE/EM) or ROE/(1 − t) divided by EM. Substituting this expression into Equation 4.4 for ROA to find the Target NIM needed for a given ROE gives:

$$\text{Target } NIM = \{[ROE / (1 - t)] / EM\} + PLL\% + \text{Burden}\% \qquad [4.7]$$

Equation 4.7 indicates that a bank's target NIM is also a function of its financial leverage. A fall in the equity multiplier or rise in equity to assets (that is, a decline in financial leverage) requires an off-setting rise in NIM to achieve a given ROE goal. Note also that since Assets / Equity is the reciprocal of Equity / Assets, the equation could be expressed as:

$$\text{Target } NIM = \{[ROE / (1 - t)] \times (\text{Equity / Assets})\} + PLL\% + \text{Burden}\%$$

To find a target NIM, given an ROE goal, suppose Bank Star has set a target ROE of 18 percent. Assume also that the bank's equity capital to assets ratio is 8 percent, the Burden% is 1 percent, the expected PLL% is 0 percent, and the marginal tax rate is 34 percent. What target NIM does Bank Star need to achieve?

$$\text{Target } NIM = \{[18\% / (1 - 0.34)] \times 0.08\} + 0\% + 1\% = 3.18\%$$

The minimum NIM necessary to achieve the target ROE is 3.18 percent. However, if the desired equity-to-capital ratio falls to 6 percent (i.e., an equity multiplier of 1 / 0.06, which equals 16.67), a much lower target NIM will allow the bank to generate the same 18 percent ROE:

$$\text{Target } NIM = \{[18\% / (1 - 0.34)] \times 0.06\} + 0\% + 1\% = 2.64\%$$

This difference demonstrates that financial leverage is an important component in daily bank decisions to determine the NIM needed to achieve a target return for bank stockholders. The effect of financial leverage on bank profitability can be more closely examined by looking at the relationships among ROA, the equity multiplier, and ROE over time.

Trends in ROA, EM, and ROE Over Time

Table 4.4 shows trends in ROA, EM, and ROE from 1990 to the third quarter of 2003. From 1990 to 1992, the U.S. economy suffered a severe recession. Bank ROAs were low then, but ROEs stayed in the low but respectable range because of high equity multipliers. For instance, a low 0.49 percent ROA times a high equity multiplier of 15.59 resulted in a ROE of 7.64 percent in 1990.

table **4.4** TRENDS IN ROA (NPM AND AU) AND ROE (ROA AND EM) FOR U.S. BANKS, 1990 TO 2003

Commercial bank ROAs improved over the latter 1990s as NPMs improved, despite a slight decline in asset utilization (AU).

All Banks	Net Profit Margin	Asset Utilization	Return on Assets	Equity Multiplier	Return on Equity
1990	4.39%	0.1117	0.49%	15.59	7.64%
1991	4.94	0.1093	0.54	14.91	8.05
1992	9.65	0.0984	0.95	14.23	13.24
1993	13.38	0.0852	1.14	12.77	14.56
1994	13.32	0.0878	1.17	12.50	14.63
1995	12.64	0.0941	1.19	12.37	14.72
1996	12.86	0.0964	1.24	12.06	14.95
1997	13.35	0.0974	1.30	11.89	15.46
1998	12.64	0.0973	1.23	11.60	14.27
1999	13.92	0.0977	1.36	11.67	15.87
2000	12.10	0.1008	1.22	11.65	14.21
2001	13.13	0.0929	1.22	11.18	13.64
2002	16.75	0.0806	1.35	10.86	14.66
2003	19.64	0.0713	1.40	10.99	15.39

Sources: Figures calculated by Authors from reports published in William B. English and William R. Nelson. "Profits and Balance Sheet Developments at U.S. Commercial Banks in 1997." Federal Reserve Bulletin *(June 1998): 391–419; and* "Profits and Balance Sheet Developments at U.S. Commercial Banks in 2001." Federal Reserve Bulletin *(June 2001), 259–269; also available at* http://www.federal-reserve.gov/pubs/bulletin/2002/0602lead.pdf. *Also, the Authors used data from FDIC Statistics on Depository Institutions, All Commercial Banks Nationwide, December 30, 2002; and December 30, 2003 from Statistics on Banking on the FDIC Website* http://www2.fdic.gov/SDI/SOB/

FDICIA raised capital requirements in 1991, and the EM fell for banks after 1992. However, an economic expansion brought increasing ROAs. In 1997, the EM was only 11.89, but the ROA of 1.30 percent resulted in a ROE of 15.46 percent, 102 percent higher than in 1990. From 1996 to 2002, bank equity-to-asset ratios rose with greater profitability allowing larger retained earnings. Hence, the equity multiplier fell from 12.06 (equity to assets of 8.29 percent) in 1996 to 10.86 (equity to assets of 9.21 percent) in 2002. Higher ROAs compensated for the lower equity multiplier in 1999, 2002, and 2003, producing higher ROEs in those years.

Trends in NPM and AU Over Time

The reason for the rise in bank ROAs in the late 1990s can be examined more closely by looking at their net profit margins (NPMs), which measure cost management (the net income produced from revenues), and asset utilization (AU) ratios (the revenue produced from assets), which measure revenue management. The well-known DuPont system for ratio analysis multiplies NPM by AU to get ROA:

$$ROA = NPM \times AU \qquad [4.8]$$

Net Income / Assets *(ROA)* = (Net Income / Revenues) *(NPM)* × (Revenues / Assets) *(AU)*

Table 4.4 shows trends in NPM and AU for U.S. banks from 1990 to the fourth quarter of 2003. Low ROAs in 1990 and 1991 can be explained by very low net profit margins. Asset utilization ratios (note AU for banks equals IR% plus NIR%) fell slightly after 1991, but NPMs after 1991 improved immensely, rising from 4.94 percent in 1991 to 13.35 percent in 1997. This change dramatically improved ROA, which rose 145 percent from 0.51 percent in 1991 to 1.25 percent in 1997. A fall in AU also occurred during 2000 to 2003. However, ROA rose over this period, with a rise in NPM from 12.10 percent in 2000 to 19.64 percent in 2003. Thus, a combination of cost management measured by NPM, revenue management reflected by AU, and financial leverage demonstrated by EM affect a bank's ROE:

$$ROE = NPM \times AU \times EM \qquad [4.9]$$

1 How can a bank's pretax operating ROA be calculated? What are the three key elements to examine?

2 What trends have occurred in bank noninterest revenues and noninterest expenses? What are some sources of bank noninterest revenues and noninterest expenses?

3 What is a simple formula to forecast a target NIM, given ROA, PLL%, and Burden%?

4 What trends have occurred in NPM, AU, and EM over time?

Overview of a Depository Institution's Performance using a UBPR

DuPont Analysis

Figure 4.8 outlines the major criteria for analyzing a depository institution's profitability. As previously noted, DuPont analysis suggests evaluating return on equity (ROE) as a function of cost management, indicated by a bank's net profit margin (NPM) and its revenue management, or asset utilization (AU) ratio. Accordingly, the change in an NPM can be examined by looking at trends in the NIM, Burden, PLL, and their components, along with net security gains and losses and extraordinary items.

Analyzing NIM (Margin Analysis)

An analysis of changes in NIM can be performed by doing what is often called a margin analysis: examining the reasons for changes in interest revenue to assets (IR%) and changes in interest expense to assets (IE%). These changes are a function of: (1) balance sheet composition or mix changes, (2) rate changes on individual balance sheet items, and (3) volume changes in the growth of the banks assets and/or the percentage of interest-paying (earning) assets and interest-paying liabilities that a bank has.

For example, suppose a bank's NIM has fallen, with the IR% (the average rate on assets) falling more than IE% (the average cost of liabilities). You'd like to explain why the IR% fell more than IE%, thereby reducing the NIM. By examining changes in the mix of the bank's assets, you find that the bank's percentage of earning assets (the percentage of assets that earn interest) has fallen from 70 percent to 60 percent, with a fall in the percentage of loans to assets the bank holds, that is, a fall in asset utilization. In addition, you examine the yield on loans, and find the average yield received by the bank on loans fell from 10 percent to 8 percent. The bank's loan growth rate was −10 percent. Putting these together, the significant fall in the IR% was the result of the combined fall in the average interest rate on loans (rate effect), the unfavorable change in asset mix (drop in the percentage of loans), and an unfavorable volume effect (the shrinkage in the size of the bank's loan portfolio). Meanwhile, you examine for changes in the liability mix as well, and find that the average rate on liabilities fell from 6 percent to 5 percent (not as large a drop as the average yield on loans). Also, the bank's liability mix changes to holding more expensive noncore deposits (uninsured liabilities) and a lower percentage of core deposits (insured demand deposits, NOW, MMDAs, savings deposits, and time deposits under $100,000). Hence, the IE% fell less than the IR%, because of both a lower drop in the average rate paid on liabilities and also an unfavorable mix effect, with the bank taking on a larger percentage of more expensive types of liabilities. The combined unfavorable rate, mix, and volume effects for assets and unfavorable mix effect for liabilities contributed to the larger fall in the IR% than IE% and the lower NIM.

The following sections present the major elements of UBPRs for both performance and risk analysis, with key ratios from these reports summarized in Tables 4.5 and 4.6, respectively, followed by an illustration of a performance and risk analysis using UBPR information for Wells Fargo Bank in San Francisco.

A More Detailed Analysis of a Depository Institution using UBPRs

Typical performance ratios on UBPRs are summarized in Table 4.5. The FFIEC Website has a UBPR User's Guide (Section III: Definition of UBPR Items) that you can print out. (Note, for this section, you

figure **4.8** DUPONT ANALYSIS FOR DEPOSITORY INSTITUTIONS

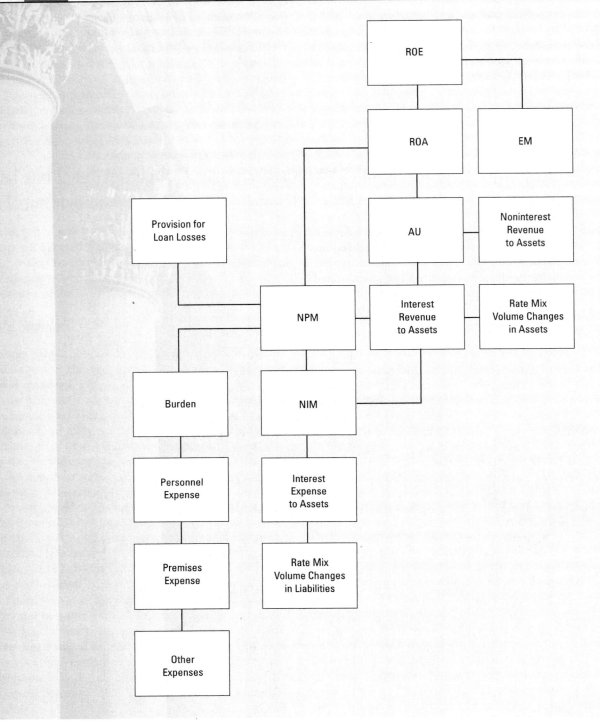

might want to go ahead and print out one for Wells Fargo Bank in San Francisco, following the instructions on Figure 4.1, to follow along.) These items sometimes change from year to year, but common sense will help you figure out any new items. Each UBPR has a Table of Contents that contains the following information:

1. **Income Statement Information (Earnings and Profitability Section),** including dollar statements and common size statement items (items as a percentage of total assets), and an analysis of yields (rates) on assets and costs (rates paid) on liabilities;

2. **Balance Sheet Information,** including dollar statements and common size statement items to analyze mix changes in assets and liabilities and off-balance sheet items, and an analysis of credit, interest rate risk analysis, liquidity, and capital risks; and

3. **A State Average Summary page giving some ratios for banks in a bank's state.**

Note the UBPRs are often twenty-five pages or longer, so don't be overwhelmed. Lots of additional information is provided, so you may need to sift through a bit to find the information that you want. **Average Total Assets** are used for common size statements and financial ratios. Average assets are calculated using the average assets (summing assets for all the quarters reported divided by the number of quarters). When not available, total assets at the end of the year can be used. By averaging assets, effects of seasonality or end of the year window dressing are avoided. Also, note that peer comparisons are given for similar size banks in the FDIC's four different size categories, which are quite broad ($100 million or less; greater than $100 million to $1 billion; $1 billion but less than $10 billion; and greater than $10 billion), so peer comparisons need to be taken with a grain of salt, since a bank with $1 billion in assets, for instance, may be quite different from a bank with $9 billion in assets. Also, peer comparisons are national comparisons, so a bank may be operating in a region that has more economic problems than average. The state peer comparison ratios help with this problem, although fewer comparisons are given. Key sections for analysis are discussed in the following separate sections.

II. Earnings and Profitability Analysis

An Earnings and Profitability Analysis appears on page 2 of each UBPR, after the Table of Contents. Similar to the earlier analysis in the chapter, key elements of the income statement are presented as a percentage of average assets to analyze the components of ROA (net income / average assets) including the IR% (interest revenue to average assets), IE% (interest expense to average assets), NIR% (noninterest revenue to average assets), NIE% (noninterest expense to average assets), PLL% (provision for loan losses to average assets), and Net Security Gains/Losses to average assets, as shown in Table 4.5. Using these ratios, you can analyze why ROA changed over time or is lower or higher than peer banks. As mentioned earlier, asset utilizations (revenues to assets) can be calculated as the IR% plus NIR%.

III. (NIM) Margin Analysis

A Margin Analysis follows the Earnings and Profitability Analysis on page 2. It gives a more precise net interest margin and IR% and IE% as a percentage of earning assets (assets that pay interest), providing a better measure of the average yield on assets and rate paid on liabilities. Also, asset utilization can be examined by looking at changes in IR% and NIR% and peer comparisons for the percentage of earning assets that a bank has.

IV. Yield or Cost of Analysis

To examine more closely why the IR% (interest revenue to assets) and the IE% (interest expense to assets) went down or up (i.e., rate effects), the yields on different types of assets and interest rate paid on different liabilities are provided (often on page 4) of the UBPR. This analysis needs to be compared with the different types of assets and liabilities (composition or mix of assets) and change in that mix as mentioned earlier as well.

V. Balance Sheet % Composition of Assets and Liabilities

On page 9 or so of the UBPR is a common size balance sheet (percentage composition of assets and liabilities to make it easy to identify changes in asset and liability mix and their respective effects on the IR% and IE% and, hence, the NIM). As mentioned earlier, moving into higher- (lower-) yielding assets increases (reduces) interest revenues, while moving into more (less) expensive liabilities increases (reduces) interest expense.

VI. Analysis of Noninterest Expenses as a Percent of Average Assets

On page 4 or so of the UBPR, an analysis of noninterest expenses as a percentage of average assets is provided, including personnel, occupancy, and other expenses, and total overhead expense. Total overhead expense is defined as the sum of personnel, occupancy, goodwill impairment, other intangible amortization, and other operating expenses. By looking at trends or peer comparisons, you can examine

table 4.5 TYPICAL PROFITABILITY PERFORMANCE MEASURES ANALYZING ROA AND ROE

I. Overall Profitability Ratios (DuPont Analysis)

Return on Equity (ROE) = Net Income / Equity

Net Profit Margin (NPM) = Net Income / Revenues

Equity Multiplier (EM) = Assets / Equity

Return on Assets (ROA) = Net Income / Assets

Asset Utilization (AU) = Revenues / Assets

II. Earnings and Profitability Analysis: Income Statement Items as a Percent of Average Assets: UBPR

Interest Income (Revenue) to Assets (IR%) = Interest Revenue / Assets

Interest Expense to Assets (IE%) = Interest Expense / Assets

Net Interest Income to Assets (NIM) = IR% − IE%

Noninterest Income (Revenue) to Assets (NIR%) = Noninterest Revenue / Assets

Noninterest Expense to Assets (NIE%) = Noninterest Expense / Assets

Provision for Loan and Lease Losses to Assets (PLL%) = Provision for Loan Loss Expense / Assets

Pretax Operating Income to Assets (Pretax Operating ROA) = NIM + NIR% − NIE% − PLL%

Realized Gains and Losses on Securities to Assets = Net Gains or Losses on Securities / Assets

Net Income to Assets (ROA) = Net Income / Assets

III. (NIM) Margin Analysis: UBPR

Average Earning Assets to Average Assets = Sum All Assets That Pay Interest / Average Assets

Average Interest-Bearing Funds to Average Assets = Sum All Liabilities That Pay Interest / Average Assets

Interest Income (Revenue) to Average Earning Assets = Interest Revenue / Average Earning Assets

Interest Expense to Average Earning Assets = Interest Expense / Average Earning Assets

Net Interest Income to Average Earning Assets (NIM) = (IR − IE) / Average Earning Assets

IV. Yield or Cost of Analysis: UBPR

Yield on Assets:

Yield Total Loans and Leases (Tax Equivalent) = Interest Revenue on Loans & Leases / Total Loans and Leases

Yield Individual Types of Loans and Securities = Interest Revenue on Particular Asset / Individual Asset

Yield on Total Investment Securities (TE) = Interest Revenue on Investment Securities / Investment Securities

Cost of Analysis (Interest Rate Bank Pays On):

Rate Paid on Total Interest-Bearing Deposits = Interest Expense on Interest-Paying Deposits / Total Interest-Paying Deposits

Rate Paid on Individual Types of Deposit or Liability = Interest Expense on a Particular Liability / That Type of Liability

Rate on All Interest-Bearing Funds = Interest Expense on All Liabilities Paying Interest / All Liabilities Paying Interest

why the NIE% and NIR% and, hence, the Burden was higher or lower. Other operating efficiency ratios include:

Efficiency Ratio = Total Overhead Expense / (Net Interest Income + Noninterest Income)

where Net Interest Income is interest revenue less interest expense, and Noninterest Income is generally noninterest revenue.

Average Personnel Expense per Employee ($ Thousands)

Assets per Employee ($ Millions)

The efficiency ratio is widely used by bank managers and analysts. The ratio represents the fraction of cost that operating expenses represents for each dollar of net revenue the bank produces. It is often listed as a percentage. A lower ratio indicates better operating efficiency. In 2003, FDIC-insured banks had the following average efficiency ratios:

All insured Commercial Banks:	55.00 percent
Small Banks with assets of less than $100 million:	68.16 percent

table 4.5   TYPICAL PROFITABILITY PERFORMANCE MEASURES ANALYZING ROA AND ROE (CONTINUED)

V. Balance Sheet % Composition of Assets and Liabilities: UBPR

Assets Percent of Average Assets (Balance Sheet as a % of Average Assets):

% Net Loans & Leases = Total Loans and Leases / Average Assets

% Each Type of Short-term Security = Each Type of Security / Average Assets

% Total Securities = Total Securities / Average Assets

% Total Earning Assets = All Earning Assets / Average Assets

% Premises & Equipment = Premise & Equipment / Average Assets

Liabilities, Percent of Average Assets:

% Demand Deposits = Demand Deposits / Average Assets

% Each Type of Insured Deposit = Type of Deposit / Average Assets

% Total Core Deposits = (Total Demand, NOW, MMDA, Savings and Time Deposits < $100M) / Average Assets

% Time Deposits of $100 million or more = Time Deposits of $100M or more / Average Assets

% Total Deposits = Total Deposits / Average Assets

% Nondeposit Borrowing = Total Nondeposit Borrowing / Average Assets

% Total Liabilities = Total Liabilities / Average Assets

% All Common & Preferred Equity Capital = (Com. Stock + Ret. Earnings + Pref. Stock) / Average Assets

VI. Analysis of Noninterest Expenses (Efficiency), Percent of Average Assets

% Personnel Expense = Personnel Expenses / Average Assets

% Total Overhead Expense = Overhead Expenses / Average Assets

% Overhead Expense less Noninterest Revenue = Overhead Expenses − Noninterest Revenue / Average Assets

Other Efficiency Ratios:

Efficiency Ratio = Total Overhead Expense / (Net Interest Income + Noninterest Income)

Average Personnel Expense per Employee ($ Thousands) = Total Personnel Expense / Total # Employees

Assets Per Employee ($ Millions) = Total Assets / Total # Employees

Banks with assets of $100 million to $1 billion:	62.79 percent
Banks with assets of $1 billion to $10 billion:	55.26 percent
Banks with assets of $10 billion or larger:	55.41 percent

In 1992, the average efficiency ratio for all insured banks in the United States was about 66 percent; hence, efficiency ratios have improved dramatically for the banking industry, largely because of higher noninterest revenues. As noted above, the efficiency gap between very large banks and small banks is large and has been widening. The FDIC reported similar efficiency ratios of 63 percent for banks greater than $1 billion in 1993, which has fallen (improved) to 55 percent at year-end 2003. In contrast, the efficiency ratios for banks less than $1 billion has risen from 65 percent in 1993 to 66 percent on average a decade later.

The average personnel expense per employee and assets per employee are also indicators of efficiency, with lower figures as indicators of more efficiency. Care needs to be taken when comparing these ratios over different types of banks or after mergers of a bank with an investment firm or other type of financial services firm. Different financial services businesses have different average ratios. For instance, investment banks have very highly paid employees that may work eighty hours a week versus less highly paid employees at banks who may work fifty or sixty hours a week, so a comparison between the two would be like comparing apples to oranges, in terms of efficiency. Similarly, an Internet bank would have low assets per employee compared with a bank with a large branching network.

UBPR Risk Ratios

Table 4.6 lists typical risk ratios found in UBPR reports, many mentioned earlier in Chapter 2 for credit risk, liquidity risk, interest rate risk, and capital risk. Rather than thinking of these ratios as something

table 4.6 SELECTED RISK RATIOS FOR DEPOSITORY INSTITUTIONS

I. Credit Risk (Risk of Defaults or Nonpayment on Loans)

A. *Asset Composition or Mix Ratios*

Growth Rate in Loans and Leases = [Current Loans and Leases / Previous Loans and Leases] − 1

Net Loans and Leases to Total Assets = Net Loans and Leases / Assets

Composition of Loan Portfolio (Types of Loans and Diversification) = Loan Type / Loans

B. *Net Loss Rates, Net Charge-offs on Loans, and Noncurrent Loan Rates to Assets*

Net Loss to Average Loans and Leases = Net Losses / Average Loans and Leases

Net Charge-offs to Total Loans and Leases = Net Charge-offs / Loans and Leases

Noncurrent Assets Plus OREO to Assets = (Noncurrent Assets + OREO) / Assets

C. *Provisioning by the Bank for Future Loan Losses*

Loan Loss Provision to Average Loans = Loan Loss Provision / Average Loans

Loan Loss Allowance to Total Loans = Loan Loss Allowance / Loans

Earnings Coverage of Net Losses = Net Operating Income (Before Taxes, Net Security Gains/Losses, Extraordinary Items Plus Provision for Loan and Lease Losses) / Net Loan and Lease Losses

II. Liquidity Risk (Risk of Not Being Able to Meet Upcoming Liabilities of Future Loan Demand)

A. *Asset Indicators: Net loans and Leases to Total Assets = Net Loans and Leases / Total Assets*

Net Loans and Leases to Deposits = Net Loans and Leases / Total Deposits

Short-term Securities to Total Assets = Short-term Securities / Total Assets

Short-term Securities to Volatile Liabilities = Short-term Securities / Noncore Deposits and Borrowed Funds

Growth Rate Short-term (S.T.) Investments = [Current S.T. Investments / Previous S.T. Investments] − 1

Market-to-Book Security Ratio = Market Value of Securities / Book Value of Securities

B. *Liability Indicators: Core Deposits to Total Assets = Total Core (Insured Deposits Less Than $100,000) / Total Assets*

Net Noncore Fund Dependence = (Noncore Liabilities − Short-term Investments) / Long-term Assets

C. *Off-Balance-Sheet Indicators: Outstanding Loan Commitments / Total Assets*
Market Rating on Commercial Paper or Other Types of Debt

III. Capital and Market Indicators (for Liquidity and Capital Risk)

Equity (Tier 1) Capital to Assets = Equity Capital / Total Assets

Growth Rate in Equity Capital = [Current Equity Capital / Previous Equity Capital] − 1

Market Value to Book Value of Equity = Market Value of Equity / Book Value of Equity

Retained Earnings to Average Total Equity = Retained Earnings (Undivided Profits) / Equity

Cash Dividends to Net Income = Cash Dividends / Net Income

IV. Interest Rate Risk (Risk of a Loss in NIM or Market Value with a Change in Interest Rates)

Repricing (Funding) Gap = Repricable Assets − Repricable Liabilities

Rate-sensitive Assets to Rate-sensitive Liabilities = Repricable Assets / Repricable Liabilities

Loans and Securities Over 1 Year = Loans and Securities with Maturities Greater Than 1 Year

Liabilities Over 1 Year = All Liabilities with Maturities Greater Than 1 Year

Net Over 1 Year Position = Loans & Securities over 1 Year − Liabilities Over 1 Year

Net Over 3 Year Position = Loans & Securities over 3 Years − Liabilities Over 3 Years

Volatility of NIM = Standard Deviation of NIM over Time or Subjective Look at Volatility

to memorize, it's better to think of them as ways of looking at bank risk. There are many different measures, and you can choose among them for the most appropriate measures in a given situation.

I. Credit Risk

Credit risk indicators generally consist of three major types of ratios:

A. The Composition of the Bank's Asset Portfolio: Does the bank have a larger loan portfolio (higher loans to assets) and a faster growth rate in loans than peer banks? Since loans have greater credit risk but also have higher rates than other assets, a higher loan-to-asset ratio is an indicator of higher asset utilization but also greater credit risk. It is also an indicator of higher liquidity risk, since the bank will be holding fewer liquid assets. Similarly, higher growth rates in loans may indicate less selectivity in underwriting loans, suggesting greater credit risk. Some types of loans have more credit risk by their nature, such as commercial real estate loans and consumer loans, which may expose banks to higher bad debt losses on average than other types of loans. If a bank has a diversified loan portfolio, it may have lower credit risk. UBPRs have a section analyzing credit allowance and loan mix (as a percentage of total assets and total loans) to examine whether a bank has more or less risky types of loans and diversification.

B. Net Loan Rates, Net Charge-offs on Loans, and Noncurrent Loan Rates to Assets: The UBPR provides an analysis of net loan losses by loan types for a bank that can be compared to peer banks and previous trends. Higher ratios relative to total loans or total assets for a bank's historical loan losses, nonaccruing (not earning interest), or noncurrent loans to assets indicate greater credit risk for different types of loans.

C. Loan Loss Provision, Earnings Coverage, and Loan Loss Allowance Ratios: How much a bank provisions for future loan losses is also an indicator of its protection against future credit risk. If a bank has a larger loan-to-asset ratio than peers or has increased its loan-to-asset ratio, it would be expected to have a larger loan loss allowance to total loans. Similarly, higher earnings coverage for losses provides greater security for the bank that it can cover current and future losses.

II. Liquidity Risk

As shown in Table 4.6 and discussed in Chapter 2, liquidity risk is also generally measured using four different types of ratios measuring liquidity on the asset side, liability side, off-balance-sheet (contingent commitments for liquidity) indicators, and using market value measures. Larger holdings of short-term securities and a higher market value for securities to their book value indicate greater liquidity (lower liquidity risk) on the asset side. A larger percentage of net loans to assets indicates greater liquidity risk, since loans are less liquid assets. Larger holdings of core deposits (insured, more stable deposits) and higher debt ratings indicate lower liquidity risk on the liability side. A larger percentage of off-balance-sheet (contingent) commitments indicate greater off-balance-sheet liquidity risk. To have a good sense of the liquidity risk of a bank, all three sides should be examined.

III. Capital and Market Indicators for Liquidity and Capital Risk

Since banks that are better capitalized are better able to quickly borrow funds for liquidity needs, capital ratios are also often used as measures of liquidity, as well as indicating a bank's capital adequacy, that is, its capital cushion to absorb potential losses. Table 4.6 shows a number of different ratios, including the equity capital to assets ratio (where equity capital generally includes common stock, retained earnings [undivided profits] and preferred stock accounts). Note that some analysts include preferred stock whereas others don't. The growth rate in equity capital compared with the growth rate in assets and the percentage of retained earnings and retained earnings growth rates are frequently used

Concept Questions

1 Why is the NIM affected by a combination of rate, mix, and volume effects? Give an example of a rate effect on the IR%, IE%, and NIM. Give an example of an asset and a liability mix change that could cause the NIM to go down.

2 What does a high efficiency ratio indicate? Why has this ratio improved for banks in the last decade?

3 Why does liquidity risk need to be examined on three sides: asset, liability, and off-balance sheet? Give some examples of risk measure for each.

4 What are some credit risk measures? Capital risk measures? Interest rate risk measures?

as indicators of the building up of capital by a bank. The dividend payout ratio (dividends to net income) is also useful as an indicator of the opposite, with less internal equity capital being built up when the dividend payout ratio is high. For publicly traded firms, the market value to book value is a good ratio, with a higher ratio indicating a greater ability for a bank to raise funds more easily by issuing new common stock (external equity). The larger the other types of risks that a bank holds the higher its capital ratio should be. Chapter 6 discusses capital ratio regulatory requirements in more detail. As noted earlier, the average bank capital ratio in the early 2000s was greater than regulatory requirements.

A Performance and Risk Evaluation Illustrated for Wells Fargo

The best way to learn how to do a performance analysis is to do one. This section presents financial performance data for Wells Fargo in San Francisco, California, from its September 30, 2003 UBPR. Wells Fargo & Company is the fourth largest diversified financial services company in the United States with $391 billion in assets, providing banking, insurance investments, mortgages, and consumer finance from more than 5,400 stores. Wells Fargo also has a leading Internet site for the industry (*http://www.wellsfargo.com*). Wells Fargo experienced more than 1,500 mergers in its 150-year history, including a $31.4 billion merger agreement with Norwest Bank of Minneapolis in 1998. Wells Fargo began a unique branching scheme in 1990, putting 922 mini-branches in supermarkets. Prior to its merger with Norwest, it won a hostile takeover battle for First Interstate Bancorp in 1996. Wells Fargo struggled to integrate its own culture of a traditional, very centralized commercial lending bank with that of First Interstate, a retail bank specializing in consumer lending. Wells Fargo eliminated 12,000 jobs, creating major defections and morale problems for a time. It also lost many customers who were upset about initially poor service during a painful integration. However, in the later 1990s and early 2000s, Wells Fargo created a strong customer service orientation, established a larger branch network in Safeway grocery stores, and established a solid reputation for good service, including excellent online banking services. Wells Fargo has a number of different bank subsidiaries across the Western United States. The sections of a UBPR report (along with some calculations made using information on the report) are for one of Wells Fargo's largest bank subsidiaries, Wells Fargo Bank, National Association in San Francisco, California, with average assets of $224.7 billion in the third quarter of 2003.[3]

Wells Fargo Peer Comparison for 2002 and 2003: DuPont Analysis

As shown at the top of Table 4.7, Wells Fargo had much higher ROEs and ROAs than the Peer average for each year. The equity multiplier was lower in 2002, but much higher in 2003, also contributing to the higher ROE in that year. The higher ROAs were primarily the result of higher net profit margins (NPM) for Wells Fargo than the Peers each year and slightly higher asset utilization ratios.

Earnings and Profitability Analysis: Peer Comparison 2002 and 2003

Looking at the Earnings and Profitability Analysis, which shows the NIM, noninterest revenue %, noninterest expense %, and the PLL%, we can examine the reasons for the higher NPMs and slightly higher asset utilization more closely. Wells Fargo had higher NIMs each year than its peer banks, a lower burden in 2002 (similar burden in 2003), and a lower PLL% each year. Hence, the higher NPMs for Wells Fargo were the result particularly of higher NIMs and lower PLLs each year, and in 2002 a lower burden. We can examine each of these in more detail to see Wells Fargo's strengths and weaknesses.

NIM Overview

Look more closely under the Earnings and Profitability Analysis. Wells Fargo's higher NIMs were the result of a lower interest expense to assets (IE%) ratio each year (2002: 1.02 versus 1.77 percent; 2003: 0.78 versus 1.31 percent). In contrast, Wells Fargo's interest revenue to assets (IR%) ratio was lower in

---

3 Matt Murray. "Norwest, Wells Fargo Agree to a Merger." *The Wall Street Journal* (June 9, 1998), A2, A6; and also see Wells Fargo's Website: *http://www.wellsfargo.com.*

2002 and similar in 2003 to the Peers (2002: 4.85 versus 5.18 percent; 2003: 4.46 versus 4.44 percent). The margin analysis below the Earnings and Profitability Analysis shows Wells Fargo to have a lower percentage of earning assets to average assets than its peers each year (for 2003, 85.79 percent versus 90.34 percent), but a higher average loan rate (interest income to average earning assets). Wells Fargo has a lower percentage of interest-bearing funds (liabilities) to average assets in 2002 (similar in 2003), and a lower average interest expense to average earning assets (2003: 0.91 versus 1.40 percent), explaining its much lower IE% than the Peers. Hence, a key strength of Wells Fargo is its low interest expense to assets, resulting in its higher NIM each year.

Since NIM is a function of rate and mix effects, we can examine these more closely by looking down Table 4.7 to the Yield or Cost Analysis, looking first at Yields on Assets and then Costs of Liabilities and then looking below at the Mix of Assets and Liabilities.

Yields on Assets: The average yield on total loans for Wells Fargo is higher than Peers in 2002 (6.38 versus 6.23 percent), but lower in 2003 (5.38 versus 5.46 percent). Apparently rates fell in 2003, and the

table **4.7** UBPR FOR WELLS FARGO BANK, NATIONAL ASSOCIATION, SAN FRANCISCO, CALIFORNIA, SEPTEMBER 30, 2003

I. Overall Profitability (DuPont Analysis)

	9/30/2003		9/30/2002	
	Bank	**Peer**	**Bank**	**Peer**
Return on equity	26.45%	18.56%	24.06%	18.83%
Return on assets	1.62%	1.29%	1.74%	1.34%
Net profit margin	22.59%	19.88%	22.62%	18.61%
Asset utilization	0.0717	0.0649	0.0805	0.0720
Equity multiplier	16.33	14.39	13.83	14.05

Earnings and Profitability Analysis	9/30/2003		9/30/2002		
	Bank	**Peer**	**Bank**	**Peer**	
Percent of Average Assets					
Interest income (TE):	4.46	4.44	4.85	5.18	IR%
− interest expense	0.78	1.31	1.02	1.77	IE%
Net interest income (TE):	3.68	3.13	3.83	3.41	**NIM%**
+ noninterest income	2.71	2.05	3.20	2.05	NIR%
− noninterest expense	3.65	3.02	4.05	3.07	NIE%
Burden	0.94	0.97	0.85	1.02	**Burden%**
− provision loan losses	0.19	0.30	0.19	0.44	**PLL%**
= pretax operating income	2.55	1.86	2.79	1.95	Pretax operating ROA%
+ net gains/losses securities	0.03	0.09	0.05	0.10	
= net pretax operating income	2.58	1.95	2.84	2.05	Pretax ROA after sec. gains & losses
Net income after taxes & adjmts.	1.62	1.29	1.74	1.34	ROA%

table 4.7 UBPR FOR WELLS FARGO BANK, NATIONAL ASSOCIATION, SAN FRANCISCO, CALIFORNIA, SEPTEMBER 30, 2003 (CONT.)

	9/30/2003		9/30/2002	
Margin Analysis	**Bank**	**Peer**	**Bank**	**Peer**
Ave. earning assets to average assets	85.79	90.34	80.12	90.07
Ave. int.-bearing funds to average assets	80.99	81.34	71.95	80.40
Interest income to average earning assets	5.20	4.92	6.05	5.76
Interest expense to average earning assets	0.91	1.40	1.28	1.94
Net interest income to average earning assets	4.29	3.47	4.78	3.80

Yield or Cost of Analysis

	9/30/2003		9/30/2002	
Yield on Assets	**Bank**	**Peer**	**Bank**	**Peer**
Total loans & leases	5.38	5.46	6.38	6.23
Real estate	5.14	5.49	5.98	6.42
Commercial & industrial	6.55	5.21	7.63	5.72
Consumer (Individual)	5.73	6.41	6.57	7.31
Agricultural	3.82	4.47	4.59	5.09
Total investment securities	7.14	4.52	7.17	5.63
Cost of (interest rate paid on):				
Total int.-bearing deposits	.82	1.31	1.17	1.91
Transaction deposits	0.17	0.74	1.21	0.95
Other savings deposits	0.42	0.72	0.68	1.11
Time deposits over $100M	1.31	2.48	2.20	3.15
All other time deposits	2.20	2.83	2.86	3.60
Fed fund purchased & repos	1.14	1.26	1.71	1.82
Other borrowed money	0.99	3.09	1.91	3.96
Subord. notes & debentures	2.73	3.29	3.12	3.39
All interest-bearing funds	0.97	1.55	1.42	2.19

Analysis of Noninterest Expense	9/30/2003		9/30/2002	
Percent of Average Assets	**Bank**	**Peer**	**Bank**	**Peer**
Personnel expense	2.18	1.43	2.15	1.45
Occupancy expense	0.42	0.39	0.50	0.40
Other operating expense	1.06	1.19	1.40	1.22
Total overhead expense	**3.65**	**3.04**	**4.05**	**3.09**
Overhead − noninterest income	**0.93**	**0.93**	**0.85**	**1.02**
Efficiency ratio	**57.09**	**58.04**	**57.63**	**56.74**
Ave. person. exp./empl. ($000)	73.25	62.99	59.90	61.22
Assets per employee ($M)	3.66	4.83	3.15	4.92

table 4.7 UBPR FOR WELLS FARGO BANK, NATIONAL ASSOCIATION, SAN FRANCISCO, CALIFORNIA, SEPTEMBER 30, 2003 (CONT.)

Asset and Liability Mix Analysis (% Balance Sheet Composition)

Assets, Percent of Average Assets	9/30/2003 Bank	9/30/2003 Peer	9/30/2002 Bank	9/30/2002 Peer
Net loans and leases	**77.13**	**58.79**	**67.55**	**60.66**
Loan mix % average gross loans & leases				
Construction & development	3.25	5.11	4.68	5.18
1-4 family residential	58.72	30.64	42.35	27.44
Home equity loans	12.94	6.72	6.05	5.52
Other real estate loans	11.01	15.50	16.40	14.22
Total real estate	**72.98**	**53.76**	**63.43**	**49.37**
Financial institution loans	0.41	1.84	0.50	1.41
Agricultural loans	1.53	0.40	2.27	0.40
Commercial & industrial loans	14.53	19.85	21.99	22.24
Loans to individuals	6.90	9.88	5.88	9.87
Credit card loans	0.00	0.70	0.03	0.62
Municipal loans	0.12	0.36	0.14	0.38
Foreign office loans & leases	0.01	1.65	0.02	1.92
All other loans	0.99	2.43	1.27	2.63
Lease financing receivables	2.54	3.49	4.90	3.98
Interest-bearing bank balances	0.82	1.30	2.94	0.95
Federal funds sold & resales	0.40	3.58	0.73	4.25
Trading account assets	3.51	1.31	3.21	1.35
Held-to-maturity securities	0.00	0.72	0.00	0.52
Available for sale securities	3.49	19.55	4.32	17.23
Total earnings assets	85.35	88.77	78.75	88.55
Noninterest cash and due from banks	4.22	3.60	5.45	3.65
Premises, fixed assets & CAP leases	0.78	1.02	1.09	1.03
Other real estate owned	0.04	0.05	0.06	0.04
Acceptances & other assets	9.61	6.41	14.66	6.50
Total nonearning assets	14.65	11.23	21.25	11.45

average loan rate fell more for Wells Fargo than for the Peers. In 2002 and 2003, Wells Fargo earned a much lower average rate for real estate, consumer, and agricultural loans than Peers, but a higher average rate for commercial and industrial loans, and investment securities.

Cost of (Interest Paid on) Liability Rates: For deposits, the average rate on interest-bearing deposits and all interest-bearing funds was generally much lower than the Peers, as are the rates on each type of deposits, explaining Wells Fargo's low interest expense to assets. With a Aaa credit rating, even uninsured liabilities have low rates.

table 4.7   UBPR FOR WELLS FARGO BANK, NATIONAL ASSOCIATION, SAN FRANCISCO, CALIFORNIA, SEPTEMBER 30, 2003 (CONT.)

Liability Mix Analysis

Liabilities, Percent of Avg. Assets	9/30/2003		9/30/2002	
	Bank	Peer	Bank	Peer
Demand deposits	4.09	7.22	10.22	7.62
All NOW & ATS accounts	0.39	1.53	0.41	1.29
Money market deposit accounts	13.56	24.05	14.93	22.09
Other savings deposits	18.94	9.56	18.19	8.93
Time dep. less than $100M	2.57	8.98	3.86	10.00
Core deposits	**39.54**	**54.70**	**47.61**	**55.03**
Time dep. of $100M or more	11.44	6.68	5.66	6.78
Deposits in foreign offices	8.78	4.26	5.73	4.31
Total deposits	59.76	67.52	59.00	66.31
Federal funds purchased & repos	15.54	9.04	14.45	8.81
Total fed home loan borrowings	0.00	3.81	0.00	4.06
Total other borrowings	8.70	4.77	7.11	5.74
Short-term noncore funding	41.03	22.24	29.62	24.18
Acceptances & other liabilities	3.71	3.16	4.84	3.14
Total liabilities	87.71	90.29	85.39	90.12
Subordinated notes & debentures	2.97	1.25	3.39	1.40
All common & preferred equity capital	9.32	8.32	11.22	8.32

Asset and Liability Mix Analysis (% Balance Sheet Composition)

Analyzing mix differences between Wells Fargo and the Peers for respectively assets and liabilities can also help to explain Wells Fargo's lower IR% but higher IE%.

Asset Mix: Wells Fargo has much larger percentage of net loans and leases than Peers (2002: 67.55 versus 60.66 percent; 2003: 77.13 versus 58.79 percent), despite its earlier lower percentage of earning assets). By having lower average loan rates, Wells Fargo appears to be attracting a larger volume of loans relative to assets. Examining the loan mix, we see that Wells Fargo has predominantly real estate loans (2002: 63.43 versus 49.37 percent; 2003: 72.98 versus 53.76 percent for Peers), and particularly a much larger percentage of home mortgage (1-4 family residential) loans (2002: 42.35 versus 27.44 percent; 2003: 58.72 versus 30.64 percent). Home mortgage loans have lower default risk and also lower interest rates, and are subject to greater loan prepayments and refinancing by customers to lower rates when interest rates fall. With falling rates in 2002 and 2003, Wells Fargo may have had such refinancing, contributing to its lower IR% than Peers in 2002.

Liability Mix Analysis: In terms of liability mix, Wells Fargo surprisingly has a less favorable mix than its peers, with a lower percentage of core deposits (2002: 47.61 percent versus 55.03 percent; 2003; 39.54 versus 54.70 percent). However, its core deposit mix is very favorable with a large percentage of savings deposits that pay relatively lower rates. In 2002, Wells Fargo had a larger percentage of demand deposits that do not pay interest, as well. Given its larger percentage of noncore deposits, Wells Fargo's lower IE% appears to be predominantly the result of its much lower rates offered on deposits, rather than a favorable mix effect relative to Peers. By being a home mortgage lender, Wells Fargo may be better able to maintain less interest rate sensitive customers that are willing to accept lower interest rates in return for the convenience of supermarket branches and benefits of having their home mortgage (with favorable rates) and deposit accounts at the same bank.

Burden

Returning back up to the top of the table to the Earnings and Profitability Analysis, we can examine the burden more closely by looking at the noninterest revenue to assets (NIR%) and noninterest expense to assets (NIE%). Wells Fargo had a significantly higher NIR% each year than Peers (2002: 3.20 versus 2.05 percent; 2003: 2.71 versus 2.05 percent). However, its NIE% was significantly higher than the Peers each year (2002: 4.05 versus 3.07 percent; 2003: 3.65 versus 3.02 percent). The net effect was a lower burden percentage in 2002 and similar burden in 2003 (2002: 0.85 versus 1.02; 2003: 0.94 versus 0.97) than the Peers. Wells Fargo has a strength in higher NIR%, but a weakness in its higher NIE%. Often to generate higher noninterest revenues, a bank will have higher noninterest expenses. An analysis of noninterest expenses further down the table can help us to analyze these differences. Personnel expense, particularly, is much higher each year for Wells Fargo (2002: 2.15 versus 1.45 percent; 2003: 2.18 versus 1.43 percent). Overhead expenses less noninterest income is, however, lower for Wells Fargo in 2002 and similar to the Peers in 2003. The efficiency ratio is similar each year to the Peers. With Wells Fargo's strategy of having thousands of banks in grocery stores, assets per employee is lower for Wells Fargo than the Peers each year (2002: 3.15 versus 4.92; 2003: 3.66 versus 4.83). The average personnel expense per employee is much higher in 2003, emphasizing higher personnel costs as a weakness or perhaps a part of the cost of its strategy of generating higher noninterest revenues, resulting in a similar overall burden percentage to Peers in 2003.

Risk Comparison with Peers

Table 4.8 provides a risk comparison with Peers from various UBPR ratios.

Credit Risk

Credit risk, as noted in Chapter 2, involves looking at the provisions and loan allowance that the bank has taken in relationship to how risky its loan portfolio is. The percentage of loans its has, its loan growth rate, and the type (mix) of loans it has helps to determine its overall credit risk. Actual net loan losses also indicate how well it has been doing in managing its loan portfolio and underwriting credit risks. As noted above, in analyzing asset mix, Wells Fargo has a much larger percentage of net loans and leases and a much higher growth rate in loans than the Peers, but it also has a larger percentage of home mortgage (a less risky mix of loans). Hence, Wells Fargo appears to be able to take a lower loss provision and loan loss allowance to loans than the Peers each year. Although not shown, the UBPR report contains additional pages that show loan losses, noncurrent, and nonaccrual loans by loan type. The largest loan losses and noncurrent loans generally occur for construction and land development loans, followed by commercial real estate loans, loans to individuals, commercial loans, and home real estate loans. By having a lower percentage of more risky loans, Wells Fargo can take a lower provision for loan losses. Wells Fargo also has a higher earnings coverage to net loans ratio than Peers. Thus, its credit risk exposure seems comparable to the Peers.

Liquidity Risk

Wells Fargo is more loaned up than its peers and it holds a lower percentage of securities to assets. Short-term assets relative to short-term liabilities and to noncore deposits (uninsured liabilities) are lower than the Peers. Thus, on the asset side Wells Fargo has greater liquidity risk. On the liability side, Wells Fargo also has greater liquidity risk with higher dependence on noncore deposits (uninsured financing) and a larger percentage of short-term liabilities to assets than Peers. On the office-balance sheet side, Wells Fargo has a larger percentage of outstanding loan and lease commitments than Peers, suggesting greater off-balance-sheet liquidity risk. Wells Fargo, as an entire holding company, does have good access to future borrowing on the liability side with an excellent bank debt rating by Moody's Investor Service of Aaa. As noted in the off-balance-sheet section at the end of the table, Wells Fargo is heavily engaged in securitization activities (pooling loans together and packaging them as securities that are sold to the public as pass-through, mortgage securities). Securitization activities provide servicing and fee income and additional liquidity for Wells Fargo.

table 4.8   WELLS FARGO UBPR SELECTED RISK RATIO COMPARISONS

	9/30/2003		9/30/2002	
	Bank	**Peer**	**Bank**	**Peer**
I. Credit Risk				
Net loans and leases to assets	76.89	58.77	69.63	60.15
Growth rate in loans and leases	49.39	8.46	38.99	9.83
Loss provision to average assets	0.19	0.32	0.18	0.45
Net loss to average loans & leases	0.30	0.49	0.43	0.69
Loan loss allowance to loans & leases	0.73	1.54	1.14	1.56
Loan loss allowance to net losses	2.60	3.73	3.05	2.83
Loan loss to nonaccrual loans & leases	1.84	2.19	2.13	1.86
Earnings coverage of net loans & leases	11.56	9.26	10.00	7.57
II. Liquidity Risk				
Net loans and leases to assets	76.89	58.77	69.63	60.15
Net loans and leases to deposits	124.10	87.34	111.70	92.63
Short-term assets to S.T. liabs.	79.54	104.48	95.24	91.22
Short-term invs. to S.T. noncore funds	11.76	43.74	11.34	34.74
Net noncore fund dependence	54.01	32.31	42.37	34.68
Net S.T. liabs. to assets	9.46	3.05	1.76	4.15
Brokered deposits to deposits	25.14	3.15	11.39	3.43
Outstanding loan & lease commitments	31.26	29.18	35.49	28.55
Moody's Investor Service: Wells Fargo Bank debt rating raised in 2002 to "Aaa."				
III. Capital Risk				
Tier 1 (equity capital) to assets	6.12	6.95	7.23	7.12
Cash dividends to net income	19.98	57.69	49.63	62.98
Retained earnings to total equity	14.17	5.71	7.70	4.42
Growth rate in equity capital	24.31	8.81	17.79	13.48
Growth rate in assets	35.28	7.74	28.28	13.24

	9/30/2003		9/30/2002	
	Bank	**Peer**	**Bank**	**Peer**
V. Interest Rate Risk Ratios				
Total loans & securities > 15 years	5.24	8.26	3.17	8.42
Total loans & securities 5 to 15 years	15.51	11.46	14.78	10.30
Loans & securities over 3 years	30.28	34.49	25.40	30.90
Liabilities over 3 years	0.83	4.05	0.36	4.13
Net 3-year position	29.46	29.81	25.05	26.46
Loans & securities over 1 year	36.08	46.12	27.98	42.46
Liabilities over 1 year	1.38	9.68	1.17	10.04
Net over 1-year position	34.71	35.78	26.81	31.91

| table | 4.8 | WELLS FARGO UBPR SELECTED RISK RATIO COMPARISONS (CONTINUED) |

Off-Balance-Sheet Items

Outstanding as % of Total	9/30/2003		9/30/2002	
Total Off-Balance-Sheet Items ($000)	**$251,845,000**		**$222,978,000**	
	Bank	**Peer**	**Bank**	**Peer**
Outstanding loan & lease commitments	31.26	29.18	35.49	28.55
Standby letters of credit	2.63	3.66	2.90	3.88
Assets securitized or sold with recourse	74.10	4.26	91.09	4.68
Amount of recourse exposure	0.07	0.27	0.02	0.29
Credit Derivatives Banks as Beneficiary	0.64	0.83	0.73	0.42
All Other Off-Balance-Sheet Items	2.83	5.19	3.17	5.14
Total Off-Balance-Sheet Items to Assets	112.24	52.58	134.44	51.41
Securitization Activities % Total Assets	71.21	91.06	76.94	92.45
% securitization 1–4 family residential loans	67.71	85.45	72.91	84.47
Derivatives contracts notional amounts to total assets	325.64%		665.29%	
Interest rate contracts %	316.98%		657.71%	
Foreign exchange contracts %	8.05%		6.97%	
Equity, commodity, & other contracts %	0.62%		0.62%	
Futures and forward contracts %	134.765%		179.67%	
Swaps %	38.75%		45.88%	
Derivative contracts 1 year or less	163.83%		331.64%	

Capital Risk

The equity capital to assets entry shows that Wells Fargo was better capitalized than the Peers in 2002, but had a lower equity capital to assets ratio in 2003 (2002: 7.23 percent versus 7.12 percent; 2003: 6.12 percent versus 6.95 percent). Wells Fargo has been building up internal equity as indicated by its lower dividend payout ratio, higher retained earnings to total equity ratio, and higher growth rate in equity capital than Peers each year. Wells Fargo's growth rate in assets, however, was much larger than its growth rate in equity capital, resulting in a decline in equity to assets in 2003. Wells Fargo's capital risk appears to be somewhat higher than the Peers. However, by being one of the nation's largest banks and having securitization activities, a higher credit rating, and predominantly home mortgage loans, Wells Fargo's managers may feel that its capitalization can be lower than the Peers. In addition to equity capital ratios, regulators also use risk-based capital ratios, discussed in Chapter 6.

Interest Rate Risk

By holding predominantly home mortgage securities, which customers generally prefer to have as longer-term, fixed rate loans, Wells Fargo is likely to have significant interest rate exposure to rising rates (a fall in the market value of fixed rate loans when interest rates rise) and prepayment risk when interest rates fall (the risk of customers prepaying loans to refinance at lower interest rates). Compared to the interest rate risk ratios of Peers, Wells Fargo has a larger percentage of loans and securities with maturities of five to fifteen years, but a lower percentage of really long-term assets with maturities greater than fifteen years. The UBPR compares the percentage of loans and securities and respectively liabilities held with different maturities (> 15 years, 5 to 15 years, > 3 years). It also shows the net 3-year and 1-year position (difference in total assets and liabilities over three years and one year, respectively), i.e., a type of maturity gap. If this net position is positive, the bank has a greater percentage of long-term assets versus long-term liabilities, comparable to a negative repricing gap (or, what we'll talk about later in the text, a positive maturity or duration gap), indicating risk of a lower NIM if interest rates rise. Both Wells Fargo and Peers have positive net positions, indicating exposure to risk of lower profits if interest rates rise, typical of banks holding a large percentage of home mortgage loans. Wells Fargo's positions are slightly lower than the Peers in both years.

Off-Balance-Sheet Activities That Reduce Interest Rate and Liquidity Risk

The off-balance-sheet items in the lower part of Table 4.8 show that Wells Fargo has a large percentage of securitization activities relative to total assets, as mentioned earlier under liquidity risk. By removing fixed rate assets through securitizations, its interest rate and liquidity risk are also reduced.

Interest Rate Derivative Off-Balance-Sheet (OBS) Items

Although Wells Fargo has high interest rate risk as a home mortgage lender, in addition to securitization activities and loan sales activities that reduce this risk and increase liquidity, Wells Fargo (and other banks) engage in hedging activities with derivatives. As mentioned in Chapter 1, derivatives include futures, forwards, and swaps, which will be discussed in more detail later in the text. Basically, a bank takes a derivative position with interest rate futures that produce a gain to offset a loss if interest rates go in an unfavorable direction. Forward and swap arrangements ensure against losses that could occur with interest rate changes. As noted at the bottom of Table 4.8, Wells Fargo has a large percentage of off-balance-sheet interest rate contracts. Although large banks also serve as dealers for contracts for customers, it is likely that many of these contracts are set up by Wells Fargo for hedging purposes, that is, to reduce its interest rate risk. Other credit derivatives, also among Wells Fargo's off-balance-sheet items, provide gains in the event of credit losses to reduce credit risk as well. As noted earlier in the text, often very large banks serve as dealers for interest rate and credit derivatives, increasing their operational risk, as well as using these for their own hedging purposes. A summary of OBS items is found in Appendix 4A.

State Peer Bank Comparison

UBPRs also give state bank comparisons for the earnings and profitability analysis, margin analysis, loan and lease analysis, liquidity, capitalization, and growth rates. These comparisons are brief, but allow a comparison to peers in a bank's state that are facing the same economic conditions. This comparison can be a little biased, since a bank like Wells Fargo would be larger compared to all banks in California, large and small. If you look up Wells Fargo in San Francisco's UBPR, you'll see this one-page analysis on page 22 (always toward the back of the UBPR). On average, Californian banks had a much lower ROA of 0.97 in 2002 and 1.08 in 2003, with higher NIMs each year (2002: 4.38 and 2003: 4.16 percent), similar PLL%s, but much higher burdens (2002: 2.81; 2003: 2.63 percent) with very low noninterest income to assets (2002: 0.97; 2003: 0.99 percent) compared with Wells Fargo. State bank averages showed lower liquidity and capital risk with larger percentages of short-term securities and core deposits and higher equity to capital ratios. From this comparison, Wells Fargo as one of the largest banks in the United States appears to be a different animal on average, by offering diverse products and generating a large part of its revenues from noninterest activities.

Summary of Analysis of Wells Fargo's Performance and Risk Relative to the Peer Average

Wells Fargo has performed better than the Peer average in 2003 and 2002 with a higher ROE resulting from a higher ROA each year and higher EM in 2003. The higher ROA is the result of a higher NPM and also a slightly higher asset utilization ratio. The higher NPM is the result of a higher NIM, slightly

Concept Questions

1 What type of risks does Wells Fargo have as a home mortgage lender? How has Wells Fargo attempted to reduce these risks?

2 What advantages on the deposit side does Wells Fargo have as a home mortgage lender?

3 Do a trend performance analysis to determine the reason for the rise in Wells Fargo's ROE, but fall in ROA from 2002 to 2003. Do a careful analysis of the trends in NIM, looking at rate and mix effects, as well as a careful analysis of the burden, PLL, and net gains and losses on securities.

4 Do a risk analysis for the trends in Wells Fargo's risk between 2002 and 2003. Were there any changes in liquidity, interest rate, credit, capital, operational costs, or off-balance-sheet risks? Try these first without peeking at the answers that will be discussed in the following section.

lower burden, and lower PLL. The higher NIM is the result of significantly lower interest expenses to assets for Wells Fargo. Although Wells Fargo is more loaned up than Peers, it offers on average lower loan rates and much lower deposit rates. Wells Fargo also generated higher noninterest revenues to assets that offset higher noninterest expense to assets, with higher personnel costs to assets. Wells Fargo is predominantly a home mortgage lender; hence, it has considerable interest rate risk and liquidity risk, but lower credit risk. By engaging in securitization and hedging activities, Wells Fargo appears to be reducing (taking a risk management approach) to lower these risks. Relative to Peer banks, its risks seem comparable, although Wells Fargo has greater liquidity and capital risk by holding fewer liquid assets and having a lower percentage of noncore liabilities, along with a lower equity capital to assets ratio. On the liability side, Wells Fargo has an excellent credit rating for short-term borrowing, as a source of ready liquidity. Wells Fargo also has more outstanding loan commitments, suggesting greater off-balance-sheet liquidity risk than Peers.

Trend Analysis for Wells Fargo in 2002 and 2003

Explaining the Lower ROA

You have probably tried to do a trend analysis to answer Concept Question 4. We'll now walk through a final quick trend analysis using Tables 4.7 and 4.8. Wells Fargo's ROE rose in 2003, just because of a higher equity multiplier, since its ROA fell from 1.74 to 1.62 percent in 2003. The lower ROA was the result of lower asset utilization (fall from 0.0805 to 0.0717) and a very small change in the NPM (from 22.62 to 22.59 percent). Although these changes are small, given a small ROA any small change can have a big effect on ROA. Examining the earnings and profitability analysis, the NIM fell from 3.83 in 2002 to 3.68 percent in 2003. The burden rose slightly from 0.85 percent in 2002 to 0.94 percent in 2003, as the result of a larger decline in noninterest revenue to assets relative to the fall in noninterest expenses to assets. The PLL% remained steady. There was also a slight drop in the net securities gain to assets in 2003, all adding up to the 0.12 percent, or 12-basis-point, drop in ROA. The Analysis of Noninterest Expense shows that overall total overhead expenses to assets fell in 2003, but overhead relative to non-interest income rose slightly with a larger fall in noninterest revenue to assets. In 2003, occupancy expenses to assets went down, but personnel expense, average personnel expense to employee, and assets per employee rose.

The Decline in the NIM

The margin analysis shows a rise in average earning assets to average assets but also a larger rise in average interest-bearing funds to average assets. The average rate on earning assets fell from 6.05 percent in 2002 to 5.20 in 2003 (85 basis points), while the average interest expense to earning assets only fell from 1.28 percent in 2002 to 0.91 in 2003 (37 basis points), resulting in the lower NIM. Apparently, interest rates fell during this period, but rates fell more on liabilities than assets on average. The Yield or Cost Analysis further down Table 4.7 shows that the average rates on loans fell as did the average rates on interest-bearing deposits, but the average rates on loans fell by a larger amount.

Examining the changes in the Composition of Assets for mix changes, we see that total net loans and leases rose in 2003, a positive mix effect, with the largest rise for real estate loans, particularly home mortgage and home equity loans, while the percentage of commercial and industrial loans fell. Despite the increase in the percentage of loans, the fall in loan rates, particularly with a drop in the average real estate loan from 5.98 percent in 2002 to 5.14 percent in 2003 (84 basis points) resulted in the lower IR%. Customers may have been refinancing loans at lower rates during this period, resulting in this large fall.

Comparing mix changes in liabilities under margin analysis, the percentage of interest-bearing funds to assets rose for Wells Fargo in 2003, which would have a dampening effect on interest expense to assets under liability mix. The percentage of core deposits also fell in 2003, with a particularly large decline in the percentage of demand deposits, the cheapest type of deposits. Apparently, the interest rate on assets fell more than the interest rate on liabilities (despite any positive mix effects and with some negative mix effects on the liability side), resulting in the net decline in the NIM. Given Wells Fargo's large percentage of home mortgage loans, it's likely that considerable refinancing by customers at this time contributed to its lower IR% at this time with falling rates, despite its overall negative refinancing gap, which would benefit from falling rates.

Trends in Risk Ratios

Trends in risk ratios in Table 4.8 suggest a slight rise in credit risk, with a larger percentage of loans to assets, a more rapid growth rate in loans, and a lower loan loss allowance to loans. However, the earnings coverage to loan losses ratio rose and the net loss to average loans fell. With the larger percentage of net loans and leases to assets (also net loans and leases to deposits) and a lower percentage of short-term investments, liquidity risk on the asset side rose in 2003 as well. Noncore fund dependence also rose, as did the percentage of brokered deposits, indicating greater liquidity risk on the liability side as well. Outstanding loan loss commitments fell, suggesting slightly lower off-balance-sheet risk. With a lower equity capital to assets ratio (higher equity multiplier) in 2003, capital risk also rose, although the internal growth rate in equity rose with a lower dividend payout and higher retained earnings to total equity. The growth rate in assets less the growth rate in equity capital provided a similar figure, somewhat over 10 percent in both years, indicating a reduction in equity financing each year. In terms of interest rate risk, the net one-year and three-year positions were both a bit larger in 2003, indicating a slight rise in Wells Fargo's negative repricing gap (positive maturity gap) position.

Summary of Trends

Wells Fargo's trend from 2002 to 2003 shows a fall in ROA due to a fall in its NIM with a fall in interest rates, resulting in a larger fall in the average rate on assets versus the average rate in deposits. This may reflect loan prepayments and refinancing by Wells Fargo customers for the home mortgage loans that Wells Fargo specializes in. While the provision for loan losses to assets remained stable, the burden percentage rose slightly with a larger decline in noninterest revenue to assets than noninterest expense to assets. Wells Fargo's liquidity, credit, interest rate, and capital risk indicators also showed a slight rise in all risks that managers should watch carefully. Overall, however, Wells Fargo performed very well with a very high ROE, ROA, and NPM, as well as a very good NIM, low burden, and low provision for loan losses compared to Peers. It's worth noting that the Peer ROA fell much more than Wells Fargo's in 2003, suggesting that the drop in ROA for Wells Fargo may have partly reflected economic conditions facing all very large U.S. banks.

Summary

Financial performance evaluation for a depository institution is a multifaceted procedure involving ratio analysis, common size financial statements, trend analysis, and consideration of additional data not always found in published financial reports. Analysts look behind the reported numbers, because financial statements are prepared using accounting rules that may disguise important developments. Relationships among different financial ratios and between financial and nonfinancial data must also be considered.

Integrated models, such as the DuPont analysis model presented in Figure 4.8, help observers to analyze and determine exactly why a bank's performance has improved or deteriorated in comparison to peers or its own past record. Return on equity is decomposed as a function of a bank's cost management (as measured by its net profit margin), its revenue management (as measured by its asset utilization), and its financial leverage (as measured by its equity multi-

plier). Further analysis of net profit margin can pinpoint cost problems by focusing on net interest margin, burden, and provision for loan losses as a percentage of total assets or revenues. A bank's net interest margin can be examined more closely by reviewing its asset mix and the yields it earns on assets, both determinants of interest revenue to assets, and its liability mix and rates paid, which determine its interest expense to assets.

Trend analysis shows whether the depository's performance has changed over time, a judgment as important as knowing the current position of the institution. Analysts should also look at off-balance-sheet items that may affect projections of future performance.

This chapter focused on commercial banks. However, the financial analysis methods discussed apply also to thrifts (savings and loans and savings banks) and to credit unions (CUs). Thrifts and CUs will be discussed in greater detail next in Chapter 5.

Questions

1. Randi Briscoe asks you the following questions. Please answer them for Randi. What are the major sources of revenues and expenses for banks? What are a bank's major assets and liabilities? How has the composition of bank assets and liabilities changed over time?

2. Laura Clifton is curious about Fed Funds and asks you the following questions. Please answer. What are Fed Funds purchased and Fed Funds sold? What are repos? If the Fed Funds rate is high, what does this condition imply about banks' need for short-term funds?

3. Dave Bailey asks you the following questions: What are provisions for loan losses on a bank's income statement and how is this related to the bank's allowance for loan losses on its balance sheet, i.e., how is the allowance for loan losses adjusted each year?

4. Eddie Greenberg wants to know what types of loans banks typically hold on their balance sheets. Why do real estate loans expose banks to more interest rate risk than other loans?

5. Dave Ingram would like to know about bank deposits. What types of deposits does a bank accept? What are the differences between NOW accounts, business checking accounts, MMDAs, retail CDs, jumbo CDs, and negotiable CDs? What is the difference between core deposits and volatile (noncore) liabilities?

6. Liz Ingram is interested in overall bank profitability. How do a bank's NPM, AU, and EM interact to affect its ROE? What do each of these figures indicate about a bank's management? Why did bank's ROEs improve in the late 1990s and early 2000s? Why did banks' EMs fall in the early 1990s? What effect does an EM fall have on ROE?

7. Tom Tomori and David Walsh ask you to explain the DuPont analysis method laid out in Figure 4.8 for analyzing a bank's profitability. Explain what indicators an analyst considers to evaluate a bank's profitability.

8. Marcella and Michael Moy ask you to explain how rate, mix, and volume of assets and liabilities affect a bank's NIM.

9. Explain to Chris North what the key components are to look for in analyzing a bank's NPM.

10. Explain to Ed Kramer what the different types of risks for a bank are and how they can be analyzed.

11. Joel and Paula Mazzoline ask why enhancing operating efficiency gained importance in recent years. Explain. What is the efficiency ratio? What does a bank's efficiency ratio tell an analyst?

Problems

1. First Caroline Bank and Trust Company has this year-end financial data for the most recent period: ROA, 0.99 percent; ROE, 12.57 percent; net income, $11,798,000.
   a. Calculate the bank's equity multiplier and equity-to-assets ratio.
   b. Calculate the bank's total assets and equity.
   c. Suppose that the bank increases total liabilities by $10 million and reduces equity by the same amount. Given a higher interest expense, suppose net income goes down by $35 million. What will be the new ROE? What do these changes reveal about the impact of financial leverage?

2. The board of directors of The First National Bank of Sydney Elizabeth have approved these target rates of return for shareholders:

   - Target ROE: 16 percent
   - Target EM: 12
   - Tax Rate (t): 35 percent
   - Total assets: $850 million

   - Interest expense: $80 million
   - Net noninterest expense: $11.5 million
   - Provision for loan losses: $1 million

   a. What should be the bank's target NIM for the planning period?
   b. What target interest revenues must First National earn to meet its financial goals?
   c. Suppose interest expenses rise 10 percent above target. What return on equity will the bank actually earn?

3. Alby Singleton, a management trainee at Bank Sussman in San Francisco, is to examine the institution's ROE under the following conditions: NIM, 4.2 percent; EM, 11; marginal tax rate, 35 percent; total assets, $1,750 million; burden, $40 million; provision for loan loss, $0.
   a. What will be the bank's ROE?
   b. If the bank's board of directors decides to increase the equity multiplier to 12 and hold other factors constant, what will be the expected ROE?

4. Terrell Savings Bank is preparing a financial plan based on the following data: target ROE, 15 percent; tax rate (t), 35%; total assets, $700 million; total liabilities, $640 million; provision for loan losses, $1 million.

   a. What is the bank's current equity multiplier?

   b. Given this EM, what before-tax income must the bank earn to reach its target ROE?

   c. What is the bank's NIM, assuming that the burden is 1.1 percent of total assets?

5. The board of directors of the Oakleigh-Elizabeth Regional Bank has requested a presentation on the relationship between financial leverage and return on equity. The bank has assets of $2 billion and an equity multiplier of 10. Net income in the coming year is expected to be between 1.2 percent and 2.0 percent of total assets.

   a. At the bank's current capital level, what is the expected range for ROE?

   b. The new chief financial officer (CFO) hopes to persuade the directors to operate aggressively by increasing the equity multiplier to 12. If they do, interest expense will rise because of the increased reliance on borrowed funds. The estimated range of ROA changes runs from a low of 0.5 percent to a high of 1.9 percent. What will be the resulting range for ROE?

   c. Based on these estimates, what recommendation should the directors follow?

6. Roscoe-Yuko Savings Bank, a savings bank in New York, has total assets of $500 million and an equity multiplier of 10. A competitor of equal size has 8 percent equity to assets. Both managers are estimating returns, and both forecast interest revenues ranging from 7 percent to 13 percent of total assets. Interest costs for both firms are expected to average 9 percent of total liabilities. Both banks have a burden to assets ratio of 1.5% and PLL to assets ratio of 0.40%, and a marginal tax rate of 30%.

   a. Calculate the potential range of net income and ROE for each bank.

   b. Graph the relationship between IR/TA and ROE for each bank.

   c. Which shareholders would be better off in an economic downturn? Which owners would benefit in a strong economy?

   d. If shareholders placed a high probability on earning interest revenues equal to 13 percent of total assets, which capitalization plan should they prefer?

7. Do a financial analysis for First National Bank of Maryland compared with its peers in 1994, given the information in Table P4.1, and a risk analysis compared with its peers using Table P4.2. Be sure to do a detailed analysis as in the chapter example. Also do a trend analysis for 1993 and 1994.

8. Do the same analysis for Nations Bank using Tables P4.3 and P4.4.

Case/Web Exercise

Look up the UBPR for a bank you are interested in at *http://www.ffiec.gov.* Do a financial and risk analysis for the bank compared with its peers and a trend analysis for the last two years. If you don't have a particular bank in mind, try JPMorgan Chase in New York City, New York, or CoBiz, a bank holding company in Denver, Colorado.

table   **P4.1**   SUMMARY PERFORMANCE RATIO MEASURES EXAMPLE FOR FIRST NATIONAL BANK OF MARYLAND, SEPTEMBER 30, 1993 AND 1994

	1994	Peers	1993	Peers
Overall Profitability Ratios				
Return on equity (net income to equity)	15.25%	17.26%	18.80%	17.32%
Return on assets (net income to assets)	1.02%	1.30%	1.13%	1.28%
Equity multiplier (assets to equity)	14.95	13.28	16.64	13.53
Common Size Income Statement to Assets				
Interest revenue (tax equivalent)	6.21%	6.61%	6.47%	6.76%
Interest expense	2.34	2.57	2.30	2.49
Net interest margin (NIM)	**3.87**	**4.04**	**4.17**	**4.27**
Noninterest revenue	1.96	1.62	1.80	1.66
Noninterest expense	4.34	3.67	4.05	3.79
Types of noninterest expenses				
Personnel expense	2.44	1.46	2.23	1.49
Occupancy expense	0.74	0.44	0.69	0.46
Other operating expense	1.17	1.66	1.13	1.74
Burden	**2.38**	**2.05**	**2.25**	**2.13**
Provision for loan losses	**0.04**	**0.17**	**0.24**	**0.37**
Net income before gains and taxes	1.45	1.82	1.68	1.76
Gains/losses on securities	0.21	0.00	0.36	0.02
Net income after taxes (ROA)	**1.02**	**1.30**	**1.13**	**1.28**
Common Size Balance Sheet to Assets				
Assets				
Deposits at other banks	0.08	0.12	0.10	0.35
Fed funds sold and repos	5.83	2.56	3.43	2.85
Securities	**31.49**	**20.07**	**34.38**	**22.57**
Gross loans and leases	53.24	61.51	51.88	60.46
Allowance for loan and lease losses	1.57	1.30	1.67	1.48
Net loans and leases	**51.67**	**61.08**	**50.21**	**59.98**
Real estate loans	48.31	43.70	46.03	42.82
Commercial loans	28.14	20.70	30.10	22.37
Consumer loans	6.57	23.27	8.05	22.52
Other loans	16.98	12.23	15.82	12.29
Liabilities				
Demand deposits	22.96	14.94	23.51	15.09
Total deposits	79.35	74.17	79.32	77.14
Core deposits	69.28	66.09	71.31	68.92
Volatile liabilities	20.55	23.35	20.65	21.54

table P4.1 SUMMARY PERFORMANCE RATIO MEASURES EXAMPLE FOR FIRST NATIONAL BANK OF MARYLAND, SEPTEMBER 30, 1993 AND 1994 (CONTINUED)

	1994	Peers	1993	Peers
Average Yields Earned on Different Types of Assets				
Average yield on securities	6.18	5.74	7.28	6.29
Average yield on loans and leases	7.44	8.05	7.55	8.19
Average yield on real estate loans	7.58	7.88	7.78	7.98
Average yield on commercial loans	8.08	7.50	7.48	7.09
Average yield on consumer loans	7.85	9.26	8.93	9.95
Average Rates Paid on Different Types of Liabilities				
Average rate on interest-bearing deposits	3.23	3.23	4.31	3.59
Average rate on large uninsured CDs	4.56	4.05	3.56	3.87
Average rate on other borrowed funds	6.59	3.88	4.35	3.14
Average rate on all interest-bearing liabilities	3.47	3.39	3.45	3.24

	1994	Peers	1993	Peers	1994	Peers
Types of Noninterest Expenses as Percentage of Assets						
Personnel expense	2.44	1.46	2.23	1.49	2.22	1.48
Occupancy expense	0.74	0.44	0.69	0.46	0.70	0.45
Other operating expense	1.17	1.66	1.13	1.74	1.16	1.75
Total overhead expense	4.34	3.67	4.05	3.79	4.08	3.81

table **P4.2** SUMMARY OF RISK MEASURES FOR FIRST NATIONAL BANK OF MARYLAND, SEPTEMBER 30, 1993 AND 1994

	1994	Peers	1993	Peers
Credit Risk Measures				
Net loans and leases to assets	51.67%	61.08%	50.21%	59.98%
Loan loss provision to average total loans and leases	0.08	0.27	0.52	0.61
Loan loss allowance to total loans and leases	2.73	2.09	3.11	2.50
Loan loss allowance to nonaccrual loans	2.88	3.14	1.53	2.07
Loan loss allowance to net losses	35.17	7.31	10.42	5.13
Noncurrent loans and leases to gross loans and leases	1.02	1.02	2.15	1.82
Earnings coverage to net losses	30.20	13.52	11.25	7.49
Net loss to average loans and leases	0.08	0.27	0.31	0.53
Growth rate in net loans and leases	11.34	13.56	3.23	7.01
Liquidity Ratios				
Net loans and leases to assets	51.67	61.08	50.21	59.98
Net loans and leases to total deposits	69.54	85.08	63.00	80.53
Securities with maturities less than 1 year to total assets	12.53	10.57	5.04	11.61
Volatile liabilities to assets	20.54	24.72	19.99	22.82
Core deposits to assets	69.14	64.36	71.79	67.48
(Securities with maturities less than 1 year volatile liabilities) to assets	28.01	213.58	214.95	210.31
Unused loan and lease commitments to assets	33.64	27.39	30.17	23.87
Standby letters of credit to assets	5.55	1.84	5.16	2.07
Interest Rate Risk				
(Rate earned on sensitive assets − rate paid on sensitive liabilities) to assets				
Within 3 months	11.27	26.00	NA	NA
Within 1 year	11.19	25.62	NA	NA
Rate earned on sensitive assets to rate paid on sensitive liabilities				
Within 3 months	1.36	0.854	NA	NA
Within 1 year	1.298	0.90	NA	NA
Capital Risk				
Equity (Tier 1 capital) average assets	6.69	7.53	6.01	7.39
Cash dividends to net income	27.04	42.42	38.46	36.44
Tier 1 capital to risk-weighted assets	8.32	10.66	8.10	10.60
Tier 1 and Tier 2 capital to risk-weighted assets	10.55	12.51	10.52	12.65
Growth rate in Tier 1 equity capital	8.12	9.37	6.19	14.65
Growth rate in assets	0.03	9.22	7.91	7.81
Equity growth less asset growth rate	8.09	0.86	21.72	6.04
Operating Efficiency Measures				
Average personnel expense per employee ($000)	$50.09	$36.47	$43.45	$35.41
Assets per employee ($M)	$02.10	$02.66	$02.04	$02.55
Total overhead expense to assets	4.34%	3.67%	4.05%	3.79%
Personnel expense to average assets	2.44%	1.46%	2.23%	1.49%
Occupancy expense to average assets	0.74%	0.44%	0.69%	0.46%

table **P4.3** FINANCIAL ANALYSIS FOR NATIONSBANK, SEPTEMBER 30, 1993 AND 1994

	1994	Peers	1993	Peers
Overall Profitability Ratios				
Return on equity (net income to equity)	16.29%	16.41%	18.80%	17.32%
Return on assets (net income to assets)	1.43	1.14	1.13	1.28
Equity multiplier (assets to equity)	11.39	14.39	16.64	13.53
Common Size Income Statement to Assets				
Interest revenue (tax equivalent)	6.34%	6.25%	5.33%	6.76%
Interest expense	2.28	2.47	2.21	2.49
Net interest margin (NIM)	**4.06**	**3.78**	**3.12**	**4.27**
Noninterest revenue	1.65	1.87	1.05	1.66
Noninterest expense	3.91	3.72	3.41	3.79
Types of noninterest expenses				
Personnel expense	1.50	1.59	1.05	1.49
Occupancy expense	0.51	0.50	0.39	0.46
Other operating expense	1.89	1.59	1.97	1.74
Burden	**2.26**	**1.85**	**2.36**	**2.13**
Provision for loan losses	20.71	0.15	0.21	0.37
Net income before gains and taxes	2.51	1.79	0.55	1.86
Gains/losses on securities	0.00	0.00	0.01	0.02
Net income after taxes	**1.43**	**1.14**	**0.34**	**1.28**
Common Size Balance Sheet to Assets				
Assets				
Deposits at other banks	0.00	1.56	0.00	0.35
Fed funds sold and repos	8.95	3.61	19.27	2.85
Securities	**27.06**	**18.19**	**30.44**	**22.57**
Gross loans and leases	55.22	59.76	42.53	60.46
Allowance for loan and lease losses	3.38	1.37	2.09	1.48
Net loans and leases	**51.84**	**58.39**	**40.44**	**58.98**
Total loans and leases (as a percentage of gross loans and leases)				
Real estate loans	46.20	34.34	57.86	42.82
Commercial loans	18.80	27.49	16.10	22.37
Consumer loans	23.74	21.87	25.23	22.52
Other loans	11.26	16.30	0.81	12.29
Liabilities				
Demand deposits	18.44	15.36	16.85	15.09
Total deposits	68.80	68.54	79.21	77.14
Core deposits	64.20	55.20	75.29	68.92
Volatile liabilities	20.47	31.45	16.69	21.54
Average Yields Earned on Different Types of Assets				
Average yield on securities	4.92	5.96	5.24	6.29
Average yield on loans and leases	8.29	7.68	8.12	8.19
Average yield on real estate loans	7.92	7.74	7.79	7.98
Average yield on commercial loans	9.19	7.38	8.68	7.09
Average yield on consumer loans	11.63	9.26	9.46	9.95
Average Rates Paid on Different Types of Liabilities				
Average rate on interest-bearing deposits	2.77	3.02	3.04	3.25
Average rate on large, uninsured CDs	3.11	3.75	3.18	3.87
Average rate on other borrowed funds	3.79	4.05	2.15	3.14
Average rate on all interest-bearing liabilities	3.18	3.29	2.98	3.24

table **P4.4** RISK MEASURES FOR NATIONSBANK, SEPTEMBER 30, 1993 AND 1994

	1994	**Peers**	**1993**	**Peers**
Credit Risk Measures				
Net loans and leases to assets	52.06%	59.22%	38.75%	59.98%
Loan loss provision to average total loans and leases	21.27	0.25	0.52	0.61
Loan loss allowance to total loans and leases	5.65	2.30	5.30	2.50
Loan loss allowance to nonaccrual loans	2.69	2.49	1.31	2.07
Loan loss allowance to net losses	181.08	8.50	19.75	5.13
Noncurrent loans and leases to gross loans and leases	2.42	1.26	4.13	1.82
Earnings coverage to net losses	100.77	13.70	7.22	7.49
Net loss to average loans and leases	0.03	0.31	0.26	0.53
Growth rate in net loans and leases	518.81	9.91	218.34	7.01
Liquidity Ratios				
Net loans and leases to assets	52.06	59.22	38.75	59.98
Net loans and leases to total deposits	74.42	86.49	49.09	80.53
Securities with maturities less than 1 year to total assets	15.63	14.04	31.23	11.61
Volatile liabilities to assets	20.35	32.13	17.11	22.82
Core deposits to assets	64.88	53.78	75.62	67.48
(Securities with maturities less than 1 year volatile liabilities) to assets	24.72	216.94	14.12	210.31
Unused loan and lease commitments to assets	20.01	38.11	17.22	23.87
Standby letters of credit to assets	3.67	5.37	3.82	2.07
Interest Rate Risk				
(Rate-sensitive assets to rate-sensitive liabilities) to assets				
Within 3 months	5.22	5.84	NA	NA
Within 1 year	6.64	8.79	NA	NA
Rate-sensitive assets to rate-sensitive liabilities				
Within 3 months	1.14	1.16	NA	NA
Within 1 year	1.15	1.18	NA	NA
Capital Risk				
Equity (Tier 1 capital) average assets	8.78	6.95	6.12	7.39
Cash dividends to net income	157.60	57.49	0.00	36.44
Tier 1 capital to risk-weighted assets	NA	NA	NA	NA
Tier 1 and Tier 2 capital to risk-weighted assets	NA	NA	NA	NA
Growth rate in Tier 1 equity capital	501.31	10.37	4.03	14.91
Growth rate in assets	360.58	10.10	22.04	7.81
Equity growth less asset growth rate	140.73	0.37	6.07	7.10
Operating Efficiency Measures				
Average personnel expense per employee ($000)	$40.32	$43.59	$38.09	$35.41
Assets per employee ($M)	$02.70	$03.05	$03.38	$02.55
Total overhead expense to assets	3.91	3.72	3.41	3.79
Personnel expense to average assets	1.50	1.59	1.05	1.49
Occupancy expense to average assets	0.51	0.50	0.39	0.46

Selected References

Hempel, George H., Donald G. Simonson, and Alan B. Coleman. *Bank Management: Text and Cases,* 4th ed. New York: John Wiley & Sons, 1994.

Koch, Timothy W. *Bank Management,* 3rd ed. Fort Worth, TX: Dryden Press, 1995.

Sinkey, Joseph F., Jr. *Commercial Bank Financial Management,* 5th ed. Englewood Cliffs, NJ: Prentice Hall, 1998.

internet *exercise*

FINDING AND PRINTING THE UBPR FOR JPMORGAN CHASE BANK

The following steps show you how to access the UBPR for any bank or savings institution:

1   Go to *http://www.ffiec.gov/* or *http://www.fdic.gov/bank/statistical/index.html*.

2   These Websites have different menus, but they should both have a link to UBPRs. Click on "Uniform Bank Performance Report (UBPR)."

3   Next, depending on which Website you start from, you'll either need to click "Search for a Uniform Bank Performance Report," or you will automatically be taken to a screen asking you to type in a bank's FDIC number or its name, city, and state. When you get to that screen, type in at least the name and state as follows, and then click "Find":

Institution Name: **JPMorgan Chase Bank**
City: (Optional)

State: **New York**

4   A screen will appear, displaying "FFIEC: These Institutions Matched the Criteria Entered."

Institution Name City State Zip County	Certificate Number Date
JPMorgan Chase Bank New York City 10017 New York	628 9/30/03

Click on the name of the institution that you want to review (in this case, JPMorgan Chase Bank). (Note: Often, if a bank has subsidiaries in different cities or states, a search will come up with several different banks with the same name but in different locations. The name, city, and state search is very sensitive, so don't be surprised if you can't immediately find the bank you want. Just recheck the search criteria and try again. If you still can't find your bank, go back to the FFIEC home page and click on the FDIC Institution Directory. After you type in the bank's name and state, it will give you the institution's FDIC certificate number, which you can then use in the search outlined in the previous steps.)

5   After selecting the bank you want, a screen will display the following information (for JPMorgan Chase Bank in this example):

Bank: JPMorgan Chase Bank

Location: 270 Park Avenue New York City, NY 10017-0000

Certificate #: 628

Select UBPR Format: Choose Standard unless you desire a custom report.

Select Report Date: Select the date/year you want using the arrows (9/30/03 in our example).

Click "Generate Report."

6   The UBPR Table of Contents will be displayed: You can either click "EXPORT" or "PRINT" at the top of the screen. If you click "PRINT," you'll be able print the entire UBPR report or individual sections. If you click "EXPORT," a screen will allow you to download the entire report or individual pages to a disk. It will advise you to save the report as a ".txt" extension file to allow data to be stored in text format that can be opened in any text editor.

This process sometimes can be tricky if you don't have exactly the right name or state for an institution, but it is well worth it; you'll have very good information for financial analysis and peer comparisons for the latest data that the bank has submitted.

EXPLORING THE NATIONAL INFORMATION CENTER WEBSITE

Go to *http://www.ffiec.gov/nic* or use the Quick Link on *http://www.ffiec.gov* to get to the National Information Center home page. You'll see a number of different tabs at the top: Institution Search, Institutional History, Organization Hierarchy, Financial & Performance Reports (for financial call reports, you'll need Adobe Acrobat Reader, which can be downloaded for free from this site and others), Top 50 BHCs/Banks, FAQ, and FFIEC Home. Look at the Top 50 BHCs/Banks; you'll be surprised to see Charles Schwab Corporation on this list (CSC has a bank subsidiary). If you click on one of the listed top fifty banks, such as Wells Fargo, you can get more information in terms of the organization hierarchy and financial reports of different types. You can also search for a bank and find out its current status (what happened to this bank) or who it took over (acquisition history).

EXPLORING THE FDIC INSTITUTION DIRECTOR

The FDIC Institution Directory provides a convenient online way to compare a bank or bank holding com-
pany with its peer institutions. Go to the FDIC Institution Directory at *http://www3.fdic.gov/idasp/main .asp.* (A Quick Link is also provided at *http://www .ffiec.gov.*) Type in Wells Fargo and click "Find." You'll be shown all the different subsidiaries of Wells Fargo. Find Wells Fargo in San Francisco, California, and click on it to get financial and other information. In addition, you might want to check *http://www.wellsfargo.com* to see what Wells Fargo's Website looks like and check out the different services and products it offers.

Appendix 4A

Overview of Selective Off-Balance-Sheet Items

Table 4A.1 shows off-balance-sheet items for all banks in 2003, with derivative off-balance-sheet activity alone having a notional value of over $67 trillion, much larger than the total industry assets for commercial banks at year-end 2003 of about $7.6 trillion. Off-balance-sheet items are often activities that create potential or contingent liabilities in the future.[1] These items include contingent loan commitments, such as unused loan commitments, letters of credit, securities borrowed and lent, participation in acceptances, securities committed to be purchased or sold, nonrecourse mortgage sales, futures contracts (financial, foreign exchange, and others), interest rate swap agreements, and option contracts.

Because of the tremendous growth in off-balance-sheet items, the FDICIA of 1991 required regulators and managers to focus attention on these emerging areas and mandated new financial reporting methods. Regulators have been especially concerned with contingent liabilities and other instruments that might increase the riskiness of an institution and in turn threaten deposit insurance funds. Some off-balance-sheet contracts, however, such as interest rate contracts and foreign exchange contracts, actually help banks to hedge risk and produce noninterest revenues (including fee income) to offset potential losses for on-balance-sheet items. Each of the major off-balance-sheet items listed is briefly described in the following paragraphs. Throughout the text, other off-balance-sheet activities, including securitization and different types of derivatives, will be discussed in more detail as well.

table A4.1   SELECTED OFF-BALANCE-SHEET ITEMS FOR FDIC-INSURED COMMERCIAL BANKS, 2003

($ millions and % of Average Total Assets)

	Total Commercial Banks	% of Assets	Banks with Assets of Less Than $100 Million	% of Assets	Banks with Assets of $100 Million to $1 Billion	% of Assets	Banks with Assets of More Than $1 Billion	% of Assets
Unused loan commitments	$5,527,516	73.95%	$98,502	48.25%	$597,320	65.80%	4,831,694	75.94%
Letters of credit	336,624	4.5%	524	0.26%	6,112	0.67%	329,988	5.19%
Securities lent	767,576	10.27%	46	0.02%	223	0.02%	767,307	12.06%
All other OBS Liabilities	58,140	0.78%	216	0.11%	1,610	0.18%	56,314	0.89%
Derivatives								
Total Notational Value	**67,795,956**	**906.65%**	**92**	**0.05%**	**7,363**	**0.81%**	**67,758,501**	**1,064.99%**
Credit Derivatives	869,001	11.63%	0	0.00%	670	0.07%	868,332	13.65%
Interest rate Contracts	58,274,567	779.66%	50	0.02%	6,445	0.71%	58,268,071	915.83%
Foreign Exchange Contracts	7,563,259	101.19%	0.32	0.00%	16	0.00%	7,563,243	118.87%
Contracts on other commodities & equities	1,059,129	14.17%	41	0.02%	232	0.03%	1,058,856	16.64%

Loan Commitments

This category of off-balance-sheet liabilities includes bank commitments for revolving lines of credit, credit lines backing the commercial paper of large corporations, and note issuance facilities, in which banks agree to buy short-term notes if a borrower is unable to sell them elsewhere. In 2003 **unused** loan commitments were over $5.5 trillion, about 74 percent of total U.S. bank assets for all banks. For banks less than $1 billion, they represent the majority of off-balance-sheet items. Like standby letters, loan commitments are often activated only if borrowers' financial situations deteriorate. Ideally, they should be considered by external analysts in assessing an institution's total risk. Unused loan commitments often serve as one measure of a bank's liquidity risk. A high proportion of unused loan commitments indicates high potential liquidity needs, if borrowers call on these commitments.

Letters of Credit

Commercial letters of credit are often used in international trade when lenders agree to provide financing for customers to purchase specific goods. Upon documentation of the completion of a transaction between the customer and a third party, the bank fully expects to advance funds. A standby letter of credit is a similar instrument with an important difference. Rather than making a definite commitment to finance a transaction, the bank states its obligation to pay a third party *only if the bank's customer defaults.* Standby letters are used not only in commercial transactions but also to enhance the marketability of municipal bonds or to guarantee performance on construction contracts. They act as insurance for risk-averse third parties. Ideally, banks provide this insurance only for the obligations of customers with little likelihood of nonperformance. The bank charges a fee for the commitment and, most importantly, assumes that standby letters will expire unused. Because they require no advance commitment of funds, standby letters are not included as liabilities on issuing banks' balance sheets, but they are considered contingent liabilities. The volume of commitments made with standby letters of credit more than quadruped in the 1980s to $300 billion, falling somewhat to $242 billion in 1996 and rising to $336.6 billion in 2003. Banks with $1 billion or more in assets issue 97 percent of these letters.

Securities Lent or Borrowed (Often Associated with When-Issued Securities)

This class of off-balance-sheet items is associated with banks' security dealer and underwriting activities. It reflects commitments to purchase or sell securities in the future. Often banks involved in investment banking activities make commitments to buy and sell securities prior to an issue, exposing them to the risk of a fall in market value with changes in interest rates or market conditions. Banks that are U.S. Government Dealers engage in these activities with weekly auctions.

Other OBS Liabilities

Other OBS liabilities include loans sold with recourse whereby banks have some liability remaining associated with a loan sale, among other items that leave the bank with the potential of some future commitment. All other off-balance-sheet items are items that are not large enough to fit into their own separate category.

Interest Rate Contracts

These contracts are associated predominantly with hedging activities intended to reduce interest rate risk. Generally, with the exception of very large (greater than $1 billion), well-capitalized firms, banks and thrifts are allowed to engage in financial futures transactions only for hedging purposes. Hedges are accompanied by exposure to basis risk, the risk that prices on contracts used to hedge a position on the bank's balance sheet will not move with the prices of the balance sheet items. Such a mismatch could result in an imperfect hedge and losses. It is difficult to assess a depository's involvement in hedging by looking at published statements. Ordinarily, an analyst must consult regulatory sources to get specific information, although institutions must now provide more information on their annual reports than they once gave. However, they still often give only aggregated information. Very large banks earn fees acting as brokers/dealers for interest rate contracts for other parties, representing the majority of the notional value of interest rate contracts. In addition, as shown, banks engage in hedging credit risk with credit derivatives and also act as brokers/dealers for these contracts.

Foreign Exchange Contracts

These contracts set terms for future exchanges of foreign currency. Many large banks deal in forward contracts for foreign currencies, agreeing with customers to buy or sell foreign currencies in the future at currently agreed upon rates. Contracts on other commodities and equity are similarly futures or forward contracts dealing with purchases or sales of commodities or stock in the future at currently agreed upon prices.

Questions

1. Why is the examination of off-balance-sheet (OBS) items important for a bank financial analyst? Why are OBS items termed *contingent commitments*? What contingencies affect them?

2. What are unused loan commitments? How do they reflect the future liquidity needs of banks?

3. What is a standby letter of credit?

4. What are interest rate contracts and foreign exchange contracts?

5. Although bank regulators are greatly concerned about the risk of OBS items, in what ways do some of these items reduce a bank's risk?

Selected References for Off-Balance-Sheet Activities

Andrews, Suzanna, and Henny Sender. "Off-Balance Sheet Risk: Where Is It Leading the Banks?" *Institutional Investor* 20 (January 1986), 75–84.

Bennett, Barbara. "Off-Balance Sheet Risk in Banking: The Case of Standby Letters of Credit." *Economic Review* (Federal Reserve Bank of San Francisco) (Winter 1986), 19–29.

Benveniste, Lawrence M., and Allen N. Berger. "An Empirical Analysis of Standby Letters of Credit." In *Proceedings of a Conference on Bank Structure and Competition*. Chicago: Federal Reserve Bank of Chicago, 1996, 387–412.

Chessen, James. "Off-Balance Sheet Activity: A Growing Concern?" In *Proceedings of a Conference on Bank Structure and Competition*. Chicago: Federal Reserve Bank of Chicago, 1986.

James, Christopher. "Off-Balance Sheet Banking." *Economic Review* (Federal Reserve Bank of San Francisco) (Fall 1987), 5–19.

Koppenhaver, Gary D. "Standby Letters of Credit." *Economic Perspectives* (Federal Reserve Bank of Chicago) 11 (July/August 1987), 28–38.

Saunders, Anthony. *Financial Institutions Management: A Modern Perspective*, 2nd ed. Burr Ridge, IL: Irwin, 1997.

Saunders, Anthony, and Marcia Million Cornett. *Financial Institutions Management: A Risk Management Approach*, 4th ed. Burr Ridge, Il.: McGraw-Hill Irwin, 2003.

Notes

[1] See the primary source for this information, the *Economic Policy Review* (Federal Reserve Bank of New York) (July 1995): 22–42. Also, for informative articles and more detailed information, see the other sources cited in Appendix 4A's Selected References.

Credit Unions and Savings Institutions

5

"I prefer credit unions. Credit unions treat members well and offer the lowest average fees and the most competitive rates on deposits and on loans."

ELEANOR SWANSON, Professor at Regis University and Credit Union Member (2004).

"The credit unions have enjoyed a free ride on the nation's taxpayers. The credit unions have overstepped their common bonds."

BARBARA WALKER, Executive Director of the Independent Bankers of Colorado, "Credit Unions Launch Intense Lobbying Effort: Supreme Court Decision Prompts Action." Denver Business Journal, February 27–March 5, 1998, 5A.

"The thrift segment has been particularly hard hit. From 1960 to the beginning of 1993, the number of thrifts dropped from 6,835 to 2,529. By the end of the century . . . the distinctions between thrifts and banks will probably have disappeared."

RICHARD D. CRAWFORD, New Visions Financial, Inc.; William W. Sihler, Professor, Darden School, University of Virginia, Financial Service Organizations: Cases in Strategic Management. New York: HarperCollins College Publishers, 1994, 1.9.

"Fannie Mae and the creation of Freddie Mac marked the beginning of a new era for thrifts in the financial system. Today the functions of origination and servicing are still lodged in thrifts (although real estate brokers and finance companies are competing for this business), but over 50% of all new residential mortgage originations flow into the secondary market and the market continues to grow."

PROFESSORS CARLISS Y. BALDWIN AND BENJAMIN C. ESTY, Harvard University, "Lessons from the Thrift Crisis." In Financial Services: Perspectives and Challenges, ed. by Samuel L. Hayes, III. Boston, MA: Harvard Business School Press, 1993, 39.

On February 27, 1998, many credit unions (CUs) and consumer advocates were shocked by the Supreme Court's decision that the National Credit Union Administration (NCUA) had exceeded its jurisdiction by allowing federal CUs to expand their original "common bond" requirement for membership. In 1982, the NCUA had reinterpreted the Federal Credit Union Act of 1934 to permit federal CUs to diversify their membership to serve other local employee groups and associations and to set up their own definitions for membership. NCUA felt that this expansion of CUs' "common bond" was vital for their subsequent success and continued operations. During the severe recession of the early 1980s, many CUs faced potential liquidation when their sponsor firms experienced financial problems. Moreover, unless several businesses were allowed under one CU, a number of businesses were too small to start their own CUs. NCUA's new policy gave CUs a more diversified member base, and CUs expanded rapidly between 1983 to 1998, with a large commitment to capital improvements, branch expansion, and additions of personnel and equipment.

Community bankers challenged this expansion of membership as unfair, since tax-exempt CUs were acting like, but not being taxed like, banks. Some CUs, such as the AT&T Family Federal Credit Union, for instance, had members from 150 unrelated companies, with only 35 percent of its members employed by AT&T and its affiliates.[1]

The Supreme Court's 1998 decision threatened CUs with grave consequences, since almost a third of the industry had committed to large capital improvements, allowing greater economies of scale and the ability to provide a larger variety of services to credit union members. In response to a letter-writing campaign by credit union members and an appeal by CUs that this decision threatened their existence, the U.S. House of Representatives passed H.R. 411-8 in April 1998; this bill was intended to open credit union membership to multiple groups. In July of 1998, the Senate voted 92 to 6 in favor of a bill granting CUs limited authority to expand their

Learning Objectives:

After completing this chapter, you will be able to:

1. Discuss the history of savings institutions and credit unions and how they differ from commercial banks.

2. Understand how regulations have changed for both thrifts and credit unions over time to allow them to compete.

3. Follow recent changes and developments in the savings institutions and credit union industries.

4. Understand differences in the assets and liabilities of the different depository institutions and how this and other differences affect their interest rate and credit risks and profitability.

5. As a case analysis, understand the causes and resolution of the U.S. S&L crisis and the problem of contagion associated with depository institution failures.

memberships. This bill was adopted by the House as an amendment and signed into law by President Bill Clinton in early August, 1998. The NCUA approved new field of membership rules in early 1999, and they continue to be controversial.[2]

Thrifts faced legislative challenges in the 1990s as well. After major losses and failures in the 1980s and more stringent regulations under the Financial Institutions Reform, Recovery, and Enforcement Act (FIRREA) of 1989, thrifts underwent a major restructuring and consolidation. In 1997 alone, 107 thrift acquisitions were announced, totaling $130 billion in assets and a price-to-earnings multiple of about 25. The viability of thrifts was threatened by house legislation that included a 1995 proposal to eliminate the thrift charter altogether and force stock thrifts to convert to banks. Other legislation, under the Financial Services Modernization Act of 1999, attacked the greater diversification ability that unitary savings and loan holding companies had enjoyed over bank holding companies by disallowing any new unitary thrift holding company charters. Furthermore, tax legislation enacted under the Small Business Jobs Protection Act of 1996 eliminated tax impediments for thrift-to-bank conversions, making bank acquisitions and conversions

---

1 Phillip C. Meyer. "High Court Decision Is Awaited on Credit Union 'Common Bond.'" *Banking Policy Report* 16 (October 20, 1997), 1, 12–14.

2 Banking groups have continued with lawsuits for common bond extensions that at the time of this writing had been settled in favor of allowing credit union extensions. See Linda Greenhouse. "Supreme Court Rules for Banks in a Fight to Limit Credit Unions." *New York Times* (February 26, 1998), A1–C2; Edward Felsenthal and Matt Murray. "Justices Deal Credit Unions Major Set Back." *The Wall Street Journal* (February 26, 1998), A3; John R. Wilke. "Senate Passes Bill Allowing Credit-Union Growth." *The Wall Street Journal* (July 29, 1998), A4; Donald Blount. "Credit Union Growth OK'd." *Denver Post* (July 29, 1998), C1; "House Votes to Let Credit Unions Expand Their Memberships." *New York Times* (April 2, 1998), C5; Paul Nylian. "House OKs New Growth for Credit Unions." *Rocky Mountain News* (April 2, 1998), 16b; "Bankers Ready Themselves to Stage Another Fight Against Credit Unions." *Banking Policy Report* 17 (August 17, 1998), 2–3; and "NCUA's D'Amours Says Field of Membership Rule Needs Improvement." *Banking Policy Report* 18 (March 1, 1999), 6–7.

of thrifts to banks more attractive. Legislative proposals were defeated in the late 1990s to eliminate the federal thrift charter and having thrifts convert to bank charters, but this issue continues to be debated. Thus, thrifts, like CUs, are subject to regulatory and legislative uncertainties.[3]

Thrifts were originally chartered to provide home mortgages, a need that was not being served by other financial institutions. Today, however, thrifts face increased competition, not only from commercial banks, mortgage banks, and finance companies, which have increased their home mortgage lending, but also from government-owned or sponsored enterprises that originate and securitize (package and sell as securities) mortgage loans. The latter include the Government National Mortgage Association (Ginnie Mae) and the publicly owned Federal National Mortgage Association (Fannie Mae). These institutions have lower costs, since they are not subject to reserve requirements, deposit insurance premiums, capital requirements, and other more stringent regulations of depository institutions. As government or quasi-government agencies, they also have low financing costs and compete with thrifts for home mortgage loans. As Baldwin and Esty (1993) point out, new technology and standardization that allowed the creation of national mortgage markets and mortgage securitization dramatically changed the role of thrifts.[4] Many thrifts now operate more like mortgage banks, originating and then selling or securitizing home mort-

gages and receiving fee income for servicing loans. These activities require a great deal more sophistication on the part of managers. Thrifts have merged to cut costs and gain economies to compete with other financial service providers. A number of very large thrift holding companies compete well, however, with other large commercial banks and other financial institutions, such as Washington Mutual (WaMu) in Seattle, Washington. WaMu has branches in twenty-eight of the fifty largest metropolitan areas across the western United States as well as on the East Coast in New York. Another very large thrift, Greenpoint Financial Corporation in New York City, was listed on the Federal Reserve System's National Information Center (NIC) Website among the top fifty bank holding companies (BHCs) in 2003. Large thrift holding companies, such as WaMu, with over $268 billion in assets, still specialize in home mortgage lending but have diversified into personal consumer and business banking services, as well as investment and insurance services, providing formidable competition to large commercial banks.

This chapter provides a brief history of the development of CUs and thrifts and describes the industry structure, operations, and balance sheet and income statement differences among banks, CUs, and thrifts. The chapter also discusses trends in profitability for the different types of depository institutions over time, along with trends in depository institution failures and government concerns over potential deposit market contagion.

Savings Institutions: A Brief History and Recent Regulatory Changes

Savings institutions, often called thrifts, are the second largest type of depository institution. As of the last quarter of 2003, about 1,425 thrifts with over 12,000 total branches existed, holding more than $1.47 trillion in assets. As the name suggests, thrifts traditionally promote "thriftiness" and cater to individual small savers, in contrast to commercial banks, which were originally established to cater to larger commercial customers. Two major types of thrifts exist: savings banks, often called mutual savings banks, and savings and loans (S&Ls). The differences between the two and their brief histories are discussed in the following sections.[5]

---

3 Cynthia J. Nickerson. "Mergers and Acquisitions: 1997 Acquisitions Cross Industries and Signal New Strategies." *Banking Policy Report* (January 19, 1998), 7; "Financial Restructuring: Thrift Charter Is Still Under Siege in Budget Debate and Separate Bills." *Banking Policy Report* (December 18, 1995), 5; Thomas P. Vartanian, Alan S. Kaden, and Matthew P. Haskins. "Tearing Down the Tax Wall Between Banks and Thrift Institutions." *Banking Policy Report* (October 16, 1995), 1; Ira L. Tannenbaum. "Thrift Powers: House Legislation Attacks Diversified Savings and Loan Holding Companies." *Banking Policy Report* (November 6, 1995), 2–4; and Ira L. Tannenbaum. "Bad Debt Legislation Clears Way for Thrifts Converting to Banks." *Banking Policy Report* (August 19, 1996), 15–18.

4 Carliss Y. Baldwin and Benjamin C. Esty. "Lessons from the Thrift Crisis." In *Financial Services Perspectives and Challenges*, ed. by Samuel L. Hayes, III. Boston, MA: Harvard Business School Press, 1993, 39.

5 FDIC historical statistics on the FDIC Website, *http://www.fdic.gov*.

Differences Between Savings Banks and S&Ls

Savings banks arose in other countries in the 1700s and in the United States in the early 1800s because no existing institutions were willing to accept savings deposits from a growing population of workers. The first savings banks were founded in the United States in 1816, the Provident Institution for Savings in Boston and the Philadelphia Savings Fund Society. By the time the U.S. population moved west, commercial banks had turned their attention to individuals as well as business customers, so the savings bank movement was never established outside the Northeast. Many of the savings banks in the Northeast, however, became quite large, such as Greenpoint Financial Corporation and Astoria Financial Corporation in New York City. Furthermore, a new type of institution with a dual interest in promoting thrift and home ownership emerged by the mid-1800s; this was the forerunner of the modern savings and loan (S&L). S&Ls originally were formed as building societies with members pooling funds to buy houses. The first building and loan in the United States was organized in 1831, the Oxford Provident Building Association, to enable its mutual owners/depositors who were primarily textile workers to build or purchases homes. Originally, S&Ls planned to liquidate after their mission of providing financing for the members was completed; however, this type of disbanding had operational problems and prevented expansion, so self-perpetuating mutual S&Ls evolved. This new institution spread nationwide with the population.[6]

Important regulatory and operating differences have separated S&Ls and savings banks for most of their history. Savings banks could issue demand deposits and make commercial loans in limited amounts. Unlike other depositories, they could also invest in corporate stock. In contrast, S&Ls' asset choices were greatly restricted until 1980 because a combination of regulations and tax laws virtually assured that more than 80 percent of their assets were mortgage-related. Under the Depository Institution Deregulation and Monetary Control Act (DIDMCA) and the Garn–St. Germain Depository Institution Act (G–St. G), both types of thrifts could invest a small percentage of their assets in commercial loans and issue traditional demand deposits. With minor exceptions, however, thrifts, like commercial banks, are now prohibited from investing in corporate stock. In the 1980s, however, many state-chartered unitary thrift holding companies (i.e., holding companies with one savings and loan) in liberally regulated states could invest through service corporations in the equity of other companies. Financial Corporation of America (FCA) in 1984, for instance, had large stock investments in the Disney Corporation. With FIRREA, such privileges were removed, and state-chartered thrifts had to abide by regulations similar to those governing federally chartered institutions.[7]

In the past, chartering and insurance regulations differed markedly for the two types of thrifts. In 1989, FIRREA's overhaul of the regulatory structure produced further changes. Both the Federal Home Loan Bank Board (FHLBB), the previous chief regulator of savings and loans, and the Federal Savings and Loan Insurance Corporation (FSLIC) were replaced by new entities. The Office of Thrift Supervision (OTS) was created as the regulator and chartering agency of federal, FDIC-insured savings institutions. Also, two new insurance funds were established under the FDIC: BIF (the Bank Insurance Fund), insuring banks and state-chartered savings banks; and SAIF (the Savings Insurance Fund), for federally chartered thrifts. States may still charter both types of thrifts, although the activities allowed by states for state-chartered thrifts may be no more permissive than those allowed to comparable federally chartered thrifts.

Of the 1,425 U.S. FDIC-insured savings institutions operating at the end of the third quarter of 2003, there were 936 OTS-supervised savings institutions (42 BIF members and 894 SAIF members). There were also 489 FDIC-supervised state savings banks (301 BIF-members and 188 SAIF members). The differences between being under SAIF versus BIF used to be significant. FIRREA imposed higher deposit insurance premiums initially under SAIF than BIF, mandating that thrifts formerly insured by the Federal Savings and Loan Insurance Corporation (FSLIC) (and now insured by SAIF) had to partially pay the cost of cleaning up the industry. This cost for S&Ls included paying for the outstanding Financing Corporation bonds used to finance S&L bailouts under the Competitive Equality in Banking Act (CEBA) of 1987. To prevent existing federal thrifts from switching en masse to become state-

---

6 See Williams (2002). Also, for more details on the history of thrifts used as sources in this chapter, see Barth (1991), White (1991), Brumbaugh (1988), and Kane (1989).

7 Ibid.

chartered savings banks, FIRREA also imposed a five-year moratorium on switching insurance funds, except in special circumstances specifically approved by FDIC officials.

With higher premium costs for S&Ls, thrifts initially lost deposits as they faced a competitive disadvantage compared with banks and BIF thrifts and a "backlash" from the S&L crisis. To avoid further S&L losses, Congress passed legislation assessing a large one-time insurance premium on all savings institutions in 1996. This hurt the profitability for thrifts in 1996 but reduced premiums for future years. At the end of the third quarter of 2003, SAIF actually had better funding relative to insured deposits with a reserve ratio (insurance fund balance to insured deposits) of 1.40 percent versus 1.31 percent for BIF. Only five SAIF thrifts were assisted or closed during 1998 to 2003 versus 92 BIF-insured saving institutions and commercial banks.[8]

Thrift Industry Structure

The structure of the thrift industry is interesting, consisting of mutual and stock organizations and huge thrifts along with small ones. Hundreds of thrifts are subsidiaries of bank holding or insurance holding companies while others are part of thrift holding companies or larger financial holding companies (FHCs) and even some nonfinancial holding companies. Some are cyber-thrifts. Thrifts, like commercial banks, also come in a variety of sizes. In 2003, of 1,425 thrift institutions, 480 (33.7 percent) had assets less than $100 million, 766 (53.8 percent) assets of $100 million to $1 billion, and only 159 (12.5 percent) assets greater than $1 billion. Hence, by the definition of a community depository institution as having less than $1 billion in assets, 87.5 percent are community thrifts. However, the largest 159 thrifts hold the majority of thrift assets, and the ten largest thrifts have assets comparable to very large banks. The ten largest thrifts by assets in 2003 include (1) Washington Mutual ($268 billion), Golden West Financial Corporation ($68.41 billion), Sovereign Bancorp, Inc. ($39.5 billion), Greenpoint Financial Corporation ($21.8 billion), Astoria Financial Corporation ($21.7 billion), Guaranty Bank ($17.5 billion), Hudson City Bancorp, Inc. ($14.15 billion), E*Trade Bank ($13.9 billion), Webster Financial Corporation ($13.47 billion), and Commercial Federal Corporation ($13.08 billion).[9]

Mutual and Stock Thrift Trends

The thrift industry has been interesting since thrifts started out as mutual organizations. Unlike stockholder-owned institutions, mutually owned thrifts are "owned" by their customers, that is their "depositors." Depositors become owners when they initiate business relationships with the institutions. Many thrift institutions were formed by emigrant groups that were not being served by commercial banks who pooled their funds together to help each other save and purchase homes. The Garn–St Germain Act of 1982 removed a thirty-year moratorium that had prohibited mutual to stock conversions for federal thrifts. As noted in Chapters 1 and 3, thrifts had severe financial problems in the 1970s and 1980s resulting from having significant interest rate risk with long-term fixed rate assets financed by short-term deposits. With inflation and interest rates rising in the late 1970s, hundreds had large losses. To allow these thrifts a source of new capital, regulators encouraged thrifts to convert to stock ownership. To protect managers, who might otherwise not want to convert, from takeovers, regulations for conversions incorporated an antitakeover rule in which any beneficial ownership of an individual could be no more than 10 percent for any class of equity security for three years following conversion. Limits were also placed on the amount of stock that could be offered during this period: (a) to 5 percent for any person or identified group; and (b) to 15 to 25 percent for all officer and directors. With these antitakeover provisions, managers of mutual thrifts converting to stock ownership did not have to worry about losing their jobs right after conversion to stock ownership with a takeover.[10]

For thrifts struggling to meet higher capital requirements in the early 1990s, conversion to stock ownership was a way to meet new higher capital requirements and, if desired, to facilitate a merger with

---

8 *FDIC Quarterly Banking Profile,* Third Quarter 2003, p. 13; Vartanian, Kaden, and Haskins, "Tearing Down the Tax Wall," 1; and *Banking Policy Report* (March 15, 1999), 3–8.

9 See Insurance Information Institute, Financial Service Industry Facts, 2003 *(http://financialservicefacts.org)*, and FDIC Statistics on Depository Institutions, September 30, 2003, on the FDIC Website, *http://www2.fdic.gov/sdi.*

10 See Cordell, MacDonald, and Wohar (1993); and Cebenoyan, Cooperman, and Register (1999).

another thrift or commercial bank. Over 1,353 federal thrifts converted to stock ownership from 1972 to 2002, with the majority of conversions occurring in the mid-1980s and early 1990s. As a result, the percentage of federal mutual thrifts fell from 54 percent in 1987 to 51 percent in 1994, to about 46.5 percent in 2003. Hundreds of thrifts also merged during the 1990s. As shown in Figure 5.1, the number of both stock and mutual firms has declined. During 1994 to 2003, the number of mutual thrifts fell from 1,148 in 1994 to 662 in 2003; and the number of stock thrifts from 1,091 to 763. In 1998 to 2002, the deal value for thrift mergers was $53.3 billion for 340 mergers. With conversions and mergers, total assets of mutual thrifts fell by 19.4 percent, from $196 billion in 1994 to $158 billion in 2003. However, total assets of stock thrifts grew dramatically by 63 percent from $801 billion in 1994 to $1.313 trillion in 2003. It's interesting to note the performance of mutual versus stock savings institutions in recent years, shown in Figure 5.2. Although mutual and stock thrifts had similar performance for ROA during the latter 1990s, in the early 2000s stock thrifts had much higher average ROAs and ROEs each year than mutuals.[11]

---

figure **5.1**   TRENDS IN MUTUAL AND STOCK THRIFTS, 1994 TO 2003

PANEL A: NUMBER OF MUTUAL AND STOCK SAVINGS INSTITUTIONS

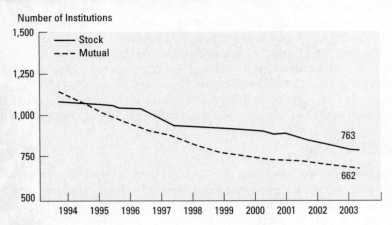

PANEL B: ASSETS OF MUTUAL AND STOCK SAVINGS INSTITUTIONS

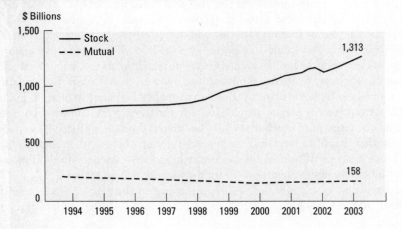

Source: FDIC Quarterly Banking Profile, Graph Book, http://www2.fdic.gov/qbp.

---

11 See FDIC Quarterly Banking Profile Graph Book on the FDIC Website *(http://www2.fdic.gov/qbp/grgraph.asp)* and the Office of Thrift Supervision Savings Institution Fact Book, 2002 *(http://www.ots.treas.gov/).*

figure   5.2   TRENDS IN PERFORMANCE MEASURES FOR MUTUAL AND STOCK THRIFTS, 1994 TO 2003

PANEL A: QUARTERLY RETURN ON ASSETS (ROA), ANNUALIZED MUTUAL AND STOCK SAVINGS INSTITUTIONS

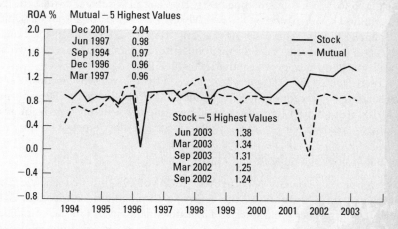

PANEL B: QUARTERLY RETURN ON EQUITY (ROE), ANNUALIZED MUTUAL AND STOCK SAVINGS INSTITUTIONS

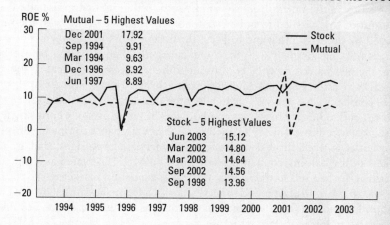

Source: FDIC Quarterly Banking Profile, Graph Book, http://www2.fdic.gov/qbp.

Unitary Thrift Holding Companies

Unitary (one savings and loan) holding companies have been an extremely popular organizational form for S&Ls. Under the SLHC Act of 1968, Congress allowed unitary thrift holding companies to engage in almost any type of activity, as long as they held primarily home mortgage-related assets. Interestingly, this act allowed nonfinancial firms to own thrifts, permitting such companies as Ford Motor Company, Southwest Gas, and Household International Finance Company to own networks of thrifts in the 1980s. In 1997, about forty to fifty diversified unitary thrift holding companies engaged to some degree in activities impermissible to BHCs, including real estate development and general manufacturing. These included unitary thrift holding companies owned by Prudential Insurance Company, United Services Automobile Association (USAA), Hawaiian Electric Industries, Inc., B. A. T. Industries, and American Mutual Life Insurance Company. Congress and regulators were concerned over the potential threat of diverse activities on the risk of federal deposit insurance funds, particularly with a number of different companies applying for thrift charters in the late 1970s including cyberthrifts. Legislators were concerned about the mix of financial and nonfinancial activities for unitary thrift holding companies owned by nonfinancial firms.

Under the Financial Services Modernization (Gramm-Leach-Bliley) Act (GLBA) of 1999, the unitary thrift holding company charter was removed for any new charters. Previous companies were grandfathered (allowed to continue to operate) but could not be sold to nonfinancial firms. Thrifts desiring to form a holding company structure are now subject to the same restrictions on activities as BHCs and FHCs regulated by the Fed. Thrifts can be part of a joint bank and thrift holding company or financial holding company. At the same time GLBA extended the range of activities allowed for BHCs and reduced the range for thrift holding companies to make the two holding company activities more equivalent, as approved activities by the Fed.

As reported by the OTS for OTS-regulated thrifts, in 1993, 748 thrift holding companies operated, representing 35 percent of the OTS-regulated thrift industry. By 2002, this number grew by 29 percent to 1,010 thrift holding companies. Holding company structures can be quite complicated, with a larger holding company having numerous other thrift and other types of holding companies as subsidiaries.[12]

Mutual Holding Companies for Thrifts

The Competitive Equality Banking Act (CEBA) of 1987 allowed a new organizational form for mutually owned thrift institutions, the ability to form holding companies. A mutual holding company (MHC) is a mix between a stock and a mutual company. A mutual holding company allows a separate stock subsidiary to be established that can issue stock. In this unusual procedure, a mutual thrift first transfers assets, insured liabilities, and capital to a newly formed, stockholder-owned subsidiary. Common stock in the new subsidiary can be sold to the public to raise additional capital. The maximum amount of stock issued to public shareholders is 49.9 percent, with the remaining majority of shares owned by the MHC that the original thrift depositors jointly own. The mutual institution (now the parent holding company with the same management and board as before) can retain operating control over the new bank simply by continuing to hold at least 51 percent of the shares. The parent company can also invest in other stockholder-owned thrifts. The advantages of this form (which mutual insurance companies have as well) is to allow the mutual organization to raise additional capital to finance growth and to be able to attract good officers by allowing stock bonuses and options as compensation. Also, it can be more quickly formed to raise capital than a complete conversion of a mutual to a stock firm. At each stage, thrift depositors and insiders are given rights that are nontransferable to purchase shares in the holding company. Sometimes, an MHC is created as a first step for a second stage conversion later to a full stock company. The first successful market test of the provision was conducted by Peoples Bank in Bridgeport, Connecticut, which formed a mutual holding company in 1989, attracting $55 million in new equity capital in the process. After this, it was not until 1992 that mutual thrifts began to adopt an MHC structure, with a moderate number of MHCs formed, about sixty-four between 1992 and 2000, as noted in a study by Carow, Cox, and Roden (2003), as reported by SNL Securities.[13]

Although depositors are joint owners when an MHC is formed, as noted by Carow, Cox, and Roden (2003), depositors do not individually have access to any of the accumulated equity in the stock subsidiary. Consumer activists have been concerned that depositors are deprived of benefits of ownership at the expense of managers who benefit from stock option compensation while protected from takeovers. As part of a comprehensive review of the treatment of mutual thrifts in 2002, the OTS proposed rule changes to encourage mutual associations seeking new capital to consider the mutual holding company form of organization as an alternative to full conversion to stock organizations. In response to public comments, the OTS placed an additional restriction on the amount of stock permitted to be allocated at the time of a reorganization to management benefit plans (except for stock

---

12 See Office of Thrift Supervision Savings Institution Fact Book, 2002 *(http://www.ots.treas.gov/)*. For information on unitary holding companies and regulatory changes, see Williams (2002); Brumbaugh (1988); and Tannenbaum, "Thrift Powers," 2–4; "GE Unit Seeks Shift to Federal S&L." *New York Times* (December 25, 1997), C6; Stephen E. Frank. "Brokers, Insurers Queue Up for Thrift Charters." *The Wall Street Journal* (September 24, 1997), C1; and "OTS Says New Thrift Can Operate in Cyberspace." *Bank Policy Report* 16 (December 15, 1997), 6.

13 See Williams (2002); Kenneth A. Carow, Steven R. Cox, and Dianne M. Roden. "Evidence of Managerial Opportunism During Mutual-to-Stock Conversions." Working Paper, Indiana University: Indianapolis, 2003; Haluk Unal. "Regulatory Misconceptions in Pricing Thrift Conversions: A Closer Look at the Appraisal Process." *Journal of Financial Services Research* 11 (1997), 239–254; "The Competitive Equality Banking Act of 1997." *Special Management Bulletin, U.S. League of Savings Institutions,* October 16, 1987; Resa W. King. "The Shape of Thrifts to Come?" *Business Week* (September 18, 1989), 102; "Mutual Holding Companies May Be a Growing Trend." *Savings Institutions* 110 (December 1989); 6–7; Tom Parliment. "To Raise Capital, Consider a Mutual Holding Company." *Savings Institutions* 112 (May 1991), 52–53; Phillip Britt. "Mutual Holding Companies Unlock Needed Capital." *Savings Institutions* (January 1992), 9; and Brian Nixon. "Goring Full Stock or Mutual Stock." *Savings and Community Banker* 2 (February 1993), 22–26.

option plans) to no more than 25 percent of the number of shares issued to minority shareholders in the public offering. Some credit unions have considered converting to MHCs to allow greater flexibility in business lending.[14]

Windfall Concerns and Regulations for Thrift Conversions from Mutual to Stock Ownership

As noted in the discussion of mutual holding companies, consumers have had concerns about managers taking advantage of depository/owners with conversions to mutual holding companies, as well as conversions to full stock organizations. The primary method of converting from a mutual to a stock organization is through an initial public offering (IPO). New shares are offered for sale first to eligible depositors, managers, employees, and then the general public. In addition to needing two-thirds of the board of directors of a mutual thrift to vote to approve a plan of conversion, federal and state regulators for federally-chartered and state-chartered thrifts, respectively, must approval the plan. Often the reasons for conversion, a post-conversion business plan for at least three years, a stock marketing and sales plan, and the proposed use for the conversion proceeds are required.

As noted in previous research studies including Colantuoni's (1999) *FDIC Banking Review* study, initial purchasers of shares in thrift conversion IPOs have had significant windfalls, with shares issued in 1995 to 1997 and the first half of 1998 rising by an average of 24 percent on the first day of trading. Colantuoni notes an even more dramatic rise for thirteen conversions that took place in early 1998, having one-day average returns of 59 percent, with higher returns for larger thrifts.

A number of different regulations have been passed to have better initial appraisals of thrifts to avoid undervaluation and, hence underpricing of new stock thrift shares. In 1994, for instance, guidelines were revised to ensure accurate appraisal and selling of thrift stock shares at their "pro forma market value," to eliminate such windfall distributions of converting institutions. Colantuoni (1999) notes that windfall gains may be more related to the unique characteristics of mutual-to-stock conversions reflecting the value of the preexisting net worth that become more valuable with the public offering exceeding its book value.[15]

Risky Behavior?

With a very healthy thrift industry after 1993 to 2003, researchers have generally concluded that allowing mutual thrifts to convert to stock thrifts to raise additional capital, grow, and acquire or be acquired by other banks or thrifts has improved the health of the thrift industry. However, in light of the Sarbanes-Oxley Act and financial debacles such as Enron, as well as the U.S. savings and loan crisis of the later 1980s, financial economists have questioned whether managers of stock-owned firms take on greater risk or engage in fraudulent activities more often, to maximize the value of their stock-related compensation, than managers of mutually owned organizations. Alternatively, with more diffuse ownership by depositors and protection from takeovers for mutual managers, mutual managers may have greater opportunities to engage in expense preference behavior (i.e., maximizing their own objectives for perquisites, expensive behavior, risk aversion, and other personal goals) than stock managers. Researchers generally have found evidence of greater risk-taking behavior for stock versus mutual thrifts. Some researchers have argued that in a complex, competitive environment, however, mutual managers may be too risk-averse in taking on new, sometimes more risky, ventures, which can make it difficult for mutual firms to compete.[16]

---

14 See Carow, Cox, and Roden, "Evidence of Managerial Opportunism," Lynn W. Adkins, Executive Editor, The Bank Place, The BankPlace@aol.com. "OTS Unveils Revised Proposal to Enhance Mutual Thrift Charter." (April 8, 2002). Also see OTS Rules on the Office of Thrift Supervision Website at *http://www.ots.treas.gov/*.

15 See Joseph A. Colantuoni (1999); also see the Illinois State Office of Banks and Real Estate, Bureau of Residential Finance, Thrift Division, Mutual to Stock Conversions Purpose, Business Plan, Community Offering for Illinois State-Chartered Mutual Savings Banks, July 12, 2001, *http://www.obre.state.il.us.*

16 Studies and discussion of the relative efficiency of mutual versus stock thrift include Mester (1989a, b), Cebenoyan, Cooperman, Register, and Hudgins (1993), and Sfirdis and Daniels (2004). Research on expense preference behavior of bank and thrift managers include Verbrugge and Jahera (1981) and Akella and Greenbaum (1988). Studies examining relative risk-taking of stock versus mutual thrifts and stock owned versus manager-owned thrifts include Esty (1997); Brewer and Saidenberg (1996); Cebenoyan, Cooperman, and Register (1995, 1999); Cole and Mehran (1991); and Cordell, MacDonald, and Wohar (1993). A number of studies have also examined the role of principal-agent conflict on the 1980s thrift crisis including Cole and Eisenbeis (1996), and Akerlof and Romer (1993). Many other bank studies have examined the relationship between managerial ownership and risk-taking including Galloway, Lee, and Roden (1997); Gorton and Rosen (1995); Allen and Cebenoyan (1991); and Saunders, Strock, and Travlos (1990), among others.

Changing Legislation to Ease Restrictions and Foster Conversions: Qualified Thrift Lender Requirements

The Competitive Equality in Banking Act (CEBA) of 1987 specified that in order for a unitary thrift holding company to be given greater freedom and flexibility, a subsidiary thrift needed to satisfy a qualified thrift lender (QTL) test. Under a QTL test, the majority of the thrift's assets had to be in home mortgage activities. FIRREA of 1989 made the consequences of not meeting the QTL test more burdensome in terms of the thrift's access to loans from the Federal Home Loan Bank System. Also, it required that the subsidiary thrift conform its activities and branching to that of a national bank and that the thrift holding company be treated as if it were a bank holding company. The IRS had its own QTL test for thrifts to be permitted a larger tax deduction for bad debt reserves for thrifts, as much as 8 percent of their income, allowing a larger bad debt reserve deduction than commercial banks. The logic of this special treatment was to promote home lending, but in fact the QTL limited thrifts' diversification and their ability to convert to banks, since excess bad debt tax deductions would have to be recaptured.[17]

In 1996, provisions were passed under the Small Business Jobs Protection Act (SBJPA) of 1996 to promote S&L conversions to banks. Under the new tax legislation, the preferential bad debt reserve treatment previously available to S&Ls under Section 593 of the Internal Revenue Code was repealed. S&Ls are now subject to the same federal tax provisions as commercial banks of the same size, and excess bad debt tax deductions had to be recaptured for all thrifts over the six-year period after 1996. With this legislation, the number of S&Ls converting to banks rose significantly. With GLBA of 1999 and IBBEA of 1994 providing greater product and geographical freedom for banks and SPJPA of 1996 allowing easier conversion of thrifts to banks, a large wave of conversions of thrifts to banks and mergers with banks occurred.[18]

The Economic Growth and Regulatory Paperwork Reduction Act (EGRPRA) of 1996, which brought SAIF back to full funding, also amended the investment restrictions of the Home Owners' Loan Act (HOLA) and the FHLBB's QTL test to allow federally chartered thrifts to originate credit card and educational loans without investment restrictions. S&Ls can invest an additional 10 percent of their assets in loans to small businesses and farms while maintaining their current authority to invest 10 percent of their assets in commercial loans and up to 400 percent of capital in loans secured by commercial real estate. EGRPRA key reforms to the QTL included small business loans and credit card loans and credit card accounts, and educational loans to count in unlimited amounts as qualified thrift investments. Consumer loans, other than credit card and education loans, may count as qualified investments up to 20 percent of a thrift's portfolio assets. Savings institutions were also allowed to choose between the revised QTL test or compliance with the federal tax code for a "domestic building and loan associations" (DBLA) test, which is somewhat more restrictive, to satisfy QTL requirements. EGRPRA also added flexibility to federal thrifts' already very liberal interstate branching powers. On September 30, 1996, the OTS amended its lending regulations to reduce regulatory burden, including

---

Concept Questions

1. What are the primary differences between savings and loans and savings banks?

2. Who are the chief regulators of savings institutions? What is BIF? SAIF?

3. What is a unitary thrift holding company, and why were new charters forbidden under GLBA of 1999?

4. What is a mutual holding company? Why have regulators and consumers been concerned about the process for mutual-to-stock conversions and conversions to mutual holding companies?

5. What advantages do stock thrifts have over mutual thrifts? Why would stock or mutual thrift managers be more likely to take on greater risk or expense preference behavior?

6. What reduction in product restrictions occurred for thrifts in 1996? Why were there more conversions of thrifts to banks in the later 1990s?

---

17 See Williams (2002), Chapter 14, "Qualified Thrift Lender Test," 14-1 to 14-20.

18 Tannenbaum, "Bad Debt Legislation," 15–18. Tannenbaum (1996) reports that experts estimate that approximately 80 percent of all excess bad debt reserves for taxes for thrifts as a group are pre-1988 reserves. The recapture of excess reserves could be deferred for 1996 and 1997 for thrifts meeting a newly developed residential mortgage origination test during these years. Also see Williams (2002). In a recent study by Cebenoyan, Cebenoyan, and Cooperman (2004), between 1990 to 1993, there were more than 218 thrift mergers, 59 percent with banks, and in 1994 to 2000, more than 399 thrift mergers, over 70 percent with banks.

no longer aggregating the commercial loans of service corporations with those of the parent thrift for the purpose of computing the maximum commercial lending limits for federally chartered thrifts. Hence, federal S&Ls that wish to act more like community banks can adjust their assets and business to do so. As Williams (2002, Chapter 14, p. 14-2) notes, "While once the QTL test may have pointed thrifts to a concentration in mortgage finance, as the test has evolved, it now easily accommodates a diversified range of consumer-oriented financial products and services."[19]

A Brief History of Credit Unions

Credit unions originated in the mid-nineteenth century in Germany; the concept was brought to the United States in the early 1900s. The first CU gained legal status in Manchester, New Hampshire, through a special act of the state legislature; Massachusetts passed a similar act the same year, 1909. CUs were set up as "cooperative associations" to promote thrift among their members. During the 1920s and the Great Depression of the 1930s, CUs grew quickly, reflecting the rapid development of consumer activism and labor organizations under a "common bond" concept. CUs provided an alternative to loan sharks and traditional thrifts and banks. In 1934, Congress passed the Federal Credit Union Act to charter federal CUs. CUs at this time were often no more than groups of farmers who pooled their money to make each other tractor loans or groups of servicemen who could not leave their military base to go to a traditional bank. Because CU profits go to individual members in the form of dividends, cheap loans, and higher interest rates on deposits, CUs are not taxed. During the first three years of their existence, federal CUs paid state taxes, but technical differences between CU shares and deposits meant that their tax burden was quite high in some states. In 1937, Congress decided that the cooperative movement was best served by exempting federal CUs from taxation. This tax exemption has been under renewed scrutiny in recent years, but it survived attempted tax reforms in 1986, 1993, and 1996. Opponents argue that the increasingly loose common bond requirements for credit union membership have eroded the principal reason for their not-for-profit status and that CUs' exemption from taxes represents a subsidy by taxpayers.[20]

Membership Requirements and Regulations

To join a CU, a person must be within its field of membership. Typical fields of membership include employee groups, associations, religious or fraternal affiliations, and residential areas. Many CUs depend heavily on volunteer labor and donated facilities. Like other depositories, CUs may choose either state or federal charters. Federally chartered CUs are regulated by the National Credit Union Administration (NCUA) and insured by the National Credit Union Share Insurance Fund (NCUSIF), as are state-chartered CUs, a fund similar to the FDIC. Deposits of credit unions are referred to as member "shares." As of 1970, all CUs must be insured under the law creating NCUSIF. The NCUSIF is funded by fees and assessments from CUs. NCUA also provides a Central Liquidity Facility (CLF) as a lender of last resort. As a quasi-public organization, the CLF has the authority to borrow from public sources and has a credit line with the U.S. Treasury department. Congress also charges the NCUA with enforcing a broad range of federal consumer laws and regulations for federally chartered CUs and also, in certain instances, state-chartered credit unions.

HR 411–8 passed in August 1998, allowing CUs extensions of their common bond requirement and extended member business loans up to 12.25 percent of CU assets. Accordingly, it also contains prompt corrective action provisious comparable to those for banks and thrifts under the Federal Deposit Insurance Corporation Improvement Act (FDICIA).

As nonprofit, untaxed organizations, CUs can offer lower average fees and more competitive rates on deposits, loans, and other products. The Bank Rate Monitor in North Palm Beach, Florida, for instance, a monitor of industry rates, found that banks paid on average lower annual rates on interest-bearing checking accounts and that loan rates for CUs were typically more competitive than bank loan rates. The Credit Union National Association (CUNA), the largest trade and support organization for

---

19 See Williams (2002), Chapter 14, "Qualified Thrift Lender Test," 14-1 to 14-20.

20 See citations in Note 2.

credit unions, also reported a large percentage of CUs offered free checking, while most banks charge customers for falling below required minimum balances.[21]

Many large CUs offer services that rival those at many large banks, including credit cards, ATMs, mutual funds, stock/bond brokerage, life insurance, and formal financial planning. Through corporate CUs, smaller CUs are also able to offer many of these services as well. In addition, CUNA has a mortgage corporation, a service corporation, a brokerage corporation, and an insurance agency. The thirty-two federally insured corporate credit unions across the country provide investment, liquidity, and payment services for their member credit unions. State CU organizations also provide services. For instance, the estimated 1.3 million members of state CUs in Colorado can access a statewide ATM network, use state CU service centers for financial planning, and apply for CU leasing, credit cards, and debit cards. CUs' market shares for consumer loans have grown significantly, although banks and finance companies continue to have the largest and second largest shares, respectively.

Credit Union Support Systems

Credit unions enjoy the benefits of strong trade organizations. Because so many CUs are small, they often need facilities and managerial expertise that larger depositories develop in-house. Figure 5.3 shows the pyramid support structure for CUs. The largest of the trade organizations is the Credit Union National Association and its affiliates. Among the most important affiliates is the Corporate Credit Union (CCU) Network, a group of CUs for CUs, with about $20.481 billion in assets at the end of 1996. Individual CUs own interest-earning shares in CCUs; the latter pool the funds of small CUs and invest in money and capital market instruments. CCUs also function similarly to correspondent banks, offering advice, cash management, check processing, and the assistance necessary for the operation of individual CUs.

They also act as bankers' banks, accepting deposits and lending to CUs as needed. Further up the support ladder is the U.S. Central Credit Union (USC), established in the 1990s in Overland Park,

figure **5.3** NCUA ORGANIZATIONAL CHART

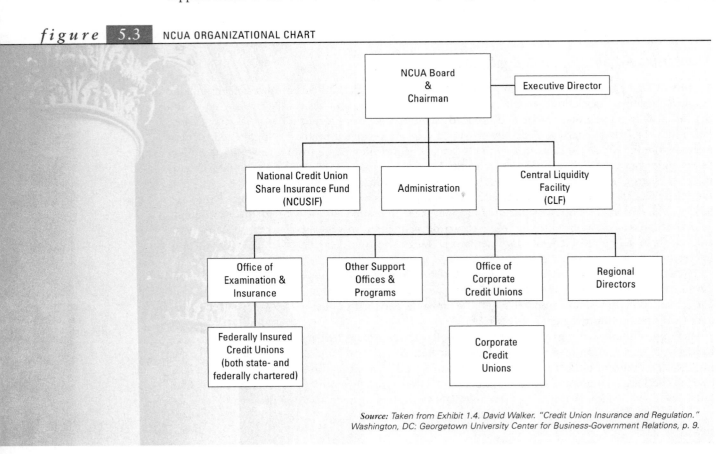

Source: Taken from Exhibit 1.4. David Walker. *"Credit Union Insurance and Regulation."*
Washington, DC: Georgetown University Center for Business-Government Relations, p. 9.

---

21 Karen Hube and Matt Murray. "Credit Unions Still Top Banks on Deals for Basic Service." *The Wall Street Journal* (March 3, 1998), C1, C25; and *Credit Union Report, 1996, Year-end.* Madison, WI: CUNA & Affiliates, 1997.

Kansas, of which CCUs are themselves members. The USC and the forty-two CUs are often referred to as the Corporate Network. This large CCU, with assets of more than $18 billion, manages investments and provides a wide array of other services for CUs, including liquidity, custody, and payment services, as well as product research and development.[22]

Size and Industry Structure

As of June 30, 2003, the National Credit Union Administration (NCUA) was supervising and insuring 9,529 credit unions (5,864 federal and 3,665 state-chartered). With thousands of mergers between credit unions, this represents a 20 percent decline in the 1996 total of 11,887 CUs (7,149 federal and 4,738 state). At the beginning of 2003, CUs had a total of 80.9 million members and assets of $0.557 trillion ($0.301 trillion in assets for federally chartered CUs with 44.6 million members; $0.256 trillion in assets for federally insured state-chartered CUs with 36.3 million members). As shown in Table 5.1,

table **5.1**   TEN-YEAR SUMMARY: FEDERAL AND STATE-CHARTERED CREDIT UNIONS, 1983 TO 2002

PANEL A: FEDERAL CREDIT UNIONS, DECEMBER 31 ($ MILLIONS)

December	1993	1994	1995	1996	1997	1998	1999	2000	2001	2002
Number of credit unions	7,696	7,498	7,329	7,152	6,981	6,815	6,566	6,336	6,118	5,953
Number of members	39,755,596	40,837,392	42,162,627	43,545,541	43,500,553	43,864,851	44,076,428	43,883,106	43,816,877	44,610,949
Assets	$172,854	$182,529	$193,781	$206,692	$215,097	$231,904	$239,316	$242,881	$270,125	301,238
Loans outstanding	94,640	110,090	120,514	134,120	140,100	144,849	155,172	163,851	170,326	181,767
Shares	153,506	160,226	170,300	180,964	187,817	202,651	207,614	210,188	235,202	261,819
Reserves	6,976	7,616	8,351	9,092	9,371	9,837	10,314	10,837	11,339	12,227
Undivided earnings	8,338	9,584	11,445	13,087	14,365	15,468	16,546	17,279	18,596	20,855
Gross income	12,946	13,496	15,276	16,645	17,404	18,137	18,530	19,456	20,042	19,676
Operating expenses	5,578	5,964	6,468	7,246	7,793	8,241	8,551	8,721	9,287	10,158
Dividends	5,038	5,208	6,506	7,087	7,425	7,760	7,698	8,120	8,277	6,369
Reserve transfers	186	245	262	240	201	211	323			
Net Income	2,282	2,149	2,136	2,232	2,113	2,081	2,184	2,470	2,436	3,082

PANEL B: FEDERALLY INSURED STATE-CHARTERED CREDIT UNIONS, DECEMBER 31 ($ MILLIONS)

December	1993	1994	1995	1996	1997	1998	1999	2000	2001	2002
Number of credit unions	4,621	4,493	4,358	4,240	4,257	4,180	4,062	3,980	3,866	3,735
Number of members	23,996,75	24,294,761	24,926,666	25,665,783	27,921,882	29,673,998	31,307,907	33,704,772	35,532,391	36,336,258
Assets	$104,316	$106,937	$112,861	$120,176	$136,107	$156,787	$172,086	$195,363	$231,280	$255,838
Loans outstanding	57,695	65,769	71,606	79,651	92,117	100,890	116,366	137,485	152,014	160,881
Shares	93,482	94,797	99,838	105,728	119,359	137,347	149,305	169,053	201,807	222,377
Reserves	4,754	4,908	5,246	5,689	6,421	7,125	7,946	9,120	10,266	11,105
Undivided earnings	4,862	5,563	6,645	7,490	8,779	9,876	11,060	12,830	14,563	16,229
Gross income	7,878	7,955	8,932	9,736	11,124	12,309	13,413	15,714	17,385	17,075
Operating expenses	3,302	3,473	3,770	4,198	4,939	5,548	6,165	7,024	8,053	8,990
Dividends	3,109	3,145	3,889	3,367	3,790	4,229	4,315	5,256	5,547	4,020
Reserve transfers	114	144	147	143	138	161	190			
Net income	1,462	1,289	1,241	1,298	1,381	1,424	1,566	1,859	2,060	2,594

Source: 2002 Annual Report, National Credit Union Administration (http://www.ncua.gov), *58–59.*

---

22 See Walker (1997); CUNA and Affiliates Annual Report, 1996, 1997, 2002, Madison, WI; and Barbara A. Good. "The Credit Union Industry—An Overview."
   Economic Commentary (Federal Reserve Bank of Cleveland) (May 15, 1998), 1–4.

although CUs are the smallest of the three types of depository institutions, they have grown enormously, with total CU assets growing 58.69 percent since 1997, a healthy 9.68 percent a year.

In the early 1980s, a number of CUs were liquidated as a result of the recession-related financial problems of employers. In contrast, after 1982, with the extension of the common bond requirement by the NCUA, much of the decline in the numbers of CUs resulted from consolidation as CUs attempted to gain greater economies of scale and to offer a greater variety of services to compete with other banks and nonbank institutions. The number of both federal and state CUs fell from a peak of 17,507 in 1979 to 11,659 in 1997 and then to 9,529 in June 2003. Between 1983 to 1997, there was a 39 percent decline in numbers, but an asset growth of 299 percent. Similarly, between 1997 and 2002, although the total number of CUs fell by almost 18 percent, total CU assets rose 58.69 percent. During 1998 to 2002 alone, there were 1,410 federal credit union mergers and 126 liquidations.

While the average size of CUs has risen, only about 2.5 percent have assets greater than $500 million. In terms of size from smallest to largest: (1) about 19 percent have assets less than $2 million; (2) 30 percent assets between $2 million and $10 million; (3) 31 percent assets between $10 million and $50 million; (4) 8.5 percent assets between $50 million and $100 million; (5) 9 percent assets between $100 million to $500 million; and (6) about 2.5 percent assets greater than $500 million. Hence, about 97.5 percent of CUs have assets less than $500 million, and they are generally much smaller than banks or thrifts. However, there are very large institutions, such as the Navy Federal Credit Union in Vienna, Virginia, which had $19.884 billion in assets in 2003. Hence, the largest CUs have gotten larger, and the number of small CUs has fallen.[23]

Recent Developments

New Credit Union Conversion Rule

On November 19, 1998, the National Credit Union Administration revised the agency's regulations on the conversion of federal credit unions to mutual savings banks to make the process more simple and to reduce the regulatory burden for insured credit unions to convert. Credit union members must approve such a conversion but now a credit union only has to notify the NCUA of its plans to convert ninety days before the membership vote, whereas previously it needed prior NCUA approval. Many credit unions have begun considering conversions in order to raise capital for growth, have greater consumer awareness, and have greater flexibility in being allowed a larger percentage of business lending and other types of activities.[24]

Community Development Credit Unions (CDCUs)

CDCUs are a special type of credit union intended to serve specific communities. In order to be designated a CDCU, organizers must define a field of membership in which over half of its prospective members fall into at least one of four categories: (1) a member of a household with an income less than 80 percent of the median household income for the nation; (2) a member of a household in a public housing project that has qualified for such a residency on the basis of income; (3) a recipient in a community action program (CAP); or (4) a full- or part-time student in a high school, vocational school, college, or university. While credit unions that are not CDCUs must raise capital directly from members, a CDCU is allowed to accept nonmember deposits from institutions such as banks, insurance companies, and utilities, which can be beneficial in the early years of the credit union's operations. Banks and savings institutions receive Community Reinvestment Act Credit by pledging deposits for a period of time, making grants to cover the CDCU's operating expenses, donating equipment, or donating the services of personnel to help guide the CDCU. Since CDCUs generally provide basic financial services to low-income consumers and make small loans, CDCUs are not really competing with such banks and savings institutions.

---

23 See 2002 Annual Report, National Credit Union Administration *(http://www.ncua.gov)*; and Navy Credit Union's call report by clicking on "Financial and Performance Reports" on the NIC-Federal Reserve System Website *(http://www.ffiec.gov/nic)*.

24 See Lynne Montgomery. "Recent Developments Affecting Depository Institutions." *FDIC Banking Review* (1999), 30; CU Financial Services: Strategic Planning and Implementation Services for Credit Unions, "Credit Union: Conversions to the Mutual Bank Charter—Business Lending Programs—Mergers and Acquisitions." *(http://www.cufinancial.com)*.

Unlike other depository institutions, there is no minimum level of capitalization to start a credit union or CDCU, but generally at least $150,000 in deposits are needed to be viable, pledged as part of a CDCU application by perspective depositors. Generally, at least 350 members are needed to be viable. A CDCU also needs a dedicated core of volunteer organizers to commit the time needed and a suitable location, such as a church or community development corporation facility and place for funds' safe-keeping, along with a computer for financial records. The entire chartering process generally takes about eighteen months. Organizers are expected to meet on a regular basis and develop a thorough business plan including realistic projections of expenses and revenues for the first three years of operation. Approvals are made for state-chartered CDCUs by State Departments of Banking and Insurance. Examples of successful CDCUs include: (1) Alternatives Federal Credit Union in Ithaca, New York, which started in 1978 and has been innovative in providing traditional credit union products to socially conscious and/or low-income members, now with more than $36 million in assets; (2) Brooklyn Ecumenical FCU in Brooklyn, New York, with $3 million in assets, which began in 1983 and now offers small business loans and assistance in running a small business; and (3) Boone County Community Credit Union in Boone, Iowa, which helped its community after thousands of individual homes were destroyed by tornadoes, rainstorms, and floods in the late 1990s. Low-income designated credit unions are also a unique form of credit union to serve primarily low-income members in distressed and financially underserved areas. NCUA manages a Revolving Loan Fund to provide technical assistance grants to low-income designated credit unions.[25]

Expanding to a Community Charter

The Credit Union Membership Access Act of 1998 allows credit unions meeting community size and other certain criteria the option of expanding to a community charter. Community credit unions agree to serve an entire community, including having a wide market area to seek members, in return for serving the entire community including extending services to all regardless of economic status or financial sophistication. Advantages of expanding a credit union's field of membership to a community charter include: (1) growing and diversifying the membership base for more flexibility in dealing with the mobility of the U.S. workforce; (2) expanding services; (3) developing broader economies of scale; and (4) streamlining the NCUA application process. However, such an expansion changes the way a CU operates and is a more difficult business model to operate including both greater complexity as well as new opportunities for marketing, product, and branding decisions. Community charters also have more rigorous requirements for calculating return on investments. Examples of credit unions that expanded in this way include: (1) Telephone Credit Union of New Hampshire, a $209 million CU, which expanded from a communication industry employee CU to cover all of New Hampshire in 2001; (2) Denver Community Federal Credit Union, with $183 million in assets, which began on January 5, 2004; and (3) Truwest Credit Union, a $632 million, fifty-year-old CU in Tempe, Arizona, which was formerly Motorola Employees Credit Union-West. Since 1998, the number of federal community charters

Concept Questions

1 How did credit unions begin? What requirements do they have? Why are they exempt from taxes?

2 In terms of asset size, how do credit unions compare to thrifts and commercial banks? What changes have occurred in the number and size of credit unions? How were CUs able to extend their common bond requirements? How did banks react to this extension?

3 What regulators and support group do credit unions have? What kind of services can they offer?

4 How do credit union deposit and loan rates generally compare with other depository institutions? What is the goal of credit unions? What aspects of a credit union allow it to offer lower loan rates and higher deposit rates?

5 Why would credit unions want to convert to mutual thrifts or mutual thrift holding companies?

6 What is a community development credit union? What is a community credit union charter, and what are its obligations?

25 See "Organizing a Community Development Credit Union." New Jersey Division of Banking, 2004 *(http://www.state.nj.us/dobi/cdcus.htm)*; "Making an Impact: Stories from the CDCU Movement." Profiles-National Federation of Community Development Credit Unions, 2004 *(http://www.natfed.org)*; and National Credit Union Administration. "About Credit Unions." and 2002 Annual Report, National Credit Union Administration *(http://www.ncua.gov)*.

more than doubled from 421 in 1998 to 900 in 2004. Under an "Access to America Initiative," all federal credit unions may include communities in their field of membership, regardless of location, to meet the definition of an underserved area. For 2002, the NCUA reported in its annual report that more than 23.5 million people in underserved areas gained access to a credit union and the opportunity of access to affordable financial services.[26]

Comparison of Assets and Liabilities: Banks, Thrifts, and Credit Unions

Comparison of Assets, Liabilities, and Equity

Comparison Overview

Figure 5.4 compares the overall types of assets and liabilities held by banks, thrifts, and CUs in 2003. Thrifts on average were the most loaned up, with net loans and leases of about 66 percent of total assets, compared to about 58.6 percent on average for federal credit unions and 57 percent for banks. Thrifts also hold the least cash and due with 2.67 percent, while federal CUs were the most liquid with 11 per-

figure **5.4** BALANCE SHEET PERCENTAGES FOR DEPOSITORY INSTITUTIONS, 2003 MIDYEAR

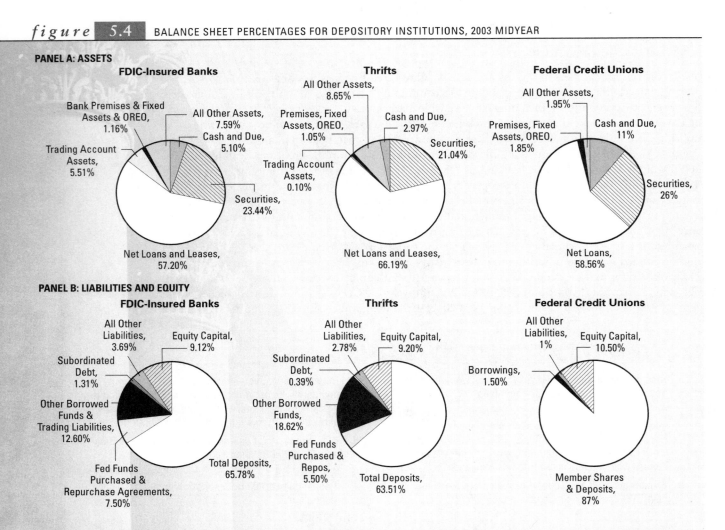

Source: Created by the Authors from FDIC Statistics on Banking, 2003, for banks and thrifts and mid-year 2003 NCUA Annual Report for Credit Unions.

---

26 See "Expanding to a Community Charter: Key Success Factors." Creditunions.com; NCUA News Release—Matz to Community Credit Unions: "Be Inclusive as Possible"; and 2002 Annual Report, National Credit Union Administration *(http://www.ncua.gov).*

cent, followed by commercial banks with 5.1 percent. Credit unions, which are required to hold a larger percentage of securities, held on average 26 percent versus about 23 percent for commercial banks and 21 percent for thrifts. Banks and thrifts had a larger percentage of premises, fixed assets, trading accounts, and other assets on average than CUs, reflecting less complexity and often less need for large premises for many credit unions.

In terms of overall liability structure, CUs have the largest percentage of deposit (called member shares) financing of 87 percent on average versus about 66 percent on average for commercial banks and 63.5 percent for thrifts. Thrifts and commercial banks both had a large percentage of other types of nondeposit liabilities. Banks had a small but larger percentage of subordinated debt financing (1.31 percent versus 0.39 percent for thrifts and 0 percent for federal credit unions). Federal credit unions had the highest average equity capital ratio of 10.50 percent, followed by thrifts with 9.20 percent, and commercial banks with 9.12 percent, all above regulatory equity capital to asset requirements.

More Detailed Comparison of Types of Loans for CUs, Thrifts, and Commercial Banks

Commercial banks can freely invest in all different types of loans, so are more diversified than credit unions and thrifts, which generally have restrictions on the types of loans that they can offer. Thrifts are home mortgage loan specialists and credit unions are consumer loan and more recently home mortgage specialists. In 2003, comparing the average commercial bank, savings institution, and federal credit union, their percentages of different types of loans are as follows:

	Commercial Banks	Thrifts	Federal Credit Unions
Gross Loans & Leases	58.25%	66.78%	59.04%
Real Estate Loans	30.40%	57.90%	25.81%
Commercial Loans	11.76%	3.59%	0.00%
Consumer Loans	9.36%	4.94%	29.77%
Other Loans & Leases	6.11%	0.32%	3.46%
Farm Loans	0.62%	0.03%	0.00%

As noted earlier, commercial banks have moved more into real estate loans but are more diversified on average than thrifts, who are predominantly in real estate (especially home mortgage) lending. On average, in 2003, only small percentages of total thrift loans were commercial or consumer loans (on average, about 8.5 percent). Hence, thrifts have greater interest rate risk than commercial banks, since real estate loans tend to be fixed rate with long maturities. However, thrifts have lower credit risk on average, since home mortgage loans tend to have low default rates. Credit unions have diversified, offering credit union members real estate loans (predominantly home mortgage loans) and consumer loans (predominantly credit card loans and new and used vehicle loans). This diversification provides CUs with lower default and interest rate risk. Also, since particularly smaller CUs know their members and, in the case of occupational credit unions, can often garnish members' wages if loans aren't paid, they tend to have lower loan losses on average. CUs have not entered commercial lending, although, as noted earlier, liberalized rules allow limited business loans. CUs often lend to small businesses indirectly by providing second mortgage loans, home equity, and credit card loans to member/depositor entrepreneurs.

More Detailed Comparison of Types of Liabilities and Equity by CUs, Thrifts, and Commercial Banks

Commercial banks as generally larger institutions on average have more diversified liabilities than CUs and thrifts. A comparison of the different liabilities (as a percent of total assets) of the three depository institutions are shown below:

	Commercial Banks	Thrifts	Federal Credit Unions
Total Deposits	65.78%	63.51%	87.00%
Business Demand Deposits	6.84%	0.00%	0.00%
Transaction Deposits (includes DD)	9.29%	6.35%	10.70% (share drafts)
Savings & Time Deposits	39.07%	51.97%	76.30%
Large Uninsured Time Deposits	8.15%	5.19%	N/A
Core (Retail Deposits)	48.40%	47.31%	87.00%

These rough figures come from FDIC Statistics on Depository Institutions (*http://www2.fdic.gov/SDI/ SOB/*) for all federally insured commercial banks and thrifts, third quarter 2003, and the consolidated balance sheet for the NCUA mid-year 2003 Annual Report. They emphasize the advantage that credit unions have of cheaper deposit funding by holding a much larger percentage of retail (core, insured deposits). Only banks have commercial demand deposits that do not pay interest. However, banks generally provide services to businesses of sweeping funds from higher yielding savings and time deposits to transactions accounts as needed for businesses, so the businesses receive interest for as long as possible before being put in a purely transaction (demand deposit) account. Legislation was proposed in Congress in 2004 to remove the restriction of not paying interest on business demand accounts. CUs do have small amounts of nondeposit borrowings and other liabilities, averaging about 2.4 percent in mid-2003. They also have small amounts of nonmember deposits, averaging only 0.20 percent in mid-2003. Thrifts and banks, as noted in Figure 5.4, have a larger percentage of other borrowings, uninsured time deposits, and other nondeposit liabilities. All three have small percentages of IRAs and Keogh plan accounts held as deposits, for thrifts in 2003, about 3.79 percent of assets and for CUs about 7.56 percent.

CUs and thrifts have similar types of deposits to banks (see Chapter 4). However, CU deposits are typically called *shares*, rather than deposits. Transaction deposits, equivalent to Negotiated Order of Withdrawal (NOW) accounts, are called *share drafts*, and certificates of deposit, *share certificates*. CUs also offer money market accounts and savings accounts. Thrifts, like banks, can offer NOWs, Money Market Deposit Accounts (MMDAs), passbook accounts, and CDs of all types. Because depositories reduced passbook savings in favor of market-sensitive deposits, the cost of funds to thrifts skyrocketed during the 1980s, when market interest rates were relatively high compared with previous decades. With lower interest rates in the 1990s and early 2000s, bank and thrift NIMs, and profitability, improved tremendously, with record ROAs and ROEs in 2003.

Thrifts have greater liquidity problems relative to CUs and banks, since in the eyes of depositors, a thrift's liabilities are highly liquid, whereas its assets, in the eyes of homeowners whose mortgages are those assets, are quite illiquid. Managing the net interest margin and interest rate risk of a thrift is clearly a challenge in a volatile interest rate environment.

The major component of other liabilities for borrowed money for S&Ls is advances from the regulators, especially the Federal Home Loan Banks. These advances are used to meet liquidity and other operating needs. Banks and CUs have also been allowed FHLB borrowing privileges if they qualify as members.

Mutually owned thrifts are permitted to issue long-term debt securities called mutual capital certificates (MCCs). MCCs are securities with a minimum denomination of $100,000 and a minimum maturity of ten years. They are similar to subordinated notes and debentures and were first authorized under DIDMCA. Their claim in income and assets is subordinate to that of depositors and other creditors. MCCs were intended to supplement undivided profits and reserves as a source of net worth for a mutually owned institution. However, regulators deemed them to be less effective than common stock or retained earnings in protecting the interests of the insurance funds. Thus, they serve a relatively minor role in institutional management.

Comparison of Equity-to-Asset Ratios and Trends for Banks, Thrifts, and CUs

Components of Equity Capital for Credit Unions

Like mutual savings institutions, credit unions have only internal equity (retained earnings and reserves) taken from net income each year and accumulated to build equity capital. Hence, they rely on the generation of retained earnings for growth. Because of their not-for-profit form of organization and the common bond requirement, CUs have limited access to funds except through the savings of members or retained earnings. Like other depositories, the balance sheets of CUs contain reserve accounts, or portions of retained earnings designated to serve as cushions against which future loan and investment losses can be charged. Earnings retained in excess of those officially designated as reserves are called undivided earnings, similar to undivided profits in commercial banks. The total of reserves and undivided earnings is equal to the capital or net worth of the CU. Credit union equity to total asset ratios are often referred to as the Credit union net worth ratio.

Components of Equity for Thrifts

Equity or net worth (since many thrifts are mutual) includes the reserves and retained earnings accounts of all institutions as well as the common stock, preferred stock, and paid-in capital accounts of stockholder-owned institutions. For mutual thrifts, retained earnings (or undivided profits or reserves) serve an identical function to common equity in a shareholder-owned firm. Although preferred stock issues have historically been more popular for banks than for thrifts, in 1984, the FHLBB enabled mutual as well as stockholder-owned S&Ls to sell preferred stock through affiliated service corporations. Many have done so. As noted in more detail in Chapter 6, which discusses depository institution capital and regulatory capital requirements, for banks and thrift capital requirements, only 25 percent of Tier 1 (equity capital) can be perpetual preferred stock, although it can used in unlimited amounts for Tier 2 capital, which also allows loan loss reserves, specified subordinated debt to be included as secondary capital.

Trends in Equity Capital Ratios over Time

With improved profitability and higher regulatory capital requirements, common equity to total asset ratios have risen dramatically for all three types of depository institutions in the 1990s and early 2000s, and particularly for thrifts that were extremely undercapitalized in the early 1990s. The trend in average equity to assets for each of the three depository institutions is shown below:

Equity to Total Asset Trends

	Commercial Banks	Thrifts	Federal Credit Unions
1991	6.3%	4.1%	7.6%
1996	8.0%	8.0%	11.0%
Mid-2003	9.1%	9.2%	10.5%

In 1991, the equity-to-asset ratio for CUs was 7.6 percent, 4.1 percent for thrifts, and about 6.3 percent for banks. With higher capital requirements under FIRREA of 1989 for thrifts and FDICIA of 1991 for banks, along with improved profitability in the later 1990s and early 2000s, equity-to-asset ratios improved dramatically. In 1996 and continuing in mid-2003, average equity to total asset ratios were higher than regulatory requirements, with a significant rise particularly on average for commercial banks and thrifts. In 2003, each of the depository institutions had equity-to-asset ratios greater than 9 percent, with CUs, the highest ratio of 10.5 percent.

Capital Accounting Gimmicks for Thrifts in the 1980s

In the 1980s, equity also included regulatory net certificates, which were used by regulators to keep technically insolvent thrifts from failing, along with accounting gimmicks that produced positive capital ratios under regulatory accounting practices (RAP). But according to Generally Accepted Accounting Principles (GAAP), hundreds of thrifts in the 1980s were technically insolvent, many with tangible equity-to-assets ratios lower than 220 percent. RAP superseded GAAP to allow what Kane (1989) calls "zombie" thrifts to continue to operate. In 1985, for instance, about 461 S&Ls had negative equity-to-asset ratios as evaluated by GAAP. RAP equity included goodwill, net worth certificates (NWCs), fees on loans, and appraisal items, among other gimmicks, while GAAP equity included only tangible equity capital consisting of retained earnings and common stock accounts.[27] Regulators gave NWCs that counted as capital to failing thrifts that met established guidelines in exchange for a promissory note from the insurer.[28] To encourage healthy thrifts to take over failing thrifts, they were allowed to include a large amount of tangible goodwill as an asset from the acquisition boosting equity (value of assets less liabilities). Under FIRREA and FDICIA, RAP accounting practices were abolished, and thrifts were required to meet the same capital requirements as commercial banks. Significant goodwill as an asset was phased out, which caused some thrifts significant problems. An example is Glendale Federal, which lost $800 million in assets and equity with this ruling. Ten years later, in 1999, a federal judge ordered the United States to pay $908.9 million to Glendale based on a previous promise of goodwill when Glendale took over a failing S&L in the 1980s (see Schmitt, 1999). With lower interest rates in the 1990s,

---

27 See Kane (1989), Barth (1991), White (1991), and Benston (1985) for a more detailed discussion of the capital of thrifts.

28 As a thrift's earnings improved, it could repay the promissory note and this liability would be removed, as would the NWC. For greater detail on the accounting provisions for capital for thrifts, see Barth (1991), Brumbaugh (1988), and White (1991). Also see Lee Berton. "Accounting at Thrifts Provokes Controversy as Gimmickry Mounts." *The Wall Street Journal* (March 29, 1985), 1, 13.

an economic expansion, closures of technically insolvent thrifts, and consolidation and recapitalization of the industry, thrifts had a much healthier 8 percent average equity-to-asset ratio at the end of 1996, which continued to be high, with a 9.2 percent ratio in mid-2003.

Trends in Market-to-Book Values for Thrifts

Figure 5.5 shows the trends in market-to-book values for large publicly traded thrifts between 1987 and 1995. Market value is equal to the stock price for thrift times its number of outstanding shares; book values are the equity values for thrifts reported on thrifts' balance sheets. With book value accounting in the 1980s, market values, which reflected what investors thought about thrifts, were much lower than book values. Thrifts had market-to-book values less than 1 from 1987 until 1992. In contrast, during this period nonfinancial firms always had market-to-book values greater than 1. With the abolishment of RAP accounting, closures of less solvent thrifts, lower interest rates, and improved profitability, market-to-book values rose dramatically in the 1990s, indicating more favorable assessments for thrifts by investors. Recent empirical studies find thrifts and banks with low charter values (proxied by market-to-book values below 1) take on greater risk than other depository institutions. This suggests that market values of equity are more relevant measures of capital than book values and that low market-to-book institutions have a greater propensity to take on excessive risk under a federal deposit insurance system. Studies also found stock-chartered thrifts with low charter values took on greater risk in the mid- to late 1980s and early 1990s.[29]

figure **5.5** MARKET-TO-BOOK VALUES FOR LARGE PUBLICLY TRADED THRIFTS, 1987 TO 1995

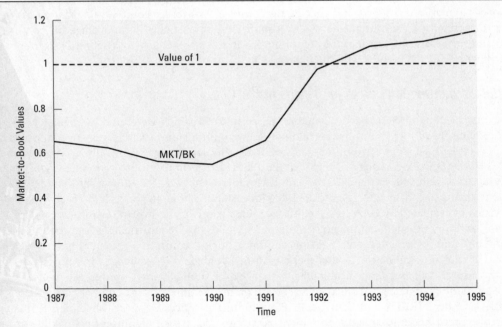

Source: Cebenoyan, A. S., E. S. Cooperman, and C. A. Register. "Ownership Structure, Charter Value, and Risk-Taking Behavior for Thrifts," *Financial Management*, Volume 28, No. 1, Spring 1999, 43–60. Ratios are for samples of large publicly traded thrifts. Ratios represent the aggregate market values of all corporations in each sample divided by the aggregate book value year-end.

---

29 See Keeley (1990) and Galloway, Lee, and Roden (1997) for market-to-book values for bank holding companies; and Cebenoyan, Cooperman, and Register (1998) for thrifts during these periods.

Performance of Depositories: A Comparison

Annual Compound Growth Rates in Assets

Banks

Bank assets at the end of 2003, were $7.603 trillion. As shown in Table 5.2, the three types of depositories have experienced different rates of asset growth over time from 1990 to 2003. Although not shown, from 1985 to 1990, both domestic commercial banks and thrifts had a significant fall in their average annual growth rate. The asset growth of banks slowed to an annual compound rate of 5.85 percent between 1985 and 1990, and a rash of bank failures led to a decline in the industry's growth. During the decade from 1980 to 1989, 1,082 banks failed (Table 5.2, Panel B). Bank failures were particularly dramatic among some of the nation's biggest banks in Texas and New England. With an expansion following the early recession of the 1990s, the average annual growth rate in bank assets for banks rose to 7.05 percent in 1990 to 1996 and stabilized to about 6.50 percent in 1996 to 2003. In the early to mid-1990s, banks expanded by purchasing thrifts under FIRREA's liberalized acquisitions rules. Asset growth rates for banks do not include off-balance-sheet items, which have grown tremendously for the nation's largest banks. Hence, the average bank growth rates are significantly understated in the 1990s to 2003.

table **5.2**   COMPARISON OF DEPOSITORY PERFORMANCE

PANEL A: ANNUAL COMPOUND GROWTH RATES IN ASSETS OF U.S. DEPOSITORIES, 1960 TO 2003

	1960–65	1965–75	1975–80	1980–85	1985–90	1990–96	1996–2003
Banks—Domestic	8.36%	8.91%	10.02%	9.47%	5.85%	7.06%	6.50%
Savings & Loans	12.25%	10.09%	13.32%	11.20%	0.72%		
Savings Banks	7.57%	7.44%	7.48%	4.55%	3.98%	−3.35%*	5.67%
Credit Unions	11.88%	12.85%	12.87%	14.75%	10.04%	8.69%	9.68%

*1990–96 and 1996–2003 figures are combined for S&Ls and savings banks.

Sources: Data from Board of Governors of the Federal Reserve System, Flow of Funds Accounts, CUNA and NCUA Annual Reports, and figures cited in David A. Walker, "Credit Union Insurance and Regulation," Georgetown University, 1997, 7; and FDIC Quarterly Bank Profiles. Estimated annual compound growth rates from given asset figures.

PANEL B: TRENDS IN BANK FAILURES 1933 TO 1996

Year	Number of Bank Failures
1933	4,004
1940–49	99
1950–59	28
1960–69	46
1970–79	76
1980–89	1,082
1990–92	208
1994–96	22
1996–2003, III	32

Commercial bank failures were their highest during the Great Depression of 1933, with 4,004 failures. In the 1980s, the second largest number of failures occurred with 1,082 failures between 1980 and 1989. With a more prosperous economy in the 1990s, bank failures fell. In 1991, 88 percent of banks were profitable. By 1996, 96 percent were profitable.

Sources: Sheshunoff Bank and S&L Quarterly, various issues, Austin, TX: Sheshunoff Information Services, Inc.; George H. Hempel, Donald G. Simonson, and Alan B. Coleman. Bank Management, 4th ed. New York: John Wiley & Sons, Inc., 1994; and FDIC Statistics at a Glance, Number of Failures for BIF-insured Institutions, September 30, 2003 (http://www.fdic.gov).

Savings Institutions

Thrift assets including S&Ls and savings banks were $1.474 trillion at yea-end 2003. Annual asset growth among S&Ls during recent decades has been extremely variable, ranging from a high of 13.3 percent in the late 1970s to a low of −3.35 percent for all thrifts between 1990 and 1996. S&Ls had a particularly high growth rate in the late 1970s and 1980s. The "go-go" days for S&Ls subsided, and the industry shrank in response to regulatory closures of insolvent S&Ls under FIRREA of 1989.

Credit Unions

As of June 30, 2003, CUs had total assets of $0.557 trillion. Between 1990 and 1996, CUs grew at a 7.66 percent annual compound growth rate. In 1997, assets grew 7.1 percent, although the number of CUs fell about 2 percent with mergers. Although CUs grew at the fastest rate of depository institutions, as the smallest depository, CU growth in dollars did not exceed the dollar asset increases at banks.

Thrift and Credit Union Closures

Figure 5.6 graphs S&L and CU closures over time. CUs have had a very low number of failures in the 1980s to 1990 relative to thrifts, yet the number, although small, has been larger than that for thrifts since 1990, after the thrift crisis was resolved. About 320 S&Ls were closed in 1990 and about 230 in 1991. Thrifts attempting to meet higher capital requirements in the 1990s also merged with other thrifts and commercial banks. Other thrifts converted to bank charters. Between 1988 and 1996, the total assets of S&Ls fell from a peak of $1.391 trillion in 1988 to $769 billion, a decline of about 81 percent. In 1997, assets grew only 1.04 percent to $777 billion, and the number of S&Ls fell 14.4 percent to 1,211 with about 205 mergers with banks and other thrifts and conversions to banks. From 1996 to 2003, however, with liberalization of thrift product restrictions and generally prosperous economic conditions and low interest rates, thrift assets grew at an annual growth rate of 5.67 percent to about $1.4 trillion.

figure 5.6 THRIFT AND CREDIT UNION FAILURES, 1990 TO 2002

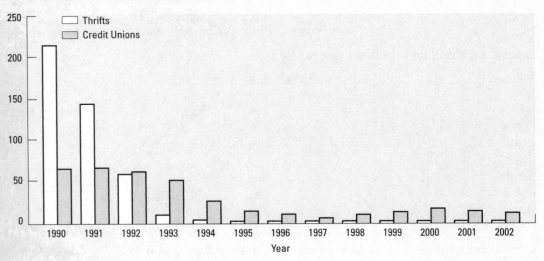

Sources: Created by the Authors using information from Sheshunoff Bank and S&L Quarterly, various issues, Austin, TX: Sheshunoff Information Services; David Walker. "Credit Union Insurance and Regulation." Washington, DC: Georgetown University; NCUA Annual Reports 2000 to 2003; and FDIC Historical Statistics for Banks and Savings Institutions, 2003.

Relative Profitability of Depository Institutions

Thrifts Decline in the 1980s and Rebound in the 1990s

Profitability has been the greatest difference among depositories. Figure 5.7 presents the return on assets (ROA) for S&Ls, banks, and federal CUs from 1990 to 2003. The profitability of S&Ls was negative at worst in 1990 following the S&L crisis of the late 1980s. In contrast, by the time S&Ls hit the bottom of the earnings charts in 1990, banks had rebounded from their earlier low. Credit unions had the highest return on assets in the early 1990s. With the clean-up of the S&L crisis, mergers of thrifts, and low interest rates and an economic expansion, profitability improved for thrifts throughout the 1990s with slight dips in 1996 and 2000. By 1998, thrifts had similar ROAs to credit unions and then surpassed the average CU ROA in the early 2000s. Banks had rising ROAs throughout the 1990s and 2000s, with a couple of dips in 1998 and the economic downturn of 2000 to 2001, and the highest average ROA of the three depositories from 1994 to 2003. The average CU ROA reached a peak in 1992 and then fell a bit until 1997. Thereafter, the average CU ROA remained very stable, showing the least volatility of the three depository institutions. Overall, all depository institutions showed good profitability, benefiting from low interest rates and general economic expansion after 1993, with the exception of a dip during the recession in the early 2000s. At the end of 2003, both thrifts and banks had record average industry ROAs and ROEs for the last thirteen years, benefiting from low interest rates and improving economic conditions.

Several additional reasons can be offered for the poor profitability of thrifts in the early 1980s and early 1990s. Changes in the regulatory and economic environment for depositories did not affect the net interest margin (NIM) of all institutions equally. Thrifts with asset maturities substantially longer than liability maturities had more volatility in ROA with volatility in interest rates. In the 1990s, with generally falling interest rates and general economic prosperity, thrift and bank NIMs were healthy. Banks and thrifts also improved their efficiency over time and increased their noninterest revenue to assets to provide diversification to net interest income.

figure 5.7   PROFITABILITY OF DEPOSITORY INSTITUTIONS, 1990 TO 2003

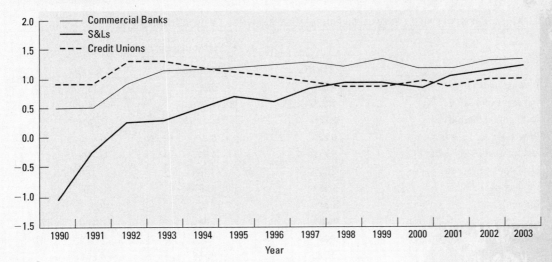

Source: Prepared by the Authors from National Credit Union Administration Annual Reports, Federal Reserve Bulletins, Sheshunoff Bank and S&L Quarterly, CUNA & Affiliates Credit Union Reports, and FDIC Quarterly Bank Statistics.

Comparison of Simplified Income Statements by Depository Institution Type

To understand the reasons for differences in ROAs among thrifts, banks, and CUs, it is helpful to compare the simplified income statements for mid-2003 shown in Table 5.3. Thrifts had a before-tax and adjustments (operating) ROA of 1.46 percent compared with 1.04 percent for CUs and 2.44 percent for banks. To explain why banks performed better, it is helpful to look at the components of operating ROA: NIM, the PLL%, and the Burden%.

Analysis of NIM

Of the three depository institutions, CUs have the highest NIM as the result of a higher interest income to assets (IR%) and the second lowest interest expense to assets (IE%). By having a large percentage of consumer loans that pay higher rates, CUs have the highest yield on assets. Banks had the second highest IR% and lowest IE%, resulting in the second highest NIM. Thrifts, however, had a much lower IR%, since they hold predominantly fixed rate home mortgage loans that offer low rates. Also, with interest rates falling, thrifts suffered prepayments when home mortgage customers refinanced for lower rates. Since thrifts have a larger percentage of savings and time deposits versus transaction accounts, they also had the highest interest expense to assets of the three depository institutions. CUs have a mission to pay higher interest rates on deposits for member/depositors so had a higher interest expense to assets than banks.

Analysis of PLL%

In terms of PLL, by holding home mortgage assets that have low default risk, thrifts were able to have the lowest provision for loan losses to assets, followed by credit unions, which tend to have low defaults on member loans, and then banks, who had the highest average provision percentage (PLL%).

Analysis of the Burden%

Although banks had the highest noninterest expense to assets (NIE%), banks had the lowest average burden percentage, by having the highest average noninterest income to assets (NIR%). As noted in Chapter 4, banks and thrifts have moved into new noninterest revenue-generating ventures that produce fee income to offset volatility in NIMs. Thrifts had the next highest NIR%, followed by CUs,

table **5.3** COMPARISON OF SIMPLIFIED COMMON SIZE INCOME STATEMENTS OF DEPOSITORY INSTITUTIONS, MID-2003

	PERCENTAGE OF AVERAGE ASSETS		
	% Thrifts	% Credit Unions	% Banks
Interest Income	4.93%	6.26%	5.18%
Interest Expense	1.95%	1.77%	1.44%
Net Interest Margin	**2.97%**	**4.49%**	**3.74%**
Provisions for Loan Losses	**0.20%**	**0.32%**	**0.41%**
Net Interest Margin after PLL	2.77%	4.17%	3.33%
Noninterest Expense	2.36%	3.18%	3.89%
Noninterest Income	1.05%	0.05%	3.00%
Burden	**1.31%**	**3.13%**	**0.89%**
ROA before Taxes/Adjustmts.	**1.46%**	**1.04%**	**2.44%**
ROA after Taxes/Adjustmts.	1.29%	1.04%	1.38%
Equity Multiplier	10.88	10.96	11.01
ROE	14.04%	9.94%	15.20%

Sources: Credit Unions represent Federal CU figures. Created by Authors from NCUA Annual Report, mid-year 2003; and FDIC Quarterly Bank Statistic, September 30, 2003.

which had very little fee income to assets (0.05 percent). Thrifts had the lowest NIE%, resulting in the second lowest burden.

Comparison of Operating ROAs

The pretax and pre-adjustment (operating) ROAs are before net loan charge-offs, security gains and losses, extraordinary items, and taxes. Banks had the highest average operating ROA, resulting from their very low average burden (as the result of the highest NIR%) and second highest average NIM (as the result of the lowest IE% and the second highest IR%). Thrifts had the next highest operating ROA with a lower PLL% and a much lower burden (as the result of higher NIR% and lower NIE%) than CUs. [Although CUs had the highest NIM, the higher burden (as the result of a negligible NIR% and higher NIE%) resulted in a lower ROA.] It is perhaps unfair to compare ROAs of banks and thrifts to those of CUs, since the goal of CUs is to minimize loan rates and maximize deposit rates for their depositor/members. However, it is surprising that CUs had the highest NIE%, since in the past volunteer labor and operating space provided by employers often reduced noninterest expenses for CUs. It is worth noting the increasing importance of noninterest income to assets for banks and thrifts. Without this fee income, banks would have had a negative ROA and thrifts a very tiny ROA. Although to be able to increase noninterest income often entails higher noninterest expenses, the burden of banks was the lowest of the three.

More on the Thrift Crisis of the 1980s

In discussing the profitability of thrifts from the 1980s to 1990s, it is important to discuss in a little more depth the thrift crisis, which resulted in a government bailout that cost taxpayers close to half a trillion dollars if interest payments are included.[30] In some ways, the crisis resembles more recent crises in the 1990s for financial institutions in Asia in terms of evidence of fraud and mismanagement by financial institutions. However, part of the thrift crisis was caused by the fact that thrifts perform a maturity intermediation function by transforming short-term deposits into long-term, fixed rate home mortgage loans. By their nature, thrifts have considerably greater interest rate risk than other financial institutions. This situation was aggravated by the fact that thrifts were not allowed to make variable rate mortgages until the early 1980s. Consequently, when interest rates rose in the inflationary environment of the 1970s and thrifts attempted to offer implicitly higher deposit rates to curb deposit disintermediation, interest expense rose but interest revenues did not.

In the early part of the 1980s, thrifts continued to suffer severe losses as the result of rising interest expenses on short-term deposits while interest revenues on fixed rate assets changed very little. In 1980, the Federal Reserve had attacked inflation by slowing the growth rate of the money supply, which caused short-term interest rates and interest rates on thrift liabilities to rise. As shown in Panel A of Table 5.4, the average NIM fell from 2.16 percent during 1976–1979 to 0.84 percent during 1980–1993. With higher noninterest expense as well, the average ROA fell from 0.68 percent to −0.24 percent. Losses resulted in a deterioration in capital, and the average equity-to-assets ratio plunged from 5.7 percent to 3 percent, that is, a rise in the equity multiplier (EM) from 17.54 to 33. The average ROE fell from 11.93 percent in 1976 to 1979 to −8 percent in 1980 to 1983.[31]

To forestall closing hundreds of insolvent thrifts, thrift regulators practiced regulatory forbearance and regulatory accounting practices (RAP), allowing net worth certificates (NWCs) and other regulatory accounting principles to give thrifts positive equity values so they could continue to operate. With dwindling insurance reserves, regulators hoped that interest rates would fall, allowing thrifts to become solvent again. Congress passed emergency powers under the Garn–St. Germain Act of 1982 that permitted failing thrifts to merge with banks and other nonthrift institutions and interstate mergers. Regulators lowered capital-to-asset requirements under RAP to 3 percent.[32]

Unfortunately, regulators created a **moral hazard** for insolvent stock thrifts. Since stockholders of technically insolvent thrifts had already lost their investment, they had nothing to lose and everything

---

30 See Cebenoyan, Cooperman, and Register (1998), Note 1. The GAO estimated a price tag including interest costs for the crisis to be $480.9 billion, with total direct bailout costs to taxpayers of $152.6 billion. *New York Times* (July 15, 1996), BB1.

31 See Barth (1991).

32 See Brumbaugh (1988).

table **5.4**   THE S&L CRISIS OF THE 1980S: TRENDS IN PROFITABILITY & LOSSES, 1980–1996

PANEL A: AVERAGE PROFITABILITY OVER DIFFERENT PERIODS

	1976–1979	CHANGE Rates	1980–1983	CHANGE Rates	1984–1987	CHANGE Rates	1988–1991	CHANGE Rates	1992–1995	CHANGE Rates	1996
Int. Rev%	7.84%	1.89%	9.73%	0.38%	10.11%	−1.45%	8.66%	−1.80%	6.86%	0.31%	7.17%
Int. Exp%	5.68%	3.21%	8.89%	−.96%	7.93%	−.79%	7.14%	−3.03%	4.11%	0.23%	4.34%
NIM %	2.16%		0.84%		2.18%		1.86%		2.75%		2.83%
Noninterest Exp.	1.21%		1.40%		1.91%		1.98%		2.27%		2.58%
Noninterest Rev.	N/G		N/G		0.48%		0.60%		0.72%		0.89%
% Reposs. Assets & Other Real Estate for last year of period:					1.54%		2.38%		0.31%		0.27%
ROA %	0.68%		−0.24%		0.07%		−0.91%		0.46%		0.64%
Eq/Assets RAP	*5.70%		3.00%		4.09%		2.84%		6.35%		7.40%
Eq/Assets GAAP			2.57%		0.79%		2.00%		6.35%		7.40%
EM*	17.54		33.33		24.43		35.21		15.75		13.51
ROE	11.93%		−8.00%		1.71%		−32.04%		7.24%		8.64%
No. S&Ls	N/G		3,544		3,242		2,951		1,807		1,416
% Not Profitable	N/G		N/G		23.75%		33.50%		9.75%		14.00%

PANEL B: STATISTICS FOR LAST YEAR IN PERIODS EXAMINED FOR INSOLVENT THRIFTS & THRIFT RESOLUTIONS

	1983	1987	1989
End-of-Period No. Insolvent Operating	16.37%	21.35%	17.96%
End-of-Period Assets of Insolvent S&Ls ($ billions)	$234	$336	$283
End-of-Period No. of S&Ls Insolvent	515	672	517
Total Number of Resolutions for Period	138	145	242
Total Assets ($ billions)	$37.659	$33.796	$110.322
Estimated Present Value of Cost ($ billions)	$2.004	$8.491	$36.788

*Estimated based on Regulatory Accounting Principles. Under GAAP, ratios would be lower.

Sources: George J. Benston. "An Analysis of the Causes of Savings and Loan Association Failures." *Monograph Series in Finance and Economics*, Salomon Brothers Center for the Study of Financial Institutions, New York University, 1985, 11; Barth (1991) and Kane (1989). Other Sources: Sheshunoff Bank and S&L Quarterly. *Sheshunoff Information Services, Austin, Texas. Federal Home Loan Bank Board and U.S. League of Savings Associations, before 1988, Office of Thrift Supervision after 1988 for early years as cited in Exhibit 18.1, Kidwell, Peterson, and Blackwell. Financial Institutions, Markets, & Money, 5th ed. New York: Dryden Press, 1993; James R. Barth. The Great Savings and Loan Debacle. Washington, DC: AEI Press, 1991. See Barth (1991) Table 3.1 for greater detail concerning thrift resolutions and insolvencies, cited in this table.*

to gain by taking on risky assets under **"bet the bank"** strategies and rapidly expanding to grow their way out of insolvency. Moreover, low capital requirements meant that owner-managers had the potential to make an exorbitant return on a small equity investment.

State regulators in several states, including California, Florida, Texas, and Ohio, adopted lenient laws concerning the types of investments a thrift could engage in. In California, for instance, state-chartered thrifts could invest in service corporations for real estate, land loans, construction development loans, and direct equity investments.[33] Consequently, low capital thrifts in these states had opportunities to take on risky nontraditional assets. These assets and high growth were often financed with insured jumbo deposits of $100,000 that offered above market yields. Many large thrifts marketed these deposits nationwide through brokers. Since these "brokered deposits" were insured, investors were willing to put funds into weak institutions in return for high yields. To match high deposit yields, thrifts were pressured to invest in even riskier assets. Owner-managers of severely insolvent thrifts also had incentives for looting types of behavior, such as paying high dividends, salaries, and other perks, and

---

33 See Benston (1985), Kane (1989), Akerlof and Romer (1993), and Day (1993).

engaging in outright fraud, knowing that their thrift would eventually close and put this cost to the deposit insurer.[34]

In the mid-1980s losses on risky assets finally came to light. In 1984, the nation's largest thrift, FCA, suffered severe loan losses as well as losses on interest rate gambles. As a result, severe deposit runs by uninsured and "jumbo" depositors ensued. FCA's crisis threatened the solvency of the FSLIC, which had insufficient reserves. The FSLIC at this time also faced difficulties finding merger partners for failed thrifts, since with the entry of nonbank banks taking over a failed thrift became a less attractive entry option. To resolve this crisis and the crisis of many other large insolvent thrifts in the mid-1980s, regulators instituted a Management Consignment Program whereby federal regulators replaced managers with regulator-picked CEOs or placed insolvent thrifts under the management of solvent S&Ls.[35]

Despite such measures to conserve FSLIC funds, in 1987 the Government Accounting Office (GAO) announced that the FSLIC was technically insolvent. By 1987, 672 (21.35 percent) S&Ls were technically insolvent, the percentage of repossessed assets rose to 1.54 percent on average per year from 1984 to 1987, and the average GAAP equity-to-asset ratio fell to 0.79 percent. Panel A of Table 5.5 shows that the FSLIC between 1980 and 1988 had used funds to liquidate or assist in 91 liquidations, 541 assisted mergers, 333 supervised mergers, and 95 management consignment cases. Despite Band-Aid measures to recapitalize the FSLIC, by 1988 the situation was so severe that a huge bailout was required.

President Bush ordered insolvent thrifts to be closed, and in 1989 Congress passed FIRREA, which formalized the bailout and a forced recapitalization of the industry. FIRREA mandated closures of severely undercapitalized thrifts that could not meet higher capital requirements by 1991. Despite over 200 thrift closures in 1988, 517 insolvent S&Ls (17.96 percent of the industry) continued to operate in 1989. The Resolution Trust Company faced a tremendous challenge to resolve the problem of the enormous number of insolvent S&Ls. Panel B Table 5.5 shows that, between 1988 and 1996, more than 1,001

table **5.5**   ATTRITION OF FEDERALLY INSURED S&LS, 1934 TO 1988

PANEL A: ATTRITION OF FEDERALLY INSURED S&LS, 1934 TO 1988

Year	Liquidated	Assisted Mergers	Supervised Mergers	Management Consignment	Nonfailed Voluntary Mergers	Total Attrition
1934–79	13	130	0	0	0	143
1980	0	11	21	0	63	95
1981	1	27	54	0	215	297
1982	1	62	184	0	215	462
1983	5	31	34	0	83	153
1984	9	13	14	0	31	67
1985	9	22	10	23	47	111
1986	10	36	5	29	45	125
1987	17	30	5	25	74	151
1988	26	179	6	18	25	254
Total	91	541	333	95	798	1,858

Source: James R. Barth. The Great Savings and Loan Debacle. *Washington, DC: AEI Press, 1991, 32–33.*

PANEL B: CLOSURES OF S&LS & FEDERALLY ASSISTED TRANSACTIONS, 1988–1996

	1988	1989	1990	1991	1992	1993	1994	1995	1996	Total
Assisted Transactions	207	54	246	153	42	19	34	0	0	755
Closures	26	6	68	78	26	8	30	2	2	246
Total	233	60	314	231	68	27	64	2	2	1,001

Source: Sheshunoff Bank and S&L Quarterly, *1990–1996. Austin, TX: Sheshunoff Information Services, Inc.*

---

34 See Kane (1989) and Akerlof and Romer (1993).

35 See Brumbaugh (1988) and Cooperman, Wolfe, Verbrugge, and Lee (1998).

thrifts exited, either through assisted transactions or closures, with the majority occurring in 1988, 1990, and 1991. In 1995 and 1996, with the industry profitable again, only two thrifts were closed each year, and in 1997 no thrifts were closed.[36]

Are Depository Institution Failures Contagious?

The thrift crisis of the 1980s and the failures of several large banks during this time have created concern over whether public deposit runs will occur at other banks or thrifts if a large bank or S&L fails. Weaknesses in deposit insurance funds for both banks and thrifts in the 1980s have increased concerns over potential contagion. Although federal insurance funds incorporate an implicit guarantee by the government to rescue insurance agencies if they fail, this guarantee has been kept off the budget, and until CEBA of 1997, this implicit guarantee was not explicitly stated. Concern over possible contagion also occurred for thrifts because of their very low or negative capitalization in the 1980s.

Several studies have found evidence of risk premiums on jumbo CDs for low capital thrifts in the 1980s, suggesting that depositors demanded a higher rate for greater institution risk for low-capital thrifts, even for insured deposits. As Kane (1989) notes, when insurance funds and depository institutions are undercapitalized, depositor confidence may waver and silent runs, or the threat of silent runs, may occur for less solvent banks and S&Ls. If a small percentage of depositors threaten to withdraw funds, poorly capitalized banks and S&Ls may be able to retain funds by paying a higher deposit rate, which makes "customers willing to live with their growing doubts." A study of FCA's crisis found some evidence to suggest investor contagion for other Western thrifts with insured deposits during the period when the FSLIC's insolvency was threatened. Similarly, another study finds a sudden rise in federally insured CD-rate premiums for Ohio thrifts during the privately insured Ohio thrift crisis in 1985.[37]

For commercial banks, as the largest type of depository, the possibility of deposit market contagion is often considered undesirable for the financial system as a whole. This view arises from fears of a public run on other depository institutions when one fails, forcing solvent institutions to close, not because their net worth has vanished but because they lack the cash to pay off all depositors on demand. Fear of contagion was especially high in the 1980s, when 1,082 banks failed, including a number of very large banks. For this reason, prior to FDICIA, bank regulators implicitly adopted a "too big to fail" (TBTF) policy, generally rescuing mega-banks from failure.

An example is Continental Illinois's crisis in 1984, a few months before that of FCA. Continental Illinois National, one of the ten largest banks in the United States at that time, had assets exceeding $40 billion. Like FCA, Continental Illinois engaged in liability management, depending on short-term borrowings and uninsured deposits for liquidity. When bad news in terms of large loan losses appeared for the bank, Continental Illinois lost large uninsured deposits and was unable to get short-term borrowings renewed, suffering a severe liquidity crisis and teetering on the brink of failure.[38]

Rather than closing the bank, federal regulators kept it afloat by the FDIC purchase of $1 billion of Continental preferred stock to shore up the bank's net worth. The insurance agency also purchased several billion dollars' worth of problem loans from Continental, enabling it to strengthen its balance sheet. This type of regulatory assistance was almost unprecedented and was interpreted to mean that the nation's largest banks would not be allowed to fail.[39] This federal assistance was given despite widespread belief that the bank's top management executives, all of whom were later removed from office, were responsible for the bank's precarious financial condition.

Similarly, in 1988, the FDIC provided an interim financial assistance package of $1 billion and provided assurances of protection to all bank depositors and creditors to rescue the two largest subsidiaries

---

36 See Barth (1991) and *Sheshunuoff Bank and S&L Quarterly.*

37 See Kane (1989); Cooperman, Wolfe, Verbrugge, and Lee (1998); and Cooperman, Lee, and Wolfe (1992). See also Flannery (1998), which provides a survey of studies of market discipline. Studies of market discipline during the thrift crisis include Golding, Hannan, and Liang (1989); Hirschhorn (1989); Cook and Spellman (1991); Cooperman, Lee, and Wolfe (1992); and Park and Peristiani (1998).

38 Wall and Peterson (1990) and Swary (1986). Swary finds some evidence of deposit market contagion for other large liability-managed, less well-capitalized banks during the pre-rescue period of the Continental Illinois crisis. Wall and Peterson, however, find such contagion to be informationally based for other banks with problems similar to Continental Illinois.

39 Comptroller of the Currency C. Todd Conover stated in congressional testimony on September 9, 1984, that none of the eleven largest banks would be allowed to fail. Tim Carrington. "U.S. Won't Let 11 Biggest Banks in Nation Fail." *The Wall Street Journal* (September 20, 1984), 2. See O'Hara and Shaw (1990). O'Hara and Shaw find a positive stock price wealth effect for these "11" biggest banks on the days surrounding this announcement.

Concept Questions

1 What are the major types of assets and loans held by banks, CUs, and thrifts? Why do thrifts have the most interest rate risk of the three depositories? Why do CUs tend to have low default risk? Which of the three hold a larger percentage of liquid assets? Why?

2 Why do CUs garner a larger percentage of core (retail) deposits than banks and thrifts? Despite this, as noted in Table 5.3, CUs have a higher interest income to assets than banks and thrifts. Explain why.

3 Explain why equity to total assets was so much higher for all depository institutions in 2003 than 1991.

4 Why did regulators in the 1980s allow thrifts to have accounting gimmicks? How did investors feel about

thrifts in the 1980s in terms of market value to book ratios? Why did these ratios improve in the 1990s?

5 Which of the three depository institutions is the largest? Fastest growing? Most profitable between 1996 to 2003? Why were banks more profitable in 2003 compared to CUs and thrifts?

6 What were the causes of the thrift crisis of the 1980s? How did regulators attempt to prevent this crisis from happening again? How did regulators create a moral hazard for managers of insolvent thrifts that were allowed to continue to operate?

7 Why are regulators worried about depository institution failures being contagious?

of First Republic Bank Corporation of Dallas, which had forty-one subsidiary banks and assets of $32.5 billion, making it the largest BHC in Texas and the fourteenth largest in the United States. When it became clear that the bank could not recover on its own, the FDIC entered into an agreement with NCNB Corporation (now part of Bank of America), to create NCNB Texas National Bank. This **bridge bank** was to be managed by NCNB. New equity capital of $1.05 billion was invested, with 80 percent provided by the FDIC and 20 percent by NCNB. The North Carolina bank was given an exclusive five-year option to buy out the FDIC's 80 percent share. Regulators appeared to endorse the position that the failure of large institutions is more detrimental to the financial industry than the failure of small ones.

Research examining abnormal stock market reactions surrounding large bank failures generally finds evidence of stock market declines for banks with similar problems to a large failing bank, but not for other banks. This suggests that investors or depositors act on new information concerning problems at their individual bank but do not sell shares or remove deposits for unrelated solvent banks.[40]

Regulatory capital requirements are partly based on the fear of possible contagion by depositors. Under FIRREA of 1989 for thrifts and FDICIA of 1991 for banks, the previous TBTF policy of regulators was eliminated, and regulators were mandated to close all severely undercapitalized banks and thrifts under "prompt corrective action" mandates. With the emergence of mega-banks in the late 1990s, such as Citigroup, analysts are concerned that given the economic importance of these large institutions regulators may have to relapse to TBTF policies. These acts also imposed a system of new risk-based capital requirements. These requirements will be discussed in greater detail in Chapter 6.

Summary

This chapter focuses on thrifts and CUs by providing a brief history and describing regulatory changes and trends that affect these institutions intermixed with a continued discussion of banks. A comparison is made among the industry structures of growth rates, balance sheets, income statements, failure rates, and financial performance of the three types of depository institutions. In contrast to banks and CUs, thrifts have had severe profitability problems as the result of their maturity intermediation function of making long-term, fixed rate loans for home mortgages financed by short-term deposits. They also face increased competition for originating home mortgages from government and quasi-government specialized mortgage agencies as well as from banks and other nonthrift

40 See Kaufman (1994) and Aharony and Swary (1996). Aharony and Swary find that distance and capital adequacy are negatively related to the magnitude of the contagion effect for abnormal stock market returns for thirty-three Southwestern BHCs in response to large bank failures in the Southwest in the mid-1980s. Kaufman (1994) provides an excellent review of studies investigating contagion.

institutions. In the 1980s, thrifts suffered a severe financial crisis. Hundreds of thrifts were closed and hundreds of mergers have occurred. In the 1990s, after regulatory closures, mergers, and restructuring, thrifts have generally become profitable again. Thrifts had on average very good profitability during the mid to latter 1990s and early 2000s, with a rise in noninterest revenue to assets, lower noninterest expenses to assets, and a lower provision for loan losses, with few failures, as well as a healthy NIM.

Credit unions, in contrast, which make short-term consumer loans financed by short-term deposits, have low interest rate risk. They also have closer relations with customers, who are employees of the same firm or members of a group with a common bond, so have lower credit risk. Under an extended common bond definition, CUs have grown rapidly and are generally profitable nonprofit organizations, passing on returns to depositor/owners in the form of higher deposit rates and lower loan rates. Many small CUs, however, do not have the professional expertise that professional managers of thrifts and banks have. CCUs allow smaller CUs to offer products that other depositories offer, although sometimes with not as high a level of sophistication.

The chapter also discusses the thrift crisis, which was magnified in the 1980s by regulators who allowed technically insolvent thrifts to continue to operate, creating moral hazard problems. Many owners of thrifts took on risky assets in attempts to bet the bank and regain solvency. Despite the fact that the GAO estimates that taxpayers ultimately paid almost $0.5 trillion to resolve the S&L failures alone, the thrift industry became profitable again after the implementation of more stringent regulatory policies and a cleanup by the Resolution Trust Corporation in the early 1990s. With similar financial crises occurring in Asia in the late 1990s and a banking crisis in Russia, lessons can be learned from the causes and cure for the thrift crisis of the 1980s in the United States.

Questions

1. Your friends Ed Kramer and Chris Woods ask you about the differences among banks, thrifts, and CUs. Explain how they are different in their operations including differences in terms of the types of loans they make, and their typical liabilities.
2. Mike Woods and Chris North are curious about why thrifts have more interest rate risk than CUs and banks. Explain why they have greater interest rate risk. Was this a good thing during periods of the 1990s and early 2000s when interest rates were falling? How did this risk contribute to the S&L crisis of the later 1980s? What recent regulatory changes also enhanced thrifts' greater product flexibility?
3. Eleanor Swanson and Bud Fogerty are curious about why banks have objected to the NCUA's extended common bond requirement for CUs. Why did the NCUA extend the common bond requirement for CUs in 1982? What are the arguments for and against this extension?
4. Dave and Laura Arberman have been talking with you about recent CU, bank, and thrift mergers and growth rates. Why have respectively banks, CUs, and thrifts had so many mergers in recent years? What legislative changes made it easier for thrifts to convert to banks and merger with banks? What motivation do CUs have to merger?
5. Celestine Abeyta asks you about what threats the thrift charter has faced. Why did Congress get rid of the unitary thrift holding company charter under the GLBA of 1999? What advantage did unitary thrift holding companies have?
6. Ken Bettenhausen is curious about CUs and asks you, what kind of regulatory and support groups do CUs have? What is a CCU, and what services does a CCU provide?
7. Dave and Jen Cather ask you to explain what factors resulted in improved performance for banks and thrifts and CUs in the early 2000s. Explain why banks had the best performance in 2003 of the three for operating ROA. Do you expect these trends to continue or to change in the near future? How important was noninterest revenue in 2003 to the profitability of banks?
8. Sherry Lenert asks you about the difference between mutual and stock thrifts. Explain how they differ and why there have been so many conversions of mutuals to stock ownership. What is a mutual holding company and why have they been controversial?
9. Betsy Katz has been very interested in the thrift crisis and the significant undercapitalization of thrifts in the 1980s. Why did regulators allow thrifts to remain so undercapitalized in the 1980s? What effect did regulatory gimmicks to keep "zombie" thrifts solvent have on thrift risk-taking?
10. Bob Harmon has been very curious about bank runs and contagion. Discuss with Bob the notion of *deposit market* or *investor contagion*. Have empirical studies found evidence of contagion? Why did regulators in the 1980s adopt TBTF policies? How was this changed

under FDICIA of 1991? With really large (mega) financial institutions today, can regulators afford to let these huge institutions fail, even though there is a mandate to do so?

Suggested Case Study for Thrifts: Financial Analysis and Changing Role of Thrifts

"Metropolitan Savings and Loans." Harvard Business School Publishing. This case provides an opportunity for financial analysis and also deals with the changing nature of thrifts. Three former investment bankers have purchased the thrift in 1989 and are attempting to transform it into more of a mortgage bank, originating and securitizing mortgage loans and attracting nationwide deposits, yet still attempting to meet Community Reinvestment Act requirements.

Suggested Case Study for Credit Unions

Capital Management: Navy Credit Union (Darden), formerly in Crawford and Sihler (1994, currently out of print).

Sources for Cases: Harvard Business School Publishing Co., *http://www.hbsp.harvard.edu*, 1-800-545-7685. Also contact *dardencases@virginia.edu*; Internet: *http://www.darden .virginia.edu/case/bib*; 1-800-246-3367 for Darden Case Bibliography, University of Virginia, Management Cases and Notes.

Selected References

Aharony, J., and I. Swary. "Additional Evidence on the Information-based Contagion Effects of Bank Failures." *Journal of Banking and Finance,* Vol. 20, No. 1 (January 1996), 57–69.

Akella, S. R., and S. I. Greenbaum. "Savings and Loan Ownership Structure and Expense-Preference." *Journal of Banking and Finance* 12 (September 1988), 419–437.

Akerlof, G. A., and P. M. Romer. "Looting: The Economic Underworld of Bankruptcy for Profit." *Brookings Papers on Economic Activity,* 1993, 1–73.

Allen, L., and A. S. Cebenoyan. "Bank Acquisitions and Ownership Structure: Theory and Evidence." *Journal of Banking and Finance* 15 (1991), 425–448.

Baldwin, Carliss Y., and Benjamin Esty. "Lessons from the Thrift Crisis." In *Financial Services Perspectives and Challenges,* ed. by Samuel L. Hayes, III. Boston, MA: Harvard Business School Press, 1993.

Barth, J. R. *The Great Savings and Loan Debacle.* Washington, DC: The American Enterprise Institute, 1991.

Benston, G. J. *An Analysis of the Causes of Savings and Loan Association Failures.* New York University Graduate School of Business, Salomon Brothers Center for the Study of Financial Institutions Monograph Series, No. 4/5, 1985.

Brewer, E., and M. R. Saidenberg. "Franchise Value, Ownership Structure, and Risk at Savings Institutions." *Working Paper,* Federal Reserve Bank of New York, 1996.

Brickley, J. A., and C. M. James. "Access to Deposit Insurance, Insolvency Rules, and the Stock Returns of Financial Institutions." *Journal of Financial Economics* (July 1986), 345–371.

Brumbaugh, R. D., Jr. *Thrifts Under Siege: Restoring Order to American Banking.* Cambridge, MA: Ballinger Publishing Co, 1988.

Cebenoyan, A. S., F. Cebenoyan, and E. S. Cooperman. "Regulatory Regimes and Takeovers of U.S. Thrifts." *Working Paper,* University of Colorado at Denver, 2004.

Cebenoyan, A. S., E. S. Cooperman, and C. A. Register. "Deregulation, Reregulation, Equity Ownership, and S&L Risk Taking." *Financial Management* 24 (Autumn 1995), 63–76.

Cebenoyan, A. S., E. S. Cooperman, and C. A. Register. "Ownership Structure, Charter Value, and Risk-Taking Behavior for Thrifts." *Financial Management,* Vol. 28, No. 1 (Spring 1999), 43–60.

Cebenoyan, A. S., E. S. Cooperman, C. A. Register, and S. C. Hudgins. "The Relative Efficiency of Stock versus Mutual S&Ls: A Stochastic Cost Frontier Approach." *Journal of Financial Services Research* (1993), 151–170.

Colantuoni, Joseph A. "Mutual-to-Stock Conversions: Problems with the Pricing of Initial Public Offerings." *FDIC Banking Review* (1999), 1–9.

Cole, R. A., and R. A. Eisenbeis. "The Role of Principal-Agent Conflicts in the 1990s Thrift Crisis." Federal Reserve Board, Finance and Economics Discussion Series, Division of Research and Statistics Division of Monetary Affairs, Working Paper 95–27, 1996.

Cole, R. A., and H. Mehran. "Executive Compensation and Corporate Performance: Evidence from Thrift Institutions: Proceedings of a Conference on Bank Structure and Competition." Chicago: Federal Reserve Bank of Chicago, 1991, 227–247.

Cook, D. O., and L. J. Spellman. "Federal Financial Guarantees and the Occasional Market Pricing of Default Risk." *Journal of Banking and Finance* 15 (1991), 1113–1130.

Cooperman, E. S., W. B. Lee, and G. A. Wolfe. "The 1985 Ohio Thrift Crisis, The FSLIC's Solvency, and Rate Contagion for Retail CDs." *Journal of Finance* 57 (July 1992), 919–941.

Cooperman, E. S., G. A. Wolfe, J. A. Verbrugge, and W. B. Lee. "Further Evidence on Equity Market Contagion: The FSLIC's Solvency and the Liquidity Crisis of Financial Corporation of America." *The Financial Review* 33 (November 1998), 93–106.

Cordell, Lawrence R., Gregor D. MacDonald, and Mark E. Wohar. "Corporate Ownership and the Thrift Crisis." *Journal of Law and Economics* 36 (1993), 719–756.

Crawford, Richard D., and William W. Sihler. *Financial Service Organizations: Cases in Strategic Management.* New York: HarperCollins College Publishers, 1994.

Day, Kathleen. *S&L Hell: The People and the Politics Behind the $1 Trillion Savings and Loan Scandal.* New York: W. W. Norton, 1993.

Esty, Benjamin C. "A Case Study of Organizational Form and Risk Shifting in the Savings and Loan Industry." *Journal of Financial Economics* 18, (April 1997), 57–76.

Flannery, Mark J. "Using Market Information in Prudential Bank Supervision: A Review of the U.S. Empirical Evidence." *Journal of Money, Credit and Banking* 30 (August 1998, Part 1), 273–305.

Galloway, T. M., W. B. Lee, and D. M. Roden. "Bank's Changing Incentives and Opportunities for Risk Taking." *Journal of Banking and Finance* 21 (April 1997), 509–527.

Golding, E. L., T. H. Hannan, and J. N. Liang. "Do FSLIC-Insured Institutions Pay Risk Premia for Insured Deposits?" Working Paper, Federal Reserve Board, 1989.

Gorton, G., and R. Rosen. "Corporate Control, Portfolio Choice, and the Decline of Banking." *Journal of Finance* 50 (December 1995), 1377–1420.

Hirschhorn, E. "Depositor Risk Perceptions and the Insolvency of the FSLIC." Working Paper, Office of Thrift Supervision, 1989.

Kane, E. J. *The S&L Insurance Mess: How Did It Happen?* Washington, DC: Urban Institute Press, 1989.

Kaufman, G. G. "Bank Contagion: A Review of the Theory and Evidence." *Journal of Financial Services Research,* Vol. 8, No. 2 (1994), 123–150.

———. "Capital in Banking: Past, Present, and Future." *Journal of Financial Services Research,* Vol. 5, No. 4 (1992), 385–402.

Keeley, M. C. "Deposit Insurance, Risk, and Market Power in Banking." *American Economic Review* (December 1990), 1183–1200.

Mester, L. J. "Owners versus Managers: Who Controls the Bank?" *Business Review* (Federal Reserve Bank of Philadelphia) (May/June 1989a), 13–22.

———. "Testing for Expense Preference Behavior: Mutual versus Stock Savings and Loans." *Rand Journal of Economics* 20 (Winter 1989b), 483–499.

O'Hara, M., and W. Shaw. "Deposit Insurance and Wealth Effects: The Value of Being Too Big to Fail." *Journal of Finance* (December 1990), 1587–1600.

Park, Sangkyun, and Stavros Peristiani. "Market Discipline by Thrift Depositors." *Journal of Money, Credit and Banking* 30 (August 1998, Part 1), 347–364.

Saunders, A., E. Strock, and N. G. Travlos. "Ownership Structure, Deregulation, and Bank Risk Taking." *Journal of Finance* 45 (June 1990), 643–654.

Schmitt, Richard B. "Judge Orders U.S. to Pay $908.9 Million to California Thrift Glendale Federal." *The Wall Street Journal* (April 12, 1999), A4.

Sfirdis, James M., and Kenneth N. Daniels. "The Relative Cost Efficiency of Stock versus Mutual Thrifts: A Bayesian Approach." *The Financial Review* 39 (February 2004), 153–178.

Swary, I. "Stock Market Reaction to Regulatory Action in the Continental Illinois Crisis." *Journal of Business* (July 1986), 451–473.

Verbrugge, J. A., and J. S. Jahera, Jr. "Expense Preference Behavior in the Savings and Loan Industry." *Journal of Money, Credit, and Banking* 13 (November 1981), 465–476.

Walker, David A., Principal Investigator. "Credit Union Insurance and Regulation." Center for Business-Government Relations, Georgetown University, 1997.

Wall, L. D., and D. R. Peterson. "The Effect of Continental Illinois' Failure on the Financial Performance of Other Banks." *Journal of Monetary Economics* (August 1990), 77–99.

White, Lawrence J. *The S&L Debacle: Public Lessons for Bank and Thrift Regulation.* New York: Oxford University Press, 1991.

Williams, Julie L. *Savings Institutions: Mergers, Acquisitions, and Conversions.* New York: Law Journal Press, 2002.

EXPLORING CREDIT UNION AND THRIFT ANNUAL REPORTS

Look up on the Internet the annual reports for a large thrift or credit union. For instance, Washington Mutual is at *http://www.wamu.com* and Navy Federal Credit Union is at *http://www.navyfcu.org.* On Washington Mutual's corporate home page, on the left, notice "About WaMu" has a pull-down arrow offering menu choices; choose "Investors Relations." Once you're on the Investors Relations menu, on the left-hand side in green you'll see additional menu choices; select "Annual Report & 10K." Choose the annual report for the latest year. These are generally in PDF form (instructions to download Adobe Acrobat Reader will be given if you don't have it). (Note: Websites change—but, in general, you can get an annual report online by selecting "Investors Relations" and then following the menu). Similarly, for the Navy Federal Credit Union, from the home page, click on "About Navy Federal," and then select "Navy Federal's Annual Report" on the next menu. Once you've printed out the annual reports, do a financial analysis of trends in profitability for the past two years and explain why return on assets went up or down in detail including components of NIM, Burden, and PLL, along with security gains/losses and other extraordinary items, as discussed in the performance analysis in Chapter 4. Also analyze the risk of the respective organization, using the risk ratios that are provided and discussed in Chapter 4.

EXPLORING CREDIT UNION AND THRIFT FINANCIAL PERFORMANCE REPORTS

For credit unions that do not have financial data on their Websites, you can also get less detailed call reports (basic income and balance sheet statements) on the
NCUA Website (http://www.ncua.gov) *and on the NIC-Federal Reserve System Website* (http://www.ffiec.gov/nic) *under financial performance reports, as discussed in Chapter 4. Uniform bank performance reports for thrifts are also available at* http://www.ffiec.gov *(follow the menu). Detailed instructions are also discussed in Chapter 4 for assessing UBPRs.*

USEFUL LINKS FOR FINANCIAL INSTITUTION DATA

Credit Unions

Federal Credit Union Act

http://www.ncua.gov/ref/fcu_act/fcu_act.html

Credit Union National Association

http://www.cuna.org/

National Credit Union Administration

http://www.ncua.gov/

Thrift Sites

Federal Home Loan Bank

http://www.fhlbanks.com/

Office of Thrift Supervision

http://www.ots.treas.gov/

6 Capital Regulations and Management

"Because of banks' multiple functions, the great degree of leverage they employ in carrying out their economic role and their access to the safety net, society has a keen interest in the health and well-being of the banking system. . . . Only in recent decades, however, have U.S. banking agencies established specific standards for capital in relation to the risk of loss rather than simply commenting on institutions' capital adequacy to managers and boards of directors on a case-by-case basis, often in qualitative terms."

"Capital Standards for Banks: The Evolving Basel Accord." Federal Reserve Bulletin, *Vol. 89, No. 9 (September 2003), p. 1 (adapted from testimony presented by Federal Reserve Board Vice Chairman Roger W. Ferguson, Jr., to House and Senate Committees on Banking and Financial Services, June 18–19, 2003).*

Capital provides a crucial cushion against potential losses on financial assets, as well as other operating losses for financial institutions, and is very important from a regulatory perspective in ensuring the integrity of the payments system. In response to the large number of bank failures and the thrift crisis of the 1980s, new regulatory capital requirements were instituted for banks and thrifts in the 1990s, with depository institutions scrambling to obtain capital. Later in the 1990s, capital was an important factor in helping to support mergers. By their nature, financial institutions have high financial leverage (low capital ratios), which magnifies their profits but also increases their risk of bankruptcy. Hence, the management of financial institution capital is crucial from both a profitability and safety standpoint. This chapter discusses the role of capital, capital regulatory requirements, new proposed capital requirements, and other capital management considerations, focusing on depository institutions that have the most stringent capital regulations.

The following sections discuss market versus book value definitions of capital, preferences of different agents, theories for the optimal amount of capital, and the role of regulatory and market forces in determining bank capital ratios. The next sections discuss regulatory definitions of capital, and requirements under Basel I that apply to the major-

Learning Objectives

After completing this chapter, you will be able to:

1 Understand the difference between book value and market value capital ratios and why capital is important for financial institutions.

2 Describe different preferences for financial leverage by different agents.

3 Understand the reasons for recent trends in capital ratios.

4 Explain the regulatory definitions for different types of bank capital.

5 Calculate risk-weighted assets and the different regulatory capital ratios for a bank and determine its regulatory capital classification.

6 Discuss regulations under Basel I and proposed changes and the framework of Basel II for very large banks.

7 Explain other practical considerations for determining a bank's capital ratio and dividend policies.

8 Understand the effect of capital mix on a bank's weighted average cost of capital.

ity of U.S. banks, along with requirements under Basel II that apply to about twenty of the largest U.S. international banks. The final sections outline capital management and dividend policy considerations and risk-adjusted return on capital (RAROC).

Defining Capital: Market versus Book Values

With the exception of securities firms, financial institutions hold the majority of their assets and liabilities for financial statements at their book (historical) rather than market values. With equity capital defined as the difference between total assets less total liabilities, the book value of equity may differ markedly from the market value of equity. This is particularly the case for depository institutions that hold the majority of their assets as loans and the majority of liabilities as deposits whose market values change with changes in interest rates. Only investments held for sale and trading securities are held at their true market values. Consequently, book equity-to-asset ratios are deceptive and often do not really reflect the economic realities facing the bank.

Figure 6.1 shows the difference between using book and market values to measure the capital for the Market King Bank. For simplicity, the Market King Bank has three assets: cash, three-month Treasury bills (T-bills), and consumer automobile loans with a four-year maturity and 10 percent rate. For this example, all deposits are variable rate, so the market value of liabilities will always remain the same as their book values.

In Panel A using book value accounting, equity capital is measured as the book value of assets less the book value of liabilities. Market King Bank has $4.2 million in equity and $70 million in assets, giving the bank a book value equity-to-asset ratio of 6 percent.

In Panel B using market value accounting, equity capital is measured as the market value of assets less the market value of liabilities (that is, the present value of cash flows on assets less the present value of cash flows on liabilities). Panel B assumes that after the loans were made, the market rate for auto loans rose to 13 percent. With a higher discount rate for the present value of future loan payments, the

figure 6.1   BOOK VALUE VERSUS THE MARKET VALUE OF CAPITAL

The market value of assets (and, therefore, of equity) reflects changing economic conditions. In this example, changing interest rates cause the market value of loans to fall (Panel B) or to rise (Panel C) when compared with their book value. Equity worth falls or rises correspondingly.

PANEL A: BOOK VALUE ACCOUNTING

Assets		Liabilities and Equity	
$ 1,000,000	Cash	$ 65,800,000	Deposits
19,000,000	T-Bills	4,200,000	Equity
50,000,000	10% Loans[a]		
$ 70,000,000	Total	$ 70,000,000	Total

Equity / Total Assets = 6.00%

a Amortizing these loans over forty-eight months at a monthly rate of 10% / 12 = 0.833% results in expected monthly payments of $1,268,129.20. That is, the present value of $1,268,129.20, discounted at 0.833 percent for forty-eight months, is $50,000,000.

PANEL B: MARKET VALUE ACCOUNTING (LOAN RATES RISE TO 13%)

Assets		Liabilities and Equity	
$ 1,000,000	Cash	$ 65,800,000	Deposits
19,000,000	T-Bills	1,469,757	Equity
47,269,757	10% Loans[b]		
$ 67,269,757	Total	$ 70,000,000	Total

Equity / Total Assets = 2.18%

b The present value of the monthly payments discounted at 13% / 12 = 1.0833%.

PANEL C: MARKET VALUE ACCOUNTING (LOAN RATES FALL TO 7.5%)

Assets		Liabilities and Equity	
$ 1,000,000	Cash	$ 65,800,000	Deposits
19,000,000	T-Bills	6,647,757	Equity
52,447,757	10% Loans[c]		
$ 72,447,757	Total	$ 72,447,757	Total

Equity / Total Assets = 9.18%

c The present value of the monthly payments discounted at 7.5% / 12 = 0.625%.

market value of the loans falls from $50,000,000 to $47,269,757. With the market value for the liabilities unchanged, the market value of equity (market value of assets less market value of liabilities) falls from $4,200,000 to $1,469,757, or by $2,730,243, a decline of about 65 percent! If Market King sold its loans, it would have a significant loss. The market value equity-to-asset ratio is now 2.18 percent versus a 6 percent book value-to-equity ratio.

Similarly, as shown in Panel C, if loan rates on similar auto loans fell to 7.5 percent, the market value (present value of future cash flows) for Market King's loans would rise significantly to $52,447,757, resulting in a rise in the market value of equity to $6,647,757, a 58 percent rise over the book value shown in Panel A. The bank's new market value equity-to-asset ratio would rise to 9.18 percent versus the book value-to-equity ratio that investors see, with book value accounting for only 6 percent.

Difficulties in Calculating Market Values

As Figure 6.1 shows, market value capital measures are superior to book measures, since they reflect market realities. For instance, in reality, if loan rates rise, Market King's low yielding loans have dropped in value and would have to be sold at a loss. Market King could only sell its loans for a much lower amount. However, problems exist in calculating the market value of assets and liabilities. Some assets, for instance, may have no markets. For a stockholder-owned institution, the market value of common stock can be used (stock price × number of shares). However, many community depository institutions are privately held or their stock is infrequently traded, so the market/book value assessments are unavailable.

The Financial Accounting Standards Board (FASB) embarked on a study of market value accounting in 1986. The first result of its efforts was FASB Rule 107, issued in 1991 and effective for financial statements prepared by large firms on or after December 15, 1992. The rule required banks, other financial institutions, and nonfinancial firms with assets of $150 million or greater to disclose in footnotes to their financial statements the fair market value of all financial instruments on their balance sheets—assets as well as liabilities. Smaller firms had three extra years before complying under the new rules. In early 1993, FASB issued another final rule requiring market value accounting for investments held for sale, which in 2003 represented 93 percent of total U.S. bank securities. Only securities being held to maturity (currently about 7 percent) can be reported under historical cost accounting rules. Other real estate owned similarly must be reported at market value. The market values of derivatives must also be reported. Accounting rules are particularly challenging for banks and other financial institutions because of the large proportion of financial assets they hold. Pressures for greater market value accounting for depository institutions will continue in the future.[1]

Why Capital?

Capital is important for many reasons including: (1) serving as a cushion against future losses; (2) protecting deposit insurance funds in the event of insolvency and ensuring the integrity of the payments system; (3) providing long-term funds for long-term investment and growth in assets, including future acquisitions of other firms; (4) providing confidence for uninsured depositors and debtholders; (5) avoiding regulatory interference by meeting regulatory capital requirements; (6) contributing to higher credit ratings by rating agencies, allowing a lower cost of financing; (7) providing extra borrowing capacity in terms of the debt-to-equity mix; and (8) providing an optimal capital structure that provides a lower weighted average cost of capital for a financial institution.[2]

The Role of Capital as a Cushion against Losses

To understand the role of capital as a cushion against losses, observe the following balance sheet for the Majestic Savings Bank:

Majestic Savings Bank Balance Sheet

Assets	Deposits & Capital
Treasury bills: $30 million	Deposits: $92 million ($80 million insured)
Mortgage loans: $70 million	Capital: $8 million
Total: $100 million	Total: $100 million

Suppose a major employer in town announces that it is transferring out of state, and many employees who have home mortgages with Majestic will lose their jobs. Majestic Bank's uninsured depositors may begin to evaluate whether their thrift could fail if delinquent loan payments reduce mortgage income and the value of loans, which would result in a fall in the value of the thrift's equity. They may think about pulling out their deposits but may be reassured by Majestic's $8 million in capital. The value of Majestic's assets would have to fall by $8 million (i.e., $8 million / $70 million, or 11.43 percent) before the depositors' interests would be threatened. Since such a large percentage decline in the value of Majestic's assets is unlikely, depositors may stay put.

If Majestic had only $2 million in capital, however, a small change in the value of assets ($2 million / $70 million, or 2.86 percent) would wipe out the thrift's equity. Hence, large depositors would be more

1 See Mondschean (1992); Moore (1992); David Siegel. "Disclosures to Herald Accounting's New Age." *American Banker* (September 21, 1992), 1, 18; Ford S. Worth. "The Battle of the Bean Counters." *Fortune* (June 1, 1992), 117–126; Lee Berton. "FASB Adopts Rule Requiring Updated Values." *The Wall Street Journal* (December 17, 1991), A3, A4; Mengle and Walter (1991); Kane and Unal (1990); Berger, Kuester, and O'Brien (1989); and Benston (1989).

2 Ibid. Also see Saunders and Cornett (2003).

likely to withdraw funds. Majestic would have a liquidity crisis if this happened and would have to liquidate assets to meet large deposit withdrawals or try to find some alternative borrowing sources. A large percentage of illiquid loans and low confidence would make finding other borrowing sources difficult, and Majestic could fail before managers had time to resolve the thrift's financial problems. In 1995, Continental Illinois suffered a similar liquidity crisis that led to its closure and takeover by regulators.

Although higher capital provides a cushion against losses and greater confidence for depositors, different parties have different preferences for how much capital should be held by a financial institution. Capital also has other uses: It supports growth and long-term fixed investments as well as reduces moral hazard. Different agents involved in a financial institution also have different preferences for more or less capital. These preferences and uses are discussed in the following section.

Preferences by Different Agents for Capital

Preferences of Stockholders for Higher Financial Leverage

As noted in Chapter 4, with higher financial leverage a firm's equity multiplier (EM) (assets / equity) rises, which, holding other factors constant, has a positive effect on return on equity (ROE; i.e, the DuPont relationship ROE = ROA × EM discussed in Chapter 4), so stockholders are often thought to prefer higher equity multipliers, allowing them higher potential returns on a smaller equity investment, (i.e., an option on the residual value of the firm after debtholders are paid that rises in value with greater financial leverage). The after-tax cost of debt is also cheaper than the cost of equity, with the tax deductibility of debt. In addition, insured deposits provide a subsidy to banks, since the interest rate on insured deposits is low (no risk premium required on this insured debt). This deposit insurance subsidy rises in value the more risky, less capitalized an insured institution. Studies show that the average equity-to-asset ratio for banks prior to deposit insurance was about 30 percent compared with 9 percent today. The fact that stockholders of insured depository institutions prefer greater financial leverage, that is, greater capital risk, creates a moral hazard problem for the deposit insurer.[3]

Moral Hazard Problems with Deposit Insurance

Given there is no check by debtholders in terms of a higher interest rate on insured deposits for greater firm risk-taking, stockholders have stronger incentives to take on greater risk, creating a moral hazard problem. Consider the Fairweather Bank (FB) with the following start-up scenario:

Assets: $5 million in cash   *Equity Capital: $5 million*

FB has $5 million of cash financed totally by the owners' investment of $5 million in equity capital. The cash can be used to make loans with a 50 percent probability of default and a 50 percent probability of producing a $5 million profit after all expenses are paid. Stockholders have a 50 percent probability of losing their entire $5 million investment, and the expected dollar return on the loans and the stockholders' investment is

$$0.50 (\$5 \text{ million}) + 0.50 (-\$5 \text{ million}) = \$0$$

The expected rate of return to stockholders is 0 percent; thus stockholders would encourage managers to seek better investments.

However, suppose the depository institution is funded by $4 million in insured deposits at a cost of 10 percent (resulting in a $0.4 million interest expense) and $1 million in equity capital. Since debt financing is being used, the most the stockholders could lose is $1 million. Stockholders' expected dollar profit on the loans is now:

$$0.50 (\$5 \text{ million} - \$0.4 \text{ million}) + 0.50 (-\$1 \text{ million}) = \$1.8 \text{ million}$$

---

3 See Buser, Chen, and Kane (1981) and Merton (1977). Also, see Kaufman (1992); and the *Journal of Banking and Finance* 19 (1995) (*Special Issue on Bank Capital*) for surveys of research on the effect of deposit insurance on bank capital.

The stockholders' expected rate of return is now 180 percent ($1.8 million / $1 million), not 0 percent, even though the investment is the same. The lower the amount of capital, the less incentive stockholders have to monitor the actions of management to prevent excessive risk-taking, with more to gain if things go well and less to lose if things go poorly. Similarly, insured depositors would have little concern about the risk involved since they are insured and, hence, would have little incentive to monitor the bank. Thus, less-capitalized banks have greater incentives for risk than better-capitalized institutions.[4]

Purposes of Capital and Some Incentives for Stockholders to Hold Capital

On the other hand, from a current stockholder's perspective, retaining earnings and increasing equity capital permits a depository to grow and acquire other firms without having to issue additional external equity, which can be expensive and dilute current stockholders' earnings. It also prevents greater regulatory interference concerning branching or merger decisions. Using capital to finance additional fixed assets or additional growth is also less risky than financing long-term assets with short-term deposits. Paying for permanent assets with short-term liabilities would be unwise because it would require additional long-term capital, which can be more expensive for less well capitalized depositories. Studies also show that better-capitalized banks have a lower cost of uninsured funds and a lower weighted average cost of capital as well as generating higher ROEs than other banks. A significant positive relation between market-to-book values and capitalization for banks appeared in the 1980s, suggesting that better-capitalized banks sell at a larger premium than other banks.[5]

Preferences of Uninsured Debtholders, Managers, and Regulators

In contrast to stockholders, who generally prefer lower capital ratios, uninsured debtholders prefer higher capital ratios to protect against potential loss of the funds they lent to the bank. Institutional investors also may be forbidden to invest in low capital stocks under a "prudent man" rule. Consequently, undercapitalized institutions may be penalized by uninsured investors, often large institutional investors, such as insurance companies and pension funds, and have to offer a risk premium to attract uninsured debt. As mentioned in Chapter 3, the Financial Services Modernization (Gramm-Leach-Bliley [GLB]) Act of 1999 mandated that the top 100 bank holding companies have an issue of subordinated debt, based on the premise that uninsured debtholders will provide monitoring and market discipline. Similarly, Basel II, proposed capital requirements for large international banks, put an emphasis on market discipline.

Managers may also fear losing their jobs if their institution fails and so may generally prefer higher capital ratios as a cushion against loss and may demand higher salaries to work for a less well capitalized bank. Some studies suggest, however, that the interests of managers become aligned with those of external stockholders for lower capital if managers have significant stock ownership or are under a compensation plan that is based on stock performance.[6]

Regulators prefer greater capital to protect deposit insurance funds and taxpayers' money and to ensure the integrity of the payments system. Because capital promotes confidence, it is more likely that depositors will not remove deposits all at once from a bank if the bank receives bad news. Because capital suppliers have a subordinate claim on the depository's income and assets, their investment helps to reassure uninsured creditors. Even if the institution has financial difficulty, uninsured depositors know the extent to which the value of assets can shrink before they are in danger of not recovering all their funds: that amount is equal to the total capital of the institution. The more capital, the more protection is afforded to uninsured depositors, federal deposit insurance funds, and other short-term creditors—making a run on the institution less likely, that might result in contagious runs for other weaker banks suffering similar types of problems and a disruption of the payments system. Accordingly,

---

4 This illustration is similar to one used by Furlong and Keran (1984).

5 See Kaufman (1992) for a survey of these studies.

6 For instance, John and John (1993) suggest that higher regulatory capital should be required for banks with managerial compensation plans tied to a bank's stock price since managers under these plans have stronger incentives for risk-taking. Cebenoyan, Cooperman, and Register (1995) find evidence of higher risk-taking by thrifts with greater managerial ownership in the late 1980s when thrifts were significantly undercapitalized, but not in the early 1990s, a period of regulatory stringency and higher capital requirements.

regulators are more likely to interfere in an institution's plans for an acquisition or additional branches or other activities if the institution is not well capitalized. Under risk-based capital requirements implemented in 1993, to be discussed later in the chapter, banks are categorized into different capital categories, with greater privileges for well-capitalized institutions and greater regulatory scrutiny and discipline for banks that are below well-capitalized definitions.

As incentives to have banks (as well as thrifts) better capitalized, a risk-based deposit insurance program was implemented in 1993 and amended in 1997. Under this program, well-capitalized banks pay lower deposit insurance premiums (0 cents per $100) than adequately capitalized banks (3 cents per $100), and undercapitalized banks (10 cents per $100). However, if institutions are a supervisory concern, these premiums rise substantially for each category the greater the supervisory concern. Under FDICIA of 1991, regulators were required under "prompt and corrective action" mandates to close severely undercapitalized banks and thrifts.[7]

The Optimal Capital Structure: Balancing Shareholders' and Regulators' Interests

Based on the stockholders' preferences we've just discussed, Buser, Chen, and Kane (1981) provide a theoretical model for the optimal regulatory capital requirement that regulators impose, illustrated in a modified Figure 6.2. Since bank stockholders, as discussed earlier, prefer greater financial leverage to increase the value of the firm, they would opt for having a very high debt to total assets ratio, close to 100 percent, resulting in a value for the firm at V_L (above the optimum debt for a firm without a deposit insurance subsidy, which instead would be at a lower point D_O, with a lower firm value at V_O). Regulators want to protect deposit insurance funds and will demand a lower debt-to-asset ratio, desiring a point like D^*. However, regulators are also concerned that banks will opt out of the insurance system altogether, so regulators are willing to accept a regulatory minimum debt-to-asset ratio at a higher level (D_R, providing a bank value of V_R) that banks will find acceptable in return for their federal deposit insurance subsidy. In a study of bank holding company (BHC) capital targets in the early 1990s, Wall and Peterson (1995) found BHCs to hold capital ratios close to the minimum regulatory requirements, consistent with this model. In the early 2000s bank equity capital ratios on average, in contrast, have exceeded regulatory requirements.[8]

Changes in the Nature of Banking: Other Views on Bank Capital

A more recent view of bank capital adequacy regulations suggests that regulatory capital adequacy regulation may not be as necessary today as in the past, with greater transparency in bank operations and market forces demanding higher capital for banks as they undertake more risk. Flannery and Rangan (2002) found a significant capital build-up for the largest 100 U.S. publicly traded banks over 1986 to 2000, with capital ratios much higher than regulatory minimums and correlated with the volatility of bank earnings. As banks took on new risks, they tended to increase the capital that they held for these risks. Allen and Gale (2002) similarly provide a model that shows that in the absence of other externalities, banks are likely to choose socially optimal capital structures on their own. Froot (2001) suggests that the role of large financial service firms has changed significantly from serving in warehouse capacities (making loans and holding on to them) to becoming diversified firms in non-warehouse capacities as originators and distributors of financial services (securitization and other fee-based activities). With this change, he points out that there is much more market transparency and pricing involved in their activities, making banks more efficient in terms of information production. This has resulted in great reliance on market pricing and the markets to provide liquidity, as well as a greater

---

7 See Saunders and Cornett (2003), Chapter 10, 487. Saunders and Cornett point out that as of January 1, 1997, if a bank had weaknesses that if not corrected could result in a significant risk to the insurance fund, it would have to pay a premium. Within each of the categories, well-capitalized banks would have to pay 3 cents per $100; adequately capitalized banks, 10 cents per $100; and undercapitalized banks, 24 cents per $100. If banks were a substantial supervisory concern, premiums for each category would rise to 17 cents per $100 for well-capitalized banks, 24 cents per $100 for adequately capitalized banks, and 27 cents per $100 for undercapitalized banks. Beginning in January 1997, all insured banks were also required to pay a charge of 1.3 cents per $100 of deposits to assist in the payoff of FICO bonds that were issued to help the FDIC's restructuring operations in the 1990s. Also see the FDIC Website (*http://www.fdic.gov;* select Regulations and Examinations) for information and updates on regulations.

8 See Buser, Chen, and Kane (1981). Also, see Larry D. Wall and David R. Peterson. "Bank Holding Company Capital Targets in the Early 1990s: The Regulators versus the Markets." *Journal of Banking and Finance* 19 (1995), 563–574.

figure 6.2   RELATIONSHIP BETWEEN CAPITAL STRUCTURE AND VALUE

Many finance theorists believe that there is an optimal capital structure. Too little or too much debt capital can result in a lower value for the firm than if managers find the ideal range. The optimal capital structure in depositories is also influenced by the deposit insurance system and capital regulations.

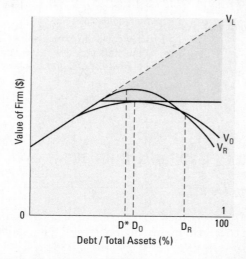

V_L = optimal capital structure (debt / assets) with insured debt financing and no regulatory interference.

V_0 = optimal capital structure with uninsured debt financing, whereby the cost of funds rises and value of the firm falls as it takes on too much debt.

V_R = optimal capital structure based on regulatory interference, insured deposits, and regulatory minimum capital requirements.

Source: Adapted from Buser, Stephen A., Andrew H. Chen, and Edward J. Kane. "Federal Deposit Insurance, Regulatory Policy, and Optimal Bank Capital." Journal of Finance, *36 (March 1981), 51–60.*

large customer dependence. Thus, he argues that the only sensible definition for capital in financial institutions must include "the difference between the market value of assets and the default-free value of customer liabilities" (versus simply the value of investor liabilities) since any loss to liabilities of margin customers can result in a serious loss of confidence for the firm.

Others, including the U.S. Shadow Financial Regulatory Committee, a group of financial economists that follows the Fed's policies and makes policy recommendations, have encouraged the requirement of the use of subordinated debt to ensure market discipline for banks and provide valuable market information to bank supervisors. Such a proposal was suggested by Evanoff and Wall (2002), whereby with the mandated use of subordinated debt by banks, the market price of subordinated debt could provide useful information on an individual bank risk. Flannery (2002) proposed as well a new financial instrument, "reverse convertible debentures," that would provide discipline by automatically converting to common equity if the market capital of a bank fell below a given stated value, forcing stockholders "to bear the full cost of their risk-taking activities." Accordingly, the Basel II proposal, to be discussed a little later in the chapter, puts an emphasis on market discipline from both an uninsured debt and equity market perspective. As noted by FDIC Chairman Donald E. Powell (2004), "The challenge on this issue is really no different than what regulators have to deal with every day: we must strike the right balance between the principle of letting the market work and the principle of stability, soundness, and responsible regulation." The FDIC is considering developing specialized financial instruments, such as bond or reinsurance contracts to use the market to help regulators "measure and manage the unique risks posed" by having a two-tiered banking system including very large bank and financial holding companies and smaller community banks in the U.S.[9]

9 See Powell (2004); Allen and Gale (2003); Froot (2001); Flannery (2002); Flannery and Rangan (2002); and Flannery and Nikolova (2004). Also see "Reforming Bank Capital Regulation: A Proposal by the U.S. Shadow Financial Regulatory Committee" (cited in the reference section).

1 Why are financial institutions particularly prone to changes in the market value of their assets and liabilities and equity? Why is capital particularly important to depository institutions?

2 Why does deposit insurance lead to a moral hazard problem for depository institutions?

3 How do the preferences of stockholders, uninsured debtholders, and regulators interact to arrive at an optimal regulatory capital-to-asset ratio?

4 How have financial economists changed their view about the necessity of regulatory capital requirements versus greater use of market discipline? How has the nature of banking changed for very large banks to allow greater market discipline?

5 How could the mandated use of subordinated banks by regulators provide greater information to help regulators be aware of changes in individual bank risk?

Changes in Regulatory Capital Requirements over Time

Equity-to-Asset Declining Trends

Before 1985, regulatory agencies generally set capital requirements on a case-by-case basis, allowing larger banks, as more diversified institutions, to have lower capital ratios. Consequently, capital ratios fell dramatically for large banks, from about 8.7 percent in 1984 to a little over 6 percent in 1980. Congressional concern over lower capital ratios led to the requirement of minimum capital to total assets ratios of 6 percent for large U.S. banks under the International Lending Supervision Act of 1983. As a result, capital ratios for large banks in the United States rose to an average of about 7 percent by 1988. Many large banks, however, shifted to off-balance-sheet activities that did not, at that time, have capital requirements. International banks that competed with each other on a global basis had very different capital requirements, making it difficult for banks in countries that imposed more stringent capital regulations to compete. Regulators were also concerned about weaker international banks.

Basel I and FDICIA as a Response

In response to these concerns, regulators for twelve major industrial nations agreed to introduce risk-based capital requirements for large international banks for Belgium, Canada, France, Germany, Italy, Japan, Luxembourg, The Netherlands, Sweden, Switzerland, the United Kingdom, and the United States. This agreement, known as the Basel Accord of 1987, or Basel (or Basle) I, was implemented during 1990 to 1992.[10] In the spirit of reducing moral hazard problems and preventing excessive risk-taking, risk-based capital requirements based on the risk of a bank's assets were put into place, as well as risk-based capital requirements for off-balance-sheet items. These capital requirements were also put into place for all U.S. banks and thrifts under FDICIA of 1991, which was implemented in January 1993. As mentioned in Chapter 3, FDICIA of 1991 made U.S. depository institutions subject to Prompt Corrective Action (PCA) requirements, whereby institutions are classified into categories based on their regulatory capital ratios. Institutions that fall below minimum capital ratios are mandated to be closed by regulators under PCA, and institutions that are less than well capitalized are subject to restrictions or conditions on certain activities that they may engage in, greater regulatory supervision, and are subject to supervisory actions.

The BIS Market Risk Amendment and Basel II

Subsequently, the Basel Committee of the Bank of International Settlements (BIS) proposed altering different requirements and risk-based weightings, and there has been debate over the capital requirements for different on- and off-balance-sheet items. In 1996, a Market Risk Amendment was passed and put into place by 1998 that requires international banks with significant trading activity to calculate a capital charge for market risk using either their own internal risk measurement model or a stan-

10 See the BIS Website *(http://www.bis.org)* for details on Basel I and the proposed Basel II Accord.

dardized process developed by the committee. Many banks use a value at risk (VAR) approach discussed in Chapter 2. A new Basel Capital Accord (Basel II; see *http://www.bis.org*), proposed in 2001 to be implemented in 2006 for large international banks, emphasizes a more risk-sensitive capital framework with a range of capital required for specific risks faced by particular banks (discussed along with Basel I, later in this chapter) based on internal measures of a bank's overall credit and operational risks. Thus, the capital regulation of banks has undergone dramatic change.[11]

Equity-to-Asset Trends Following Basel I

Since the implementation of Basel I, equity capital to total asset ratios have risen dramatically as shown in the following list. Equity to total assets on average rose for U.S. commercial banks from 6.23 percent in 1989 to 9.23 percent in 2002, with a fall to 9.10 percent as of year-end 2003, with a similar rise for U.S. savings institutions (2003 equity-to-asset ratio of 9.41 percent). This rise in capital ratios may be a combined result of a better economic climate and higher returns on assets and equity as noted below, resulting in the generation of higher internal equity from retained earnings; the higher capital requirements and desire of banks to be well capitalized to avoid regulatory sanctions; attempts by banks to avoid being penalized by uninsured creditors, ratings agencies, and shareholders; and the desire after the banking crisis of the 1980s of bank managers to have a larger capital cushion, among other explanations.

U.S. Commercial Bank Income and Capital Growth, Year-End, 1989 to 2003

	Assets (bils.)	ROA	Equity-to-Assets Ratio	ROE
2003	$7,602	1.41%	9.10%	15.53%
2002	7,077	1.23%	9.15%	13.44%
2001	6,820	1.22%	9.13%	13.64%
2000	6,475	1.22%	8.56%	14.21%
1999	5,973	1.36%	8.44%	15.87%
1998	5,669	1.23%	8.58%	14.27%
1997	5,229	1.30%	8.41%	15.46%
1996	4,810	1.24%	8.29%	14.95%
1995	4,540	1.19%	8.08%	14.72%
1994	4,219	1.17%	8.00%	14.63%
1993	3,911	1.14%	7.83%	14.56%
1992	3,486	0.93%	7.19%	12.94%
1991	3,414	0.53%	6.75%	8.01%
1990	3,369	0.50%	6.47%	7.89%
1989	3,288	0.51%	6.23%	7.82%

Sources: Sheshunoff Bank and S&L Quarterly, *1992, 1997, 1992, and* FDIC Reports of Conditional Income and Historical Statistics *and* FDIC Statistics at a Glance, *December 31, 2003. Similarly, thrift ROAs, ROEs, and equity capital ratios rose in the later 1990s and early 2000s.*

---

11 See Glantz (2003) and Chorafas (1998) for details on the Basel Market Risk Amendment implemented in 1998. Also, see the BIS Website (*http://www.bis.org*), Basel Committee on Banking Supervision section of the Website, which contains announcements, modifications to the market risk amendment of 1996, press releases, and working papers on the Basel Market Risk Amendment, among others. Under modifications to the market risk amendment, banks can use models to base their specific risk capital charge for trading risk if the general qualitative and quantitative requirements for risk models are met as well as additional criteria including being able to explain the historical price variation in the portfolio, being able to demonstrate the magnitude and change in composition (capture concentration) and models are validated using back testing to assess whether specific risk is accurately being captured, and having methodologies in place to adequately capture event and default risk for its traded-debt and equity positions. See Cornett and Saunders, 2003, Chapter 10, for a discussion of back testing, which involves a historic (back simulation) model. As they note, back simulation models provide a worst case scenario and do not need an assumption of a normal distribution of asset returns. Monte Carlo simulation models are also often used to generate additional observations, in the event of limited data. If banks can not meet these criteria, they are required to base specific risk capital charges on the full amount of a standardized specific risk charges, which are often higher than those of internal bank models. See Saunders and Allen (2002) for a more detailed discussion of other types of credit risk measures used and new approaches to value at risk. The Basel Committee, Models Task Force, did a study, "Performance of Models-Based Capital Charges for Market Risk," September 1999 (cited in the references on the BIS Website, *http://www.bis.org*). The survey of over 40 banks, subject to the capital charge for market risk with significant trading activity, operating in nine countries, suggested that capital charges using the internal models approach did provide a buffer that was adequate against trading losses during a period of high market volatility, the third and fourth quarters of 1998 (based on 99th percentile value at risk [VAR] estimates).

Is Basel II Needed?

A recent FDIC report, "Basel and the Evolution of Capital Regulation: Moving Forward, Looking Back," asks the question, given the high equity-to-asset ratios and very low failure rate for depository institutions in the last decade, why is there a need for the new Basel II Accord? This report shows that although over 97 percent of banks are classified as well capitalized today versus 86 percent in 1990, the average bank's credit portfolio risk has risen as well, as shown by higher average net charge-off to total loans and higher loan-to-asset ratios. Annual net charge-offs as a percentage of average loans rose from about .85 percent in 1985 to over 1.55 percent in 1990, falling in 1995 to close to .50 percent, and rising to close to .90 percent in 2000. Similarly, total loans and security-to-assets ratios have risen over time to close to 80 percent in the early 2000s. In addition, the FDIC report notes that bank derivatives, among other off-balance-sheet items, have risen dramatically in the last decade from a notional value of $7 trillion in 1990 to $45 trillion in 2001. Also, with banking consolidation, the banking payment system depends on fewer, larger banks: The top fifty bank holding companies (BHCs) held 55 percent of total bank domestic deposits in 2000 (versus 36 percent in 1990), and the top five BHCs hold 21 percent of total domestic deposits (versus only 8 percent in 1990). As noted by Powell (2004), by early 2004 the top ten banking organizations held 40 percent of industry deposits versus 16 percent in 1985. Hence, Basel II, which focuses on a more risk-sensitive capital framework for the specific risks of larger international banks, appears to be needed. With greater complexity for the world's largest international banks, regulators have had more difficulty understanding the complex internal operations and inherent risk in these operations. The report notes, moreover, that "the increasing size and complexity of the largest banks has made it more important for bank supervisors to enhance their ability to enforce capital adequacy by harnessing two key tools, market discipline and the risk metrics employed by banks themselves."[12]

Before discussing the current capital regulations and capital calculations for U.S. depository institutions, first we need to understand the definitions of bank capital, which are quite unique, including core (Tier 1) and supplementary (Tier 2) forms of capital.

Regulatory Definitions of Capital

Depository institutions have traditionally been allowed by regulators to hold two types of capital: **Tier 1, Core or Tangible Equity Capital**, and **Tier 2, Supplemental Capital**. These two types of capital and restrictions on each type are described in detail in Table 6.1 and in the following simplified form.

Tier 1 (Core) Capital = Common Stock Accounts and Retained Earnings (Common Equity)

Qualifying cumulative and noncumulative perpetual preferred stock (up to 25 percent of Tier 1 capital)

Minority interest in equity accounts of consolidated subsidiaries

Less ineligible intangible assets (goodwill on books after March 12, 1988)

Tier 2 (Supplementary) Capital = Any Additional Perpetual Preferred Stock Not Allowed in Tier 1

Subordinated notes and debentures (up to 50 percent of Tier 2 capital)

[original maturities of five years or more, amortized as they mature]

Allowance for loan and lease losses (up to 1.25 percent of risk-weighted assets)

Mandatory convertible subordinated debt

Immediate-term preferred stock (original weighted average maturity of five years or more)

Tier 1 capital is defined as common stockholders' equity (common stock and retained earnings) plus perpetual preferred stock less any new goodwill incurred after new rules came into effect. **Tier 1 capi-**

---

12 See FDIC FYI (2003). Also see Flannery and Rangan (2002), who studied 100 of the largest U.S. BHCs from 1986 to 2000. They found a significant rise in the capital ratios, well over required regulatory capital ratios for these BHCs, but also found higher capital ratios to reflect greater portfolio risk for these BHCs. They attribute the higher capital ratios to a rise in market incentives by market participants to monitor and price the default risk of large BHCs. Also see the Basel II proposal on the BIS Website (*http://www.bis.org*).

table **6.1** DEFINITIONS FOR TIER 1 AND TIER 2 CAPITAL

U.S. banking regulators, along with regulators in eleven other nations, have agreed on the definitions of core and supplementary items used to determine institutions' capital adequacy.

Item	Description
Core (Tier 1) Capital	
Common stock	Aggregate par or stated value of outstanding common stock
Perpetual preferred stock	Aggregate par or stated value of outstanding perpetual preferred stock. Preferred stock is a form of ownership interest in a bank or other company that entitles its holders to some preference or priority over the owners of common stock, usually with respect to dividends or asset distributions in a liquidation. Perpetual preferred stock does not have a stated maturity date and cannot be redeemed at the option of the holder. It includes those issues that are automatically converted into common stock at a stated date.
Surplus	Amount received from the sale of common or perpetual preferred stock in excess of its par or stated value
Undivided profits	Accumulated dollar value of profits after taxes that have not been distributed to shareholders of common and preferred stock as dividends
Capital reserves	Contingency and other capital reserves. Reserves for contingencies include amounts set aside for possible unforeseen or indeterminate liabilities not otherwise reflected on the bank's books and not covered by insurance. Capital reserves include amounts set aside for cash dividends on common and preferred stock not yet declared and amounts allocated for retirement of limited-life preferred stock and debentures subordinated to deposits.
Minority interest in consolidated subsidiaries	Sum of the equity of the subsidiaries in which the bank has minority interest multiplied by the percentage ownership of the bank in the subsidiaries
Intangible assets[a]	Purchased credit card relationships and purchased mortgage servicing rights
Minus:	
All other intangible assets (primarily goodwill)	Generally these other intangible assets represent the difference between the purchase price and the book value of acquired institutions.
Supplementary (Tier 2) Capital[b]	
Limited-life preferred stock	Preferred stock with an original maturity of 5 years or more
Subordinated notes and debentures[c]	Debt obligations of issuer, with original maturities of 5 years or more, that are subordinated to depositors in case of insolvency. Subordinated notes and debentures issued by depository institutions are not insured by the federal deposit insurance agencies.
Reserves for loan and lease losses	Amount set aside to absorb anticipated losses. All charge-offs of loans and leases are charged to this capital amount, and recoveries on loans and leases previously charged off are credited to this capital account
Mandatory convertible subordinated debt	Debt issues that mandate conversion to common or perpetual preferred stock at some future date
Other items accepted as capital in international banking	Items such as "undisclosed reserves" that are similar to retained earnings but are not revealed on the balance sheet using accounting practices accepted in some nations

a *The intangible assets regulators allow banks to include cannot total more than 50 percent of an institution's Tier 1 capital.*

b *Total supplementary capital cannot exceed the total of Tier 1 items.*

c *Subordinated debt may not exceed 50 percent of supplementary capital.*

tal must be at least 50 percent of total capital. Supplemental capital (Tier 2 capital) is included by regulators since it is subordinated to depositors in case of insolvency. Restrictions also exist concerning how much of different types of capital can be used. Perpetual preferred stock can only be up to 25 percent of Tier 1 capital, and subordinated debentures can be no more than 50 percent of Tier 2 capital. Reserves for loan losses can be included only up to 1.25 percent of risk-based assets.[13]

---

13 See the Federal Reserve Board of Governors press release for January 1989, Attachment II, for a summary of definitions of qualifying capital for BHCs. Also see Saunders and Cornett (2003), 525. Other deductions may be made from the sum of Tier 1 and Tier 2 capital including other subsidiaries or joint ventures as determined by the supervisory (regulatory) authority, investments in unconsolidated subsidiaries, and the reciprocal of holdings of banking organizations capital securities.

Regulatory Capital Ratios and Definitions of Capital Adequacy

Regulatory Capital Ratios

In addition to the risk-based standards, U.S. bank regulators have identified levels of capital characterizing well-capitalized and undercapitalized banks. Capitalization categories are based are three different capital ratios as follows:

$$\text{Leverage Ratio (for adequacy): Minimum Tier 1 capital to total assets ratio} = 4\% \quad [6.1]$$

$$\text{Tier 1 capital to total risk-based assets ratio} = 4\% \quad [6.2]$$

$$\text{Total Tier 1} + \text{Tier 2 capital to total risk-based assets ratio} = 8\% \quad [6.3]$$

The first leverage ratio is based on core (Tier 1) equity capital to total assets. The second two ratios are Tier 1 capital divided by risk-based assets and combined Tier 1 and Tier 2 capital divided by risk-based assets. Regulators classify assets into risk-based categories based on their credit risk. The dollar amount of each asset category is multiplied by a weight from 0 percent to 100 percent based on the asset's risk. These weighted dollar values are then summed to get total on-balance-sheet risk-based assets. A similar procedure is used for off-balance-sheet items, which are first converted to dollar amounts as if they were on-balance-sheet based on their contingent risk. The sum of risk-based on- and off-balance-sheet assets equals total risk-based assets, the denominator for Equations 6.2 and 6.3. The calculation of risk-based assets, which includes converted risk-based off-balance-sheet assets, is discussed in the following section.

Regulatory Definitions of Capital Adequacy

Table 6.2 provides regulatory definitions of capital adequacy. Banks and thrifts in any of the three undercapitalized categories face severe penalties, higher deposit insurance premiums, and regulatory intervention. Banks just meeting minimum standards are considered adequately capitalized. To determine the proper amount of capital a bank needs, regulatory supervisors also evaluate a depository institution's **Capital, Asset Quality, Management, Earnings, Liquidity, and Interest Rate Sensitivity (CAMELS)** rating, among other factors including the growth rate of bank assets. Undercapitalized banks must restrict growth, prepare plans to restore capital, and receive approval from regulators before expanding operations, making acquisitions, or opening new branches. Significantly undercapitalized banks face more strict limitations, including prohibitions on increases in compensation to senior executives. Finally, Congress requires regulators to take prompt corrective action against critically undercapitalized banks. If managers cannot correct deficiencies, regulators are required to place banks in receivership (**Federal Deposit Insurance Corporation [FDIC] control**) within ninety days. These policies reflect the view that severely undercapitalized institutions have little incentive to control risk and thus expose the deposit insurance system to substantial moral hazard.

In practice, there are currently three categories for risk-based deposit insurance assessments based on capital adequacy: Group 1, Well Capitalized; Group 2, Adequately Capitalized; and Group 3, Undercapitalized. Supervisory evaluations based on examinations, offsite information, and the institution's risk profile are also used to assign banks to appropriate supervisory subgroups of A, B, or C. Subgroup A includes banks with top CAMELS ratings of 1 or 2, subgroup B, ratings of 3, and subgroup C, with ratings of 4 or 5, with higher premiums for less well capitalized banks. In recent years, the majority of banks (95 to 97 percent) have been well capitalized.[14]

Calculating Risk-Based Assets and Risk-Based Capital Ratios

Under the Basel I risk-based capital requirements, capital is required to be held on assets based on their credit risk. Assets are classified into four risk categories that have higher or lower weights according to

---

14 See FDIC Financial Institution Letters, "Determination of Assessment Risk Classification," and "Deposit Insurance Assessments," on the FDIC Website (*http://www.fdic.gov/news/news/financial/2003/fil0390a.html*). Also see footnote 7. See Walker (1997) for a discussion of capital adequacy considerations for Credit Unions, which similarly use CAMELS ratings to help assess capital for CUs.

table **6.2** DEFINITIONS OF CAPITAL ADEQUACY

Regulators have identified levels of capital characterizing well-capitalized and undercapitalized banks. Banks in any of three undercapitalized categories face severe penalties and regulatory intervention.

Category	Tier 1 & Tier 2 Ratio (Tier 1 + Tier 2) to RBA[a]		Tier 1 Ratio Tier 1 to RBA[b]		Leverage Ratio Tier 1 to Total Assets[c]
Well Capitalized	10% or higher	and	6% or higher	and	5% or higher
Adequately Capitalized	8% but less than 10%	and	4% but less than 6%	and	4% but less than 5%
Undercapitalized	6% but less than 8%	or	3% but less than 4%	or	Less than 4%
Significantly Undercapitalized	Less than 6%	or	Less than 3%	or	More than 2% but less than 3%
Critically Undercapitalized	2% or under	or	2% or under	or	2% or under

a (Tier 1 capital + Tier 2 capital) / risk-adjusted assets.

b Tier 1 (core) capital / risk-adjusted assets.

c Tier 1 (core) capital / average total assets. Institutions with poor CAMEL ratings must have higher leverage ratios.

Sources: *Richard Cantor and Ronald Johnson. "Bank Capital Ratios, Asset Growth, and the Stock Market."* Quarterly Review *(Federal Reserve Bank of New York) 17 (Autumn 1992), 11–12; Kenneth H. Bacon. "FDIC Proposed Curbs on Banks' Loans for Real Estate, Seek Capital Levels."* The Wall Street Journal *(June 24, 1992), A5; and Catherine Lemieux. "FDICIA Mandated Capital Zones and the Bank Industry."* Financial Industry Trends *(Federal Reserve Bank of Kansas City) (1993), 11–14.*

their credit risk. Risk-based assets are equal to the sum of the total assets for each risk class times their respective risk weights. The four risk categories have respective weights of 0 percent, 20 percent, 50 percent, and 100 percent. Thus, depository institutions do not have to hold any capital for risk-free assets with 0 percent weights, only capital for 20 percent of assets with low risk, only capital for 50 percent of assets with moderate risk, and capital on 100 percent on more risky assets. The following list describes the basic types of assets that fit into each of the four categories:

Category 1 (0 percent weight): Federal Reserve balances, U.S. government securities, Organization for Economic and Cooperation and Development (OECD) government securities, and some U.S. agency securities including GNMA (Ginnie Mae) mortgage-backed securities.

Category 2 (20 percent weight): Cash items in the process of collection, OECD interbank deposits and guaranteed claims, some non-OECD bank and government deposits and securities, General Obligation Municipal Bonds, Fed Funds Sold, some mortgage-backed securities, claims collateralized (backed) by the U.S. Treasury, FHLMC and FNMA mortgage-backed securities, and some other government securities. Current proposals are being discussed for including privately backed (issued) mortgage-backed securities and other securitization issues with AAA ratings (at the time of this writing in the 100 percent class).

Category 3 (50 percent weight): Other municipal revenue bonds, secured mortgage loans on 1-4 family residential properties, fully secured by first liens.

Category 4 (100 percent weight): All other on-balance-sheet assets. These include commercial and consumer loans, corporate bonds, commercial paper, and other assets not included in other categories.

To calculate risk-based on-balance-sheet assets, the dollar amounts of total assets in each category are multiplied by their respective fraction weights and the sum is taken. Risk-based off-balance-sheet assets must also be calculated and added to get total risk-based assets for risk-based capital ratios. To do this, off-balance-sheet items must first be converted to credit-equivalent assets.[15] These credit-equivalent assets are then placed in respective risk-based categories, like other assets. The risk-based categories for off-balance-sheet items are generally as follows:

Category 1 (0 percent risk weight): For unused commitments with an original maturity of one year or less or conditionally cancellable commitments (under Basel II, proposed to be put in the 20 percent risk weight category).

Category 2 (20 percent risk weight): For commercial letters of credit, banker's acceptances conveyed, and other short-term self-liquidating trade-related items.

Category 3 (50 percent risk weight): For standby letters of credit, other performance warranties and unused portions of loan commitments with original maturities exceeding one year, and revolving underwriting facilities.

Category 4 (100 percent risk weight): For direct credit substitutes including general guarantees, sale and repurchase agreements with recourse, and forward agreements to purchase assets.

There has been controversy over risk-based categories for particular types of assets and off-balance-sheet items, particularly since general weights are given to particular types of assets and off-balance-sheet items regardless of their particular credit and interest rate risks or their use, in the case of off-balance-sheet items, for hedging and liquidity purposes.

Illustration: Calculating Tier 1 and Tier 2 Capital for Victory Bank

To illustrate Victory Bank's calculation of Tier 1 and Tier 2 capital, dollar capital figures are shown in the following table:

Tier 1 Capital ($000)	
Common Equity	$1,880,937
Less Ineligible Intangible Assets	291,335
Net Tier 1	$1,589,602

Tier 2 Capital ($000)	
+ Allowable Subordinated Debt	$0
+ Cumulative Preferred Stock	0
+ Mandatory Convertible Debt	0
+ Allowable Loan & Lease Loss Allowance	$161,113
Net Eligible Tier 2	$161,113 for Tier 1 capital
Total Tier 1 and Tier 2 Capital	$1,750,715

Victory Bank had no perpetual preferred stock, but it did have some ineligible intangibles to subtract, giving the bank $1,589,602 million in Tier 1 capital. For Tier 2 capital, Victory Bank did not have any allowable subordinated debt, preferred stock, or convertible debt, only an allowable allowance for loan losses, providing $161,113 million in additional Tier 2 capital. Hence, over 90 percent of Victory Bank's total capital is Tier 1. Thus, total regulatory capital for Victory Bank is $1,750,715.

---

15 For details on how individual off-balance-sheet items are converted into equivalent on-balance-sheet items, see Saunders (1997), Chapter 19. For loan commitments and letters of credit, regulators generally give a conversion factor for individual off-balance-sheet contingent or guaranty contracts. The conversion factor for a direct credit substitute standby letter of credit is 100 percent; for a performance-related standby letter of credit, 50 percent; for the unused portion of loan commitments with original maturities of more than one year, 50 percent; for commercial letters of credit, 20 percent; for banker's acceptances conveyed, 20 percent; and for other loan commitments, 0 percent. Once credit-equivalent amounts are calculated, off-balance-sheet items are placed in risk categories and multiplied by risk weights to get risk-based asset amounts. For other off-balance-sheet items, conversions are much more technical. Details can be found in Saunders (1997), 411–414; and Saunders and Cornett (2003), Chapter 20.

Illustration: Finding Risk-Based Assets for Victory Bank

To illustrate calculating risk-based assets, Victory Bank classified its on-balance-sheet risk-based assets as follows:

Victory Bank

On Balance Sheet ($000)	Assets in This Category	Risk-Weighted Assets
Category 1: 0% weight	$ 2,879,181	$ 0
Category 2: 20% weight	6,126,605	1,225,321
Category 3: 50% weight	806,398	403,199
Category 4: 100% weight	9,539,784	9,539,784
Total On-Balance-Sheet Risk-Based Assets		$11,168,304

Multiplying the amounts in each category by their appropriate weights, the risk-based assets for each category are calculated and then summed, resulting in total on-balance-sheet risk-based assets of about $11.168 billion.

Credit-equivalent amounts of off-balance-sheet items are then calculated and placed in similar risk-weighted categories:

Victory Bank Equivalent (Converted) Off-Balance-Sheet (OBS) Items ($000)

Risk Category	Equivalent OBS	Weight-Equivalent OBS
Category 1: 0%	$ 12,139	$ 0
Category 2: 20%	73,180	14,636
Category 3: 50%	27,252	13,626
Category 4: 100%	1,983,830	1,983,830
Total Off-Balance-Sheet Risk-Based Assets		$2,012,092

Multiplying each of the risk-based classes of off-balance-sheet items by the appropriate weights and summing them, the total off-balance-sheet risk-based assets equals about $2.012 billion. Taking the sum of both on- and off-balance-sheet risk-based assets, the total is

Total Risk-Based Assets before Adjustments = Balance Sheet Risk-Based Assets + Off-Balance-Sheet Risk-Based Assets

$11,168,304 + $ 2,012,092 = $13,180,396

In reality, Victory Bank also had some very technical adjustments to make that resulted in somewhat fewer risk-based assets and total assets as follows:

Total Risk-Based Assets after Adjustments = $12,465,170

Total Assets after Adjustments = $18,756,337

Risk-based assets are much less than total assets. The next section calculates the regulatory capital ratios for Victory Bank by using the three required ratios shown in Equations 6.1, 6.2, and 6.3.

Example: Finding Capital Ratios for Victory Bank

By using the risk-based assets and total assets for Victory Bank and its Tier 1 and Tier 2 and Total Tier 1 and Tier 2 capital calculated earlier, Victory Bank's capital ratios can be expressed as

Tier 1 to Risk-Based Assets [6.1]

$1.5896 / $12.465 = 0.1275, or 12.75%

Tier 1 to Total Assets [6.2]

$1.5896 / $18.756 = 8.48%

(Tier 1 + Tier 2) to Risk-Based Assets [6.3]

$1.7507 / $12.465 = 14.04\%$

Thus, Victory Bank has ratios considerably above the minimum regulatory ratios. As you can see, Victory Bank is well-capitalized, with a total capital ratio of 10 percent or higher, Tier 1 capital ratio greater than 6 percent, and leverage ratio greater than 5 percent. Table 6.3 provides an additional example for calculating risk-weighted assets and the Tier 1 capital ratio for Mega Bank. Mega Bank (in thous.) has $5,000 in Tier 1 capital. Its total risk-based assets are $75,000, so its Tier 1 to risk-based assets ratio is $5,000 / $75,000, or 6.67 percent.

Criticisms of Basel I

As noted earlier, Basel I has been successful from the perspective of better capitalization for U.S. commercial banks with about 97 percent in the well-capitalized category. Basel I has been criticized, however, for not including interest rate and operating risk and for having very broad risk categories that do not consider the credit risk of particular loans within these categories. For instance, a bank has to hold 100 percent capital on commercial loans, regardless of whether each loan is an A-rated or a C-rated loan. Concerns have been voiced that higher capital requirements for commercial banks were related to the capital crunch of the early 1990s. Also, many nonbank activities of banks are not included. As noted in a recent FDIC report, the risks of large, complex FHCs and BHCs often cannot be understood in the Basel I framework or even through intensive supervisory review of their loan portfolios, since many other, unobservable types of risk are involved. As pointed out in a recent speech by FDIC Chairman Donald E. Powell (2004), Basel I also ignored the superior information that risk management models of the largest banks provide, which Basel II proposes to include.[16]

---

table 6.3 CALCULATING A RISK-BASED CAPITAL RATIO FOR MEGA BANK

Capital standards are based in part on the riskiness of an institution's assets and on the degree of its off-balance-sheet involvement. Depositories with lower-risk assets and lower-risk off-balance-sheet activities will have more favorable capital ratios than higher-risk institutions.

(1) Risk Category	(2) Amount (in thousands)	(3) Risk Weight	(2) × (3) Risk-Based
On-Balance-Sheet Assets			
Cash and Treasury securities	$ 20,000	0.00	$ 0
Repos and Fed Funds	30,000	0.20	6,000
Mortgages	10,000	0.50	5,000
Commercial loans and fixed assets	40,000		40,000
Total on-balance-sheet items	$100,000		$51,000
Contingent Liabilities (Off-Balance-Sheet Items)			
Cancellable short-term loan commitments	$ 5,000	0.00	$ 0
Commercial letters of credit	20,000	0.20	4,000
Long-term loan commitments	10,000	0.50	5,000
Selected forward agreements	15,000	1.00	15,000
Total off-balance-sheet items	$ 50,000		$24,000
Total risk-weighted value			$75,000
Core (Tier 1) capital	$ 5,000		
Risk-based total assets ($5,000 / $75,000)	6.67%		

---

16 For a discussion of the relationship between the implementation of Basel I and the credit crunch of the early 1990s, see Wagster (1999). As a source and for a discussion of the weaknesses of Basel I for large, complex banks, see FDIC FYI, "Basel and the Evolution of Capital Regulation" (2003), cited in the reference section. Also see Powell (2004).

Concept Questions

1. How did Basel I and FDICIA respond to declining capital ratios in the 1980s? How did capital ratios for banks on average change in the later 1990s and early 2000s?

2. Define bank Tier 1 (core) and Tier 2 (supplementary) regulatory capital. Why are banks allowed to include subordinated debt as supplementary capital?

3. What are the three regulatory capital ratios for capital adequacy? What ranges must these ratios be in for a bank to be well capitalized? Adequately capitalized? How are capital ratios used along with CAMELS ratings for risk-based deposit insurance assessments?

4. What are the different categories for putting assets into different risk-based buckets? How are total risk-based assets calculated? Why are off-balance-sheet items used as additional converted risk-based assets?

5. What are some criticisms of Basel I?

The Evolving Basel II Accord for Very Large International and Top Ten U.S. Banks

With greater complexity for very large, complex FHCs and BHCs, Basel II provides a new philosophy on the regulation of very large banks. The majority of large banks have in the past developed their own internal risk measures using a value at risk (VAR), along with other more complex internal risk ratings and systems for quantifying their risk exposure. Under the 1998 Market Risk Amendment to the Basel Accord, qualifying banks with securities activities already have internal models to assist them in determining their capital requirements for market risk. Basel II (planned to be phased in by 2006 after its final revisions and approval) for large international banks also requires internal risk measures to set capital requirements for credit and other operational risks as well. As noted by Vice Chairman Roger W. Ferguson, Basel II takes the position of modern asset-pricing theory in finance by thinking of measuring overall portfolio risk for a bank and measuring risk in quantifiable ways. He notes that Basel II, "at least in its more advanced form, is as much a proposal for strengthening risk management as it is a proposal for improving capital standards."[17]

Basel II's proposed revisions, which apply currently only to large international banks (including currently the top ten U.S. banks, with another ten very large banks likely to opt in), include three mutually reinforcing "pillars."

(1) **Pillar 1: Capital Charges against Market Risk, Operational Risk, and Credit Risk.** Basel II includes capital charges for operational and credit risk, as well as market risk for banks with trading activities. As in the Basel 1998 amendment, capital charges for credit risk continue to be 8 percent of risk-weighted assets, but the computation of risk weights is done using a Basel II Advanced IRB (internal ratings-based) model that allows banks themselves to estimate the amount of capital (capital charge) that they need to support their "unique set of risks." Only very large BHCs that demonstrate their ability to conduct this model are eligible to participate in the IRB approach.

FDIC staff calculations based on "Quantitative Impact Study 3: Technical Guidance" (Basel Committee on Banking Supervision, October 2002, available at *http://www.bis.org*) were used to create the following comparisons, which outline the range of minimum capital charges for a few sample credit quality buckets under Basel II versus fixed buckets under pre-1982 and Basel I.

Minimum capital required for a $100 commercial loan of quality:

		AAA	BBB-	B
Pre-1982	All Judgmental by Regulators			
Basel I (Current Rules)		$8	$8	$8
Basel II Advanced IRB		$0.37 to $4.45	$1.01 to $14.13	$3.97 to $41.65

Notes: The quality of loans refers to one-year default probabilities corresponding to the historical average for a given credit rating, in this case an unsecured credit with an assumed loss given a default (LGD) of 45 percent. The one-year probability of default used is 0.03 percent for AAA, 0.35 percent for BBB, 8.38 percent for B, based on a maturity of 2.5 years. Lower bounds reflect an LGD of 10 percent for high recovery for a one-year loan and 90 percent for a five-year loan. All Basel II capital calculations (standardized and IRB) include an operational risk charge (under the Basic Indicator Approach, the operational capital charge is equal to 15 percent of the institution's average gross income over the previous three years). As a proxy for gross income, the calculations in this table use the current industry average ROA (1.41% × the amount of the loan, $100) for an estimated operational risk charge of $0.21 (15 percent of $1.41).

---

17 See "The Federal Reserve Board: Remarks by Vice Chairman Roger W. Ferguson, Jr., at the ICBI Risk Management 2003 Conference, Geneva, Switzerland, December 2, 2003." *(http://www.federalreserve.gov/boarddocs/speeches/2003/20031202/default.htm).*

Under Basel II, credit ratings become vitally important in determining the capital charge for different loan quality categories, with a wide range across categories based on the quality of loans in each category. The ranges of capital required include an operational risk charge in addition to the credit risk charge. While Basel I has a uniform 8 percent capital requirement for commercial loans, Basel II has a wide range, for instance, for the best quality AAA loans, a range of only 0.37 percent to 4.45 percent. Hence, capital requirements could rise for some banks holding riskier loans but could decrease significantly for banks holding high-quality loans that implement internal rate-based (IRB) programs that are rigorous enough to quantify and monitor risks. Capital requirements for credit risk include greater risk sensitivity and flexibility.

(2) **Pillar 2: An Effective Supervisory Review Process.** Under Pillar 2, supervisors are mandated to review banks' internal assessments of their individual capital allocation and adequacy and to determine if they are sufficient. Supervisors may intervene when approaches are deemed insufficient and will also examine banks' overall risk management practices and internal controls.

(3) **Pillar 3: Market Discipline.** Under Pillar 3, the risk and capital positions of banks are to be made more transparent to allow market discipline to reinforce the efforts of the other pillars. Banks are encouraged to disclose all the information to the public that market participants need to monitor banking institutions. Market discipline goes along with greater use of bank credit ratings by rating agencies for uninsured debt and proposed mandates for large banks to have issues of subordinated debt, as earlier mandated under the U.S. Financial Services Modernization Act of 1999 for the top fifty U.S. BHCs.

As pointed out in the 2003 FDIC FYI report, "Basel and the Evolution of Capital Regulation," the practices in Basel II present a change in the traditional philosophy of bank capital regulation with: (1) the very largest banks operating under a completely different, formal set of capital regulations than other smaller banks, which could affect the competition among banks of various sizes; and (2) the reliance on large banks' own internal risk estimates for capital requirements for credit risk, which necessitates both a "sophisticated quantitative and operational risk management infrastructure to ensure the integrity of their risk estimates." This represents a significant challenge for regulators to develop new examination procedures for the largest banks to evaluate the integrity of internal ratings at a significant level of detail under Basel II. The report notes that there is also considerable human judgment included in Basel II in validating assumptions and in forming estimates of the correct capital amounts required for different credit categories for specific banks.[18]

Very Large U.S. Bank Participation for Basel II: Two Regulatory Systems

Operations and Other Large Banks That Opt In

Basel II creates what regulators note as a "formal bifurcation" (two-pronged) system of regulation, with different regulations for very large versus less large, medium-sized, and smaller (community) banks in the United States. In a speech in 2003 by Federal Reserve Board Governor Mark W. Olson, "Basel II: Its Implications for Second-Tier and Community-Size Banks," Governor Olson notes that bank supervisors in the United States intend that only the most risk-sensitive approaches under Basel II, notably the Advanced Internal Ratings-Based (A-IRB) option for credit risk and Advanced Measurement Approach (AMA) for operational risk would be applied, likely mandated for the ten or so most complex, internationally active banking organizations (with meaningfully cross-border exposures of at least $10 billion and other large banks with assets of at least $250 billion). Other large U.S. banks (another ten or more banks) meeting the "qualifying internal infrastructure standards" for risk measurement and management are likely to voluntarily opt in to apply their models under Basel II. Since the majority of U.S. banks are well capitalized and well managed under the current, modified Basel I, only these few participants would be required to be under the new Basel II Accord, given the high costs versus the benefits of implementing a more complex system. Hence, other banks would continue under Basel I regu-

---

18 Information for this section comes from FDIC FYI, "Basel and the Evolution of Capital Regulation" (2003), cited in the reference section; FDIC Press Releases 2003, "FDIC to Demystify Basel II Capital Regulation." *(http://www.fdic.gov/news/news/press/2003/pr0303.html)*; "FDIC: Proposed Implementation of the New Basel Capital Accord in the U.S.," 2004. *(http://www.fdic.gov/regulations/laws/publiccomments/basel/index.html)*; and "Advance Notice of Proposed Rulemaking Regarding Risk-Based Capital Guidelines: Implementation of New Basel Capital Accord." *(http://www.fdic.gov/regulations/laws/publiccomments/basel/riskbasedcap.pdf)*.

latory capital requirements. As noted, although Basel II will not be used by the majority of U.S. banks, the top ten banking organizations in the United States hold 40 percent of industry deposits.[19]

Advanced Internal Ratings-Based (A-IRB) Approach for Credit Risk and Advanced Measurement Approach (AMA) for Operational Risk

Under both approaches, key risk elements provide the primary inputs for capital calculations. For the A-IRB approach, in general, formulas or risk weight functions use the bank-estimated inputs, including the probability of default (PD), the loss given default (LGD), and the exposure at default (EAD) and, for certain portfolios, maturity (M) in deriving specific capital requirements. In the earlier discussion under Pillar 1, with the illustration comparing capital requirements under Basel II to Basel I, the loss given default (LGD) was used to calculate the Basel II requirements. Assumptions of formulas depend on statistical or probability-based assessments of defaults for different asset categories and maturities. The total capital requirements include capital calculated for both credit risk under the A-IRB and operational risk under the AMA methods. The formulas also derive a risk-weighted asset equivalent by multiplying the dollar amount of the calculated capital charge by a 12.5 conversion factor (the reciprocal of the 8 percent minimum capital requirement). Banks applying the A-IRB must assign assets into one of three portfolios: (1) wholesale (corporate, interbank, and sovereign); (2) retail; and (3) equities.

Banks adopting the AMA and A-IRB approaches must have the highest level and quality of internal risk measurement and management systems including developing and maintaining qualifying loss and default data for portfolios under the A-IRB framework and subject to strict internal control processes, stress testing and validation programs, independent review and oversight, among other qualitative standards. Similarly strict standards are required for the measurement and management of operational risks, with the capital charge for operational risk resting heavily on supervisory judgment.[20]

Advance Notice of Proposed Rulemaking (ANPR) Guidelines

In the ANPR guideline distributed by regulators, key components include active federal supervision, independent auditors, effective internal controls, and strong bank management. Increased disclosures, especially regarding a bank's use of the A-IRB approach for credit risk and the AMA for operational risk, were intended to allow private sector stakeholders to more fully evaluate a BHC's financial condition, including its adequacy, with greater transparency improving shareholder and debtholder monitoring to allow greater market discipline and encourage better risk management procedures and controls. If a BHC fails to meet the minimum disclosure requirements and this is not corrected, the firm will become ineligible to use the advanced approaches.[21]

Guidelines for Measuring Operational Risk

Operational risks include (1) **"process risk,** the breakdown in established processes, failure to follow processes, or inadequate process mapping within business lines; (2) **people risk,** management failure, organizational structure or other human failures, which may be exacerbated by poor training, inadequate controls, poor staffing resources, or other factors; (3) **systems risk,** the disruption and outright system failures in both internal and outsourced operations, and (4) **external events risk,** natural disasters, terrorism, and vandalism, as well as legal risk, the risk of loss from failure to comply with laws as well as prudent ethical standards and contractual obligations." Strategic and reputational risks are excluded. The operational risk exposure is generated by a BHC's internal operational risk measurement

---

19 See Powell (2004) and "The Federal Reserve Board: Remarks by Governor Mark W. Olson, Basel: Its Implications for Second-Tier and Community-Size Banks," at the Banking Institute, Center for Banking and Finance, University of North Carolina, Charlotte, North Carolina, April 10, 2003; and "The Federal Reserve Board: Remarks by Vice Chairman Roger W. Ferguson, Jr., at the ICBI Risk Management 2003 Conference, Geneva, Switzerland, December 2, 2003." *(http://www.federalreserve.gov/boarddocs/speeches/2003/20031202/default.htm).*

20 The material throughout this section comes from "FDIC: Proposed Implementation of the New Basel Capital Accord in the U.S.," 2004. *(http://www.fdic .gov/regulations/laws/publiccomments/basel/index.html).*

21 The material throughout this section comes from "Advance Notice of Proposed Rulemaking Regarding Risk-Based Capital Guidelines: Implementation of New Basel Capital Accord." *(http://www.fdic.gov/regulations/laws/publiccomments/basel/riskbasedcap.pdf).*

system, which needs to incorporate internal loss data, relevant external loss data, assessments of internal controls, the business environment; and scenario analysis that includes potential expected and unexpected aggregate operational losses at a 99.9 percent confidence level, over a one-year period. The total expected losses are converted to an equivalent amount of risk-weighted assets by multiplying by 12.5 (reciprocal of an 8 percent capital requirement).

Guidelines for Measuring Credit Risk under an IRB Approach

Institutions are expected under Basel II to have a system that assigns ratings and validates their accuracy, and that quantifies and translates risk ratings into IRB parameters. An interdependent system of controls should include independence, transparency, accountability, use of ratings, a rating system review, an internal audit, and board and senior management oversight. Checks and balances should be included to ensure the IRB system's integrity. Capital calculations are similar but have individual different types of parameters and formulas for exposures for (1) wholesale exposures; (2) small and medium-sized enterprise exposures; (3) specialized lending including (a) project finance for large, complex, expensive installations that produce goods or services for sale, such as power plants or transportation infrastructure where repayment sources are primarily revenues generated by these sales or services; (b) object finance for the acquisition of large (but typically moveable) assets, such as aircraft; (c) commodities finance, the structured short-term financing of reserves, inventories, or receivables; and commercial real estate (CRE) exposure where the prospects for repayment depend primarily on cash flows generated by the lease, rental, or sale of real estate including low and high volatility CRE; (4) retail exposure (residential mortgages, qualifying revolving retail exposures, and other exposures); (5) equity exposures; (6) purchased receivables; (7) securitization exposures (on- and off-balance-sheet); and (8) credit migration exposures for collateral and guarantees (where credit ratings migrate or change), among others. The ANPR guidelines give the following example of the capital calculations for credit risk for commercial and industrial loans (wholesale exposures) using an IRB system. These appear to be and are complex, but can programmed in for very large banks.

Four primary inputs are needed by banks for each individual exposure: (1) the **probability of default (PD)** for each internal rating grade; (2) the **loss given default (LGD)** based on an assessment of the dollar amount of loan that would be recovered if there were a default, expressed as a percentage of the total defaulted exposure based on historical recovery rates; (3) **exposure at default (EAD),** the expected gross exposure of the facility in the event that the borrower defaults; and (4) the effective **remaining maturity (M) based on the weighted average remaining maturity** of cash flows in years and borrower size. The IRB capital requirement for a particular wholesale exposure is calculated by (1) calculating the relevant asset correlation assumption, R, based on PD and size; (2) calculating the capital requirement assuming a maturity of one year, which is a function of PD, LGD, EAD, and the asset correlation; and (3) applying maturity adjustments for differences in the true maturity, which is a function of PD and M. Asset correlations are subject to a formula with correlations changing with lower credit quality, since these types of assets are more likely to be idiosyncratic. The general (spreadsheet/calculator format, where * is equivalent to times) formulas used for some of the different types of calculations for each type of exposure are provided by the Board of Governors of the Federal Reserve System, FDIC, and OCC (Joint Release, January 16, 2001, and in more detail in the full BIS document on the BIS Website, at *http://www.bis.org*) are briefly shown next. As an example for calculating capital under the Commercial and Industrial (C&I) Risk Weight function, the first step in calculating the asset correlation, R, is

$$\text{Assets Correlation } (R) = 0.12*(1 - \text{EXP}(-50*\text{PD})) + 0.24*[1 - (1 - \text{EXP}(-50*\text{PD}))]$$

where EXP is the natural exponential function (e^x on a calculator). Higher asset correlations imply that average defaults are more likely to occur together ("in clumps"), necessitating higher capital requirements. Under this wholesale IRB framework (proposed by the Basel Committee and being considered by the agencies), this asset correlation parameter, R, is not a fixed amount, instead varying as a function of the probability of default (PD), which reduces the speed of the rise in the capital requirement as the PD rises. For all wholesale (commercial) exposures (with the exception of high-volatility commercial real estate exposure), the asset correlation, R, has an upper bound value of 24 percent for very low PD values and a lower bound of 12 percent for very high PD values. The values of R are then used in the second step to calculate K_1, the one-year maturity capital requirement:

$$K_1 = \text{EAD}*\text{LGD}*N[(1 - R)^{\wedge}0.5*G(\text{PD}) + (R / (1 - R))^{\wedge} - 0.5*G(0.999)]$$

where N is the standard normal cumulative distribution function and G(x) is the inverse of the standard normal cumulative distribution function, used widely in statistics and commonly available in computer spreadsheet programs (found in the help function of most spreadsheet programs or in standard statistics textbooks). This gives the dollar amount of capital needed to cover the extreme scenario (99.9th percentile) of credit losses likely to occur in one year in a portfolio of identical exposures, given the correlation R and other specific assumptions. Since this formula rises linearly with increase in EAD or LGD, a doubling of either EAD or LGD results in double the capital requirement. Similarly, as LGD estimates approach zero, capital requirements approach zero.

The third step adjusts the IRB capital requirement to reflect the exposure's effective remaining maturity (M) by multiplying the one-year maturity capital requirement (K_1) by a factor depending on both M and PD, with a greater proportional need for maturity adjustments for exposures with low PD values with a greater potential for a deterioration in credit quality. This calculation of the capital requirement (K) is

$$K = K_1 * [(M - 2.5)*(1 + b)] / [-1.5*(1 + b)], \text{ where } b = (0.08451 - 0.05898*LN(PD))^2$$

Here the b determines the slope of the maturity adjustment and is a function of PD. Note, if M is set equal to 1, the maturity adjustment will also equal 1, so K will be equal to K_1. This gives the total dollar minimum capital requirement for this individual exposure. Since the minimum capital requirement is by definition 8 percent of risk-weighted assets, the risk-weighted assets value can be obtained by multiplying by 12.5 (i.e., the reciprocal, 1/0.08), that is, **Risk-Weighted Assets = 12.5*K.**

Finally, the risk weight for the exposure is found by dividing its risk-weighted assets by the exposure amount, which is equal to **(Risk-Weighted Assets) / EAD.** The total capital required for any exposure can be divided into two parts, the "expected loss" and the "unexpected loss," where the expected loss component of capital (EL) equals EAD*LGD*PD, the amount of loss that on average is expected to occur for this particular type of exposure in a one-year time horizon. Hence, the IRB method for Basel II is more complex than Basel I but is facilitated by computer programs set up for these calculations. There are other individual, detailed, specific calculations for the other types of loans and off-balance-sheet items mentioned earlier.

FDIC Study of the Expected Effects with Basel II and Other Criticisms

The FDIC conducted a study, known as QIS-3, of the effects on bank capital held by very large banks with Basel II. On average, at the end of 2002, U.S. banks held 6.34 percent of their total assets as capital, well above the required 5 percent under Basel I. Using Basel II models, the FDIC noted a significant decline in capital required to be held by the twenty largest U.S. banks, which ranged from 2.5 percent to 4 percent. This represented a likely 17 percent reduction in the credit risk-based capital requirements for the twenty largest U.S. international banks, although this reduction would fall by an increased operational risk capital charge of 11 percent, resulting in a likely net 6 percent decline in capital required. While U.S. regulators would prefer a capital floor (minimum capital requirement) to the Basel II Accord, European regulators have firmly opposed such a floor. Other banks, as well as some regulators, have complained that proposed standards under Basel II might be unfair, favoring the twenty largest U.S. banks and creating a two-tiered regulatory system, favoring very large banks who would have lower capital requirements under Basel II. Financial economists have noted that Basel II moves in the right direction by allocating capital based on the risk of different activities and emphasizing market discipline. However, some financial economists worry about the lack of a theoretical framework behind Basel II. Allen and Gale (2003) note that the Basel Accords make practitioners "become experts at the details of a highly complex system for which there is no widely agreed rationale based in economic theory." Froot (2001) points out that the Basel II proposals are a significant move forward, but "lag behind" the evolution of banks from "primary warehousers of risk to diversified originators and distributors of financial services" and "may lead to considerable regulatory distortions as a result." As noted in a speech in early 2004 by Richard E. Powell, Chairman of the FDIC, however, regulators are concerned that Basel II will result in much lower risk-based capital requirements for the world's largest and most complex banking organizations. In contrast, to recent theory that suggests that regulation of bank capital is not needed, he notes that "getting capital right is the cornerstone of any responsible regulatory approach to the continuing trend of banking industry consolidation," with capital providing "an indispensable

1 How does Basel II compare to Basel I in terms of the difficulty of computing risk-based capital requirements? What types of different risks are included for very large international banks?

2 What are the three pillars of Basel II?

3 What is the Advanced Rating Based (A-IRB) Method for Credit Risk? What is the Advanced Measurement Approach (AMA) for Operational Risk?

4 Why are only about the twenty largest U.S. banks involved in Basel II? Why do other banks think Basel II may give these very large banks a capital advantage? What do FDIC studies expect in terms of changes in capital required under Basel II?

cushion against unexpected events and unanticipated shifts in the marketplace," and compensating for errors that might occur even under "sophisticated risk-management techniques."[22]

Beyond Regulatory Requirements: Management of Capital and Growth with RAROC

From a real-world standpoint, how much capital is adequate for a depository institution depends on a combination of (1) regulatory requirements, (2) an institution's risk profile, and (3) other practical considerations. In a discussion of capital management for banks, Donald Davis and Kevin Lee (1997) of Bank of America point out that the process of developing an optimal capital structure for banks encompasses the economic risk of banks and regulatory requirements as well as practical considerations. **Economic risk** is the risk of a bank having significant losses. The amount of capital a bank needs to hold depends on its credit risk, market risk, business risk, and targeted equivalent bond rating. Banks with a higher risk profile than similar-size (peer) banks need to hold higher capital ratios. Very large money center banks often employ an **RAROC (risk-adjusted return on capital)** approach. Under RAROC, each asset is given a capital charge based on the amount of capital that needs to be held on the asset according to its risk, with a higher equity-to-asset percentage allocated to more risky assets. Hence, more risky assets require a higher return to cover the cost of the extra capital that has to be held for them. An example of RAROC pricing for a bank's commercial loans is shown in the following table.[23]

Example: RAROC Pricing of Commercial Loans for the Hard Rock Bank

Source	Component	Example
Funds Transfer Cost of Funds	5.00%	Funds Transfer Pricing System
Required Loan Loss Provision	1.25%	Credit Risk Model
Plus:		
Direct Expense	0.80	Customer/Product Cost
Indirect Expense	0.40	Accounting System
Overhead	0.50	
Total Charges before Capital Charge	7.95%	
Plus:		
Capital Charge (RAROC)	3.00%*	
*Allocated Equity / Asset = 12.00%		
Total Required Loan Rate	10.95%	

*RAROC: allocated equity / assets = 12%; opportunity cost of equity = 15%; after-tax capital charge = 15% × 0.12 = 1.80%; marginal tax rate = 40%; pretax capital charge = 1.80% / 0.6 = 3.0%

---

22 See Powell (2004); Froot (2001); Allen and Gale (2003); and Rebecca Christie. "Rules on Bank Capital Draw Fire." *The Wall Street Journal* (December 8, 2003), B8; and see Alexander (2003) for detailed discussions of operational risk. Copies of the FDIC study can be found in "Advance Notice of Proposed Rulemaking Regarding Risk-Based Capital Guidelines: Implementation of the New Basel Capital Accord," on the FDIC's Website as well as samples of calculations at *http://www.fdic.gov/regulations/laws/publiccomments/basel/riskbasedcap.pdf* and *http://www.bis.org/bcbs/qis/qis3.htm*.

23 See Kimball (1998). For a more detailed discussion of a practical application for RAROC, see Zaik, Walter, Kelling, and James (1996); and Donald Davis and Kevin Lee (1997).

As shown in the preceding table, to price its commercial loans, the Hard Rock Bank has allocated to the loan a transfer cost of funds that includes a profit markup, a loan loss provision, and other administrative expenses that must be covered, plus an RAROC charge based on capital that must be held on commercial loans. With a 100 percent equity capital requirement for commercial loans under risk-based capital requirements and an additional allocation for the estimated market risk of commercial loans, a target equity-to-capital ratio is set for the loans of 12 percent. Based on an expected after-tax cost of equity capital of 15 percent, the after-tax capital charge for the loans is equal to 15 percent $\times$ 0.12, or 1.80 percent. Since the bank's marginal tax rate is 40 percent, this becomes 1.80 percent divided by $(1 - 0.40)$, or 3 percent on a before-tax basis. Adding the 3 percent capital charge to the other costs that must be covered, including a profit markup, the required loan rate is 11.25 percent. Whether a bank could charge this rate or not would depend on competitive conditions and the rates that other banks offer.

Because of higher capital requirements, banks must earn a higher return on traditional commercial lending activities than for government securities or home mortgage loans, which would have a lower risk-based capital allocation. This makes traditional lending less attractive than other types of activities, such as brokerage and investment banking, which have much higher spreads, averaging about 20 percent. Hence, it is not surprising that banks have been active in entering nontraditional activities.[24]

Other Capital Allocation Techniques for RAROC

While very large money center banks use detailed historical market data to determine equity-to-asset allocations under RAROC, different capital allocation methods are used by other banks. In a Federal Reserve Bank of Boston *New England Economic Review* article, Ralph Kimball (1998) provides the following examples of similar methods for allocating equity to assets according to the risk of a bank's different business lines. For instance, a bank might allocate equity that needs to be held for a particular line based on the average equity-to-asset ratio held by peer banks in that business. Such a peer group approach for the Consolidated Amalgamated Bank is shown in the following table.[25]

Line of Business	Assets	Equity	Equity to Assets
Credit Cards	$10,000	$1,000	10%
Mortgage Banking	20,000	4,000	20%
Subprime Lending	5,000	1,500	30%
Total	$35,000	$6,500	18.57%

In the preceding table, capital is allocated according to the average equity-to-asset ratio maintained by peer groups in each of the respective businesses. The overall equity-to-asset ratio for the bank is total equity / total assets, which equals $6,500 / $35,000 or 18.57 percent. This approach is somewhat ad hoc, since it is based on commonly held equity-to-asset ratios by businesses in each line, which may not really reflect the line's solvency risk. Alternatively, Kimball notes an allocation method could use the standard deviation of the ROA for a particular line of business and a bank's probability of insolvency ratio (Z), defined as

$$Z = (ROA^* + K) / \text{Std } (ROA) \qquad [6.4]$$

where ROA^* is the pretax expected ROA, K is the ratio of equity capital to assets, and Std (ROA) is the standard deviation of ROA. The Z-ratio gives the number of standard deviations by which ROA would have to fall before the bank's book value of equity capital would be exhausted, with a lower Z-ratio showing greater insolvency risk. If a bank knows the Z-ratio it is willing to accept for a given probability of no default (such as 95 percent), the desired equity to assets (K^*) for each line can be solved for as

$$K^* = [Z \times \text{Std } (ROA)] - ROA^* \qquad [6.5]$$

For instance, suppose the acceptable Z for each line is 10, and the respective expected hypothetical ROAs for each line of business are 5 percent (1 percent STD), for the credit card line, 10 percent (2 percent STD) for the mortgage banking, and 30 (5 percent STD) percent for the subprime lending. The respective K^* would be 5 percent for the credit card line, 10 percent for the mortgage banking line, and

---

24 This material and examples similar to these come from Kimball (1998).

25 Ibid.

20 percent for the subprime lending. Multiplying each required capital ratio, K*, by the assets for each category equals a total dollar capital requirement of $10,000 × 0.05 + $20,000 × 0.10 + $5,000 × 0.20 equals a $3,500 million total capital requirement or an average equity-to-capital ratio of $3,500 / $35,000 or 10 percent, in this case lower than the $5,633 million capital (18.57 percent) required based on typical equity-to-asset ratios for each line. To adjust for diversification between the three lines of businesses, correlations could be calculated and a deduction taken for any reduction in the total standard deviation of the loan portfolio with diversification.

The equity allocated for less risky types of asset is also significantly lower for use with an RAROC-type pricing. Since banks must price loans competitively, this type of allocation is very important. If the allocation of equity to assets is too high and results in too high a price, the loan may not be priced competitively. Similarly, in strategic decision making, when allocating scarce resources or when deciding to enter or exit a business line, managers compare the expected ROE for the business to its cost of equity considering the amount of equity capital that needs to be allocated to that business line.

These allocation methods are used for the purpose of illustration. Other types of allocations of capital are used that range from highly technical methods based on the distribution of a business line's historical returns to simple allocation methods based on subjective consensus estimates of a business unit's risk. As these examples illustrate, such allocation methods may provide dramatically different allocations of equity for different lines of business.

A Practical Approach to Capital Structure

Davis and Lee (1997) point out that in practice depository institution managers consider practical factors in setting target capital ratios as well as including the capital ratios of peers, the risk appetite of the bank, maintaining good debt ratings, comfortable margins over regulatory minimums, protections based for earnings volatility for individual operations (i.e., as in RAROC); and considering the firm's sustainable growth, [i.e., its internal equity generation capacity for growth, g^* equal to $(ROE)(1 − D)$, where D is the firm's dividend payout ratio] and future needs for external capital. The optimal capital mix to minimize the firm's weighted cost of capital and maximize firm value also should be considered.[26]

Defining an Optimal (Minimum) Weighted Average Cost of Capital

Related to the last point, since certain types of regulatory capital (equity, for instance) are more expensive than other types (the after-tax cost of subordinated debt), banks may want to take on the maximum allowed of the cheaper types of regulatory capital to minimize their weighted average cost of capital. Crawford and Sihler (1994) identify the maximum/minimum capital structure weights for different types of regulatory capital to still be in line with regulatory requirements but minimize the weighted average cost of capital. Based on regulatory restrictions, the percentages that would be optimal to have the lowest weighted average cost of capital could be illustrated as follows.

Capital Structure Weights

Class of Capital	Percent of Tier 2	Percent of Tier 1 & Tier 2 Capital
Loan Loss Reserve	31.25%	15.625%
Subordinated Debt	50.00%	25.000%
Balance: Other Types of Capital	18.75%	9.375%
Tier 2 Capital	100.00%	50.000%

Class of Capital	Percent of Tier 1	Percent of Tier 1 & Tier 2 Capital
Perpetual Preferred Stock	25.00%	12.500%
Common Equity	75.00%	37.500%
Tier 1 Capital	100.00%	50.000%

Based on regulatory limits, 75 percent of Tier 1 capital or 37.5 percent of total capital must be common equity. A maximum of 50 percent of Tier 2 capital can be subordinated debt or 25 percent of total

---

26 See Davis and Lee (1997).

capital. Based on a maximum Tier 2 capital-to-asset ratio of 4 percent for a total capital ratio of 8 percent and a maximum loan loss reserve of 1.25 percent of total assets, the maximum loan loss reserve would be approximately 1.25 percent / 4 percent, or 31.25 percent of total Tier 2 capital. Thus, there are limits to holdings of cheaper debt capital, which has a tax subsidy. Equity capital and additional loan loss reserves, in contrast, have a higher opportunity cost for stockholders and a higher cost of capital. A bank's weighted after-tax cost of capital can be calculated by taking the sum of the fraction of each type of capital relative to total capital times its respective cost. The following table provides an example. The bank has calculated the following costs of capital for each type of capital. The bank is holding its maximum allowable subordinated debt and preferred stock as cheaper forms of capital. The weighted average cost of capital is 10.656 percent.[27]

Weighted Average Cost of Capital

Capital Component	Weight	Cost of Capital Component	Weighted Cost
Loan Loss Reserve	15.625%	12%	1.875%
Subordinated Debt	25.000%	5%	1.2500%
Preferred Stock	21.875%	8%	1.7500%
Common Equity	37.500%	12%	*4.5000*%
Sum Weighted Average Cost of Capital 9.375%			

Dividend and Stock Repurchase Trends

Under corporate dividend theory, financial markets favor stable dividend policies, with changes in dividends, other than special dividends, often signaling changes in a firm's earnings prospects. Banks, like utility firms in the past, as relatively mature industries generally have had stockholder clienteles that prefer large dividend payouts. Also, many banks are closely owned, and owners depend on dividends for income.

As shown in Figure 6.3, banks have had very high average dividend payout ratios (dividends / net income), on average 68.81 percent over the last thirteen years. The lowest payout was 43.93 percent in

figure **6.3**   EARNINGS AND COMMON STOCK DIVIDENDS FOR COMMERCIAL BANKS, 1990 TO 2002

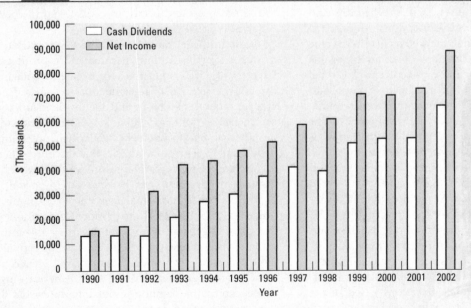

Source: FDIC Historical Statistics on Banking, http://www2.fdic.gov/hsob. *Put in figure form by the Authors.*

27 See Crawford and Sihler (1994), Case 16.1 and Note to Case 16.1, National Bank of Los Angeles.

Concept Questions

1 Why might banks want to hold more capital than required by regulators?

2 Why have RAROC models become very popular for large banks? What is the purpose of these models?

3 Why in RAROC models is it important to examine the correlations between different lines of businesses?

4 What do Davis and Lee (1997) suggest as practical implications for determining the proper economic amount of capital needed by a bank?

5 How can banks minimize their weighted average cost of capital in terms of holding the cheapest types of regulatory capital required? Would banks want to do this? Why or why not?

6 What are recent trends in bank dividend payouts and stock repurchases? Why do you think bank dividend payouts are so high on average compared with nonfinancial firms?

1992 and the highest was 86.14 percent in 1990. In 2002, the payout ratio was 74.86 percent, and in 2003, 75.88 percent.

Similarly, with rising profitability in the latter 1990s and excess capital generated for many large banks, almost all of the twenty-five largest banks had stock buyback (repurchase) programs to adjust capital ratios to defined targets, attempt stock price corrections when management felt the stock price was too low, and return capital to stockholders when marginal investment opportunities fell below the bank's relevant cost of capital. Stock repurchases have an advantage over dividends in terms of allowing the choice of selling or not selling their shares and only being taxed on cash they receive if they sell their shares.

From the standpoint of regulators, dividend payout is constrained by capital adequacy requirements and the ability of the bank to maintain sufficient capital given its risk. If banks are not undercapitalized, regulators have the right to mandate that dividend payouts be lowered. With the majority of banks in 2003 well capitalized, this has not been a recent problem.

Summary

This chapter examines capital regulations and management for depository institutions, the purposes of capital, market versus book value capital, and preferences of different agents within a firm for more or less capital. Capital management became increasingly important for banks and thrifts in the early 1990s as they were required to meet more stringent regulatory capital requirements. The optimal capital structure for a depository institution is affected by deposit insurance, which provides a larger subsidy for firms with high financial leverage. Risk-based capital regulations are presented under Basel I and the proposed new capital requirements for very large, international banks under Basel II (affecting about 10 to 20 very large U.S. banks), which is planned to be phased in by 2006. The chapter presents a practical framework for determining a depository institution's optimal capital structure, which includes keeping a comfortable cushion of capital above well-capitalized regulatory standards, capital allocations based on an RAROC approach, and other workable considerations such as capital ratios of peer banks, achieving a given bond rating, future prospects and needs for capital, and the best mix of different types of capital.

Capital-to-asset ratios rose in the 1990s and early 2000s; as depository institutions became more profitable, many larger banks faced the unusual problem of having excess capital. Consequently, larger institutions devised new policies for stock repurchases and higher dividend payouts to return excess capital to stockholders. Bank dividend policies are affected by stockholders, who often prefer high dividends, and by regulatory policies that discourage higher dividend payouts, particularly for undercapitalized institutions. Capital management has become an important part of depository institution management to maximize shareholder value. In the 1990s, with more efficient use of capital through the generation of revenues from off-balance-sheet activities, the "velocity" or efficient use of capital by very large depository institutions has increased. Hence, managers of very large banks, such as Bank of America, suggest that excess capital that cannot be put into endeavors that offer higher returns than a bank's marginal cost of capital should be returned to stockholders.

Questions

1. Why is the market value of equity so different from the book value of equity for depository institutions? What happens to the market value of equity if interest rates rise and a bank has long-term assets financed by short-term deposits? Explain why.

2. What is the purpose of capital? Why is capital particularly important for depository institutions?

3. What are the different preferences of stockholders, managers, regulators, and insured and uninsured depositors for how much capital banks should have? Why does deposit insurance create a moral hazard problem?

4. Briefly discuss Buser, Chen, and Kane's (1981) theory of the optimal debt ratio that will occur under deposit insurance. Discuss other recent theories, how the nature of banking has changed according to these theories to allow for greater market capital discipline and perhaps, according to theory, less need for regulatory capital requirements.

5. Briefly discuss how capital requirements for banks have changed over time. Can you explain why?

6. What is Tier 1 capital? Tier 2 capital? Why are banks allowed to hold Tier 2 capital for regulatory requirements?

7. In your own words, describe how risk-based assets and off-balance-sheet assets are calculated. What are the current minimum leverage ratio and Tier 1 and Tier 2 risk-based capital ratios? What ratios do banks have to have to be well capitalized? Adequately capitalized? What enforcement measures can be taken if institutions are undercapitalized?

8. What is Basel II, and to which banks does it apply? What are some weaknesses of both Basel I and Basel II?

9. What is RAROC? How does RAROC help in allocating capital for a bank's economic risks? How is it used to price loans? Discuss the peer group method versus the volatility method for allocating capital-to-asset ratios for different lines of a bank's business. What are the respective advantages and disadvantages of each method?

10. What practical considerations need to be made by a bank in considering the best capital structure?

11. Why did large banks wish to reduce their excess capital in the 1990s? How did dividend payout policies change in the 1990s? What are some factors that need to be considered by banks in setting their dividend policies?

Problems

1. The Kelly and Mark Savings Bank has the following balance sheet (book values):

Assets		Liabilities & Equity	
Cash	$ 300,000	Deposits	$40,500,000
T-bills	7,000,000	Equity	1,800,000
Consumer Loans	35,000,000	Total	$42,300,000
Total	$42,300,000		

All consumer loans have a 12 percent annual rate with amortized monthly payments (1 percent monthly rate) and are three-year loans (i.e., for thirty-six months).

a. If the market rate for similar consumer loans rises to 15 percent, what is the new market value of the consumer loans? If the market value for liabilities remains the same, what is the new market value of equity?

b. What is the book value of equity to assets? What is the new market value of equity to assets? Explain why they differ.

c. Answer parts a and b again, but assume that similar consumer loans fall from the initial 12 percent rate to an 8 percent rate.

2. The bank owned by Ann and Albert, The Railroad Bill Bank, has Tier 1 capital of $60 million and Tier 2 capital of $15 million. The bank's assets and off-balance-sheet items are listed in the following table:

Assets ($000)	Risk-Based Assets	Risk Weights
Cash	$ 10,000	
Short-term Treasury Securities	28,000	
Long-term Treasury Securities	243,500	
Municipal Bonds (GOs)	150,000	
Other Long-term Securities	50,000	
Residential Mortgages	400,000	
Consumer Loans	200,000	
Commercial Loans	520,000	
Off-Balance-Sheet Items:		
Long-term Loan Commitments	$200,000	0.50
Interest Rate Swap Agreements	30,000	0.50
Total Risk-Based Assets $		

a. Fill in the risk weights in the preceding table for assets, and calculate the bank's risk-based assets and off-balance-sheet items.

b. Calculate Tier 1 capital to assets, Tier 1 capital to risk-based assets, and Tier 1 + Tier 2 capital to risk-based assets.

c. In which category of capital adequacy does The Railroad Bill Bank fall? What advice would you give to management?

3. The Precipice Savings and Loan has the following balance sheet (in millions):

Assets		Liabilities & Equity	
Cash & Reserves	$ 20	Deposits	$850
Treasury Securities	75	Subordinated Debt	15
Mortgages	740	Common Stock	10
Fixed Assets	70	Retained Earnings	30
Total	$905		$905

Off-Balance-Sheet Items (assume 50% risk-based weights):

Long-term Loan Commitments	$500 million
Interest Rate Swap Agreement	$100 million

Because of severe economic difficulties in the S&L's region, $50 million of the mortgages are in default.

a. Calculate the risk-based assets, Tier 1 capital, Tier 2 capital, risk-adjusted capital, and leverage ratios. Is the S&L adequately capitalized?

b. Suppose Precipice S&L's reduced its long-term loan commitments to $100 million. What would its new capital ratios be?

4. The Oakleigh-Roscoe-Yuko Bank, with total assets of $850 million and an assets / equity multiplier (EM) of 11.5, expects to earn an ROE of 15 percent. Dividends will be 40 percent of net income, which is projected at $9 million. Risk-based off-balance-sheet items total $200 million. The bank has $150 million in cash and Treasury securities. All other assets are commercial loans and fixed assets.

a. What is the bank's equity to risk-based asset ratio and leverage ratio? Is the bank adequately capitalized?

b. What internal growth rate in equity is expected $[(ROE)(1 - D)]$?

c. If deposits increase by 7 percent, what asset growth rate is expected? If these expectations materialize, explain why, without doing any calculations, the EM will be higher or lower than 11.5 next year. Calculate the EM and see if you are correct.

d. If the bank paid out a 0 percent dividend, what would the new EM be? What would the EM be with a 100 percent dividend?

e. If the bank pays a dividend payout of 40 percent and any new assets are invested in commercial loans with no new off-balance-sheet items, what will be the new equity to risk-based asset ratio? Explain why the results change compared with part a.

5. The management of the Gail and Mike Savings and Loan forecasts a 5 percent growth in assets for the coming year and a 5.5 percent growth in liabilities.

a. The equity to total assets ratio is now 8 percent. What rate of growth in equity is expected next year? At this rate, will the EM rise, fall, or remain the same? Do these plans make sense?

b. Suppose instead that asset growth is planned at 7.5 percent. If liabilities grow 2 percent, how much must equity grow to achieve this planned asset growth? If liabilities grow 10 percent, how much must equity grow to achieve the planned asset growth? Do you see any parallels between the results of this analysis and the financial condition of some thrifts in the late 1980s? Explain.

6. The management of the Caroline-Lizzie Bank and Trust is pleased about the bank's capital adequacy. Therefore, management has decided to increase the rate of growth in assets for the coming year by pursuing more aggressive liability management. A 15 percent growth rate in liabilities is projected, and a stable dividend payout ratio is projected.

Last year, the firm earned net income of $18 million and paid dividends of $12 million. It expects the same ROE and payout to prevail this year. Management will invest all new funds in consumer loans during the coming year. Total assets are $1.5 billion ($350 million in cash and Treasury securities, with the rest in consumer loans); total liabilities are $1.4 billion; equity is $100 million.

a. What is the current capital to risk-adjusted assets ratio?

b. Calculate the expected growth in percentages and dollars in equity and assets.

c. What capital to risk-based assets ratio is expected next year?

d. If this ratio is unacceptably low to management, suggest ways to improve it.

7. The Terrell-Alby Bank has a marginal tax rate of 35 percent, a current dividend of $2.00, and an expected growth rate of 5 percent. The stock is selling for $30. The yield to maturity for subordinated debt is 8 percent. Preferred stock has a price of $100 and a dividend of $8.00. The bank's Tier 1 and Tier 2 capital is given in the following table:

% of Total Capital	Cost of Capital
Common Equity	$300,000,000
Perpetual Preferred Stock	100,000,000
Subordinated Debt	50,000,000
Loan Loss Reserve	50,000,000

a. Calculate the percentage of each type of capital to total capital, the cost of each type of capital, and the weighted average cost of capital.

b. Suppose management has $70 million of subordinated debt and equity of $150 million. Recalculate the weighted average cost of capital.

Suggested Case Studies Dealing with Capital Requirements

Cost of Capital and Strategies

"National Bank of Los Angeles." (Darden Case), in Richard D. Crawford and William W. Sihler. *Financial Service Organizations: Cases in Strategic Management.* New York: Harper Collins College Publishers, 1994, 16.1. (Currently out of print, but case should be available from Darden.) This case provides an opportunity for bank financial analysis and computing risk-based capital requirements and the cost of capital for a large bank in Los Angeles attempting to implement new risk-based capital requirements.

Bank/Basel Capital Requirements

"Royal Bank of Canada: Capital Options." L. Wynant and H. Fraser (Richard Ivy School of Business: Ivy Case, The University of Western Ontario, 1999). This case goes through Royal Bank of Canada's optimal capital structure decision making and choices of capital with the implementation of the Basel I requirements in the early 1990s.

Selected References

Alexander, Carol, ed. *Operational Risk: Regulation, Analysis and Management.* London: FT (Financial Times) Prentice Hall (Pearson Education), 2003.

Allen, Franklin, and Douglas Gale. "Capital Adequacy Regulation: In Search of a Rationale." Wharton Financial Institutions Center Working Paper (-3-07), 2003 (*http://fic.wharton.upenn.edu/fic/wfic.html*).

Basel Committee on Banking Supervision Consultative Document. "Overview of the New Basel Capital Accord." Issued for Comment by July 31, 2003 (April 2003). Bank for International Settlements, BIS Website, *http://www.bis.org*.

Basel Committee on Banking Supervision. "Performance of Models-Based Capital Charges for Market Risk." (1 July-31 December 1998), September 1999; and "Modifications to the Market Risk Amendment, Textual Changes to the Amendment in the Basel Capital Accord of January, 1996." Documents under the Basel Committee on the BIS Website, *http://www.bis.org*.

Benston, George J. "Market-Value Accounting: Benefits, Costs, and Incentives." In *Proceedings of a Conference on Bank Structure and Competition.* Chicago: Federal Reserve Bank of Chicago, 1989, 547–563.

Berger, Allen N., Kathleen A. Kuester, and James M. O'Brien. "Some Red Flags Concerning Market Value Accounting." In *Proceedings of a Conference on Bank Structure and Competition.* Chicago: Federal Reserve Bank of Chicago, 1989, 515–546.

Buser, Stephen A., Andrew H. Chen, and Edward J. Kane. "Federal Deposit Insurance, Regulatory Policy, and Optimal Bank Capital." *Journal of Finance* 36 (March 1981), 51–60.

Caouette, John B., Edward I. Altman, and Paul Narayanan. *Managing Credit Risk: The Next Great Financial Challenge.* New York: Wiley Frontiers in Finance, 1998.

"Capital Standards for Banks: The Evolving Basel Accord." *Federal Reserve Bulletin,* Vol. 89, No. 9 (September 2003), 395–405.

Cebenoyan, A. S., E. S. Cooperman, and C. A. Register. "Deregulation, Reregulation, Equity Ownership, and S&L Risk Taking." *Financial Management* (Autumn 1995), 63–76.

Chorafas, Dimitris N. *The Market Risk Amendment: Understanding the Marking-to-Model and Value-at-Risk.* Chicago: Irwin McGraw-Hill, 1998.

Cline, Kenneth. "The Velocity of Capital." *Banking Strategies* (November/December 1996), 37–42.

Coulter, David. "Managing for Shareholder Value at Bank of America." *Bank of America Journal of Applied Corporate Finance* 10 (Summer 1997), 68–71.

Crawford, Richard D., and William W. Sihler. *Financial Service Organizations: Cases in Strategic Management.* New York: Harper Collins College Publishers, 1994 (currently out of print).

Davis, Donald, and Kevin Lee. "A Practical Approach to Capital Structure for Banks." *Bank of America Journal of Applied Corporate Finance* 10 (Spring 1997), 33–43.

Evanoff, Douglas D., and Larry D. Wall. "Subordinated Debt as Bank Capital: A Proposal for Regulatory Reform." *Economic Perspectives* (Federal Reserve Bank of Atlanta) (Second Quarter 2000), 40–53.

FDIC FYI. "Basel and the Evolution of Capital Regulation: Moving Forward, Looking Back." *FDIC FYI: An Update on Emerging Issues in Banking,* January 14, 2003. Susan Burhouse, John Feid, George French, and Keith Logan (principal authors). FDIC Website, *http://www.fdic.gov/bank/analytical/fyi/2003/011403fyi.html*.

Flannery, Mark J. "No Pain, No Gain? Effecting Market Discipline via 'Reverse Convertible Debentures'." Working Paper, University of Florida Graduate School of Business Administration, November 2002.

Flannery, Mark J., and Kasturi P. Rangan. "Market Forces at Work in the Banking Industry: Evidence from the Capital Buildup of the 1990's," University of Florida Working Paper, 2002.

Flannery, Mark J., and Stanislava Nikolova. "Market Discipline of U.S. Financial Firms: Recent Evidence and Research Issues." Forthcoming in William C. Hunter, George G. Kaufman, Claudio Borio, and Kostas Tsatsaronis (eds.). *Market Discipline Across Countries and Industries.* Cambridge: MIT Press, 2004.

Froot, Kenneth A. "Bank Capital and Risk Management: Issues for Banks and Regulators." Working Paper, Harvard University and NBER, June 2001, prepared for the International Financial

Risk Institute (IFCI) Risk Round Table, Geneva, Switzerland, April 5 and 6, 2001.

Furlong, Frederick T., and Michael W. Keran. "The Federal Safety Net for Commercial Banks: Part II." *Weekly Letter* (Federal Reserve Bank of San Francisco) (August 3, 1984).

Glantz, Morton. *Managing Bank Risk: An Introduction to Broad-Base Credit Engineering.* New York: Academic Press, 2003.

Hirtle, Beverly. "Bank Holding Company Capital Ratios and Shareholder Payouts." *Current Issues in Economics and Finance* (Federal Reserve Bank of New York) 4 (September 1998), 1–5.

John, Kose, and Teresa A. John. "Top Management Compensation and Capital Structure." *Journal of Finance* 48(3) (1993), 949–974.

Kane, Edward J., and Haluk Unal. "Modeling Structural and Temporal Variation in the Market's Valuation of Banking Firms." *Journal of Finance* 45 (March 1990), 113–136.

Kaufman, George G. "Capital in Banking: Past, Present, and Future." *Journal of Financial Services Research* 5 (April 1992), 385–402.

Kimball, Ralph C. "Economic Profit and Performance Measurement in Banking." *New England Economic Review* (Federal Reserve Bank of Boston) (July/August 1998), 35–53.

Lopez, Jose A. "Methods for Evaluating Value at Risk Estimates." *Economic Policy Review* (Federal Reserve Bank of New York) (October 1998), 119–124.

Marshall, Christopher. *Measuring and Managing Operational Risks in Financial Institutions.* New York: John Wiley & Sons, 2001.

McCoy, John B., Larry A. Frieder, and Robert B. Hedges. *Bottom Line Banking.* Chicago: Probus Publishing Company, 1994.

Mengle, David L., and John R. Walter. "How Market Value Accounting Would Affect Banks." In *Proceedings of the Conference on Bank Structure and Competition.* Chicago: Federal Reserve Bank of Chicago, 1991, 511–533.

Merton, R. C. "Analytic Derivation and the Cost of Deposit Insurance and Loan Guarantees." *Journal of Banking and Finance* (June 1977), 3–11.

Mondschean, Thomas. "Market Value Accounting for Commercial Banks." *Economic Perspectives* (Federal Reserve Bank of Chicago) 16 (January/February 1992), 16–31.

Moore, Robert R. "The Role of Bank Capital in Bank Loan Growth: Can the Market Tell Us Anything That Accountants Don't?" *Financial Industry Studies* (Federal Reserve Bank of Dallas) (December 1992), 11–18.

Powell, Donald E., Chairman, FDIC. "Remarks Before the National Association for Business Economics, March 26, 2004." Washington, DC, FDIC Press Release, PR-30-2004 (3-26-2004). See *www.fdic.gov/news/news/press/2004* for current press releases.

"Reforming Bank Capital Regulation: A Proposal by the U.S. Shadow Financial Regulatory Committee." George G. Kaufman, Robert E. Litan, Richard C. Aspinwall, George J. Benston, Charles W. Calomiris, Franklin R. Edwards, Scott E. Harrington, Richard J. Herring, Paul M. Horvitz, Roberta Romano, Hal S. Scott, Kenneth E. Scott, and Peter J. Wallison. Washington, DC: AEI Press, March 2000.

Saidenberg, Marc, and Til Schuermann. "*The New Basel Capital Accord and Questions for Research.*" Working Paper, Wharton Financial Institutions Center, 03-14, 2003.

Saunders, Anthony. *Financial Institutions Management: A Modern Perspective,* 2nd ed. Chicago: Irwin, 1997.

Saunders, Anthony, and Linda Allen. *Credit Risk Measurement: New Approaches to Value at Risk and Other Paradigms,* 2nd ed. New York: John Wiley & Sons, 2002.

Saunders, Anthony, and Marcia Millon Cornett. *Financial Institution Management: A Risk Management Approach,* 4th ed. Chicago: Irwin McGraw-Hill, 2003.

Wagster, J. D. "The Basle Accord of 1988 and the International Credit Crunch of 1989–1992." *Journal of Financial Services Research* 15 (March 1999), 123–143.

Walker, David A. Principal Investigator. "Credit Union Insurance and Regulation." Washington, DC: Center for Business-Government Relations, Georgetown University, 1997.

Zaik, Edward, John Walter, Gabriela Kelling, and Christopher James. "RAROC at Bank of America: From Theory to Practice." *Bank of America Journal of Applied Corporate Finance* 9 (Summer 1996), 83–93.

CAPITAL REGULATION AND MANAGEMENT

RISK-BASED CAPITAL MODEL FOR BANKERS

The Risk-Based Capital (RBC) Model for Bankers, a microcomputer-based program to estimate a national bank's risk-based capital ratio, is available from the OCC. The model has been revised to reflect recent changes to the regulation and proposed changes to the call reports. The model operates in a Microsoft Windows environment.

1   To access this program, go to the Risk-Based Capital Model for Bankers 2001 Version 1.05 Web page at the OCC at *http://www.occ.treas.gov/rbc.htm*. The download procedure seems a bit complex but for bank managers it is worth the time involved as this program is helpful for banks to calculate their risk-based capital.

2   To get an idea of the process involved in filling out call report data, you can go to the FFIEC Website (*http://www.ffiec.gov*) and use the dollar value information from the uniform bank performance report (UBPR) for Wells Fargo or another bank (as discussed in Chapter 4) to calculate its capital ratios yourself as an exercise.

OTHER USEFUL SITES FOR FINANCIAL INSTITUTION DATA

Darryll Hendricks and Beverly Hirtle. "Bank Capital Requirements for Market Risk: The Internal Models Approach."

http://www.newyorkfed.org/research/epr/97v03n4/ 9712hend.pdf

Basel Committee on Banking Supervision Consultative Document: Overview of the New Basel Capital Accord

http://www.bis.org

Choose among the documents listed under Publications including this consultative document overview or more detailed documents. The full document, titled "The New Basel Capital Accord," as well as an overview, is available at http://www.bis.org/bcbs/bcbscp3.htm. You can also search for a particular topic for announcements and research articles.

Federal Reserve Board Website

http://www.federalreserve.gov

White papers and many other documents related to Basel II are available on the Board's Website; see in particular http://www.federalreserve.gov/generalinfo/basel2/ default.htm. On a link on the http://www.federalreserve .gov home page, you can also go to the Federal Reserve Bulletin's *Website and see copies of* Bulletin *articles, such as "Capital Standards for Banks: The Evolving Basel Accord,"* Federal Reserve Bulletin, *September 2003.*

FDIC Proposed Implementation of the New Basel Capital Accord in the United States

http://www.fdic.gov/regulations/laws/publiccomments/ basel/index.html

7 Changes with Technology

Securitization, Structured Financing, Internet Banking,
and the Role of Financial Institutions in E-Commerce

"How the Internet will affect banking is one of the most intriguing questions in the ongoing evolution of the U.S. banking industry. . . . But Internet banking remains a work in progress, and for many U.S. banks the initial Internet experience has been disappointing."

ROBERT DEYOUNG, Senior Economist, Federal Reserve Bank of Chicago, "The Internet's Place in the Banking Industry," Chicago Fed Letter *(The Federal Reserve Bank of Chicago) 163 (March 2001), p. 1.*

"Technology has also had a remarkable impact on the ways in which financial services do business. . . . Since the arrival of commercial satellite communications, financial and informational data can be transmitted around the globe within seconds."

JOHN B. MCCOY, LARRY A. FRIEDER, AND ROBERT B. HEDGES, JR. Bottomline Banking: Meeting the Challenges for Survival and Success. *Chicago, Illinois: Probus Publishing Company, 1994, p. 258.*

I nnovations and technology have dramatically changed the way financial institutions operate, increasing efficiency, expanding services, and providing more convenience and products, and increasing the speed of the payments system. However, as indicated in the chapter opening quotation, not all financial institutions have had an easy time dealing with new technology, and new technological risks have also evolved. This chapter provides a brief overview of some of the changes that have occurred with technology and how these changes have dramatically reshaped the landscape for financial institutions, focusing on loan sales and securitization, Internet banking, changes in the payment mechanism, and the role of financial institutions in E-commerce.

Learning Objectives

After completing this chapter, you will be able to:

1 Discuss the tremendous growth in loan securitization and understand the mechanics of securitization.

2 Understand how structured finance is used in different types of applications including asset-backed commercial paper, project financing, and catastrophic risk securities.

3 Understand the economic reasons for the rapid growth in securitization and loans sales.

4 Explain the effect of the Enron scandal on the regulatory view of securitization.

5 Understand trends in Internet banking and banks' role in E-commerce.

6 Understand trends in the ATM and debit card industry.

Loan Securitization and Sales

Although loan sales and securitization are now widespread for financial institutions, securitization, as an innovation, is relatively new, beginning in the 1970s and growing dramatically in the 1980s and 1990s and on through the 2000s. In order to perform extensive loan sales and securitizations, numerous records and information have to be stored, so the advent of the information age in the 1990s gave securitization a tremendous boost. With securitizations, loans are packaged into portfolios, sold off-balance sheet to a specialized securitization enterprise, and passed on to a trust organization to be repackaged as participating securities with cash flows received by investors on principal and interest. Meanwhile the bank that originated (underwrote) the loans often maintains the servicing right and receives fees for continuing to collect interest and principal payments from the loan customers, which, in turn, are passed through to the trust organization to pass on to investors in the mortgage (pass-through) securities. Hence, the process involves a great deal of information processing and record-keeping that has been facilitated by new technology.

Government-Sponsored Enterprises (GSEs), discussed in Chapter 1, initiated the first home mortgage loan securitizations. Banks and savings institutions sell loans to the GSEs, who repackage them as securities. Banks and thrifts benefit by having more liquid funds available to make new home mortgages, increasing the availability of home mortgages and hence home ownership to the public. The first securitization began in 1970 when the Government National Mortgage Association (GNMA, or Ginnie Mae) developed the first mortgage-backed security that passed through interest and principal payments for 1-4 family home mortgage loans. These securities, backed by pools of home mortgages, are known as mortgage-backed securities (MBS) or pass-through securities. In 1991, the Federal Home Loan Mortgage Corporation (FHLMC, or Freddie Mac) followed by developing similar pass-through securities, and later the Federal National Mortgage Association (FNMA, or Fannie Mae) followed with its own pass-through securities in 1981.[1]

Private sector securitization began in 1977 when Bank of America first began securitizing conventional mortgages. Other private sector firm securitizations include Certificates of Automobile Receivables (CARs) and Credit Card Receivables, known as Certificates of Amortizing Revolving Debts (CARDs). Large, specialized credit card banks, such as MBNA in Delaware, have been innovative in designing new types of securitizations for credit cards and other consumer loans. Home equity and even subprime loans are securitized today. In February 2004, ABS Market Statistics reported an estimated total of $61.3 trillion in asset-backed securities (ABS) outstanding worldwide, a rise from $60.4 trillion

---

1 See Arshadi and Karels (1997), 86–89, and Saunders and Cornett (2003), Chapter 28, 733–768.

for the prior year.[2] The Banc One Capital Markets, Inc., Structured Debt yearbook for 2004 reported $416.06 billion in U.S. public issuance of asset-backed securities in 2003 compared with only $46.78 billion ABS issued in 1990. This is a phenomenal 789 percent growth rate in issuance from 1990 to 2003, or an average annual growth rate of about 18 percent each year. The different types of ABS reported by Banc One Capital Markets in 2003 include securities backed by the following types of loans: automobile (18.77 percent), credit cards (15.49 percent), residential mortgage ABS (51.81 percent), manufactured housing loans (0.15 percent), student loans (8.87 percent), and other (4.91 percent). Hence, residential mortgage asset-backed securities continue to be the largest percentage of total U.S. asset-backed securities. In terms of coupon type, 31 percent of U.S. ABS in 2003 had fixed rates and 69 percent, floating rates.[3]

The Banc One Capital Markets Report cited the largest issuers of the 544 ABS deals made in 2003 to include: GMAC with 11 percent of the total dollar amount, Ameriquest with 7 percent, Sallie Mae (the Student Loan Marketing Association) with 6 percent, JPMorgan Chase Bank with 4 percent, Lehman Brothers with 4 percent, and the remaining 68 percent from other issuers including Citibank, Countrywide Financial, Credit Suisse First Boston, Banc One, and Capital One. Hence, a variety of financial institutions and GSEs are actively involved in securitizations.[4]

Public securitizations generally have part of their issuance insured or have standby letters of commitment from large, very creditworthy banks to guarantee part of the issue in the event of default for a fee. The Banc One Capital Markets Report in 2004 reported that about 11 percent of ABS issues had insurance. The top four insurers as a percentage of insured market share included MBIA, FGIC, AMBAC, and Fannie Mae. In addition to asset-backed securities, asset-backed commercial paper (ABCP) has become very popular. Estimated issuance of ABCP was $719.8 billion at the end of the second quarter of 2003, a rise from $46.9 billion in 1992. Ongoing securitization can be very profitable for financial institutions as discussed in the following section.[5]

Mechanics of Securitization

Loan securitization, which is similar to loan sales, involves removing loans from a bank's balance sheet and selling them to investors. However, before being sold, the loans are packaged into securities with characteristics that make them attractive to large and small investors. The mechanics of securitization are subject to a variety of tax, securities, regulatory, and accounting laws.

Structure of a Securitization

Figure 7.1 shows a brief outline of the mechanics for securitizing automobile loans. On a nonrecourse basis (where an institution sells loans with no legal recourse for losses), a depository institution originating the loans sells a pool of loans and collateral values to a limited-purpose corporation. The limited-purpose corporation (specialized enterprise vehicle), often a subsidiary of the investment bank setting up the deal or a special subsidiary of the originating bank, exists solely to act as an intermediary between the buyer and seller to transfer assets to a trust. The trust purchases loans from the limited-purpose company and packages the loans into certificates that can be sold to investors. If the trust has no recourse with the originating bank for loan losses, the bank can then remove the loans sold from its balance sheet. To make the certificates that represent "fractional and undivided" interests in the pool of assets more attractive to investors, an insurance company surety bond or a bank letter of credit is purchased to guarantee a portion of the loan pool.

The trust generally also asks an agency to rate the certificates. With a portion of the pool guaranteed and the originating bank putting aside part of its future servicing income from the loan as security to back the pool, a high rating (AA or AAA required by many investors) is often given if the loans are randomly selected and of decent quality. Standard and Poor's often requires for an AAA rating

---

2 Asset-Backed Alert: The Weekly Update on Worldwide Securitization, ABS Market Statistics for February 18, 2004, at *http://www.abalert.com/public/market-place/marketstatistics/index.cfm*, or *http://www.abalert.com*, click on "ABS Market Statistics" on right-hand side of the home page.

3 Banc One Capital Markets, Inc. *ABS Structured Debt Yearbook, 2004*, 68 *(http://www.bocmsdr.com)*.

4 Ibid, 71, 73.

5 Ibid, 87–89.

figure **7.1**   MECHANICS OF SECURITIZATION

STRUCTURE OF AN AUTOMOBILE LOAN SECURITIZATION

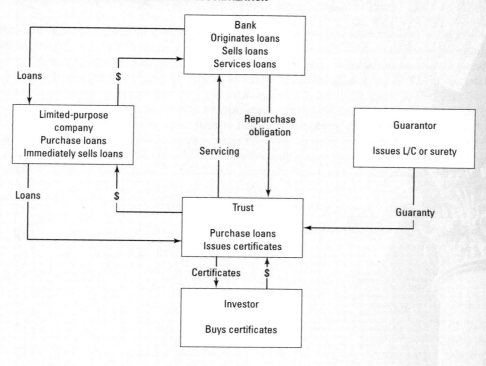

CASH FLOWS OF HYPOTHETICAL AUTOMOBILE LOAN SECURITIZATION

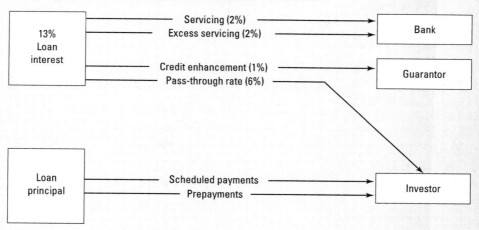

Source: Adapted by authors, using examples from Bank Performance Annual. *(1988), illustration, as presented in packets of materials at a seminar on Securitization in Baltimore, MD, 1989, Figure 3, p. 108, and Figure 4, p. 109*

that the third-party credit enhancement and excess servicing fee put in trust be at least 8 percent of the value of the underlying loan portfolio if a bank has a history of losses of about 40 basis points per year. The trust generally hires an underwriter to set the initial price and market the securities to the public. The bank continues to service the loans and collect servicing fees for doing this. Collections of principal and interest net of the originating bank's servicing fees are deposited each month with the trustee, which in turn passes payments to investors as interest. All principal payments are passed on to the investor as well. Mortgage loans are securitized in a similar way (discussed in greater detail in Chapter 14). However, often government agencies such as the Government National Mortgage Association or quasi-government agencies such as the Federal National Mortgage Association or Federal Home Loan Mortgage Corporation provide the trust, investment banker, and guarantor roles.

Example of Cash Flows in a Hypothetical Securitization

The lower panel of Figure 7.1 shows the mechanics of a securitization. Automobile loans with an 11 percent interest rate are sold. The originating bank receives 2 percent of the loan amount for servicing the loans plus a 2 percent excess servicing fee that is reserved for future losses on the loans. If losses do not occur over the life of the securities, the bank is entitled to this excess fee as well. The guarantor receives 1 percent for the letter of credit. The remaining 6 percent is the pass-through interest rate that investors receive who purchase the certificates for automobile receivables (CARS).[6]

Table 7.1 shows the cash proceeds based on automobile receivables of $500 million with a coupon rate of 6 percent with monthly payments and a maximum maturity of four years. The average life of the CARS is actually only two years, because borrowers are likely to prepay their loans early, particularly if rates fall. Hence, investors in effect are purchasing securities that have an expected life of two

table 7.1 PRICING SUMMARY OF HYPOTHETICAL AUTOMOBILE LOAN SECURITIZATION

Collateral	
Type	Automobile receivables
Face amount	$500 Million
Amortization method	Effective interest
Weighted average APR	11%
Servicing fee	2%
Excess servicing fee	2%
Payment frequency	Monthly
Maturity range	18–48 Months
Weighted average maturity	24 Months
Asset-Backed Security	
Face amount	$500 Million
Coupon	6% (Monthly)
Maximum maturity	4 Years
Average life	2 Years
Proceeds	
Gross (sold at par)	$ 500,000,000
Underwriting fee	−2,500,000
Issuing expenses	−1,250,000
First-year credit enhancement	−500,000[1]
	$ 495,750,000
Net	
Present value of excess servicing flows	+20,800,000[2]
Net present value	$516,550,000[3]

[1]*Assumes a letter of credit for 10 percent of the transaction size at a cost of 1 percent.*

[2]*This can be reported as income at the time of sale under GAAP (but not RAP) after deduction of appropriate loan loss and prepayment provisions.*

[3]*This figure would be slightly less after deduction for cost of subsequent credit enhancement. This added cost would be a function of the amount of actual outstandings in years two, three, or four.*

Source: Example created by authors, based on Bank Performance Annual *(1988) as presented in packets of materials at a seminar on Securitization in Baltimore, MD, 1989, Table 2, p. 110.*

6 This example was created by the authors similar to commonly used examples, including an example from *Bank Performance Annual*, 1988, 107–111; the information in the previous section also comes from this source.

years. There is some prepayment risk because if the security is prepaid the investors will have to rein-vest the principal payments that they receive early at a lower rate. This prepayment risk is particularly serious for mortgage securities, so investors will generally demand a premium on the rate they receive over comparable securities.

The originating bank sells the loans for $500,000,000. After paying $2,500,000 for the underwriting fee, $1,250,000 for issuing expenses, and $500,000 for the first-year credit enhancement, the bank receives a net of $495,750,000. However, taking the present value of future excess servicing fees and adding this to the net, the bank actually receives a net present value for the securitization of $516,550,000. This exam-ple shows securitizations to be quite profitable. In addition, banks no longer have to hold capital on these loans or pay interest on the deposits used to finance such loans. The bank has newfound liquidity and has cash to make new loans if it wishes. Banks can also get rid of long-term loans, such as home mortgage loans, to adjust their interest rate gaps and reduce their interest rate risk positions. For the loans to be completely off the bank's balance sheet for regulatory and accounting purposes, the loans must be sold with no recourse. Because packaged loans must have similar maturities, loan rates, and other characteris-tics, commercial loans that are tailor-made are difficult to securitize. Congress has recently discussed the possibility of developing agencies to help securitize small business loans to make more capital available from banks to small businesses. Securitizations are packaged in many innovative ways to make them more attractive to investors with different maturity and prepayment risk preferences. Collateralized Mortgage Obligations (CMOs; pass-through securities backed by mortgage obligations) are just such a package; they are organized in *tranches,* classes of stated maturities that investors can choose based on their maturity preferences, and are discussed in more detail in Chapter 14.[7]

Structured Finance Transactions

As noted by Barbara Kavanagh in an FMA Online article in 2002, all structured transactions include certain common features: (1) a separate entity (a special-purpose vehicle, SPV) from the bank to hold a portfolio of assets; and (2) a separate trust that issues debt or equity securities to investors with claims on the cash flows of the assets held by the first SPV. The trust also monitors reports by the loan servicer on the pool performance, takes in cash flows collected by the servicer, and distributes cash flows passed on to investors. By having a separate SPV and trust to monitor activities, isolating assets from the orig-inator bank, a "true sale" of the assets occurs, which allows sales accounting treatment under Generally Accepted Accounting Principles (GAAP). Also, by having a credit enhancer, as discussed earlier, with a standby letter of credit by an AAA–rated bank or a percentage of the assets insured or funds put in a special reserve against future losses, the securities can have a higher credit rating than the originating bank. In addition to traditional securitizations, banks have used structured securitizations to provide financing to businesses in creative ways that avoid limitations placed on banks in terms of the maxi-mum that can be lent to a borrower as a percentage of total capital and other regulatory restrictions. Three examples she notes of structured transactions are asset-backed commercial paper, structured project financing, and catastrophe-linked securities ("Cat Bonds").[8]

Asset-Backed Commercial Paper

Asset-backed commercial paper has been used as such a vehicle for off-balance-sheet lending, where accounts receivables of multiple corporate clients of banks are put in an SPV. A trust in turn issues high-quality commercial paper backed by the underlying accounts receivables, often backed by credit and liquidity lines from a bank or group of banks as a credit enhancer. The proceeds of the commer-cial paper are passed on to the corporate clients for their liquidity needs and to pay for the accounts

---

7 Ibid. Also see Saunders and Cornett (2003), Chapter 28, and Koch and MacDonald (2000), Chapter 19, for more details on securitization and different types of collateralized mortgage securities (CMOs). Fixed-rate mortgage-backed securities are subject to prepayment risk, which results in the principal coming back and the maturity (or more technically the duration) of the security falling. Accordingly, estimates of the security's prepayment risk, such as the prepayment model developed by the Public Securities Association (PSA), are used in the estimation of the likely prepayment of a security issue to calculate the required interest spread of a pass-through security over a Treasury security with a similar expected maturity. Calculations are based on the estimated prepayment risk of the security. CMOs are created generally by the trust that issues the CMOs, which issues different classes of securities based on their degree of pre-payment protections, with earlier classes (A, B, etc.) having bonds retired first, while the last class, Z, accrues interest, like a zero-coupon bond, and has the longest maturity, being paid only after the other classes of bonds have been repaid.

8 See Barbara T. Kavanagh. "Securitization and Structured Finance: Legitimate Business Management Tools." *FMA Online,* Fall 2002. See *http://www.fma.org* (FMAI archives on Risk Management) or *http://207.36.165.114/FMAOnline/Securitization.pdf.* The information in the following section is based on this source.

receivables that were sold. Corporate clients receive both a low cost of financing and access to commercial paper markets that normally would require high credit ratings. Banks in return receive fee income and enhanced customer lending relationships.

Structured Project Finance Securitization

Similarly, project financing (for large public or capital-intensive projects) that entails extensive financing needs has also been transformed by using structured finance, with the creation of an SPV to issue debt serviced by cash flows from underlying assets held by the SPV. Typically, isolated or at times multiple diversified long-term bank project loans are put in an SPV. The SPV in turn issues senior and subordinated debt that will be serviced by cash flows that come from underlying projects. While a bank may initiate the construction of a plant, for instance, for a two-year phase, the SPV will take on the loan, thereafter removing loans from the bank's balance sheet. Since banks don't like to take on permanent, long-term financing of projects, the project financing securitization alleviates this problem.. It also offers the company seeking the financing, such as a utility firm, cheaper fixed-rate financing than a two-stage process, where a bank finances the first stage, and a long-term lender, such as an insurance firm takes over the loan and finances the second stage, often at a higher interest rate.[9]

Catastrophe-Linked Securities

A final example of a structured finance transaction, as described by Barbara Kavanagh, is catastrophe-linked securities. An insurance company may surmise that, given its expected income stream and balance sheet, it can only handle $150 million in losses. Accordingly, the insurer could get reinsurance by passing premiums to another insurer for any losses greater than $150 million up to perhaps $250 million. However, reinsurance is not always available. Consequently, an alternative, structured finance transaction, CAT bonds, was developed. As a structured transaction, a remote SPV is established backed by collateral provided by the insurance firm. The SPV issues securities that represent the risk of a catastrophic loss above the typical, expected risk for a particular risk and region (i.e., earthquakes in California). The excess coupon on the securities is set at a rate greater than the return on the collateral paid by excess premiums from the insurer. The SPV serves to issue a reinsurance contract to the insurance firm, in the event of a greater loss than expected. The cash proceeds from the security issuance would generally be invested in high-quality, fixed-income investments (i.e., U.S. Treasuries) to provide payments against security claims that could occur in excess of a specified benchmark and/or to provide a source of principal repayment to bondholders. The yield that the bondholders receive will be conditional on whether the insurance company files claims for excess losses above the expected (attachment) point.[10]

Loan Sales

Banks have been active in the past decade as loan brokers, negotiating large loans and selling them or selling portions of them to other financial institutions, including pension funds, insurance companies, and other depository institutions that have longer-term investment horizons than the bank. Loan sales benefit customers by allowing them to maintain their relationship with their bank, which goes through

---

Concept Questions

1 What are the steps involved in doing a securitization? How is the risk of the securitization reduced? What types of loans are frequently securitized today?

2 How does a bank make money from securitizations?

3 Explain the special features of structured finance.

4 Briefly explain how asset-backed commercial paper, project financing, and catastrophe-linked securities each provide benefits over traditional financing methods.

---

9 Ibid.

10 Ibid.

the credit analysis and loan approval process. The bank benefits by allowing it to take longer-term loans off its balance sheet, reducing the bank's interest rate risk, yet at the same time satisfying customers who want longer-term loans. Also, by selling the loan without recourse, legally, the bank is no longer responsible for the loan and is no longer subject to the credit risk associated with the loan. By acting as a broker, the bank also receives fee income, and the loan that it has made has no effect on the required capital the bank must hold on assets if the loan is sold without recourse.[11]

Other economic justifications for loan sales include actively managing a bank's credit risk exposure by both selling and buying loans for risk management purposes. Banks can reduce their exposure to certain industry or geographic sectors by selling portions of these loans and buying loans from other banks from other industry sectors or regions. Hence, theoretically, a bank's overall loan portfolio can become less risky and more diversified. Studies of large banks that buy and sell loans have not been able to examine diversification effects, because data on diversification has not been available. A recent study be Cebenoyan and Strahan (2004) examining large bank holding companies (BHCs) that are actively involved in both buying and selling loans actually finds that these BHCs tend to make more risky loans and hold less capital as a percentage of total loans than other banks, suggesting other motives for these transactions.

Types of Loan Sales

There are different types of loan sales. The most common form is *the **participation**,* whereby the originating bank continues to hold the formal contract between the bank and the borrower. The originating bank continues to service the loan, collecting payments, overseeing the collateral, and keeping the books. In the case of a silent participation, the borrower may not be aware of the sale. A less common type is *the **assignment**,* in which the debtor-creditor relationship is transferred to the loan buyer, which gives the purchaser the right to take actions against the borrower if payments are not made. The originating bank, however, may retain the lien on any collateral backing the loan or some other obligations. The **novation,** the least common type of arrangement, transfers all rights and obligations of the selling bank to the buyer, and the originator is completely free from any legal obligations to either the borrower or the loan buyer. Nonetheless, selling a loan is generally less of a "clean break" than the sale of other types of assets. Even if loans are sold without recourse, banks implicitly have responsibilities to the buyer of the loan in terms of maintaining the reputation of the bank. If a bank simply sold its worst loans to other institutions, it would certainly lose its reputation and goodwill with the institutions it sold "bad" loans to.[12]

Banks can also sell troubled loans to investors at large discounts. For instance, in the mid-1980s banks that had excessive loan exposure to Latin America and Mexico sold loans to other financial institutions and investors, taking a significant loss. To make such loans more sellable, the U.S. government has provided loan guarantees for several years to investors purchasing such loans. Under the U.S. Treasury's 1989 Brady plan, countries were also allowed to exchange original, nonconforming loans at U.S. banks for long-term bonds with longer maturities and more favorable terms. These **debt-to-debt swaps** are known as **Brady Bonds.** By the mid-1980s, a strong secondary market for trading less-developed country debt emerged with large commercial banks and investment banks serving as brokers and dealers. Less-developed country debt brokers also made arrangements to swap debt for equity investments that could benefit foreign investors who wished to make fixed capital investments in their respective countries. The volume of Brady Bonds has declined in recent years.[13]

Economic Benefits and Reasons for the Rapid Growth in Loan Sales and Securitization Activities

There has been much debate over the years about securitization and its benefits and risks. A number of economic reasons have been given for this rapid growth including, initially, avoidance of

---

11 See Koch and MacDonald (2000) and Joseph G. Haubrich. "The Evolving Loan Sales Market." *Economic Commentary* (Federal Reserve Bank of Cleveland) (July 15, 1993), 1–5.

12 Ibid.

13 See Saunders and Cornett (2003), Chapter 16, 412–416, for a more detailed discussion of Brady Bonds.

bank regulations—with loans removed from the balance sheet no longer requiring capital or deposit insurance fees for their financing with deposits. The rapid growth is also attributed to improvements in information technology, which made securitization more cost effective for financial institutions, as well as nonfinancial institutions; diversification of an institution's loan portfolio; significant noninterest (fee) income with continuing servicing income for banks once loans are sold or securitized; a significant source of liquidity; and reducing a financial institution's interest rate risk by removing long-term fixed rate assets from its balance sheet. Large banks and thrifts have been heavily involved in securitization activities, receiving fee income for continued servicing of loans, as noted in the previous example of securitization, as well as fees for credit enhancement for securitizations of other banks, among other activities.[14]

The Enron Scandal Backlash on Securitization Activities

The scandal at Enron in 2000, whereby managers of Enron set up structured finance special-purpose entities (SPEs), often called special-purpose vehicles (SPVs), to illegally hide its large debt liabilities from financial analysts, led to a backlash against securitization activities and greater regulatory scrutiny. As noted by Schwarcz (2004) in an article titled "Securitization Post-Enron," this happened despite the fact that Enron's deals using SPVs were only superficially similar to securitization activities. New accounting, regulatory, and legal rulings were enacted focusing on greater disclosure that particularly affected the asset-backed commercial paper market. For instance, as pointed out by the Banc One Capital Markets' *ABS Structured Debt Yearbook 2004*, under the Sarbanes-Oxley Act of 2002, public companies must disclose their participation in all structured financing activities in the Management Discussion and Analysis Section of quarterly financial reports that they file with the SEC. The Financial Accounting Standards Board (FASB) also struggled with improving the accounting of firms for off-balance-sheet special-purpose vehicles, and passed a new rule (Interpretation No. 46, FIN 46) in January of 2003 that created some technical difficulties for the reporting of variable interest special entities, requiring consolidation of all related parties at risk in the event of the bankruptcy of the originator of the loans. Threats for securitization have included possible judicial decisions concerning the existence of contingent risk for SPVs if a loan sale is not a "true sale," and the SPV would be at risk if the originator of the loans goes bankrupt.[15]

Regulators have also been concerned about covenants attached to securitizations, such as a transfer of servicing rights for an originating bank in the event of a regulatory CAMELS downgrade—that, in turn, could create liquidity problems for a banking organization. Under a 2003 supervisory ruling (Rule 2002-34), banking organizations are asked to make sure that such covenants related to supervisory actions are not included in documents for securitizations. Other supervisory rulings in 2002 provided guidance to ensure that asset securitizations are "true sales" for banks by not including any implied or moral support or residual interests by the originating bank beyond contractual obligations, when loans are sold to SPVs for securitization. Under Basel I, banks that have securitizations with any recourse for the originating bank must hold additional risk-based capital for such off-balance-sheet obligations. Under Basel II for large international banks, at the time of this writing, the Basel Committee would allow both originating and investing banks with securitization-related exposures for unrated asset-backed commercial paper SPVs to map their internal risk assessments to comparable external credit ratings to determine comparable risk-based weights for capital requirements for unrated securitization exposures, with higher base risk weights for more risky comparable exposures.[16]

---

14 See Charles T. Carlstrom and Katherine A. Samolyk. "Securitization: More than Just a Regulatory Artifact." *Economic Commentary* (Federal Reserve Bank of Cleveland) (May 1, 1992), 1–4.

15 Steven L. Schwarcz. "Securitization Post-Enron." In the Symposium Issue on "Threats to Secured Lending and Asset Securitization," *Cardozo Law Review*, Vol. 25, forthcoming 2004. Also see the PDF working paper at *http://www.securitization.net/pdf/duke_enron_052303.pdf*. Banc One Capital Market, Inc., ABS Yearbook 2004, 4–6, can be found at *http://www.bocmsdr.com*.

16 "Banking Supervision and Regulation: Credit Card Securitizations, Interagency Advisory on Accounting for Accrued Interest Receivables Related to Credit Card Securitizations (SR 02-22)." Federal Reserve Bank of San Francisco, December 11, 2002; "Implicit Recourse Provided to Asset Securitization (SR 02-15)." Board of Governors of the Federal Reserve System, May 23, 2002; "Securitization Covenants Linked to Supervisory Actions or Thresholds (RU 2002-34)." Regulatory News for Financial Institutions in the Seventh Federal Reserve District, *Chicago Fed Regulatory Update*, Vol. 5, No. 8, June 13, 2002; "Continued Progress Toward Basel II." Bank for International Settlements, Press Release, January 15, 2004 (*http://www.bis.org/press/p040115.htm*).

Similarly, there have been concerns about too much risk taken on by government-sponsored enterprises (GSEs) in their role in buying up mortgages worth billions and repackaging them as securities. Fed regulators, including Alan Greenspan, have warned that their growth has been so rapid and they have taken on so much debt in their roles that they can no longer hedge against potential financial crises. Fannie Mae and Freddie Mac currently hold about $2 trillion in security obligations tied to home mortgages. Although they are private companies, as quasi-government enterprises, regulators are concerned that lenders and investors expect that the U.S. government would bail Fannie Mae and Freddie Mac out in the event of a financial crisis. Consequently, as Alan Greenspan notes, this creates a moral hazard danger, whereby Fannie Mae and Freddie Mac may be tempted to assume increased risks, given low-cost (implicitly subsidized) financing regardless of the risks they undertake. Thus, some regulators have argued for tighter regulatory control for Fannie Mae and Freddie Mac. Critics have also been concerned about their rapid growth and large debt exposures. Because of questionable accounting practices (including a $1.1 billion accounting error by Fannie Mae in October 2003 and similar problems with Freddie Mac), as well as less transparency in accounting than other financial institutions, critics have been concerned about their outdated accounting systems as well.[17]

Internet Banks and Other Internet Financial Institutions

How Widespread Are Internet Banks and Other Financial Institutions?

With the advent of the information age, many predictions were thrown around in the early to mid-1990s that banks would no longer have any need for branches and that Internet banking would predominate. This event has not come to pass in the early twenty-first century. Banks have actually been expanding their branching systems, and Internet banking appears to be a complement rather than a substitute for bank branches. As of March 1, 2004, the "Online Banking Report: Internet Strategies for Financial Institutions" reported thirty true Web banks and credit unions in the United States; true meaning that they operate only on the Internet with no branches. An overview on a special OBR report on the first seven and a half years of Web banking ("Online Banking by the Numbers 2003") notes a dramatic increase, however, in complementary Web banking services worldwide, as well as Web usage in general. In 1995, only one Web financial institution operated. By the end of 2002, 6,000 Web financial institutions operated worldwide. Similarly, the survey shows tremendous growth in financial institution Websites, growing from only 50 in 1995 to 14,000 today. The total of online banking households in the United States jumped from 300,000 in 1995 to 28 million in 2002. Also, monthly bank and credit card Web traffic rose from 100,000 to 50 million. There has also been a fivefold increase in U.S. households accessing bank accounts and paying bills online. Hence, although *brick and mortar* banking continues to be the dominant channel for financial service firm activities, online banking has emerged as a very popular channel in the United States and worldwide. A recent Federal Reserve article, "U.S. Consumers and Electronic Banking, 1995-2003," examining recent surveys of consumers also finds that in the U.S. ninety percent of U.S. households have a bank account and 93 percent of those with bank accounts have one or more of different electronic transfer features including direct deposit, ATM, debit

---

Concept Questions

1 Describe the characteristics of different types of loan sales, including participation, assignment, and novation. Which type of sale is used most frequently?

2 What are the economic benefits of loan sales and securitization?

3 How did the Enron scandal create a backlash for securitizations? What are a few accounting and regulatory concerns about securitizations?

4 Why are regulators particularly concerned about Freddie Mac and Fannie Mae?

---

17 See "Fed Chief Warns of a Risk to Taxpayers: Fannie Mae and Freddie Mac Cannot Hedge Against Financial Crises, He Says." *New York Times* (February 25, 2004), C1, C8; "Fannie Scolded for Obsolete Accounting System." *The Wall Street Journal* (February 26, 2004), A2; Frame and White (2004); and Frame and Wall (2002).

cards, or computer banking in association with their accounts, and the proportion of households in the survey that used computer banking rose from 4 percent in 1995 to 32 percent in 2003.[18]

How Widely Used Are Internet Financial Services by Financial Professionals?

The Association for Financial Professionals (AFP) surveyed treasury professionals in 2002 to see how practitioners used the Internet in their treasury and finance operations. Eighty percent of the companies surveyed used the Internet to obtain information on financial services and 64 percent to communicate with financial services institutions about financial products. The most widely used Internet service was cash management services, followed by investments and foreign exchange. The biggest benefit treasury and finance professionals cited was their ability to perform more of their own data inquiries and to have greater access to real-time information, while the biggest barrier was security concerns and the inability to verify the identity of a counterparty. Concerns by more than 90 percent of respondents also included the enforceability of contracts and problems integrating data obtained with their internal systems.

The following list indicates the percentage of respondents who use the Internet for particular financial services:

Cash management	86 percent
Investments	52 percent
Foreign exchange	45 percent
Bank loans	39 percent
Letters of credit	32 percent
Insurance	31 percent
Bonds and commercial paper issuance	29 percent
Derivatives/hedging	21 percent

When asked whether firms increased or decreased their use of the Internet over the previous year, the majority of respondents noted that their usage was about the same. Seventy-one percent of respondents also expected to increase their use of the Internet for their cash management services in the next year.[19]

Strategic Choices for Banks in Using the Internet as a Delivery Channel

How financial services firms and particularly how banks use the Internet in providing services and products is a question that almost all financial service firms have had to deal with in the past decade. As noted by Robert DeYoung, Senior Economist at the Chicago Fed in a *Chicago Fed Letter,* "The Internet's Place in the Banking Industry," the Internet offers a delivery channel for "virtually any type of banking service," with the exception of "providing cash to almost any place at almost any time," and its future and profitability for banks will depend more on the quality of the bank's products and services. Similarly, it will also depend on how the Internet is integrated with a bank's more traditional channels. Despite predictions that "brick and mortar banks" would be a thing of the past in the mid-1990s, bank branches have increased dramatically, as have banking kiosks and ATMs (automated teller machines). As noted in a recent *Federal Reserve Bulletin* article, more than 75 percent of households participating in surveys, reported that they continued to do banking in person at their bank. As DeYoung notes, rather than being a replacement, the Internet has served as a complementary distribution mechanism, extending the geographic reach of banks. Banks with Internet banking capabilities provide new services and greater convenience, allowing customers to make loans, receive approvals through credit scoring, and pay their bills. With the passage of the Financial Modernization Act, banks can offer other financial services on the Internet as well, including insurance and securities activities. For commercial customers, working capital management services and assistance in E-commerce can also be provided.

---

18 See Online Banking Report: Internet Strategies for Financial Institutions at *http://www.onlinebankingreport.com.* From the menu, click "Resources" for information on online banks. See particularly, "OBR Special Reports: Online Banking by the Numbers 2003: Overview." A full (414-page) report can be purchased from Online Banking at their Website. Also, see Anguelov, Hilgert, and Hogarth (2004).

19 Association for Financial Professionals (AFP). "The Internet and the Changing Financial Services Marketplace: Results of the 2002 Survey." Prepared by AFP Research, September 2002, *http://www.afponline.org/pub/pdf2002_AFP_Internet_Survey.pdf.*

Although new services are offered, as DeYoung notes, the Internet is more of a distribution network, rather than a product itself. Hence, a bank's success ultimately depends on the quality of its products and services. Although the Internet reduces a bank's transaction costs, depending on the quality and nature of services, the Internet as a distribution network may create greater distance between a bank and its customers, and a perception of inferior service unless the quality of internet service is very high. Hence, he points out banks need to decide their own particular best distribution strategy in using the Internet along with other distribution mechanisms.[20]

In a more detailed research paper, DeYoung and Hunter (2002) note that the Internet can add value for both very large banks and community banks. For large banks the Internet serves to improve the market presence, cost advantages, and scale of their operations, while for community banks the Internet can actually improve the service quality that they can offer to their customers thereby reducing the cost disadvantages that they have compared to very large banks. The Internet, if used well, may allow banks to cross-sell different products. This, in turn, can make customers more loyal to the bank by increasing the convenience of having access to a broad variety of services within one institution, creating a stronger relationship with the bank, and increasing customer switching costs.[21]

The Performance of Pure Play Internet Banks

Although "pure play," totally Internet banks were highly touted in the early stages of Internet banking, as noted previously, there are relatively small numbers of reported purely Internet banks compared to total banks operating worldwide. As noted by DeYoung (2000, 2001a), Internet-only banks often provide limited types of Internet services, focusing on a customer niche characterized by greater Internet sophistication. Often pure, or virtual, Internet banks use ATMs to augment their services. The results of early studies of the profitability of Internet banks by the OCC (Furst, Lang, and Nolle, 2000) and the Federal Reserve Bank of Kansas City (Sullivan, 2000), find pure Internet banks to have similar or higher profitability than traditional banks. However, a third study at the Federal Reserve Bank of Chicago (DeYoung, 2001b) looking at twelve pure Internet banks and thrifts operating between 1997 and 2000, compared to other branching banks and thrifts and controlling for other factors, finds pure Internet depository institutions to be less profitable. This lower profitability was related to difficulties of Internet banks in generating deposit funding, along with higher labor expenses and lower fee income.

On a caveat, DeYoung (2001b) notes that pure Internet banks and their customers may be experiencing a learning curve, so pure Internet banks may yet become more efficient and profitable. He points out that a large number of Internet-only banks are specialty-niche banks. Examples include the BMW Bank, a pure Internet bank that focuses on wealthy BMW customers associated with BMW auto dealerships, and the E*Trade Bank, which has a niche for customers making stock transactions electronically via E*Trade. However, some very large banks or other financial institutions have purchased or launched Internet-only banks and attempted to give them a high profile, such as the pure Internet bank owned by Citigroup. Other prominent pure Internet banks have associated with large insurance companies or finance firms including ING Direct and American Express Membership Banking. Large banks, such as Royal Bank of Canada and Citigroup, have established or purchased Internet banks that also allow Internet customers access to their traditional bank networks. As noted by DeYoung (2001b), many pure Internet banks that started before 2000 have either been closed by regulators, been acquired, or have voluntarily liquidated as they struggled as de novo (start-up) banks for profitability. Others established in 1999 or later are still experiencing a learning curve.[22]

Advantages and Disadvantages to Customers of Pure Internet Banks

One advantage of totally virtual Internet banks is that they can have low overhead costs, since they exist on the Internet and don't have buildings and branches. With the lower overhead and not having to pay tellers and other personnel, they at times can be competitive by offering higher yields on funds

---

20 See DeYoung (March 2001a) and Anguelov, Hilgert, and Hogarth (2004).

21 DeYoung and Hunter (2002).

22 See DeYoung (2001a, 2001b); Furst, Lang, and Nolle (2000); and Sullivan (2000). Also see, "True Web Banks and Credit Unions," as posted on the Online Banking Report: Internet Strategies for Financial Institutions: Resources Search *(http://www.onlinebankingreport.com)*.

deposited and lower fee and loan rates to customers. However, they often must rely on the ATMs of other banks, which requires heavy surcharges, or they don't accept deposits through ATMs and can only receive deposits by customer checks through the mail or via electronic or automated clearinghouse transfers (ACH) from other accounts. A fall survey of 1,300 checking accounts by Bankrate.com in 2002 found in comparing fees and yields that Internet checking accounts had lower fees and higher yields than traditional banks. For the survey, the average yield was 1.5 percent on checking accounts at Internet banks compared with 0.57 percent by traditional banks, admittedly low rates for both given very low interest rates in 2002. The survey also found that many E-checking accounts provided free services, such as bill paying as long as customers maintained a minimum balance, but free services often expired after ninety days. Also, the average minimum to open an account and earn interest at a pure Internet bank was nearly a third higher than that at a traditional bank to partly offset the expense of paying a higher rate. The survey notes that some customers may feel uncomfortable with an Internet bank, particularly with a growing number of Internet hackers. Customers may also be concerned about fraud on the Internet. Accordingly, the FDIC has posted tips for safe banking over the Internet including ways to confirm that an online bank is really an FDIC-insured bank. The OCC has also amended its regulations to facilitate the conduct of business by national banks using electronic technologies that are consistent with safety and soundness.[23]

The Supporting Role of Banks in Business-to-Business Electronic Commerce

John Wenninger, Assistant Vice President in the Payments Studies Function of the Research and Market Analysis Group of the Federal Reserve Bank of New York, wrote two excellent essays (1999, 2000) on E-commerce and the role of banks in E-commerce. Businesses have traditionally used computers to manage product and customer data but due to technological advances, they are now expanding their markets, providing better customer service, and increasing productivity with faster exchange of information and lower costs for transactions with their suppliers, distribution network, and customers. With rapidly growing technology, financial services firms are constantly innovating new services and greater access to information and efficiency for business customers.

Traditional Bank Facilitation of Business Cash Management

Banks have also traditionally provided reconciliation services for business customers for accounts receivables and accounts payables, often managing a customer's accounts receivables and accounts payable. Similarly, bank cash management services have been a standard function of banks, including lockbox services (whereby customers of a firm send payments to a post office box managed by a bank, which opens, processes, collects, and deposits checks within an hour of their receipt, so interest can be earned on checks as quickly as possible). Firms using lockboxes receive a fax or electronic notification from the bank immediately after deposits are made, so they can manage their cash balances each day.

Banks also provide many personalized services for both large and small companies, moving (sweeping) funds from savings accounts that earn interest to transaction accounts that do not earn interest as firms need to make disbursements. Bank employees monitor customers' accounts and contact them when additional funds are needed for upcoming disbursements and make daily EFTs for customers as needed. Large corporate customers often have cash concentration systems with lockboxes at key banks or branches with a national presence in different customer locations. These banks, in turn, routinely transfer funds to a centrally located concentration bank. This allows corporate cash managers a larger available pool to manage and makes funds at one central location easier to keep track of and manage.[24]

---

23 See "Better Deals From Internet Banks." Reported on the Kiplinger.com Website *(http://www.kiplinger.com/basics/archives/2002/10/story24.html)*, October 24, 2002 (search on Internet Banks); and "What Is Online Banking?" Reported on the Bankrate.com Website (Bank Rate Monitor) at *http://www.bankrate .com/brm/green/ob/ob1.asp*, February 26, 2004; "Safe Internet Banking: Tips for Save Banking Over the Internet." FDIC Website *(www.fdic.gov/bank/indi- vidual/online/safe.html)*; and "Department of the Treasury: Office of the Comptroller of the Currency." 12 CFR, Part 7, [Docket No. 02-07], RIN 1557-AB76: Electronic Activities], *Federal Register,* Vol. 67, No. 96/Friday, May 17, 2002/Rules and Regulations, 34992 to 35006.

24 See Ross, Westerfield, and Jordan (1996), 436–490, and Maness and Zietlow (2002) for a discussion of bank concentration systems and banks' role in assist- ing payments in Treasury cash management.

Banks' Role in Facilitating Payments and Financial Information Exchange Electronically

Many depository institutions have broadened their range of corporate services to include management consulting, data processing, and information systems or other technological services. As noted by McCoy Frieder, and Hedges (1994) in discussing changes in banking, "Innovative commercial banks have recognized the value of customers by providing real-time access to both financial information and their transaction accounts. Today, a significant proportion of corporate banking activities is conducted from computer terminals in the office of corporate treasurers." Even the owners of small businesses have new electronic corporate financial services provided by banks.[25] Management consulting services allow corporate customers to purchase expert advice addressing a variety of management problems. Information systems and software marketed by banks assist clients in collecting, analyzing, and reporting data effectively and efficiently. Among the most popular new technological services are **electronic data interchange (EDI) systems,** which generally refer to the practice of direct electronic information exchange between all types of businesses. Financial EDI allows the electronic transfer of financial information and funds between parties and financial institutions. Thus, corporations can exchange accounts receivable and accounts payable records electronically as well as transfer funds automatically to settle these accounts. This eliminates the cost of handling, mailing, and issuing paper checks. For payrolls, for instance, a bank can be authorized to take funds electronically from a corporation's checking account each month and deposit checks electronically through the **Automated Clearinghouse System** within minutes to employees' accounts. EDI allows bills to be sent electronically as well, reducing mailing costs and time. Banks, in turn, receive fee income for these services. Corporate service activities provide more consistent fee income than other noninterest revenue activities, since fees are steady and less cyclical. Bank of New York, for instance, has a securities- and cash-processing business that constitutes 40 percent of its earnings. Although these types of services may not appear as exciting to bank managers as other activities that utilize technology, such as global foreign exchange and security trading, in the later part of 1998, when other banks faced severe trading losses from volatility in global markets, Bank of New York's had high and stable earnings from its cash processing businesses. EDI for businesses allows firms to manage their supply chains electronically by having vendors and buyers communicate and exchange information through centralized electronic mailboxes, increasing the speed, accuracy, and efficiency of exchanges. However, centralized EDI networks have not grown as much as expected because of the costs and technological demands involved, including problems transferring data from computers designed only to store data to electronic networks. Without large volumes of transactions, this becomes an expensive task. Less centralized networks can have problems including compatibility of computer languages and security risk. **Financial EDI (FEDI)** allows the exchange of business information electronically between a company and its banks including reports on the firm's daily balance, its monthly account analysis reports, and lockbox informational reports. With extensive information passed from the bank to the firm electronically, firms can improve their cash and other working capital management practices, including facilitating more efficient management of accounts payables and receivables. Treasury workstations, "an automated system of software modules" that provide support for the management of corporate treasury operations, are also used by corporations to smooth processes of FEDI, and also assist in the management of a corporation's investment portfolio transactions and decision. In addition to more sophisticated electronic services, corporations rely on banks for direct deposits through Automated Clearing House (ACH) systems. As noted in a recent Federal Reserve Bulletin article, almost two-thirds of all employers have salary payments directly deposited into employee bank accounts.[26]

Banks' Emerging Role in E-Commerce

As noted by Wenninger (2000) banks have a big stake in facilitating E-commerce for businesses and establishing a presence on the Internet to be able to more effectively market, develop, and sell the new

---

25 See McCoy, Frieder, and Hedges (1994), p. 258.

26 See Maness and Zietlow (2002, pp. 607 to 612) for a more detailed discussion of EDI and Financial EDI and the bank's role. Also see Wenninger (1999, 2000); and Paul Beckett. "Bank of New York Stands Out Among Rivals by Dint of Scoring with Pedestrian Businesses." *The Wall Street Journal* (October 9, 1998), A2. Also, see Anguelov, Hilgert, and Hogarth (2004).

products that E-commerce participants seek. Many banks have been responding to E-commerce demands in recent years by beginning to use the Internet as a supplementary distribution channel for delivering traditional products to consumers and businesses, and to some extent designing new products for E-commerce. Some of these products that Wenninger (2000) notes include:

1. **Internet portals or "supersites,"** where many business sellers can display their product lines together to lead a larger volume of potential buyers to sites offering a broad range of financial and nonfinancial products;

2. **Identity verification,** where banks use encryption technology to develop products to verify the identity of parties, protecting E-commerce participants against fraud associated with misrepresented identities;

3. **Assistance for small businesses entering into E-commerce,** where electronic bill presentment and collection services are developed to enhance current cash management and accounts receivable and accounts payable processing services for companies with substantial volumes of recurring bills, whereby banks can use Internet capabilities to send out bills and the interbank payment networks to electronically process payments;

4. **Facilitating business-to-business E-commerce,** where large banks have attempted to automate the complete informational flow associated with procuring and distributing services and goods between businesses;

5. **Issuing electronic money and checks,** such as "smart cards," that store electronic money and can be read on computers with "smart card readers," allowing consumers to spend money on the Internet, or similarly, electronic checks that could be electronically endorsed and forwarded to a seller's bank for electronic collection from a buyer's bank; and

6. **The integration of the ATM and Internet networks,** where customers can access the Internet and bank Websites from ATMs, allowing them to engage in E-commerce activities and conduct their banking in a flexible bank Website environment.

As Wenninger (2000) notes, banks have reputational "brand name" advantages over other potential competitors, and, by taking advantage of E-commerce opportunities, they can benefit greatly by stronger customer relationships, cross-selling of products and services, and avoid the "encroachment" of other technology companies that have already entered bill-paying and other related financial service areas. Banks have to be careful, however, of risk implications from both a strategic and operational perspective and should set up risk management practices, including value at risk measures to understand and reduce the degree of risk that they are undertaking. As noted under the new Basel II regulations, regulators, aware of these new risks, are now requiring very large banks with international operations to set aside capital for operational risk.[27]

ATM and Debit Cards and Changes in the Payments System

In a recent Federal Reserve Bank of Kansas City study of the ATM and debit card industry, Hayashi, Sullivan, and Weinter (2003) note dramatic changes that have occurred in the automated teller machine (ATM) and debit card industries. These innovations, they say, likely foreshadow future changes that may occur in terms of greater use of electronic forms of payment versus paper checks, which have, to the surprise of many, remained the major source of payments in the United States. The study finds a rapid rise in ATM growth in recent years, with a rise in the annual average growth rate of new ATMs during 1996 to 2002 to 15.5 percent from an annual average growth rate of 9.3 percent for new ATMs during 1983 to 1995. Much of this increase was accounted for by the development of off-premise ATMs (in locations other than bank offices). In 2003, off-premise ATMs accounted for 64 percent of all ATMs compared with only 26 percent of total U.S. ATMs in 1994. By 2003, approximately 902 million ATM transactions were processed each month.[28]

Debit cards (cards with computer chips that store information, sometimes called "check cards") are swiped through credit-card sized devices at the point of sale (POS) when a customer makes a purchase.

---

27 See Wenninger (1999, 2000).

28 See Hayashi, Sullivan, and Weiner (2003), Chapter 1, "Introduction," 1–4. For an excellent overview and details of changes in the ATM and debit card industries, please see the full Kansas City Federal Reserve Bank report, as noted in the Selected References. Also, see Anguelov, Hilgert, and Hogarth (2004).

The cost of the purchase is automatically deducted from the customer's bank account. Debit cards can also be used at ATMs and over the Internet. Because of this flexibility in terms of multiple uses, they have become very popular. Debit card use has grown dramatically, about 42 percent a year since 1995, with POS transactions rising 21 percent in 2003 from 2002 to 495 million per month. POS debit cards have grown most dramatically for any type of payment in the United States, accounting for almost 12 percent of all retail, noncash payments. Debit cards have been used both online (using PIN-based numbers) and off line (using signature), with off-line debits growing at a faster rate (annual growth of 36 percent versus 29 percent for online debits). Preauthorized debit cards are also used to let customers automatically pay for regularly reoccurring bills on specific dates, with automatic debits on a particular date, for instance for loan or lease payments, with money transferred from a customer's account to the account of "the payee or creditor."[29]

Of concern to federal regulators is the fact that the payment infrastructure for ATM/debit cards has undergone tremendous change with great consolidation, ownership by nonbanks, and a larger volume of transaction processing by nonbank (third-party) processors. Since these nonbanks are less regulated, this could lead to abuse of power and even loss of innovation and perhaps greater risk to the payments system. As the Kansas City Fed Report notes, in 2002, the three largest regional networks (Star, NYCE, and Pulse) had a 70 percent market share in terms of switch volume compared with only a 39 percent market share for the three largest networks in 1995. With increased consolidation expected, such as a potential merger of First Data Corporation and Concord EFS, which could result in a combination of the network subsidiaries NYCE and Star, control of the payments networks become increasingly dominated by a few nonbank networks. As the report points out, in 2002, nonbank companies owned five of the ten largest networks compared to 1985, when banking associations were the owners of all of the top ten networks. The largest nonbank providers have also had strategies of expanding their operational scope, with larger firms such as Concord EFS and First Data acquiring the networks of smaller firms, such as E*Trade and eFunds, giving them an expanded ownership of ATMs or the ATMs that they service. The dominance by nonbanks also resulted in a change in the strategy and structure of pricing, including surcharges for more than 88 percent of ATMs to users who have access cards not associated with the ATM's owner. A number of consumer advocates have attacked the idea of these surcharges. Similarly, fees for online debits by financial institutions to encourage off-line debits instead have annoyed consumers and spurred lawsuits. The study notes other criticisms as well including volume discounts provided by some networks that may put smaller users at a competitive disadvantage. Other innovations for using debit cards for payments on the Internet may also increase their use.[30]

It's interesting to note the widespread use of debit cards in the United States today, relative to resistance in the past while such "smart cards" have been in wide use in Europe for some time. Credit cards have always had advantages in terms of float in the United States, meaning customers are billed later versus debited immediately from bank accounts for their purchases. Similarly, check writing has a longer float time for customers. With lower interest rates in the 1990s and early 2000s, this float may not be as important to customers, and debit cards may offer greater convenience. The use of E-cash, where funds can be transferred from bank accounts easily to pay for goods on Internet sites, has been

Concept Questions

1 How widespread are Internet banks? What is a pure play Internet bank? How widespread are they?

2 How widespread is use of the Internet for financial services by financial professionals in treasury management? Discuss some of these uses.

3 How have banks facilitated businesses in their commerce and E-commerce activities? Discuss some of the services that banks offer and plan to offer.

4 Why has debit card and ATM usage grown so rapidly? What are some regulators' concerns over the dominance of nonbank companies in this business?

5 What are some recent trends in spending on technology by financial services firms?

29 Ibid.

30 Ibid.

initiated but has not been widely used. David Chaum of Amsterdam created DigiCash, which relies on doubly encrypted credit information as an alternative currency allowing customers to buy products on the Internet from vendors that accept this form of electronic currency. The first commercial use of DigiCash occurred in November 1995, when Mark Twain Bancshares in Missouri advertised an Internet account called "The Mint" to issue "Digibucks." Anyone with a real account at Mark Twain could transfer funds to a DigiCash account to pay for purchases on an Internet site. If the merchant also had an account at Mark Twain, the transaction could be completed through a transfer between accounts upon delivery of the product to the customer. As pointed out by Martin Mayer (1997) in an excellent book entitled *The Bankers: The Next Generation*, electronic money or E-cash represents an alternative payment system for the future that could be issued perhaps not only by banks but also by technology firms, creating a dual monetary system. For instance, Microsoft could offer accounts in whatever currency Bill Gates might wish to create.[31]

Recent Trends in Technology for Financial Service Firms

As noted in the *Financial Service Fact Book, 2004,* published by the Insurance Information Institute, Information technology (IT) spending has increased for all the different types of financial services firms. In 2003 IT spending was $33.8 billion, with expected spending to be as much as $38 billion as estimated by the TowerGroup, based an annual growth rate of 3.3 percent. Insurance IT spending by life insurance companies was $19.5 billion and by property liability firms $18 billion in recent years. For security firms, technology spending in 2003 totaled about $25.6 billion, with 29 percent spent on institutional sales and trading, 27 percent on brokerage back-office activities, 21 percent on retail brokerage, 17 percent on asset management, and 6 percent on clearing and custody activities. Other trends in use of technology included an increase in bank internet loan offerings. In 2003, approximately 2,619 banks had Internet lending offerings, with an expected 3,735 (or about 50 percent) of banks expected to have offerings in 2005. For securities firms, E-commerce revenue associated with securities and commodity contracts rose to 1.8 percent of total revenue. Wireless banking and brokerage services also grew rapidly, but peaked in 2001 at over 200,000 user units and has fallen since that time by over 50,000 units, despite popular use initially by consumers to conduct financial service transactions.[32]

Summary

Technology has dramatically changed the way financial services firms operate, involving a greater expense for technology, but at the same time creating new products and distribution opportunities. Securitization and loan sales have helped to reduce liquidity and interest rate and credit risk of financial institutions and provides a large source of noninterest income for many institutions through continued loan servicing arrangements. Securitization also provides financial institutions the opportunity to increase the availability of credit by being able to increase the volume of loans they underwrite. It also provides an alternative loan portfolio–backed investment for investors. Structured finance innovations reduce risk for financial institutions and allow more risky finance of large projects, among other uses. The Internet has changed distribution methods for banks and has helped them to develop new strategies, many to help businesses in E-commerce endeavors. The payment mechanism has also changed dramatically with greater use of debit cards and ATM transactions. Regulators have expressed concern over new risks involved with technology and electronic transfers of funds and have attempted to develop new policies to encourage the measurement of operational risks for banks to manage and control these risks.

---

31 Mayer (1997). Examples come from Mayer and other news articles.

32 *The Financial Services Fact Book, 2004.* Washington, D.C. Insurance Information Institute, also in pdf form on the Insurance Information Institute Website, (*http://www.iii.org*).

Questions

1. How has securitization changed the business model of many banks, thrifts, and other financial institutions, such as mortgage banks? Is the new business model healthy for these institutions? Is it healthy for the economy? Explain why or why not.

2. Why have regulators been so concerned about Fannie Mae and Freddie Mac? What benefits and risks do these quasi-GSEs pose? Find a recent article in the financial press or on the Internet about these institutions. What are the most recent developments?

3. What is structured finance? How can it be beneficial as a risk management tool? What risks does structured finance entail? Look up Enron on the Internet (use a search engine such as *http://www.google.com*). Find an article on Enron. How did Enron use structured finance to hide its large debt liabilities from financial analysts and regulators?

4. How have banks been using the Internet to boost profitability? Look up a bank you know on the Internet (such as JPMorgan Chase). How attractive and useful is their Internet bank site? Are many cross-products being advertised to help customers with different concerns?

5. What is a pure play Internet bank? What advantages and disadvantages do pure Internet banks have compared to traditional banks? Why do you think many pure play Internet banks in the past have failed?

6. What strategic choices do banks have in their use of the Internet? Compare how a very large bank like Citigroup can use the Internet to enhance profitability versus a smaller community bank. Does your bank have Internet banking services? Do you use them? Explain why or why not.

7. Discuss how banks are engaged in facilitating transactions for businesses. What new types of products are some large banks developing to facilitate E-commerce for businesses? Do you think this is a good idea? Explain why or why not.

8. Explain the recent trends in ATMs and debit cards. Why do you think debit cards have been so popular recently in the United States? What advantages and disadvantages do ATMs and debit cards have for banks? What advantages and disadvantages do ATMs and debit cards have for consumers?

Selected References

Anguelov, Christoslav E. Marianne A. Hilgrt, and Jeanne M. Hogarth, "U.S. Consumers and Electronic Banking, 1995–2003," *Federal Reserve Bulletin,* 90 (1), Winter 2004, 1–18.

Arshadi, Nasser, and Gordon V. Karels. *Modern Financial Intermediaries and Markets.* Upper Saddle River, NJ: Prentice Hall, 1997.

Carlstrom, Charles T., and Katherine A. Samolyk. "Securitization: More than Just a Regulatory Artifact." *Economic Commentary* (Federal Reserve Bank of Cleveland) (May 1, 1992), 1–4.

Cebenoyan, A. Sinan and Philip E. Strahan. Risk Management, Capital Structure, and Lending at Banks. *Journal of Banking and Finance,* Vol. 28, Issue 1 (January 2004), 19–43.

DeYoung, Robert. "The Internet's Place in the Banking Industry." *Chicago Fed Letter* (The Federal Reserve Bank of Chicago) 163 (March 2001a), 1–4.

———. "Learning-by-Doing, Scale Efficiencies, and Financial Performance at Internet-Only Banks." Working Paper, Federal Reserve Bank of Chicago, WP 2001-06, 2001b.

DeYoung, Robert, and William C. Hunter. "Deregulation, the Internet, and the Competitive Viability of Large Banks and Community Banks." In *The Future of Banking,* ed. by Benton Gup. Westport, CT: Greenwood Press, Quorum Books, 2002.

Frame, W. Scott, and Larry D. Wall. "Fannie Mae's and Freddie Mac's Voluntary Initiatives: Lessons from Banking." *Economic Review* (Federal Reserve Bank of Atlanta) (First Quarter 2002), 45–59.

Frame, W. Scott, and Lawrence J. White. "Emerging Competition and Risk-Taking Incentives at Fannie Mae and Freddie Mac." Working Paper Series, Federal Reserve Bank of Atlanta, WP 2004-04, February 2004.

Furst, Karen, William W. Lang, and Daniel E. Nolle. "Who Offers Internet Banking." *Quarterly Journal* (Office of the Comptroller of the Currency), Vol. 19, No. 1 (June 2000), 1–21.

Hayashi, F., Richard Sullivan, and Stuart E. Weiner. *A Guide to the ATM and Debit Card Industry.* Kansas City, MO: Federal Reserve Bank of Kansas City, Payments System Research, 2003.

Koch, Timothy W., and S. Scott MacDonald. *Bank Management,* 4th ed. Cincinnati, OH: Southwestern/Thomson Publishing, 2000.

McCoy, John B., Larry A. Frieder, and Robert B. Hedges, Jr. *Bottomline Banking: Meeting the Challenges for Survival and Success.* Chicago, IL: Probus Publishing Company, 1994.

Maness, Terry S., and John T. Zietlow. *Short-term Financial Management,* 2nd ed. Cincinnati, OH: Southwestern/Thomson Publishing, 2002.

Mayer, Martin. *The Bankers: The Next Generation.* New York: Truman Talley Books/Plume, 1997.

Ross, Stephen A., Randolph W. Westerfield, and Bradford D. Jordan. *Essentials of Corporate Finance.* Chicago: Irwin, 1996.

Saunders, Anthony, and Marcia Millon Cornett. *Financial Institutions Management: A Risk Management Approach,* 4th ed. Burr Ridge, IL: McGraw-Hill Irwin, 2003.

Schwarcz, Steven L. "Securitization Post-Enron." *Cardozo Law Review,* Symposium Issue on Trends in Secured Lending and Asset Securitization, Vol. 25, forthcoming, 2004.

Sullivan, Richard J. "How Has the Adoption of Internet Banking Affected the Performance and Risk in Banks?" *Financial Industry Perspective* (Federal Reserve Bank of Kansas City) (December 2000), 1–16.

Wenninger, John. "Business-to-Business Electronic Commerce." *Current Issues in Economics and Finance* (Federal Reserve Bank of New York) Vol. 5, No. 10 (June 1999), 1–6.

———. "The Emerging Role of Banks in E-Commerce." *Current Issues in Economics and Finance* (Federal Reserve Bank of New York) Vol. 6, No. 3 (March 2000), 1–6.

internet *exercise*

1 Visit the Securitization.Net Website, which provides free structured finance information, at

http://www.securitization.net/knowledge/index.asp

You can also just go to *http://www.securitization.net* and follow the menu instructions for different types of information on its knowledge bank. On the right-hand side are a number of links to information including Intro to Securitization, Legal, Rating Agency, Rating Criteria, Special Purpose Vehicles, and Transactions, among others. Click on "Intro to Securitization." You'll find a number of different sources of news, information, and articles that you can download or print out on securitization (many are PDFs, so they will require Adobe Acrobat Reader). Look at the different reports and statistics, such as the JPMorgan and Bank One ABS (asset-backed security) statistics.

"Securitization Post-Enron" by Steven L. Schwarcz is a good article that had a link on this Website at the time of this writing:

http://www.securitization.net/pdf/duke_enron_052303.pdf

Schwarcz is a Professor of Law at Duke University School of Law, and this article is from the Cardozo Law Review, 2003, Symposium on "Threats to Secured Lending and Asset Securitization." Excellent detailed information on all aspects of securitization can be found on this Website.

Another useful source for securitization activity is the Website for Asset-Backed Alert: The Weekly Update on Worldwide Securitization, which gives year-to-date volume statistics on worldwide ABS issuance at

http://www.abalert.com/public/marketplace/marketstatistics/index.cfm

or you can use the menu on the main Website at *http://www.abalert.com* and click on "ABS Market Statistics."

2 There are many helpful Websites that give information on Internet financial services and strategies in Internet banking and E-commerce for financial institutions. The Bank Rate Monitor Website at

http://www.bankrate.com/brm

contains all sorts of information on Internet financial services institution products including Internet banks, thrifts, and credit unions. The BRM also provides listings and rate comparisons and does its own safety and soundness ratings (note these are private ratings, not regulatory ratings). There is also information on Internet securities firms and trading, Internet insurance companies, and primers on online banking basics including understanding online banking services, E-mail payments, online shopping for loans and mortgages, insurance, auctions, and stock trading. Another useful Website to get information on financial institutions from a consumer perspective is

http://www.kiplinger.com (Enter "banking" in the search box).

3 Online banking journals also provide very useful information and statistics, such as *The Journal of Internet Banking and Commerce,* which contains useful academic and practitioner articles published by Array Development. Their Website is

http://www.arraydev.com/commerce/jibc

The Online Banking Report provides information on strategies for financial services firms on the Internet and other interesting articles and statistics at

http://www.onlinebankingreport.com

4 For information on the use of banking relationships for Corporate Treasury Areas including articles on cash management, E-commerce, the Certified Treasury Professional designation (CTP), and the payments system, see the Association for Financial Professionals (AFP) Website:

http://www.afponline.org

AFP also has valuable information about careers, and, at the time of this writing, if you are a student Financial Management Association member, you may apply for student membership in the AFP as well.

Interest Rate & Foreign Exchange Environments

8 Interest Rates, Exchange Rates, and Inflation

Theories and Forecasting

"The rise of interest rates and market yields to record levels in the 1970s and early 1980s [such as the three-month Treasury bills rates rising to 15.5% in 1981] cannot be understood without reference to inflation and the economic concept of real interest rates. If a lender considers that a 4% real return, that is, a 4% gain in purchasing power or in dollars of constant value, is required in order to justify lending $100 for one year, then that lender will demand a nominal interest rate of 14.4% if the expected rate of inflation in that year is 10%."

"The United States in the Twentieth Century: 1900–1945," from Sidney Homer and Richard Sylla. A History of Interest Rates, *3rd ed. New Brunswick: Rutgers University Press, (1991), 429.*

"With inflation rates now quite low in the United States, some have expressed concern that we may soon face a new problem—the danger of deflation, or falling prices. That this concern is not purely hypothetical is brought home to us whenever we read newspaper reports about Japan, where what seems to be a relatively moderate deflation—a decline in consumer prices of about 1 percent per year—has been associated with years of painfully slow growth, rising joblessness, and apparently intractable financial problems in the banking and corporate sectors. While it is difficult to sort out cause from effect, the consensus view is that deflation has been an important negative factor in the Japanese slump."

"Remarks by Governor Ben S. Bernanke, Before the National Economics Club," Washington, D.C., November 21, 2002.

Preceding chapters introduce unique characteristics of financial institutions, including the predominance of financial assets and liabilities and the resulting emphasis on the net interest margin (NIM). The interest rate environment is one of the most important influences on asset/liability decisions and institutional performance. Key determinants of success are managers' abilities to understand movements in interest rates and inflation and to interpret forecasts. And, although all financial institution managers must respond to interest rate changes, the growing globalization of financial markets creates additional requirements for some; they must make asset/liability decisions in reaction to changes in the value of the dollar compared with other currencies. Fortunately, managers have access to a growing array of risk management tools; but they must first understand the theories underlying interest rate and exchange rate movements. Similarly, managers must be able to calculate rates on different types of financial instruments. This chapter looks at trends in interest rates and exchange rates and discusses theories that help managers of financial institutions to make critical decisions concerning future trends. The chapter also presents the calculation of yields on different types of money market instruments and quotations for money market rates and foreign exchange rates. Finally, implications of the introduction of the Euro for financial institutions are briefly discussed. The first section discusses why theories are important to managers.

Learning Objectives

After completing this chapter, you will be able to:

Part A: Theories of Interest Rates

1 Understand why theories of interest rates and exchange rates are important to managers.

2 Follow trends in interest rates and interest spreads over the past three decades.

3 Understand how the supply and demand for funds in an economy affect the real rate of interest under the loanable funds theory.

4 Understand Fisher's theory and how investors set nominal interest rates based on inflation expectations and explain the difference between ex ante and ex post real rates.

5 Calculate yields and prices for money market securities.

Part B: Currency Exchange Rates

6 Interpret exchange rate quotations in the financial news, including the difference between spot and forward exchange rates.

7 Understand how relative interest rates, inflation rates, and supply and demand for a country's goods affect its exchange rate.

8 Calculate gains and losses for transactions in different currencies.

PART A: THEORIES OF INTEREST RATES

Interest rates have been an important factor in individuals' and financial institutions' lives throughout history and are subject to great volatility. Exchange rates have also been very important for international trade and have become critical with globalization trends. Hence, they also have a critical effect on the business of financial institutions. Exchange rates can be exceptionally volatile, as noted in recent years. For instance, the exchange rate between the U.S. dollar and the Euro was 1.00 in November of 2002. During 2003, the value of the U.S. dollar relative to the Euro fell by 17 percent, with a Euro worth $1.20 (or $1 worth only about 0.83 of a Euro) by December 1, 2003.

Foreign exchange rate changes can also be volatile over short time periods. On August 26, 1998, in response to Russian economic problems, the Russian ruble fell 69 percent relative to the German mark. With a similar plunge in the ruble's dollar value, the Russian government halted dollar trading.[1] In reaction to the 1998 Asian economic crisis, currencies in Korea, Malaysia, Thailand, and Indonesia also fell dramatically relative to the U.S. dollar (for the Indonesian rupiah, a drop of almost 70 percent). Such declines resulted in government imposition of currency controls in some countries, such as Malaysia. In contrast, the Mexican peso rose 24 percent relative to the dollar during 1998. Hence, in

---

1 Andrew Higgins and Mark Whitehouse. "Russia Quits Fight to Back the Ruble: Moscow Halts Dollar Trading; Currency Drops 69% vs. Mark." *The Wall Street Journal* (August 27, 1998), A8; Christopher Rhoads. "European Bank Stocks Again Hit by Russia Woes." *The Wall Street Journal* (August 27, 1998), A8.

1998, financial institutions with long positions in financial instruments denominated in falling currencies experienced tremendous losses, whereas institutions with short positions received extraordinary gains. Financial institution managers learned difficult lessons concerning the severity of foreign exchange risk. With the gradual phasing out of the different currencies of participating European Monetary Union members by July 1, 2002, the transitional period and the risk entailed with the gradual curtailment of individual currencies called for considerable operational efforts as well.[2]

As noted in the quotes at the beginning of the chapter, central bankers have also been greatly concerned about inflation, a rise in the prices of goods and services, which can seriously hurt an economy. Inflation was a serious problem in the United States in the 1970s and early 1980s, resulting in very high interest rates to compensate investors for loss of purchasing power. In many emerging countries, inflation continues to be a serious problem, creating great economic hardship and financial instability. In the early 2000s, however, central bankers in China, Japan, and the United States, among others, were concerned about the opposite problem, deflation, the danger of an unexpected general fall in an economy's prices. As noted by Federal Reserve Governor Ben S. Bernanke in the recent speech cited earlier, Japan in the late 1990s and early 2000s faced an economic recession associated with deflation, where general prices constantly fell. In October 2003, after four years of falling consumer prices and recession, Japan's core consumer price index rose 0.1 percent from a year earlier, suggesting a turnaround for the economy and an end of falling prices. Deflation can be a side effect of a collapse of aggregate demand that becomes so severe that producers have to cut prices on an ongoing basis in order to find buyers, leading to recession with rising unemployment and financial distress. Central bankers can encounter severe problems when attempting to relieve a deflation-based recession, since nominal interest rates may become zero-bound, by declining to zero or close to zero. This removes the central bankers' option of stimulating an economy by lowering target short-term interest rates. Lending will also decline in an economy suffering severe deflation, since a zero interest rate is unattractive. Also, if prices for goods and services are plunging, borrowers will not even want to borrow at a 0 percent interest rate, since they will, in effect, be paying the rate of the decline in future prices. For instance, if prices are expected to fall 10 percent, borrowers would pay a 10 percent rate over their real cost of funds. Hence, economies can be disrupted by both unexpected inflation and unexpected deflation. As noted in the first quote, investors and lenders adjust the interest rates they demand based on inflationary or deflationary expectations to maintain their purchasing power. Similarly, exchange rates are affected by the relative inflation of different countries. Countries with higher relative inflation, holding other factors constant, generally have lower exchange rates. In December 2003, after previously worrying about deflation, and with the U.S. economy improving, the Fed began expressing concerns about inflation versus deflation once again.[3]

Why Theories Are Important to Managers

Managers are rarely theoreticians; instead, they spend their time analyzing and making decisions critical to the future of their institutions. These decisions rely on often-conflicting opinions about the direction of the economy and interest rates, nationally and internationally. To make better decisions, managers must be able to evaluate available data and forecasts. Those evaluations, in turn, require knowledge of the principles on which forecasts are based.

For example, the manager of the investment portfolio of a life insurance company can invest in variable-coupon bonds, zero-coupon bonds, or traditional fixed-rate instruments, among many other choices. The manager's expectations about interest rate movements will certainly influence the decision. In a period of declining rates, a variable-coupon instrument will be unattractive, but a zero-coupon bond (a bond that only makes a maturity payment) will lock in a higher rate if intermediate cash flows are not important. A bond denominated in British pounds will be undesirable to the life

---

2 Darren McDermott and Karby Leggett. "Jitters Grow over Currencies of Asia's Giants." *The Wall Street Journal* (June 12, 1998), A8; Bill Spindle. "Yen Falls Again Against Dollar: Data Awaited." *The Wall Street Journal* (June 12, 1998), A8; Darren McDermott and Leslie Lopez. "Malaysia Imposes Sweeping Currency Controls." *The Wall Street Journal* (September 2, 1998), A10; and Paul S. Tufaro. "European Economic and Monetary Union: A Continuity of Contracts." *Banking Policy Report* 17 (July 6, 1998), 1, 13.

3 See "Japan's Consumer Price Index Rose in October," *The Wall Street Journal*, November 28, 2003, A6, and "Remarks by Governor Ben S. Bernanke, Before the National Economics Club," Washington, D.C., November 21, 2002.

insurance company as an investor if the value of the pound is expected to fall. Similarly, raising funds also must be guided by forecasts.

Often economists are unable to agree about the future direction of economic variables, and managers must exercise judgment in evaluating available forecasts. Theories concerning the economic, political, and behavioral factors that influence interest rates and exchange rates provide the foundation on which economic forecasters base their expectations about interest and exchange rate changes, which also affect managerial evaluation and decision making.

A Historical Look at Interest Rates

As shown in Figure 8.1 (which shows trends in rates for different classes of securities over time), interest rates are constantly changing and have been particularly volatile in recent decades. The shaded areas in Panel B indicate recessionary periods. In the United States, interest rates peaked in the early 1980s, reaching historically high levels, only to fall ten years later in the early 1990s to their lowest levels since the Great Depression. After rising again somewhat in the late 1990s, rates fell in the early 2000s to even lower historical levels, with the three-month Treasury bill rate falling at times below 1 percent. As shown, the rates on different types of bonds tend to follow each other, but the spread (difference) between risk-free (U.S. government securities) and more risky corporate bonds changes dramatically over time, generally becoming larger as economic recessions approach and smaller during expansions, when corporations have lower earnings risk.

Interest rates also generally fall during recessions, such as 1981–1982 and 1990–1992, and 2001, and rise during expansions. However, exceptions exist. For instance, 1997 and 1998, years encompassing the ten-year expansion the National Bureau of Economic Research cites as lasting from March 1991 to March 2001, were characterized by low inflation, and interest rates fell dramatically. Short-term rates also often lead long-term rates in terms of rising and falling, such as in 1990–1991, when short-term rates fell dramatically, but long-term rates did not fall until 1992–1993. However, in 1997-1998, long-term rates fell dramatically, whereas short-term rates remained stable.

Interest rates incorporate the real rate of interest that investors expect to receive in return for lending their money and a premium for expected loss of purchasing power for inflation. What we call the nominal interest rates includes a real rate and a premium for expected inflation. Hence, when inflation expectations are high, nominal interest rates rise. Panel A clearly demonstrates this by the general upward trend in rates that began in the late 1960s, with some dips in the 1970s, to a peak in the early 1980s. At this time rises in interest rate were fueled by expectations of high inflation and government deficits.

As discussed in the Appendix to Chapter 3, the Federal Reserve System's famous temporary policy change away from targeting interest rates as a part of monetary policy from October 1979 to October 1982 also led to greater rate volatility during the early 1980s. Even though yields declined in 1982, as inflation subsided, the volatility continued through the end of the decade. In the early 1990s and early 2000s, with declining interest rates, as noted earlier, the Fed was concerned about deflation, a decline in expected general prices, instead. With falling interest rates in the early 1990s and early 2000s, many depository institutions and mortgage banks holding fixed rate assets and variable rate liabilities benefited with the decline in their interest expenses. Generally, net interest margins for depository institutions rose. However, they also experienced significant customer prepayments of loans and refinancing to lower rates. Although such refinancing provides significant noninterest (fee) income, it also leaves depository institutions with lower rates on the fixed interest loans on their balance sheets for the future revenue streams.

Rates are very difficult to predict and vary enormously, even on a weekly or monthly basis. Figure 8.2, Panel A shows weekly changes in short-term and long-term rates for 1998 to 2003, which were quite volatile. Similarly, the difference in yields (yield spreads) between corporate bonds and the three-month Treasury bill changed dramatically over this period, especially the spreads for more risky (unrated) high yield bonds. Panel B shows more recent trends in short-term and long-term interest rates; although short-term rates are generally more volatile than long-term rates, long-term rates were extremely volatile in recent years.

The spread between corporate and Treasury bonds widens during financial crises. Panel A of Figure 8.2 illustrates this concept for late 1998, when professional investors fled to Treasury bonds as a safe

figure **8.1** TRENDS IN INTEREST RATES

Over time, interest rates are variable. Although there are many different financial markets, interest rates in all markets tend to move in the same general direction at the same time.

PANEL A: LONG-TERM BOND YIELDS (PERIODIC AVERAGES)

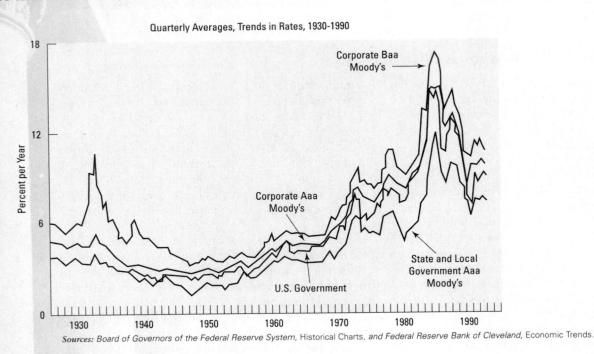

Quarterly Averages, Trends in Rates, 1930-1990

Sources: Board of Governors of the Federal Reserve System, Historical Charts, and Federal Reserve Bank of Cleveland, Economic Trends.

PANEL B: TRENDS IN RATES, 1985 TO 2003

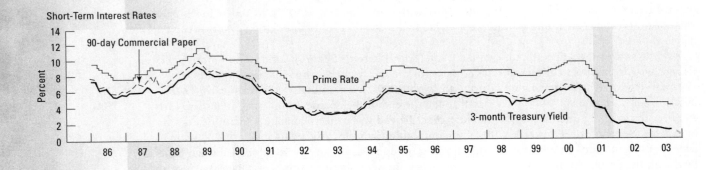

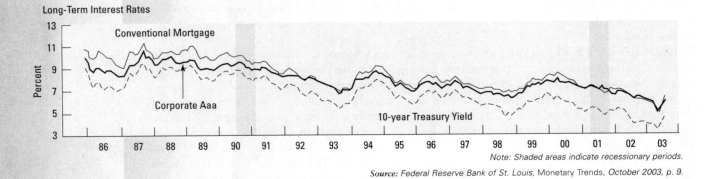

Note: Shaded areas indicate recessionary periods.

Source: Federal Reserve Bank of St. Louis, Monetary Trends, October 2003, p. 9.

figure 8.2 RECENT TRENDS IN YIELDS

PANEL A: PERCENT WEEKLY AVERAGE RATES AND YIELD SPREADS

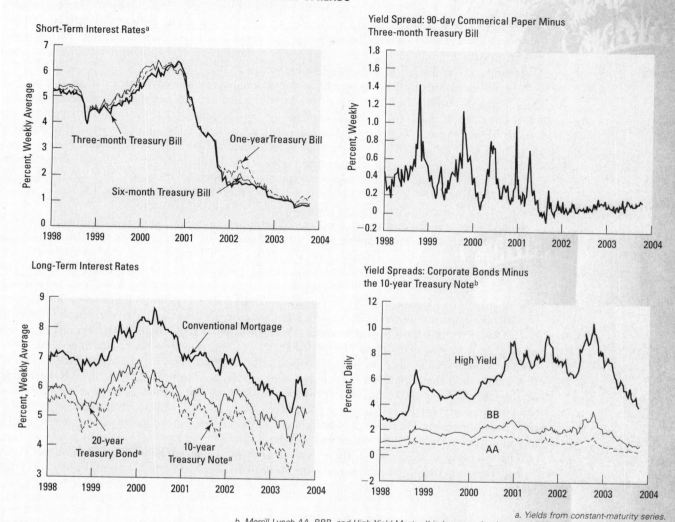

a. Yields from constant-maturity series.
b. Merrill Lynch AA, BBB, and High Yield Master II indexes, each minus the yield on the ten-year Treasury note.

Source: Board of Governors of the Federal Reserve System, "Selected Interest Rates," H. 15, Federal Reserve Statistical Releases; and Bloomberg Financial Information Services. From Federal Reserve Bank of Cleveland, Economic Trends, November 2003, p. 5.

PANEL B: TRENDS IN YIELD SPREADS

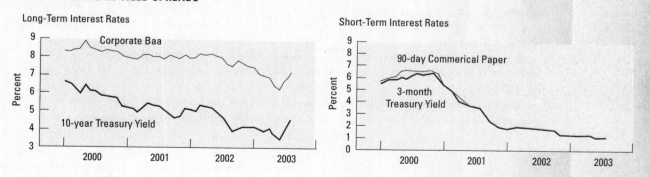

Source: Federal Reserve Bank of St. Louis, Monetary Trends, October 2003, p. 9.

investment following the financial crises in Russia and Asia. These financial crises also had a seemingly contagious effect on Latin American financial markets. Such a "flight to quality" created a liquidity crunch for investors holding corporate bonds, who found bidders for the long-term bonds that they held scarce at the end of September 1998. Liquidity for high-quality corporate bonds gradually improved in November of that year.[4] Traders speculating on risk spreads between Treasury and corporate bonds also experienced large losses during this period. Investment bankers hoping to assist corporations in issuing bonds or initial public offerings of stock faced very unreceptive markets and high borrowing costs, making firms reluctant to issue securities.

Hence, financial institution managers find the volatile interest rate environment a continuing challenge. Some institutions have maintained good performance records, but many firms have faltered or failed. For example, at the end of 1987, First Bank System, Inc., at that time the nation's sixteenth largest bank holding company (now part of U.S. Bancorp), announced a loss on its investment portfolio of more than $700 million. What was the reason? According to *The Wall Street Journal*, management's mistake was "betting heavily the wrong way on interest rates." Fortunately, the outlook is almost always brighter for institutions that successfully navigate choppy interest rate waters. In 1992, for example, Boatmen's Bancshares, Inc., of St. Louis enjoyed hefty profits because, according to Chairman Andrew Craig, "We structured the balance sheet in anticipation of a downturn in rates."

Financial institutions continue to speculate on interest rate and exchange rate movements. In 1998, investment firms Long-Term Capital and Paloma Partners, LLC, hedge-funds that invest in stocks, bonds, currencies, and other financial instruments for wealthy investors, suffered severe losses from interest rate bets that went bad in volatile domestic and international bond markets. Bankers Trust (now part of Deutsche Bank), Citicorp, JPMorgan, Morgan Stanley Dean Witter, Barclays, Nomura Securities, and other large financial institutions that engaged actively in bond trading suffered severe losses.

Many of these losses were associated with foreign exchange rates as well. When the ruble plunged on August 26, 1998, the exposure of U.S. banks to Russia was about $6.8 billion, not including hedge-fund lending. In addition, many large European banks including Deutsche Bank, Dresdner Bank, Commerzbank, and Credit Suisse, with large loan exposure in Russia, experienced stock price plunges on that date. Also, at that time, investment banks, such as Salomon Smith Barney, that held Russian treasury bonds, known as GKOs, received only about 20 to 25 percent of the face value of the debt under the Russian government's restructuring plan. Given the risk that financial institutions face, managers must have a theoretical knowledge of both interest rates and exchange rates to assist them in predicting the advent of sudden interest rate and currency changes.[5]

The following sections discuss theories of interest rates that are helpful for financial institution managers as they attempt to decipher possible movements in interest rates that significantly affect their institutions' performance.

The General Level of Interest Rates

Theories of interest rate determination follow several conventions. First, models usually focus on determination of the *equilibrium* level of interest. Equilibrium is a state of rest or the absence of forces for change. Actually, the financial markets are seldom, if ever, in equilibrium but are in the process of approaching equilibrium as they respond to the numerous factors that cause an imbalance between supply and demand.

Second, economic models rely on several assumptions required to simplify the real world. The objective is to develop a useful explanation without omitting factors crucial to achieving the purpose of the model.

Finally, theories explaining the general level of interest rates do just that: They focus on *the* rate of interest. Obviously, there are many interest rates for different types of securities. This chapter points

---

4 Gregory Zuckerman and Greg Ip. "Ripple Effect: It Isn't Just Investors Who Are Smarting from Liquidity Crunch." *The Wall Street Journal* (November 6, 1998), A1, A9.

5 Jeff Bailey. "First Bank System Says Bond Portfolio Fell $700 Million as Interest Rates Rose." *The Wall Street Journal* (October 14, 1987), 17; Fred R. Bleakley. "Banks, Thrifts Scored as Interest Rates Fell, But Difficulties Loom." *The Wall Street Journal* (February 2, 1992), A1, A6; Peter Truell. "5 Big Lenders Report Losses from Russia: At Citicorp, Profit Drain of $200 Million Is Seen." *New York Times* (September 2, 1998), C1; and Christopher Rhoads. "European Bank Stocks Again Hit by Russia Woes." *The Wall Street Journal* (August 27, 1998), A8.

Concept Questions

1 Explain what deflation and inflation are, and how they can be harmful to an economy.

2 Do interest rates tend to rise or fall in an expansion? In a recession?

3 Which type of rates (short-term or long-term) tend to lead to changes in the other type?

4 Why is it important for financial managers to understand theories of interest rates?

5 What generally happens to interest rate spreads for more risky bonds during a recession?

out how differences in yields reflect term to maturity, default risk, taxability, and other characteristics of the underlying security. Still, compared over time, yields on securities tend to move in the same general direction. Although the correlation is not perfect, it is strong enough that economists are justified in focusing on *one* interest rate to build a model that explains movement in *all* rates.

Loanable Funds Theory

Several compatible theories attempt to explain interest rate movements, although they are not equally useful for forecasting changes in rates. The loanable funds theory focuses on the amount of funds available for investment (the supply of loanable funds) and the amount of funds that borrowers want (the demand for loanable funds). It is particularly adaptable for use in forecasting and, therefore, is the one on which this discussion concentrates.

The Supply of Loanable Funds

The **loanable funds theory** categorizes borrowers and lenders into five distinct types: households or consumers; businesses; governments; the central bank, which has control over changes in the money supply; and the foreign sector. Governments supply almost no loanable funds, but it is important to understand the forces affecting the savings decisions of individuals, businesses, and foreign investors.

The Expected Rate of Return and the Decision to Save

Economic units always have several choices for disposition of funds. They can *spend* money on consumable goods; they can *save* money by investing in financial assets; or they can choose to hold, or *hoard,* money. The motivation for consumption is self-evident. But once the amount of consumption has been determined, there is still a choice between investing and holding money.

A key motivation for saving is the expected rate of return. Because investors have a **time preference for consumption,** they will reduce current consumption to save money only if they receive some reward for doing so. That reward is the expected rate of interest, which must always be positive to induce substantial postponement of consumption.

Economists have also identified several other motivations for savings, discussed shortly, which suggest that some funds will be saved even if the expected rate of interest is zero.

Holding, or hoarding, cash requires postponement of consumption but, unlike saving, does not provide a positive rate of return. So why does anyone hold cash balances? Three motivations have been identified: the **transactions demand,** the **precautionary demand,** and the **speculative demand.**[6] Because individuals and businesses cannot always assume that the timing of cash inflows and cash

---

6 These motivations for holding cash were introduced by the renowned economist John Maynard Keynes in *The General Theory of Employment, Interest, and Money* (1936). Actually, Keynes used them in the liquidity preference theory, an explanation of interest rates that is separate but compatible with the loanable funds theory. The liquidity preference theory focuses on the supply and demand for money, whereas the loanable funds theory focuses on the supply and demand for credit. Once consumption is determined, a household's decisions to hold cash (demand money) or to lend (supply credit) are not independent of one another; deciding to do more of one means deciding to do less of the other. Thus, it is easy to see how theories on the determination of interest rates can be approached by looking at either money or loanable funds.

expenditures will coincide, they usually need to maintain ready access to cash to handle transactions. Also, some cash will be held as a precaution against unforeseen contingencies. Neither of these motivations is tied to the expected rate of interest.

The third demand for money—the speculative motivation—is sensitive to expected interest rates and is therefore especially important in understanding the supply of loanable funds. In the face of high expected rates on financial assets, funds suppliers will reduce cash balances as they invest; with low expected rates of return, they will hold cash in anticipation of better opportunities to come. Thus, the expected rate of return is important in the decision to reduce speculative cash balances, which in turn increases the supply of loanable funds.

Other Factors Influencing Households

These relationships lead to a better but still incomplete understanding of the amount of funds available for borrowing. Factors other than interest rates affect the savings decision. For example, most people voluntarily save for future needs, either because they recognize that illness or other emergencies could jeopardize their financial position or because they will need funds to support themselves after retirement. Other people may be involved in involuntary savings programs, such as social security or required retirement programs for state and federal employees.

The household income is also significant. Low-income families often spend all available funds on the basic necessities of life, leaving nothing for alternative uses. At the opposite end of the spectrum, high-income families may be unable to consume all available funds even if they wanted to, so they must invest regardless of the expected interest rate.

Other Factors Influencing Businesses

Although businesses are usually demanders, they also supply some loanable funds. The primary sources of these funds are the depreciation tax shield and retained earnings from profitable past operations. Expected interest rates may have some bearing on the decisions of businesses to save by investing in financial assets, but other important factors are potential real asset investments, the nature of the business enterprise, and the philosophy of the firm's managers and owners.

The Money Supply

The supply of loanable funds is affected by changes in the total money supply (ΔM), which is influenced by Fed policy. An increase in the money supply makes more funds available for saving after consumption is satisfied.

The Foreign Sector

Funds available domestically are also influenced by the behavior of foreign investors. The key factor influencing funds provided by the foreign sector is not simply the expected rate of interest in the United States, but the difference between that rate and the expected rate available in other countries. Also, the stability of a country's currency may make investments in that country's securities more attractive to international investors. These relationships will be explained in more detail later.

The Supply of Loanable Funds Illustrated

The combined impact of these influences on the supply of loanable funds is shown in Figure 8.3. The supply curve (S_{LF}) is positively related to the expected rate of interest; that is, the quantity supplied is larger as the interest rate increases, but only moderately so. Even at a zero rate of interest, the supply of loanable funds exceeds zero because of nonrate factors influencing the savings decision.

The household sector is the only *net* supplier of loanable funds; that is, in a given period, households save more than they demand in the credit markets. For that reason, the borrowings of the household sector are usually netted against savings, and the S_{LF} curve is net of loanable funds demanded by households. Using this approach, household savings equals income minus consumption minus household borrowing.

figure   **8.3**   SUPPLY OF LOANABLE FUNDS

The willingness of households, businesses, governments, and the foreign sector to supply loanable funds increases as the expected interest rate increases.

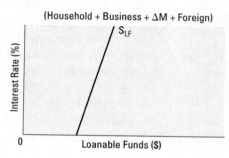

The Demand for Loanable Funds

The forces determining the demand for loanable funds—the total funds that households, businesses, government units, and the foreign sector want to borrow—is tied much more closely to expected interest rates than is the supply.

The Effect of Expected Interest Rates on Borrowing

Most business borrowing is sensitive to expected interest rates. The funds raised by nonfinancial firms will depend on their optimal budgets for investment in real assets. An optimal capital budget reflects a firm's investment opportunities. It occurs at the point where the marginal returns from investing in real assets are equal to the marginal costs of raising the funds, and the net present value of incremental investments is zero. At lower rates of interest, the capital budget will be larger, because a lower discount rate will be used for calculating net present value (the present value of the cash flows less the initial outlay cost of the project). The investment opportunity schedule and the resulting demand for loanable funds (D_{LF}) are inversely related to expected interest rates.

Noninterest Factors

As with the supply of loanable funds, noninterest factors motivate the demand for borrowing. For example, government units at the local, state, and federal levels often must borrow regardless of interest rates. Governments borrow whenever they face budget deficits or when they need to finance major construction of roads or government buildings.[7] In fact, government demand for credit is relatively inelastic with respect to interest rates.

Demand by the Foreign Sector

Foreign borrowers also seek funds in the domestic credit markets. Foreign business borrowers are motivated by the same factors that affect domestic firms, but differences between interest rates in the United States and those abroad will determine where borrowing actually occurs. Foreign governments also borrow in U.S. markets for the same reasons that U.S. governmental units borrow. Recently, in fact, the domestic demand for loanable funds by foreign governments has been substantial.[8]

---

7 Many experts argue that the relationship between borrowing and interest rates is not the same for state and local governments as it is for the federal government, under the assumption that the former are more flexible in spending decisions and may postpone some projects to be financed by borrowing if interest rates are high. In addition, some state or municipal statutes actually prohibit government units from borrowing if expected interest rates exceed a certain critical level. For further discussion, see Polakoff (1981), 494.

8 In recent years, the foreign sector as a whole has been a net supplier of funds to the U.S. credit market. In the past, however, it was a net borrower. See Board of Governors of the Federal Reserve System. *Flow of Funds Accounts, Financial Assets and Liabilities* (First Quarter, 1992).

figure **8.4** DEMAND FOR LOANABLE FUNDS

The willingness of businesses, governments, and the foreign sector to borrow funds decreases as the expected interest rate increases.

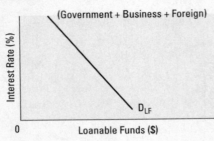

The Demand for Loanable Funds Illustrated

The demand schedule (D_{LF}) for loanable funds in Figure 8.4 is for total business, government, and foreign borrowing. As noted earlier, households do borrow, but their demand is usually netted against the funds they supply and is not included in the aggregate demand for loanable funds.

Loanable Funds Theory and Interest Rate Forecasting

The loanable funds theory follows classical supply/demand analysis and explains the equilibrium rate of interest as the point of intersection of the supply and demand schedules. In Figure 8.5, i^* and Q^* represent the equilibrium rate of interest and the equilibrium quantity of loanable funds, respectively. Many analysts use the loanable funds framework to explain and anticipate the movement of interest rates.

Because the loanable funds theory explains the rate of interest as the point of intersection between supply and demand curves, the political, economic, or behavioral factors that shift either curve are expected to result in a change in interest rates.

Changes in Supply or Demand

What forces could shift the supply or the demand curves? Government fiscal policy is one important force. The size of the federal budget deficit affects the demand for loanable funds. The more federal expenditures exceed federal revenues, the more frequently the government must enter the credit markets. Unless the change in government borrowing is offset by an equal and opposite change in demand

figure **8.5** EQUILIBRIUM RATE OF INTEREST

The equilibrium level of interest rates is the rate at which the quantity of loanable funds demanded equals the quantity of loanable funds supplied.

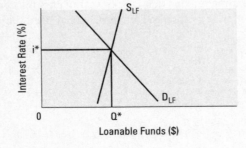

for loanable funds by other sectors, the demand curve must shift, and the rate of interest will be higher. Furthermore, the supply curve may also be affected, as anticipated increases in government borrowing cause funds suppliers to increase their speculative balances in anticipation of higher interest rates.

Another fiscal policy, taxation, also has the potential for shifting the supply or demand curves. For example, an increase in corporate taxes reduces after-tax profits and thereby reduces the incentive for additional business spending. Smaller capital budgets lower the demand for borrowed funds.

Monetary policy, through its effect on the money supply, also affects interest rates. For example, an increase in the money supply relative to money demand leads to higher levels of savings, shifting the supply curve to the right. This subsequently leads to a lower interest rate, at least in the short run.[9] Research suggests another monetary policy effect: Volatility in money growth may lead to higher interest rates because it precipitates a reduction in the supply of loanable funds. High variability in monetary growth increases investors' uncertainty about future rates of return on financial assets. In response to that uncertainty, the suppliers of loanable funds will choose to hold more money, and the supply curve will shift to the left. Borrowers may also respond by reducing their demand for funds as they grow more uncertain about their borrowing costs.[10]

A shift in the demand curve could also result from a change in the state of the economy. As the economy moves into a recession, customer demand drops off, inventory surpluses accumulate, and expansion plans are postponed. Capital expenditures and the need for funds to support them decline.

Forecast of Future Interest Rates Illustrated

Suppose a recession is anticipated. The forecaster expects the quantity of funds required by the business community to decline in anticipation of reduced consumer demand. At the same time, estimates of lower federal tax revenues, as unemployment rises, lead to a forecast of larger deficits. The government sector, therefore, will demand more loanable funds.

In practice, an interest rate forecast requires detailed identification of all potential changes and their magnitude. As shown in Figure 8.6 (left panel), if the increase in the government's demand for funds is greater than the decrease in demand by the business sector, net demand will increase, and the demand curve (D_{LF}) will shift to the right to $D_{LF'}$. Thus, the new equilibrium interest rate (i') will be higher.

figure **8.6**   SHIFTS IN THE DEMAND CURVE AND CHANGES IN THE EQUILIBRIUM RATE OF INTEREST

If the demand for loanable funds increases, the equilibrium level of interest rates will increase. If the demand for loanable funds decreases, the equilibrium level of interest rates will fall.

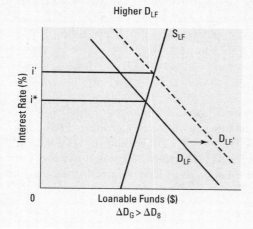
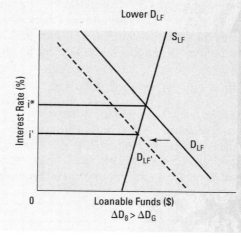

---

9 This effect is somewhat controversial; some analysts argue that growth in the money supply will lead to higher inflation so that the long-term effect on interest rates is uncertain. The effects of inflation are examined in subsequent sections.

10 Mascaro and Meltzer (1983).

1 What factors affect the supply of funds in an economy?

2 What factors affect the demand for funds?

3 How are interest rates determined under the loanable funds theory?

4 If the supply of funds increases (or decreases), what happens to the real rate of interest?

5 If the demand for funds increases (or decreases), what happens to the real rate of interest?

However, as shown in the right panel, if the decrease in business demand is greater than the increase in government demand, aggregate demand for loanable funds will decline, and the demand curve will shift to the left. Hence, the forecast will be for a new lower equilibrium rate of interest. The supply curve also may shift as a result of changing conditions. This, too, would affect anticipated movements in interest rates.

Inflation and the Level of Interest Rates

The rate of inflation was of particular concern in the 1980s because of the volatility in and high levels of several different measures of price changes. By the early 1990s and later in the early 2000s, a decline in annual inflation rates had some economists studying and writing about **disinflation,** or a reduction in the inflation rate to zero.[11] Because anticipated changes in the purchasing power of the dollar affect investors' yields, price-level changes have a role in theories of the general level of interest rates.

To illustrate, suppose a student's parents are saving for a graduation gift to be presented in one year. They are considering a one-year $2,000 bank certificate of deposit (CD) in a federally insured institution that is expected to yield 10 percent. The expected yield at the time of investment is the nominal return. If there is no inflation during the coming year, the ex post real return will also be 10 percent. But if the price level increases during the year, say 5 percent, the $2,200 that the student receives is worth 5 percent less. Deflating the $2,200 by dividing by 1.05, it is worth only $2,095.24 in terms of real purchasing power. Thus, the ex post return on the investment in terms of what the student received in real terms over what his or her parents invested is only 4.76 percent [($2,095.24 − $2,000) / $2,000 = 0.0476, or 4.76 percent], instead of the ex ante return expected of 10 percent.

Looking at this from a more practical perspective, suppose that a year prior to the investment, a compact disc cost $10. A year later, a compact disc now costs 5 percent more, or $10(1.05) = $10.50. With $2,000, the amount his or her parents invested, the student a year before could have bought 200 (i.e., $2,000 / $10) compact discs. However, because of the 5 percent price rise over the year, when the student receives the $2,200 earned on the investment a year later, he or she can buy only $2,200 / $10.50 = 209.52 compact discs (209 compact discs with some change left over). The profit on the investment in terms of additional purchasing is only 9.52 more compact discs, a return in terms of purchasing power of just 4.76 percent (i.e., 9.52 compact discs / 200 compact discs).

Inflation and Financial Innovation

If inflation were uncommon, participants in the financial markets would pay relatively little attention to it in forecasting future events. Charts of historical movements in the Consumer Price Index (CPI) and the Producer Price Index (PPI) in Figure 8.7, Panel A for 1975 to 1990 and Panel B for 1986 to 2003 demonstrate, however, that neither borrowers nor lenders can afford to ignore price levels and their potential impact on returns and costs.[12] Although inflation rates have subsided in recent years, CPI

---

11 Croushore (1992) reviews the arguments for and against the Fed's trying to reduce inflation to 0 percent and provides a comprehensive bibliography. See also Lawrence B. Lindsey. "The Case for Disinflation." *Economic Commentary: Federal Reserve Bank of Cleveland,* (March 15, 1992).

12 There is no general agreement on how to measure inflation. The most widely used measures are the CPI, the PPI, and the implicit Gross National Product (GNP) Price Deflator. The first two track changes in the price level of "market baskets" of goods; the third attempts to reflect price changes in all components of the GNP. Wallace and Cullison (1979) provide a good discussion of the PPI and the GNP Price Deflator. For a description of the current components of the CPI, which has been undergoing revisions since 1981, see the monthly issues of "The CPI Detailed Report" from the U.S. Department of Labor, Bureau of Labor Statistics.

figure 8.7 MEASURES OF EXPECTED INFLATION

PANEL A: COMPREHENSIVE PRICE MEASURES: CPI AND PPI

Inflation rates change over time. There are also many different ways of measuring inflation, such as the CPI, which focuses on the prices of goods most important to households, and the PPI, which tracks prices of goods especially important to businesses.

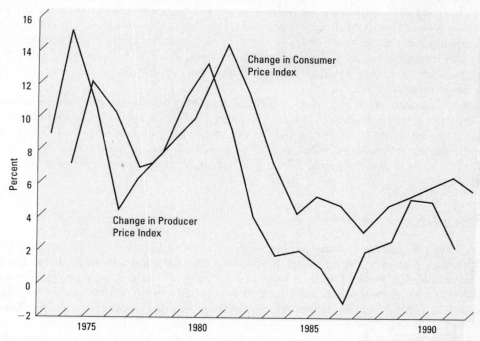

Source: Federal Reserve Bank of St. Louis, Annual U.S. Economic Data.

PANEL B: INFLATION AND INFLATION EXPECTATIONS

The shaded region shows the Humphrey-Hawkins CPI inflation range. Beginning in January 2000, the Humphrey-Hawkins inflation range was reported using the personal consumption expenditures (PCE) price index and therefore is not shown on this graph. CPI inflation is the percentage change from a year ago in the consumer price index. Inflation expectations measures include the quarterly Federal Bank of Philadelphia Survey of Professional Forecasters, the monthly University of Michigan Research Center's Survey of Consumers, and Federal Open Market Committee ranges reported to Congress in testimony for the Humphrey-Hawkins Act.

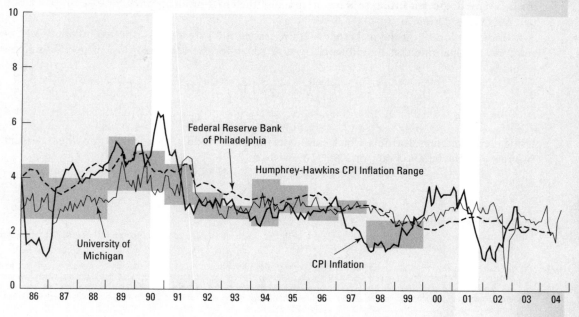

Source: Federal Reserve Bank of St. Louis, Monetary Trends, *October 2003, p. 8.*

inflation rates were close to 14 percent in 1975 in the United States and continue to be high in many countries. Many observers note that the demand for new financial products in the 1970s and 1980s can be attributed at least partially to expectations of inflation. Examples are adjustable-rate bonds and mortgages, zero-coupon bonds, deposit accounts that pay variable rates of interest, universal life insurance policies, interest rate swaps, inflation-adjusted Treasury securities, and inflation futures contracts. An entirely new type of financial instrument, the money market mutual fund, was created to allow investors to obtain yields that vary with daily changes in market conditions. Major deregulation of the financial system, through the Depository Institutions Deregulation and Monetary Control Act (DIDMCA), the Garn–St. Germain Act, and changes in state laws permitted institutions to meet this inflation-driven demand.

Inflation has deleterious effects on an economy. Hence, there are a number of different measures calculated for expected inflation (Figure 8.7, Panel B), including the Federal Bank of Philadelphia's survey of professional forecasters, the Federal Open Market Committee inflation range reported to Congress annually under the Humphrey-Hawkins Act, and the University of Michigan Research Center's Survey of Consumers. As Panel B shows, expected inflation and actual inflation as estimated by the CPI index often differ.

The Fisher Effect

Although the basic principles of this real/nominal effect were first suggested in the eighteenth century, a twentieth-century economist, Irving Fisher, is widely credited with laying the foundation for the study of the relationship between interest rates and expected inflation.[13] Suppose, for instance, investors wanted a 2 percent real return, and inflation was expected to be 12 percent over the year. Basically, investors will demand a higher interest rate (an inflation premium) for expected lost purchasing power over the period of an investment. That relationship, frequently called the Fisher effect, is summarized as follows: The nominal rate of interest reflects the real rate of inflation and a premium based on the expected rate of inflation.[14] Stated as an equation:

$$(1 + i_N) = (1 + i_R)(1 + \text{Expected Inflation Rate}) \qquad [8.1]$$

Thus,

$$i_N = [(1 + i_R)(1 + \text{Expected Inflation Rate})] - 1$$

where i_N is the nominal interest rate demanded and i_R is the real rate of return desired. Note that when multiplying rates 1 is added to each rate and then subtracted. In effect, multiplying this out, the nominal rate asked will be a function of the real rate, the inflation rate, and the cross-product terms, the interaction terms between the real rate and the inflation rate. In practice, many analysts simply solve for $i_N = i_R + \textbf{Expected Inflation Rate,}$ eliminating the cross-product terms for ease of calculation if precision is not desired.

Using Equation 8.1, if the real rate of return desired is 2 percent and expected inflation is 12 percent, the nominal rate that should be charged to adjust for the 12 percent loss of purchasing power would be

$$(1 + i_N) = (1.02)(1.12) = 1.1424$$

and

$$i_N = 1.1424 - 1 = 0.142, \text{ or } 14.2\%$$

Using the approximate formula, which eliminates the cross-product, the nominal rate would be just the real rate plus the inflation rate, or 2% + 12% = 14%.

---

13 This discussion draws on the work of Santoni and Stone (March, 1981). For a discussion of the development of the theory of real and nominal rates, including Fisher's forerunners and his own contributions, see Humphrey (1983).

14 Economists have studied several relationships between yields and price levels. Fisher was interested in the relationship between security yields and *changes* in the price level. Another researcher, A. H. Gibson, studied the relationship between the actual level of prices and yields, noting that when prices are relatively high, so are interest rates, and when prices are low, yields also tend to be low. No conclusion has been reached about whether the Gibson relation is consistent with or in conflict with the Fisher effect. See Gibson (1923); Shiller and Siegel (1977); and John H. Wood and Norma L. Wood. *Financial Markets.* San Diego, CA: Harcourt Brace Jovanovich (1985), 579–586.

The **real ex post return** that an investor actually gets, based on the actual inflation that occurred over the year, can be solved for by using Equation 8.1 as follows:

$$i_R = [(1 + i_N) / (1 + \text{Actual Inflation Rate})] - 1 \qquad [8.2]$$

Equation 8.2 shows that if inflation turned out to be 12 percent and the investor had charged 14.2 percent, the ex post real return would be equal to the desired return as follows:

$$i_R = [(1.142) / (1.12)] - 1 = 0.02, \text{ or } 2\%$$

Expected Inflation and the Loanable Funds Theory

Changes in nominal interest rates can be examined in the context of the loanable funds theory. As shown in Figure 8.8, Panel A, an anticipated increase in price levels means that savers (the suppliers of loanable funds) will require a higher nominal rate of return equal to approximately the real rate plus the expected inflation rate at every quantity of loanable funds supplied. This change means that the original curve S_{LF} must shift to the left, to $S_{LF'}$. At the same time, however, borrowers (the demanders of loanable funds) will be willing to pay the higher nominal rate, realizing that they will be repaying their loans in "cheaper dollars," so the demand curve D_{LF} will shift to $D_{LF'}$. The result is a new point of intersection at a higher nominal rate of interest, with the increase in nominal interest rates, or the inflationary premium, equal to the expected rate of inflation. A key point is that the real rate of interest remains unchanged. The Fisher theory implicitly assumes that even in the face of inflationary expectations, the real rate, or the rate at which goods can be exchanged for goods, is unaffected.

Stability of the Real Rate

Alternatively, challengers to the stability of the real rate under the Fisher theory argue that real rates will not stay constant and will be affected by expected inflation, as shown in Panel B of Figure 8.8. With higher expected inflation, investors will reduce their cash holdings in the short run to avoid an even greater loss of purchasing power and invest in a larger amount of interest-bearing assets. The additional money available for investments will increase the supply of funds available, causing the supply curve to

figure **8.8**   EFFECT OF INFLATION ON INTEREST RATES

PANEL A: INFLATION AND THE EQUILIBRIUM RATE OF INTEREST

According to the Fisher theory of interest rates and inflation, if inflation is anticipated, the nominal equilibrium level of interest rates (i_N) will equal the real rate (i_R) plus a premium equal to the expected rate of inflation [E(P)].

PANEL B: INFLATIONARY EXPECTATIONS AND THE REAL RATE OF INTEREST

Challengers of the Fisher theory argue that real rates are also affected by expected inflation. Thus, the supply of loanable funds may increase if inflation is anticipated, resulting in a decrease in the real rate.

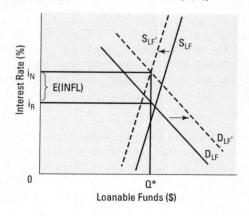

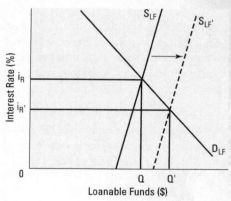

shift to the right to $(S_{LF'})$. Under this scenario, the real rate of interest falls from i_R to $i_{R'}$.[15] Hence, if Equation 8.1 is used to estimate the new nominal rate, expected inflation would be adjusted to using a lower real rate, not the original one, and investors would set a lower nominal rate adjusted for inflation than under the Fisher theory, in which the real rate remains the same.

Further Evaluation of the Fisher Theory

Fisher's theory is intuitively appealing and widely cited. During the 1980s, as inflation approached a modern peak of 13.6 percent in 1980 and Treasury bill (T-bill) yields were on their way to levels as high as 15.51 percent in the summer of 1981, the link between the two was emphasized even more than usual. Without actual reference to the Fisher theory, Fed officials publicly blamed high interest rates on inflation. Then Chairman Paul Volcker stated, "When the money supply is brought clearly under control and expectations of inflation dissipate, interest rates will tend to decline." His predecessor, G. William Miller, made a similar reference, stating, ". . . the recent and expected inflation also has been an extremely important factor underlying the increase in interest rates. . . ."[16] The Bush administration's chief economist, Michael Boskin, also acknowledged the linkage, stating, "The best step we can take to reduce pressure on inflation and interest rates is to negotiate a credible deficit-reduction package promptly."[17] (This statement is an implicit acceptance of the loanable funds theory.)

Historical Relationships

Empirical research on past interest rate movements and the rate of inflation has also been used to support the Fisher theory. Tracking historical changes in a rate-of-inflation measure such as the CPI against an interest rate measure almost always results in a positive correlation. For example, during the period 1966–1979, the correlation coefficient between the prime rate and the GNP Price Deflator was 0.70; when the commercial paper rate was used as the measure of interest rates, the correlation was 0.81.[18] Although the relationship has been stronger in some periods than others, it encourages belief in the Fisher effect. However, observed correlation does not guarantee causality, because some unknown factor or factors could be affecting both interest rates and inflation in a similar fashion so that they appear to be related to one another but are actually both related to other things. In addition, these findings focus on historical inflation rates, whereas the Fisher effect addresses expected inflation rates.

Measurement Problems

Other studies, including those by Fisher himself, have calculated ex post real rates of return by subtracting ex post inflation rates from nominal rates to solve for the real rate of return (i.e., real rate = nominal rate − ex post rate of inflation). Fisher found that ex post real rates were not stable, which suggests that inflationary expectations by investors were consistently incorrect. In later tests, he concluded that the inflation premiums imposed by the markets were strongly influenced by past rates of inflation and that past price changes were inadequate estimates of future inflation.[19]

Historical Ex Post Analysis

Recent ex post analyses confirm that if the Fisher theory is true, inaccurate inflationary expectations persist. For example, Panel A of Figure 8.9 shows that during the period 1960–1986, the ex post real rate on three-month T-bills was sometimes negative. This means that nominal rates were less than actual rates of inflation in some years. However, investors appeared to have gained a lesson from these years and demanded higher nominal rates in most years in the later 1980s, with positive ex post real rates

15 Mundell (1963) and Tobin (1965). Recent empirical work also casts doubt on the stability of the real rate. See Rose (1988).

16 See Cox (1980).

17 David Wessel and Tom Herman. "Interest Rates Head Up Across the Board, but Brady Discounts New Inflation Fears." *The Wall Street Journal* (February 24, 1989), A2.

18 See Cox (1980), 22.

19 A review of Fisher's initial empirical research is provided in Humphrey (1983).

figure **8.9** TRENDS IN INFLATION AND INTEREST RATES

PANEL A: EX POST NOMINAL AND REAL INTEREST RATES ON THREE-MONTH T-BILLS, 1960–1986

If the actual (ex post) rate of inflation during a period exceeds the premium for expected (ex ante) inflation incorporated in nominal interest rates, the ex post real rate will be negative.

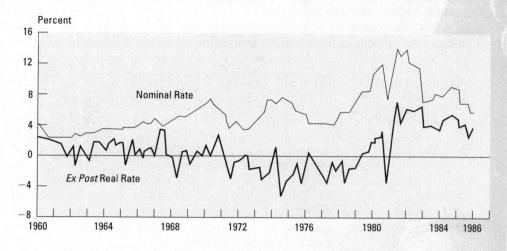

Source: Adapted from Carl E. Walsh, "Three Questions Concerning Nominal and Real Interest Rates,"
Economic Review *(Federal Reserve Bank of San Francisco) (Fall 1987): 7.*

PANEL B: ACTUAL INFLATION IN RECENT YEARS, 1977–2003

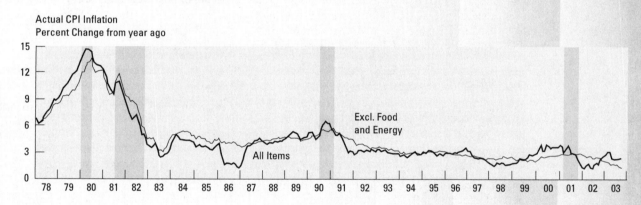

Source: Federal Reserve Bank of St. Louis, Monetary Trends, *November 2003, p. 8.*

PANEL C: TREND IN REAL INTEREST RATES, 1981–2003 (EX POST RATES)

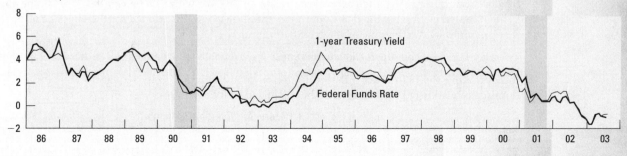

Note: Real interest rates are ex post measures, equal to nominal rates minus CPI inflation.

Source: Federal Reserve Bank of St. Louis, Monetary Trends, *October 2003, p. 8.*

shown, to cover the higher inflationary expectations that were realized. Panel B shows trends in actual inflation, measured by the CPI Index from 1977 to 2003, and Panel C shows trends in real (ex post) interest rates from 1985 to 2003. Real ex post interest rates have been positive since the 1980s through the 2000s covering actual inflation rises.

Interest Rate Behavior Adjustments for Deflation?

At the beginning of 2003, as shown in Panels B and C of Figure 8.9, it is interesting to note that the CPI fell significantly in 2002, indicating a general fall in consumer prices. The real interest rate also fell significantly at the end of 2002, which perhaps could reflect some deflationary price expectations by investors, although other factors were involved. In Figure 8.10, the components of the CPI separated out by the CPI for core services and the CPI for core goods are illustrated for 1995 to 2003 in the upper left. It's interesting to note that prices rose for core services but fell for core goods during 2001. In particular, as shown in the top right figure, the reason for the difference in prices for goods and services can be reflected in falling prices for imported consumer goods with a rise in the U.S. exchange rate, resulting in a decline in the overall CPI in 2001. Hence, with globalization, actual and expected inflation or deflation rates are also affected by how much a country imports and the exchange rates for imports.

Although nominal rates rose to compensate for lost purchasing power in the 1980s to the early 2000s, Fisher's theory is based on ex ante expectations. Researchers have had difficulty calculating desired ex ante real rates of return by investors, since neither the real rate of interest nor the expected rate of inflation is empirically observable. In general, expert observers assume the real rate of interest to be in the range of 2 percent to 4 percent, based on the average growth rate in the GNP. Estimates of real rates have included yields on T-bills, high-grade corporate bonds, and equity securities. Actual figures or lagged averages of one of several inflation measures, such as CPI or the GNP Price Deflator, have been used to estimate the inflationary premium. Not surprisingly, there is no uniform agreement on measurement or methodology, and the research findings are contradictory.[20]

Adjusting for the Tax Effect

Another complicating factor is income taxes, which are levied on nominal rather than real returns. For example, suppose that the before-tax ex ante real return is 4 percent. For an investor in the 28 percent marginal tax bracket, an after-tax real rate of 2.88 percent [4% $\times$ (1 − 0.28) = 2.88%] would be expected in the absence of inflation.[21]

Now suppose that inflation is expected to be 4 percent, so ignoring the Fisher theory cross-product terms, investors ask for an approximate nominal rate of 8 percent (4 percent before-tax real rate + 4 percent expected inflation rate). However, since the investor will be taxed on the entire nominal rate, he or she will be taxed on the inflation premium as well as the real rate. Thus, the expected approximate real after-tax return would be the nominal rate after tax less the expected inflation rate, or [8% $\times$ (1 − 0.28) − 4%], which is only 1.76 percent versus the 2.88 percent desired. Anticipation of this tax effect exerts a new upward pressure on the nominal rate, suggesting that the change in nominal yields will actually be greater than that predicted by Fisher to compensate for the tax on the investors' inflation premium. To protect after-tax real returns to an investor with a 28 percent tax rate (t), the approximate nominal yield must include a before-tax inflation premium inflated for the tax to be imposed on that premium by dividing the expected inflation ratio by (1 − t), that is,

$$\text{Before-Tax Inflation Premium} = [\text{Expected Inflation Rate}] / (1 - t) \qquad [8.3]$$

Incorporating the before-tax inflation premium in the original Fisher equation (Equation 8.1), the nominal rate adjusted for taxes would be calculated as follows:

$$i_N = [(1 + i_R)(1 + \text{Before-Tax Inflation Premium})] - 1 \qquad [8.4]$$

---

20 Examples of attempts to measure inflationary expectations and/or the real rate can be found in Fama (1975), Carlson (1977), Mullineaux and Protopapadakis (1984), and Leonard and Solt (1986).

21 Key proponents of the tax effect are Darby (1975) and Feldstein (1976). A discussion of the potential effect of changing inflationary expectations on the real rate and the subsequent tax effects is provided in Holland (1984).

figure **8.10**   TRENDS IN CORE CPIS SEPARATED INTO GOODS AND SERVICES AND IMPORT PRICE INDEXES

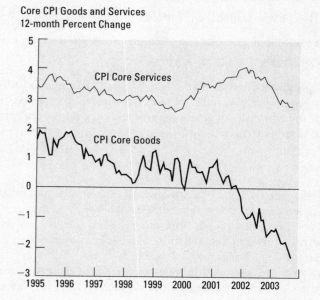

Core CPI Goods and Services
12-month Percent Change

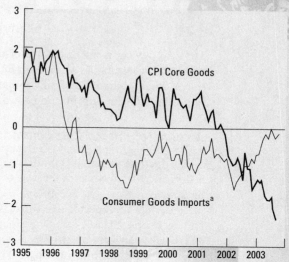

Core CPI Goods and Consumer Goods Import Price Indexes
12-month Percent Change

Prices of Consumer Goods Imports[a]

	Share Percent	Percent Change, Last		
		3 mo.[b]	12 mo.	36 mo.[b]
Nondurables	48.5	−0.40	0.20	−0.03
Apparel and Footware	31.9	0.0	0.71	−0.23
Other	16.6	−1.18	−0.79	0.27
Durables	46.2	−1.24	−0.62	−1.18
Household Goods	20.3	−0.82	0.0	−0.81
Recreational	10.8	0.41	−0.10	−0.97
Home Entertainment	10.6	−2.65	−4.31	−3.65
Other	4.5	−3.74	4.01	2.42
Other	5.5	−0.88	−0.28	−1.41

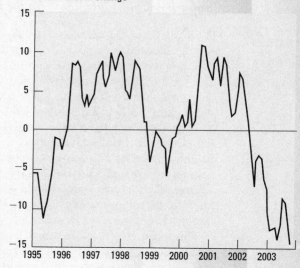

Major Currency Index
12-month Percent Change

a. Excluding automotives.

b. Annualized.

Source: *U.S. Department of Labor, Bureau of Labor Statistics; and Board of Governors of the Federal Reserve System, "Foreign Exchange Rates," H.10, Federal Reserve Statistical Releases. From Federal Reserve Bank of Cleveland,* Economic Trends, *November 2003, p. 3.*

where i_N = the nominal return before taxes and i_R = the real rate expected before taxes.

For the previous example, using Equation 8.3, the before-tax inflation premium would be

$$0.04 / (1 − 0.28) = 5.556\%$$

and using Equation 8.4, the nominal rate that investors would charge would be

$$i_N = (1.04)(1.0556) − 1 = 9.782\%$$

To prove that the tax-adjusted nominal rate compensates for both inflation and its tax effect, Equation 8.4 can be used to solve for the after-tax real return, $i_R(1 - t)$:

$$i_R(1 - t) = \{[(1 + i_N) / (1 + \text{Before-Tax Inflation Premium})] - 1\}(1 - t) \qquad [8.5]$$

If 4 percent inflation actually occurs, the ex post rate after taxes that the investor will receive will be

$$i_R(1 - t) = \{[(1.0978) / (1.0556)] - 1\}(0.72) = 0.0288, \text{ or } 2.88\%$$

The 2.88 percent is the original after-tax real rate of return the investor desired. The inflation adjustments, however, are based on ex ante rather than ex post inflation rates. Thus, again, if expected inflation is different than actual inflation, the investor may not get this desired ex post after-tax real return. Thus, the problem of protecting ex ante after-tax yields remains.[22]

Accuracy of Interest Rate Forecasting

As the opening paragraphs to this chapter suggest, the life of a forecaster of interest rates and inflation is difficult. Many variables must be considered before rates are predicted, and each variable is a possible source of error. Another problem is that forecasters cannot stop with a prediction of the real rate of interest; they are expected to estimate several different rates. At commercial banks, movements in T-bill and negotiable CD rates are of great concern. At a savings institution, trends in mortgage rates are just as crucial. Managers of insurance companies are interested in long-term bond yields, as are mutual fund and pension fund managers. Finance company managers focus on interest rates on consumer credit and commercial paper.

Professional Forecasts Based on the Loanable Funds Theory

The loanable funds framework is widely used by professional forecasters. They project changes in interest rates based on an analysis of credit demand by sector and by type of security offered as well as on the amount of loanable funds supplied and the types of securities investors will prefer. Resulting forecasts are crucial to managers who must choose what securities to issue or to purchase from among a variety with fixed and variable rates and different maturities.

Salomon Brothers' annual *Prospects for the Credit Markets* is perhaps the most widely quoted example of this approach to rate forecasting, but the American Council of Life Insurance, Morgan Guaranty Trust Company, Prudential Insurance Company, and others also make their forecasts available to financial intermediaries. Other analysts supply forecasts only on a proprietary basis. Large financial institutions often have staff economists who develop forecasts for managers. Managers of smaller firms gather information from many professional forecasters to assist in formulating asset/liability strategies appropriate for the interest rate environment. Economists use other more sophisticated time series or regression models for forecasts as well.[23]

This section discussed factors that are important in understanding and predicting the movements of interest rates. Before discussing theories for exchange rates, the following sections discuss how to read and calculate interest rates or yields for short-term money market securities, with which individual investors are often unfamiliar.

---

22 For more discussion, see Gordon J. Alexander and William Sharpe. *Fundamentals of Investments.* Englewood Cliffs, NJ: Prentice Hall (1989), 102, and Peek (1988).

23 VAR (vector autoregressive) models are discussed and illustrated in Eugeni, Evans, and Strongin (1992), and in "The Future Is Not What It Used To Be." *The Economist* (June 13, 1992), 75. Other models that have been used are multivariate regression models, in which the expected change in rate is a function of the unexpected change in a money supply measure, the unexpected change in the CPI, the unexpected change in the PPI, the unexpected change in the unemployment rate, the unexpected change in industrial production, the unexpected change in the trade balance, an intercept term, and a random error term. The model attempts to explain interest rate changes by using measures of the money supply, inflation, the level of business activity, and activity involving the foreign sector—all important components of the theoretical interest rate models discussed earlier in the chapter. See Dwyer and Hafer (1989). The perils of economic forecasting are discussed in more detail in Van Dyke (1986) and Taylor (1982). A recent study at the Federal Reserve Bank of Cleveland showed that households' forecasts of inflation are more accurate than forecasts of professional economists. Some argue, however, that economists are improving through the use of techniques such as VAR. See Bryan and Gavin (1986). Many argue that in reasonably efficient markets, only those participants with private sources of information or with superior information-processing models unknown to other participants are in a position to earn potentially superior profits. Thus, if an economist is an exceptionally successful forecaster, it is not in his or her best interest to reveal that fact to others. See Urang (1988, 1989); Tom Herman. "How to Profit from Economists' Forecasts." *The Wall Street Journal* (January 22, 1993), C1, C6; Ronald Bailey. "Them That Can, Do; Them That Can't, Forecast." *Forbes* (December 26, 1988), 94–100; and Belongia (1987).

1 Under Fisher's theory, if inflationary expectations rise, what is generally the effect on nominal interest rates?

2 Explain mathematically how investors set nominal rates to compensate for expected inflation.

3 Explain how adjustments can be made mathematically for the fact that nominal yields will be taxed to ensure that the nominal rate is high enough to compensate for both

expected inflation and the tax on the inflation premium that investors demand.

4 Explain the difference between ex ante and ex post real interest rates.

5 Given a nominal interest rate on a bond and the actual rate of inflation that occurred, how can the ex post real rate be solved for?

Calculating Effective Annual Yields

In its simplest form, a *yield is what you earned divided by what you paid for a security adjusted for how many times you could earn this yield during a year.* Since securities have different maturities, holding periods, and cash flows, *effective annual yields* are calculated to facilitate comparisons. The effective annual yield (y^*) on an investment is the compound rate of return an investor would earn, given the asset's cash flow characteristics if the investor held it for exactly 365 days (366 days in leap years) and received the return at the end of that year. For long-term securities, in general, the effective annual yield is calculated as the discount rate that makes the price of the security equal to the present value of its future cash flows, a definition with which students of financial management are familiar.[24]

Money market securities are unique in that they are short-term securities with maturities less than one year that generally sell as discount securities, requiring a single cash outflow from the investor, followed by a single cash inflow at a later date (much like a zero-coupon bond that simply pays a maturity value). However, money market securities have maturities that are less than one year in maturity, so their yields have to be annualized for the number of times a year an investor could earn that yield. For instance, if an investor invests in a three-month T-bill, the investor could earn that yield 365 days / 90 days = 4.06 times a year. Hence, formally, the equation for the annual yield, often called **coupon equivalent yield,** for a money market security is basically what the investor received over what he or she paid times the number of times a year this could occur:

$$y = \frac{[\text{Par (or } P_1) - P_0]}{P_0} \times (365/n) \qquad \frac{1000-150}{150} \qquad [8.6]$$

where P_0 is the amount initially invested, Par (or P_1) is the par value at maturity (Par) or price (P_1) received if sold before maturity, and n is the number of days until maturity or until sold.

If the possibility of compounding over a full year is also considered, an **effective annual yield (y^*)** can be calculated as follows:

$$y^* = \left[1 + \frac{\text{Par (or } P_1) - P_0}{P_0} \right]^{(365/n)} - 1 \qquad [8.7]$$

or simply

$$y^* = [\text{Par (or } P_1) / P_0]^{365/n} - 1$$

This equation implicitly assumes that any money received will be reinvested at the given annual rate during the year, resulting in a higher effective annual rate at the end of the year. Hence, y^* will always be greater than y.

In the real world, the yield on money market securities is generally quoted, however, as a percentage of the securities par (maturity) value of 100 percent. This is called a **bank discount yield.** This traditional method for quoting bills yields dates to 1929, when T-bills were first sold. At that time, traders

---

24 The yield to maturity on a bond, for instance, is the discount rate that makes the bond's price equal to coupon payment (PVIFAn) + Maturity Value (PVIFn), where PVIFA = the present value annuity factor and PVIF, the single sum present value factor. See Arthur J. Keown, David F. Scott, John D. Martin, and J. William Petty. *Basic Financial Management*, 8th ed., Upper Saddle River, NJ: Prentice Hall, 1999, Chapter 7.

found it easier to make computations considering a year as 360 days, and calculating yields as a fraction of 100 percent (par value) versus price (P_O). The formula for calculating the bank discount yield (d) on T-bills is

$$d = \frac{[\text{Par (or } P_1) - P_0]}{\text{Par}} \times (360/n) \qquad [8.8]$$

Note that because bank discount yields are a fraction of par value versus price, discount yields (d) will always be lower then annual yield (y) or effective annual yields (y*).

Solving for the T-bill's price (P_O) by using Equation 8.8,

$$P_0 = \text{Par} \times \left[1 - \frac{(d \times n)}{360} \right] \qquad [8.9]$$

The bill's price is the par value of 100 percent less the discount rate times (n/360), adjusting for the T-bill's maturity in days relative to a 360-day year. Given the security's price (P_O), y and y* can then be calculated by using Equations 8.6 and 8.7.

Example of Price and Yield Calculations

Money market securities are sold in both primary (original issuance) and secondary (for resale) markets. T-bills, for instance, are usually issued with one of three original maturity dates—92, 182, or 364 days—with typical minimum denominations of $10,000. Weekly auctions are conducted by the Federal Reserve Bank of New York, with bids quoted as discount yields as a percentage of par value, as calculated in Equation 8.8. Approximately forty large government security dealers (large banks and investment banks) authorized by the U.S. Treasury stand ready to purchase Treasury securities at every auction and often act as buyers and sellers in the secondary market. Thus, these dealers are frequently involved in trades for Fed open market operations.[25]

Figure 8.11, Panel A shows the results of a typical T-bill auction as reported in *The Wall Street Journal*. Information for T-bill auctions are published on Tuesday after regularly scheduled Monday auctions. These data are for a T-bill auction on Monday, November 24, 2003. In this auction, as usual, many more bids were submitted than could be accepted, based on the volume of bills the Treasury had decided to sell. Noncompetitive bidders are assured of receiving bills, but the price they pay is determined by the average competitive bid that is ultimately accepted. Winning competitive bidders are those willing to pay the highest percentage of par value. Thus, noncompetitive bidders know their bids will be accepted but are unsure of the price, whereas competitive bidders know the price they will pay if they win but have no guarantee of delivery.

Published information on T-bill auctions includes the average price and high, median, and low rate bid for the bills, along with the total applied for and accepted, including noncompetitive bids.

The auction price (rate) for the 3-month (91-day) T-bill is 99.768 (0.920 percent median rate). The 99.768 rate is the price as a percentage of par, that is, 99.768 percent. The 0.920 percent median rate is the discount yield. Based on the discount yield of 0.920 percent for 13-week (91-day) T-bills, the T-bill's price was calculated using Equation 8.9:

$$P_0 = \text{Par} \times \left[1 - \frac{d \times n}{360} \right] = 100\% \times \left[1 - \frac{(0.0092 \times 91)}{360} \right] = 99.768\% \text{ of par}$$

So, the price that must be paid is $10,000(0.99768), or $9,976.80.

---

25 Primary dealers are involved in about 75 percent of the daily volume in T-bill trading, so they receive significant price information that provides them with a competitive advantage over other traders. In 1991, Salomon Brothers misused its power by submitting false bids in its customers' names to win more than 90 percent of a two-year Treasury note issue, in spite of the fact that Treasury auction rules are intended to prevent a single bidder from receiving more than 35 percent of any issue. Salomon was fined $290 million; these actions hurt the firm's reputation and, hence, profitability for many years. In 1992, the Fed instituted a single-price, or Dutch auction, system for selected two-year and five-year notes. This entails that all winning bidders in the auction pay the same price, unlike a traditional auction, in which securities are allocated to the highest bidders in descending order of price until all securities are allocated. Many experts believe that the traditional bidding system encourages primary dealers, who must bid at every auction, to collude in their efforts to minimize the "winners' curse." The Dutch auction system reduces such problems. In 1998, the U.S. Treasury announced that Treasury bond and note sales would be based on a Dutch auction format, with all bonds sold at the price offered by the highest bidder. Consumers can more easily purchase Treasury notes directly from the government under a recent Treasury Direct program by calling the Bureau of Public Debt at (202) 874–4000 and punching in 1 and then 241 to receive documents; by phoning (800) 722-2678; or by visiting the Bureau's Website at *http://www.publicdebt.treas.gov*. Five-year notes are issued quarterly with interest on the notes paid semiannually and taxed in the year received. See Robert Heady. "'Safe' Options for Your Dollar." *The Denver Post* (November 15, 1998), 13L.

figure   **8.11**   PUBLISHED INFORMATION ON TREASURY BILLS

PANEL A: RESULTS OF WEEKLY T-BILL AUCTIONS PUBLISHED IN *THE WALL STREET JOURNAL*, NOVEMBER 25, 2003

Data include the average price and the discount (d) and coupon equivalent yields to purchasers.

PANEL B: DAILY DATA ON SECONDARY MARKET YIELDS FOR T-BILLS

Information includes the maturity date and the bid discount at which investors must pay dealers. The Ask Yield is the bond equivalent yield (y) based on the asked price.

Prices for Monday, November 24, 2003

Here are the results of yesterday's Treasury auction of three- and six-month bills:

(000 omitted in dollar figures)

	3-Mo. Bills	6-Mo. Bills
Price	99.768	99.492
High Rate	0.930	1.010
Investment Rate	0.946	1.032
Low Rate	0.900	0.990
Median Rate	0.920	1.000
Total applied for	$45,256,192	$40,779,916
Accepted	$21,968,509	$21,867,186
Noncompetitive	$1,396,492	$992,345

Both issues are dated Nov. 28. The three-month bills mature on Feb. 26, and the six-month bills on May 27.

TREASURY BILLS

Date	Bid	Ask	Chg	Yield
Nov 27 03	0.94	0.93	+0.04	0.94
Dec 04 03	0.89	0.88	+0.02	0.89
Dec 11 03	0.89	0.88	+0.01	0.89
Dec 18 03	0.91	0.90	+0.01	0.91
Dec 26 03	0.92	0.91	+0.02	0.92
Jan 02 04	0.92	0.91	+0.02	0.92
Jan 08 04	0.89	0.88	+0.01	0.89
Jan 15 04	0.90	0.89	+0.02	0.90
Jan 22 04	0.89	0.88	+0.01	0.89
Jan 29 04	0.89	0.88	+0.01	0.89
Feb 05 04	0.91	0.90	+0.01	0.91
Feb 12 04	0.92	0.91	+0.01	0.92
Feb 19 04	0.92	0.91	+0.01	0.93
Feb 26 04	0.92	0.91	+0.01	0.93
Mar 01 04	0.93	0.92	+0.01	0.94
Mar 04 04	0.90	0.89	...	0.91
Mar 11 04	0.91	0.90	...	0.92
Mar 18 04	0.93	0.92	+0.01	0.94
Mar 25 04	0.91	0.90	...	0.92
Apr 08 04	0.93	0.92	+0.01	0.94
Apr 15 04	0.94	0.93	+0.01	0.95
Apr 22 04	0.94	0.93	+0.01	0.95
Apr 29 04	0.96	0.95	+0.01	0.97
May 06 04	0.97	0.96	+0.01	0.98
May 13 04	0.97	0.96	+0.01	0.98
May 20 04	0.99	0.98	+0.01	1.00
May 27 04	1.01	1.00	+0.01	1.02

Source: The Wall Street Journal, *November 25, 2003, C9, C12.*

The coupon equivalent (or annual yield) for the T-bill given as a percent can be calculated by using Equation 8.6:

$$y = \frac{[\text{Par (or } P_1) - P_0]}{P_0} \times (365/n) = \frac{[100\% - 99.768\%]}{99.768\%} \times (365/91) = 0.933\%$$

The effective annual yield for the T-bill is not given but can be calculated by using Equation 8.7:

$$y^* = [\text{Par (or } P_1) / P_0]^{(365/n)} - 1 = [100\% / 99.768\%]^{(365/91)} - 1 = .00936, \text{ or } 0.936\%$$

Panel B of Figure 8.11 shows data on T-bill yields in the secondary market for the same date, November 24, 2003. Besides the maturity date and days to security, the discount yield at which dealers are willing to buy (the bid price) and sell them (the asked price) are given on a bank discount basis. The dealer makes a profit on the spread between the asked and bid prices. Because there is an inverse relationship between bill prices and yields, dealers sell bills at higher prices (lower yields to buyers) than the prices at which they are willing to buy them. Given the January 29, 2004, maturity date bill shown in Panel B with 66 days to maturity and an asked discount rate of 0.88%, its price can be calculated by using Equation 8.9:

$$P_0 = \text{Par} \times \left[1 - \frac{(d \times n)}{360}\right] = 100\% \times \left[1 - \frac{(0.0088 \times 66)}{360}\right] = 99.839\% \text{ of par}$$

So, the price that must be paid is $10,000 × 0.99839, or $9,983.90.

Hence, the effective annual rate (y*) for the bill can be computed by using Equation 8.7:

$$y^* = [\text{Par (or } P_1) / P_0]^{(365/n)} - 1 = [100\% / 99.839\%]^{(365/66)} - 1 = 0.00895, \text{ or } 0.895\%$$

Differences in Yields for Money Market Securities

Differences in yields on securities reflect differences in default risk, liquidity, denomination size, and maturity. Because Treasury securities are backed by the taxing and money-creation power of the federal government, they are in this sense free of default risk. The existence of secondary markets for investments and the size of those markets also affect an investor's assessment of risk. An investor wishing to sell a financial asset quickly obviously needs a market in which to sell it. The larger the market, the greater the seller's opportunity to obtain cash easily without substantial loss of value—that is, the greater the **liquidity.** As short-term securities maturing in less than a year, money market securities are subject to low price risk in terms of the present values of their cash flows falling with a change in rates. Securities with higher minimum denominations, such as money market securities, also tend to pay higher rates.

Figure 8.12 shows money rates for different types of money market securities including commercial paper, CDs, banker's acceptances, repurchase agreements, and T-bills. These securities are similar in that they mature in less than one year, have low or no default risk, and generally are very liquid; that is, they can be sold easily with little or no loss of value. Since these money market securities are relatively homogeneous and substitutable, their rates tend to be close to each other. For instance, as shown on Figure 8.12, on November 25, 2003, the three-month certificates of deposit (CD) rate was 1.11 percent; the 90-day commercial paper, 1.10 percent; 90-day banker's acceptances, 1.09 percent; and the 90-day Eurodollars rate, 1.11 percent. Differences reflect differences in default risk, maturity, minimum

---

figure 8.12 MONEY MARKET YIELD QUOTATIONS

Money Rates

Tuesday, November 25, 2003

The key U.S. and foreign annual interest rates below are a guide to general levels but don't always represent actual transactions.

Commercial Paper

Yields paid by corporations for short-term financing, typically for daily operation

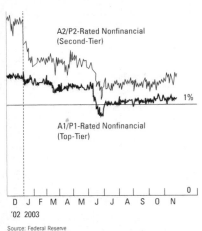

A2/P2-Rated Nonfinancial (Second-Tier)

A1/P1-Rated Nonfinancial (Top-Tier)

1%

D J F M A M J J A S O N   0
'02 2003

Source: Federal Reserve

Prime Rate: 4.00% (effective 06/27/03). The base rate on corporate loans posted by at least 75% of the nation's 30 largest banks.

Discount Rate (Primary): 2.00% (effective 06/25/03).

Federal Funds: 1.125% high, 0.969% low, 1.000% near closing bid, 1.063% offered. Effective rate: 1.03%. Source: Prebon Yamane (USA) Inc. Federal-funds target rate: 1.000% (effective 06/25/03).

Call Money: 2.75% (effective 06/30/03).

Commercial Paper: Placed directly by General Electric Capital Corp.: 0.80% 30 to 41 days; 1.09% 42 to 84 days; 1.10% 85 to 120 days; 0.90% 121 to

132 days; 1.12% 133 to 160 days; 1.14% 161 to 224 days; 1.20% 225 to 270 days.

Euro Commercial Paper: Placed directly by General Electric Capital Corp.: 2.02% 30 days; 2.10% two months; 2.11% three months; 2.11% four months; 2.15% five months; 2.17% six months.

Dealer Commercial Paper: High-grade unsecured notes sold through dealers by major corporations: 1.04% 30 days; 1.09% 60 days; 1.10% 90 days.

Certificates of Deposit: 1.05% one month; 1.11% three months; 1.14% six months.

Bankers Acceptances: 1.06% 30 days; 1.09% 60 days; 1.09% 90 days; 1.10% 120 days; 1.13% 150 days; 1.15% 180 days. Source: Prebon Yamane (USA) Inc.

Eurodollars: 1.08% - 1.06% one month; 1.09% - 1.06% two months; 1.10% - 1.08% three months; 1.11% - 1.09% four months; 1.16% - 1.13% five months; 1.18% - 1.15% six months. Source: Prebon Yamane (USA) Inc.

London Interbank Offered Rates (Libor): 1.11875% one month; 1.1700% three months; 1.233375% six months; 1.50438% one year. Effective rate for contracts entered into two days from date appearing at top of this column.

Euro Libor: 2.08375% one month; 2.15025% three months; 2.21625% six months; 2.41150% one year. Effective rate for contracts entered into two days from date appearing at top of this column.

Euro Interbank Offered Rates (Euribor): 2.068% one month; 2.152% three months; 2.220% six months; 2.402% one year. Source: Reuters.

Foreign Prime Rates: Canada 4.50%; European Central Bank 2.00%; Japan 1.375%; Switzerland 2.13%; Britain 3.75%.

Treasury Bills: Results of the Monday, November 24, 2003, auction of short-term U.S. government bills, sold at a discount from face value in units of $1,000 to $1 million: 0.930% 13 weeks; 1.010% 26 weeks. Tuesday, November 25, 2003 auction: 0.940% 4 weeks.

Overnight Repurchase Rate: 1.01%. Source: Garban Intercapital.

Freddie Mac: Posted yields on 30-year mortgage commitments. Delivery within 30 days 5.54%, 60 days 5.61%, standard conventional fixed-rate mortgages: 3.375%, 2% rate capped one-year adjustable rate mortgages.

Fannie Mae: Posted yields on 30-year mortgage commitments (priced at par) for delivery within 30 days 5.62%, 60 days 5.70%, standard conventional fixed-rate mortgages; 3.00%, 6/2 rate capped one-year adjustable rate mortgages. Constant Maturity Debt Index: 1.100% three months; 1.150% six months; 1.392% one year.

Merrill Lynch Ready Assets Trust: 0.53%.

Consumer Price Index: October, 185.0, up 2.0% from a year ago. Bureau of Labor Statistics.

Key Rates

Percent	Yesterday	Day Ago	Year Ago
Prime rate	4.00	4.00	4.75
Federal Funds	1.00	0.98	1.26
3-month Libor	1.17	1.17	1.42
3-month T-bills	0.93	0.93	1.20
6-month T-bills	1.00	1.01	1.25
10-yr. T-infl.	1.90	1.80	2.48
10-yr. T-note	4.19	4.23	4.07
30-yr. T-bond	5.03	5.07	4.93
Telephone bd.	6.13	6.15	6.29
Municipal bds.	4.84	4.86	5.11

Sources: *Bloomberg News; Telerate; The Bond Buyer; British Bankers' Assoc.*

Source: The Wall Street Journal, *November 26, 2003, C10.*
Source: New York Times, *November 26, 2003, C7.*

denomination, and the marketability of different securities in terms of having a strong or weak secondary market for trading.

Money market securities have large minimum denominations. For instance, the minimum T-bill has a face value of $10,000. Commercial paper ranges from a minimum of $25,000 upward. Negotiable CDs have a legal minimum of $100,000 but in practice usually are more than $1 million, and banker's acceptances come in denominations of $100,000 to $500,000. Consequently, small investors may choose to hold shares in a money market fund (holding a portfolio of money market securities) with a $500 to $2,500 minimum. The different types of securities are summarized in Table 8.1.

Figure 8.13 shows how a banker's acceptance is created, a process with which individual investors are often unfamiliar. Basically, an importer arranges with his or her bank to have a letter of credit (L/C) from the bank guaranteeing that the importer will pay. This L/C is delivered to the exporter's bank,

table **8.1** SUMMARY OF CHARACTERISTICS: DIFFERENT TYPES OF MONEY MARKET SECURITIES

REPURCHASE AGREEMENTS

Repurchase agreements are money market transactions in which securities (usually Treasury securities) are sold by one party to another, with the agreement that the seller will repurchase the securities at a specified price on a specified date. For the seller, the transaction is called a repo and for the buyer, a reverse repo. Repurchase agreements are commonly used by large government security dealers to finance their inventories. The daily volume of repurchase agreements sometimes reaches $1 trillion, with many transactions as short as one day. Repos are used by the Fed as part of open market operations to temporarily decrease the amount of reserves available in the banking system by selling Treasury securities with agreements to repurchase them later or to increase reserves by buying Treasury securities from banks under agreements that the banks will repurchase them later. In the mid-1980s, crises occurred in the repo market with the collapse of government security dealers with large reverse repos with financial institutions. There is no secondary market for reverse repos.

COMMERCIAL PAPER

Commercial paper are corporate short-term borrowings in the open market by major and lesser known companies. Commercial paper has a maturity of less than nine months; issues of longer maturity sold in the United States must be registered with the SEC, which increases the borrower's cost and time required to raise funds. Commercial banks, S&Ls, insurance companies, mutual funds, and other large financial institutions are the main purchasers of commercial paper. The paper, like T-bills, is bought on a discount basis and redeemed at par on maturity. Minimum denominations range from $25,000 up, depending on whether the purchase is made through a dealer or directly from the borrowing firm. Finance companies are large issuers. Most commercial paper is held to maturity, and the secondary market is somewhat limited compared with T-bills, but the growth of money market funds enlarged the market.

BANKER'S ACCEPTANCE

Banker's acceptances are negotiable securities that arise out of bankers' accepting payment in association with international trade. Thus, banker's acceptances serve not only as short-term assets to money market investors but also as short-term sources of funds to large banks that finance international transactions. Similar to T-bills, banker's acceptances are sold to money market investors at a discount from the face value, and yields are quoted on a banker's discount basis.

NEGOTIABLE CERTIFICATES OF DEPOSIT

Negotiable CDs developed as a loophole to Regulation Q, which prevented banks from offering market rates on deposits. Negotiable CDs have face values with a legal minimum of $100,000, but in practice are usually more than $1 million. They can be sold in secondary markets. Innovations in the CD market include variable-rate CDs, on which the maturity is fixed but the interest rate varies every thirty days. Also, Eurodollar CDs—which are dollar-denominated negotiable CDs issued primarily by London-based branches of American, Japanese, British, or other foreign banks—are popular. The secondary market for Eurodollar CDs is smaller than the secondary market for negotiable CDs issued in the United States. Because the first $100,000 of each domestic negotiable CD is eligible for federal deposit insurance, but Eurodollar CDs are uninsured, yields are usually higher on Eurodollar CDs than domestic CDs.

FEDERAL FUNDS

Excess reserves required by the Fed lent by one institution to another are federal funds (Fed Funds). They are the assets of the lending institution and liabilities of the borrowing firm. Typically, Fed Funds transactions are very short-term; in fact, many are overnight, similar to repo/reverse repos. Fed Funds are borrowed either through direct negotiation with the lending institution or through New York brokers. The lending institution instructs the Fed or its own bank to transfer the agreed-on balances to the borrower. Because most Fed Funds transactions are overnight, the transaction is reversed the next day, including one day's interest. The Fed Funds rate is extremely important in monetary policy decisions on a daily basis. To make short-term adjustments in the supply of funds, the New York Fed will be instructed by the Fed to keep the Fed Funds within a desired range by buying or selling funds.

Source: See Marcia Stigum. The Money Market. *Homewood, IL: Dow Jones-Irwin, 1990; and Marcia Stigum.* Money Market Calculations: Yields, Breakevens, and Arbitrage. *Homewood, IL: Dow Jones-Irwin, 1981 for in-depth discussions of money market securities and yields.*

figure   **8.13**   EXAMPLE OF BANKER'S ACCEPTANCE FINANCING OF U.S. IMPORTS: A BANKER'S ACCEPTANCE IS CREATED, DISCOUNTED, SOLD, AND PAID AT MATURITY

Mechanically speaking, banker's acceptances are among the most complex money market instruments. In this example, a banker's acceptance is created as a result of a purchase of imported goods by a U.S. firm. The purchaser's bank, assumed to be Chase Manhattan, initially extends credit to pay for the goods. Chase, in turn, borrows the funds from a money market investor by issuing a banker's acceptance. When the acceptance matures, Chase repays the investor, using funds repaid to it by the importer.

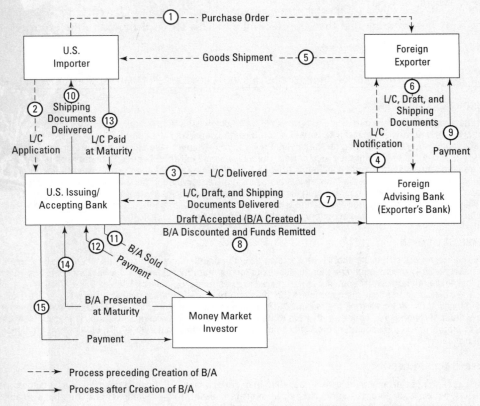

- - - -▸ Process preceding Creation of B/A

———▸ Process after Creation of B/A

Source: Adapted by the authors from Eric Hill, "Bankers' Acceptances," in Instruments of the Money Market *(Richmond, VA: Federal Reserve Bank of Richmond, 1986), 127.*

which notifies the exporter, upon which the exporter sends the goods to the importer, along with shipping documents and a time draft, asking for payment in a certain number of days. When the bank accepts this draft, it becomes a banker's acceptance. If the bank pays the draft, the importer owes the bank this sum. The banker's acceptance can be sold by the bank at a discount and traded among investors like other money market securities, to be paid after the bank is paid by the importer at maturity.

Calculating Yields for Negotiable CDs and Fed Funds

Some money market securities, including Fed Funds and negotiable CDs, rather than selling for a discount and paying a higher maturity value, sell at par value and pay interest and principal at maturity. Effective rates are calculated similar to those for T-bills. In this case P_O is the par value of amount invested and P_1 is the amount received at maturity, equal to the interest earned at the quoted rate (d) on the CD as a function of a 360-day year, as follows:

$$P_1 = \text{Amount Invested} \left[1 + \frac{(d \times n)}{360} \right] \qquad [8.10]$$

1 How do you calculate an annual yield for a Treasury bill?

2 What is the difference between a discount yield, a coupon equivalent yield, and an effective annual yield?

3 Given a discount yield quotation, how do you find the price of a T-bill?

4 What are the general characteristics of money market securities, and why do their rates tend to move close together?

5 Briefly describe the characteristics of a negotiable CD, a banker's acceptance, a Eurodollar CD, and commercial paper.

For example, if a 180-day negotiable CD had a face value of $1 million and a coupon rate (d) of 3.5 percent, the investor would receive at maturity P_1, as follows:

$$P_1 = \$1 \text{ million} \left[1 + \frac{(0.035 \times 180)}{360} \right] = \$1.0175 \text{ million}$$

Once you have the maturity value (P_1) for the negotiable CD, the coupon equivalent yield and effective annual are calculated just as before for T-bills, using P_1 in place of the Par value. For instance, the effective annual yield (y^*) for the bill can be computed by using Equation 8.7:

$$y^* = [Par \text{ (or } P_1) / P_0]^{(365/n)} - 1 = [1.0175 \text{ mil.} / 1 \text{ mil.}]^{(365/180)} - 1 = 0.03581, \text{ or } 3.581\%$$

PART B: CURRENCY EXCHANGE RATES

Financial institutions active in international markets face **exchange rate risk,** or variability in NIM (net interest margin) caused by fluctuations in currency exchange rates. Exchange rate risk increased significantly in 1971 when, as explained in the Appendix to Chapter 3, the United States officially abandoned the gold standard and allowed its currency exchange rate to float. Although many other currencies had been pegged to the value of the U.S. dollar, since 1973 most have been allowed to float. As a result, institutions that have foreign branches, issue banker's acceptances, purchase foreign securities, accept deposits in foreign currencies, or provide loans in the international markets are exposed to exchange rate risk.

Figure 8.14 tracks real effective exchange rates for four countries against that country's trading partners from 1986 through 2003. The fluctuations illustrate the uncertainty faced in international finance, with great volatility in effective exchange rates for the Euro area, the United States, Japan, and the United Kingdom. For instance, the United States had an index close to 180 in 1985, but less than 100 in 1995, representing an 80 percent fall in ten years. As noted when discussing interest rates, these effective exchange rates affect the prices that countries pay for goods from other countries, which in turn affects expected inflation rates and nominal interest rates. Figure 8.15 tracks exchange rates for three foreign currencies against the U.S. dollar and the U.S. dollar against its trade-weighted trading partners from 1999 to 2003. The darker line reflects the exchange rates and the lighter line the area's inflation differential. The fluctuations in exchange rates illustrate the uncertainty faced in international finance. For example, during this relatively short period, the graph shows that a U.S. dollar was worth more than 1.10 Euros in mid-2001, but fell to be worth 0.85 Euros in mid-2003. Similarly, a U.S. dollar could have been exchanged for over 130 yen in early 2002, but fell to be worth less than 120 yen in 2003. The rates plotted are **spot rates,** or rates for immediate exchanges between currencies. In the foreign exchange markets, spot rates are distinguished from forward rates, which are agreed on today for currency exchanges that will occur at a future date. Differences between forward and spot rates are discussed later.[26]

---

26 Even more dramatic changes in exchange rates occurred during the Russian and Asian currency crises that occurred in 1998. For information on these crises, see Marianne Sullivan. "Russia's Crisis Affects Latin America As Several Currencies There Weaken." *The Wall Street Journal* (August 27, 1998), C17; Andrew Higgins and Mark Whitehouse. "Russia Quits Fight to Back the Ruble." *The Wall Street Journal International Edition* (August 27, 1998), C1; Darren McDermott and Leslie Lopez. "Malaysia Imposes Sweeping Currency Controls." *The Wall Street Journal International* (September 2, 1998), A10; Darren McDermott and Raphael Pura. "Malaysian Currency Controls Roil Asia Markets." *The Wall Street Journal International* (September 3, 1998), A14; and "Japan's 6-Month T-Bill Yield Is Negative." *The Wall Street Journal* (November 6, 1998), C1, C19.

figure 8.14 SPOT EXCHANGE RATE TRENDS

Exchange rates among currencies fluctuate, sometimes considerably. In recent years, the value of the U.S. dollar has changed frequently in relation to other major currencies.

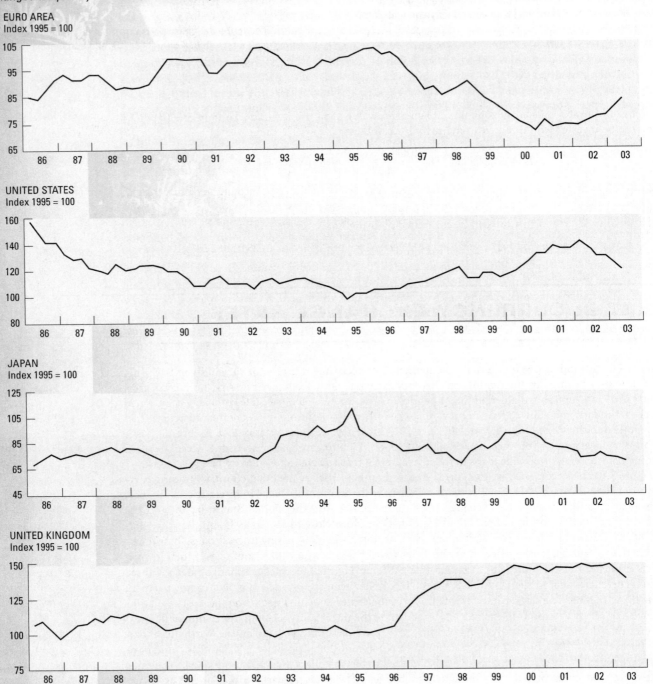

Note: Real effective exchange rates use normalized unit labor costs in manufacturing. The weighting scheme used to construct the rates, for all except the Euro area, is based on disaggregated data for trade among twenty-one industrial countries in manufactured goods for 1995. For the Euro area the weights relate to the trade of the Euro area with the other countries. The weights reflect the relative importance of a country's trading partners in its direct bilateral trade relations and competition in third markets. Normalized unit labor costs in manufacturing are calculated by dividing an index of actual hourly compensation per worker by a five-year moving average index of output per man-hour.

Source: *Federal Reserve Bank of St. Louis,* International Economic Trends, *November 2003, pp. 9, 15, 32, 38, 46.*

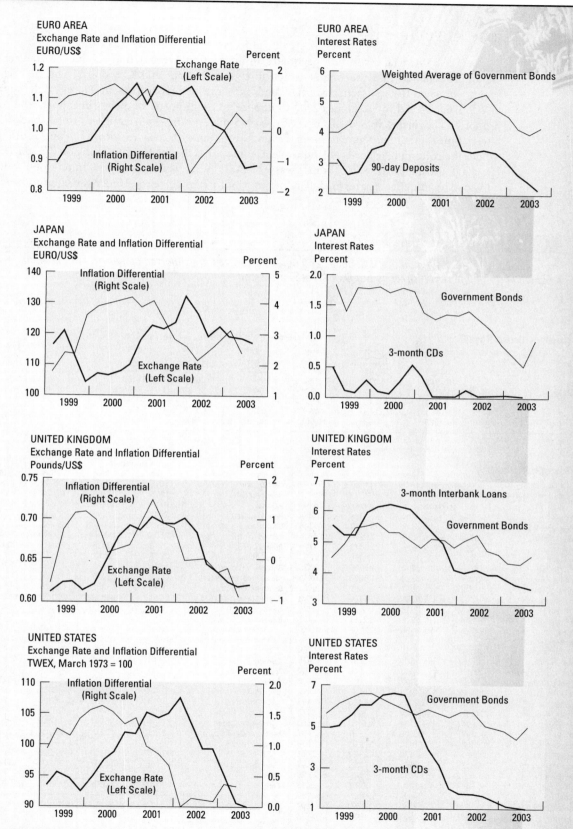

Note: The exchange rate for all countries except the United States is expressed as units of local currency per U.S. dollar. For the United States the trade-weighted exchange rate, TWEX, is used. This is a weighted average of the exchange value of the U.S. dollar relative to the major international currencies—the Euro, Canadian dollar, Japanese yen, British pound, Swiss franc, Australian dollar, and Swedish kronor. Prior to 1999, the currencies of the Euro area countries (with the exception of Greece) are used instead of the Euro. Inflation differential = Foreign inflation less U.S. inflation.

Source: *Federal Reserve Bank of St. Louis,* International Economic Trends, *November 2003, pp. 12, 29, 35, 41, 42.*

Exchange Rate Risk

Whenever a financial institution negotiates an international transaction involving a transfer of funds at a later date, so that the rate at which foreign currencies and U.S. dollars will be exchanged is unknown when the transaction is negotiated, exchange rate risk is present. For example, suppose that a U.S. bank agreed in December 2002 to finance a U.S. importer of Swiss chocolates. The cost of the imported chocolates, in Swiss francs (SF), was 25 million; the exporter agreed to pay back the loan in Swiss francs and did not have to pay back funds until June 19, 2003. As shown in Panel A of Figure 8.16 under the column labeled "U.S. $ Equivalent," the spot exchange rate prevailing on Tuesday, December 10, 2002, for the Switzerland (Franc) was 0.6844. In other words, one Swiss franc would buy $0.6844 U.S. dollars, the **direct rate,** or dollars per unit of foreign currency. Under the column headed "Cur-

figure **8.16** FOREIGN EXCHANGE RATES

Spot and forward exchange rates between the U.S. dollar and other currencies are reported daily in the financial pages. Both direct (U.S. $ Equivalent) and indirect (Currency per U.S. $) rates are listed.

PANEL A:

Key Currency Cross Rates

Late New York Trading Tuesday, December 10, 2002

	Dollar	Euro	Pound	SFranc	Peso	Yen	CdnDlr
Canada	1.5605	1.5735	2.4513	1.0680	.15345	.01260	...
Japan	123.81	124.84	194.48	84.734	12.174	...	79.336
Mexico	10.1698	10.2542	15.975	6.9602	...	.08214	6.5168
Switzerland	1.4611	1.4733	2.2951	...	.14367	.01180	.9363
U.K.	.63660	.6419	...	.4357	.06260	.00514	.40794
Euro	.99180	...	1.5579	.67877	.09752	.00801	.63553
U.S.	...	1.0083	1.5708	.68440	.09833	.00808	.64080

Source: Reuters

Exchange Rates

The foreign exchange mid-range rates below apply to trading among banks in amounts of $1 million and more, as quoted at 4 p.m. Eastern time by Reuters and other sources. Retail transactions provide fewer units of foreign currency per dollar.

	U.S. $ EQUIVALENT		CURRENCY PER U.S. $	
Country	Tue	Mon	Tue	Mon
Argentina (Peso)-y	.2845	.2829	3.5149	3.5348
Australia (Dollar)	.5594	.5639	1.7876	1.7734
Bahrain (Dinar)	2.6524	2.6526	.3770	.3770
Brazil (Real)	.2627	.2639	3.8066	3.7893
Canada (Dollar)	.6408	.6400	1.5605	1.5625
1-month forward	.6400	.6392	1.5625	1.5645
3-months forward	.6385	.6377	1.5662	1.5681
6-months forward	.6361	.6354	1.5721	1.5738
Chile (Peso)	.001424	.001418	702.25	705.22
China (Renminbi)	.1208	.1208	8.2781	8.2781
Colombia (Peso)	.0003544	.0003556	2821.67	2812.15
Czech. Rep. (Koruna)				
Commercial rate	.03238	.03250	30.883	30.769
Denmark (Krone)	.1357	.1361	7.3692	7.3475
Ecuador (US Dollar)	1.0000	1.0000	1.0000	1.0000
Hong Kong (Dollar)	.1282	.1282	7.8003	7.8003
Hungary (Forint)	.0004268	.004275	234.30	233.92
India (Rupee)	.02075	.02075	48.193	48.193
Indonesia (Rupiah)	.0001114	.0001114	8977	8977
Israel (Shekel)	.2142	.2134	4.6685	4.6860
Japan (Yen)	.008077	.008106	123.81	123.37
1-month forward	.008089	.008118	123.62	123.18
3-months forward	.008106	.008136	123.37	122.91
6-months forward	.008136	.008165	122.91	122.47
Jordan (Dinar)	1.4092	1.4092	.7096	.7096
Kuwait (Dinar)	3.3167	3.3187	.3015	.3013
Lebanon (Pound)	.0006634	.0006634	1507.39	1507.39
Malaysia (Ringgit)-b	.2632	.2632	3.7994	3.7994
Malta (Lira)	2.4261	2.4328	.4122	.4110
Mexico (Peso)				
Floating rate	.0983	.0979	10.1698	10.2176

	U.S. $ EQUIVALENT		CURRENCY PER U.S. $	
Country	Tue	Mon	Tue	Mon
New Zealand (Dollar)	.5015	.5032	1.9940	1.9873
Norway (Krone)	.1375	.1382	7.2727	7.2359
Pakistan (Rupee)	.01713	.01714	58.377	58.343
Peru (new Sol)	.2841	.2840	3.5199	3.5211
Philippines (Peso)	.01875	.01877	53.333	53.277
Poland (Zloty)	.2528	.2536	3.9557	3.9432
Russia (Ruble)-a	.03138	.03138	31.867	31.867
Saudi Arabia (Riyal)	.2666	.2667	3.7509	3.7495
Singapore (Dollar)	.5662	.5669	1.7662	1.7640
Slovak Rep. (Koruna)	.02415	.02420	41.408	41.322
South Africa (Rand)	.1112	.1101	8.9928	9.0827
South Korea (Won)	.0008251	.0008282	1211.97	1207.44
Sweden (Krona)	.1111	.1112	9.0009	8.9928
Switzerland (Franc)	.6844	.6861	1.4611	1.4575
1-month forward	.6849	.6866	1.4601	1.4565
3-months forward	.6857	.6874	1.4584	1.4548
6-months forward	.6871	.6887	1.4554	1.4520
Taiwan (Dollar)	.02878	.02881	34.746	34.710
Thailand (Baht)	.02305	.02304	43.384	43.403
Turkey (Lira)	.00000064	.00000064	1562500	1562500
U.K. (Pound)	1.5708	1.5794	.6366	.6332
1-month forward	1.5673	1.5758	.6380	.6346
3-months forward	1.5609	1.5695	.6407	.6371
6-months forward	1.5511	1.5597	.6447	.6411
United Arab (Dirham)	.2723	.2723	3.6724	3.6724
Uruguay (Peso)				
Financial	.03650	.3650	27.397	27.397
Venezuela (Bolivar)	.000771	.000767	1297.02	1303.78
SDR	1.3337	1.3261	.7498	.7541
Euro	1.0083	1.0106	.9918	.9895

Special Drawing Rights (SDR) are based on exchange rates for the U.S., British, and Japanese currencies. Source: International Monetary Fund.
a-Russian Central Bank rate. b-Government rate. y-Floating rate.

Source: The Wall Street Journal, *December 11, 2002, C13.*

rency per U.S. $," the spot rate is quoted as an **indirect rate,** or units of foreign currency per dollar: SF/$1.4611. Thus, one U.S. dollar would buy 1.4611 Swiss francs. Direct and indirect rates are reciprocals.

The Swiss funds that the bank lent to the importer in dollars on December 10, 2002, would have cost the bank SF25,000,000 × $0.6844 = $17,110,000. The bank faced uncertainty because the SF25,000,000 would be paid back approximately two months later, and the actual dollar value of the Swiss currency that the bank would receive could be worth more or less than **$17,110,000.** In fact, Panel B of Figure 8.16 shows that on Thursday, June 19, 2003, the direct spot rate was 0.7609 and the indirect spot rate was 1.3142. The value of the dollar had fallen, and SF25,000,000 received from the customer would now be worth SF25,000,000 × $0.7609 = **$19,022,500.** In this example, the bank benefited from the rise in the Swiss franc relative to the dollar, **receiving $1,912,500 more back than it lent** ($19,022,500 received − $17,110,000 lent). However, the bank could just as easily have seen a fall in the value of the Swiss franc and received less than it lent, if the value of the Swiss franc had fallen relative to the dollar over this

figure 8.16 FOREIGN EXCHANGE RATES (CONTINUED)

PANEL B:

Key Currency Cross Rates

Late New York Trading Thursday, June 19, 2003

	Dollar	Euro	Pound	SFranc	Peso	Yen	CdnDlr
Canada	1.3432	1.5745	2.2549	1.0220	.12792	.01135	...
Japan	118.32	138.69	198.63	90.026	11.268	...	88.086
Mexico	10.4998	12.3079	17.627	7.9893	...	.08874	7.8171
Switzerland	1.3142	1.5405	2.2063	...	.12517	.01111	.9784
U.K.	.59570	.6982	...	.4532	.05673	.00503	.44347
Euro	.85310	...	1.4322	.64912	.08125	.00721	.63513
U.S.	...	1.1722	1.6788	.76090	.09524	.00845	.74450

Source: Reuters

Exchange Rates

The foreign exchange mid-range rates below apply to trading among banks in amounts of $1 million and more, as quoted at 4 p.m. Eastern time by Reuters and other sources. Retail transactions provide fewer units of foreign currency per dollar.

Country	U.S. $ EQUIVALENT Thu	Wed	CURRENCY PER U.S. $ Thu	Wed
Argentina (Peso)-y	.3568	.3568	2.8027	2.8027
Australia (Dollar)	.6713	.6729	1.4896	1.4861
Bahrain (Dinar)	2.6523	2.6522	.3770	.3770
Brazil (Real)	.3463	.3463	2.8877	2.8877
Canada (Dollar)	.7445	.7481	1.3432	1.3367
1-month forward	.7430	.7467	1.3459	1.3392
3-months forward	.7402	.7440	1.3510	1.3441
6-months forward	.7366	.7403	1.3576	1.3508
Chile (Peso)	.001416	.001414	706.21	707.21
China (Renminbi)	.1208	.1208	8.2781	8.2781
Colombia (Peso)	.0003534	.0003540	2829.65	2824.86
Czech. Rep. (Koruna)				
Commercial rate	.03718	.03711	26.896	26.947
Denmark (Krone)	.1579	.1574	6.3331	6.3532
Ecuador (US Dollar)	1.0000	1.0000	1.0000	1.0000
Egypt (Pound)	.1671	.1670	5.9852	5.9898
Hong Kong (Dollar)	.1282	.1282	7.8003	7.8003
Hungary (Forint)	.004427	.004365	225.89	229.10
India (Rupee)	.02150	.02150	46.512	46.512
Indonesia (Rupiah)	.0001212	.0001215	8251	8230
Israel (Shekel)	.2279	.2279	4.3879	4.3879
Japan (Yen)	.008452	.008488	118.32	117.81
1-month forward	.008460	.008496	118.20	117.70
3-months forward	.008474	.008511	118.01	117.50
6-months forward	.008493	.008532	117.74	117.21
Jordan (Dinar)	1.4104	1.4104	.7090	.7090
Kuwait (Dinar)	3.3487	3.3448	.2985	.2990
Lebanon (Pound)	.0006634	.0006634	1507.39	1507.39
Malaysia (Ringgit)-b	.2632	.2632	3.7994	3.7994
Malta (Lira)	2.7370	2.7315	.3654	.3661
Mexico (Peso)				
Floating rate	.0952	.0942	10.4998	10.6180

Country	U.S. $ EQUIVALENT Thu	Wed	CURRENCY PER U.S. $ Thu	Wed
New Zealand (Dollar)	.5837	.5842	1.7132	1.7117
Norway (Krone)	.1436	.1432	6.9638	6.9832
Pakistan (Rupee)	.01733	.01734	57.703	57.670
Peru (new Sol)	.2881	.2881	3.4710	3.4710
Philippines (Peso)	.01877	.01872	53.277	53.419
Poland (Zloty)	.2618	.2634	3.8197	3.7965
Russia (Ruble)-a	.03292	.03291	30.377	30.386
Saudi Arabia (Riyal)	.2667	.2666	3.7495	3.7509
Singapore (Dollar)	.5783	.5777	1.7292	1.7310
Slovak Rep. (Koruna)	.02810	.02806	35.587	35.638
South Africa (Rand)	.1263	.1262	7.9177	7.9239
South Korea (Won)	.0008344	.0008432	1198.47	1185.96
Sweden (Krona)	.1290	.1291	7.7519	7.7459
Switzerland (Franc)	.7609	.7557	1.3142	1.3233
1-month forward	.7614	.7563	1.3134	1.3222
3-months forward	.7622	.7572	1.3120	1.3207
6-months forward	.7634	.7585	1.3099	1.3184
Taiwan (Dollar)	.02894	.02899	34.554	34.495
Thailand (Baht)	.02406	.02403	41.563	41.615
Turkey (Lira)	.00000070	.00000071	1428571	1408451
U.K. (Pound)	1.6788	1.6788	.5957	.5957
1-month forward	1.6752	1.6752	.5969	.5969
3-months forward	1.6678	1.6678	.5996	.5996
6-months forward	1.6577	1.6577	.6032	.6032
United Arab (Dirham)	.2723	.2722	3.6724	3.6738
Uruguay (Peso)				
Financial	.03810	.03810	26.247	26.247
Venezuela (Bolivar)	.000626	.000626	1597.44	1597.44
SDR	1.4190	1.4234	.7047	.7025
Euro	1.1722	1.1688	.8531	.8556

Special Drawing Rights (SDR) are based on exchange rates for the U.S., British, and Japanese currencies, Source: International Monetary Fund.
a-Russian Central Bank rate. b-Government rate. y-Floating rate.

Source: The Wall Street Journal, *June 20, 2003, C14.*

period. We will explain in a later section that changes in relative interest rates among major economies often lead to changes in the relative values of their currencies on the worldwide market. In this instance, the U.S. dollar fell in value relative to other currencies, perhaps partially because the Federal Reserve lowered its target interest rate over this period to stimulate the economy and the United States went to war in Iraq, among many other factors that resulted in the fall in the U.S. exchange rate. Because they can rarely forecast with precision the actions of regulators or other market participants over whom they have no control, financial institution managers face exchange rate variability, such as that illustrated here, whenever they engage in international commerce.[27]

The Forward Currency Market

A discussion of exchange rate risk would be incomplete without mention of a mechanism heavily used by investors, nonfinancial firms, and financial institutions to reduce the uncertainty about exchange rates during a planning period—the **forward currency market.** A forward exchange is an agreement between two parties to exchange a specified amount of one currency for another, at a specified future date and a specified rate of exchange. The forward rate that is agreed on may differ from the spot rate at the time of negotiation and also from the spot rate at the time the exchange actually occurs.

Forward rates are quoted daily along with spot rates. For many currencies, rates for 30-, 90-, and 180-day forward exchanges are reported. In Figure 8.16, all three forward rates are quoted for the Swiss franc. As of December 10, 2002, the direct forward rates for 1-month, 3-months, and 6-months forward were more than the spot rate. If the U.S. bank, in its agreement to finance the Swiss chocolate importer, had wanted to lock in a rate in the forward market to protect against a fall in the value of the Swiss franc relative to the dollar, it could have negotiated an agreement. Since the loan was due in about six months, the bank would have wished to negotiate a forward contract for 180 days (six months later) at 0.6871, guaranteeing that given direct forward exchange rate. Locking in this rate, the bank would have been able to convert the SF25,000,000 × $0.6871 U.S. $ equivalent to $17,177,500, closer to the dollar value of the funds lent on December 10, 2003, of $17,110,000. The forward rate is favorable compared with December's spot rate, and the bank could base its plans on this figure. The uncertainty about the dollar commitment to be received in June would have been eliminated. A forward transaction could, however, lock a financial institution into an exchange rate less desirable than the spot rate that actually prevailed on December 10, 2003. Still, the potential for a favorable movement in rates could have been traded for certain knowledge of the rate of exchange. Of course, as things turned out on June 19, 2003, the bank was happy that it did not lock in this forward rate. However, if the direct rate for the Swiss franc had fallen during this period, the bank might have had losses as large as its current gains.

On average, forward rates are reasonably good indicators of future spot rates, so in this instance managers might have predicted that spot rates in June for the Swiss francs would be greater than that in December. But averages, by definition, are based on the results of many transactions occurring above and below the mean. In this case, in fact, spot rates in June were actually higher for the Swiss franc than for the 30- or 90-day forward rates predicted in December. As these examples suggest, to determine whether spot or forward exchange transactions are appropriate, managers must understand the reasons behind exchange rate fluctuations.

Theories of Exchange Rate Determination

Exchange rate variability has been the focus of much academic research. Some theories focus on supply/demand relationships for goods and services; others focus more specifically on comparative inflation rates or interest rates among nations.

Supply and Demand for Goods and Services

A fundamental factor influencing exchange rates is the demand for goods and services produced in one country relative to the demand for goods and services produced in another. Imbalances may lead to

---

27 Details on the microstructure of foreign exchange markets and illustrative transactions (using the colorful vocabulary of the markets) are found in Flood (1991).

trade or balance-of-payments deficits that eventually affect currency exchange rates. Suppose, for example, that the demand for California wine in France is greater than the demand for French wine in the United States. The demand for U.S. dollars with which to buy California wine will exceed Americans' demand for French francs to buy French wine. An excess supply of French francs will develop in the currency markets, and the value of the franc will fall. The reverse would apply if Americans demanded relatively more French wine; the value of the dollar would fall compared with the franc. In brief, an increase in the demand for a country's goods and services should lead to an increase in the value of that country's currency, and a decrease in demand for its goods and services should lead to currency depreciation.

Under a managed floating exchange rate system, such as that described in the Appendix of Chapter 3, trade imbalances leading to exchange rate fluctuations are somewhat self-correcting. If the value of the French franc falls because the French are exchanging their money to buy California wine, California wine will begin to seem more expensive. Even if the dollar price of California wine does not change, subsequent wine purchases by the French will cost more because more francs will be required to purchase the same amount of dollars. Eventually, the demand for California wine may diminish among the French and they will begin to purchase more French wine. As fewer francs are changed into dollars, the supply of francs in the currency markets will fall, and the value of francs will rise relative to the dollar.

Floating Exchange Rates as Adjusters for International Monetary Surpluses and Deficits

Floating exchange rates serve to help adjust countries' monetary surpluses and deficits, which also affect the exchange rate for its currency. If a country has a large international deficit, it tends to import more from other countries and export less, resulting in more demand for the currency of other countries and less for its own currency. Economic forces for trading partners of countries with floating exchange rates help to make adjustments, since as a country's exchange rate for its currency falls, its goods become relatively cheaper, increasing demand for that country's goods and increasing exporting. When a trading partner, however, has a pegged versus floating exchange rate, such an economic adjustment cannot happen. For example, in 2003, China, a major trading partner of the United States, pegged the yuan to the dollar, keeping the exchange rate for the yuan low, despite the fact that the floating exchange rate for the dollar was falling. Hence, Chinese products would remain cheap, encouraging importing by consumers in the United States, while U.S. products would remain expensive for Chinese consumers, discouraging exporting from the United States to China. As noted in Figure 8.10, this may help to partially explain the fall in the core CPI for consumer goods in the United States in 2002 and 2003, with import prices falling at this time.

Relative Inflation Rates

The California wine illustration assumes no change in the dollar prices of California wines, but changes in the prices of goods *do* occur. The **purchasing power parity theorem** ties exchange rates to differential inflation rates across countries. The theorem states that relatively high inflation in one country will be accompanied by a *depreciation* of its currency relative to currencies in countries with lower inflation rates. In other words, there is an inverse relationship between differences in inflation rates and changes in currency values.

Suppose that a drought in the western United States greatly reduces harvests on most agricultural products, including Chardonnay grapes, which are used to produce some of California's finest white wines. Even with no increase in demand, the price of California wine will increase, along with the price of most goods dependent on agriculture. More francs must be exchanged to import California wines and other U.S. products, not because the exchange rate has changed, but because U.S. prices have increased. If French goods of comparable quality are less expensive because they escape the drought, French *and* U.S. citizens will increase their demand for French products. As more dollars are exchanged for francs and fewer francs are exchanged for dollars, the value of the dollar will fall. The purchasing power parity theorem holds that the value of the dollar will decline because inflation in the United States exceeds that in France.

Graphical Evidence of the Effect of Relative Inflation on Exchange Rates

The left panel of Figure 8.15 provides graphs of not only exchange rates but also inflation differentials (foreign inflation less U.S. inflation). For the graphs for the Euro and Japan, there is a clear relationship with higher exchange rates, particularly in 2002, when the differential inflation is lower. A similar relationship is shown for U.S. exchange rates in 2002, although the relationship for the United Kingdom is less clear.

Relative Interest Rates

Yet another theory suggests that exchange rates are closely tied to interest rates. The previous two theories have focused on consumption goods and services, but currencies also travel among countries as a result of the purchase and sale of financial assets. The **interest rate parity theorem** asserts that interest rates and exchange rates are interdependent: If interest rates in one country differ from those in another, supply and demand for the currencies of the two countries can be affected. According to this theory, when interest rates in the United States are high relative to those in other countries, foreign investors will demand U.S. dollars so that they can take advantage of more desirable rates of return. Exchange rates will then adjust to reflect the interest rate differentials; in this example, the value of the dollar will increase as demand exceeds supply.

Figure 8.17 provides a concrete example of the workings of interest rate parity. As the left panel shows, for many months before September 1992, the German discount rate had been rising as Japanese and U.S. central bank rates were falling. Market rates in the three countries followed the lead of central bank rates (right panel). Thus, investors all over the world were changing U.S. dollars into Deutschmarks to take advantage of high yields on German securities. Central banks in other European countries had also kept their interest rates high to maintain their currencies' value relative to the Deutschmark. But many of these currencies were mired in recessions, so the higher rates were hurting them domestically even as they helped in the foreign exchange markets. Finally, under pressure from its G-7 trading partners (the United States, Canada, France, Great Britain, Italy, Japan, and Germany, which agreed to coordinate efforts to keep the U.S. dollar within a specified trading range relative to other currencies), the German central bank cut its discount rate by 1/4% (not shown in Figure 8.17). Because the spread between U.S. and German rates narrowed, the immediate reaction in world mar-

figure **8.17**   RELATIVE INTEREST RATES IN GERMANY, JAPAN, AND THE UNITED STATES

During the early 1990s, the German central bank raised its discount rate as central banks in the United States and Japan lowered theirs. Market interest rates in the three countries followed the lead of central bank rates. These differences in interest rates affected currency exchange rates.

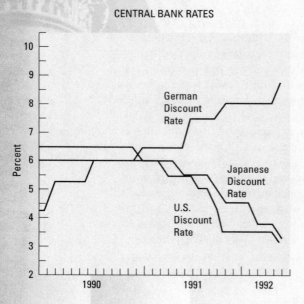

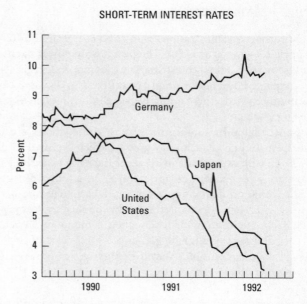

Source: Federal Reserve Bank of Cleveland, Economic Trends, *August 1992, p. 18.*

kets was to increase the value of the U.S. dollar. Although the long-term effects of the German bank's action are more complex and beyond the intent of this chapter, the importance of relative interest rates to exchange rate determination is clear.

Prior to the advent of the Euro, participating countries started to coordinate central bank actions. In a surprise move, on December 3, 1998, the central banks of the eleven countries participating in the coming European Monetary Union issued coordinated lower interest rates in response to softening economic conditions. Italy lowered its interest rate to 3.5 percent, with a promise of a further reduction in the weeks ahead. The other ten countries lowered their key interest rates to 3 percent. This was the first joint act of the new monetary union prior to the introduction of the Euro on January 1, 1999. Since that time, the European Union (EU) member states have expanded. Figure 8.18 shows the members and their location in Europe as of November 2003. At this time, twelve of the EU's fifteen member states share a single currency. The European Central Bank (ECB), set up in 1998 under the Treaty on the European Union, introduces and manages the Euro, including conducting foreign exchange operations and ensuring a smooth payment system. The ECB also frames and implements the EU's economic and monetary policy, working with the European System of Central Banks (ESCB) covering all fifteen EU countries. The ECB has a target to keep inflation under control, ensuring a year-by-year consumer

figure   **8.18**   EUROPEAN UNION MEMBER STATES

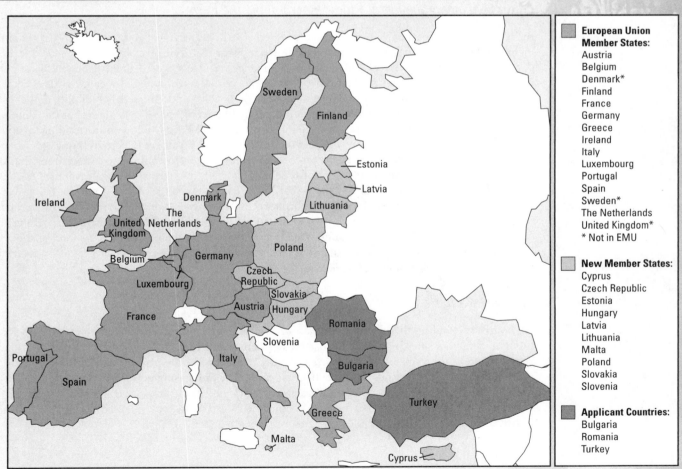

Note: Each country's name and place names are in the local language. Twelve of the EU's fifteen member states share a single currency (excluding the United Kingdom, Sweden, and Denmark).

Map source: Adapted from Europa—The E.U. at a Glance, http://europa.eu.int/abc/maps/index_en.htm.
© European Communities, 1995–2004.

price increase of less than 2 percent by controlling the money supply and monitoring price trends to assess the risk posed to price stability in the Euro area.[28]

Graphical Evidence of the Effect of Relative Interest Rates on Exchange Rates

The right panel of Figure 8.15 shows graphs of interest rates over time for the different countries. Although the relationships are less clear for other countries, the dramatic fall in short-term interest rates in 2002 and 2003 correspond to the fall in the U.S. exchange rate in 2002 and 2003. Again, relationships are complex, but the graphs do depict somewhat the effect of relative inflation and relative interest rates on exchange rates.

Controlling Inflation for the Euro

The European Monetary Union (EMU) marked significant progress in regulating inflation and by having a common currency reducing exchange rate problems across the twelve European member states in the EMU (Austria, Belgium, Finland, France, Germany, Greece, Ireland, Italy, Luxembourg, Portugal, Spain, and The Netherlands). To avoid inflation for the Euro, EMU countries were required to keep their budgets in surplus or run a deficit of no more than 3 percent. When the Euro was introduced in 1999 and 2000, years when the world economy was doing well, all twelve countries managed to comply. However, in tougher economic times, the fiscal rules became constraining for some countries.

Politics Changing the Fiscal Rules Underpinning the Euro

By 2003, a few of the EMU countries had problems with excessive deficits over the 3 percent limit including Portugal, France, and Germany, as shown in Figure 8.19. Given economic problems for these countries, after much political debate, Europe's finance ministers agreed to suspend the fiscal rules underpinning the Euro. They made this decision despite criticism from the European Central Bank that this suspension could have "serious dangers" and risk that could "undermine the credibility of the institutional framework and the confidence in sound public finances." Accordingly, the European Union in late November 2003 suspended the fiscal rules underpinning the Euro to allow countries time to reduce their deficits. Whether a relaxation will hurt the stability of the Euro and the credit ratings of some of the twelve nations using the Euro has yet to be seen. Surprisingly, in contrast to expectations that the relaxation would hurt the exchange rate for the Euro, just after this relaxation, on November 28, 2003, the Euro rose to its highest level in its five-year history to an exchange rate of one Euro being worth $1.20, and rose even higher to $1.2703 on February 6, 2004. Analysts pointed out that this rise may have reflected the fact that the pact, which limited deficits of the twelve members of the EMU to 3 percent of their gross domestic product, could actually hurt growth in these countries by forcing them to "undertake draconian budget cuts" at times when they needed fiscal policies of expansion to revive demand for products in their countries.[29]

A Complex Puzzle

Obviously, integrating these three explanations of changes in currency exchange rates requires some thought. Thus far, one can conclude that greater demand for a nation's goods and services leads to appreciation in the value of its currency, assuming no change in the price level. But this limited scenario is insufficient when inflation or deflation occurs. The purchasing power parity theorem says that higher inflation in one country will lead to a *depreciation* of its currency, and the interest rate parity theorem states that higher interest rates in a country will lead to an *appreciation* of its currency. Yet the Fisher effect says that inflation rates and interest rates are directly related!

---

28 See Europa Website *(http://europa.eu.int/institutions/ecb/index_en.htm)*.

29 Under the terms of the stability pact, EMU countries were subject to a lengthy procedure of warnings and heavy fines if they failed to get deficits under the 3 percent ceiling. Mark Landler and Paul Meller, "France and Germany Given Time to Curb Deficits," *New York Times*, November 26, 2003, C1, C7; G. Thomas Sims, "EU Members Call for Review of Budget Pact," *The Wall Street Journal*, November 28, 2003, A6; Mark Landler, "Politics Rescue Euro from Stability Agreement," November 29, 2003, B1, B3; and "Euro Breaks $1.20 for First Time in History," *Denver Post*, November 29, 2003, 5C.

figure   8.19   EXCESSIVE DEFICITS OF EUROPEAN MONTEARY UNION COUNTRIES IN THE EARLY 2000s

PANEL A: SOME EMU COUNTRIES HAD DEFICITS EXCEEDING AGREED-ON 3 PERCENT BOUNDARY IN LATE 2003

OUT OF BOUNDS

As they prepared for monetary union, the 12 Euro nations agreed to keep their budgets in surplus, or run a deficit of no more than 3 percent. All 12 managed to comply in 1999 and 2000, when the common Euro currency was introduced and the world economy was thriving. But in recent years, first Portugal and then the union's two largest economies, France and Germany, have run deficits that broke the rules, and the European Union expects Italy to follow suit soon.

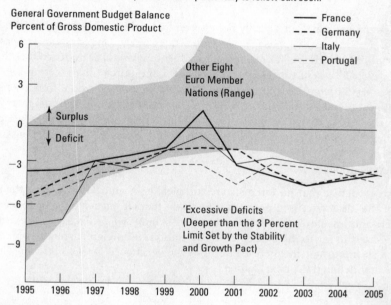

Source: Mark Landler and Paul Meller, "France and Germany Given More Time to Curb Deficits," New York Times, *November 26, 2003, C1.*

PANEL B: RISE IN THE EURO TO $1.20 IN 2003

CURRENCIES

| Currency | Yesterday | | Year | |
	Close	Change	to Date	52 Weeks
British pound (in U.S. dollars)	1.7216	+.0102	+6.83%	+11.29%
Canadian dollar (per U.S. dollar)	1.2983	−.0056	−17.50	−17.52
Euro (per U.S. dollar)	.8342	−.0037	−12.38	−17.40
Japanese yen (per U.S. dollar)	109.55	+.57	−7.74	−10.46
Mexican peso (per U.S. dollar)	11.3780	+.0335	+9.53	+12.26
South Korean won (per U.S. dollar)	1202.40	−.00	+1.40	2.41
U.S. Dollar Index	90.28	−.44	−12.18	−15.23

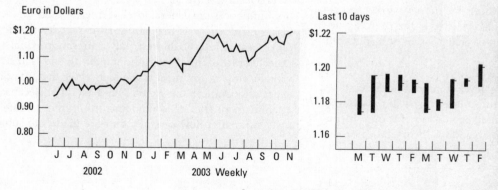

Source: New York Times, *Business Section November 29, 2003, p. B3.*

Concept Questions

1 What are three major factors that affect exchange rates? Provide examples of each of their effects.

2 Why do financial institution managers need to worry about exchange rate risk?

3 What is the difference between a spot and forward exchange rate price?

4 Given an example of how politics can have a significant effect on exchange rates.

What may seem confusing can actually be resolved by recalling Fisher's distinction between nominal and real rates of interest. Suppose that nominal rates in the United States increase as a result of expected inflation. Although the interest rate parity theorem would seem to predict that the U.S. dollar would appreciate as a result of higher interest rates, the purchasing power parity theorem helps managers recognize that increases in interest rates caused by inflation will ultimately result in depreciation, not appreciation, of the U.S. dollar. However, relatively high U.S. nominal rates that result from an increase in the real rate, signifying greater potential return on investment in goods and services, should strengthen the value of the dollar as investment in U.S. assets is seen as being more desirable.[30]

The Role of Expectations

Finance experts recognize that no forecasts are complete without acknowledging the role of expectations. Some of the ideas discussed previously focus on market participants' reactions to what *is*, but both consumers and investors also react to what they believe *will be*. Indeed, the existence of the forward market is a testimony to the influence of expectations in foreign currency exchanges. The role of expectations is so important in interest rate (and thus exchange rate) forecasting, in fact, that it is explored in greater detail in the next chapter.

Summary

ecause the net interest margin is the key variable in asset/liability management, understanding the behavior of interest rates is important. In increasingly global markets, the NIM is also affected by the value of one currency relative to others. This chapter discusses the general level of interest rates and currency exchange rates. It also discusses institutional details concerning money market securities and their prices and yields as well as exchange rate pricing. A brief overview is given of changes that occurred with the introduction of the Euro.

Because all interest rates tend to move in the same direction, a forecast for the general level of interest rates is a starting point for estimating future rates on specific assets and liabilities. The most widely used explanation for movements in the general level is the loanable funds theory, based on the

motivations for saving and borrowing. Although other factors also affect the decision, the dollar amount individuals are willing to save is positively related to interest rates, and the demand for borrowing is inversely related to interest rates. The equilibrium general level of interest rates is determined by the intersection of the supply and demand curves for loanable funds.

Economists have also hypothesized that expected inflation influences the general level of interest rates. In fact, the Fisher effect suggests that nominal market rates of interest reflect a real rate of interest plus a premium equal to the expected rate of inflation. Although this theory is difficult to validate empirically, most researchers agree that inflationary expectations affect the general level of rates. Because they attempt to predict an unknown future, interest rate forecasts, no matter how carefully they are made, are subject to

---

30 Further discussion of the parity theorems is found in Kubarych (1983), Shapiro (1983), and Giddy and Dufey (1975). Reconciling the theories is considered in Reuven Glick. "Global Interest Rate Linkages." *Weekly Letter, Federal Reserve Bank of San Francisco* (May 25, 1990); and Strongin (1990).

error. So, besides theories, financial institution managers must be aware of techniques to minimize the impact of forecasting errors on their institution's performance.

Exchange rate risk, or the rate variability at which one currency can be converted to another, is significant for all institutions participating in international markets, particularly for those that negotiate transactions today for execution at a later date. Such transactions may occur either at subsequent spot rates or at forward rates determined today.

Several theories have been advanced to explain exchange rate variability. In general, the value of a nation's currency should increase if demand increases for its goods and services or if interest rates are relatively high compared with those in other countries. The value of a country's currency should decrease, however, if its rate of inflation is relatively high. Both interest rates and exchange rates are influenced not only by contemporary developments but also by market participants' expectations of the future.

Questions

1. The Greg, Mary, and Verity McArthur Investment Company runs a bond mutual fund. Describe the direction and volatility of interest rate movements during the past two years. Discuss the expected effects of this interest rate environment on the management of their bond fund.

2. What choices are available to Greg, Mary, and Verity's bond fund for their use of funds? Why would the fund hold cash balances? Do interest rates affect these motives? If so, how?

3. Explain to Greg, Mary, and Verity what economic sector is a net supplier of loanable funds. How are the savings decisions of this sector affected by noninterest factors?

4. As a financial economist for a major bank, suppose you see a survey of consumer savings patterns in the United States revealing that Americans are saving less disposable income than in the past. Based on your knowledge of the loanable funds theory, explain to the bank's president, Marilyn Taylor, the potential effect of this trend on U.S. interest rates (assuming no increase in loanable funds from international investors).

5. Continuing as the financial economist for the major bank, explain to Bob Taylor, the bank's investment manager, why the federal government's demand for loanable funds is relatively inelastic with respect to interest rates.

6. Baine Kerr, the comptroller of the major bank, asks you how the business sector's demand for loanable funds relates to interest rates. Explain this to Baine. If corporate taxes are lowered, also explain to Baine how the demand curve for loanable funds would be affected.

7. You are a financial planner. A client, Patty Hamilton, asks you to explain the difference between the nominal rate and the real rate of interest. She also asks how inflation affects the real, ex post rate of return to investors. Explain this to Patty.

8. Beverly Walker, an artist and client of your financial planning firm, astutely asks you if the ex post real rate could be negative. Give an example to Beverly of this happening.

9. Explain to Gail Welply, president of a diversified financial firm in France, Fisher's theory of the relationship between the nominal rate of interest and expected inflation. Why would this relationship be important for Gail to know? Also, explain why Fisher's belief that the ex ante real rate of interest is constant has become controversial.

10. Doug Walker, your boss at the Rock Island Railroad Bank, has criticized you for your recent interest rate forecast. Explain some of the difficulties economists face in developing forecasts.

11. Your friend Carl Weeks is thinking of investing in a money market mutual fund. Explain to Carl the difference between money market securities and longer-term capital market securities. What special characteristics do money market securities have? What affects differences in yields for different types of money market securities?

12. Carl, your friend and a business college student, also asks you the following questions: What is a yield? How is it calculated for a money market security? What is the difference between a discount yield, annual yield, and effective annual yield? Answer his questions.

13. Explain to Bud Fogerty, owner of a Colorado importing firm, what a banker's acceptance is and how it is created. Why is this information important to Bud?

14. Hugh Ruppersburg, a Georgia exporter, asks you the difference between spot and forward rates in the foreign currency markets. He also asks you how a forward exchange agreement could assist him in reducing his exchange rate risk exposure. Explain this to Hugh.

15. How do changes in the supply of and demand for goods and services affect exchange rates between the currencies of two countries? How do relative changes in interest rates and inflation effect exchange rates between the currency of two countries? Why would these relations be important for Hugh, an exporter, to know?

Problems

1. Graph the supply and demand curves for loanable funds. What is meant by the equilibrium rate of interest?

2. Using the graph from Problem 1, show the effect on the equilibrium rate of interest if government borrowing increases while the demand for loanable funds from other sectors remains constant.

3. If the demand for loanable funds by the business sector decreases because of a recession and the demand for loanable funds by the government increases but by a smaller amount, how will the equilibrium interest rate be affected? Sketch the change on the same graph used in Problems 1 and 2.

4. Within the framework of the loanable funds theory, illustrate how inflation affects the equilibrium rate of interest.

5. Ignoring taxes, use the Fisher equation to calculate the nominal yield required by investors when the real rate of interest is 4 percent and the expected inflation rate is 5 percent. What will be the ex post real rate of return to an investor if inflation actually turns out to be 8 percent?

6. Redo Problem 5 assuming you want a 4 percent real rate of return after taxes and considering the investor has a marginal tax rate of 28 percent.

7. Suppose your favorite uncle expected to earn a real after-tax rate of return of 4.5 percent and demanded a nominal rate of 12.79 percent. (His marginal tax rate is 28 percent.)
   a. What rate of inflation was he expecting?
   b. Considering the fact that his actual after-tax real rate of return was only 2.5 percent, what was the ex post rate of inflation?

8. Several years ago, a Texas bank offered a thirty-year CD with an annual return indexed to inflation. The rate offered was the annual percentage increase in the CPI plus 4 percent. Suppose that you are in the 28 percent marginal tax bracket and require a 5 percent real return after taxes. Suppose also that the annual inflation rate last year was 3 percent, so this year's annual rate on the CD investment is set at 7 percent.
   a. Show the after-tax real return you would earn, assuming that the inflation rate stays at 3 percent and the CD rate offered is 7 percent.
   b. What ex ante nominal rate should you require instead to keep your after-tax real yield at 5 percent?

9. State College's Credit Union bid noncompetitively for a $10,000, 91-day T-bill. The average discount yield for the auction was 3.4 percent.
   a. What price did the credit union pay for the T-bill?
   b. What was the annual effective yield for the T-bill? What was its annual yield?

10. What is the effective annual yield on a 52-week T-bill selling at 93.27 percent of par with a 100 percent par value? What is the bank discount yield?

11. The discount yield on a ten-day, $100,000 reverse repurchase agreement is quoted in the market as 5.95 percent. Calculate the expected annual yield and effective annual yield for the reverse repo.

12. Robert Cooperman, president of Snow City Bank, plans to invest $4 million in a negotiable CD for 180 days. The bank offers a discount rate of 6.2 percent. What is the effective annual yield on the CD?

13. Refer to the exchange rates reported in Figure 8.16.
   a. Suppose that on December 10, 2002, your firm needed to pay a French exporter for goods received. The bill was 750,000 Euro. The direct exchange rate for the Euro, shown on Panel A of Figure 8.16, was one Euro equals $1.0083. What was the cost in dollars on December 10, 2002?
   b. If, on the same day, a Japanese corporation needed to pay your firm $3.5 million, what was the cost in yen? The direct rate for Japanese yen, shown on Panel A of Figure 18.16, was $0.008077.
   c. If the bill in part a was due on June 19, 2003, what would be the dollar value of 750,000 French francs with the direct rate for the Euro now $1.1722, as shown in Panel B of Figure 8.16? What would be the change in the dollar value of the bill from the direct rates quoted in part a?
   d. If the bill in part b was also due on June 19, 2003, what would be the cost in yen of the $3.5 million that the Japanese firm had to pay, with the direct rate for Japanese yen now $0.008452, as shown in Panel B of Figure 18.16? What would be the change in the yen value of the bill from the direct rate quoted in part b?

14. Suppose a Midwestern auto dealer must convert $2 million into yen to buy Japanese cars currently priced at 220 million yen. Calculate the implied direct rate of exchange between dollars and yen given these prices and the implied indirect exchange rate.

15. Suppose that the importer in Problem 14 had earlier locked in a forward exchange agreement at a direct rate for the yen of $0.0094. Under that agreement, how many U.S. dollars must be converted to cover the cost of the imported automobiles?

16. Suppose it is December 11, 2002, and the Crazy Boris Export Company plans to receive 200,000 British pounds in late June 2003. Based on the December 10, 2002 United Kingdom (UK) direct exchange rate of $1.5708 quoted from Figure 8.16, Panel A, what does the company expect to receive? Looking at the same panel, what would the firm receive in dollars if it took out a three-months forward contract for this amount? Note that the three-months forward direct rate is $1.5609 per British pound. What would it receive in dollars if it did not take out a contract and instead received the pounds on June 19, 2003? Note that the direct rate for the pound has changed to $1.6788 in June.

Selected References

Barth, James R., and Michael D. Bradley. "On Interest Rates, Inflationary Expectations and Tax Rates." *Journal of Banking and Finance* 12 (June, 1988), 210–220.

Belongia, Michael T. "Predicting Interest Rates: A Comparison of Professional and Market-Based Forecasts." *Review* (Federal Reserve Bank of St. Louis) 69 (March 1987), 915.

Bryan, Michael F., and William T. Gavin. "Comparing Inflation Expectations of Households and Economists: Is a Little Knowledge a Dangerous Thing?" *Economic Review* (Federal Reserve Bank of Cleveland) (Quarter 3, 1986), 1419.

Carlson, John A. "Short-Term Interest Rates as Predictors of Inflation: Comment." *American Economic Review* 67 (June 1977), 469–475.

Clarida, Richard D., and Benjamin M. Friedman. "The Behavior of U.S. Short-Term Interest Rates since October, 1979." *Journal of Finance* 39 (July 1984), 671–682.

Cox, William N., III. "Interest Rates and Inflation: What Drives What?" *Economic Review* (Federal Reserve Bank of Atlanta) 65 (May/June 1980), 20–23.

Croushore, Dean. "What Are the Costs of Disinflation?" *Business Review* (Federal Reserve Bank of Philadelphia) (May/June 1992), 3.

Darby, Michael R. "The Financial and Tax Effects of Monetary Policy on Interest Rates." *Economic Inquiry* 12 (June 1975), 266–276.

Dwyer, Gerald P., Jr., and R. W. Hafer. "Interest Rates and Economic Announcements." *Review* (Federal Reserve Bank of St. Louis) 71 (March/April 1989), 34–46.

Eugeni, Francesca, Charles Evans, and Steven Strongin. "Making Sense of Economic Indicators: A Consumer's Guide to Indicators of Real Economic Activity." *Economic Perspectives* (Federal Reserve Bank of Chicago) 16 (September/October 1992), 232.

Fama, Eugene A. "Short-Term Interest Rates as Predictors of Inflation." *American Economic Review* 65 (June 1975), 269–282.

Feldstein, Martin. "Inflation, Income Taxes and the Rate of Interest: A Theoretical Analysis." *American Economic Review* 66 (December 1976), 809–820.

Fisher, Irving. *The Theory of Interest.* New York: Macmillan, 1930.

Flood, Mark D. "Microstructure Theory and the Foreign Exchange Market." *Review* (Federal Reserve Bank of St. Louis) 73 (November/December 1991), 52–70.

Friedman, Benjamin. "Price Inflation, Portfolio Choice and Nominal Interest Rates." *American Economic Review* 70 (March 1980), 32–48.

Gibson, A. H. "The Future Course of High Class Investment Values." *Bankers Magazine* (London) 115 (January 1923), 15–34.

Giddy, Ian H., and Gunter Dufey. "The Random Behavior of Flexible Exchange Rates." *Journal of International Business Studies* 6 (Spring 1975), 1–32.

Hakkio, Craig S. "Interest Rates and Exchange Rates—What Is the Relationship?" *Economic Review* (Federal Reserve Bank of Kansas City) 71 (November 1986), 33–43.

Holland, A. Steven. "Real Interest Rates: What Accounts for Their Recent Rise?" *Review* (Federal Reserve Bank of St. Louis) 66 (December 1984), 18–29.

Humphrey, Thomas M. "The Early History of the Real/Nominal Interest Rate Relationship." *Economic Review* (Federal Reserve Bank of Richmond) 69 (May/June 1983), 2–10.

Keane, Michael P., and David E. Runkle. "Are Economic Forecasts Rational?" *Quarterly Review* (Federal Reserve Bank of Minneapolis) 13 (Spring 1989), 26–33.

Keynes, John Maynard. *The General Theory of Employment, Interest, and Money.* New York: Harcourt, Brace, and World (1936).

Kubarych, Roger M. *Foreign Exchange Markets in the United States,* 2nd ed. New York: Federal Reserve Bank of New York, 1983.

Leonard, David C., and Michael E. Solt. "Recent Evidence on the Accuracy and Rationality of Popular Inflation Forecasts." *Journal of Financial Research* 9 (Winter 1986), 281–290.

Mascaro, Angelo, and Allen H. Meltzer. "Long- and Short-Term Interest Rates in a Risky World." *Journal of Monetary Economics* 12 (November 1983), 485–518.

McNees, Stephen K. "Consensus Forecasts: Tyranny of the Majority?" *New England Economic Review* (Federal Reserve Bank of Boston) (November/December 1987), 15–21.

Mullineaux, Donald J., and Aris Protopapadakis. "Revealing Real Interest Rates: Let the Market Do It." *Business Review* (Federal Reserve Bank of Philadelphia) (March/April 1984), 3–8.

Mundell, Robert. "Inflation and Real Interest." *Journal of Political Economy* 71 (June 1963), 280–283.

Peek, Joe. "Inflation and the Excess Taxation of Personal Interest Income." *New England Economic Review* (Federal Reserve Bank of Boston) (March/April 1988), 46–52.

Polakoff, Murray E. "Loanable Funds Theory and Interest Rate Determination." In *Financial Institutions and Markets.* 2nd ed. Edited by Murray E. Polakoff and Thomas A. Durkin. Boston: Houghton Mifflin, 1981, 483–510.

Rose, Andrew K. "Is the Real Rate Stable?" *Journal of Finance* 43 (December 1988), 1095–1112.

Rosenblum, Harvey, and Steven Strongin. "Interest Rate Volatility in Historical Perspective." *Economic Perspectives* (Federal Reserve Bank of Chicago) 7 (January/February 1983), 10–19.

Santoni, G. J., and Courtenay C. Stone. "Navigating Through the Interest Rate Morass: Some Basic Principles." *Economic Review* (Federal Reserve Bank of St. Louis) 63 (March 1981), 11–18.

Santoni, G. J., and Courtenay Stone. "What Really Happened to Interest Rates?" *Economic Review* (Federal Reserve Bank of St. Louis) 63 (November 1981), 3–14.

Shapiro, Alan C. "What Does Purchasing Power Parity Mean?" *Journal of International Money and Finance* (December 1983), 295–318.

Shiller, Robert J., and Jeremy J. Siegel. "The Gibson Paradox and Historical Movements in Real Interest Rates." *Journal of Political Economy* 85 (October 1977), 891–907.

Strongin, Steven. "International Credit Market Connections." *Economic Perspectives* 14 (July/August 1990), 2–10.

Taylor, Herbert. "Interest Rates: How Much Does Expected Inflation Matter?" Business Review (Federal Reserve Bank of Philadelphia) (July/August 1982), 3–12.

"The Livingston Surveys: A History of Hopes and Fears." Business Review (Federal Reserve Bank of Philadelphia) (January/February 1992), 15–27.

Tobin, James. "Money and Economic Growth." *Econometrica* 33 (October 1965), 671–684.

Urang, Sally. "The Economists' Scoreboard." *Institutional Investor* 22 (March 1988), 251–256, and 23 (March 1989), 211–216.

Van Dyke, Daniel T. "Why Economists Make Mistakes." *Bankers Magazine* 169 (May/June 1986), 69–75.

Van Horne, James C. *Financial Market Rates and Flows,* 2nd ed. Englewood Cliffs, NJ: Prentice Hall, 1984.

Wallace, William H., and William E. Cullison. *Measuring Price Changes,* 4th ed. Richmond, VA: Federal Reserve Bank, 1979.

Wood, John H. "Interest Rates and Inflation." *Economic Perspectives* (Federal Reserve Bank of Chicago) 5 (May/June 1981), 3–12.

Yohe, William P., and Denis Karnosky. "Interest Rates and Price Level Changes, 1952–1969." *Review* (Federal Reserve Bank of St. Louis) 51 (December 1969), 18–39.

internet *exercise*

INTEREST RATES, EXCHANGE RATES, AND INFLATION: THEORIES AND FORECASTING

1. St. Louis Federal Reserve Economic Data (FRED): *http://www.stls.frb.org/fred2/*

    The St. Louis Federal Reserve Bank has an excellent economic database called FRED with graphs and data on CPIs, PPIs, interest rates, bank data, and other economic information. Go to http://www.stls .frb.org/fred2/. You'll see a menu with different data categories. Click on Interest Rates and then choose the first interest rate series, which will give you graphs and trends. Return to the home page and then click on Consumer Price Index (CPI), and you'll see a graph of CPI trends and the latest change in the Consumer Price Index. Similarly, if you click on Producer Price Index (PPI), you'll see a corresponding graph and recent changes in the Producer Price Index. Explore this site, and you'll find lots of interesting and useful data.

2. Cleveland Federal Reserve Economic Research and Data: *http://www.clevelandfed.org/index.cfm*

    The Cleveland Federal Reserve Bank also has excellent economic data. Go to *http://www.clevelandfed. org/index.cfm* and select Economic Research & Data on the menu. Click and you'll have a choice of economic data and research to look at. Click on CPI, and you'll find the latest changes in the CPI.

3. Survey of Professional Forecasters: *http://www.phil .frb.org/econ/spf/index.html*

    The Survey of Professional Forecasters is the oldest quarterly survey of macroeconomic forecasts in the United States. The survey began in 1968 and was conducted by the American Statistical Association and the National Bureau of Economic Research. The Federal Reserve Bank of Philadelphia took over the survey in 1990. To get the most recent forecast summary, click on the highlighted quarter under Most Current Release. This will provide a short summary of the forecasters' consensus on economic growth, interest rates, inflation expectations, and long-term expectations for real GDP growth and productivity. The main site also includes links for historical data on median forecasts, the forecasts by individual forecaster, and mean forecasts. Since the data go back to 1968, some of the files are available only in zipped format. In addition, there are tables for short-term inflation forecasts (over the next year) and long-term forecasts (over the next ten years). Finally, there is a useful bibliography of academic articles using the data from the survey.

USEFUL LINKS

NBER Macrohistory Database: Historical economic data for the United States

http://www.nber.org/databases/macrohistory/contents/ index.html

Fed in Print: An index to articles published by the Federal Reserve System

http://www.frbsf.org/publications/fedinprint/index.html

The Europa Website: Information, maps, historical information, and news on the European Union

http://europa.eu.int/abc/governments/index_en.htm

The Federal Reserve Bank of Cleveland Website: Download Economic Trends, providing graphs of exchange rates, interest rates, and other economic historical information

http://www.clevelandfed.org/Research/index.htm

The Federal Reserve Bank of St. Louis Website: Download St. Louis *Monetary Trends,* providing graphs of exchange rate, interest rates, and other economic historical information

http://www.stlouisfed.org/research

The Bureau of Economic Analysis (U.S. Department of Commerce): Detailed economic data including national and regional data

http://www.bea.doc.gov

SHORT INVESTIGATIVE PAPER EXERCISE

Using the Internet or other sources, look up articles on the Japanese economy and the problems it faced with deflation during 1998 to 2003, including recent articles. How did the government solve these problems?

The Term Structure of Interest Rates

9

"If I had to pick one indicator, it would be the yield curve. It hasn't missed in a century. Every time the yield curve is inverted, a contraction has followed on average a year later."

RAYMOND DALIO, Bridgewater Group (1989)

"A flatter yield curve indicates investors may be expecting a significant slowing of the economy."

JONATHAN FUERBRINGER, New York Times, *December 10, 1998, C10.*

A n investor with idle funds in mid-1989 would have faced nothing but frustration in soliciting professional advice about how long to invest those funds. Consider the recommendations given simultaneously to a reporter for *The Wall Street Journal:* "Shorter is better right now," said Michael D. Hirsch, chief investment officer of Republic Bank of New York. "People should be lengthening their maturities now," advised James Riepe, director of investment services at T. Rowe Price, a large mutual fund group. "Intermediate-term bonds offer the possibility of price appreciation and good rates," opined William E. Donoghue, chairman of Donoghue Organization, an investment research group. What's the reason behind the confusion? The yield curve, often used as an indicator of the course of future interest rates, was "flat"—that is, expected rates of return were almost equal regardless of how long one invested one's money. Similarly, a decade later, in 1998, over the course of the year, the yield curve flattened somewhat for securities with maturities from one to ten years.[1] This situation in both 1989 and 1998 made economic forecasting even more difficult than usual. In the 2000s, yield curves were upward-sloping, but interest rates started falling to their lowest levels in forty-five years by the summer of 2003. Investors in bonds at that time, after years of falling rates, wondered whether rates would continue to fall or, as the upward yield curve suggested, begin to rise again.

The previous chapter points to the importance of understanding how both the supply and demand for

Learning Objectives

After completing this chapter, you will be able to:

1 Understand how a yield curve is constructed and what it tells you about the term structure of interest rates.

2 Follow historical trends in yield curves and explain differences between upward-sloping, flat, and downward-sloping yield curves and where they often appear during business cycles.

3 Understand the different theories for the shape of yield curves including the expectations, liquidity premium, modified expectations, segmented markets, and preferred habitat theories.

credit and inflationary expectations affects the general level of interest rates. The preceding paragraph, as well as the opening quotations, point to another important influence on institutional performance—the **term structure of interest rates,** often called the **yield curve.** All else equal, the term structure of interest rates is the relationship, at a specific time, between yields on securities and their maturities. For example, yields on 182-day Treasury bills (T-bills) almost always differ from those on 25-year Treasury bonds (T-bonds).

Just as there are theories explaining how the general level of interest rates is determined, there are also theories explaining the term structure. Because financial institutions simultaneously participate in the markets for securities of many different maturities, theories of the term structure can assist managers in making decisions that commonly confront them. Some of these decisions are illustrated later in the chapter.

The Term Structure Defined: A Closer Look

As noted, the term structure of interest rates is the relationship between security yields and maturities, *all else equal.* "All else equal" is an important qualifying phrase. To isolate the effect of maturity on yield, one must remove the potential effects of other factors. Comparing a bank's existing yields on a 6-month T-bill and a 20-year loan to a developing nation would say little about the effect of maturity on yields but a great deal about default risk. It would also be misleading to compare a T-bill yield with the tax-exempt yield on bonds of the City of Dallas or to compare General Motors' 90-day commercial paper rate with the yield on its preferred stock and then draw conclusions about the effect of maturity on expected return.

Identifying the Existing Term Structure

It is generally agreed that comparing yields on Treasury securities of different maturities is the best way to control for extraneous factors. Existing term structures are obtained by observing spot rates, that is, current market yields, on T-bills, Treasury notes (T-notes), and T-bonds. A daily listing of yields and maturities is found in the "Treasury Issues" column of major newspapers; an example is shown in Figure 9.1. The few Treasury issues that are callable or have special estate tax features, called flower bonds,

---

1 Georgette Jasen. "High-Yield Hunters Now Face a Decision." *The Wall Street Journal* (May 3, 1989), C1.

figure **9.1**

Yields of Treasury securities of varying maturities are found in the daily financial pages. These data are the basis for estimating the current shape of the yield curve.

TREASURY BILLS, BONDS AND NOTES

TUESDAY, NOVEMBER 25, 2003

TREASURY BILLS

Date	Bid	Ask	Chg	Yield
Nov 27 03	0.95	0.94	+0.01	0.95
Dec 04 03	0.90	0.89	+0.01	0.90
Dec 11 03	0.89	0.88	...	0.89
Dec 18 03	0.91	0.90	...	0.91
Dec 26 03	0.93	0.92	+0.01	0.93
Jan 02 04	0.92	0.91	...	0.92
Jan 08 04	0.89	0.88	...	0.89
Jan 15 04	0.90	0.89	...	0.90
Jan 22 04	0.88	0.87	-0.01	0.88
Jan 29 04	0.89	0.88	...	0.89
Feb 05 04	0.91	0.90	...	0.91
Feb 12 04	0.91	0.90	-0.01	0.91
Feb 19 04	0.90	0.89	-0.02	0.90
Feb 26 04	0.92	0.91	...	0.93
Mar 01 04	0.93	0.92	...	0.94
Mar 04 04	0.91	0.90	+0.01	0.92
Mar 11 04	0.91	0.90	...	0.92
Mar 18 04	0.93	0.92	...	0.94
Mar 25 04	0.91	0.90	...	0.92
Apr 08 04	0.93	0.92	...	0.94
Apr 15 04	0.95	0.94	+0.01	0.96
Apr 22 04	0.95	0.94	+0.01	0.96
Apr 29 04	0.95	0.94	-0.01	0.96
May 06 04	0.97	0.96	...	0.98
May 13 04	0.97	0.96	...	0.98
May 20 04	0.99	0.98	...	1.00
May 27 04	1.00	0.99	-0.01	1.01

BONDS AND NOTES

Month		Rate	Bid	Ask	Chg	Yld
Nov 03	p	3	100.00	100.01	-0.01	...
Dec 03	p	$3\frac{1}{4}$	100.07	100.08	...	0.46
Jan 04	p	3	100.11	100.12	...	0.74
Feb 04	p	$4\frac{3}{4}$	100.26	100.27	...	0.73
Feb 04	p	$5\frac{7}{8}$	101.02	101.03	...	0.76
Feb 04	p	3	100.16	100.17	-0.01	0.85
Mar 04	p	$3\frac{5}{8}$	100.29	100.30	...	0.84
Apr 04	p	$3\frac{3}{8}$	101.00	101.01	...	0.93
May 04		$12\frac{3}{8}$	105.09	105.10	-0.01	0.88
May 04	p	$5\frac{1}{4}$	101.31	102.00	...	0.92
May 04	p	$7\frac{1}{4}$	102.28	102.29	-0.01	0.93
May 04	p	$3\frac{1}{4}$	101.03	101.04	...	0.98
Jun 04	p	$2\frac{7}{8}$	101.02	101.03	...	1.01
Jul 04	p	$2\frac{1}{4}$	100.24	100.25	...	1.08
Aug 04	p	6	103.14	103.15	...	1.09
Aug 04	p	$7\frac{1}{4}$	104.11	104.12	...	1.08
Aug 04		$13\frac{3}{4}$	108.31	109.00	-0.01	1.05
Aug 04	p	$2\frac{1}{8}$	100.23	100.24	...	1.10
Sep 04	p	$1\frac{7}{8}$	100.18	100.19	...	1.16
Oct 04	p	$2\frac{1}{8}$	100.25	100.26	...	1.22
Nov 04	p	$5\frac{7}{8}$	104.12	104.13	...	1.25
Nov 04	p	$7\frac{7}{8}$	106.09	106.10	-0.01	1.25
Nov 04	k	$11\frac{5}{8}$	109.29	109.30	...	1.23
Nov 04	p	2	100.22	100.23	...	1.26
Dec 04	p	$1\frac{3}{4}$	100.14	100.15	...	1.30
Jan 05	p	$1\frac{5}{8}$	100.09	100.10	+0.01	1.34
Feb 05	p	$7\frac{1}{2}$	107.12	107.13	...	1.32
Feb 05	p	$1\frac{1}{2}$	100.03	100.04	+0.01	1.39
Mar 05	p	$1\frac{5}{8}$	100.06	100.07	+0.01	1.45
Apr 05	p	$1\frac{5}{8}$	100.05	100.06	+0.02	1.49
May 05	p	$6\frac{1}{2}$	107.07	107.08	+0.01	1.48
May 05	p	$6\frac{3}{4}$	107.18	107.19	+0.02	1.49

Month		Rate	Bid	Ask	Chg	Yld
May 05	k	12	115.10	115.11	+0.01	1.37
May 05	p	$1\frac{1}{4}$	99.17	99.18	+0.02	1.53
Jun 05	p	$1\frac{1}{8}$	99.07	99.08	+0.02	1.59
Jul 05	p	$1\frac{1}{2}$	99.23	99.24	+0.02	1.65
Aug 05	p	$6\frac{1}{2}$	108.04	108.05	+0.02	1.64
Aug 05	k	$10\frac{3}{4}$	115.09	115.10	+0.02	1.64
Aug 05	p	2	100.15	100.16	+0.03	1.71
Sep 05	p	$1\frac{5}{8}$	99.23	99.24	+0.02	1.75
Oct 05	p	$1\frac{5}{8}$	99.19	99.20	+0.03	1.82
Nov 05	p	$5\frac{3}{4}$	107.16	107.17	+0.02	1.82
Nov 05	p	$5\frac{7}{8}$	107.24	107.25	+0.02	1.82
Feb 06	p	$5\frac{5}{8}$	107.29	107.30	+0.03	1.94
Feb 06	k	$9\frac{3}{8}$	116.00	116.01	+0.02	1.93
May 06	p	2	99.24	99.25	+0.03	2.09
May 06	p	$4\frac{5}{8}$	106.00	106.01	+0.03	2.09
May 06	p	$6\frac{7}{8}$	111.12	111.13	+0.03	2.10
Jul 06	p	7	112.06	112.07	+0.03	2.19
Aug 06	p	$2\frac{3}{8}$	100.10	100.11	+0.03	2.24
Oct 06	p	$6\frac{1}{2}$	111.18	111.19	+0.03	2.31
Nov 06	p	$2\frac{5}{8}$	100.22	100.23	+0.04	2.37
Nov 06	p	$3\frac{1}{2}$	103.07	103.08	+0.02	2.35
Feb 07	p	$6\frac{1}{4}$	111.21	111.22	+0.03	2.44
May 07	p	$4\frac{3}{8}$	105.27	105.28	+0.03	2.59
May 07	p	$6\frac{5}{8}$	113.11	113.12	+0.04	2.57
Aug 07	p	$3\frac{1}{4}$	101.28	101.29	+0.03	2.70
Aug 07	p	$6\frac{1}{8}$	112.04	112.05	+0.04	2.66
Nov 07	p	3	100.24	100.25	+0.04	2.79
Feb 08	p	3	100.14	100.15	+0.05	2.88
Feb 08	p	$5\frac{1}{2}$	110.14	110.15	+0.05	2.84
May 08	p	$2\frac{5}{8}$	98.13	98.14	+0.05	3.00
May 08	p	$5\frac{5}{8}$	110.31	111.00	+0.05	2.97
Aug 08	p	$3\frac{1}{4}$	100.19	100.20	+0.05	3.10
Sep 08	p	$3\frac{1}{8}$	99.30	99.31	+0.04	3.13
Oct 08	p	$3\frac{1}{8}$	99.27	99.28	+0.05	3.15
Nov 08	p	$3\frac{3}{8}$	100.28	100.29	+0.06	3.18
Nov 08	p	$4\frac{3}{4}$	107.08	107.09	+0.05	3.15
May 09	p	$5\frac{1}{2}$	111.13	111.14	+0.06	3.20
May 04–09	p	$9\frac{1}{8}$	103.25	103.26	-0.01	0.84
Aug 09	p	6	113.18	113.19	+0.06	3.36
Nov 04–09		$10\frac{3}{8}$	108.17	108.18	-0.01	1.39
Feb 10	p	$6\frac{1}{2}$	116.19	116.20	+0.08	3.50
Feb 05–10		$11\frac{3}{4}$	112.12	112.12	...	1.41
May 05–10		10	112.02	112.03	+0.01	1.60
Aug 10	p	$5\frac{3}{4}$	112.16	112.17	+0.07	3.63
Nov 05–10		$12\frac{3}{4}$	120.25	120.26	+0.02	1.90
Feb 11	p	5	107.23	107.24	+0.07	3.76
May 06–11		$13\frac{7}{8}$	128.01	128.02	+0.02	2.12
Aug 11	p	5	107.15	107.16	+0.08	3.87
Nov 06–11		14	133.12	133.14	+0.03	2.27
Feb 12	p	$4\frac{7}{8}$	106.10	106.11	+0.07	3.96
Aug 12	p	$4\frac{3}{8}$	102.15	102.16	+0.09	4.03
Nov 12	p	4	99.15	99.16	+0.09	4.07
Nov 07–12		$10\frac{3}{8}$	128.04	128.05	+0.05	2.82
Feb 13	p	$3\frac{7}{8}$	98.09	98.10	+0.09	4.10
May 13	p	$3\frac{5}{8}$	96.29	96.30	+0.08	4.01
Aug 13	p	$4\frac{1}{4}$	100.20	100.21	+0.09	4.17
Aug 08–13		12	138.27	138.29	+0.05	3.07
Nov 13	p	$4\frac{1}{4}$	100.16	100.18	+0.09	4.18
May 09–14		$13\frac{1}{4}$	149.20	149.22	+0.07	3.25
Aug 09–14	k	$12\frac{1}{2}$	147.05	147.07	+0.07	3.35
Nov 09–14	k	$11\frac{3}{4}$	144.11	144.13	+0.07	3.45
Feb 15	k	$11\frac{1}{4}$	161.04	161.06	+0.13	4.31
Aug 15	k	$10\frac{5}{8}$	156.22	156.24	+0.14	4.38
Nov 15	k	$9\frac{7}{8}$	150.01	150.04	+0.12	4.43
Feb 16	k	$9\frac{1}{4}$	144.14	144.16	+0.13	4.48
May 16	k	$7\frac{1}{4}$	125.14	125.16	+0.12	4.55
Nov 16	k	$7\frac{1}{2}$	128.00	128.01	+0.12	4.60
May 17	k	$8\frac{3}{4}$	140.30	141.00	+0.14	4.63
Aug 17	k	$8\frac{7}{8}$	142.12	142.15	+0.14	4.65

Month		Rate	Bid	Ask	Chg	Yld
May 18	k	$9\frac{1}{8}$	145.28	145.30	+0.16	4.71
Nov 18	k	9	145.01	145.04	+0.15	4.75
Feb 19	k	$8\frac{7}{8}$	143.26	143.28	+0.16	4.78
Aug 19	k	$8\frac{1}{8}$	135.27	135.29	+0.16	4.84
Feb 20	k	$8\frac{1}{2}$	140.15	140.17	+0.16	4.86
May 20	k	$8\frac{3}{4}$	143.21	143.23	+0.17	4.86
Aug 20	k	$8\frac{3}{4}$	143.28	143.30	+0.17	4.87
Feb 21	k	$7\frac{7}{8}$	133.26	133.28	+0.18	4.93
May 21	k	$8\frac{1}{8}$	137.01	137.03	+0.18	4.93
Aug 21	k	$8\frac{1}{8}$	137.04	137.06	+0.18	4.95
Nov 21	k	8	135.26	135.29	+0.18	4.96
Aug 22	k	$7\frac{1}{4}$	126.30	127.00	+0.18	5.01
Nov 22	k	$7\frac{5}{8}$	131.24	131.26	+0.18	5.01
Feb 23	k	$7\frac{1}{8}$	125.17	125.19	+0.18	5.03
Aug 23	k	$6\frac{1}{4}$	114.19	114.21	+0.16	5.06
Nov 24	k	$7\frac{1}{2}$	131.07	131.08	+0.20	5.06
Feb 25	k	$7\frac{5}{8}$	132.28	132.30	+0.20	5.07
Aug 25	k	$6\frac{7}{8}$	123.03	123.05	+0.20	5.10
Feb 26	k	6	111.20	111.22	+0.18	5.11
Aug 26	k	$6\frac{3}{4}$	121.24	121.26	+0.18	5.11
Nov 26	k	$6\frac{1}{2}$	118.13	118.15	+0.18	5.12
Feb 27	k	$6\frac{5}{8}$	120.07	120.09	+0.19	5.12
Aug 27	k	$6\frac{3}{8}$	116.28	116.30	+0.17	5.13
Nov 27	k	$6\frac{1}{8}$	113.15	113.17	+0.17	5.14
Aug 28	k	$5\frac{1}{2}$	104.27	104.29	+0.16	5.14
Nov 28	k	$5\frac{1}{4}$	101.13	101.15	+0.15	5.14
Feb 29	k	$5\frac{1}{4}$	101.18	101.20	+0.16	5.13
Aug 29	k	$6\frac{1}{8}$	114.03	114.05	+0.18	5.13
May 30	k	$6\frac{1}{4}$	116.06	116.08	+0.18	5.12
Feb 31	k	$5\frac{3}{8}$	105.01	105.02	+0.15	5.03

Source: Street Software/Bear Stearns via The Associated Press

Treasury Yield Curve

Yields of selected Treasury securities. Short-term maturities are shown on a bond-equivalent basis. Horizontal scale is a ratio scale.

Percent

(Chart plotting "Yesterday" (filled circles) and "One Month Ago" (open circles) against maturities of 3, 6 Months; 2, 3, 5, 10 Years; 30 Maturities. Vertical axis 0 to 6.0 Percent.)

Source: New York Times

Source: New York Times, *November 26, 2003, C7, C12.*

must be eliminated. Standardized calculations must be used so that bank discount yields for T-bills with maturities of one year or less are not erroneously compared with bond-equivalent yields.[2]

A Historical Look at Term Structures

Just as the general level of interest rates differs over time, so does the term structure. In March 1989, for example, yields on short-term Treasury securities exceeded those on long-term Treasuries. A plot of this relationship is shown in Figure 9.2. A yield curve with this shape is often described as **downward-sloping** or **inverted.** In contrast, Figure 9.3 shows an upward-sloping relationship in March 1992. Figure 9.4 shows an almost constant (flat) relationship between yields and maturities in December 1988.

Figure 9.5 gives a long-term view of short- and long-term rates, showing yields on T-bills and T-bonds over a period of approximately twenty-eight years. During this period, no single relationship

---

figure **9.2** YIELDS OF TREASURY SECURITIES, MARCH 31, 1989

The yield curve in March 1989 was downward-sloping, or inverted: Short-term rates were higher than long-term rates.

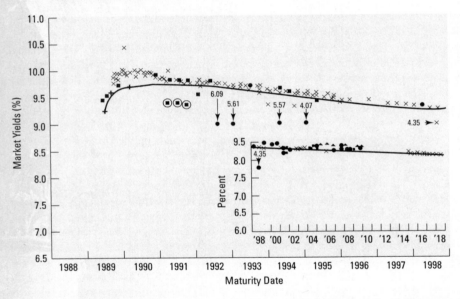

Note: The curve is fitted by eye and is based only on most actively traded issues. Market yields on coupon issues due in less than three months are excluded.

✕ *Fixed maturity coupon issues less than 12%*
■ *Fixed maturity coupon issues of 12% or more*
● *Callable coupon issues less than 12%*
▲ *Callable coupon issues of 12% or more*
Note: Callable issues are plotted to the earliest call date when prices are above par and to maturity when prices are at par or below.
+ *Bills. Coupon equivalent yield of the latest 13-week, 26-week, 52-week bills.*

Source: Treasury Bulletin, *June 1989, 55.*

---

2 For a theoretically correct determination of the "true" term structure, the securities used should all be pure discount, zero-coupon bonds of varying maturities. The growing market for stripped Treasury securities may eventually introduce new practices, but currently coupon-bearing as well as discount security yields are used to estimate existing term structures, especially when the analyst is fitting a curve visually. Also, bonds with different coupon rates are usually used to construct a yield curve, causing some distortion. The yields and prices for T-bills are discussed in Chapter 8. The prices for T-bonds in Figure 9.1 are prices at 100 percent of par value. For example, an ask price of $100^1/_{32}$ would be 100.03125 percent times the bond's par value. The yield for a long-term bond is its "yields to maturity" (YTM), the rate that makes the present value of the bond's coupon payments and maturity value equal to its current ask price. This implied discount rate can be calculated using a financial calculator or trial-and-error approach.

figure **9.3**   YIELDS OF TREASURY SECURITIES, MARCH 31, 1992

The yield curve in early 1992 was upward-sloping, or normal: Short-term rates were lower than long-term rates.

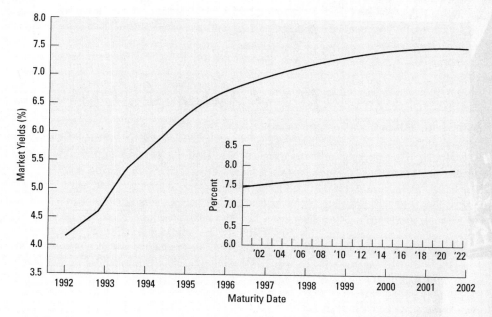

Note: The curve is fitted by eye and based only on most actively traded issues.
Market yields on coupon issues due in less than three months are excluded.

Source: Treasury Bulletin, *June 1992, 78.*

between short- and long-term rates prevailed, although long-term rates exceeded short-term rates most of the time. In fact, the prevalence of upward-sloping yield curves during much of the early twentieth century led to them being dubbed **"normal" yield curves,** which is why downward-sloping curves have been called "inverted."[3]

Figure 9.6 shows more recent changes in yield curves during the second half of 1998 and the early 2000s. The yield curve changed dramatically from June to December of 1998, flattening in August and September and becoming steeper in October. It is interesting to note that on several dates, such as November 6, 1998, securities with maturities of two to five years actually had lower yields than three-month T-bills, whereas securities with maturities of ten years or greater had consistently higher yields. To be able to anticipate changes in interest rates, financial institution managers need to understand relations between yield curves and different stages of the business cycle. In contrast, in the early 2000s, interest rates tended to be low, but the yield curve tended to be upward-sloping, such as the yield curve shown for November 26, 2003.

The Term Structure and the General Level of Interest Rates

Another feature of Figure 9.5 is important because it suggests a historical relationship between the general level of economic activity and the shape of the yield curve. The dates labeled on the graph denote months when there were peaks in the business cycle.[4] A downward-sloping yield curve often appears at these peaks, such as during November 1973. At this point, investors seemed to be anticipating the end of an expansion and beginning of a recession that would result in a lower demand for funds and a fall in rates. During periods of sluggish economic performance but toward the end of a recession, such as

---

3 Inverted yield curves appeared more frequently in the 1970s and early 1980s than in previous periods, although they are not evident in Figure 9.5, which shows only annual averages.

4 Peaks shown are as delineated by the National Bureau of Economic Research, U.S. Department of Commerce, *Business Conditions Digest.*

figure **9.4** YIELDS OF TREASURY SECURITIES, DECEMBER 31, 1988

The yield curve in late 1988 was almost flat: Short-term and long-term rates were approximately equal.

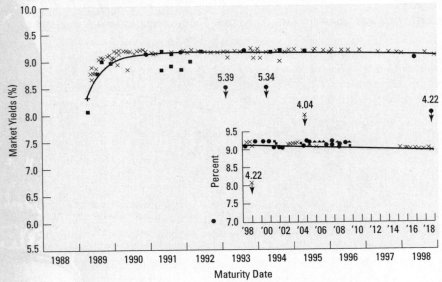

Note: The curve is fitted by eye and based only on most actively traded issues.
Market yields on coupon issues due in less than three months are excluded.

× Fixed maturity coupon issues less than 12%
■ Fixed maturity coupon issues of 12% or more
● Callable coupon issues less than 12%
▲ Callable coupon issues of 12% or more
Note: Callable issues are plotted to the earliest call date when prices are above par and to maturity when prices are at par or below.
+ Bills. Coupon equivalent yield of the latest 13-week, 26-week, 52-week bills.

Source: Treasury Bulletin, *March 1989, 59.*

figure **9.5** LONG- AND SHORT-TERM INTEREST RATES

Short-term rates have been lower than long-term rates for most of the twentieth century and on into the twenty-first century. Periods when short-term rates were higher have often coincided with peaks in the business cycle, leading to subsequent recessions.

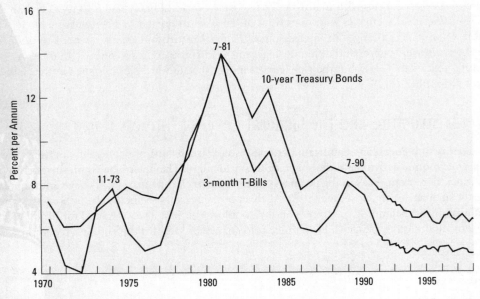

Source: Board of Governors of the Federal Reserve System, Federal Reserve Bulletin, *various issues.*

figure   9.6   YIELD CURVES DURING 1998 AND EARLY 2000S

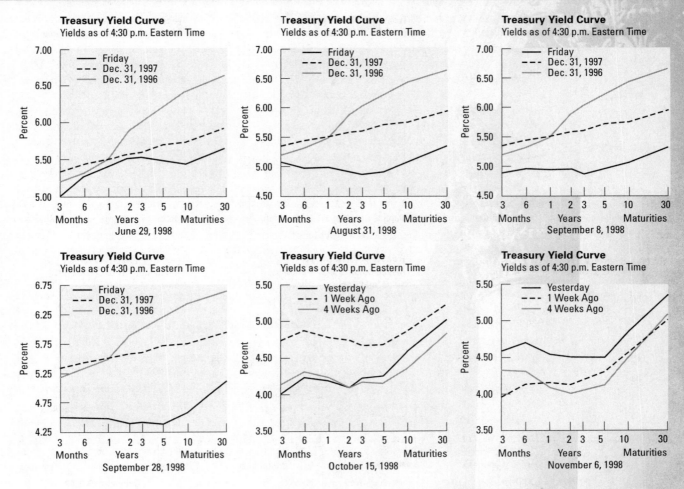

Source: The Wall Street Journal, *for the dates given, C17, C17, C23, C19, C21, C19, C22, C20, C17, C10, C2, C2.*

the mid-1970s, the yield curve has often been upward-sloping as investors anticipated the end of a recession and a rise in future rates. This same pattern occurred in anticipation of the recession of 1981–1982 with a downward-sloping curve prior to July 1981, followed by an upward-sloping curve as the economy moved out of the recession.[5]

The next downward-sloping curve appeared for a brief period in 1989 (recall Figure 9.2). At the time, some economists suggested that an inverted term structure might no longer signal a recession. Previously, recessions were the only times that market participants seemed to expect interest rates to decline. But surveys of financial institution managers at this time revealed expectations of a prolonged decline in the rate of inflation, particularly relative to inflation in the early part of the decade. Some experts suggested that the downward-sloping curve meant only that a smaller inflationary premium would be built into future short-term rates, not that a recession was at hand.[6] This alternative inter-pretation of the inverted yield curve proved, of course, to be incorrect. The U.S. economy fell into a pro-longed recession in the early 1990s, confirming once again the difficulties encountered by economic forecasters. Yield curves again became steeper and upward-sloping toward the end of the 1990–1991 recession, with short-term rates falling more than long-term rates, and the economy expanded.

---

5 From the beginning of World War II until 1951, Federal Reserve policies actually kept the term structure independent of the level of economic activity. Controls were lifted under President Harry Truman, and rates were free to move according to the supply of and demand for funds. For more discussion of this policy and the accord that brought it to an end, see Wallich and Keir (1979).

6 See Furlong (1989) and Stevens (1989).

figure **9.6** YIELD CURVES DURING 1998 AND EARLY 2000S (CONTINUED)

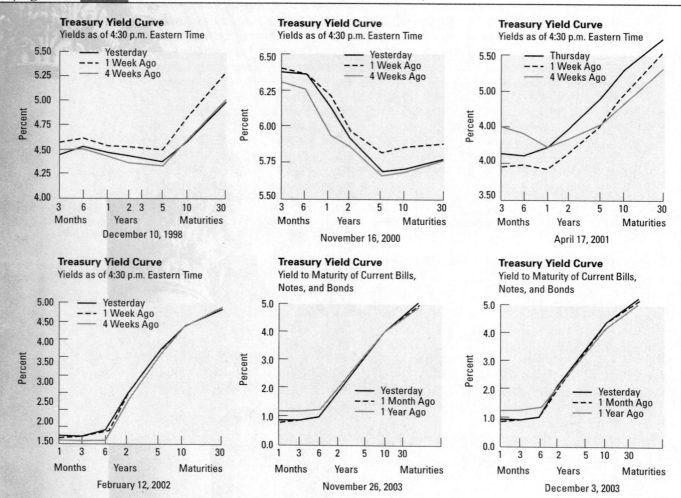

Source: The Wall Street Journal, *for the dates given, C17, C17, C23, C19, C21, C19, C22, C20, C17, C10, C2, C2.*

Another perspective on historical term structures is shown in Figure 9.7. When the general level of rates has been relatively high, term structures have tended to slope downward, and they have sloped upward when the general level has been relatively low. From 1900 to 1929, as the general level of rates drifted upward, yield curves gradually changed shape from flat to inverted. From 1930 to 1981, as rates gradually moved higher, yield curves also shifted from upward-sloping to downward-sloping. Scholars have inferred from these historical curves that the financial markets may periodically revise their opinions of what represents a high general level of rates. Before the 1930s, for example, a 7 percent short-term rate may have been considered high, but by the 1970s such a rate was considered relatively low. In this context, the 1982 normal curve was an aberration from recent history. As Figures 9.2, 9.3, and 9.4 indicate, during the late 1980s and early 1990s the general level of interest rates fell, and yield curve levels appeared similar to those from the 1960s and 1970s.

One important difference observed in the early 1990s, however, was the extremely steep slope of the yield curve. As shown in Figure 9.8, although short-term interest rate levels were similar to those prevailing in the 1960s, the relative differential between short-term and long-term rates was most unusual. By August 1992, when the yield on 3-month T-bills was just above 3 percent, the yield on 30-year T-bonds was more than twice that, at 7.3 percent. Experts attributed this differential to investor uncertainties about long-term economic conditions, including the outlook for inflation and stability in the world currency markets.[7]

---

7 For more discussion, see Wood (1983), Blalock (1993), and Cogley (1993).

figure **9.7** YIELD CURVES FOR HIGH-GRADE CORPORATE BONDS, 1900–1929 AND 1930–1982

When the general level of interest rates is relatively high, yield curves are usually downward-sloping. When the general level is relatively low, the yield curve often slopes upward.

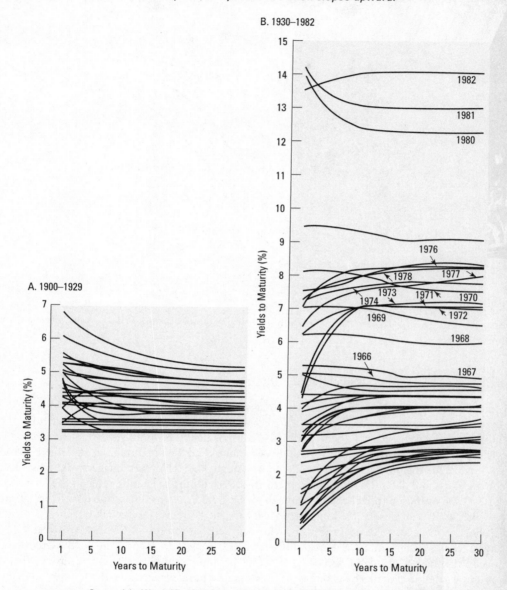

Source: John Wood, "Do Yield Curves Normally Slope Up? The Term Structure of Interest Rates, 1862–1982," Economic Perspectives (Federal Reserve Bank of Chicago) 7 (July/August 1983): 18.

Concept Questions

1 Historically, at the beginning of a recession, what type of yield curve often appears?

2 Historically, at the beginning of an expansion, what type of yield curve typically appears?

3 Can you explain why these particular types of yield curves would appear at these times?

4 What typical shape does a yield curve have?

figure **9.8** YIELDS OF TREASURY SECURITIES, 1991 AND 1992

The term structure of interest rates exhibited a very steep slope in 1991 and 1992, presenting a strong contrast to earlier periods when the differential between short-term and long-term rates was much smaller.

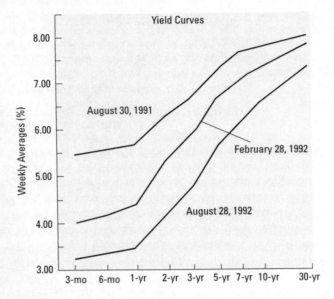

Source: Economic Trends *(Federal Reserve Bank of Cleveland) (September 1992): 5.*

Unbiased (Pure) Expectations Theory

Historical patterns and the reasons for their existence provide clues about when to expect shifts in the term structure, but they are no substitute for a theoretical understanding of the yield curve. Understanding how the term structure is determined is complicated by economists' lack of agreement on any single explanation. The existence of several theories should not be discouraging, however, because each provides insights the others lack. The body of knowledge is valuable for managers who make decisions involving assets and liabilities of different maturities. Perhaps the most influential of the term structure theories is the **unbiased (pure) expectations theory,** hereafter referred to as the pure expectations theory, which holds that observable long-term yields are the average of expected, but directly unobservable, short-term yields.[8] For example, this theory argues that the spot rate on twenty-year T-bonds is the average of expected annual yields on short-term Treasury securities over the next twenty years. Theoretically, there is no best definition of "short term" or "long term." For simplicity, most of the following examples define short term as one year; however, the pure expectations theory also holds that the observed yield on one-year securities is the average of expected rates on shorter-maturity securities during the year. *Short-* and *long-term* can therefore be defined however the decision maker desires.

Assumptions of the Pure Expectations Theory

The pure expectations theory rests on the following important assumptions about investors (lenders or demanders of securities) and markets:

1. All else equal, investors are indifferent between owning a single long-term security or a series of short-term securities over the same time period. In other words, maturity alone does not affect investors' choice of investments.

2. All investors hold common expectations about the course of short-term rates.

---

8 Irving Fisher, discussed in Chapter 8 in connection with inflation and the general level of rates, is often credited with the first statement of the pure expectations hypothesis in 1896. The theory was not fully developed until several decades later, however, when both J. R. Hicks (1946) and Frederick Lutz (1940) pursued it. More recent discussions are found in Malkiel (1966) and Meiselman (1962).

3. On average, investors are able to predict rates accurately. Their expectations about future rates are unbiased in the *statistical* sense, that is, they are neither consistently low nor consistently high.

4. There are no taxes, information costs, or transaction costs in the financial markets. Investors are free to exchange securities of varying maturities quickly and without penalty.

The main implication of the pure expectations theory follows directly from these assumptions. *For a given holding period, the average expected annual yields on all combinations of maturities will be equal.*[9] For example, the theory holds that the average annual yield on a series of one-year investments over a specific five-year period will be the same as the average annual yield on a single three-year investment followed by two one-year investments *and* the same as the average annual yield on a single five-year security. Because investors are assumed to be indifferent about the maturity of their holdings and because they have common and accurate predictions about future rates, they will demand securities at prices that equalize average annual yields over the period. Investors simply have no incentive to prefer one combination of maturities over another. Annual yields currently available on long-term securities will be the average of expected annual yields on shorter-term instruments.

Mathematics of the Pure Expectations Theory

Mathematically, the theory is expressed by the following formula:

$$1 + {}_1r_n = [(1 + {}_1r_1)(1 + {}_2\gamma_1) \ldots (1 + {}_n\gamma_1)]^{1/n} \qquad [9.1]$$

The "average" of rates referred to earlier is not the simple arithmetic average, but a **geometric average** that is equal to the nth root (or 1/n power) product of 1 plus the current r and 1 plus the expected [γ] short-term interest rates during the life of the long-term bond issued today with n years to maturity. Rates are fractions, so 1 is added to each of the rates before taking the product and added to the long-term rate on the left-hand side of the equation as well. The left subscript in each term identifies the beginning of a particular time period. The right subscript in each term indicates the maturity to which a particular yield applies. Thus, for example, the term $({}_1r_1)$ refers to the observed yield of a one-year security (right subscript) at the beginning of period 1 (left subscript). The term ${}_2\gamma_1$ refers to the expected yield of a one-year security (right subscript) at the beginning of period 2 (left subscript), where the r term refers to actual rates and the γ term to expected rates. Equation 9.1 states that the *observed* yield in period 1 for a security with n years to maturity $({}_1r_n)$ is the **geometric average** of a series of one-year current and *expected* yields over this period.[10]

Table 9.1 contains investors' expectations for one-year yields during a hypothetical period of January 2005 to January 2008. The first three columns are used in the following examples. The fourth column of liquidity premiums is used later.

table **9.1**   OBSERVED AND EXPECTED ONE-YEAR YIELDS AND PREMIUMS AS OF JANUARY 2005

These hypothetical data on observed and expected one-year rates and liquidity premiums can be used to estimate the shape of a yield curve.

Bill Purchased	Bill Matures	Observed or Expected Annual Yield (%)	Liquidity Premium (%)
January 2005	January 2006	8.50% observed $({}_1r_1)$	0.00% (on 1-year security)
January 2006	January 2007	9.50% expected $({}_2r_1)$	0.35% (on 2-year security)
January 2007	January 2008	11.00% expected $({}_3r_1)$	0.45% (on 3-year security)
January 2008	January 2009	11.75% expected $({}_4r_1)$	0.50% (on 4-year security)

---

9 Recently, some scholars have argued that this implication holds strictly only for a specific holding period of instantaneous duration and that it is incompatible with other versions of the expectations hypothesis, such as the statement that long-term spot rates are the average of expected short-term rates. See Cox, Ingersoll, and Ross (1981).

10 The notation for pure expectations mathematics is invariably confusing. Present and compound value calculations usually emphasize end-of-period cash flows, so t = 1 usually means the end of period 1, and t = n means the end of period n. That usage prevails in most chapters in this book. The pure expectations theory focuses on beginning-of-period expectations; however, t = 1 means the beginning of period 1 (or the end of period 0), and the notation t = n means the beginning of period n.

According to the unbiased expectations theory and from these expectations alone, Equation 9.1 can be used to calculate the required yield to maturity on a four-year Treasury security bought in January 2005 (the beginning of period 1) and maturing in January 2009:

$$1 + {}_1r_n = [(1 + {}_1\gamma_1)(1 + {}_2r_1) \ldots (1 + {}_n\gamma_1)]^{1/n}$$

$$1 + {}_1r_4 = [(1 + {}_1r_1)(1 + {}_2\gamma_2)(1 + {}_3\gamma_1)(1 + {}_4\gamma_1)]^{1/n}$$

$$1 + {}_1r_4 = [(1.0850)(1.0950)(1.1100)(1.1175)]^{1/n}$$

$${}_1r_4 = 1.10180 - 1 = 0.10180 = 10.180\%$$

Using Equation 9.1, it is possible to calculate the spot yields on securities with two- and three-year maturities as of January 2005 as follows:

$$1 + {}_1r_2 = [(1 + {}_1r_1)(1 + {}_2\gamma_1)]^{1/2}$$

$$1 + {}_1r_2 = [(1.0850)(1.0950)]^{1/2}$$

$${}_1r_2 = 1.08999 - 1 = 0.08999 = 8.999\%$$

$$1 + {}_1r_3 = [(1 + {}_1r_1)(1 + {}_2\gamma_1)(1 + {}_3\gamma_1)]^{1/3}$$

$$1 + {}_1r_3 = [(1.0850)(1.0950)(1.1100)]^{1/3}$$

$${}_1r_3 = 1.09662 - 1 = 0.09662 = 9.662\%$$

As shown in Figure 9.9, the pure expectations theory implies that investors' expectations of rising short-term yields will result in an upward-sloping yield curve for Treasury securities as of January 2005.

If the pure expectations theory is correct, the average annual yield an investor could obtain over the period 2005–2009 is the same, regardless of the investment strategy chosen. If the investor decides to buy four one-year securities, the average annual yield over the holding period (i_H) will be 10.180 percent. If, instead, the investments are a two-year security in January 2005 (annual yield of 8.999 percent) and two successive one-year T-bills in 2007 and 2008 (expected yields of 11.000 percent and 11.750 percent, respectively), the average annual yield for this strategy is as follows:

$$1 + i_H = [(1.08999)(1.08999)(1.1100)(1.1175)]^{1/4}$$

$$i_H = 1.10180 - 1 = 10.180\%$$

---

figure **9.9** HYPOTHETICAL OBSERVED YIELD CURVE, JANUARY 2005

Because long-term yields are the average of expected short-term yields, if short-term rates are expected to increase, the pure expectations theory holds that the term structure will be upward-sloping.

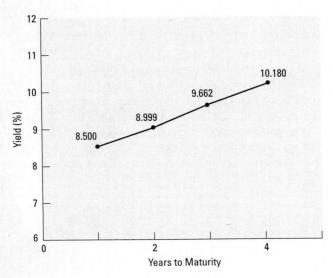

Or, if an investor buys a three-year T-note in 2005 (annual yield of 9.662 percent), followed by a one-year bill in 2008 (11.750 percent expected yield), the average annual yield for the holding period is as follows:

$$1 + i_H = [(1.09662)(1.09662)(1.09662)(1.1175)]^{1/4}$$

$$i_H = 1.10180 - 1 = 10.180\%$$

Under the assumptions of investor indifference to maturity and unbiased expectations of future short-term rates, any combination of maturities over the period will result in an average annual yield of 10.180 percent. This will be true as long as all proceeds are reinvested and expectations of future rates remain constant during the period. In other words, the 10.180 percent average four-year yield would be expected as long as investors do not revise their one-year predictions for 2007, for example, at some point after 2005.

Modifications of the Unbiased Expectations Theory

The unbiased expectations theory succinctly explains the shape of any term structure: Lenders' expectations of rising short-term rates produce an observable upward-sloping yield curve; expectations of falling short-term rates produce a downward-sloping term structure; and expectations of unchanging rates produce a flat yield curve. Changes in the shape of the curve over time can easily be explained by changes in expectations. Also, the theory appeals to researchers because its mathematical form provides testable hypotheses as well as the opportunity to develop models for predicting interest rates.

Criticisms of the Pure Expectations Theory

The pure expectations theory is not without its critics, however, who focus on its restrictive assumptions as serious shortcomings. In particular, investors' assumed indifference between short- and long-term securities ignores the fact that a long-term investment may be riskier than a series of short-term investments. Risk, brought about by the passage of time alone, is rarely a matter of indifference. Even for two securities of the same issuer with equal initial default risk, the probability of default may increase on the long-term security over time. Furthermore, investors are never certain that personal circumstances will allow them to follow initial investment strategies throughout the holding period. If emergencies arise, they may have to sell long-term securities at a loss.[11]

A second assumption that troubles critics is that, according to the theory, issuers of securities have no influence on the term structure. This appears to contradict the negotiation process that actually occurs between borrowers and lenders in many financial markets. It is important to remember that no theory should be judged on the realism of its assumptions. The test of a theory is how well it explains "real-world" relationships, and the theory enjoys some qualified empirical support. However, these criticisms have led to some theoretical modifications.

The Liquidity Premium Hypothesis

The belief that most investors find long-term securities to be riskier than short-term securities has led to the **liquidity premium hypothesis.** According to this theory, today's long-term rates reflect the geometric average of intervening expected short-term rates *plus* a premium that investors demand for holding long-term securities instead of a series of short-term, less risky investments. The hypothesized effect of these liquidity premiums, also called **term premiums,** can be illustrated by looking at the fourth column of Table 9.1.[12]

In the previous example using the pure expectations theory, spot rates of 8.99 percent, 9.66 percent, and 10.18 percent were calculated earlier for two-, three-, and four-year maturities. According to the

---

11 For an investor who holds the investment throughout the planned holding period, another element of risk must be considered: the potential for unexpected changes in short-term yields. If such changes occur, the investor faces uncertainty from periodic reinvestment rates. This source of risk is discussed in more detail in Chapter 10.

12 Presentations of the liquidity premium hypothesis can be found in Hicks (1946) and Kessel (1965). Although it is easy to incorporate given liquidity premiums into the basic pure expectations equation, it is more difficult to specify the structure of liquidity premiums themselves. Scholars disagree about how to model them, but for illustrative purposes, liquidity premiums in these examples are considered to increase with time. A brief review of alternative specifications is provided later in the chapter.

figure 9.10 PURE EXPECTATIONS AND LIQUIDITY PREMIUMS

If short-term rates are expected to decrease sharply and if investors also demand a premium for holding long-term securities, the slope of the yield curve will be less steep than if expectations alone are considered.

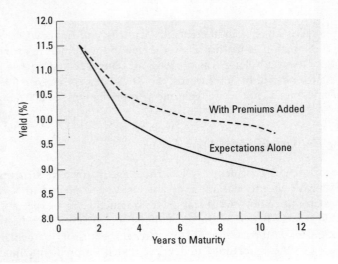

figure 9.11 TRANSFORMATION OF AN INVERTED CURVE

If short-term rates are expected to decrease slightly, and if investors also demand a premium for holding long-term securities, the yield curve could be slightly upward-sloping.

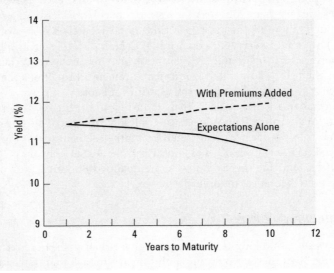

liquidity premium hypothesis, you would instead expect the following yields, using Equation 9.1 with the liquidity premiums added:

$$1 + {}_1r_2 = [(1.0850)(1.0950 + 0.0035)]^{1/2}$$

$${}_1r_2 = 1.0917 - 1 = 0.0917 = 9.17\%$$

$$1 + {}_1r_3 = [(1.0850)(1.0950 + 0.0035)(1.1100 + 0.0045)]^{1/3}$$

$${}_1r_3 = 1.0993 - 1 = 0.0993 = 9.93\%$$

$$1 + {}_1r_4 = [(1.0850)(1.0950 + 0.0035)(1.1100 + 0.0045)(1.1175 + 0.0050)]^{1/4}$$

$$= 0.1050 = 10.50\%$$

figure **9.12**   HYPOTHETICAL YIELD CURVE WITH LIQUIDITY PREMIUMS

If short-term rates are expected to increase, and if investors demand a premium for holding long-term securities, long-term yields will be higher than if expectations alone are considered.

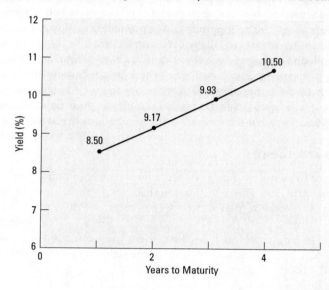

Because investors are no longer indifferent among maturities, the same expectations are supplemented by a premium for holding long-term securities. As shown in Figures 9.10, 9.11, and 9.12, this term structure has a steeper slope than curves based on the same expectations but assumed no liquidity premiums.

A general restatement of the term structure including liquidity premiums is seen in Equation 9.2:

$$1 + {}_1r_n = [(1 + {}_1r_1)(1 + {}_t\gamma_1 + L_t)]^{1/n} \qquad [9.2]$$

where L_t = liquidity premium for holding a t-period security instead of a one-year security. By definition, $Ld_1 = 0$, since investors will not demand a liquidity premium for a one-year security.

The liquidity premium hypothesis does not rule out the possibility of downward-sloping yield curves, although some economists believe that it explains why they are less common. If investors expect future short-term rates to fall sharply, the pure expectations theory holds that a steeply downward-sloping curve should be observed in the spot markets. If investors also demand a premium for investing long-term, the observed yield curve might still be inverted, but it would be more gently sloped than if determined by expectations alone, as shown in Figure 9.10.

It is even possible, according to the liquidity premium hypothesis, that a yield curve reflecting expectations of falling rates could appear to be upward-sloping if investors demanded a relatively high premium on long-term issues. Such a situation is illustrated in Figure 9.11.

Incorporating the Role of Lenders

Other theories of the term structure are distinguished from the pure expectations approach because they include a role for lenders in the determination of spot rates, and they discard the assumption of indifference between maturities.

The Modified Expectations Theory

One theory is sometimes called the **modified expectations theory** to reflect support for the idea that expectations of future rates do, in fact, determine today's yields.[13] As this argument goes, if interest rates

13 Smith (1960). The modified expectations theory produces the same mathematical model as the pure expectations theory (Equation 9.1).

are expected to rise in the future, lenders may wish to lend short term to avoid locking in today's lower spot rates. Such a long-term commitment would not only prevent reinvestment of principal at the expected higher rates, but it also would subject lenders to capital losses should they sell their investments before maturity. However, borrowers will wish to borrow long-term to avoid expected higher interest costs.

According to the theory, the common expectations of borrowers and lenders and their conflicting maturity preferences put pressure on long-term rates, producing an upward-sloping curve. Conversely, when all parties expect interest rates to fall, lenders wish to lend long, but borrowers prefer to roll over a series of short-term loans at progressively lower expected rates. This places upward pressure on short-term rates, resulting in an inverted term structure. Thus, the conclusions of the modified expectations theory are the same as those for the unbiased expectations theory: Expectations of rising rates produce an upward-sloping curve, whereas expectations of falling rates produce a downward-sloping relationship. The main difference between the theories is the motivations that determine spot rates.

The Segmented Markets Theory

Relying heavily on the existence of market imperfections, the **segmented markets theory** argues that there really is no term structure. The segmentation theory has gained especially strong support among market participants.[14] It suggests that different spot rates on long- and short-term securities are explained not by any common set of market expectations, or by a liquidity premium to induce lenders to switch from short- to long-term securities, but rather by separate supply/demand interactions in the financial markets. According to this theory, short-term yields result from interactions of individuals and institutions in the short-term market segment; the same is true of yields on long-term securities. Because laws, regulations, or institutional objectives prevent many market participants from borrowing or lending in every segment, some maturities are of little concern.

One justification for the segmented markets theory is that it reflects the preference of financial institutions to match the maturities of their assets and liabilities. Commercial banks, for example, have traditionally concentrated on lending in the short-term markets while obtaining funds from depositors in that same segment of the market. Similar segmented supply/demand factors may affect long-term rates. Life insurance firms expect long-term payment inflows from customers and invest those funds heavily in instruments with long maturities.

According to the segmented markets theory, what might seem to be a downward-sloping yield curve is really many distinct—and theoretically unrelated—market interactions, as shown in Figure 9.13. Notice the similarities between this hypothetical curve and the actual term structure of interest rates shown in Figure 9.14. For example, proponents of the market segmentation theory believe that the yield curve on December 31, 1969, clearly reveals distinct financial market segments. This theory has implications for interest rate forecasting that are quite distinct from those of the expectations hypothesis. It returns forecasting solely to supply/demand in market segments and relies on forecasting methods similar to those discussed in Chapter 8.

The Preferred Habitat Theory

Closely related to the segmented markets theory is the **preferred habitat theory,** which assumes that although investors may strongly prefer particular segments of the market, they are not necessarily locked into those segments. These strong preferences for certain maturities arise not from legal or regulatory reasons but, rather, from *consumption preferences.*[15] In other words, investors' time preferences for spending versus saving influence their choice among securities. They will lend in markets other than their preferred one, but only if a premium exists to induce them to switch. This argument differs from the liquidity premium theory in that it does not assume that all lenders prefer short-term securities to long-term ones. There may well be lenders who prefer to lend long but who can be induced to lend short for a yield premium, or vice versa.

Although the preferred habitat theory recognizes that some lenders may not be persuaded to depart from their preferred habitats at any price, it holds that the markets are only partially segmented because

---

14 See Culbertson (1957).

15 See Modigliani and Sutch (1966). Cox, Ingersoll, and Ross (1981) argue instead that risk aversion, not time-related consumption preferences, will create preferred habitats. In particular, they interpreted a habitat "as a stronger or weaker tendency to hedge against changes in the interest rate" (p. 786).

figure 9.13 YIELDS IN SEGMENTED MARKETS

The segmented markets theory holds that the term structure is not continuous. Instead, supply and demand in separate financial markets determine the yields in those markets.

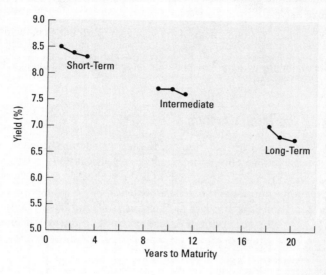

figure 9.14 YIELDS OF TREASURY SECURITIES, DECEMBER 31, 1969

The shape of the yield curve in December 1969 has been used by some as support for the segmented markets theory; yields seemed to cluster rather than being continuously distributed across the spectrum of maturities.

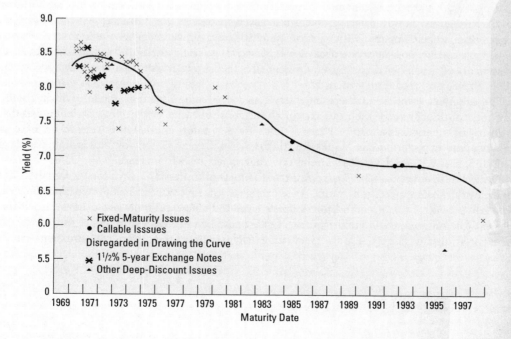

Source: Treasury Bulletin, *January 1970, 83.*

many participants are willing to switch maturities if properly rewarded. Short- and long-term yield differentials are only partially explained by the expectations hypothesis; supply/demand imbalances in various markets may result in positive or negative premiums added to the pure expectations rate to induce shifts from one segment to another. Thus, the preferred habitat theory differs from the segmented markets theory in the following ways:

1. It relies less on the maturity preferences of the suppliers of securities in the determination of spot rates.
2. It acknowledges that many investors consider developments across the spectrum of maturities before making their decisions.

Emerging Theories of the Term Structure

Since the mid-1980s, several new formulations of the term structure have emerged. Although still in their formative stages and yielding conflicting results in empirical tests, these models are gaining support in some circles at the expense of the expectations theory and its modifications.[16] They have by no means supplanted the more traditional theories, however.

Best known of the new models is the work of Cox, Ingersoll, and Ross. Their model bears some similarity to the expectations theory in that it, too, recognizes the influence of interest rate expectations. The newer approach, however, focuses on the factors determining those expectations, such as inflation, uncertainty, and productivity.

Researchers continue to explore adjustments, applications of, and empirical verification of the new models, although their complexity has made empirical testing difficult. Experts agree that investigation of these term structure theories will continue to be a fertile area of research.

Empirical Tests of the Term Structure Theories

A full review of empirical tests of term structure theories would fill a book, because research interest in the subject spans almost a century. Nonetheless, no single theory has prevailed.

A Familiar Research Problem: Measuring Expectations

As the oldest of the theories, the pure expectations model has received the greatest attention. Particularly troublesome, however, is a problem also faced in tests of the Fisher effect: measuring market expectations to be compared with subsequent actual rates. Researchers have used several alternatives. Some have used ex post rates as a proxy for expected rates. The conclusions are similar to those drawn by students of the Fisher theory: Even though, after the fact, expectations are not always correct, they still influence observed term structures.[17]

For example, some researchers have developed an "error learning" model, which argues that investors continually revise their expectations in response to earlier errors. This model implies that past and present experiences affect investors' response to new information. Other researchers have argued that investors' expectations are "regressive," that is, when the general level of rates is high, people expect them to fall, and when the general level is low, they expect rates to increase.

Quite a different approach uses interest rate forecasts of professional investors and analysts as proxies for interest rate expectations. Some researchers have also recognized that the financial futures markets may provide a good method for estimating interest rate expectations and have turned to those markets for continuation of empirical tests. Others have investigated the influence of monetary policy on expectations and the slope of the yield curve.[18] Regardless of the chosen measurement, many stud-

---

16 See Cox, Ingersoll, and Ross (1981, 1985) and Ho and Lee (1986). Abken (1990) offers a comprehensive summary and evaluation of the newer models and results of empirical tests.

17 Examples of these studies include Van Horne (1965), Kessel (1965), Meiselman (1962), Wood (1983), Walz and Spencer (1989), Froot (1989), and Dua (1991).

18 See Kane and Malkiel (1967), Friedman (1979), Hafer and Hein (1989), and Cook and Hahn (1990).

ies of the U.S. Treasury securities market have concluded that expectations play a major role in determining the term structure.[19]

Research on the expectations theory increasingly reflects globalization of financial markets. Scholars have noted that investors' expectations may be directed not only toward rates in their home country but also toward rates in other financial markets in which they customarily interact. Thus, some recent studies have tested the expectations theory on contemporaneous data from several countries. Although the evidence by no means supports a definite conclusion that long-term rates in one country reflect expectations of short-term rates in other countries, this avenue of term structure research will undoubtedly be continued in the next decade.[20]

Evidence on Liquidity Premiums

Many researchers have concluded that investors also demand liquidity premiums, although they do not agree on the nature of these premiums. The disagreement centers on whether the premium demanded by investors is affected by the general level of interest rates (i.e., whether the premium increases or decreases when rates are considered to be relatively high or low) and whether it is stable or rises monotonically with maturity. There is considerable evidence that the liquidity premium *does* vary with the general level of interest rates, but there is no agreement on whether the relationship is positive or negative.[21] In other words, some research indicates that when rates are higher than normal, the liquidity premium required by investors is smaller than usual, whereas other results suggest that it is larger.

The debate over the nature of the liquidity premium has implications for tests of the expectations hypothesis and for its usefulness as a forecasting model. Because it is difficult to determine the size and pattern of liquidity premiums, it is difficult to isolate an expected "pure" interest rate from a premium attached to it. Some research has suggested that liquidity premiums range from 0.54 percent to 1.56 percent, but other studies have concluded that premiums are less than 0.50 percent, even for long maturities. Some researchers have even concluded that liquidity premiums decrease, rather than increase, with maturity.[22]

Research on Segmented Markets and Preferred Habitats

Research on the segmented markets and preferred habitat theories is extremely contradictory. Some researchers have reported findings of discontinuities in the yield curve, supporting the market segmentation theory; some have concluded that preferred habitats exist.[23] In contrast, other studies, including those supporting the expectations and liquidity premium theories, argue that the financial markets function more efficiently than the segmented markets theory or preferred habitat theory recognizes. In other words, investors are more willing to move funds back and forth between maturities to maximize returns than either of these theories implies.

Concept Questions

1 If a yield curve is downward-sloping, under the pure expectations theory, what are short-term rates expected to do in the future (rise, fall, or stay the same)?

2 For the same scenario outlined in question 1, what are short-term rates expected to do under the liquidity premium theory?

3 What are the differences between the modified expectations theory, the segmented market theory, and the preferred habitat theory? How do they each incorporate the role of lenders (investors)?

---

19 There are serious critics. For example, one study concludes that the use of the simple expectations theory "to forecast the direction of future changes in the interest rate seems worthless." See Schiller, Campbell, and Schoenholtz (1983). Belongia and Koedik (1988) also fail to find support for the expectations hypothesis.

20 See Belongia and Koedik (1988) and Kool and Tatom (1988).21 See Nelson (1972), Van Horne (1965), Friedman (1979), and Dua (1991).

22 For further information on empirical research addressing the liquidity premium hypothesis, see McCulloch (1975); Lee, Maness, and Tuttle (1980); Roll (1970); and Throop (1981).

23 See Modigliani and Sutch (1966). Also see Dobson, Sutch, and Vanderford (1976); Echols and Elliott (1976); Roley (1981); and Heuson (1988).

Applying Term Structure Theories to Financial Institutions Management

Most managers do not personally intend to resolve these theoretical and empirical debates, but they are interested in using the fruits of research to make better decisions. Fortunately, although no one has written the definitive word on yield curves, ample insights are available from existing theory to assist a knowledgeable manager. Some of the most important problems for which term structure theories are useful are illustrated in the following discussion.

It is important to appreciate the perspective from which managers view the term structure. Instead of confronting the raw material of yield curves—investors' expectations, liquidity premiums, and supply/demand relationships in the financial markets—managers observe the finished products, such as the actual term structures depicted in Figures 9.2 through 9.4. Term structure theories attempt to explain how observed term structures came about. The information a manager obtains by applying theory to an existing yield curve can assist in making decisions, such as forecasting interest rates, setting a mortgage loan rate, or trading securities for the institution's portfolio.

Interest Rate Forecasting

Of particular importance to interest rate forecasting is the pure expectations theory. The mathematical expression of the pure expectations theory itself provides a forecasting model. To illustrate, suppose that in June 2005, the spot Treasury yields shown in Table 9.2 for a five-year maturity horizon are observed.

Forward Rates

If it is currently June 2005, according to the pure expectations theory, the two-year spot rate (i.e., the existing yield on a security maturing in June 2007) is the geometric average of the expected yield on a one-year Treasury security (a rate that can be directly observed from the existing yield curve maturing in 2006) and the expected annual yield on one-year securities issued a year later in June 2007 (a rate not directly observable). That relationship was modeled mathematically in Equation 9.1.

Using data from Table 9.2,

$$1 + {}_1r_2 = [(1 + {}_1r_1)(1 + {}_2\gamma_1)]^{1/2}$$
$$1 + 0.1185 = [(1.1250)(1 + {}_2\gamma_1)]^{1/2}$$

where ${}_2\gamma_1$ = unobservable expected one-year rate at the beginning of period 2.

If the pure expectations theory is correct, one can infer the expected one-year rate at the beginning of period 2 by solving Equation 9.1 for ${}_2\gamma_1$:

$$(1 + {}_2\gamma_1) = (1 + {}_1r_2)^2 / (1 + {}_1r_1) \qquad [9.3]$$
$$(1 + {}_2\gamma_1) = (1.1185)^2 / (1.1250)$$
$$(1 + {}_2\gamma_1) = 1.1120 - 1 = 0.1120 = 11.20\%$$

An implied expected rate calculated from an existing yield curve is a **forward rate**. The one-year forward rate, or expected rate, at the beginning of period 2 is 11.20 percent. This rate is expected to pre-

table **9.2**   HYPOTHETICAL SPOT RATES ON TREASURY SECURITIES AS OF JUNE 2005

These hypothetical data on observed yields can be used to infer one-year forward rates.

Maturity Date	Spot Yield (%)	Notation
June 2006	12.50%	${}_1r_1$
June 2007	11.85%	${}_1r_2$
June 2008	11.00%	${}_1r_3$
June 2009	10.90%	${}_1r_4$
June 2010	10.50%	${}_1r_5$

vail on investments made in June 2006 and maturing in June 2007. It is lower than the one-year T-bill yield in 2005 because the spot yields in Table 9.2 suggest market expectations for falling rates. If an institution's managers use the pure expectations theory, this forward rate can serve as a specific forecast for short-term T-bill rates for future years.

The general formula for a one-year forward rate as of the beginning of period t is as follows, where observable bond rates with n years to maturity are used.

$$(1 + {}_t\gamma_1) = (1 + {}_1r_n)^n / (1 + {}_1r_{n-1})^{n-1} \qquad [9.4]$$

Equation 9.4 allows calculation of the one-year forward rate as of the beginning of any future period (t). It is more useful than Equation 9.3, which solves only for the one-year forward rate as of the beginning of period 2.

Incorporating Liquidity Premiums

Many managers may not accept the unbiased expectations theory as the only explanation for the term structure. Fortunately, it is possible to incorporate liquidity premiums into a forecasting model. If liquidity premiums exist, spot rates for two-, three-, four-, and five-year securities in Table 9.2 are affected not only by expectations but also by premiums on long-term investments.

For example, suppose a manager believes that investors expect a premium of 0.5 percent for holding a two-year security in 2005. That belief can be incorporated into a forecast of future short-term rates by solving Equation 9.2 for the forward rate as of the beginning of period 2:

$$1 + {}_1r_2 = [(1 + {}_1r_1)(1 + {}_2\gamma_1 + L_2)]^{1/2} \qquad [9.5]$$

$$1 + {}_2\gamma_1 = [(1 + {}_1r_2)^2 / (1 + {}_1r_1)] - L_2$$

Under the assumption of liquidity premiums, the estimate for the forward rate in June 2006 becomes the following:

$$(1.1185)^2 = (1.1250)(1 + {}_2\gamma_1 + 0.005)$$

$$1 + {}_2\gamma_1 + 0.005 = (1.1185)^2 / (1.1250)$$

$$1 + {}_2\gamma_1 + 0.005 = 1.1120$$

$$1 + {}_2\gamma_1 = 1.1120 - 0.005 = 1.1070$$

$${}_2\gamma_1 = 0.1070 = 10.70\%$$

This one-year rate expected to prevail in 2006 is lower than the forward rate of 11.20 percent calculated earlier with only the pure expectations theory as a basis for forecasting. The difference is the assumed liquidity premium required for two-year loans. If liquidity premiums exist, their effect on actual long-term rates will cause the results of Equations 9.3 or 9.4 to be biased upward. Equation 9.5 adjusts for that bias.

Using the pure expectations theory with liquidity premiums, the general equation for calculating the one-year forward rate in period t is as follows:

$$1 + {}_t\gamma_1 = [(1 + {}_1r_n)^n / (1 + {}_1r_{n-1})^{n-1}] - L_t \qquad [9.6]$$

Equation 9.6 allows estimation of the forward rate as of the beginning of any future period, adjusted for a liquidity premium. In contrast, Equation 9.5 applies only to the forward rate as of the beginning of period 2.

Setting Institutional Interest Rates

A financial institution manager frequently faces simultaneous decisions about short- and long-term interest rates. For example, if short-term deposits such as one-year certificates of deposit (CDs) are to be used to finance long-term assets such as mortgages, care must be taken to establish both rates so that the cost of financing does not exceed the yield on the mortgages. Using the pure expectations theory, a manager who observes an upward-sloping Treasury security term structure can infer that most investors expect increasing short-term rates over the next several periods. The cost of one-year CDs is therefore likely to increase during the period when mortgage loans made today have a constant yield.

According to the liquidity premium theory, existing Treasury rates may also include liquidity premiums, and the manager may also believe that a premium for default risk should be required for holding mortgages instead of Treasury securities. Furthermore, the segmented markets and preferred habitat theories suggest that competitive pressures from other depository institutions should be considered in setting both rates. For example, if there is strong competition for one-year CDs, a savings and loan association (S&L) may be forced to pay an even higher yield than the expectations hypothesis would suggest.

Estimating the Cost of Deposits

Sample calculations and estimations involved in this decision are provided in Table 9.3. For simplicity, it is assumed that mortgages made today will mature in five years. Because the source of funds is one-year CDs, the manager would begin by calculating a series of one-year forward rates implied in the existing yield curve by using Equation 9.4. Using Equation 9.6, liquidity premiums embedded in the current term structure would be removed to avoid overestimating expected one-year CD rates in future periods. Because the institution plans to issue one-year CDs each year, it would not have to offer liquidity premiums to its depositors.

The resulting series of forward rates (given in Column 5) is used to set initial and anticipated one-year CD rates. Specifically, the initial CD rate is based on the first rate in this series (8 percent), with subsequent forward rates serving as the basis for estimating the future annual interest cost of the deposits. After obtaining these costs, the manager would increase them as needed to account for the administrative costs of servicing deposits (Column 6). In addition, adjustments might be made to account for premiums necessary to meet competitors' offerings. Column 6 contains estimated total interest plus noninterest costs of issuing one-year CDs each year for five years.

table 9.3   USING TERM STRUCTURE THEORIES TO SET INSTITUTIONAL INTEREST RATES

These hypothetical data on observed yields, liquidity premiums, administrative costs, risk premiums, and profit markups can be used to estimate the appropriate rate to charge on a mortgage loan.

(1) Maturity (years)	(2) Observed Yield on Treasury Securities	(3) Unadjusted 1-year Forward Rate (from Equation 9.4)	(4) Estimated Liquidity Premium	(5) Estimated 1-year Rate with Liquidity Premium Removed (Column 3 − Column 4)
1	0.0800	0.0800	0.0000	0.0800
2	0.0825	0.0850	0.0050	0.0800
3	0.0950	0.1204	0.0100	0.1104
4	0.1025	0.1253	0.0250	0.1003
5	0.1100	0.1405	0.0350	0.1055

(6) Annual CD Cost (Column 5 + Administrative Markup of 0.25% Per Year)	(7) Estimated Premium Required to Hold Mortgages	(8) Estimated Annual Required Return (Column 6 + Column 7 + Profit Markup of 0.75% Per Year)
0.0825	0.0100	0.1000
0.0825	0.0250	0.1150
0.1129	0.0300	0.1504
0.1028	0.0400	0.1503
0.1080	0.0450	0.1605

(9)
Estimation of Required Annual Yield on Mortgages
(using Equation 9.1 on Data from Column 8)

$$i_m = \sqrt[5]{(1.1000)(1.1150)(1.1504)(1.1503)(1.1605)} - 1$$

$$i_m = 0.1350 = 13.50\%$$

Setting the Mortgage Rate

The manager would then set the five-year mortgage rate by estimating the risk premium necessary to compensate the institution for holding mortgages (Column 7). Finally, a desired profit markup of 0.75 percent per year is added to allow for a return to owners in a stockholder-owned firm or to provide for additions to net worth in a mutual institution. The resulting figures in Column 8 are the estimated annual returns required to cover all costs, including the cost of funds, noninterest costs, and a target rate of profit. Finally, the geometric average of the five rates is calculated by using Equation 9.1. This rate, 13.50 percent in Table 9.3, is the appropriate annual interest rate to charge on a mortgage made at the beginning of the five-year period. If the institution earns 13.50 percent annually for five years and if actual costs equal estimates, the desired profit markup over the life of the mortgage will be earned. Of course, an institution's ability to charge this rate is constrained by competition, but competing institutions would also be aware of the need to recover long-term costs.

It is important to remember that even such careful forecasting and rate setting include a great deal of uncertainty. As the review of empirical research suggests, expectations embedded in the term structure are not always fulfilled, and additional sources of error are introduced in the estimation of the liquidity premium. Such errors can be costly, because once the long-term mortgage rate has been established, it may not be subject to renegotiation, and profits will disappear if interest rates move to such a high level that costs cannot be recovered. Many thrift institutions, in particular, learned this lesson the hard way in the early 1980s. Institutions must also maintain sufficient flexibility to respond when forecasts prove to be incorrect. Increasingly sophisticated techniques for managing interest rate risk are discussed in the chapters that follow.

Using Forward Rates Estimated from Yield Curves to Set Loan Credit Risk Premiums

Another use for yield curves is to set risk premiums for loans based on risk premiums set in bond markets for corporate bonds.[24] Under this technique, which is based on the pure expectations theory of interest rates, Equation 9.3 is used to calculate the one-year expected rates, that is, forward rates, for next year's one-year Treasury bond and a corporate bond with some credit classification (for instance, BBB). The probability of no default for the BBB bond is then calculated by taking the ratio between (1 + forward rate for the Treasuries) / (1 + forward rate for the corporate bonds). For example, hypothetically suppose in the year 2002, you are a loan pricing analyst, and *The Wall Street Journal* quotes a two-year Treasury bond to have a 4.62 percent yield and a one-year Treasury bond to have a 4.28 percent yield. Similarly, *The Wall Street Journal* shows a two-year BBB Corporate bond to have a 5.18 percent yield and a one-year corporate BBB bond to have a 5.00 percent yield. By using Equation 9.3, the respective forward rates for one-year Treasury and corporate bonds issued next year can be calculated, as follows:

$$(1 + {_2}r_1) = (1 + {_1}r_2)^2 / (1 + {_1}r_1)$$

$$\text{Expected 1-yr T-bill} = (1.0462)^2 / (1.0428) - 1 = 4.961\%$$

$$\text{Expected 1-yr Corporate rate} = (1.0518)^2 / (1.0500) - 1 = 5.360\%$$

By taking the ratio of 1 plus the Treasury forward rate to 1 plus the risky bond rate, the expected probability of the corporate bond defaulting can be calculated. Taking the ratio of (1 + Treasury forward rate) / (1 + corporate forward rate) is equal to the following:

$$(1.04961) / (1.0536) = 0.9962$$

Hence, the expected probability of the BBB corporate bond of defaulting is $1 - 0.9962 = 0.0038$, or 0.38 percent. Based on this, the risk premium for similar one-year loans with a probability of default of only 0.38 percent should be similar to the risk premium for the corporate bond over the Treasury bond of about (5.36 percent − 4.961 percent) = 0.40 percent, or 40 basis points (1 basis point = 0.01 percent). For longer-term bonds, risk premiums can be calculated by finding the respective forward rates for each year and the ratio of forward rates to find the probability of no default for each year. The joint probabilities, that is, the product of the probabilities of no default for each year, can then be cal-

---

24 This use of forward rates to calculate probabilities of bonds not defaulting comes from Saunders (1997), who provides a detailed description of the term structure derivation of credit risk.

culated for the life of the bond, and the joint probability of default $[1 - (p_1)(p_2)$, and so on] can be calculated for bonds of different maturities. A term structure of default risk can then be graphed to show the increase in default risk for securities of different maturities.

Managing the Securities Portfolio

Term structure theories are also useful in managing the institution's securities portfolio. A common trading strategy is searching for undervalued or overvalued securities. This strategy assumes that, although the pure expectations theory applies in general and investors price securities to make the expected annual yield the same regardless of the maturities selected over a holding period, the markets are sometimes in temporary disequilibrium. According to this line of thinking, if a security's yield exceeds those on securities of equal maturity and risk, the security is underpriced. If the institution does not own the security, it can purchase it immediately. When the market returns to equilibrium, the price of the security should rise, lowering its yield to the appropriate level. The institution can expect to profit from the capital gain.

Conversely, if a security's yield is less than those on securities of comparable maturity, the security is overpriced and should be sold. The pure expectations theory suggests that its price will fall as the market returns its yield to the level proper for its maturity. Analysts sometimes attempt to identify under- or overvalued securities in the Treasury market, for example, by studying yield curves such as the one in Figure 9.2. The issues circled left of the center of the graph have lower yields than securities of similar maturity (approximately two years). A manager who believed that the market was in temporary disequilibrium would sell the issues before the anticipated drop in price increased their yields.

Such a strategy would reflect not only a belief that the pure expectations theory correctly describes interest rate movements in the long run but also a recognition of the role of **arbitrage** in the financial markets. Arbitrage is trading to profit from temporary price discrepancies in otherwise identical assets. As noted, the pure expectations theory assumes that investors are indifferent among equally risky securities of varying maturities. If the theory were correct, investors holding the relatively lower-yielding two-year securities circled in Figure 9.2 would possess arbitrage opportunities. They could attempt to improve returns by selling the circled securities and either purchasing higher-yielding two-year securities *or* purchasing a series of shorter-term securities over a two-year period. These arbitrage selling and buying activities would, in turn, cause the price of the circled securities to decline and the prices of purchased securities to rise. Because of the inverse relationship between prices and yields, the expected return to subsequent owners of the circled securities would rise. Ultimately, then, the actions of arbitrage traders should cause the yields on securities of similar maturity to converge.[25] The relationship between prices and yields is explored further in Chapter 10.

Concept Questions

1 How can the expectations theory be used to set long-term interest rates?

2 How can the liquidity premium theory be used to adjust the setting of long-term interest rates?

3 How can forward rates be calculated and used in setting short-term CD rates?

4 How can forward rates be used to set long-term mortgage rates?

5 How can forward rates be used to set credit risk premiums?

6 Ideally, how would a financial institution manage a securities portfolio using yield curves as signals for the business cycle? What restrictions often prevent this ideal strategy?

---

25 This discussion refers to arbitrage in general and not to a specific trading strategy used by some securities firms called "yield-curve arbitrage." The latter phrase refers to simultaneous trading in short-term interest rate futures and long-term bonds to profit from the fact that short-term interest rates (thus, the "short" end of the yield curve) fluctuate more than long-term rates. For more information, see Craig Torres. "'Yield-Curve Arbitrage' Rewards the Skillful." *The Wall Street Journal* (July 27, 1989), C1, C10. For the sake of brevity, basic applications are considered here for financial institutions. As noted in the introduction to the chapter, yield curves are commonly used to forecast stages of the business cycle and the future movements of rates as well. For instance, in the past the end of a business expansion has often been accompanied by a downward-sloping yield curve. Although the downward slope is not always a reliable indicator, it would suggest that a financial institution might think about investing in long-term bonds, because under the expectations theory, investors are expecting rates to fall. Similarly, a rising yield curve is often present at the end of a recession (start of an expansion), which under the expectations theory suggests that investors are expecting rates to rise. If this is thought to be the case, a financial institution might want to shorten the maturity of its securities to avoid capital losses on fixed income securities. If an expansion does begin, it will often be accompanied by rising rates as the demand for funds by businesses grows.

Summary

The term structure of interest rates is the relationship at a specific time between the yields and maturities of securities of comparable default risk. Historically, this relationship has varied. The variation is related both to the general level of interest rates and to the pace of economic activity.

Economists have developed several theories to explain term structures. Researchers agree that the financial markets' expectations of future short-term rates play a large role in determining existing yields on long-term securities. Other factors, such as investors' varying preferences for liquidity, their policies and attitudes, or regulation in the financial markets, appear to have less influence on the term structure.

Knowledge of term structure relationships is useful in asset/liability management. Understanding the role of expectations allows managers to develop interest rate forecasts to use in institutional planning and in trading strategies for the securities portfolio. Also, knowledge of expectations, liquidity preferences, and supply/demand interactions can help managers establish the prices of financial products such as deposits and loans.

Questions

Suppose you are interviewing for a job with a mutual fund company. Jim Moser, the financial economist interviewing you, wants to see if you understand how yield curves are created and used. Answer the following questions for him.

1. Explain the term structure of interest rates and the relationships measured. Why must all securities plotted on a given term structure have equal default risk?
2. Historically, what has been the relationship between the slope of the yield curve and the level of economic activity? Between the slope of the yield curve and the general level of interest rates?
3. In a recent issue of *The Wall Street Journal* or other major newspaper, find yield quotations for U.S. Treasury securities. Using data for T-bills, bonds, and notes, sketch the prevailing term structure.
4. According to the pure expectations theory, what determines the slope of the term structure of interest rates? On what important assumptions is this theory based? Using this theory, what expectations about future interest rates are reflected in the term structure you plotted for Question 3?
5. An investor who accepts the pure expectations theory and its underlying assumptions has been offered two six-year investment plans. One plan is a series of three two-year instruments, whereas the other plan is a series of six one-year T-bill purchases. Ignoring any fees and assuming no liquidity premiums, which alternative would be preferable? Why?
6. Explain how the liquidity premium hypothesis differs from the pure expectations theory. Which of the pure expectations assumptions is rejected under the liquidity premium hypothesis?
7. Assume that the yield curve you plotted in Question 3 includes liquidity premiums that gradually increase as maturity increases. Sketch an estimate of the prevailing pure expectations term structure.
8. According to the modified expectations theory, what role do borrowers play in determining the relationship between short-term and long-term interest rates?
9. What market imperfections are recognized in the segmented markets hypothesis? What are its assumptions about the maturity preferences of borrowers and lenders?
10. How does the preferred habitat theory characterize the maturity preferences of borrowers and lenders? Under what conditions will investors switch from one maturity to another? Does the preferred habitat theory support the concept of a continuous yield curve? Why or why not?
11. Which theory of the term structure do you find most plausible? Which is the least plausible? By integrating ideas from all term structure theories, state briefly how you believe the term structure is determined.
12. Briefly summarize the difficulties in measuring interest rate expectations and liquidity premiums for tests of the pure expectations theory.
13. Explain how financial institution managers may use estimates of forward rates as they set long-term loan and deposit rates.
14. How are estimates of forward rates used to set risk premiums for loans?

Problems

1. Jeff and Lori Cooperman, your financial planning consultants, have adopted the followed expectations for short-term interest rates:

   1-year rate prevailing January 2005: 6.7%
   1-year rate prevailing January 2006: 7.8%

   Based on these expectations and assuming no liquidity premiums, what rate do your consultants expect you to earn on a two-year security purchased in January 2005?

2. Your mother, who watches her investments closely, has sent a newsletter reporting yields currently available on various Treasury securities. As of January 1, 2005, a T-bond with exactly three years to maturity carries a yield of 7.65 percent, while a four-year bond (maturing January 1, 2009) offers a yield of 7.30 percent. Assuming no liquidity premiums, what is the one-year forward rate expected to prevail as of January 1, 2008 (the beginning of year 4)?

3. If you estimate that a liquidity premium of 0.0025 (0.25 percent) on a four-year investment is included in the yields quoted in Problem 2, what is your revised estimate of the one-year forward rate expected to prevail at the beginning of year 4?

4.

TREASURY BILL PURCHASED	TREASURY BILL MATURES	EXPECTED ANNUAL RATE %
January 2005	January 2006	9.35% (observed)
January 2006	January 2007	8.95
January 2007	January 2008	8.15
January 2008	January 2009	7.50

   a. Using the preceding information and the pure expectations hypothesis, calculate the yield to maturity as of January 2005 for each of the following:
   1) a two-year security
   2) a three-year security
   3) a four-year security

   b. Using your calculations in part a, sketch the term structure of interest rates prevailing in January 2005.

   c. Calculate the expected average annual yield for each of the following investment strategies:
   1) investment in a two-year security followed by investment in a second two-year security
   2) investment in a series of four one-year T-bills

   d. Explain how your answers to part c support the pure expectations theory.

5.

TREASURY BILL PURCHASED	TREASURY BILL MATURES	EXPECTED ANNUAL RATE %	LIQUIDITY PREMIUM AS OF JUNE 2005 %
June 2005	June 2006	4.25% (observed)	0.00%
June 2006	June 2007	5.95	0.15 (on 2-year security)
June 2007	June 2008	6.75	0.25 (on 3-year security)
June 2008	June 2009	7.95	0.30 (on 4-year security)

   a. Based on the preceding information and using the pure expectations and liquidity premium hypotheses, calculate the yield to maturity as of June 2005 for each of the following:
   1) a two-year Treasury security
   2) a three-year security
   3) a four-year security

   b. Using your calculations in part a, sketch the observed term structure of interest rates as of June 2005.

   c. Calculate the expected average annual yield for each of the following investment strategies:
   1) investment in a four-year Treasury security
   2) purchase of a one-year T-bill followed by investment in a three-year Treasury security
   3) investment in a series of four one-year T-bills

6.

TREASURY BILL PURCHASED	TREASURY BILL MATURES	EXPECTED ANNUAL RATE %
June 2005	June 2006	6.75% (observed)
June 2006	June 2007	7.30
June 2007	June 2008	8.05
June 2008	June 2009	8.95

   a. Calculate the expected average annual yield for each of the following investment strategies:
   1) investment in a series of three one-year securities, with the investments made in June of each year from 2005 through 2007 (beginning of the month)
   2) investment in a two-year security in June 2005 followed by investment in a one-year T-bill in June 2007

   b. Calculate the expected average annual yield for each of the following investment strategies:
   1) investment in a one-year security in June 2005 followed by investment in a three-year security in June 2006
   2) investment in a series of four one-year T-bills, with the investment made in June of each year from 2005 through 2008

c. Recalculate your answers for parts a and b under the liquidity premium hypothesis, given the following liquidity premiums as of June 2005:

MATURITY OF SECURITY	LIQUIDITY PREMIUM
1 Year	0.00%
2 Years	0.12
3 Years	0.18
4 Years	0.22

7. Assume it is now May 2006 and that the following yields prevail:

TREASURY SECURITY MATURITY DATE	SPOT YIELD AS OF MAY 2006 %
May 2007	11.05%
May 2008	10.50
May 2009	10.05
May 2010	9.45
May 2011	8.95

a. Calculate the one-year forward rate as of May 2010 (the beginning of Period 4).

b. Calculate the one-year forward rate as of May 2009 (the beginning of Period 3).

8. For these problems, use the information on maturity dates and spot yields from Problem 7 and the liquidity premiums in the following table:

a. Calculate the one-year forward rate with liquidity premium removed as of May 2010 (the beginning of Period 4).

b. Calculate the one-year forward rate with liquidity premium removed as of May 2009 (the beginning of Period 3).

MATURITY OF SECURITY	LIQUIDITY PREMIUM AS OF MAY 1995 %
1 Year	0.00%
2 Years	0.15
3 Years	0.21
4 Years	0.26
5 Years	0.29

9. Charles Register, president of the Alligator Bank of Trust, is in the process of setting rates on one-year certificates of deposit and on four-year, fixed-rate automobile loans, in which newly acquired funds will be invested. The yield curve is presently upward-sloping, suggesting that these fixed-rate loans should be priced carefully. Based on the following information and the pure expectations hypothesis, what rate should the bank charge on a four-year loan? (Hint: Calculate the expected rates for future one-year CDs first.) Assume liquidity premiums equal 0.

TREASURY SECURITIES

MATURITY	OBSERVED ANNUAL YIELD %
1 Year	4.50
2 Years	5.25
3 Years	5.75
4 Years	6.50

Administrative Markup:
1% per year

Risk Premium Required for Holding Auto Loans:

Year 1	2.0%
Year 2	2.5
Year 3	3.0
Year 4	3.5

10. Sinan Cebenoyan of the Big Apple National Bank is evaluating the bank's charges on five-year balloon mortgages. The mortgage rate is fixed for five years, but the bank acquires funds primarily by issuing one-year CDs. Using the following information, estimate rates for future CDs and the appropriate five-year mortgage rate. In addition to this information, bank management estimates that the following liquidity premiums are included in observed long-term yields:

TREASURY SECURITIES

MATURITY	OBSERVED YIELD
1 Year	9.00%
2 Years	9.75
3 Years	10.15
4 Years	10.95
5 Years	11.40

Administrative Cost Percentage (Markup) on CDs:
1% per year

ESTIMATED RISK PREMIUMS REQUIRED FOR HOLDING MORTGAGES:

Year 1	1.0%
Year 2	1.8
Year 3	2.5
Year 4	3.2
Year 5	3.8

In addition to this information, bank management estimates that the following liquidity premiums are included in observed long-term yields:

MATURITY	PREMIUM
1 Year	0.00%
2 Years	0.10
3 Years	0.16
4 Years	0.21
5 Years	0.25

Selected References

Abken, Peter. "Innovations in Modeling the Term Structure of Interest Rates." *Economic Review* (Federal Reserve Bank of Atlanta) 65 (July/August 1990), 2–27.

Belongia, Michael T., and Kees G. Koedik. "Testing the Expectations Model of the Term Structure: Some Conjectures on the Effects of Institutional Changes." *Review* (Federal Reserve Bank of St. Louis) 70 (September/October 1988), 37–45.

Blalock, Joseph. "Whither the Yield Curve?" *Savings and Community Banker* 2 (April 1993), 36–38.

Cogley, Timothy. "Interpreting the Term Structure of Interest Rates." *Weekly Letter* (Federal Reserve Bank of San Francisco) (April 16, 1993).

Cook, Timothy, and Thomas Hahn. "Interest Rate Expectations and the Slope of the Money Market Yield Curve." *Economic Review* (Federal Reserve Bank of Richmond) 76 (September/October 1990), 3–26.

Cox, John C., Jonathan E. Ingersoll, Jr., and Stephen A. Ross. "A Re-Examination of Traditional Hypotheses about the Term Structure of Interest Rates." *Journal of Finance* 36 (September 1981), 769–799.

Cox, John C., Jonathan E. Ingersoll, Jr., and Stephen A. Ross. "A Theory of the Term Structure of Interest Rates." *Econometrica* 53 (March 1985), 385–408.

Culbertson, John M. "The Term Structure of Interest Rates." *Quarterly Journal of Economics* 71 (November 1957), 485–517.

Dobson, Steven W., Richard C. Sutch, and David E. Vanderford. "An Evaluation of Alternative Empirical Models of the Term Structure of Interest Rates." *Journal of Finance* 31 (September 1976), 1035–1065.

Dua, Pami. "Survey Evidence on the Term Structure of Interest Rates." *Journal of Economics and Business* 43 (1991), 133–142.

Echols, Michael E., and J. Walter Elliott. "Rational Expectations in a Disequilibrium Model of the Term Structure." *American Economic Review* 66 (March 1976), 28–44.

Friedman, Benjamin M. "Interest Rate Expectations versus Forward Rates: Evidence from an Expectations Survey." *Journal of Finance* 34 (September 1979), 965–973.

Froot, Kenneth A. "New Hope for the Expectations Hypothesis of the Term Structure of Interest Rates." *Journal of Finance* 44 (June 1989), 283–305.

Furlong, Frederick T. "The Yield Curve and Recessions." *Weekly Letter* (Federal Reserve Bank of San Francisco) (March 10, 1989).

Hafer, R. W., and Scott E. Hein. "Comparing Futures and Survey Forecasts of Near-Term Treasury Bill Rates." *Review* (Federal Reserve Bank of St. Louis) 71 (May/June 1989), 33–42.

Heuson, Andrea J. "The Term Premia Relationship Implicit in the Term Structure of Treasury Bills." *Journal of Financial Research* 11 (Spring 1988), 13–20.

Hicks, J. R. *Value and Capital.* London: Oxford University Press, 1946.

Ho, Thomas, and Sang-Bin Lee. "Term Structure Movements and Pricing Interest Rate Contingent Claims." *Journal of Finance* 41 (December 1986), 1011–1029.

Kane, Edward J., and Burton G. Malkiel. "The Term Structure of Interest Rates: An Analysis of a Survey of Interest Rate Expectations." *Review of Economics and Statistics* 49 (August 1967), 343–355.

Kessel, Reuben A. *The Cyclical Behavior of the Term Structure.* New York: National Bureau of Economic Research, 1965.

Kool, Clemens J. M., and John A. Tatom. "International Linkages in the Term Structure of Interest Rates." *Review* (Federal Reserve Bank of St. Louis) 70 (July/August 1988), 30–42.

Lee, Wayne, Terry S. Maness, and Donald Tuttle. "Non-Speculative Behavior and the Term Structure." *Journal of Financial and Quantitative Analysis* 15 (March 1980), 53–83.

Lutz, Frederick. "The Structure of Interest Rates." *Quarterly Journal of Economics* 30 (November 1940), 36–63.

Malkiel, Burton. *The Term Structure of Interest Rates: Theory, Empirical Evidence, and Applications.* Princeton, NJ: Princeton University Press, 1966.

McCulloch, Huston J. "An Estimation of the Liquidity Premium Hypothesis." *Journal of Political Economy* 83 (January/February 1975), 95–119.

Meiselman, David. *The Term Structure of Interest Rates.* Englewood Cliffs, NJ: Prentice Hall, 1962.

Modigliani, Franco, and Richard Sutch. "Innovation in Interest Rate Policy." *American Economic Review* 66 (May 1966), 178–197.

Nelson, Charles R. *The Term Structure of Interest Rates.* New York: Basic Books, 1972.

Roley, V. Vance. "The Determinants of the Treasury Yield Curve." *Journal of Finance* 36 (December 1981), 1103–1126.

Roll, Richard. *The Behavior of Interest Rates.* New York: Basic Books, 1970.

Saunders, Anthony. *Financial Institutions Management: A Modern Perspective,* 2d ed. Burr Ridge, IL: Irwin, 1997.

Schiller, Robert J., John Y. Campbell, and Kermit L. Schoenholtz. "Forward Rates and Future Policy: Interpreting the Term Structure of Interest Rates." In *Brookings Papers on Economic Activity, I: 1982.* Washington, DC: Brookings Institution, 1983, 173–223.

Smith, Warren L. *Debt Management in the United States.* Study Paper 19, Joint Economic Committee of the 86th Congress (January 1960).

Stevens, E. J. "Is There a Message in the Yield Curve?" *Economic Commentary* (Federal Reserve Bank of Cleveland) (March 15, 1989).

Throop, Adrian. "Interest Rate Forecasts and Market Efficiency." *Economic Review* (Federal Reserve Bank of San Francisco) (Spring 1981), 29–43.

Van Horne, James. "Interest Rate Risk and the Term Structure of Interest Rates." *Journal of Political Economy* 73 (August 1965), 344–351.

Wallich, Henry C., and Peter M. Keir. "The Role of Operating Guides in U.S. Monetary Policy: A Historical Review." *Federal Reserve Bulletin* 65 (September 1979), 679–691.

Walz, Daniel T., and Roger W. Spencer. "The Informational Content of Forward Rates: Further Evidence." *Journal of Financial Research* 12 (Spring 1989), 69–81.

Wood, John H. "Do Yield Curves Normally Slope Up? The Term Structure of Interest Rates, 1862–1982." *Economic Perspectives* (Federal Reserve Bank of Chicago) 7 (July/August 1983), 17–23.

THE TERM STRUCTURE OF INTEREST RATES

Risk Library International Finance and Commodities Institute (IFCI)
IFCI site is designed to help the user navigate through the sea of regulatory documents on international finance. IFCI's Advisory Committee has selected online documents that are regarded as essential to understanding the current status of various aspects of financial regulation and risk management. They provide the answers to the "why and how of where we are" and point to future trends in international finance.

1. Go to *http://risk.ifci.ch/RiskDocuments.HTM.*

2. From the Risk Library page, click on "Core Documents."
    The table provides a linked list of articles on international finance. In the columns, the key finance concepts discussed in the article are marked with an "X." For example, the article "Sound Practices for Loan Accounting, Credit Risk Disclosure, and Related Matters," published by the Basle Committee of the Bank for International Settlements (BIS), discusses the concepts of credit risk, risk control, and accounting and disclosure. This site provides a wealth of information about key concepts in international finance and articles that can help you understand the real-world application of those concepts.

ESTIMATING THE TERM STRUCTURE OF INTEREST RATES

1. Go to *http://www.bundesbank.de/index.en.php.*
    The German Central Bank (Bundesbank) provides information on a new way to estimate the term structure of interest rates. The term structure of interest rates shows the relation between the interest rates and maturities of zero-coupon bonds without risk of default. In the monetary policy context, it is primarily of interest as an indicator of the market's expectations regarding interest rates and inflation rates. Its slope can provide information about the expected changes in interest rates or inflation rates. Hitherto, this constellation was captured by way of approximation in the publications of the Deutsche Bundesbank by an (estimated) yield curve. From now on that approach is to be replaced by a direct estimation of the term structure of interest rates. This approach is being adopted increasingly in the international context. In principle, it allows a more precise presentation and analysis of expectations and ensures enhanced cross-country comparability of the estimation results. Moreover, (implied) forward rates can be calculated directly from the term structure of (spot) rates. Although such forward rates contain the same information as the term structure of interest rates, in principle they make it easier to separate expectations for the short, medium, and long term.

(continued)

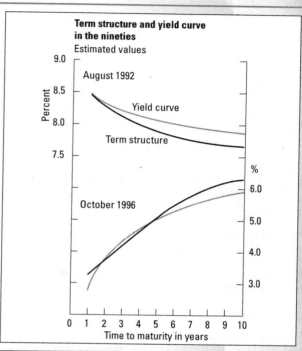

Term structure and yield curve in the nineties
Estimated values

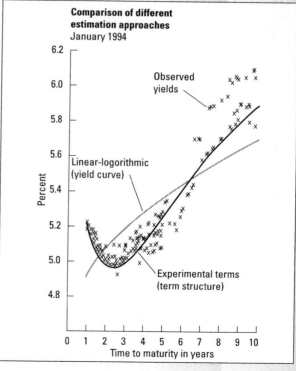

Comparison of different estimation approaches
January 1994

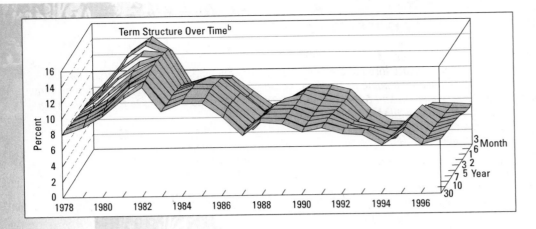

Term Structure Over Time[b]

TERM STRUCTURE OF INTEREST RATES OVER TIME

1. Go to *http://www.clevelandfed.org/research/ aug96et/ charts/intrat1c.HTM.*
   Tracking the yield curve is fundamentally a three-dimensional problem, because the curve both twists and shifts up and down over time. A 3-D perspective indicates that the big rise in 1994 was not a parallel shift. It also shows how the high but inverted curve of 1981 first steepened in 1982 and then dropped downward. On the other hand, it allows us to see how inversions occurred as a result of short rates rising, not long rates falling.

USEFUL LINKS

FinanceWise Website: FinanceWise does not aim to index the Internet in its entirety, only sites that possess content of interest to the financial world.

http://www.financewise.com/

Federal Reserve Bank of Atlanta Economic Review: From the main menu, click on Economic Review and view the latest articles or search for back articles on topics of interest. You can click on Research Economists and find the latest working papers (often an Adobe Reader is needed for pdfs; follow instructions to download if you don't have it).

http://www.frbatlanta.org

Federal Reserve Bank of Philadelphia Research Working Papers: Follow the menu to research and read Working Papers by economists on latest issues

http://www.phil.frb.org

Interest Rate Risk Measurement and Immunization Using Duration

10

"*A 30-year zero is probably three times as volatile as a common stock. It's like a roller coaster. You'll finish the ride with a dizzy head and woozy walk and wonder what hit you.*"

WILLIAM H. GROSS, Managing Director, Pacific Management Investment Company (1985)

"*How much risk to take on interest rates is one of the biggest decisions a bank makes.*"

STEVEN ELLIOTT, Chief Financial Officer, Mellon Bank (1992)

"*The Federal Reserve speaks today, and the bond market anxiously awaits the latest word on interest rates and the economy. . . . Because of the uncertainty about the magnitude of the Fed move, expectations for short-term rates will likely snap one way or the other based on the size of the expected move.*"

AARON LUCCHETTI, "The Fed Sharpens Rate-Cut Shears Again: Bond Market Awaits Fed's Move on Interest Rates, with Traders Expecting a Cut but Split on Size," The Wall Street Journal, June 25, 2003, C1.

As the preceding quotations suggest, managing interest rate risk is a crucial part of managing a financial institution, and interest rates are volatile and difficult to predict. Many managers faced a critical dilemma in the early 1990s as market rates fell to levels not seen in three decades or more, while the upward-sloping term structure was much steeper than usual; that is, the spread between what could be earned on long- versus short-term assets was relatively large. Decision makers at Collective Savings Bank in Egg Harbor, New Jersey, decided to structure the institution's assets on the assumption that the rate decline was temporary: They chose a preponderance of short-term investments so as not to be "locked in" if rates rose suddenly. But managers of other depositories, such as Boatmen's Bancshares in St. Louis, took an entirely opposite tack and lengthened asset maturities to take advantage of the high spread between long- and short-term rates.

Considering how many of each bank's asset returns and liability costs were affected by these decisions about an unknowable future, the risks of betting wrong were enormous for both groups of managers. In 1998, investors experienced a similar flat yield curve for securities with three-month to five-year maturities, with yields on five-year securities below yields on shorter-term securities, but a steeper rising slope for securities with maturities longer than five years. Interest rate movements were volatile and difficult to predict, and a number of securities firms and banks involved in securities activities suffered large losses in 1998 as a result of incorrect predictions for movements in interest rates. In the early 2000s, bond fund managers experienced continuous interest rate drops, including interest rates falling to their lowest level in forty-five years in the summer of 2003, after a rate cut by the Fed. As noted by Douglas Fore, an economist and principal research fellow for the TIAA-CREF Institute, "These low

rates meant both good news and bad news for investors. For homeowners, it was certainly good news: Huge numbers of Americans refinanced their mortgages. . . . But if you're investing in interest-rate sensitive instruments such as bond or money market funds or lending your money to a bank through certificates of deposits (CDs), the low rates weren't so beneficial."[1]

This chapter examines concepts of interest rate risk for financial institutions, including reinvestment risk and market price risk. It also discusses duration, an overall measure of interest rate risk and applications for financial institution management. The first section begins by discussing interest rate yields.

Learning Objectives

After completing this chapter, you will be able to:

1 Understand the inverse relationship between prices and yields.

2 Calculate ex post (actual) effective annual yields.

3 Understand the two types of interest rate risk: reinvestment and price risk.

4 Understand bond theorems and their implications.

5 Follow the effect of interest rate changes on common stock.

6 Understand duration as a measure of both reinvestment and price risk and how to calculate it.

7 Estimate percentage price changes and interest rate elasticity using duration.

8 Understand the concept of portfolio immunization using duration and its opportunity cost.

9 Calculate a financial institution's duration gap and, using the duration, calculate the change in the value of the institution's equity with a change in interest rates.

10 Explain the use of simulation and scenario analysis to provide an estimate of the current exposure of a financial institution to interest rate risk.

Interest Rate Risk Defined

Risk is a fact of life. Risk for securities is the potential variation in the returns from an investment. This chapter explains and illustrates one of the most significant risks faced by financial institutions today: potential variation in returns caused by unexpected changes in interest rates, or **interest rate risk.**

1 Fred R. Bleakley. "Banks, Thrifts Scored as Interest Rates Fell, But Difficulties Loom." *The Wall Street Journal* (February 12, 1992), A1, A6; Steven Vames. "Bond Prices Fall Despite Favorable CPI Report." *The Wall Street Journal* (December 16, 1998), C20; Jonathan Fuerbringer. "A Flatter Yield Curve Indicates Investors May Be Expecting a Significant Slowing of the Economy." *New York Times* (December 10, 1998), C9; and Douglas Fore, "How Interest Rates Can Affect Your Investments," *TIAA-CREF Participant*, November 2003, 7.

Note the use of the word *unexpected.* Investors can and do incorporate expected changes in interest rates into their investment decisions. The risk they face, then, arises not from changes they correctly anticipate at the time investment decisions are made, but from changes they do not anticipate. Because even the most astute forecasters err, no investors are protected against potential variation in returns, even if forecasting is a part of their decision making.

The Price/Yield Connection

Although unexpected changes in interest rates affect virtually all financial institutions, they do not affect them equally. Differences in interest rate risk occur because of the type of instrument, maturity, size and timing of cash inflows, and planned holding period relative to the asset's maturity. To understand interest rate risk, however, it is first necessary to understand the fundamental principles of financial asset prices. Financial markets are characterized by many participants and much publicly available information. Generally, an individual investor, as only one of many buyers and sellers, is unable to influence the price of a financial asset. A manager considering the purchase of a Treasury bill (T-bill) knows that an institution must pay the going market price. The supply and demand for an asset is also important (see the loanable funds theory in Chapter 8). Risk aversion is also critical. All else equal, the price of a riskier asset will be lower than that of a less risky one because most financial market participants are risk averse. Risk aversion causes investors to demand higher expected rates of return from riskier investments.

Putting Them Together

The effects of these influences on security prices are incorporated in the general equation for the effective annual yield on a financial asset:

$$P_0 = \sum_{t=1}^{n} \frac{C_t}{(1 + y^*)^t}$$

[10.1]

where y^* is the discount rate that makes the sum of the present value of the assets' cash flows (C_t) equal to its price (P_O). This expression reveals the relationship between price and yield. It is evident that, all else equal, price changes must be accompanied by yield changes, and vice versa, with prices and yields changing simultaneously in the opposite directions. If the price of an asset falls (rises), its yield rises (falls). Similarly, if y^* rises, which will usually occur when investors become more risk averse and require a higher market rate, the price of the security falls. If y^* falls, for example, as the result of a rise in the supply of loanable funds, the price of the security rises.

The Price/Yield Relationship Illustrated

Calculating Ex Ante Effective Annual Yield (y*) for Bonds

For a bond, the yield to maturity or ex ante effective annual yield (y^*) that an investor expects to receive over the life of the bond is the discount rate that makes the present value of the bond's future cash flows equal to its current price. For a coupon bond, solving for y^* entails using the bond price formula as follows:

$$P_0 = \text{Coupon Payment (PVIFA } y^*, n) + \text{Maturity Value (PVIF } y^*, n)$$

[10.2]

where P_O is the price (market value of the bond), PVIFA is the present value of the annuity factor $\{\{1 - [1 / (1 + y^*)^n]\} / y^*\}$ (used to find the present value of the coupon payments), and PVIF is the present value factor $[1 / (1 + y^*)^n]$ (used to find the present value of the maturity value). This yield assumes that the bond will be held to maturity and that each coupon payment will be invested at the y^* rate over the life of the bond.[2]

As an example, see the price information for bonds traded on Monday, December 1, 2003, presented in Figure 10.1. Under NYSE bonds, find the highlighted IBM bond maturing in 2013 (ten-year maturity) that has a coupon rate of $7\frac{1}{2}$ percent and sells for a price of $118\frac{1}{4}$ percent of its par value of $1,000, or $1,182.50 ($1.1825 \times \$1,000$). The yield listed is the coupon yield of 6.3 percent (the coupon payment divided by the bond's price, not y^*). The effective annual yield (y^*) for the bond is the discount rate that makes the present value of the coupon payments and maturity value equal to $1,182.50:

$$\$1,182.50 = \$75 \text{ (PVIFA } y^*, 10) + \$1,000 \text{ (PVIF } y^*, 10)$$

Because the bond is selling at a higher price than its par value, we know that $y^* < 7.5$ percent, the annual coupon rate. Using trial and error or a financial calculator, y^* can be found to be 5.123 percent. At about a 5.123 percent discount rate, the bond's price is equal to the present value of its cash flows:

$$\$75 \text{ (7.67578)} + \$1,000 \text{ (0.60677)} = \$1,182.50$$

However, an investor will only receive an annual effective yield of 5.123 percent if this bond is held to maturity and coupons can be reinvested at a 5.123 percent rate each year.

Calculating Ex Post (Actual) Effective Annual Yield

The premise that an investor will receive an actual effective annual yield of 5.123 percent if he or she holds the bond until maturity and reinvests the coupon payments at 5.123 percent can be demonstrated by solving for the ex post effective annual yield (EAY). The ex post EAY is the future value (FV) of all cash flows from our investment divided by the price we paid, annualized by taking this to the 1/nth power and then subtracting 1 to subtract out our original investment that was included as part of our future value, as follows:

$$\text{EAY} = (\text{FV} / P_0)^{1/n} - 1 \qquad \text{[10.3]}$$

The FV of the cash flows received at the end of the life of a bond includes the future value of all the coupons reinvested at some rate y^* each year plus the bond's maturity value:

$$\text{FV} = \text{Coupon PMT (FVIFA } y^*, n) + \text{Maturity Value} \qquad \text{[10.4]}$$

$$\text{FV} = \$75 \text{ (FVIFA 5.123\%, 10)} + \$1,000$$

$$= \$75 \text{ (12.650)} + \$1,000 = \$1,948.75$$

where FVIFA is the future value of an annuity factor $\{[(1 + y^*)^n - 1] / y^*\}$. Here we are assuming that y^* stays the same over the life of the bond, and the coupons can be reinvested each year at that market rate of 5.123 percent.

Hence, the investor will receive $1,948.75 at the end of ten years if the bond is held until maturity and the coupon payments are reinvested each year at 5.123 percent. Using Equation 10.3 to solve for the realized annual effective rate (EAY) shows that it is indeed equal to 5.123 percent:

$$\text{EAY} = (\$1,948.75 / \$1,182.50)^{1/10} - 1$$

$$\text{EAY} = (1.64799)^{0.10} - 1 = 0.05123, \text{ or } 5.123\%$$

---

2 To find the approximate rate by using the trial-and-error method, an approximation formula can be initially used, where

$$\text{YTM} = \frac{\text{Coupon Payment} + [(\text{Maturity Value} - \text{Price}) / n]}{(\text{Maturity Value} + \text{Price}) / 2}$$

This represents the approximate yearly benefit received from a bond divided by its average price over its life. This YTM (yield to maturity) should be plugged into the bond formula to see if it is correct, which is more likely if the bond is selling close to par value. Otherwise, it is a good starting point. Interpolation can also be used, in which the bond's price is calculated at a high and too low rate (i.e., by using a discount rate in which the bond's price is too low and by using a lower discount rate in which the bond's price is too high). Through interpolation, the yield can be found between these two rates as the following:

$$\text{The Low Rate} + \frac{(\text{High Price} - \text{Price}) \times 1\%}{(\text{High Price} - \text{Low Price})}$$

figure **10.1**   SAMPLE BOND PRICES, DECEMBER 1, 2003

Yields of Treasury Securities of varying maturities are found in the daily financial pages. These data are the basis for estimating the current shape of the yield curve.

STOCK EXCHANGE BOND TRADING

MONDAY, DECEMBER 1, 2003

NYSE BONDS

Company	Cur. Yld	Vol	Price	Chg
AMR 9s16	11.3	280	$79^3/_8$	$+ ^3/_8$
AT&T $7^1/_2$04	7.4	78	$101^5/_8$	$- ^3/_8$
AT&T 7s05	6.6	20	$105^1/_2$	$+ ^1/_8$
AT&T $7^3/_4$07	6.9	47	$111^7/_8$	$- ^1/_2$
AT&T 6_s09	5.7	110	$105^3/_4$	-1
AT&T $6^1/_2$13	6.3	128	$103^5/_8$	-1
AT&T 8.35s25	7.8	1	$107^1/_2$	$- ^1/_4$
AT&T $6^1/_2$29	6.6	273	$98^1/_4$	$- ^3/_8$
ATTBdb $8^3/_8$13	7.0	199	$119^7/_8$	$-1^3/_4$
ATTBdb 9.45s22	7.1	401	$133^5/_8$	$-1^1/_2$
BauschL $6^3/_4$04	6.5	30	104	$+1^1/_2$
BellsoT $5^7/_8$09	5.4	126	$108^3/_8$	$- ^5/_8$
BellsoT 7s25	6.3	40	$110^3/_4$	$- ^1/_2$
BellsoT $6^3/_4$33	6.6	63	102	...
BellsoT $7^5/_8$35	7.1	100	$107^1/_2$	$+ ^5/_8$
BlockF $6^3/_4$04	6.5	10	$103^3/_4$	$- ^1/_{16}$
BordCh $8^3/_8$16	9.9	27	85	$-3^3/_4$
CallonP 11s05	10.8	10	102	$+1^3/_8$
Chkpnt $5^1/_4$05	cv	7	$105^5/_8$	$+4^3/_8$
ChespkE $8^1/_8$11	7.5	3	$107^3/_4$	...
CSFB $6^1/_8$11	5.7	55	$107^5/_8$	$-1^1/_8$
CrwnCk $7^3/_8$26	8.1	10	$90^1/_2$	$- ^1/_2$
Deere 6s09	5.5	50	$109^1/_8$	$+ ^1/_8$
Deere 6.55s28	6.3	15	$104^1/_4$	$-1^3/_4$
DevonE 4.9_s08	cv	10	$102^1/_4$	$- ^5/_8$

Company	Cur. Yld	Vol	Price	Chg
FordCr $6^3/_8$08	6.3	97	$102^1/_8$	$+ ^3/_8$
GE Glob 7s26	6.6	5	$106^1/_2$	$+ ^3/_8$
GMA $6^5/_8$05	6.3	215	$105^7/_8$	$- ^3/_8$
GEICap $7^7/_8$06	6.9	7	$113^5/_8$	...
GMA $8^3/_4$05	8.1	10	$108^1/_8$	$+ ^1/_8$
GMA $6^1/_8$08	5.8	5	105	$- ^1/_4$
GMA dc6s11	6.0	85	$99^1/_4$	$- ^1/_2$
GMA zr 12	...	26	542	$-2^1/_4$
GMA zr 15	...	50	$440^1/_8$	$-4^7/_8$
GoldmS 7.35s09	6.4	12	$114^1/_2$	$-1^1/_4$
GoldmS 7.8s10	6.7	95	$116^1/_2$	$-1^1/_2$
Honywll zr07	...	10	$86^1/_2$	...
IBM $5^3/_8$09	5.1	10	$106^3/_8$	$-1^3/_8$
IBM $7^1/_2$13	6.3	5	$118^1/_4$	-2
IBM $8^3/_8$19	6.5	5	129	$- ^3/_8$
IBM 6.22s27	5.8	20	$107^1/_2$	$+3^1/_4$
IntShip $7^3/_4$07	7.9	210	$98^3/_4$	$- ^1/_4$
KCS En $8^7/_8$06	8.6	5	103	$+ ^1/_2$
K&B Hm $7^3/_4$04	7.5	10	$103^{25}/_{32}$	$- ^1/_{16}$
Leucadia $8^1/_4$05	7.8	10	106	$- ^7/_8$
Loews $3^1/_8$07	cv	10	$93^1/_8$	$- ^3/_8$
Lucent $7^1/_4$06	7.1	160	$101^3/_8$	$+ ^3/_4$
Lucent $5^1/_2$08	6.0	120	92	$+1^1/_8$
Lucent $6^1/_2$28	8.4	33	$77^1/_4$	$+ ^7/_8$
Lucent 6.45s29	8.4	4	$76^1/_2$	$+ ^1/_2$
MBNA 8.28s26	7.7	205	$107^1/_2$	$-1^3/_8$
Malan $9^1/_2$04	cv	3	$100^1/_2$	$+ ^1/_2$
McDnl 8 11	7.1	25	125	$+1$
McDnl 7.05s25	6.7	9	105	$-1^1/_2$
McDnl 7.31s27	6.8	10	107	...
ML PubSt 7s07	6.8	30	103	...
NRurU 6.2s08	5.7	3	$109^5/_8$	$- ^7/_8$

Company	Cur. Yld	Vol	Price	Chg
NETelTel $6^7/_8$23	6.7	3	103	$+ ^1/_2$
NETelTel $7^7/_8$29	6.6	40	$118^1/_2$	$+ ^1/_2$
NYTel 6.70s23	6.6	29	102	...
NYTel 7s25	6.8	35	$102^3/_8$	...
NYTel 7s33	6.7	50	$104^5/_8$	$+ ^1/_8$
Noram 6s12	cv	10	98	$- ^1/_4$
OcciP $10^1/_8$09	8.0	8	126	$-3^1/_2$
PECO $7^3/_8$28	7.4	10	100	...
ParkerD $5^1/_2$04	cv	46	$99^1/_{16}$	$- ^7/_{16}$
PSEG $9^1/_8$05	8.3	500	110	$+ ^3/_8$
PSvEG 7s24	6.8	16	$102^3/_4$	$- ^1/_2$
ReynTob $8^3/_4$05	8.3	2	$105^1/_2$	$- ^5/_8$
ReynTob $9^1/_4$13	8.2	5	113	$+3^5/_8$
RoyCarib zr2-21	...	53	46	$+1$
Sequa 9s09	8.4	35	$107^3/_4$	$+ ^5/_8$
SvcCorp $6^3/_4$08	cv	50	105	$- ^1/_2$
SilicnGr $5^1/_4$04	cv	326	$106^1/_4$	$+5^1/_2$
Solectrn zrN20	...	30	$57^1/_4$	$+2^3/_4$
Sprint $6^7/_8$28	7.3	80	$93^3/_4$	$- ^3/_4$
TVA $6^7/_8$43	6.6	33	$104^1/_4$	$+ ^1/_4$
TVA 6.23s45	6.0	30	$103^7/_8$	$+ ^1/_8$
Tenet 8s05	7.9	69	101	$- ^7/_8$
Tenet $5^3/_8$06	5.5	86	97	$- ^1/_4$
Tenet $6^3/_8$11	6.9	8	$93^3/_4$	$- ^1/_4$
TmeWar 7.48s08	6.6	5	$113^1/_2$	$- ^1/_2$
TmeWar $9^1/_8$13	7.3	5	$124^3/_8$	$-1^3/_4$
TmeWar 9.15s23	7.2	5	127	...
THilfig 6.85s08	6.7	42	$102^5/_8$	$+ ^7/_8$
US Timb $9^5/_8$07f		20	$58^1/_2$	$+ ^1/_2$
XeroxCr 7.2s12	7.2	487	100	$- ^1/_2$

AMEX BONDS

Company	Cur. Yld	Vol	Price	Chg
GB Prop 11s05	16.8	4	$65^3/_8$	$-4^5/_8$
GS S&P2-13	...	9	$104^7/_8$	$+ ^1/_2$
GS S&P4-13	...	15	103	...
JPM S&P10-08	...	10	93	...
LehDJA 8-07	...	100	$102^3/_8$	$- ^1/_8$
Leh Prudents04	...	10	$96^7/_8$	...
Leh Prudents06	...	2	$104^1/_8$	$+ ^3/_8$
MS INTC 10	...	130	100	$+ ^1/_4$
MS WMT 10	...	125	$96^1/_2$	$+ ^1/_4$
MS S&P12-10	...	60	$93^1/_8$	$-1^3/_8$
SelNoteC 6-33	...	1	95	...
TmsLux $7^1/_2$06	cv	30	93	$-1^3/_8$
UBS S&P07	...	209	$103^1/_8$	$+1^1/_8$
WellsF bsk08	...	35	$98^5/_8$	$+1^3/_8$
WellsF SP08	...	18	$102^3/_4$	$+ ^1/_2$
WellsF DJ10	...	7	$96^1/_2$	$-1^3/_8$

BOND TABLES EXPLAINED

Bonds are interest-bearing debt certificates. Their value is usually quoted as a percentage, with 100 equaling par, or face value. This table shows the issuing company, then the original coupon rate (interest rate) and the last two digits of the maturity year.

Current yield represents the annual percentage return to the purchaser at the current price. The **Price** column refers to the bond's closing price, and **Chg** is the difference between the day's closing price and the previous daily closing price. A majority of bonds, and all municipal or tax-exempt bonds, are not listed on exchanges; rather they are traded over the counter

Other footnotes:

cv	Bond is convertible into stock under specified conditions	**rp**	Reduced principal
cld	Called	**st**	Stamped
dc	Selling at a discounted price	**t**	Floating rate
f	Deal in flat—traded without accrued interest	**x**	Ex interest
k	Treasury bond, non-resident aliens exempt from withholding tax	**vj**	In bankruptcy or receivership or being reorganized under the Bankruptcy Act, or securities assumed by such companies
m	Matured bonds	**wd**	When distributed
na	No accrual of interest	**wi**	When issued
p	Treasury note, non-resident aliens exempt from withholding tax	**zr**	Zero coupon issue
r	Registered		

Source: New York Times, *December 2, 2003, C13.*

Thus, if all coupon payments are reinvested at the y^* rate and the bond is held until maturity, the EAY will be equal to the ex ante effective annual rate, y^*.

Reinvestment and Price Risk

The ex ante effective annual rate y^* will only equal the realized rate EAY, however, if the bond is held to maturity and all coupons can be reinvested at the y^* rate. If this is not the case, the realized return that the investor will receive can be quite different. If the investor has to sell the bond prior to maturity, he or she may sell the bond for a gain or loss and receive more or less than the maturity value. Similarly, if interest rates fall or rise, the investor may receive more or less interest income than expected on reinvesting coupon payments by the end of year 10. Thus, investors in fixed-income securities always face interest rate risk, that is, the risk of not achieving their desired ex ante yield y^*.

The Two Sides of Interest Rate Risk

Interest rate risk consists of two components:

1. **Reinvestment risk,** the risk of interest rates falling and having to reinvest coupon payments at a lower rate than y^*, resulting in a lower ex post yield, and
2. **Price or market value risk,** the risk of rates rising and the market price of the bond falling if the bond must be sold prior to maturity, also resulting in a lower ex post yield.

Example of Reinvestment Risk

Looking at the bond in the previous example, suppose that market rates fall after the purchase of the bond and that rates are, on average, only 4 percent over the life of that bond.[3] The FV at the end of ten years can now be calculated as follows:

$$FV = \$75 \ (FVIFA \ 4\%, 10) + \$1,000$$

$$= \$75 \ (12.006) + \$1,000 = \$1,900.45$$

The ex post EAY (using Equation 10.3) now becomes

$$EAY = (1,900.45 \ / \ \$1,182.50)^{1/10} - 1 = 0.04859, \text{ or } 4.859\%$$

Thus, because of reinvestment risk, the investor has a lower ex post yield on his or her bond than the expected y^* of 5.123 percent. This yield may not seem very much lower, but if the portfolio manager invested in 1,000 bonds, or (1,000 bonds $\times$ \$1,182.50) = \$1.1825 million in bonds, the portfolio manager would expect to have his or her investment grow at about 5.123 percent a year, so he or she would expect to have \$1.1825 million $(1.05123)^{10}$ = \$1.94885 million at the end of year 10. However, with an average yield of only 4.86 percent a year, the investment only grows 4.86 percent on average each year, and he or she will only have \$1.1825 million $(1.04859)^{10}$ = \$1.90046 million at the end of year 10, or (\$1.94885 million $-$ \$1.90046 million) = 0.04839 million, or a \$48,390 difference. If the investor was the portfolio manager of a fixed-income portfolio for a mutual fund, a pension fund, or an insurance fund with a guaranteed income certificate (GIC) promising a given annual return of 5.123 percent to investors, he or she would have to make up this \$48,390 shortfall.

Example of Market Price Risk

Suppose for the bond discussed in the preceding section that rates instead stay at 5.123 percent on average for the first five years of the bond but rise to 6.5 percent at the end of year 5. Also, suppose that the investor needs to sell the bond at the end of year 5. Because of the rise in interest rates, the bond's price will fall in year 5 to:

$$Price = Coupon \ Payment \ (PVIFA \ r, n) + Maturity \ Value \ (PVIF \ r, n)$$

$$Price \ year \ 5 = \$75 \ (PVIFA \ 6.5\%, 5) + \$1,000 \ (PVIF \ 6.5\%, 5)$$

$$= \$75 \ (4.1557) + \$1,000 \ (0.7299) = \$1,041.58$$

Thus, the investor has a capital loss of \$1,182.50 $-$ \$1,041.58 = a loss of \$140.92. Again, this may not seem like a significant loss, but for a portfolio manager invested in 1,000 bonds at the initial \$1,182.50 price, or \$1.1825 million in bonds, the loss would be a potentially significant \$140.92 $\times$ 1,000 bonds = \$140,920.

Based on the assumption that the investor reinvested the coupon payments at the 5.123 percent rate for five years and then sold the bond for \$1,041.58 at the end of year 5, the terminal FV that the investor received is as follows:

$$FV = \$75 \ (FVIFA \ 5.123\%, 5) + \$1,041.58$$

$$= \$75 \ (5.5392) + \$1,041.58 = \$1,457.02$$

---

3 This is a very simplified assumption, but the same results can be demonstrated if one assumes that the market rate changes each year over the life of the bond.

Concept Questions

1 If rates are falling, which type of interest rate risk would investors be concerned about? Explain why.

2 If rates are rising, which type of interest rate risk would investors be concerned about?

3 For a bond to receive the yield to maturity that is expected when an investor buys a bond, at what rate would the coupon payments have to be invested over the life of the bond?

4 What is the price of a bond with a par value of $1,000 that sells for a price quote of 109? 98?

5 If a bond has an 8% coupon rate and interest rates on similar bonds go up to 10%, what will happen to the bond's price? What will happen to the bond's price if interest rates on similar bonds go down to 6%?

and the ex post EAY (using Equation 10.3) now becomes

$$EAY = (\$1,457.02 \,/\, \$1,182.50)^{1/5} - 1$$

$$EAY = (1.2322)^{0.20} - 1 = 0.04265, \text{ or } 4.265\%$$

Because of market price risk, the annual effective yield the investor received ex post of 4.265 percent for the first five years was 0.86 percent, or 86 basis points lower than the expected annual effective yield of 5.123 percent.

Reinvestment Risk versus Price Risk

Thus, interest rate risk has two facets: potential variation from unexpected changes in the rate at which intermediate cash flows can be reinvested—**reinvestment risk**—and potential variation from unexpected changes in market prices of financial assets—**market value** or **price risk.** For a given change in market conditions, the two types of interest rate risk have opposite effects. A decline in market rates lowers reinvestment income but increases prices (potential capital gains); an increase in market rates improves reinvestment income but decreases prices (potential capital losses). It is not surprising, then, that interest rate risk is so hard to manage successfully.

Because interest rate risk is so difficult to manage, it is important to understand as much as we can about how joint effects of reinvestment and price risk affect the prices of fixed income securities. Some well-known bond theorems can lay a foundation for understanding duration, an overall measure of interest rate risk for such securities. These theorems are discussed in the following sections.

Bond Theorems

In 1962, as part of an article on the term structure of interest rates, Burton Malkiel proposed and proved mathematically a series of theorems on the relationship between the yields and prices of fixed-income securities. These theorems have become known as "the bond theorems." By using calculus, Malkiel differentiated a bond price equation with respect to yield and maturity and drew the following conclusions:[4]

Theorem I. Bond prices must move inversely to bond yields. The implications of Theorem I were explained earlier in the chapter. When bond prices rise (fall), yields fall (rise), and vice versa.

Theorem II. Holding the coupon rate constant, for a given change in market yields, percentage changes in bond prices are greater the longer the term to maturity of a bond.[5] In informal terms, with a change in interest rates longer-term bonds will have bigger capital losses and capital gains than short-term bonds. Longer-term bonds have cash flows further into the future, so the present value of their cash flows and, hence, their market values, fall and rise more with a change in rates than do shorter-term bonds.

Theorem III. The percentage price change for a bond will increase at a decreasing rate as N increases. The longer the time to maturity, the less the difference in percentage price changes. For

---

4 The bond theorems are discussed and proven in Malkiel (1962), pp. 201–206.

5 Theorem II is true for bonds selling at or above par at the time of a change in market yields but not for all discount bonds. Malkiel observed this but did not examine why it was so, as other authors have done subsequently.

example, when yields change, the price of fifteen-year bonds will change by a greater percentage than the prices of ten-year bonds, but the difference is less than the difference between the price changes of a five-year bond and a ten-year bond.

Theorem IV (Convexity Theorem). Starting with a given market yield y^*, holding other factors constant, the rise in price with a fall in y^* will be greater than the fall in price with the same absolute value rise in y^*. Price changes in bonds with a change in rates are asymmetric. For a given change in y^*, a fall in rates will result in a larger capital gain than the capital loss with the same absolute value rise in y^*. This property is known as *convexity*. This relation benefits investors, because for a given change in rates, capital gains will be greater than capital losses.[6]

Theorem V. Holding N constant and starting from the same y^*, the higher the coupon rate, the smaller the percentage change in price for a given change in yield.[7] This principle is illustrated in Figure 10.2, which shows the percentage price changes of three eight-year bonds plotted against changes in yields, starting from a 12 percent base. As yields drop (rise) from a 12 percent level, the percentage changes in the price of a 6 percent coupon rate, eight-year bond are greater than the percentage price changes for a 12 percent or 18 percent coupon-rate bond of comparable maturity. Hence, lower coupon bonds have greater interest rate risk.

Implications of the Bond Theorems

The bond theorems show that changes in market rates will not affect all bond portfolios in the same way. In periods of volatile market rates, portfolios heavily invested in long-term securities have greater

		BOND THEOREM V: AS COUPON RATE INCREASES, PERCENTAGE PRICE CHANGES DECREASE
figure	10.2	AS YIELDS CHANGE

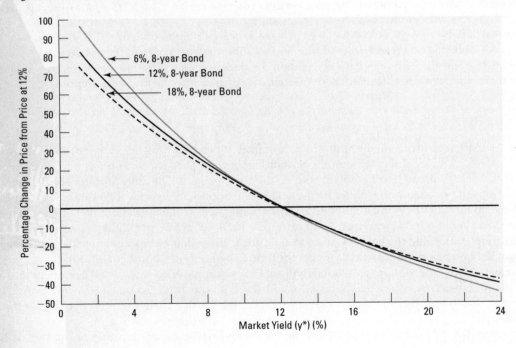

With term to maturity held constant, the higher the coupon rates, the lower the percentage price changes on bonds as market yields change.

6 Although coupon bonds have positive convexity, mortgage securities can actually have negative convexity because if rates fall dramatically, prepayments will be reducing the present value of the security's future cash flows. Thus, any rise in value with a fall in rates will be dampened by the fall in value associated with greater mortgage prepayments.

7 Theorem V holds for all bonds except perpetuities and bonds with one period to maturity.

price fluctuations than portfolios concentrated in money market securities. The value of portfolios heavily invested in low-coupon instruments is more changeable than portfolios of high-coupon bonds. If (a big if) managers forecast market changes correctly and understand the bond theorems, they can position their institutions to profit from anticipated rate movements. Judging a bond's interest rate risk depends on the current level of market rates (y^*) and the coupon rate of a bond as well as its time to maturity. The concept of duration enables a manager to develop an overall measure of interest rate risk that includes the effect of coupon rate, level of interest rates, and time to maturity, discussed later in the chapter.

Implications for Financial Institutions

Financial institutions have so many interest-bearing assets and liabilities that the effect of changing market interest rates is very important to them. For instance, higher reinvestment rates for investors mean changing costs for financial institutions. However, if market yields fall unexpectedly, the interest costs of a financial institution will fall if it has incurred variable rate liabilities. If market rates rise unexpectedly, the reverse is true. Either way, the net interest margin is subject to unexpected variation.

As mentioned in Chapter 2, a financial institution's funding gap is presented as rate-sensitive (repricable) assets − rate-sensitive (repricable) liabilities. This serves as a measure of an institution's reinvestment (refinancing) risk for a given time period. Recall that if the funding gap is positive, the financial institution risks a lower net interest income (NII) if interest rates fall, because interest revenues will fall more than interest expenses. If the funding gap is negative, the financial institution risks a lower NII if interest rates rise, because interest expenses will rise more than interest revenues. The approximate change in NII with a change in interest rates was described as

$$\Delta NII = (\Delta Interest\ Rate) \times (Funding\ Gap)$$

The funding gap, however, only measures one side of interest rate risk for a financial institution: reinvestment (refinancing) risk. It does not consider the time value of money and the effect of a change in the market value of assets and liabilities on a financial institution's balance sheet. Financial institutions that hold long-term financial assets and liabilities also have market price risk, that is, the risk of a decline in the market value of assets being greater than the decline in the market value of liabilities and, hence, a decline in the market value of equity (equal to the market value of assets − market value of liabilities). A duration gap, discussed later in the chapter, provides a better overall measure of interest rate risk including market price as well as reinvestment risk.

Effects of Interest Rate Changes on Common Stock

"Fed Move Ignites Explosive Stock, Bond Rallies," read a *Wall Street Journal* headline on Friday, April 10, 1992.[8] The story centered on the behavior of common stock prices after the Fed's April 9, 1992, cut in the discount rate. Similar stories followed the Fed's cuts in October 1998 and in July 2003 (see the chapter opening quote). Because common stocks are financial assets, their prices behave similarly to those of bonds. As market yields fall, yields on common stock also fall and their prices rise. As market yields rise for other financial assets, the yields on common stock rise and their prices fall. In 1998, analysts suggested one reason for the booming stock market was that low interest rates on bonds prompted investors to seek better returns elsewhere. Similarly, analysts in the final quarter of 2003 often mentioned low interest rates as contributing to the stock market's rise. These analysts theorized that investors were willing to take on more risk by investing in stock and to put a low price on that risk because their alternative investment bonds offered very low yields.[9] Research shows that financial institutions and other nonfinancial firms that have more fixed rate assets than liabilities (i.e., larger interest

---

8 Randall Smith and Robert Steiner. "Fed Move Ignites Explosive Stock, Bond Rallies." *The Wall Street Journal* (April 10, 1992), C1. The Dow's reactions to discount rates over a twenty-year period are discussed and illustrated in Douglas R. Sease. "Are Five Fed Rate Cuts Enough?" *The Wall Street Journal* (December 2, 1991), C1, C2.

9 Greg Ip. "Low Interest Rates Pave the Road to Risk." *The Wall Street Journal* (December 14, 1998), A1.

1 If you own a ten-year bond and a five-year bond with the same coupon rates, which has more interest rate risk? Explain why.

2 If you own two ten-year bonds and one has a coupon rate of 4 percent and the other a coupon rate of 8 percent, which has more interest rate risk? Explain why.

3 What is meant by the convexity theorem (IV) for bonds? How does it benefit investors?

4 What type of interest rate risk does a funding gap represent (reinvestment risk or price risk)? Explain what type of risk is not included in funding gap measures.

5 Holding other factors constant, if interest rates fall, what is likely to happen to common stock prices? What types of companies are likely to have a bigger change in stock prices with changes in interest rates?

rate risk) are more sensitive to unexpected changes in interest rates than other firms. Hence, for financial institutions, the relationship between interest rates and stock prices is particularly important.[10]

Duration: An Idea Ahead of Its Time

Duration is a measure of overall interest rate risk. It is difficult to find a recent scholarly article on financial institution management that does not mention duration, and many fixed-income mutual funds are listed as high- or low-duration funds. It would be easy to conclude that duration is a new idea, but, in fact, Frederick Macaulay first developed it more than fifty years ago. Similar concepts were developed shortly thereafter, but Macaulay's duration has only recently been widely appreciated for the power it brings to the management of interest rate risk.[11]

Duration Defined

Duration is the weighted average time over which the cash flows from an investment are expected, where the weights are the relative time-adjusted present values of the cash flows. It is an alternative to maturity for expressing the time dimension of an investment. Focusing on maturity ignores the fact that, for most securities, some cash benefits are received before the maturity date. Benefits that are received before maturity are often substantial, especially for bonds with relatively high coupon rates or annuities. It can be argued, therefore, that ignoring the time dimension of cash benefits before maturity is unwise.

The importance of the time dimension is evident in the basic expression for the market value (P_o) of an investment shown earlier (Equation 10.1):

$$P_0 = \sum_{t=1}^{N} \frac{C_t}{(1 + y^*)^t}$$

Because the market value of an investment equals the present value of expected benefits and because the discount factors $(1 + y)^t$ are exponential functions of time, early payments are discounted less than those received later. Differences in discounted value become more pronounced as t increases. In essence, the *effective* maturity—that is, the time period over which the investor receives cash flows with relatively high present value—may differ from the *contractual*, or legally specified, maturity. Duration is a measure of this effective maturity. Duration is also a measure of the interest rate risk or responsiveness of a bond's market price to a change in market rates. Securities with higher durations will have a greater change in market value with a change in market rates.

10 See Fogler (1981) Christie (1981), Flannery and James (1984), and Sweeney and Warga (1986). Flannery and James found that the interest rate sensitivity of a firm's common stock is related to the net fixed-rate asset position of the firm, or the amount by which long-term, fixed-rate assets exceed long-term, fixed-rate liabilities. The effect was confirmed in Scott and Peterson (1986) and Bae (1990). Neuberger (1992) found that commercial real estate loans have a strong effect on bank stock returns. In the 1990s banks made greater use of interest rate hedging strategies; therefore, more recent studies find that many banks have less interest rate sensitivity for stocks.

11 Macaulay (1938). One early work based on a property similar to duration was Samuelson (1945). Several scholars have also attributed an idea virtually identical to duration to J. R. Hicks in his *Value and Capital* (1939). For a review of the intellectual history of duration, see Weil (1973).

The formula for duration is shown as follows:

$$\text{DUR} = \cfrac{\displaystyle\sum_{t=1}^{N} \cfrac{tC_t}{(1 + y^*)^t}}{\displaystyle\sum_{t=1}^{N} \cfrac{C_t}{(1 + y^*)^t}}$$ [10.5]

The equation used to solve for duration is the sum of the weighted present value of a bond's cash flows, each weighted by being multiplied by t, the time each cash flow comes in, divided by the sum of the present value of the cash flows (i.e., the bond's price, P_O). Duration can also be calculated as the sum of the [(present value of each cash flow / P_O) × t]. Hence, duration represents the weighted contribution of a cash flow to the market value or present value of a bond. A bond with larger cash flows coming in later will have a higher duration than a bond with larger cash flows coming in earlier that can be reinvested earlier at the market rate (y^*) by the investor.

Example: Calculating Bond Duration

Duration is perhaps best understood through examples. Consider the following three bonds:

- Bond 1 has an 8 percent coupon rate, $1,000 maturity value, n = 6 years.
- Bond 2 is a zero-coupon bond with a $1,000 maturity value, n = 6 years.
- Bond 3 has a 6 percent coupon rate, $1,000 maturity value, n = 6 years.

The market rate y^* for bonds of similar risk to these bonds is 8 percent. Which bond has the least overall interest rate risk, that is, the shortest duration?

Calculating duration is often easiest by using a table, as in the following:

Bond 1: 8% coupon rate, $1,000 maturity value, 6 years to maturity, y^* = 8%

Year	Cash Flow	PVIF 8%	PV Cash Flow	t × PV Cash Flow
1	$80	0.9259	$74.07	$74.07
2	80	0.8573	68.58	137.16
3	80	0.7938	63.50	190.50
4	80	0.7350	58.80	235.20
5	80	0.6806	54.45	272.25
6	1080	0.6302	680.62	4,083.72
Sum			$1,000.00	4,992.90

Duration = Sum (t × PV Cash Flow) / Sum (PV Cash Flow) = 4,992.90 / $1,000 = 4.993 years

Bond 2: $1,000 maturity value, no coupons, 6 years to maturity, y^* = 8%

Year	Cash Flow	PVIF 8%	PV Cash Flow	t × PV Cash Flow
1	$0	0.9259	0	0
2	0	0.8573	0	0
3	0	0.7938	0	0
4	0	0.7350	0	0
5	0	0.6806	0	0
6	$1,000	0.6302	$630.20	$3,781.20
Sum			$630.20	$3,781.20

Duration = $3,781.2 / $630.20 = 6 years

Bond 3: 6% coupon rate, $1,000 maturity value, 6 years to maturity, $y^* = 8\%$

Year	Cash Flow	PVIF 8%	PV Cash Flow	$t \times$ PV Cash Flow
1	$60	0.9259	$55.55	$55.55
2	60	0.8573	51.44	102.88
3	60	0.7938	47.63	142.89
4	60	0.7350	44.10	176.40
5	60	0.6806	40.84	204.18
6	1,060	0.6302	668.01	4,008.07
Sum			$907.57	$4,689.97

Duration = $4,689.97 / $907.57 = 5.17 years

All three bonds have the same maturity, but they have different durations. Of the three bonds, Bond 2, the zero coupon, has the highest duration of 6 years, which is equal to its maturity. The duration of a zero-coupon bond will always be equal to its maturity, because all cash flows come in at that time. Bond 3 has a higher duration (5.17 years) than Bond 1 (4.993 years) because Bond 3 has a much lower coupon rate than Bond 1, so investors will get their money back later. Because of Bond 1's high coupon rate, its duration is almost a year less than its maturity value. Those investing in this bond will have lower interest rate risk than with Bond 2 or Bond 3. By capturing each of the factors mentioned in the bond theorems (maturity, current market rates, and coupon payments), duration is an overall measure of both reinvestment and price risk.

Note that duration is a negative function of a bond's coupon payment or cash flows. It gets smaller as the coupon payment or cash flow per year gets larger. It is a positive function of a bond's time to maturity, but it is a negative function of y^*, the market rate on similar bonds. With higher market rates, investors can reinvest coupon payments at a higher rate and get their money back sooner.

Alternative Formula for Duration to Use for Long-term Securities

At times it is clumsy to calculate duration, particularly if you are trying to find the duration of a very long-term bond and do not have a spreadsheet set up. Fortunately, through mathematical analysis of Macaulay's original work, researchers have derived a simplified formula for calculating bond duration:

$$\text{DUR} = N - \{[\text{Coupon Payment} / (P_0 \times y^*)] \times [N - (1 + y^*) (\text{PVIFA } y^*, M)]\} \quad [10.6]$$

where

$$\text{PVIFA} = \text{the present value annuity factor} = \frac{[1 - (1 / (1 + y^*)^N)]}{y^*}$$

For example, for Bond 1, with N = 6 years, Coupon Payment = $80, and $y^* = 8$ percent, the PVIFA factor for 6 years, 8 percent is 4.6229; by using Equation 10.6, duration is equal to 4.993 years:[12]

$$\text{DUR} = 6 - \{[\$80 / \$80] \times [6 - (1.08) (4.6229)]\} = 6 - 1.0073 = 4.993 \text{ years},$$
the same as the duration calculated using the regular formula.

Measuring Interest Rate Risk: The Relationship Between Duration and Price Changes

Why is duration important in assessing an institution's interest rate risk? The answer is direct: For a given change in market yields, percentage changes in asset prices are proportional to the asset's duration. This is a powerful statement, because duration is a complex variable that considers relationships among the size of cash flows, their timing, and current market expectations. Although coupon rate, maturity value, and market rates allow an analyst to anticipate price changes based on one characteristic at a time, the relationship between duration and price changes considers all characteristics simultaneously. Note that a fixed income security's duration is dynamic. It changes any time market rates y^* change.

---

12 This equation was developed by Caks et al. (1985) and is designed for bonds paying interest annually. It is possible to modify the equation for bonds paying interest more than once a year; see Moser and Lindley (1989). Other simplified formulas are presented in Chua (1984), Bierwag (1987), and Smith (1988). In practice, most professional analysts have access to microcomputers or to bond duration tables that present durations for many combinations of yield, coupon rate, and maturity.

Estimating Percentage Price Changes

The relationship between duration and the percentage price change expected from a change in market yield is closely approximated by the following equation[13]:

$$\%\Delta P_0 = \Delta P_0 / P_0 = -\text{DUR}\,[\Delta y^*\% / (1 + y^*)] \qquad [10.7]$$

where the change in rate is expressed as a percentage in the numerator, but y^*, the original market rate prior to the change, is expressed as a fraction with 1 added to it.

To illustrate, consider Bond 1, which has a duration of 4.993 years, market price (P_O) of $1,000, and y^* of 8 percent. If rates rise from 8 percent to 8.5 percent, that is, a rise of 0.50 percent, then by using Equation 10.7, the approximate percent change in price for Bond 1 will be as follows:

$$\%\Delta P_0 = \Delta P_0 / P_0 = -\text{DUR}\,[\Delta y^*\% / (1 + y^*)]$$
$$= -4.99\,[0.50\% / (1.08)] = -2.31\%$$

Multiplying $0.023 \times \$1,000$, the bond's price would fall by approximately $23.10.

Note that this is only the approximate change in price. Duration assumes a linear relation between price changes and changes in y^*. Actually, because of the property known as convexity for bond prices, this relation is not really linear, but curves (see Figure 10.2). Bond price changes actually follow a convex pattern with changes in y^*. When market interest rates rise, the capital loss on a bond will be smaller than the capital gain on the bond for the absolute value for a fall in rates (i.e., bond theorem IV).

Thus, duration somewhat overestimates the percent fall in price with a rise in rates and underestimates the percent rise in price with a fall in rates. For small changes in y^*, the difference is minuscule, but for large rate changes, convexity should be taken into account.[14] As shown in the footnote below, a convexity term can be calculated and added to adjust for convexity.

Estimating Interest Rate Elasticity

It is only a short step from Equation 10.7 to a measure of interest rate elasticity (E) for a financial asset, which may serve as a reasonable proxy for the interest rate risk of holding the asset. Earlier, the interest

---

13 See Saunders (1997), p. 108, for a full derivation. Basically, the first derivative with respect to a change in rate is taken by using the bond price formula, and the change in price with a change in $y^* / (1 + y^*)$ is solved for.

14 See Fabozzi (1993), pp. 78–87, for a detailed derivation and discussion of convexity. Also, see Hempel, Simonson, and Coleman (1995) and Saunders (1997). Convexity measures the curvature, or error, in estimating the change in a bond's price with a change in y^*. Dollar convexity is the second derivative of the bond price equation with respect to a change in $y^*(d^2P / dy^2)$. When dollar convexity is divided by the price of the bond, it becomes a measure of the percentage change in the price of the bond due to convexity $[(d^2P / dy^2) \times 1 / P]$, or $dP / P = 1.2\,(\text{Convexity})(dy)^2$. To calculate convexity, a general formula is as follows:

$$\text{Convexity} = \text{Sum}\,[\text{PVCFs} \times (t^2 + t)] / \text{Sum}\,(\text{PVCFs}) \times (1 + y^*)^2$$

For instance, the duration and convexity for a five-year bond with an 8 percent coupon and $y^* = 8$ percent can be calculated by using a table as follows:

Year	Cash Flow	PVIF 8%	PV CF	t (PV CF)	$t^2 + t$	$t^2 + t$ (PV CF)
1	$80	0.9259	$74.07	$74.07	2	148.14
2	80	0.8573	68.58	137.16	6	411.48
3	80	0.7938	63.50	190.50	12	762.00
4	80	0.7350	58.80	235.20	20	1,176.00
5	1,080	0.6806	735.05	3,675.25	30	22,051.15
		Sum	$1,000.00	$4,312.18		$24,548.77

$$\text{Duration} = \$4,312.18 / \$1,000 = 4.312$$

$$\text{Convexity} = \$24,548.77 / [1000^* (1.08)^2] = 24,548.77 / 1166.40 = 21.05$$

Adjusting the duration formula for the approximate change in the price of a bond is equal to the following:

$$-\text{DUR}\,[\Delta y^*/(1 + y^*)] + 0.5(\text{Convexity})[\Delta y^{*2}]$$

Hence, for a 1 percent rise in rates, the approximate change in the price of the bond would be as follows:

$$-4.312[0.01 / 1.08] + 0.5(21.05)(0.01)^2 = -0.0462 + 0.0014 = -4.48\%$$

Here, convexity adjusts for the fact that with a rise in rates, the actual loss in the price in the bond is smaller than predicted under duration (in this case, 0.14 percent smaller). Third-order derivatives can also be taken to anticipate shifts in the slope of the yield curve. Fixed-income portfolio managers with billion dollar portfolios are very concerned about higher-order duration measures.

rate elasticity of a financial asset was defined as the percentage price change expected for a 1 percent change in market yields. Thus,[15]

$$E = -\text{DUR} [y^* / (1 + y^*)$$ [10.8]

To interpret the results of Equation 10.8, it is important to know what is meant by a "1 percent change." A 1 percent change in yields is a change equal to 1 percent of the existing yield; that is, if the present yield is 8.00 percent, a 1 percent change is an increase or decrease of 0.08 percent or 8 basis points (0.01×8 percent), not an increase to 9 percent or a decrease to 7 percent (that is, not a 100-basis-point change). By using Equation 10.8, the respective elasticity on Bonds 1, 2, and 3 can be calculated:

Bond 1: $E = -4.993 (0.08 / 1.08) = -0.3699$

Bond 2: $E = -6 (0.08 / 1.08) = -0.4444$

Bond 3: $E = -5.17 (0.08 / 1.08) = -0.3830$

For Bond 1, for every 1 percent change in the bond's yield of 8.00 percent, the bondholder could have expected a price change of 0.3699 percent in the opposite direction of the yield change. Bonds 2 and 3 are shown to have higher elasticity than Bond 1, which implies greater interest rate risk. In this case, the ranking of the elasticity of the bonds provides the same risk rankings as their relative durations, because each bond has the same market yield (y^*) of 8 percent. However, if market yields are different, calculating elasticities provides a better comparison of different securities' relative interest rate risk. Equation 10.8 provides more general assistance for decision making, because no specific change in yields has to be predicted.

Modified Duration

Since the approximate change in the value of an asset or liability can be calculated as $-\text{DUR} \times [(\Delta y^*) / (1 + y^*)]$, as shown in Equation 10.7, investors often calculate the modified duration (MD) of an asset. This calculation makes it easier to calculate approximate changes in prices based on hypothetical rate changes, where

$$\text{Modified Duration (MD)} = \text{DUR} / (1 + y^*)$$ [10.9]

Multiplying the modified duration by any Δy^* gives the approximate change in the value of that fixed rate asset or liability with a change in y^*. Modified duration is often used in risk-adjusted return on capital (RAROC) models to estimate the expected loss in value of individual fixed-income securities on loans with an expected change in y^*. It is also used in regulatory models to measure the overall risk of a financial institution in terms of the expected change in the value of assets and liabilities and, hence, the expected change in the market value of the firm's equity with an estimated change in y^*.[16]

Limitations of a Duration-Based Measure of Interest Rate Risk

As with all tools that help to manage an unknown future, a duration-based risk measure has imperfections. Perhaps the most important is an assumption that when interest rates change, there will be a parallel shift in the yield curve, so that for a given level of default risk, yields across the entire term struc-

---

15 Equation 10.8 can be derived as follows from Equation 10.7. First, note that the mathematical definition of interest rate elasticity is as follows:

$$E = \frac{\Delta P_0}{\Delta y^*} = \frac{\Delta P_0 / P_0}{\Delta y^* / y^*}$$

Therefore, Equation 10.7 can be divided by y^* / y^* to obtain an expression for E:

$$E = \frac{\Delta P_0 / P_0}{\Delta y^* / y^*} = \frac{-\text{DUR} [\Delta y^* / (1 + y^*)]}{\Delta y^* / y^*}$$

After the right side of this expression is simplified and E is substituted for the left side, Equation 10.8 results.

16 See Saunders (1997) for a detailed discussion of the regulatory interest rate risk models proposed by the Federal Reserve and Office of Thrift Supervision in the early 1990s. In the models, assets and liabilities were classified by asset types, and their modified durations were calculated to estimate expected change in price with a given change in y^*. The total change in the value of assets and liabilities was summed to find the expected percent change in the value of equity with a 1 percent rise in rates. In its original proposal, the Fed assumed that an equity loss-to-asset ratio greater than 1 percent was potentially dangerous. Under JPM's (JPMorgan's) RiskMetrics model, the daily price volatility for bonds, similarly, is equal to (the modified duration for a bond) × (the expected adverse daily yield move). Similarly, the Bankers' Trust RAROC model calculates the dollar capital risk exposure or loss amount for a loan as the duration of the loan × (the size of the loan) × [dy^* / (1 + y^*)]. See Saunders (1997).

ture change equally. Some research indicates that parallel shifts in the yield curve are unusual and that relative volatility in yields, as well as duration, affects price changes. Because the formula for interest rate elasticity involves both yield and duration, this conclusion is not surprising. Duration also generally assumes a flat yield curve, because the same y^* discount rate is used for early and late cash flows. Adjustments, however, can be made to account for an upward-sloping yield curve by discounting cash flows for different years at different rates when taking the present value used to calculate duration. Duration is also a dynamic concept; as market rate (y^*) changes, so will a security's duration.[17]

Other research on the historical relationship between duration and rates of return on Treasury securities indicates that factors besides duration are needed to explain variations in returns. In addition, the return/duration relationship is not always linear, as discussed earlier. Nonetheless, many experts view the benefits of duration-based interest rate risk measures to be far greater than their shortcomings.[18] Duration is also widely used. For instance, fixed-rate security mutual funds are now often defined by their duration, that is, as short or longer-term duration mutual funds. Similarly, depository institutions are asked to report their duration gap to regulators. Most successful managers find it essential to understand duration.

Applying Duration to Asset/Liability Management

Duration and related measures of interest rate risk are relevant for almost every financial institution. The most common applications are discussed here.

Duration and the Term Structure

Some analysts argue that the term structure of interest rates is best viewed as the relationship between yield and duration, not yield and maturity. Forward rates could be calculated from the duration-based curve for use in forecasting future yields. For example, Figure 10.3 shows two sets of yield curves for Treasury securities. The left panel plots yield against maturity, and the right panel plots yield against duration. Although the curves have similar shapes, as is expected from the general duration/maturity relationship, the appropriate managerial response might be quite different.[19]

The yield/maturity panel indicates that the maximum maturity of Treasury securities increased between the two dates. But the duration/yield relationship shows that the maximum duration of Treasury securities decreased. Because of the high general level of interest rates in 1980, new Treasury issues had high coupons and relatively short durations, even though the contractual maturities of new issues were not shortened. A duration measure reveals that investors in long-term Treasury bonds (T-bonds) were exposed to less, not more, interest rate risk in 1980 than they were in 1979; the traditional yield/maturity relationship would have suggested otherwise. Major investors in the Treasury market may have had lower exposure to interest rate risk in 1980 than many realized.

---

17 See Saunders (1997) for a more detailed discussion of the limitations of duration.

18 See Yawitz (1977), Reilly and Sidhu (1980), Kaufman (1984), Leibowitz (1983), and Hess (1982).

19 These insights are provided in Bisignano and Dvorak (1981), from which the yield curves in Figure 10.3 are taken.

figure **10.3** THE YIELD CURVE: DURATION VERSUS MATURITY AS A MEASURE OF TIME

These duration-based yield curves are more gently sloped than maturity-based curves plotted at the same time, suggesting that investors faced less interest rate risk than they might have thought.

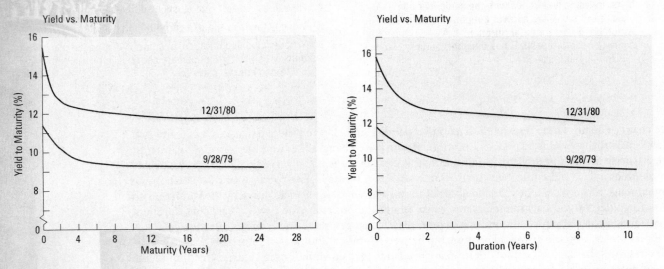

Source: Joseph Bisignano and Brian Dvorak, "Risk and Duration," Weekly Letter *(Federal Reserve Bank of San Francisco), April 3, 1981.*

Portfolio Immunization

Interest rate risk, both with respect to changing market values and reinvestment rates, means that the realized yield on an investment will often differ from the expected yield at the time of investment. For some investors, accepting this risk may be extremely unappealing if they have financial goals or obligations that depend on attaining a certain amount of cash at the end of a holding period. For example, a pension fund may have known obligations to retirees, and cash must be accumulated by the due date. Or an individual may retain the services of a bank trust department and require that his or her funds increase enough by a given date that they will cover the cost of a child's Harvard education.

In the 1970s, a duration-based strategy for portfolio management was introduced and has since been widely adopted by financial institutions.[20] The strategy is known as **immunization** because it makes a portfolio "immune" to the "disease" of interest rate risk over a given holding period. Immunization is a portfolio management strategy to achieve a realized annual rate of return at the end of a holding period that is no less than the expected annual yield at the beginning of the period. Within the constraints addressed later in the chapter, a portfolio is immunized if its duration is equal to the holding period.

Immunization Illustrated

Suppose an insurance company issues a $1 million guaranteed investment contract that guarantees an annual effective yield (y^*) of 8 percent for five years. In other words, the investor is promised that he or she will receive $1 million$(1.08)^5$ = $1.4693 million in five years, that is, an 8 percent annual realized return on the investment:

$$r = (FV / PV)^{1/n} - 1 = (1.4693 / 1 \text{ mil.})^{1/5} - 1 = 0.08, \text{ or } 8\%.$$

---

20 Fisher and Weil (1971). The authors acknowledge their indebtedness to the ideas of writers dating back to the 1970s. In an interesting history of the use of immunization by institutional portfolio managers, Leibowitz (1983) notes that despite previous academic research, immunization was not put into practice until financial markets faced unprecedented events in the late 1970s. Academics, however, benefited from the use of the technique in the real world. Advanced applications are discussed in more detail in Leibowitz (1981) and Bierwag (1987).

The company is considering two alternatives:

1. **Bond 1: six-year bonds with an 8% coupon rate** and $1,000 par value, which sell for $1,000 per bond, with $y^* = 8\%$.

2. **Bond 2: five-year bonds with an 8% coupon rate** and $1,000 par value, which sell for $1,000 per bond, with $y^* = 8\%$.

The duration for Bond 1, as we calculated earlier, is equal to 4.993 years. The duration for Bond 2 can be calculated by using a table as follows:

Year	Cash Flow	PVIF 8%	PV Cash Flow	$t \times$ PV Cash Flow
1	$80	0.9259	$74.07	$74.07
2	80	0.8573	68.58	137.16
3	80	0.7938	63.50	190.50
4	80	0.7350	58.80	235.20
5	1080	0.6806	735.05	3,675.25
			Sum $1,000.00	$4,312.18

DUR = $4,312.18 / $1,000 = 4.312

or you can use the short Equation 10.6:

$$\text{DUR} = N - \{[\text{Coupon pmt} / (P_0 \times y^*)] [N - (1 + y^*) (\text{PVIFA } y^*, N)]\}$$

$$= 5 - \{(80 / 80) \times [5 - (1.08)(3.9927)]\} = 5 - 0.68788 = 4.312$$

If the insurance company's portfolio manager selected a maturity match strategy, Bond 2 would be selected. In contrast, Bond 1 would be selected under a duration match strategy.

To see which choice immunizes the portfolio manager's investment to ensure an 8 percent effective annual yield, we need to calculate the ex post effective annual rate (EAY) for each bond under different interest rate scenarios. These are shown in Table 10.1. The first panel shows the duration matching strategy. Under this strategy, the six-year bond will be held until the end of year 5 and then sold for a price equal to the present value of the remaining coupon and maturity value at that time [$1080 / (1 + y^*)]. Under each of the scenarios (rates staying the same, rates rising, or rates falling) the ex post effective annual (realized) rate will be 8 percent. This is because reinvestment risk exactly offsets market price risk for each of the strategies. For instance, in Scenario 2, if rates rise, the portfolio receives higher reinvestment income from the coupons for the first five years, but the bond will be sold for a loss that just offsets the rise in reinvestment income, leaving a realized return of 8 percent. In Scenario 3, if rates fall, the portfolio receives lower reinvestment income from the coupons for the first five years; however, the bonds can be sold for a gain at the end of year 5, offsetting the lower reinvestment income. Thus, an effective annual yield of 8 percent is again realized. In effect, with duration matching the bond portfolio is immunized and an 8 percent effective annual return is locked in. Of course, there is an opportunity cost associated with Scenario 2, in which the higher reinvestment income is offset by the lower price that the bond is sold for at the end of year 5.

The second panel of Table 10.1 shows the results of Strategy 2: maturity matching. Under this strategy, the portfolio achieves a greater than 8 percent realized annual rate if interest rates rise, as in Scenario 2, because at the end of year 5, the portfolio receives higher reinvestment income from the coupon payments plus the maturity value. However, if interest rates fall (Scenario 3), the portfolio will receive a lower realized annual yield as the result of lower reinvestment income (with no offsetting capital gain) as in the duration matching strategy.

Hence, only under the duration matching strategy is the bond portfolio immunized. For a portfolio of bonds with several different durations, the weighted average duration of the bond portfolio would be constructed to be equal to the desired holding period horizon.[21]

Immunization: Assumptions and Limitations

Under certain assumptions, a bond with a duration equal to the desired holding period results in exactly offsetting market value and reinvestment risks, as suggested for Bond 1 in the previous illustration. With

---

21 The weighted average duration would simply be the sum of (the market value of each bond / total market value of the portfolio) (its duration). For development and proof of the additive property of duration, see Bierwag (1987), pp. 84–86 and 109–110.

t a b l e **10.1** ILLUSTRATION: DURATION AND PORTFOLIO IMMUNIZATION

With immunization, the expected return on a portfolio is protected from both reinvestment and market value risk. In this example, holding bonds with a duration of five years will lock in an annual rate of return of 8% over a holding period of five years. Suppose, for instance, that an insurance company issues a $1 million guaranteed investment contract (GIC) that guarantees an annual effective yield of 8% (y*) for five years. The portfolio manager would like to immunize this yield regardless of what interest rates do.

STRATEGY 1: DURATION MATCH; BUY 8% BOND WITH AN APPROXIMATELY 5-YEAR DURATION

Bond 1: six-year bonds, with an 8% coupon rate, and $1,000 par value that sells for $1,000/bond, with $y^* = 8\%$, Dur = 4.993 years.

Coupon payments reinvested at y^* and bond sold at end of year 5.

Scenario (1) Market interest rates stay at $y^* = 8\%$ for the five years.

   Ex post effective annual rate for Bond 1:

FV of cash flows per bond at end of year 5 = $80 (FVIFA 5, 8%) + $1,080 / (1.08) = $80 (5.8666) + $1,000 = $1,469.33

   Ex post effective annual rate is $(1469.33 / 1000)^{0.20} - 1 = 0.08$, or 8%.

Scenario (2) Market interest rates rise to $y^* = 9\%$ for the five years.

   Ex post effective annual rate for Bond 1:

FV of cash flows per bond at end of year 5 = $80 (FVIFA 5, 9%) + $1,080 / (1.09) = $80 (5.9847) + $990.83 = $1,469.61

   Ex post effective annual rate is $(1469.61 / 1000)^{0.20} - 1 = 0.08$. or 8%.

Scenario (3) Market interest rates fall to $y^* = 7\%$ for the five years.

   Ex post effective annual rate for Bond 1:

FV of cash flows per bond at end of year 5 = $80 (FVIFA 5, 7%) + $1,080 / (1.07) = $80 (5.7507) + $1,009.35 = $1,469.41

   Ex post effective annual rate is $(1469.41 / 1000)^{0.20} - 1 = 0.08$, or 8%.

Summary for Duration Matching Strategy: Regardless of the yield scenario, the duration matching strategy achieves an annual effective yield of 8%, because reinvestment and price risk offset one another.

STRATEGY 2: MATURITY MATCH; BUY 8% BOND WITH A MATURITY OF FIVE YEARS

Bond 2: five-year bonds, with an 8% coupon rate, and $1,000 par value that sells for $1,000/bond, with $y^* = 8\%$, Dur = 4.312 years.

Coupon payments reinvested at y^* and bond held to maturity

Scenario (1) Market interest rates stay at $y^* = 8\%$ for the five years.

   Ex post effective annual rate for Bond 2:

FV of cash flows per bond at end of year 5 = $80 (FVIFA 5, 8%) + $1,000 = $80 (5.8666) + $1,000 = $1,469.33

   Ex post effective annual rate is $(1469.33 / 1000)^{0.20} - 1 = 0.08$, or 8%.

Scenario (2) Market interest rates rise to $y^* = 9\%$ for the five years.

   Ex post effective annual rate for Bond 2:

FV of cash flows per bond at end of year 5 = $80 (FVIFA 5, 9%) + $1,000 = $80 (5.9847) + $1,000 = $1,478.78

   Ex post effective annual rate is $(1478.78 / 1000)^{0.20} - 1 = 0.0814$, or 8.14%.

Scenario (3) Market interest rates fall to $y^* = 7\%$ for the five years.

   Ex post effective annual rate for Bond 2:

FV of cash flows per bond at end of year 5 = $80 (FVIFA 5, 7%) + $1,000 = $80 (5.7507) + $1,000 = $1,460.06

   Ex post effective annual rate is $(1460.06 / 1000)^{0.20} - 1 = 0.0786$, or 7.86%.

Summary for Maturity Matching Strategy: The portfolio manager will not achieve an 8% effective annual yield if rates fall, because of lower reinvestment income on coupon payments. Hence, a maturity matching strategy does not immunize the bond against reinvestment risk if interest rates fall.

a flat initial yield curve and with only one unexpected parallel shift in the curve immediately after the beginning of the period, the realized annual return over the holding period will exactly equal the expected annual yield. However, market yield changes can occur in the middle of the investment period, and an investor may be less than perfectly immunized. Also, although not considered in the example, interest rate changes are so common and so unpredictable that single parallel shifts in the yield curve are the exception rather than the rule.[22] Still, empirical tests of duration and maturity

---

22 See Yawitz (1977); Bierwag, Kaufman, and Toevs (1983); and Ott (1988).

strategies over forty-four years suggest that the dispersion of realized returns is consistently smaller when durations rather than maturities are matched with holding periods.

Another limitation of immunization is that it is difficult to find an investment with a duration exceeding ten years.[23] Thus, investors with lengthy desired holding periods may be unable to use the strategy. Although zero-coupon bonds may not be available, the stripped securities introduced in 1982 by divisions of Merrill Lynch and Salomon Brothers have alleviated this limitation. Stripped securities are created when the originators "strip" ordinary T-bonds of their coupon payments and sell one or more coupon payments or the par value separately to investors wanting single cash inflows at specified dates. The acronyms given to these securities include CATS (Certificates of Accrual on Treasury Securities), Salomon Brothers' version of a strip, and TIGRS (Merrill Lynch's Treasury Investment Growth Receipts), among others.[24] In 1985, to facilitate the issuance of strips, the Treasury Department decided that each coupon payment on specified Treasury issues may be registered in a separate name. The program is called Separate Trading of Registered Interest and Principal of Securities (STRIPS). Treasury issues eligible for the program may be presented to the Treasury for stripping; subsequently, each expected cash flow may be sold as if it were a separate security. This broadening and deepening of the market reduced the liquidity risk of owning strips for investors forced to sell before maturity. As expected, STRIPS have been exceptionally popular, with outstanding volume exceeding $113 billion by the end of 1990.[25] The Tax Reform Act of 1986 allowed the stripping of municipal bonds for the first time, and large securities firms began doing so within minutes of the signing of the law. Mortgage lenders have fashioned stripped securities based on cash flows from expected mortgage payments. Each new type of strip has addressed a market need, such as the desire to minimize taxes or to immunize particular kinds of cash flow obligations.[26]

Financial Institutions and Immunization

Immunization of Security Portfolios

As the previous example illustrates, one way in which financial institutions use immunization is to offer it as part of an array of portfolio management services to customers. Commercial bank trust departments, securities firms, and investment companies are among those institutions for which knowledge of immunization is important. Yet even institutions that do not sell portfolio management services can benefit from understanding immunization. If an institution has promised to make cash payments to others at specified dates in the future, as is the case with pension funds and life insurance companies, a way to enhance the probability that cash will be available to meet those payments is to invest in assets with a weighted average duration equal to that of future cash obligations. Asset portfolios selected for their duration and designed to help meet future cash outflows are called **dedicated portfolios.**

Despite its usefulness, immunization presents difficulties for institutions. Ideally, immunization locks in a yield for a desired holding period by protecting against both sides of interest rate risk. But immunized portfolios are not protected from default risk, nor is there a guarantee against changes in anticipated yields as a result of unanticipated changes in tax laws. Finally, immunization eliminates the possibility of unexpected gains when interest rates change. In other words, it is a hedging, or risk-minimization, strategy, not a profit-maximization strategy. If rates rise to 9 percent, as in the example, the second strategy is the most desirable, but an immunizer forgoes that opportunity. Thus, immunization is appropriate for portfolio managers who wish to avoid rate forecasting or who are willing to trade potential unexpected gains for protection from potential unexpected losses.

---

23 The behavior of duration for bonds with very long maturities is discussed and illustrated in Fisher and Weil (1971). They note that for bonds selling at or above par, duration is bounded by $(y^* + m) / (m \times y^*)$, so the maximum duration for a bond paying interest twice a year $(m = 2)$ with a yield of 10 percent, regardless of coupon or maturity, would be $(0.10 + 2)(2 \times 0.10) = 2.10 / 0.20 = 10.5$ years. For bonds selling at a discount, duration actually decreases for maturities of more than about fifty years. The mathematical expression of the maximum duration for a discount bond is more complex and is presented in Hopewell and Kaufman (1973). Because, as a practical matter, few institutions have investment planning periods exceeding fifty years and because few, if any, bonds with contractual maturities of more than fifty years are available, the limitations of this property are not considered further.

24 See Becketti (1988).

25 See Livingston and Gregory (1989) and Gregory and Livingston (1992).

26 Ann Monroe. "Goldman Sachs and Salomon Brothers Scramble for Sales of Stripped Municipal Bonds." *The Wall Street Journal* (October 23, 1986), 50; and Sherlock and Chen (1987).

1 How is duration a better measure of interest rate risk than term to maturity?

2 How can duration be used to provide portfolio immunization?

3 What are some limitations for using duration for portfolio immunization?

4 What is a dedicated portfolio?

Duration Gap: Measuring an Institution's Overall Interest Rate Risk

In addition to locking in returns on fixed-income portfolios through immunization, depository institutions also use their duration gap as an overall measure of the bank's interest rate risk and to immunize the market value of equity for the institution. A depository institution's duration gap has an advantage over its funding gap by considering not only reinvestment (refinancing) risk and the effect of possible changes in NII with a change in rates but also market value risk. The market value risk is the effect of possible change in interest rates on the market value of the depository institution's assets and liabilities, as well as potential changes in the market value of the institution's equity (market value of assets − market value of liabilities).

A depository institution's duration gap (DGAP) is the difference between the duration of its assets (DUR_A) minus the duration of its liabilities (DUR_L) multiplied by the fraction of liabilities held to assets:

$$\text{DGAP} = \text{DUR}_A - \left[\left(\frac{\text{Liabilities}}{\text{Assets}} \right) \times (\text{DUR}_L) \right] \qquad [10.10]$$

Hence, a depository institution's duration gap is a function of the duration of its assets, the duration of its liabilities, and the percentage of the institution's debt financing. If the institution has a positive duration gap, it has assets with a higher duration (more interest rate risk) than its liabilities. If interest rates rise, the market value of its assets will fall more than the market value of liabilities, and the value of equity will fall. Similarly, if interest rates fall, the market value of equity will rise. If the institution has a negative duration gap, its liabilities will have a higher duration than its assets, and if interest rates rise, the value of its equity will rise; in contrast, if interest rates fall, the value of equity will fall. Note that a positive duration gap implies a negative funding gap (more long-term assets and fewer rate-sensitive assets than liabilities). Similarly, a negative duration gap implies a positive funding gap (more long-term liabilities and fewer rate-sensitive liabilities than assets). A percentage change in the value of the depository institution's equity-to-assets ratio can be found just as one would find a change in any other security:

$$\Delta \text{Value Equity} / \text{Total Assets} = -\text{DGAP} \left[\Delta y^* / (1 + y^*) \right] \qquad [10.11]$$

where y^* is the average rate on assets. The Duration of Assets for a balance sheet is the weighted average of the duration of the assets as follows:

$$\text{DUR}_A = \text{DUR}_{A1} \left(\frac{A_1}{\text{TA}} \right) + \text{DUR}_{A2} \left(\frac{A_2}{\text{TA}} \right) + \ldots + \text{DUR A}_i \left(\frac{A_i}{\text{TA}} \right) \ldots \text{DUR}_{An} \left(\frac{A_n}{\text{TA}} \right) \qquad [10.12]$$

where A_i is the dollar value of Asset$_i$ to the last type of Asset$_n$ and TA is the total dollar value of assets.

Similarly, the Duration of Liabilities for a balance sheet is the weighted average of the duration of the liabilities:

$$\text{DUR}_L = \text{DUR}_{L1} \left(\frac{L_1}{\text{TL}} \right) + \text{DUR}_{L2} \left(\frac{L_2}{\text{TL}} \right) + \ldots + \text{DUR}_{Li} \left(\frac{L_i}{\text{TL}} \right) \ldots \text{DUR}_{Ln} \left(\frac{L_n}{\text{TL}} \right) \qquad [10.13]$$

where L_i is the dollar value of Liability$_I$ and TL is the total dollar value of liabilities.

Difficulties in Calculating Durations

Durations are often difficult to calculate for some depository institution balance sheet items. For instance, do demand deposits have a duration of 0, because they mature at any time, or a duration of the average time they turn over in a year? What is the duration of a variable-rate loan? Often the time frame to which the loan is subject to change is used; thus, a variable-rate loan, subject to change every six months, would have a duration of 0.50 years. Also, remember that with any market rate change, the duration of an asset or liability will also change, so durations must be constantly updated and monitored.

Example: Calculating a Bank's Duration Gap

Information for Excelsior Bank is shown on Table 10.2, Panel A, and as follows.

Calculating the Duration Gap for a Simplified Bank, Excelsior (in Mils.)

Assets

Cash	DUR = 0	$ 10,000
6-month T-bills y* = 6%	DUR = maturity = 0.5 years	$40,000
10-year Fixed-Rate Loans, 10%	DUR = ?	$50,000
amortized	Total Assets	$100,000

Liabilities and Equity

Transaction Deposits rate = 2%	DUR = 0	$40,000
1-Year CDs*, rate = 7%	DUR = 1	50,000
Equity		$10,000
	Total Liabilities and Equity	$100,000

*Interest and principal paid at maturity for 1-year CDs.

Duration of Excelsior's Assets

To calculate the duration of Excelsior's assets, we first calculate the duration of the ten-year amortized loans with equal loan payments of $8,137.27 per year as follows. First, we calculate the duration of the ten-year amortized loans with an annual loan rate of 10 percent, where the loan payment is

$$PMT = \text{Loan Amount} / (\text{PVIFA } 10\%, 10) = \$50,000 / 6.1446 = \$8,137.27 \text{ per year:}$$

Year	Cash Flow	PVIF 10%	PV Cash Flow	$t \times$ PV Cash Flow
1	$8,137.27	0.9091	$7,397.59	$7,397.59
2	8,137.27	0.8264	6,724.65	13,449.28
3	8,137.27	0.7513	6,113.53	18,340.59
4	8,137.27	0.6830	5,557.76	22,231.02
5	8,137.27	0.6209	5,052.43	25,262.16
6	8,137.27	0.5645	4,593.49	27,560.93
7	8,137.27	0.5132	4,176.05	29,232.33
8	8,137.27	0.4665	3,796.04	30,368.29
9	8,137.27	0.4241	3,451.02	31,059.15
10	8,137.27	0.3855	$3,136.92	$31,369.18
		Sum* $50,000.00		$236,270.52

Duration of Loans = $236,270.52 / $50,000 = **4.73 years**

*Note: The present value of the loan should be $50,000, but because of PVIF rounding errors, the sum when adding up the PVCFs is slightly off.

Similarly, the formula for short duration (Equation 10.6) could be used, as follows:

$$DUR = N - \{[\text{Coupon Payment} / \text{Loan Amount} \times y^*] \times [N - (1 + y^*)(\text{PVIFA } y^*, N)]\}$$

$$DUR = 10 - \{[8.137.27 / (50,000 \times 0.10)] \times [10 - (1.10)(6.1446)]\}$$

$$= 10 - [1.6275 (3.241)] = 4.73 \text{ years}$$

Because the loan is amortized, paying equal amounts each year, in contrast with a bond that pays only interest and then principal the final year, the duration years of the loan are much lower than the loan's maturity. The duration of the T-bills is six months, because all cash flows are paid at maturity,

table **10.2** ILLUSTRATION OF IMMUNIZING A BANK'S DURATION GAP

PANEL A: BANK EXCELSIOR'S BALANCE SHEET (UNIMMUNIZED)

Assets	Maturity	Rate y*	Duration	Mkt Value	Liabs/Eq.	Maturity	Rate y*	Duration	Mkt Value
Cash	0	0%	0 years	$10,000	Tran. Deps	0	2%	0 years	$40,000
T-bills	6 months	6%	0.5 years	40,000	1Yr CDs	1 year	7%	1 year	50,000
Loans	10 years	10%	4.73 years	50,000	Equity				10,000
Total Assets				$100,000	Total Liabilities & Equity				$100,000

Information on Assets: T-bills pay interest & principal at maturity, so Duration = 0.5 years

Loans are amortized, so Annual Loan PMT = $50,000 / (PVIFA 10%, 10) = $50,000 / 6.1446 = $8,137.27

Information on Liabilities: CDs pay interest and principal at maturity, so duration = 1

Assume 0 maturity and duration for transaction deposits.

Sample Duration Calculation for Loans:

$DUR = N - [Loan\ PMT / (P_0 \times y^*)] \times [N - (1 + y^*) (PVIFA\ y^*, N)]$

$DUR = 10 - \{[8137.27 / (50,000 \times .10)] \times [10 - (1.10)(6.1446)]\} = 4.73$ years

Calculation of DGAP:

$DURAssets = (10,000 / 100,000)\ 0 + (40,000 / 100,000)\ .5 + (50,000 / 100,000)\ 4.73 = 2.565$ years

$DURLiabs = (40,000 / 90,000)\ 0 + (50,000 / 90,000)\ 1 = .5556$ years

$DGAP = DURAssets - (Liabilities/Assets) \times DURLiabs = 2.565$ years $- (90,000 / 100,000)\ 0.5556$ years $= 2.065$ years

Expected Net Interest Income = 40,000(.06) + 50,000(.10) − 40,000(.02) − 50,000(.07) = $7,400 − $4,300 = $3,100 mil.

6-month funding gap = RSA − RSL = $40,000 − 0 = $40,000

1-year funding gap = $40,000 − $50,000 = −$10,000

PANEL B: HYPOTHETICAL RISE IN INTEREST RATES 100 BASIS POINTS (1%): NEW BALANCE SHEET (MILS.)

Assets	Maturity	Rate y*	Duration	Mkt Value	Liabs/Eq.	Maturity	Rate y*	Duration	Mkt Value
Cash	0	0%	0 years	$10,000	Tran. Deps	0	2%	0 years	$40,000
T-bills	6 months	7%	0.5 year	39,807	1 Yr CDs	1 year	8%	1 year	49,537
Loans	10 years	11%	4.73 years	47,922	Equity				8,192
Total Assets				$97,729	Total Liabilities & Equity				$97,729

Approximate Change in Equity Using DGAP = −DGAP (Δy*) / (1 + y*) × Total Assets = −2.065 (.01) / (1.074) × $100,000 = −$1,922.72

Actual Change in Value of Equity = Change in Value of Assets − Change in Value of Liabilities = −2,271 − (−463) = −$1,808

New Net Interest Income = $40,000(.03) + 40,000(1.03)(.035) + 50,000(.10) − 40,000(.02) − 50,000(.07) = $7,642 − $4,300 = $3,342 [$3,342 − $3,100 = $242 higher net interest income]

*In this scenario with a positive 6-month funding gap, NII went up when rates rose. However, with a positive duration gap, the market value of equity fell when rates rose.

Note: Changes in balance sheet items are calculated by taking the present value of future cash flows for each item. See Koch (1995) for a more thorough example of Duration Gap immunization, from which this example is derived.

and the duration of cash is zero. Thus, the **weighted average duration of Bank Excelsior's assets, DUR_A**, using Equation 10.12 is as follows:

$$DUR_A = (\$10,000 / \$100,000)\ 0 + (\$40,000 / \$100,000)\ 0.5 + (\$50,000 / \$100,000)\ 4.73$$

$$= (0.10)\ 0 + (0.40)\ 0.5 + (0.50)\ 4.73 = 2.565\ \text{years}$$

Duration of Excelsior's Liabilities

The **weighted average duration of Bank Excelsior's liabilities, DUR_L**, can be calculated by using Equation 10.13:

$$DUR_L = (40,000 / 90,000)\ 0 + (50,000 / 90,000)\ 1 = 0.5556\ \text{years}$$

table   **10.2**   ILLUSTRATION OF IMMUNIZING A BANK'S DURATION GAP (CONTINUED)

PANEL C: IMMUNIZED BALANCE SHEET FOR EXCELSIOR BANK (MILS.)

Assets	Maturity	Rate y*	Duration	Mkt Value	Liabs/Eq.	Maturity	Rate y*	Duration	Mkt Value
Cash	0	0%	0 years	$10,000	Tran. Deps	0	2%	0 years	$40,000
T-bills	6 months	6%	0.5 years	40,000	5 Yr CDs	5 years	8%	5 years	50,000
Loans	10 years	10%	4.73 years	50,000	Equity				10,000
Total Assets				$100,000	Total Liabilities & Equity				$100,000

DURAssets = same as previously, no change = 2.565 years

DURLiabs = (40,000 / 90,000) 0 + (50,000 / 90,000) 5 = 2.78 years

DGAP = DURAssets − (Liabilities/Assets) × DURLiabs = 2.565 − (90,000 / 100,000) 2.78 years = 2.565 − 2.502 = 0.063

Expected NII = 40,000(.06) + 50,000(.10) − 40,000(.02) − 50,000(.08) = $7,400 − $4,800 = $2,600 mil.

6-month & 1-year funding gaps = $40,000 − 0 = $40,000

PANEL D: HYPOTHETICAL RISE IN RATES OF 1% BASED ON IMMUNIZED BALANCE SHEET

Assets	Maturity	Rate y*	Duration	Mkt Value	Liabs/Eq.	Maturity	Rate y*	Duration	Mkt Value
Cash	0	0%	0 years	$10,000	Tran. Deps	0	2%	0 years	$40,000
T-bills	6 months	7%	0.5 years	39,807	1 Yr CDs	1 year	9%	1 year	47,749
Loans	10 years	11%	4.73 years	47,922	Equity				9,980
Total Assets				$97,729	Total Liabilities & Equity				$97,729

Approximate Change in Equity Using DGAP = −0.063 (0.01 / 1.074) × $100,000 = $58.65

Actual Change in Value of Equity = −$2,271 − (−2,251) = − $20

Net Interest Income = Interest Revenue − Interest Expense

NII = $40,000(.03) + 40,000(1.03)(.035) + 50,000(.10) − 40,000(.02) − 50,000(.08) = $7,642 − $4,800 = $2,842

In this scenario, the value of equity is much better protected, but at the cost of a higher interest expense and a lower net interest income.

Duration Gap for Excelsior

The duration gap for Excelsior can be calculated by using Equation 10.14:

$$DGAP = DUR_A - \left(\frac{\text{Liabilities}}{\text{Assets}}\right) DUR_L \qquad [10.14]$$

$$= 2.565 \text{ years} - (90,000 / 100,000)\, 0.5556 \text{ years} = 2.065 \text{ years}$$

Effect on the Value of Equity of a 1% Rise in Rates

Table 10.2, Panel B, shows the actual effect on the balance sheet and the value of equity for Excelsior if interest rates rise 1 percent. A 1 percent rise in interest rates means that the change in value of equity for Excelsior will be as follows:

$$\$\Delta\text{Value Equity to Total Assets} = -DGAP\, [\Delta y^* / (1 + y^*)]$$

$$\$\Delta\text{Value Equity to Total Assets} = -2.065\, (0.01 \times 1.074) = -0.0192, \text{ or } -1.92\%$$

Note: the weighted average rate on assets = (0.4)6 percent + (0.5)10 percent = 7.4 percent should be used for y*. Multiplying the fraction change by Total Assets, we get the following:

$$\$\Delta\text{Value Equity} \approx (-0.0192) \times \$100,000 \text{ mil.} = -\$1,920 \text{ mil.}$$

With a positive duration gap of 2.065, the market value of Excelsior's equity will fall by about $1,920 million, or $1.92 billion, for the $100 billion bank. Note that the actual change in the market value of equity is −$1,808 million (see Table 10.2, Panel B). The duration gap formula, which does not adjust for convexity, somewhat overestimates the fall in the bank's equity value.

Concept Questions

1 What is a financial institution's duration gap?

2 How is a duration gap a better overall measure of interest rate risk than a funding gap?

3 If a financial institution has a positive duration gap and if interest rates rise, what happens to the value of equity? If interest rates fall, what happens to the value of equity?

4 If a financial institution has a positive duration gap, what type of funding gap is it likely to have (positive or negative)? If a financial institution has a negative duration gap, what type of funding gap is it likely to have?

5 If two financial institutions, A and B, have the same duration of assets and duration of liabilities, but institution B has high financial leverage (i.e., a higher liabilities-to-assets ratio), which will have the larger duration gap?

Immunization and Its Cost

If Bank Excelsior's managers expect rates to rise and want to have a duration gap closer to zero, they have several alternatives. They could shorten the duration of the bank's assets, such as by issuing variable-rate loans. Alternatively, they could issue longer-term certificates of deposit (CDs) to lengthen the bank's liabilities. However, there is a price to pay for either strategy. If Bank Excelsior issues variable-rate loans, its customers will demand a lower loan rate, because they will in effect be taking on the upcoming interest rate risk. This will lower Bank Excelsior's interest revenues and NII. Similarly, if Bank Excelsior lengthens the duration of its liabilities to match that of its assets, it will have to offer a higher CD rate for longer-term deposits for customers to be willing to take on the additional interest rate risk of locking into a longer-term CD rate when rates might rise.

Panel C of Table 10.2 shows a scenario of immunizing the balance sheet by lengthening the duration of liabilities so the duration gap is closer to zero. As shown in Panel D, the bank switched to longer-term, five-year CDs. The duration of liabilities rises to 2.78, and the Duration Gap is now 0.063. Under this scenario the value of equity does not change very much with a rise in rates. However, the net interest revenue for the bank is lower than when it had a positive duration gap because of the higher interest expense for five-year CDs of 8 percent versus 7 percent for one-year CDs used in Panel A.

With immunization, the bank misses any opportunities of a higher value of equity if interest rates fall instead. Thus, bank balance sheet immunization brings with it an opportunity cost. Hence, many bank managers do not aim for a zero gap but rather position the bank with a duration gap based on their confidence in interest rate forecasts. For instance, a number of banks in the 1990s, a period of low, falling interest rates, had positive duration gaps. Other banks have gaps that hinge largely on customer preferences for different types of assets and liabilities, accepting interest rate risk as part of the risk/reward of banking. Still, other banks hedge using off-balance-sheet methods, including securitization, discussed earlier, and derivatives (futures, options, interest rate swaps, caps, collars, and floors), which are discussed in Chapters 11 and 12.

Simulation and Scenario Analysis

One weakness of both funding gaps and duration gaps is the assumption that assets and liabilities remain the same after an interest rate rise or fall. In reality, with a fall in rates, for instance, loan customers may prepay their fixed loans and refinance at their bank or with another bank. Thus, the bank's mix of loans may change considerably if rates fall significantly. Similarly, deposit customers may withdraw funds from CDs and be willing to take withdrawal penalties to be able to reinvest funds in higher-yielding assets when rates rise. However, with static duration and funding gap measures, mix and volume changes in assets and liabilities are not considered.

Hence, most depository institutions use simulation or scenario analysis packages that consider mix and volume changes in assets and liabilities and changes in the institution's net interest margin under different scenarios. Sheshunoff, for instance, has such a package.[27] Similarly, regulators ask institutions to perform such an analysis with the interest rate sensitivity (S) component of their regulatory CAMELS rating (Capital, Assets, Management Quality, Earnings, and Liquidity). Table 10.3 shows such

---

27 Sheshunoff Information Services, Inc., Austin, Texas.

table 10.3

PANEL A: EARNINGS AND ECONOMIC EXPOSURE TO CHANGES IN INTEREST RATES—MARCH 31, 1997

1997 NET INCOME

Change in Basis Points	Net Income	% Change
−200	947,285	−9.73%
−150	974,583	−7.13%
−100	1,002,811	−4.44%
−50	1,030,674	−1.79%
0	1,049,407	0.00%
50	1,090,599	3.93%
100	1,130,970	7.77%
150	1,169,383	11.43%
200	1,207,417	15.06%

1998 NET INCOME

Change in Basis Points	Net Income	% Change
−200	1,049,435	−17.42%
−150	1,093,400	−13.96%
−100	1,156,205	−9.01%
−50	1,219,582	−4.03%
0	1,270,749	0.00%
50	1,353,001	6.47%
100	1,417,080	11.52%
150	1,474,793	16.06%
200	1,531,015	20.48%

PRESENT VALUE EQUITY

Change in Basis Points	Net Income	% Change
−200	8,229,473	−4.13%
−150	8,342,986	−2.81%
−100	8,454,402	−1.51%
−50	8,555,311	−0.33%
0	8,583,900	0.00%
50	8,698,321	1.33%
100	8,809,193	2.62%
150	8,900,457	3.69%
200	8,982,353	4.64%

1997 NET INCOME PROJECTIONS

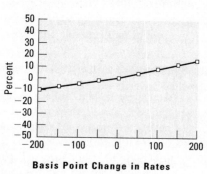

Basis Point Change in Rates

1998 NET INCOME PROJECTIONS

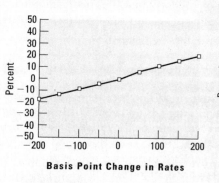

Basis Point Change in Rates

PRESENT VALUE EQUITY

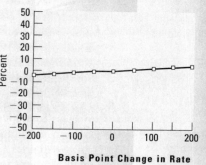

Basis Point Change in Rate

PANEL B: CURRENT EXPOSURE / RISK LIMIT ANALYSIS—MARCH 31, 1997

Net Interest Income Exposure	
Current Rolling 12-month NII Exposure (−200 bp)	6.1%
Current Net Interest Income Limit	N/A
Exposure to Limit Ratio	N/A

Present Value Equity Exposure	
Current Present Value Equity Exposure (−200 bp)	4.1%
Current Present Value Equity Limit	N/A
Exposure to Limit Ratio	N/A

Income Exposure Analysis
EXPOSURE TO FALLING RATES

	Base Case	−200 Bp	Exposure
Net Interest Income	3,777,812	3,548,569	6.1%
Net Income	1,175,915	1,022,323	13.1%
ROA	1.89%	1.65%	13.0%
ROE	16.70%	14.66%	12.2%

Present Value Equity Exposure Analysis

1) The change in economic value, given a 200-basis-point change in rate	354,427
2) The change in economic value as a percentage of total assets	0.58%
3) The change in economic value as a percentage of total market value equity	4.13%
4) Pre-shock present value ratio: Present value equity as a percentage of present value assets	13.99%
5) Post-shock (200 bp) present value ratio: Post-shock present value equity as a percentage of present value assets	13.42%
6) Change in present value ratio (#4 − #5)	0.58%

Concept Questions

1 How can a financial institution that has fixed-rate loans for assets and variable-rate deposits for liabilities change its asset or liability composition to achieve a duration gap closer to zero?

2 What is the cost of immunization for a financial institution, that is, having a duration gap that is close to zero?

3 What is a weakness of both a funding gap and a duration gap as a measure of interest rate risk?

4 How can simulation and scenario analysis be used by a financial institution to determine the degree of its economic exposure to a change in interest rates?

an interest rate scenario analysis. Note that net income is projected, and the present value of equity for different interest rate scenarios, from 22 percent (200-basis-point fall) to a 12 percent (200-basis-point rise), is included. The lower panel quantifies the effect on return on assets and return on equity based on a 200-basis-point change in rates, along with the percentage of the value of equity relative to total assets with a 2 percent change in rates. The exposure to falling rates is shown in the bottom panel for this bank, which has a positive funding gap and, hence, a negative duration gap.

Summary

Managing interest rate risk is a crucial part of financial management for a financial institution. Managers need to understand interest rate risk and to have an overall method of measuring that risk. Interest rate risk can be divided into two components: reinvestment risk and market value (or price) risk. Reinvestment risk is most serious when an investor plans to hold an asset to maturity. Market value risk can be severe when an investor plans to sell an asset before maturity. Changes in market yields cause changes in market value in the opposite direction. The bond theorems further define the effect of interest rate changes on market value. The magnitude of fluctuations in value for a given change in market yields varies with the term to maturity, size of the security's coupon rate, and direction of the change in yields. The theorems hold important implications for financial institutions: In managing a given asset/liability mix, one must recognize varying degrees of sensitivity to shifts in market yields.

Equity securities are also sensitive to changes in interest rates, but the nature of the relationship is more difficult to identify. Recent research indicates an inverse relationship between shifts in interest rates and prices of common stock, so even institutions primarily involved with the management of equity portfolios are susceptible to interest rate risk.

Duration is the foundation for analyzing an investor's and a financial institution's overall exposure to both reinvestment and market price risks. It is a measure superior to contractual maturity for comparing the risk of debt instruments because it also captures the effects of differing coupon rates and market yields. An important property of duration is that it is directly proportional to percentage changes in asset prices that result from a change in market yields. Thus, duration can be used to calculate an investment's interest rate elasticity.

Portfolio immunization is a strategy that balances reinvestment risk and market risk to protect a portfolio from the effects of an unexpected shift in interest rates. An immunized portfolio is one with a duration equal to the planned holding period for the investment. The demand for immunization through longer-duration assets has led to the development of a new type of financial asset: the stripped Treasury security.

Duration is also used to calculate the duration gap as a comprehensive measure for the overall interest rate risk of a depository institution. The duration gap for an institution is the duration of its assets less the duration of its liabilities times the proportion of assets financed by liabilities. In contrast to the traditional funding gap measure, which considers only reinvestment (refinancing) risk, the duration gap considers both reinvestment and market price risk.

Depository institutions also use scenario and simulation analysis in their analysis of interest rate risk. Scenario and simulation analysis allow for potential mix and volume changes in an institution's assets and liabilities that neither the funding nor duration gap measures include. Regulators now require institutions to specify under the S, the "sensitiv-ity to interest" rate measure of CAMELS, what will happen to their net interest margin, net income, and market values of equity with a 200-basis-point rise or fall in rates. Sheshunoff and other private bank services offer packages for such simulations.

Questions

1. Suppose you are a bond portfolio manager for a major insurance company and are training a new assistant. Explain how the ex ante annual effective yield to maturity differs from a bond's ex post (realized) ex ante yield. Also explain under what assumptions the two are the same.

2. What are the two components of interest rate risk? If a portfolio manager has invested in ten-year bonds to be held until maturity and the proceeds expected of $1 million will be needed for a new corporate venture, explain how this position is exposed to interest rate risk.

3. A small insurance company's board of directors has asked for an explanation of the effect of interest rate changes on bond values and on the choices between high- and low-coupon bonds or between long- and short-term maturities. Based on the bond theorems, what should the directors be told about the ideal composition of a bond portfolio when market yields are rising? When they are falling?

4. Using the bond theorems, but without doing any calculations, explain which bonds would fluctuate more assuming their other characteristics are the same (high or low coupon bonds, short- or long-term maturity bonds, or zero-coupon bonds) given a rise or fall in market rates of 2 percent. If rates are expected to fall, will it be better to have a longer- or shorter-term bond?

5. What is the relationship between interest rates and stock prices? Why do the bond theorems not provide a sufficient explanation of this relationship? Why do the stock prices of financial firms tend to be more affected by changes in market interest rates than other stocks?

6. In your own words, explain what duration measures are and why duration is more useful than time to maturity for evaluating the interest rate risk of an investment.

7. Under what circumstances are the duration of a bond and its contractual maturity the same? Why?

8. How can a security's interest rate elasticity be calculated by using its duration? Explain what a security's interest rate elasticity is. What is modified duration, and how is it used?

9. What are the limitations of duration? What adjustments can be made for these? What is the property of convexity for bonds?

10. How can duration be used to immunize a fixed-income bond portfolio? Explain how a given rate of return is locked in. Why will a maturity matching strategy not work in terms of immunizing a portfolio from interest rate risk?

11. The bond portfolio manager of a small life insurance company emphasizes immunization as a primary goal. Explain whether the manager is following a hedging or a profit-maximizing approach. Identify the limitations that prevent immunization from providing total protection against interest rate risk. What is a dedicated portfolio? When is a dedicated portfolio useful?

12. What are STRIPS? Why are STRIPS and zero-coupon bonds popular choices for immunized portfolios?

13. Explain the difference between a depository institution's funding gap and its duration gap. Why is the duration gap a better overall measure? How is a duration gap calculated?

14. What limitations do both funding gaps and duration gaps have in terms of changes in volume and mix in assets and liabilities for a depository institution when interest rates change? How can simulation and scenario analysis provide a depository institution with a better picture of its overall interest rate risk?

15. Explain the options available to managers for restructuring the balance sheet under either funding gap or duration gap immunization. What are the advantages and disadvantages of each? How do customers' preferences influence a depository institution's ability to manage its gap?

16. For an institution with a positive funding gap (negative duration gap) that uses active GAP management (adjusting the gap to make larger profits when interest rates rise or fall), what adjustments should managers make under expectations of declining rates? Under expectations of rising rates?

17. Explain how a depository institution's efforts to manage interest rate sensitivity through the loan portfolio might also affect its profits and default risk exposure. If you were a depository institution manager, would you try to achieve a zero gap for the institution? Why or why not?

Problems

1. Your broker, Sue Tracy, has brought three bond portfolios to your attention. Each has annual interest payments, a 9 percent rate, and a par value of $1,000. The portfolios differ in that they are for 10-, 20-, and 30-year bonds. Calculate and compare the change in values in each of the bonds with a fall in rates from 9 percent to 6 percent.

2. Hostess International Corporation issued zero-coupon bonds ten years ago with an initial time to maturity of twenty-five years and a par value of $1,000. Today, ten years later, you can buy one of these bonds for $23.455.
   a. What yield to maturity (y^*) is the market expecting on the bonds today?
   b. What will the percentage change in price in the bond be if market yields rise to 14 percent immediately after you buy the bonds?
   c. Explain why a zero-coupon bond is particularly exposed to market price risk but not reinvestment risk if it must be sold prior to maturity.

3. You purchase a 13.5 percent coupon rate bond with annual interest payments and a market value of $1,170, par value of $1,000, and yield to maturity of 10.49 percent and plan to hold it for nine years when it matures. If market yields change just after you buy the bond and fall drastically to 8 percent, what will be your ex post (realized) annual return on the investment? Explain why the realized yield is lower than the expected yield to maturity when you bought the bond.

4. Your father is preparing for his twenty-fifth wedding anniversary celebration. He wants to have $5,000 on July 1, 2010, and has set up an annuity to reach that goal. He will invest $869.46 on July 1 of each of five years from 2006 to 2010 and estimates that he will earn an average annual yield of 7 percent.
   a. Show that if market yields of 7 percent prevail, your father will reach his investment goal of $5,000 by July 1, 2010.
   b. Suppose that market yields drop to 5 percent immediately after the first $869.46 investment and that they remain there until July 1, 2010. Calculate the future value of the investment and realized return. What type of risk does this problem demonstrate?

5. Calculate the duration of the following bonds with $1,000 par values, annual interest payments, and $y^* = 8$ percent to determine which bond has the most interest rate risk:
   a. 6 percent coupon rate, three years to maturity, market price = $94.846
   b. 10 percent coupon rate, two years to maturity, market price = $103.567
   c. 14 percent coupon rate, five years to maturity, market price = $123.956

6. A bond mutual fund manager is considering adding two bonds to the portfolio: (a) a 4 percent coupon rate bond trading at 85 and (b) a 5 percent coupon rate bond trading at 94. Both bonds have nine years remaining until maturity, annual interest payments, and a par value of $1,000. Calculate the duration of each bond and its elasticity. Which bond has greater interest rate risk?

7. As a new analyst for a large insurance firm's investment division, you have been assigned to assist the firm's asset/liability management committee. Durations are calculated for all assets to evaluate risk. As your first assignment, estimate duration and interest rate elasticities for the following corporate real estate loans ($y^* = 9$ percent):
   a. $10,000, five-year amortized loan with a 9 percent annual interest rate
   b. $10,000, five-year loan with a 9 percent annual interest rate. This loan is not amortized. It pays interest only at the end of each year and then the $10,000 principal at the end of year 5.
   Which loan has more interest rate risk? Why?

8. Suppose you need to earn 7.18 percent on your investment portfolio of $100,000 each year to reach a goal of $200,049 in ten years. You have a choice between the following bonds with annual coupon payments:
   a. 7.18 percent coupon bond that matures in ten years, with $1,000 par value, selling at par value now (i.e., $y^* = 7.18$ percent)
   b. 7.18 percent coupon bond that matures in sixteen years, with $1,000 par value, also selling at par value now (i.e., $y^* = 7.18$ percent)
   c. 7.18 percent zero-coupon bond that matures in ten years
   Find the duration for each bond. Also find the realized annual yield that you would earn under each strategy if rates fall to 6 percent after you purchased the bond and remain at 6 percent for the next ten years. Which strategies would be appropriate to immunize your annual 7.18 percent return, regardless of what interest rates do? Explain why.

9. Texas Independence Bank has the following balance sheet in millions:

Assets		Liabilities and Equity	
3-year fixed rate loans (9%)	$35	Demand Deposits (0%)	$12
		Fed Funds Purchased (7%)	30
30-year fixed rate mortgages (10%)	11	Equity	8
Land and Buildings	4		
Total Assets	$50	Total Liabilities and Equity	$50

   a. What is the bank's expected NII next year?
   b. What is its one-year funding gap? How large is this gap relative to assets? Without doing any calculations but looking at the maturity of assets and liabilities, decide whether the bank has a positive or negative duration gap.

c. Assuming Fed Funds Purchased have an average 0.50 (half a year duration), and Demand Deposits a 0 duration, what is the duration of the bank's liabilities?

d. Suppose both the three-year and thirty-year loans are amortized loans. Find their annual loan payments and durations (assume $y^* =$ the rate given for each loan). Assuming the land and buildings have 0 duration, what is the duration of the bank's assets, and what is the bank's duration gap?

e. If interest rates rise 1 percent over the year, what will be the effect on NII and net interest margin? Based on the bank's duration gap, what will be the effect on the value of assets relative to the value of liabilities and the value of the bank's equity?

10. A balance sheet analysis and the average duration of each account for the Blumberg Savings Bank is shown in the following table:

The Blumberg Savings Bank

Balance Sheet Analysis (mils.)

Assets		Liabilities and Net Worth	
Short-term securities and adjustable-rate loans		Short-term and floating-rate funds	
Duration: 3 months	$210	Duration: 1 month	$580
Fixed-rate loans:		Fixed-rate funds:	
Duration: 8 years	650	Duration: 35 months	280
Nonearning assets	80	Core capital (net worth)	80
Total Assets	$940	Total Liabilities and Net Worth	$940

a. Calculate the bank's duration of assets and liabilities and its duration gap.

b. Currently, the average rate of return on assets is 10 percent. If the general level of interest rates increases by 1 percent, how much will the value of the bank's net worth change?

c. Suppose that the expected change in the value of net worth is unacceptable to management. Suggest several actions that could be taken to counteract this expected change. What are the advantages and disadvantages of each action?

d. Show the effect on the bank's capital if interest rates fall by 1 percent instead.

11. The Sofia National Bank has the following balance sheet (in mils):

Assets		Liabilities and Net Worth	
Short-term securities and adjustable-rate loans		Short-term and floating-rate funds	
Duration: 3 months	$660	Duration: 1 month	$210
Fixed-rate loans:		Fixed-rate funds:	
Duration: 8 years	220	Duration: 35 months	650
Nonearning assets	80	Core capital (net worth)	80
Total Assets	$940	Total Liabilities and Net Worth	$940

a. Calculate Sofia's duration gap.

b. If the average rate on Sofia's assets is 10 percent and the general level of interest rates increases by 100 basis points (1 percent), by how much will Sofia's net worth change? If you were the bank manager, would you be pleased with this result? Why or why not?

c. Now suppose that interest rates fell sharply by 300 basis points. By how much will Sofia's net worth change? If you were Sofia's manager, would you be pleased with this result? Why or why not?

d. Notice that Sofia National's assets and net worth are identical to the assets and net worth of the Blumberg Savings Bank in Problem 10, as are the durations of both institutions' assets and liabilities. Compare the results for the two banks. Can you see why managing institutions with large positive duration gaps can be stressful?

12. Consider the Mardi Gras National Bank's balance sheet:

The Mardi Gras National Bank

Assets		Rate	Liabilities and Equity		Rate
Cash	$441.67		Demand Deposits	$2,000	
Consumer Loans	$4,814.55	0.10	CDs	$12,000	0.08
Commercial Loans	$9,743.78		Equity	$1,000	
Total Assets	$15,000		Total Liabilities and Equity	$15,000	

Each of the loans is amortized and has equal payments of principal and interest each period. The consumer loans pay $2,774.10 per year for two years, and the commercial loans pay $2,570.92 per year for five years.

On the liability side, the CDs have a one-year maturity and pay principal of $12,000 and the annual interest payment at maturity in one year.

a. Calculate the duration of each of the assets and liabilities.

b. Calculate Mardi Gras Bank's duration of assets, duration of liabilities, duration gap, and the expected change in the value of equity if rates rise by 1 percent.

c. How could the bank reduce its duration gap? What would be the effect on profits?

Selected References

Bae, Sung C. "Interest Rate Changes and Common Stock Returns of Financial Institutions: Revisited." *Journal of Financial Research* 13 (Spring 1990), 71–79.

Becketti, Sean. "The Role of Stripped Securities in Portfolio Management." *Economic Review* (Federal Reserve Bank of Kansas City) 73 (May 1988), 20–31.

Benesh, Gary A., and Stephen E. Celec. "A Simplified Approach for Calculating Bond Duration." *Financial Review* 19 (November 1984), 394–396.

Bierwag, Gerald O. *Duration Analysis.* Cambridge, MA: Ballinger Publishing Co., 1987.

Bierwag, Gerald O., George G. Kaufman, and Alden Toevs. "Bond Portfolio Immunization and Stochastic Process Risk." *Journal of Bank Research* 13 (Winter 1983), 282–291.

Bisignano, Joseph, and Brian Dvorak. "Risk and Duration." *Weekly Letter* (Federal Reserve Bank of San Francisco) (April 3, 1981).

Caks, John, et al. "A Simple Formula for Duration." *Journal of Financial Research* 8 (Fall 1985), 245–249.

Christie, Andrew A. "The Stochastic Behavior of Common Stock Variances: Value, Leverage, and Interest Rate Effects." *Journal of Financial Economics* 5 (December 1981), 407–432.

Chua, Jess B. "A Closed-Form Formula for Calculating Bond Duration." *Financial Analysts Journal* 40 (May-June 1984), 76–78.

Dietz, Peter O., H. Russell Fogler, and Anthony U. Rivers. "Duration, Non-Linearity, and Bond-Portfolio Performance." *Journal of Portfolio Management* 7 (Spring 1981), 37–41.

Fabozzi, Frank J. *Bond Markets, Analysis and Strategies,* 2d ed. Englewood Cliffs, NJ: Prentice Hall, 1993.

Fisher, Lawrence. "An Algorithm for Finding Exact Rates of Return." *Journal of Business* 39 (January 1966), 111–118.

Fisher, Lawrence, and Roman Weil. "Coping with the Risk of Interest Rate Fluctuation: Returns to Bondholders from Naive and Optimal Strategies." *Journal of Business* 44 (October 1971), 408–431.

Flannery, Mark J., and Christopher M. James. "The Effect of Interest Rate Changes on the Common Stock Returns of Financial Institutions." *Journal of Finance* 39 (September 1984), 1141–1153.

Fogler, Russell H. "Bond Portfolio Immunization, Inflation, and the Fisher Equation." *Journal of Risk and Insurance* 51 (June 1984), 244–264.

Gregory, Deborah W., and Miles Livingston. "Development of the Market for U.S. Treasury Strips." *Financial Analysts Journal* 48 (March-April 1992), 68–74.

Hempel, George H., Donald G. Simonson, and Alan B. Coleman. *Bank Management: Text and Cases,* 4th ed. New York: John Wiley & Sons, 1995.

Hess, Alan C. "Duration Analysis for Savings and Loan Associations." *Federal Home Loan Bank Board Journal* 15 (October 1982), 12–14.

Hicks, J. R. *Value and Capital.* Oxford: Clarendon Press, 1939.

Hopewell, Michael C., and George G. Kaufman. "Bond Price Volatility and Term to Maturity: A Generalized Respecification." *American Economic Review* 63 (September 1973), 749–753.

Kaufman, George G. "Measuring and Managing Interest Rate Risk: A Primer." *Economic Perspectives* (Federal Reserve Bank of Chicago) 8 (January/February 1984), 16–29.

Kaufman, George G., G. O. Bierwag, and Alden Toevs, eds. *Innovations in Bond Portfolio Management: Duration Analysis and Immunization.* Greenwich, CT: JAI Press, 1983.

Koch, Timothy W. *Bank Management,* 3rd ed. Fort Worth, TX: Harcourt Brace, 1995.

Leibowitz, Martin L. "Bond Immunization: A Procedure for Realizing Target Levels of Return." In *Financial Markets: Instruments and Concepts,* ed. John R. Brick. Richmond, VA: Robert F. Dame, 1981, pp. 443–454.

Leibowitz, Martin L. "Financial Theory Evolves into the Real World—or Not: The Case of Duration and Immunization." *Financial Review* 18 (November 1983), 271–280.

Leibowitz, Martin, et al. "A Total Differential Approach to Equity Duration." *Financial Analysts Journal* 45 (September/October 1989), 30–37.

Livingston, Miles, and Deborah Wright Gregory. *The Stripping of U.S. Treasury Securities.* New York: Salomon Brothers Center for the Study of Financial Institutions, 1989.

Macaulay, Frederick R. *Some Theoretical Problems Suggested by the Movements of Interest Rates, Bond Yields, and Stock Prices in the U.S. since 1856.* New York: National Bureau of Economic Research, 1938.

Malkiel, Burton, G. "Expectations, Bond Prices, and the Term Structure of Interest Rates." *Quarterly Journal of Economics* 76 (May 1962), 197–218.

Moser, James T., and James T. Lindley. "A Simple Formula for Duration: An Extension." *Financial Review* 24 (November 1989), 611–615.

Neuberger, Jonathan A. "Bank Holding Company Stock Risk and the Composition of Bank Asset Portfolios." *Economic Review* (Federal Reserve Bank of San Francisco) 3 (1992), 53–62.

Ott, Robert A., Jr. "Duration Analysis and Minimizing Interest Rate Risk." In *Managing Interest Rate Risk: Selected Readings.* Atlanta: Federal Home Loan Bank of Atlanta, 1988, pp. 31–34.

Reilly, Frank K., and Rupinder S. Sidhu. "The Many Uses of Bond Duration." *Financial Analysts Journal* 36 (July-August 1980), 58–72.

Rosenberg, Joel L. "The Joys of Duration." *Bankers Magazine* 169 (March-April 1986), 62–67.

Samuelson, Paul. "The Effects of Interest Rate Increases on the Banking System." *American Economic Review* 35 (March 1945), 16–27.

Saunders, Anthony. *Financial Institutions Management: A Modern Perspective,* 2d ed. Burr Ridge, IL: Irwin, 1997.

Scott, William L., and Richard L. Peterson. "Interest Rate Risk and Equity Values of Hedged and Unhedged Financial Intermediaries." *Journal of Financial Research* 9 (Winter 1986), 325–329.

Sherlock, Patricia M., and Le In Chen. "Stripped Mortgage Backed Securities: The Sum Is Greater than the Parts." *Mortgage Banking* 47 (June 1987), 61–68.

Smith, Donald J. "The Duration of a Bond as a Price Elasticity and as a Fulcrum." *Journal of Financial Education* 17 (Fall 1988), 26–38.

Sweeney, Richard J., and Arthur D. Warga. "The Pricing of Interest Rate Risk: Evidence from the Stock Market." *Journal of Finance* 41 (June 1986), 393–410.

Weil, Roman L. "Macaulay's Duration: An Appreciation." *Journal of Business* 46 (October 1973), 589–592.

Yawitz, Jess B. "The Relative Importance of Duration and Yield Volatility on Bond Price Volatility." *Journal of Money, Credit, and Banking* 9 (February 1977), 97–102.

internet *exercise*

INTEREST RATE RISK MEASUREMENT AND IMMUNIZATION USING DURATION

1. To see an example of the common use of duration by bond investment firms, go to the PIMCO Bonds Website at *http://www.pimco.com.* From the home page, you'll have a choice of countries; choose U.S. From the U.S. Website menus, go to the very bottom and click Products & Services. A products and services screen will list products on the left-hand side. Click on either Long Duration or Short-Term and you'll see the bond management strategies using duration. If you go to *http://www.google.com* or another search engine and search for Immunization and Duration, you'll also find other articles and applications. Duration is commonly used for bond mutual funds and by bond managers for securities firms and other financial institutions.

2. The Bank for International Settlements site *(http://www.bis.org)* provides a number of useful publications. Especially important are those authored by the BIS standing committees such as the Basle Committee on Banking Supervision, the Committee on Payment and Settlement Systems, and the Euro-currency Standing Committee. The publications are available in either HTML or Adobe PDF. For example, the Committee on Banking Supervision has policy pieces on public disclosure of derivatives activities of banks and securities firms, market risk, the supervision of financial conglomerates, operational risk management, and enhancing bank transparency.

USEFUL LINKS

Finance Sites

http://www.cob.ohio-state.edu/~fin/journal/jofsites .htm#edres or http://fisher.osu.edu/fin/journal/jofsites.htm

Chicago Mercantile Exchange

http://www.cme.com/

11 Interest Rate Risk Management

Interest Rates and Foreign Currency Futures

"The creation of futures and options in Chicago created a legion of people who have learned to manage risk in ways they never before could have dreamed of."

WILLIAM J. BRODSKY, President, Chicago Mercantile Exchange (1992)

"The technological advances and financial innovations of recent years, of which derivatives are but one prominent example, today allow many banks and other financial and non-financial firms to adjust risk profiles quite rapidly. These institutions can limit the likelihood of substantial losses from adverse changes in market conditions by promptly liquidating or hedging the risk exposures."

SUSAN PHILLIPS, Former Member of the Board of Governors of the Federal Reserve System, from an address at the Chicago Fed's Conference on Derivatives and Public Policy; quoted in Banking Strategies (September/October 1996), 40.

rofessor Merton Miller, winner of the Nobel Prize for financial economics and recognized for his contributions to the development of financial futures, once commented to a *Chicago Tribune* reporter in the early 1990s that the innovations in the financial market were so phenomenal that if a banker fell asleep in the 1970s and awoke in the 1990s, his astonishment would rival that of Rip Van Winkle waking after twenty years. Similarly, in the twenty-first century, we live in a radically changing financial environment where the rapidity with which new markets and instruments are introduced is challenging even to those who are wide awake!

In 1992, the futures markets embraced another major technological innovation. In a joint venture, the Chicago Board of Trade (CBOT) and the Chicago Mercantile Exchange (CME) inaugurated **Globex,** a computerized futures trading system designed to link futures markets around the world with twenty-four-hour trading. As the first bid and offer popped onto his screen, a New York trader described the system as similar to a video game, except with real money involved. But Globex is very different from the chaos of the "live" trading pits, and some participants find it challenging to remain alert all night. Globex has resulted in a more exciting environment with increased volume and market participants, but some European traders were less than excited about the prospect of being asked to work the "graveyard shift." Globex started with a small average daily volume trading of only 2,063 futures contracts on its first day of business. Today, on average over one million contracts change hands a day, accounting for 44 percent of the total CME's volume in the first quarter of 2003. Nonetheless, computer screen-based systems have also rapidly developed in Europe for derivatives, including the German-Swiss exchange **Eurex,** which opened in 1990. On February 8, 2004, **Eurex US** opened, offering services to the U.S. derivatives marketplace as well. **CBOT/Eurex Alliance, L.L.C.,** was formed in 1999 to create an alliance and joint venture company to operate a single global electronic trading system, allowing members and customers to trade the most active futures and options products in the world electronically from a single screen. In November 2003, CBOT transitioned into a new **e-cbot®** **electronic trading platform** (LIFFE CONNECT®) with a landmark agreement with the CME to form a common electronic clearing platform to

Learning Objectives

After completing this chapter, you will be able to:

1 Follow the historical trends in the use of derivatives by financial institutions and trends in trading derivatives including globalization and electronic trading.

2 Understand how futures prices are quoted and how to calculate the gain or loss on a futures transaction.

3 Explain the advantages and disadvantages of hedging with forward contracts versus futures contracts.

4 Understand when short and long hedges should be used to hedge, respectively, against reinvestment and market price risk on spot positions.

5 Describe the risks of hedging including basis risk, cross-hedging risk, opportunity costs, and regulatory concerns.

6 Determine the proper number of futures contracts to use to set up a hedge.

7 Understand the difference between a macro and micro hedge and be aware of accounting concerns with macro hedges.

allow more efficiency and ease for electronic trading and clearing of futures contracts.[1]

Although twenty-four-hour international trading markets may require some schedule adjustments for traders, no one doubts that automation and globalization will continue to bring changes to the financial markets and will make the futures markets an ever more integral part of every financial manager's daily environment. In fact, in a complex economic environment, financial institutions and their managers need complex strategies; and duration, discussed in the preceding chapter, is only one of many essential risk management techniques.

Other risk management techniques that this chapter and the following chapter explore include financial futures contracts and options on financial futures. All are relatively new compared to many other financial instruments; for example, the interest rate futures contract was created in 1975 at the CBOT, and stock index futures began trading in 1982. Since the introduction of futures and options, financial institutions have recognized their potential for improving asset/liability management. This chapter

1 Chicago Tribune (January 20, 1992), Section 4, 1, 2; William B. Crawford, Jr. "Globex Takes Off." *Chicago Tribune* (June 26, 1992), Section 3, 1, 3; Terzah Ewing. "'Open-Outcry' Trading Faces Threat from Electronic Rivals." *The Wall Street Journal* (December 24, 1998), C1; CME Website, "Welcome to Globex: History of Globex," *(http://www.cme.com)*; CBOT Website, "How the e-cbot Market Works" *(http://www.cbot.com)*; Eurex US Website *(http://www.eurexus.com/index.html)*; Eurex Website *(http://www.eurexchange.com/index.html)*; and "Action in the Marketplace," CBOT Publication (free on its Website, *http://www.cbot.com*), pp. 6–7.

focuses on interest rate and foreign currency futures.

Futures are not without their own risks. The inherent dangers have attracted the attention of regulators and legislators and, in some cases, have resulted in restrictions on their use by financial institutions. A number of financial institutions, including Banc One and Bankers Trust, had large losses associated with the use of derivatives in the early 1990s. Scandals were associated with the misuse of derivatives for Orange County, California, and Barings, Inc., in London, which consequently failed. Futures have also presented some new financial reporting problems. In 1990, in response to early concerns, the Financial Accounting Standards Board (FASB)

issued **FAS 105,** which requires firms and financial institutions to disclose their exposure in derivative instruments. After June 15, 2000, **FAS 133** (Accounting for Derivative Instruments and Hedging Activities) also became effective, mandating more stringent accounting for the hedging of derivatives and making the accounting for derivatives somewhat more onerous.[2] In 2003, Fannie Mae and Freddie Mac were associated with scandals regarding their accounting for derivative hedges, leading to greater supervision of these government-sponsored enterprises. Thus, the integration of futures into asset/liability management has, by necessity, moved somewhat slowly, with the largest institutions often serving as the trendsetters.

Financial Institutions and Financial Futures

Although financial futures have received a great deal of attention, in 1997 only about 400 U.S. commercial banks actually held a position in the interest rate futures market. As Carter and Sinkey (1998) point out, however, by mid-1997, the notional amount of derivatives held by all commercial banks was a phenomenal $15.8 trillion, with banks holding almost 68 percent of the $23.3 trillion total derivatives outstanding. The notional derivatives amount is the contractual amount that serves as the basis for calculating cash flows under a contract, such as $1 million for a Treasury bill futures contract. Twenty-five of the nation's largest banks held 98.6 percent of the total outstanding bank derivatives. Medium-sized banks increased their use of derivatives in the early 1990s, but only for about 279 large community banks.

The phenomenal growth in the notional value of derivatives held by insured commercial bank portfolios has continued to increase. For the first quarter of 2003, the Office of the Controller of the Currency (OCC) reported a notional amount of derivatives held for all insured commercial banks of $61.4 trillion (see Figure 11.1, Panel A), with derivatives held by banks growing by an astounding 289 percent since 1997. As shown in Figure 11.1, Panel B, 87 percent of the bank-held derivatives were interest rate contracts ($53.4 trillion in 2003). The number of commercial banks holding derivatives also rose to 488 banks in 2003; however, 25 banks still held 99 percent of the notional value of contracts, with 7 of the largest banks holding 96 percent of the notional value. It is interesting to note for the top twenty-five derivative holders, the small relative size of their total assets to their notional value of derivatives held (see Figure 11.2). The largest holder, JPMorgan Chase Bank, had derivatives holdings of $30.7 trillion, forty-nine times larger than its $621.7 billion in total assets on its balance sheet.

As Figure 11.3 shows, the notional holdings of derivatives by the twenty-five largest holders are primarily **dealer notionals,** derivatives traded for customers and other parties, whereby these largest holders take on an intermediary role to earn fee income. **End-user notionals,** for a bank's own risk management needs, are only about 3.7 percent of total derivatives held, totaling about $2.4 trillion for all insured banks in the first quarter of 2003. A decline in the end-user notional value in the early 2000s reflected uncertainties associated with the impact of new accounting standards for derivatives, **FAS 133**

2 For a summary of the Orange County crisis, see Keith Sill. "The Economic Benefits and Risks of Derivative Securities." *Federal Reserve Bank of Philadelphia Business Review* (January/February 1997), 15–25. The Orange County Investment Pool (OCIP) for Orange County, California, had losses amounting eventually to $1.7 billion, resulting in the county declaring bankruptcy. OCIP's losses were largely the result of bad bets on interest rates staying the same or falling, whereby the fund would profit by borrowing short-term funds at a low rate to buy higher yielding long-term bonds. When interest rates rose in 1994, this strategy resulted in severe losses in the value of bonds and higher short-term borrowing costs. OCIP also invested in interest rate derivative securities called inverse floaters, which gain value when interest rates fall and lose value when they rise. See Chaudhry and Reichert (1998) for a summary of FASB concerns. FASB recommends that firms and institutions provide detailed information regarding the specific transactions for which risk is being hedged but contains no specific guidelines identifying the degree of risk inherent in various types of derivatives activities.

figure **11.1** TRENDS IN THE NOTIONAL VALUE OF DERIVATIVE HOLDINGS BY COMMERCIAL BANKS

PANEL A: DERIVATIVE CONTRACTS BY PRODUCT TYPE (BILS.)*

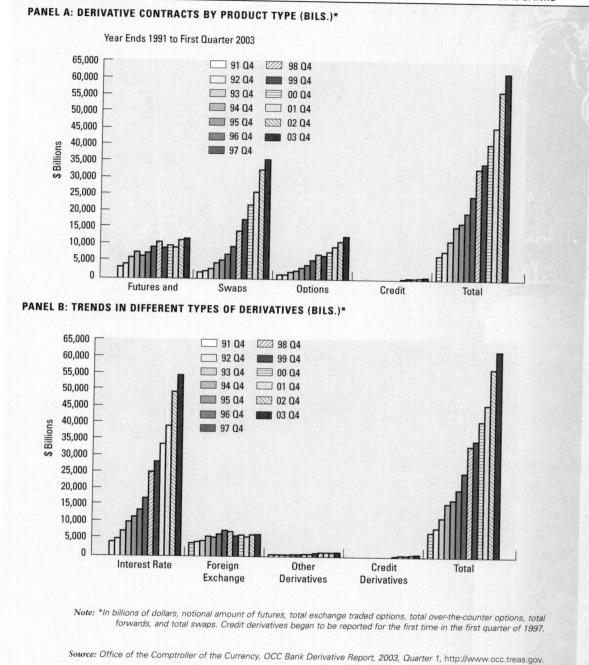

PANEL B: TRENDS IN DIFFERENT TYPES OF DERIVATIVES (BILS.)*

Note: *In billions of dollars, notional amount of futures, total exchange traded options, total over-the-counter options, total forwards, and total swaps. Credit derivatives began to be reported for the first time in the first quarter of 1997.

Source: Office of the Comptroller of the Currency, OCC Bank Derivative Report, 2003, Quarter 1, http://www.occ.treas.gov.

(Accounting for Derivative Instruments and Hedging Activities), which became effective after June 15, 2000. Regulations have often tended to discourage smaller- and medium-sized banks from taking on derivatives, except for risk management purposes. Smaller institutions often purchase risk management products from larger institutions, such as caps, collars, and floors (discussed in Chapter 12), where larger financial institutions take on the hedging activities and associated risks for the smaller firms.[3]

3 See Carter and Sinkey (1998). Also, see Jeffery W. Guntherand Thomas F. Siems. "Who's Capitalizing on Derivatives?" *Federal Reserve Bank of Dallas Financial Industry Studies* (July 1995), 1–8. Also see "OCC Bank Derivatives Report: First Quarter 2003," *(http://www.occ.treas.gov/ftp/deriv/dq103.pdf).*

figure 11.2 TOTAL ASSETS AND TOTAL DERIVATIVES ($ MILLIONS) HELD BY TWENTY-FIVE BANKS AND THRIFTS HOLDING
MOST DERIVATIVES, MARCH 31, 2003

RANK	BANK NAME	STATE	TOTAL ASSETS	TOTAL DERIVATIVES
1	JPMORGAN CHASE BANK	NY	621,696	30,649,328
2	BANK OF AMERICA NA	NC	574,410	13,014,291
3	CITIBANK NATIONAL ASSN	NY	514,803	10,120,507
4	WACHOVIA BANK NATIONAL ASSN	NC	323,783	2,261,049
5	BANK ONE NATIONAL ASSN	IL	226,331	1,141,244
6	HSBC BANK USA	NY	85,936	847,557
7	WELLS FARGO BANK NA	CA	196,755	752,316
8	FLEET NATIONAL BANK	RI	192,100	508,176
9	BANK OF NEW YORK	NY	76,683	461,947
10	STATE STREET BANK & TRUST CO	MA	71,787	269,690
11	NATIONAL CITY BANK	OH	43,814	184,802
12	NATIONAL CITY BANK OF IN	IN	47,656	129,180
13	MELLON BANK NATIONAL ASSN	PA	26,450	123,909
14	STANDARD FEDERAL BANK NA	MI	47,623	111,482
15	LASALLE BANK NATIONAL ASSN	IL	60,497	97,575
16	KEYBANK NATIONAL ASSN	OH	76,669	85,564
17	SUNTRUST BANK	GA	118,315	77,083
18	FIRST TENNESSEE BANK NA	TN	24,350	50,424
19	U S BANK NATIONAL ASSN	OH	177,979	45,252
20	PNC BANK NATIONAL ASSN	PA	62,331	44,844
21	DEUTSCHE BANK TR CO AMERICAS	NY	38,488	35,633
22	MERRILL LYNCH BANK USA	UT	64,468	29,246
23	COMERICA BANK	MI	41,688	19,980
24	IRWIN UNION BANK & TRUST CO	IN	5,061	18,876
25	UNION BANK OF CALIFORNIA NA	CA	39,834	18,747

TOP 25 COMMERCIAL BANKS & TCs WITH DERIVATIVES	$3,759,506	$61,098,701
OTHER 463 COMMERCIAL BANKS & TCs WITH DERIVATIVES	$1,938,474	$324,514
TOTAL AMOUNTS FOR ALL 488 BKS & TCs WITH DERIVATIVES	$5,697,980	$61,423,215

Source: Office of the Comptroller of the Currency, *OCC Bank Derivative Report, 2003, Quarter 1,* http://www.occ.treas.gov.

figure 11.3 DERIVATIVES, NOTIONALS BY TYPE OF USER

For insured commercial banks, dealer notionals signify bank holdings in a dealer capacity for customers versus their own use.

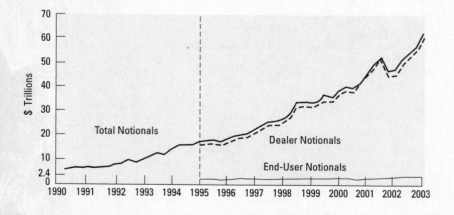

Source: Office of the Comptroller of the Currency, *OCC Bank Derivative Report, 2003, Quarter 1,* http://www.occ.treas.gov.

Figure 11.4, Panel A compares the total derivative holdings of the top seven holders of derivatives versus other insured banks of different types of derivatives, demonstrating a clear dominance by these top seven. This list includes **JPMorgan Chase, Bank of America, Citibank, Wachovia, Banc One, HSBC Bank USA,** and **Wells Fargo.** Figure 11.4, Panel B shows the trading revenue as a percentage of their total gross revenue for each of the seven banks for 1999 to 2003. This was a relatively large source

figure **11.4** DERIVATIVE HOLDINGS OF SEVEN BANKS DOMINATING HOLDINGS, FIRST QUARTER 2003

PANEL A: TYPES OF DERIVATIVE HOLDINGS BY TOP BANKS AND OTHER BANKS

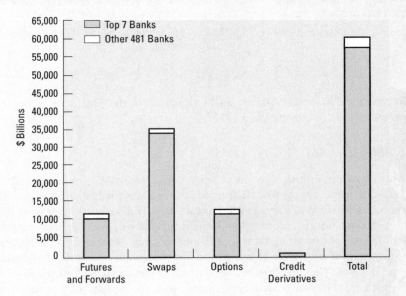

PANEL B: TRADING REVENUE AS A PERCENTAGE OF GROSS REVENUE

TOP COMMERCIAL BANKS WITH DERIVATIVES, FIRST QUARTER 2003, RANKING RATIOS IN %*

Third Quarter

	99Q1	99Q2	99Q3	99Q4	00Q1	00Q2	00Q3	00Q4	01Q1	01Q2	01Q3	01Q4	02Q1	02Q2	02Q3	02Q4	03Q1
JPMorgan Chase (JPM)	11.2	8.8	7.4	6.9	13.2	10.7	7.0	5.9	9.0	7.5	11.99	10.6	16.2,	12.5	6.0	6.1	13.5
Bank of America (BAC)	3.3	2.9	2.1	1.7	5.2	2.1	1.3	1.2	4.1	2.6	2.9	6.5	4.6	4.9	2.6	3.0	2.1
Citibank (C)	8.7	6.6	7.0	6.4	7.7	7.7	7.6	8.2	10.7	8.3	9.8	7.1	7.5	8.4	8.1	5.1	7.5
Wachovia (WB)	1.9	1.5	0.2	1.3	1.4	1.6	1.1	1.3	1.0	2.4	1.1	0.9	1.4	1.2	−0.4	0.1	1.8
Banc One (ONE)	4.0	3.0	2.9	1.1	3.2	1.7	1.7	2.5	1.8	1.8	2.8	1.3	0.6	2.9	4.5	0.1	2.0
HSBC Bank USA				0.4	3.2	1.5	1.7	2.5	2.7	4.4	4.6	2.4	2.3	−3.3	1.7	0.8	3.7
Wells Fargo (WFC)	1.3	1.4	0.6	0.7	0.8	0.8	0.7	1.4	1.6	2.1	2.1	2.2	2.0	1.5	0.4	1.9	1.7
Total % (Top Banks)	9.6	5.8	5.7	5.4	8.3	6.2	5.5	5.0	7.1	5.8	7.0	5.9	6.9	6.8	4.4	3.3	5.8
Total % (All Banks)	3.7	2.2	2.1	2.3	3.5	2.7	2.4	2.3	3.4	2.6	3.3	2.6	3.1	3.3	2.3	1.8	3.0

Note: *The third quarter 1999 call report used to collect the data reflects the merger of Bank of America and Nations Bank, the fourth quarter, First Chicago and Banc One, and the fourth quarter 2001, the merger of Chase and JPMorgan.

Source: Office of the Comptroller of the Currency, OCC Bank Derivative Report, 2003, Quarter 1, http://www.occ.treas.gov.

of revenues, particularly for the largest holder, JPMorgan Chase, which had derivative trading revenue of 13.5 percent of total gross revenues in the first quarter of 2003. Other financial services firms including the insurance and pension fund industries also participate in the futures markets. As is true in the commercial banking industry, the evidence indicates that large institutions are the major players. Commercial banks primarily have transactions as hedgers or dealers, with derivatives concentrated at dealer banks. The majority of hedging contracts used by depository institutions are interest rate swap contracts (where institutions exchange fixed and variable rate cash flows) to hedge their interest rate risk.[4]

Futures Contracts

Futures contracts on agricultural products have existed for more than a century; the first organized market for them was the CBOT, also the birthplace of the interest rate futures contract, in October

---

4 See Koppenhaver (1990); Booth, Smith, and Stolz (1984); Hurtz and Gardner (1984); Lamm-Tennant (1989); Hoyt (1992); Puwalski (2003); and OCC Bank Derivatives Report, Quarter 1, 2003.

1 How many insured banks hold derivatives in the United States? Why are the largest institutions primarily involved?

2 List the top seven institutions holding 96 percent of derivatives in 2003.

3 What is the largest type of derivatives used for hedging purposes by commercial banks?

4 Explain the difference between dealer notionals and end-user notionals.

1975. The International Monetary Market (IMM), a branch of the CME, introduced the first financial futures contracts on foreign currencies in 1972.[5]

Futures Contracts Defined

A **futures contract** is a commitment to buy or sell a specific commodity of designated quality at a specified price and date in the future (**the delivery date**). The specified price is an estimate of the commodity price that is expected to prevail at that future time. A distinguishing feature of futures trading is that the two sides of a futures contract do not trade directly with one another but, rather, with a clearinghouse. This feature of futures markets is explained in more detail later in the chapter.

A commodity may fall into one of many categories; the number continues to expand in these innovative markets. However, five categories, three of which are financial, include the vast majority of commodities on which contracts are traded: agricultural products, metallurgical products, interest-bearing assets, stock indexes and other market indexes, and foreign currencies. The last two, although not specifically focused on interest rate risk, have emerged as tools of asset/liability management for some institutions. Foreign currency futures are discussed later in this chapter, and stock index futures are discussed in Chapter 12.

Hedging versus Speculation

One reason that futures contracts developed is to avoid risk. Wheat or soybean farmers can use futures agreements to reduce uncertainty about the prices they will receive for their products. A grower, by agreeing through a futures contract to deliver a certain amount of wheat at a specified future date and for a specified price, avoids exposure to unfavorable price movements during the intervening period. Thus, futures contracts, like immunization (discussed in Chapter 10), can be used to hedge, or minimize, risk.

On the other side of the farmer's contract may be a **speculator**, someone willing to accept the risk of price fluctuations with the intention of profiting from them. The counterparty to the farmer could also be a hedger who needs the farmer's wheat at the designated time and is minimizing the risk that wheat will be in short supply at the time. Alternatively, both parties in a futures contract could be speculators, each hoping to profit from price fluctuations.

Thus, the distinction between hedging and speculation comes not from the side of a futures contract one takes but from the motivation for entering into the contract. With few exceptions, because of regulatory limitations, smaller- and medium-sized depository institutions use the financial futures markets as end-users only for hedging. However, as noted in the first section of the chapter, the twenty-five largest financial institutions holding derivatives do engage actively in trading activities for customers, as well as, to some extent, particularly for large diversified financial service firms, some trading for their own accounts.

Financial Futures Contracts

In a financial futures contract, the underlying commodity promised for future delivery is one of three financial commodities: an interest-bearing asset, a stock or bond index, or a foreign currency. Since 1972, contracts on many financial assets have been introduced with varying levels of success. For example, contracts on Treasury bills (T-bills) have been widely accepted, but futures contracts on commercial paper were tried without success. Interest-bearing or discount securities on which contracts are writ-

5 For details on the birth of the first financial futures contract at the International Monetary Market, see Miller (1986).

ten include T-bills, Treasury notes (T-notes), Treasury bonds (T-bonds), and Eurodollar deposits, among others. The instruments span the entire yield curve, giving managers important flexibility.

Role of the Clearinghouse

All trading is conducted through the **clearinghouse** of each exchange. In effect, the clearinghouse acts as a buyer to every seller and a seller to every buyer; it does not simply match buy and sell orders. This procedure eliminates the need for direct contact between traders. The clearinghouse guarantees the performance of the contract and, instead of the seller, assumes responsibility for the creditworthiness of buyers. The willingness of participants to rely on the financial stability of the clearinghouse is an important characteristic of the futures markets, and the fact that the clearinghouses have so far consistently performed as promised testifies to the validity of their role. At the end of each trading day, the clearinghouse settles all accounts, paying profits earned by some traders and collecting payments due from others.

Because the contracts are standardized and default risk is assumed by the clearinghouse, the original owner of a futures contract can easily offset or cancel the contract before its delivery date. Few financial futures contracts (less than 2 percent) are carried to an actual physical transfer of assets. Instead traders make an offsetting trade to close out their positions rather than delivering or accepting the commodity (i.e., if a trader has a contract to buy, he will purchase the offsetting contract to sell, and take the gain or loss).[6] The exchange clearinghouse handles the bookkeeping and associated transactions.

If the commodity is an agricultural product, movements in the market price of the product affect the contract value. If the commodity is a T-bill, a change in short-term interest rates affects the price of bills in the spot market and also affects the value of a T-bill contract. Similarly, the value of bond futures contracts is tied to changes in long-term yields.

The standardization of futures contracts allows the market to function efficiently. For interest rate futures, the contract size, maturity, and (except for discount securities) coupon rate are predetermined to facilitate efficient trading. For example, a T-bill and a Eurodollar CD futures contract are traded in a standard size of $1 million, based only on a ninety-day (three-month) maturity. Similarly, a futures standard contract for T-bonds is a contractual value of $100,000 with a 6 percent coupon. The contract size is the face value of the underlying securities. Recently, the CBOT and CME also began offering **mini-sized futures** for many different types of contracts, providing a smaller contractual value than the standard contracts. For instance, the CBOT offers a mini-sized Eurodollar futures contract for Eurodollar time deposits with a contractual value of $500,000.

The Developing Global Marketplace

The rapid growth in the volume of futures contract trading on the exchanges in Chicago has not gone unnoticed in other countries. In the 1980s, in fact, international markets for trading futures and other risk management securities opened in strategic locations around the world; at least eighteen have originated since 1985. Newer exchanges include the **London International Financial Futures Exchange (LIFFE),** the **Marché a Terme International de France (MATIF),** the **Tokyo International Financial Futures Exchange (TIFFE),** the **Singapore International Monetary Exchange (SIME),** and the **Sydney Futures Exchange (SFE).** The **Deutsche Terminbourse (DTB)** opened in Frankfurt in 1990, along with futures exchanges in Austria, Belgium, and Italy. Other new exchanges opened up in the later 1990s including the **Taiwan Futures Exchange (TAIFEX)** in 1998 and the **Korea Futures Exchange (KOFEX)** in 1999. Many recent exchanges have developed as electronic, computer-based systems that compete with the more traditional "open outcry" trading of the CBOT, the CME, and the relatively high-tech Chicago Board Options Exchange. As noted in the opening paragraph, in the United States the CME and CBOT have also gone electronic. The CBOT is operating a joint venture, **Eurex US,** with the successful all-electronic German-Swiss exchange Eurex, which provides a single global electronic trading system, offering services to the U.S. derivatives marketplace.[7]

---

6 The Chicago Board of Trade. *A Guide to Financial Futures at the Chicago Board of Trade,* 29.

7 Terzah Ewing. "'Open-Outcry' Trading Faces Threat from Electronic Rivals." *The Wall Street Journal* (December 24, 1998), C1.

Several of the international exchanges offer greater flexibility in terms of the currency of exchange. For example, LIFFE allows traders to settle their positions in a variety of currencies, whereas the Chicago markets are almost entirely dollar-based. Market participants responded favorably to this flexibility, and, by 1992, the volume of financial futures trading in Europe was beginning to challenge the dominance of the Chicago markets. Accordingly, *Futures Industry* (February/March 2001, p. 39) reported the top ten global futures exchanges by trading volume as Eurex, CME, CBOT, LIFFE, the New York Mercantile Exchange, BM&F Brasil, the Paris Bourse, the London Metal Exchange, the Tokyo Commodity Exchange, and the Euronext Brussels Derivatives Market in Belgium.

For the most part, expert observers view the emergence of these new markets as a positive development for market participants. The increased competition across international borders has brought the exchanges under pressure to control transaction costs, making futures trading more efficient for participants. Traders can now participate in more than one market simultaneously and enjoy greater liquidity and longer trading hours. In addition, the new exchanges are highly automated and are setting new standards for the use of technology in futures trading.

Besides the advantages noted previously, futures market expansion carries increased risks, most notably the potential for problems in the clearing process. Although all international futures exchanges have clearinghouses, the settlement of claims may involve counterparties operating under different legal and payment systems. In the view of most experts, however, the increased opportunities clearly outweigh the additional risk exposure.[8]

Characteristics of Financial Futures Transactions

Financial futures markets have several unique features, as explained in the following sections.

The Margin

Futures traders are required to post an initial margin to support their positions. The margin serves as a deposit in good faith. It may be in the form of cash, a bank letter of credit, or short-term Treasury securities. The margin required is quite small in comparison with the face value of the securities underlying the financial futures contract; the initial deposit is often no more than 5 percent of the contract face value. The margin is set by the exchange; it depends on the type of contract and whether the trader is a hedger or speculator. The price volatility of the underlying instrument is an influencing factor on the margin: The higher the volatility in the underlying instrument, the higher the margin. The CBOT (*http://www.cbt.com*) and CME (*http://www.cme.com*) provide information on their Websites for the maintenance and initial margins on different contracts that are subject to change. The initial margin is the amount that must be placed in a brokerage account to protect against losses. Some, but not all, brokers will allow it to earn interest. At the end of each day, there is a **daily resettlement.** Daily losses are taken against this margin. Daily gains are added to the margin and can be taken out by the trader. If the amount of the margin goes below a somewhat lower maintenance margin, additional funds must be put in to bring the account back up to the initial margin. In 2003, for instance, a $100,000 T-bond futures contract had a maintenance margin of $2,250, with an initial margin per contract of $3,038. For a mini-sized $50,000 T-bond futures contract, the maintenance margin was half this amount, $1,125. The CBOT requires the same initial and maintenance margin of $2,250 for hedging versus speculative contracts for Treasury bonds, but for some contracts, lower hedging margins are posted.[9]

Hence, trading in futures involves some cash flow on every trading day, and many observers believe that the daily resettlement makes the futures markets much safer than they would be otherwise. The

8 For more information on the development of international markets, see Remolona (1992–1993); Napoli (1992); Scarlata (1992); Abken (1991); David Greising. "Has Chicago Lost Its Edge?" *Business Week* (March 9, 1992), 76–78; William B. Crawford, Jr. "London's Exchange to Sign On to Globex." *Chicago Tribune* (September 28, 1992), Section 4, 1, 2; Jeffery Taylor. "Globex System Is Vexed by Low Trading Volume, Overseas Competition, and Technology Glitches." *The Wall Street Journal* (December 14, 1992), C1; and Peter J. W. Elstrom. "Sleepy Globex May Start Trading Earlier." *Crain's Chicago Business* (January 18, 1993), 3. Also see CME Website, "Welcome to Globex: History of Globex," (*http://www.cme.com*); CBOT Website, "How the e-cbot Market Works" (*http://www.cbot.com*); Eurex US Website (*http://www.eurexus.com/index.html*); Eurex Website (*http://www.eurexchange.com/index.html*); and "Action in the Marketplace," CBOT Publication (free on its Website, *http://www.cbot.com*), pp. 6–7.

9 Legislation pending in Congress in late 1992 would transfer to the Federal Reserve Board the authority to set margins for some types of futures contracts. The CBOT and CME opposed the legislation containing this provision.

1 What is a financial futures contract? How is a futures contract different from a forward contract?

2 What role does the clearinghouse of each exchange play? How does this reduce risk for traders?

3 What is the difference between a hedger and a speculator?

4 As futures contract trading becomes more electronic and global, what do you think the effect will be on the efficiency and risk of the futures market?

daily resettlement or "mark to market" is also viewed as a justification for the relatively small initial cash required to trade contracts with a much higher face value. Nevertheless, managers of institutions trading futures contracts must manage cash carefully, because they must be ready each day to make deposits into their margin accounts.

Limits on Price Changes

To control traders' exposure to risk, the exchanges set a maximum amount by which the price of a contract is allowed to change. When that limit is reached on a given day, the price cannot move farther, and subsequent trades will take place only if they are within the limits. Risk exposure still exists, however. At times the exchanges will set a maximum price fluctuation on the maximum price fluctuation allowed, so the price will not move by more than that amount on any one day. For example for ten-year Agency Note Futures contracts, the CME in December of 2003 had a $3,000 price limit above or below the previous settlement price. Several days of "limit moves" in a row could add up to substantial losses.

Interest Rate Futures

For most **interest rate futures contracts,** interest-bearing or discount securities are the underlying commodity. Recently, contracts based on movements in an interest rate such as the Fed Funds rate have been developed. Should a trader hold such contracts to maturity, they would be settled in cash rather than by delivery of an underlying security. Because they are an important component of asset/liability management, techniques involving interest rate futures trading will be examined in detail. First, however, it is important to introduce the characteristics of contracts commonly traded by financial institutions.

Terms of Selected Interest Rate Futures Contracts

As in any field in which change is the rule rather than the exception, a comprehensive list of interest rate futures contracts is virtually impossible. Undoubtedly, contracts that were unheard of—perhaps even unimagined—at the time this book was written may be traded regularly by the time it is read. Nonetheless, it is clear that certain interest rate futures contracts, such as those for Treasury securities, have had staying power over the years, and it seems reasonable to assume that they will continue to be popular. Table 11.1 summarizes features of selected popular contracts based on underlying cash-based instruments. The features change with changes in interest rates and market conditions, and new innovations often appear that can be found on the Websites of the future exchanges.

Although the importance of individual features will become clear as applications of futures in asset/liability management are presented, the table shows that interest rate futures contracts are available in a wide range of face values on underlying instruments or indexes with a variety of maturities. The table also indicates that futures contracts have standardized delivery dates in the rare event that delivery is actually made or taken. By convention, then, a contract with a delivery date of the last trading day in June is known as a "June contract." For about 99 percent of trading for interest rate futures contracts, traders simply reverse their positions and take the gain or loss versus actually delivering securities. As noted in the table, many contracts allow no delivery. The varied features provide important flexibility for interest rate risk management in financial institutions.

table **11.1** FEATURES OF SELECTED INTEREST RATE FUTURES CONTRACTS

Interest rate futures are available on a variety of underlying instruments. Face values and other specifications differ, and the choice of contract depends on the cash instrument to be hedged. These are just a few of the most popular interest rate futures contracts.

Name of Contract	Underlying Instrument	Face Value of Contract	Price Quote and Minimum Price Fluctuation	Delivery Months
T-bill futures (CME)	13-week T-bills	$1 million	[100 − discount rate] 1/2 bp = 0.005 = $12.50 1 bp = 0.01 = $25.00	March, June, September, December
3-month Euro-dollar futures (CME)	None; settled in cash based on prevailing rate on 3-month Eurodollar time deposits	$1 million	[100 − IMM Index] 1/2 bp = 0.005 = $12.50 1 bp = 0.01 = $25.00	March, June, September, December
3-month Euro-dollar mini-futures (CBOT)	None, settled in cash based on prevailing British Bankers' Association Interest Settlement Rate	$500,000	[100 − 3-month Eurodollar Yield] 1/2 of 1 bp = $6.25	March, June, September, December
T-note futures (CBOT)	2-year, 5-year, or 10-year T-notes	$100,000 or $200,000	Points (Par 100 points) 1/32 of a point = $15.625	March, June, September, December
Mini-sized 10-year U.S. T-notes (CBOT)	10-year T-notes (delivery T-notes of at least 6.5 yrs. but no greater than 10 yrs.)	$50,000	Points (Par 100 points) 1/2 of 1/32 of a point = $7.8125	March, June, September, December
T-bond futures (CBOT)	6% T-bonds, minimum maturity of at least 15 years	$100,000	Points ($1,000) 1/32 of a point = $31.25	March, June, September, December
10-Yr. Municipal Note Index Futures (CBOT)	None; settled in cash based on a synthetic 10-year municipal note that pays a fixed semiannual coupon of 5%	$1,000 times value of index	Points ($1,000) 1/32 of a point = $31.25	March, June, September, December
30-day Fed Funds futures (CBOT)	None; settled in cash based on monthly average of daily Fed Funds rate	$5 million	100 − Ave. Daily Fed Funds Overnight Rate for the Delivery Month (i.e., a 7.25% rate = 92.75)	Every month
LIBOR[a] (CME)	None; settled in cash based on prevailing LIBOR rate on 1-month Eurodollar time deposit with a principal value of $3,000,000	$3 million	100 − the LIBOR rate for 1-month Eurodollar time deposit 1/2 bp = $12.50	First 12 consecutive calendar months
10-year Agency Notes (CME)	$100,000 face value of the 10-year Fannie Mae Benchmark Notes or Freddie Mac Reference Notes	$100,000	Globex: Regular 0.015625 = $15,625	March, June, September, December
Euroyen (CME)	100,000,000 Euroyen time deposit with a 3-month maturity	100,000,000 Japanese yen	100 − IMM 3-month Euroyen Index 0.005 = 1,250 yen	March, June, September, December

a LIBOR is an acronym for the London Interbank Offered Rate, a short-term European interest rate, which is the best (cheapest, prime) rate for interbank dollar loans between international banks in the Eurodollar market for a given maturity.

Source: *Adapted from Patrick J. Catania, ed. Commodity Trading Manual (Chicago: Chicago Board of Trade, 1989), updated by authors; Chicago Board of Trade, "30-Day Interest Rate Futures," 1992; Chicago Mercantile Exchange, "CME Interest Rate Futures," 1991; and updated using 2003 Chicago Board of Trade (http://www.cbt.com) and Chicago Mercantile Exchange (http://www.cme.com) Websites. See the respective CBOT and CME Websites for updates and further explanations.*

Interest Rate Futures as a Hedging Device

By definition, a hedge is a position taken in the futures market to offset risk in the cash or spot market position. The preceding chapters stressed the inverse relationship between changes in market values of interest-earning assets and changes in market yields. Because the value of a futures contract depends on the market value of its underlying commodity, the prices of interest rate futures contracts also change inversely with interest rates. Thus, a financial institution can use futures to reduce its exposure to adverse rate changes.

For example, a decline in interest rates, which lowers the reinvestment rate on an insurance company's bond portfolio, increases the price of interest rate futures contracts. Profits from the futures transactions could reduce the negative effect of the interest rate reduction on the bond portfolio. **To protect (hedge) against reinvestment risk of a fall in interest rates and an opportunity loss on such a spot position, a futures hedge would involve taking a long position in futures (contract to buy securities in the future at the current futures price).** If interest rates fall, and, hence, the price to buy bonds rises on the spot market, the gain on the futures contract (contract to buy at a lower price that can be offset with a contract to sell at the now higher price) will offset this spot market loss. Futures can provide similar protection in times of interest rate increases. A fixed-income portfolio manager may want to protect a bond portfolio, for instance, against a loss in market value if interest rates rise. **To hedge against the risk of a rise in interest rates (price risk) and a loss on such a spot position, a futures hedge would involve taking a short position in futures (contract to sell securities at the current futures price).** If interest rates rise, the portfolio manager will have a loss in the value of her portfolio but will have a gain on her futures contracts (contract to sell at a higher price that can be offset with a contract to buy at the now lower price) that will offsets the spot loss on the portfolio. The next section provides an illustration of each of these hedges.

Futures Prices and Market Yields: An Illustration

When interest rates rose in 2003 between mid-June and early December, the prices on Treasury securities fell, as did the prices of outstanding futures contracts. Portions of *The Wall Street Journal* quotations of futures prices for June 17, 2003, and December 1, 2003, are shown in Figure 11.5. Interest rate T-bond futures prices are quoted in the financial press in the following format:

INTEREST RATE FUTURES: JUNE 2003

Treasury Bonds (CBT) $1000,000 pts. 32nds of 100%

	Open	High	Low	Settle	Change	Lifetime High	Lifetime Low	Open Interest
December	120-17	120-17	119-03	119-07	−36	121-18	106-04	21,904

The first open price is the opening price for that day, followed by the high and low and settle (closing) prices, the change in prices, lifetime high and low for the contract, and open interest, or the number of contracts outstanding. On June 17, a T-bond contract for December 2003 delivery had a settlement "Settle" price" of 119-07. The settle price is a representative closing price for that date. The open interest reflects the volume of contracts outstanding for that contract.

Futures contracts on T-bonds and T-notes, like the prices of their underlying instruments, are quoted in 32nds of a percent, so 119–07 means 119.2188 percent of the face value of a contract, or $119,218.80 on a $100,000 contract. (Recall that Table 11.1 indicates the face value of T-bond and T-note contracts as $100,000.) Each 1/32 change is a dollar change of $31.25 [i.e., $100,000 (1/32 × 0.01)]. At the close of trading on December 1, 2003, the December contract price was 108–27, that is, 108.8438 percent, or a face value of $108,843.80. Hence, the price fell by 119.2188% − 108.8438% = 10.375% from June to December. The dollar change was $100,000 × 0.10375 = $10,375.. With the rise in interest rates and fall in the price of the bond futures contract, traders who had short positions (contracts to sell T-bonds at the June price) made gains on their positions. Traders with long positions (to buy T-bonds at the June price) suffered losses on their positions. Those who lost on their positions were required to settle with the clearinghouse, possibly having to add cash to their margin accounts if the loss eroded their balances below acceptable levels.

Prices for shorter-term money market security futures are listed near the bottom of Figure 11.5. Very few T-bill futures were offered at this time, for example, only one September T-bill futures contract is listed on June 17. T-bill futures are quoted as discount yields (d), with the quoted price as (100% − d). For June 17, the September 2003 T-bill futures contract had a discount yield settle of 0.77 percent and

figure **11.5** INTEREST RATE FUTURES PRICES: JUNE 17, AND DECEMBER 1, 2003

Information on interest rate and other futures contracts is reported daily in the financial pages of major newspapers. The most recent prices and the total volume of contracts outstanding (open interest) are included.

June 17, 2003

Interest Rate Futures

Treasury Bonds (CBT)-$100,000; pts 32nds of 100%

	OPEN	HIGH	LOW	SETTLE	CHG	LIFETIME HIGH	LIFETIME LOW	OPEN INTEREST
June	123-06	123-12	121-27	121-31	-35	124-12	105-00	57,187
Sept	121-23	122-04	120-14	120-19	-36	123-03	106-02	531,423
Dec	120-17	120-17	119-03	119-07	-36	121-18	106-04	21,904

Est vol 245,327; vol Mon 233,163; open int 610,570, +3,335.

Treasury Notes (CBT)-$100,000; pts 32nds of 100%

June	120-11	120-12	119-15	19-185	-23.5	121-16	109-10	47,485
Sept	119-22	119-27	118-26	18-295	-24.0	120-14	10-055	962,118

Est vol 583,371; vol Mon 454,021; open int 1,022,117, +8,122.

10 Yr. Agency Notes (CBT)-$100,000; pts 32nds of 100%

June	...	...	117-03	-21.0	18-005	109-10	2,265

Est vol 28; vol Mon 0; open int 6,426, unch.

5 Yr. Treasury Notes (CBT)-$100,000; pts 32nds of 100%

June	117-08	117-10	116-22	16-235	-16.0	17-255	10-125	82,268

Est vol 253,923; vol Mon 246,060; open int 837,210, +7,088.

2 Yr. Treasury Notes (CBT)-$200,000; pts 32nds of 100%

June	08-195	108-20	08-177	08-177	-5.0	108-27	07-015	10,910

Est vol 7,858; vol Mon 15,695; open int 122,449, +1,003.

30 Day Federal Funds (CBT)-$5,000,000; 100 — daily avg.

June	98.815	98.815	98.810	98.815	-.005	99.010	98.480	88,874
July	99.15	99.15	99.10	99.10	-.06	99.17	98.48	175,535
Aug	99.18	99.18	99.12	99.13	-.05	99.20	98.44	79,853
Sept	99.19	99.20	99.14	99.15	-.05	99.22	98.21	32,970

Est vol 86,017; vol Mon 72,526; open int 421,930, +12,468.

10 Yr. Interest Rate Swaps (CBT)-$100,000; pts 32nds of 100%

June	...	...	121-13	...	121-19	110-04	7,977

Est vol 617; vol Mon 7,365; open int 54,957, -5,269.

10 Yr. Muni Note Index (CBT)-$1,000 × index

June	108-00	108-02	107-25	107-25	-18	108-29	100-18	1,013

Est vol 714; vol Mon 246; open int 4,300, -62.
Index: Close 107-18; Yield 4.072.

	OPEN	HIGH	LOW	SETTLE	CHG	YIELD	CHG	OPEN INT
13 Week Treasury Bills (CME)-$1,000,000; pts of 100%								
Sept	...	...	...	99.23	...	0.77	...	3

Est vol 0; vol Mon 0; open int 1,392, unch.

1 Month Libor (CME)-$3,000,000; pts of 100%

July	99.03	99.03	98.99	98.99	-.04	1.01	.04	33,549
Aug	99.06	99.06	99.03	99.03	-.04	0.97	.04	7,809
Sept	99.06	99.06	99.05	99.06	-.03	0.94	.03	4,134

Est vol 3,702; vol Mon 6,167; open in 64,440, +3,307.

Eurodollar (CME)-$1,000,000; pts of 100%

July	99.04	99.04	98.99	99.00	-.05	1.00	.05	106,628
Aug	99.06	99.06	99.01	99.02	-.04	0.98	.04	10,084
Sept	99.07	99.07	99.01	99.02	-.06	0.98	.06	862,488
Dec	99.03	99.03	98.96	98.97	-.07	1.03	.07	777,355
Mr04	98.95	99.04	98.86	98.87	-.08	1.13	.08	716,876
June	98.75	98.76	98.66	98.66	-.09	1.34	.09	454,594
Sept	98.50	98.51	98.38	98.39	-.11	1.61	.11	399,042
Dec	98.25	98.25	98.10	98.10	-.14	1.90	.14	451,959
Mr05	98.01	98.01	97.85	97.86	-.14	2.14	.14	231,280
June	97.78	97.79	97.62	97.63	-.15	2.37	.15	186,003
Sept	97.58	97.58	97.41	97.42	-.15	2.58	.15	176,170
Dec	97.37	97.38	97.20	97.21	-.15	2.79	.15	134,387
Mr06	97.11	97.18	97.01	97.02	-.15	2.98	.15	147,531
June	96.97	96.98	96.81	96.82	-.15	3.18	.15	101,167
Sept	96.71	96.79	96.63	96.63	-.15	3.37	.15	81,903
Dec	96.50	96.60	96.44	96.44	-.14	3.56	.14	65,241
Mr07	96.34	96.42	96.27	96.27	-.14	3.73	.14	75,076
June	96.25	96.25	96.10	96.10	-.13	3.90	.13	48,121
Sept	96.01	96.09	95.95	95.95	-.13	4.05	.13	40,306

December 1, 2003

Interest Rate Futures

Treasury Bonds (CBT)-$100,000; pts 32nds of 100%

	OPEN	HIGH	LOW	SETTLE	CHG	LIFETIME HIGH	LIFETIME LOW	OPEN INTEREST
Dec	109-06	109-08	107-31	108-27	-14	121-18	102-14	247,222
Mr04	107-23	107-25	106-16	107-12	-15	116-23	101-05	266,122
June	106-07	106-07	105-09	106-00	-15	116-15	104-00	568

Est vol 345,983; vol Fri 142,914; open int 514,298, -7,665.

Treasury Notes (CBT)-$100,000; pts 32nds of 100%

Dec	12-095	112-11	111-14	111-31	-14.0	171-17	107-16	396,649
Mr04	110-26	10-265	09-255	10-125	-16.0	116-10	106-29	660,046
June	08-285	108-31	108-15	08-275	-17.5	111-08	107-13	29

Est vol 989,110; vol Fri 508,932; open int 1,056,724, -24,763.

10 Yr. Agency Notes (CBT)-$100,000; pts 32nds of 100%

Dec	...	...	...	108-12	-14.5	110-27	104-08	997

Est vol 0; vol Fri 0; open int 997, unch,

5 Yr. Treasury Notes (CBT)-$100,000; pts 32nds of 100%

Dec	11-195	11-195	11-005	11-115	-9.5	115-01	108-27	360,882

Est vol 548,573; vol Fri 278,814; open int 926,180, +13,134.

2 Yr. Treasury Notes (CBT)-$200,000; pts 32nds of 100%

Dec	07-022	07-022	106-28	107-00	-3.2	07-287	106-06	60,435

Est vol 42,600; vol Fri 20,518; open int 157,209, +3,870.

30 Day Federal Notes (CBT)-$5,000,000; 100 — daily avg.

Dec	98.990	98.995	98.990	98.990	...	99.230	98.400	46,328
Ja04	98.99	98.99	98.98	98.99	...	99.24	98.66	36,869
Feb	98.97	98.97	98.95	98.96	-.01	99.22	98.70	64.355
Mar	98.91	98.91	98.89	98.90	-.01	99.16	98.74	40,355
Apr	98.82	98.83	98.81	98.83	.01	99.17	89.96	38,917
May	98.69	98.70	98.68	98.68	-.03	99.79	98.40	16,946
June	98.66	98.66	98.65	98.65	-.03	98.96	98.38	14,047
July	98.46	98.47	98.37	98.44	-.05	98.89	98.20	3,559

Est vol 22,536; vol Fri 9,786; open int 310,646, +2,801.

10 Yr. Interest Rate Swaps (CBT)-$100,000; pts 32nds of 100%

Dec	109-25	109-26	108-27	109-09	-23	110-31	105-10	27,608

Est vol 13,170; vol Fri 2,705; open int 41,416, +554.

10 Yr. Muni Note Index (CBT)-$1,000 × index

Dec	102-10	102-11	101-22	101-30	-13	103-14	97-13	2,059

Est vol 306; vol Fri 183; open int 2,281, -13.
Index: Close 102-24; Yield 4.653.

	OPEN	HIGH	LOW	SETTLE	CHG	YIELD	CHG	OPEN INT
13 Week Treasury Bills (CME)-$1,000,000; pts of 100%								
Dec	...	...	...	n.a.	...	...	...	0

Est vol n.a.; vol Fri 0; open int 0, unch.

1 Month Libor (CME)-$3,000,000; pts of 100%

Dec	98.82	98.83	98.82	98.83	...	1.17	...	13,883
Ja04	98.84	98.84	98.83	98.84	-.01	1.16	.01	8,686
Feb	98.80	98.81	98.79	98.79	...	1.21	...	19,996
Apr	98.62	98.63	98.61	98.62	-.02	1.38	.02	3,525
May	98.55	98.55	98.51	98.53	-.04	1.47	.04	298

Est vol 9,478; vol Fri 1,896; open int 59,915, +38.

Eurodollar (CME)-$1,000,000; pts of 100%

Dec	98.81	98.81	98.80	98.80	-.01	1.20	.01	624,869
Ja04	98.76	98.76	98.75	98.76	-.01	1.24	.01	38,482
Feb	98.69	98.69	98.68	98.69	-.01	1.31	.01	11,472
Mar	98.60	98.62	98.57	98.60	-.02	1.40	.02	704,163
Apr	98.48	98.48	98.45	98.47	-.04	1.53	.04	10,672
June	98.23	98.27	98.18	98.21	-.04	1.79	.04	667,777
Sept	97.82	97.81	97.73	97.77	-.06	2.23	.06	581,955
Dec	97.38	97.34	97.25	97.29	-.08	2.71	.08	556,408
Mr05	96.93	96.94	96.83	96.88	-.10	3.12	.10	346,194
June	96.58	96.58	96.47	96.52	-.10	3.48	.10	281,393
Sept	96.28	96.28	96.15	96.21	-.10	3.79	.10	225,783
Dec	96.03	96.03	95.87	95.95	-.10	4.05	.10	177,241
Mr06	95.80	95.80	95.67	95.73	-.10	4.27	.10	135,825
June	95.57	95.58	95.45	95.53	-.11	4.47	.11	116,858
Sept	95.39	95.40	95.29	95.34	-.11	4.66	.11	93,642
Dec	95.22	95.22	95.11	95.17	-.11	4.83	.11	86,039
Mr07	95.08	95.08	94.96	95.02	-.12	4.98	.12	78,179
June	94.93	94.94	94.83	94.88	-.12	5.12	.12	63,259
Sept	94.82	94.82	94.70	94.75	-.12	5.25	.12	56,703
Dec	94.68	94.68	94.56	94.62	-.12	5.38	.12	47,762
Mr08	94.58	94.58	94.46	94.53	-.12	5.47	.12	39,919
June	94.47	94.47	94.36	94.43	-.12	5.57	.12	41,475
Sept	94.38	94.39	94.27	94.34	-.12	5.66	.12	27,768
Dec	94.32	94.32	94.24	94.25	-.11	5.75	.11	14,144
Mr09	94.24	94.24	94.16	94.18	-.11	5.82	.11	14,691
Sept	94.00	94.03	94.00	94.04	-.10	5.96	.10	9,443
Ju10	93.80	93.83	93.80	93.84	-.09	6.16	.09	6,136

Est vol 1,030,723; vol Fri 418,902; open int 5,100,938, +73,633.

Source: The Wall Street Journal, *June 18, 2003, C13; and December 2, 2003, C14.*

a quoted price of 99.23 percent. The actual price for a $1 million contract, just like the spot price for T-bills, equals the par value $\times [1 - (dn/360)]$, where (n) is the number of days to maturity. Since T-bill futures are based on ninety-day maturity T-bills, the actual price for the September contract on June 17 was $1 million $[1 - (0.0077)(90/360)] = \$998,075$. The approximate change in price with a change in the discount rate for T-bills can also be approximated as $25 \times$ the number of basis points change in the discount rate. Hence, if the discount rate rose from 0.77 percent to 2 percent, hypothetically, the change in the value of the futures contract would be 2.00 percent $-$ 0.77 percent $=$ 1.23 percent, or 123 basis points $\times$ $25 per basis point $= \$3,075$ (a gain for a short position since the interest rate rose and a loss for a long position). Note as a proof that the new price for the T-bill with a rise in the discount rate to 2 percent would be equal to $1 million $[1 - (0.02 \times 90/360)] = \$995,000$, that is, a gain for a short position of $998,075 $-$ $995,000 $=\$3,075$, with the arranged futures contract selling price of $998,075. The contract owner with this short position would reverse the trade by contracting to buy the contract at the new lower price of $995,000 and make the $3,075 gain.

As noted in Figure 11.5, three-month Eurodollars had many more futures contract offerings in June and December of 2003. Eurodollar CD future contracts are based on three-month Eurodollar time deposits with a $1,000,000 par value. They are priced as 100% $-$ IMM Eurodollar Index (similar to a T-bill discount rate). Similar to T-bill futures, each 1-basis-point change in the IMM index is equal to $25.00. For example, as shown on Figure 11.5, a December Eurodollar futures contract has a settle price of 98.97 percent on June 17, 2003. Suppose on that date a trader took a long position to buy Eurodollar CDs in December at 98.97 percent. Later in December 1, 2003, the trader would see the new settle price of 98.80 percent. Since rates rose slightly during this period and the IMM index price fell, the trader would suffer a small loss. The loss incurred would be equal to the basis point change in the IMM index $\times$ $25. That change is -0.17 percent (98.8% $-$ 98.97%). So, the loss would be 17 basis points $\times$ $25 = ($425).

Short versus Long Hedges

A financial institution using futures to hedge can choose either a short hedge or a long hedge. **A short hedge means that the trader *sells* a futures contract, incurring an obligation either to deliver the underlying securities at some future point or close out the position through the clearinghouse before the delivery date by buying an offsetting contract.** When interest rates rise, as they did in December 2003, the value of both interest-earning assets (spot prices) and outstanding futures contracts (futures prices) fall. A trader who has contracts to sell T-bonds in the future can reverse her trade to buy them at the lower price for an immediate profit or buy the T-bonds in the spot market at the lower price to deliver them for sale on the delivery date. **Either way, the trader benefits from a short position if interest rates rise.** As noted in Table 11.1, which describes different futures contracts, many do not allow deliveries from spot market purchases or sales. Instead, trades are simply reversed and a gain or loss is taken. For about 99 percent of financial futures trades, spot deliveries are not made, instead trades are simply reversed and gains or losses are taken by traders.

In contrast to a short hedge, a long hedge means that the trader buys a futures contract, incurring an obligation either to take delivery of the securities at the pre-established price on some future date (if allowed for the contract) or to sell the contract, closing out the position through the clearinghouse before the delivery date. If interest rates fall in the intervening period, either obligation can be met at a profit. A trader who actually takes delivery on securities can sell them at an immediate profit over the purchase price written into the futures contract. If, instead, the futures contract is sold before the delivery date, the contract selling price will be higher than the purchase price. **Either way, the trader benefits from a long position if interest rates decline.**

It is important to emphasize that neither the long nor the short position is a hedge unless the futures transaction is undertaken to offset interest rate risk in an existing portfolio. Traders also should know that transaction costs and brokers' commissions reduce the proceeds of both long and short hedges. **The net hedging error that a trader has equals the opportunity gain or loss on the spot (hedged) position less the gain or loss on the futures position.** If the error is equal to zero, this is often called a perfect hedge. In the real world, the transaction costs including the brokerage fee to purchase the futures contract and the opportunity cost of holding the margin requirement would also be deducted.

The Long Hedge Illustrated

Suppose that in June 2008 the manager of a money market portfolio expected interest rates to decline. New funds, to be received and invested in ninety days (September 2008), will suffer from the drop in yields, and the manager would like to reduce the effect on portfolio returns. The appropriate strategy under this forecast is a long hedge, because long futures positions profit from falling rates.

Gains and losses on cash and futures market transactions are summarized in Table 11.2. The money manager expects an inflow of $10 million in September. The discount yield currently available on 91-day T-bills is 10 percent, and the goal is to establish a yield of 10 percent on the anticipated funds. Because contracts on 91-day T-bills have face values of $1 million, ten contracts are needed to hedge the cash position. Assuming that the initial margin requirement is 2 percent of the contract price, the cash required for the margin for the contracts in June will be slightly less than $20,000 ($2,000 × 10 contracts). The market value of the contracts purchased for future delivery in September is $9,750,000 million. If the funds were available now for the T-bill investment at a discount yield of 10 percent, the cost would be $9,747,222.

Suppose interest rates have fallen by the time the new funds arrive in September. The 91-day T-bill yield is down to 8 percent, and it now costs $9,797,778 to purchase bills with a face value of $10 mil-

---

table **11.2**   THE LONG HEDGE (FORECAST: FALLING INTEREST RATES)

A long hedge is chosen in anticipation of interest rate declines and requires the purchase of interest rate futures contracts. If the forecast is correct, the profit on the hedge helps to offset losses in the cash market.

I.

Cash Market	Futures Market
June	
T-bill discount yield at 10%	Buy 10 T-bill contracts for September delivery
Price of 91-day T-bills, $10 million par:	at 10% discount yield
$9,747,222[a]	Value of contracts:
	$9,750,000[b]
September	
T-bill discount yield at 8%	Sell 10 September T-bill contracts at 8%
Price of 91-day T-bills, $10 million par:	discount yield
$9,797,778	Value of contracts:
	$9,800,000

II.

Cash Market Loss		Futures Market Gain	
June cost	$9,747,222	September sale	$9,800,000
September cost	$9,797,778	June purchase	$9,750,000
Loss	($ 50,556)	Gain	$ 50,000
	Net Loss: ($556)		

III.

Effective Discount Yield with the Hedge

$$\frac{\$10,000,000 - (9,797,778 - 50,000)}{\$10,000,000} \times \frac{360}{91} = 9.978\%$$

a At a discount yield of 10%, the price of a 91-day T-bill is

$$P_0 = \$10,000,000 \left[\frac{1 - 0.10(91)}{360} \right] = \$9,747,222$$

b T-bill futures contracts are standardized at 90-day maturities, resulting in a price different from the one calculated in the cash market.

lion. The higher price results in an "opportunity loss" to the portfolio manager of $50,556, but the long futures hedge offsets most of that loss. With the decline in market yields, the September futures contracts have risen in value from $9.75 million to $9.8 million. Their sale provides a gain of $50,000 (the difference between the actual new and old prices) or $25 × the 200 basis-point-change in the discount yield (ten contracts), which almost equals the loss in the cash market. Hence, there is a net hedging error of ($556), the opportunity loss in the spot market less the futures gain of $50,000 = ($556). The effective discount yield on T-bills purchased, including the effect of the hedge (calculated as the net amount earned as a percentage of par value × the number of times this could be earned a year) is 9.978 percent, very close to the desired discount yield of 10 percent.

By definition, a hedge is undertaken to offset potential losses in an institution's existing or planned portfolio of financial assets. Buying long futures contracts when no future investment in T-bills was planned would be speculation, not hedging, because the contract purchase would be an attempt to earn a pure profit on futures.

The Short Hedge Illustrated

If a financial institution stands to lose under forecasts of rising rates, it can undertake a short hedge. For depository institutions, many liability costs are tied to yields on short-term Treasury securities, and an increase in interest rates can raise the cost of funds significantly. Profits on a short hedge may be used to lock in a lower cost of funds.

For deposit costs pegged to the T-bill rate, T-bill futures provide a good vehicle for the short hedge. Suppose that in September a savings institution wants to hedge $5 million in short-term certificates of deposit (CDs) whose owners are expected to roll them over in ninety days. If market yields go up, the thrift must offer a higher rate on its CDs to remain competitive, reducing the net interest margin (NIM). The asset/liability manager can reduce these losses by the sale of T-bill futures contracts. With a subsequent increase in rates, the value of contracts declines, and when the position is closed out through the clearinghouse, a profit will be realized to offset the higher interest expense on the CDs with the rise in rates.[10]

The short hedge illustrated in Table 11.3 is designed to offset the increase in CD rates from 7 percent to 9 percent; the interest paid on the CDs will increase by $25,000 for the three-month period. In September, the savings and loan association (S&L) sells five December contracts at a discount yield of 7 percent. To close out the position in December, after rates have risen to 9 percent, the hedger buys five T-bill contracts from the clearinghouse. They have declined in value, resulting in a $25,000 profit on the futures position. In the simplified world of this example, the institution's returns are protected from interest rate fluctuations because the higher dollar interest cost for the quarter, netted against the gain on the futures hedge, is equal to zero (a zero net hedging error). Taking the new interest cost less the gain on the futures contract as a percentage of the $5 million in CDs issued annualized by dividing by 360 / 90, the effective rate on the CDs is locked in at the desired 7 percent. Again, transaction costs, brokers' fees, and the opportunity cost of the margin deposit are not included.

As with the long hedge, the short hedge is undertaken only to protect an existing financial position. Attempting to gain a pure profit from rising rates would be speculation.

Concept Questions

1 What is the difference between a long and a short hedge?

2 Which type of hedge should be undertaken if a trader wants to protect against a spot loss if interest rates rise?

3 Which type of hedge should be undertaken if a trader wants to protect against a spot loss if interest rates fall?

4 How do you calculate the net hedging error?

---

10 This example assumes that the thrift has at least $5 million more short-term liabilities than short-term assets and thus meets regulatory requirements for hedges. This example also ignores the tax consequences of short hedges, which worsened after an IRS ruling in early 1993. See William B. Crawford, Jr. "IRS Rule Change Putting Futures Hedging at Risk." *Chicago Tribune* (February 21, 1993), Section 7, 1, 10.

table **11.3** THE SHORT HEDGE (FORECAST: RISING INTEREST RATES)

A short hedge is chosen in anticipation of interest rate increases and requires the sale of interest rate futures contracts. If the forecast is correct, the profit on the hedge helps to offset losses in the cash market.

I.

Cash Market	Futures Market
September	
CD rate: 7%	Sell 5 T-bill contracts for December delivery at 7% discount yield
Interest cost on $5 million in deposits (3 months):	Value of contracts:
$87,500	$4,912,500
December	
CD rate: 9%	Buy 5 December T-bill contracts at 9% discount yield
Interest cost on $5 million in deposits (3 months):	Value of contracts:
$112,500	$4,887,500

II.

Cash Market Loss		Futures Market Gain	
September interest	$87,500	September sale	$4,912,500
December interest	112,500	December purchase	−4,887,500
Loss	($25,000)	Gain	$ 25,000
	Net Result of Hedge: $0		

III.

Net Interest Cost and Effective CD Rate

$112,500 − $25,000 = $87,500

$$\frac{\$87,500}{\$5,000,000} \times \frac{360}{90} = 0.07 = 7.0\%$$

Risk and the Financial Futures Markets

The preceding scenarios are extremely simplified. For example, they assume that the changes in spot and futures yields are identical. They also do not address several decisions that investors must make before entering the market, such as the type and number of contracts to be purchased or sold and the length of the hedge. The examples also assume that the interest rate forecasts are accurate and timely. The more complex aspects of hedging and the risks they introduce are discussed in this section.

Incorrect Rate Forecasts

The preceding examples illustrate that rate forecasts are an integral part of every hedge but that their accuracy determines management's satisfaction with the results. The assumption made in Table 11.2 was that interest rates would fall and that funds received and invested after three months would earn a lower yield. If interest rates had not fallen, the portfolio manager could have maintained or even increased returns through the cash market position alone. The long hedge would result in a loss, because the contracts owned would decline in value. The loss on the futures hedge would reduce the otherwise favorable returns on the securities investment. The protective hedge limits the institution's loss from an unfavorable interest rate change, but it also limits the potential gains from a favorable movement in rates. Thus, hedging is indeed a risk-minimization strategy that is intended to reduce potential variation in the NIM.

Basis Risk

An influence on both the type and number of contracts to be traded is the **basis.** Basis is the difference between the spot price (P_{St}) of the underlying financial asset and the price of a futures contract (P_{Ft}) at time t:

$$\text{Basis} = P_{St} - P_{Ft} \qquad\qquad [11.1]$$

To execute a perfect hedge, one in which the cash market loss is exactly offset by the futures market profit, the hedger must predict the basis accurately and adjust the size of the hedge accordingly. In the simplified world of Table 11.2, the discount yield on the T-bills equals the effective discount yield at which the T-bill contract traded. The difference in the cash and futures market results arose from the futures market convention of pricing T-bill contracts based on ninety rather than ninety-one days. In reality, however, although cash yields and futures market yields are closely related, they are not perfectly correlated because each market has its own supply/demand interactions. The possibility of unexpected changes in the relationship between spot and futures market prices introduces another element of risk, known as **basis risk.**

Basis Risk Illustrated[11]

When a hedger closes out cash and futures positions, the gains and losses from each are netted. These calculations are shown at the end of Tables 11.2 and 11.3. Presenting them in a different format clarifies the importance of the basis.

At the close of a hedge, the results from the cash market transactions are determined by the number of securities bought or sold (Q) times their cost, or $Q(P_{St})$. In Table 11.2, the trader bought ten bills with a total par value of $1 million:

$$Q\,(P_{St}) = 10 \times \$979,777.80 = \$9,797,778$$

The result of the futures transaction alone is the proceeds from the offsetting sale of futures contracts (at time $t = 1$) minus the cost of the purchase of futures contacts at $(t = 0)$:

$$Q\,(P_{F1}) - Q\,(P_{F0}) = Q\,(P_{F1} - P_{F0})$$

For the long hedge,

$$Q\,(P_{F1} - P_{F0}) = 10 \times (\$980,000 - \$975,000) = 10 \times \$5,000 = \$50,000$$

The net cost of the bills purchased can be expressed as the difference between their spot price in September—the amount the institution would actually pay for the bills—and the profits from the futures trade:

$$\text{Net Cost} = Q\,(P_{S1}) - Q\,(P_{F1} - P_{F0}) \qquad\qquad [11.2]$$

$$= 10(\$979,777.80) - 10\,[\$980,000 - \$975,000] = \$9,797,778 - \$50,000 = \$9,747,778$$

Rearranging, the net cost is also

$$\text{Net Cost} = Q\,(P_{S1} - P_{F1}) + Q\,(P_{F0})$$

$$= 10(\$979,777.80 - \$980,000.00) + (10 \times \$975,000.00)$$

$$= -\$2,222 + \$9,750,000 = \$9,747,778$$

In other words, the basis at the time the position is closed out—the quantity $(P_{S1} - P_{F1})$—determines the success or failure of the hedge. If there were no uncertainty about the basis, a hedge in the futures market would involve much less risk. In reality, at the time the hedge is undertaken, the trader does not know P_{S1} or P_{F1} or the difference between the two that will prevail in the future. As the basis fluctuates, so does the potential gain or loss on the hedge.

The top panel of Figure 11.6 shows prices on a popular futures instrument, T-bond contracts, as well as prices on T-bonds during the period 1978–1988. The high positive correlation in price movements is evident from the bottom line, which is the basis over that period. Although the basis does not fluctuate greatly, it is not stable. **Traders who hedge positions in the cash markets with futures incur basis risk, a fact that must be considered in the hedging decision.** As the top panel of Figure 11.6 illustrates, however, basis risk exposure on the futures position may be lower than price risk exposure in the cash market, especially when the cash and futures instruments are identical or very closely related. The variability in the basis in the top panel is clearly much smaller than the variability in prices on thirty-year T-bonds.

---

11 The following section draws on Van Horne (1990), 160–161.

figure **11.6** PRICES OF 30-YEAR BONDS AND T-BOND FUTURES CONTRACTS

The basis is the difference between the current price of a hedged asset and the current price of a futures contract. The more nearly identical the characteristics of the hedged asset and the futures contract, the more stable the basis.

Prices of 30-Year Treasury Bonds and Treasury Bond Future Contracts 1978–1988

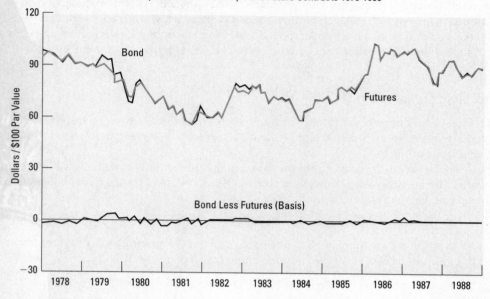

Prices of 30-Year Corporate Bonds and Treasury Bond Futures Contracts 1979–1988

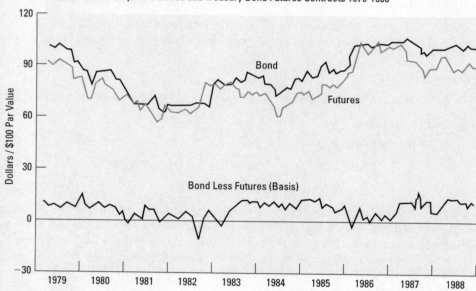

Source: Adapted from Charles S. Morris. "Managing Interest Rate Risk with Interest Rate Futures," Economic Review (Federal Reserve Bank of Kansas City) 74 (March 1989): 13.

The Cross Hedge and Basis Risk

In Table 11.2, the money market portfolio manager protected yields on an anticipated T-bill investment with a T-bill futures contract. In many hedging decisions, however, the limited variety of futures contracts available makes it impossible to hedge a cash instrument with a contract for future delivery of the same security. Whenever a futures hedge is constructed on an instrument other than the cash market security, as would be the case when hedging a corporate bond portfolio, the hedge is considered a **cross hedge.** The basis risk for these positions is even greater than when the same security is involved in both sides of the transaction, as the bottom panel of Figure 11.6 demonstrates.

Figure 11.6 shows that from 1979 to 1988, the prices of T-bond futures contracts and the prices of a typical high-grade corporate bond differed more than the prices of T-bond futures and T-bonds. If a portfolio manager had hedged a corporate bond portfolio with T-bond futures during this period, the basis risk would have been higher than if the manager were hedging a T-bond portfolio. The basis in the cross hedge, however, would still have been less variable over the period than the price of the unhedged corporate bond.

If a short-term instrument were hedged with a futures contract on a long-term security, or vice versa, the basis risk would be even greater. A change in the slope of the yield curve would produce changes of differing magnitudes for long- and short-term yields. In that case, the changes in spot and futures values would certainly diverge, and, consequently, the effectiveness of the hedge would be more uncertain.

The cross hedge exposes the hedger to basis risk for another important reason. Even if the changes in yields were the same on two securities, the resulting price changes could very well differ. The bond theorems and duration discussions in Chapter 10 demonstrate that a given basis point change in yields will not affect the prices of securities in the same way if they have different coupon rates or terms to maturity, differences likely to occur in a cross hedge. As market interest rates fluctuate, the goal of a hedge—minimizing NIM fluctuations by realizing a profit on the futures trade that exactly offsets the cash market loss—is difficult to achieve with a cross hedge.

Choosing the Optimal Number of Contracts

An asset/liability manager faces additional uncertainties in determining the size of the futures position. The objective of hedging is to offset, as closely as possible, potential losses on a cash instrument with gains on futures, but price changes on the two types of instruments are seldom exactly proportional to one another. Therefore, simply dividing the total value of the cash portfolio to be hedged by the face value of a single futures contract on an appropriate instrument would give a misleading signal about the number of futures contracts a hedger should buy or sell. Selecting the number of contracts to trade is particularly difficult in a cross hedge, because face value, coupon, and maturity characteristics may all differ between cash and futures instruments.

The first step in structuring the hedge is to identify the assets or liabilities (or both) to be protected. The volume and interest rate characteristics of the instrument to be hedged are the foundation for the futures decision.[12]

The Hedge Ratio

Before the optimal position in the futures market can be determined, a **hedge ratio** must be estimated. Although there are other ways of defining a hedge ratio, many experts prefer a definition that focuses on the relative variability of the prices of the cash and futures instrument involved in a contemplated hedge. This definition assumes that the objective of the hedge is to minimize the variability in price/yield changes to which the hedger is exposed:[13]

$$HR = \frac{Cov\,(\Delta P_S, \Delta P_F)}{\sigma^2\,\Delta P_F} \qquad [11.3]$$

where HR is the hedge ratio, Cov $(\Delta P_S, \Delta P_F)$ is the covariance between changes in spot prices and change in future prices, and $\sigma^2\,\Delta P_F$ is the variance in changes in future prices.

The covariance is a statistic that measures the extent to which two variables move together. Students of regression analysis may also realize that the covariance between two variables divided by the variance

---

12 The development of an institutional hedging strategy is a major aspect of asset/liability management. The futures position may revolve around either a macro or micro hedge, terms that refer to the magnitude of the futures position in relation to the institution's balance sheet.

13 For further discussion of hedge ratios, including alternative definitions, see Kolb (1988); Schwartz, Hill, and Schneeweis (1986); and Chance (1989).

of one of the variables is the beta coefficient in a simple regression model between the two variables. Thus, the hedge ratio as defined previously can be estimated by regressing past price changes in the cash instrument to be hedged against past price changes in a futures instrument. The beta of such a regression is the hedge ratio for the proposed hedge.[14]

Suppose that a securities portfolio manager, anticipating a decline in interest rates over the next three months, wishes to protect the yield on an investment of $15 million in T-bills and that a T-bill futures contract is now selling for $989,500. If the hedge ratio between price changes in T-bills and T-bill futures contracts has been estimated through regression to be 0.93, the number of contracts to be used in the hedge can be determined by

$$N_F = \frac{V \times HR}{F}$$

[11.4]

where

N_F = the number of futures contracts to be purchased or sold,

V = the total market value of securities to be hedged, and

F = the market value of a single futures contract.

In this example, the number of contracts to be purchased (a long position is needed because the forecast is for falling rates) based on a $15,000,000 T-bill portfolio to be hedged (V), the price for a T-bill futures contract of $989,500 ($F$), and a hedge ratio of 0.93 (HR) is as follows:

$$N_F = (\$15,000,000 / \$989,500) \times 0.93 = 14.098, \text{ or about 14 futures contracts}$$

Several factors will affect the outcome of the hedge. If the *past* covariance between changes in T-bill prices and changes in T-bill futures prices is not the same as the covariance between those price changes *during* the hedge, the number of contracts calculated by using Equation 11.4 will not result in a position that minimizes the hedger's risk exposure. Also, it is not possible to trade fractional amounts of futures contracts, so the hedger in this instance would need to purchase fourteen contracts. Thus, even if past and future covariances between price changes were equal, the manager would still expect a less-than-perfect hedge. This inability to trade fractional futures units or, for that matter, fractions of a T-bill, explains why the hedge results in Table 11.2 are imperfect. Although many financial theories assume perfect divisibility of financial assets, it seldom exists in practice.

Appendix 11A shows an alternative hedge ratio model using the relative durations of spot and future positions as a type of hedge ratio in calculating the appropriate number of futures contracts (N_{DUR}), which can be a better hedge ratio for hedging long-term bond portfolios.

Futures as a Supplement to Gap Management

Macro Hedges versus Micro Hedges

The hedging examples described have been **micro** hedges, designed to hedge the risk of a loss in the spot market for a particular asset or liability. For instance, suppose a bond portfolio manager has some bonds maturing in three months that he or she wants to reinvest in the bond market but fears that interest rates will fall and the prices of bonds will rise over this time period. The bond manager could set up a micro hedge for the dollar worth of the bonds to be purchased by purchasing futures contracts

---

Concept Questions

1 What is the basis in hedging with futures contracts and what is basis risk?

2 Why does basis risk increase with cross hedging?

3 What is the opportunity loss that can occur with hedging?

4 How do you calculate the optimal number of futures contracts to hedge a particular spot position?

---

14 Note the similarity between this process and estimating the beta coefficient on common stock.

to buy bonds at a given price in three months. If bond prices rise, the futures contract will have a gain that will offset the higher cost of the bonds in the spot market three months from now. Similarly, suppose the manager of a depository institution expects to make a loan in three months and is concerned that the interest rate of CDs used to fund the loan will rise during that time. He or she could set up a micro hedge for the dollar worth of the CDs to be financed by purchasing futures contracts to sell CDs (or T-bills of similar maturity) at a given price in three months. If CD rates rise (prices fall), the futures contract will have a gain that will offset the higher interest expense for the CDs three months from now.

An institution, however, may be more concerned over its overall interest rate risk as reflected by its funding gap or duration gap and wish to hedge this entire gap, in other words, use a **macro** hedge. If an institution has a negative funding gap (i.e., a positive duration gap), if interest rates rise, the institution's net interest income will fall, and its market value of its equity will fall.

With a proper number of futures contracts, the financial institution could hedge this loss by taking a short position in futures that would produce a gain equal to the institution's expected loss if interest rates rise. Similarly, if the institution had a positive funding gap (i.e., a negative duration gap), exposing it to losses if interest rates fall, it could hedge this loss by taking a long position in futures that would produce a gain equal to the institution's expected gain if interest rates fall.

Example of a Macro Hedge: Hedging a Funding Gap

Suppose a bank has a funding gap of −$100 million over the next three months. This implies that if interest rates rise 100 basis points (1 percent), its loss in net interest income will be Funding Gap × Change in y^* = −$100 million × (0.01 × 90 days/360) = $25,000. By using Equation 11.4, hedging with future contracts on three-month T-bills and assuming a hedge ratio of 1, the bank manager would purchase 100 contracts to sell T-bills in three months at a given discount rate of 8.55 percent. If, three months later, both spot and futures rates rose 100 basis points, the approximate gain on the futures with a discount rate of 9.55 percent now would be $25.00 per basis point rise, or 100 basis points × $25 × 100 contracts = $25,000. Here, we are assuming a perfect hedge, which of course may not be the case if spot and futures prices do not move by the same amount over this period. Naturally, the bank also has an opportunity cost with this hedge if interest rates fall, whereby its gain in net interest income will be offset by an equal loss on its futures position. A duration gap hedge could also be implemented. Note that a macro hedge requires detailed knowledge of a bank's total exposure to interest rate risk and requires a relatively large transaction in the futures market because it is designed to protect the value of or the earnings generated by the entire asset and liability portfolio. The institution makes a significant commitment to its interest rate forecast.[15]

Interest Rate Futures: Regulatory Restrictions and Financial Reporting

The risks accompanying the futures markets have led regulators to focus attention on policies governing institutional involvement. For state-regulated institutions, there may be as many different policies as there are state regulators. In contrast, federally chartered or federally insured institutions in each industry do have uniform regulations. In general, regulators disapprove of futures transactions that increase the institution's risk exposure. Instead, they expect an institution to assume a futures position that will desensitize the balance sheet to interest rate changes. Because commercial bank balance sheets are less homogeneous than thrift balance sheets, thrift regulators have set more specific rules on the use of futures. Bank regulators have followed a model similar to that used by securities industry regulators by emphasizing a self-policing approach.

In any case, depositories cannot use futures as income-generating investments for speculative purposes. Regulators also expect a high-level management committee, often including members of the board of directors, to establish a hedging policy for the institution that contains a set of guidelines for establishing hedges and monitoring the results.

---

15 See Saunders (1997) for more details on hedging a duration gap. Similar to the Appendix 11A equation, the number of duration-based contracts would be calculated with the average rate of the bank's used for the expected yield, the duration gap used for the duration, and the total assets of the bank the instrument to be hedged.

In addition to futures, options and other derivatives (financial instruments whose value derives from an underlying security) are traded by security firms. With the Financial Modernization Act allowing investment firms, banks, and insurance firms to operate together, regulators have been concerned about the dealer derivative risks of their operations. As noted earlier in the chapter, twenty-five large financial services firms have the majority of derivative holdings by notional value, with the majority of derivatives held for trading for customers and other parties.

In the 1990s, there were several highly publicized crises caused by rogue traders incurring large losses from trading for Barings, Inc., in London, which failed, and Daiwa in Japan. Similarly, Long-Term Capital Management, L.P., an investment hedge fund, had severe losses in 1998, requiring a $3.6 billion Federal Reserve-brokered bailout. In response to such operational risks, the new Basel II Accord requires greater capital to be held for operational risk, as well as a Market Risk Amendment in 1996.

Congress and regulators since the mid-1990s have contemplated greater oversight over the derivatives market and financial institutions' use of derivatives. Regulators have also established examiner guidance on bank derivatives activities, including Federal Reserve Guidelines issued in 1993 that are applied to all trading activities, such as derivatives and other financial instruments. Examiners also began assigning a formal rating to a bank's overall risk management capabilities as part of the management component of the CAMELS (regulatory ratings on Capital, Asset Quality, Management, Earnings, and Liquidity) rating for safety and soundness. Similarly, examiners for the Office of the Comptroller of the Currency are required to determine whether bank managers understand the risks associated with derivatives.

Managers are required to implement controls to quantify and manage these risks effectively. Such controls include written policies setting limits on various risks and procedures and internal controls to ensure that policy limits are enforced. They also include a risk management system to quantify the risks associated with a position and to provide the means to manage that risk effectively. Examiners must ensure the accuracy of the models used to measure and monitor the risk, including analyzing earnings of the position (i.e., the gains and losses associated with given hedges) and comparing them with the expected result. Internal and external audits also must be performed, focusing particularly on the effectiveness of internal controls and the adequacy of the management information system.[16]

Accounting Rules

Guidelines for reporting futures transactions have also received much attention. The accounting profession has addressed two areas of controversy: what distinguishes a hedge from a speculative trade and how to report a futures position. FASB rules designate a futures transaction as a hedge when two conditions are met:[17]

1. The asset or liability to be hedged exposes the institution to interest rate risk.
2. The futures contract chosen reduces interest rate risk, is designated as a hedge, and has price movements highly correlated with the instrument being hedged.

FASB recommends more favorable accounting methods for future hedges linked to identifiable cash market instruments (micro hedges) than for more general hedges (macro hedges). In other words, hedging a portfolio of six-month adjustable rate mortgages with T-bill futures contracts (a micro hedge) qualifies for more favorable reporting than a macro hedge that lowers the total rate of the institution but cannot be linked to a specific asset or liability.

Unless an institution can identify a specific asset or liability for which a hedge has been selected, accounting rules require the results of the hedge to be reported as gains or losses on the income state-

---

16 For more details on the guidelines established for commercial banks and bank holding companies, see Chicago Board of Trade (1990), 94–95; Parkinson and Spindt (1985), 469–474; and Koppenhaver (1984). Also see Chorafas (1998); Dominic Casserley and Greg Wilson. "Managing Derivatives-Related Regulatory Risk." *Bank Management* (July/August, 1994), 27–32; and Susan M. Phillips. "Derivatives and Trading: No Quarantine Necessary." *Banking Strategies* (September/October, 1996), 39–42.

17 See Drabenstott and McDonley (1984), 24–25, and Chicago Board of Trade (1990), 100–101. The FASB rules became effective December 31, 1984. Also see Chorafas (1998) for details of the 1996 Market Risk Amendment by the Basel Committee of Banking Supervision, which includes a section on hedge accounting and more sophisticated hedge ratios.

ments before the final futures position is closed out. Because changes in interest rates during the course of a hedge may produce temporary losses that are ultimately recovered, reporting hedging results before the position is closed can increase variability in reported earnings. The results of micro hedges, in contrast, now require that both gains and losses on the spot and futures assets be reported, providing some netting out. Not surprisingly, managers often favor micro hedges for accounting reasons alone as well as for the flexibility to structure bank services to meet the needs of a particularly desirable customer.

Some regulators prefer contemporaneous reporting and require institutions to use a mark-to-market approach. For example, the Comptroller of the Currency requires national banks to report the market value of their futures positions before closure and thus before any gains or losses are realized. During the course of a hedge, the value of a futures contract may fluctuate substantially as financial market conditions change, although the institution's financial position is not actually affected until a contract is closed out. Thus, many bank managers believe that mark-to-market futures reporting may provide misleading information.

The risks inherent in the interest rate futures markets, as well as additional regulatory and accounting standards, mean that futures strategies require careful planning and monitoring after they are implemented. Most financial institutions that are successful hedgers have established objectives and safeguards to control the additional risk exposure.

More Detailed Reporting Under FAS 133

New, more detailed reported for hedging became effective on June 15, 2000, under the Financial Accounting Standards Board's FAS 133 and its amending statement FAS 138. Qualifying hedges are not required under these guidelines to be marked to market and recorded at fair value on the financial statements of hedging companies. One problem with the new regulations for banks and other corporations is that changes must be recorded without offsetting changes to the spot position that is being hedged unless the transaction can be defined as a qualifying hedge. For nonqualifying hedges, hence, the firm's financial statements are exposed to potential viability. As noted by Maness and Zietlow (2002, pp. 595–596), there are four key rules under FAS 133:

1. All "standalone and qualifying embedded derivatives" must be marked to market and reported on the balance sheet.
2. Gains and losses for changes in the value of derivatives must be reported to earnings immediately unless the derivative is part of a qualifying hedge (based on meeting rigorous criteria regarding its effectiveness).
3. If a hedge is considered qualified but is not perfect, the amount that is not perfect must be reported on the firm's income statement.
4. Firms must fully describe their derivative and hedging activities in the footnotes of their financial statements.

Since complying with FAS 133 is very complex and requires quite detailed forms, a number of consulting firms, such as PricewaterhouseCoopers, have established Websites to help document and prepare FAS 133 reports for firms.. As noted by Jay Glacy, in an overview of FAS 133 in *Derivatives Week* (April 10, 2000, v. 9, p. 6), the key changes of FAS 133 are that all derivatives are recognized in the balance sheet at fair value. For fair value hedges, the hedged items also need to be adjusted on the balance sheet to preserve the hedging effect in the income statement. Portions of the hedge that are considered as ineffective must be recognized in earnings versus being deferred, creating volatility in earnings. Gains and losses on derivatives that qualify as cash flow hedges are initially recognized in other comprehensive income (OCI), creating additional volatility in equity. Also, new and somewhat onerous qualification criteria for hedge accounting were established, although the new rules for foreign currency hedging are more flexible. With FAS 133, hedge accounting became more of a hurdle for banks, since macro hedging does not get hedge accounting treatment. It also could increase earnings volatility due to the marking of the hedge to market if "hedged" assets or liabilities can't also be marked to market. Hence, Puwalski (2003) notes some institutions might use a trading account and hold both the derivative hedge and the hedged balance sheet items in a trading portfolio where both are market to market instead. Executives at both financial and nonfinancial institutions have complained about the complexity of rules under FAS 133, particularly mortgage bankers who use forward contracts, considered as derivatives as well by FAS 133, in their securitization activities.[18]

Regulators' Risk Concerns for Derivative Activities of Financial Institutions

Regulators have been concerned about the risks of financial institutions with derivatives activities. As noted in a recent report by Puwalski (2003), senior financial analyst at the FDIC, the risk associated with the use of derivatives by financial institutions can vary substantially, including risks for hedging, dealing, or speculating. Poorly managed operational risk can lead to losses no matter what the type of derivatives activity. The risk of hedging depends on the potential of the hedge ratio changing (i.e., the historical relationships used to create the hedge ratio changing after the hedge was constructed). The majority of very large banks (about 339, or 77 percent) use derivatives solely for hedging purposes to hedge interest rate risk. The risk of this derivatives activity depends on how well the hedge is constructed, and if historical relations on which the hedge was constructed continue to hold during the hedge. For example, the downfall of the large hedge fund Long-Term Capital Management (LTCM) in late 1998 was brought about by the default of Russia on its debt at that time. The spread between mortgage rates and ten-year Treasury securities widened significantly in ways that weren't predicted when LTCM originally took its positions. Similarly, hedgers of mortgage-related products often depend on the stability in the relationship between different rates. With sudden, unpredicted change in spreads, hedgers can experience losses on both their derivatives contracts and on the spot assets that they are trying to hedge. If hedges are constructed well and unpredicted changes don't occur in the basis (spread between spot rates and future rates), in contrast, financial institutions can reduce their interest rate risk.

The majority of the notional value for insured commercial banks is dealer notionals by seven of the largest banks; these derivatives are part of their total trading operations that entail market, credit, and operational risk, with the majority of losses associated with operational risk. Major deals are required to set capital for trading assets using internal value at risk (VAR) models, holding greater capital with greater value at risk, reflecting the risk of loss due to unlikely events. The primary federal supervisors and the FDIC, through its dedicated examiner program, closely monitor the major derivatives dealers for their derivatives activities and risk management systems and require greater risk-based capital for longer and more volatile contracts and contracts with greater counterparty risk. Basel II focuses on the measurement of international banks' operational risks and additional capital requirements for operational risk.[19]

Limitations of Futures in Asset/Liability Management

Setting the appropriate hedge ratio and selecting the most effective futures instrument are difficult problems for any type of hedge. For many assets held by depositories, no futures contracts exist, forcing institutions to cross hedge and increase basis risk. These decisions are less complex for a micro hedge, however, because only one instrument and one maturity are involved. Monitoring the institution's futures position is also time-consuming, especially in a micro strategy that may involve many individual hedges. Finally, the daily cash settlements required for futures trading place additional liq-

Concept Questions

1 What is a macro hedge? Give an example for a bank hedging its interest rate risk.

2 Why do accounting regulations discourage macro hedges?

3 Discuss the main provisions of FAS 133.

4 What are some of the risks and limitations of using futures in asset/liability management for financial institutions?

---

18 Jay Glacy. "Overview of FAS 133," *Derivatives Week*, April 10, 2000, v. 9, p. 6; Puwalski (2003); Adam Tempkin. "Morass of Regulatory Woes Engulfs Mart: Market Grapples with Pooling of Interest, FAS 133 and ERISA," *Mortgage-Backed Securities Letter*, September 25, 2000; and Karen Brettell. "Fed Staffer Says FAS 133 Is Not Working," *Derivatives Week*, September 29, 2003, v. 1, p. 11.

19 This section comes from Puwalski (2003).

uidity demands on the institution, especially if rate forecasts prove to be incorrect. The disadvantages must be weighed against the additional flexibility that futures provide.

Other synthetic or derivative techniques used for hedging—including interest rate swaps, caps, collars, floors, and options on interest rate futures—are discussed in Chapter 12.

Foreign Currency Futures

Financial institutions active in international markets face exchange rate risk, or variability in NIM caused by fluctuations in currency exchange rates. Foreign currency futures are instruments used to hedge exchange rate risk, just as interest rate futures are used to hedge interest rate risk. Hedging strategies useful to institutions financing international transactions are similar to the choices available for hedging against interest rate fluctuations.

Figure 11.7, Panel A shows futures contracts prices on December 2, 2003. A number of different futures contracts were available on exchange rates between the U.S. dollar and the Japanese yen, the Canadian dollar, the British pound, the Swiss franc, the Australian dollar, the Mexican peso, and the Euro to the U.S. dollar. Currency futures contract prices are quoted as direct rates, or dollars per unit of the foreign currency (i.e., the value of a foreign currency in U.S. dollars). Thus, the value of a foreign currency in dollars and, hence, the value of a futures contract in that currency, rises when the value of that currency rises relative to the U.S. dollar, that is, rises when the value of the dollar falls.

In early 1992, the CME introduced futures contracts on currency **cross rates.** (Cross rates are rates of exchange between two non-U.S. currencies.) The first contract of this type approved for trading was the mark/yen futures contract. The contract price is quoted as yen per mark; contracts are settled in yen. With the end of the mark and the advent of the Euro, the contract is now Euro/Japanese yen as shown in Figure 11.7. As the value of the Euro increases against the yen, the Euro/yen contract price rises; when the yen appreciates against the Euro, the price of the contract falls. A Euro/British pound contract is listed as a futures contract as well.

Comparison of Forward and Futures Markets

In Panel B of Figure 11.7, exchange rates for December 2, 2003, are listed for different currencies relative to the U.S. dollar, with forward contracts listed below for some currencies, such as Switzerland (the franc). Like foreign currency futures, forward markets provide a mechanism for avoiding the uncertainty of exchange rate fluctuations over a given planning period. Before illustrating the use of foreign currency futures to hedge exchange rate risk, it is useful to distinguish between futures and forward contracts.

Forward contracts are not standardized; rather they can be customized to the needs of each trader. For example, they can be negotiated in any currency, in any denomination, and for any maturity. In contrast, currency futures contracts, like interest rate futures contracts, are available only in standard denominations and maturities. Forward contracts are arranged electronically by means of a foreign currency dealer or through large financial institutions, especially money center banks. Currency futures contracts are traded on the futures exchanges. As a result, the holder of a forward contract faces default risk, whereas the clearinghouse assumes that risk in the futures markets. Because there is no secondary market for forward contracts, they are less liquid than currency futures, a position that can be offset before maturity. However, as with interest rate futures, currency futures contracts require that a trader's margin account be marked to market daily (i.e., losses must be taken against the margin deposited on a contract). Nonetheless, because traders face default and liquidity risks in the forward markets, usually only very large traders participate.

Currency Futures Illustrated

Suppose a U.S. bank made a formal commitment on December 2, 2003, to loan a Swiss customer 1 million Swiss francs on January 2, 2003 (i.e., in one month). At that time, the bank plans to convert U.S. dollars into Swiss francs, but management recognizes the risk of exchange rate fluctuations over the period. Figure 11.7, Panel B shows the direct exchange rate between Swiss francs and dollars was $0.7760; the indirect rate (the reciprocal) was 1.2887 Swiss francs per dollar. In other words, one Swiss franc is worth $0.7760, and one U.S. dollar would buy 1.2887 Swiss francs. Hence, under the current

figure **11.7** FOREIGN EXCHANGE RATES AND FUTURES PRICES

Key Currency Cross Rates

Late New York Trading Tuesday, December 2, 2003

	Dollar	Euro	Pound	SFranc	Peso	Yen	CdnDir
Canada	1.2979	1.5674	2.2440	1.0071	.11473	.01195	. . .
Japan	108.65	131.21	187.85	84.311	9.605	. . .	83.714
Mexico	11.3122	13.6618	19.559	8.7783	. . .	.10412	8.7161
Switzerland	1.2887	1.5563	2.2281	. . .	.11392	.01186	.9929
U.K.	.57840	.6985	. . .	.4488	.05113	.00532	.44563
Euro	.82800	. . .	1.4316	.64254	.07320	.00762	.63799
U.S.	. . .	1.2077	1.7290	.77600	.08840	.00920	.77050

PANEL A: FOREIGN CURRENCY FUTURES PRICES

Prices and other information on futures contracts are reported daily in the financial pages.

PANEL B: FOREIGN CURRENCY EXCHANGE RATES BETWEEN THE U.S. DOLLAR AND OTHER CURRENCIES

Both direct (U.S. $Equivalent) and indirect (Currency per U.S. $) rates for December 2, 2003, are listed.

FUTURES

Tuesday, December 2, 2003

Currency Futures

	OPEN	HIGH	LOW	SETTLE	CHG	LIFETIME HIGH	LIFETIME LOW	OPEN INT
Japanese Yen (CME)-¥12,500,000; $ per ¥								
Dec	.9142	.9217	.9110	.9209	.0075	.9305	.8318	132,439
Mr04	.9183	.9243	.9139	.9237	.0075	.9323	.8240	2,988
June	.9217	.9256	.9217	.9266	.0075	.9315	.8496	208

Est vol 12,468; vol Mon 23,021; open int 135,688, +976.

	OPEN	HIGH	LOW	SETTLE	CHG	LIFETIME HIGH	LIFETIME LOW	OPEN INT
Canadian Dollar (CME)-CAD 100,000; $ per CAD								
Dec	.7669	.7714	.7638	.7693	.0026	.7726	.6160	72,651
Mr04	.7630	.7685	.7611	.7663	.0025	.7691	.6150	7,591
June	.7640	.7650	.7595	.7638	.0025	.7660	.6201	1,366
Sept	.7584	.7635	.7582	.7615	.0025	.7635	.6505	726
Dec	.7595	.7610	.7560	.7592	.0025	.7610	.6940	257

Est vol 8,958; vol Mon 16,231; open int 82,606, −166.

	OPEN	HIGH	LOW	SETTLE	CHG	LIFETIME HIGH	LIFETIME LOW	OPEN INT
British Pound (CME)- £62,500; $ per £								
Dec	1.7176	1.7295	1.7154	1.7272	.0094	1.7295	1.5000	69,579
Mr04	1.7036	1.7172	1.7034	1.7150	.0094	1.7172	1.5654	1,877

Est vol 4,957; vol Mon 12,038; open int 71,464, −673.

	OPEN	HIGH	LOW	SETTLE	CHG	LIFETIME HIGH	LIFETIME LOW	OPEN INT
Swiss Franc (CME)-CHF 125,000; $ per CHF								
Dec	.7709	.7788	.7673	.7766	.0054	.7835	.6773	66,418
Mr04	.7718	.7803	.7692	.7783	.0054	.7815	.7060	2,508
June	.7730	.7810	.7730	.7799	.0054	.7810	.7117	127

Est vol 6,670; vol Mon 10,033; open int 69,106, +285.

	OPEN	HIGH	LOW	SETTLE	CHG	LIFETIME HIGH	LIFETIME LOW	OPEN INT
Australian Dollar (CME)-AUD 100,000; $ per AUD								
Dec	.7266	.7317	.7255	.7298	.0036	.7317	.5025	58,859
Mr04	.7195	.7239	.7179	.7222	.0036	.7239	.5193	2,777

Est vol 3,045; vol Mon 5,822; open int 61,962, +421.

	OPEN	HIGH	LOW	SETTLE	CHG	LIFETIME HIGH	LIFETIME LOW	OPEN INT
Mexican Peso (CME)-MXN 500,000; $ per MXN								
Dec	.08775	.08845	.08765	.08812	.00055	.09590	.08330	35,764
Mr04	.08655	.08700	.08655	.08697	.00055	.09330	.08600	6,972

Est vol 4,592; vol Mon 4,299; open int 43,183, −336.

	OPEN	HIGH	LOW	SETTLE	CHG	LIFETIME HIGH	LIFETIME LOW	OPEN INT
Euro/US Dollar (CME)-€125,000; $ per €								
Dec	1.1966	1.2088	1.1939	1.2077	.0109	1.2088	.9551	123,612
Mr04	1.1930	1.2058	1.1910	1.2047	.0108	1.2058	1.0425	4,282

Est vol 29,136; vol Mon 54,328; open int 128,332, −3,510.

	OPEN	HIGH	LOW	SETTLE	CHG	LIFETIME HIGH	LIFETIME LOW	OPEN INT
Euro/US Dollar (FINEX)- €200,000; $ per €								
Dec	. . .	. . .	. . .	1.2076	.0108	1.2012	.9551	471

Est vol 295; vol Mon 334; open int 477, −35.

	OPEN	HIGH	LOW	SETTLE	CHG	LIFETIME HIGH	LIFETIME LOW	OPEN INT
Euro/Japanese Yen (FINEX)- €100,000; ¥ per €								
Dec	130.85	131.23	130.85	131.12	.11	132.05	124.10	8,977

Est vol 489; vol Mon 235; open int 8,987, −267.

	OPEN	HIGH	LOW	SETTLE	CHG	LIFETIME HIGH	LIFETIME LOW	OPEN INT
Euro/British Pound (FINEX)- €100,000; £ per €								
Dec	. . .	. . .	. . .	.6994	.0025	.7131	.6832	2,525

Est vol 71; vol Mon 46; open int 2,526, −45.

Exchange Rates

The foreign exchange mid-range rates below apply to trading among banks in amounts of $1 million and more, as quoted at 4 p.m. Eastern time by Reuters and other sources. Retail transactions provide fewer units of foreign currency per dollar.

COUCOUNTRY	U.S. $ EQUIVALENT TUE	U.S. $ EQUIVALENT MON	CURRENCY PER U.S. $ TUE	CURRENCY PER U.S. $ MON
Argentina (Peso)-y	.3359	.3359	2.9771	2.9771
Australia (Dollar)	.7312	.7280	1.3676	1.3736
Bahrain (Dinar)	2.6526	2.6526	.3770	.3770
Brazil (Real)	.3411	.3422	2.9317	2.9223
Canada (Dollar)	.7705	.7671	1.2979	1.3036
1-month forward	.7693	.7661	1.2999	1.3053
3-months forward	.7673	.7641	1.3033	1.3087
6-months forward	.7646	.7614	1.3079	1.3134
Chile (Peso)	.001633	.001617	612.37	618.43
China (Renminbi)	.1208	.1208	8.2781	8.2781
Colombia (Peso)	.0003532	.0003539	2831.26	2825.66
Czech. Rep. (Koruna)				
Commercial rate	.03735	.03704	26.774	26.998
Denmark (Krone)	.1623	.1609	6.1614	6.2150
Ecuador (US Dollar)	1.0000	1.0000	1.0000	1.0000
Egypt (Pound)-y	.1633	.1625	6.1226	6.1550
Hong Kong (Dollar)	.1288	.1288	7.7640	7.7640
Hungary (Forint)	.004450	.004411	224.72	226.71
India (Rupee)	.02187	.02188	45.725	45.704
Indonesia (Rupiah)	.0001178	.0001176	8489	8503
Israel (Shekel)	.2260	.2258	4.4248	4.4287
Japan (Yen)	.009204	.009146	108.65	109.34
1-month forward	.009214	.009156	108.53	109.22
3-months forward	.009231	.009173	108.33	109.02
6-months forward	.009262	.009204	107.97	108.65
Jordan (Dinar)	1.4104	1.4104	.7090	.7090
Kuwait (Dinar)	3.3959	3.3957	.2945	.2945
Lebanon (Pound)	.0006596	.0006594	1516.07	1516.53
Malaysia (Ringgit)-b	.2632	.2632	3.7994	3.7994
Malta (Lira)	2.8128	2.7925	.3555	.3581
Mexico (Peso)				
Floating rate	.0884	.0879	11.3122	11.3753
New Zealand (Dollar)	.6464	.6439	1.5470	1.5530
Norway (Krone)	.1479	.1466	6.7613	6.8213
Pakistan (Rupee)	.01750	.01745	57.143	57.307
Peru (new Sol)	.2875	.2875	3.4783	3.4783
Philippines (Peso)	.01802	.01801	55.494	55.525
Poland (Zloty)	.2591	.2567	3.8595	3.8956
Russia (Ruble)-a	.03367	.03367	29.700	29.700
Saudi Arabia (Riyal)	.2667	.2667	3.7495	3.7495
Singapore (Dollar)	.5813	.5800	1.7203	1.7241
Slovak Rep. (Koruna)	.02935	.02919	34.072	34.258
South Africa (Rand)	.1584	.1569	6.3131	6.3735
South Korea (Won)	.0008365	.0008326	1195.46	1201.06
Sweden (Krona)	.1339	.1328	7.4683	7.5301
Switzerland (Franc)	.7760	.7706	1.2887	1.2977
1-month forward	.7766	.7712	1.2877	1.2967
3-months forward	.7778	.7723	1.2857	1.2948
6-months forward	.7794	.7739	1.2830	1.2922
Taiwan (Dollar)	.02933	.02933	34.095	34.095
Thailand (Baht)	.02504	.02505	39.936	39.920
Turkey (Lira)	.00000069	.00000069	1449275	1449275
U.K. (Pound)	1.7290	1.7189	.5784	.5818
1-month forward	1.7250	1.7147	.5797	.5832
3-months forward	1.7171	1.7069	.5824	.5859
6-months forward	1.7043	1.6942	.5868	.5902
United Arab (Dirham)	.2723	.2723	3.6724	3.6724
Uruguay (Peso)				
Financial	.03440	.03460	29.070	28.902
Venezuela (Bolivar)	.000626	.000626	1597.44	1597.44
SDR	1.4470	1.4509	.6911	.6892
Euro	1.2077	1.1975	.8280	.8351

Source: The Wall Street Journal, *December 3, 2003, C14.*

exchange rate, the U.S. dollar value of the loan (spot position) is $776,000 (1 million SF × $0.7760). The bank could lock in a rate close to this rate by negotiating a one-month forward rate, currently quoted as $0.7766 for large banks in amounts of $1 million or more.

Instead of negotiating a forward contract to allow the exchange of Swiss francs to U.S. dollars at a known rate thirty days hence, suppose the bank decides to use futures contracts to hedge against the risk of appreciation in the value of the Swiss franc. Because the hedge is undertaken to protect against the appreciation of the Swiss franc (i.e., against decline in the value of the dollar), a long futures position is indicated; i.e., if the dollar falls, the value of the Swiss franc rises, and there will be a rise in the value of the contract to purchase Swiss francs at the lower rate on the long futures contract). Figure 11.7, Panel A shows that on December 2, 2003, the settlement price for a March 2004 futures contract for Swiss francs was 0.7783. Each Swiss franc futures contract has a face value of SF125,000, so eight contracts (1,000,000SF / 125,000SF per contract = 8) will be required to hedge against the entire SF1,000,000 transaction. The value of the futures contract would hence be $778,300 (125,000 × 8 × $0.7783). Table 11.4 presents the details of the hedge.

Suppose for the results of the hedge, as shown in Table 11.4, that the actual spot exchange rate on January 2nd, in 2004 rose to 0.8883 dollars per Swiss franc (or 1.12575 Swiss francs per dollar). The Swiss franc had appreciated relative to the dollar, as the bank managers feared, resulting in a higher dollar cost of the $888,300 loan. Suppose the price of the Swiss franc for the futures contract, also shown in Table 11.4, rose to 0.8893, so the new value of the futures contract is also higher at $889,300 (125,000 × 8 × $0.8893). If the bank management had chosen not to hedge, the institution would have had a higher cost of $112,300 ($888,300 − $776,000) to convert the dollars to Swiss francs. However, the bank receives a gain on the futures contract of $111,000 ($889,300 − $778,300). This results in a net hedging error of ($1,300), because the gain on the futures contract is less than the higher dollar cost

table **11.4**   HEDGING WITH CURRENCY FUTURES CONTRACTS (FORECAST: FALLING DOLLAR)

Currency futures contracts may be used to protect against a decline in the value of the dollar. A long hedge, requiring the purchase of currency futures, results in a gain if the value of the dollar falls against the currency on which the futures contract is written but results in a loss when the value of the dollar strengthens.

I. HEDGING IN DECEMBER

Cash Market	Futures Market
December 2	
Dollars required to purchase 1 million Swiss francs at $0.7760:	Buy 8 March contracts at $0.7783
$776,000	Value of contracts:
	125,000 × 8 × $0.7783 = $778,300
Results in January	
January 2	
Dollars required to purchase 1 million Swiss francs at $0.8883:	Sell 8 September contracts at $0.8893
$888,300	Value of contracts:
	125,000 × 8 × $0.8893 = $889,300

II. NET RESULTS OF HEDGE IN JANUARY

Cash Market Gain		Futures Market Loss	
December "cost"	$776,000	December purchase	$778,300
January cost	−888,300	January sale	889,300
Loss	−112,300	Gain	$111,000
Net Hedging Error: ($1,300)			

Note: This hedge assumes that in January, the Swiss franc rose in the spot market to $0.8883 and the futures contract price for the Swiss franc rose to $0.8893.

Concept Questions

1 Are foreign currency futures quoted as direct rates or indirect rates?

2 If a business is concerned about the value of a currency appreciating relative to the U.S. dollar (i.e., the dollar depreciating), should it take a long or short position in a futures contract for that currency?

3 If a business is concerned about the value of a currency depreciating relative to the U.S. dollar (i.e., the dollar appreciating), should it take a long or short position in a futures contract for that currency?

4 What are the advantages and disadvantages in hedging with foreign currency using a forward contract versus a futures contract?

for the Swiss francs. The firm is still much better off with the hedge. Of course, if the Swiss franc had fallen in value instead, the firm would have been better off not hedging. It is important to remember that in December no one knew whether the Swiss franc would appreciate or depreciate relative to the dollar. This uncertainty is precisely the reason for a hedge.[20]

Exchange Rate Volatility in Recent Years

Hedging has become very important in recent years, with great exchange rate volatility marking the late 1900s and early 2000s. Figure 11.8 shows the volatility in the exchange rate of the Euro to the U.S. dollar from its beginning in 1999 to 2003. At its launch, the Euro had a value of $1.17 to the U.S. dollar, but it fell to below $1 by the end of the year. At the end of 2000, it hit a record low below $0.83 and then began a gradual but bumpy rise and fall, finally rising significantly in 2002 and 2003 to a record high in its first five years of $1.20 on December 1, 2003, as well as another rise in the first two months of 2004 to $1.27 on February 20, 2004. Recall the interest rate parity theory of exchange rates in Chapter 8. Central bank interest rates for the United States were lowered significantly, as shown in Panel A, over the 2001–2003 period in order to stimulate the U.S. economy. Cuts in interest rates in the EU and Britain lagged those of the United States over this time period.

figure **11.8** TRENDS IN CENTRAL BANK INTEREST RATES AND TRENDS IN THE EURO FOR ITS FIRST FIVE YEARS

PANEL A: TRENDS IN CENTRAL BANK INTEREST RATES, 2001 TO 2003

Central Bank interest rates fell dramatically during 2001 to 2003, with frequent lowering by Central Bankers in Britain, the EU, and U.S.

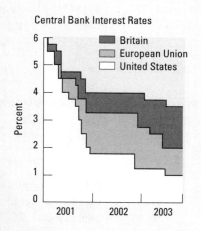

Central Bank Interest Rates

- Britain
- European Union
- United States

Source: New York Times, *December 5, 2003, C4.*

---

20 For more information on currency futures, see Kolb (1988) and Fieleke (1985).

figure **11.8** TRENDS IN CENTRAL BANK INTEREST RATES AND TRENDS IN THE EURO FOR ITS FIRST FIVE YEARS (CONT.)

PANEL B: TRENDS IN STOCK MARKET INDEXES, GOLD FUTURES PRICES, AND THE EURO, 1999 TO 2003

The Euro began with an initial value of $1.17 on January 1, 1999, fell continuously until 2001, and then began rising to a lifetime high of $1.20 on December 1, 2003. The U.S. stock market was also volatile, generally falling during 2001–2002, and rising in 2003. Gold futures prices fell generally before 2001 and then generally rose.

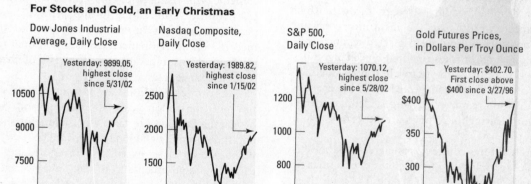

A Day of Market Milestones

For Stocks and Gold, an Early Christmas

Dow Jones Industrial Average, Daily Close — Yesterday: 9899.05, highest close since 5/31/02

Nasdaq Composite, Daily Close — Yesterday: 1989.82, highest close since 1/15/02

S&P 500, Daily Close — Yesterday: 1070.12, highest close since 5/28/02

Gold Futures Prices, in Dollars Per Troy Ounce — Yesterday: $402.70. First close above $400 since 3/27/96

High Point for Euro's Five-Year Ride

Since its launch in January 1999, the Euro at times has absorbed a pummeling vs. the dollar, but it now has recovered to hit record highs in recent days.

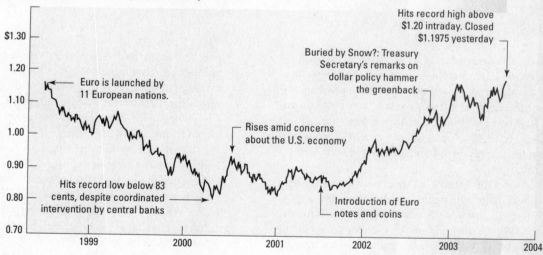

Source: Michael R. Sesit, Tom Holland, and Michael M. Phillips. "As Euro Touches Another Record, Dollar's Weakness May Persist," The Wall Street Journal, December 2, 2003, C1.

Summary

Tools for managing interest rate risk include two types of financial futures: interest rate and foreign currency futures. They allow managers to adopt a hedging strategy, through which expected profits on the institution's existing financial position are protected against unfavorable changes in interest rates or foreign exchange rates. Hedging is a risk-minimization approach; it does not allow an institution to profit from unexpected favorable changes. Futures are traded on organized exchanges, facilitating their liquidity, and the clearinghouse plays an important role in transactions.

An interest rate futures contract is an agreement between a buyer and seller to exchange a fixed quantity of a financial asset at a specified price on a specified date. The buyer has a long futures position and purchases a contract when interest rates are expected to fall. The seller of a futures contract takes a short position in anticipation of rising rates. Because the prices of futures contracts move in the same direction as prices on underlying financial assets, falling interest rates coincide with rising prices for futures contracts, and rising rates coincide with falling futures prices. The hedger uses profits earned on futures transactions to offset losses incurred on other financial assets. Additional markets permit institutions to hedge against the risk of changes in currency exchange rates.

The most compelling reasons to use futures contracts are the low transaction costs of initiating and closing out a hedge, the flexibility to take either a long or short position, and the minimal default risk exposure because of the clearinghouse. Problems faced in futures hedging include the cash flow requirements from daily margin calls, basis risk, and the difficulty of determining the best hedge ratio. Financial institutions must also be careful to follow regulatory and accounting rules governing the use of futures contracts.

Questions

1. Describe the characteristics of an interest rate futures contract. Consult a current issue of *The Wall Street Journal* or another major newspaper to find price quotations on interest rate futures contracts. Are there contracts written on any financial instruments not shown in Table 11.1? How have interest rate futures prices changed for futures on T-bonds compared with December 1, 2003?

2. What features of futures contracts distinguish them from other financial instruments? What are the important differences between forward markets and futures markets? What is the role of the clearinghouse in the futures market? Why do clearinghouses set margin requirements?

3. Explain the difference between using financial futures in a hedging strategy and using futures to speculate. Explain why futures are called derivatives. With the Orange County and Long-Term Capital Hedge Fund crises, derivatives were used to place interest rate bets. How can futures be used to speculate if the consensus is that interest rates are expected to fall? If interest rates are expected to rise?

4. Identify interest rate forecasts or investment situations in which each of the following would be appropriate: (a) short hedge, (b) long hedge, and (c) cross hedge.

5. Find a current article on one or more of the futures exchanges located outside the United States. (Note a good place to look is on the Web using Google or another search engine). What is the rate of growth in trading volume? How do policies and trading mechanisms compare with those in U.S. markets such as the CBOT or CME? How much closer are we to a truly global futures market?

6. What is meant by the term *basis risk*? What types of hedges have the greatest exposure to basis risk?

7. What does the hedge ratio measure? Why is the hedge ratio needed to determine the number of contracts to trade? What factors make it difficult to construct a perfect hedge? What is the difference between a micro and a macro hedge?

8. What types of restrictions have regulators and accountants developed to control the risk exposure of financial institutions participating in futures markets? Why in recent years have regulators asked banks to have an overall risk management strategy for derivatives?

9. If you were charged with managing exchange rate risk for a U.S. commercial bank operating in international markets, in which types of situations might you prefer to enter into a forward contract? Trade foreign currency futures contracts? What different risks would you face with forward contracts versus futures contracts?

10. Consult the financial pages of *The Wall Street Journal* or another major newspaper. Find the price quotations for foreign currency futures contracts. Have any new cur-

rencies been added to those shown in Figure 11.7, Panel A? How has the settle price changed for the Euro since December 1, 2003? Based on the current settlement prices you find, is the value of the dollar higher or lower against foreign currencies than it was on December 1, 2003?

11. Suppose it is your responsibility to manage exchange rate risk for a large German bank with activities in the European Community, the United States, and Asia. How does the development of cross rate futures contracts facilitate the bank's exchange rate risk management?

12. What are some limitations in using futures to hedge a financial institution's overall risk that might explain why the majority of users of futures are very large financial institutions? If a depository institution performs an overall macro hedge for a negative funding gap, would the institution take a long or short position? What would happen to the basis risk of the hedge if rates go down and mortgage customers prepay their mortgages (i.e., if overall volume or mix changes occur that change the institution's funding gap during the hedging period)?

Problems

1. A portfolio manager will trade futures contracts to protect the value of a $150 million portfolio invested in short-term securities. Calculate the number of contracts that should be traded for the following instruments and hedge ratio estimates. Refer to Table 11.1 to determine the face value (minimum amount) for each of the different types of contracts: (a) T-bond contracts, hedge ratio = 0.85; (b) T-bill contracts, hedge ratio = 0.82; and (c) thirty-day Fed Funds futures contracts, hedge ratio = 0.91.

2. A money market portfolio manager needs to hedge against an expected drop in interest rates that could occur before a large inflow of funds is received and invested. The manager plans to buy ten T-bill futures contracts at a price of 97 percent (i.e., 1 less the discount yield). If the contracts are sold three months later at 96.25 percent, what will be the gain or loss on the futures position? What if the contracts are sold at 97.63 percent?

3. The manager of a large savings and loan corporation forecasts an increase in interest rates over the next two months. The thrift currently has $20 million in CDs costing 6 percent. The manager hedges against the expected increase in interest rates by trading twenty T-bill futures contracts (based on a ninety-day T-bill) with a minimum contract value of $1 million.
   a. Should a long or short hedge be used? Why?
   b. Based on the following information, calculate the net gain or loss on the hedge.

	CD Cost	T-Bill Futures Settlement Price
Current	6.0%	$983,750
Futures (2 months later)	7.5%	$979,950

4. The executive vice president of a large bank believes that a forecasted increase in T-bill rates will occur, forcing the bank to pay higher interest on its MMDAs (money market demand accounts). She decides to hedge $20 million of the bank's deposit accounts by trading T-bill futures contracts.

a. Should the executive vice president assume a long or short futures position?
b. If she estimates a hedge ratio of 0.97, how many contracts should she buy or sell?
c. Suppose the T-bill futures contracts are trading at 98.13 percent today but are priced at 98.01 percent one month from today, when the position is closed out. What will be the profit or loss on the futures transactions?
d. Suppose the bank's MMDA costs rise from 2 percent to 8 percent between the beginning and end of the one-month period. What will be the net effect on the monthly interest cost for the institution resulting from the hedge and the change in interest rates?

5. After studying market forecasts, the investment manager of a property/liability insurer anticipates an interest rate decline over the next three months. He expects to receive $100 million in new funds in ninety days, which he will invest in T-bills. In an effort to avoid the adverse effect of the interest rate decline on expected yield, he hedges in the futures market.
   a. Should he assume a short or a long position?
   b. Based on the following information, calculate the resulting gain or loss on the hedge.

	T-Bill Discount Yield	T-Bill Futures Settlement Price
January	9.85%	$979,200
April	8.80%	$982,000

   c. Suppose the manager's interest rate forecast is incorrect and interest rates increase. By April the discount yield on T-bills is 10.50 percent, and the settlement price on the contracts held is 97.75. What is the resulting gain or loss on the hedge?

6. A finance company is planning to issue $50 million in commercial paper in four months. Forecasts of interest rate movements over the intervening period are contradictory, so the firm's manager decides a T-bill futures hedge should be assumed. Fifty T-bill futures contracts

are sold at 98.94. The firm estimates that the rate currently required on its commercial paper is 7 percent. Four months later, when the finance company closes out its futures position, the contracts are trading at 98.80 and the company issues commercial paper at a rate of 8.45 percent. Calculate the net interest cost to the firm on its thirty-day paper and the effective interest rate it is paying on this short-term debt.

7. Metropolitan National Bank regularly extends loans to importer/exporter customers. In March, management agrees to finance a shipment of cameras for an importer who does not have to pay for the merchandise until it arrives in June. The current cost of the cameras in Japanese yen is 200 million yen. The prevailing exchange rate is one yen = $0.008639 and one U.S. dollar = 115.75 yen. The bank's economists anticipate that the value of the dollar will fall over the next three months and recommend a hedge with yen currency futures. Using the following information, calculate the gain or loss on the hedge.

   a. The most recent settlement price on a June yen futures contract was 0.008642, and the standard size of a Japanese yen futures contract is 12.5 million yen. Given the economists' forecasts, what position should management assume in the futures market to hedge its foreign currency risk? How many contracts will be traded?

   b. In June, the bank closes out its position. The spot rate ($/yen) is 0.008333, and June yen futures are trading at 0.008345. Calculate the gain or loss on the hedge. Did the hedge work as expected?

   c. Suppose instead that the June spot rate is 0.008929 $/yen and yen futures trade at 0.008928. Calculate the results of the hedge. Did the bank benefit from the hedge?

8. A German exporter will receive payment in U.S. dollars for a candle shipment made to an American firm. The current spot rate between the Euro and dollars (Euro's value in U.S. dollars) is 1 Euro = $1.20, and the U.S. dollar equivalent rate (value of a dollar in Euros) is 1 U.S. dollar = 0.8333 Euros. The German exporter will receive $5 million in exactly two months (July) that he'll want to convert to Euros to use in his operations. Given the uncertainty about the Euro exchange rate that will prevail in July, the German firm decides to hedge with Euro currency futures.

   a. Anticipating a decline in the value of the dollar (rise in the value of the Euro), will the German firm buy or sell Euro futures? The prevailing price on Euro futures is $1.2077. How many contracts will be traded? Euro futures contracts are written for 125,000 Euro.

   b. In July, the spot rate is 1 Euro = $1.00, and Euro futures trade at a futures price of 1 Euro = $1.05. Calculate the gain or loss on the hedge.

   c. In general, what position should you take on currency futures (short or long) if you have a long position (for instance, have a portfolio of bonds in Euros) in a foreign currency? If you have a short position in a foreign currency (such as you owe someone Euros to pay a bill)? Explain your reasoning.

9. An American importer buys Swiss wine. The wine shipment will arrive in thirty days, at which time payment is due. Currently, the Swiss franc is worth $0.7760, and the 1-month forward rate is $0.7766. If the payment due is SF4 million and the value of the dollar is expected to fall, how could the importer use the forward currency market to hedge? What cost, in U.S. dollars, would the firm be obligated to pay based on the forward contract? What risks is the firm assuming by using the forward market? If the spot rate between dollars and Swiss francs at the time payment is due is 0.8800 $/Swiss franc, would the forward agreement achieve its purpose? Explain.

10. Turn to the duration-based hedging example in Appendix 11A. Suppose that the initial price of the instrument (bond) to be hedged is $955. The expected position of the cash instrument is a yield to maturity of 10.14 percent and a price of $1,008.76 with a duration of 4.148, the same as in Table 11A.1. Suppose that in May 2005, the expected duration of T-bond futures is 10.06 and the expected yield on futures is 8.50 percent. The expected futures price is 96–24. Calculate the number of futures contracts needed as well as the results of the new hedge.

Suggested Case Study: Macro Hedging for a Depository Institution

Esty, Ben, Peter Tufano, and Jonathan Headley. "Banc One Corporation: Asset and Liability Management." *Bank of America Journal of Applied Corporate Finance* 7 (Fall 1994), 33–65. (This is also a Harvard Business Case Study.) This case illustrates problems that large financial institutions have when financial analysts do not understand the nature of complex hedges and interpret them instead as entailing greater versus lower risk for the institution.

Selected References

Abken, Peter A. "Globalization of Stock, Futures, and Options Markets." *Economic Review* (Federal Reserve Bank of Atlanta) 76 (July/August 1991), 1–22.

Booth, James R., Richard L. Smith, and Richard W. Stolz. "Use of Interest Rate Futures by Financial Institutions." *Journal of Bank Research* 14 (Spring 1984), 15–20.

Carter, David A., and Joseph F. Sinkey, Jr. "The Use of Interest Rate Derivatives by End-users: The Case of Large Community Banks." *Journal of Financial Services Research* 14 (July 1998), 17–34.

Chance, Don M. *An Introduction to Options and Futures,* 2nd ed. Hinsdale, IL: The Dryden Press, 1992.

Chaudhry, Mukesh K., and Alan K. Reichert. "Interest Rate Derivatives and Bank Risk." Working Paper, Cleveland State University, 1998.

Chicago Board of Trade. *Treasury Futures for Institutional Investors.* Chicago: Board of Trade of the City of Chicago, 1990.

Chicago Mercantile Exchange. *Trading and Hedging with Currency Futures and Options.* Chicago: Chicago Mercantile Exchange, 1985.

Chorafas, Dimitris N. *The Market Risk Amendment: Understanding the Marking-to-Model and Value at Risk.* New York: McGraw-Hill, 1998.

Drabenstott, Mark, and Anne O'Mara McDonley. "Futures Markets: A Primer for Financial Institutions." *Economic Review* (Federal Reserve Bank of Kansas City) 69 (November 1984), 17–33.

Esty, Ben, Peter Tufano, and Jonathan Headley. "Banc One Corporation: Asset and Liability Management." *Bank of America Journal of Applied Corporate Finance* 7 (Fall 1994), 33–65.

Federal Reserve Bank of New York. *Clearing and Settlement Through the Board of Trade Clearing Corporation.* New York, 1990.

Fieleke, Norman S. "The Rise of the Foreign Currency Futures Markets." *New England Economic Review* (Federal Reserve Bank of Boston) (March/April 1985), 38–47.

Goldstein, Henry S. "Foreign Currency Futures: Some Further Aspects." *Economic Perspectives* (Federal Reserve Bank of Chicago) 7 (November/December 1983), 3–13.

Hansell, Saul. "The Computer That Ate Chicago." *Institutional Investor* 23 (February 1989), 181–188.

Hieronymous, Thomas A. *Economics of Futures Trading.* New York: Commodity Research Bureau, Inc., 1971.

Howard, Charles T., and Louis J. D'Antonio. "Treasury Bill Futures as a Hedging Tool: A Risk-Return Approach." *Journal of Financial Research* 9 (Spring 1986), 25–39.

Hoyt, Robert E. "Use of Financial Futures by Life Insurers." *Journal of Risk and Insurance* 56 (December 1992), 740–748.

Hurtz, Rebecca M., and Mona J. Gardner. "Surviving in a New Environment." *Best's Review (Life/Health Edition)* 85 (September 1984).

Kolb, Robert W. *Understanding Futures Markets.* Glenview, IL: Scott, Foresman and Co., 1988.

Kolb, Robert W., and Raymond Chiang. "Improving Hedging Performance Using Interest Rate Futures." *Financial Management* 10 (Autumn 1981), 72–79.

————. "Duration, Immunization and Hedging with Interest Rate Futures." *Journal of Financial Research* 5 (Summer 1982), 161–170.

Koppenhaver, Gary D. "An Empirical Analysis of Bank Hedging in Futures Markets." *Journal of Futures Markets* 10 (February 1990), 1–12.

————. "Futures Market Regulation." *Economic Perspectives* (Federal Reserve Bank of Chicago) 11 (January/February 1987), 3–15.

————. "Trimming the Hedges: Regulators, Banks and Financial Futures." *Economic Perspectives* (Federal Reserve Bank of Chicago) 8 (November/December 1984), 3–12.

Lamm-Tennant, Joan. "Asset/Liability Management for the Life Insurer: Situation Analysis and Strategy Formulation." *Journal of Risk and Insurance* (September 1989), 501–517.

Maness, Terry S., and John T. Zietlow. *Short-Term Financial Management,* 2nd ed. Mason, OH: South-Western Thomson Learning, 2002.

Miller, Merton H. "Financial Innovation: The Last Twenty Years and the Next." *Journal of Financial and Quantitative Analysis* 21 (December 1986), 459–471.

Morris, Charles S. "Managing Interest Rate Risk with Interest Rate Futures." *Economic Review* (Federal Reserve Bank of Kansas City) 74 (March 1989), 3–20.

Napoli, Janet A. "Derivative Markets and Competitiveness." *Economic Perspectives* (Federal Reserve Bank of Chicago) 16 (July/August 1992), 13–24.

Parkinson, Patrick, and Paul Spindt. "The Use of Interest Rate Futures by Commercial Banks." In *Proceedings of a Conference on Bank Structure and Competition.* Chicago: Federal Reserve Bank of Chicago (1985), 457–489.

Puwalski, Allen C. "Derivative Risk in Commercial Banking." *FDIC Report,* March 24, 2003 (*http://www.fdic.gov*) [Search under Derivatives].

Remolona, Eli M. "The Recent Growth of Financial Derivative Markets." *Quarterly Review* (Federal Reserve Bank of New York) 17 (Winter 1992–1993), 28–43.

Saunders, Anthony. *Financial Institutions Management: A Modern Perspective,* 2nd ed. Burr Ridge, IL: Irwin, 1997.

Scarlata, Jodi G. "Institutionalization Developments in the Globalization of Securities and Futures Markets." *Economic Review* (Federal Reserve Bank of St. Louis) 74 (January/February 1992), 17–30.

Schwartz, Edward D., Joanne M. Hill, and Thomas Schneeweis. *Financial Futures: Fundamentals, Strategies, and Applications.* Homewood, IL: Dow Jones-Irwin, 1986.

Smirlock, Michael C. "Hedging Bank Borrowing Costs with Financial Futures." *Business Review* (Federal Reserve Bank of Philadelphia) (May-June 1986), 13–23.

Van Horne, James. *Financial Market Rates and Flows,* 3rd ed. Englewood Cliffs, NJ: Prentice Hall, 1990.

EXPLORING THE CHICAGO BOARD OF TRADE WEBSITE

Go to *http://www.cbot.com.* You'll find a menu at the top of the screen with tabs to click on for product information, education, and news, among others. Click on the "Products" tab. From the pull-down menu, select Interest Rate. You'll come to a page that lists all the different interest rate futures products that the CBOT offers. Click one of the interest rate products. One side of the screen will provide links for all sorts of information for that product including charts, margin requirements, and other information. Click on "Chart" and a chart will come up showing the yearly, monthly, and daily trends. Look at different charts for different interest rate futures products; explore and see the wealth of information about the product. Also, click on the "Education" tab at the top and note the publications that are offered for different products including

interest rate futures (PDF files can be downloaded, requires Adobe Acrobat Reader; or pamphlets can be ordered). If you click the "News" tab at the top, you'll also find lots of information about new products and what's happening on the exchange. Similarly, the Chicago Mercantile Exchange has an excellent Website with lots of great information at *http://www.cme.com.*

USEFUL WEBSITES

http://www.cbot.com

http://www.cme.com

http://www.eurexus.com

http://www.eurexchange.com

Appendix 11A

A Duration-Based Futures Hedge

In a cross hedge, Equation 11.4, used for calculating the appropriate number of futures contracts to trade, could suggest an inappropriate number of contracts because of the unequal price reactions in instruments with different coupons and maturities, even if yields are perfectly correlated. Including the duration of the cash and futures instruments provides a better estimate of the required number of contracts:

$$N_{DUR} = \frac{R_F P_C D_C}{R_C FP_F D_F} \qquad [11A.1]$$

where

N_{DUR} = the number of contracts to be traded for each cash market instrument being hedged,

R_F = 1 + the rate expected to prevail on the instrument underlying the futures contract,

R_C = 1 + the expected yield to maturity on the asset to be hedged,

F_{PF} = the price agreed on in the futures contract,

P_C = the expected spot price of the asset to be hedged as of the hedge termination date,

D_C = the expected duration of the asset to be hedged as of the termination date, and

D_F = the expected duration of the instrument underlying the futures contract as of the termination date.

This approach to estimating N_{DUR} was developed in Kolb and Chiang (1981, 1982). For additional discussion, see Chance (1992).

The duration-based equation adjusts the size of the futures position for potential differences in the maturity and coupon rates of the cash and futures securities. For example, consider the decision facing a bond portfolio manager in February 2005, when he anticipates an $8 million cash inflow in May 2005 and forecasts a decline in corporate bond yields over the intervening period. The manager is watching a bond issue that matures in 2005; he expects the yield on these bonds to be 10.14 percent in May, down from the February level of 11.14 percent. At that yield, their duration in May would be 4.148 years. If funds were available in February, 8,231 bonds ($8 million / $971.83 per bond) could be purchased at the current market price. By May, however, the price is expected to have risen to $1,008.76, and $8 million will buy only 7,930 bonds.

Table 11A.1 shows the calculation of a duration-based hedge position to fit this situation. Because there are no futures contracts on corporate bonds, a cross hedge is required. T-bond futures are a reasonable choice. However, because they are standardized at an 8 percent coupon (for this particular example, assuming interest rates on bonds were higher than in 2003) with at least fifteen-year maturities, the duration of the cash and futures securities will differ. Constructing a hedge by simply comparing the market values of the cash and futures instruments would lead to a less than optimal hedge. The appropriate long position for this hedge is to buy forty-one T-bond contracts, which can later be sold at a profit if rates fall.

Table 11A.2 shows the results of a long hedge with forty-one T-bond contracts. Assuming the manager's expectations are perfectly fulfilled, the net gain on the hedge is $13,779, more than offsetting the opportunity loss from the decline in market yields during the period in which investment must be delayed. Nothing guarantees a perfect hedge, but performance is improved if the coupon and maturity of the instrument to be hedged are matched closely to the security underlying the futures contract. As with any duration measure, the hedge protects against only one interest rate movement, so it must be adjusted frequently as market conditions change.

table **11A.1** DURATION-BASED ESTIMATION OF THE FUTURES POSITION

Expected Cash Inflow (May 2005)	$8,000,000
Cash Instrument to be Hedged	Corporate bonds: 10 3/8 of 05
	Current YTM (February 2005): 11.14%
	Current price: $971.83
Number of Bonds if Purchased at Current Price	8,231
Expected Position of Cash Instrument in May 2005	Expected YTM: 10.14% ($R_C = 1 + 0.1014$)
	Expected market price: $1,008.76 ($P_C$)
	Duration at expected YTM: 4,148 (D_C)
February 2005 Price on T-Bond Futures (10.12% Yield)	83–24 = 83.75% of par = $83,750 ($FP_F$)
Expected Position of T-Bond Futures in May 2005	Price: 91–16 = 91.5% of par = $91,500
	Yield: 9.12% ($R_F = 1 + 0.0912$)
	Duration: 9.871 (D_F)

Duration-Based Number of Contracts

$$N_{DUR} = \frac{R_F\,P_C\,D_C}{R_C\,FP_F\,D_F} \qquad [11A.1]$$

$$N_{DUR} = \frac{(1.0912)\,(\$1{,}008.76)\,(4.148)}{(1.014)\,(\$83{,}750)\,(9.871)} = 0.005015 \text{ per cash instrument}$$

Total Number of Contracts = $0.005015(8{,}231) = 41.28 = 41$ contracts

---

table **11A.2** RESULTS OF THE DURATION-BASED HEDGE

I.

Cash Market	Futures Market
February	
Corporate bond yield: 11.14%	Buy 41 T-bond contracts for September delivery
Price: $971.83	at 83–24
Total available if purchased in February 2005:	Yield: 10.12%
8,231 bonds	Cost: $3,433,750
May	
Funds received and invested: $8,000,000	Sell 41 September T-bond contracts at 91–16
Corporate bond yield: 10.14%	Yield: 9.12%
Price: $1,008.76	Price: $3,751,500
Total purchase: 7,930 bonds	

II.

Cash Market Loss		Futures Market Gain	
February cost (8,231 bonds)	$7,999,133	May sale	$3,751,500
May cost (8,231 bonds)	−8,303,104	February purchase	−3,433,750
Loss	($303,971)	Gain	$317,750
	Net Gain: $13,779		

Interest Rate Risk Management

Index Futures, Options, Swaps, and Other Derivatives

12

"In financial markets, risk is neither created nor destroyed. It is simply repackaged—shifted from one form to another so as to change the profile of an instrument's risk and return."

Steven Bloom, Member, New Products Team, American Stock Exchange (1992)

"Bank regulators clearly recognize the power of derivatives to manage risk. Yet, they also understand the risks associated with using derivatives must likewise be managed carefully and proactively. Thus, any management team that considers using derivatives to manage the bank's risk, improve performance, and/or serve customers must convincingly demonstrate its competence to do so."

Dominic Casserley and Greg Wilson, McKinsey & Company, Washington, DC. "Managing Derivatives-Related Regulatory Risk." Bank Management 70 (June/August, 1994), 27–32.

I n the early 1990s, members of the financial press anointed a small group of securities experts as Wall Street "Rocket Scientists" or "Financial Engineers." These experts—most of whom work for securities exchanges or securities firms—are a new breed of inventors who study financial markets, sources of risk, and the needs of market participants. These "scientists" then devote their creative energy to developing financial instruments capable of satisfying these needs.

For the most part, the rocket scientists are working with **derivatives**, the name given to instruments whose value is derived from prices and price fluctuations in some underlying asset. Financial futures contracts on Treasury bills (T-bills) and bonds (T-bonds), introduced in Chapter 11, are just one category of derivative securities; futures contracts and options are now available on many other instruments. As the financial engineers continue their inventive work into the 2000s, new derivatives are introduced almost daily.

What continues to drive these innovations? The most important factor is risk. Uncertainty about interest rates, exchange rates, price fluctuations in stock and bond markets around the world, even air pollution—all are categories of risk that market participants want to escape. The financial engineers

are constantly searching for a better means of allowing them to do so. This chapter continues the discussion of hedging techniques begun in Chapter 11 by introducing a variety of new derivative instruments and compares and contrasts several strategies used for managing risk by financial institutions.[1]

Learning Objectives

After completing this chapter, you will be able to:

1 Understand stock indexes and stock index futures and their particular characteristics.

2 Understand when a short and when a long hedge should be used by a stock portfolio manager with stock index futures.

3 Calculate the appropriate number of contracts for a stock portfolio hedge and the risks involved.

4 Understand program trading and how it has been used.

5 Understand how call and put options are used and priced.

6 Explain the advantages and disadvantages of using options versus options on futures for hedging.

7 Understand other types of interest rate derivatives including swaps, swaptions, caps, collars, and floors and credit derivatives, and how they are used for hedging.

Stock Index Futures

Like interest rate and currency futures, **stock index futures** are instruments for hedging exposure to changes in market values, specifically exposure to the change of values in equity portfolios. Participants in the stock index futures markets include commercial bank trust departments, insurance companies, pension funds, equity mutual funds, and securities firms. In contrast to the contracts discussed in Chapter 11, stock index futures do not protect against changes in interest rates, but instead their value is pegged to movements in one of several aggregate measures of stock market performance. Their origins in the wild and woolly commodities markets, coupled with their appeal to conservative financial institutions, led to an early nickname of "pin-striped pork bellies."[2]

As of 1993, futures contracts were traded regularly on groups of domestic stocks such as the Standard & Poor's (S&P) 500, the New York Stock Exchange (NYSE) Index, the Value Line Composite Index, the Mini Value Line Index, and the Major Market Index (MMI) of twenty large firms. Each of these were designed to emulate the Dow Jones Industrial Average (DJIA). In 2003, an even greater variety of index futures contracts were traded including the Dow Jones Industrial Average and Mini DJ Industrial Average by the Chicago Board of Trade (CBOT), the S&P 500 Index, Mini S&P Index, S&P MidCap 400, Nasdaq 100, Mini Nasdaq 100, and Russell 2000 Indexes by the Chicago Mercantile

---

1 Donald Katz. "Wall Street Rocket Scientists." *Worth* (February/March, 1992), 68–74; "Derivatives Sprout Bells and Whistles." *Euromoney* (August 1992), 29–39.

2 Kathleen Kerwin. "Pin-Striped Pork Bellies: Why Stock Index Futures Are Red Hot." *Barron's* 14 (February 14, 1983), 32–34.

Exchange (CME) among others. Tracking the performance of non-U.S. equities have also been introduced by the CME—most notably the Nikkei 225 Stock Average. In 2003, the *Wall Street Journal* and *New York Times* listed prices for eighteen different types of stock index futures. Other international exchanges offer stock index futures including those on the DAX (index of German stocks), FTSE (index of United Kingdom stocks), Nikkei (index of Japanese stocks), Hang Seng (index of Korean stocks), Swiss SMI (index of Switzerland stocks), and Aussie (index of Australian stocks), among others.

As is true of interest rate futures, developments in the stock index futures market are rapid. New contracts come into the market and old ones leave relatively often, and the array of available contracts is likely to change with time. An example is the development in 1998 by the Kansas City Board of Trade of futures and options contracts on the ISDEX, an index of fifty stocks that receive their revenues from the Internet. International futures exchanges also have initiated stock index futures in another currency, such as Eurex's offering of Dow Jones Euro STOXX 50 Futures. New stock index futures are constantly being created as well. For instance, in 2003, the Taiwan Futures Exchange (TAIFEX) planned to diversify its product line by launching TSEC Taiwan 50 Stock Index Futures. In addition to futures on more diversified stock indexes, such as the S&P 500, there are also stock index futures based on industry-specific sector indexes within the S&P 500 Index. SPCTR Futures offered by the Chicago Mercantile Exchange (CME), for example, are futures on particular industry sectors within the S&P 500, including Financial SPCTR Futures, the financial sector; and Technology SPCTR Futures, the technology sector (see *http://www.cme.com*).

Theoretical Basis of Stock Index Futures

Stock index futures are based on capital market theory as reflected in the capital asset pricing model (CAPM) and the **efficient markets hypothesis (EMH)**. CAPM models the price of an individual asset or portfolio as a function of its beta coefficient, which, in turn, is a function of the covariance between the asset's expected returns and the expected returns on the market portfolio. The market portfolio, with a beta of 1, is a fully diversified combination of assets that represents the standard of comparison for all others. EMH argues that given the wide availability of information to market participants and the speed with which prices react to it, investors with well-diversified portfolios cannot consistently earn returns higher than those on the market portfolio. Investors who choose portfolios with more or less risk than the market portfolio, as measured by beta, should expect to earn a return commensurate with the risk of the portfolio they choose. The EMH hypotheses has been challenged in recent years with cases of fraud, accounting misrepresentation, and insider trading, yet diversification remains an important principle for reducing an investor's risk, particularly in light of scandals for individual stocks, such as Enron, and downturns for particular industry sectors, such as the technology sector in the early twenty-first century.

Although not perfect, some stock indexes are used as surrogates for the stock market as a whole; the portfolio of stocks underlying such an index is assumed to have a beta of 1. The performance of many professional portfolio managers is evaluated through comparison to a market index, and those who earn lower returns are soundly criticized. Other indexes may reflect a segment of the market. For example, the Chicago Mercantile Exchange (CME) introduced the S&P MidCap 400 Index in 1992, tracking the performance of a portfolio of firms with market values between $300 million and $5 billion. Smaller investors, who may be prevented by brokerage fees, commissions, or funds limitations from holding a well-diversified portfolio, often use "the market" or a market segment as a standard of comparison for interpreting their own results, or may compare the results of their shares in a diversified mutual fund to the performance of a market index. Later examples indicate why using a stock index as a benchmark of performance is useful to managers hedging equity portfolios.

History and Characteristics of Stock Index Futures

The first stock index futures contract, based on the Value Line Composite Index, was traded on the Kansas City Board of Trade in February 1982. Within three months, an S&P 500 contract was trading at the CME, and a NYSE contract was trading on the New York Futures Exchange. The indexes are similar in that they are composite measures of the prices of several stocks, but there are also important differences. Table 12.1 compares the composition and calculation of several indexes, including some

t a b l e **12.1** COMPOSITION OF SELECTED STOCK MARKET INDEXES

Some popular futures contracts and options are based on commonly watched indicators of general stock market activity. A wide variety of market indexes is regularly published in the financial pages. Each index is based on a different group of securities. There are many ways of calculating index values.

Index	Composition
S&P 500 Index	Measures value of 500 representative stocks listed on national and regional exchanges. The index is a weighted average; the weights reflect the total market value of all outstanding shares.
NYSE Composite Index	Measures the value of all common stocks listed on the NYSE (more than 1,500 stocks). The index is a weighted average; the weights reflect the total market value of all outstanding shares.
Value Line Composite Index	Measures the value of most stocks listed on the NYSE and some traded on other regional exchanges or the over-the-counter markets. The index is a geometric average; all values are equally weighted.
Dow Jones Industrial Average	Measures the value of 30 blue-chip industrial stocks. The index is a simple average; all prices are equally weighted, with the divisor adjusted for stock splits and stock dividends.
Major Market Index (MMI)	Measures the price of 20 blue-chip stocks traded on the NYSE, 17 of which are in the DJIA. The index is a simple average.
AMEX Market Value Index	Measures value of all stocks traded on the American Stock Exchange (approximately 850).
S&P 100 Index	Measures value of 100 stocks selected from and designed to mirror the S&P 500. The index is value-weighted.
Wilshire Index	Measures the value of all NYSE and AMEX stocks plus the most actively traded over-the-counter stocks. The index is a weighted average; the weights reflect the total market value of all outstanding shares.
Nasdaq 100 Index	Measures the value of the 100 largest nonfinancial firms traded over the counter.
S&P MidCap 400 Index	Measures value of 400 stocks—none of which is included in the S&P 500—with firm market values between $300 million and $5 billion. The index includes firms in four main industrial groups. The index is a weighted average like the S&P 500 but is quoted as a percentage of its base value on December 31, 1990.
Nikkei 225 Index	Measures the value of 225 large publicly traded Japanese firms. Historically the index was price-weighted, but it was recently revised to reflect market value weights.
Dow Jones World Stock Index	Measures value of 2,200 stocks traded in 10 countries. The index is calculated in four major currencies: dollar, mark, pound, and yen. It is value-weighted and quoted as a percentage of its base value on December 31, 1991.

developed expressly for use in the index futures and options markets. Because the indexes are not identical, they do not behave identically, although their movements are similar. For example, during the period 1987 through 1991, the MMI had a 0.99 correlation with the DJIA.[3]

Impossibility of Delivery

In comparison with almost all other futures contracts, stock index futures have a distinguishing characteristic: It is not possible to make or take physical delivery of an index, so cash settlements are made. If closure does not occur before the delivery month, the contract's settlement level is the same as the level of the index on a given date for contracts in March, June, September, or December, the four months during the year when index futures contracts expire. As with other futures contracts, a trader's account is marked to market daily and cash settlement is required. Final settlement days are given for each contract and posted on the exchange Website. For instance, the final settlement day for the CBOT DJIA futures contract is defined as the third Friday of the contract month; or if the DJIA is not published for that day, the first preceding business day for which the DJIA is scheduled to be published.

Value of a Contract

The value of a stock index contract is calculated as the level of the index multiplied by an established amount, which varies by index. For instance, the CBOT Dow Jones Industrial Average Index's unit of trading is $10 times the DJIA, a price-weighted composite index of thirty stocks. The dollar multiplier for each index is given in daily price quotations in major newspapers. For example, Figure 12.1, Panel A shows data for index futures for December 3, 2003, and December 15, 2003, from *The Wall Street Jour-*

---

3 Chicago Board of Trade. *MMI Futures and Options* (1991).

figure   **12.1**   STOCK INDEX FUTURES AND STOCK MARKET INDEXES

PANEL A: INDEX FUTURES PRICES

Aiming High
The Nasdaq Composite Index made a brief visit above the 2000 milestone yesterday, for the first time since Jan. 15, 2002, while the Dow Jones Industrial Average spent much of the day above 9900–the last step before a possible return to the 10000 mark. But both indexes fell short of their milestone goals.

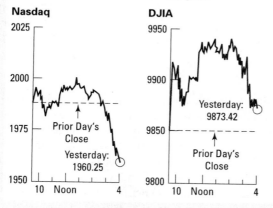

Nasdaq / **DJIA**

December 3, 2003

	Open	High	Low	Settle	Chg	Lifetime High	Low	Open Int

Index Futures

DJ Industrial Average (CBT)-$10 x index
Dec   9851   9940   9865   9870   15   11490   7675   34,747
Mr04   9855   9970   9845   9845   16   9910   8580   3,506
Est vol 6,808; vol Tue 7,866; open int 38,256, –442.
Idx prl: Hi 9942.01; Lo 9851.42; Close 9873.42, +19.78.

Mini DJ Industrial Average (CBT)-$5 x Index
Dec   9854   9939   9845   9870   15   9939   8442   41,269
Vol Wed 39,464; open int 47,563, –1,065.

DJ-AIG Commodity Index (CBT)-$100 x index
Dec   424.0   423.4   424.5   3.0   424.0   389.5   3,349
Est vol 430; vol Tue 424; open int 3,573, –200.
Idx prl: Hi 132.208; Lo 130.585; Close 132.102, +.958.

S&P 500 Index (CME)-$250 x index
Dec   106650   107400   106430   106510   –180   122650   77400   520,267
Mr04   106900   107220   106300   106380   –170   123950   77700   81,591
Est vol 98,495; vol Tue 58,084; open int 606,717, +941.
Idx prl: Hi 1074.30; Lo 1064.63; Close 1064.73, –1.89.

Mini S&P 500 (CME)-$50 x index
Dec   106650   107425   106425   106500   –200   107425   95700   526,070
Vol Wed 574,538; open int 542,506, +23,346.

S&P Midcap 400 (CME)-$500 x index
Dec   577.00   577.50   568.25   568.40   –6.60   577.50   386.45   16,417
Est vol 2,683; vol Tue 874; open int 16,418, +83.
Idx prl: Hi 577.34; Lo 568.79; Close 569.25, –5.46.

Nasdaq 100 (CME)-$100 x index
Dec   143500   145300   141750   141800   –1750   145800   102950   76,847
Est vol 13,956; vol Tue 12,086; open int 80,154, +492.
Idx prl: Hi 1452.03; Lo 1419.77; Close 1419.77, –12.12.

Mini Nasdaq 100 (CME)-$20 x index
Dec   1434.5   1453.0   1417.5   1418.0   –17.5   1458.5   1183.5   252,432
Vol Wed 217,073; open int 254.708, +8,839.

GSCI (CME)-$250 x nearby index
Dec   252.50   255.50   250.50   255.50   2.40   257.00   222.00   12,572
Est Vol 145; vol Tue 130; open int 13,093, +18.
Idx prl: Hi 255.00; Lo 250.89; Close 254.98, +2.45.

TRAKRS Long-Short Tech (CME)-$1 x index
JI05   41.15   41.15   40.01   40.01   –.82   41.41   19.76   432,049
Est vol 625; vol Tue 240; open int 432,049, +240.
Idx prl: Hi 40.03; Lo 38.56; Close 38.62, –.95.

Russell 2000 (CME)-$500 x index
Dec   556.25   557.25   543.50   543.50   –10.15   557.50   347.25   21,582
Est vol 3,599; vol Tue 2,150; open int 21,918, +95.
Idx prl: Hi 556.74; Lo 545.05; Close 545.19, –8.41.

December 15, 2003

	Open	High	Low	Settle	Chg	Lifetime High	Low	Open Int

Index Futures

DJ Industrial Average (CBT)-$10 x index
Dec   10160   10190   10015   10025   –10   11490   7675   26,734
Mr04   10157   10166   9992   10000   –10   10166   8580   17,813
Est vol 19,286; vol Fri 14,199; open int 44,554, +1,149.
Idx prl: Hi 10139.63; Lo 10021.64; Close 10022.82, –19.34.

Mini DJ Industrial Average (CBT)-$5 x index
Dec   10160   10190   10018   10026   –9   10190   8442   44,415
Vol Mon 66,862; open int 64,063, +3,486.

DJ-AIG Commodity Index (CBT)-$100 x index
Dec   —   —   437.2   –2.1   433.0   389.5   30
Est vol 6; vol Fri 200; open int 2,528, unch.
Idx prl: Hi 136.328; Lo 134.740; Close 136.328, –.298.

S&P 500 Index (CME)-$250 x index
Dec   108450   108520   106750   106880   –510   122650   77400   239,452
Mr04   108690   108890   106650   106740   –520   123950   77700   428,894
Est vol 242,418; vol Fri 240,565; open int 679,595, –302.
Idx prl: Hi 1082.79; Lo 1068.00; Close 1068.04, –6.10.

Mini S&P 500 (CME)-$50 x index
Dec   108725   109025   106775   106875   –525   109025   95700   470,663
Vol Mon 578,239; open int 690,998, +18,861.

S&P Midcap 400 (CME)-$500 x index
Dec   571.50   571.50   558.25   557.55   –7.80   577.50   386.45   8,755
Est vol 7,008; vol Fri 5,363; open int 19,374, +556.
Idx prl: Hi 570.58; Lo 558.43; Close 558.47, –7.37

Nasdaq 100 (CME)-$100 x index
Dec   144500   144500   139400   139950   –2000   145800   102950   66,219
Mr04   —   —   140250   –2000   144800   —   45,993
Est vol 43,948; vol Fri 40,871; open int 112,259, +6,338.
Idx prl: Hi 1442.65; Lo 1396.82; Close 1396.82, –20.45.

Mini Nasdaq 100 (CME)-$20 x index
Dec   1446.5   1452.5   1393.0   1399.5   –20.0   1458.5   1183.5   249,650
Vol Mon 281,188; open int 342,762, –1,711.

GSCI (CME)-$250 x nearby index
Dec   264.30   267.50   262.70   na   na   268.60   222.00   490
Ja04   262.50   268.75   262.50   268.30   —   268.50   235.70   13,522
Est vol 72; vol Fri 295; open int 14,016, +89.
Idx prl: Hi 267.74; Lo 263.10; Close 267.57, –1.04.

TRAKRS Long-Short Tech (CME)-$1 x index
JI05   —   —   37.78   –.62   41.41   19.76   431,334
Est vol 0; vol Fri 895; open int 431,334, unch. Idx prl: Hi 38.40; Lo 36.46;
Close 36.52, –.82.

Russell 2000 (CME)-$500 x index
Dec   555.00   555.00   533.50   533.90   –12.95   557.50   347.25   12,463
Mr04   —   —   533.65   –12.95   555.25   —   14,713
Est vol 8,728; vol Fri 9,316; open int 27,176, +1,487.
Idx prl: Hi 553.38; Lo 535.25; Close 535.25, –12.34.

Sources: The Wall Street Journal, *December 4, 2003, C1, C14; and December 16, 2003, C14.*

PANEL B: STOCK MARKET INDEXES (SPOT MARKET)

December 3, 2003

STOCK MARKET INDEXES

	High	Low	Close	Chg	% Chg	52 Wk % Chg	YTD % Chg
DOW JONES							
Industrials	9974.53	9824.23	9873.42	+ 19.78	+ 0.20	+ 13.00	+ 18.36
Transportation	2980.30	2919.70	2939.51	+ 3.15	+ 0.11	+ 25.33	+ 27.25
Utilities	254.77	250.93	252.16	– 0.73	– 0.29	+ 26.69	+ 17.19
Composite	2892.89	2845.07	2860.67	+ 2.51	+ 0.09	+ 18.29	+ 20.45
STANDARD & POOR'S							
100 Stocks	529.03	524.36	524.42	– 0.29	– 0.06	+ 12.05	+ 17.91
500 Stocks	1074.30	1064.63	1064.73	– 1.89	– 0.18	16.04	+ 21.02
Mid-Cap 400	577.34	568.79	569.25	– 5.46	– 0.95	+ 29.10	+ 32.45
Small-Cap 600	270.62	265.29	265.29	– 3.94	– 1.46	+ 31.23	+ 34.93
NEW YORK STOCK EXCHANGE							
Composite	6181.12	6139.50	6142.78	+ 3.16	+ 0.05	+ 19.15	+ 22.86
Industrial	708.77	703.45	703.59	– 0.78	– 0.11	+ 16.44	+ 20.49
Transportation	504.73	500.30	500.55	+ 0.03	+ 0.01	+ 23.66	+ 26.46
Utility	252.36	250.86	250.91	– 1.04	– 0.41	+ 8.06	+ 7.65
Finance	636.48	632.34	632.42	– 1.55	– 0.24	+ 19.96	+ 28.89
NASDAQ							
Nasdaq 100	1452.03	1419.77	1419.77	– 12.12	– 0.85	+ 32.75	+ 44.23
Composite	2000.92	1960.13	1960.25	– 19.82	– 1.00	+ 37.05	+ 46.78
Industrials	1619.57	1581.45	1581.74	– 26.31	– 1.64	+ 45.37	+ 53.61
Banks	2901.27	2864.02	2864.97	– 27.79	– 0.96	+ 27.99	+ 28.40
Insurance	2757.77	2728.33	2730.02	– 17.76	– 0.65	+ 16.33	+ 18.39
Other Finance	3234.46	3197.31	3205.80	– 4.14	– 0.13	+ 63.03	+ 65.40
Telecommunications	175.61	171.81	171.81	– 1.55	– 0.89	+ 48.69	+ 57.93
Computer	939.00	918.07	918.16	– 6.06	– 0.66	+ 32.77	+ 47.47

December 3, 2003

STOCK MARKET INDEXES

	High	Low	Close	Chg	% Chg	52 Wk % Chg	YTD % Chg
DOW JONES							
Industrials	10181.34	9994.38	10022.82	– 19.34	– 0.19	+ 16.17	+ 20.15
Transportation	3028.00	2942.41	2950.77	– 32.64	– 1.09	+ 25.09	+ 27.74
Utilities	256.94	253.25	254.34	+ 0.09	+ 0.04	+ 20.33	+ 18.20
Composite	2942.76	2882.87	2891.81	– 11.54	– 0.40	+ 19.15	+ 21.76
STANDARD & POOR'S							
100 Stocks	536.53	530.42	530.47	– 1.31	– 0.25	+ 14.51	+ 19.27
500 Stocks	1082.79	1068.00	1068.04	– 6.10	– 0.57	+ 17.32	+ 21.39
Mid-Cap 400	570.58	558.43	558.47	– 7.37	– 1.30	+ 27.05	+ 29.94
Small-Cap 600	269.05	261.41	261.41	– 4.98	– 1.87	+ 29.19	+ 32.95
NEW YORK STOCK EXCHANGE							
Composite	6240.26	6171.85	6172.02	– 24.27	– 0.39	+ 20.12	+ 23.44
Industrial	715.86	707.22	707.23	– 3.83	– 0.54	+ 17.86	+ 21.11
Transportation	516.41	509.76	509.80	– 1.28	– 0.25	+ 25.37	+ 28.80
Utility	256.76	254.77	254.83	– 0.06	– 0.02	+ 7.91	+ 9.33
Finance	638.32	630.41	630.42	– 3.80	– 0.60	+ 19.62	+ 23.50
NASDAQ							
Nasdaq 100	1442.65	1396.82	1396.82	– 20.45	– 1.44	+ 34.00	+ 41.90
Composite	1979.78	1918.26	1918.26	– 30.74	– 1.58	+ 36.99	+ 43.63
Industrials	1588.96	1531.96	1531.96	– 30.88	– 1.98	+ 43.15	+ 48.78
Banks	2897.17	2834.66	2835.12	– 48.51	– 1.68	+ 25.30	+ 27.06
Insurance	2753.05	2702.31	2702.85	– 33.31	– 1.22	+ 15.31	+ 17.21
Other Finance	3248.19	3148.33	3148.37	– 57.12	– 1.78	+ 60.35	+ 62.47
Telecommunications	176.34	170.73	170.81	– 2.67	– 1.54	+ 48.80	+ 57.01
Computer	927.76	896.86	897.34	– 13.39	– 1.47	+ 35.26	+ 44.13

Sources: New York Times, *December 4, 2003, C12; and December 16, 2003, C13.*

nal. Panel B shows the actual (spot market) indexes for some of these stock market indexes. On December 3, 2003, the Dow Jones Industrial Average closed at 9873.42, as shown in Panel B. For the same day, the CBOT posted a settle price of 9870 for a December futures contract and a 9845 settle price for a March 2004 contract, suggesting expectation of a future fall in the DJIA. The multiplier for the DJIA futures contract is $10 × the Index, so the settlement price for the December contract is 9870 × $10, which equals $98,700. Note that each type of futures contract has its own multiplier. For instance, the futures contract offered by the CME for the S&P 500 Index has a multiplier of $250 × the Index, while the CME's Mini S&P 500 contract has a multiplier of $50 × the Index. Also, note that the spot stock market indexes, as shown in Panel B, must be used as reference points, with the proper decimal places inserted. For instance, for the S&P 500 December futures contract, the settle price is given in Panel A as 106510, which is based on the spot close index for the S&P 500 of 1064.73, as shown in Panel B. This actually implies a settle price of 1065.10 for the futures contract, with the proper decimal point inserted.

Limits on Price Movements

Until after the stock market crash of 1987, stock index futures contracts had no limits on daily price movements. Since the crash, however, most index futures contracts have been subject to daily trading limits. Each exchange has handled the limits somewhat differently. The limits on S&P 500 futures contracts, for example, are pegged to price movements on the underlying stocks. In contrast, daily limits on other indexes at times are based in part on movements away from the previous day's contract settlement price and in part on movements in the DJIA. Limits on other stock index futures contracts are different still. Like other futures contracts, there are also margin requirements. For instance, in 2003, the CBOT required an initial margin of $5,000 and maintenance margin of $4,000 for the futures contract on the DJIA. Margin requirements and limits are posted for each contract on the CME and CBOT Websites *(http://www.cme.com; http://www.cbot.com).*

Besides overall price movement limits, most contracts also require minimum price movements from trade to trade. In general, the limit is 5 percent. For example, the minimum movement on the CME's regular S&P 500 Index contract traded on Globex was listed as 5 percent, or $50, in 2003. Futures and options also have related trading halts. The trading halts are coordinated with trading halts on the NYSE, often referred to as circuit breakers. As noted on the Chicago Board of Trade Website, successive NYSE trading halts are triggered when intraday declines of the DJIA from its previous closing value fall by 10 percent, 20 percent, and 30 percent. Specifically, circuit-breaker threshold levels are calculated at the end of every quarter as 10 percent, 20 percent, and 30 percent of the average daily closing value of the DJIA for the preceding calendar month, with new circuit-breaker levels announced on the first day of January, April, July, and October. The CBOT Dow Jones futures price limits are set equal to the NYSE quarterly circuit-breaker thresholds for both contracts traded in open outcry and on the CBOT electronic trading system.[4]

Greater Price Volatility

Observers of stock index futures have identified another distinguishing characteristic. The price volatility of each index futures contract, measured by the standard deviation of daily percentage price changes, is greater than the volatility of the underlying index. Such a relationship suggests that basis risk exposure can be significant for institutions using index futures to hedge their equity portfolios.[5] These early findings, however, have not dampened investor interest in these markets.

Financial Institutions and Stock Index Futures

Because of regulatory restrictions and unfamiliarity with index futures, institutions at first engaged in only limited trading. As risk management strategies used by financial institutions have become increasingly sophisticated, their involvement in the index futures markets has accelerated.

---

4 Chicago Board of Trade. *MMI Futures and Options* (1991) and *CBOT and CME Websites,* 2003.

5 See Hill, Jain, and Ward (1987), 10–11.

1 What is a stock index futures contract, and how is its value calculated?

2 Why do the exchanges place limits on price movements and require margin requirements for stock index futures?

3 Why do you think stock index futures prices are more volatile than underlying stock indexes?

4 Name a few different types of stock indexes, the underlying instruments behind them, and their multipliers. Why do you think there are so many different types? Give an example of a mini stock index contract.

Hedging against a Decline in the Market (A Short Hedge)

A direct use of stock index futures is as a hedge for an equity portfolio, designed to protect against swings in the market that could reduce returns. The most obvious need for a hedge occurs when a market downturn is anticipated. The manager of a large equity position naturally wants to avoid a substantial decline in portfolio value if a **bear market** is forecast—one in which prices in general are expected to fall.

One way to avoid losses is to sell large portions of the portfolio before the decline, but transactions costs could be considerable. Another drawback is the time required to choose the stocks to be sold. As an alternative, the manager could hedge against market price declines with a short hedge by selling stock index futures. If the market indexes do indeed fall, so will the value of the contracts, resulting in a profit on the futures contracts when the position is closed out and offsetting losses in the stock portfolio. Of course, if the stock index rises instead, there will be a loss on the short futures contracts (with the contracted selling price on the futures contract now below the new futures contract buying price). However, there will be a corresponding gain on the stock portfolio to offset this loss. Hence, the portfolio manager would have an opportunity loss, but at the same time, his portfolio will maintain a stable value regardless whether stock prices go up or down if the hedge is done correctly and there is no basis risk (futures contract and stock index prices move together).

Importance of the Number of Contracts

A main determinant of the effectiveness of the hedge, as in any other futures position, is the number of futures contracts used. Besides the size of the portfolio, the number of contracts is affected by the volatility of returns on the portfolio relative to the market indexes on which futures contracts are available. Beta is a relative measure of volatility. Because the portfolio of stocks underlying a market index is assumed to have a beta of 1, if the portfolio to be hedged has a beta greater or less than 1, changes in the value of the hedged portfolio will be more or less than changes in the index underlying the futures contract. Thus, the number of contracts must be adjusted to structure an effective hedge.

The Number of Contracts When Portfolio Beta Is 1

Suppose that a pension fund manager holds a stock portfolio of $500 million on December 4 and that, as shown on Figure 12.1, Panel B, the DJIA Index is at 9873.42. The equity market had been on an upswing, but some analysts predict a downturn in December. Thus, the pension fund manager is concerned about a fall in the value of the pension fund's stock portfolio. Rather than liquidating portions of the portfolio, the manager chooses to take a short position, that is, sell DJIA stock index futures. As noted in Panel A of Figure 12.1, the settle price for the DJIA Index December futures contract for the previous day is 9870, with a multiplier of $10 × the Index. Assuming that the portfolio beta (Bp) is 1, the number of contracts to sell is

$$N_F = \frac{\text{Value of Portfolio}}{\text{Futures Index} \times \text{Multiplier}} \times \text{Bp}$$

[12.1]

So

$$N_F = \frac{\$500,000,000}{9870 \times \$10} \times 1 = \frac{\$500,000,000}{\$98,700} = 5,066 \text{ contracts}$$

Equation 12.1 divides the value of the portfolio the manager is attempting to hedge by the value of one index futures contract at the current settlement level. It then adjusts for the relative risk of the cash portfolio as compared with the risk of the market index. In this case, the cash portfolio has a beta of 1, as does the DJIA Index.

Now suppose that on December 15, before the final settlement date of the third Friday of the contract month (in this case December 19, 2003), the portfolio manager looks in *The Wall Street Journal,* as shown on Figure 12.1, Panel A, and sees a new settlement price for the December contract of 10,025, or a change in price of 155 (10,025 − 9,870), which is a 1.57 percent rise (155 / 9870 = 0.0157) in the futures price. With a multiplier of $10, this implies a loss on each futures contract of 155 × $10 multiplier = $1550. So, for 5,066 contracts, the loss would be $1550 × 5,066 contracts = ($7,852,300). However, assume that the pension fund's equity portfolio's value rose the same amount as the change in the spot DJIA shown in Figure 12.1, Panel B, from 9873.42 on December 3, 2003, to 10022.82 on December 15, 2003 [10022.82 - 9873.42 = 149.4, a percentage change in value of 149.4 / 9873.42 equal to 0.0151, or 1.51 percent]. Hence, the $500,000,000 portfolio would rise in value by $500,000,000 (0.0151), which equals a spot position gain of $7,550,000.

If the portfolio manager reversed his trades, closing the position out, the net hedging loss before transactions costs would be the gain in the spot positions of $7,550,000 less the loss on the futures position of (7,852,300), or a net hedging error of ($302,300). Table 12.2 summarizes the results of the hedge. Because the hedge wasn't perfect, in this particular case, the portfolio manager had a positive hedging error. The hedge was not perfect because apparently the beta of the portfolio and the futures contract were not the same as predicted using the hedge. Also, hedges are often not perfect because fractional contracts cannot be traded, hence, the rounding to get the proper number of contracts can also affect results.

Basis Risk

As noted in the previous example, the portfolio manager made a mistake in the hedge ratio, since the beta of the futures index and the spot index and, hence, the price movements in the futures and spot market position, were not the same. Consequently, since stock prices rose, the portfolio manager would be quite unhappy with a ($302,300) net hedging loss on the hedge, particularly give the opportunity loss of the $7.55 million on the portfolio's gain if he had not engaged in the hedge. Of course, if stock prices had fallen instead, the portfolio manager would have been more pleased with a $302,300 net hedging gain, along with the elimination of the $7,550,000 portfolio loss with the gain on the futures contract. Hence, if the market had fallen instead as he had expected, he would have been very glad to have the hedge. Hedging ideally should keep the value of the portfolio stable, at the expense of opportunity losses if the market goes the opposite way the portfolio manager expected. Given the large potential opportunity loss of the market rising, the portfolio manager may want to only immunize (hedge) part of the equity portfolio.

A better hedge position to try to get a zero net hedging error would adjust for a larger historical change in the futures price versus the market prices in this instance. Suppose, typically, the spot DJIA moves about 0.9613, as much as the DJIA futures index. This suggests a beta coefficient (spot/market) of 0.9613. Using this beta, the adjusted number of futures contracts would be

$$N_F = \frac{\$500,000,000}{9870 \times \$10} \times 0.9613 = \frac{\$500,000,000}{\$98,700} \times 0.9613 = 4,870 \text{ contracts}$$

As shown in Table 12.3, with a short hedge of 4,870 futures contracts, the loss on the futures contract will now be $1550 × 4,870 contracts = ($7,548,500) loss on the futures contracts against a gain of $7,550,000 on the portfolio, resulting in a much smaller net hedging loss of ($1,500). This emphasizes the importance of the estimated beta or hedge ratio between the spot prices and futures prices and, hence, basis risk. Risk can actually be increased, as noted in the earlier hedge, by having an incorrect hedge.

Hedging When an Upturn Is Anticipated That Will Result in a Loss (Long Hedge)

A stock index futures hedge in anticipation of a stronger equity market would be more unusual but still possible. For example, a long hedge may be undertaken when a trust department has good reason to expect a large inflow of funds at some future point, funds that can be invested only after an expected

t a b l e **12.2** THE SHORT HEDGE: PORTFOLIO BETA OF 1.0 (FORECAST: BEAR MARKET)

A short hedge with index futures is used when falling securities prices are forecast. The profit on the short futures position can be used to offset losses in a portfolio of stocks.

Cash Market	Futures Market
December 4, 2003	**December 4, 2003**
DJIA Index: 9873.42	DJIA Index settlement level: 9870 (Dec. contract)
Stock portfolio value:	Sell 5,066 contracts
$500,000,000	9870 × $10 =$98,700 × 5,066 contracts = $500,014,200
December 15, 2003	**December 15, 2003**
Forecast Was Incorrect; Stock Prices Rose Instead (Bull Market)	
DJIA Index: 10022.82	DJIA Index settlement level: 10,025
% rise in DJIA stocks	Close out position by buying 5,066 contracts (reverse trade):
= (10022.82 − 9873.42) / 9873.42	Futures Price DJIA has risen 1.57%
= 0.0151, or 1.51%	Loss on Futures Contract = (9870 − 10,025) × $10 multiplier
Gain on Portfolio = $500,000,000 (0.0151)	× 5,066 contracts = ($7,852,300)
= $7,550,000	

Cash Market Gain		Futures Market Loss	
December 4, 2003, value	$500,000,000	December 4, 2003, Contract to Sell (Short Position)	$500,014,200
December 15, 2003, value	507,550,000	December 15, 2003, Contract to Buy (reverse trade)	507,866,500
Gain in Portfolio	$ 7,550,000	Loss on Futures Contracts	($ 7,852,300)

Net Hedging Loss ($302,300)

Note: If stock prices had fallen instead, as predicted, this would be a net hedging gain, with a corresponding gain on the futures contract and a gain on the portfolio.

t a b l e **12.3** THE SHORT HEDGE: PORTFOLIO BETA OF 0.9613 (FORECAST: BEAR MARKET)

Short hedges with index futures must take into account the market risk (as measured by beta) of the hedged portfolio. Portfolios with high betas must be hedged with a larger number of index futures contracts than portfolios with lower betas.

Cash Market	Futures Market
December 4, 2003	**December 4, 2003**
DJIA Index: 9873.42	DJIA Index settlement level: 9870 (Dec. contract)
Stock portfolio value:	Sell 4,870 contracts
$500,000,000	9870 × $10 =$98,700 × 4,870 contracts = $480,669,000
December 15, 2003	**December 15, 2003**
Forecast Was Incorrect; Stock Prices Rose Instead (Bull Market)	
Portfolio rises by 1.51%	DJIA Index futures settlement level: 10,025 (rise of 1.57%)
Rise in stock portfolio value:	Close out position by buying 4,870 contracts (reverse trade):
Gain =$500,000,000 (0.0151) = $7,550,000	Loss on Futures Contract = (9870 − 10,025) × $10 multiplier
	× 4,870 contracts = ($7,548,500)

Cash Market Gain		Futures Market Loss	
December 4, 2003, value	$500,000,000	December 4, 2003, Contract to Sell (Short Position)	$480,669,000
December 15, 2003, value	507,550,000	December 15, 2003, Contract to Buy (reverse trade)	488,217,500
Gain in Portfolio	$ 7,550,000	Loss on Futures Contracts	($ 7,548,500)

Net Hedging Loss ($1,500)

Note: If stock prices had fallen instead, as predicted, this would be a net hedging gain, with a corresponding gain on the futures contract and a gain on the portfolio.

1 When would a portfolio manager want to use a short hedge using stock index futures? When would a portfolio manager want to use a long hedge?

2 How is the correct number of contracts for a hedge using stock index futures calculated?

3 Why is it particularly important to have the correct number of contracts constructed for a hedge using stock index futures? Use the previous example as an illustration of the basis risk associated with stock index futures. Why do you think stock index futures prices tend to move more than their underlying spot indexes?

upswing. The invested funds will miss the benefits of the **bull market,** one in which price increases are anticipated. If the manager buys stock index futures contracts, they will increase in value during the bull market. When the position is later closed out by selling the contracts, the increase in value produces a profit that compensates for the higher prices at which new stock must be purchased. Once again, the effectiveness of the hedge is based on the price volatility of the stock purchased relative to the price volatility of the futures contract. In the previous example, based on the DJIA futures prices for December 3 and December 15, 2003, if a portfolio manager planned on purchasing $500,000,000 worth of stocks with funds that were coming in later in December and wanted to hedge against a higher cost of buying stocks, he could have purchased long futures contracts. Given the same number of contracts and price changes in the earlier example, with a 1.51 percent rise in the cost of stocks (based on the rise in the spot DJIA) between December 4 and December 15, he would have had to pay $7,550,000 more for the stocks. However, if he purchased the 4,870 long futures contracts on the DJIA, he would have a gain on the futures contracts of $7,548,500 to offset the higher cost of purchasing the stock, with a net gain of $1,500 on the hedge.

Program Trading: Index Arbitrage

The term **program trading** encompasses several modern investment strategies. The narrowest definition is the simultaneous placement of buy and sell orders for groups of stocks totaling $1 million or more. A common and controversial form of program trading is the simultaneous trading of stock and stock index futures to profit from changes in the spread between the two, sometimes called **index arbitrage.**[6]

Table 12.4 illustrates a simple example of index arbitrage using the MMI (see Table 12.1), which was used widely for arbitrage in the late 1980s. Suppose that on February 26, a manager buys 2,000 shares of each stock in the MMI, simultaneously selling 18 MMI futures contracts. Hypothetically, the MMI is at 311.74, and the futures settlement level is 313.55 on that date. The contracts expire on March 21, and the manager knows, as is true of all index futures, that the contract settlement level and the MMI itself will converge by the expiration date, even though they differ on February 26.

On March 21, the stock portfolio will be liquidated and the short futures position closed out. Regardless of the actual level of stock prices on that day, the manager profits. If prices rise, the value of the stock will increase more than the loss on the futures contract, resulting in a net profit. If prices fall, the value of the stock will fall to less than the value of the futures contracts. This is true because both the index and the contract settlement value must be the same on March 21, but the contract settlement value is higher on February 26. The gain on the futures contracts will exceed losses on the stock portfolio, again resulting in a net profit.

Index arbitrage and other forms of program trading differ from hedging because hedgers use futures to offset adverse changes in a portfolio held in the normal course of operations. Index arbitragers, however, choose and manage portfolios based solely on the characteristics of available futures contracts, with the intention of profiting from fluctuations in the basis.

Program Trading and the Crash of 1987

Because program trading involves buying and selling large quantities of stocks, it has been blamed for wide fluctuations in stock prices in recent years. In the early days of index arbitrage, price swings were

---

6 These and other definitions can be found in "The Realities of Program Trading." *Market Perspectives* (Chicago Mercantile Exchange) (January/February, 1990). The example in Table 12.4 is similar to one in Jeffrey Laderman. "Those Big Swings on Wall Street." *Business Week* (April 7, 1986), 32–36.

table **12.4**   INDEX ARBITRAGE

Index arbitrage *is the simultaneous trading of index futures and stocks composing the underlying index. Computer programs are used to determine when stocks and futures should be bought or sold to profit from temporary price discrepancies in the two markets.*

Cash Market		**Futures Market**	
February 26			
MMI: 311.74		MMI settlement level: 313.55	
		Sell 18 contracts:	
Buy 2,000 shares of each MMI stock:		$313.55 \times \$500 \times 18 = \$2,821,950$	
Value = $2,749,000			
If Prices Increase by March 21			
MMI increase = 5.238%		MMI settlement level:	
MMI: 328.07		328.07, an increase of 4.631%	
		Close out position by buying 18 contracts:	
Stock portfolio value: $2,893,000		$328.07 \times \$500 \times 18 = \$2,952,630$	

Cash Market Loss		**Futures Market Gain**	
3/21 value	$2,893,000	2/26 sale	$2,821,950
2/26 value	$2,749,000	3/21 purchase	$2,952,630
Gain	$ 144,000	Loss	($ 130,680)

Net Gain $13,320

If Prices Decrease by March 21			
MMI decrease = 5.238%		MMI settlement level: 295.41, a decrease of 5.785%	
MMI: 295.41		Close out position by buying 18 contracts:	
Stock portfolio value: $2,605,000		$295.41 \times \$500 \times 18 = \$2,658,690$	

Cash Market Loss		**Futures Market Gain**	
3/21 value	$2,605,000	2/26 sale	$2,821,950
2/26 value	$2,749,000	3/21 purchase	$2,658,690
Loss	($ 144,000)	Gain	$ 163,260

Net Gain $19,260

particularly noticeable on the four trading days each year in which stock index futures contracts expired, as large numbers of traders closed out positions in stocks, index futures, or both. A widely quoted study in 1986 concluded, however, that small investors could potentially benefit from institutions' use of program trading because small investors would know in advance when price volatility would be high and could avoid the market on those days.[7]

When the DJIA fell by 508 points to 1,738.74 (a 22.6 percent drop) on October 19, 1987, the debate over the effect of program trading on stock price volatility escalated. The **Brady Commission,** a blue-ribbon panel appointed by President Reagan to investigate causes of the crash, concluded in 1988 that computerized trading by large institutions played a major role in the downward spiral of the market. The commission recommended that the stock and futures markets be brought under a single regulator (the Federal Reserve System [the Fed]) and that the two markets institute coordinated "circuit-breaker" programs to halt trading in both markets when price movements exceeded specified limits. Other observers suggested that the Securities and Exchange Commission (SEC) be given oversight authority for both stock and stock index futures markets. Some critics even called for a complete regulatory ban on computerized trading.

Other experts have come to very different conclusions. They believe that the computerized trading of stocks and stock index futures improves the liquidity of the markets and contend that the 1987 crash was actually caused by the NYSE's antiquated system of trading. As stock prices fell during the day on

---

7 See Stoll and Whaley (1986). Other studies have questioned the conclusion that program trading increases price volatility. See James T. Moser. "Trading Activity, Program Trading, and the Volatility of Stock Returns." Unpublished Working Paper, Research Department, Federal Reserve Bank of Chicago (September 1992).

October 19, traders who wished to purchase stock at "cheap" prices were unable to do so because their orders could not be executed. Had the NYSE's computers been more up-to-date, these observers argue, the market decline would have been considerably slowed.[8]

Since 1987, the debate over program trading has continued. In fact, it escalated in 1990 when Japanese investors and officials blamed U.S. securities firms for contributing to the steep decline in the Tokyo stock market by using index arbitrage. Some large securities firms, although not condemning the practice, succumbed to pressure from politicians and regulators and curtailed—or even abandoned—index arbitrage for their own accounts. (Many will still engage in it on behalf of clients.) Still, by 1993, no formal ban on program trading had been contemplated. Most experts recognize that financial and technological innovations, and the regulatory avoidance they spawn, virtually ensure that no amount of regulation will eliminate institutions' efforts to profit from market opportunities. Instead, it is likely that regulators' efforts will focus on potential abuse of innovation rather than its elimination. In fact, as technology and innovation have increased market efficiency, potential profits from program trading have declined, and the volume of activity has declined as well.

Other Index Futures

An institution's ability to hedge against portfolio declines through index futures is not limited to stock index futures. For example, the CBOT introduced Bond Buyer Municipal Bond Index futures contracts in 1985. This contract was motivated by the relatively poor historical results for cross hedges of municipal bond portfolios that used T-bond futures. Using a recently created index of forty municipal bonds, daily settlement prices are calculated as $1,000 times the index level. Institutions with diversified holdings of municipals, such as commercial banks, mutual funds, securities firms, and property/liability insurers, view the contracts as holding much promise for protecting against broad-based declines in the bond markets.

Other index futures contracts have been developed to protect investors against exchange rate risk in general, that is, for those not wishing to hedge against a particular currency (U.S. Dollar Index and DJ Euro STOXX 50 Index), as well as against changes in the value of precious metals or commodity prices (DJ-AIG Commodity Index). Stock index futures for stocks traded on the London, Sydney, Tokyo, Singapore, and Hong Kong exchanges, among others, have also been developed; most are traded only on foreign stock exchanges, but several are approved on U.S. exchanges.

Options on Financial Assets

Another financial innovation, the **option,** is enjoying greater acceptance as a hedging instrument for financial institutions, including options on stock indexes and stock index futures, T-bonds and T-bond futures, and foreign currencies. Although options are similar to futures contracts, important differences separate the two types of hedging mechanisms. Like futures, options can be used for speculation, but this discussion emphasizes hedging.

Concept Questions

1 What is program trading and how was it involved in the stock market crash of 1987?

2 Give some examples of other types of index futures and how they could be used for a hedge.

3 If the stock market is expected to fall, what type of position would a portfolio manager who has a large equity portfolio want to have?

4 If the stock market is expected to rise, what type of position would a portfolio manager who plans to buy stocks in the near future want to have?

5 Why is the beta (relative movement of changes in spot stock market indexes to future stock market indexes) crucial to having a good hedge? Using this beta, how does a portfolio manager determine the correct number of futures contracts for a hedge?

8 Excerpts from the Brady Commission Report, as well as analyses by the commission's critics, can be found in Barro, et al. (1989).

Options on individual stocks have existed for some time. When they were concentrated in the over-the-counter markets, trading was relatively infrequent. The move in 1973 to offer standardized instruments on the organized exchanges has improved liquidity, and newer types of options have attracted a wider group of market participants.

Options Defined

An option is an agreement giving its holder the right to buy or sell a specified asset, over a limited time period, at a specified price. The option itself is created by an **option writer,** someone who stands ready to buy or sell the asset when the holder wishes to make a transaction. The price written into the option agreement is the **exercise** (or **strike**) **price.** Because options are traded on organized exchanges, they may also be sold to other investors before they expire.

Although options are similar to futures agreements, there are differences. As the name suggests, an option does not obligate the holder to undertake the purchase or sale. Depending on movements in the value of the underlying asset, the holder may choose not to exercise the option to buy or sell. If so, the option expires at maturity and becomes worthless. Another difference is that most options (those called **American options**) can be exercised at any point during their lives; with futures contracts, in contrast, an exchange of securities takes place only on the specified delivery date. (A few options, including options on the S&P 500 Index, are **European options** that can be exercised only at expiration.) **Options are also written on futures contracts,** with options to exercise or not the futures contracts. This can provide an opportunity cost advantage, since, as in the case of the portfolio manager with the futures contracts losses, they would not have to be exercised. In return the portfolio manager would pay a premium to purchase the options, offering the right but not the requirement to exercise.

Call Options

A **call option** is an agreement in which the option writer sells the holder the right to **buy** a specified asset on or before a future date. The buyer of a call option expects the price of the asset to increase over the life of the option, eventually exceeding the exercise price. If the asset price rises, the value of the option also rises, and the option holder has the additional opportunity to sell it at a profit before it expires.

Put Options

A **put option** is the opposite of a call. Puts give the holder the right to **sell** an asset at the strike price, and the option writer is obligated to buy it if the holder desires to sell. The buyer of a put option expects the asset's price to fall below the strike price. If the price falls, the put option becomes increasingly valuable.

Premiums

If market prices do not move as the option buyer forecasts, the option is allowed to expire. There is no obligation to exercise it if market conditions make it unprofitable to do so. The cost, however, is the original price (the **premium**) of the option. If the option is not exercised, that cost cannot be recovered; the writer of the option, that is, the seller, realizes a gain.

Option Values Illustrated

The value of an option over time is influenced by the difference between the market and exercise prices of the underlying asset. Other influences are the time to expiration of the option and the volatility in the price of the underlying asset.

Figure 12.2, Panel A shows the value of options on several indexes at the close of trading on December 4, 2003, and December 15, 2003. As with futures contracts on indexes, it is not possible for investors to take physical delivery of the index when an option or an option on a futures contract is exercised; therefore, index options are settled with cash. The holder of a call option on a stock index is really purchasing the right to "buy" cash, based on the difference between the strike price (in this case a designated value for the DJIA Index) and the actual value of the index at the end of trading on the expiration date. The amount the holder receives in cash is determined by the difference between the actual index value and the strike price times the dollar multiplier assigned to that index. For options on

figure **12.2** INFORMATION ON STOCK INDEX OPTION FUTURES AND TRENDS IN THE DOW JONES INDUSTRIAL AVERAGE

PANEL A: FUTURES INDEX OPTIONS FOR DECEMBER 4 AND DECEMBER 15, 2003

December 4, 2003

Futures Index Options

Index	Calls			Puts		

DJ Industrial Avg (CBOT)

$100 times premium

Price	Dec	Jan	Feb	Dec	Jan	Feb
97	25.50	30.15	...	3.50	11.00	18.50
98	17.50	24.00	...	5.50	14.00	22.00
99	11.00	18.00	26.00	9.00	18.00	26.00
100	6.25	12.50	20.00	14.00	...	30.75
101	3.00	8.00	16.00	21.00	...	...
102	1.25	5.00	12.00	...	...	...

Est vol 580 Wd 1,654 calls 322 puts

Op int Wed 10,312 calls 7,232 puts

S&P 500 Stock Index (CME)

$250 times premium

Price	Dec	Jan	Feb	Dec	Jan	Feb
1060	17.90	26.00	34.80	8.50	17.90	26.70
1065	14.70	23.00	...	10.30	19.90	...
1070	11.80	20.10	28.90	12.40	22.00	30.80
1075	9.30	17.60	26.30	14.90	24.50	33.20
1080	7.30	15.30	23.70	17.90	27.20	...
1085	5.50	13.10	...	21.10	30.00	...

Est vol 11,488 Wd 5,984 calls 12,519 puts

Op in Wed 96,668 calls 224,329 puts

Other Options

Nasdaq 100 (CME)

$100 times NASDAQ 100 Index

Price	Dec	Jan	Mar	Dec	Jan	Mar
1430	29.75	52.50	...	26.75	46.00	...

Est vol 14 Wd 13 calls 12 puts

Op int Wed 3,391 calls 327 puts

NYSE Composite (NYFE)

$50 times premium

Price	Dec	Jan	Feb	Dec	Jan	Feb
6160	na	na	na	na	na	na

Est vol na Wd 0 calls 240 puts

Op in Wed 0 calls 4,798 puts

December 15, 2003

Futures Index Options

Index	Calls			Puts		

DJ Industrial Avg (CBOT)

$100 times premium

Price	Dec	Jan	Feb	Dec	Jan	Feb
98	23.50	29.00	...	1.00	9.00	17.00
99	15.00	22.00	31.00	2.00	12.00	21.00
100	7.00	16.00	25.00	4.50	16.00	25.00
101	2.50	11.00	20.00	10.50	21.00	...
102	1.00	7.00	15.00	18.00	...	...
103	0.50	4.00	11.00	...	...	...

Est vol 4,554 Fr 810 calls 114 puts

Op int Fri 13,513 calls 9,092 puts

S&P 500 Stock Index (CME)

$250 times premium

Price	Dec	Jan	Feb	Dec	Jan	Feb
1060	12.70	23.20	32.70	3.90	15.80	25.30
1065	9.00	20.20	29.70	5.20	17.80	27.30
1070	6.40	17.40	26.90	7.60	20.00	29.50
1075	4.30	14.90	24.30	10.50	22.50	31.90
1080	2.80	12.70	21.90	14.00	25.30	34.50
1085	1.70	10.70	19.50	17.90	28.30	...

Est vol 26,676 Fr 4,019 calls 10,206 puts

Op int Fri 103,380 calls 254,849 puts

Other Options

Nasdaq 100 (CME)

$100 times NASDAQ 100 Index

Price	Dec	Jan	Mar	Dec	Jan	Mar
1400	12.50	43.80	72.50	13.00	41.30	70.00

Est vol 44 Fr 7 calls 3 puts

Op int Fri 4,040 calls 387 puts

NYSE Composite (NYFE)

$50 times premium

Price	Dec	Jan	Feb	Dec	Jan	Feb
6180	2700	7900	12700	3450	9650	14450

Est vol 0 Fr 0 calls 0 puts

Op int Fri 0 calls 6,803 puts

Sources: The Wall Street Journal, *December 5, 2003, C11; December 16, 2003, C14.*

PANEL B: THE PUT-CALL RATIO AS A MARKET INDICATOR

Consolidated Trading/Wednesday, December 3, 2003

Market Gauge: Put-Call Ratio

Ratio of daily volume of put and call options on Standard & Poor's 100. The ratio is a contrary indicator; high pessimism is viewed as bullish, high optimism as bearish.

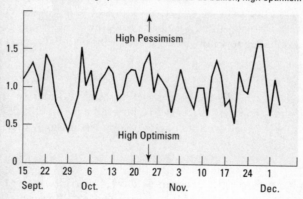

Source: New York Times, *December 4, 2003, C12.*

indexes, by far the most common dollar multiplier is $100, as shown for the options on the DJIA Index. Call options are listed for December, January, and February, followed by Put Options for the same settlement months.

In Figure 12.2, call options for the DJIA Index are shown with strike prices ranging from 97 to 102 (implying, given the spot DJIA Index of 9873.42 at this time, shown in Figure 12.1, Panel B, strike prices of 9700 to 10,200). On December 4, 2003, the call option with a strike price of 97 and an expiration date of December 19, 2003, traded for a premium index of 25.50, or a total premium cost of 25.50 × $100 multiplier = $2,500. The underlying contract for the call option is the strike index of 9700 (97 × 100) times the $100 index multiplier for a settlement price for the DJIA futures contract of $97,000. Hence, the $2,500 premium cost is about 2.577 percent (2500 / 97,000 = 0.02577) of the value of the futures contract settlement price. As shown in Figure 12.1, Panel A, the DJIA December futures contract prices rose by December 15, 2003, to a settle price of $100,250 (10,025 index × $10 multiplier). Hence, the holder of the option would exercise the option for the long position on the DJIA futures contract and upon settlement would receive the net gain of $10 × (10,025 - 9,700) = $3,250 less the $2,500 premium paid, which equals a net gain on the exercised call of $750. If there was a loss instead, the call would not be exercised, so the maximum loss on the call would be the premium price of $2,500.

A call option, such as this one, with a strike price on December 3, 2003, of 9700, below the spot DJIA market index value at that time of 9873.42, is said to be **in the money;** when the strike price of a call option is greater than the index value, the call is **out of the money.**[9] In Figure 12.2, even call options that are out of the money have a positive value, indicating the possibility that by the expiration date the index value could rise above the strike price.

Call Option Values, Strike Prices, and Expiration Dates

Given an underlying asset or index and holding the expiration date constant, call options with higher strike prices have lower values. For example, as shown in Figure 12.2 on December 15, 2003, premiums for call options on the DJIA expiring in January 2004 ranged in value from 29.00 × $100 = $2,900 for a strike price of 98 (9800 index) to 4 × $100 = $400 for a strike price of 103 (10,300 index). The higher the strike price, the less likely the index value will rise above the strike price, so the less valuable the option.

Holding strike price constant, call options with more distant expiration dates are more valuable. For the single strike price of 100 (10,000 index), the call option value ranged from 7 ($700) for a December expiration to 25 ($2500) for a February expiration. The longer time to maturity increases the chances that the actual index value will eventually exceed the strike price.[10]

A final factor that influences option prices in general is unobservable in the data for the DJIA options in Figure 12.2. All else equal, the greater the price volatility of an underlying asset, the greater the value of an option on that asset. For a call option, for example, the greater the asset price volatility, the greater the probability that the price will eventually exceed the strike price; and the higher the asset's price, the higher the value of the option. Yet the minimum value to which an option can fall, no matter how volatile the price of the underlying asset, is zero.

As shown in Panel A of Figure 12.3, if an option's value falls to zero, the holder will simply not exercise it, losing the premium but nothing else. A call option on a futures contract is similar to a long futures hedge, except the call does not have to be exercised. Hence, the call option has unlimited potential gains, but its loss is limited to the premium cost, since the option holder will not exercise the option if there is a loss. In contrast with a long futures hedge, the gain/loss on the futures contract must be taken. However, with a futures hedge, there is no premium cost to reduce the futures contract gain.

Put Option Values, Strike Prices, and Expiration Dates

For put options, holding the expiration date constant, the higher the strike price, the higher the value of the put option; this is in contrast to call options. Puts on physical assets give the holder the right to sell an asset at the option strike price if its market value falls below the strike price. Because one cannot sell an index, the holder of a put option on an index buys the right to receive cash if the index value falls below the strike price by the expiration date.

In Figure 12.2, the premium cost of a put on the DJIA Index on December 15, 2003, with a January 2004 expiration date ranged from 9.00 ($900) at a strike price of 98 (9800 index) to 21 ($2,100) for a strike price of 101 (10,100 index). The higher the exercise price, the more likely it will be above the actual index value at the expiration date. As with call options, however, holding strike price constant, put values are higher for more distant expiration dates. Note the premiums for February contracts for each strike price are much higher than for the January contracts. Again, the chance that the option will eventually be profitable for the holder is greater the longer the time to maturity. The value of put options is also positively related to volatility in the price of the underlying asset.

As shown in Figure 12.3, just as with call options, hedging with put options have unlimited gains but a loss limited to the premium cost, since the option will not be exercised if there is a loss on the contract.

---

9 Because put holders benefit when underlying asset or index values fall, put options are in the money when their strike prices exceed the market value of the underlying asset or index; puts are out of the money when the value of the asset or index exceeds the put strike price.

10 The increase in value with more distant expiration dates holds for most options, with exceptions. For more details, see Chance (1992), Chapter 3.

figure   **12.3**   COMPARISON OF RISK EXPOSURE IN FUTURES AND OPTIONS HEDGES

Panels A and C show that the losses to option holders are limited to the option premium, whereas profits are limited only by movements in the underlying asset's price. In contrast, Panels B and D illustrate that losses, as well as profits, on futures contracts depend on the price behavior of the underlying asset.

Forecast of Falling Prices, Falling Rates

PANEL A: THE CALL OPTION

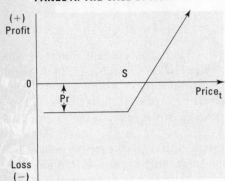

PANEL B: THE LONG FUTURES HEDGE

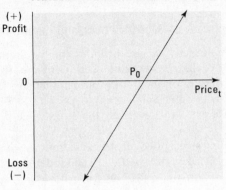

Forecast of Falling Prices, Rising Rates

PANEL C: THE PUT OPTION

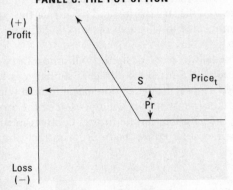

PANEL D: THE SHORT FUTURES HEDGE

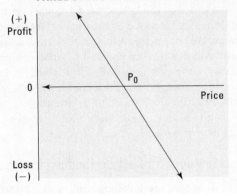

Hence, a portfolio manager, for instance, can keep the opportunity gain on a spot position without having to take the loss on a futures contract, if the market goes the opposite way than expected. This again contrasts with a short futures hedge where the loss on the futures contract must be taken. However, with a put option hedging strategy, the gain will be reduced by the cost of the premium. With a futures contract hedge, there is no premium cost deduction against the gain on the futures contract.

Options and Financial Institutions

Options on assets other than common stock originated in 1982. Table 12.5 lists many of the nonstock options that have been traded. Options are written both on various financial assets (such as bonds or stock) and on a variety of futures contracts. The list of options on financial instruments is in a state of flux. Based on trading volume, stock index options often attract the largest group of traders, but this, too, may well change as the markets mature.

table   12.5   OPTION INSTRUMENTS AND MARKETS

Options are available on financial assets and on futures contracts. New options come and go according to the needs of the marketplace. The table lists a representative group of options traded on financial assets.

Options on Financial Assets	Options on Financial Futures Contracts
Interest Rate Options	**Options on Interest Rate Futures**
Chicago Board Options Exchange	CBOT
Short-term Interest Rates	T-bonds
Long-term Interest Rates	Municipal Bond Index
Stock Index Options	2-year T-notes
American Stock Exchange	5-year T-notes
LEAPS MMI	CME
Computer Technology Index	Eurodollar
Eurotop 100 Index	LIBOR
Institutional Index	T-bills
S&P MidCap Index	London International Financial Futures Exchange
Japan Index	Eurodollar
Chicago Board Options Exchange	Long Gilt
Russell 2000	
S&P 100 Index	**Options on Stock Index Futures**
S&P 500 Index	CBOT
LEAPS—S&P 500 Index	MMI
LEAPS—S&P 100 Index	CME
CAPS—S&P 500 Index	S&P 500 Index
CAPS—S&P 100 Index	Nikkei 225 Stock Average
NYSE	S&P MidCap 400
NYSE Index	New York Futures Exchange
Philadelphia Exchange	NYSE Composite Index
Gold/Silver Index	
Value Line Index	**Options on Foreign Currency Futures**
O-T-C Index	CME
Pacific Exchange	Australian dollars
Financial News Index	British pounds
Wilshire Index	Deutschmarks
	Swiss francs
Foreign Currency Options	Japanese yen
Philadelphia Exchange	Canadian dollars
Australian dollars	Euro/Yen Cross Rate
British pounds	FINEX
British pound/German mark cross rate	U.S. Dollar Index
Canadian dollars	Japanese yen
	Euro
	Swiss francs

Source: The Wall Street Journal, *various issues.*

Regulation of Options Trading

Writers and holders can both use options for speculative purposes. Either party can profit by correctly forecasting price movements on the underlying asset. Some financial institutions, however, may use options only to hedge against adverse movements in the prices of existing assets. As with futures, federal bank regulators disapprove of options trading that increases risk exposure. For example, buying stock options without owning stock would increase risk and thus be disallowed. Also, regulators may question banks that write, rather than buy, options.

Thrifts are permitted broader authority both to write and to purchase options as long as they report their positions to regulators and as long as the positions are related to financial instruments in which an institution can legally invest. Federal credit union regulations permit purchase of put options written on several categories of secondary mortgage market securities. Thus, credit unions making mortgage loans are able to hedge against increases in market rates.[11]

Hedging with Options versus Futures

Examples of Using Options for Hedging by Financial Institutions

The manager of an equity mutual fund might hedge with options on stock indexes or options on stock index futures. A put option position is equivalent to a short position in futures and a call option is equivalent to a long position. As in the previous examples for stock index futures, a portfolio manager worrying about the value of her stock portfolio falling has a choice of a short stock index futures position or a put option on a stock market index or on a stock index futures contract. Similarly, if the portfolio manager is concerned about having to pay a higher price for stocks she wants to purchase in a few months, she can get a long futures position or a call option on the stock market index or on a stock index futures contract.

For managers protecting the value of interest-bearing assets, options on debt instruments or interest rate futures are a logical choice that similarly can be hedged with a call option or long futures position if losses will occur with falling rates (rising prices) and a put option or short futures position if losses will occur with rising rates (falling prices), as shown in Figure 12.3.

Examples of hedging needs that can be accommodated with options by financial institutions are, hence, similar to those for hedging with futures in Chapter 11. Options are a particularly good hedging choice when a financial institution faces potential declines in profitability at the discretion of its customers, such as customers likely to act on their loan commitments set at earlier fixed rates and take out loans in periods of rising rates, but not to act on fixed rate loan commitments if rates fall below the set fixed rate for the commitment. Similarly, if mortgage rates are expected to decline, existing customers may choose to prepay their mortgages, borrowing at new lower rates and lowering a depository institution's interest revenues.

A bank can hedge its commitment to lend in the future by buying a put option on a T-bond. If rates go up, bond values will fall, and the bank can exercise its right to sell bonds at the strike price. The profit on the hedge can be used to offset liability costs that will increase as market rates increase. However, if rates decline, the value of T-bonds will rise, and the bank will not exercise the put. The option premium is the price the lender pays for protecting the spread against rising rates. Since a large price change is necessary to cover the cost of the option premium, instruments with large expected price changes are better to hedge with options. Futures, in contrast, do not have a premium cost, so do not need as large a price change to be profitable.

Similarly, a thrift can protect itself against potential mortgage prepayments in the face of falling rates by purchasing a call option on T-bonds. As rates fall and the value of bonds rises, the call option will also rise in value. Profits from selling the option can be used to offset a decline in interest revenues as mortgages are prepaid. If rates rise instead, the option premium is the price paid for attempting to protect the spread.

---

11 See Koppenhaver (1986) and Christopher (1989).

LEAPS

Options on equity securities are a relatively short-term hedge; most expire within ninety days. Some institutional investors, however, have desired an alternative offering longer-term protection. In the early 1990s, a new instrument was introduced to meet that need. These options (calls and puts)—called long-term equity anticipation securities, or LEAPS—are traded on approximately 100 stocks and several stock indexes including the DJIA and S&P 500 Index. LEAPS have expiration dates several years into the future (generally up to three years) and have less price volatility than traditional options. The longer maturity also gives investors more time to determine the best course of action for managing an options hedge (i.e., selling or exercising the option). LEAPS long-term options often do not have as much trading at times as regular options. For instance, for December 18, 2003, the call volume on the DJIA for the CBOT for regular options was 13,263 and the put volume was 15,154. For LEAPS on the DJIA, the call volume was 3 and put volume was 294.[12]

Since puts reflect short positions (opinions in the market that prices will fall) and calls reflect long positions (opinions that prices will rise), put-call ratios, as shown in Figure 12.2, Panel B, provide the ratio of daily volume of put and call options off stock option indexes and are often used as a contrary indicator. A high ratio reflects high pessimism, indicating more traders engaged in put strategies than traders engaged in call strategies. A low ratio, in contrast, reflects high optimism. The ratio is a contrary indicator since high pessimism is viewed as bullish and high optimism as bearish (that is, the opposite of the average expectations of traders). In early December 2003, the indicator was closer to 1.0, reflecting uncertainty with a fairly equal volume in calls and puts on the Standard & Poor 100 Index.

Hedging with Options versus Futures: An Illustration

Hedging with Options

Suppose that in June 2006, the bond portfolio manager for a large insurance firm forecasts a sharp decline in interest rates over the next three months. Because of several new products developed by the company, a large inflow from sales of insurance policies in August is also expected. The manager wants to hedge the opportunity loss on the investment of those premiums.

On the other side of town, however, the manager of a money market fund holds the opposite expectation for interest rate movements; she is willing to write a call option on T-bond futures contracts. Suppose T-bond futures for September delivery ($100,000 face value) are currently trading at 75.5 (75.5 percent of face value). The call option has a strike price of 76, a premium of $1,187.50, and an expiration date of August 2006. Table 12.6 summarizes the effect of the hedge on the position of the insurance company under three different interest rate scenarios.[13]

First, if interest rates go up instead of down, the bond manager will not exercise the option because the market value of the futures contract will be less than the strike price. The company will lose the $1,187.50 option premium. Second, if interest rates do fall, but not by a significant amount, the value of the T-bond futures and the T-bond futures option will increase. But the rise in value—for example, to 77—will be insufficient to recover the entire purchase premium. The bond manager will suffer an opportunity cost on the investment of the new funds received in August, and this cost will be increased by the gain on the option less the premium cost ($187.50).

Finally, suppose interest rates drop sharply. The value of the T-bond futures contract rises sharply to 81. The bond portfolio manager exercises the call at 76 and immediately resells the futures contracts at 81, for a $5,000 profit. That profit is still offset somewhat by the cost of the option, but the hedge has now provided a net gain of $3,812.50, compensating for the lower return on the newly invested funds. The larger the drop in interest rates, the higher the profits earned. The bond manager could also choose

---

12 Stanley W. Angrist. "Taking Leaps with Treasuries to Buffer Sell-Off." *The Wall Street Journal* (June 5, 1992), C1, C14; Joan Warner. "A Different Kind of Hedge." *Business Week* (September 7, 1992), 94–95; Chicago Board of Trade Website, OneChicago Glossary *(http://www.onechicago.com/000000_misc/oc_000010.html); The Wall Street Journal*, December 18, 2003, C12.

13 Theoretically, losses on futures contracts are halted when the value of the contract falls to zero.

table 12.6 HEDGING WITH OPTIONS ON T-BOND FUTURES CONTRACTS (LONG HEDGE)

An option provides the opportunity to limit losses to the amount of the option premium if forecasts are incorrect. If forecasts are correct, gains on a hedge can be used to offset losses in cash markets.

Treasury Bond Call Option

Premium:	$1,187.50
Strike price:	76
Expiration date:	August 2006
Security:	Treasury bond futures contract for September delivery
	$100,000 face value
	Current market value: 75.5

Scenario 1: Interest Rates Rise

T-bond futures contract market value: <76

Call option not exercised

Results of hedge: −$1,187.50 (premium)

Scenario 2: Interest Rates Fall Slightly

T-bond futures contract market value: 77

Call option exercised: Contract purchased at 76 and sold at 77

Results of hedge:

$1,000.00	Profit on futures trade
−$1,187.50	Premium
($187.50)	Loss

Scenario 3: Interest Rates Fall Significantly

T-bond futures contract market value: 81

Call option exercised: Contract purchased at 76 and sold at 81

Results of hedge:

$5,000.00	Profit on futures trade
−$1,187.50	Premium
$3,812.50	Gain

to sell the option before its expiration date, also at a profit, although that hedge would require the purchase of a larger number of options. Finally, the manager could retain ownership of the futures contracts and take delivery on the T-bonds at a yield reflecting the higher levels that were available in June.

Options and Futures Hedging: A Comparison

The financial institution manager mentioned previously could, instead of using options, hedge with futures. She has to consider, among other things: (1) the investment required—futures do not require a premium cost, only a broker's fee and the opportunity cost of holding the margin requirement with a broker in a low or nonearning account; (2) liquidity and choice of contracts in the market—options markets sometimes are not as liquid as futures or options on futures contracts; (3) how large the premium cost of the options contract is; and (4) the volatility of prices—with volatility the premium cost of the option is more likely to be covered if it is exercised.[14]

---

14 Another reason for preferring one type of option to another is the difficulty of determining the appropriate size of the hedge. Because T-bond futures contracts are standardized with a designated coupon, they sometimes trade at deep discounts, and the number of contracts (or options on contracts) must be adjusted to reflect that discount. For options on the T-bonds themselves, however, the difference between coupon and current market rates is seldom as large, because T-bond and T-note options are traded on issues with many different coupons. Specifications on options vary considerably. Options on T-bond futures contracts expire in the month before the futures contract delivery month. See Chicago Board of Trade (1986b).

The insurance company manager with a forecast of falling rates could have assumed a long hedge in T-bond futures, buying at a price of 75.5. The results of the futures hedge are summarized in Table 12.7. If interest rates move against the manager's forecasts, his losses have no ceiling, except for those imposed by the movement of interest rates. If interest rates rise sharply and the contract value falls to, for example, 70, there will be a significant loss when the position is closed. The greater the increase in interest rates, the greater the loss on the long hedge. Losses on the hedge will offset the returns gained from investing the new funds at the higher market rates.

However, if the manager's forecasts for lower interest rates are correct, there is no purchase premium to reduce the profits from the hedge. If the value of the T-bond futures contract rises to 81, there will be a profit of $5,500 per contract for Scenario 3 instead of the gain of $3,812.50 shown in Table 12.6.

Thus, hedging with futures offers a higher potential profit in terms of no offsetting premium costs, but at the same time, there is a higher opportunity loss if interest rates go the opposite way than expected, since the loss on the futures contract must be taken. With a loss, the options won't be exercised, resulting in a maximum loss of the premium cost for the option. Generally, in volatile markets where prices could go up or down, with sufficient volatility likely to cover the premium cost of the option, options strategies if available would be preferred. However, if prices are likely to go in the direction of the hedge, and premium costs are very high, a futures contract strategy will result in a higher net gain on the futures contract to offset the loss in the spot market.

Interest Rate Swaps

Investors' thirst for new risk management strategies may be unquenchable. Despite the wide range of alternatives offered by futures, options, and options on futures, new hedging techniques are constantly

table **12.7** HEDGING WITH T-BOND FUTURES CONTRACTS (LONG HEDGE)

Futures hedges also provide opportunities to gain if forecasts are correct. If forecasts are incorrect, however, losses on a futures position can be larger than losses on comparable options hedging strategies.

The Long Hedge

T-bond futures contract

$100,000 face value

Current market value: 75.5

Scenario 1: Interest Rates Rise

T-bond futures contract market value: 70

Position closed at loss of 5.5 per contract

Results of hedge: −$5,500

Scenario 2: Interest Rates Fall Slightly

T-bond futures contract market value: 77

Position closed at profit of 1.5 per contract

Results of hedge: $1,500 profit

Scenario 3: Interest Rates Fall Significantly

T-bond futures contract market value: 81

Position closed at profit of 5.5 per contract

Results of hedge: $5,500 profit

under development and finding a place in the financial management policies of financial institutions. One of these—**interest rate swaps**—had become a mainstay of risk management by the early 1990s. In fact, interest rate swaps account for the majority of derivative activity by banks.[15] A swap agreement, in its basic form, is an exchange of cash flows between two parties (or **counterparties,** in the standard terminology of swaps). An interest rate swap is a transaction in which each of two parties agrees to pay the interest obligations on a specified debt obligation of the other party. In the simplest type of interest rate swap, one counterparty exchanges a fixed rate payment obligation for one with a floating rate, while the other counterparty exchanges floating for fixed.[16]

Motivations for Swaps

A government agency introduced interest rate swaps to the United States, although currency swaps had previously been introduced in international markets. The Student Loan Marketing Association, known as Sallie Mae, pioneered swap programs in the United States in 1982 because of an asset structure heavily dominated by floating-rate student loans and advances. Investors supplying funds to Sallie Mae preferred to lock in the high rates prevailing at that time. The agency preferred to fund its rate-sensitive assets with sources of funds of a similar nature. Hence, Sallie Mae sought a swap to meet both its and its investors' needs. In the intervening years, the popularity of interest rate swaps has increased at a phenomenal rate. By 1992, the interest rate swap market, including financial and nonfinancial institutions, was estimated to involve liabilities with principal values of almost $3 trillion. The market for all swaps and swap-related products increased by 50 percent between 1989 and 1991, with phenomenal growth thereafter, with over $35 trillion of notational swap holdings by commercial banks in the first quarter of 2003 alone![17]

For a financial institution, the objective of an interest rate swap is to trade one form of rate sensitivity on liabilities for another that better matches its asset structure. Federal savings and loans (S&Ls), for example, are permitted by regulation to seek swaps only to trade rate-sensitive deposit costs for fixed costs, and not the reverse. A swap allows a thrift to reduce its rate sensitivity and to lock in a spread on long-term, fixed rate assets. Conversely, a multinational commercial bank that borrows in the long-term Eurodollar market may, if most of its assets are rate-sensitive, prefer to swap fixed rate interest obligations on Eurodollar deposits for floating-rate payments.

For commercial banks, as noted in Chapter 11, interest rate swaps have been by far the most popular derivative. The OCC reported in the first quarter of 2003 that interest rate swaps had a $35.7 trillion notional value versus $11.9 trillion for futures and forwards, and $13.089 trillion for options. Since interest rate swaps can be used for long-term hedging purposes and require less liquidity and maintenance in terms of having to watch margin requirements, they have been particularly popular. Also, large commercial banks often serve as intermediaries for swaps. The risk of swaps for banks is the fact that they are long-term. A bank's interest rate risk position could change over the life of the swap, for instance, if rates fall and there are loan prepayments removing fixed rate loans from a bank's balance sheet. Hence, the bank could be stuck in a swap that it no longer needs, unless there is a provision to get out of the swap or trade the swap with another institution.

Nonfinancial firms also participate in the interest rate swaps market; they benefit from the ability to tailor interest obligations to suit their cash flow patterns without having to restructure existing balance sheets. This flexibility may save substantial transactions costs. Also, nonfinancial firms, if they find a substantial rate differential between short-term and long-term interest rates, often engage in interest

---

15 See David A. Carter and Joseph F. Sinkey, Jr. "The Use of Interest Rate Derivatives by End-users: The Case of Large Community Banks." *Journal of Financial Services Research* 14 (July 1998), 17–34. For their sample of banks between $100 million and $1 billion, swaps accounted for 69 percent of bank derivative activity, options for 23 percent, and futures/forwards for 8 percent. Other studies have also shown that interest rates swaps have been used more often in hedging activities by very large banks as well.

16 Further discussions on the development and purposes of swaps are provided in Brown and Smith (1993); Abken (1991[a and b]); Smith, Smithson, and Wakeman (1991); Litzenberger (1992); Marshall (1990–1991); Wall, Pringle, and McNulty (1990); Wall and Pringle (1988, 1989); Smith, Smithson, and Wakeman (1988); Felgran (1987); Whittaker (1987); Bicksler and Chen (1986); Loeys (1985); Hutchinson (1985); Baldoni and Isele (1986); and Roy C. Smith. "Swaps and Synthetic Securities." *Working Paper Series* Number 489, Salomon Brothers Center for the Study of Financial Institutions, New York University (September, 1988).

17 Remolona (1992–1993); Pat Widder. "Trillions at Stake in the Swaps Market." *Chicago Tribune* (June 22, 1992), Section 4, 1, 2; and William Glasgall. "Swap Fever: Big Money, Big Risks." *Business Week* (June 1, 1992), 102–106. See the OCC Website for statistics on commercial banks' use of derivatives *(http://www.occ.treas.gov)*. Search under research on derivatives at the FDIC Website *(http://www.fdic.gov)*.

rate swaps to reduce the effective cost of borrowing. By swapping interest payments with a counter-party experiencing similar but opposite rate differentials, a firm can lower the costs of its liabilities.

Swaps as a Hedging Tool

Plain Vanilla Swap

The most basic type of interest rate swap is known as a **plain vanilla swap.** The mechanics of a swap of this type are shown in Figure 12.4. The example involves a savings institution that has interest rate risk from a large proportion of fixed rate mortgages on its balance sheet. The S&L needs a source of funds with similar interest rate characteristics, but its liabilities are primarily short-term with floating rates. The S&L finds a large commercial bank counterparty with the ability to borrow at fixed rates. The S&L and bank agree to swap interest rate obligations on $50 million of liabilities, called the **notional principal** of a swap.

Exchanging Interest Obligations

The flow of funds is evident in Figure 12.4. The S&L agrees to pay interest on the notional principal at a rate of 8.5 percent; it will receive cash flows from the bank at the London Interbank Offered Rate (LIBOR) plus 25 basis points. Initially, this floating rate will probably be lower than the fixed rate of 8.5 percent. That relationship could change over the life of the swap as interest rate levels fluctuate. The swap allows the S&L to lock in its cost of liabilities, resulting in a more stable net interest margin on its fixed rate mortgage portfolio.

Costs and Benefits of a Swap Agreement

As with any hedging tool, interest rate shifts can make a swap agreement costly or beneficial. Also, as noted previously, it is quite common for the fixed rate agreed on when the swap is initiated to be higher than the floating rate. In the context of this example, that differential is the "insurance premium" paid by the thrift to transfer interest rate risk exposure to its commercial bank counterparty.

figure   **12.4**   EXCHANGE OF OBLIGATIONS IN AN INTEREST RATE SWAP

This swap involves an S&L that exchanges its variable-rate interest obligations for the fixed rate interest obligations of a counterparty commercial bank. The cost of the swap is the initially higher interest payments the S&L must make.

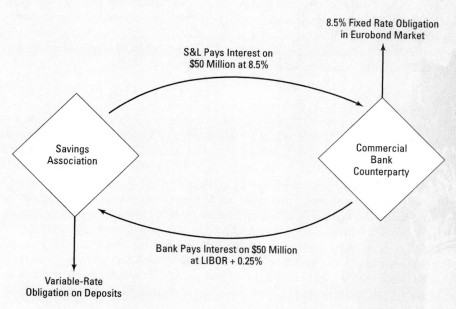

Important Factors in a Swap

Maturity

The maturity of an interest rate exchange can vary from a relatively short period to as long as twenty years. The longer maturities available in the swap market make swaps suitable hedges when futures or options contracts are not. If interest rate forecasts underlying the swap prove to be incorrect, however, five or ten years is a long time to pay for one's mistakes. For this reason, shorter swaps are more popular, and termination clauses are usually included in the original agreement. The party that "unwinds" (the swap market term for ending a swap early) must pay a penalty, but that may be cheaper than the consequences of continuing the swap under an unfavorable interest rate scenario. Many participants in the swap market make arrangements to reverse a swap, in the event of unfavorable rate movements, by agreeing to a swap that offsets the original one. The growing market for options on swaps, discussed later in this chapter, presents an increasingly popular alternative for early termination. A secondary market in swap agreements has also developed.

Interest Rate Index

Another important issue for negotiation is the index by which floating-rate interest payments will be adjusted. In the example, the S&L would prefer a payment stream positively correlated with the rate on its short-term deposits and at least equal to the average deposit cost. There is no guarantee that the anticipated relationship will materialize.

The LIBOR rate is the predominant index, but the T-bill rate and the prime rate, among others, are also used. Increased competition for deposits may change the effectiveness of a given index.

The Role of Brokers and Dealers

Interest rate swaps are often arranged through brokers or dealers. Although it is possible for a small depository to find a swap partner on its own, the process is time-consuming and may be expensive. Most market participants prefer to use an intermediary.

In 1984, the Federal Home Loan Bank Board (FHLBB) formally recognized the potential benefits of swaps for thrift institutions and allowed the district FHL banks to serve as brokers and counterparties to member institutions. Thus, member associations can take advantage of reduced transactions costs if they work through the FHLB system.

Many large banks in the United States and Great Britain, as well as large Japanese securities firms, act as brokers and dealers in the swap markets, earning substantial fees for arranging and servicing swaps. As brokers, institutions bring two parties together, but as dealers they may even take the position of counterparty in a swap agreement. In many dealer arrangements, the intermediary guarantees the continuation of the cash flows for the swap, even if one counterparty defaults on the agreement. Thus, the dealer may be exposed to considerable credit risk, while the individual counterparties benefit from greater confidence that their cash flows will be uninterrupted.

Credit Risk

A financial institution must evaluate the counterparty's credit position, because some confidence is needed that there will be no default. When a dealer actually becomes a principal in an agreement or guarantees the payment streams, the financial position of the dealer is the most important issue.

Concern about controlling credit risk escalated when Beverly Hills Savings and Loan failed in 1985. It had previously made a swap with one of the subsidiaries of Renault, the French automaker. When the thrift failed, the Federal Savings and Loan Insurance Corporation (FSLIC) and Renault disagreed about who had claim to the $2 million in collateral pledged by Beverly Hills to secure the swap. Although counterparties with weak financial positions had become accustomed to pledging collateral to improve their chances of finding swap partners, the Beverly Hills incident provoked concern from stronger market participants and regulators about access to assets pledged. In the early 1990s, regulators' apprehensions about the swap market were rekindled in the aftermath of the failures of the Bank of New England and Drexel Burnham Lambert, Inc. These two failures alone left behind swaps with more than $30 billion in notional value, and one European official claimed that the entire global payments system was almost upset.[18]

Although debate continues about the legal and systemic risk exposure in swap agreements, credit risk does appear to be limited. If a counterparty defaults on an agreement, the other party has responsibility only for its own debt obligations, not for the counterparty's. If the default occurs in an unfavorable interest rate environment, however, the loss of the protective hedge could be expensive.

Asset Swaps and Liability Swaps

The preceding example showed an exchange of payments on liabilities. An asset swap can be set up as well with an exchange of payments on assets. For instance, counterparty A may have fixed rate assets and desire a variable-rate asset to match up with its variable-rate liabilities (e.g., a thrift). Counterparty B may have variable-rate assets and desire fixed rate assets to match up with its fixed rate liabilities (e.g., an insurance company). By swapping the payments on their assets with each other, they both benefit by receiving the type of cash flows they desire on their assets: Counterparty B gets a fixed rate cash flow, while counterparty A gets a variable-rate cash flow, reducing the interest rate risk for both parties since they match up with the cash flow of their liabilities.

Liability Swaps Used to Reduce Interest Costs

Swaps are also used by institutions to gain more favorable interest rates. For instance, counterparty A may have a cost advantage in the fixed rate bond market, while counterparty B may have a cost advantage in the variable-rate bond market; however, counterparty A may want to have a variable-rate liability and counterparty B a fixed rate liability. By having a liability swap with A issuing fixed rate bonds and B issuing variable-rate bonds, where they have a cost advantage and then swapping payments, the two counterparties gain the best of both worlds. Both get a lower cost of funds as well as the type of liability that they desire. Putting numbers to this example, suppose the fixed rate bond costs are 6 percent for counterparty A and 7 percent for counterparty B, and the variable-rate bond costs are 5 percent for counterparty A and 4 percent for counterparty B. By exchanging payments, each counterparty will save 1 percent in its respective variable-rate and fixed rate interest costs. This is a very simple example; more complex arrangements can be made, but, in general, it shows how companies can gain a liability cost advantage with swaps for their preferred type of financing to match the type of cash flows coming in from their assets.

Currency Swaps Used to Reduce Foreign Exchange Risk

Similarly, foreign currency swaps are made between different firms to help reduce their foreign exchange risk. For instance, a Japanese bank doing business in the United States may be receiving interest revenues in dollars from loans in U.S. dollars but be financing this loan with debt in Japan denominated in yen. To reduce its foreign exchange risk, the Japanese bank could arrange a currency swap of payments through an intermediary broker with another institution that has the opposite problem, receiving interest revenues, for instance, in Japanese yen and paying expenses for financing in U.S. dollars.

Regulatory and Accounting Issues

As swaps have grown in popularity, regulators and accountants have focused attention on appropriate means for controlling and reporting the potential risk to which swap counterparties are exposed. Regulatory controls on depositories' swap activities have been imposed in the form of the risk-based capital standards discussed earlier in Chapter 6. The Financial Accounting Standards Board now requires that firms involved in financial agreements with off-balance-sheet risk, including interest rate swaps, disclose details about these agreements and the potential loss that could occur should a counterparty fail to perform. Since 1993, firms have been required to disclose unrealized gains and losses from swap agreements.

---

18 For more discussion of the risks in the swap market, see Hansell and Muering (1992); Glasgall. "Swap Fever."; and Jonathan R. Laing. "The Next Meltdown?" *Barron's* (June 7, 1993), 10–11, 30–34.

Stock Price Risk Issues

One interesting risk that Banc One encountered was the risk of investors not understanding the institution's use of interest rate swaps. Analysts reported concern over Banc One's interest rate swap exposure. This, in turn, led to a decline in the bank's stock price in April 1993, from a high of $48 to just $36, as well as a fall in the corporation's credit rating based on its derivative exposure. Esty, Tufano, and Headley report in a case study on Banc One that one analyst stated that "Banc One's investors are uncomfortable with so much derivative exposure. Buyers of regional banks do not expect derivatives involvement. . . . Heavy swaps usage clouds Banc One's financial image [and is] extremely confusing. . . . It is virtually impossible for anyone on the outside to assess the risks being assumed." These reports occurred despite the consistent reporting by Banc One of unrealized losses and gains on its swap portfolio and its sending a brochure explaining its swap activity to investors. Nevertheless, Banc One's use of swaps for hedging was considered by some analysts to be speculative.[19] Hence, public misconceptions of speculative derivative activity by a large regional bank using interest rates swap for macro hedging did cause some market valuation problems.

More Exotic Swaps

Market participants have recognized the swap concept as one of the most flexible and effective tools for managing many types of financial risks. As a result, many innovations have appeared. A representative (but not exhaustive) sample of those available in the early 1990s is presented in Table 12.8. The variety and complexity of the swap market are apparent.

Two emerging categories of swaps not shown in the table are **commodity swaps** and **equity swaps.** Commodity swaps allow exchange of risks due to price fluctuations of raw materials or other production inputs. One or both counterparties may lock in a price on future commodity purchases, depending on the terms with the swap dealer. The equity swap allows a portfolio manager to convert interest flows on a debt portfolio to cash flows linked to an equity index, such as the S&P 500. Thus, managers can realize the benefit of returns on different asset categories without paying transactions costs.

Swaps versus Futures Hedging

Table 12.9 summarizes important differences between hedging with futures and hedging with interest rate swaps. In general, the swap market is less complex, and agreements do not require the daily monitoring necessary in futures trading. Swaps allow management more flexibility in negotiating the initial size and maturity of a hedge, but futures hedges are easier and less costly to reverse once in place. Currently, the futures markets are larger, more liquid, and more competitive, although growth in dealer activity and development of a secondary market are facilitating the use of swaps. Thus, the choice between futures and swaps depends on the expertise of managers and the regularity with which hedges will be managed.

Swap Options and Futures

Despite the fact that many market participants use swaps as a hedging tool, swap dealers and some counterparties continue to feel the effect of interest rate risk exposure. Consequently, mechanisms in the form of swap options—**swaptions**—and futures are now available to assist in more precise management of those risks. As is true of other options, swaptions provide the buyer with the right to exercise some choice during the life of the option. In the early 1990s, options on plain vanilla swaps were most common; the swaptions market had reached a volume of almost $100 billion by 1990.

A call swaption gives the buyer an opportunity to enter into a swap agreement in the future to receive a fixed rate and pay a floating rate. A put swaption gives the buyer the right to make a future swap agreement to receive a floating rate of interest while paying a fixed rate. If a swaption is exercised,

---

19 See Ben Esty, Peter Tufano, and Jonathan Headley. "Banc One Corporation: Asset and Liability Management." *Bank of America Journal of Applied Corporate Finance* 7 (Fall 1994), 33–65. The quotation used in this paragraph is from George Salem. "Rating for Banc One Reduced to Hold from Buy Based on Confusion from Heavy Exposure to Interest Rate Swaps." *Prudential Securities* (November 1993), 2.

table 12.8 VARIETIES OF INTEREST RATE AND CURRENCY SWAPS

By the early 1990s, swap dealers and brokers were offering a vast array of agreements, all much more complex than the original plain vanilla swap.

Type of Swap	Description
Interest Rate Swaps	
Amortizing swap	Used to hedge interest rate risk on mortgages or other amortized loans; the notional principal diminishes over the life of the swap
Accreting swap	Used to hedge interest rate risk on agreements with a rising principal value, such as construction loans; notional principal increases over the life of the swap
Seasonal swap	Notional principal may vary up or down over the life of the swap; also known as roller coaster swap
Basis swap	Exchange of floating rate payments between counterparties, but with interest rates based on different indexes
Zero-coupon swap	All cash flows of the swap occur at the end of the life of the agreement; payment obligations are compounded to future maturity
Yield curve swap	A subset of the basis swap; involves exchange of interest payments indexed to a short-term rate for payments indexed to a long-term rate
Participating swap	Allows the fixed rate to be adjusted downward during the life of the swap, depending on the level of the floating-rate index; allows counterparty paying fixed to participate in benefit of declining rates
Reversible swap	Allows counterparty to change status from floating-rate payor to fixed rate payor, and vice versa
Asset swap	Effectively transforms an asset into an asset of another type, such as converting a fixed rate bond into a floating-rate bond; results in what is known as a "synthetic security"
Forward swap	Used when new debt is to be issued at a future date; allows issuer to hedge against an undesirable increase in rates before the securities are issued
Forward rate swap	Reduces default risk by establishing, at the time the swap is executed, a schedule for adjusting the fixed rate over the life of the swap
Mark-to-market swap	Reduces default risk by allowing the fixed rate to be reset when fixed and floating rates diverge substantially after the beginning of the swap
Currency Swaps	
Currency-coupon swap	Used to hedge currency and interest rate risk; a fixed rate is paid in one currency while a floating rate is paid in another
Euro-swap	Used to transform principal and coupon payments denominated in European Currency Units into another currency, and vice versa

Source: Adapted from Abken (1991[a and b]), Litzenberger (1992), and Brown and Smith (1993).

table 12.9 COMPARING INTEREST RATE FUTURES AND INTEREST RATE SWAPS

These comparisons show that swaps are more flexible hedging tools than futures, but futures markets are larger, more well-developed, and more standardized.

Feature	Futures	Swaps
Maturities available	$1\frac{1}{2}$ to 2 years	1 month to 20 years
Costs	Margins and commissions	Brokers' or dealers' fees
Size of hedges available	Standardized contract values	Any amount over $1 million
Contract expiration dates	Fixed quarterly cycle	Any dates
Difficulty of management	Complex	Simple
Termination of positions	Closed out with opposite contract	Unwound or reversed
Transactions completed through	Organized exchanges	Commercial or investment banks

Source: Adapted from Robert Baldoni and Gerhard Isele. "A Simple Guide to Choosing between Futures and Swaps." Intermarket 3 (October 1986), 16; and Vivian Lewis. "Stop and Swap." Bankers Monthly 106 (October 1989), 82–84.

the swap will begin at a stipulated future date with a predetermined rate of interest. Most swaptions are of the European variety, meaning that they can only be exercised at the option's expiration date.

A put swaption would be exercised if the option would allow the buyer to pay a rate of interest lower than the level of interest rates prevailing on similar swaps at the swaption's maturity. If the buyer does not really need the swap agreement, the low fixed rate swap could be sold at a gain to another counterparty.

The swaption market also effectively gives counterparties the opportunity to cancel or otherwise alter a swap agreement before maturity, if interest rate movements are unfavorable. This method of cancellation can be less costly than unwinding a swap before the end of the agreement. A swap can be bundled together with a swaption to allow the holder to terminate the agreement. For example, a counterparty paying the fixed rate can bundle the swap with a call swaption; if interest rates have declined by the time the swaption matures, the swaption can be exercised and the agreement cancelled. Such a combination is known as a **callable swap.** Other types of swaptions allow the holder to exercise the right to extend a swap agreement (**extendable swaps**) or reverse the obligation to pay floating and fixed rates (another way to achieve a reversible swap).

Swap Futures

The CBOT introduced a swap futures contract in 1991. The "cash instruments" on which such futures contracts are based are generic, plain vanilla swaps with three- or five-year lives, with a variable rate indexed to LIBOR. The price of the futures contract reflects expectations about the fixed rate required for such a swap. At maturity, the price of a swap futures contract is determined by the prevailing fixed rate on swap agreements at that point in time.

Swap futures were primarily designed to offer protection to swap dealers, who face risk exposure in many swap agreements. Dealers, besides assisting in structuring agreements, often serve as counterparties. As such, they face risk from unfavorable fluctuations in interest rates, as well as credit risk from potential nonperformance of counterparties. The swap futures contracts provide a mechanism for managing the interest rate risk exposure of the counterparty paying the fixed rate.[20]

Interest Rate Caps, Floors, and Collars

The final interest rate risk management tool introduced in this chapter is a group of relatively new products called **interest rate caps, floors,** and **collars.** These are designed to limit exposure to interest rate fluctuations on existing assets, liabilities, or payment obligations in a swap agreement. For example, institutions can purchase interest rate caps to limit increases in their cost of funds in a volatile rate environment. Likewise, a cap could serve as an effective ceiling to limit potential increases in floating rate payments required by an existing swap agreement.

Concept Questions

1 What are the particular characteristics of call options? Put options? What do they cost?

2 What are the advantages and disadvantages of hedging with options versus futures?

3 To hedge against a spot loss with a rise in interest rates, what type of option should be used (call or put)? To hedge against a spot loss with a fall in interest rates, what type of option should be used?

4 What is an interest rate swap? What advantages and disadvantages do interest rate swaps have for hedging over futures and options? Given an example of a swap.

5 What is a swap future? What is a swaption? Why would these have advantages over a regular swap?

---

20 Unfortunately, because swaptions are relatively new compared to many other contracts, terminology may not always be standardized. Readers may even find conflicting definitions in different sources. For more information on these emerging markets, see Beidleman (1991); Chicago Board of Trade. *CBOT Swap Futures: The Reference Guide.* Chicago: Chicago Board of Trade, 1991; William B. Crawford, Jr. "CBOT's Planting a New Hedge." *Chicago Tribune* (June 18, 1991), Section 4, 1, 4; Abken (1991[a and b]); and Brown and Smith (1991).

Interest rate caps are similar to call options. The purchaser pays a premium for the right to limit the cost of its liabilities to a specified rate (the strike level), just as purchasers of call options pay a premium for the right to buy an asset at the strike price. If the current rate on the index underlying the cap (usually the LIBOR rate, the prime, the T-bill rate, the prime commercial paper rate, or a certificate of deposit index) rises above the strike level, it will be profitable to exercise the cap. If interest rates remain below the strike level, the cap expires unused, and its price serves as an insurance premium.

Alternatively, interest rate floors can be purchased to protect against the possibility that returns on variable-rate instruments will fall so low that they no longer exceed the cost of funding sources. Floors could also be used to protect against the possibility that floating payments received from a swap agreement fall below the existing fixed obligations. Floors are similar to put options. For a premium, institutions that purchase floors own the right to receive interest payments at the strike level, just as put buyers own the right to receive a specified sales price for an underlying asset. If interest rates fall below the strike level, it becomes profitable for the floor owner to exercise the option. If interest rates remain above the strike level, the floor expires unused.

For example, consider a swap agreement with a fixed rate of 7.5 percent. As interest rates rise, the floating rate could easily reach a level several hundred basis points above the fixed rate. By purchasing a cap, the floating-rate counterparty could effectively limit the rate paid to, say, 9 percent. If the indexed rate rises above 9 percent, the cap is exercised and the party who sold it is obligated to pay the difference between the cap rate and the actual rate.

An interest rate floor can protect the recipient of the floating-rate payments. The floor would be exercised if the index rate falls below the strike rate, and the writer of the interest rate floor would again be obligated to pay an amount sufficient to cover the shortfall. Buyers of caps and floors pay a premium, just as is true in the purchase of options.

Finally, some market participants may purchase both caps *and* floors or may purchase a cap and sell a floor. These strategies hedge against both increases and decreases in interest rates or provide some premium income to offset the cost of purchasing the cap. Such arrangements, known as **interest rate collars,** attempt to stabilize the net interest margin within a defined range.

Risks in the Market for Caps and Floors

The market for interest rate caps and floors is similar to the interest rate swap market, in that it is over the counter and dominated by large commercial and investment banks acting as dealers or brokers. Many of these dealer/broker institutions purchase caps and floors as part of their own interest rate risk management plans and also write caps and floors for others. Like swaps, caps and floors are tailored to individual user's needs. For every cap or floor purchaser entitled to receive payments if the cap or floor goes in the money, there is a cap or floor writer (seller) who is obligated to make those payments. Thus, the purchaser faces the possibility that the writer may default on the promised obligations. Furthermore, the purchaser also faces basis risk when attempting to hedge assets or liabilities whose returns or costs are not perfectly correlated with an index on which caps or floors are available.

Data on the volume of caps and floors outstanding are sparse, but most purchasers appear to be banks and other financial institutions, as well as nonfinancial firms using caps to hedge against increases in short-term borrowing costs. Transactions are large, with a typical minimum notional principal amount of $5,000,000. Thus, many purchasers are highly sophisticated businesses whose managers are aware of the risks inherent in the market. Interestingly, however, caps can also be attractive hedging vehicles for weaker institutions with poor credit ratings that are unable to find a willing counterparty in the interest rate swap market. Because the writer of a cap bears no default risk, the credit standing of the purchaser is of no consequence.

Given their relatively low risk levels, caps and floors are enjoying increasing acceptance among financial institution managers. The market has been strengthened by their association with swap agreements. Along with swaptions and swap futures contracts, caps, floors, and collars are the most recent examples of financial innovation and engineering.[21]

---

21 For more information on caps, floors, and collars, see Remolona (1992–1993); Abken (1991[a and b]); Abken (1989); and Spahr, Luytjes, and Edwards (1988).

Other New Derivatives for Financial Institution Management

Financial innovations are constantly being made to assist managers of financial institutions. Two new types of derivatives that do this are insurance derivatives as a new hedging tool for the insurance industry and credit derivatives, including credit swaps, to assist financial institutions in managing their credit risk for loans.

Insurance Derivatives

Options Contracts for Insured Losses from Catastrophic Events

On September 29, 1995, the CBOT began trading options contracts that are based on the Property Claims Services (PCS) indices, which track the aggregate amount of insured losses that result from catastrophic events that occur in given regions and risk periods. Each index represents total losses that occur in a region during a risk period. For an index based on seasonal catastrophes, the risk period is quarterly and the options trade in March, June, September, and December. For regions with nonseasonal catastrophes, such as earthquakes, the risk period is annual, with only a December contract traded. The index begins at zero and rises one point for each $100 million of insured property damage that occurs over a time period. Contracts are also available for trading in a "loss development" period of either six or twelve months after a risk period. Options can be traded on "small cap" or "large cap" contracts, where small cap options track aggregate insured losses from $0 to $20 billion, and large cap options track losses from $20 billion to $50 billion. Caps limit the amount of losses that are included under each contract, protecting the seller of an uncovered call. For instance, if the damage in a region is $25 billion (250 index points), the seller of a 150 call will need to pay only $10,000 $[(200 - 150) \times$ $\$200]$ for each call spread written versus $20,000 $[(250 - 150) \times \$200]$. These caps play an important role since traders otherwise would not be willing to write out-of-the-money calls for a small premium while bearing the risk of unlimited losses. Market participants, however, recognize that even these caps do not provide enough protection against large losses. They commonly trade call spreads, in which a seller sells a call at one strike value and simultaneously buys another call of the same expiration at a higher strike value, limiting the potential loss to the difference between the strike prices of the two options. Puts can be traded on all indices, but they are rarely traded. There are also no underlying futures contracts for trading the PCS catastrophe indices, making PCS options the first contracts ever listed on the CBOT that lack an underlying futures contract. Insurance derivatives are an alternative for property-casualty (p/c) insurers to buying a traditional layer of reinsurance from a reinsurer (another insurance company whose business is to insure some of other insurers' risk), reducing the p/c companies' exposure to the credit risk of the reinsurer. Similarly, reinsurers could purchase PCS options to reduce their layers of risk.[22]

Credit Derivatives

New risk management tools that transfer credit risk from one party to another are called credit derivatives. Credit derivatives were first introduced in the early 1990s by banks for the purpose of reducing risks for banks that had a high concentration of risk for loans from one geographic area, industry group, or borrowers with similar types of risk exposures. In effect, banks find counterparties that are willing to assume the credit risk in return for a fee, while the banks keep the loans on their books. Credit derivatives are derived from an underlying asset such as a loan, bond, or portfolio of these. Credit derivatives can be tailored for any part of the credit risk exposure of the loans including the

---

22 This section is based on Canter, Cole, and Sandor (1997). Other derivative-type instruments to reduce p/c insurers' risk are catastrophe-linked bonds (cat bonds), which constitute an exchange of principal for periodic coupon payments whereby the payment of the coupon and/or return of the principal are linked to the occurrence of a specified catastrophic event. An insurance company establishes an offshore special purpose vehicle (SPV) reinsurer from which it will buy a reinsurance contract. In turn, the SPV issues a bond that cedes that reinsured risk to the capital markets. The insurance company pays a reinsurance premium to the SPV, which is passed on as a premium to investors in the form of a coupon. In return, investors pay the notional amount of the bond equal to the maximum loss, which is placed in a trust invested in short-term Treasuries. Hence, the risk that the investors bear is fully collateralized, eliminating any credit risk. If a catastrophic event occurs that exceeds a given amount in a given region, the investors lose a portion or all of their principal. If not, the investor will earn the coupon plus the risk-free rate. The buyer of the bonds in effect is writing a call spread, whereby the investor shares proportionately in the maximum loss of a catastrophic event. Also see Doherty (1997).

amount, rate of recovery, and maturity, or even an event, such as a downgrade in a credit rating versus a default. As pointed out by Caouette, Altman, and Narayanan (1998), credit derivatives actually are quite similar to traditional standby letters of credit and loan guarantees. Consequently, regulators often treat credit swaps similarly to letters of credit. Credit derivatives are arranged by brokers over the counter and come in different types, but they all have common features in terms of retaining assets on the books of originating institutions while transferring some portion of the credit exposure underlying these assets to other parties. Typical amounts are $10 to $50 million with maturities of one to ten years. Credit derivatives have advantages in terms of not requiring the sale of assets, which would weaken relationships with borrowers. Also, credit derivatives allow the reshaping of an institution's credit exposure by improving diversification, such as when an institution has too large a loss exposure in one region. A credit risk swap, for instance, reduces the institution's concentration in that area, allowing the firm's loan portfolio to be more diversified. Two of the major types of credit derivatives are total return swaps and credit swaps. Figure 12.5 illustrates each of these types of swaps.[23]

Total Return Swaps

With a total return swap, shown in Panel A of Figure 12.5, cash flows are exchanged between a total return payor and a total return receiver. The total return payor pays out a return based on the return from its holdings of a risky debt obligation or portfolio of risky debt obligations, based on an interest income stream and changes in the market value of debt. If a bond defaults, returns from the bond and its market value will be affected. The counterparty, the total return receiver, bases what it pays on a default-free obligation less a negotiated compensation for taking on the exposure to risky debt and receives the return from the underlying risky debt. In essence, the total return payor receives an income stream appropriate for a default-free obligation and the total return receiver obtains the income stream appropriate for holdings of risky debt. The income stream reconfiguration occurs contractually without any exchange of assets. The swap allows participation in the return stream of the underlying debt without having to purchase a risky bond itself.

figure   12.5   EXCHANGE OF OBLIGATIONS IN A TOTAL RETURN SWAP AND CREDIT SWAP

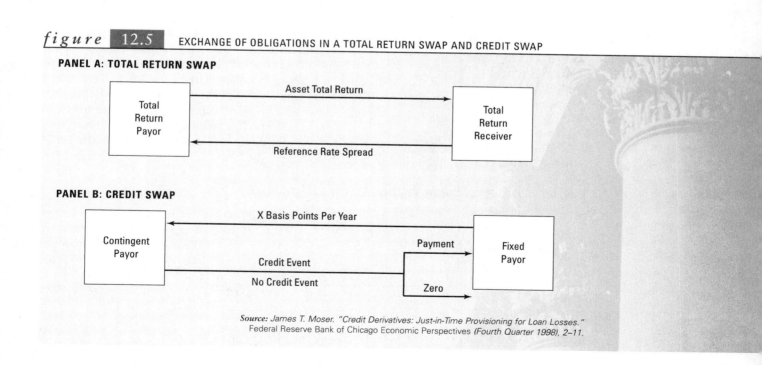

Source: James T. Moser. *"Credit Derivatives: Just-in-Time Provisioning for Loan Losses."* Federal Reserve Bank of Chicago Economic Perspectives *(Fourth Quarter 1998), 2–11.*

23 This and the following sections comes from Moser (1998), with some additions from Caouette, Altman, and Narayanan (1998), Chapter 20, "Credit Derivatives." Also see Wall and Shrikhande (1998).

Credit Swaps

Compared with return swaps, credit swaps are more like insurance contracts, whereby a fixed payor insures against credit events by periodically paying a fixed percentage of the loan's par value, as shown in Panel B of Figure 12.5. If a credit event such as a loan default occurs, the contingent payor makes a payment that compensates the insured for part of its loss, but otherwise the contingent pays zero. As Moser (1998) points out, credit swaps are in effect a technique of just-in-time loan provisioning. Instead of holding liquid assets against future loan losses, financial institutions could use credit swaps, whereby a portion of their credit risk is in effect insured against losses. This derivative method of provisioning may be more cost effective in many cases, although regulators, in their treatment of credit derivatives, do not currently view them as a means of reducing risk; thus, institutions receive limited relief from capital requirements.

Differences between a Total Rate of Return Swap and a Credit Swap

As noted by Caouette, Altman, and Narayanan (1998), unlike a credit swap, the total rate of return swap (often called a TR or TROR swap) has periodic changes of cash flows (much like an interest rate swap) regardless of whether there is a default or not. Hence, a bank no longer has to worry about the risk of an asset without actually having to sell it. For instance, the risk seller (bank wanting to remove the credit risk) might make an exchange with a risk buyer (bank that agrees to protect the seller) by exchanging periodic cash flows, where the risk seller gives the risky buyer cash flows from the loans, and the risk buyer gives the risk seller a predetermined safe cash flow of LIBOR or some other index plus 75 basis points.[24]

Other Types of Credit Swaps

Caouette, Altman, and Narayanan (1998) point out other types of credit swaps including **credit-linked notes, first-to-default swaps,** and **index swaps.** With a **credit-linked note,** a risk-seller bank, for instance, sets up a trust (special purpose vehicle) separate from the bank to issue notes or security certificates. The proceeds from the security issue are invested to build up cash collateral for an amount to protect the buyers. The yields from the loans or other collateral plus fees paid to the protection buyers are passed on to the investors. In the event of a default, the cash collateral is liquidated to protect the buyer with any remaining proceeds passed on to investors. With **first-to-default** swaps, a credit swap is developed based on a whole basket of assets, with the default event triggered by any of the assets in the basket. An **index swap** combines both a bond and a credit option allowing coupon or principal payments to be recalculated (lowered) in the event of a change in expected credit defaults. For instance, a finance company that finances its loans with fixed rate bonds could have a credit option attached that allows the finance company to reduce the coupon payment by a given number of basis points for every increase in the national rate of past due loans or loan defaults. This credit option provides protection for the finance company, since if its loan revenues fall with greater loan defaults, it will still have sufficient revenues to repay its bonds that were issued to finance the loans.

Valuation and Current Pricing Practices for Credit Derivatives

The valuation of credit derivatives is generally based on an expected cash flow analysis of the characteristics of the credit risk assets and the probability of default, at times using scenario analysis or even a stochastic Monte Carlo simulation. Comparisons can also be made to risk spreads and the cost for other types of credit protection. As relatively new instruments, their pricing is also evolving, with pricing often similar to that of an asset swap since credit derivatives are often very similar. A credit derivative, however, has more asset risk than an asset swap, so, as Caouette, Altman, and Narayanan (1998) note, it will generally pay more given the uncertainty of a default event.

Notional Size of Credit Swaps Used by U.S. Banks and Regulatory Concerns

The global size of the primarily "privately negotiated" credit derivatives market was about $100 to $200 billion by the end of 1996. It has grown dramatically since that time. In the first quarter of 2003, the

---

24 This discussion and the following sections are based on material from Caouette, Altman, and Narayanan (1998) and Moser (1998).

OCC reported the notional amount of credit derived by insured U.S. banks alone was $710 billion, with the notional amount of $320 billion for the nineteen commercial insured institutions that sold credit protection (i.e., assumed credit risk) to other parties, and the notional amount of $390 billion for the twenty-two commercial banks that purchased credit protection to hedge credit risk from other parties. Still, relative to the total U.S. loan market, the amount is relatively small. The users of credit derivatives by banks remains concentrated among large financial institutions. In 2002, there was concern in the financial community with large credit derivative losses by German banks, leading to the S&P cutting its rating on Commerzbank, resulting in a large dive in its stock price. The BIS has also been concerned about the risk of the banking system with the use of credit derivatives and has formulated new capital regulations for the protection of credit sellers. As of May 2003, under the Basel II proposals, new guidelines were put into place listing eligible protection providers as sovereign entities, privately sponsored entities, banks, and securities firms that had a lower risk weight than the counterparty and other entities with ratings of A− or better. By definition, a credit derivative has to be a direct claim on the protection seller that is unconditional and irrevocable. Basel II also has new criteria for credit derivatives allowing some capital relief to the protection buyer and a capital charge to the protection seller. Regulators have been particularly concerned about the buyers of credit risk. On the other hand, Alan Greenspan, among others, has noted that credit derivatives can reduce systemic risk for the banking industry by spreading risk across a number of different entities, reducing the concentration of risk and, hence, chance of default risk for individual banks.[25]

Example of a Plain Vanilla Credit Swap

Bank Florida has had a $5 million credit exposure with Alligator Swamp Corporation, a large tourist corporation in Florida, for five years. Now Bank Florida would like to sell off part of the loan to reduce its risk, but Alligator Swamp Corporation does not want part of its loan sold, since it likes dealing with Bank Florida. Bank New York has examined Alligator Swamp's loan and realizes that it's a good credit risk. They agree to enter into a credit swap arrangement in exchange for a fixed fee every year of 50 basis points (0.0050 × $5 million = $25,000 a year fee). Bank New York agrees that if Alligator Swamp Corporation defaults on its loan, Bank New York will pay Bank Florida a given sum representing the loss that Bank Florida has taken. Bank New York may want to have some diversification by having business in Florida, gain fee income, and may feel more confident given its information about Alligator Swamp Corporation than Bank Florida does, hence, valuing the risk of the loans a little differently than Bank Florida. The period for the arrangement could be the full five years or less. If Alligator Swamp Corporation does not default, Bank New York just gets the fees without having to pay anything to Bank Florida. If Alligator Swamp Corporation defaults and Bank Florida gets only $2.5 million of its money back, Bank New York would have to pay Bank Florida the loss of $2.5 million.

Concept Questions

1 What is an interest rate cap, floor, and collar? What are the advantages and disadvantages of each of these types of derivatives?

2 How are large financial institutions able to create caps, floors, and collars? In return, what type of fee income do they receive?

3 What risks are entailed with caps, collars, and floors?

4 What is an insurance derivative? Give an example where an insurance derivative might be used for a hedge.

5 Describe some different types of credit derivatives and explain how they can reduce a financial institution's risk.

---

25 See Tavakoli (1998), who provides a detailed guide for credit derivatives. Also see *http://www.credit-deriv.com/bisproposals.htm* for a summary of the Basel II proposals on credit derivatives, along with the BIS Website *(http://www.bis.org)*.

Summary

This chapter concludes the material on tools for managing interest rate risk by discussing index futures; options; interest rate and other swaps; swaptions; swap futures; and interest rate caps, floors, and collars and other new derivatives. Like other financial futures, stock index futures are used to hedge against declines in existing financial positions, especially in equity portfolios. Procedures governing their use are similar to those for all futures contracts. Futures contracts have also been developed for market indexes on other financial instruments.

Options are also available for hedging. An option enables the holder to purchase or sell a financial asset or a futures contract at the strike price. A call option is purchased in anticipation of rising asset prices or falling interest rates. If the forecast is incorrect, losses are limited to the option premium. In contrast to the call option, the holder purchases a put in anticipation of falling asset prices or rising interest rates.

Hedging with futures and hedging with options are popular risk management tools. In general, financial futures present more risk to the hedger but can be more profitable.

Interest rate swaps allow two parties to exchange cash flows on debt obligations. The most common form of such agreements involves an exchange of fixed rate payment obligations for floating-rate payments. Swaps allow market participants to manage exposure to interest rate uncertainties. Many forms of interest rate swaps have been developed; currency, commodity, and equity swaps are also increasingly popular risk management tools. Although the futures markets continue to have a higher volume of participation, swap market volume grew exponentially in the late 1980s and early 1990s.

Two very new risk management tools complement the swaps market: swaptions and swap futures contracts. Swaptions are a form of option agreement; when exercised, the holder has the right to enter into a swap with a predetermined fixed rate. Depending on interest rate changes after the option is written, swaptions may provide beneficial interest rate terms for the holder. The swaps futures contract, introduced in 1991, has a value determined by expectations about the fixed rate available on a hypothetical three- or five-year swap agreement.

Finally, interest rate caps, collars, and floors allow risk managers to limit their exposure to interest rate fluctuations. Caps can be used to create a ceiling for the costs of deposits or other liabilities of financial institutions. They can also be used to limit increases in floating-rate obligations of a rate swap. An interest rate floor serves the opposite function, limiting potential decreases in returns on variable-rate assets or in the floating-rate payments to be received in a swap agreement.

New types of financial innovations are constantly appearing. Recent innovations include options to insure against catastrophic events, which help managers of p/c insurers to reduce their risk, and credit derivatives, which help to insure the risk of credit losses for financial institutions.

Questions

1. Give an example of a stock index and another market index. Why are these indexes computed, and what benefits do they offer to financial market participants? Look in *The Wall Street Journal* and find the current level for the stock index in your example.

2. What are stock index futures contracts and how can they be used for hedging? Compare and contrast their use by financial institutions for interest rate risk management with the use of interest rate futures contracts.

3. Explain the importance of the correlation between movements in an institution's stock portfolio and movements in the stock index used for hedging. How are the risks posed by this relationship similar to the risks posed by a cross hedge in the interest rate futures market?

4. Given a forecast of a bear market, why might the manager of an equity portfolio hedge with stock index futures rather than adjusting the cash portfolio? What are the advantages and disadvantages of each strategy?

5. Compare and contrast the delivery terms of stock index and interest rate futures contracts. How do the delivery characteristics of stock index futures affect hedging positions in those markets?

6. Suppose that a portfolio manager structures a stock index futures hedge based on an estimated portfolio beta equal to 1. What is the implicit assumption about the volatility of the returns on the portfolio? If the portfolio beta was 1.25, would the number of contracts traded rise, fall, or remain the same? Why?

7. What is meant by the term *index arbitrage*? Could this trading technique work in the T-bill or T-bond futures market? Why? What conclusion did the Brady Commission draw about the relationship between program trading and the stock market crash in 1987? What alternative explanation have proponents of program trading offered?

8. Describe the characteristics of an option. Compare a call option and a put option. Under what equity market forecast would a hedger buy a call option? A put option? Why?

9. What is the difference between American and European options?

10. Two call options have equal strike prices, but one has a more distant expiration date. Which option would trade at a higher value? Why? Is price volatility of the underlying asset positively or negatively related to option values? Why?

11. Under what interest rate forecast would a hedger buy a call option on debt instruments such as T-bonds? A put option? Why?

12. Explain why an asset/liability manager might choose a financial futures hedge rather than an options hedge. When is the options hedge preferred? Compare the risk exposure of the two alternatives.

13. What is the maximum loss exposure to the purchaser of a call option? To the writer of a call option?

14. Describe in your own words a plain vanilla interest rate swap. Draw a simple diagram of a typical swap agreement. Explain the terms *notional principal* and *counterparty.*

15. Examine recent forecasts of interest rates for the coming year. How might the manager of a large savings institution heavily invested in fixed rate mortgages use a swap agreement to hedge interest rate risk? What additional risks may be encountered?

16. Compare and contrast the credit risk exposure in swap agreements and futures contracts.

17. Explain how the market for interest rate swaps is organized, and describe the roles of brokers and dealers.

18. Suppose you were charged with managing interest rate risk exposure for a large commercial bank that is heavily invested in intermediate term securities and loans (i.e., those with maturities of approximately five years). Evaluate the relative advantages and disadvantages of hedging with futures versus swaps.

19. Explain a basic call swaption. Does the holder of a call swaption benefit from an interest rate increase or decrease? Give an example.

20. Explain how a swaption and a swap can be combined to give a market participant flexibility in terminating a swap obligation.

21. Describe the interest rate forecast under which it would be beneficial to buy a call option on an interest rate futures contract. Is this the same forecast under which you would buy a call swaption? Why or why not?

22. What is a swap futures contract? What determines the changes in value of swap futures?

23. What are caps and floors? Discuss the similarities between these instruments and options. Give an example of a scenario in which a financial institution manager might buy an interest rate cap.

24. What is an interest rate collar? What is its role in risk management? Could a similar hedge be structured using swaps and swaptions? Explain.

25. Briefly explain how an option contract for insured losses from catastrophic events works. How does a credit swap work? What is a return swap?

Problems

1. John Turner of the Risk-Be-Gone Property/Liability Insurance Company manages a $700 million stock portfolio. On December 15, 2003, he is watching the stock market carefully and anticipates a downturn in the next two months. He knows that liquidating part of the portfolio will involve transactions costs, so he instead chooses a hedge with stock index futures. The S&P 500 stock index is at 1068.04 on December 15, 2003 (see Figure 12.1, Panel B). Yesterday's settlement level for a March 2004 S&P index futures (see Figure 12.1, Panel A) was 1067.40. John expects the market index and futures prices to fall by 6.5 percent over the next two months. He has estimated that the company's portfolio has a beta of 1.25.

   a. Calculate the number of contracts required and the resulting gain or loss on the hedge, assuming that the market index and futures prices fall by 6.5 percent as predicted.

   b. Suppose futures prices and cash prices are not perfectly correlated so that futures prices fall by 6.2 percent when the market falls by 6.5 percent. Recalculate the gain or loss on the hedge.

   c. Now suppose that John's forecast is incorrect and that stock prices rise by 2 percent after he places the hedge. Assuming a 2 percent rise in futures prices as well, calculate the gain or loss on the hedge. What potential disadvantages of hedging are revealed by this situation?

d. Now suppose again that cash and futures positions are not perfectly correlated and that futures rise by 3 percent when stock prices rise by 2 percent. Recalculate the net results of the hedge. If John anticipated this possibility, what might he do at the time the hedge is placed?

2. Pam Lowry, Titan Corporation's pension fund manager, is expecting a $50 million cash inflow three months from now that she must invest in the equity market. Economists forecast an upswing in the stock market over the next three months. Knowing that the expected funds will miss the upswing and resulting benefits, Pam has decided to hedge by using stock index futures. The DJIA Index currently stands at 9311.19. Yesterday's settlement level for the DJIA (CBOT) futures index for settlement in three months was 9377, and economists predict an increase of 4.5 percent in the index during the same period. The average beta of the stocks in which the incoming funds will be invested is 0.87.
   a. Recommend the number of futures contracts to be traded.
   b. Calculate the gain or loss on the hedge if the economists' forecasts are correct.
   c. Calculate the gain or loss if the market falls by 4 percent and futures fall by 5 percent.

3. Lisa Brown, a commercial loan officer, has made a commitment to one of her best clients to provide a fixed rate loan for $100,000 in three months at the rate prevailing today. However, she forecasts rising rates in the interim. She recommends to the bank's portfolio manager that the position be hedged by buying a put option on T-bond futures contracts. Assume Lisa's bank will exercise the put if it is profitable to do so. The following information is available:

T-bond futures	Face value: $100,000
	Current price: 97–16
Put option	Strike price: 97–12
	Premium: $2,000

   Calculate the gain or loss on the hedge under the following conditions:
   a. Interest rates decrease; T-bond futures rise to 99.
   b. Interest rates increase; T-bond futures fall to 95–28.
   c. Interest rates increase; T-bond futures fall to 94.

4. Suppose John Turner, whose situation is described in Problem 1, can buy a stock index futures put option for a premium of $1,000 with a strike price of 1065. Assume the number of options purchased is equal to the number of contracts that would be involved in a futures hedge. Also, assume a multiplier for the strike price of $250.

a. Calculate the gain or loss on the options transaction under each of the following conditions that could prevail when options expire:
   1) The index futures continue to trade at 1067.
   2) The index futures settlement level drops to 1000.
   3) The index futures settlement level rises to 1134.
b. Calculate the gain or loss on the futures hedge described in part a of Problem 1 under each of the three scenarios in part a of this problem.
c. Compare the futures results to the gains or losses on the options hedge and assess the risk exposure of the two alternatives.

Note: This problem does not require you to calculate the net result of the options or futures hedges; that is, no calculations are required for the stock portfolio results.

5. Return to the index arbitrage example in Table 12.4. Show that the portfolio manager will gain on the transaction even if the market falls by 20 percent before the expiration date. (Hint: Remember that the futures settlement level and the index must be equal at expiration.)

6. Calculate the cash flows that each party receives for the following swap for each year. The notional value of the swap is $5 million for five years. Party A, a thrift, has fixed rate assets paying a fixed rate of 8 percent and wants variable-rate cash flows. Party B, a pension fund, has variable-rate assets with a variable rate of LIBOR + 5% and wants fixed rate cash flows. The two parties will swap the payments each year, with the net difference passed on to the party with the higher rate. LIBOR for each of the five years is given as Yr. 1: 2%; Yr. 2: 2.5%; Yr. 3: 3%; Yr. 4: 3.5%; Yr. 5: 4%. Explain which party benefited most from the swap and why the other party would still be content with the swap. What type of risk is being hedged with the swap?

7. A small bank has purchased a five-year cap from a large commercial bank with a strike rate of 8 percent and a notional value of $500,000. What will be the cash flows to the small bank if rates for each year are as follows? Yr. 1: 7%; Yr. 2: 8%; Yr. 3: 9%; Yr. 4: 8.5%; Yr. 5: 9%. Another bank purchased a five-year floor with a strike rate of 8 percent. What would be the cash flows to that bank given the same rates for each year?

Suggested Case Study

Esty, Ben, Peter Tufano, and Jonathan Headley. "Banc One Corporation: Asset and Liability Management." *Bank of America Journal of Applied Corporate Finance* 7 (Fall, 1994), 33–65 (This is also a Harvard Business Case Study). This case examines Banc One's interest swap strategy and its solution to the dramatic fall in its stock price related to analysts' opinion of its swap exposure.

Chapter 12 Minicase: Singleton Funds in Colorado

On December 5, 2003, Alby, Terrell, Caroline, and Lizzie Singleton, the dynamic quartet portfolio managers for Singleton Funds in Colorado Springs, Colorado, have a fixed income Treasury bond portfolio with a par value of $100,000,000. It currently has a market value of $109,000,000, which they want to hedge against interest rates rising and the value of the T-bond portfolio falling, since they plan on selling the bonds on December 17, 2003. They are considering a choice of January Treasury bond interest rate futures or options on T-bond futures as shown in Panel A of Figure 12A.1. Both the futures and options have underlying contracts of $100,000 per contract. Notice the settle price for the T-bond futures contract from the previous day is quoted on December 5, 2003, in *The Wall Street Journal* as 109–01 (in 32nds of 100). Under Futures Options Prices, there is a call option and a put option on a futures contract for January 2004 with a strike price of 109, as well. The strike price for the put option is quoted as 2–03 (in 64ths of 100) per $100,000 contract, which is $2\,{}^3\!/_{64}$% of $100,000 or 2.04688 percent. Hence, the premium cost is $100,000 $\times$ 0.0204688, or a $2,046.88 premium. The premium for the call option at this strike price is quoted as 0–41 (41/64 of 100) per $100,000 contract, which is 0.6406% of $100,000 (0.006406 $\times$ $100,000) or a $640.60 premium. For the hedge, the Singletons plan on cashing out on either position (reversing their trade for the futures position) or selling their option (if exercised).

a. Suppose the Singletons decide to hedge with the option on a futures strategy. Should they get a January call or put option on futures contracts to hedge against interest rates rising and the bond portfolio prices falling? How many options will they need? (Assume an equal duration, i.e., hedge ratio of 1 for the bond portfolio and the futures contracts.)

b. Based on your answer in part a, look at the new options prices in Figure 12A.1, Panel B on December 17, 2003. Should they exercise their options or not? Note the new call premium for a January contract with a strike price of 109 is 1–21 for a call and 0–23 for a put. With the premium for the call going up and the premium for the put going down, what does this imply about bond prices and interest rates between December 4 and December 17?

c. Assuming the same percentage change in T-bond prices for their portfolio as the futures prices for December contracts between December 4 and December 17, what will be the gain or loss on their T-bond portfolio? Based on your decision to exercise or not (and if you exercise, use the change in the option premiums to find a gain or loss on the options), what will be the net hedging result?

d. Suppose the Singletons had decided instead to hedge with December Treasury Bond future contracts shown in Panel A on December 4, 2003, with a settle price of 109–01, which are priced in 32nds for an underlying $100,000 T-bond, implying a quoted price of 109.03125% or a settle price of ($100,000 $\times$ 1.0903125) or $109,031.25. How many futures contracts did they need to get and what position should they have taken (short or long)?

e. Given the future prices quoted for December 17 in *The Wall Street Journal,* shown in Figure 12A.1, Panel B, with a new settle price of 111–14, what is the new settle price in dollars, and what would their gain or loss on the futures contracts be? Assuming the same percentage change in value in their portfolio as the percentage change in futures prices (between December 4 and December 17), what will be the net hedging error?

f. Based on your net hedging results, explain which strategy worked out best and why.

Selected References

Abken, Peter. "Interest-Rate Caps, Collars, and Floors." *CME Financial Strategy Paper.* Chicago Mercantile Exchange, 1991a.

———. "Beyond Plain Vanilla: A Taxonomy of Swaps." *Economic Review* (Federal Reserve Bank of Atlanta) 76 (March/April 1991b), 12–29.

———. "Interest-Rate Caps, Collars, and Floors." *Economic Review* (Federal Reserve Bank of Atlanta) 74 (November/December 1989), 2–24.

Baldoni, Robert, and Gerhard Isele. "A Simple Guide to Choosing between Futures and Swaps." *Intermarket* 3 (October 1986), 15–22.

Barro, Robert J., et al. *Black Monday and the Future of Financial Markets.* Homewood, IL: Richard D. Irwin, 1989.

Beidleman, Carl R., ed. *Interest Rate Swaps.* Homewood, IL: Business One Irwin, 1991.

Bicksler, James, and Andrew H. Chen. "An Economic Analysis of Interest Rate Swaps." *Journal of Finance* 41 (July 1986), 645–655.

Brown, Keith C., and Donald J. Smith. "Default Risk and Innovations in the Design of Interest Rate Swaps." *Financial Management* 22 (Summer 1993), 94–105.

figure   **12A.1**   SELECTED INTEREST RATE FUTURES AND FUTURES OPTIONS

PANEL A: FUTURES AND FUTURES OPTIONS PRICES FOR DECEMBER 4, 2003

December 4, 2003

FUTURES

	OPEN	HIGH	LOW	SETTLE	CHG	YIELD	CHG	OPEN INT
Interest Rate Futures								

Treasury Bonds (CBT)-$100,000; pts 32nds of 100%

Dec	108-17	109-06	108.10	109-01	17	121-18	102-14	157,468
Mr04	107-01	107-23	106-26	107-19	18	116-23	101-05	342,470
June	105-21	106-10	105-21	106-07	18	116-15	104-00	1,881

Est vol 256,404; vol Wed 328,891; open int 502,223, +4,330.

Treasury Notes (CBT)-$100,000; pts 32nds of 100%

Dec	111-28	112-12	11-235	112-09	13.5	171-17	107-16	195,830
Mr04	110-10	110-27	10-045	110-24	15.0	116-10	106-29	825,789
June	109-03	09-085	109-02	109-07	14.5	111-08	107-13	30

Est vol 575,207; vol Wed 151,362; open int 1,021,649, +2,454.

10 Yr. Agency Notes (CBT)-$100,000; pts 32nds of 100%

Dec	...	...	...	108-13	15.0	110-27	104-08	967

Est vol 0; vol Wed 0; open int 967, unch.

5 Yr. Treasury Notes (CBT)-$100,000; pts 32nds of 100%

Dec	11-115	11-215	111-08	11-195	7.5	115-01	108-27	222,382

Est vol 373,285; vol Wed 462,233; open int 965,116, +3,672.

2 Yr. Treasury Notes (CBT)-$200,000; pts 32nds of 100%

Dec	06-307	107-03	06-302	07-027	2.5	07-287	106-06	34,744

Est vol 34,024; vol Wed 36,601; open int 153,870, −963.

30 Day Federal Funds (CBT)-$5,000,000; 100 − daily avg.

Dec	98.990	98.995	98.990	98.990	...	99.230	98.400	47,154
Ja04	98.99	98.99	98.99	98.99	...	99.24	98.66	42,545
Feb	98.96	98.97	98.96	98.97	.01	99.22	98.70	69,104
Mar	98.91	98.93	98.90	98.93	.02	99.16	98.74	44,694
Apr	98.95	98.88	98.84	98.88	.04	99.17	89.96	40,313
May	98.68	98.73	98.67	98.73	.04	99.79	98.40	16,623
June	98.66	98.70	98.66	98.70	.05	98.96	98.38	13,991
July	98.46	98.46	98.46	98.49	.04	98.89	98.20	3,583

Est vol 18,202; vol Wed 32,609; open int 280,520, +3,457.

10 Yr. Interest Rate Swaps (CBT)-$100,000; pts 32nds of 100%

Dec	109-03	109-24	109-03	109-21	18	110-31	105-10	18,456

Est vol 16,813; vol Wed 8,688; open int 43,428, +959.

10 Yr. Muni Note Index (CBT)-$1,000 x index

Dec	101-24	102-09	101-24	102-05	12	103-14	97-13	1,575

Est vol 158; vol Wed 1,172; open int 2,397, +79.

Index: Close 102-21; Yield 4,666.

December 4, 2003

FUTURES OPTIONS PRICES

STRIKE	CALLS-SETTLE			PUTS-SETTLE		
Interest Rate						

T-Bonds (CBT)
$100,000; points and 64ths of 100%

PRICE	JAN	FEB	MAR	JAN	FEB	MAR
107	1-36	2-16	2-56	0-62	1-42	2-18
108	1-02	1-47	2-22	1-28	2-09	2-48
109	0-41	1-19	1-57	2-03	2-45	3-19
110	0-24	0-60	1-32	2-50	3-22	3-58
111	0-13	0-42	1-11	3-39	4-04	4-36
112	0-07	0-29	0-58	4-32	4-54	5-19

Est vol 24,443;
Wd vol 27,840 calls 10,016 puts
Op int Wed 359,146 calls 229,830 puts

T-Notes (CBT)
$100,000; points and 64ths of 100%

PRICE	JAN	FEB	MAR	JAN	FEB	MAR
110	1-27	1-58	2-20	0-43	1-10	1-36
111	0-55	1-23	1-49	1-07	1-39	2-01
112	0-30	0-59	1-20	1-46	2-11	2-36
113	0-15	0-38	0-61	2-31	2-54	3-13
114	0-07	0-24	0-43	3-23	3-40	3-58
115	0-03	0-14	0-29	4-19	4-29	...

Est vol 116,051 Wd 67,289 calls 59,354 puts
Op int Wed 661,388 calls 721,435 puts

5 Yr Treas Notes (CBT)
$100,000; points and 64ths of 100%

PRICE	JAN	FEB	MAR	JAN	FEB	MAR
11050	0-34	0-54	1-07	0-48	1-04	1-21
11100	0-21	0-40	0-57	1-03	...	1-39
11150	0-13	0-29	0-44	1-27	1-43	1-58
11200	0-07	...	0-34	...	...	...
11250	0-04	0-14	0-26	...	...	...
11300	0-02	...	0-19	...	...	...

Est vol 90,085 Wd 6,658 calls 38,943 puts
Op int Wed 99,608 calls 292,361 puts

30 Day Federal Funds (CBT)
$5,000,000; 100 minus daily average

PRICE	DEC	JAN	FEB	DEC	JAN	FEB
988750	...	...	.110	.005	...	.020
989375	...	...	.060	.007	...	.030
990000	.005	.007	.010	.015	.017	.045
990625	.002	...	...	...	...	...
991250	.002	.002	.002	.137	...	...

Source: The Wall Street Journal, *December 5, 2003, C11.*

————. "Forward Swaps, Swap Options, and the Management of Callable Debt." In *New Developments in Commercial Banking,* ed. Donald Chew. Cambridge, MA: Blackwell Publishers, 1991.

Canter, Michael S., Joseph B. Cole, and Richard L. Sandor. "Insurance Derivatives: A New Asset Class for the Capital Markets and a New Hedging Tool for the Insurance Industry." *Bank of America Journal of Applied Corporate Finance* 10 (Fall 1997), 69–83.

Caouette, John B., Edward I. Altman, and Paul Narayanan. *Managing Credit Risk: The Next Great Financial Challenge.* New York: John Wiley & Sons, 1998.

Chance, Don M. *An Introduction to Options and Futures,* 2nd ed. Chicago: Dryden Press, 1992.

Chicago Board of Trade. *Commodity Trading Manual.* Chicago: Board of Trade of the City of Chicago, 1989.

————. *MMI Futures and Options.* Chicago: Board of Trade of the City of Chicago, 1991.

————. *Stock Index Futures.* Chicago: Board of Trade of the City of Chicago, 1987.

————. *NASDAQ-100 Index Futures.* Chicago: Board of Trade of the City of Chicago, 1986a.

————. *An Introduction to Options on Treasury Bond Futures.* Chicago: Board of Trade of the City of Chicago, 1986b.

————. *Options on U.S. Treasury Bond Futures for Institutional Investors.* Chicago: Board of Trade of the City of Chicago, 1985.

Chicago Mercantile Exchange. *Using S&P Index Futures and Options.* Chicago: Chicago Mercantile Exchange, 1985.

Christopher, Benjamin B. "Recent Developments Affecting Depository Institutions." *FDIC Banking Review* 2 (Spring/Summer 1989), 37.

Doherty, Neil A. "Financial Innovation in the Management of Catastrophe Risk." *Bank of America Journal of Applied Corporate Finance* 10 (Fall 1997), 84–95.

Felgran, Steven D. "Interest Rate Swaps: Use, Risk, and Prices." *New England Economic Review* (Federal Reserve Bank of Boston) (November/December 1987), 22–32.

Goodman, Laurie. "New Options Markets." *Quarterly Review* (Federal Reserve Bank of New York) 8 (Autumn 1983), 35–47.

figure **12A.1** SELECTED INTEREST RATE FUTURES AND FUTURES OPTIONS (CONTINUED)

PANEL B: FUTURES AND FUTURES OPTIONS PRICES FOR DECEMBER 17, 2003

December 17, 2003

FUTURES
Interest Rate Futures

Treasury Bonds (CBT)-$100,000; pts 32nds of 100%

Dec	111-04	111-29	111-04	111-14	23	121-18	102-14	57,162
Mr04	109-14	110-14	109-13	109-31	23	116-23	101-05	396,846
June	108-14	109-00	108-14	108-18	23	116-15	104-00	9,828

Est vol 190,926; vol Tue 182,095; open int 464,253, +852.

Treasury Notes (CBT)-$100,000; pts 32nds of 100%

Dec	13-295	114-09	13-275	113-31	9.0	117-17	107-16	29,596
Mr04	112-11	112-30	112-11	112-19	11.5	116-10	106-29	892,590
June	10-235	111-13	10-235	111-02	11.5	111-13	104-13	61

Est vol 438,889; vol Tue 471,950; open int 922,247, -10.206.

10 Yr. Agency Notes (CBT)-$100,000; pts 32nds of 100%

Dec	...	...	...	10-095	11.5	110-27	104-08	962

Est vol 0; vol Tue 0; open int 962, unch.

5 Yr. Treasury Notes (CBT)-$100,000; pts 32nds of 100%

Dec	12-225	113-00	12-235	112-25	3.5	115-01	108-27	48,097

Est vol 182,975; vol Tue 268,394; open int 862,804, -10,968.

2 Yr. Treasury Notes (CBT)-$200,000; pts 32nds of 100%

Dec	07-202	107-22	07-192	07-197	1.0	07-287	106-06	12,676

Est vol 14,807; vol Tue 8,631; open int 148,799, -343.

30 Day Federal Funds (CBT)-$5,000,000; 100 - daily avg.

Dec	98.995	98.995	98.995	98.995	...	99.230	98.400	44,912
Ja04	98.99	98.99	98.99	98.99	...	99.24	98.66	50,781
Feb	98.99	98.99	98.98	98.99	...	99.22	98.70	79,117
Mar	98.97	98.98	98.97	98.97	...	99.16	98.74	50,434
Apr	98.95	98.96	98.95	98.95	...	99.17	89.96	55,928
May	98.88	98.89	98.88	98.88	...	99.79	98.40	23,066
June	98.86	98.86	98.86	98.86	...	98.96	98.38	15,955
July	98.77	98.77	98.74	98.75	...	98.89	98.20	8,836

Est vol 10,122; vol Tue 17,731; open int 331,515, +1,867.

10 Yr. Interest Rate Swaps (CBT)-$100,000; pts 32nds of 100%

Mar	110-13	110-21	110-10	110-11	12	110-21	107-20	35,318

Est vol 606; vol Tue 1,195; open int 42,414, +141.

10 Yr. Muni Note Index (CBT)-$1,000 x index

Dec	103-28	104-03	103-27	103-27	9	104-03	97-13	511

Est vol 195; vol Tue 235; open int 2,315, +31.

Index: Close 104-00; Yield 4.497.

December 17, 2003

FUTURES OPTIONS PRICES

STRIKE	CALLS-SETTLE	PUTS-SETTLE

Interest Rate

T-Bonds (CBT)
$100,000; points and 64ths of 100%

PRICE	JAN	FEB	MAR	JAN	FEB	MAR
109	1-21	2-08	2-48	0-23	1-10	1-50
110	0-45	1-36	2-13	0-47	1-38	2-15
111	0-20	1-07	1-47	1-22	2-09	2-49
112	0-08	0-48	1-21	2-10	2-50	3-22
113	0-03	0-31	1-01	...	3-32	4-02
114	0-01	0-19	0-47	4-03	...	4-48

Est vol 55,335;
Tu vol 22,047 calls 18,509 puts
Op int Tues 409,464 calls 276,961 puts

T-Notes (CBT)
$100,000; points and 64ths of 100%

PRICE	JAN	FEB	MAR	JAN	FEB	MAR
112	0-59	1-31	1-62	0-21	0-57	1-24
113	0-23	0-61	1-27	0-49	1-23	1-53
114	0-07	0-36	0-63	1-33	1-62	2-25
115	0-01	0-19	0-42	2-27	2-45	...
116	0-01	0-09	0-27	...	...	3-53
117	0-01	0-04	0-17	...	...	...

Est vol 226,376 Tu 39,409 calls 69,238 puts
Op int Tues 737,097 calls 818,437 puts

5 Yr Treas Notes (CBT)
$100,000; points and 64ths of 100%

PRICE	JAN	FEB	MAR	JAN	FEB	MAR
11200	0-14	0-37	0-56	0-37	0-61	1-15
11250	0-06	0-25	0-42	...	...	...
11300	0-03	0-15	0-31	...	...	...
11350	0-01	0-09	0-22	...	...	...
11400	0-01	0-05	0-16	...	...	...
11450	0-01	0-03	0-11	...	...	...

Est vol 30,854 Tu 6,831 calls 12,671 puts
Op int Tues 122,745 calls 351,954 puts

30 Day Federal Funds (CBT)
$5,000,000; 100 minus daily average

PRICE	DEC	JAN	FEB	DEC	JAN	FEB
988750	...	...	.120	.002	...	.010
989375	...	...	.060	.002	...	0.15
990000	.005	.005	.007	.010	.015	.022
990625	.002	...	...	...	...	...
991250	.002	.002	.002	.132	...	...

Source: The Wall Street Journal, *December 18, 2003, C13.*

Hansell, Saul, and Kevin Muehring. "Why Derivatives Rattle the Regulators." *Institutional Investor* (September 1992).

Hill, Joanne M., Anshuman Jain, and Robert A. Ward, Jr. *Portfolio Insurance: Volatility Risk and Futures Mispricing.* New York: Kidder Peabody and Co., 1987.

Hutchinson, Michael M. "Swaps." *Weekly Letter* (Federal Reserve Bank of San Francisco) (May 3, 1985).

Koppenhaver, G. D. "Futures Options and Their Use by Financial Intermediaries." *Economic Perspectives* (Federal Reserve Bank of Chicago) 10 (January/February 1986), 18–31.

Litzenberger, Robert. "Swaps: Plain and Fanciful." *Journal of Finance* 47 (July 1992), 831–850.

Loeys, Jan G. "Interest Rate Swaps: A New Tool for Managing Risk." *Business Review* (Federal Reserve Bank of Philadelphia) (May/June 1985), 17–25.

Marshall, John F. "Futures Versus Swaps: Some Considerations for the Thrift Industry." *Review of Business* 12 (Winter 1990–1991), 15–22, 44.

Merrick, John J., Jr. "Fact and Fantasy about Stock Index Futures Program Trading." *Business Review* (Federal Reserve Bank of Philadelphia) (September/October 1987), 13–25.

Moser, James T. "Credit Derivatives: Just-in-time Provisioning for Loan Losses." *Economic Perspectives* (Federal Reserve Bank of Chicago) (Fourth Quarter 1998), 2–11.

Napoli, Janet A. "Derivative Markets and Competitiveness." *Economic Perspectives* (Federal Reserve Bank of Chicago) 16 (July/August 1992), 13–24.

Remolona, Eli M. "The Recent Growth of Financial Derivative Markets." *Quarterly Review* (Federal Reserve Bank of New York) 17 (Winter 1992–1993), 28–43.

Smith, Clifford W., Jr., Charles W. Smithson, and Lee Macdonald Wakeman. "The Market for Interest Rate Swaps." *Financial Management* 18 (Winter 1988), 34–44.

———. "The Evolving Market for Swaps." In *New Developments in Commercial Banking,* ed. by Donald Chew. Cambridge, MA: Blackwell Publishers, 1991.

Spahr, Ronald W., Jan E. Luytjes, and Donald G. Edwards. "The Use of Caps as Deposit Hedges for Financial Institutions." *Issues in Bank Regulation* 12 (Summer 1988), 17–23.

Stoll, Hans R., and Robert E. Whaley. *Expiration Day Effects of Index Futures and Options.* New York: Salomon Brothers Center for the Study of Financial Institutions, 1986.

Tavakoli, Janet M. *Credit Derivatives: A Guide to Instruments and Applications.* New York: John Wiley & Sons, 1998.

Wall, Larry D., and John J. Pringle. "Interest Rate Swaps: A Review of the Issues." *Economic Review* (Federal Reserve Bank of Atlanta) 73 (November/December 1988), 22–40.

———. "Alternative Explanations of Interest Rate Swaps: A Theoretical and Empirical Analysis." *Financial Management* 18 (Summer 1989), 59–73.

Wall, Larry D., John J. Pringle, and James E. McNulty. "Capital Requirements for Interest Rate and Foreign-Exchange Hedges."

Economic Review (Federal Reserve Bank of Atlanta) 75 (May/June 1990), 14–29.

Wall, Larry D., and Milind M. Shrikhande. "Credit Derivatives." *Working Paper* (Federal Reserve Bank of Atlanta) (Fall 1998).

Whittaker, J. Gregg. "Interest Rate Swaps: Risk and Regulation." *Economic Review* (Federal Reserve Bank of Kansas City) 72 (March 1987), 3–13.

internet *exercise*

INTEREST RATE RISK MANAGEMENT: INDEX FUTURES, OPTIONS, SWAPS, AND OTHER DERIVATIVES

CHICAGO BOARD OF TRADE (CBOT) INTEREST RATE SWAP FUTURES

The CBOT began trading a 10-Year Interest Rate Swap Futures Contract in 2001. To see information on this contract, go to *http://www.cbot.com*. Once you get to the home page, go to the top and click on "Products." From the menu choices given, pick "Interest Rate." A new menu choice will show all the CBOT's interest rate products in a list on the left; click on "Swaps." Once you're on the Swap page, look toward the bottom of the page and you'll see lots of different choices including Product Strategies. Select "Hedging a Fixed-Income Portfolio with Swap Futures." This will give you a detailed article on hedging. Different uses for interest rate swap futures are also given, along with articles by researchers on swaps. You can also click on "Chart" and see a chart of prices for the 10-Year Interest Rate Swap Futures.

BUSINESS.COM: SEARCHING FOR ARTICLES ON CREDIT DERIVATIES

Business.com is a nice search engine that gives you listings of items on the Web for different topics, including research topics. Go to http://www.business.com. From this Website, you can search for anything you're looking for by typing in words or phrases in the box at the top of the screen. Type in "Credit Derivatives Research." From among the choices that appear, click on "Credit Derivatives Research & Reference." A list of articles on credit risk and derivatives will appear. One excellent article on the list is an introductory article on credit derivatives by Don Chance. Click on this link and the article will appear. A number of different articles on different topics provide

detailed information on credit derivative swaps, pricing, credit-linked notes, among others. You can also search for other topics and find articles on swaptions and other types of derivaties as well.

BANKWEST AND OTHER BANK WEBSITE INTEREST RATE PRODUCTS

Go to *http://www.bankwest.com.au/business/Business_ Services/Financial_Markets/Interest_Rate_Products/* or, if you prefer, go to *http://www.bankwest.com.au* and work through the links to get to the Interest Rate Products page. This Website provides an explanation of interest rate swaps, swaptions, swaption collars, caps and collars, and sample PDF case studies for each (requires Adobe Acrobat Reader). If you search on *http://www.google.com* or another search engine for interest rate swaps or interest rate derivatives, you will find links to other financial institutions that offer services and information on different types of interest rate derivatives as well.

USEFUL LINKS FOR FINANCIAL INSTITUTION DATA

Applied Derivatives Trading Magazine

http://www.appliederivates.com/

Chicago Board Options Exchange

http://www.cboe.com/

Coffee, Sugar & Cocoa Exchange, Inc.

http://www.csce.com/

IV

Asset and Liability Management Problems for Depository Institutions

13 Asset Management

Commercial, Consumer, and Mortgage Lending

"Revolutionary changes are taking place in the management of credit risk. When a loan was made in the past, the associated credit risk remained on the lender's balance sheet until the debt was repaid or written off. Today, the loan and the risk are just as likely to be resold and/or reconfigured for incorporation into a structured financing that serves as an intermediary between the saving and borrowing sectors. Traditionally, lenders viewed credit risk as a cost of doing business—a hazard to defend against. Today, they see credit risk as something of value that can be packaged and traded."

JOHN CAOUETTE, EDWARD I. ALTMAN, AND PAUL NARAYANAN, Managing Credit Risk: The Next Great Financial Challenge, *New York: Wiley Frontiers in Finance, 1998, ix.*

he years of the early twenty-first century were generally good years for banks with low loan losses and healthy profitability on lending operations. Five years earlier, however, in 1998, banks in many countries faced severe problems from loan losses, which in turn often had a significant effect on that country's economy. In Indonesia, Korea, Japan, Russia, and Thailand, banks and finance companies faced the results of speculative commercial real estate and other risky loans made during the early 1990s that later soured. Large commercial banks in the United States that had international loan exposure also faced large losses. Factors often listed in the financial press to explain bank failures in Asia and Russia include (1) close, relaxed relationships between banks and industries in bank-oriented financial systems; (2) lax regulation, fraud, and bribery by regulators; and (3) cronyism including powerful families who own banks and use them as "private finance houses for their business empires;" and (4) poor lending practices.[1] Later into the early 2000s, large banks in Japan and Germany suffered large loan losses that worried regulators as well.

In the early 1990s, analysts had predicted a continued long-term decline in bank lending in the United States, with large corporate customers disintermediating to the direct lending markets. However, bank lending rose dramatically in the mid- to late-1990s and continues to be a dominant activity for most

Learning Objectives

After completing this chapter, you will be able to in:

Part A: Lending Trends Policies, and Management Trends in Types of Loans

1 Follow trends in bank lending and explain the reasons for these trends.

2 Understand the functions of the credit process used by financial institutions to protect against default risk and credit policies.

3 List some of the most important bank regulations that are associated with making loans.

Part B: Evaluating and Structuring Bank Loans to Manage Credit Risk

4 Understand basic quantitative credit scoring models

5 Create a simple loan presentation and analyze a loan decision.

6 Define the terms associated with a loan including pricing (rate and noninterest terms) and restrictive covenants and know how terms should be set to help ensure profitability and loan repayment.

7 Explain the special considerations and typical terms associated with different types of loans.

8 Understand loan monitoring and review procedures and other lending considerations.

U.S. depository institutions. This chapter examines bank lending, focusing on U.S. banks. The first section is Part A: Lending Trends, Policies and Management; followed by Part B: Evaluating and Structuring Bank Loans to Manage Bank Risk.

PART A: LENDING TRENDS, POLICIES, AND MANAGEMENT

Trends in Types of Loans

As of August 2003, U.S. commercial banks had $4.448 trillion of loans (an increase of greater than $1 trillion since 1998) on their balance sheets, amounting to about 57 percent of total assets of $7.8035 trillion. As shown in Figure 13.1, of these loans, 20 percent were commercial loans and 50 percent were real estate loans, with about 11 percent of these being home equity loans. Consumer loans were 13 percent of total loans. The remaining 17 percent of loans consisted of security loans, other loans and leases, and interbank loans. Hence, commercial banks have moved more into consumer and mortgage lending. The following sections discuss key factors for the three primary types of lending for depository institutions and finance companies: commercial, consumer, and mortgage lending, beginning with brief overviews of trends in each of these areas.

---

1 See Seth Mydans. "Indonesia Begins the Rescue and Consolidation of Banks." *New York Times* (January 20, 1998), C2; Joseph Kahn. "Thailand Nationalizes Three Faltering Private Banks." *New York Times* (February 7, 1998), 13–3B; Namju Cho. "In South Korea, Bad Loans Soar to $6.1 Billion," *The Wall Street Journal* (February 27, 1998), A11; Betsy McKay. "Russia's Banks Planted Seeds of Their Own Problems." *The Wall Street Journal* (August 31, 1998), A10; and Sheryl WuDunn. "Tokyo Tries to Calm Fears on Bad Loans." *New York Times* (November 13, 1998), C1–C5.

---

figure **13.1**   TYPES OF COMMERCIAL BANK LOANS, NOVEMBER 2003

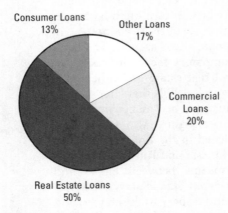

Total Loans, August 2003: *$4,448 trillion*

Source: Compiled by Authors from Federal Reserve Bulletin, *November 2003, Table 1.26, A15.*

Commercial Lending: Recent Trends

Figure 13.2 shows trends in bank credit from 1994 to 2003. Loan growth for banks generally rises during expansions and falls during recessions. Credit growth peaked at about 12 percent in mid-2000 and then fell during the recession of 2001 (defined by the National Bureau of Economic Research as starting in March 2001 and ending in November 2001). Growth in bank credit rose with the recovery in 2002 to a peak of about 13 percent in 2003, followed by a moderate downturn. Growth in bank credit securities (such as mortgage-backed credit card receivables and automobile-loan-backed securities), total loans and leases, and commercial and industrial loans, as shown in the lower panels, followed a similar trend. The decline in growth for commercial and industrial loans was very significant, becoming negative in 2001 and continuing to be negative in 2002 and 2003.

Unique Aspects of Bank Lending to Small to Medium-Sized Firms

With the information and technological age from 1970 on, the "special role" of depository institutions in assessing relevant information on large borrowers, information that is readily available to investors, has become less important. The availability of information makes it easier for large corporations to issue bonds and commercial paper in the direct markets, reducing the special role of banks in lending to large corporations in the United States.

However, depository institutions continue to play an important information role for the financing of small to medium-sized firms where information is not readily available. It is difficult for investors to obtain information on small to medium-sized privately held firms, creating significant information asymmetries between borrowers and lenders. The cost of monitoring individual borrowers' behavior can also be substantial. Depositories reduce monitoring costs by entering into financial contracts with (lending to) many borrowers on similar contract terms, then using specialized personnel and resources that can be devoted entirely to enforcing the contracts. Depositories can, in the context of a lending relationship, exert direct influence on a borrower's financial conduct and decisions. Also, once relevant data on a borrower has been collected and an initial loan application processed, cost economies are associated with the next application from that borrower. Information asymmetry is reduced because the lender knows more about the borrower's ability and intention to pay than at the time of the first application. Cost reductions can be significant for depositories that cultivate a strong clientele of regular borrowers. These depositories can, in turn, pass the cost savings to their depositors and shareholders.

Borrowers, too, benefit from information reusability and reduction of information asymmetry. For example, applying for a loan becomes less arduous as more financial contracts are made with the same

figure 13.2 TRENDS IN BANK CREDIT, 1994 TO 2003

Bank Credit
Percent Change from Year Ago

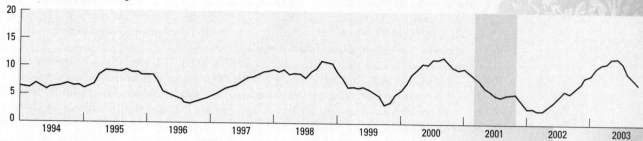

Investment Securities in Bank Credit at Commercial Banks
Percent Change from Year Ago

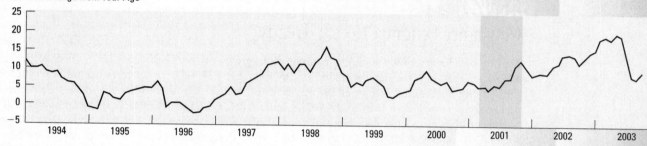

Total Loans and Leases in Bank Credit at Commercial Banks
Percent Change from Year Ago

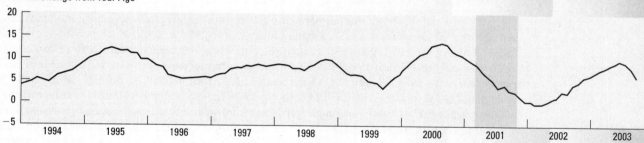

Commercial and Industrial Loans at Commercial Banks
Percent Change from Year Ago

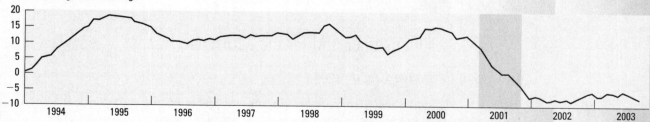

Source: The Federal Reserve Bank of St. Louis Monetary Trends, *November 2003, 14.*

lender. Further, research shows that a corporate borrower's shareholders bid up the firm's stock price after the firm announces it is undertaking new bank borrowing. If a commercial bank, with its "inside" knowledge, is willing to give a firm its "seal of approval," the securities markets appear to interpret that fact as reducing their need to monitor that same firm. Hence, depositories are indeed still special, and banks have increased their lending to small and medium-sized businesses. Lending to smaller firms has higher credit analysis and monitoring costs. But by being willing to provide additional liquidity, being flexible, and solving problems when they arise, many banks have been able to differentiate themselves from the impersonality of the direct finance marketplace.

The issue took on added significance in the early 1990s when many would-be borrowers accused banks of creating a "credit crunch" in response to tightening regulation and supervision during 1990–1992, a time when bank loan growth was close to zero. Some small and medium-sized business applicants claimed they could not get loans because banks' credit standards had become so unreasonable that no one could qualify. Many community banks continued to serve their small and medium-sized customers. Bank relationships continue to be "special" for small and medium-sized firms in the United States, implying that if banks cut off funds to this group, few alternative funding sources would arise. Many large banks have also set up special divisions that specialize in small firm lending.

Consumer Lending: Recent Trends

As shown in Figure 13.3, Panel A, consumer credit grew at a very fast rate in the last decade, peaking in 1995 and again in 2000. Regulators in the 1980s and early 1990s were concerned about a very low ratio for personal income relative to credit market debt, with U.S. household credit market debt nearly 81 percent of personal income by mid-1998. A Federal Reserve Bank of St. Louis study noted that this may have been the result of consumers feeling wealthier with a rising stock market, as well as changes in societal attitudes toward personal indebtedness from both borrower and lender perspectives.[2]

Growth Rates in Nonperforming Loans as a Risk Measure, 1984 to 2002

Figure 13.3, Panel B, shows the nonperforming loan ratio (aggregate nonperforming loans as a percentage of total loans) for the U.S. banking industry from 1984 to 2002, which peaked in 1991, during the recession of the early 1990s, particularly for commercial real estate lenders with the real estate market's collapse at that time. After 1991, the percentage of nonperforming loans fell dramatically to just 1 percent in 1994, rising modestly by 0.5 percent to 1.5 percent in 2002. As noted in an article by Stiroh and Metli (2003) in *Current Issues in Economics and Finance*, banks were much healthier in the early 2000s than the early 1990s by having larger reserves for loan losses and larger equity-to-asset ratios as a buffer against future loan charge-offs. Examining nonperforming loan ratios over time by loan type in Panel C, rising nonperforming loans in the early 1990s were primarily associated with several different industry sectors including commercial and industrial and real estate loans. The recent rise in nonperforming loans in 2002 was concentrated in commercial loans to the telecommunications industry by large banks, with the broadcast and telecommunications industry accounting for nearly one-quarter of the aggregate ratios.[3]

Who Makes Consumer and Home Mortgage Loans?

Holders of Consumer Credit

Figure 13.4 shows the major suppliers of consumer credit as of July 2003. Surprisingly, securitized pools, as discussed in Chapter 7 (where loans are packaged in pools and sold as securities to investors) were the largest holders (35 percent), along with commercial banks (33 percent), followed by finance

---

2 See William R. Emmons. "Is Household Debt Too High?" The Federal Reserve Bank of St. Louis *Monetary Trends* (December 1998), 1; and Ana M. Aizcorbe, Arthur B. Kennickell, and Kevin B. Moore. "Recent Changes in U.S. Family Finances: Evidence from the 1998 and 2001 Survey of Consumer Finances." *Federal Reserve Bulletin*, January 2003, 1–32.

3 Kevin J. Stiroh and Christopher Metli. "Now and Then: The Evolution of Loan Quality for U.S. Banks." Federal Reserve Bank of New York: *Current Issues in Economics and Finance*, Volume 9, No. 4, April 2003, 1–6.

companies (13 percent), credit unions (12 percent), savings institutions (4 percent), and nonfinancial firms (3 percent). Credit card banks, commercial banks, and finance companies, such as General Motors Acceptance Corporation (GMAC), are large securitizers of consumer debt. In 1992, the percentage of securitized consumer debt was only 15 percent! Hence, banks have a great deal of competition.

Holders of Mortgage Debt

As shown in Figure 13.5, securitized mortgage pools are also the largest holder of mortgage debt (49 percent), followed by commercial banks (24 percent), savings institutions (10 percent), federal and related agencies (5 percent), and life insurance companies (3 percent). Mortgage pools and trusts are generated by the Government National Mortgage Association (GNMA), Federal Home Loan Mortgage Association (FHLMC), Federal National Mortgage Association (FNMA), and the Farm Home Administration (FHA), as well as private mortgage pools. GNMA, FHLMC, and FNMA held about 76 percent of the assets in the mortgage pools and trusts as of July 2003. These agencies also held 5 percent of mortgages outside of pools. Depository institutions continue to be large holders of mortgage debt and also large suppliers for securitizations.

figure **13.3**   TRENDS IN CONSUMER LENDING AND NONPERFORMING LOANS BY LOAN TYPE

PANEL A: GROWTH RATES IN CONSUMER CREDIT

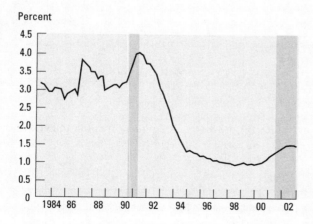

Source: Federal Reserve Bank of St. Louis Monetary Trends, *November 2003, 7.*

PANEL B: THE NONPERFORMING LOAN RATIO FOR THE U.S. BANKING INDUSTRY, 1984 TO 2002

Notes: *The nonperforming loan ratio is defined as aggregate nonperforming loans as a percentage of total loans. Shaded areas indicate periods designated recessions by the National Bureau of Economic Research.*

Source: *Kevin J. Stiroh and Christopher Metli. "Now and Then: The Evolution of Loan Quality for U.S. Banks." Federal Reserve Bank of New York: Current Issues in Economics and Finance, Volume 9, No. 4, April 2003, p. 2, Chart 1.*

figure **13.3** TRENDS IN CONSUMER LENDING AND NONPERFORMING LOANS BY LOAN TYPE (CONTINUED)

PANEL C: DECOMPOSITION OF THE NONPERFORMING LOAN RATIOS BY MAJOR LOAN RATIO TYPE, 1984 TO 2002

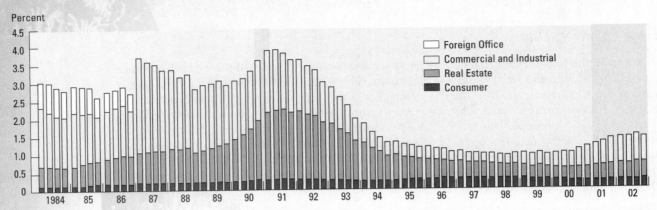

Notes: The contribution of each loan type to the aggregate nonperforming loan (NPL) ratio equals the share-weighted NPL ratio of that loan type. Foreign office loans are broken out only for first-quarter 1984 to fourth-quarter 1986; after that period, they are classified by loan type. Shaded areas indicate periods designated recessions by the National Bureau of Economic Research.

Source: Kevin J. Stiroh and Christopher Metli. "Now and Then: The Evolution of Loan Quality for U.S. Banks." Federal Reserve Bank of New York: Current Issues in Economics and Finance, Volume 9, No. 4, April 2003, p. 3, Chart 2.

PANEL D: DECOMPOSITION OF THE NONPERFORMING LOAN RATIOS BY BANK SIZE, 1984 TO 2002

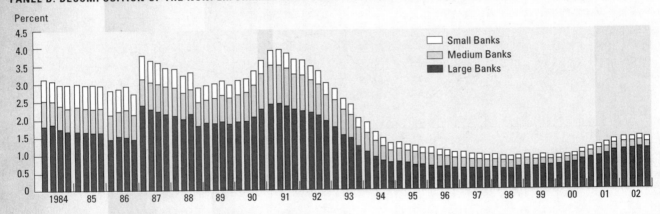

Notes: The contribution of each size class to the aggregate nonperforming loan (NPL) ratio equals the share-weighted NPL ratio of that group of banks. Small banks have assets less than $500 million; medium banks, assets between $500 million and $10 billion; and large banks, assets greater than $10 billion (all values are in constant 2002 dollars). Shaded areas indicate periods designated recessions by the National Bureau of Economic Research.

Source: Kevin J. Stiroh and Christopher Metli. "Now and Then: The Evolution of Loan Quality for U.S. Banks." Federal Reserve Bank of New York: Current Issues in Economics and Finance, Volume 9, No. 4, April 2003, p. 3, Chart 3.

The following sections discuss the overall credit process including its function, policies and objectives, and credit analysis, and the pricing and structure for different types of loans.

Concept Questions

1 What are the percentages of different types of loans held by commercial banks in 2003? Why do you think commercial banks have taken on fewer commercial loans and more of other types of loans?

2 Discuss trends in the growth of bank credit in recent years. Why did the percentage of nonperforming loans go

up in the early 2000s? What industry sectors were involved?

3 Who are the primary suppliers of consumer and mortgage credit? Why have securitized loans taken a bigger role?

figure   **13.4**   SUPPLIERS OF CONSUMER CREDIT, 2003

Total Consumer Credit, July 2003: $1.763 trillion

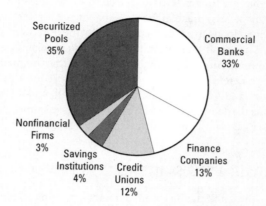

Source: Federal Reserve Bulletin, *November 2003, A34.*

figure   **13.5**   HOLDERS OF MORTGAGE DEBT, FIRST QUARTER 2003

Mortgage Pools or Trusts

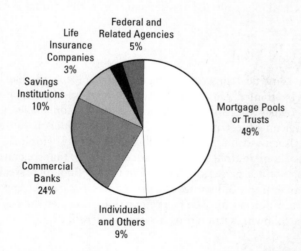

Note: Mortgage Debt Outstanding includes one- to four-family residences, multifamily residences, nonfarm residences, and farm mortgages. Mortgage Pools or Trusts include GNMA, FHLMC, FNMA, and FHA pools, along with private mortgage pools.

Source: Federal Reserve Bulletin, *November 2003, A34.*

Functions of the Credit Process: The Credit Process as Protection against Default Risk

Financial institutions want to underwrite (structure) loans to reduce the risk to the institution. Credit policies also need to be uniform and fair to all lenders, and to follow the strategic policies of the institution, including the types of loans the institution wants to makes. Risks of loans include default risk as the result of firm-specific practices, such as mismanagement and dishonesty and economic and industry-related factors that might lead to a firm's bankruptcy, such as problems in the telecommunications industry in the early 2000s. In addition, longer-term, fixed rate loans have greater interest rate risk than variable-rate loans, although variable-rate loans have greater default risk (since borrowers may not be able to pay rising rates) if they are longer-term and fixed rate. Variable-rate loans have less interest rate risk, but since borrowers will have to make higher loan payments if interest rates rise, they have greater default risk. The structuring of loans to ensure repayment by the borrower is one of the keys to an effective bank lending process. The credit evaluation process is also crucial.

To protect the bank and maximize the profitability of loans that are made, banks must have a credit process in place including a carefully written loan policy, loan request procedures and a process for credit analysis, a process for credit execution and administration, and a credit review process to identify problems early for loans that have been made. The loan process must also conform to a large number of lending regulations, discussed in more detail in a later section.

The Role of the Credit Process in Business Development

In addition to protecting the bank against nonpayment, the bank credit process includes business development for the bank. This includes loan call programs, advertising, marketing, and developing relationships. Several decisions have to be made including what areas will be targeted for potential business, what the forecast demand for bank services is, and how employees will be trained regarding all bank products. Loan officers have become more market-oriented, gathering business for the bank including becoming active in community organizations and calling on desirable firms to get their business for the bank. Lenders must also be trained in cross-selling other products, such as cash management products including online banking services, sweep accounts, lockboxes, automatic check deposits, and bill paying services, among others. Credit analysts assist the loan officer in obtaining financial statements, credit reports and ratings, and in performing financial statement analysis. Bank procedures ensure that credit information is collected and presented in a uniform fashion.

Loan Committee Review

Loan officers are given some flexibility depending on their seniority and bank policies in determining whether loans should be granted. Larger loans must be approved by a loan committee consisting of loan officers, often the bank's regulatory compliance officer, and, for smaller banks, often the chief officers of the bank. The loan officer presents the loan request information and the weaknesses and strengths of the loan. Usually, loan officers have close relationships with loan customers, so they act as the advocate for their customers at the loan committee meetings. In turn, bank officers and other lending officers grill the loan officer presenting the loan in terms of potential weaknesses or problems that the loan might have. An example of loan request procedures is shown in Appendix 13A. Underwriting guidelines have a uniform format for ease of presentation, discussed later in the chapter. Before presenting procedures, the following section provides an overview of a bank's overall written loan policies.

Banks' Written Loan Policies

A bank's overall loan policy reflects long-term strategic planning for the overall asset portfolio including setting general guidelines for the size of the loan portfolio, its composition, and the maximum acceptable level of default risk. For example, in a commercial bank, decisions must be made about the proportion of loan funds to be invested in different types of loans. These decisions influence the way a depository advertises its services, the customers whose loan applications will be given preference, and many other aspects of lending. Specific industries or markets that the bank wishes to target where lending officers have expertise are also included. Goals for loan volume and loan quality balances with a bank's liquidity, capital, and rate of return objectives are also incorporated, along with systems and controls to reduce credit risk. In addition, standards and procedures are included in terms of loan quality and procedures for documenting and reviewing loans and loan pricing.

Compliance Policies

Loan policies and procedures for complying with lending regulations also need to be put in place. Some of the major consumer lending regulations are as follows:

- The **Equal Credit Opportunity Act (Reg B)**, whereby the bank is forbidden to discriminate in lending on the basis of race, color, national origin, sex, age, religion, marital status, and/or receipt of public assistance.

- The **Fair Housing Act**, which forbids discrimination based on any handicap or family status.

- The **Fair Credit Reporting Act of 1970**, which requires consumer credit reporting agencies to stress accuracy, correct errors promptly, and release individuals' consumer histories only for legitimate purposes. Customers also must be told why they are not given loans and have the right to know of any discrepancies in their credit reports.

- **Truth in Lending (TIL)**, which requires that a bank must quote its rates as annual percentage rates (APRs).

- **Reg Z**, which sets standards for disclosing the terms and costs of a consumer credit agreement before the borrower becomes obligated, establishes a period during which a consumer may cancel a transaction and procedures through which a consumer can challenge billing errors on revolving credit agreements. Institutions must comply with both state and federal legislation; if there are any contradictions between the two, federal statutes prevail.

There are many mortgage lending regulations as well, including the following:

- A **Uniform Residential Loan Application (FNMA)** for home purchase or refinancing of home purchase of the applicant's principal dwelling where that dwelling will be used as collateral also must be provided, along with a notice of the right to receive a copy of the appraisal if applicable.

- The **Real Estate Settlement Procedures Act (RESPA)**, which provides servicing transfer disclosure and a good faith estimate (GFE) within three business days of receipt of a completed application, the provision of a settlement cost brochure for home purchases only, and a **HUD-1** or **HUD-A1A Settlement Statement** provided at loan closing that must be prepared and available prior to loan closing.

- The **Home Mortgage Disclosure Act (HMDA)**, which obligates a bank to obtain HMDA information (race, sex, national origin) for home purchases, home improvement, or refinance applications.

- The **Community Reinvestment Act (CRA)**, which requires that the bank meet the credit needs of its area, especially low and moderate-income areas.

Examinations for CRA have become increasingly rigorous in recent years. Since July 1990, institutions have been required to disclose the CRA ratings they receive from examiners from outstanding to substantial noncompliance. These evaluations are available for any bank on the OCC Website (*http://www.occ.treas.gov/cra/crasrch.htm*), or you can go to *http://www.occ.treas.gov*, their home page, and select CRAEvalSearch on the menu to get to the CRA Database search page.

Since 1992, lenders have been required to analyze their lending on a detailed geographic basis, correlating the location of borrowers to whom they give loans against demographic data for that location, such as income, percent of minority population, and so on. Although the historical focus of CRA enforcement has been mortgage lending, commercial lending to small businesses is also under scrutiny. Institutions failing to demonstrate community reinvestment can face denial when they seek regulators' permission to branch, merge, or acquire another institution.[4]

- **Loans to Insiders Act (Reg O)**, which says that banks are not allowed to give preferential loan terms to insiders. Loans given to insiders are limited, must be submitted to regulators, and require prior board approval.

- **Limits on lending to one party as a percentage of total capital**, which means that banks are not allowed to make loans to one individual or firm greater than 15 percent of capital, 25 percent if collateralized by safe securities.

---

4 New rules came in the wake of a Fed study in 1990 that found minority mortgage applicants to be rejected four times more often than nonminority applicants. Lenders responded that the study failed to control for applicants' credit histories and existing debt, but many institutions subsequently reexamined their loan approval practices to eliminate policies that may have resulted in discrimination, even if inadvertent. See Paulette Thomas. "Mortgage Rejection Rate for Minorities Is Quadruple That of Whites, Study Finds." *The Wall Street Journal* (October 21, 1991), A2; "CRA Policy Released." *Fedwire* (Federal Reserve Bank of Chicago), January 1992; and Garwood and Smith (1993).

There are a number of different regulations for different types of loans as well. The FDIC Website (*http://www.fdic.gov/regulations/laws/rules*) provides details for each of these regulations.

Credit Execution Policies

Policies also include an overview of the credit execution and administration process in terms of loan committee reviews, collateral, and documents required for loans and loan reviews and the follow-up procedures for loans once they have been made. From these policies specific procedures for the credit analysis, credit execution and administration, and credit review process are put in place. Policies also include a **code of ethics and conflict of interest policy** for boards of directors and senior management including treatment of confidential information from customers.

Lender Compensation Policies

In addition to policies for the bank's overall lending strategy and regulatory compliance policies, banks also have lender compensation policies that are crucial to the bank's business development process. In the 1990s, compensation policies for lenders became more performance-based. Bonuses were given based on how well lenders performed in bringing in new loans, having low loan losses on the loans that they made, serving current loan customers, and in cross-selling other bank products such as working capital management services.

PART B: EVALUATING AND STRUCTURING BANK LOANS TO MANAGE CREDIT RISK

Loan Request Procedures

Appendix 13A shows a sample of loan request procedures for loan officers used by Signet Bank (which now is a part of Wachovia Bank) that remain typical today. The loan request procedures are the implementation of the bank's overall lending policy. The procedures make loan presentations uniform and accessible to loan committee members. The procedures include the following:

1. The source of the business
2. The principal contacts for the loan
3. The participation structure (if other banks are participating in the loan)
4. The amount and reason for the loan request
5. Brief history and operations of the firm
6. Optional industry analysis if needed
7. Profile of managers and their experience and expertise
8. Financial statement analysis, including historical and pro formas and ratios focusing on the company's ability to repay its debt
9. Collateral/risk analysis, summarizing collateral available and risks involved in the loan, such as barriers for entry into a particular industry
10. Loan review and rating recommendation by the loan officer, which includes whether the loan would be categorized as A, B, or C, from excellent to average or below ratings, based on the bank's classification of ratings for loans
11. Conclusion and opinion: favorable or unfavorable factors for the loan

Basically, the loan procedures focus on the risks inherent in the business of the loan applicant, how risks have been mitigated, the use and amount of the loan, the ability of the borrower to repay the loan in terms of cash flow, and secondary sources of repayment including collateral.

The framework of this presentation basically includes what bankers call the **5 Cs of Credit:**

1. **Character (the willingness of a customer to pay).** Often loan officers use their experience to evaluate the character of individuals during a loan interview. Other evidence of character includes past credit history, credit ratings of firms, and reputation from customers and suppliers.

2. **Capacity (the ability of a customer to pay in terms of cash flow).** Capacity can be shown by looking at current and projected cash flow statements of corporate customers to determine if cash flow will be adequate to cover loan payments. For consumer loans, annual income from tax returns and an employment contract and paystubs can be used. For mortgage loans, comparing the borrower's gross monthly income with the monthly loan payment is widely used to assess the burden on the borrower. The payment is sometimes adjusted to include homeowners' insurance and property taxes, although research has shown this payment-to-income ratio is not a reliable predictor of default.

3. **Capital (the soundness of a borrower's financial position in terms of equity).** The net worth, or equity position, of a corporate borrower relative to assets provides information on the cushion that the borrower has to absorb potential losses. For consumer customers, net worth is estimated as personal assets less personal liabilities.

4. **Conditions (the industry and economic conditions that may affect a firm's ability to repay a loan).** Particularly for corporate customers, external conditions related to the industry and economic environment of the firm are particularly important for the loan officer to analyze. Lenders in the Southeastern United States, for instance, did not consider the effect of a fall in oil prices for firms they lent to in the 1980s, which later plunged otherwise healthy companies in the oil industry into bankruptcy. Similarly, during recessions, mortgage loan delinquencies also tend to rise.

5. **Collateral (secondary sources of repayment,** now often called **asset-based lending).** Collateral and at times personal guarantees against personal assets by a corporate lender are used as a secondary source of payment for the bank, particularly for more risky loans. However, taking possession of the collateral is expensive, so lenders rely on cash flow for primary payment, with the hope of not having to take possession.

With asset-based lending, rules of thumb are often used, such as lending from 40 percent to 60 percent against raw materials and finished goods inventory, which are easier to collect on; 50 percent to 80 percent against accounts receivables depending on the aging schedule and collection experience. Since asset-based lending often incorporates costly monitoring, loan rates are often higher than safer, unsecured loans, often 2 percent to 6 percent above a bank's basic lending rate.

Collateral is generally matched with the use for the loan. For instance, a working capital loan to finance seasonal inventory and accounts receivables is often collateralized by those assets, whereas a term loan to purchase equipment is collateralized by the equipment to be purchased. Maintaining accurate records, known as *loan documentation,* is important when examiners are assessing the quality of outstanding loans, especially under FDICIA's tripwire provisions.

One important form of self-protection for lenders of consumer and mortgage loans is to make sure that the value of the property at the time of application exceeds the loan amount by enough to protect the lender in case of default. Also, this provides an incentive for the borrower not to default. Research indicates that the initial **loan-to-value ratio** is positively related to both delinquency and default. The difference between the outstanding loan balance and the value of the property is the borrower's equity in the home. When the loan-to-value ratio is high (the maximum initially allowed by most lenders is 95 percent), the borrower has only a small personal investment, and if the market value of the property falls, the reduction in the borrower's equity may contribute to default even several years after the loan agreement is made. To estimate property values, lenders hire trained real estate appraisers. As noted in a previous chapter, FNMA and FHLMC often require certain loan-to-value ratios before being willing to securitize mortgage loans or mortgage insurance if loan-to-value ratios do not meet these stipulations.

Quantitative Credit Scoring Models

Zeta Models for Commercial Loans

Many lenders, particularly large lenders, use quantitative credit scoring models to integrate information from a variety of sources. Data on an applicant are weighted according to predetermined standards, and a score for creditworthiness is calculated. Applicants falling below a predetermined minimum acceptable score are rejected or given more attention in the loan application process before loans can be made. In the past two decades, credit scoring models have become widely used, particularly by

Concept Questions

1 How has the role of the loan officer changed in terms of including business development functions?

2 Why are loan committee review and bank loan policies important in the credit underwriting process?

3 What are some lending regulations that banks must comply with when they make loans?

4 Why is it important for banks to have a code of ethics and conflict of interest policy included in their credit execution policies?

5 How can lender compensation policies increase the risk of a bank? Give an example.

6 List eleven important items that should be included in loan request procedures.

7 What is the loan-to-value ratio for a loan, and why is it important?

large banks, to analyze loans. With widespread loan securitizations, this facilitates the quickness in underwriting loans, making credit scoring models a way of life for large banks.

Example of Commercial Loan Credit Scoring Models and Their Uses

One of the most popular classification models for commercial loans is **Zeta Analysis,** designed by Edward Altman at New York University in 1968, which has endured and been refined over the past three decades. This model uses a multiple discriminant analysis technique to identify important ratios used to classify firms likely to fail from those that are not likely to fail. For instance, in an early model for manufacturing firms, significant ratios included **working capital to total assets (WC),** (current assets less current liabilities) / total assets; **retained earnings to total assets (RE); return on assets based on operational earnings (ROA),** [Earnings Before Interest and Taxes (EBIT) / Total Assets]; a firm's **market value of equity to book value of debt ratio (Equity);** and **asset turnover (AT),** sales to total assets. Given statistically determined weights for each of the ratios, a Zeta, or Z-score, can be calculated by plugging in a firm's ratios (as decimals ratios), as follows:

$$Z = 1.2 \, WC + 1.4 \, RE + 3.3 \, ROA + 0.6 \, Equity + 0.999 \, AT$$

For instance, if a firm had a WC of 0.41, an RE of 0.355, operating ROA of 0.154, an Equity ratio of 2.48, and an AT of 2.84, its Zeta score would be

$$Z = 1.2 \, (0.41) + 1.4 \, (0.335) + 3.3 \, (0.154) + 0.6 \, (2.48) + 0.999 \, (2.84) = 5.794$$

If the score is greater or equal to the cutoff score of about 2.675, as clearly the score above is, the firm is more like the nonfailed group, and the loan is less likely to default. The lower bound Zeta score of 1.81 (failed) and upper bound of 2.99 (nonfailed) are optimal, with any score in between this zone being more in the zone of ignorance. The Z-score model's classification accuracy based on a development sample was 95 percent a year before bankruptcy and 82 percent two years before. Type II errors (classifying healthy firms as bankrupt) ranged from 15 to 20 percent in secondary samples.

Classification models, such as the Zeta model, can be purchased by banks as computer packages or developed in-house. Brief descriptions of more complex credit risk classification models including neural networks, expert systems, and credit risk models based on a firm's stock price, such as the KMV model, are provided in Appendix 13D.[5]

Example of a Consumer Credit Scoring Model

Consumer credit scoring models are attempts to assess all important factors about an applicant and to simultaneously evaluate all applicants objectively by the same standards to comply with Regulation B. Hence, credit scoring models are widely used by consumer lenders.

---

5 See Altman (1968; 1981, 1983); Altman, Hartzell, and Peck (1997), Altman, Haldeman, and Narayanan (1997) and Caouette, Altman, and Narayanan (1998) provide excellent in-depth analysis of other Zeta models for service firms, firms in emerging markets, and other credit models. Many banks and GSEs have also implemented credit scoring for home mortgages; see Robert B. Avery, Raphael W. Bostic, Paul S. Calem, and Glenn B. Canner. "Credit Risk, Credit Scoring, and the Performance of Home Mortgages." *Federal Reserve Bulletin* (July 1996), 621–648.

Table 13.1 provides information on a hypothetical credit scoring system for consumer loans. The first step in developing a model is to determine, from past data, borrower characteristics most often associated with bad and good loans, where "bad" is defined as slow-paying, delinquent, or in default. Typical characteristics include how long the applicant has been employed at his or her current job, whether the credit history is good, number of dependents, whether the applicant rents or owns a home, and his or her income and occupation. Points are assigned to new applicants based on these characteristics. For example, a borrower with a higher income would be assigned more points on that characteristic than one with a lower income. In Table 13.1, some characteristics have higher points than others as determined by statistical analysis of historical data, such as by using discriminant analysis. As shown at the bottom of Table 13.1, scores greater than 90 are closer to the profile of a "good" customer, while scores lower than 50 fall closer to that of a "bad" customer. In between 50 and 90 is an overlap range. Consequently, lenders would have to use more judgment for these cases. For most institutions, the costs (including cash losses and the penalties of regulatory displeasure) of accepting a "bad" applicant are higher than the opportunity costs of rejecting a "good" one. Caouette, Altman, and Narayanan (1998) point out that models are often developed using both credit bureau reports, such as those generated by TRW, TransUnion, Equifax, and CBI, credit information clearinghouses. Credit bureaus often provide an index of the likelihood of charge-offs or bankruptcy based on an individual's previous account history or activity.[6]

Performance and Limitations of Credit Scoring Models

Research indicates that the accuracy of classifying loan applicants improves when a combination of statistical credit scoring models and judgmentally determined decision rules is used. The experience of some institutions provides even stronger endorsement for quantitative models. Some banks use credit scoring models for virtually all its consumer loan applications but allows loan officers to override a score with approval from supervisors. One study showed that the delinquency rate for loans granted on the basis of loan-officer overrides was seven times higher than for loans approved solely on the basis of credit scores. Such findings will lead, undoubtedly, to the refinement of expert systems for consumer lending. One application of the credit scoring concept is behavior scoring, which attempts to predict the behavior of borrowers in the future rather than simply scoring the acceptability of a current loan applicant. Credit scoring and behavior scoring are also being used more frequently to evaluate mortgage applicants, particularly for affordable loan programs that attempt to provide home mortgage loans for low- to moderate-income borrowers.

Like all models, credit scoring schemes have limitations. The statistical complications of gray ranges are one problem. Also, models focus only on default risk and may ignore such information as deposit or other service relationships with the customer. They also must be carefully structured to comply with Regulation B: Applicant characteristics included in a model must be "demonstrably and statistically sound," as defined by the Fed. But despite these limitations, major consumer lenders, especially retailers, regularly use the models, as do many depositories offering credit cards.

CreditMetrics and Other Portfolio Approaches

In recent years, bank managers have attempted to develop measures of a financial institution's credit risk more from an overall portfolio approach, looking at the total diversification of a bank's loan or total asset portfolio. In 1997, JPMorgan with several other large banks released to the public a model for quantifying portfolio risk based on a **value at risk (VAR)** approach discussed in Chapter 2. The **CreditMetrics** approach estimates changes in the market value of a bank's loan portfolio as well as other financial instruments in the event of a credit upgrade or downgrade as well as potential loan defaults. Probabilities based on historical data are calculated for the occurrence of such events. Using these probabilities, the expected change in the value of loans, value at risk, for a given confidence level can be calculated. Correlations between the value at risk for different loans and other financial instruments can be used to derive an aggregate measure of the volatility or value at risk for a bank's entire

---

6 See Caouette, Altman, and Narayanan (1998), pp. 154–171, for a detailed discussion of consumer finance models, which this section draws from, which also expands upon other decision tree and neural network models and other quantitative consumer models and the advantages and disadvantages of credit scoring models. Also, a thorough review of the theory, history, and statistical properties of credit scoring models can be found in Altman (1981). Another good source is Capon (1982).

table 13.1 HYPOTHETICAL CREDIT SCORING SYSTEM

Credit scoring models are designed to allow lenders to classify credit applicants into "good" or "bad" risks based on past credit history, employment history, and other variables. The table illustrates a typical scoring system.

Applicant Characteristics	Allotted Points	Applicant Characteristics	Allotted Points
Own or rent		Checking or savings account	
Own	41	Neither	0
Rent	0	Either	13
Other finance company		Both	19
Yes	−12	Applicant age	
No	0	30 years or less	6
Bank credit card		30+ to 40 years	11
Yes	29	40+ to 50 years	8
No	0	Older than 50 years	16
Applicant occupation		Years on job	
Professional and officials	27	5 or less	0
Technical and managers	5	5+ to 15	6
Proprietor	−3	More than 15	18
Clerical and sales	12		
Craftsman and nonfarm-laborer	0		
Foreman and operative	26		
Service worker	14		
Farm worker	3		

Source: Adapted from Gilbert A. Churchill, Jr., et al. "The Role of Credit Scoring in the Loan Decision." The Credit World 65 (March 1977): 7. Reprinted with the permission of ACA International, http://www.acainternational.org.

EVALUATING CREDIT SCORES

Difficulty arises when an applicant's score does not fall clearly into either group. Lenders must then decide between the opportunity cost of not giving credit to a potentially "good" customer and the risk of loaning to a "bad" one.

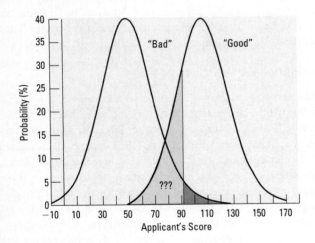

loan portfolio and other instruments, such as swaps, futures, and forward contracts. This approach is fairly new and is primarily used by very large banks that have borrowers with publicly rated debt. It is important because it is one of the first formal models to incorporate the overall risk of a bank's loan portfolio including diversification effects. CreditMetrics basically looks at the probability of rating migrations over time and their effect on the value of nontradable loans or private placements if their probability of default or credit rating changes. Just like value at risk, the present values of the loans in a portfolio are calculated (i.e., a re-valuation) under different downgrade scenarios. The discount rate for each scenario rises with a downgrade in a loan's (or a bond's) credit rating, resulting in a decline in the valuation as the grade goes lower (for instance, from an A rating to a B rating, etc.). The discount rate for the re-valuation is typically equal to the risk-free rate plus the typical rate spread based on the default risk for particular credit ratings. Based on the scenario analysis, a probability distribution is created by CreditMetrics based on two value at risk (VAR) measures based on the normal distribution of loan values and the actual distribution. Having calculated the present value of the loan for different future states and ascertained the probability of each state, the expected value of the loan is calculated along with the standard deviation. If a normal distribution is assumed, for instance, a 5 percent probability of the worst case, the VAR for the loan is $1.65 \times STD$; for 1 percent probability, the VAR is $2.33 \times STD$. If the distribution is not normal, a table for that particular distribution can be used for the appropriate multiplier. Hence, CreditMetrics is a very similar concept to value at risk for market value changes, measuring the amount of maximum expected potential loss with a rating change (VAR), but it entails a longer time period in which such a change could occur, such as in a year or more, versus the daily earning at risk (DEAR) used to measure market risk. Similar to value at risk, correlations can also be taken into consideration, to calculate a total portfolio measure of portfolio credit value at risk.[7]

Commercial Lending: Financial Statement Analysis

For commercial loans, financial statement analysis by credit analysts and lenders is crucial not only in deciding whether a loan should be granted but also in determining the proper structure for the loan.

Types of Information Required

The evaluation of a loan is based on information from a number of sources. If the applicant is not a new customer, the loan officer already has much reusable information, including the borrower's previous payment record, past financial statements, and personal contacts. For new applicants, the credit analyst-loan officer will need some or all of the following:

- Past financial statements for the firm that can be put into common size statements (i.e., put the income statement items as a percentage of total revenues and the balance sheet statement as a percentage of total assets) to be able to see trends more easily
- Personal financial information from the owner, if the firm is not large, with diversified ownership
- Projections of the future financial position (i.e., pro forma statements)
- A credit report
- Financial performance measures for similar firms as a basis of comparison
- Personal contact with the potential borrower and a personal visit to the business
- Economic projections

Concept Questions

1   Why have quantitative credit scoring models become very popular in the last two decades?

2   What advantages and disadvantages do you think credit scoring models have for lenders and borrowers?

3   What does a Zeta score tell you?

4   What are limitations of credit scoring models?

5   What does CreditMetrics measure? How is it similar to value at risk (VAR)?

---

7 See Caouette, Altman, and Narayanan (1998), pp. 285–293. For a more detailed discussion of CreditMetrics, see Saunders and Cornett (2003), pp. 303–306.

Financial institutions generally have software that the credit analyst uses to facilitate the credit analysis, putting statements into common size statements, calculating financial ratios, and setting up a uniform presentation for the financial analysis of a loan.

External Sources of Information

Several other sources of information supplement the information provided by the applicant. For example, other creditors of the firm, such as suppliers, may be willing to discuss the firm's payment record. The lender can also purchase a Dun & Bradstreet (D&B) Business Information Report, which includes D&B's own assessment of a firm's creditworthiness and other details about its operations, owners, and management.

If the firm has a credit relationship with another commercial lender, information can be requested from that institution. Robert Morris Associates (RMA), the national trade organization for commercial loan officers, has developed a code of ethics to guide the exchange of information among lenders. RMA also publishes Annual Statement Studies containing standard performance measures for more than 300 lines of business. Other industry average ratios are found in other publications, such as *D&B's Key Business Ratios,* among other private and government sources, as well as information by analysts and many Internet sources with financial statements on Websites and analyst reports for publicly traded firms.

In all cases, industry averages must be interpreted with care, because an individual loan applicant is likely to have unique characteristics requiring the lending officer's judgment. After a credit analyst or lending officer has tapped available information sources, the hardest task is ahead—organizing the data, rating the applicant on each dimension of the institution's risk-rating system, and recommending approval or denial. Data on an applicant are weighted according to predetermined standards, and a risk category for credit quality is determined (such as A = excellent, B = good, and C = average credit). Applicants falling below a predetermined minimum acceptable risk category are rejected. Generally, loan officers are given dollar limits for discretion; larger loans above this limit must be discussed and approved by a loan committee of bank officers, which has weekly or more frequent meetings. Most banks also have a loan compliance officer, often a lawyer with a specialty in regulatory law, who attends these meetings to make sure federal and state regulations are abided by and to ensure compliance to CRA requirements.

If the loan is approved, the risk category to which the borrower is assigned has important ramifications for other aspects of the lending decision, including the interest rate; whether collateral is required; and whether financial standards, such as minimum working capital ratios, are imposed on the firm over the life of the loan. The structuring of the loan will be designed to ensure repayment of the loan and compensation to the lender for the risk that it has taken on.

Evaluating Risk

Evaluating creditworthiness requires more than financial analysis. Commercial loan officers should learn as much as possible about a business and the way it is managed. Some experts suggest that good risk analysis asks, "What could go wrong?" and investigates all aspects of the business in an attempt to find out. Careful investigation serves another purpose as well. The more complete and accurate the information collected on a loan, the better the lender's position when regulatory examiners review the institution's loan portfolio. As noted earlier, maintaining accurate records, known as loan documentation, is important when examiners are assessing the quality of outstanding loans, especially under the FDICIA's tripwire provisions.

Financial statement analysis includes an analysis of historical trends in financial statements including common size income statements (put as a percentage of revenues), balance sheets (put as percentage of assets), and cash flow statements. In addition, pro forma statements showing whether cash flow is adequate to repay a loan need to be reviewed. Financial ratios are also calculated and compared with trends and peer industry ratios. Pro forma (projected) financial statements provided by the borrower or created by the lender are carefully looked over to determine the ability of the borrower to repay the loan from future cash flows. The credit analyst should carefully look at the assumptions used to create the pro forma analysis. Are the assumptions realistic is a key question that needs to be answered in making adjustments to the pro forma statements. For instance, a borrower may assume a 20 percent growth rate in revenues, when revenue growth in the past for the firm and the industry has only been

10 percent on average. Similarly, inventory may be forecast using an assumption of inventory turnover of five times, when the firm on average has only had inventory turnover of two times. Cost of goods sold to sales may be projected as 75 percent of sales, when the past average CGS to sales ratio was a much higher 85 percent of sales. Pro forma assumptions need to be closely examined for realism, and, if necessary, new pro formas created using more realistic assumptions. Often scenario analysis is used with best, average, and worst case scenarios, and future industry conditions are taken into consideration as well. Table 13.2 reviews financial ratios used in analyzing loans including overall profitability ratios, cost efficiency (profit margin) ratios, asset utilization (revenue generated from assets), days cash cycle, debt and debt coverage ratios, and stored liquidity ratios.

A DuPont financial analysis that decomposes the reasons for changes in overall profitability can be a particularly helpful framework as discussed in Chapter 4. Return on equity (ROE) is decomposed into its components to determine the reason for a firm's profitability as follows:

$$ROE = NPM \times AU \times EM \qquad [13.1]$$

where

NPM = net profit margin (net income / revenues), a measure of cost efficiency,

AU = asset utilization (revenues / total assets), a measure of revenue generation or asset efficiency, and

EM = equity multiplier (assets / total equity), a measure of financial leverage.

By examining trends in ROE, ROA, and their components, the credit analyst can determine why overall profitability changed over time. A firm, for instance, might have had good cost efficiency (a high NPM) but poor asset efficiency (low asset utilization) because it holds too large a quantity of working capital in terms of inventory and accounts receivables. This can be revealed by analyzing particular asset utilization ratios including accounts receivables, inventory, and fixed asset turnover. The bank might want to require the firm to reduce its accounts receivables and inventory turnover to the industry averages as part of the provisions for granting the loan. Similarly, a firm might have good asset utilization

table 13.2   REVIEW OF IMPORTANT FINANCIAL RATIOS

Overall Profitability:	Return on Equity = Net Income / Equity
	Return on Assets = Net Income / Assets
Cost Efficiency:	Net Profit Margin = Net Income / Revenues
	Operating Profit Margin = Operating Income / Revenues
	Gross Profit Margin = Gross Income / Revenues
Revenue Generation:	Total Asset Turnover = Revenues / Assets
	Fixed Asset Turnover = Revenues / Fixed Assets
	Inventory Turnover = Cost of Goods Sold / Inventory
	Accounts Receivables Turnover = Revenues / Accounts Receivables
Days Cash Cycle:	Inventory Days = 365 / Inventory Turnover
	Average Collection Period or Accounts Receivables Days = 365 / AR Turnover
	Accounts Payable Days = 365 / (CGS / Accounts Payable)
Days Cash to Cash Cycle = Average Collection Period + Days Inventory − Days Accounts Payable	
Debt and Debt Coverage Ratios:	Debt to Assets = Total Debt / (Total Assets)
	Interest Coverage = EBIT / Interest Expense
	Fixed Charge Coverage = (EBIT + Fixed Charges) / (Interest Expense + Fixed Charges)
	Cash Flow to Total Debt = Operating Cash Flow / Total Debt
Cash Flow to Maturing Long-Term Debt = Operating Cash Flow / Maturing Long-Term Debt (Previous Period)	
Liquidity Ratios:	Current Ratio = Current Assets / Current Liabilities
	Quick Ratio = (Current Assets − Inventory) / Current Liabilities

but a poor net profit margin. By examining other profit margins including the operating profit margin (OPM = EBIT to Revenues) and gross profit margin [(Sales − CGS) to Revenues], as well as the common size income statement, the credit analyst could determine the reason for the cost efficiency problem. For instance, the firm may have had a good GPM but a low OPM, with a problem controlling its administrative expenses. Similarly, the firm may have a good GPM and OPM but low NPM, indicating perhaps a problem with high interest expenses due to high financial leverage, as indicated by a high debt ratio or equity multiplier. This, in turn, could affect the covenants that the bank may require prior to making the loan.

In addition, credit analysis includes analyzing trends in cash cycle, bankruptcy risk, and liquidity ratios to ensure that the loan can be repaid, as shown in Table 13.2. The analysis for the lender includes analyzing the ability of a firm to repay the loan, so debt coverage ratios based on cash flow are particularly important, such as the cash flow to maturing long-term debt ratio (operating cash flow / maturing debt). Often banks calculate operating income as net operating income after taxes (NOPAT) equal to net income plus depreciation and amortization plus interest expense. Net cash flow is then calculated as NOPAT less debt service based on the proposed loan structure. Alternatively, cash flow from a direct or indirect cash flow statement can be used. The debt coverage ratio is then calculated as NOPAT divided by debt service. Appendix 13B, which provides a fictional sample loan presentation, calculates the debt coverage ratio in this way. For instance, in 2003, the debt coverage ratio equals NOPAT / debt service, which equals $214,188 / 101,784, which equals 2.10. The firm is able to cover its debt payments two times from its net operating income. Other debt servicing ratios include other upcoming external financing obligations as well, such as (1) cash flow from operations divided by dividends and previous current maturing long-term debt; (2) cash flow from operations divided by all of the above in (1) and short-term debt; (3) cash flow from operations divided by dividends and previous current maturing long-term debt and currently maturing short-term debt. Other obligations could be included as well, with the goal of determining how well the firm is able to meet its upcoming external financing obligations. Cash flow analysis is particularly important, and careful financial analysis is needed in light of accounting deception and fraud found in firms such as Enron, where accounting innovations were used to hide expenses and include revenues that were accounting transactions as opposed to cash revenues that had actually been received. Using cash flow statements, the proper amount of the loan can also be solved for. Sometimes firms ask for too large a loan. By looking carefully at pro forma financial statements and adjusting them for proper assumptions, the loan amount requested may be less than the amount a firm requests. By adjusting the loan amount, a loan that might not have been feasible to grant to a company can become feasible.

Sample Loan Presentation

Appendix 13B shows an example of a short sample loan presentation in mid-2007 for a loan renewal request from the Great Euphoria Bank of New York City by the Big Apple Real Estate & Storage Company, a real estate and storage company partnership operating in New York City. The company's loan officer, Eleanor Winters, presents the loan request at the weekly loan committee meeting of the bank attended by Phil Lerner, CEO; Roslyn Lerner, President; Albert Singleton, the Regulatory Compliance Officer; and other senior loan officers at the bank including Ann Fox, Robert Cooperman, Leendert Van Der Pool, Patty Moran, and Gary Patterson.

Background and Request

Eleanor Winters' report, shown in Appendix 13B, includes **background** on the company and its partners and the nature of the **loan request,** along with a repayment analysis based on the proposed loan structure. This loan request from the Big Apple Real Estate & Storage Company of New York City is to renew its current term debt of about $830,000 on the company's facility in downtown Manhattan, which will be maturing later in the year in 2007.

Repayment Analysis

Based on the proposed loan structure, Patty Moran has prepared a repayment analysis for the loan based on historical figures for the past four years. **Net operating income (NOI)** is calculated by adding back depreciation and amortization and interest expense to net income. The debt service (loan payment) for the amortized mortgage loan has been estimated to be $101,784 including interest and principal. Subtracting the debt service from NOI gives **net cash flow.** Dividing NOI by the debt service gives a debt coverage ratio of greater than 2 for each of the previous four years.

For commercial real estate loans, occupancy rates are also very important. As noted in the repayment analysis, the storage facility has had a high level of 95 percent occupancy in the summer to a low of 87 percent. Hence, based on the operating expenses of $282,579 in 2006, rental income would have to drop by over 40 percent of $174,666 for the company to fall below a break-even point (i.e., have a loss). Other points made in the repayment analysis are that revenue growth over the past three years has been the result of rate increases and that the average occupancy rates for the storage facility have been relatively stable. In 2005, expenses rose on a one-time basis because of the need to temporarily replace a manager who was hospitalized. Projections for 2007 reflect annualized revenue similar to 2006, with seasonality considerations taken into account.

Secondary and Tertiary Sources of Repayment

Other sources of repayment are presented next. The primary partner is the only guarantor of the loan. The financial statements of the guarantor show sufficient secondary strength to be considered. The tertiary repayment will be the refinance or sale of the subject property. A collateral section is provided with an independent appraisal of the market value of the property.

Financial Analysis Summary

A financial analysis summary is presented based on the attached CPA-reviewed spreadsheets of the company for the past four years. The spreadsheets include common size and dollar financial statements including income statements, balance sheets, and cash flow statements, along with summary key ratios. The presentation includes the key points from these statements.

Balance Sheet

For the **balance sheet,** after the sale of assets in 2005 and early 2006, assets dropped while net worth rose. Cash balances and liquidity have improved in 2006. It is interesting to note on the balance sheet that net worth was negative in 2002 to 2004, which reflects accumulated depreciation of real estate assets and the amortization of goodwill, which reduced assets in those years making liabilities greater than assets. With the sale of assets in later years, net worth became positive in 2005 and 2006. This demonstrates the importance for the credit analyst to understand such factors that affect balance sheets for real estate companies. Otherwise, the negative net worth figures would be particularly alarming.

Income Statement

Highlights for the **income statement** include fluctuating revenue and operating margins over the past five years as the firm grew and sold off assets. Operating profits are expected to return to their normal range of 40 to 50 percent in 2007. Net profits have been strong for the past two years as the result of gains realized from the sale of partnership interests.

Guarantor and Collateral

The final portion of the presentation includes more detailed information on the **guarantor and collateral** as secondary and tertiary sources of repayment. Reviewing the assets of John Jahera, the guarantor of the loan, indicates a strong annual cash after debt service for other partnerships. A review of the collateral reveals a fair market value appraisal of $1.6 million for the property and a valuation of $2.21 million based on a net income valuation approach (using net income divided by a capitalization rate of 12.5 percent). With the $2.21 million valuation ratio, the loan-to-value ratio would be 38 percent. If a less conservative discount rate of 10 percent is used, the valuation is $2.76 million, or a loan-to-value ratio of 30 percent for the approximately $0.830 million loan.

An environmental property audit was performed on the property used as collateral and did not indicate any potential hazards, although a gas station across the street had an unknown disposition.

Risk Analysis and Recommendation

Based on the financial analysis, the loan was rated 1-C (average risk) based on the bank's ranking system. Risks mentioned included inherent economic and market risk associated with a real estate investment as well as limited information supplied by the chief guarantor. However, the firm had a profitable history, experience, financial strength in the guarantor, and a solid collateral position, so the loan officer recommended approval.

Proposed Loan Structure

Eleanor Winters presented a proposed loan structure that sets the original loan to be renewed for five years at a fixed rate equal to the current five-year Treasury bond plus a 2.65 percent premium, plus a loan fee of 1/2 percent. The collateral for the loan would be the first deed of trust on the company's downtown New York City facility.

After much discussion about the loan and some concerns about the collateral for the loan and the financial condition of the guarantor, the loan was unanimously approved by the committee, based on the solid cash flow and the very good current and future prospects for the Big Apple Real Estate & Storage Company operating in a brisk real estate market in New York City.

Establishing Loan Terms

Terms of individual loans are particularly important for a lender's financial performance. The dominance of loans in institutions' asset portfolios suggests that keeping loan rates at approximate levels is a prerequisite to earning a target NIM and target ROE. Loan terms include the lending rate, noninterest terms and fees for the loan, the maturity and timing of payments, the loan amount, collateral or other secondary sources of payment, and any restrictive covenants associated with the loan.

The base lending rate for the loan plus a premium to cover expected default risk, administrative costs, and the bank's desired spread to achieve its NIM and ROE targets is discussed in the following section.

Base Lending Rates

Base lending rates are established at the institutional level and are used as benchmarks for determining specific loan rates. Very good customers may be offered a lower rate, and higher-risk customers are charged a higher rate. But the base sets the boundaries within which the loan officer can exercise discretion.[8]

Earlier chapters introduced the relationship between the target ROE and the target NIM. Although interest revenues earned on the loan portfolio are an important influence on the NIM, other assets also must be considered in the base loan rate calculation. For example, suppose the hypothetical institution shown in Table 13.3 has nonearning assets equal to 10 percent of total assets. Also, suppose that 30 percent of the institution's total assets are invested in securities on which the before-tax average rate of return is 10.5 percent. The remaining 60 percent of total assets are invested in loans. The mix of assets

---

Concept Questions

1 When loan officers analyze a loan, what are they trying to determine?

2 Discuss why an overall DuPont ratio analysis is useful for analyzing whether to grant a loan application.

3 If a firm had poor working capital asset turnover ratios (low days inventory and average collection period),

explain why this could signal potential difficulties in terms of repaying a loan for a firm.

4 Why are cost efficiency (profit ratios) an important indicator, along with cash flow measures, of the ability of a firm to repay a loan?

---

8 Historically, the base rate at commercial banks was known as the "prime" lending rate. For reasons explained later in the chapter, the terms *base rate* and *prime rate* are no longer always synonymous; rather, a bank's base rates reflects its average cost of funds.

table   13.3   THE BASE LENDING RATE REQUIRED TO MEET TARGET RATES OF RETURN

A base lending rate is established after considering an institution's target NIM, its target RONW, and its asset mix. The base rate is the starting point from which loan terms for individual borrowers are established.

I. BALANCE SHEET AND PLANNING ASSUMPTIONS

Assets (in mils.)		Liabilities and Net Worth	
Securities	$ 30	Liabilities	$92
Loans	60		
Nonearning assets	10	Net worth	$8
Total	$100	Total	$100

Return on securities: 10.5%

Return on nonearning assets: 0%

Target NIM: 3.2%

t = 34%

Base loan rate: 13.88% (as calculated in text)

Average cost of liabilities: 9%

Net worth multiplier: 12.5

Target ROE: 18%

II. PRO FORMA INCOME STATEMENT

Interest revenues:

 $10.50\% \times \$30 = \$3.150$

 $13.88\% \times \$60 = 8.328$

 $0.00\% \times \$10 = 0.000$

Total	$11.478

Interest expense:

 $9.00\% \times \$92 =$ $(8.280)

Spread $ 3.198

Less net noninterest expenses:

 $1.00\% \times \$100 =$ (1.000)

Income before taxes $ 2.198

Less income taxes (0.34) (0.747)

Net income $ 1.451

NIM = $3.2 / $100 = 3.2%

ROE = $1.451 / $8 = 18%

and rates of return, as well as the fact that some assets are nonearning, must be considered in planning for the total spread, Interest Revenues − Interest Expenses (IR − IE), as shown in the following equation:

$$R - IE = [\Sigma r_i \times A_i] - (c \times TL) \qquad [13.2]$$

where

r_i = the interest rate earned on asset category i,

A_i = total dollar investment in asset category i,

c   = average interest cost of financial liabilities, and

TL = total liabilities.

Note that the first term equals total interest revenues and the second term equals total interest expense. Equation 13.1 can be used to solve for the base loan rate r_L.

Table 13.3 notes that the average cost of liabilities is 9 percent and that liabilities total $92 million. If the target NIM—a calculation based on total assets—is 3.2 percent, the necessary spread between interest revenues and interest cost of liabilities is $3.2 million. Using Equation 13.2, the target spread is expressed in millions as follows:

$$\text{Spread} = [(0\% \times \$10) + (10.5\% \times \$30) + (r_L \times \$60)] - \$8.28$$

Solving for r_L:

$$r_L = \$8.33 / \$60)] = 0.1388 \text{ or } 13.88\%$$

Because nonearning assets and securities contribute to the target NIM at a lower rate than do loans, interest earned on loans must provide a higher than average return for the institution's financial objectives to be achieved. The pro forma (projected) income statement at the bottom of Table 13.3 illustrates this point. The base rate of 13.88 percent is appropriate only for customers of average cost and average risk; it is a starting point for loan officers in setting loan rates for individual customers. Competitive conditions including loan rates offered by other banks also affect such lending rates.

Noninterest Terms and Conditions

Commercial lenders use more than the interest rate to determine the effective yield on loans. A term commonly used to describe the evaluation of the total institutional relationship with a loan customer is customer profitability analysis. It involves examining the funds received from and the nonlending services provided to a customer as well as a specific loan application. For example, a customer voluntarily keeping large demand deposit balances is a valuable one, because no explicit interest is paid on these balances. Similarly, customers using the institution's cash management services or those whose pension fund balances are managed by the bank's trust department are also valuable. These factors can affect noninterest loan terms and conditions, the most common of which are compensating balances, commitments and commitment fees, discounting, and collateral.

Compensating balance requirements require that the borrower keep a minimum noninterest-earning deposit balance with the institution, which guarantees the lender access to inexpensive funds and liquidity. In turn, the borrower has a higher effective cost of funds equal to interest expense divided by the loan less the compensating balance. Banks at times allow compensating balances to be kept in low-interest time deposits, which avoids reserve requirements. Banks generally offer two pricing schemes, one with compensating balances and one with alternative fees and/or a higher loan rate for customers who prefer to pay separately for loan and deposit services.

Lines of credit and commitments are agreements to extend funds to the borrower over some pre-arranged time period. A line of credit is an informal arrangement like a credit card arrangement with loan rates determined at the time of borrowing if funds are available. In contrast, a loan commitment is a formal arrangement with a legal guarantee that funds will be available at a given rate, amount, and maturity. With a commitment, the customer can borrow or "take down" some, all, or none of the authorized funds. The terms of the commitment usually require the borrower to pay a **commitment fee** based on any amount of unused credit over the life of the agreement and to pay interest on funds actually taken down. The fee compensates the lender for the liquidity that must be provided. The most common type of commitment is a revolving commitment, guaranteeing that funds can be borrowed, repaid, and borrowed again over an extended period, often as long as three years. The interest rate may be fixed or pegged to a reference market rate. The lender assumes risk of a potential financial deterioration of the borrower during the period, so the commitment fee will be higher. Some banks include protective clauses to avoid a commitment if the borrower's condition significantly deteriorates. It is not uncommon for commitments to require a compensating balance as well.

Effect of Noninterest Terms on a Lender's Expected Return

Table 13.4 illustrates the combined effect of interest and noninterest terms on the lender's total return from a loan commitment.[9] The base rate plus the appropriate risk premium is 11.5 percent, with a 0.25 percent commitment fee on the unused portion of the commitment, an 8 percent compensating balance on the entire commitment, and a 4 percent compensating balance on the amount actually borrowed. To estimate the bank's effective rate of return, the portion of the line that will actually be taken down on average over the commitment period is estimated to be 60 percent of the $2 million commitment during the next one-year period.

---

9 This example draws on a presentation in Brick (1984).

table **13.4** EFFECT OF NONINTEREST TERMS ON THE LENDER'S EXPECTED RETURN

The cost to a borrower and the yield to the lender can be significantly affected by noninterest loan terms. The table illustrates how a commitment fee on a line of credit can increase an institution's rate of return.

Stated interest rate	11.5% (base rate plus risk premium)
Commitment fee	0.25% on unused portion of the commitment
Term	1 year
Compensating balances	8% of commitment plus 4% of borrowed funds
Estimated average loan balance	60% of commitment
Maximum line of credit	$2,000,000

Loan Interest and Noninterest Revenues

Interest [$2,000,000(0.6)(0.115)]	$138,000
Fees [$2,000,000(0.4)(0.0025)]	2,000
Total revenues	$140,000

Net Funds Invested

Average loan balance	$1,200,000
Portion offset by compensating demand deposit balances	
$2,000,000(0.08)	$(160,000)
$1,200,000(0.04)	(48,000)
Deduct reserve requirements [10% × ($160,000 + $48,000)]	$20,800
Total offsetting funds	(187,200)
Net invested funds	$1,012,800

Total Expected Return

$$\frac{\text{Interest and Noninterest Revenues}}{\text{Net Invested Funds}} = \frac{\$140,000}{\$1,012,800} = 13.82\%$$

The commitment fee of 0.25 percent will be paid on $800,000 (the 40 percent of the commitment expected to be unused), and the interest rate of 11.5 percent will be paid on the portion taken down, or $1,200,000. The lender earns total interest and fee revenues of $140,000. Net funds extended, however, are $187,200 less than $1,200,000, or $1,012,800, because of compensating balances after adjustments for a 10 percent marginal reserve requirement. As shown in Table 13.4, the expected yield is 13.82 percent. The lending institution also incurs implicit costs not included here, such as additional uncertainty about the timing and quantity of funds demanded. No one knows when, or in what quantity, the borrower will actually request the committed funds.

Discounted Loans

A lending practice that also increases the return to the lender beyond the stated interest rate is discounting. With discounting the first interest payment is paid at the beginning of the loan period by being deducted before loan funds are made available to the borrower. In effect, the borrower's effective rate is the interest expense based on the entire loan divided by the actual amount borrowed less the first interest payment. For instance, if the borrower borrowed $100,000 with a 10 percent annual rate, the actual effective annual rate would be $10,000 / $90,000 = 11.11 percent. Thus, discounting increases the lender's yield and the borrower's cost.

Similarly, for mortgage loans, lenders customarily charge initial service fees, known as points, at the time of the loan origination. A point is 1 percent of the principal of the loan. Points are similar to discounted loans with the point amount deducted up front from the loan, increasing the effective cost for the borrower and the effective return to the lender. Points were originally established to compensate lenders for not being allowed to charge market rates because of mortgage usury ceilings (ceilings on loan rates) established in many states. Although mortgage usury ceilings were eliminated in most states after DIDMCA, points still influence the pricing of mortgages of all types.[10]

Customer Pricing Using Profitability Analysis

Based on the relationship that a customer has including noninterest terms, banks often set a loan rate for a customer based on the total net income brought in by a relationship. The loan rate including noninterest factors is set based on the total revenues and expenses of a customer, so that total expenses plus a given profit are equal to the total revenues generated from the loan.

Appendix 13C shows a profitability analysis used to price the loan to the Big Apple Real Estate & Storage Company presented earlier. The loan amount authorized by the bank was $820,487. Subtracting the average demand deposits held by the customer less float and reserve requirements, the amount actually given to the customer equals $748,514. With a 9.15 percent annual loan rate on the loan amount of $820,487 plus a $835 fee, the gross income on the loan per year is $75,910 less the cost of the $600 the bank spends for maintenance and setup expenses, resulting in net income of $75,310. Hence, the relationship yield that the bank is getting is $75,310 / $748,514 = 0.1006, or 10.06 percent, if a 9.15 percent loan rate is charged with a $835 fee.

Based on a profitability index analysis at the bottom of Appendix 13C, the bank wants to make its marginal cost of funds of 5.25 percent plus a profit spread of 4.35 percent plus a 1 percent adjustment for risk equal to a minimum required yield of 10.6 percent. With the 10.06 percent yield based on the preceding pricing analysis, the bank reaches just 94.917 percent of its required yield. To achieve 10.6 percent, either the fee would have to be raised, additional basis points added to the loan, or an additional compensating balance would need to be required.

Quoted Base Rates on Commercial Loans

As shown in the preceding profitability analysis, commercial loan officers often tailor the terms of a loan to fit customers' preferences and the needs of the lending institution. Rates are often set off a bank's marginal cost of funds as noted in the preceding example. As noted in Chapters 2 and 6, for large banks loan rates are also set with a premium added for the risk-adjusted return on capital (RAROC) based on the likelihood of losses for that loan. In setting rates, particularly variable rates, however, an index is often used, such as the five-year Treasury rate in the loan presentation example or the prime rate.

Historically, the **prime rate** was the interest rate charged on short-term loans to a bank's most creditworthy customers and was used in the early 1970s often as an economic indicator of business activity. In the later 1970s, financial managers began issuing commercial paper, bonds, or Eurobonds in place of taking on bank loans, and many large money center banks began to link their prime rates to the commercial paper rate. Later these banks returned to an administered prime rate, with prime rates differing for money market and other regional banks. However, at times, banks used the practice of offering below prime rates. This has at times led to lawsuits by customers who were quoted a bank's prime rate, which was not the bank's lowest rate.[11]

Use of Cost of Funds as a Base Rate

As a result of these lawsuits, institutions have redefined the prime or, perhaps more accurately, have given it a "nondefinition." Morgan Guaranty Trust, for example, announced that the "bank's prime shall mean the rate of interest publicly announced by the bank in New York from time to time as the prime

---

10 A point is equal to 1 percent of the principal of the loan. Thus, for a ten-year, annual payment mortgage loan of $100,000, 1 point would be equal to (0.01) $100,000 = $1,000; 2 points = $2,000, and so on. If the rate on the loan was 6 percent, then the loan payment would be $100,000 divided by the present value of annuity factor (PVIFA) for ten years, 6 percent, equal to 7.360, resulting in a loan payment of $100,000 / 7.36 = $13,587. Setting the actual amount given for the loan with 2 points, $98,000 = $13,587 (PVIFA y, 10 years) and solving for the yield using trial and error or a financial calculator, the effective annual yield is about 6.43 percent.

11 An early example was in 1984, when First Atlanta Bank in Atlanta, Georgia, which gave a customer a rate cited as 1 plus prime, but advertised lower rates later for its best customers. The customer sued First Atlanta when it refused to give the customer the lower rate. First Atlanta finally settled to avoid the law suit, offering plaintiffs the lower rate. Subsequently, in the next few years more than forty lawsuits were filed against other commercial banks based on the definition of "prime."

rate." At many institutions, base rate replaces the prior usage of the prime rate, with different base rates based on customer preferences, such as LIBOR for large borrowers with access to funds in the international as well as the domestic markets. Other rates announced as prime may actually reflect a bank's average cost of funds with a risk premium added. By using the average versus marginal cost of funds as a base, small borrowers who may be unable to bear the risk associated with highly volatile interest rates benefit, as do lenders who avoid the administrative cost of frequent rate changes and who can maintain higher loan yields for a longer period if rates fall.[12] By using an index such as the Treasury rate, lenders can also help borrowers who want to hedge their interest rate risk. Interest rate futures are traded on Treasury bill rates, so borrowers would not have to cross hedge.[13]

Risk Premiums on Loans

Determining the risk premium to be added to a loan is a controversial issue. As noted in discussing RAROC pricing in Chapter 2, risk premiums can be added based on the expected losses of the loan. Other strategies for risk premiums include rating loans and using similar risk premiums to those between different grade bonds and Treasury bonds in bond markets. For instance, the rate spread between a Treasury security and a BBB corporate bond might be 50 basis points, so such a premium would be used for a loan that the bank gives a "Good" BBB rating. Other premiums may be based on rules of thumb, such as 10 basis points for a loan with a very high rating with higher basis points added for higher risk loans, as commonly practiced in the industry. Additional risk premiums might be added for credit, maturity, and collateral risk, as well. Loans were typically underpriced for risk in the 1980s, so the proper pricing of loans for risk is an important issue. Of course, competitive rates must be considered as well.

Other Terms: Collateral

Collateral was discussed briefly earlier in the chapter. By requiring collateral, a lender can service customers who would be too risky for an unsecured loan. But because lenders do not want to be forced to take possession of the borrower's assets, credit analysis is just as important (if not more so) for a secured loan agreement as for an unsecured one. Small banks are more likely to make collateralized loans than their larger counterparts. Asset-based lending adds several important dimensions to loan analysis:

1. Determining the value of the assets to be pledged as collateral;
2. Meeting all legal requirements for securing those assets; and
3. Monitoring the condition of the collateral during the loan period.

The legal agreement assigning the assets as collateral is called the **security agreement.** The Uniform Commercial Code, a body of law adopted individually by states but containing many common provisions across states, establishes guidelines under which these agreements are drawn. Different types of collateral arrangements include a **floating lien,** which gives the lender recourse to the borrower's entire inventory, even if portions are acquired after the loan is made. In the case of riskier loans, **warehouse receipts** place specific inventory items assigned as collateral under the control of a third party, and the goods are often physically transferred to a bonded public warehouse for safekeeping. **Floor planning,** often used by automobile dealers, allows the borrower to retain possession of the collateral. It is an agreement often used to finance expensive retail items such as major appliances or heavy equipment that can be distinguished by serial number or description.

In the case of accounts receivable financing, the collateral may be either pledged or actually sold to the lender. The latter arrangement is called **factoring** and means the bank assumes default risk and responsibility for collection. Whether pledged or factored, the loan amount should always be less than the face value of the receivables.

---

12 See Koch and MacDonald (2000) for a more detailed discussion of base rates including the liability cost transfer price systems used at large banks for pricing loans.

13 Using an index such as the T-bill rate associated with the bank's cost of funds is sometimes called a "synthetic fixed rate loan." See Brady (1985), pp. 12–13. For a more detailed discussion of loan pricing including pricing for risk, see Saunders (1997) and Sinkey (1998).

Restrictive Covenants

Banks often protect their interests as well by establishing restrictive covenants, such as minimum liquidity or debt ratios or a borrower taking on additional debt. Covenants may require life insurance on a key person in a firm, that the bank be notified if any change in management occurs, that the bank be sent quarterly statements from the firm, as well as many other covenants structured to protect the bank's interests. The loan may state that if covenants are not met the loan will be called.

Other Considerations

Type of Loan and Proper Structuring and Maturity

A loan is structured in terms of when payments are made to ensure that loan customers will be able to make these payments. Banks must also be careful to lend the proper amount. Often companies request a loan larger or smaller than they actually need. With too large a loan, a company may have difficulty paying the loan back, and with too small a loan, the company may find itself having liquidity difficulties. By forecasting financial statements including a source or use statement or cash flow statements, the proper amount needed for a loan can be determined, as the missing use that makes total sources equal total uses. Projected monthly cash flow statements also can be used to determine when a loan can be repaid and the proper payment structure.

Special Considerations for Different Types of Loans

Seasonal Working Capital Loans

Seasonal working capital loans are generally repaid within one year once inventory has been sold and accounts receivables have been collected. Often seasonal working capital loans are given out as lines of credit that can be repaid over the year. To determine the approximate loan amount needed for a seasonal working capital loan, quarterly balance sheet statements need to be projected. Performing a sources and uses statement based on the differences between the balance sheet for the peak and low seasons will determine the total uses and sources needed, with the difference between uses and sources as the approximate amount of the loan needed from the bank or another external source.

A rule-of-thumb method for determining the amount of a working capital loan needed is often calculated as a firm's cash to cash cycle times its daily average cost of goods sold (CGS / 365). A firm's cash to cash cycle is typically calculated as:

Cash to Cash Cycle = Days Inventory + Average Collection Period − Days Accounts Payable   [13.3]

where

Days Inventory	= 365 / (CGS / Inventory),
Average Collection Period (ACP)	= 365 / (Credit Sales / Accounts Receivables), and
Days Accounts Payable	= 365 / (CGS / Accounts Payable).

Concept Questions

1. List the different noninterest terms that are included in the structuring of a loan and their effect on a lender's expected return.

2. Explain the concept of profitability analysis. How is it used to price a loan?

3. What other rates are often used to price loans, and how is a risk premium determined?

4. What types of collateral are used for a working capital loan? For a term loan?

5. What are restrictive covenants? Why are they used? Give an example of a restrictive covenant.

For example, if a firm had a Days Inventory of 60 days, an ACP of 30 days, and a Days Accounts Payable of 20 days, the Cash to Cash Cycle would be 70 days. If its daily average cost of goods sold was $1 million, its approximate working capital loan needs would be approximately $70 million. The cash cycle points out the effect of firm working capital policies. If a firm can shorten its inventory cycle by holding less inventory, for instance to 30 days, the cash cycle would only be 40 days and approximately only $40 million of working capital financing would be needed. Since this is just an approximation, it is better for a lender to use cash flow statements to determine the exact amount of the loan that is needed. Quarterly cash flow statements are helpful for determining the financing needed for particular quarters. Seasonal working capital loans are typically collateralized by inventory and accounts receivable.

Term Loans

Term loans used to purchase depreciable assets have maturities that generally vary from one to seven years. The amount of term loans is usually based on the purchase price of an asset and the loan is often amortized to generate a gradual cash repayment of interest and principal over the life of the loan. The collateral for a term loan is typically the machinery and equipment that is being purchased with the loan or other fixed assets. Alternative structures include balloon payments, where everything is paid at maturity, or a bullet loan, which is like a bond paying periodic interest payments with principal paid at maturity. Loans can also be structured to be renewable after a certain number of years.

Commercial Real Estate Loans

Commercial real estate loans or construction loans with real property as collateral often involve interim (temporary) financing by a bank with a **takeout commitment** from a long-term lender such as a life insurance company or pension fund after completion of a project or a certain number of years. Bankers have to be very careful to ensure that the takeout commitment protects the bank from being stuck with a long-term loan. Projected vacancy rates are important to reduce the risk of the project failing. Bankers also need to work with reliable developers, have third-party appraisals, and demand up-front fees to reduce their risk. Fees must be amortized over the life of the loan for accounting purposes. Often construction loans have higher rates as well, usually 1 percent to 1.5 percent above typical commercial loan rates to compensate for the greater risk of these loans. Surety bonds are also necessary to ensure completion of a project.[14]

Agricultural Loans

Agricultural loans are also often collateralized by land and equipment and are very cyclical and seasonal, providing seasonal funds for planting that are repaid at harvest time, as well as providing long-term loans for land and equipment. Lenders learned after large loan defaults in the 1980s to lend on **cash flow** versus real estate values. In 1984 to 1986, about 40 percent of bank failures were agriculture banks that lent on collateral that dropped incredibly in value as more farms went bankrupt with a tremendous fall in commodity prices at that time.

A number of government-sponsored agencies also provide loans to farms, including production credit associations, which are part of the cooperative Farm Credit System; the Farmers Home Administration, which is a federal government agency that provides guarantees for farm loans made by banks and also provides direct lending; and the Commodity Credit Corporation, which is also a government agency and which provides price support and crop storage loans. Rural banks make approximately half of all the farm loans made by commercial banks.[15]

---

14 See Koch and MacDonald (2000) and Hempel, Simonson, and Coleman (1994). Prior to the early 1980s, banks and thrifts were allowed to report fee income up front, which often inflated earnings and capital for institutions that made commercial real estate and construction loans.

15 Ibid. See Hempel, Simonson, and Coleman (1994) for a more detailed discussion of agriculture loans.

Consumer Loans

Consumer loans are usually short term, between one and four years, and often have fixed rates paid in installments. As mentioned earlier in the chapter, consumer loans often have a higher default rate than other types of loans, and in recent years regulators have been concerned about widespread consumer borrowing. Consumer loans are also subject to numerous regulations discussed previously. Bankruptcy laws, which are currently being discussed for revision, have also been more lenient with the implementation of the **Bankruptcy Reform Act in 1980.** A surge of personal bankruptcy filings occurred in the 1980s. In 1984, the Bankruptcy Amendments and Federal Judgeship Act were passed, designed to prevent abuse of the bankruptcy acts with lower limits placed on the amount of property protected from creditors and an improved monitoring system. If a judge believes an individual is abusing the law, the case can be dismissed. One provision welcomed by consumer lenders requires debtors to be responsible for debts incurred shortly before bankruptcy, discouraging individuals from increasing debts with no intention of repaying them. With less of a stigma on personal bankruptcies and attorneys advertising to provide consumers with a means to escape debts, personal bankruptcy rates continue to be a problem for lenders.[16]

Credit Card Loans

One popular type of consumer credit is through **credit cards,** known as **revolving credit,** on which the lender designates a prearranged interest rate and maximum line of credit. The cardholder chooses when and whether to borrow, repaying the lender partially or in full on receipt of a monthly statement. The annual fee most borrowers pay is analogous to a commitment fee in commercial lending. Depository institutions receive fee income from credit cards, and institutions that process credit transactions and bill customers for other depositories are able to earn additional revenues. Finally, the credit card issuing bank charges merchants accepting bank cards fees usually ranging from 2 percent to 5 percent of a transaction. Under the **Fair Credit and Charge Disclosure Act of 1988,** regulations require card issuers to disclose interest rates, grace periods, and other terms and conditions at the time of application. The disclosure must be in the form of a chart so that comparison among lenders is facilitated.

Risks in Credit Cards

Because credit cards carry pre-established lines of credit, consumers may accumulate substantial borrowings before the card issuer knows financial problems have developed. Mass mailing has increased such risks. Although credit cards often offer a 2 percent to 3 percent net return after administrative costs, expected loan losses, and the interest cost of funds, they also entail higher risk. In the early 1990s, some banks introduced **secured cards,** which require customers with poor credit risk to leave a security deposit at a bank to become a cardholder, and higher interest rates and fees were charged.[17]

Installment Loans

Other types of consumer loans are often made on an installment basis. Annual percentage rates (APRs) must be quoted on these loans, which were targeted particularly by Congress, because of confusion in stated rates. In an installment agreement, the borrower makes equal periodic payments. In addition, many automobile and other consumer loans use the add-on interest method. The interest on the full amount borrowed must be paid for each year of the loan term, even though the entire balance is not outstanding for the full term. For example, suppose a couple decides to buy a new car priced at $12,000.

---

16 An individual declaring bankruptcy can seek two forms of protection from creditors. One form, Chapter 7, seeks complete absolution from indebtedness. The other, Chapter 13, seeks protection from creditors while the debtor works under a court-approved plan to repay obligations. Chapter 7 filings have increased in recent years and present the greatest potential for loss.

17 There are many bank and nonbank competitors for credit card loans including credit cards banks, such as MBNA, which offer affinity cards to members of special groups, and other nonbank competitors, such as General Electric, American Express, among many others. With competition, return on assets on credit card business has fallen.

After making a $2,000 down payment, they approach their CU for a $10,000 loan and are quoted an add-on rate of 9 percent for four years. They will repay a total of:

$$\$10,000 \ (0.09) \ (4) + \$10,000 = \$13,600$$

The repayment schedule will be $13,600 / 48 = $283.33 per month, resulting in a monthly interest rate of 1.3322 percent and an annual percentage rate (APR) of just under 16 percent, based on setting the $10,000 = $283.33 (PVIFA 48 periods). Using a financial calculator or trial and error, the monthly rate is 1.3322 percent $\times$ 12 $\approx$ 16 percent annually. Note with an add-on rate, the effective rate is a little less than double the quoted rate. Reg Z requires lenders to disclose the APR to borrowers. The Fed defines the APR as the periodic rate multiplied by, not compounded by, the number of periods in a year. Thus, the APR is a legal definition of an interest rate and is not the effective annual yield to the lender.[18]

The Rule of 78s as a Prepayment Penalty for Installment Loans

When a borrower repays an installment loan before the original maturity date, lenders often apply the rule of 78s to calculate the remaining principal balance. This approach, also called the sum-of-digits, involves adding together the digits for the number of payments to be made. The 78 in the name is derived from the sum of digits for a twelve-month loan:

$$12 + 11 + 10 + 9 + 8 + 7 + 6 + 5 + 4 + 3 + 2 + 1 = 78$$

For a four-year (forty-eight-month) automobile loan, the sum of digits is 1,176 $[(N / 2) \times (N + 1)]$, where N is the number of payments. According to the rule of 78s, were the borrowers to pay off the loan early, they would be charged for 48 / 1,176 of their total interest payment owed in the first month, 47 / 1,176 in the second month, and so on, as interest. For instance, if the borrowers repaid the loan after one year, after twelve payments of $283.33, they have paid $3,399.96. Under the rule of 78s, they would be charged with (510 / 1,176), or 0.43367 of the total interest payment of $3,600 {[$10,000 (0.09) $\times$ 4] $\times$ 0.43367 = $1,561.22} as interest. The numerator 510 is the sum of 48, 47, 46, and so on, through 37. Subtracting this $1,561.22 of interest from the total payment gives us $3,399.96 − $1,561.22 = $1,838.74, which would be considered as repaid principal. To discharge their obligation, the borrowers would have to pay the credit union $10,000 − $1,838.74 = $8,161.26. The rule of 78s is controversial because it specifies a balance for repayment higher than the balance indicated by an amortization schedule based on an APR of 16 percent. In most states, however, lenders are permitted to use this rule, although a few states have adopted laws specifically prohibiting it. Lenders argue that it is justified because it helps them recover fixed lending costs, although consumer advocates argue that the rule of 78s is unfair to borrowers.[19]

Home Equity Loans

The Tax Reform Act of 1986 spurred intense interest in home equity loans, a type of credit with characteristics of both mortgage and nonmortgage consumer lending. The Tax Reform Act phased out the tax deductibility of interest expenses for consumer borrowers with the exception of interest on home mortgage loans and home equity loans (*hels*). Hels are different from second mortgages, which are additional loans backed by the property on which a first mortgage has been issued, with fixed dollar amounts, specified maturity dates, and a higher interest rate than first mortgages. The amount that homeowners can borrow is limited by the amount of equity they have accumulated in their homes. A hel, in contrast, is a revolving line of credit against which a homeowner can borrow. The maximum amount the homeowner is allowed to borrow is 70 percent to 85 percent of the equity the borrower has in the home. Because the lender has the security of a junior lien on the borrower's home in case of default, hels are offered at lower interest rates than credit card or unsecured consumer loans. Interest rates are variable, sometimes changing monthly and often tied to movements in a prime rate or T-bill index. Repayment schedules are more flexible than second mortgages, and the borrower often may

---

18 Board of Governors of the Federal Reserve System, "Official Staff Commentary on Regulation Z Truth-in-Lending as Amended April 1, 1990" (June 1990).

19 Thanks to Jim McNulty for assistance with this discussion. See "The Rule of 78's or What May Happen When You Pay Off a Loan Early." Federal Reserve Bank of Philadelphia, *Department of Consumer Affairs Pamphlet*, 1986.

Concept Questions

1 What is the difference between a seasonal working capital loan and a term loan? What type of collateral is used for each?

2 Why is a takeout commitment important for banks making commercial real estate loans?

3 What is an installment loan? What is Regulation Z, and how does it protect consumers from quoted add-on interest rates? What is the rule of 78s as a prepayment penalty for installment loans?

4 What is a home equity loan, and what is the maximum amount that can be borrowed against the equity a borrower has in a home?

draw on unused but approved credit simply by writing a check. In response to consumer organization pressure for stricter regulation of hels, in 1987 the Competitive Equality Banking Act (CEBA) mandated that hels must have lifetime interest rate caps. In 1988, Congress passed the Home Equity Loan Consumer Protection Act. It specifies rigid disclosure rules and restricts the right of creditors to change loan terms after a hel has been approved. Thus, the flexibility in hel terms was reduced.[20]

Special Considerations of Mortgage Loans

ARMS

There are many special regulations for mortgage loans including adjustable rate mortgage loans (ARMs). National banks have only three choices: indexes of long-term mortgage rates, T-bill rates, or Treasury bond rates. Thrifts may use any interest rate series that is widely published, verifiable by the borrower, and not in the direct control of an individual lender. The lender must explain to the borrower exactly how the loan interest rate is related to the index and how it will be adjusted as the index changes. A fifteen-year history of the index must be provided. Often the one-year Treasury index is popular, since it tends to vary with lenders' average cost of funds index. Federal regulations allow thrifts to offer ARM plans with any frequency of rate adjustments, but national banks may not change the mortgage interest rate more than once every six months.

Banks also have limits called **caps** on the size of the periodic rate adjustment, with an overall rate cap required by federal law. Federal regulations prohibit prepayment penalties on ARMs. Convertible ARMs have also been developed whereby borrowers may switch their ARMs to FRMs during a specified period.[21]

Due on Sale Clauses

Increasingly common for mortgage loans is the due on sale clause, in which the lender can require the borrower to repay the outstanding loan balance when the mortgage property is sold. Mortgages without due on sale clauses are assumable by the new homeowner.[22] Due on sale clauses protect the lender by allowing the lender to evaluate the financial position of the new owner before deciding to continue the loan and allowing a higher interest rate if necessary than the original loan. The Garn-St. Germain Act of 1982 gave lender the authority to enforce due on sale clauses in all mortgage agreements originated thereafter.

Innovative Mortgages

Other innovative mortgages are **graduated payment mortgages (GPM)** where monthly payments are set at a low level in the early years, then payments increase according to a known schedule before sta-

---

20 Information on this section was drawn from several excellent articles, including Thomas A. Durkin. "Home Equity Credit Lines in Perspective." *Finance Facts* (June-July 1987); "Home Equity Lines of Credit Revisited." *Finance Facts* (August 1987); Canner, Fergus, and Luckett (1998); Canner and Fergus (1988); Canner and Luckett (1989); John Meehan. "It's Like Being on the Edge of a Precipice." *Business Week* (July 6, 1992), 56–58; Steve Rodgers. "CUs Gain Home Equity Market Share." *Credit Union Magazine* (June 1992), 20–24.

21 See Mills and Gardner (1986); Carroll (1989); and Peck (1990).

22 Federal agency policies require that VA and FHA mortgages be assumable; conventional mortgages usually have a due on sale clause. Federal regulations carefully define sale for purposes of enforcement of due on sale clauses. For a review of the technicalities, see Priess (1983).

bilizing. **Reverse annuity mortgages (RAMs)** for elderly homeowners that face cash shortages allow borrowers to receive cash payments from a depository institution, with the depository institution gradually becoming the owner of the property. At a specified maturity date, or when the homeowner with a RAM moves or dies, the property is sold and the lender receives the repayment with interest from the proceeds. With **growing equity mortgages (GEMs)** initial payments are set at the level that would amortize the mortgage over thirty years, but scheduled increases in payments result in a shorter actual maturity. **Price-level adjusted mortgages (PLAMs)** have an adjustable interest rate tied to an inflation index rather than an interest rate index, whereby a borrower pays for actual versus expected inflation and benefits from lower initial interest costs that are not adjusted for expected inflation.

Small Business Loans

Small lending grew rapidly in the 1990s with many large banks, such as Wells Fargo, Key Bank, and others setting up special divisions to help small businesses with loans, working capital management, and other needs, often associated with Community Reinvestment Act lending activities. Also, community banks have become specialists in small business lending.

Banks often become designated as small business lenders, with the ability to make **Small Business Administration (SBA) loans.** To be eligible to apply for an SBA loan, a borrower must first be denied a conventional loan. A borrower can then apply for an SBA loan through a designated lender. The SBA guarantees a portion of the loan, so the lender is protected against default risk, which allows the lender the ability to take on a loan to a small business, which can entail considerable risk. The SBA-guaranteed portions of SBA-guaranteed loans, however, are securitized with yields close to those of government-issued securities.[23]

Types of Higher Risk Lending

Subprime Lending

During the expansion of the later 1990s, a greater number of banks and finance companies took on high-risk (subprime), higher interest-rate lending to more risky consumer borrowers. The higher rates make subprime loans profitable in good times if rates charged are high enough to cover the higher average loan loss rates and overhead costs associated with the underwriting, servicing, and collection for the loans. With a newfound ability to sell and securitize subprime loans at a profit, while retaining the servicing rights and associated fee income for servicing, financial institutions found this type of lending attractive. Often large financial institutions formed subsidiaries for subprime lending to high-risk borrowers for loans that a bank would not normally be allowed to make. This type of high-risk lending was of concern to regulators, particularly in 1999, when unfavorable market events resulted in large losses for many subprime lenders. In addition, many subprime lenders faced lawsuits by customers for predatory lending, whereby lenders pressured borrowers with weak credit histories to take on loans and/or did not inform them of the risk (such as losing their homes) with such loans. Accordingly, in March 1999, the Federal Reserve Board issued a letter to examiners and detailed interagency guidance for the Federal Reserve, FDIC, OCC, and OTS on subprime lending that can be found at *http://www .federalreserve.gov/boarddocs/SRLetters/1999.* In this guide, "subprime lending" was defined "as extending credit to borrowers who exhibit characteristics indicating a significantly higher risk of default than traditional bank lending customers." The guide was intended to increase examiner and financial awareness of some of the pitfalls and hazards of subprime lending and to provide examination guidance. In general, the guide recommended that institutions that engaged in subprime lending in a significant way should have policies and procedures, as well as internal controls, to identify, monitor, and control the additional risks. Firms with a smaller volume should have systems in place commensurate with their level of risk. Capital, staff expertise, collection loan administration, loan review and monitoring, consumer protection, and risk assessment planning should increase with the additional risk of subprime lending. For securitizations, key assumptions used to value subprime pools of debt should be

---

23 See Hempel, Simonson, and Coleman (1994) for more details concerning the securitization and profits from securitization of SBA loans. Congress has debated legislation to attempt to develop greater securitization of other small business loans to increase funds available for small businesses.

conservative and appropriate for the risk of these pools. Financial institutions should also periodically reevaluate whether the subprime lending program has met profitability, risk, and performance goals. The evaluation should include estimates of costs, losses, and profit projections; any support required to maintain the quality and performance of securitized loan pools; whether the risks inherent in subprime lending are properly identified, measured, monitored, and controlled; and whether community credit needs were being met. Examiners were urged to evaluate how adequately managers planned for subprime lending activities; had the financial capacity, lending standards, and skills to conduct this high-risk activity; and had adequate contingency plans to address alternative funding sources, back-up purchasers of the securities or attendant servicing functions, and methods of raising additional capital during periods of volatile financial markets and economic downturns. Securitization transactions also need to comply with FAS 125, including the financial institution's support to maintain the credit quality of loan pools that it securitized. Financial institution managers also needed to be responsive to adverse performance trends, including higher than expected prepayments, delinquencies, charge-offs, customer complaints and expenses, and to have a compliance program that effectively managed the fair lending and consumer protection compliance risks associated with subprime lending operations.[24]

Leveraged Buyouts

Especially harsh criticisms have been leveled at bank lenders in **leveraged buyouts (LBOs)** particularly in the late 1980s and early 1990s. LBOs are transactions in which a group of investors, often including a firm's managers, buys a firm by using huge amounts of debt capital and relatively little net worth. At year-end 1988, LBOs and related loans accounted for over 10 percent of the commercial loan portfolios at sixty of the largest commercial banks.[25] Few LBOs occurred before the mid-1980s, when the economy was comparatively robust; however, weakening economic indicators in the late 1980s and early 1990s caused many observers to be concerned that LBO borrowers would not be able to meet their debt obligations in the future, thereby putting their lenders substantially at risk. Although most observers believe that additional regulation against bank and thrift involvement in LBOs is not needed, most also believe that the practice should be confined to lenders with high levels of capital.

Mezzanine Lending

Some commercial banks have approached participation in highly leveraged transactions through the practice of mezzanine lending. Mezzanine loans are longer-term, unsecured loans in which a firm's cash flow is the major source of repayment; in addition, the financial contract contains an option through which the lender can share in the increased value of the business if the venture is particularly successful. The potentially high return on the option is designed to compensate for the relatively high risk of the loan. The option is used in place of a higher interest rate, which might increase the probability of borrower default in the short run. Mezzanine financing often contains layers of investors with senior and junior debt including warrants attached that allow future equity stakes in a firm. Bond financing is privately placed. With mezzanine financing, different layers appeal to different preferences for risk by groups of investors. Venture capital is often involved. Also, bonds issued with **payment in kind (PIK)** are similar to a zero-coupon bond with interest accumulating, so the principal that must be repaid at maturity gets larger and larger. By providing additional financing to growing firms that may not be large enough to issue public debt, such as junk bonds, mezzanine financing serves as a good example of financial innovation at work.[26]

---

24 See FRB: Supervisory SR 99-6 (GEN) on Subprime Lending—March 5, 1999 *(http://www.federalreserve.gov/boarddocs/SRletters/1999/SR9906.htm)* and Intra-gency Guidance on Subprime Lending *(http://www.federalreserve.gov/boarddocs/SRLetters/1999)*. Also see Federal Trade Commission Release, September 19, 2002, "Citicorp Settles FTC Charges Against the Associates Record-Setting $215 Million for Subprime Lending Victims," *http://www.ftc.gov/opa/2002/09/associates.htm;* and FTC Subprime Lending Cases (since 1998) *(http://www.ftc.gov/opa/2002/09/subprimelendingcases.htm)*.

25 See Wolfson and McLaughlin (1989), 464.

26 For more details, see Stacy (1988); and "Roundtable Discussion of Issues in Commercial Banking." *Bank of America Journal of Applied Corporate Finance* 9 (Summer 1996), 24–51.

Lending to Hedge Funds

Previous chapters discuss huge losses for banks in 1998 from loans made to Long-Term Capital Management, L.P., a highly leveraged giant investment fund for wealthy private investors, known as a hedge fund. The potential failure of Long-Term Capital led to a Fed-arranged $3.625 billion bailout by fourteen banks and securities firms. In response to this bailout, the Federal Reserve Board in 1999 told banks to tighten their standards for lending to hedge funds and to avoid focusing too much on easy profits while ignoring credit risks posed by some funds. The Fed also issued guidelines to regulators for assessing bank lending to hedge funds including self-imposed limits by banks on the amount of their loans to hedge funds and improving their models for credit risks. The OCC also issued guidelines and recommendations for monitoring risk for hedge fund loans, as did a leading group of international bankers in 1999. A number of securities firms including Goldman Sachs, Merrill Lynch, and Morgan Stanley Dean Witter & Co. formed an industry group in 1999 to develop risk standards for financial institutions extending credit in global markets.[27]

Loan Monitoring and Review

Despite even the best credit analysis and loan policies, problems occur. Monitoring procedures are designed to identify problems early enough to circumvent a need for legal action later. A comprehensive loan review system also serves to monitor the effectiveness of an institution's loan officers by providing incentives for them to make good decisions initially and then periodically to assess the borrower's subsequent financial position. Research suggest that banks have significant investments in loan monitoring and that the investment is positively related to the risk of the loan portfolio.[28]

As previously noted, many lending institutions assign a special group of personnel to workouts (when loans are going bad and need to be restructured) in an effort to avoid default. Workout specialists know that most of the financial problems of borrowers are traced to mismanagement arising from inadequate training and experience or perhaps even fraud.

Problems are accelerated by the state of the local or national economy or by the condition of a particular industry. Consider, for example, the effect of declining oil prices on energy-related industries throughout the 1980s. Similarly, overbuilding of commercial properties in many of the nation's largest cities posed severe problems for thrifts that invested directly in these properties or lent to the developers. As banks increased their commercial real estate lending, some were faced with prospects of problem loans. Unfortunately for lenders, even secured loans provide little protection under those conditions, because the property obtained on default has usually declined in value.

Loan Monitoring, Regulation, and Financial Reporting

Loan monitoring has important ramifications for financial reporting to the public and to regulatory agencies. Loans are often classified as **past due** for 30 to 89 days, **nonperforming** if they are past due for 90 or more days, and **nonaccruing** when payments are not received. As explained in Chapter 4, institutions estimate problem loans and report them in the **allowance for possible loan losses** account on their balance sheet. The loan loss allowance account is increased by current estimates of anticipated loan losses (**the provision for loan losses**) and reduced by **actual net loan charge-offs** (actual loans charged off as losses less any actual loan recoveries). Thus, the allowance account is always an estimate of future loan losses, not a record of past losses.

Estimating future loan losses for planning purposes is of considerable concern to depositories. To estimate losses with a reasonable degree of accuracy, lenders develop procedures to identify when a borrower moves into the "questionable" category. Regulators expect these policies to accomplish their purpose; when they do not, disciplinary actions may be taken. Examiners in periodically reviewing a

---

27 Matt Murray. "Fed Tells Banks to Tighten Standards for Loans They Extend to Hedge Funds." *The Wall Street Journal* (February 2, 1999), A4.

28 Gregory F. Udell. "Loan Quality, Commercial Loan Review, and Loan Officer Contracting." Salomon Brothers Center for the Study of Financial Institutions, Working Paper No. 459 (March 1988).

bank's loans will classify problem loans into categories of substandard, doubtful, and loss. Accordingly, regulators may ask banks to write down their capital for loans that are likely to be losses and for a percentage of likely losses such as 20 percent for substandard loans and 50 percent for doubtful loans.[29] In the late 1980s and early 1990s, some banks felt regulators were unduly harsh in writing down loan losses. Maryland National Bank in Baltimore, for instance, was forced to write down a large number of its loans as losses, which severely hurt its capital position and led the bank to sell to the public its profitable credit card and securitization subsidiary, MBNA, and also led to the bank's ultimate merger with Nationsbank (which later merged with Bank of America).

Delinquent Loans

Despite careful scrutiny of loan applications, some borrowers inevitably will be unable or unwilling to meet their repayment schedules. When a borrower is seriously delinquent, management of the loan moves from the loan officer to those responsible for collection. In all cases, collection personnel want to avoid legal action, because it consumes resources and time. For example, a savings institution does not really want to foreclose on a mortgage loan; the legal expenses are large, and the institution must sell or maintain the repossessed property. Lenders will usually work closely with borrowers to set up revised repayment plans, suggest general financial counseling, or provide advice on financial management. Such efforts, as mentioned earlier, are often termed **workouts**.

Monitoring collateral can be difficult in some cases. When vehicle loans become delinquent, the lender must move quickly—because the collateral is mobile! As with other aspects of loan management, the more resources committed to the collection effort, the greater the protection against instability in the NIM but also the greater the addition to net noninterest expenses. A close relationship with borrowers helps the bank to discover problems and provide assistance before they become too overwhelming. Small and medium-sized banks often have an advantage in this respect, and many banks have instituted policies that loan officers must contact and visit their previous customers as a condition for compensation.

Other Lending Considerations

Loan Participations and Syndications

A **loan participation** is an arrangement by two or more lenders to share a loan in some agreed-on proportion. A lead institution initiates the loan and usually has all of the contact with the borrower. Closely related to participations are **loan syndications,** in which several lenders simultaneously lend to a single borrower, and all lenders have a direct relationship with the borrower. Participations and syndications are often necessary in large loans because of regulatory limitations placed on the amount a commercial bank may loan to a single borrower as a percentage of the depository's capital. For commercial banks with federal charters a bank may lend to one borrower an unsecured amount not to exceed 15 percent of capital and surplus or 25 percent if "readily marketable collateral" is pledged as securities. Loan participations and syndications allow institutions to accommodate large borrowers and share the risk.

Loan participations and syndications allow smaller institutions to enlarge their loan portfolios, especially if they lack ready access to a business community large enough to support a direct lending program. Such agreements also permit lenders to diversify geographically. But they can lead to severe problems, especially if the participants do not perform their own credit analysis. Publicity surrounded the heavy losses incurred by Continental Illinois, Chase Manhattan, and other commercial lenders on loan participations with Penn Square Bank of Oklahoma City, which failed in 1982 when most of its loans to energy-related companies went into default. Fed data suggest that fewer than 15 percent of commercial loans result from participation agreements.

---

29 See Koch and MacDonald (2000).

Lender Liability Including Environmental Liability

A growing problem for commercial lenders is the threat of a suit by a borrower if the borrower is in financial difficulty. A recent study of lender liability showed that most suits arose because an institution has refused to advance funds or has attempted to take possession of collateral. In addition, lawsuits have appeared in which a lender failed to renew a loan, which defendants claim led to their firms' failures. Lenders are also often cited in environmental liability suits if collateral used for loans is associated with environmental hazards. Consequently, lenders perform environmental audits on land or buildings used as collateral, as shown in the loan presentation for the Big Apple Real Estate & Storage Company discussed earlier. Lawsuits are expensive for lenders even if they win cases. Consequently, most experts caution lenders that the best way to prevent lawsuits is to follow institutional monitoring and foreclosure procedures scrupulously, to give ample notice to borrowers if credit is not to be extended, and to keep excellent records.

But even careful record keeping may not be enough. Courts have interpreted lending contracts in inconsistent, even contradictory, ways. For example, some lenders have been fined for failing to provide advance notice that a line of credit will not be renewed, whereas others have been sued for "threatening" borrowers by providing just such notice! Some financial economists have concluded that the specter of being held liable for monitoring borrowers' actions may eventually result in credit rationing against borrowers whom lenders believe are most likely to need monitoring. At best, such high-risk borrowers may pay even higher interest rates to compensate lenders for the extra cost of being sued. Although acknowledging that borrowers are entitled to protection from the capricious act of lenders, these experts conclude that lending markets are sufficiently competitive and the permissible construction of financial contracts is sufficiently flexible that borrowers already enjoy adequate protection without having to sue banks. Thus, the lender liability battleground is likely to be a lively one for the rest of this decade.

Community Reinvestment Act Revisions

The Community Reinvestment Act (CRA) of 1977, introduced earlier, requires regulators to encourage depositories to meet the credit needs of their local communities, including low- and moderate-income neighborhoods. The act is enforced primarily through regulators' examinations of credit policies and practices. Examinations have become increasingly rigorous in recent years. Institutions may be required to provide evidence that personnel have met with community leaders to determine credit needs, that they have taken an active role in economic development, and that they have responded to past complaints about credit allocation in the community.

In the 1990s, both lenders and community leaders criticized the focus of CRA performance evaluations on process and paperwork versus actual results of efforts made by a financial institution to serve its local community. Other criticisms included the failure of CRA ratings to distinguish between banks that performed well and those that performed poorly. Very few institutions received high or low evaluations. In response to these concerns, in July 1993 President Clinton asked supervisory agencies to reform the regulations that implement CRA.

In May 1995, new regulations were presented to make CRA assessments "more performance-based, more objective, and less burdensome for covered institutions." The original regulation had twelve assessment factors. The new regulations substitute three performance measures in terms of **lending, investment,** and **service.** The **lending tests** measure lending activity for a variety of loan types including small business and small farm loans. Assessment criteria includes the geographic distribution of lending, the distribution of lending across different types of borrowers, the extent of community development lending, and the use of innovative or flexible lending practices to address the needs of low- or moderate-income individuals or areas. The **investment test** considers the institution's involvement with qualified investments, such as providing capital for an investment group in the community that invests in low-income areas. A qualified investment includes an investment, deposit, or grant that benefits the institution's assessment area or a broader statewide or regional area. The **service test** considers the institution's availability and responsiveness for delivering retail banking services and judges the extent of its community development services and their degree of innovation. Alternative systems for delivering services to low- and moderate-income areas, for instance, are considered, as well as the provision of community development services. Some banks developed traveling loan offices to provide information to low-income areas about the bank's lending services and community low-income loan grants. In assessing CRA compliance, evaluations are made in the context of information about the lending institutions and its community competitors and peers. The capacity and constraints of an institution are considered as well as economic and demographic characteristics of the local service areas and the institution's business strategy. CRA disclosure information for each financial institution is available for purchase through the Federal Financial Institutions Examination Council (FFIEC) in CD-ROM or hard copy form through the FFIEC's Website at *http://www.ffiec.gov,* or by calling the CRA Assistance Line at (202) 872–7584. The FDIC Website, *http://www.fdic.gov,* has a quick link for consumers that includes a search locator for CRA ratings for particular institutions.[30]

Sales of Commercial Loans and Some Securitizations

Early chapters discussed loan sales and securitization as sources of noninterest revenues and as investment securities for depository institutions. Many large banks have turned away from so-called **portfolio lending**—in which financial contracts are written with the intent that the lender will hold the loan until maturity. This trend has important implications for the future of the banking industry. Although purchasers of loans, including small non-money-center banks, can benefit from the resulting diversification, issues of information reusability and asymmetry become somewhat more complicated. For example, if the original lender has no intention of holding a loan to maturity, will credit analysis be as rigorous as before? Will originating lenders conclude that it is in their best interests to sell weaker credit and to retain only the less risky loans for themselves? If so, are purchasers—especially less sophisticated banks or even thrifts—equipped to evaluate the risk exposure they assume, particularly when the information required to make proper evaluations in one instance may not be reusable in another? Although the selling of loans of all types is undoubtedly one of the most important asset/liability management tools today, it brings up a new set of unanswered issues. Because commercial loans are less homogeneous than other loans, being tailored and negotiated in terms of size, rate, and maturity, they are not in as many securitized pools as often as other types of loans. Yet, the securitization of commercial loans has grown dramatically. JPMorgan Chase, for instance, securitized $5.5 billion of commercial loans in 2001, along with $7.9 billion of residential mortgage loans, $6 billion of credit card loans, and $2.5 billion of automobile loans, resulting in pretax gains on securitizations of $341 million.

Providing One-Stop Shopping for All Corporate Needs

Many large banks have also changed their traditional lending focus from being simply "product-oriented" institutions to solution-oriented companies, providing expertise and innovative ways to find tailor-made solutions that are unique to the particular circumstances of a company. For instance, banks have developed products like mezzanine debt for unrated firms to anchor relationships in the middle market. Many larger banks have also transformed themselves into firms that can offer one-stop shopping for all kinds of financial products from investment services to banking to working capital management. Lending relationships have become more than just lending relationships. Commercial banks have streamlined the loan process, allowing customers to get loans online, with online mortgage loans growing rapidly.

Improvement in Credit Risk Management

Banks have attempted to improve their risk management. One aspect of this focus is the growing use of **risk-adjusted return on capital (RAROC)** to measure how much risk the bank is taking and to determine whether returns are providing adequate compensation for risk. RAROC is also used to determine whether the bank is providing shareholders with value added through its participation in that business. Although RAROC has only become popular in the last decade, it was introduced by Bankers Trust in the late 1970s in association with trading portfolios. As defined by Bankers Trust and noted by Caouette, Altman, and Narayanan (1998), RAROC allocates a capital cost or charger to a line of busi-

---

30 For a summary of the new CRA regulations, see Raphael W. Bostic and Glenn B. Canner. "New Information on Lending to Small Businesses and Small Farms: The 1996 CRA Data." *Federal Reserve Bulletin* (January 1998), 1–21.

Concept Questions

1 What are ARMS, caps, due on sale clauses, graduated payment mortgages, reverse annuity mortgages, growing equity mortgages, price-level adjusted mortgages, and SBA loans?

2 Why have banks gotten into subprime lending, and why have regulators been concerned about these trends?

3 What are leveraged buyouts, and why are they risky? What is mezzanine financing? What is a hedge fund?

4 Why is loan monitoring and review of great importance to banks? What are some different measures for loan problems?

5 What are some provisions of the Community Reinvestment Act?

6 What is RAROC? Given an example of its use.

ness at an amount equal to the maximum expected loss (at a 99 percent confidence level) over a period of a year on an after-tax basis. The greater the volatility of an asset's returns, the more capital must be allocated. Capital accordingly is allocated to a business in proportion to the risk contribution of that business. For instance, Bank of America had a stated policy of having enough capital to support any given activity to cover 99.97 percent of the unexpected losses in that business. RAROC is calculated as the expected yearly income for a loan divided by the amount of supporting economic capital (representing the expected loss on the loan).

Alternatively, RAROC can be calculated as the expected net income per dollar on an activity (subtracting out interest and noninterest expenses and expected losses) divided by the expected loss rate on the loan, which includes funds that can be recaptured through collateral or other sources. For instance, if the expected income per dollar on the loan less its interest costs and administrative fees was 50 basis points, or 0.50 percent, and the expected losses for this type of loan was 5 percent for a 99.97 percent confidence level, with 80 percent likely not to be recaptured through collateral, RAROC would be 0.005 / (0.05)(0.80), or 12.5 percent. Accordingly, loans or other activities with RAROCs lower than a bank's cost of capital would not be acceptable.[31]

Summary

Loans are the largest category of assets of depository institutions. Although depository institutions specialize in different types of loans, all depositories share important elements of successful lending. In fact, lending is one of the functions that makes depositories "special" financial institutions in regulators' eyes. Lending policies must incorporate specific objectives for the size, composition, maturity, interest rate characteristics, and default risk of the loan portfolio.

Procedures for evaluating and approving loan applications must then be devised to achieve those objectives. A major step is to establish a base lending rate from which individual loan-pricing decisions follow. The process of evaluating and approving a loan includes decisions regarding what rate to charge a given customer, how often the rate will change, and whether special terms and conditions should be attached. Finally, procedures must be developed to monitor the loan's performance to avoid borrower default.

Loans to businesses are of particular interest to commercial banks, although thrifts have begun to enter the market in small numbers in recent years. Of special importance in commercial lending is an analysis of the borrower's financial condition. Applicants must be categorized according to the level of default risk to which the institution is exposed. Credit scoring systems have often played a part in this screening. New risk-based pricing techniques including RAROC have also become popular.

After analysis of an applicant's financial condition, specific loan terms must be determined. In the past, the standard pricing practice was to charge the institution's best customers the prime rate and to scale other loan rates upward from there. Today, a more two-tiered pricing system has emerged for large and small borrowers. Further decisions involve compensating balances, commitments, discounting,

---

31 See "Roundtable Discussion on Current Issues in Banking." *Bank of America Journal of Applied Corporate Finance* 9 (Summer 1996), 24–41; "Click for a Mortgage." *The Wall Street Journal* (February 4, 1999), A1; and Carlos Tejada. "Guide to On-Line Mortgages, Refinancing." *The Wall Street Journal* (February 6, 1998), B8. Online sites also give information on the best mortgage rates, such as E-Loan, at *http://www.eloan.com*.

and collateral. The expected yield to the depository will reflect all these decisions. Some institutions choose loan participation or syndication agreements originated by a lead bank instead of, or in addition to, direct lending, and many banks have become loan originators and servicers entering the loan sales market. Environmental liability and Community Reinvestment Act assessments have also become very important considerations for lenders.

Questions

1. Why have bank loans to large corporations fallen, and why has real estate lending risen? How are banks still special to medium-sized and small firms?

2. Why are regulators concerned about increased consumer lending by depository institutions? What factors have contributed to the growth in consumer credit in the United States from the 1970s to the 1990s?

3. Why did loan losses fall for banks in the mid- and later 1990s? What are past due loans, nonperforming loans, and nonaccruing loans? Why do some banks feel that regulators were harsh in forcing banks to write down loan losses in the early 1990s? What was the credit crunch of the early 1990s? What factors contributed to it?

4. Who are the primary suppliers of consumer loans and primary suppliers of mortgage debt? Why do you think the percentage of securitized consumer and mortgage debt grew so rapidly in the 1990s and 2000s?

5. Why do banks need an overall lending policy? What does a bank's lending policy include? Explain the lender's role in bringing business into the bank. How can this role conflict with the lender's credit analysis role? How have lender compensation policies changed to encourage lenders to make "good" loans?

6. Briefly give the major provisions for the Equal Credit Opportunity Act (Reg B), the Fair Housing Act, the Fair Credit Reporting Act, the Truth in Lending Act, Reg Z, the Uniform Residential Loan Application, the Real Estate Settlement Procedures Act, the Home Mortgage Disclosure Act, the Community Reinvestment Act, and the Loans to Insiders Act (Reg O). Why are lenders subject to so many regulations?

7. Why are codes of ethics and conflict of interest policies particularly important for financial institutions? Can you give an example of an institution whose failure within the last two decades was related to ethical problems?

8. Briefly list the typical items that are included in a loan request procedure. What are the 5 C's of Credit? How many can be measured objectively?

9. Discuss rules of thumb for lending on collateral. Why are loan to collateral value ratios important? Why do collateralized loans typically have higher rates?

10. Explain what a quantitative scoring model is, such as Zeta Analysis or a Consumer Scoring Model. What type of information does corporate and consumer loan scoring models emphasize? Why have they been popular? What are their limitations?

11. What is CreditMetrics? What advantage does this approach have?

12. What is a depository institution's base lending rate? Using Equation 13.2, explain how to solve for this rate. How do competitive conditions also affect loan pricing?

13. What are some noninterest terms and conditions of a loan including compensating balance requirements, loan commitments, and discounts (or points)? How do noninterest terms affect loan rates? How are loans priced using profitability analysis?

14. What has been the historical definition of the term *prime rate*? How has this changed?

15. Why are indexes such as Treasury rates used often by lenders as a base rate?

16. How are risk premiums on loans set? Explain what RAROC is and how it is calculated. How do restrictive covenants help to protect a lender?

17. Briefly define the following types of loans: seasonal working capital loans, term loans, commercial real estate/construction loans, and agricultural loans. What special considerations need to be made for each of these respective loans?

18. How do bankruptcy acts affect the risk of consumer loans? How do banks make profits on credit card loans? What are the risks and trends in credit card loans?

19. Discuss how the rates on consumer installment loans are set. How are these rates converted to annual percentage rates (APRs)? What is the rule of 78s?

20. Explain how home equity loans differ from second mortgages. What provisions does the Home Equity Consumer Protection Act have to protect consumers taking out home equity loans?

21. What rules does a lender have to abide by in setting rates on ARMs? What are due on sales clauses? What is a GPM? RAM? GEM? PLAM?

22. Why have banks increased their lending to small businesses? How can a Small Business Administration (SBA) loan be securitized?

23. Explain what leveraged buyout lending, mezzanine lending, and hedge fund lending are. Why are these types of loans risky?

24. What are loan participations and syndications? Who do banks compete against for this type of lending?

25. Why has lender liability, including environmental liability, become an important issue for banks? How can banks protect against these types of liabilities?

26. Briefly discuss revisions in the Community Reinvestment Act. How do the new provisions respond to criticisms of previous CRA procedures?

Problems

1. Minicase: The Bronco Badges Company Loan Application. Refer to Table P13.1 showing projected financial statements for 2006 and current balance sheet for 2005, along with projected financial ratios for 2006 and answer these questions about the Bronco Badges Company.

   a. Fill in the missing items in the sources and uses statement and statement of changes in cash flow. How much does the firm need to borrow in 2006?

   b. Based on the uses (increases in assets in this case) for funds in 2006 shown in the sources and uses statement, how would you structure the loan in terms of short-term notes payable (one year or less maturity) and long-term debt?

   c. Analyze the projected key ratios compared with last year's ratios and the industry averages. What strengths and weaknesses does Bronco Badges Company have?

   d. As a lender, what other types of information would you like to know about the company or its managers in determining whether to grant the loan?

   e. How would you price this loan? What kind of loan structure (maturity, terms, loan covenants, and collateral) would you suggest?

table **P13.1**   CURRENT BALANCE SHEET 2005 AND PROJECTED BALANCE SHEET FOR 2006 BRONCO BADGES CO.

Income Statement (mils.)	2006	Balance Sheets	2006	2005	Source	Use
Sales	$3,000	Cash	$500	$450		50
CGS	$1,000	Accts. Rec.	1,000	900		100
Gross Profit	2,000	Inventory	1,500	1,350		150
Depreciation	500	Net Fixed Assets	2,000	1,800		200
Operating Costs	$500	Accts. Payable	500	450	50	
Operating Profit	1,000	Accruals	500	450	50	
Interest Expense	$200	Notes Payable	?	142	?	
Earnings Before Tax	800	Long-term Debt	?	500	?	
Taxes (30%)	$240	Common Stock	2,000	2,000		
Net Income	$560	Retained Earnings	1,138	958	$180	
Dividend	$380	Total			$500	$500
Add to Ret. Erngs.	$180					

Statement of Changes in Cash Flow:

Beg. Cash	$450

Cash Flow from Operating Activities:

Net Income	$560
+ Depreciation Expense	$500
Accounting Cash Flow	$1,060
• − Rise in Accounts Receivable	−100
• − Rise in Inventory	−150
• + Rise in Accounts Payable	+50
• + Rise in Accruals	+50
Net Sources/Uses Oper. Activities	−150
Cash flow from Operations	**$910**

table **P13.1** CURRENT BALANCE SHEET 2005 AND PROJECTED BALANCE SHEET FOR 2006 BRONCO BADGES CO. (CONT.)

Cash Flow from Investing Activities:

Change in Gross Fixed Assets = Change in Net Fixed Assets + Depreciation

Cash Flow from Investing Activities = 200 + $500 = $700

Cash flow from Financing Activities:

- – Dividends Paid — $380
- + Increase in Notes Payable ?
- + Increase in Long-term Debt ?

Cash Flow from Financing = ?

Change in Cash = $910 – $700 – ? = $50

Ending Cash Balance = $500

Key Information and Financial Ratios for Bronco Badges

Sales 2005 = $2,700   Projected Sales 2006 = $3,000   Projected growth rate = 11.11%

Total Assets 2005 = $4,500   Total Assets Projected 2006 = $5,000

Projected growth rate assets = ($5,000 / $4,500) – 1 = 11.11%

Overall Profitability:	Projected 2006	2005	Peer Average
Return on Equity (ROE)	17.8%	21.3%	25%
Return on Assets (ROA)	11.2%	14.0%	15%
Debt to Assets	37.2%	34.2%	40%
Equity Multiplier (Assets / Equity)	1.59 ×	1.52 ×	1.67 ×
Cost Efficiency:			
Net Profit Margin (NPM)	18.67%	23.33%	30%
Operating Profit Margin (OPM)	33.33%	40.00%	45%
Gross Profit Margin (GPM)	66.67%	70.00%	80%
Asset Utilization:			
Total Asset Turnover	0.6 ×	0.6 ×	0.5 ×
Fixed Asset Turnover	1.5 ×	1.5 ×	1.2 ×
Inventory Turnover	0.67 ×	0.6 ×	0.7 ×
Average Collection Period	122 days	122 days	120 days
Bankruptcy Risk:			
Times Interest Earned Ratio	5 ×	6 ×	5 ×
Liquidity Risk:			
Current Ratio	3 ×	3 ×	3.5 ×
Quick Ratio	1.5 ×	1.5 ×	2.0 ×

2. Find the cash to cash cycle for Bronco Badges projected in 2006. Based on the firm's daily average cost of goods sold in 2006, what is the approximate working capital loan need for the firm in 2006?

3. Using the sample Zeta model example, what is the Zeta score for Bronco Badges in 2006?

4. Based on the lending rate(s) and terms that you decide for any loans to Bronco Badges, what will be the expected interest expense for Bronco Badges in 2006? How will this affect the firm's projected TIE and Net Income for 2006? How many times could the new interest expense be paid from Cash Flow from Operations in 2006?

5. The Imperial Ski Bank in Imperial, Colorado, is considering a loan application from Dean Taylor, an avid skier, who wants to purchase a video store and needs $50,000. The bank's best loan officer, René Gash, considers the loan to be of above-average risk and will add a 2 percent risk and administrative cost premium to the bank's base rate. The bank's total assets are $200 million, interest expense is $14 million, net noninterest expense is $2 million, and the marginal tax rate is 35 percent. The target NIM is 3.8 percent, and the bank's asset structure is as follows:

Securities: $35 million; average yield, 9.45 percent

Loans: $120 million

Nonearning Assets: $15 million

a. Based on this information and using Equation 13.2, what is the bank's base lending rate, and what loan rate will Dean be offered?

b. Prepare a pro forma income statement, assuming that the bank earns, on average, the base rate you calculated in part a on its loan portfolio. Calculate the NIM under this assumption.

c. What ROE is expected if the equity multiplier is 12?

d. How would the base rate you calculated in part a change if the yield on securities fell to 8.5 percent? If the yield on securities rose to 10.5 percent?

6. The Remarkable Bank of Gold Creek in Gold Creek, Colorado, has total assets of $140 million, an equity multiplier of 12.5, and net noninterest expense of $1.5 million. Its target NIM is 2.9 percent, and its liability cost averages 8 percent annually. Assets are distributed as follows:

Securities: $25 million; average yield: 8.25 percent
Mortgages and consumer loans: $110 million
Nonearning assets: $5 million

a. Bank president Robert Remarkable asks you to calculate the base lending rate Remarkable Bank must earn to achieve its target NIM. What is that rate?

b. Prepare a pro forma income statement, assuming that Remarkable Bank earns the base rate on its loans. Show that this rate will allow the bank to earn its desired NIM.

c. What ROE is expected if the marginal tax rate is 35 percent?

d. Suppose that Remarkable Bank reduces its target NIM to 2 percent, what base rate must be earned to achieve this target?

e. Suppose the average liability rate rises to 9 percent, what base rate is needed to achieve a 2.5 percent NIM? What is the significance of this for banks with negative funding gaps?

7. Larry Cunningham is negotiating a $4 million line of credit for his ski board business with the Enchanted Bank of Santa Fe, New Mexico. The one-year agreement requires a 0.20 percent commitment fee, with a 12 percent compensating balance on the entire commitment and an additional 5 percent on funds actually borrowed. The stated rate of interest is 11 percent, and J. C. Bosch, the bank's extraordinary loan officer, estimates that Larry will use on average 85 percent of the line.

a. Calculate the total expected dollar return and rate of return for the Enchanted Bank, assuming a 10 percent marginal reserve requirement.

b. What would be the expected dollar return and rate of return for the Enchanted Bank if Larry borrowed on average 70 percent of the line? 90 percent of the line?

8. Suppose Woody Eckerd, the superb loan officer of the Superlative Bank of Santa Fe, instead offers Larry Cunningham (in Problem 7) the $4 million line of credit with a stated rate of 11.9 percent, a 6 percent compensating balance requirement on the total line, and an additional 4 percent compensating balance on the amount borrowed. If other terms stay the same, does the Superlative Bank expect to earn more or less on the agreement than the Enchanted Bank of Santa Fe?

9. Your loan officers, Woody and Chris Woods of the Wonder Woods Bank are willing to offer a $1 million line of credit for one year to help you establish your own consulting firm. The agreement requires a 0.15 percent commitment fee, a 10 percent compensating balance on the entire commitment, and 4 percent more on funds actually borrowed. The stated rate is 12 percent, and you have told the bank that you probably will not need more than an average of 60 percent of the line.

a. Calculate the expected dollar return and rate of return for the bank, assuming a 10 percent marginal reserve requirement.

b. What would be the expected dollar return and rate of return for the bank if you drew down your line by 80 percent? Is the bank better off if you borrow more or less of your line? Explain why.

10. Ann Singleton of Singleton Savings asks you what is the annual yield on a one-year loan if interest is discounted and the stated rate is 10 percent. If it is 13 percent? If it is 9.6 percent?

11. What is the effective annual rate that Marcelle Arak is paying for a home mortgage loan for $100,000 with annual loan payments for fifteen years and a stated annual rate of 6 percent, if she has two points on the loan?

12. Jim Morris is purchasing a new van priced at $24,000 and has saved enough money to make a 20 percent down payment. His credit union will finance the remaining balance at an 11 percent add-on rate for four years (forty-eight months).

a. Calculate the annual percentage rate.

b. Would Jim be better off borrowing from his bank for only thirty-six months?

13. Rich Foster has decided to purchase a recreational vehicle to have fun with in the mountains. The RV costs $30,000, and Rich is able to make an $8,000 down payment. The bank has quoted an add-on rate of 14 percent, with sixty months to finance the remaining balance.

a. Based on this information, what are Rich's monthly payments?

b. If Rich prepays the loan after fifteen months, using the rule of 78s, what would Rich have to pay to pay off the loan?

c. If instead, Rich negotiates a 14 percent, sixty-month loan without add-on interest, how much would each monthly payment be? If the rule of 78s does not apply to this new loan, how much principal would remain after fifteen months? (Hint: To find the remaining principal without preparing an amortization schedule, compute the present value of the remaining forty-five payments.) Compare your answers with parts a and b.

d. If the rule of 78s does apply to the loan in part c, how much would Rich owe after fifteen months? Based on your comparisons, does the rule of 78s or the add-on interest provision make a greater difference in Rich's rate of principal repayment?

14. Ajeyo Banerjee is buying a super sports car. After extensive negotiations, he has agreed on a price of $40,000. He plans to make a down payment of $10,000 and will finance the remaining balance over a forty-eight-month period. The bank has offered an add-on rate of 6.75 percent. The car manufacturer's subsidiary, however, is offering four-year loans at an annual percentage rate of 6 percent. Compare the APRs on the two loans and decide which one Ajeyo should accept.

15. Sylvia Hudgins is planning on buying a condo in Crested Butte, Colorado, for $300,000. She plans to borrow $250,000 from the Mountain Beauty Bank at a 6.5 percent interest rate. The bank offers a standard thirty-year, fixed rate loan or a quicker fifteen-year loan with annual loan payments.
    a. Calculate the monthly payments under each loan.
    b. How much total interest will Sylvia pay under each loan?

c. Assuming Sylvia can comfortably meet either monthly payment, which loan should she choose? Why?

Suggested Case Study: See Darden School and Harvard Business School Case Catalogs

Darden Cases: Padgett Blank Book Company, structuring a term loan; **Hoosier Hose Company,** restructuring a troubled seasonal loan; and **Patriots Hall,** evaluating a proposed commercial mortgage (previously in Richard D. Crawford and William W. Sihler. *Financial Service Organizations: Cases in Strategic Management.* New York: HarperCollins College Publisher, 1994, currently out of print); Harvard Business School: **U.S. Bank of Washington Case** by Elizabeth R. Lawrence, Case 9-292-057, loan analysis for Reedhook Ale Brewery.

Selected References

Allen, Linda, Jacob Boudoukh, and Anthony Saunders. *Understanding Market, Credit, and Operational Risks: The Value at Risk Approach.* London: Blackwell Publishing, 2003.

Altman, Edward I. "Financial Ratios, Discriminant Analysis, and the Prediction of Corporate Bankruptcy." *Journal of Finance* 23 (September 1968), 589–609.

Altman, Edward I., et al. *Application of Classification Techniques in Business, Banking, and Finance.* Greenwich, CT: JAI Press, 1981.

Altman, E. I. *Corporate Financial Distress.* New York: John Wiley, 1983.

Altman, E. I., R. G. Haldeman, and P. Narayanan. ZETA Analysis: A New Model to Identify Bankruptcy Risk of Corporations, *Journal of Banking and Finance*, 1997, 1–29.

Altman, E. I., J. Hartzell, and M. Peck. *Emerging Markets Corporate Bonds: A Scoring System.* New York: Salomon Brothers, 1995. Reprinted in *Emerging Market Capital Flows,* edited by R. Levich. Amsterdam: Kluwer Publishing, 1997.

Brady, Thomas F. "Changes in Loan Pricing and Business Lending at Commercial Banks," *Federal Reserve Bulletin* 71 (January 1985): 1–13.

Brick, John R. "Pricing Commercial Loans." *Journal of Commercial Bank Lending* 66 (January 1984), 49–52.

Canner, Glenn B. and James T. Fergus. "Home Equity Lines of Credit—How Well Do They Fit the Needs of Consumers and Creditors?" *Journal of Retail Banking* 10 (Summer 1988): 19–23.

Canner, Glenn B., James T. Fergus, and Charles A. Luckett. "Home Equity Lines of Credit," *Federal Reserve Bulletin* 74 (June 1988): 361–373.

Canner, Glenn B., and Charles A. Luckett. "Home Equity Lending," *Federal Reserve Bulletin* 75 (May 1989): 333–344.

Caouette, John B., Edward I. Altman, and Paul Narayanan. *Managing Credit Risk: The Next Great Financial Challenge.* New York: Wiley Frontiers in Finance, 1998.

Capon, Noel. "Credit Scoring Systems: A Critical Analysis." *Journal of Marketing* 46 (Spring 1982), 82–91.

Carroll, David. "Benchmark Pricing Enhances ARM Design." *Savings Institutions* 110 (February 1989), 69–74.

Garwood, Griffith L. and Dolores S. Smith. "The Community Reinvestment Act: Evolution and Current Issues," *Federal Reserve Bulletin* 79 (April 1993): 251–267.

Glantz, Morton. *Managing Bank Risk: An Introduction to Broad-Base Credit Engineering.* New York: Academic Press, 2003.

Hempel, George H., Donald G. Simonson, and Alan B. Coleman. *Bank Management: Text and Cases.* New York: John Wiley & Sons, 1994.

Koch, Timothy W., and S. Scott MacDonald. *Bank Management,* 4th ed. Cincinnati, OH: Southwestern/Thomson Publishing, 2000.

Marshall, Christopher. *Measuring and Managing Operational Risks in Financial Institutions.* New York: John Wiley & Sons, 2001.

Mills, Dixie L., and Mona J. Gardner. "Consumer Response to Adjustable Rate Mortgages: Implications of the Evidence from Illinois and Wisconsin." *Journal of Consumer Affairs* (Summer 1986), 77–105.

Peek, Joe. "A Call to ARMS, Adjustable Rate Mortgages in the 1980s." *New England Economic Review* (Federal Reserve Bank of Boston) (March/April 1990), 47–61.

Priess, Beth. "The Garn–St. Germain Act and Due-on-Sale-Clause Enforcement," *Housing Finance Review* 2 (October 1983): 360–377.

Saunders, Anthony. *Financial Institution Management: A Modern Approach.* Chicago: Irwin, 1997.

Saunders, Anthony, and Marcia Millon Cornett. *Financial Institution Management: A Risk Management Approach,* 4th ed, Chicago: Irwin McGraw-Hill, 2003.

Saunders, Anthony, and Linda Allen. *Credit Risk Measurement: New Approaches to Value at Risk and Other Paradigms,* 2nd ed, New York: John Wiley & Sons, 2002.

Sinkey, Joseph F., Jr. *Commercial Bank Financial Management,* 5th ed. Upper Saddle River, NJ: Prentice Hall, 1998.

Stacy, Ronald L. "Mezzanine Lending: A Primer for Asset-Based Lenders," *Journal of Commercial Bank Lending* 71 (October 1988): 54–66.

Walter, John R. "Loan Loss Reserves." *Economic Review* (Federal Reserve Bank of Richmond) 77 (July/August 1991), 20–30.

Wolfson, Martin H., and Mary M. McLaughlin. "Recent Developments in the Profitability and Lending Practices of Commercial Banks." *Federal Reserve Bulletin* 75 (July 1989), 461–484.

internet *exercise*

The Bank Rate Monitor has a useful discussion, with an example, of credit scoring at http://www.bankrate.com/brm/news/pf/19981204b.asp. In his article "A Credit Score Can Make—or Break—a Would-Be Borrower," Michael D. Larson notes that credit scoring is perhaps the most important technological advance of all for the countless Americans who try to borrow money every day. Some examples of credit scores are given at http://www.bankrate.com/brm/news/pf/19981204.asp. Named for credit scoring industry leader Fair, Isaac and Co., the FICO score is derived in part from a borrower's past credit history, says David Shellenberger, product manager for the company's credit bureau products. The company's software and services take that history and measure it against a database of habits in the general borrowing population. That, in turn, determines whether the borrower's tendencies match those of borrowers who default on debt, declare bankruptcy, or end up in other types of financial trouble.

CRA SCORE FOR YOUR BANK

Go to the OCC's Website, *http://www.occ.treas.gov/crainfo.htm.* On the left-hand menu on the home page, click CRA Eval Search. This will take you to the CRA Database Search page. Alternatively, go directly to this page at *http://www.occ.treas.gov/cra/crasrch.htm.* Fill in your bank's name and state as directed at the bottom of the page and click Search. You can also do this for all the banks in your state by just entering the state. A list with the evaluation will be given. Some evaluations may be in PDF form (so to download, you will need to download Adobe Reader as instructed).

USEFUL LINKS

Government National Mortgage Association (Ginnie Mae)

http://www.ginniemae.gov/

Federal National Mortgage Association (Fannie Mae)

http://fanniemae.com/

Federal Home Loan Mortgage Corporation (Freddie Mac)

http://www.freddiemac.com/

USEFUL LINKS FOR FINANCIAL ANALYSIS AND MARKET INFORMATION (AMONG MANY OTHERS)

http://finance.yahoo.com

http://www.sec.gov

http://www.sec.gov/edgarhp.htm

http://www.cbs.marketwatch.com

http://www.quicken.com

http://www.smartmoney.com

Sample Loan Underwriting Guidelines

Signet Bank

Presented by Michael B. Bronfein, Senior Vice Pres. Com. Finance Division

The following outline provides the standard form to be used when preparing a credit memo and also explains the minimum requirements for underwriting issues that must be addressed. The loan officer should use discretion to determine whether additional information is necessary. If so, then it should be added to the form.

The credit memo should be titled "Credit Memorandum" with the company's name listed directly below. Next, the Bank unit and division in which the credit will be housed should be listed. Directly under that, "Prepared by" should be inserted with a colon and the account officer's name as well as the date prepared.

Thereafter, the following Roman numeral structure should be employed:

I. Source of Business (Referral source—new or existing customer)

II. Principal Contacts (The one or two contacts with which the bank communicates on a regular basis)

III. Participation Structure (Optional)

If the credit accommodation is either a bought or sold participation, all of the salient details of the participation should be clearly articulated. This information should include the lead bank, what its role will be in the management of the credit (if it is a bought participation), and all other participants. Additionally, each participant's share should be highlighted as well as the effective yield that the Bank will enjoy on the credit accommodation.

When the requested accommodation is a bought participation, information should be provided about the lead bank and its experience in leading participants. References from other banks who have bought participations from the proposed lead lender should be obtained if Signet does not have prior experience with the lead bank.

In the case of a lead position by Signet, all fees attendant to the transaction, including rate overrides on the participant's portion of the loans, should be clearly shown and utilized in the computation of the yield analysis.

Loan closing fees should be amortized over the term of the commitment when calculating yield. The amortization period shall be noted.

Finally, this section should also indicate the voting rights and the operational structure of the participation so that the loan committee has a clear understanding of what rights Signet shall obtain or convey in the course of the loan participation.

IV. Requested Accommodation

There should be two subsections. Section A should contain the reason for the requested accommodation (i.e., LBO, refinance, equipment acquisitions) and should articulate the structure of the transaction including a general narrative about the rationale for the transaction and structure, as well as complete delineation with regard to all components of the capital structure (i.e., both debt and equity).

Section B should be a Sources and Uses statement of funds relative to the transaction. This section should clearly demonstrate to the reader that Signet and any other source of funds provide the financing necessary to accomplish the contemplated transaction.

V. History and Operations

First, the history of the company should be given including how and when it was formed; general background about the company's products, services, and markets; and how it has evolved over time. Thereafter, there should be a detailed explanation of the company's operations, including the market it serves (geographical customers), the products its sells, and the competitive environment in which it operates. This section should address competitive advantages or disadvantages the company enjoys and how they relate to the overall economic environment in which the company operates.

In general, this section should give the reader a sense of the company's mission, how it relates to the general economic conditions with regard to both its industry and the geographic region in which it operates, and the resultant competitive situation it enjoys.

VI. Industry Analysis (Optional)

In cases of large credit requests, unusual credit requests, or a credit request in which the Bank/Division has a large concentration, an Industry Analysis should be provided.

Sources of information for the industry analysis could include trade associations, trade journals, the Credit Administration Department's *computer-based information services,* recognized industry experts, and, lastly, the customer. The credibility of the industry analysis to a large extent will be based on the source of the information utilized in providing the analysis and therefore should be as independent as possible.

VII. Management Performance/Profiles

This section should contain "practical resumes" of the executive management of the company. It should also contain a section that provides editorial comments about the account officer's assessment of management, their professional accomplishments, and their overall capabilities.

The information needed for this narrative should be one of the primary focuses of the underwriting effort (i.e., assessment of management).

VIII. Financial Performance

A. Historical Financial Performance

This section should include a Historical Financial Performance heading with these subsections: Income Statement, Balance Sheet, and Uniform Cash Flow.

The income statement section should provide a narrative as to the trends that are occurring with insightful analysis as to why the trends are either negative or positive. It should also examine the mix of sales, if applicable, and the complexion of the cost of sales.

Operating expenses should be closely examined for negative trends on a common size basis and explanations therefore should be provided. Any unusual or extraordinary expenses or revenues should be clearly explained. The reader of this section should have a clear indication that the account officer is conversant with the company's earning capabilities or lack thereof as a result of the income statement analysis.

The balance sheet section should contain explanations for all major accounts on the balance sheets and changes thereto. There should also be insightful trend analysis with regard to asset turnover with specific emphasis on accounts receivable, inventory, accounts payable, and accruals.

There should also be an explanation as to the rationale for the existing capital structure and discussion as to whether or not it is appropriate to the company's operating strategy.

Analysis of the uniform cash flow should provide the reader with insight to the sources and uses of cash and the *company's ability to generate sufficient cash flow to sustain its growth and/or repay its debt.*

B. Future Prospects/Projections

This section should contain two subsections: (1) Future Prospects—a narrative about the future prospects of the company as it relates to its markets, products, competition, management, and general capabilities; and (2) Financial Projections—an analysis of the projected operating results *with reconciliation of the projected operating results to the historical operating results.* In this section, there should be a clear indication of any operating changes that are being contemplated, why they are being contemplated, and the effect on operating results.

The reconciliation between the past and the future is imperative as it relates to the credibility with which the loan committee will view the attainability of the company's projected results.

Whenever possible, the "Cash Forecasting" monthly model should be used for projection purposes. The monthly model is preferred for working capital or related transactions; however, where a multi-year commitment is being requested, the "Cash Forecasting" annual model should also be prepared.

It is imperative that the model be used as structured and that no significant format changes be made to the cells within the Excel spreadsheet model. In order for loan administration to allow this model to be utilized, we must be responsible and thereby ensure the integrity of the underlying architecture.

IX. Collateral/Risk Analysis

This section should contain three subsections: A, a narrative on the collateral; B, a liquidation analysis (Micro); and C, a general risk analysis (Macro).

A. Collateral

The first subsection should contain a narrative about the accounting systems, their integrity, and their competency. It should then list the collateral that is securing the obligation and the nature of that collateral. Information from the auditor's preliminary audit should be utilized in writing this section and should reconcile with the Collateral Analysis Sheet performed by the auditors.

When the account officer's analysis of the collateral and the attendant advance rates on current asset collateral differs from the auditors, then a paragraph should be included to discuss the differences and the loan officer's rationale for his or her position.

This subsection should provide the reader with significant detail with regard to the nature and quality of the collateral being taken. This section should also include a Sources and Uses statement of cash, specifically an availability schedule relative to the current asset availability that is being generated under the loan formula, how much of that availability will be used for closing, and the amount of estimated excess availability at the closing date. This analysis should indicate that there is sufficient availability to pay off all existing indebtedness (required to be paid), closing costs, and any past due payables.

B. Liquidation Analysis

The second subsection should be a detailed liquidation analysis (when applicable) of what the writer expects to be the mode of liquidation, the realization of liquidation values on the collateral, and the expenses associated with liquidation. In this section there should also be a schedule of events that would occur in a liquidation scenario.

C. Risk Analysis

The third subsection, Risk Analysis, should be a general summation of the risk as viewed by the loan officer. This section should take into account the barriers to entry for this particular industry, the quality of management, the quality of the products and services offered, the "franchise" value of the assets, and other factors that may impact the company's ability to operate in the future.

The conclusion of the section should clearly demonstrate to the loan committee members that the loan is either fully collateralized or that a gap exists. When a gap exists, rationale should be provided for why the bank should entertain such a risk.

X. Loan Review Recommendation

In this section, the writer should recommend the loan review rating that is appropriate to the requested accommodation.

XI. Conclusion

In this section, there should be a summation of all of the salient items that lead the writer to conclude that this is a reasonable risk for the organization to enter into. There should be a *Favorable* column and an *Unfavorable* column, and only the most salient points should fall into each category.

Appendix 13B

Fictional Sample Loan Presentation

I. Background

The Big Apple Real Estate & Storage Company was organized in 1990 to acquire, hold, and operate transportation storage facilities in downtown Manhattan. The firm is a general partnership, and the guarantor, John Jahera, owns 60 percent of the partnership. Other partners own 20 percent, 10 percent, and 10 percent shares in the partnership. The partnership owns 100 percent of three other transportation storage facilities. The company has had a loan with the bank since 2002. At that time, the company was much larger. Since that time it has scaled down, selling two facilities that it owned.

II. Request

The request is for the renewal of its term debt, which originated in 2002, on its facility in downtown New York. It should be noted that the mortgage on another facility matures in 2008, which may be a future business opportunity for the Bank.

III. Repayment Analysis

Primary repayment is from cash flows from property. Based on notes to the firm's CPA-reviewed statements, a summary cash flow of the downtown New York facility on a standalone basis is as follows:

(In Thousands)	2003	2004	2005	2006
Revenue	$365,298	$396,783	$414,524	$428,161
Operating Expense	266,921	289,486	316,959	282,579
Net Income	$78,377	$107,297	$97,565	$145,582
+ Deprec. & Amortiz.	45,214	44,630	44,871	44,883
+ Interest Expense	90,597	89,265	87,231	85,985
(NOPAT) Net Operating Income	214,188	241,192	229,667	276,450
Less: Debt Service*	101,784	101,784	101,784	101,784
Net Cash Flow	112,404	139,408	127,883	174,666
Debt Coverage Ratio	2.10	2.37	2.26	2.72

*Based on proposed loan structure

Historic debt service coverage is more than adequate in the years reviewed. The facility operates between a high level of 95 percent occupancy in the summer to a low of 87. Based on 2006 operating expenses, rental income would have to drop by over 40 percent (or $174,666) to fall below break-even.

Revenue growth over the past three years is attributed solely to rate increases, as average occupancy rates have been relatively stable. Expenses jumped somewhat in 2005, in the form of wages due to large one-time expenses for a replacement for a hospitalized manager, while continuing to pay for the hospitalized employee.

A four-month interim Income Statement ending April 30, 2007, on the downtown New York facility reflects annualized revenue of $408,501, which is on par with 2006 with seasonality taken into account.

Secondary Source

Secondary repayment will look to the partners. The primary partner is the only guarantor on the loan and is considered to provide ample secondary strength, so another guarantor is not needed.

Tertiary Source

Tertiary repayment will be the refinance or sale of the subject property (see Collateral section).

Financial Analysis

Attached are spreadsheets for the company for 2002 through 2006. The statements are CPA-reviewed. In each of the years examined, the Accountants Review Report notes a GAAP (Generally Accepted Accounting Practices) exception in the firm's accounting practices. The company has been amortizing its nonpurchased goodwill because management believes there has been no diminution of value. GAAP requires amortization of goodwill over the lesser of its estimated useful life or forty years.

Balance Sheet

- Over the past five years, the firm's balance sheet has improved considerably, particularly after the sale of assets in 2005 and early 2006. Total Assets dropped from $7.06MM in 2002 to $3.16MM in 2006, while Net Worth rose from ($732M) to $978M.

- The firm's leverage position has gradually improved from an upside-down position in 2002 to a Debt/Tangible Net Worth of 4.27× for year-end 2006 with over $1.44MM in cash distributions taken in 2005 and 2006.

- The firm's cash balances grew from $196M for the end of 2002 to $847M at the end of 2006, substantially improving its Current and Quick ratios, which reached 3.9× and 3.65×, respectively, at year-end 2006.

Income Statement

- Revenue and Operating Margins have fluctuated over the past five years as the firm grew and sold off assets.

- Operating profits dropped off in 2006 as a result of extra professional expenses incurred with the aforementioned sales and are expected to return to their normal range of 40 percent to 50 percent. The partnership has always turned a healthy Operating Profit in the periods reviewed.

- Net Profits were particularly strong in the last two years as a result of the gains realized from the sale of the partnership interests. The 2006 property distribution was recorded with the resulting gain reflected in Gain on Sale of Assets.

Guarantor

John Jahera submitted a Personal Financial Statement. The statement reflects an outside net worth of $2.65 million. Liabilities consist of a minimal amount of revolving credit card debt and mortgage debt of $352,000. Assets are centered around real estate and partnership interests, and a substantial $880,000 in cash and marketable securities. Federal tax returns for 2006 are on extension. John Jahera submitted his 2005 tax return to the Bank, which reflects an aggregated gross income of $1.65 million centered around $0.437 million in capital gains and $0.892 million in Schedule E S-Corp/Partnership Income. However, a true cash flow picture cannot be ascertained as K-1's on Jahera's 20 S-Corps and Partnerships were not available for analysis, and the majority of capital gain income was from the sale of business property, which is not a solid source of recurring income. Nevertheless, based on a relatively minimal $49,000 in annual debt service and the known distributions from the firm, Jahera's annual cash after debt service is estimated to be quite strong—as evidenced by his personal savings.

Collateral

The Bank has a first mortgage on the downtown New York Transportation Storage Center. The property consists of a 15,600-square-foot lot containing a 62,687-square-foot building with an 8,000-square-foot basement. Moving Company originally built this building circa 1925. The building is several stories tall, and the original open warehouse space on each floor has been finished with individual storage spaces. Two large freight elevators are located in the center of the building. There is office space on the first floor where John Jahera conducts business for his various partnerships.

An appraisal was prepared in 2006 for our bank by James Gilkeson of Gilkeson & Sons assigning a fair value of $1.6MM to the property. The valuation was based primarily on an Income approach, utilizing a cap rate of 12.5 percent. Based on FY06 net income capitalized at 12.5 percent, which is considered to be very conservative for current market conditions, the property values at $2.21 million—a respective LTV of 38 percent. At a more updated cap rate of 10 percent, the property values at $2.76 million for an LTV of 30 percent. An updated appraisal is not considered necessary by this Officer as there have been no adverse changes in market conditions or physical aspects of the property that would threaten the Bank's collateral position.

A Phase I was performed by Environmental Property Audits, Inc., on September 11, 2006, which came up clean. Present and past use of the property did not reveal any potential hazards. It was noted, however, that a gas station was located across the street from 1979 to 1987, for which there were no records or knowledge available regarding its disposition.

Risk Analysis & Recommendation

There is inherent economic and market risk associated with real estate investment, as well as the fact that personal income information supplied by the Guarantor is somewhat limited. However, these risks are mitigated by a profitable history, the extensive experience and strong liquid strength of the guarantor, and a solid collateral position.

Recommend approval as presented at a Grade of 1-C.

Proposed Loan Structure

Credit Request: Renewal—Real Estate Loan Grade: 1-C

Amount: $835,314

Rate/Index: 5-yr. Treasuries + 2.65 percent, fixed* (*currently at 10 percent)

Loan Fees: 1/2 percent

Renewal of existing real estate debt and continue amortization. Loan matures November 2007.

Requesting a 5-year renewal plus number of months remaining until maturity

Approximately 15 years remaining amortization (original amortization was 20 years)

Collateral: First deed of trust on downtown Manhattan Facility

BIG APPLE REAL ESTATE & STORAGE

Statement in $ Thousands	Review Dec. 31 2003	Review Dec. 31 2004	Review Dec. 31 2005	Review Dec. 31 2006
INDIRECT METHOD—FASB 95 CASH FLOW				
Net Income	159	326	1,188	1,234
Adjustments to Reconcile				
Depreciation & Amortization	247	245	179	113
Other Adjustments	0	0	0	0
Changes in Assets/Liabilities				
Change in Accounts Receivable	(41)	12	54	13
Change in Inventory	0	0	0	0
Change in Prepaids	(33)	6	58	8
Change in A/P & Accrued Exp.	(39)	179	(57)	(275)
Change in Interest Payable	0	0	0	0
Change in Income Taxes Payable	0	0	0	0
Change in Deferred Taxes	0	0	0	0
Change in Other Assets/Liab.	(94)	(279)	(300)	(21)
Total Adjustments	40	163	(66)	(162)
Net Cash Provided by				
Operating Activities	199	489	1,122	1,072
Cash Flows from Investing Activities				
Capital Expenditures	(38)	(40)	2,309	1,415
Change in Long-term Investments	0	0	0	0
Net Cash Used—Investing	(38)	(40)	2,309	1,415
Cash Flows from Financing Activities				
Current Portion Long-term Debt	(2)	0	0	0
Change in Short-term Debt	0	0	0	0
Change in Long-term Debt	(95)	(153)	(2,563)	(1,832)
Change in Contributed Capital	123	42	55	0
Oth. Chgs in Retained Earnings	1	(1)	1	(1)
Dividends or Owners' Withdrawals	0	0	(838)	(579)
Change in Dividends Payable	0	0	0	0
Net Cash Provided by				
Financing Activities	27	(112)	(3,345)	(2,412)
Change in Cash & Equivalents	188	337	86	75
Cash & Equivalents—Beginning	233	421	758	844
Cash & Equivalents—Ending	421	758	844	919

BIG APPLE REAL ESTATE & STORAGE

Statement in $ Thousands	Review Dec. 31 2002		Review Dec. 31 2003		Review Dec. 31 2004		Review Dec. 31 2005		Review Dec. 31 2006	
ASSETS COMMON SIZED										
Cash	196	2.8	362	5.1	668	9.2	774	16.6	847	26.8
Escrow	37	0.5	59	0.8	90	1.2	70	1.5	72	2.3
Trade Accounts Receivable	34	0.5	41	0.5	40	0.6	32	0.7	20	0.6
Other Accounts Receivable	47	0.7	81	1.1	70	1.0	24	0.5	23	0.7
Net Accounts Receivable	81	1.1	122	1.7	110	1.5	56	1.2	43	1.4
Prepaid Expenses	80	1.1	113	1.6	107	1.5	49	1.1	41	1.3
Total Current Assets	394	5.6	656	9.2	976	13.6	949	20.4	1,003	31.8
Land	1,937	27.4	1,937	27.2	1,937	26.8	1,230	26.5	492	15.6
Buildings	5,941	84.2	5,941	83.3	5,945	82.3	3,600	77.4	2,605	82.5
Furniture & Fixtures	107	1.5	91	1.3	95	1.3	59	1.3	49	1.6
Gross Fixed Assets	7,985	113.1	7,969	111.7	7,977	110.5	4,889	105.1	3,146	99.6
Accumulated Depreciation (−)	(1,876)	(26.6)	(2,069)	(29.0)	(2,282)	(31.6)	(1,682)	(36.2)	(1,467)	(46.4)
Net Fixed Assets	6,109	86.6	5,900	82.7	5,695	78.9	3,207	69.0	1,679	53.1
Other Assets	88	1.2	111	1.6	85	1.2	27	0.6	10	0.3
Nonpurchased Goodwill*	467	6.6	467	6.5	467	6.5	467	10.0	467	14.8
TOTAL ASSETS	7,058	100.0	7,134	100.0	7,222	100.0	4,650	100.0	3,159	100.0
LIABILITIES COMMON SIZED										
Current Portion Capital Leases	2	0.0	0	0.0	0	0.0	0	0.0	0	0.0
Accounts Payable & Accruals	374	5.3	335	4.7	514	7.1	457	9.6	182	5.8
Security Deposits	25	0.4	28	0.4	28	0.4	10	0.2	8	0.3
Prepaid Rental Income	81	1.1	123	1.7	122	1.7	96	2.1	67	2.1
Total Current Liabilities	482	6.8	486	6.8	664	9.2	563	12.1	257	8.1
Mortgage Notes Payable	6,567	93.0	6,472	90.7	6,319	87.5	3,756	80.8	1,924	60.9
Due to Related Parties	724	10.3	519	8.7	314	4.3	0	0.0	0	0.0
Deferred Income	11	0.2	0	0.0	0	0.0	0	0.0	0	0.0
Minority Interest	7	0.1	6	0.1	7	0.1	7	0.2	0	0.0
Other Liabilities	(1)	0.0	0	0.0	0	0.0	0	0.0	0	0.0
Total Liabilities	7,790	110.4	7,583	106.3	7,304	101.1	4,326	93.0	2,181	69.0
Minority Interest	(220)	(3.1)	(97)	(1.4)	(55)	(0.8)	0	0.0	0	0.0
Partners' Equity	(512)	(7.3)	(357)	(4.9)	(27)	(0.4)	324	7.0	978	31.0
Total Net Worth	(732)	(10.4)	(449)	(6.3)	(82)	(1.1)	324	7.0	978	31.0
TOTAL LIABILITIES & NET WORTH	7,058	100.0	7,134	100.0	7,222	100.0	4,650	100.0	3,159	100.0

BIG APPLE REAL ESTATE & STORAGE

Statement in $ Thousands	Review Dec. 31 2002		Review Dec. 31 2003		Review Dec. 31 2004		Review Dec. 31 2005		Review Dec. 31 2006	
INCOME STATEMENT COMMON SIZED										
Rent	1,354	77.4	1,524	77.5	1,729	79.7	1,349	72.9	800	78.4
Mgmt. & Consulting Fees	188	10.7	196	10.0	222	10.2	197	10.6	106	10.4
Late Charges & Other	207	11.8	246	12.5	218	10.1	305	16.5	114	11.2
Total Sales	1,749	100.0	1,966	100.0	2,169	100.0	1,851	100.0	1,020	100.0
Gross Profit	1,749	100.0	1,966	100.0	2,169	100.0	1,851	100.0	1,020	100.0
Guaranteed Payments to Partners	120	6.9	129	6.6	135	6.2	135	7.3	135	13.2
Other Operating Expenses	696	39.8	747	38.0	731	33.7	667	36.0	464	45.5
Depreciation & Amortization	285	16.3	247	12.6	245	11.3	179	9.7	113	11.1
Operating Expenses	1,101	63.0	1,123	57.1	1,111	51.2	981	53.0	712	69.8
Operating Profit	648	37.0	843	42.9	1,058	48.8	870	47.0	308	30.2
Gain on Sale of Assets	0	0.0	0	0.0	0	0.0	1,734	93.7	1,133	111.1
Income—Minority Interest	28	1.6	0	0.0	0	0.0	0	0.0	0	0.0
Total Other Income	28	1.6	0	0.0	0	0.0	1,734	93.7	1,133	111.1
Interest Expense	783	44.8	651	33.1	656	30.2	493	26.6	207	20.3
Other Expense	0	0.0	0	0.0	0	0.0	36	1.9	0	0.0
Loss—Minority Interest	0	0.0	33	1.7	76	3.5	887	47.9	0	0.0
Total Other Expenses	783	44.8	684	34.8	732	33.7	1,416	76.5	207	20.3
Profit before Tax	(107)	(6.1)	159	8.1	326	15.0	1,188	64.2	1,234	121.0
NET INCOME	(107)	(6.1)	159	8.1	326	15.0	1,188	64.2	1,234	121.0
RECON. OF NET WORTH COMMON SIZED										
Beginning Net Worth	(625)	85.4	(732)	163.0	(449)	547.6	(82)	(25.3)	324	33.1
Changes in Retained Earnings:										
Net Income (Loss)	(107)	14.6	159	(35.4)	326	(397.6)	1,188	366.7	1,234	126.2
Cash Dividends	0	0.0	0	0.0	0	0.0	838	258.6	579	59.2
Other Incr (Decr) to RE	0	0.0	1	(0.2)	(1)	1.2	1	0.3	(1)	(0.1)
Total Change in RE	(107)	14.6	160	(35.6)	325	(396.3)	361	108.3	654	66.9
Changes in Other NW										
Other Equity	0	0.0	123	(27.4)	42	(51.2)	55	17.0	0	0.0
Ending Total Net Worth	(732)	100.0	(449)	100.0	(82)	100.0	324	100.0	978	100.0

BIG APPLE REAL ESTATE & STORAGE

Statement in $ Thousands	Review Dec. 31 2002	Review Dec. 31 2003	Review Dec. 31 2004	Review Dec. 31 2005	Review Dec. 31 2006
HIGHLIGHTS					
Income Statement:					
Sales	1,749	1,966	2,169	1,851	1,020
Gross Margin	1,749	1,966	2,169	1,851	1,020
Operating Expenses	1,101	1,123	1,111	981	712
NPBT	(107)	159	326	1,188	1,234
NPAT	(107)	159	326	1,188	1,234
Cash Dividends	0	0	0	838	579
Balance Sheet:					
Total Current Assets	394	656	975	949	1,003
Net Fixed Assets	6,109	5,900	5,695	3,207	1,679
Total Assets	7,058	7,134	7,222	4,650	3,159
Short-term Obligations	2	0	0	0	0
Total Current Liabilities	482	486	664	563	257
Long-term Debt	6,567	6,472	6,319	3,756	1,924
Total Liabilities	7,790	7,583	7,304	4,326	2,181
Net Worth	(732)	(449)	(82)	324	978
Ratios:					
Sales Growth		12.41%	10.33%	(14.66%)	(44.89%)
Gross Margin	100.00%	100.00%	100.00%	100.00%	100.00%
Profit Margin	(6.12%)	8.09%	15.03%	64.18%	120.98%
Current Ratio	0.82	1.35	1.47	1.69	3.90
Quick Ratio	0.55	0.95	1.20	1.56	3.65
Working Capital	(88)	170	311	386	746
Age of Receivables	7	8	7	6	7
Days Supply in Inventory	0	0	0	0	0
Age of Payables	0	0	0	0	0
Debt/Tangible Net Worth	(6.50)	(8.28)	(13.30)	(30.25)	4.27
Breakeven Sales—Cash Basis		1,741	1,741	758	(402)
Actual Sales/Breakeven Sales		1.13	1.25	2.44	(2.54)
Cash Flow: Incr. (Decr.) in Cash					
Cash from Sales		1,959	2,170	1,859	1,032
Cash from Trading		1,920	2,349	1,802	757
Net Cash after Operations		873	1,119	1,557	1,262
Cash after Financing Costs		222	463	226	476
Cash after Debt Amortization		220	463	226	476
Capital Expenditures		(38)	(40)	2,309	1,415
Financing Surplus (Requirement)		159	449	2,593	1,908

BIG APPLE REAL ESTATE & STORAGE

Statement in $ Thousands	Review Dec. 31 2002	Review Dec. 31 2003	Review Dec. 31 2004	Review Dec. 31 2005	Review Dec. 31 2006
RATIOS					
Operating Ratios:					
Sales Growth		12.41%	10.33%	(14.66%)	(44.89%)
Pretax Profit Margin	(6.12%)	8.09%	15.03%	64.18%	120.98%
Profit Margin	(6.12%)	8.09%	15.03%	64.18%	120.98%
Return on Assets (ROA)	(1.52%)	2.23%	4.51%	25.55%	39.06%
Return on Equity (ROE)	(8.92%)	17.36%	59.38%	830.77%	241.49%
Asset Turnover	0.25	0.28	0.30	0.40	0.32
Current Position:					
Current Ratio	0.82	1.35	1.47	1.69	3.90
Quick Ratio	0.55	0.95	1.20	1.56	3.65
Working Capital	(88)	170	311	386	746
Working Capital/Assets	(1.25%)	2.38%	4.31%	8.30%	23.62%
Working Capital Turnover	(19.88)	11.56	6.97	4.80	1.37
Receivable Turnover	51.44	47.95	54.23	57.84	51.00
Age of Receivables	7	8	7	6	7
Inventory Turnover					
Days Supply in Inventory	0	0	0	0	0
Payable Turnover					
Age of Payables	0	0	0	0	0
Equity Position:					
Owner Equity/Assets	(10.37%)	(6.29%)	(1.14%)	6.97%	30.96%
Creditor Equity/Assets	110.37%	106.29%	101.14%	93.03%	69.04%
Debt/Tangible Net Worth	(6.50)	(8.28)	(13.30)	(30.25)	4.27
Fixed Assets/Long-term Debt	83.59%	83.13%	85.77%	85.22%	87.27%
Fixed Assets/Tangible Net Worth	(509.51%)	(644.10%)	(1,037.34%)	(2,242.66%)	328.57%
Plant Turnover	0.29	0.33	0.38	0.58	0.61
Other:					
Interest Coverage (NPBT)	0.86	1.24	1.50	3.41	6.96
Prin. & Interest Coverage (NPBT)		1.24	1.50	3.41	6.96
Interest Coverage (Operating Cash)		1.34	1.71	3.16	6.10
Prin. & Interest Coverage (OC)		1.34	1.71	3.16	6.10
Sustainable Growth Rate	9.09%	(13.96%)	(35.71%)	(68.77%)	(1,183.31%)
Breakeven Sales—Cash Basis		1,741	1,741	758	(402)
Actual Sales/Breakeven Sales		1.13	1.25	2.44	(2.54)
Bankruptcy Ratio: Z value	0.44	0.58	0.75	1.67	2.36
Z < 1.23 Weak; > 2.90 Strong					

Example Commercial Loan Pricing Formula— Customer Name: Big Apple Real Estate & Storage

Period of Analysis: (Historical/Projected?)	**Projected**			
Today's Prime Rate:	8.50%			
Average Balance THIS LOAN:	$820,487	SOP =	0.65%	$75,075
Average Balance LOAN #2:	$0	SOP =	0.00%	$0
Average Balance LOAN #3:	$0	SOP =	0.00%	$0
Total # Loans:	1			
I. Source and Use of Funds				
1. Average Loan and/or Line Balance			$820,487	
2. Ledger Demand Deposit Balances (NOT on analysis)		$81,857		
3. Less: Reserve (12% of Ledger)		$9,823		
Float (historic avg. or 15%)		$61		
4. Available Balances			$71,973	
5. Savings & NOW Accounts Deposits		$0		
6. Less Reserves (3%)		$0		
7. Available Balances			$0	
8. Net Funds Needed	91.23%		$748,514	
II. Loan/Line Income/Expense (Relationship Costs)				
9. Gross Loan Interest: Relationship a.n.y. =		9.15%	$75,075	
10. Account Analysis Profit (applicable to time period of analysis)			$0	
11. Fees (applicable to time period of analysis)			$835	
12. MMA Margin on balance of:	$0		$0	
13. Total Gross Income			$75,910	
14. Account Analysis Loss (applicable to time period of analysis)		$____		
15. Time Deposit Costs (based on 5.5% interest paid)		$0		
16. Maintenance and Setup Expenses ($600 per loan above)		$600		
17. Other Costs (T & E, overhead, etc.)		——		
18. Total Loan Costs			$600	
19. Net Income			$75,310	
20. Relationship Yield			10.06%	

III. Profitability Index

21. Marginal Cost of Funds (as set by Sr. Mgmt or ALCO)	5.25%
22. Margin (asset/liability management spread)	4.35%
23. Risk Adjustment (inclusive of allocation for loan loss provision: $-1 < RA < 3$)	1.00%
24. Minimum Required Yield	10.60%
25. Profitability Index (Target > 100%)	94.917%

Additional/(Less) Ledger Demand Balances Required to Achieve 100% P.I. = $56,783

Additional/(Less) Fees Required to Achieve 100% P.I. = $4,033

Additional/(Less) BASIS POINTS Needed on THIS LOAN to Achieve 100% P.I. = 0.004915

Overview of Credit Risk Models Including KMV Model

Expert Systems

Expert systems are computerized approaches, not just to process data but to help make actual commercial bank lending decisions. These systems use algorithms based on step-by-step chartering of the stages of a decision, as illustrated in Figure 13D.1 for a commercial lending decision.

Note that Figure 13D.1 includes all relevant stages of credit analysis. Once the decision-making process is clearly understood, a computer program is developed that mimics, as closely as possible, the thinking process of decision makers recognized for their expertise in applying judgment at each stage of the flowchart. Expert systems incorporate the ability to perform calculations necessary to evaluate a credit application (such as financial ratios, which enter the model in Stage D in Figure 13D.1). They also incorporate the capacity to interpret the results of those calculations as seasoned loan officers would, then to make decisions (Stage F in the figure) based on interpretation of results from previous stages. At appropriate stages in the decision, users of expert systems technology can interact with the computer to provide additional data or to perform supplementary calculations that may improve the system's ability to make the right decision.

Supporters of expert systems point to their tremendous cost-saving potential. Once they are online, they never take vacations, never enter the hospital (although they may be subject to viruses), and are never lured away from the institutions for higher paying jobs. Cautious observers note, however, that the true test of expert systems will be their success in making lending decisions that are as profitable, at a comparable level of risk, as those made by human loan officers. In general, expert systems are used as a supplement rather a replacement for decision makers. Unlike quantitative scoring models, they are not widely used for making loan decisions. However, nonfinancial as well as financial institutions have used expert systems for customer credit and credit card decisions (granting a customer a credit card or not).

Neural Network Models

Artificial neural networks are computer models based on artificial intelligence, copying the way simple processing units operate in the brain. The system recognizes similarities in new input patterns and predicts an output pattern. Different types of neural network applications can be grouped into categories of (1) pattern recognition and assignment to different classes (such as a handwritten symbol); (2) clustering, or recognizing similarities in patterns and placing similar ones in clusters; (3) approximations of functions, or finding an estimate of an unknown function; and (4) prediction, or forecasting some future values of time-sequenced data. Neural networks have been used by some banks and credit card companies in their application screening process similar to expert systems, and consulting companies have developed to help financial institutions apply neural networks (see MAKHFI.com, *http://www.makhfi.com/tutorial/introduction.htm;* ERISK.com, *http://erisk.com*). Neural network applications have included loan approvals, credit card approvals, financial market predictions, bankruptcy predictions, and potential customer analysis for the creation of mailing lists involving learning and statistical trends. They are also helpful in other applications by filtering out noise for other applications (*http://www.dacs.dtic.mil/techs/neural/neural1.html*).

As pointed out by Caouette, Altman, and Narayanan (1998, p. 128), neural network analysis is similar to nonlinear discriminant analysis by no longer assuming that variables used to predict financial distress are linearly and independently related. Rather, neural network models of credit risk examine hidden correlations among predictive variables as additional variables in the nonlinear distress function. Just like the brain that contains a collection of interconnected neurons, a neural network contains a collection of simple computational elements that are interconnected. Inputs can be a financial ratio, a market trend, or any other

figure **13D.1** MODEL OF THE COMMERCIAL LENDING DECISION-MAKING PROCESS

Expert systems for loan analysis begin with a detailed diagram of the stages in the lending decision. Then a computer program that emulates the thinking of a skilled loan officer is developed.

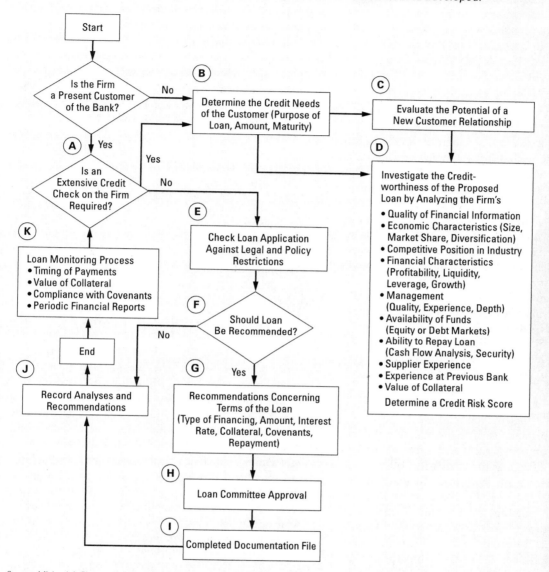

Source: Michael J. Shaw and James A. Gentry. "Using an Expert System with Inductive Learning to Evaluate Business Loans." Financial Management 17 (Autumn 1988), 47.

input variable. Inputs that respond less to the received stimuli, X, are removed, much as in discriminant analysis, with a learning stage that can be supervised or unsupervised. Different layers of hidden variables can be increased if the network is unable to reach a target accuracy rate. Learning stages, however, may have a number of problems including needing a huge number of cycles and the fact that a system may not work well if actual conditions differ from test conditions, and the analysis may have weightings that are so complex they are difficult to interpret. As Caouette, Altman, and Narayana (1998, p. 133) wisely state, artificial intelli-

gence systems have currently played more of a role as an assistant, helping an analyst be disciplined in making decisions rather than taking over decisions. As they note, "Although artificial intelligence (AI) systems hold promise in the credit evaluation area, they have yet to live up to this promise—apart from a few specialized applications in selected instances. One reason for the limited success of AI is that the nature of credit risk itself is changing in the global financial system. Even human experts become obsolete quickly, and an automated expert runs the same risk. AI models may need frequent retooling and redesign. New technology has made a stronger contribution to progress in other aspects of the banking business, making it possible for institutions to increase their vigilance on credit exposure and to be more flexible in extending credit because of better information systems."

Credit Models Based on Stock Price

Moody's KMV Model

Moody's KMV (MKMV) is a subsidiary of Moody's Corporation and a leading provider of financial software, credit training, and both quantitative and judgmental credit risk assessment models. MKMV has special models designed for private firms of different countries including Korea, Nordic countries, Singapore, Austria, Italy, Portugal, The Netherlands, Australia, Belgium, UK, France, Mexico, Spain, Germany, and the United States among others *(http://riskcalc .moodysrms.com/us/research/crm.asp)*. MKMV also has a leading stock-market-based credit measure for expected default frequency, as well as a portfolio management model, and specializes in measuring the probability of default of all publicly traded companies worldwide.

The KMV model is an asset value model for assessing the risk of a corporation's debt based on the option pricing models of Black and Scholes and Merton to calculate an Expected Default Frequency (EDF) credit measure. As noted in an article of *Credit Today,* "U.S. Credit Risk Is Rising Sharply and Approaching a Modern All-Time High," January 1, 2001 *(http://www.CreditToday.net)*, the KMV measures the risk of default using an Expected Default Frequency (EDF) statistic. Three primary variables drive EDF: debt, the market value of the company, and the volatility of market value. The more debt a firm has the greater its likelihood of default. Also, the greater a firm's stock price fluctuations, the greater its default risk. The model is based on an efficient market, at least in the long-term that in the past has been able to predict downturns. Critics have argued that if stock prices are inflated, such as during the dot.com era, this may not be the case. The model consists of estimating the market value of total assets and its volatility and finding the distance to default using a default database to calculate actual probabilities of default. The model has advantages by being a forward-looking measure for particular firms. As pointed out by Caouette, Altman, and Narayanan (1998, pp. 144–147), under the KMV option-based approach, the market value of equity can be expressed as a call option on the residual value of the firm (Assets − Liabilities) as follows:

$$\text{Market Value of Equity} =$$
$$f(\text{Book value of liabilities, market value of assets,}$$
$$\text{volatility of assets, time horizon}) \qquad [13C.1]$$

They note that although KMV uses a special (undisclosed) form of the options pricing approach, the model can be made more concrete by substituting the Black-Scholes options formula as they show, which follows:

$$E = VN(d_1) - De^{-t}N(d_2) \qquad [13C.1]$$

where

E	=	the market value of equity (option value),
D	=	the book value of liabilities (strike price),
V	=	the market value of assets,
t	=	the time horizon,
r	=	the risk-free borrowing and lending rate,
STD	=	the percentage standard deviation of asset value, and
N	=	the cumulative normal distribution function whose value is calculated for d_1 and d_2 where

$$d_1 = [\ln(V/D) + (r + \tfrac{1}{2}STD^2)\,t]/STD\sqrt{t}$$
$$d_2 = d_1 + STD\sqrt{t}$$

Two variables are unknown, the market of assets (V) and the volatility of assets (STD). However, by differentiating both sides of each equation and taking the mathematical expectation, the volatility of equity can be solved for as in [13C.1]. Accordingly using the Black-Scholes formula for an example, after taking the first derivative and applying "the expectation operator," the standard deviation of equity is equal to

$$\text{STD of Equity} = N(d_1)\,V\,STD/E \qquad [13C.2]$$

Since there are now two unknowns and two equations, a solution can be found. The second step is to find the expected asset value for the time horizon based on the historic asset market returns less the firm's payouts to investors of interest and dividends, and the point of default, when a firm's market value equals the book value of its liabilities. Beyond this point, the firm would default. Using a measure of systematic risk for a firm's assets, an expected return based on a firm's historic asset market returns is then determined by KMV, which is reduced by the firm's expected interest and dividend payments. By applying this expected return to the firm's current asset value, an expected future value of an asset and default point is calculated. As Caouette, Altman, and Narayanan (1998, pp. 144–147) note, KMV found firms to have a higher default likelihood when a firm's value was about equal to its current liabilities plus 50 percent of long-term liabilities. Based on a firm's expected value and its horizon default point, KMV estimates the percentage drop a firm would have to have in its firm value to bring it to the default point, such as 75 percent. They also note that KMV calculates the distance to default as follows:

$$\text{Distance from Default} =$$
$$\frac{(\text{Exp. Mkt. Value of Assets} - \text{Default Point})}{(\text{Exp. Mkt. Value of Assets})(STD - \text{Assets})} \qquad [13C.3]$$

This distance from default metric as a normalized measure can be used to compare one company to another. KMV then determines an expected default frequency as a function of distance from default by comparing the distances that were calculated from default to actual historic default rates for a group of firms, fitting an expected default frequency curve based on the distance from default.

Caouette, Altman, and Narayanan (1998) point out that KMV also has models for private firms by comparing reported characteristics of private firms based on accounting data with firms that have been rated using public data. For private firms, the market value of the firm is modeled using its operating value (Earnings Before Interest Taxes and Depreciation, EBITDA) times a multiplier (based on similar publicly traded firms in the same industry and country) and its liquidating value. Hence, the default probabilities depend on the mappings of similar publicly traded firms. For more details, see Caouette, Altman, and Narayanan (1998, pp. 146–147). Glantz (2003) notes that expected default frequency (EDF) credit measures are viewed and analyzed with a software product, Credit Monitor™ (CM) that allows users to see a term structure of EDF values over five years. The KMV model's predictive power depends on the assumption that the current market value of the firm is a good predictor of future values, which is derived from the firm's equity value. Thus, the model depends totally on stock prices and, hence, an efficient market, for its information and, hence, predictions. If the market is efficient, analysts would expect EDF values to be timely.

Portfolio Risk Considerations and Models

The preceding models have generally looked at individual loans versus the entire loan portfolio risk of a financial institution. In the theory of finance, diversification is a key concept in reducing overall investor risk and increasing the expected return of the portfolio. As Caouette, Altman, and Narayanan (1998, Chapter 9, "Application of Portfolio Approaches," pp. 267–303) note, the amount of diversification of a portfolio depends on the correlation between default risks within the portfolio and how much of an asset is held in the portfolio. Hence, the improvement of a portfolio's performance depends on including large numbers of assets and keeping weights of each asset in line with the return contribution of that asset to the overall portfolio return. As noted in previous chapters, the risk of a bank's portfolio can be reduced by asset securitization or loan sales and by the use of market and credit derivatives. Major banking institutions mark to market their portfolios and adjust for changes in ratings and credit/market spreads to be able to better see correlations between assets. CreditMetrics, mentioned earlier in the chapter, which measures the risk of default rate changes on the value of assets, developed a comprehensive framework including correlations in this risk. The risk for each asset or loan balance is calculated and then given a bond rating or, if no rating is available, an associated rating based on its risk of migration to a lower rating. The state to which each asset can move to is given a transition probability, and a transition matrix for the different grades is created. Standard deviations are used to measure the volatility of an asset's value, along with the value of the distribution

corresponding to a state with a 1 percent probability of transition. The correlation of the future asset values is calculated using a spreadsheet of industry returns and correlations. Using a Monte Carlo simulation approach, the total risk of the portfolio can be estimated.

Other models that use an efficient frontier for loans include the **KMV Portfolio Manager,** which uses a similar type of approach based on the correlation of default risks between loans made to borrowers including the expected return on loans less expected losses, the standard deviation of the loan's default rate around its expected value, and the correlations between the systematic risk of the asset returns across borrowers (see Saunders and Cornett, 2003, Chapter 12, pp. 310–320). **The Credit Risk+ Model** of Credit Suisse Financial Products also uses a portfolio approach that includes the default rate as a continuous random variable and the volatility of default rates dividing portfolios into homogeneous sections where borrowers in these sectors have the same amount of systematic risk (for instance, by geography or industry) whereby different sectors have different loss distributions. **McKinsey & Co.** also developed a model, known as the **Wilson model** by its inventor, that analyzes portfolio risk and returns using Monte Carlo simulation, which attempts to incorporate more realistic conditions facing financial institutions, including results that are conditional on the state of the economy and uncertainty regarding recovery rates and losses from country risk (see Caouette, Alman, and Narayanan, 1998, pp. 296–297).

As pointed out by Saunders and Cornett (2003, p. 317), with the exception of major, very large ones, many financial institutions have difficulties acquiring the data or expertise to apply modern portfolio theory to their loan portfolios. They can, however, use call reports, peer data, and data on shared national credits (a national database on commercial loans classifying loan volume by two-digit SIC codes) as benchmarks to see how their percentages of different types of loans in different major lending sectors compare. Since research has found many bank failures in the past to be associated with overconcentration in a regional economy or industry sector, an analysis of the diversification of a bank's portfolio can be an important exercise. With loan sales and purchases, as well as credit derivatives, there are greater means today to reduce the risk of having great systematic risk by being concentrated in one sector.

Source: Appendix 13D draws heavily and primarily from Caouette, Altman, and Narayanan (1998), Chapter 11, pp. 139–147, and secondarily from Saunders and Cornett (2003), as well as Glantz (2003) for the KMV model. Please see these sources for a more detailed discussion and overview. Also, see Morton Glantz (2003), pp. 504 to 516 for a detailed discussion and application of the KMV model; and Saunders and Allen (2002), Allen, Boudoukh, and Saunders (2003), and Marshall (2001) for technical details for these and other models used to measure and manage operational and credit risks. Caouette, et al. also provided details on several different portfolio models.

14 Asset Management

Liquidity Reserves and the Securities Portfolio

"[M]any regional banks maintain large, low-yielding securities portfolios for liquidity and balance sheet structure reasons. In today's capital market environment, this problem [liquidity] is probably much more imagined than real."

JOHN B. McCOY, CEO Banc One; Larry A Frieder, Professor, Florida A&M University; and Robert B. Hedges, Jr., Executive Vice President, Consumer Banking Group, Shawmut National Corporation. Bottomline Banking (1994), 11.

Banking organizations provide liquidity intermediation services for depositors by taking deposits and being ready to provide funds back to depositors at any time. Hence, liquidity management is important for the viability of all banking organizations and one key component of regulatory ratings, that is, the "L" in CAMELS ratings. Liquidity management involves both asset and liability management. Asset management for liquidity is in terms of the investments that banks invest in for stored liquidity and the amount and maturity of these, as well as operations for many large banks in ongoing loan securitizations and/or loan sales. Investment management has changed dramatically for financial institutions in the past two decades. In the mid to late 1980s, with deregulation and rising interest expense costs, many depository institution managers took on high risk investments to gamble for high returns. Unfortunately, some of these institutions made "bad bets" and failed. Columbia Savings and Loan in Beverly Hills, California, for example, had at its zenith over 40 percent of its assets in high yielding, noninvestment grade junk bonds (a practice allowed at the time for state-chartered thrifts in California). By 1990, the junk market collapsed, resulting in a $1 billion decline in Columbia's junk bond portfolio, and Congress outlawed junk bonds as thrift investments. In 1991, Columbia closed, costing taxpayers $2 billion, and its CEO, Thomas Spiegel, awaited trial on a fiftyfive-count indictment on charges of misappropriation, fraud, and lying to federal regulators.[1] Similar stories have occurred for other types of financial institutions, including insurance firms such as First Executive that took on high-risk investments in the 1980s, which contributed to large losses, or, in the case of First Executive, its demise.[2]

Almost all financial institutions, by their nature, are subject to investment management and liquidity problems related to potential withdrawals by liabil-

Learning Objectives

After completing this chapter, you will be able to:

1 Understand the importance of liquidity for depository institutions from both a regulatory and operational perspective.

2 Calculate regulatory reserve requirements.

3 Understand discretionary and nondiscretionary factors affecting liquidity and how liquidity needs are generally estimated.

4 Explain the risk/return trade-off associated with using stored liquidity versus liability management.

5 Understand the multiple objectives of a depository institution's investment portfolio and the need for a sound framework for managing liquidity.

6 Understand ladder, barbell, and hybrid investment maturity strategies.

7 Explain real-world and strategic considerations in investment strategies.

8 Follow trends in security holdings by depository institutions and be familiar with the special characteristics of mortgage-backed securities.

ity holders, including policyholders for insurance companies, depositors for depository institutions, and investors for mutual funds and securities firms. How managers respond to new asset investment opportunities and how they manage liquidity are both determined by the institution's long-term goals, and decisions are influenced by the preferences of shareholders, regulators, customers, and managers themselves. In this chapter reserve, liquidity, security investment management, and liability management are examined, focusing predominantly on depository institutions, which face the greatest liquidity risk and challenges in these areas in terms of satisfying a nexus of regulations. In Chapter 15, which follows, deposit and liability management are discussed in greater detail.

Importance of Liquidity in Depository Institutions

As one expert explained, depository institution liquidity is "the ability . . . to raise a certain amount of funds at a certain cost within a certain amount of time."[3] Access to cash is important in the financial management of all businesses, but because providing liquidity for customers is an intermediation function, a depository institution's own liquidity is even more important. Institutions obtain many deposits

---

1 Kathleen Kerwin. "He Who Lives by the Junk Bond. . . ." *Business Week* (December 25, 1989), 46–47; Richard B. Schmitt. "Spiegel Indicted in Case Stemming from S&L Failure." *The Wall Street Journal* (June 25, 1992), B4.

2 George W. Fenn and Rebel A. Cole. "Announcements of Asset-Quality Problems and Contagion Effects in the Life Insurance Industry." *Journal of Financial Economics* 35 (April 1994), 181–198.

3 See Burns (1971), 1.

under the promise of immediate or almost immediate repayment on demand, so the investment and financing decisions for a depository are inseparable. In other words, obtaining deposits and deciding how to invest them are closely intertwined. Liquidity is important for depository institutions for regulatory purposes, to have sufficient liquidity for deposit transactions, and to have sufficient liquidity for future borrowing needs by a bank's customers.

Because deposits—especially some transactions accounts—can be volatile, government regulatory agencies emphasize depository institution liquidity. Most depositories operate under a set of liquidity requirements established at either the state or the federal level. Also, after the Depository Institutions Deregulation and Monetary Control Act (DIDMCA) extended Federal Reserve System (Fed) reserve requirements to all depository institutions, all but the smallest institutions must meet standards set by more than one regulator—the Fed's and those of their chartering or insuring agency.

Besides the requirements of regulators, liquidity needs are affected by the expectations of depositors and borrowers. Even in annual reports, companies view liquidity as being able to meet all their current and future financial obligations including meeting depositor withdrawal demands and borrower's upcoming financial needs.[4]

Depository institutions generate most of their interest income from loans and strive to develop a strong base of loan customers. To retain the loyalty of customers, a lender must be able to provide funds for all loan applications that meet its credit standards. Often, firms make loan commitments to supply funds to customers as needed that also must be met. Thus, an institution needs to maintain liquidity to support expected loan demand in addition to meeting obligations arising from its liabilities. Also, to maintain a favorable credit rating on its uninsured deposits and other debt by rating agency, and, hence, have a lower cost of funds, a financial institution must have adequate liquidity as well.[5]

Liquidity: The Risk/Return Trade-Off

With many compelling reasons to maintain liquidity, one might think that liquidity could be easily managed by keeping a large quantity of cash or marketable securities in the asset portfolio. However, a well-recognized trade-off is that liquid assets contribute relatively little to the firm's net interest margin (NIM), because they ordinarily offer a low rate of return. The conflict between the risk of illiquidity and a desire to maintain a high NIM is the heart of liquidity management. The challenge is to maintain enough liquidity to avoid a crisis but to sacrifice no more earnings than absolutely necessary. Although the need for liquid assets arises for a variety of reasons and all demands must be met simultaneously, each need presents a separate problem. First, reserve requirements must be met, but since deposits with the Fed and cash held for reserve requirements cannot be used to meet liquidity needs for deposit withdrawals and loan demand, liquidity needed for such normal and unexpected demands must also be estimated.

Historic and Current U.S. Reserve Requirements

Reserve requirements, as mentioned in the Appendix to Chapter 3, are a tool for monetary policy. In the United States today, reserve requirements are less of a tool for monetary policy than open market operations. However, in countries that do not have well-developed financial markets, they are often a dominant tool to help stimulate a sluggish economy by reducing reserve requirements or the opposite if an economy is overheating. In the United States, reserve requirements were first placed on the deposits of commercial banks with national charters under the National Currency and National Banking Acts of 1863 and 1864.[6] These reserves, established as a percentage of deposits and other liabilities, were required as either cash or interbank deposits, depending on the location of the bank. The early rationale for reserve requirements was to protect the liquidity of the banking system to promote public confidence. The Federal Reserve Act of 1913 revised but continued reserve requirements with a

---

4 First Chicago Corporation, *1982 Annual Report*, 25.

5 Citicorp, *Citicorp Worldwide: 1988 Report*, 34.

6 For a discussion of the history of reserve requirements, on which the historical information in this chapter is based, see Feinman (1993) and Goodfriend and Hargraves (1983). An earlier survey treatment of this topic is Knight (1974). A good article arguing that no rationale for reserve requirements is convincing enough to justify them is Stevens (1991).

motivation to prevent liquidity crises, and the Fed also allowed short-term borrowing by member banks at the Fed discount window to provide short-term (emergency) liquidity. By 1931, reserve requirements were recognized as a tool for controlling the amount of credit extended by banks, and by the 1950s, they had become an important element of monetary policy. In the 1970s, the Fed was concerned because only Fed-member banks were required to hold reserves, limiting monetary policy objectives; hence, under DIDMCA of 1980, all depository institutions were required to abide by the Fed's reserve requirements.[7] Others have criticized reserve requirements as an unnecessary tax on depository institutions, which in the 1990s the Fed seemed to agree with by reducing requirements dramatically, to 0 percent in some cases. Note, however, that in less-developed countries such as Mexico, where central bank open market operations cannot take place because money markets are not very well developed, large reserve requirements for banks are more crucial for implementing monetary policy.

Although the rationale for imposing reserve requirements on depository institutions is no longer solely to protect the liquidity position of the financial system, meeting the requirements continues to be a key management issue.

Current Reserve Requirements

Under the Federal Reserve Board's Regulation D, reservable liabilities include net transaction accounts, nonpersonal time deposits, and Eurocurrency liabilities. Since December 27, 1990, however, the reserve ratio for the latter two has been zero, so effectively reservable liabilities have been net transaction accounts. The particular reserve ratio goes up (is progressive) above a certain amount of net transaction accounts, currently 3 percent at lower tranche levels, rising to 10 percent at higher levels. Also, the Garn–St. Germain Act of 1982 exempts an adjusted amount each year based on a formula that was specified in the act. The low tranche before the reserve ratio goes up (as specified under DIDMCA of 1980) also is an amount that is adjusted each year. Currently, the ratio requirement is as follows for 2004 (requirements are specified in the *Federal Reserve Bulletin* at the end of each year):

Reserve Requirements

Type of Liability	Percentage of Liabilities	Effective Date
Exemption amount for December 25, 2003: $6.6 million		
Net transaction accounts[a]		
$0 to $6.6 million[b]	0	12-25-03
More than $6.6 million to $45.4 million[c]	3	12-25-03
More than $45.4 million	10	12-25-03
Nonpersonal time deposits	0	12-27-90
Eurocurrency liabilities	0	12-27-90

[a]Total transaction accounts include demand deposits, automatic transfer service (ATS) accounts, NOW accounts, share draft accounts, telephone or preauthorized transfer accounts, ineligible banker's acceptances, and obligations that are issued by affiliates that are maturing in seven or fewer days. Net transaction accounts equal total transaction accounts less amounts due from depository institutions and less cash in the process of collection.

[b]The exemption amount (not subject to a reserve requirement) is adjusted upward by 80 percent of the previous year's (June 30) rate of increase in total reservable liabilities to all depository institutions. If liabilities decrease instead, no adjustment is made.

[c]The amount of net transaction accounts in the low-reserve (3 percent) tranche is adjusted each year by 80 percent of the previous year's (June 30) rate of increase or decrease in net transaction accounts held by all depository institutions.

Required reserves must be held in the form of vault cash or if vault cash is inadequate, also in the form of deposits with a Federal Reserve Bank for Federal Reserve System members. If an institution is not a member, it can hold deposits with a Reserve Bank or with another correspondent institution in a pass-through relationship.[8]

---

7   In one DIDMCA provision, Congress established a range of 8 percent to 14 percent for the marginal reserve requirements on transactions accounts. It gave the Fed the authority to set a higher percentage for monetary policy reasons but stipulated that the Fed must pay interest on those reserves. The authority has never been exercised. For further details, see "The Depository Institutions Deregulation and Monetary Control Act of 1980"; and Cacy and Winningham (1980).

8   See "Reserve Requirements," Federal Reserve Board Website (http://www.federalreserve.gov/monetarypolicy/ reservereq.htm), 2004, and *Federal Reserve Bulletin,* December 2003, A8. Note under Regulation D, Money Market Deposit Accounts (MMDAs) are treated as savings deposits, and do not require reserves.

Managing the Reserve Position

Required reserves must be held as vault cash or as deposits at a district Federal Reserve Bank. The Fed requires weekly reports from large depositories; a quarterly schedule applies to institutions with total deposits below an amount specified in Federal Reserve **Regulation D.** If an institution's reserves are >4 percent below the daily average minimum reserve required, it is subject to a penalty imposed by the Fed. Reserves that are 4 percent below the minimum can be carried over as a deficit into the next period, with 4 percent more reserves needed to be held that period. Similarly, if reserves are 4 percent higher than the minimum, this excess can be carried over to the next two-week reserve period. The Fed does not pay interest on reserve deposits, so reserve balances are nonearning assets for depositories. Because of the interest penalty plus regulatory intervention exacted for having too few reserves and the loss of income from having too many, depositories must estimate their reserve requirements as accurately as possible.

Reserve Requirement Calculations Using Lagged Reserve Accounting

The Fed from 1968 to early 1984 used lagged reserve accounting (LRA), which allows an institution to calculate its reserve period during an earlier two-week computation period to be held as a requirement during a later two-week maintenance period. Between 1984 and 1998, the Fed required a more complicated contemporaneous reserve accounting system for transaction deposits, making it difficult for institutions to estimate the reserves required on average for a contemporaneous period. After July 1998, the Fed returned to a LRA system, which is much easier for banks to manage.

The Fed has a detailed Maintenance Manual that lists the exact dates for computation periods and maintenance periods for the current and upcoming years. Except for small banks below an exemption amount, banks must submit detailed reports to the Fed. Banks file reports either weekly or quarterly depending on their level of deposits.[9]

Maintenance periods consist of seven consecutive days beginning on a Thursday and ending on the following Wednesday for which an institution must maintain average daily balances with the Fed to satisfy its total balance requirement. For a given computation period, the corresponding maintenance period begins on the fourth Thursday following the end of the computation period and ends on the fourth Wednesday after the close of the next computation period. The maintenance cycle runs for thirteen weeks (sometimes twelve to fourteen weeks depending on the calendar). The Fed's Reserve Maintenance Manual expresses this in a different way; the required reserves to be maintained in each of the maintenance periods in a thirteen-week cycle is based on the deposit data from the computation period that ended twenty-four days before the beginning of the first maintenance period. The Fed posts these periods in this manual. For instance, a maintenance period for the two weeks of 3/04/2004 to 3/17/2004, at the time of this writing, would be based on computation periods from the two weeks of 02/17/2004 to 02/23/2004 and 02/10/2004 to 02/16/2004.[10]

An example from the Fed's Manual (November 2003, p. V-2) is as follows:

14-day average net transaction accounts: $75.0 million

Low reserve tranche ($45.4 million less $6.6 million exemption) = $38.8 mil. × 0.03

Higher reserve tranche (> $45.4 million) = ($75 mil. − 45.4 mil.) = $29.6 mil. × 0.10

Daily Ave. Reserve Requirement = $38.8 mil. (0.03) + $29.6 mil. (0.10) = $1.164 mil. + $2.96 mil. = $4.124 mil.

Note net transaction accounts are calculated by taking total transaction accounts less any demand balances due from depository institutions in the United States less cash items in the process of collection. For example, in the calculation of the average net transaction accounts above, suppose total transactions accounts were $1,078 million less total demand balances of $14 million at other U.S. depository institutions, and cash in the process of collection was $14 million; the net total transaction accounts

9 Reports, forms, and instructions are on the Fed's Reporting and Reserves Website *(http://www.reportingandreserves.org).*

10 Ibid.

Concept Questions

1 Why is liquidity management important for depository institutions?

2 What is the liquidity/risk trade-off?

3 How has the justification for reserve requirements changed over time? What is the current justification?

4 Why do you think the Fed reduced reserve requirements in recent years and returned to a lagged reserve accounting system?

5 Why are reserve requirements more essential in countries without well-developed financial markets?

6 Explain to a friend in your own words how you would calculate a bank's reserve requirement.

would be $1,078 million less $28 million equals $1,050 million divided by 14 days equals $75 million average net transaction accounts.

To get the total balances that will have to be held at the Federal Reserve for the maintenance period, the daily average required reserve amount would be multiplied by the total days of the maintenance period. The total vault cash that was held over the two-week computation period would be subtracted since it contributes to the reserve requirement, leaving the total required reserves to be held at the Fed during the maintenance period.

Estimating Liquidity Needs above Reserve Requirements

Besides meeting standards set by government regulators, depository institutions need liquid funds to meet customer loan demand and deposit withdrawals.[11] Commercial banks, having offered transactions accounts and short-term commercial loans longer than other depositories, have traditionally been more concerned with liquidity needs arising from operations, but nonbank depositories now pay increased attention to liquidity because they, too, now offer transactions accounts. Liquidity management is closely related to liability management. If a large money center bank, for instance, has multiple sources for short-term borrowing, it requires less liquidity in terms of short-term assets on its balance sheet. However, ultimately, the amount of liquidity needed depends on predicted loan demand, deposit withdrawals adjusted for cyclical and seasonal factors, and growth. Also, the amount of liquidity needed depends on how much of a cushion a bank wants for unexpected loan demand and deposit withdrawals and the risk preferences of stakeholders in the institution.

Discretionary and Nondiscretionary Factors

The balance sheet of a depository can be divided into discretionary and nondiscretionary items.[12] Discretionary items include those over which management can exert considerable influence, such as the use of repurchase agreements. Nondiscretionary items are those beyond the short-run control of an institution, such as deposit fluctuations, loan demand, and reserve requirements. Some nondiscretionary items—such as deposit increases or maturing loans—are sources of liquidity, but others are drains on liquidity.

Managers must understand the implications of nondiscretionary items for their institutions. A depository that derives most of its revenues from loans does not really wish to deny loans to good customers based on liquidity shortages. Such actions would undermine customer relationships built over long years of service and damage profit potential. Refusing to honor customer requests for deposit withdrawals would surely have even more severe consequences. These operations-based liquidity demands are an important part of the planning process. The better an institution can predict its expected loan demand and deposit withdrawals, the lower excess liquidity it needs to hold.

---

11 This dichotomy was proposed in Luckett (1980), 12–13.

12 See Timothy W. Koch and S. Scott MacDonald. *Bank Management*, 4th ed. Fort Worth, TX: Southwestern/Thomson, 2002, Chapter 14, for a more detailed discussion of these factors..

Estimating Liquidity Needs for Operations: An Example

The estimation of liquidity needs arising from anticipated volatility in deposits and expected loan demand involves several techniques, ranging from managerial judgment to quantitative models. Table 14.1 presents a simplified example of estimating a liquidity surplus or deficit over a single planning period.[13] The first step is to estimate total balances for each main asset and funding source category.

Liquid and Illiquid Assets

Asset categories are divided into liquid or illiquid components; liquid assets in this context are those available to meet operational needs. For example, at the top of Table 14.1, the institution's total cash balances during the next period are estimated to be almost $210 million. But because of reserve requirements and daily transactions, total cash balances are never entirely available to meet deposit withdrawals or increased loan demand. In fact, management has estimated that only $21 million could be used to fulfill these needs. Within the investments category, liquid investments are those that can be

table **14.1** ESTIMATING LIQUIDITY NEEDS FOR OPERATIONS

Institutions need to forecast potential liquidity positions and plan to avoid deficits. The approach illustrated identifies the volatility of funds sources and estimates whether liquid assets could cover large outflows and meet additional loan demand.

	Total (Millions)	Liquid (%)	Liquid	Illiquid
I. Original Assumptions				
Assets				
Cash	$ 209.7	10%	$ 21.0	$ 188.7
Investments	1,037.6	59	609.4	428.2
Loans	1,214.4	0	0.0	1,214.4
Other assets	171.0	0	15.0	156.0
Total	$2,632.7		$645.4	$1,987.3

	Total (Millions)	Volatile (%)	Volatile	Nonvolatile
Funds sources				
Deposits	$1,755.0	7%	$130.0	$1,625.0
Other liabilities	674.0	82	549.7	124.3
Equity	203.7	0	0.0	203.7
Total	$2,632.7		$679.7	$1,953.0

Liquidity deficit (liquid assets − volatile funds):

$645.4 − $679.7 = ($34.3)

	Total (Millions)	Liquid (%)	Liquid	Illiquid
II. Additional Loan Demand				
Assets				
Cash	$ 209.7	10%	$ 21.0	$ 188.7
Investments	1,037.6	59	609.4	428.2
Loans	1,214.4	−1	(12.1)	1,226.5
Other assets	171.0	9	15.0	156.0
Total	$2,632.7		$633.3	$1,999.4

Liquidity deficit (liquid assets − volatile funds):

$633.3 − $679.7 = ($46.4)

---

[13] This example is similar to one in Kaufman and Lee (1977).

sold easily, without great loss of value, during the planning period. Sources of funds are also maturing securities and loans.

More about managing the securities portfolio to allow for operational liquidity appears later in the chapter. Longer-term securities are not liquid, but they can be used as a form of stored liquidity for unexpected loan demand or deposit withdrawals; however, they may have to be sold at a loss if interest rates have risen since their initial purchase.

Volatile and Nonvolatile Sources of Funds

As noted in Chapters 2 and 4, discussing measures of liquidity risk, core (insured) deposits are funds that tend to stay with a bank, since retail insured depositors are often more interested in convenience considerations and want to avoid significant switching costs (new checks, relationships, etc.) in switching their accounts to other banks. In contrast, noncore (uninsured deposits) and other short-term borrowings (often called purchased funds) tend to be volatile funds, with investors moving funds around to the institution with the highest yield or for institutional investors with high-quality ratings as well. Drains on liquidity can be estimated by examining funds sources. In this institution, most deposits are considered relatively stable, so only $130 million are judged to be volatile. In contrast, other liabilities for borrowed money, including negotiable certificates of deposit, repurchase agreements, and federal funds purchased, are quite volatile. Management assumes that most could be withdrawn or become unavailable on short notice. The equity of the institution is entirely nonvolatile in the short run.

A liquidity deficit is projected for the upcoming period because liquid assets are less than volatile funds sources by $34.3 million. If management's estimates are correct, the institution must somehow generate additional cash in that amount.

Additional Drains on Liquidity

The first panel of Table 14.1 adjusts for normal loan demand and deposit supplies. It assumes that next period's loan demand can be completely met by maturing loans or stable deposits; that is, the loan portfolio is viewed neither as a source of liquidity nor as a drain on liquidity. A more conservative approach would build in coverage for unexpected loan demand by assigning a *negative* balance to the liquid loan category, reflecting the drain on liquidity from increased loan demand. Suppose that management wishes to allow for additional loan demand equal to 1 percent of that already forecast, or a total of $12.1 million. The liquidity deficit from operations would then rise to $46.4 million (bottom panel of Table 14.1).

Other more detailed liquidity gaps estimate all funding sources and funding uses (including all maturing loans and securities, unused loan commitments, expected deposit withdrawals, and maturing deposits) to derive a more precise liquidity gap for an upcoming period, including unexpected loan demand and deposit withdrawals. The liquidity gap is then compared with contingent borrowing sources or other sources of stored liquidity.

Incorporating Quantitative Models

A more quantitative method of estimating liquidity needs is to forecast from a regression analysis of past data. For example, in the analysis of expected loan demand, management could use a model relating past loan demand, D, to time, t: $D = f(t)$. The resulting regression equation can serve as a basis for projecting a range of future demand that incorporates past volatility and knowledge of other economic or seasonal factors that may cause a change from past trends. An even better forecast might be generated with multiple regression, because loan demand is also affected by factors such as economic conditions, interest rates, and competition from other institutions, to name just a few, and each institution must identify its relevant set of variables. Similar analyses can be performed for all nondiscretionary items that affect liquidity.

Sophistication in forecasting techniques is positively related to the size of depository institutions; this is not surprising because it is expensive to employ forecasting specialists.[14] Regardless of how forecasts

---

14 A survey of forecasting techniques revealed that the percentage of large banks (deposits in excess of $400 million) that use sophisticated forecasting techniques (such as multiple regression, time series forecasting, and simulation) was higher than among smaller banks. A large number of institutions of all sizes, however, rely on managerial judgment—either alone or in combination with quantitative methods—for estimating future deposit levels and loan demand. See Giroux (1980).

are generated, they are an important part of the liquidity management solution. These estimates combine with estimates of required reserves to represent a target level of liquid funds for the planning period.

Managing the Liquidity Position

Table 14.1 presents a bank's liquidity dilemma; the bank has a potential liquidity deficiency and needs immediate access to liquid funds.[15] The institution in Table 14.1 needs liquidity as a result of operational factors. Whatever the reason, managers must act.

Borrowing versus Selling Securities

Two general liquidity management strategies are available. First, management can borrow funds, either from the regulators or from nondeposit creditors in the financial markets. Obtaining nondeposit sources of cash, a technique used more often by large commercial banks than by other depositories, is called **liability management.** Because the use of nondeposit funds, such as federal funds and Euromarket borrowing, has implications far beyond liquidity management, full discussion of liability management is deferred until Chapter 15. This chapter discusses borrowing from regulators as a source of liquidity. Larger institutions with greater sources of borrowing can engage in greater liability management than smaller institutions that are often limited to Fed Funds Purchased or borrowing from regulators.

A second strategy is to use asset management and liquidate assets from the securities portfolio. High market interest rates can make this approach undesirable. Also, depositories hold securities for purposes other than liquidity, so trade-offs are involved in this approach to liquidity management. Some of these are discussed later in the chapter.

Factors Influencing Liquidity Management

The choice between borrowing or selling securities (i.e., between liability management and asset management) is influenced by several factors, including the size of the institution, its financial stability, its industry, and the risk/return preferences of managers and owners:

- **Size and Financial Stability.** Small or financially weak institutions are especially likely to look to the securities portfolio, not to liability management, for generating liquidity. Within the asset portfolio, too, liquidity is influenced by institutional size. As discussed more fully later, active portfolio management is expensive; thus, a smaller institution is likely to keep larger proportions of readily marketable short-term securities and higher excess reserve balances. An institution's credit rating also affects its ability to issue short-term securities quickly for its financing needs. Institutional investors also often will only invest in short-term securities and uninsured deposits of institutions with excellent credit ratings.

- **Industry Membership.** Another influence over which a depository institution usually has little control is its industry. Regulatory policies governing an industry limit its operations—including the composition of its securities portfolio, the proportion of liquid assets held, and the sources of short-term loans for liquidity purposes. Recently, however, regulators have provided depository institutions with more freedom to change from one industry to another by simplifying the process of applying for new charters.

- **Risk/Return Preferences.** Managers' and owners' risk preferences also influence liquidity management. For a variety of reasons (explored in Chapter 15), liability management exposes an institution to greater risks than does a strategy of selling securities when cash is needed. Furthermore, some strategies for managing the securities portfolio are riskier than others.

---

15 Liquidity is also needed in the management of the reserve position. Depositories may also find themselves with *excess* reserves toward the end of the maintenance period. When the institution has excess reserves, management may choose to lend them in the federal funds market. The asset thus created is defined as "federal funds sold."

Borrowing from Regulators as a Source of Liquidity

The carryover privilege on Fed reserve requirements is useful in meeting small deficiencies in liquid assets. For example, if deposits fluctuate unexpectedly toward the end of the maintenance period, an institution can postpone major reserve adjustments until the next period as long as the fluctuations are not too large. However, if deficiencies are large or frequent, the institution can turn to federal regulators for other sources of cash for liquidity management.

The Discount Window

The Fed discount window was originally available only to member commercial banks, but DIDMCA opened it to all depositories subject to Fed reserve requirements. Commercial banks remain by far the largest users, because Fed policy requires other depositories to exhaust traditional sources of regulatory borrowing before turning to the discount window.

The Fed administers discount window borrowing under **Regulation A,** which permits institutions to borrow under three conditions: to meet temporary liquidity needs, such as those illustrated in Table 14.1; to meet seasonal credit demands, such as those arising around Christmas or, for many rural banks, during planting season; and for special "extended credit" purposes, often after disasters such as Hurricane Andrew or the Los Angeles riots, both in 1992, which make unforeseeable demands on institutions. The Fed may also provide extended credit if an institution experiences unusually heavy withdrawals and regulators fear a "run," such as occurred with the near-failure of Continental National Bank in 1984.

The interest cost and availability of these borrowings are major factors in the decision to use the window. Ordinarily, discount window borrowings are very short-term, used only to meet genuine liquidity emergencies and not as additional funds for expanding the loan portfolio. Officials at the Fed monitor an institution's use of the window and may ask management to discontinue borrowing should norms for the amount and frequency of borrowing be exceeded. Thus, frequent borrowing at the window has negative connotations that managers are careful to avoid.[16]

FHLB Advances

Membership in the Federal Home Loan Bank (FHLB) system used to be predominantly federal savings institutions who, when they faced a shortage of qualifying liquid assets, could apply for advances from the Federal Home Loan Banks. This FHLB lending program was originated in the Federal Home Loan Bank Act of 1932 and modeled after that of the Fed. Advances from the FHLBs tended to be longer term than the Fed's discount window loans, and the interest rate was sometimes adjusted by the Bank System in an effort to alter the volume of mortgage lending that thrifts were undertaking.

FIRREA made important changes to the FHLB advance program. Insured commercial banks, credit unions, and certain other financial institutions that make residential home mortgage loans and related community investment can become members in the FHLBank system. Members are eligible for advances from the twelve regional FHLBs. Longer-term advances in general are made only to enable an institution to meet unmet demand for mortgage loans and not to provide a more-or-less permanent source of cash. Advances must be collateralized by low-risk, generally home mortgage assets, and the volume of advances is limited by an institution's level of net worth. Furthermore, the FHLBs must consider an institution's reinvestment in the community and its willingness to lend to first-time home-buyers in deciding whether to grant a requested advance. Members are shareholders in the regional FHLBanks. In the early 1990s, there were only 2,855 system members. At the end of 2003, there were 8,092 member institutions including 5,926 commercial banks, 1,384 thrifts, 704 credit unions, and 78 insurance companies. As reported by the FHLB, the collective assets of members were $6 trillion (see *http://www.fhlbanks.com*). The use of advances by banks and thrifts has risen dramatically in the latter 1990s and early 2000s, with an annual growth rate of 8 percent a year. At the end of 2001 alone, FHLBank advances were $472.7 billion. The FHLBanks, as privately owned wholesale banks, raise money by selling Aaa/AAA-rated bonds to investors. This enables the FHLB to lend money at low cost to member banks at lower rates (smaller spreads over comparable Treasuries) than other privately

---

16 Details on the administration of the window can be found in Mengle (1986) and Spong (1990).

offered debt, providing a lower borrowing cost for its member banks and thrifts (see *http://www .fhlbanks.com,* and click "FHLBank System" on the home page). In 1999, the Financial Services Modernization Act (Gramm-Leach-Bliley) amended the authority of the FHLB to make advances secured by small enterprise loans of community financial institutions as well.

FIRREA also specified conditions under which institutions with emergency cash shortages can obtain short-term advances from the FHLBs. Eligible institutions must be solvent and must present substantial evidence that they can repay the debt. With these guidelines, Congress hoped to prevent a recurrence of the situation prevailing immediately before FIRREA, in which the insolvent portion of the industry owed regulators millions of dollars borrowed during the period of extreme forbearance, which it could never realistically repay.[17]

Sources of Borrowing for Credit Unions

For CUs, three sources of short-term funds are available, two of these from regulatory sources. Congress authorized one source of liquidity in 1978, when it approved the creation of the Central Liquidity Facility (CLF) as an arm of the National Credit Union Administration. The CLF functions as the lender of last resort for CUs voluntarily choosing to join it. In contrast to FHLB advances, CLF loans are made for liquidity purposes only. Besides interest, the CLF requires borrowing CUs to pay a commitment fee of 1 percent. Fed discount window loans are also available to CUs offering transactions deposits or nonpersonal time deposits. Finally, a CU that is a member of a Corporate Credit Union (CCU) may borrow from the CCU.[18]

The Securities Portfolio as a Source of Stored Liquidity

Managing the securities portfolio—in particular, choosing an optimal combination of liquid versus higher-yielding assets—is an integral part of liquidity management for financial institutions, particularly small and medium-sized depositories. Under a stored liquidity approach, institutions keep a pyramid of reserves, with cash above reserve requirements as **primary reserves,** short-term marketable securities that are not pledged for public deposits (such as Treasury and agency bills) as **secondary reserves,**[19] and mortgage securities and other longer-term securities as **tertiary reserves** that can be sold if necessary—although possibly at a loss if interest rates have risen since their purchase. Tertiary reserves are primarily for income-producing purposes, particularly countercyclical income when loan demand is down.

Most depository institutions use a combination of stored liquidity and liability management for their liquidity needs. Again, the more borrowing sources that an institution has and the better it can forecast its liquidity needs, the less stored liquidity it has to keep. Other ways of maintaining liquidity are securitization and loans sales, as discussed in Chapter 7.

Concept Questions

1 Why do depository institutions want to hold liquidity above reserve requirements?

2 What are some potential drains on an institution's liquidity?

3 What are some factors affecting the nature of an institution's liquidity management?

4 Why have FHLB advances become a popular source of borrowing?

5 What restrictions are there for borrowing at the Fed's discount window?

---

17 See McKenna, Conner, and Cuneo (1989), 49–50.

18 See Pearce (1984) and *NCUSIF Annual Report* (1991).

19 Institutions receiving deposits from the U.S. government and many state and municipal governments, such as tax deposits, are required to pledge collateral against deposits in excess of the $100,000 FDIC insurance ceiling, that is, invest deposits greater than $100,000 in only certain assets, such as U.S. government, state, or local securities that qualify as collateral. In addition, institutions serving as major dealers in money market assets must keep an inventory of trading account securities to make trades with customers.

Securitization of Loans and Loan Sales as Liquidity Sources

Depository institutions with institutional investor networks can sell loans for liquidity to long-term investors, such as pension funds and insurance companies. In addition to shortening their funding gaps by removing long-term fixed assets from the balance sheet and reducing credit risk if loans are sold without recourse, such loan sales provide a stream of liquidity that can be used to fund new loan demand or deposit withdrawals. Similarly, if loan securitization processes are set in place for a depository institution through a subsidiary or a correspondent bank, or for home mortgages through a government or quasi-government agency, the depository institution has a steady source of liquidity and fee income. In addition, if the depository institution removes loans from the balance sheet, it can use the funds received from securitization or loan sale to pay off deposits (i.e., shrink the size of the bank), reducing its deposits and, hence, its reserve requirements as a regulatory tax. With fewer assets, capital requirements, also as a regulatory tax, can be reduced.

Liquidity Risk of Other Financial Institutions

Although depository institutions have the largest liquidity risk of financial institutions, since deposits as liabilities have instantaneous maturities and can be withdrawn at any time, life insurance companies and other types of financial institutions have liquidity risks as well.

Insurance Companies

Although life insurance companies have long-term contracts and therefore have much lower liquidity risk than other financial institutions, they still have some liquidity risk when they have large investment losses, such as First Executive Life in 1990. Policyholders and annuity holders and investors in guaranteed investment contracts (GICs) have at times engaged in runs to cash in policies and investments to try to obtain what they could before a troubled institution's closure. Similarly, property/casualty insurance companies (P/Cs) must keep sufficient liquidity to make payouts for contingencies for damages to personal property or individuals. Since policy coverages are shorter-term than life insurance companies, P/Cs must keep a larger percentage of shorter-term assets. They are also exposed to the liquidity risk of policyholders canceling or not renewing policies, which reduces cash flow from incoming premiums, and to potential liquidity crises from catastrophic events, such as Hurricane Mitch in 1998.

Mutual Funds

Mutual funds are also subject to liquidity risk in the event of an investor panic in the expectation of a large market downturn. However, as Peter Fortune, a senior economist at the Federal Reserve of Boston, points out, research shows that even during the stock market crash of 1987, mutual fund outflows were relatively small compared with their liquidity on hand, and very few funds experienced problems. Such stability is often attributed to the relatively high-income profile of the median shareholder for mutual funds, with investments predominantly for retirement, suggesting a longer-term investment time horizon and some degree of sophistication.[20]

Open-end funds are obligated to buy back their shares in any quantity offered generally at the net asset value on the day the redemption is requested. As Fortune notes, "Thus, their shares are similar to demand deposits at financial institutions, redeemable at short notice although at a variable price."[21] To bridge the gap between the settlement period until liquidity can be replenished by selling securities, mutual funds typically hold cash-equivalent assets, such as cash and Treasury securities.

---

20 This section comes from Peter Fortune. "Mutual Funds, Part I: Reshaping the American Financial System." *Federal Reserve of Boston New England Economic Review* (July/August 1997), 1–72. According to a 1996 Investment Company Institute study, the median shareholder in a mutual fund had household income of $60,000 and held $50,000 in financial assets, with $18,000 in mutual funds. About 60 percent of shareholders had completed college and over 54 percent also held individual stocks. Over 60 percent of shareholders responding indicated that they invested for at least a six-year horizon, and 35 percent indicated a horizon of more than ten years.

21 Ibid, 64.

A number of factors have resulted in mutual funds holding lower liquidity ratios in the 1990s, falling to 5.5 percent cash equivalents to assets for equity and mixed bond/stock funds and 4 percent for bond funds at the end of 1996. These factors include a shorter settlement period (from five to three days for securities), which requires less cash to bridge the gap between redemptions and receipts from security sales; a larger average size of mutual funds, which provides economies of scale in cash balances; the availability of lines of credit with banks as a source of liquidity, which was not readily available prior to October 1987; and greater competitive pressures, which encourage fund managers to hold less liquidity to achieve higher fund returns.[22]

Other Financial Institutions

Finance companies, securities firms, and other types of financial institutions have liquidity concerns as well, since they are all highly financially levered institutions and rely on public confidence. Government security dealers, security traders, and investment bankers have to finance security inventories with short-term sources of financing such as repurchase agreements and other short-term borrowings, and thus are subject to great liquidity risk as well if securities are not sold quickly. Similarly, finance companies often finance loans with short-term borrowings and commercial paper, which must be paid back in less than a year. Better capitalized institutions and institutions with greater reputational capital are able to attract larger sources of short-term financing.

Depository Institution Investment Portfolio Management

The preceding sections have discussed different aspects of liquidity management for depository institutions, including reserve management, estimating liquidity needs, and alternative strategies for achieving liquidity through stored liquidity, securitization and loan sales, and short-term borrowing (liability management).

In contrast to other financial institutions that rely on portfolio management and other strategies taught in investment courses for investment management, depository institutions are subject to much greater regulation on the type of securities that they can hold; to pledging requirements (collateral that must be held in the form of government or other very safe securities for U.S. government and often state and municipal deposits greater than the $100,000 ceiling on deposit insurance); and to greater liquidity needs. Depository institutions are also subject to interest rate risk considerations. A depository, by its nature, often has a negative funding gap and must use its security portfolio to reduce that gap, since customer preferences may restrict an institution from shortening the duration on its loans, such as fixed rate home mortgage loans. The investment portfolio may also be used by depository institutions to reduce the institution's tax burden. As Hempel, Simonson, and Coleman state in their well-regarded text on bank management, bank managers have to establish general criteria and objectives for portfolios, including:[23]

- Providing liquidity, either through the maturing of securities or as stored liquidity;
- Providing income, particularly countercyclical income to keep funds fully employed;

Concept Questions

1 How can the securities portfolio be used as a source of stored liquidity? What are primary reserves and secondary reserves?

2 How can securitization of loans and loan sales provide a liquidity source?

3 What do insurance companies, mutual funds, and security companies need liquidity for?

---

22 Ibid, 64. For equity and mixed funds, the liquidity-to-asset ratio averaged about 10 percent during the mid to late 1980s, peaking in 1990 to 13 percent, and then dramatically falling to 5.5 percent at the end of 1996. Bond funds have typically had lower liquidity ratios, generally above 5 percent but declining to 4 percent by the end of 1996.

23 See George H. Hempel, Donald G. Simonson, and Alan B. Coleman. *Bank Management: Text and Cases*, 4th ed. New York: John Wiley & Sons, Inc., 1994.

- Satisfying pledging requirements;
- Reducing taxes through tax swaps or holding municipal securities; and
- Using the portfolio to make adjustments for the bank's asset and liability position, including the bank's overall capital and interest rate risk.

Types of Securities That Depository Institutions Can Hold

Regulatory Restrictions

Although during the 1980s permissive states allowed thrifts and, in some cases, banks that were state-chartered to hold risky securities, under the Federal Deposit Insurance Corporation Improvement Act (FDICIA) of 1991, state-chartered banks and thrifts were placed under the same rules as nationally chartered banks.

Banks are not generally allowed to hold equity securities in their investment portfolio. Consequently, their investments are predominantly fixed-income securities of different types. Regulators classify securities into three groups. The first class, or Type 1 securities, are securities that carry very low or no default risk. These include U.S. Treasuries, federal agency, and general obligation municipals that are backed by the taxing power of the state or municipal government that issues the bonds. Type 2 securities include quasi-public federal and municipal agency securities and selected state agencies associated with public projects, such as housing or universities, with the restriction that no more than 15 percent of a bank's capital plus surplus can be invested in any single issuer. Type 3 securities encompasse investment grade securities (BBB/Baa ratings or better), with no more than 10 percent of capital and surplus in any single issue invested in any single issue, and any issues underwritten or dealt in by a bank are disallowed. There are no specific restrictions on maturity, but as a rule of thumb, banks often do not like to hold securities with maturities greater than ten years, since they often have long-term loans, and long-term securities would increase their interest rate risk.[24]

Liquidity Restrictions

Since the investment portfolio is held partially for liquidity reasons, the liquidity portion of the portfolio needs to be identified. Different investment strategies are used to provide for liquidity and investment returns, including a matching cash flow, ladder of maturities, barbell strategy, and buffer portfolio strategy, which are discussed in the following sections.

Matching Cash Flows

One school of thought for protecting liquidity argues that a depository institution should carefully analyze its deposit structure and loan demand to forecast the timing and quantity of cash needs. Maturities of the investment portfolio should then be chosen to coincide with those forecasts. In other words, investments should mature, providing a cash inflow, at just the time an institution needs liquid funds. The relative proportion of primary, secondary, and tertiary sources of asset liquidity would be determined by cash flow forecasts. A problem with this policy is that forecasts contain errors, so there could still be a liquidity crisis.

Ladder of Maturities

An alternative investment strategy is the **ladder of maturities,** which spreads the maturity of securities held for liquidity purposes evenly throughout a given period. For example, suppose that a savings bank decided the maximum maturity of its tertiary reserves should be five years. In the ladder-of-maturities strategy, an equal proportion of the portfolio would mature during each planning period. Cash received at maturity would be reinvested in assets with a five-year term to maturity. One way of conceptualizing the ladder of maturities is as a conveyor belt. Assets move along the belt for five years

24 Ibid. See also Timothy W. Koch and S. Scott MacDonald. *Bank Management,* 4th ed. Fort Worth, Texas: Southwestern/Thomson, 2002, Chapter 19.

toward their maturity date; when they reach the end of the line (maturity), the funds are placed back at the beginning through reinvestment if they are not immediately needed for liquidity purposes.

Perhaps the most serious criticism of the ladder portfolio is that it does not attempt to optimize investment returns for the institution. It is a relatively passive approach to investment management; no real effort is made to distinguish between secondary and tertiary reserves. Consequently, the institution may forgo investments that could increase returns without also incurring unacceptable liquidity risks. But for institutions without personnel to manage the securities portfolio, it may be a viable strategy.

Barbell Strategy

An alternative to the ladder-of-maturities strategy is to invest funds at either end of the yield curve but not in the middle, a strategy called the **barbell** or **split-maturity** portfolio. This approach retains some very liquid assets as secondary reserves but (assuming an upward-sloping yield curve) allows a larger investment in higher-return, long-term securities. To manage a barbell portfolio efficiently, however, the institution must devote resources to interest rate forecasting, because the anticipated direction of rate movements plays an important role in the proportionate investments at either end of the yield curve.

For example, under expectations of falling rates, the portfolio manager would want to increase the investment at the long-term end of the portfolio. The manager would be locking in current high rates, and the market value of the securities would benefit from the declining rates if long-term tertiary reserves had to be liquidated. With the opposite interest rate scenario, more funds would be invested in short-term assets. Consequently, knowledge of interest rate theories, the bond theorems, and duration would play an integral role in the management of liquidity reserves.

Buffer Portfolio

A fourth alternative is the **buffer portfolio strategy,** under which most of the investment in securities is concentrated in the short-term end of the maturity schedule, allowing the portfolio to serve as a buffer against even the slightest risk of cash shortages. With this approach, most secondary reserves and even some tertiary reserves would be invested in short-maturity assets. The average maturity under this strategy is considerably lower than under either the ladder-of-maturities or barbell strategies.

Choosing a Strategy

The ladder-of-maturity, barbell, and buffer portfolio strategies are illustrated side by side in Figure 14.1 for a hypothetical $100 million securities portfolio. The choice of a strategy depends on the institution's risk and expected return objectives. Risk arises from several sources. The risk of illiquidity is obviously the primary concern. But exposure to interest rate risk under a ladder-of-maturities or buffer portfolio is quite different from that of the barbell. A ladder-of-maturities or buffer portfolio, with a regular reinvestment schedule, poses extreme exposure to reinvestment risk but little or no risk from fluctuations in market value, because securities are held to maturity. In the barbell portfolio, the exposure to market value risk could be severe, especially if the portfolio is heavily invested at the long end of the term structure. As interest rates change, returns could fluctuate significantly if it becomes necessary to liquidate securities. Yet, if managers correctly anticipate interest rate movements, adjusting portfolio maturities in advance of rate changes can allow them to take advantage of favorable price changes. Such regular monitoring of the portfolio and interest rate forecasts requires a larger commitment of resources. Smaller banks often receive investment advice from larger correspondent banks.[25]

---

25 An early discussion of the split-maturity portfolio (but called spaced maturity) is included in Robinson (1962), 370–375. Another good source on alternatives for managing liquidity through the investment portfolio is Watson (1972). The descriptions of the ladder-of-maturities and barbell portfolios also draw on Watson. A discussion geared to thrift managers is Tom Parliment. "Barbell Strategy Helps to Manage the Yield Curve." *Savings Institutions* 113 (May 1992), 38–39.

figure **14.1**   THE LADDER-OF-MATURITIES, BARBELL, AND BUFFER PORTFOLIO STRATEGIES

Depending on their risk/return objectives, depository institutions managers may choose either the ladder-of-maturities, barbell, or buffer portfolio strategies as part of liquidity management. The figure shows how a $100 million portfolio might be allocated across maturities under the three strategies.

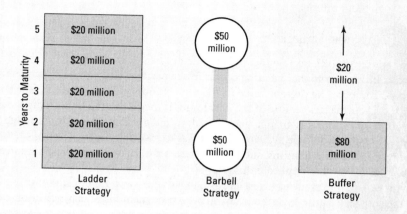

Real-World Considerations in Investment Strategies

Depository institutions face a number of real-world considerations in their investment strategies that other financial institutions do not. Depository institutions are in the business of making loans, which generally offer higher returns than securities. Consequently, a bank's loan policies restrict its investment strategies.

Limitations on Investment Maturity Strategies for Banks

During expansions, banks' security portfolios shrink and loan portfolios expand as investments are sold to meet expanding loan demand. Similarly, during recessions with lower loan demand, the investment portfolio expands as banks have more liquid funds available to invest in securities to attempt to generate countercyclical income. Typically, during the beginning of an expansion (ending of a recession) the yield curve is upward-sloping, suggesting under the expectations theory that rates are expected to rise. Ideally, under a barbell-type maturity strategy, banks would hold a larger percentage of short-term securities that could be reinvested at higher rates when loan demand picks up and interest rates rise. However, bank investment managers during such a time period may be pressured to invest in longer-term securities that offer higher yields to make up for low profitability at the end of a recession.

Similarly, at the peak of an expansion (beginning of a recession) a downward yield curve often appears, indicating that investors expect rates to fall. Ideally, an investment manager following a barbell strategy would lock in high yield by purchasing long-term bonds. However, at this time the bank will be likely loaned up, with little cash available to purchase securities. Hence, maturity strategies may not be able to be optimally implemented for many banks.[26]

---

26 See Notes 23 and 24.

Limitations on Diversification of the Investment Portfolio for Banks

Similarly, a bank investment manager may desire greater geographical diversification for the bank's portfolio, such as by purchasing municipal securities from different areas of the country. Real-world considerations may, however, limit this decision as well. For the sake of community relations, a bank may feel obligated to support its municipality or community by purchasing local municipal bonds. Also, a bank investment manager may have better knowledge of the quality of bonds within its own area versus out-of-state munies.

Limitations on Tax Swap Strategies

Strategies to reduce a bank's taxable income include tax swaps, whereby a bank sells a bond that has a loss and invests in another higher yielding bond. To see whether this would be a viable strategy, a bank manager would compare the present value of the higher coupon income of the new bond to the present value of the lower maturity value of the new bond. If the rise in the total change in present value of the coupons of the new bond is greater than the fall in the present value of the change in the maturity value (since less money would be available after losses to invest in the new bond), then this would be a viable strategy. Other considerations, such as a difference in maturity or credit risk for the new bond versus the old bond, would complicate this analysis.

In reality, a bank may hesitate to take a loss and make a tax swap that would improve the bank's profitability in the future, because investors may misinterpret such a loss as a reflection of poor management. Similarly, the bank may not have a sufficient capital cushion to absorb the losses involved with a large tax swap.

A bank may also have a strategy to reduce taxable income by investing in municipal securities, the income for which is not taxed at the federal level. Additionally, some states do not tax the income generated by state-issued municipal securities in the issuing state. Considerations include a stipulation in the Tax Reform Act of 1986 that does not allow banks to deduct the interest cost of funds raised to purchase munies. Interest rate and default risk also must be considered. Most municipals are long-term and expose an institution to considerable interest rate risk. Furthermore, there is the risk of a bond rating downgrade by rating agencies that would reduce the market value of munies. For instance, Moody's bond rating service reduced the credit ratings of more issues between 1978 and 1983 than it increased, and fear of greater default risk on municipals has discouraged investment at times.[27]

Investment Accounting Rule Restrictions

Investment accounting rules require banks to clearly distinguish between "investment" securities, presumably to be held until maturity, and "securities available for sale," which are held to earn potential profits if their prices increase. Investment securities can be shown on the balance sheet at historical cost, but securities held for sale are supposed to be shown at the lower of cost or market value. This classification somewhat reduces managers' ability to respond intelligently and prudently to changing market conditions in terms of tax or other types of swaps for securities that are classified as "held to maturity."[28]

The requirements of liquidity, regulations, and real-world considerations make depository institution investment management a challenge. However, the development of new types of securities, such as mortgage-backed securities (MBSs) and collateralized mortgage obligations (CMOs), among others, allow depository institutions a wide choice of securities. The following section provides a brief description of the average commercial bank's investment portfolio as of the end of the third quarter of 2003.

---

27 These trends are discussed in Rodrigues (1993). See also Steven Lipin. "Are Banks Playing a Dangerous Game?" *The Wall Street Journal* (June 30, 1992), C1, C9; and Fred R. Bleakley. "Banks Turn to Government Securities in Basic Reassessment of Profitability." *The Wall Street Journal* (October 1, 1991), A2.

28 Tom Parliment. "Overall, TB 52 Is a Welcome Tool for Portfolio Managers." *Savings Institutions* 113 (April 1992), 38–39; Lee Berton. "SEC Pushes Market-Value Accounting on Banks Reaping Big Investment Gains." *The Wall Street Journal* (April 29, 1992), A2, A3; Martha Brannigan. "NationsBank Is Reclassifying Part of Portfolio." *The Wall Street Journal* (June 9, 1992), A2; Lee Berton. "Accounting Body Backs Modified Rules on the Valuation of Securities by Banks." *The Wall Street Journal* (July 16, 1992), A2, A6; David Siegel. "FASB Votes to Adopt Mark-to-Market Rule." *American Banker* (April 14, 1993), 1, 20.

1 What are some general criteria and objectives for managing a bank's security portfolio?

2 What types of securities can banks hold?

3 What is the difference between a ladder-of-maturities and a barbell maturity strategy? Which has the highest potential risk and return? How can a hybrid strategy be used to gain advantages of both strategies?

4 Optimally, how would a bank adjust security strategies over the business cycle? What real-world considerations prevent such an optimal strategy?

5 What is a tax swap strategy? What are some limitations on tax strategies?

6 What is the accounting difference for investment securities held to maturity versus held for sale?

The Typical Bank Investment Portfolio

Table 14.2 shows the different types of securities held by the average commercial bank at the end of the third quarter of 2003. Securities represented 18.63 percent of total assets for all insured U.S. commercial banks, with larger holdings (almost 24 percent) of assets for banks with less than $1 billion in assets. For larger banks, the percentage of securities held was almost 18 percent. In 2003, for all insured banks the largest holdings were U.S. government securities (12.98 percent of assets), with larger holdings again by banks with less than $1 billion in assets. Of these U.S. government securities, the majority were U.S. government obligations, rather than Treasury securities. Of the 12.05 percent of U.S. government obligations as a percentage of assets, the majority, as noted in the memoranda at the bottom of the table, 9.96 percent were mortgage-backed securities including certificates of participation in pools of residential mortgages and collateralized mortgage obligations (CMOs) issued privately or by Fannie Mae or Freddie Mac. There are a small percentage of equity securities (0.21 percent). This reflects special cases as normally commercial banks are not allowed to hold equity investments.

Looking more closely at the memoranda at the bottom of Table 14.2, on average 1.36 percent of the total 18.63 percent of securities held as a percentage of total assets were listed as held to maturity (listed at book value), with a majority of 17.27 percent held for sale at fair market value. The largest banks have more assets in trading accounts.

Table 14.2, Panel C shows the percentage of securities by different maturity classes. For the mortgage pass-through securities, the maturities are quite varied. Many of these mortgage-backed securities actually have lower durations than stated with prepayments that can occur if interest rates fall. For other debt securities, the majority are less than five years, with only 2.01 percent between five to fifteen years in maturity and only 0.67 percent over fifteen years. The largest banks, on average, hold a larger percentage of their mortgage-backed securities in the over-five-year range than the medium-sized banks do.

The Typical Thrift Investment Portfolio

Table 14.3 shows a similar set of data for the security portfolio of savings institutions (savings and loans and mutual savings banks). Like commercial banks, savings institutions hold the majority of their assets in agency securities that are dominantly MBSs. In fact, for all savings institutions, the majority of the 21.04% of securities held as a percentage of total assets are held in mortgage-backed securities. Thrifts held 5.38 percent of assets in CMOs (these are discussed in the following section). The largest thrifts (those with assets greater than $1 billion) held 6.02 percent in CMOs compared with 1.79 percent for savings institutions with total assets less than $100 million and 2.72 percent for savings institutions with assets between $100 million to $1 billion. U.S. Treasuries and municipals are a very small part of the average thrift's investment portfolio. Under the FDICIA, thrifts can have no more than 35 percent of their assets invested in bonds, commercial paper, and consumer loans. Also, the average maturity of the bond portfolio is limited.

Credit Union Investment Portfolios

Federal CUs can invest in Treasury and agency securities, insured accounts at other depositories, and Eurodollar deposits and banker's acceptances without restriction. They can also invest in municipal

FDIC STATISTICS ON DEPOSITORY INSTITUTIONS REPORT: SECURITIES OF FDIC-INSURED COMMERCIAL BANKS ($ MILLIONS)

table **14.2**

PANEL A: CASH AND BALANCES DUE REPORT, SEPTEMBER 30, 2003

Percent of Assets	All Commercial Banks Column 1	Assets < $100 mil. Column 2	Assets $100 mil. to $1 bil. Column 3	Assets > $1 bil. Column 4
1 Number of institutions reporting	7812	3985	3404	423
2 Cash and due from depository institutions	5.10%	5.96%	4.47%	5.16%
By balance type:				
3 Cash items in process of collection	2.10%	0.02%	0.80%	2.35%
4 Collection in domestic offices	1.63%	0.01%	0.46%	1.84%
5 Currency and coin in domestic offices	0.44%	0.00%	0.34%	0.47%
6 Balances due from depository institutions in the U.S.	0.73%	0.04%	0.85%	0.74%
7 U.S. branches of foreign banks	0.08%	0.01%	0.01%	0.09%
8 Balances due from foreign banks	1.49%	0.01%	0.08%	1.74%
9 Foreign branches of U.S. banks	0.37%	0.00%	0.04%	0.43%
10 Balances due from FRB	0.33%	0.00%	0.36%	0.34%
Memoranda:				
11 Total noninterest-bearing balances	3.36%	4.14%	3.51%	3.31%

Percent of Assets	Column 1	Column 2	Column 3	Column 4
1 Number of institutions reporting	7812	3985	3404	423
2 Securities	18.63%	24.37%	23.20%	17.80%
3 U.S. government securities	12.98%	18.41%	17.00%	12.23%
4 U.S. Treasury securities	0.93%	1.17%	0.90%	0.93%
5 U.S. government obligations	12.05%	17.24%	16.10%	11.30%
6 Securities issued by states & political subdivisions	1.47%	4.66%	4.44%	0.95%
7 Asset-backed securities	1.28%	0.02%	0.09%	1.49%
8 Other domestic debt securities	1.80%	0.98%	1.32%	1.90%
9 Foreign debt securities	0.90%	0.00%	0.02%	1.05%
10 Equity securities	0.21%	0.31%	0.33%	0.19%
11 Less: Assets held in trading accounts for TFR Reporters	0.00%	0.00%	0.00%	0.00%
12 Less: General valuation allowances for securities for TFR Reporters	N/A	N/A	N/A	N/A
Memoranda:				
13 Pledged securities	9.35%	8.27%	9.67%	9.34%
14 Mortgage-backed securities	9.96%	5.71%	8.20%	10.35%
15 Certificates of participation in pools of residential mortgages	6.60%	4.29%	5.49%	6.83%
16 Issued or guaranteed by U.S.	6.50%	4.28%	5.48%	6.72%
17 Privately issued	0.10%	0.01%	0.01%	0.12%
18 Collateralized mortgage obligations (CMOs)	3.36%	1.41%	2.71%	3.52%
19 Issued by FNMA or FHLMC (includes REMICs)	2.17%	1.33%	2.43%	2.16%
20 Privately issued	1.19%	0.09%	0.28%	1.36%
21 Held to maturity (book value)	1.36%	4.26%	3.15%	1.01%
22 Available for sale (fair market value)	17.27%	20.12%	20.05%	16.78%
23 Total debt securities	18.41%	24.07%	22.86%	17.59%
24 Amortized cost	0.18%	0.94%	0.72%	0.08%
25 Fair value	0.18%	0.93%	0.72%	0.08%
26 Assets held in trading accounts	5.51%	0.00%	0.01%	6.48%
27 Re-valuation gains on off-balance-sheet contracts	2.62%	0.00%	0.00%	3.08%
28 Re-valuation losses on off-balance-sheet contracts	2.23%	0.00%	0.00%	2.63%

Note: Savings institutions regulated by the Office of Thrift Supervision (OTS) file a Thrift Financial Report (TFR). TFRs are quarterly reports of condition and income and are filed with the OTS as of the close of businesss on the last calendar day of each calendar quarter. Some reporting requirements are different from those of the FFIEC call reports.

table **14.2** FDIC STATISTICS ON DEPOSITORY INSTITUTIONS REPORT: SECURITIES OF FDIC-INSURED COMMERCIAL BANKS ($ MILLIONS) (CONTINUED)

PANEL B: U.S. GOVERNMENT OBLIGATIONS, SEPTEMBER 30, 2003

	Percent of Assets	All Commercial Banks Column 1	Assets < $100 mil. Column 2	Assets $100 mil. to $1 bil. Column 3	Assets > $1 bil. Column 4
1	Number of institutions reporting	7812	3985	3404	423
2	U.S. government obligations	12.05%	17.24%	16.10%	11.30%
	Nonmortgage-backed:				
3	Issued by U.S. government agencies	0.13%	0.18%	0.14%	0.13%
4	Issued by U.S. government enterprises (GSEs)	3.24%	11.45%	8.04%	2.30%
	Mortgage-backed:				
	Pass-throughs:				
5	Issued by FNMA and FHLMC	5.51%	3.42%	4.50%	5.72%
6	Issued by GNMA	0.99%	0.86%	0.98%	0.99%
	Collateralized mortgage obligations (CMOs) and REMICS:				
7	Issued by FNMA, FHLMC, and GNMA	2.17%	1.33%	2.43%	2.16%

PANEL C: MATURITIES OF DEBT SECURITIES, SEPTEMBER 30, 2003

	Percent of Assets	Column 1	Column 2	Column 3	Column 4
1	Number of institutions reporting	7812	3985	3404	423
2	Total debt securities	18.41%	24.07%	22.86%	17.59%
	Maturity and repricing data for debt securities:				
	Mortgage pass-throughs backed by closed-end first lien 1-4 residential mortgages:				
3	Three months or less	0.28%	0.34%	0.36%	0.27%
4	Over three months through twelve months	0.13%	0.32%	0.34%	0.09%
5	Over one year through three years	0.11%	0.19%	0.21%	0.10%
6	Over three years through five years	0.26%	0.71%	0.67%	0.19%
7	Over five years through fifteen years	2.12%	1.93%	2.60%	2.06%
8	Over fifteen years	3.64%	0.76%	1.25%	4.07%
	CMOs, REMICs, and stripped MBSs (excluding mortgage pass-throughs) with an expected average life of:				
9	Three years or less	1.41%	0.87%	1.73%	1.38%
10	Over three years	1.96%	0.54%	0.98%	2.14%
	Other debt securities:				
11	Three months or less	1.19%	1.27%	1.19%	1.18%
12	Over three months through twelve months	1.00%	2.08%	1.47%	0.90%
13	Over one year through three years	2.07%	4.95%	3.60%	1.76%
14	Over three years through five years	1.56%	4.14%	3.07%	1.26%
15	Over five years through fifteen years	2.01%	5.53%	4.61%	1.52%
16	Over fifteen years	0.67%	0.43%	0.79%	0.66%
	Fixed and floating-rate debt securities (included above):				
17	With remaining maturity of one year or less	1.50%	2.95%	2.34%	1.33%

Source: FDIC Bank Statistics 2003, http://www2.fdic.gov.

securities, up to 10 percent of capital plus surplus. Beyond this, federal CUs may invest only in securities of organizations providing services associated with the routine operations of CUs, up to 1 percent of capital plus surplus. In 1991, further restrictions were placed on CUs when they were prohibited from holding several types of complex MBSs. Hence, CUs hold the majority of their investments, beyond

table **14.3**

FDIC STATISTICS ON S&LS AND SAVINGS BANK INSTITUTIONS REPORT:
SECURITIES OF FDIC-INSURED SAVINGS INSTITUTIONS

PANEL A: CASH AND BALANCES DUE, SEPTEMBER 30, 2003

Percent of Assets	All Savings Institutions Column 1	Assets < $100 mil. Column 2	Assets $100 mil. to $1 bil. Column 3	Assets > $1 bil. Column 4
1 Number of institutions reporting	1425	480	786	159
2 Cash and due from depository institutions	2.97%	10.25%	5.40%	2.31%
By balance type:				
3 Cash items in process of collection	1.55%	1.44%	1.28%	1.61%
4 Collection in domestic offices	0.12%	N/A	0.17%	0.11%
5 Currency and coin in domestic offices	0.08%	N/A	0.12%	0.08%
6 Balances due from depository institutions in the U.S.	0.44%	1.58%	1.00%	0.30%
7 U.S. branches of foreign banks	0.00%	N/A	0.02%	0.00%
8 Balances due from foreign banks	0.00%	N/A	0.00%	0.00%
9 Foreign branches of U.S. banks	0.00%	N/A	0.00%	0.00%
10 Balances due from FRB	0.10%	N/A	0.18%	0.08%
Memoranda:				
11 Total noninterest-bearing balances	1.80%	1.98%	1.90%	1.77%

PANEL B: PERCENTAGE SECURITY HOLDINGS, SEPTEMBER 30, 2003

Percent of Assets	Column 1	Column 2	Column 3	Column 4
1 Number of institutions reporting	1425	480	786	159
2 Securities	21.04%	21.37%	26.70%	19.84%
3 U.S. government securities	17.31%	16.08%	20.42%	16.68%
4 U.S. Treasury securities	0.18%	0.13%	0.34%	0.15%
5 U.S. government obligations	17.13%	15.95%	20.07%	16.53%
6 Securities issued by states & political subdivisions	0.45%	0.89%	1.04%	0.32%
7 Asset-backed securities	0.05%	0.01%	0.02%	0.05%
8 Other domestic debt securities	2.54%	1.56%	3.03%	2.45%
9 Foreign debt securities	0.00%	0.00%	0.01%	0.00%
10 Equity securities	0.79%	2.86%	2.21%	0.45%
11 Less: Assets held in trading accounts for TFR Reporters	0.09%	0.02%	0.02%	0.11%
12 Less: General valuation allowances for securities for TFR Reporters	0.00%	0.00%	0.00%	0.00%
Memoranda:				
13 Pledged securities	2.20%	0.33%	1.47%	2.39%
14 Mortgage-backed securities	13.83%	9.96%	13.31%	14.02%
15 Certificates of participation in pools of residential mortgages	8.45%	8.17%	10.59%	8.00%
16 Issued or guaranteed by U.S.	7.77%	8.06%	10.41%	7.21%
17 Privately issued	0.68%	0.12%	0.18%	0.79%
18 Collateralized mortgage obligations (CMOs)	5.38%	1.79%	2.72%	6.02%
19 Issued by FNMA or FHLMC (includes REMICs)	4.82%	1.75%	2.45%	5.39%
20 Privately issued	0.56%	0.04%	0.27%	0.63%
21 Held to maturity (book value)	4.62%	8.27%	7.42%	3.96%
22 Available for sale (fair market value)	16.42%	13.10%	19.29%	15.89%
23 Total debt securities	20.35%	18.53%	24.51%	19.51%
24 Amortized cost	0.08%	0.11%	0.23%	0.05%
25 Fair value	0.08%	0.11%	0.23%	0.05%
26 Assets held in trading accounts	0.10%	0.02%	0.02%	0.12%
27 Re-valuation gains on off-balance-sheet contracts	0.00%	0.00%	0.00%	0.00%
28 Re-valuation losses on off-balance-sheet contracts	0.00%	0.00%	0.00%	0.00%

table **14.3** FDIC STATISTICS ON S&LS AND SAVINGS BANK INSTITUTIONS REPORT
SECURITIES OF FDIC-INSURED SAVINGS INSTITUTIONS (CONTINUED)

PANEL C: TOTAL DEBT SECURITIES, SEPTEMBER 30, 2003

Percent of Assets	Column 1	Column 2	Column 3	Column 4
1 Number of institutions reporting	1425	480	786	159
2 U.S. government obligations	17.13%	15.95%	0.07%	16.53%
Nonmortgage-backed:				
3 Issued by U.S. government agencies	0.01%	0.02%	0.04%	0.00%
4 Issued by U.S. government enterprises (GSEs)	1.49%	1.57%	3.96%	0.97%
Mortgage-backed:				
Pass-throughs:				
5 Issued by FNMA and FHLMC	1.76%	1.17%	3.62%	1.38%
6 Issued by GNMA	0.47%	0.43%	0.61%	0.44%
Collateralized mortgage obligations (CMOs) and REMICS:				
7 Issued by FNMA, FHLMC, and GNMA	4.82%	1.75%	2.45%	5.39%

PANEL D: MATURITIES OF DEBT SECURITIES, SEPTEMBER 30, 2003

Percent of Assets	Column 1	Column 2	Column 3	Column 4
1 Number of institutions reporting	1425	480	786	159
2 Total debt securities	20.35%	18.53%	24.51%	19.51%
Maturity and repricing data for debt securities:				
Mortgage pass-throughs backed by closed-end first lien 1-4 residential mortgages:				
3 Three months or less	0.21%	0.25%	0.36%	0.18%
4 Over three months through twelve months	0.28%	0.31%	0.39%	0.26%
5 Over one year through three years	0.08%	0.10%	0.25%	0.04%
6 Over three years through five years	0.16%	0.18%	0.50%	0.09%
7 Over five years through fifteen years	0.78%	0.45%	1.85%	0.56%
8 Over fifteen years	0.78%	0.31%	0.88%	0.76%
CMOs, REMICs, and stripped MBSs (excluding mortgage pass-throughs) with an expected average life of:				
9 Three years or less	1.02%	0.18%	0.61%	1.12%
10 Over three years	1.28%	0.31%	0.58%	1.44%
Other debt securities:				
11 Three months or less	0.43%	0.13%	0.47%	0.43%
12 Over three months through twelve months	0.31%	0.27%	0.84%	0.20%
13 Over one year through three years	0.56%	0.70%	1.94%	0.26%
14 Over three years through five years	0.45%	0.45%	1.56%	0.21%
15 Over five years through fifteen years	0.78%	0.86%	1.67%	0.59%
16 Over fifteen years	0.24%	0.08%	0.31%	0.23%
Fixed and floating-rate debt securities (included above):				
17 With remaining maturity of one year or less	0.52%	0.40%	1.17%	0.38%

Source: FDIC Savings Institutions Statistics, 2003, http://www2.fdic.gov.

cash and deposits and Fed Funds and Repos (representing 58 percent of their cash and securities portfolio), in Treasury Issues (17.9 percent) and Federal Agency Issues (23.3 percent).[29]

Since agency securities and in particular mortgage-backed agency securities were the predominant investment for depository institutions in the 1990s, they are discussed in greater detail in the following section, including peculiar characteristics that financial institution managers should be aware of.

---

29 See the Federal Credit Union Act (1983), 5–6; and National Credit Union Administration *Annual Reports* (1984 and 1991). These averages are based on 1992, but have been similar in recent years.

Agency Securities and Mortgage-Backed Securities

As shown in Tables 14.2 and 14.3, the largest holdings by banks and thrifts were predominantly mortgage-backed agency securities. There are a number of different federal agencies to achieve different purposes. These agencies are backed by the U.S. government with the primary purpose of reducing the cost and increasing the accessibility of funds to particular sectors. They are funded by the Treasury and can borrow from the Federal Financing Bank, a subdivision of the Treasury. Many of these federal agencies were later privatized and became quasi-public agencies or so-called government-sponsored agencies. Although government-sponsored agencies are owned by private investors, most investors implicitly assume that these agencies will be bailed out by the U.S. government if they get into trouble. Consequently, they generally have a lower cost of funds than other private firms. The Government National Mortgage Association (GNMA, or Ginnie Mae) is a federal government agency owned by the U.S. government, as are the Federal Housing Administration (FHA) and the Export-Import Bank. The Federal National Mortgage Association (FNMA, or Fannie Mae), and the Federal Home Loan Mortgage Corporation (FHLMC, or Freddie Mac) are privately owned, government-sponsored agencies.

GNMA, FNMA, and the FHLMC are active in the mortgage securities market. GNMA does not create mortgage securities, but since 1968 it has sponsored MBS programs instituted by banks, thrifts, and mortgage banks and provides guarantees to investors for the timely pass-through of interest and principal payments for these securities. GNMA, however, only backs mortgage loans that have their credit risk insured by any one of three government agencies, the Federal Housing Administration (FHA), the Veterans Administration (VA), or the Farmers Home Administration (FmHA), which target low-income borrowers and veterans. Maximum mortgage amounts for loans to be included in GNMA securitizations are capped, although these caps are frequently raised to adjust for higher home prices.[30]

The FNMA, created in 1938, is now a stock-owned, publicly traded firm. In contrast to GNMA, FNMA creates pass-through securities itself by purchasing conventional mortgages, as well as FHA/VA loans from banks and thrifts. Conventional loans must have 80 percent collateralization ratios (i.e., 20 percent down payments for new loans). Otherwise, they must have private credit insurance. Such purchases are financed by selling MBSs created from these mortgages to investors, including large institutional investors such as insurers, pension funds, banks, thrifts, CUs, and mutual funds that desire MBSs. Like GNMA, FNMA provides guarantees for the timely payment of interest and principal on these bonds. These guarantees make these securities very marketable in the capital markets. Although FHLMC, originally owned by the Federal Home Loan Mortgage Corporation, is now a publicly traded quasi-government agency, Congress still selects a portion of FHLMC's Board of Directors. FHLMC, like FNMA, purchases conventional and insured mortgages from financial institutions and creates MBSs. Both the FHLMC and FNMA also swap MBSs for mortgage loans with financial institutions as well. This enables institutions to have greater liquidity and geographic diversification in their asset portfolios.

Mortgage-Backed Security Securitization Process

The mechanics of the loan securitization process described in an earlier chapter is similar to the process of creating mortgage securities, illustrated in Figure 14.2. GNMA, FNMA, and FHLMC provide guarantees, in place of a private credit enhancer, shown in a credit card receivables or automobile loan securitization. A custodian is designated to maintain mortgage documentation, and a mortgage servicer (which could be the selling bank in a GNMA securitization, for instance, or another financial institution) receives payments of principal and interest from borrowers. After deducting a servicing fee, the mortgage servicer passes on these payments to the investors owning the MBSs.

Different Types of Mortgage-Backed Securities

MBSs include **mortgage-backed bonds, certificates of participation in pools of residential mortgages** (either issued or guaranteed by the U.S. government or privately issued), and **CMOs.** Mortgage-backed bonds are simply bonds collateralized by mortgages on a financial institution's balance sheet and thus are not securitizations. Banks, for instance, can offer bonds with a lower coupon rate because

---

30 See Note 24. See also Anthony Saunders. *Financial Institutions Management: A Modern Perspective,*. 2nd ed. Chicago: Irwin, 1997; Frank J. Fabozzi. *Bond Markets, Analysis and Strategies,* 2nd ed. Englewood Cliffs, NJ: Prentice Hall, 1993; Clifford E. Kirsch, ed. *The Financial Services Revolution.* Chicago: Irwin Professional Publishing, 1997; and David S. Kidwell, Richard L. Peterson, and David W. Blackwell. *Financial Institutions, Markets, and Money,* 6th ed. Fort Worth, Texas: Dryden Press, 1997.

figure **14.2**   STRUCTURE OF SECURITIZING MORTGAGE LOANS

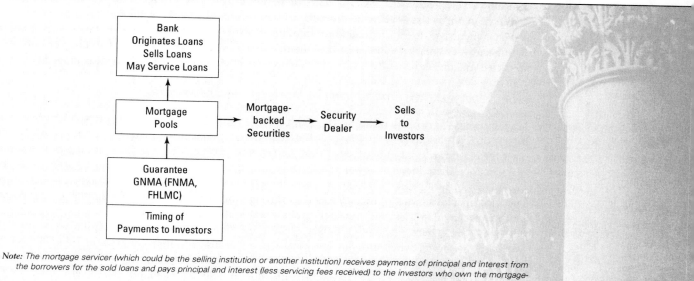

Note: The mortgage servicer (which could be the selling institution or another institution) receives payments of principal and interest from the borrowers for the sold loans and pays principal and interest (less servicing fees received) to the investors who own the mortgage-backed securities.

they are collateralized by specific mortgage assets on the bank's balance sheet. This arrangement provides investors with a primary claim on these assets if the institution goes under.

Mortgage pass-through securities or certificates of participation in pools of residential mortgages, in contrast, are securitizations (as described in the following section) whereby shares in the interest and principal payment on a pool of mortgages are passed on to investors who purchase these securities.

CMOs, like stripped securities, are securities created from mortgage pass-through securities designed to have more favorable characteristics than the pass-throughs, or they can simply be pass-throughs originally packaged into several classes (tranches) of securities with different characteristics for each tranche appealing to different types of investors. The FHLMC introduced CMOs in 1983. Under the Tax Reform Act of 1986, the IRS removed regulations that previously imposed irksome costs on the issuers and investors in CMOs, resulting in rapid growth for CMOs. An issuer of CMOs takes a pool of mortgages and converts them into different maturities: When mortgage holders prepay their mortgages in a pool of mortgages, investors holding the first class (or A-class or tranche) of bonds are repaid their principal payments first. B-class investors would be paid off next, then C-class, and so on. Consequently, A-class investors have mortgage securities with the lowest expected maturity, B-class the next, and later classes, the highest maturities. In this way, investors have less prepayment uncertainty than they would with an ordinary pass-through security. Also, investors have a better estimate in terms of the likely maturity and yield that should be offered on a particular type of CMO relative to a similar maturity Treasury security that has no prepayment risk.

Different Types of CMOs

A plain vanilla CMO may have four tranches, A, B, C, and Z, with A receiving prepayments first and having the shortest maturity, then B and C. Class Z, in contrast to A, B, and C, which receive interest payments, receives no periodic interest until the other three tranches are retired. At that time, the cash flow payments from the remaining underlying collateral (remaining mortgage pool) are utilized to pay principal plus accrued interest to investors with Z-bonds (often called accrual bonds). Hence, Z-bonds are like zero-coupon bonds that receive principal and interest, but at some unknown approximate maturity date. Z-tranches have the most interest rate risk.

A **planned amortization class (PAC)** bond is a CMO that has lower risk by having a fixed amortization schedule, so investors can better predict when a particular tranche of bonds will mature. If actual prepayment rates differ from the expected prepayment rates, principal payments to designated tranches are reduced or increased to ensure that PAC CMOs mature as scheduled.

Stripped mortgage-backed securities separate securities into classes of interest only (IO) paying securities and principal only (PO) paying securities. With prepayment risk, POs and IOs are very interest rate sensitive. If interest rates decline significantly, IOs decline in value, since the maturity of the security is shortened with prepayments, indicating fewer interest payments for the investor. In turn, if rates rise significantly, then prepayment risk will decrease significantly, and the value of the IO will rise because the expected maturity rises. When interest rates fall significantly, the market value for POs rises since the principal payments are discounted at a lower rate and are expected to come in sooner. When interest rates rise significantly, PO market value falls since the principal payments are discounted at a higher rate and are expected to come in later. Thus, IOs and POs are very risky, and regulators have discouraged their use.[31]

The Prepayment Risk and Pricing of Mortgage-Backed Securities

As mentioned previously in connection with CMOs, MBSs have considerable prepayment risk, particularly during periods of falling rates. When interest rates fall approximately 2 percent below the average mortgage rate on a pool of securities, prepayments rise for that pool as mortgage borrowers rush to refinance their loans at lower rates. Consequently, holders of pass-through mortgage securities receive a return of principal at a time when interest rates are low, and they must reinvest this return of principal at a lower rate. In this sense, a pass-through mortgage security is like a callable bond. Because of their prepayment risk, pass-through MBSs often demonstrate negative convexity, with smaller capital gains than other conventional bonds when interest rates fall, but smaller capital losses than other conventional bonds when interest rates rise. This is because although the present value of cash flows rises for MBSs when interest rates fall, their prepayment risk rises, shortening their expected duration. Similarly, when interest rates rise, the present value of cash flows fall, but the lower prepayment risk lengthens their expected duration.

Pricing Prepayment Risk

Investors in pass-through securities demand a higher coupon rate for their prepayment risk. Different factors affect how much prepayment risk a pass-through mortgage security has, including the coupon rate relative to current mortgage coupon rates, the age of the mortgage pool, the region where mortgages are originated, whether a mortgage is assumable, and the demographic characteristics of the borrowers in the pool of mortgages, among many other factors. Several models have been developed to estimate the prepayment risk of specific mortgage security pools, including the Public Securities Association model, which estimates the average prepayment risk of a pool based on the experience of previous FHA-insured mortgage pools. Accordingly, mortgage securities are priced relative to similar Treasury securities based on their prepayment risk.[32]

Investments in Mutual Funds

Table 14.2 shows a small amount of investment in mutual funds by commercial banks. Regulators have permitted banks to own mutual funds for securities that they are allowed to hold, including U.S. government and agency bonds, investment grade bonds, and MBSs. Banks are limited to holding mutual fund assets of up to 10 percent of a bank's capital and surplus. Shares must be marked to market, which has discouraged banks from investing in mutual funds despite the diversification benefits that they could reap.[33]

Decline in Investments in Government Securities

As shown in Tables 14.2 and 14.3, banks and thrifts hold a very small percentage of municipal securities today, since they no longer can deduct their interest expense for funds borrowed to purchase municipals, making municipals an unattractive investment. Other real-world considerations that have made municipals less attractive were discussed in an earlier section. U.S. Treasuries are invested in, predominantly for liquidity purposes, although as default-free securities they offer lower yields than other securities. With competition, higher liability costs, and, hence, narrower NIMs, banks have moved away from Treasury securities, which previously dominated their investment portfolios, into other types of securities, such as MBSs, which offer higher yields.

---

31 See sources cited in Note 30. For a detailed discussion of other types of CMOs, see Fabozzi (1993), as cited in Note 30.

32 See sources in Note 30.

33 See Andrew Kuritzkes. "Transforming Portfolio Management." *Banking Strategies* (July/August 1998), 57–60.

Other Changes in Bank Investment Portfolio Management

Larger banks have become much more sophisticated in their asset management, including derivatives among their investments, with swaps to protect against changes in interest rates and the yield curve to lock in spreads between asset returns and liability costs. They have also responded to the need for improved portfolio diversification, realizing that improved diversification can lower their requirements for economic capital by up to 25 percent. With increasing liquidity for banks as the result of loan sales and securitization, large banks have expanded investments in high quality, large corporate debt. As pointed out in an article in *Bank Management,* "the takeoff of credit derivatives is creating new possibilities for risk transformation through innovative structures such as credit-linked notes, default swaps and collateralized loan obligations. One example of the latter is JP Morgan's 'Bistro' deal, in which the bank essentially paid investors to assume the default risk on a $9.7 billion pool of large corporate credits."[34]

The article also points out that an important consequence of the rise in market liquidity for banks is a "convergence of traditional fixed income and corporate lending activities," whereby banks are coming to view loans and bonds as complementary products in the same asset class; and credit, bond, and derivative exposures to the same borrowers can be managed as a single portfolio. Derivatives, in turn, are being used as means for transforming credit risk, and larger banks have switched to active portfolio management models to adjust their interest rate and credit risks across their entire asset portfolio of loans and securities.[35]

Basel Committee Publication on Sound Practices for Managing Liquidity in Banking Organizations

In February of 2000, the Basel Committee published guidelines for sound practices in liquidity management *(http://www.bis.org/publ/bcbs69.htm)* in Basel Committee Publications No. 69 (February 2000) with a framework of fourteen principles including developing an overall structure for managing liquidity, measuring and monitoring net funding requirements, managing access to markets for borrowing, contingency planning, foreign currency liquidity management, internal controls, public disclosure to improve liquidity, and the role of supervisors. The guidelines go into great depth but generally support an overall strategic framework and internal controls for banking organizations in managing liquidity. With such a framework, expected and unexpected liquidity needs can be anticipated and planned for, as well as adequate systems of internal controls for a bank's risk management process to ensure that a bank has an ongoing process for measuring and monitoring its net funding requirements. By calculating net funding needs on a day-to-day basis and over specified time periods, cumulative surpluses or deficits can be calculated and anticipated and the earliest date of an anticipated deficit can be determined. Accordingly, marketable securities can be made available to be liquidated at such points in time or other sources of liquidity can be made readily available. "What if" scenario analysis can also be used to determine what needs are likely to be under best, average, and worst case scenarios, so a bank can be prepared for unanticipated liquidity needs. Banks also need to review the assumptions that they make for maturing assets and liability withdrawals to ensure that they are valid. Other details can be found in the document at *http://www.bis.org* (search on menu for liquidity management).

Concept Questions

1 What type of securities are typically held by banks and thrifts? Which have become more popular? Why?

2 What is the prepayment risk for mortgage-backed securities? What are CMOs, and how do they divide up this risk?

3 What advice does the BIS give to banks in managing their liquidity positions?

34 Andrew Kuritzkes. "Portfolio Management Strategies." *Bank Management* 70 (1994), 56–60.

35 With recent laws on derivatives, large banks and investment banks have made concerted efforts to develop risk management strategies for their investment portfolios, including derivatives.

Summary

Liquidity, or the ability to obtain cash with little risk of financial loss, is one of the most important concerns of depository institutions. Sufficient liquidity is necessary for two reasons: to meet regulatory requirements and to ensure uninterrupted operations in the face of unexpected loan demand or deposit withdrawals. With the growth of asset sales and loan securitization, many large banks have, however, been faced with excess liquidity. Liquidity can be managed by having stored liquidity in terms of holding short-term securities on a bank's balance sheet or through liability management, whereby depository institutions have many short-term borrowing sources to meet liquidity needs. Most banks use a combination of the two techniques.

The Federal Reserve Board influences institutional liquidity through reserve requirements on transactions accounts and time deposits. Besides meeting Federal Reserve specifications, some depositories must comply with liquidity requirements set by states or other federal regulators.

Depositories also require liquidity to meet unexpected loan demand or deposit withdrawals. To avoid selling assets at a loss when these needs arise, management should maintain liquid assets in excess of those required by regulators. Because liquid assets are often low yielding, however, liquidity needs must be balanced against profitability. Other financial institutions have also demonstrated the need to have sufficient liquidity in the event of unusual events including life insurers, property/casualty insurers, and mutual funds.

Unlike other financial institutions that can manage their investment portfolios to maximize returns based on a desired risk level, depository institutions must ensure that liquidity needs are met, provide countercyclical income when loan demand is down, satisfy pledging requirements for large government deposits, and use the investment portfolio to make adjustments for the bank's asset and liability position, including the bank's overall capital and interest rate risk. Depository institutions are also generally limited by regulations to hold debt securities that are investment grade or better. Consequently, depository institutions often rely on maturity strategies, such as barbell or ladder strategies, to ensure liquidity as well as to maximize returns if possible. With the investment portfolio as a complement to a depository institution's loan portfolio, depository institutions are also subject to a number of real-world limitations on their investment strategies.

In recent years, to improve returns, depository institutions have moved away from holding predominantly Treasury and municipal securities to holding MBSs, and for very large banks, to corporate debt securities as well. This movement necessitates a greater degree of sophistication from institution investment managers in terms of understanding the special risks entailed in MBSs, including considerable prepayment risk. Larger banks have also come to use derivatives more in their overall investment strategies, a practice that also necessitates greater sophistication by investment managers.

Questions

1. Providing liquidity is one of the functions of a financial intermediary. How does the intermediation role of depository institutions affect their liquidity needs?

2. Explain the historical rationale for the reserve requirements first imposed on national banks in the 1860s and continued after the creation of the Federal Reserve. Since that time, how has the Fed's monetary policy role affected the breadth and management of reserve requirements for all depository institutions? Why do other countries that do not have a strong money market have high reserve requirements for banks?

3. A key problem for depository managers is accurately estimating their liquidity needs for operations. How is this effort affected by the relative proportion of volatile and nonvolatile funds? By changes in economic conditions and return to depositors on alternative investments?

4. Depository institution managers may rely on both sides of the balance sheet to ensure adequate liquidity. Compare and contrast the potential effects on risk and return that result from asset sources of liquidity as compared with that from liability sources. How does an institution's size and financial soundness affect its liquidity management options?

5. Explain the functions of the Federal Reserve discount window. Contrast the Regulation A provisions governing use of the window to FHLB advances and to sources of CU liquidity.

6. Evaluate the differences in interest rate risk exposure from the ladder-of-maturities, the buffer, and the barbell portfolio investment strategies. Compare the relative rates of return that managers might expect from the three strategies under upward-sloping, flat, and downward-sloping yield curves.

7. Why can't bank managers simply manage a bank's investment portfolio from a risk/return respective? What are some other objectives for a bank's investment portfolio? What are some real-world considerations that prevent bank managers from focusing only on risk and return in their investment strategies?

8. What restrictions do regulators impose on banks in terms of the types of securities that they can hold? What special restrictions do thrifts and CUs have?

9. Looking at Tables 14.2 and 14.3, what are the most important distinctions between bank and thrift portfolios? Explain how differences in regulations, tax policies, and financial objectives have influenced asset holdings in banks and thrifts.

10. Do you consider the restrictions on bank and thrift investment in equity securities and junk bonds justified? What rationale would you offer for retaining or revising these regulations?

11. Explain the rationale for requiring firms—including depository institutions—to report the market value of financial assets on the balance sheet. Describe the different accounting procedures allowed by the Financial Accounting Standards Board for securities held for sale and for investment. What might be the potential effect on bank portfolio management?

12. What are GNMA, FNMA, and FHLMC? How do these agencies help increase the amount of mortgage credit available in the United States? What characteristics must mortgage loans have to be securitized? Why do depository institutions hold such a large percentage of MBSs?

13. Explain what a mortgage security is and what a CMO is and how they are created and priced. What is a PAC, an IO, and a PO? How does prepayment risk affect the value of MBSs when rates rise? When rates fall?

14. Why did very large banks in the later 1990s have so much excess liquidity to invest? How did these large banks transform their approach to portfolio management? Do you think this is a good idea? Explain.

Problems

1. J. C. Bosch, CEO, just placed you in charge of managing the Rockies Riviera Bank's reserve position. Your immediate responsibility is to calculate the total reserves that need to be held with the Fed during the upcoming maintenance period. You have been given the following information calculated from the two-week computation period:

Average vault cash	$4 million
Average net transactions balances	$625 million

a. Using the current reserve requirements, compute the average daily required reserves.

b. Given the vault cash figure, what total balances must be held at a Federal Reserve Bank for the total maintenance period?

2. a. Western Slope Bank must estimate its liquidity needs over the next two months. Using the following information given for that period, estimate the bank's liquidity surplus or deficit:

Assets	Millions	Liquid
Cash	$ 266.25	12%
Commercial loans	1,002.27	0%
Consumer loans	539.68	0%
Investments	1,317.45	45%
Other assets	217.15	17%
Total	$3,342.80	

Sources of Funds	Millions	Volatile
Deposits	$2,228.38	10%
Other liabilities	885.79	75%
Equity	258.63	0%
Total	$3,342.80	

b. Assume instead that 65 percent of investments are liquid and that 65 percent of nondeposit liabilities are volatile. Recalculate the liquidity surplus or deficit. Compare the advantages and disadvantages of this situation to that in part a.

c. Assume that Western Slope Bank wants to be prepared for an increase in commercial loan demand of 1 percent and an increase in consumer loan demand of 2 percent during the next two months. Using the data in part a, recalculate the bank's liquidity surplus or deficit under these assumptions.

3. Glenn Wolfe, a famous bank portfolio manager, holds a twelve-year, 10 percent coupon T-bond with a $1,000 maturity value; the bond's original price was $1,000, its current price is $990, and its pretax yield to maturity (YTM) is 10.15 percent. The bank has a marginal tax rate of 30 percent. A municipal bond in the bank's state has a coupon rate of 10.15 percent and sells for $1,000 with a pretax YTM of 10.15 percent. (Note that its tax equivalent coupon rate, since coupon payments are not taxed, is the coupon rate / [1 − t], or 10.15 percent / [1 − 0.30] = 14.5 percent.)

a. Calculate the tax savings if the T-bond is sold (the current price − the original price) (t), that is, the tax deduction for the loss on the bond. Add this to the $990, which will equal the total amount the bank manager will have to invest if the bond is sold.

b. Calculate the present value of the change in coupon payments for the twelve years if the T-bond is sold and the municipal bond is purchased. Assume a discount rate of 10.15 percent × (1 − t) = 10.15 percent × (1 − 0.3) = 7 percent.

c. Calculate the present value of the change in the principal payment at year 12 if the T-bond is sold, where the difference in principal payment will be the $1,000 that would have been received less the new principal payment, which will be the amount available to invest in the new bond calculated in part a.

d. Add the present value of the change in coupon payments to the present value of the change in principal payments to get the net present value for the swap decision. If it is positive, the swap will be value-enhancing. If it is negative, the swap will be value-reducing.

e. Based on your answer in part d, should the tax swap be made? What other considerations should be taken into account in determining whether to undertake this tax swap?

4. **Minicase:** The Sunny Side Bank, a small bank operating in Boca Raton, Florida, is having an investment committee meeting on Thursday, January 14, 1999, to see how it should adjust its investment portfolio. Attending the meeting are Charles A. Register, the senior vice president in charge of investments; Patty Moran, a member of an investment firm in Miami that handles many of the bank's investment orders; and Sinan Cebenoyan and Fatma Cebenoyan, the vice-president and investment manager, respectively, of the Alligator Bank of Miami. The Alligator Bank, a family-owned, but prominent regional bank in Miami, is Sunny Side's primary correspondent.

Before the meeting, Charles Register glances at the Thursday morning *Wall Street Journal* to read the report on credit markets for the previous day. Figure P14.1 summarizes the current yield curve on the page from the preceding day and the movement of interest rates that Register observes. On the preceding day, markets had been volatile in the wake of Brazil's devaluation of its currency. Consequently, many international investors shifted into Treasuries on that date to seek safety amid sizable losses in global stock markets and emerging bond markets. This resulted in a rise in Treasury security prices (fall in rates). For instance, the price for the bellwether 30-year T-bond rose $1\frac{6}{32}$, or $11.875 for a bond with a $1,000 face value, selling at $101\frac{24}{32}$, with a fall in the yield to 5.126 percent. Two-year T-note prices rose even more, by $\frac{7}{32}$, with a yield of 4.54 percent. Such a short-term flight to quality was short-lived, with

traders selling bonds when they reached market highs. However, speculation that the Brazilian situation might fuel rate cuts by the Federal Reserve resulted in a buying trend in Treasuries. But a rebound in the stock market during the day quelled buying by reducing hopes of a rate cut at the Federal Open Market Committee's next meeting. Despite the market turmoil, Freddie Mac, with Goldman Sachs and JPMorgan and Salomon Smith Barney as joint lead managers, sold $3 billion worth of five-year notes, priced to yield about 0.56 percent over U.S. Treasury yields, with 25 percent of the demand coming from international investors.

Register also glances at a recent copy of The Federal Reserve Bank of St. Louis's *Monetary Trends* showing trends in interest rates (see Figure P14.2). News on the radio that morning suggested that inflation and unemployment continued to be low in the United States. However, after such a long expansion, some security analysts predicted a downturn, and some corporations were announcing large layoffs. These analysts suggested buying long-term bonds, since if a recession occurs, interest rates tend to fall. Other analysts predicted that the U.S. economy would continue to be strong. The dollar had fallen sharply the previous week relative to the Japanese yen. As shown in the lower panel of Figure P14.2, this was the result of a rise in Japanese bond yields, resulting in a sell-off of U.S. T-bonds by Japanese investors and day traders, causing U.S. Treasury security prices to fall, and hence yields to rise. This week, however, with intervention by the Bank of Japan, the dollar had risen.

Register shakes his head in confusion. Bond market prices were much too volatile for his liking. How could a small bank manage its investment portfolio in such a global economy, where events in Brazil and Japan had a dramatic effect on Treasury security yields and, hence, the bank's investment portfolio? He had always thought of Treasuries as a risk-free investment, but in terms of interest rate risk, they certainly were not.

The investment portfolio for the Sunny Side Bank is depicted in Table P14.1, with estimated maturities, fair value, amortized cost, and weighted average yields of securities by type.

As shown by the investment portfolio unrealized gains/loss in the table, with falling rates in the 1990s the securities portfolio is posting gains. Answer the following questions based on the information supplied.

a. Based on the maturities for the securities given, does the portfolio seem to be engaged in any type of maturity strategies (i.e., barbell, ladder, or buffer)? Explain. Does Sunny Side's strategy seem appropriate for a small bank?

b. Based on trends shown in Figure P14.2, why do you think the securities portfolio is posting net gains?

c. Compare Sunny Side's percentage holdings in Treasury securities, municipals, MBSs, and corporate bonds to the percentages held by the average $100 million to $1 billion dollar bank (see Table 14.2).

d. Based on the recent information listed from the *Wall Street Journal* and from Figures P14.1 and P14.2, what do you think rates will be like during 1999 (disregard what actually happened)? How have recent international events at the time of the case affected interest rates on T-bonds? Why is it so difficult to predict interest rates?

e. Would you recommend any changes in Sunny Side's investment portfolio management strategy?

f. Would your recommendation change if you thought strongly that interest rates were going to rise? What would your recommendation be if you thought strongly that interest rates were going to fall?

g. The bank could swap a current $100,000 of eight-year T-bonds with par values of $1,000 each with 4 percent coupon rates for a recently issued eight-year T-bond with 5 percent coupon rates selling at $1,000 par. If the bank has a 30 percent marginal tax rate, should it make the swap? Assume the par value of the T-bond is $1,000. (Hint: You will need to calculate the prices of the current bond using the new 5 percent yield as the discount rate and find the present value of the change in coupons and change in maturity values.)

h. Why do you think Sunny Side, like other banks, holds a large percentage of MBSs? What benefits do MBSs have over other bonds? What disadvantages do they have?

table **P14.1**   INVESTMENT PORTFOLIO FOR SUNNY SIDE BANK

	Maturity Date				
	1999	2000	2001	2006	2007+
Tax-Exempt Securities Held to Maturity					
Amortized Cost	$76	$87	$59	$89	$38
Fair Value	$81	$91	$63	$95	$41
Weighted Ave. Yield (tax equivalent)	6.54%	7.08%	6.65%	6.50%	5.58%
All Other Securities					
Amortized Cost	$26	$9	$9	$80	
Fair Value	$27	$9	$9	$79	
Weighted Ave. Yield	6.88%	6.51%	6.83%	7.42%	
Total Amortized Cost	$102	$96	$68	$169	$38
Total Fair Value	$108	$100	$72	$174	$41
Total Unrealized Gains	$6	$4	$4	$5	$3

	Maturity Date				
	1999	2000	2001	2006	2007+
Securities Available for Sale					
U.S. Treasury Securities					
Amortized Cost	$351	$392	$452	$911	$3
Fair Value	$349	$392	$437	$904	$3
Weighted Ave. Yield	5.37%	6.24%	5.41%	6.33%	7.47%
Government-Sponsored MBSs					
Amortized Cost	$955	$1,905	$959	$1,763	$164
Fair Value	$967	$1,934	$972	$1,757	$165
Weighted Ave. Yield	6.66%	6.92%	7.19%	6.95%	7.66%
Corporate Bonds					
Amortized Cost	$9	$121	$11	$57	$92
Fair Value	$10	$121	$11	$57	$93
Weighted Ave. Yield	6.47%	6.06%	8.03%	7.48%	6.67%
Total Amortized Cost	$1,315	$2,418	$1,422	$2,731	$259
Total Fair Value	$1,326	$2,447	$1,420	$2,718	$261
Total Unrealized Gain or Loss	$11	$29	($2)	$2 ($13)	$42 ($15)
Net Unrealized Gain on Held for Sale Securities					$27

Notes: Dollar amounts are in thousands. Annual Reports and Moody's Bank & Finance Manual often provide this information.

figure **P14.1** TREASURY YIELD CURVE AND RECENT MOVEMENT IN SHORT-TERM INTEREST RATES FOR JANUARY 13, 1999

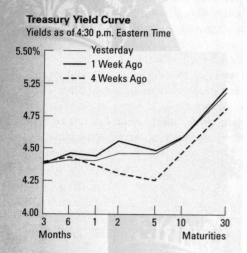

Treasury Yield Curve
Yields as of 4:30 p.m. Eastern Time

YIELD COMPARISONS

Based on Merrill Lynch Bond Indexes, priced as of midafternoon Eastern time.

	1/13	1/12	—52 WEEK— High	Low
Corp.-Govt. Master	5.36%	5.42%	6.13%	4.84%
Treasury 1-10yr	4.73	4.79	5.77	4.19
10 + yr	5.40	5.46	6.12	4.86
Agencies 1-10yr	5.40	5.46	6.19	4.71
10 + yr	5.76	5.81	6.44	5.22
Corporate				
1-10 yr High Qlty	5.46	5.52	6.27	5.08
Med Qlty	6.05	6.11	6.53	5.59
10 + yr High Qlty	6.18	6.25	6.81	5.91
Med Qlty	6.72	6.79	7.22	6.46
Yankee bonds (1)	6.24	6.30	6.69	5.87
Current-coupon mortgages (2)				
GNMA 6.00%	6.21	6.25	6.81	5.79
FNMA 6.00%	6.28	6.33	6.77	5.87
FHLMC 6.00%	6.29	6.34	6.80	5.89
High-yield corporates	10.02	9.96	10.81	8.17
Tax-Exempt Bonds				
7-12-yr G.O. (AA)	4.23	4.28	4.86	4.07
12-22-yr G.O. (AA)	4.70	4.73	5.25	4.50
22 + yr revenue (A)	4.97	5.00	5.37	4.67

Note: High quality rated AAA-AA; medium quality A-BBB/Baa; high yield, BB/Ba-C.

(1) Dollar-denominated, SEC-registered bonds of foreign issuers sold in the U.S. (2) Reflects the 52-week high and low of mortgage-backed securities indexes rather than the individual securities shown.

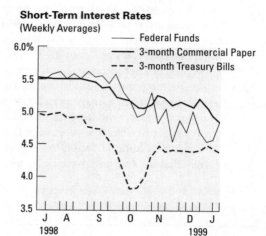

Short-Term Interest Rates
(Weekly Averages)

Increasing Treasury Troubles
A Falling Dollar...
Value of U.S. Dollar in Japanese Yen

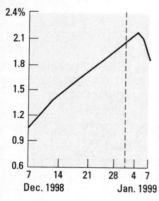

Rising Japanese Yields...
Yield on 10-year Japanese Government Bonds

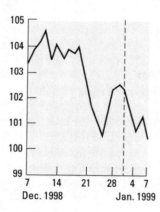

Hurt U.S. Treasurys
Price of 30-year Treasurys

Source: The Wall Street Journal *(January 14, 1999), C21.*

Source: The Wall Street Journal *(January 8, 1999), C1.*

Suggested Case Studies

"Case 3: CARs (Certificates for Automobile Receivables)." Darden School, University of Virginia: Richard D. Crawford and William W. Sihler. *Financial Service Organizations: Cases in Strategic Management.* His case provides an overview of the history of loan securitization and an introduction to the characteristics and structure of asset-backed securities, focusing on CARs.

"Case 2: Quigley Bank Corporation." Darden School, University of Virginia: This case, in addition to providing a format for financial analysis for a bank, also focuses on the investment management of a bank's portfolio and its interest rate risk, including difficulties in trying to forecast interest rates.

figure **P14.2**   TRENDS IN INTEREST RATES AS OF DECEMBER 1998

Short-Term Interest Rates
Percent

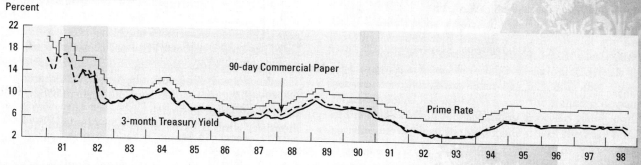

Long-Term Interest Rates
Percent

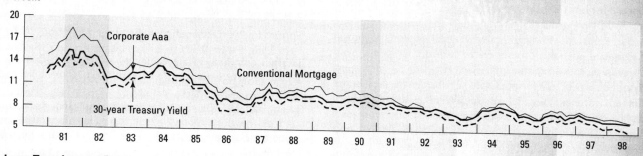

Long-Term Interest Rates
Percent

Short-Term Interest Rates
Percent

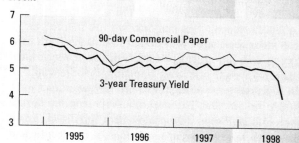

FOMC Expected Federal Funds Rate and Discount Rate
Percent

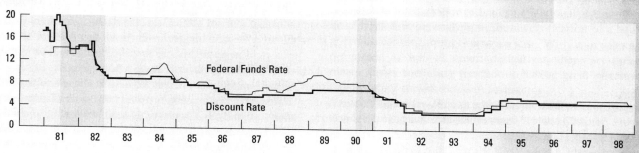

Source: Monetary Trends *(The Federal Reserve Bank of St. Louis) (December 1998).*

Selected References

Burns, Joseph E. "Bank Liquidity—A Straightforward Concept but Hard to Measure." *Business Review* (Federal Reserve Bank of Dallas) (May 1971).

Cacy, J. A., and Scott Winningham. "Reserve Requirements under the Depository Institutions Deregulation and Monetary Control Act of 1980." *Economic Review* (Federal Reserve Bank of Kansas City) 65 (September/October 1980), 3–16.

Dietz, Peter O., H. Russell Fogler, and Donald J. Hardy. "The Challenge of Analyzing Bond Portfolio Returns." *Journal of Portfolio Management* 6 (Spring 1980), 53–58.

Evanoff, Douglas D. "Reserve Account Management Behavior: Impact of the Reserve Accounting Scheme and Carry Forward Provision." Federal Reserve Bank of Chicago, Working Paper 89–12 (1989).

Feinman, Joshua N. "Reserve Requirements: History, Current Practice, and Potential Reform." *Federal Reserve Bulletin* 79 (June 1993), 569–589.

Gilbert, R. Alton. "Lagged Reserve Requirements: Implications for Monetary Control and Bank Reserve Management." *Economic Review* (Federal Reserve Bank of St. Louis) 62 (May 1980), 7–20.

Giroux, Gary. "A Survey of Forecasting Techniques Used by Commercial Banks." *Journal of Bank Research* 11 (Spring 1980), 51–53.

Goodfriend, Marvin, and Monica Hargraves. "A Historic Assessment of the Rationales and Functions of Reserve Requirements." *Economic Review* (Federal Reserve Bank of Richmond) 69 (March/April 1983), 3–21.

Haberman, Gary, and Catherine Piche. "Controlling Credit Risk Associated with Repos: Know Your Counterparty." *Economic Review* (Federal Reserve Bank of Atlanta) 70 (September 1985), 28–34.

Hamdani, Kausar. "CRR and Excess Reserves: An Early Appraisal." *Quarterly Review* (Federal Reserve Bank of New York) 9 (Autumn 1984), 16–23.

Homer, Sidney, and Martin Leibowitz. *Inside the Yield Book.* New York: Prentice Hall and the New York Institute of Finance, 1972.

Kaufman, Daniel J., Jr., and David R. Lee. "Planning Liquidity: A Practical Approach." *Magazine of Bank Administration* 53 (November 1977), 55–63.

Knight, Robert E. "Reserve Requirements, Part I: Comparative Reserve Requirements at Member and Nonmember Banks." *Monthly Review* (Federal Reserve Bank of Kansas City) 59 (April 1974), 3–20.

Luckett, Dudley G. "Approaches to Bank Liquidity Management." *Economic Review* (Federal Reserve Bank of Kansas City) 65 (March 1980), 11–27.

McKenna, Conner, and Cuneo. *An Analysis of the Financial Institutions Reform, Recovery, and Enforcement Act of 1989.* New York: McKenna, Conner, and Cuneo, 1989.

Mengle, David. "The Discount Window." *Economic Review* (Federal Reserve Bank of Richmond) 72 (May/June 1986), 2–10.

Pearce, Douglas K. "Recent Developments in the Credit Union Industry." *Economic Review* (Federal Reserve Bank of Kansas City) 69 (June 1984), 10–12.

Proctor, Allen J., and Kathleen K. Donahoo. "Commercial Bank Investment in Municipal Securities." *Quarterly Review* (Federal Reserve Bank of New York) 8 (Winter 1983–1984), 26–37.

Robinson, Roland I. *The Management of Bank Funds.* New York: McGraw-Hill, 1962.

Rodrigues, Anthony P. "Government Investments of Commercial Banks." *Quarterly Review* (Federal Reserve Bank of New York) 18 (Summer 1993), 39–53.

Rosenbaum, Mary Susan. "Contemporaneous Reserve Accounting: The New System and Its Implications for Monetary Policy." *Economic Review* (Federal Reserve Bank of Atlanta) 69 (April 1984), 46–57.

Saunders, Anthony, and Thomas Urich. "The Effects of Shifts in Monetary Policy and Reserve Accounting Regimes on Bank Reserve Management Behavior in the Federal Funds Market." *Journal of Banking and Finance* 12 (December 1988), 523–535.

Sealey, C. W., Jr. "Valuation, Capital Structure, and Shareholder Unanimity for Depository Financial Intermediaries." *Journal of Finance* 38 (June 1983), 857–871.

Spong, Kenneth. *Banking Regulation.* Kansas City: Federal Reserve Bank of Kansas City, 1990.

Stevens, E. J. "Is There Any Rationale for Reserve Requirements?" *Economic Review* (Federal Reserve Bank of Cleveland) 27 (Quarter 3, 1991), 2–17.

Stigum, Marcia. *The Money Market,* 3rd ed. Homewood, IL: Dow Jones-Irwin, 1990.

Tarhan, Vefa. "Individual Bank Reserve Management." *Economic Perspectives* (Federal Reserve Bank of Chicago) 8 (July/August 1984), 17–23.

Tschinkel, Sheila S. "Overview." *Economic Review* (Federal Reserve Bank of Atlanta) 70 (September 1985), 5–9.

Watson, Ronald D. "Bank Bond Management: The Maturity Dilemma." *Business Review* (Federal Reserve Bank of Philadelphia) (March 1972), 23–29.

internet *exercise*

Look up the Website for JPMorgan Chase or another large bank and click on investor relations to see their annual report (usually downloadable in PDF form). See what the bank says about its liquidity position in its annual report. Also, look at the section on the bank's security portfolio. What types of securities does it hold? Do you see any different trends versus previous years?

OTHER USEFUL SITES FOR FINANCIAL INSTITUTION DATA

Federal Home Loan Bank System

http://www.fhlbanks.com/

Federal Home Loan Bank of Chicago

http://www.fhlbc.com/

15 Deposit and Liability Management

"Bankers face the unappetizing choice of watching dollars run out of certificates of deposit into such alternative investments as mutual funds and annuities, or actively offering those alternatives and accelerating the trend."

DOUGLAS FREEMAN, Chief Corporate Banking Executive, Barnett Banks, Quoted in Jeffrey Marshall, "Rolling the Dice on Asset Management," U.S. Banker (March 1994), p. 33.

"Because nondeposit alternatives such as Federal Home Loan Bank borrowings, subordinated debt, and federal funds purchases consistently have higher interest costs than core deposits, . . . banks with high levels of noncore funding, on average, report lower NIMs than core-funded banks do. Increased noncore funding could lead some banks to sacrifice liquidity, extend asset maturities, or assume higher credit risk to bolster yields."

Atlanta Region Staff, Atlanta Federal Reserve Bank, Regional Perspectives, FDIC: Atlanta Regional Outlook, Fourth Quarter, 1999, p. 2.

A s the chapter opening quotes suggest, depository institutions continue to face dramatic changes in their deposit and liability management. In the 1990s and early 2000s, with interest rates falling dramatically and bank deposit rates declining to less than 1 percent, investors moved funds out of deposits with low rates into higher yielding investments, such as mutual funds. Hence, banks have had less access to cheaper core deposit financing. This trend has occurred for several decades, with bank and savings institution deposit financing falling from 92 percent of assets in 1950 to 68 percent in 1996 to 65.60 percent of assets as of December 31, 2003. Of the 65.60 percent, 8.17 percent included deposits in nondomestic offices, and 49 percent in core (insured retail) deposits. With a large percentage fall in the percentage of deposit financing and particularly core deposit financing, depository institutions, especially large financial institutions, have been forced to engage in greater noncore financing (time deposits over $100,000, foreign office deposits, and brokered deposits and other borrowed funds), which are more expensive, interest rate sensitive, and volatile than insured, "core" deposits. Regulators have been concerned about institutions taking on more risky assets to increase their asset utilization to offset higher liability interest expenses. With expectations of rising rates in the first quarter of 2004, new liability management challenges will appear, with greater interest rate sensitivity for noncore financing sources.[1]

Liability and deposit management entail the active use of deposit and nondeposit funds to meet liquidity needs, enhance profits, or achieve growth. Factors that need to be considered include trends, mix, pricing, fees for deposit services, and the operating costs of different types of financing, each discussed in this chapter.

Learning Objectives

After completing this chapter, you will be able to:

1. Understand the implications of falling interest rates on the liability mix of depository institutions.

2. Describe alternative financing sources for depository institutions with a decline in the percentage of core deposit financing.

3. Follow trends in retail deposit fees, a rise in bank offices, and other marketing and service techniques to attract deposits.

4. Understand problems that depository institutions have in setting retail deposit fees and prices and the concept of value pricing.

5. Explain the concept of the marginal cost of funds and a bank's base rate for funds.

Recent Trends in Liability Management for Depository Institutions

With declining interest rates resulting in a lower percentage of core deposit financing for depository institutions, higher technology costs for deposit operations, and changes in the payment system with greater use of ATMs, debit cards, and online banking, depository institutions have responded to these challenges with more aggressive liability management in the past decade, discussed first in the following sections.

Falling Deposit Rates and Greater Dependence on Noncore Financing

Figure 15.1 shows average deposit yields for banks and savings institutions across the United States on April 13, 2004, as presented in *The Wall Street Journal* from Bankrate.com. Bank rates were very low on this date, as they were in the early 2000s. For instance, the average yield on retail savings money market accounts (MMAs) by major New York banks was 0.49 percent. Even high-yield savings account rates were low, such as the 2.15 percent MMA yield by an Internet bank, VirtualBank. Similarly, the average for retail five-year certificates of deposit (CDs) by New York banks was only 2.99 percent. As noted in the introduction, the average percentage of deposit and core deposit financing fell for banks at this time, given very low interest rates, whereby depositors sought higher returns elsewhere. This forced managers to seek funds from noncore (wholesale) sources through jumbo certificates of deposits

---

1 *Federal Reserve Bulletin*, various issues 1997, 1998, 2002, 2004; and FDIC Website *(http://www.fdic.gov)*. See Information for Analysts and Statistics on Banking.

figure **15.1** DEPOSIT RATE QUOTES FOR BANKS IN THE WALL STREET JOURNAL, APRIL 14, 2004

BANKRATE.COM® Money Markets and CDs

Tuesday, April 13, 2004

Average Yields of Major Banks

TYPE	MMA	1-MO	2-MO	3-MO	6-MO	1-YR	2-YR	25-YR	5-YR
NEW YORK									
Savings	0.49	0.91	0.93	0.76	0.87	1.08	1.67	1.80	2.99
Jumbos	0.84	0.89	0.91	0.90	1.01	1.23	1.70	1.83	3.04
CALIFORNIA									
Savings	0.49	0.73	0.71	0.83	0.90	1.05	1.63	1.62	2.89
Jumbos	0.97	0.86	0.86	0.92	1.01	1.16	1.81	1.82	3.21
PENNSYLVANIA									
Savings	0.37	0.47	0.65	0.80	0.80	1.02	1.57	1.76	2.81
Jumbos	0.95	0.80	0.94	0.85	0.92	1.11	1.61	1.78	2.82
ILLINOIS									
Savings	0.50	0.61	0.61	0.75	0.88	1.10	1.61	1.81	3.08
Jumbos	0.79	0.74	0.74	0.85	0.98	1.21	1.87	2.07	3.26
TEXAS									
Savings	0.39	0.67	0.67	0.78	0.93	1.04	1.67	1.71	3.09
Jumbos	1.05	0.73	0.72	0.81	0.99	1.14	1.78	1.82	3.19
FLORIDA									
Savings	0.38	0.79	0.79	0.81	0.90	1.17	1.66	1.73	3.11
Jumbos	0.95	0.84	0.85	0.88	0.97	1.22	1.74	1.82	3.21
National Average									
Savings	0.43	0.69	0.70	0.79	0.90	1.13	1.68	1.78	3.03
Jumbos	0.89	0.79	0.80	0.87	0.99	1.22	1.79	1.88	3.15
WEEKLY CHANGE									
Savings	0.00	0.00	0.00	0.01	0.01	0.01	0.04	0.04	0.06
Jumbos	0.00	0.00	0.00	0.00	0.00	0.01	0.04	0.05	0.06

High Yield Savings

	Phone	Min $ to Open	Ann % Yld		Phone	Min $ to Open	Ann % Yld
Money Market Account (MMA)				**6-Month CD**			
VirtualBank (4)	(877) 998-2265	$100	2.15	Corus Bank (4)	(800) 989-5101	$10,000	2.06
Bank of Internet USA (4)	(877) 541-2634	$1,500	2.11	Ascencia Bank (4)	(877) 369-2265	$500	2.00
National InterBank Inc (4)	(888) 580-0043	$1	2.05	Quantum National Bank (4)	(800) 533-6922	$25,000	1.96
MetLife Bank, NA (3)	(866) 226-5638	$5,000	2.01	Countrywide Bank (4)	(800) 479-4221	$10,000	1.86
ING DIRECT (4)	(877) 469-0232	$1	2.00	New South Fed Svgs (3)	(866) 450-RATE	$5,000	1.85
1-Month CD				**1-Year CD**			
FirstBank of Puerto Rico (3)	(866) 822-8201	$10,000	1.25	Corus Bank (4)	(800) 989-5101	$10,000	2.27
New South Fed Svgs (3)	(866) 450-RATE	$5,000	1.25	Intervest Natl Bk (4)	(212) 218-8383	$2,500	2.25
Capital Crossing Bk (2)	(877) 976-7722	$2,500	1.21	Countrywide Bank (4)	(800) 479-4221	$10,000	2.22
Bank of Internet USA (4)	(877) 541-2634	$1,000	1.16	Bank of Internet USA (4)	(877) 541-2634	$1,000	2.21
Beal Bank (4)	(469) 467-5214	$25,000	1.15	New South Fed Svgs (3)	(866) 450-RATE	$5,000	2.20
2-Month CD				**2-Year CD**			
FirstBank of Puerto Rico (3)	(866) 822-8201	$10,000	1.30	Nova Savings Bank (2)	(877) 482-2650	$500	2.75
New South Fed Svgs (3)	(866) 450-RATE	$5,000	1.30	Countrywide Bank (4)	(800) 479-4221	$10,000	2.75
Capital Crossing Bk (2)	(877) 976-7722	$2,500	1.21	Intervest Natl Bk (4)	(212) 218-8383	$2,500	2.70
State Bank of Texas (5)	(800) 860-1887	$1,000	1.16	Bank of Internet USA (4)	(877) 541-2634	$1,000	2.70
Bank of Internet USA (4)	(877) 541-2634	$1,000	1.16	State Farm Bank (2)	(877) 734-2265	$500	2.60
3-Month CD				**5-Year CD**			
Corus Bank (4)	(800) 989-5101	$10,000	1.76	Intervest Natl Bk (4)	(212) 218-8383	$2,500	4.15
Imperial Capital Bank (4)	(877) 906-4852	$2,000	1.66	Countrywide Bank (4)	(800) 479-4221	$10,000	4.11
Stonebridge Bank (3)	(800) 807-1666	$500	1.65	Apple Bank for Savings (4)	(800) 722-6888	$500	4.10
IndyMac Bank, FSB (3)	(800) 734-6063	$5,000	1.65	Nova Savings Bank (2)	(877) 482-2650	$500	4.01
State Farm Bank (2)	(877) 734-2265	$500	1.50	MBNA America Bank (5)	(877) 229-5565	$10,000	4.00

High Yield Jumbos

	Phone	Min $ to open	Ann % Yld		Phone	Min $ to open	Ann % Yld
Money Market Account (MMA)				**6-Month CD**			
Corus Bank (4)	(800) 989-5101	$100,000	2.01	Corus Bank (4)	(800) 989-5101	$100,000	2.06
MetLife Bank, NA (3)	(866) 226-5638	$100,000	2.01	Quantum National Bank (4)	(800) 533-6922	$100,000	1.96
GMAC Bank (5)	(866) 246-2265	$100,000	2.00	Countrywide Bank (4)	(800) 479-4221	$100,000	1.86
National InterBank Inc (4)	(888) 580-0043	$100,000	2.00	New South Fed Svgs (3)	(866) 450-RATE	$100,000	1.85
ING DIRECT (4)	(877) 469-0232	$100,000	2.00	IndyMac Bank, FSB (3)	(800) 734-6063	$100,000	1.85
1-Month CD				**1-Year CD**			
FirstBank of Puerto Rico (3)	(866) 822-8201	$100,000	1.25	Corus Bank (4)	(800) 989-5101	$100,000	2.27
New South Fed Svgs (3)	(866) 450-RATE	$100,000	1.25	Intervest Natl Bk (4)	(212) 218-8383	$100,000	2.25
Capital Crossing Bk (2)	(877) 976-7722	$100,000	1.21	Countrywide Bank (4)	(800) 479-4221	$100,000	2.22
First Trade Union Bk (3)	(800) 242-0272	$100,000	1.20	Bank of Internet USA (4)	(877) 541-2634	$100,000	2.21
Bank of Internet USA (4)	(877) 541-2634	$100,000	1.16	New South Fed Svgs (3)	(866) 450-RATE	$100,000	2.20
2-Month CD				**2-Year CD**			
FirstBank of Puerto Rico (3)	(866) 822-8201	$100,000	1.30	Countrywide Bank (4)	(800) 479-4221	$100,000	2.75
New South Fed Svgs (3)	(866) 450-RATE	$100,000	1.30	Intervest Natl Bk (4)	(212) 218-8383	$100,000	2.70
Capital Crossing Bk (2)	(877) 976-7722	$100,000	1.21	Bank of Internet USA (4)	(877) 541-2634	$100,000	2.70
First Trade Union Bk (3)	(800) 242-0272	$100,000	1.20	Providian Natl Bk (4)	(800) 414-9692	$100,000	2.70
State Bank of Texas (5)	(800) 860-1887	$100,000	1.16	State Farm Bank (2)	(877) 734-2265	$100,000	2.70
3-Month CD				**5-Year CD**			
Corus Bank (4)	(800) 989-5101	$100,000	1.76	Intervest Natl Bk (4)	(212) 218-8383	$100,000	4.15
IndyMac Bank, FSB (3)	(800) 734-6063	$100,000	1.65	Countrywide Bank (4)	(800) 479-4221	$100,000	4.11
State Farm Bank (2)	(877) 734-2265	$100,000	1.60	Apple Bank for Savings (4)	(800) 722-6888	$100,000	4.10
Beal Bank (4)	(469) 467-5214	$100,000	1.50	Providian Natl Bk (4)	(800) 414-9692	$100,000	4.10
New South Fed Svgs (3)	(866) 450-RATE	$100,000	1.50	MBNA America Bank (5)	(877) 229-5565	$100,000	4.00

Accounts are federally insured up to $100,000 per person. Yields are based on method of compounding and rate stated for the lowest required opening deposit to earn interest. CD figures are for fixed rates only. **MMA:** Allows 6 third party transfers per month, 3 of which may be checks. Rates are subject to change.

Explanation of Ratings: Safe & Sound℠, (561) 627-7330 ext. 1410, evaluates the financial condition of federally insured institutions and assigns a rank of 1–5 (number in parentheses) based on 3rd quarter 2003 data from federal regulators. Information is believed to be reliable, but not guaranteed. A rank of 5 indicates the most desirable performance. A "U" rating indicates that an institution is too new to rate and is not an indication of financial strength or weakness.

Source: Bankrate.com®, a publication of Bankrate, Inc., North Palm Beach, FL 33408 Internet: www.bankrate.com

CD Yields Increased During Latest Week

NEW YORK—Yields on certificates of deposit were higher in the latest week. The average yield on six-month jumbo CDs, which typically require deposits of $95,000 or more, was unchanged from a week earlier at 0.99%, according to Bankrate.com. The yield on five-year jumbos was 3.15%, up from 3.09%, the information service said.

The average yields on small-denomination savings CDs were higher. The average six-month yield was unchanged from a week earlier at 0.9%, said Bankrate.com. The average two-year CD yield was 1.68%, up from 1.64%, and the average five-year yield was 3.03%, up from 2.97%.

This week, the experts say when rates are this low, it is tough to advise people to lock in rates.

"The trend has turned favorable in long-term CDs, as economic momentum remains positive. However, yields are still regaining the lost ground of the past four months," said Greg McBride, a financial analyst at Bankrate.com.

Source: The Wall Street Journal, *April 14, 2004, C17.*

(CDs), insured deposits of $100,000, or other uninsured types of more expensive borrowing. As shown at the top of Figure 15.1, jumbos pay higher rates, such as 3.04 percent for five-year jumbo CDs of major New York banks and at the bottom of the figure, the higher 4.15 percent offered by Intervest National Bank at this time. Similarly, other noncore types of borrowing are more expensive than core (insured NOW, MMDAs, and other types of retail savings accounts) deposits. Hence, depository institutions found themselves depending on more expensive noncore deposits and other borrowings for financing.

Cheaper Noncore Financing by Large Banks with High Credit Ratings and for Community Depository Institutions Using FHLB Advances

Although the greater use of noncore financing by banks and savings institutions put upward pressure on their interest expenses, some large banks, such as Wells Fargo, by having excellent credit ratings were able to pay low rates on jumbo CDs and other uninsured borrowings as well (see Wells Fargo performance analysis in Chapter 4). Community depository institutions also have come to rely more on cheaper noncore financing as members of the Federal Home Loan Bank (FHLB) System, through advances (loans) from the FHLB. The Federal Home Loan Banks (FHLBanks) are wholesale banks that are privately owned with the goal to provide "readily available, low-cost funding, known as advances, and other credit products to more than 8,000 stockholder members." Each member (banks, savings institutions, credit unions, and insurance companies) belong to one of twelve regional FHLBanks. The FHLBanks provide lower rates and spreads over comparable Treasury securities, by having triple-A credit ratings by Moody's and Standard & Poor's for consolidated obligations (securities) that are sold to institutional investors. In this way, the FHLB system allows local lenders to offer affordable loans to their respective communities for affordable housing, small business, community development, and agricultural loans. The FHLBanks since 1990 have also contributed 10 percent of their income to the Affordable Housing Program (AHP), which provides long-term financing subsidies for loans for very low, low-, and moderate-income families. As of December 31, 2003, the FHLB reported 8,045 financial institutions as members (5,977 commercial banks, 1,342 thrifts, 706 credit unions, and 79 insurance companies) and $514.2 billion in advances (member loans), a rise of 5 percent from the previous year. Regulators and some critics have been concerned in recent years about rural and other depository institutions taking on extra risks, given the subsidy of lower-cost FHLB financing, especially with the expansion of institutions allowed to borrow from the FHLB under the Financial Modernization Act of 1999. Legislators have continued to encourage eligibility for credit unions and others as FHLB members, as proposed as part of HR 1375, the Financial Services Regulatory Relief Act of 2004, passed by the House in April 2004 and sent to the Senate Banking Committee for consideration. In 2003 for all FDIC-insured banks and savings institutions, FHLB advances were 5.28 percent of total assets, with similar percentages in 2001 and 2002, a significant rise from 2.99 percent in 2000.[2]

Securitization as a Source of Liquidity

Another strategy to maintain liquidity to meet deposit demand and fund new loans involves the asset side. Many depository institutions engage in securitizations and loan sales, which frees up funds to make new loans and meet other liquidity needs on a continuing basis. While very large banks often have their own securitization operations through special-purpose vehicles (SPVs), smaller community banks and thrifts often sell loans to other lenders including other banks and insurance companies or government-sponsored or quasi-sponsored enterprises (GSEs) including Fannie Mae, Ginnie Mae, and Freddie Mac. The volume of securitizations has grown phenomenally. As noted in a recent *Wall Street Journal* article on Capital by David Wessel, loans and securities that commercial banks hold account "for less than 20 percent of U.S. credit-market debt these days," with loans being traded in the markets "just like stocks and bonds."[3] With the rapid growth in securitization, particularly by the GSEs, regulators have been concerned about the possibility of legislation that would reduce the government's

---

2 See Federal Home Loan Bank Website *(http://www.fhlbanks.com)*.

3 See "FYI: An Update on Emerging Issues in Banking: Assessing the Banking Industry's Exposure to an Implicit Government Guarantee of GSEs," March 1, 2004 (revised April 14, 2004). Also see David Wessel. "Financial Markets Can Look to Economy as Model of Stability." *The Wall Street Journal* (April 15, 2004), A2.

backing of GSEs in the event of bankruptcy. Banks and thrifts hold large percentages of GSE mortgage-backed securities, so such a change possibly could reduce the value of their mortgage-security holdings. A recent FDIC *FYI: Update on Emerging Issues in Banking* estimates that FDIC-insured depository institutions hold almost $300 billion, or 17 percent, of Fannie Mae and Freddie Mac outstanding direct obligations of $1.8 trillion and about $770 billion, or 40 percent, of Fannie Mae and Freddie Mac's $1.9 trillion in mortgage pools outstanding. However, Fannie Mae and Freddie Mac had top, "AAA" credit ratings in 2004, so leading chief executives of these organizations suggest that such an overhaul would have little effect on the value of their securities. In 2003, Fannie and Freddie owned or guaranteed about half of $7.3 trillion of the outstanding home mortgages in the United States.[4]

Rapid Growth in Total Deposits

Although the percentage of deposit financing of depository institutions has fallen and securitization has become commonplace, both total assets and deposits held by banks have grown phenomenally for FDIC-insured banks and thrifts, as shown in Figure 15.2. At the end of 2003, the FDIC reported $9.087 trillion in total insured bank and savings institution deposits financed by $5.959 trillion in deposits, representing a 49 percent growth rate since 2000, when total deposits were $4 trillion, and an 82 percent growth rate from 1990, when total deposits were $3.278 trillion. Hence, depository institutions are still strongly "depository" in the deposit-taking and clearing business. This business has represented the heart of a bank's operations, entailing check clearing, processing, ATMs, and customer services, which encompass a large percentage of bank activities and operating costs.[5]

figure **15.2** DEPOSITS OF FDIC-INSURED INSTITUTIONS AS OF JUNE 30, 1989 TO 2003

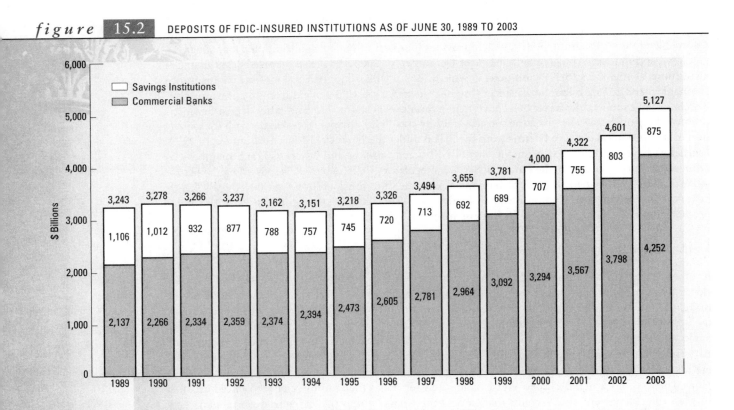

Source: FDIC Summary of Deposits, Current Charts and Graphs, April 22, 2004 (http://www2.fdic.gov/sod).

---

4 See James R. Hagerty and John D. McKinnon. "Regulators Hit Fannie, Freddie with New Assault." *The Wall Street Journal* (April 28, 2004), A1, A8; and Lynn Adler. "Update 2—Freddie CEO Sees Slim Chance of GSE Reform in '04." *Reuters Bond News* (April 22, 2004), 1–2.

5 See FDIC Statistics on Banking and Regional Outlooks on the FDIC Website.

Rise in Bank Offices to Collect Deposits

Banks have also in recent years increased their number of branches and offices to collect deposits, with 87,777 offices for FDIC-insured institutions at the end of 2003, including 13,883 branches and offices for savings institutions and 73,894 for banks, excluding U.S. branches of foreign banks. For banks, this represents an increase of 3,686 branches and offices since 1999. As shown in Figure 15.3, of these branches, 21,999 were interstate branches for banks and 2,538 for savings institutions as of June 30, 2003, representing a remarkable rise from only 30 interstate bank branches and 1,851 thrift branches in 1994. Bank of America, Wells Fargo, and other large regional and interstate banks have developed regional or national networks of branches. Other large banks, including Banc One, have taken advantage of economies of scale and gained fee income by offering deposit check writing and clearing services for nonbank financial institutions. A number of banks and thrifts, such as TeleBank Financial Corporation of Arlington, Virginia, are virtual banks, attracting deposits by mail, phone, and the Internet. Some cyberbanks and thrifts—for example, CompuBank in Houston, Texas—can offer higher deposit rates, because they do not have the cost of branches.[6]

New Marketing Innovations and Service Attractiveness

Depository institution managers in the past two decades have developed a new marketing focus to attract deposits based on convenience, access to ATMs, having a large number of branches, friendliness, and other bank products and service. Similarly, by offering cash management, personal banking, and

figure **15.3** NUMBER OF INTERSTATE BRANCHES OPERATED BY FDIC-INSURED COMMERCIAL BANKS AND SAVINGS INSTITUTIONS, 1994 TO 2003

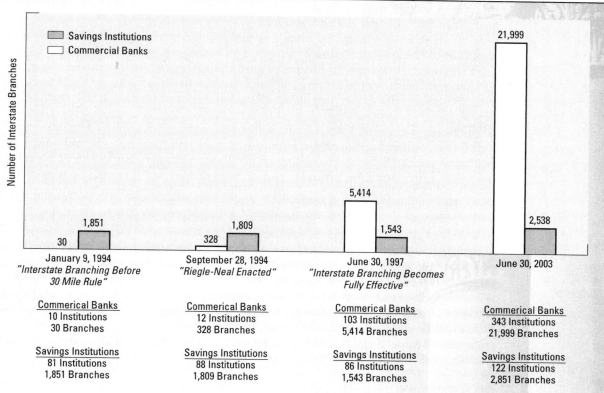

Source: FDIC Summary of Deposits, Current Charts and Graphs, April 22, 2004 (http://www2.fdic.gov/sod).

6 Ibid.

other corporate services, banks have been able to retain deposits of corporate customers. Many large banks also earn considerable fee income as correspondent banks providing check-clearing services for other banks, in competition with the Fed, and also providing lockbox and other working capital management services for companies. These services include controlled disbursement accounts, account reconciliation, lockboxes, fund transfers from different banks across the country into a centralized account, electronic funds transfer via CHIPS (Clearing House Interbank Payments System), Fedwire, or automated clearinghouses (ACHs) including the transfer of payment messages internationally by SWIFT, among other deposit services for E-commerce as discussed in Chapter 7.[7]

Depository institutions have also tried to retain retail deposit customers by offering better service, including automated twenty-four-hour telephone services that provide customers with account information. In addition to reducing labor-intensive costs of having to hire employees to answer hundreds of phone calls, this service provides a way to attract deposits and allows depository institutions to compete with mutual funds that offer such services. Although in the past larger depository institutions charged for this service, many institutions, including community banks, are now offering this service free of charge. Depository institutions have also developed new low-cost deposit-gathering mechanisms that are more conveniently placed for customers through supermarket branches. For instance, Wells Fargo Bank established supermarket kiosks in Safeway grocery stores, avoiding the expense of building new branches. Through this strategy Wells Fargo was able to collect a greater volume of deposits, while avoiding the higher operating expenses associated with building new branches. As noted in Chapter 7, ATMs have grown dramatically as well, especially those off-site. Debit cards that allow customers to have funds automatically deducted from bank accounts for sales have also become very popular, providing greater convenience for non-check payments for goods, with funds automatically deducted from their bank accounts by using their cards for payment. Other innovations include different types of savings programs and deposits. Depository institutions have become more sophisticated in their advertising and marketing campaigns, as well, and in creating favorable publicity by sponsoring community fund-raising events. National advertising including letter-writing campaigns, newspaper ads, and radio and television ads has allowed depository institutions to attract funds across the country.

Evolution in the Payments System

The payments system for banks is also evolving, with the development of check imaging systems, which significantly reduce bank costs in terms of having to compile and mail cancelled checks to customers. Banks have also become leaders in electronic check presentment (ECP), which is a hybrid, electronic/paper method of expediting check collections. Under this system, check data are exchanged in advance of presenting actual checks, speeding up the payments system and reducing banks' operational expenses. New computer systems and software allow even small community banks to reduce the cost of processing checks and speed up the check-clearing process. When you think of depository institutions clearing billions of checks each day and spending $4 billion annually just to handle checks, new systems have simplified the lives of harried bankers dramatically and lowered costs for many banks in the late 1990s and early 2000s. Recent studies suggest productivity benefits from technology.[8]

Banks have also been active in offering online banking services, as discussed in Chapter 7. The entry of banks into online banking has concerned regulators in terms of how banks will be able to handle technology risk. For instance, one of the ten banks that the GAO surveyed did not have basic virus-detection software on its systems. Consequently, the Office of the Comptroller of the Currency (OCC) issued new guidelines in 1998 for examiners to follow when reviewing a bank's technology risk management plan. Regulators have also been concerned about the significant change in the infrastructure for ATMs and debit cards, with a rise in the processing of transactions by "nonbank" (third-party) processors and continued consolidation of ATM and debit card networks and the rapid growth of off-site ATMs.[9]

7 For an excellent detailed discussion of bank working capital management services, see Maness and Zietlow (2002).

8 See Buddy Massengill and Ned Miltko. "NCHA: Private Check-Clearing Alternative." *Bank Management* (March/April 1995), 47–50; J. D. Carreker. "Electronic Check Presentment: Capturing New Technology." *Bank Management* (March/April 1995), 33–44; and William M. Randle. "Delivering the Future: Redefining the Role of Banks in a New Competitive Environment." *Bank Management* (January/February 1995), 45–48.

9 See "Electronic Banking: OCC Issues New Guidance to Ensure Banks Can Handle Technology Risks." *Banking Policy Report* 17 (March 2, 1998), 13–18. The OCC guidelines evaluate whether senior management has significant knowledge and skills to manage the bank's use of technology, including significant involvement of the board of directors in the planning process to manage the bank's technology risk. Banks also must closely scrutinize the operations of vendors to ensure that systems work properly and are secure, and that consumer information is protected. See Hayashi, Sullivan, and Weiner (2003).

Innovative Products and Implicit Interest

Also, managers have come up with innovative deposit products to attract deposit customers. Examples of such innovations include certificates of deposits (CDs) that are indexed to savings goals, such as the cost of education or inflation. For more gaming customers, depository institutions offer CDs with premiums that rise based on the results of football games, elections, or more conventional investments, such as the price of gold or stock market indexes. By offering annuities, mutual funds, and other types of investment services, depository institutions are able to retain customers who prefer one-stop investment shopping. In low interest rate markets, such as the 1990s, banks have offered CDs whose rates will rise periodically, and in booming stock markets, CDs indexed to provide extra returns if the S&P 500 rises. Although such offerings may cannibalize other deposit accounts, they generate fee income and retain some customer deposits. Other implicit interest payments include gifts. For example, a bank in Boulder, Colorado, offered VCRs and Rolex watches to customers opening new CDs. Some banks have used a combination of explicit interest and premiums such as jewelry and rare coins. Others have offered new customer accounts to participate in raffles for gifts.

Increased Use of Deposit Service Charges and Some Customer Lawsuits

Despite dramatic improvements in customer service and products, banks and thrifts have suffered from the perception that fees and low deposit rates charged are not justified from a cost perspective. With the deregulation of interest rates in the 1980s, banks and thrifts began charging explicit or implicit fees for deposit services. Additional fees were imposed in the early 1990s to 2000s to improve falling profitability. At many institutions, customers with high balances are given "free" checking and other implicit interest benefits, suggesting at times that more wealthy customers are receiving a larger "implicit" subsidy from banks. Customers with lower minimum balance accounts are often charged explicitly for each deposit or withdrawal and in some cases for simply using a teller. A study conducted for the House Banking Committee estimated that the average U.S. household faced an increase of 104 percent in the cost of basic banking services from 1979 to 1983—from $91.94 per year to $187.59. However, a study by economists at the Federal Reserve Board concluded that the overall profitability of personal checking accounts did not increase, and that banks were simply charging fees necessary to cover their costs. More recently, in the Board of Governors' Annual Report to the Congress on Retail Fees and Services of Depository Institutions in June 2002, average retail banking fees by size of institution were provided (in 2001 dollars) as follows by banks of different sizes:[10]

Type of Fee	SIZE OF INSTITUTION		
	$100 Million or Less	$100 Million to $1 Billion	Greater Than $1 Billion
Monthly Low Balance			
Fee on NOW accounts	$7.61	$8.52	$10.71
Stop Payment Order	$16.69	$19.46	$21.53
Bounced Check	$19.33	$22.05	$24.70
Deposit Items Returned	$6.82	$7.60	$5.90

A recent study of the role of community banks at the Federal Reserve Bank of Kansas City, where these figures were cited, showed that community banks, which hold larger percentages of core deposits, tend to charge lower average fees for retail services, suggesting that smaller community banks are more interested in attracting retail customers than large banks. As noted in the article, in 2003, there were more than 6,900 community banks with less than $1 billion in assets, accounting for about 20 percent of total deposits, tending to emphasize relationship-banking services. Large banks, in contrast, may prefer specializing in less personal, more transaction-based, large volume types of deposit service where they have a significant advantage with access to technology and the ability to manage a large volume of

---

10 See Keeton, Harvey, and Willis (2003), 29, Table 10, which presents this table along with discussion from the Board of Governors' Annual Report to the Congress on Retail Fees and Services of Depository Institutions, June 2002.

deposit transactions. A recent study of trends in retail fees of depository institutions from 1997 to 2001 by Timothy Hannan (2002), showed that fees tended to rise significantly on common types of depository accounts, as well as minimum balances that depositors needed to maintain to avoid fees. However, the percentage of institutions that charged for some types of ATM fees fell significantly, while other more common types of ATM fees rose significantly. Although large banks charged significantly higher fees than smaller banks, when general locations of institutions were controlled for, the differences became smaller, although still significantly different. With higher fees particularly associated with the use of ATMs outside of a bank's system, there has been much consumer lobbying to regulate these fees and in some cases consumer lawsuits.[11]

Depository institution managers have often failed to provide an adequate explanation for new fees. Consumers are not aware of regulatory costs such as the implicit cost of reserve and capital requirements and explicit cost of deposit insurance premiums that depositories must pay. With mergers resulting in larger banks, service has at times fallen for many large banks because of difficulties integrating different bank cultures and computer and ATM systems.[12]

Lifeline Banking

Concern has been raised about the ability of low-income households to afford services formerly offered as a substitute for market interest rates. Many consumer groups have called for basic (or lifeline) banking legislation at the federal level, requiring that depositories offer a minimum level of financial services to households at low or even no cost. "Basic banking" is generally considered to include the right to a checking account with a low minimum balance requirement and a limited number of free checks per month. Data from the Fed suggest that almost 50 percent of financial institutions had no-frills service packages as early as 1988 and that the proportion of households without checking accounts has not increased despite deregulation. Although many regulators opposed making lifeline banking compulsory for banks if it could not be offered at least on a break-even basis, in 1998 the U.S. government decided that welfare-related payments would only be transmitted electronically, and banks were asked to provide lifeline banking accounts for recipients.[13]

Better Customer Education of the Cost and Nature of Bank Operations

Technology is heavily involved today in the back office processes of check clearing, debiting and crediting accounts, and the assembly and mailing of customer deposit account statements. With technology also comes operating risks including potential fraud or glitches with ATMs, online banking, electronic transfer of deposit funds, encoding errors, mail processing, identity theft, PIN issuance for ATMs and debit cards, meeting courier deadlines, and check-kiting (using the payments system for fraudulent reasons) among other operational risks. These areas all need to be considered as potential costs. Banks also have additional surveillance costs for large cash deposits greater than $10,000 and must file forms with the U.S. government and have copies of IDs made for such large depositors (unless an exemption form is submitted for frequent depositors, such as gambling casinos). Suspicious activity forms must also be submitted for any questionable activities that could encompass money laundering or other illegal activities under the **Bank Secrecy Act. "Know your customer"** regulations and the role of depository institutions as "policing agents" for the government has increased in recent years under the **USA Patriot Act,** where bankers are asked to be on the alert for activities associated with terrorist activities as well, and to help to detect "money trails" that lead to terrorist activities. In lawsuits, banks are also often given subpoenas to provide copies of checks and other information and must use or hire workers to perform such an investigation in microfilming checks for disputing parties as well. A recent rash of bank robberies underscores banks' ongoing need to provide surveillance and security protections. The

---

11 See Keeton, Harvey, and Willis (2003); and Hannan (2002), and Hayashi, Sullivan, and Weiner (2003).

12 See Ingo Walter. *Mergers and Acquisitions in Banking and Finance: What Works, What Fails, and Why.* New York: Oxford University Press, 2004, for a detailed discussion of technology problems associated with merging different bank systems.

13 See Canner and Maland (1987); Board of Governors (1988), 157; Scott (1988); and Robert Trigaus. "Right or Wrong, Lifeline Battle Looms for Banks." *American Banker* (February 1, 1990), 1, 8.

Concept Questions

1 What factors have led to the decline in the percentage of core depositing by banks?

2 How has securitization helped to reduce funding needs of financial institutions?

3 What are FHLB advances and what types of depository institutions are FHLBank members?

4 Give examples of marketing techniques and implicit types of interest that have been used by banks to attract deposits.

5 Why have bank fees for deposits gone up in recent years, particularly for large institutions?

6 Why have bank credit ratings become more important for banks in recent years?

7 What mandates do banks have to meet in serving as policing agents against money laundering and other illegal activities, and in providing lifeline banking? How do these activities help prevent crime?

clearing of billions of dollars of deposits every day without errors is also an elaborate production operations process, involving tellers and ATMs for depositing and withdrawing funds, check coding, technology to sort and debit and credit accounts, separation of checks by location and bank, transporting of checks by courier to correspondent banks or the Fed for processing, finding check errors and detecting problems, notification to customers, preparing customer statements, among many other detailed processing activities. Technology has improved this process with check imaging and automatic sorting of checks, with computerized machines that also detect forgeries, but still there remain many labor-intensive services. Often customers aren't aware of the different costs involved. In recent years, banks and regulators have tried to provide better data to the public on bank costs, so the public can compare different banks' fees and also be aware of the reasonableness of fees.

Factors to Consider in Deposit and Liability Mix

Depository institution managers need to understand a number of different factors that affect the institution's deposit and liability volume, mix, and rate. These include the type of lending business that a bank is in and the loan rates the bank charges, the sophistication of its depositors, its branching system, the services and convenience it offers, its use of advertising, the reputation of the bank, the bank's ATM system, the retail fees the bank charges for ATMs and other deposit services, competing banks' deposit pricing, and operational efficiency, among many other factors. Depository institutions try to attract a favorable mix of deposits to minimize the average or marginal cost of financing. However, often the type of deposits that an institution will attract depends on the type of institution, for instance, a consumer lender, commercial lender, wholesale or retail bank, or supermarket type of bank, since customers often hold their deposits with the same bank they borrow from.

Lending Mix

Whether a bank or thrift can attract different types of deposits is affected by the type of bank it is and the market segment it serves. For instance, a bank that provides consumer loans will also attract more consumer deposits than a bank that primarily focuses on commercial loans. Similarly, a bank that offers home mortgage loans at attractive rates, such as Wells Fargo, discussed in Chapter 4, may have loyal home mortgage customers who prefer to keep their deposits at Wells Fargo and accept lower interest rates on these deposits. Credit unions are financed by consumer deposits because they make loans to consumers.

However, a bank focusing on commercial loans will attract more business demand deposits, which, at the time of this writing, are not allowed to pay interest. Banks generally give such business loan customers the choice of paying fees or holding compensating balances in the form of demand deposits (in effect charging implicit interest) or a combination of the two. Large companies often choose key banks as concentration banks where deposit funds are consolidated, through automated clearinghouse (ACH) or electronic transfers from other banks around the country (or branches of an interstate bank). Hence, firms may benefit from paying for services with compensating balances that remain with a bank, given necessary clearing times. Banks also provide sweep accounts for businesses, so they can earn interest on savings accounts until funds are needed, when they are swept to demand deposit accounts. Other wholesale banks that have few or no branches, in contrast, must rely on nondeposit funds for financing. Thus, in terms of a bank's market segment and the type of loans it makes, asset management and relationship management with customers that receive working capital management or other services are closely related to its deposit and liability management. In April of 2004, at the time of this writing, the House passed the Financial Services Regulatory Relief Act of 2004 (HR 1375), legislation that included a removal of the prohibition of paying interest on business checking accounts. This bill was sent to the Senate Banking Committee for consideration (see the FDIC Website for any regulatory updates at *http://www.fdic.gov*).

Greater Depositor Sophistication

With the deregulation of interest rates in the 1980s, the dramatic growth in money market and mutual funds, and the greater availability of information for consumers, depositors have become more sophisticated and less loyal to particular financial institutions. Consequently, retail CDs have became much more interest rate sensitive, with CD depositors willing to pull funds out despite withdrawal penalties if other institutions or funds offer higher rates. This has been particularly the case for large, insured CDs of $100,000 (often called jumbo CDs), discussed in a later section. Investors have also invested more in mutual fund bond and stock funds that have offered higher returns. Hence, banks and thrifts must competitively price such interest-sensitive deposits, which are often repriced weekly based on T-bill rates and the rates offered by competitors. The best savings rates are readily available to savers on the Internet, in published newsletters, and in magazines and newspapers. The Bank Rate Monitor collects and publishes CD rate data in a weekly report *(http://www.bankrate.com)*. As shown in Figure 15.1, in late April 2004, even the top FDIC-insured bank deposit rates were quite low, but rates varied across different lenders, with rates at historically low levels.

More National Advertising to Attract Funds Across the Country and More Competition for Funds

As Figure 15.1 illustrates, consumers have greater access to rates across the country, with top rates posted in newspapers and on the Web. Consumers may prefer to have transaction accounts in nearby depository institutions that offer convenient national automated teller machine (ATM) networks, which make branches less of a priority. With the advent of interstate banks, such as Bank of America, it is easier for depositors using such banks to deposit and cash checks nationwide. With national advertising and the advent of cyberbanks and direct banks, it is also easier for banks to attract funds from different regions. Nonbanks, such as securities firms, also offer money market funds and resource management accounts with check-writing privileges and other services. Similarly, mutual fund companies offer check writing, and some companies—including Fidelity, American Century, Dreyfus, Scudder, and USAA—offer debit cards.[14] Well-capitalized banks are allowed to use brokers who receive a commission to solicit deposits on a national or international basis, usually ensuring that jumbo CDs sold to individuals are a maximum of $100,000 each. Brokered deposits are only a small percentage of total deposits, however, only 3.62 percent at the end of 2003.[15] Credit unions, which have lower costs and are not taxed, also are formidable competitors for banks and thrifts, with the ability to offer lower fees and at times more attractive deposit rates.

Average Liability Mix for Commercial Banks and Savings Institutions

At the end of 2003, FDIC-insured banks and savings institutions had the following average liability structure as a percentage of total assets, which has remained fairly stable since 2000 (see *http://www2 .fdic.gov/sod/;* or go to *http://www.fdic.gov,* click on the Quick Link for "Analysts," and then click on

---

14 See Vanessa O'Connell. "It's a Broker! It's a Banker! It's a Mutual-Fund Group!" *The Wall Street Journal* (February 19, 1998), C1.

15 See FDIC Website, Statistics on Banking, December 30, 2003.

"Statistics on Banking" to get the FDIC Statistics on Depository Institutions Report showing the national averages and percentages for depository institution liabilities):

	Percent of Assets (12/31/2003)
Total Liabilities	90.85
Total Deposits	65.60
Interest-Bearing Deposits	54.54
Deposits Held in Domestic Offices	57.43
Time Deposits Less Than $100,000	8.06
Total Time and Savings Deposits	47.81
Total Time Deposits	16.66
Noninterest-Bearing Deposits	10.66
Interest-Bearing Deposits	46.77
Core Retail Deposits	48.15
IRAs and Keogh Plan Accounts	2.45
Brokered Deposits	3.62
Fully Insured	2.38
Deposit Accounts of $100,000 or Less	30.07
Estimated Insured Deposits	38.01
Estimated Assessable Deposits	57.04
Deposits Held in Foreign Offices	8.16
Federal Funds Purchased & Repurchase Agreements	6.84
Trading Liabilities	3.02
Other Borrowed Funds	11.34
Subordinated Debt	1.18
All Other Liabilities	2.87
Equity Capital	
Perpetual Preferred Stock	0.08
Common Stock & Surplus	5.00
Undivided Profits (Retained Earnings)	4.07

As shown in the preceding table, FDIC-insured banks and savings institutions had on average 65.60 percent of deposits to assets, with 57.43 percent held in domestic offices. About 48.15 percent included core (retail, insured) deposits with the majority of core deposits in transaction accounts (NOW, Super-NOW, and demand deposits) and 8.06 percent in time deposits of less than $100,000, with total time deposits (including times deposits of $100,000 or greater) 16.66 percent of total assets. About 46.77 percent on average of deposits to assets were interest-bearing deposits. IRA and Keogh plan accounts were 2.45 percent of assets and brokered deposits 3.62 percent (2.38 percent of these fully insured). Quarterly mutual fund sales by comparison were $3.345 billion (indicating competition that depository institutions have within their own banks for deposits).

Although not shown (available at *http://www2.fdic.gov*), for the 7,769 FDIC-insured commercial banks the percentage of deposits to assets on average was lower (56.40 percent compared with 62.77 percent) than the average for 1,413 savings institutions operating at the end of 2003. For both banks and thrifts, the larger institutions with greater than $1 billion in assets (424 banks and 157 thrifts) had a much lower average deposit-to-asset ratio (63.51 percent and 59.69 percent) compared with the average community bank and thrift (less then $1 billion in assets) with about 75 percent deposits to assets for community banks and 78 percent for community thrifts. Community banks and thrifts also held a larger percentage of cheaper core deposits (69 percent and 73 percent) with the largest percentages for the smallest (less than $100 million) category. Hence, larger banks and thrifts with greater than $1 billion in assets (424 very large banks and 157 very large thrifts) engage in greater liability management in terms of financing with a larger percentage of noncore deposit financing and other types of borrowings. As an example of the greater importance of noncore financing for particular very large banks, in 2003 JPMorgan Chase Bank's percentage of core (retail insured) deposits was only 23.87 percent compared with 52.98 percent for peer banks, suggesting that the proposed merger in 2004 with Banc One might provide benefits in terms of greater core deposit financing, often a big incentive in merger considerations.[16]

Considerations in the Pricing of Deposits

An important part of deposit management is the pricing of deposits including understanding the marginal cost of funds and weighted average marginal cost of funds to determine the types of deposits that an institution wants to attract, considerations in the setting of explicit deposit rates, and explicit costs associated with deposits.

The Marginal Cost of Funds

With declining NIMs in the latter 1980s, banks and thrifts became more aware of the need to reduce operating expenses, including the major costs entailed with administering deposit accounts. Loan rates are often priced from a bank's marginal cost of funds, which includes administrative and processing costs for deposits. When these costs can be lowered, loans can be more competitively priced. The marginal cost of funds for a bank is typically used as a base rate in pricing loans, as discussed in Chapter 13, and in calculating risk-adjusted returns on capital (RAROC), discussed in Chapter 6, to ensure that loan prices adequately reflect the true cost of bank funds. In addition to the base cost of funds based on interest expenses, depository institutions have considerable operating costs involved in collecting and servicing deposit accounts, from tellers to backroom processing and clearing of checks, to keeping accounting records of total deposits, tracking of quality (errors), employing bank guards to prevent robberies, and keeping detailed records for regulatory agencies for deposit insurance and reserve requirement assessments, among other regulatory requirements.

Setting Explicit Interest Rates

Most depository institution managers had little experience in setting rates to attract funds before 1980. The negotiable CD, Fed funds, and Eurodollar markets are national or international in scope, so even managers practicing liability management faced limited discretion in rate setting. Today, managers of all depositories are required to use judgment. One course of action is simply to follow the crowd—to establish interest rates similar to those offered by key competitors, especially ones viewed as market leaders. For many years, some depositories have used this strategy to establish loan rates, and some studies find evidence of smaller institutions following rate changes of very large institutions within metropolitan areas in the mid-1980s. However, in the late 1980s, the 1990s, and early 2000s, there is increasing evidence of expanding geographic retail banking markets.[17] Many institutions appear to take more control over the explicit prices paid for deposits. Studies of retail deposit pricing have found differences in pricing patterns about depository institutions, with individual institutions not following the crowd all the time. An individual institution would often raise or lower rates relative to its market competitors. Further, as market rates rose or fell, not all institutions adjusted rates equally quickly or in the same magnitude. Researchers have also found at times aggressive approaches to pricing consumer deposits with bank managers considering many different factors including the cost of alternative sources of wholesale funds, the rates set by competitors, and the degree to which customers would respond to changes in interest rates with managers gathering data to estimate depositors' sensitivity to pricing decisions.

---

16 Ibid.

17 See Lawrence J. Radecki. "The Expanding Geographic Reach of Retail Banking Markets." *Federal Reserve Bank of New York Policy Review* 4 (June 1998), 15–34. Studies in the early 1990s found evidence of geographical integration for the retail price-setting decisions of large depository institutions and between banks and thrifts in local markets, including Elizabeth S. Cooperman, Winson B. Lee, and James P. Lesage. "Geographical Integration and the Retail Pricing Decisions of Large Depository Institutions." *The Review of Economics and Statistics* 73 (August 1991), 546–552; and "Commercial Bank and Thrift Interdependence and Local Market Competition for Retail Certificates of Deposit." *Journal of Financial Services Research* 4 (March 1990), 37–51. For other more recent papers examining this issue, see current financial economics working papers on the Federal Reserve Board Website (*http://www.federal reserve.gov*).

Withdrawal penalties for time deposits must be priced as well. A recent study finds that the bank CD-Treasury rate spreads for 100 large commercial banks from June 1990 to 1997 were negative, averaging 41 basis points, suggesting that depositors accept lower yields on CDs in return for their withdrawal option.[18]

Costs Incurred for Specific Account-Related Services

Ideally, prices should be related to the costs incurred by the institution, so cost analysis has begun to attract more attention. Prior to 2000, the Fed provided a functional cost analysis (FCA) service that gave unit costs for different key services offered by depository institutions. However, this analysis was phased out after 2000. Sheshunoff, among other private bank information companies, as well as trade groups in each industry have been active in collecting information on unit costs in books that can be purchased by banks. Large banks also often have their own unit cost accounting systems and measures. As noted in Chapter 13 on lending, banks also use relationship pricing for large customers, providing business customers with a choice of paying for services with compensating deposits or explicit fees for services.[19]

Different Pricing Strategies

In the 1990s many depository institutions realized that they had poor pricing strategies. Paul Allen (1994, p. 57) in *Reengineering the Bank* in his introduction to Chapter 3, "The Pricing Impact of the Past," notes that banks have not understood "the true nature of their complex common cost structures" and have "woefully underpriced for: (1) transaction services to reflect the value they provide; (2) geographic differences in relative price sensitivity; and (3) the specific risk of commercial borrowers." He also points out that banks that have attempted to adjust prices to make them adequate to cover costs "must now battle both consumer advocate groups and antitrust regulators who will make repricing in the future even more difficult."[20] This view is in contrast to complaints and lawsuits about rising bank fees. He notes several different types of pricing strategies including: (1) cost-based pricing, which is the cost of an activity plus a profit margin; (2) competition-based pricing, whereby a bank follows a market leader's price; and (3) value-based pricing, which is based on customer behavior including price elasticity and then "factors in cost and competition." Paul Allen notes that the first strategies create problems because it is very difficult to allocate common costs in banking and to estimate these costs, since costs for different activities are intertwined and following the competition does not take into consideration whether a bank's cost structure can cover the costs, with neither strategy considering the price elasticity of customers (i.e., the change in demand by a customer with a percent change in price). Value-based pricing, in contrast, examines changes in customer behavior with changes in prices as a primary focus, followed then by an examination of cost and competition factors. Examining the relative sensitivity of prices includes both "financial and psychological factors," such as "amount of payment, frequency of purchase, complexity of product, pricing structure, switching cost, availability of information, and image," and local convenience factors favored by customers. In finance, until recently psychology wasn't considered a large factor in pricing considerations, but accessibility, image, quality of service, technical knowledge, reputation, customer relationships, and courtesy are often qualitative factors that affect the attractiveness of putting deposits with a particular depository institution. Many community banks have capitalized on qualitative factors and customer relationships to attract customers that felt disenfranchised by very large banks that forgot the importance of these factors, as they became more transactionally focused. Other very large banks have tried to regain a more personal focus, such as the concept of personal bankers. Paul Allen points out a particularly egregious example of banks following a cost-based strategy at the expense of considerations of customers and value-based

---

18 See James H. Gilkeson, Gary E. Porter, and Stanley D. Smith. "The Impact of the Early Withdrawal Option on Time Deposit Pricing." *Quarterly Review of Economics and Finance* 40 (2000), 107–120.

19 See Maness and Zietlow (2002) for a detailed discussion on bank relationship pricing and calculations of alternative bank pricing using compensating balances versus explicit fees by companies.

20 See Allen (1994), Chapter 3, 57–62.

pricing. Banks popularly engaged in cost-based pricing for individual customers and found that low-balance customers provided for a large percentage of costs and very low revenues. Accordingly, they attempted to charge much higher (tiered) fees for such customers and force customers to use ATMs versus bank teller lines. This approach ignored the fact that cost allocations were actually just a fictitious accounting allocation, with such customers not really increasing bank costs. This type of pricing resulted in unhappy customers, consumer protests, "significant Community Reinvestment Act" problems, and poor publicity for banks, resulting in "cost accounting overcoming common sense," and "fictional costs" begetting "aberrant pricing."[21]

Estimating the Marginal Cost of a Deposit Account

After determining the interest and servicing costs of each type of deposit account, managers must consider additional costs imposed by regulation. One model widely cited in the academic and practitioner literature estimates the marginal interest and noninterest costs of an additional deposit dollar (MCD) as follows:[22]

$$MCD = \frac{I + S + DI}{I - RR} \qquad [15.1]$$

where

I = current market interest rate on type of deposit;

S = servicing costs of deposits expressed as percentage of each dollar acquired

DI = deposit insurance premium (expressed as percentage of each insured dollar)

RR = Fed reserve requirement on type of deposit

Suppose an institution's managers have decided to pursue a retail banking strategy. They have determined that the current market interest rate on NOW accounts is 6.5 percent and the cost of servicing a basic NOW account is 3.4 percent (including unlimited transactions and the use of a teller window). Also, Fed reserve requirements on transactions accounts are 10 percent, and the deposit insurance premium is 0.254 percent. Note the Fed reserve requirement represents the nonearning percentage of that deposit, since that portion must be held in cash or deposits with the Fed for reserve requirements. In 2003, the reserve requirements for transaction deposits were 3 percent for deposits of more than $6.6 to $45.4 million, and 10 percent for deposits over $45.4 million. Thus, for the marginal cost, the reserve requirement of 10 percent would reflect that new deposits for the marginal cost would be in the latter category. Using Equation 15.1, the marginal cost of offering a NOW account in this interest rate and regulatory environment is as follows:

$$MCNOW = \frac{0.065 + 0.034 + 0.00254}{1 - 0.10} = 0.1128, \text{ or } 11.28\%$$

A similar analysis can be performed for each fund source customarily used by the institution and a weighted average of these costs can also be estimated (i.e., the sum of each marginal cost times the fraction of funds used as a percentage of total financing). The weighted marginal average cost of deposits and other liabilities is one of the main determinants of required lending rates. Marginal costs are also used in determining how to price accounts to attract the quantity of desired deposits from target customer segments. The marginal cost (expected cost of the deposits that will be involved in the actual funding of a loan) rather than the historical average cost is used, since with changes in rates and other costs, incremental costs change, so a historical average cost reflects the past, not the future.

---

21 Ibid.

22 See Watson (1977, 1978).

1 What factors affect the type of deposits that a depository institution will likely have?

2 What are some recent trends in trying to attract core deposits?

3 How do very large and smaller community banks differ in their liability structures including core deposits?

4 Why is it important to calculate the marginal cost and the weighted marginal cost of each type of liability? What types of costs are included?

5 What are different deposit pricing strategies, and which seems to be the best? Explain.

Overview of Types of Deposit and Nondeposit Borrowing

Chapter 4 provided an overview of different types of deposits and liabilities, and now this section briefly discusses some of their features.

Retail Deposit Accounts

Different types of deposit accounts often have special features. **Demand deposits** (noninterest negotiable orders of withdrawal at thrifts) as business transaction accounts do not pay interest and are subject to reserve requirements, although legislation is currently pending in Congress to remove the no-interest restriction. **NOW accounts** as retail transactions pay variable or fixed interest, offer unlimited number of transactions, and are subject to reserve requirements. **SuperNOW** accounts have a higher minimum balance (subject to the depository institution's discretion) and pay higher rates than regular NOWs. Generally, NOWs are not subject to restrictions, although institutions may reserve the right to require seven days advance notice before withdrawal (same with MMDAs and Passbook savings accounts). **Money market deposit accounts** (MMDAs) typically pay higher interest rates than NOW accounts, but preauthorized transfer to and from the account is often limited to six per month, though transfers in person or through ATMs are not limited. **Passbook savings** (savings shares at CUs) have no checking-writing privileges and pay fixed or variable rates. **Nonnegotiable (retail) certificates of deposits** (share certificates of CUs) have minimum maturity of seven days and fixed or variable interest rates, with forfeiture penalties imposed on withdrawals within the first six days and additional penalties may be imposed on nonpersonal accounts with original maturities of eighteen months or more. **Individual retirement accounts** (IRAs) have maturities depending on the type of instrument they are invested in with interest earned on accounts tax-deferred, and penalties for withdrawal before age $59\frac{1}{2}$. **Jumbo negotiable CDs** have a minimum maturity of seven days, with fixed or variable interest rates, and a $100,000 minimum denomination. The depositor can sell the negotiable CD prior to maturity with the price market determined and no federal deposit insurance on amounts over $100,000. Most negotiable CDs are issued directly to customers, although some large institutions issue them to dealers who then sell them to other investors.[23]

Other Noncore Deposits and Sources of Financing

Sources of noncore financing include the following types of funds: Fed Funds Purchased, Eurodollar Deposits, Repurchase Agreements, Mortgage-Backed Bonds, Deposit Notes and Bank Notes, and for longer-term capital, Preferred Stock and Trust Preferred Stock, among others.

   Fed Funds Purchased, unlike the discount window that is discouraged for regulators by the Fed, are used by many depositories on a daily basis. Fed Funds play a central role in reserve requirement management. The lending institution instructs the Fed or its correspondent bank to transfer agreed-upon balances to the borrower instantaneously through Fedwire, the Fed's communication system. Because most Fed Funds transactions are overnight loans, the transaction is usually reversed the next day but

---

23 See *Federal Reserve Bulletins*, various issues, and "Insured Accounts for Savers," pamphlet by Federal Reserve Bank of Richmond, April 1988, and other more recent years for descriptions of retail savings accounts and their characteristics.

includes one day's interest calculated at the Fed Funds rate. Fed Funds are readily available, but the cost is difficult to forecast giving daily changes in the Fed Funds rate. A relatively small market exists for "term" Fed Funds transactions, with maturities of one week to six months, or sometimes longer.[24]

Eurodollar Deposits (Eurodeposits) are time deposits denominated in dollars but held in banks outside the United States such as foreign branches of U.S. banks. While Eurodeposits are created in several ways, the most typical way is when a domestic customer transfers funds on deposits in the United States to a foreign bank or branch. The motivation is usually to obtain a higher rate of interest while facing no currency exchange risk, since the deposit remains in dollars. Eurodeposits become a source of funds to domestic institutions when they borrow from foreign banks or branches, creating a liability reported on the domestic bank's balance sheet as "Due to Foreign Banks or Branches." Eurodeposits may range in maturity from overnight to five years, with the average six months or less. They are nonnegotiable and are not currently subject to Fed reserve requirements or deposit insurance premiums. Traditionally, all transactions are carried out electronically over the Clearing House Interbank Payments System (CHIPS), a privately owned transfer system in New York. Funds actually never leave the home country. Eurodeposits are really nothing more than a series of accounting entries, resulting in the customer's holding a time deposit and the domestic bank's incurring a liability. Eurodollar rates are similar to alternative sources of funds; for instance, for overnight Eurodollars, the rate is close to the Fed Funds rate plus a small premium.[25]

Repurchase Agreements (repos) are the sale of marketable securities by an institution, with an agreement to repurchase at a specified higher price at a specified future date. The seller obtains cash for liquidity purposes while the buyer has the "reverse repo" as a short-term investment. As long as securities pledged against repos are U.S. government or government agency securities, repos are not subject to reserve requirements. The cost of issuing repos is ordinarily lower than the rate paid on Fed Funds or negotiable CDs with similar maturities, since default risk is lower given the security backing. Repo maturities range from overnight to thirty days or longer. If transactions are between institutions and individuals, they are called "retail repos." Since they are not deposits, they are not subject to reserve requirements and are ineligible for deposit insurance.

Mortgage-Backed Bonds are debt obligations backed by expected cash flows from an institution's general mortgage portfolio, allowing low interest rates at a slight premium above Treasury bonds. Because of administration and flotation costs, mortgage-backed bonds are usually issued with minimum face values of $100 million. To make it easier for small depositories to use mortgage-backed securities, methods have been developed by which several firms working together can pool collateral and issue bonds. Pooling has increased the participation of smaller thrift institutions in this form of liability management.

Deposit Notes and Bank Notes are medium-term sources of funds (maturities ranging from two to five years) and are designed to appeal to investors with particular risk/return preferences. **Deposit notes** are similar to negotiable CDs, in that an investor receives deposit insurance protection up to $100,000. Unlike CDs, however, deposit notes are evaluated by rating agencies and are often accompanied by a brief circular describing the financial condition of the insuring institution. Although they are not negotiable, the existence of a formal rating for the notes makes them attractive to some investors, such as insurance companies, which ordinarily do not (or cannot in some states) own unrated securities. As a result of costs associated with the rating process, deposit notes carry lower interest rates than negotiable CDs issued by the same institution.

Bank Notes are similar to deposit notes in that they carry agency ratings, but they differ in that they are uninsured and can be traded in secondary markets. Since they are uninsured, they have a higher interest rate than deposit notes but do not have to pay deposit insurance premiums. Bank notes are marketed primarily to sophisticated investors investing large amounts.

Financing Sources That Serve as Secondary Capital

As discussed in Chapter 6 on capital management, subordinated debt and preferred stock, along with convertible debentures and convertible preferred stock, can be used as secondary capital, subject to the

---

24 See Stigum (1990); Goodfriend and Whelpley (1986); and Wood and Wood (1985), Chapter 9.

25 There are also negotiable Eurodollar CDs for which there is a secondary market centered in London. This market is relatively small, so few institutions are able to raise funds by issuing these. Nonnegotiable Eurodeposits are a much more common source of funds for U.S. banks.

regulatory rules that were discussed. **Subordinated debt** has advantages in terms of the deductibility of interest providing a tax advantage and having a long-term maturity for a longer duration of liabilities to match up with the longer duration of fixed rate assets that the bank holds. Convertible debentures can be issued at lower rates, given the sweetener of the conversion option. Generally, an average convertible has a maturity of twelve years, floating rates, and the option for the issuer to redeem the debentures (call option) after four years. Convertible debentures have the disadvantages of dilution on earnings if they are converted in the future. **Preferred stock,** although not tax deductible, has the advantage if it is perpetual of being Tier 1 capital, as well as Tier 2 capital. Adjustable-rate preferred stock has been very popular (with adjustments based on changes on Treasury security rates). Preferred stock has the advantage of not diluting earnings and can be particularly advantageous as an equity financing source when a bank's common stock is underpriced. No sinking funds are necessary, reducing cash flow requirements for perpetual preferred shares as well versus debt, and similarly, convertible preferred stock can be sold at a higher price (lower yield), although the conversion creates the potential for dilution of earnings. **Trust preferred stock** has also been popular for banks in the past decade, because it allows the payment of tax-deductible dividends by having a separately established trust company sell preferred stock to investors, with the proceeds loaned to the bank. Hence, the interest that the bank pays on its loan to the trust is equal to the dividends that are paid to the preferred stockholders, providing the bank a lower after-tax cost of funds, as well as a source of Tier 1 capital.[26]

Deposit Insurance and Regulatory Considerations

With insured deposits, depository institutions have to follow many federal regulations including regulations for reserve requirements, discussed in Chapter 14, deposit insurance premium assessments, and other consumer regulations including check-clearing times.

Speed of Deposit Clearing, Pledged, and Correspondent Bank Deposits

Under the Competitive Equality Banking Act of 1987, depository institutions are required to cash government checks for customers and under Title VI (**Expedited Funds Availability Act**) to make funds from local deposits available to customers within one business day and within a reasonable time (generally within three business days) for out-of-state checks. Banks are also asked to post their deposit availability schedules. For uninsured public deposits (Treasury tax and loan accounts and local and state government accounts), banks are required to hold these in safe, qualified securities (generally government securities), as a **pledging requirement.** Banks can become qualified depositories and must generally pay a rate based on the going market repurchase rate. In some states, bids are taken with the state accepting the highest bid rate. Some states require pledging of securities against demand and time deposits for state and local governments as well. **Correspondent deposits** are also often a significant fund source, whereby banks leave compensating balances with their correspondent bank for their services including check clearance, investment advice, international entry, and loan participations. In this case, the correspondent bank needs to be sure that profits are made from funds held in the place of fees.[27]

Risk-Based Deposit Insurance Premiums

As noted in the calculation of the marginal cost of deposits, reserve requirements and assessments for deposit insurance increase the marginal cost of deposits, which needs to be carefully considered. Some financial institutions, such as credit card banks that have triple-A credit ratings, fund themselves with nondeposit funds, finding deposit funding and its corresponding regulatory requirements too expensive. The FDIC has a risk-based premium system with higher rates assessed for institutions that impose higher risks to insurance funds. To assess appropriate premiums, the FDIC puts each institution into one of nine risk categories based on a two-step process on capital ratios (the capital group assignment) and then based on other relevant information (the supervisory subgroup assignment). Capital groups

---

26 See Mark Dobbins. "Trust-Preferred Securities." *Cleveland Fed, Fourth District Conditions,* Vol. 1, Issue 2 (December 2000). Recent issues can be found on the Cleveland Fed's Website *(http://www.clevelandfed.org/bsr/conditions).* Also see Koch and MacDonald (2000), 532–533, for a more detailed discussion of trust preferred stock.

27 See Koch and MacDonald (2000).

as discussed in Chapter 6 include Group 1, well capitalized (total risk-based capital ratio equal to or greater than 10 percent, Tier 1 risk-based capital ratio equal or greater than 6 percent, and Tier 1 capital to assets equal to or greater than 5 percent); Group 2, adequate capitalization (total risk-based capital ratio equal to or greater than 8 percent, Tier 1 risk-based capital ratio equal to or greater than 4 percent, and Tier 1 leverage ratio equal to or greater than 4 percent); and Group 3, undercapitalized (not adequately capitalized). The institution's primary regulator assigns it to one of the three groups based on capital ratios and other information that is determined to be relevant. The FDIC then assigns a supervisory subgroup for each institution for each semiannual assessment period based on a number of different factors and examination reviews, as well as an examination of financial data and other pertinent information. Subgroups include A (best, only a few minor weaknesses), a CAMELS rating of 1 or 2; B (weakness that could increase the risk of loss for insurers), rating of 3; and C (substantial risk of loss unless effective action is taken), rating of 4 or 5. Premiums rates are reviewed semiannually. Initially, when the risk-based assessment system was introduced in January of 1993, annual assessment rates were between 23 to 31 cents of $100 of assessable deposits. After BIF reached the Designated Reserve Ratio (DRR) of 1.25 percent at the end of May 1995, a reduction was put in place for a range of 4 to 31 cents per $100 in assessable deposits, and in November 1995 reduced to a range of 0 to 23 cents per $100 in assessable deposits by January 1996. In 1996, SAIF assessment rates were reduced to the same amount.

The current assessment rate schedule is as follows for BIF and SAIF institutions, where bp (basis points) is cents per $100 of assessable deposits (annual rates):[28]

	SUPERVISORY SUBGROUP		
Capital Group	**A**	**B**	**C**
1. Well	0 bp	3 bp	17 bp
2. Adequate	3 bp	10 bp	24 bp
3. Under	10 bp	24 bp	27 bp

The Financing Corporation (FICO) assessments are separate from FDIC insurance assessments. FICO was established under the Competitive Equality Banking Act of 1987 as a mixed-ownership government corporation and a financing vehicle (originally to issue bonds and pay the interest to help bail out the FSLIC following the S&L crisis) that has the authority to collect funds from the FDIC-insured institutions adequate to pay interest on FICO bonds. The Deposit Insurance Funds Act of 1996 (DIFA) authorized assessments for SAIF- and BIF-insured institutions, originally with BIF-insured institutions paying one-fifth of the SAIF rate until the end of 1999, and the same rate thereafter. The assessments are adjusted quarterly; in 2004, for both BIF and SAIF at about 1.54 basis points per $100 assessable deposits per quarter.

Other Obligations to Inform the Public

As regulated institutions, depository institution managers are required to state the annual percentage rate for deposits and loans, as required under FIRREA, which became effective in 1993. The Fed's truth-in-savings rules stipulate that depositories must uniformly publish the fees, service charges, and annual yields associated with each account to promote intelligent shopping for financial services among consumers. Key provisions include a prohibition against advertising accounts as "free" if they contain any conditions, such as a minimum account balance, that might impose a fee on the customer if the conditions are violated. The annual percentage rate on accounts must be disclosed including the effect of service charges and fees, basically a calculation of what the customer pays divided by what the customer invested on an annual basis. For more complex features and longer maturity, more detailed information needs to be provided to consumers. Customers also need to be carefully informed if deposits or

---

28 See FDIC, "Risk-Based Assessment—Overview," on the FDIC Website *(http://www.fdic.gov/deposit/insurance/risk).*

other investment products are not insured. Similarly, they should be informed of the coverage rules for deposit insurance. Depositors are insured up to a maximum of $100,000, exclusive of individual retirement accounts, which are also provided up to $100,000 at a single insured institution. In addition, a family of four could possibly have deposit insurance up to $1.4 million at each institution they have a relationship with, as long as no more than $100,000 is claimed by any one legal owner. Hence, under the current system, most consumers can have full coverage for all their deposits (see *http://www.fdic .gov/deposit/deposits* for current information explaining insurance coverage to bank customers).[29]

Concept Questions

1 What are some typical core deposits of depository institutions and their characteristics?

2 What are some typical noncore types of financing? What advantages and disadvantages do they have?

3 List some important regulatory considerations for institutions as deposit collectors.

4 Describe how risk-based deposit insurance premiums are assessed. What are the current risk-premium assessments?

5 How much insurance coverage do retail depositors have? What information must be given to depositors by depository institutions?

Summary

Deposit and nondeposit liabilities for depository institutions and regulations governing their management are the subjects of this chapter. The phase-out of Reg Q gave institutions new freedom to offer a wide variety of accounts with different maturities and interest rate characteristics. Larger and more aggressive institutions also rely heavily on managed liabilities, including negotiable CDs, Eurodollar deposits, repurchase agreements, mortgage-backed securities, brokered deposits, deposit notes, and bank notes. Even contingent liabilities serve as sources of discretionary funds for some institutions.

The elimination of restrictions on institutions' access to funds has given managers new challenges. Institutions formerly relying on implicit interest payments as the only allowable form of competition now develop pricing strategies, and the choice between explicit and implicit interest affects the volatility of returns. Many firms offer flexible pricing mechanisms that provide more choices to customers and to management. Fed rules require uniform disclosure of an institution's fee structure and yields on deposits. In conjunction with pricing decisions, management must evaluate wholesale and retail market strategies and choose the mix of funds that firms will seek.

Federal deposit insurance continues to influence management decisions. Insurance reduces the risk borne by depositors and therefore reduces the potential instability of funds to insured institutions. Because insurance premiums have only recently been adjusted to reflect the relative riskiness of an institution, it is too early to know whether the substantial moral hazard, which contributed to many depository failures over the past decade, has been brought under control. Several recommendations for additional reform have been considered, but there is no doubt that some form of deposit insurance will continue to provide a buffer against loss of confidence in the financial system.

29 See Brian P. Smith. "Adding Up Truth in Savings." *Savings and Community Banker* 2 (August 1993), 46–48; "Truth in Savings." *Banking Legislation and Policy* (Federal Reserve Bank of Philadelphia) (September/October 1992), 3; Phil Roosevelt. "Banks Race Truth-in-Savings Deadline." *American Banker* (January 7, 1993), 1, 10; Francis A. Grady. "Innocent Errors Create Liability Under the Truth-in-Savings Act." *American Banker* (March 23, 1993), 4, 17. The hypothetical deposit insurance of a family includes a combination of individual accounts, joint accounts, and revocable trust accounts.

Questions

1. Celestine Abeyta and Malena Brohm are the Chairs of the Board of Directors at the UCD Bank in Denver, Colorado. They ask you as their favorite adviser to research why banks have lost their percentage of core deposit financing over the last few decades and what banks have done to try to retain retail core deposits. Why does noncore financing generally involve higher interest expenses, liquidity, and interest rate risk for a bank? Can noncore financing have advantages over financing in some cases given reserve requirements and insurance premiums for some core deposits? Explain advantages and disadvantages of each type of financing.

2. Beth Polizzotto is the CEO of the Mountain High Community Bank (MHCB) in Denver. She is looking for nondeposit sources of financing for her bank. Explain the nondeposit sources of funding MHCB could use as a community bank including ways to engage in securitization activities, FHLB advances, Fed Funds purchased, repurchase agreements, and deposit notes and bank notes.

3. Chen Ji, Barb Pelter, and Marianne Plunkert, executives at the International Mountain Bank, are trying to find the best pricing system for the bank's deposits. Explain the different pricing strategies that Paul Allen notes that banks have often used including (1) cost-based pricing, (2) competition-based pricing; and (3) value-based pricing. What are the advantages and disadvantages of the different strategies?

4. Linda Olson, Nancy Reed, and Shelley Townley are famous consumer advocates. They would like to know why retail deposit bank fees have increased. Please discuss public relations problems that banks have had in connection with public perceptions of the fees and services that banks offer and how banks can improve this image. Do you think retail fees are justified? Also, explain why community banks tend to have lower retail fees than larger banks.

5. Sueann Ambron, J. C. Bosch, and Ken Bettenhausen are owners of the Sunshine Mountain Bank, a very large bank in Colorado. Discuss with them some different types of nondeposit liabilities for very large banks. Also, explain how consumer sophistication affects the volatility of bank deposits. Compare and contrast the risks of each liability source with those of traditional deposit sources of funds.

6. Judy Chavez, Marti Mann, and JoAnna Ramirez-Darnell are, respectively, CEO, President, and CFO of the Alpine Savings and Loan in Denver. They would like to know more about ways lenders use mortgage-backed bonds to obtain new funds. Please explain to them how a mortgage-backed bond is created. Also, explain the advantages and disadvantages of subordinated debt, preferred stock, and trust preferred stock.

7. Rene Gash is the President of the Colorado Internet Bank. As president, she would like you to prepare a report on the evolution in the payments system. Explain how Internet banks are able to attract funds without having to open their own branches or ATM systems. How are they able to offer higher deposit rates than other banks? Give some examples of how the payments system has changed with technology including the greater use of debit cards and ATMs. How does this create efficiency in the banking system, but also at times higher costs?

8. Cindy Sutfin, John Daley, and John Byrd are starting a new savings institution in Durango. They would like to attract new deposits and are thinking about using brokered deposits. Explain to them what brokered deposits are and the advantages they offer to financial institutions. What are the risks involved? What requirements must banks meet to be allowed to have brokered deposits?

9. Debbie Capaldi, Resa Cooper-Morning, and Linda Theus-Lee of the Delightful Morning Credit Union are planning a big promotion to attract new depositors. Give them some good ideas and explain what implicit interest payments are and how and why depositories have been using implicit payments. How can implicit interest pricing strategies affect the stability of earnings as interest revenues change? How is the cost of implicit payments measured? Give some examples for banks and thrifts based on recent advertisements in newspapers, television, the radio, the Internet, or other sources.

10. Jamie Esparza, Ashley Feaster, and Ashley Harder are financial consultants with the Esparza-Feaster-Harder Financial Group and are preparing a report on how depository institutions determine their marginal cost of funds. Explain how interest rates, servicing costs, deposit insurance premiums, and reserve requirements are included in calculating the marginal cost of a particular type of fund. Explain how deposit insurance reduces the interest cost of funds but also can increase the noninterest costs. How is the weighted average marginal cost calculated?

11. Bob Harmon and Joel Penick have been working on a report on the Role of Bankers in Detecting Money Laundering, Fraud, and Other Suspicious Activity. Explain bankers' duties in knowing their customers and in providing a policing role for the government under the Bank Secrecy Act and proposed Know Your Cus-

tomer Rules. How does deposit-taking involve security precautions by banks? What additional costs are entailed for banks?

12. Rich Fortin, Seyed Mehdian, and Sridhar Sundaram are directors of a very large bank, the Spectacular Sky Bank of Michigan. They would like you to do a report for them on risk-based deposit insurance premiums. Explain the risk-based deposit insurance premium system and how banks and savings institutions are divided into different risk classes and what their assessments are based on these classes. What are FICO assessments in addition to these?

13. Phil Smith, Tom Kerlee, and Robert Riley, astute research consultants, would like you to discuss the benefits and disadvantages of a deposit insurance system. What are the advantages and disadvantages to depository institutions of an insurance system including both building confidence and moral hazard problems? Could the financial system survive without federal deposit insurance? Why or why not? Would your answer change if you were retired and living on social security? If you were on *Forbes* magazine's annual list of the 400 richest Americans?

14. Arnie Cowan, Dick Dowen, Edgar Norton, and Glenn Pettengill, officers of the Super MFA Bank, would like you to discuss clearing of check requirements under the Expedited Funds Availability Act. Also, discuss what a pledging requirement of government funds entails, and other obligations that depository institutions have to inform the public about their deposit accounts. For companies, banks provide many special deposit services, such as lockboxes, transfer of deposits to concentration banks, electronic transfers, online banking services, disbursement and bill-paying services, and managing accounts payables and receivables, among others. Explain the benefits to banks of offering such working capital management services associated with their role as depositories. Has this changed the role of banking? Explain.

Problems

1. Phil and Roz Lerner, the management of Euphoria Savings Bank, are analyzing the bank's cost structure. You have been asked to evaluate the effect of implicit interest payments on operating income; approximately 25 percent of fixed costs is traced to implicit interest. The following information is provided:

   Total revenues: $65 million
   Total variable costs: 80 percent of total revenues
   Total fixed costs: $8.0 million

   a. If explicit interest were substituted for implicit interest, what percentage of total revenues would variable costs be? What would total fixed costs be?

   b. Calculate the degree of operating leverage: (% change in operating income, total revenues less variable costs) / (% change in revenues), or it can be calculated as (total revenues − variable costs) / (total revenues − variable costs − fixed costs).

   c. If revenues increase by 10 percent, by how much would you expect operating income to change under the current cost structure? Under the alternative structure?

   d. If revenues decrease by 10 percent, what would operating income be under the current and alternative cost structures?

   e. What risk/return trade-off is involved with implicit versus explicit interest? How does implicit interest in terms of a larger branching system, providing greater customer convenience, help attract core deposits? How does it increase the operating leverage (percentage of fixed costs) of a bank? Why do you think banks have been increasing their branching systems (number of branches and offices) in recent years? Do you think interstate branching privileges have contributed to this rise?

2. a. Bob McDonald, the manager of Great Smoky Mountains Savings and Loan, asks you to estimate the total marginal cost of retail MMDAs. Reserve requirements are 0 percent, and the cost of deposit insurance is 0.23 percent. Competing institutions are paying 8 percent on MMDAs, and the manager estimates that servicing costs are 2.5 percent.

   b. The manager is considering a marketing campaign to attract NOWs that pay only 5.5 percent compared with 8.0 percent on MMDAs. The unlimited transactions feature of NOWs increases reserve requirements to 10 percent and servicing costs to 4 percent. Will the institution enjoy cost reductions if customers switch from MMDAs to NOWs? Explain why or why not.

3. Allison and David Cooperman, owners of The Super Staten Island Bank, are estimating the average marginal cost of its retail deposit accounts. They have collected the following data:

| | EXPLICIT | | | EXPECTED | |
	Effective Interest Rate	Servicing Cost	Insurance Premium	Reserve Requirement	Expected Total Balance ($ Billions)
Demand Deposits	0.0%	6.5%	0.23%	10%	$1.77
NOWS	5.0%	4.0%	0.23%	10%	1.27
MMDAs	8.0%	1.5%	0.23%	0%	1.92
Passbook Savings	4.5%	0.5%	0.23%	0%	0.64
CDs*	8.9%	0.25%	0.23%	0%	1.03

*(< $100,000 per account)

a. Please find the marginal cost for each type of deposit and the weighted average marginal cost for the bank for Allison and David. (Hint: Weight the total cost of each deposit by its proportion of total deposits.)

b. From the perspective of cost, should the bank seek additional dollars through the Fed Funds market or should it attempt to attract more MMDA accounts? Fed Funds are customarily purchased with three-day maturities, and the current rate is 7.75 percent. What other factors besides cost should management consider in making this decision?

4. JPMorgan Chase reported on its UBPR interest expense to assets of 3.24 percent in 2001 and 1.31 percent in 2003. Explain the reasons for JPMorgan Chase's lower interest expense, looking at rate and mix changes between 2001 and 2003 as reported in Table P15.1. How does JPMorgan Chase's liability structure differ from the average liability structure for all FDIC-insured banks and savings banks reported in the chapter? Recall that JPMorgan Chase is one of the largest U.S. banks, becoming larger with the merger of JPMorgan and Chase. JPMC engages actively in securitizations and numerous other types of off-balance-sheet activities with hundreds of overseas subsidiaries. How do these activities affect JPMC's liability structure compared with a traditional community bank?

Selected References

Allen, Paul H. *Reengineering the Bank: A Blueprint for Survival and Success.* Chicago: Richard D. Irwin, Inc., 1994.

Avery, Robert B., Gerald A. Hanweck, and Myron L. Kwast. "An Analysis of Risk-Based Deposit Insurance for Commercial Banks." In *Proceedings of the Conference on Bank Structure and Competition.* Chicago: Federal Reserve Bank of Chicago, 1985, 217–250.

Baer, Herbert, and Elijah Brewer. "Uninsured Deposits as a Source of Market Discipline." *Economic Perspectives* (Federal Reserve Bank of Chicago) 10 (September/October 1986), 23–31.

Benston, George. "Interest on Deposits and the Survival of Chartered Depository Institutions." *Economic Review* (Federal Reserve Bank of Atlanta) 69 (October 1984), 42–56.

Brigham, Eugene F. *Fundamentals of Financial Management,* 6th ed. Fort Worth, TX: Dryden Press, 1992.

Canner, Glenn B., and Ellen Maland. "Basic Banking." *Federal Reserve Bulletin* 73 (April 1987), 255–269.

Cohn, Jeffrey, and Michael E. Edleson. "Banking on the Market: Equity-Linked CDs." *AAII Journal* 15 (March 1993), 11–15.

Cook, Douglas O., and Lewis J. Spellman. "Federal Financial Guarantees and the Occasional Market Pricing of Default Risk." *Journal of Banking and Finance* 15 (1991), 1113–1130.

Cooperman, Elizabeth S., Winson B. Lee, and Glenn A. Wolfe. "The 1985 Ohio Thrift Crisis, the FSLIC's Solvency, and Rate Contagion for Retail CDs." *Journal of Finance* 47 (July 1992), 914–941.

Davis, Richard G., and Leon Korobow. "The Pricing of Consumer Deposit Products—The Non-Rate Dimensions." *Quarterly Review* (Federal Reserve Bank of New York) 11 (Winter 1986–87), 14–18.

table P15.1   JPMORGAN CHASE, SELECTED ITEMS AND PERCENTAGES CALCULATED FROM ITS 2003 UBPR REPORT

Percentage of Total Interest Expense	12/31/2003	12/31/2001
Interest Expense on Deposits Foreign Offices	22.55%	32.15%
Interest on Time Deposits > $100 Million	7.94%	6.67%
Interest on All Other Deposits	11.37%	11.55%
Interest on Fed Funds Purchased & Repos	19.43%	26.35%
Interest on Traditional Liabilities & Other Borrowings	33.35%	19.18%
Interest on Subordinated Notes & Debentures	5.36%	4.10%
Total Interest Expense ($000)	$8,327,000	$14,578,000
Total Noninterest Expense ($000)	$16,590,000	$16,203,000
Cost of (Rate on):		
Total Interest-Bearing Deposits	1.28%	3.29%
Transaction Accounts	3.24%	3.33%
Other Savings Deposits	0.75%	1.70%
Time Deposits > $100 Million	1.55%	2.69%
All Other Time Deposits	1.79%	6.33%
Foreign Office Deposits	1.61%	4.20%
Federal Funds Purchased & Repos	1.41%	5.34%
Other Borrowed Money	16.21%	27.44%
Subordinated Notes & Debentures	5.43%	8.67%
All Interest-Bearing Funds	2.02%	4.67%
Liability & Equity Mix: Total Liabilities & Capital ($000)	**$628,662,000**	**$537,826,000**
Total Core Deposits	23.87%	22.03%
Time Deposits $100M or More	6.40%	7.74%
Deposits in Foreign Offices	21.71%	22.38%
Total Deposits	**51.98%**	**52.15%**
Fed Funds Purchased & Resale	12.19%	14.87%
Other Borrowings	24.22%	19.26%
Acceptances & Other Liabilities	4.38%	5.78%
Noncore Liabilities Other Than SubNotes/Debs.	**40.79%**	**39.91%**
Total Liabilities Excluding Sub Notes & Debentures	**92.94%**	**92.06%**
Subordinated Notes and	1.28%	1.76%
All Common & Preferred Capital	5.96%	6.19%
Total SubNotes, Debentures & Equity Capital	7.24%	7.95%
Other Capital and Off-Balance-Sheet Ratios:		
Tier 1 Leverage Capital	5.27%	5.25%
Tier 1 to Risk Weighted Assets	8.05%	8.31%
Tier 1 & Tier 2 to Risk Weighted Assets	10.43%	11.20%
Total Off-Balance-Sheet Items to Assets	157.03%	121.21%
Liquidity Ratios:		
Net Noncore Fund Dependence	68.04%	71.90%
Net Loans and Leases to Assets	28.80%	32.52%
Growth Rates:		
Assets	1.01%	42.62%
Short-Term Noncore Funding	24.21%	45.90%

Davis, Richard G., Leon Korobow, and John Wenninger. "Bankers on Pricing Consumer Deposits." *Quarterly Review* (Federal Reserve Bank of New York) 11 (Winter 1986–87), 6–13.

Dotsey, Michael. "An Examination of Implicit Interest Rates on Demand Deposits." *Economic Review* (Federal Reserve Bank of Richmond) 69 (September/October 1983), 3–11.

Dotsey, Michael, and Anatoli Kuprianov. "Reforming Deposit Insurance: Lessons from the Savings and Loan Crisis." *Economic Review* (Federal Reserve Bank of Richmond) (March/April 1990), 3–28.

Elliehausen, Gregory E., and John D. Wolken. "Banking Markets and the Use of Financial Services by Households." *Federal Reserve Bulletin* 78 (March 1992), 169–184.

Elmer, Peter J. "Developing Service-Oriented Deposit Accounts." *Bankers Magazine* 168 (March/April 1985), 60–63.

Evanoff, Douglas D. "Preferred Sources of Market Discipline: Depositors vs. Subordinated Debt Holders." Working Paper, Federal Reserve Bank of Chicago, WP 1992–21, 1992.

Flannery, Mark. "Deposit Insurance Creates a Need for Bank Regulation." *Business Review* (Federal Reserve Bank of Philadelphia) (January/February 1982a), 17–24.

———. "Retail Bank Deposits as Quasi-Fixed Factors of Production." *American Economic Review* 72 (June 1982b), 527–536.

Flood, Mark D. "The Great Deposit Insurance Debate." *Economic Review* (Federal Reserve Bank of St. Louis) 74 (July/August 1992), 51–77.

Friedman, Milton. "Controls on Interest Rates Paid by Banks." *Journal of Money, Credit, and Banking* 2 (February 1970), 15–32.

Furlong, Frederick. "A View on Deposit Insurance Coverage." *Economic Review* (Federal Reserve Bank of San Francisco) (Spring 1984), 31–38.

Gardner, Mona J., and Lucille E. Lammers. "Cost Accounting in Large Banks." *Management Accounting* 69 (April 1988), 34–39.

Goodfriend, Marvin. "Eurodollars." In *Instruments of the Money Market*, 6th ed. Richmond, VA: Federal Reserve Bank of Richmond, 1986, 53–64.

Goodfriend, Marvin, and William Whelpley. "Federal Funds." In *Instruments of the Money Market*, 6th ed. Richmond, VA: Federal Reserve Bank of Richmond, 1986, 8–22.

Hannan, Timothy H. "Retail Fees of Depository Institutions, 1997–2001." *Federal Reserve Bulletin* 88, No. 9 (September 2002), 405–413.

Harless, Caroline T. "Brokered Deposits." *Economic Review* (Federal Reserve Bank of Atlanta) 69 (March 1984), 14–25.

Hayashi, Fumiko, Richard Sullivan, and Stuart E. Weiner. *A Guide to the ATM and Debit Card Industry, Federal Reserve Bank of Kansas City.* Kansas City: Payments System Research, Federal Reserve Bank of Kansas City, 2003.

Hempel, George H., Donald G. Simonson, and Allan B. Coleman. *Bank Management: Text and Cases,* 4th ed. New York: John Wiley & Sons, 1994.

Kane, Edward J. "The Three Faces of Commercial Bank Liability Management." In *The Political Economy of Policy-Making,* ed. by M. J. Dooley. Beverly Hills, CA: Sage Publications, 1979.

———. "A Six-Point Program for Deposit Insurance Reform." *Housing Finance Review* 2 (July 1983), 269–278.

———. *The Gathering Crisis in Federal Deposit Insurance.* Cambridge, MA: The MIT Press, 1985.

———. *The S&L Insurance Mess: How Did It Happen?* Washington, DC: The Urban Institute Press, 1989.

Keeley, Michael C. "Interest-Rate Deregulation." *Weekly Letter* (Federal Reserve Bank of San Francisco), January 13, 1984.

Keeley, Michael C., and Gary C. Zimmerman. "Competition for Money Market Deposit Accounts." *Economic Review* (Federal Reserve Bank of San Francisco) (Spring 1985), 5–27.

Keeton, William, Jim Harvey, and Paul Willis. "The Role of Community Banks in the U.S. Economy." *Economic Review* (Federal Reserve Bank of Kansas City) Vol. 88, No. 2 (Second Quarter 2003), 15–43.

Kidwell, David S., Richard L. Peterson, and David W. Blackwell. *Financial Institutions, Markets, and Money,* 6th ed. Fort Worth, TX: Dryden Press, 1997.

Koch, Timothy W., and S. Scott MacDonald. *Bank Management,* 4th ed. Mason, OH: Southwestern Publishing Company (Dryden Press), 2000.

Logue, James A. "Pricing Strategies for the 1980s." *Magazine of Bank Administration* 59 (September 1983), 28–34.

Mahoney, Patrick I., et al. "Responses to Deregulation: Retail Deposit Pricing from 1983 through 1985." Board of Governors of the Federal Reserve System, Staff Study Number 151, January 1987.

Maness, Terry S., and John T. Zietlow. *Short-Term Financial Management,* 2nd ed. Mason, OH: South-Western Thomson Learning, 2002.

McKinney, George W. "Liability Management: Its Costs and Uses." In *Financial Institutions and Markets in a Changing World,* ed. by Donald R. Fraser and Peter S. Rose. Dallas, TX: Business Publications, 1980, 90–104.

Moore, Robert R. "Brokered Deposits: Determinants and Implications for Thrift Distributions." *Financial Industry Studies* (Federal Reserve Bank of Dallas) December 1991, 15–27.

Murphy, Neil B., and Richard H. Kraas. "Measuring the Interest Sensitivity of Money Markets Accounts." *Magazine of Bank Administration* 60 (May 1984), 70–74.

Parliment, Tom. "Not Paying Market Is an Option." *Savings Institutions* 106 (April 1985), S12–S17.

Puglisi, Donald J., and Joseph A. McKenzie. "Capital Market Strategies for Thrift Institutions." *Federal Home Loan Bank Board Journal* 16 (November 1983), 2–8.

———. "Research on Federal Deposit Insurance." In *Proceedings of a Conference on Bank Structure and Competition.* Chicago: Federal Reserve Bank of Chicago, 1983, 196–298.

Rogowski, Robert J. "Pricing the Money Market Deposit and Super-NOW Accounts in 1983." *Journal of Bank Research* 15 (Summer 1984), 72–81.

Saunders, Anthony, and Marcia Million Cornett. *Financial Institution Management: A Risk Management Approach,* 4th ed. Burr Ridge, IL: McGraw-Hill Irwin, 2003.

Scott, Charlotte H. "Low-Income Banking Needs and Services." *Journal of Retail Banking* 10 (Fall 1988), 32–40.

Staten, Michael. "Retail Banker's Review of Laws and Regulations—Winter 1989." *Journal of Retail Banking* 11 (Winter 1989), 62–63.

Stigum, Marcia. *The Money Market,* 3rd ed. Homewood, IL: Dow Jones-Irwin, 1990.

Taggart, Robert A., Jr. "Effects of Deposit Rate Ceilings: The Evidence from Massachusetts Savings Banks." *Journal of Money, Banking, and Credit* 10 (May 1978), 139–157.

Watson, Ronald D. "Estimating the Cost of Your Bank's Funds." *Business Review* (Federal Reserve Bank of Philadelphia) (May/June 1978), 3–11.

———. "The Marginal Cost of Funds Concept in Banking." *Journal of Bank Research* 8 (Autumn 1977), 136–147.

White, Lawrence J. "Price Regulation and Quality Rivalry in a Profit Maximizing Model: The Case of Bank Branching." *Journal of Money, Credit, and Banking* 8 (February 1976), 97–106.

Willemse, Rob J. M. "Large Certificates of Deposit." In *Instruments of the Money Market,* 6th ed. Richmond, VA: Federal Reserve Bank of Richmond, 1986, 36–52.

Wood, John H., and Norma L. Wood. *Financial Markets,* Chapter 9. San Diego: Harcourt Brace Jovanovich, 1985.

Zimmerman, Gary C. "Shopping Pays." *Weekly Letter* (Federal Reserve Bank of San Francisco) (November 8, 1985).

Zimmerman, Gary C., and Michael Keeley. "Interest Checking." *Weekly Letter* (Federal Reserve Bank of San Francisco) (November 14, 1986).

Zimmerman, Gary C., and Jonathan A. Neuberger. "Interest Rate Competition." *Weekly Letter* (Federal Reserve Bank of San Francisco) (July 27, 1990).

internet *exercise*

1 The Financial Services Technology Consortium (FSTC) is a not-for-profit organization whose goal is to enhance the competitiveness of the U.S. financial services industry. Members of the consortium include banks, financial services providers, research laboratories, universities, technology companies, and government agencies. The FSTC conducts the Bank Internet Payment System Project. There are several classes of commercial transactions necessary for Internet commerce. One of the more important of these transaction classes, payment systems, enables consumer-oriented activities such as online shopping and bill payment. Payment systems also enable business activities such as invoice payment, cash management, supply chain settlement, and procurement. There are various currently available or emerging payment systems designed to provide payment transactions over the Internet. You can find a survey of Internet payments systems in Microsoft Word and a matrix in Microsoft Excel format at *http://www.fstc.org/projects/bips/survey.cfm.* It is the intent of the survey to assist perspective Internet users, merchants, and service providers in understanding the various Internet payment alternatives. The survey is meant as a starting place to learn about these payment systems. To that end, the survey provides links to more information and a matrix, or at-a-glance comparison," of some of the payment systems. The matrix shows the features of different payment systems all on one page in order to make it easier for the beginner to understand some of their similarities and differences.

2 PM Publishing offers information on daily Eurodollars option analysis at *http://www.pmpublishing.com/volatility/ed.html.* To test your ideas about options trading, go to *http://www.pmpublishing.com/price/index.html.* Here you enter trade inputs, market inputs, contract specifications, and projection increments. You can find an example of contract specifications at *http://www.pmpublishing.com/options/onspecs.html.*

USEFUL LINKS

Bank Rate Monitor

http://www.bankrate.com

Compubank

http://www.compubank.com

Netbank

http://www.netbank.com

Management Issues and Performance Analysis of Nondepository Institutions

V

16 Insurance Company Financial Management Issues

"Clearly, the most significant crisis the [insurance] industry faces right now is how to deal with catastrophes—natural disasters, hurricanes, earthquakes, and tidal waves."

GENERAL ROBERT T. HERRES, Chairman and CEO-United Services Automobile Association (USAA), in Charles B. Wendel. The New Financiers. *Chicago: Irwin Professional Publishing Co., 1996, 127.*

"The prospect of Washington's seizing a role in the regulation of insurance, which for more than 150 years has been the purview of the states, is gaining momentum."

JOSEPH R. TREASTER, New York Times *(March 18, 2004), C1.*

I n the 1980s and early 1990s, insurance companies took on greater interest rate and liquidity risk by moving into annuities and guaranteed investment contracts (GICs) that pay a specified fixed return over a specified period. To ensure a given return, investment companies often funded these investments with higher yielding, riskier investments. Consequently, annuity purchasers, as well as insurers, were subject to greater default risk. For instance, Herbert D. Engle, senior vice president of Transamerica Occidental Life Insurance, invested $100,000 in a supposedly "safe" life insurance annuity product sold by Executive Life Insurance Company (EXEC) in 1983. EXEC funded its annuities by investing in junk bonds and commercial real estate mortgages. With the collapse of the markets for these instruments in 1989, EXEC suffered huge losses and was seized by regulators in 1991. Although Mr. Engle recovered some of his investment, the investment return he received was significantly below the promised "guaranteed" rate for the annuity. With interest rates falling in the late 1990s and early 2000s due to a weak economy, it was difficult for insurance companies to generate investment income to help cover losses.[1]

As noted in the opening quote, in addition to greater risk from investing in new investment products, property/liability (P/L) insurance companies faced significant losses from catastrophic events in the 1990s and early 2000s, including the California wildfires of October 21 to November 5, 2003; terrorist attacks of September 11, 2001; Hurricanes Andrew (1992), Opal and Fran (1995), and George and Mitch (1998); and 163 tornadoes in Tennessee, Arkansas, and Missouri in January of 1999. As noted by the Insurance Information Institute (I.I.I.), on an inflation-adjusted basis, the California wildfires in 2003 cost insurers about $2 billion, terrorist attacks on the World Trade Center cost about $40 billion, Hurricane Andrew cost $15.9 billion, and 41 major catastrophes in 1996 cost $7.35 billion![2]

Despite these pressures, some major property/casualty (P/C) insurers, such as State Farm, weathered the decade's losses and even increased capital reserves during the most difficult periods. Similarly,

despite failures and losses by many life insurance companies, other life insurers, such as Massachusetts Mutual, performed well. As the result of problems in the late 1990s and early 2000s, all insurance firms face greater regulatory scrutiny. In addition, legislators focused on a number of social problems revolving around a large, growing number of U.S. citizens with no or insufficient health insurance; very high insurance rates for small businesses, resulting in a lack of insurance for a large percentage of home-based businesses and other small businesses; and a growing number of obesity-related disability insurance claims; not to mention rising worldwide disaster and terrorism risks, among other social problems.

A factor that contributes to differences in insurers' financial strength is better financial and investment management. Executive Life had concentrated more than 60 percent of its investment portfolio in junk bonds. Many P/C firms, in contrast, relied on more stable investment income to offset large

Learning Objectives

After completing this chapter, you will be able to:

1 Explain the structure of the life and property/casualty insurance industries.

2 Understand the typical items and their relative importance on an insurance company's income statement and balance sheet.

3 Follow trends in different types of premium and investment income and different types of expenses for insurance companies.

4 Understand the differences between statutory versus GAAP accounting.

5 Do a performance evaluation of an insurance company and understand special ratios used by life and P/C insurers.

6 Describe cyclical, social, and economic forces affecting insurers.

7 Understand technological changes in insurer distribution systems and different aspects of insurance operations.

8 Discuss insurance company capital and other regulations.

---

1 Richard S. Teitelbaum. "How Safe Is Your Insurance?" *Fortune* (September 9, 1991), 137–141.

2 For a discussion and listing of recent catastrophes, latest studies, and issues facing the insurance industry, see the Insurance Information Institute Website at *http://www.iii.org*. Also see Insurance Information Institute's *Financial Services Fact Book, 2003*, provided on its Website at *http://financialservicefacts.org*. See also Cornett and Saunders (1999), 91–92; and Greg Steinmetz, et al. "In Wake of Hurricane, Insurers Face Financial and Regulatory Tests." *The Wall Street Journal* (September 2, 1992), A1, A4; and *Property/Casualty Insurance Facts, 1998*. Note P/C and P/L are often used for the same type of insurance company.

catastrophic losses in the 1990s. The financial opportunities and problems that insurers face are both similar to and different from those faced by the institutions discussed in previous chapters. Like depository institutions, insurance companies hold financial assets that are subject to interest rate, liquidity, and default risk. However, they have liabilities that are potential claims against the company by policyholders or their beneficiaries.

Insurers are subject to state regulations, but under the McCarran-Ferguson Act of 1945, the federal government has the right to regulate insurance companies if states do not provide adequately enforced standards for the industry. In early 2004, there was new momentum by Congress after more than 150 years to involve greater federal oversight over state regulators. Representative Michael G. Oxley, the chairman of the House Committee on Financial Services at this time, laid out planned legislation for later in the year that would create a council of federal and state officials to oversee insurance nationally, using uniform standards and allowing market-determined insurance prices versus current prices that are generally determined by regulators.[3]

This chapter addresses similarities and differences between insurance firms and other types of financial institutions, with the recognition that in recent years insurers and depositories have entered each other's arenas. The responses of insurers to economic challenges, competition, and regulatory developments, and the accompanying financial management techniques, are addressed as well.

Before discussing in more detail a financial analysis of insurance companies, it is worthwhile to present an overview of the structure of the industry and then an overview of insurance company operations.

An Overview of Insurance Operations

The extent of insurance company operations is quite broad, as described by J. François Outreville in the *Theory and Practice of Insurance:*

1. **New product design and development to satisfy customer and market needs strategically considering** potential competition, expected losses, legal and regulatory and cost factors;

2. **Production and distribution and advertisement** for a new product;

3. **Product management** including setting the price (rate) for the product based on its risk and that covers expected losses (based on statistics and actuarial considerations), payment of claims, and other costs plus a profit markup;

4. **Underwriting** including strategically determining the risks that the company is willing to take on based on its financial capacity, technical skills and abilities, regulatory restrictions, and the availability of reinsurance and implementing these policies;

5. **Claims adjustment and settlement, which involves having integrity and "fairly and promptly"** paying for losses of claimants, which Outreville points out entails an agent who must be "a detective, a lawyer, a psychologist, a gentleman, and above all, an ambassador of good will and good public relations";

6. **Services** involving legal, loss control, risk management, policyholder and consumer and employee educational services;

7. **Administration** involving strategic planning, personnel management, branch management, accounting, and public relations; and

8. **Finance and investment** including management and valuation of the investment portfolio from a strategic and regulatory perspective, since state regulators often limit the percentage of different types of investments that can be held.[4]

---

3 See Joseph B. Treaster. "New Momentum for Letting U.S. Help Regulate Nation's Insurers." *New York Times* (March 18, 2004), C1, C8.

4 See Outreville (1998).

Overview of the Insurance Industry's Structure

Life Insurers Overview

Similar to the bank and thrift industry, the insurance industry consists of very large (mega) firms and medium-size and smaller firms. Considerable economies of scale are necessary for profitability in the life insurance industry, so firms tend to be larger. With consolidation, the insurance industry has become more concentrated. In 2002 alone, $304 billion in net acquisitions of life insurance firms occurred. At the end of 2002 in the United States, there were 1,171 life insurance companies with $3.38 trillion in assets, and $16.3 trillion of life insurance in force. From 1992 to 2002, the number of life insurers fell by 40 percent.[5]

The life insurance industry, like the thrift industry, has both stock and mutual companies. Although a number of large mutual insurance companies dominated the industry in previous years, stock firms dominate today. At the end of 2002, only 83 mutual firms (including mutual holding companies) operated, with the remaining firms stock-operated. The mutual and stock firms have about 94 percent market share in the life/health insurance industry. Other insurers include fourteen hospital-related, medical, dental, and indemnity companies and fraternal societies and the U.S. Department of Veterans Affairs, which underwrite about 6 percent of total insurance and annuities. With consolidation, large financial holding companies and mutual fund companies also own insurance firms, such as TIAA-CREF, among the top five life/health insurance companies by revenues. Similarly, large insurance companies, such as Mass Mutual Life, have diversified into pension and mutual fund management. In the United States, many large life insurers are subsidiaries of non-U.S. companies, representing 20 percent of U.S. insurers. The Netherlands, Canada, France, and then the United Kingdom are ranked the largest international owners of U.S. insurer assets.[6]

Mutual companies are implicitly owned by their policyholders. In addition, in the 1990s, a hybrid structure known as a mutual holding company developed, whereby a mutual holding company transfers assets, liabilities, and capital to a newly formed, stockholder-owned insurance company subsidiary. In this way, the new stockholder-owned subsidiary can issue common stock to the public to raise external capital and offer managers incentive-based stock compensation. Generally, under state laws, when a mutual company converts to stock form, it must first divide most accumulated profits or surplus among policyholders as compensation for giving up their ownership. However, in the late 1990s in many states, an insurer could issue stock without any payment to policyholders by setting up a series of holding companies, with policyholders remaining as the majority of owners of the company. For this reason consumer advocate lawsuits ensued in the late 1990s. Mutual holding company conversions have involved quite substantial amounts of money, such as the $12 billion surplus of Metropolitan Life and the $6 billion surplus for New York Life in 1997. Often conversions to mutual holding companies served as a transition for full conversions to stockholder-owned firms, with the dissolution of the mutual holding company.[7]

Property/Casualty Insurers Overview

Like life insurance companies, the property/casualty insurance industry consists of a number of very large firms that dominate the industry. However, with greater ease of exit and entry, there are also numerous small and medium-sized firms, with about 3,163 P/C insurance companies operating in the United States. According to the U.S. Bureau of Labor Statistics, the insurance industry as a whole provided about 2.2 million jobs in 2002 (about 2.1 percent of total U.S. employment). In terms of gross premiums for insurance companies, about 32 percent were for P/C, 13 percent for health maintenance organizations (HMOs), 46 percent for life/health insurers, 5 percent for Blue Cross/Blue Shield, 3.1 percent for other, and 0.7 percent for title insurance at the end of 2001. P/C insurers have also undergone

---

5 American Council of Life Insurers: *Life Insurers Fact Book, 2003 (http://www.acli.org)*.

6 Financial Services Fact Book, 2003 *(http://financialservicefacts.org)* and Life Insurers Fact Book, 2003 *(http://www.acli.org)*.

7 See "Mutual Insurers Lose Bid as New York Lets Holding-Firm Bill Die." New York Times (June 19, 1998), 16. See also, Leslie Scism. "Mutual-Life Insurers Going Public." The Wall Street Journal (December 9, 1997), C1; Joseph B. Treaster. "Insurers' Plan to Sell Stock Riles Consumer Advocates." New York Times (October 9, 1997), C2; Leslie Scism. "MONY Plans Switch to Stock Ownership." The Wall Street Journal (September 9, 1997), B1.

significant consolidation. Based on net premiums written, the top four insurers held about 28 percent of market share at the end of 2002. The largest fifty insurers together held almost 50 percent of market share, leaving a 21 percent share for all other insurers. The five firms with the largest total revenues include American International Group with assets of $561 billion, State Farm Insurance with assets of $117.8 billion, Berkshire Hathaway with assets of $169.5 billion, Allstate with assets of $117.4 billion, and Loews (CNA) with assets of $75.5 billion.[8]

Other Types of Nonlife Insurance Firms and Products

In addition to life, P/C, and health insurance, financial guarantees are a major insurance product, with some firms specializing in these areas. **Surety bonds** are contracts (required for large government work projects) that guarantee the performance of a specific obligation, such as the completion of a building by a contractor. In the event of the contractor's failure to complete the job on time, the insurer either makes payments for losses or finds another contractor to complete the job. **Financial Guaranty Insurance** includes surety for mortgage-backed securities, as well as state and foreign government and other bonds. These surety bonds guarantee interest and principal payments or a portion of the default risk of the mortgage pool backing a mortgage-security issue, allowing bonds to be issued at lower interest rates (often 2 to 3 percent less). Generally, financial guaranty insurers are well-capitalized companies with high credit ratings. Credit insurers have also diversified into insuring pools of credit default swaps and other structured finance transactions. In 2002, MBIA, Ambac, FSA, FGIC, and XL Capital Assurance were among the top five financial guaranty insurers. Related types of insurance include **credit insurance for short-term trade receivables,** protecting the seller against the risk of a customer's default or insolvency, serving to insure against losses above expected losses set up with bad debt reserves, allowing easier access to bank credit. Under the sponsorship of the Export-Import bank, private credit insurers also provide export credit insurance. **Private mortgage guaranty insurance (PMI)** is another product often required by banks for borrowers with down payments less than 2 percent. PMI allows borrowers to purchase homes without having to save up for a 20 percent down payment. Mortgage Guaranty Insurance Corporation and PMI are two of the largest mortgage insurers. **Reinsurance companies** insure risk for insurance companies against unexpected and extraordinary losses. The majority of reinsurance companies insuring risk for U.S. insurers are non-U.S. companies, such as General Reinsurance Corporation, the largest P/C reinsurance company in 2002, with $3.63 billion in net premiums written. Some major investment banks and insurance companies also sell alternative risk management arrangements, including **catastrophe bonds (CBs).** CBs use a special-purpose vehicle (SPV) or specialized company (reinsurer) to underwrite bonds that pay high interest rates, but investors lose all or part of the principal and interest if insurer losses go above a given threshold. This represents a form of securitization of insurer risk. An example is Swiss Re, which sponsored an SPV in Redwood with a risk amount of $194 million for earthquake peril in California. **Weather-related derivatives and insurance** have been developed to hedge the risk of weather changes that could adversely affect businesses, such as ski resorts. These are often structured as options or swaps that pay an agreed-upon amount over a specific time based on weather conditions being above or below a certain average benchmark. Weather swaps, which can be custom-tailored, allow funds to be exchanged between two different entities that experience different conditions with money exchanged for points above or below a given threshold.[9]

Overview of Insurance Company Operations

As pointed out by J. François Outreville in the *Theory and Practice of Insurance* (1998), insurance is an interesting process of financial intermediation because of its reverse production cycle with payment made before a service (the payment of claims) is provided. **Gross written premiums** provided by policyholders are used to cover the costs of commissions and administrative expenses, with the "ultimate service" or output of the firm, the claim paid, determined in the event of a loss. Because claims are not always made in the same year as premiums are received, **reserves** are put aside as commitments by the insurer for the insured policyholders and invested in securities of maturity equivalent to contracts.

---

8 See Financial Services Fact Book, 2003 (*http://financialservicefacts.org*) and other information provided on the Insurance Information Institute Website at *http://www.iii.org.*

9 Ibid.

Similarly, a portion of premiums received in a given year may be used to cover claims incurred within that year. Insurers receive income each year from **premiums** and from **returns earned on investments.** Insurers make profits whenever premium and investment income exceeds the amount needed to cover all expenses, claims, and proper provisions (reserves) for liabilities to policyholders.[10]

Source of Revenues

Table 16.1 shows typical common size income statements for life insurance and property/casualty insurance companies. On average, life insurers' premium income contributed about 70 percent in 2002, with investment income supplying 25 percent and other income the remaining 5 percent. For P/L insurers, premium income contributes a larger share of total revenues, about 90 percent of revenues in 2002, with the remaining 10 percent of revenues from net investment earnings. P/L insurers depend more on premium income because they have shorter-term (unexpected payoff) contracts and thus cannot invest in higher-yielding long-term assets as life insurers with long-term contracts can.[11]

Details on Life Insurer Revenues

For life insurance companies, premium income comes from three sources: (1) life insurance premiums; (2) health insurance premiums; and (3) annuity considerations. As shown in Table 16.2, life insurance

table **16.1** TYPICAL COMMON SIZE INCOME STATEMENTS FOR INSURANCE COMPANIES

Revenues for insurance companies primarily include premium payments and earnings from investments. Expenses for life insurance companies include benefit payments, additions to policy reserves, operating expenses, and investment expenses. Expenses for P/C insurance companies include loss expenses, operating expenses, and policyholder dividends.

LIFE INSURANCE COMPANIES			P/L INSURANCE COMPANIES		
% Total Revenues	**2001**	**2002**	**% Total Revenues**	**2001**	**2002**
Premium Payments	66%	70%	Earned Premiums	89%	90%
Gross Investment Earnings	28%	25%	Net Investment Earnings	11%	10%
Other Income*	6%	5%			

*Other income includes commissions and expense allowance on reinsurance ceded and amortization of interest maintenance reserve.

% Total Expenses			**% Total Expenses**		
Benefit Payments	60%	56%	Loss Expenses	75%	74%
Additions to Policy Reserves	25%	28%	Operating Expenses	24%	25%
Operating Expenses	11%	13%	Policyholder Dividends	1%	1%
Investment Expenses	2%	2%			
Taxes	2%	2%			
Dividends to Stockholders	2%				
Addition to Surplus	2%				

Sources: Percentages calculated by Authors from average annual report data as presented by the American Council of Life Insurers: Life Insurers Fact Book, 2003 (http://www.acli.org) and Insurance Information Institute: Property/Casualty Industry Financials and Outlook, 2003 (http://www.iii.org), presented to the public on their Websites.

Note: This represents a typical average allocation in 2001 and 2002, but percentages vary from year to year. Typically life insurers receive a third or more of revenues from investment earnings while P/L insurers receive less. The majority of life insurer expenses are benefit payments and then additions to policy reserves. Loss expenses are the largest expenses of P/L insurers.

---

10 See Outreville (1998).

11 Sources for this section and the following paragraphs are from the American Council of Life Insurers: Life Insurers Fact Book, 2003, and Insurance Information Institute: Financial Services Fact Book, 2003 (*http://financialservicefacts.org*), and other information provided on the Insurance Information Institute Website at *http://www.iii.org*.

table 16.2 TRENDS IN INCOME FOR U.S. LIFE INSURANCE COMPANIES (IN MILS.)

	1986 % Total Premiums		1997 % Total Premiums		2002 % Total Premiums	
Life Insurance Premiums	34%		28%		26%	
Annuity Considerations	43%		49%		53%	
Health Insurance Premiums	23%		23%		21%	
	1986 Income	**%Total**	**1997 Income**	**%Total**	**2002 Income**	**%Total**
Total Premium Receipts	$194,078	**68%**	$405,305	**66%**	$512,482	**70%**
Net Investment Income	$ 75,435	27%	$170,713	28%	$180,855	25%
Other Income	$ 12,744	5%	$ 34,628	6%	$ 40,676	5%
Total Income	$282,257	100%	$610,646	100%	$734,013	100%
Rate of Investment Income	**1986**		**1997**		**2002**	
Net Rate						
Total Assets	9.35%		7.17%		5.38%	
General Account Only	9.64%		7.71%		6.64%	
Gross Rate						
Total Fixed-Income Assets	11.14%		8.00%		7.13%	

Source: American Council of Life Insurance: Life Insurers Fact Books *1997, 1998, 2003.*
Note: General Accounts are undivided accounts in which life and health insurers formerly recorded all incoming funds.
Since the 1960s, life and health insurers have begun using other accounts as well. Separate accounts are asset accounts maintained independently from the insurer's general investment account that is used primarily for pension plans and variable life products. The arrangement permits wider latitude in the choice of investments, particularly in equities.

premiums over time have become a less significant percentage of total U.S. life insurance receipts, falling from 34 percent of total premiums in 1986 to 26 percent in 2002. Annuities contributed the largest share of revenues, which rose from 43 percent in 1986 to 53 percent in 2002. Health insurance premiums contributed the remaining 23 percent in 1986 and 21 percent in 2002. Although not shown in the table, premiums from individuals for life and health insurance and annuities continue to be the largest percentage of premiums (50 percent in 1997 and 60 percent in 2002). Group insurance premium income has grown over time and contributed 49 percent in 1997 and 40 percent in 2002 of premiums. The gross rate of return on life insurance assets shown in the lower panel of Table 16.2 fell significantly as interest rates fell in the 1990s and early 2000s, with the gross rate on total fixed income assets falling from 11.14 percent in 1986 to 8 percent in 1997, and 7.13 percent in 2002, reducing investment income as a source of total revenue relative to premiums.

Expenses of Insurers

Life Insurers

In contrast to depository institutions, in which the majority of expenses are interest expenses, as shown in Table 16.1, the majority of expenses for life insurers are benefit payments and additions to policy reserves. Combined, these were approximately 84 percent of total life insurer expenses in 2002. Operating expenses are a much smaller percentage of total expenses (13 percent in 2002). Dividends to stockholders of stock life insurance companies are about 2 percent of total expenses, and taxes are another 2 percent. Policyholder dividends are the return of part of premiums that policyholders made on policies that were sold on a participating basis. Hence, they reflect a portion that is not needed by the insurer after claims, additions to reserves, and administrative expenses are paid. Operating expenses include commissions to agents and costs such as depreciation, rent, and managerial salaries. Commissions to agents in 2002 were about 6 percent of total expenses, and home- and field-office expenses were about 6 percent.[12]

---

12 See note 5.

Property/Liability Insurers

As shown in Table 16.1, the majority of expenses (about 74 percent in 2002) for property/liability companies are loss expenses. Operating expenses, including commissions, are about 25 percent, and policyholder dividends, about 1 percent. Often, for many companies, total expenses are larger than revenues from premiums during periods of catastrophic losses. Consequently, P/L insurance companies often depend on investment revenues to make a profit.

Statutory Accounting for Insurers

Interpreting financial data on P/L insurers is somewhat more difficult than for other financial institutions. Insurance companies are subject to two sets of accounting rules: regulatory principles that insurers call **statutory accounting principles (SAP)** and generally accepted accounting principles (GAAP). SAP is a combination of cash-based and accrual accounting; expenses are not recognized until earned. In general, it is a more conservative way of reporting financial results than GAAP. Statutory accounting affects balance sheets and income statements for all insurers, although differences between statutory accounting and GAAP are greater for P/L insurers than life insurers. Virtually all data on life insurers are consistent with GAAP; this is not true for P/L insurers. For instance, statutory accounting for P/Ls requires unrealized gains or losses on stock holdings to be reflected on the balance sheet, directly affecting both reported asset holdings and insurers' net worth. This is in contrast with GAAP, which requires the reporting of equity security holdings as the lower of either cost or market value. Also, for statutory accounting, P/L insurers may only include admitted assets in "other assets," which are assets that could be liquidated should the insurer face a financial emergency. This procedure differs from GAAP, in which "other assets" includes cash, but not premises. Thus, the reported net worth of P/L insurers is understated by non-admitted assets that do not appear on the balance sheet. In general, while GAAP emphasizes a business as a going concern, SAP operates as if insurance companies are about to be liquidated, recognizing liabilities as having higher values and occurring earlier and recognizing assets at a lower value. SAP is based on uniform codes established by the National Association of Insurance Commissioners (NAIC). Thus, public insurers must have separate financial statements in GAAP form to report to the Securities and Exchange Commission as well. As noted in the Insurance Information Institute's *Financial Services Fact Book* for 2002, major differences in SAP include: (1) having to account for sales cost right away versus during the period when premiums are earned; (2) having to deduct policy expenses right away; (3) not being allowed to defer taxes; (4) requiring loss reserves to be discounted for tax purposes; (5) not allowing net worth to include reinsurance payments that might not be recovered, (6) not allowing certain assets, such as furniture and equipment, to be admitted; (7) demanding that most bonds be carried at their amortized value; (8) allowing subordinated surplus notes to be carried as part of policyholder surplus; and (9) allowing deferred taxes on unrealized capital gains to be included in net worth.[13]

Concept Questions

1 Why have life insurance firms converted from mutual to stock ownership?

2 What is a mutual holding company? Why have consumer groups complained about these conversions?

3 How do insurers make money? What are their two major sources of revenues?

4 What are the major expenses of P/C and life insurers, respectively?

5 What are surety bonds? Financial guaranty insurance? Private mortgage guaranty insurance? Reinsurance companies? Catastrophe bonds? Weather-related derivatives and insurance?

6 What is the difference between GAAP and SAP for insurers?

---

13 See *Property/Casualty Insurance Facts 1998.* "Total premiums written" is often referred to in the industry as "net premiums written." These are premiums collected before deducting those paid but not yet earned. Accounting rules for unearned premiums on the income statement differ from unearned premium reserves on the balance sheet, which are often calculated under the assumption that services have been rendered for only one half of the amount of premiums paid during the year. As a result, unearned premium reserves on the balance sheet are often overstated and net worth understated for the industry. Some experts estimate the extent of reserve overstatement to be as much as 35 percent. See Vaughan (1982), 109, n. 7; and Mehr (1983), 470–471. Also see American Council of Life Insurers: *Life Insurers Fact Book, 2003,* and Insurance Information Institute: *Financial Services Fact Book, 2003 (http://financialservicefacts.org),* and other information provided on the Insurance Information Institute Website at *http://www.iii.org.*

Overview of Insurance Company Balance Sheets

Life Insurer versus P/C Insurer Assets

Figure 16.1 provides an overview of common size balance sheets of U.S. life and P/C insurers at the end of 2002. For U.S. life insurers, about 93 percent of assets are financial assets. Since life insurer contracts are long-term, financial assets also tend to be long-term. About 58 percent of assets are held in government and corporate bonds and 23 percent in stocks. Other assets include policy loans—short-term loans made to policyholders—about 3 percent of assets, and mortgages and real estate, about 8 percent.

In contrast, P/C insurers held 40 percent of assets in corporate and government bonds, 20 percent in municipal securities (since P/C insurers are taxed on their investment income, unlike life insurers), 17 percent in stock, 9 percent in trade receivables, 7 percent in cash, deposits, and security repurchase agreements, and 7 percent in miscellaneous assets. Non-life insurers tend to hold a larger percentage of

---

figure **16.1** LIFE INSURERS AND P/C INSURERS: A COMPARISON OF ASSETS, OBLIGATIONS, AND NET WORTH

A notable difference in the assets of life and P/C insurers is the proportion invested in government securities and policy loans. Both types of insurers have large policy reserve liabilities, but life insurers are more highly leveraged.

PANEL A: LIFE INSURER ASSETS

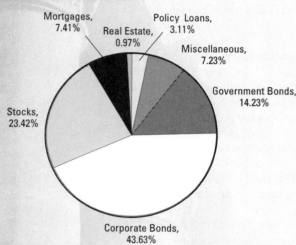

PANEL A: P/C INSURER ASSETS

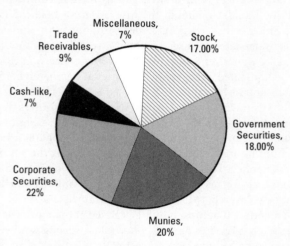

PANEL B: LIFE INSURER LIABILITIES & EQUITY

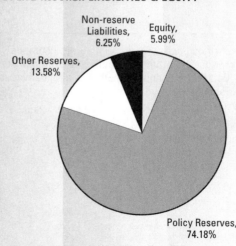

PANEL B: P/C INSURER LIABILITIES & EQUITY

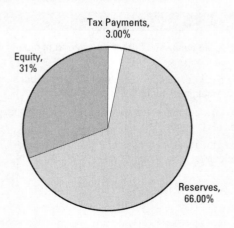

Source: Percentages calculated by the Authors from end of the year average balance sheet figures for life insurers, as cited in the American Council of Life Insurance: Life Insurers Fact Book, 2003, and balance sheet figures for non-life (P/C) insurers, as cited in the Information Insurance Institute's Financial Services Fact Book, 2003.

liquid and short-term and intermediate-term assets, since they may have to pay unexpected claims and, hence, have greater liquidity risk.

Trends in Securities Held by Life and P/L Insurers

As shown in Figure 16.1, both life insurers and P/L insurers hold the majority of their assets in fixed-income securities, notably bonds. The percentage holdings of different types of securities for life insurers changed dramatically between 1986 and 2003. In the late 1980s and early 1990s, stock holdings rose as state regulators became more flexible in allowing stock investments, and insurers took advantage of a bull stock market. With large losses from real estate loans in the early 1990s, the percentage of mortgage and real estate holdings of life insurers fell significantly, from 24 percent in 1986 to about 8.38 percent in 2003.

Life Insurer versus P/L Insurer Liabilities and Equity

As shown in Panel B of Figure 16.1, the majority of liabilities and equity for insurance companies are reserves, 74 percent for U.S. life insurers and 66 percent for P/L insurers at the end of 2002. Life insurers have policy reserves, security loss reserves, and also a dividend reserve. P/L insurers have a total loss and unearned premium reserve.[14]

Surplus and common stock (equity accounts) to assets were about 6 percent for life insurers on average, and 31 percent for P/L insurers. Because of the potential for large catastrophic losses, P/L firms hold a larger capital cushion.

Details of Life Insurer Liabilities and Surplus Funds

Life insurers have several different types of reserves and other liabilities listed as follows at the end of 2002.[15]

Policy Reserves (74.2% of total liabilities and equity)
Other Reserves (13.6% of total liabilities and equity)

Liabilities for deposit-type contracts	Policy and contract claims
Asset valuation reserve (AVR)	Funds set aside for policyholder dividends
Interest maintenance reserve (IMR)	Miscellaneous reserves

Nonreserve Liabilities (6.2% of total liabilities and equity)

Surplus funds	Book value of capital stock

Total Surplus and Capital Stock (6% of total liabilities and equity)

Policy reserves for future obligations on insurance policies are estimated by taking the total present value of future financial obligations—that is, the total present value of expected death, medical, or lifetime income benefits that the company may be required to pay to current policyholders. The amount, determined actuarially, considers: (1) mortality and morbidity (disease) rates, reflecting the reasons future claims will be made; (2) the present value of future premium payments to be received from those currently insured; and (3) the expected rate of return on the company's investments. In sum, the reserves on a life insurer's balance sheet are the present value of expected claims, net of the present value of estimated receipts of premium and investment incomes. In 2002, life insurer policy reserves included 39 percent for individual annuities, 23 percent for group annuities, 33 percent for life insurance, 4 percent for health insurance, and 1 percent for supplementary contracts. Hence, the largest percentage of outstanding reserves is often for annuity contracts.[16]

---

14 Ibid and Harrington and Niehaus (1999). Life insurer policy reserves and P/L total loss and unearned premium reserve are liabilities, in contrast to other types of reserves, which are often included as equity.

15 See Life Insurers Fact Book, 2003.

16 Ibid. Reserves for annuities are included as the largest single category of policy reserves. Most of the annuity obligations of life insurers are from group pension plans established by employers for employees, although individual annuity policies can be purchased. Annuities provide protection against the risk of outliving one's accumulated financial resources. In exchange for a lump sum payment or a series of smaller payments relatively early in a policyholder's life, insurers provide a predetermined post retirement monthly income, either fixed or variable and usually lasting for the life of the policyholders. Actuaries project the cash outflows expected under an annuity policy, based on how long the policyholder may live after annuity payments begin. In 1997 group annuities were 35 percent of policy reserves and individual annuities, 32 percent. Life insurance was 29 percent and health insurance, 4 percent.

In addition to policy reserves, life insurers have a number of other types of reserves. **Reserves for deposit-type contracts** including reserves for guaranteed interest contracts (GICs) that guarantee a fixed rate of return to investors and two statutory reserves required to absorb gains and losses for asset valuation fluctuations. The **asset valuation reserve (AVR)** is for realized and unrealized credit-related capital gains and losses including a default component for credit-related losses on fixed-income assets and an equity component for all types of equity investments. The **interest maintenance reserve (IMR)** is for realized interest-related capital gains and losses on fixed-income assets, with gains and losses amortized into income for the remaining life of the investments. A **policy dividend reserve** for mutual life insurance companies provides refunds for **participating insurance policies** on premiums paid during the year if the loss experience, operating expenses, and investment income of the insurer are better than expected at the beginning of the year. In practice, to maximize the probability that dividends can be paid regularly, premiums on participating policies are higher than premiums on nonparticipating policies that provide similar coverage but that are not entitled to dividends.

Policy dividend accumulations are past dividends that policyholders have reinvested in interest-bearing accounts; **dividend obligations payable** are policy dividends declared during the current year but not yet paid to policyholders. Because policy dividends are considered refunds of previous payments, they are not taxable to the insured when paid. **Other obligations** include accrued expenses, prepaid premiums, and mandatory reserves for fluctuations in security values.

Surplus and common stock are the equity, or capital, of the life insurance industry. The surplus account is analogous to retained earnings. The common stock account is for shareholder-owned firms. The book value of an insurer's surplus plus common stock shows how much the book value of assets can shrink before estimated claims on the insurer exceed asset values. In 2002, this figure was about 6 percent. At other times the asset valuation reserve and mandatory securities valuation reserves are included as part of capital; with these included, the average capital ratio of life insurers was 9.3 percent, falling from 10.1 percent in 2001. Without the asset valuation reserve, the capital ratio falls to 8.4 percent in 2002 versus 8.7 percent in 2001. State regulators require that insurers meet minimum capital ratios and risk-based capital ratios (discussed later in the chapter).[17]

Overview of Liabilities and Capital and Surplus for P/C Insurers

As noted in Figure 16.1, the liabilities of P/C (nonlife) insurers include taxes payable and miscellaneous liabilities. **Miscellaneous liabilities** include predominantly reserves for known and anticipated claims on policies and contracts. P/C insurers also must maintain a minimum capital (capital and surplus) ratio, known as **capacity** for underwriting risks. When large losses occur resulting from catastrophic events, capacity is reduced, with restoration of capacity coming from higher net income, investment returns, reinsurance of more risk, or raising additional external capital. Premiums tend to rise and fall as conditions change and capacity is low or high.

Performance Evaluation of Life Insurance Companies

Similar to depository institutions, key ratios can be calculated to help analysts focus on critical aspects of an insurer's financial performance and risk. One ratio common to both types of insurers is the **net**

Concept Questions

1. What are the differences between the financial assets and financial liabilities held by life insurers versus P/C insurers? What are reasons for the differences?

2. What are policy reserves? How are policy reserves determined?

3. Define the other types of reserves held by life insurers including the asset valuation reserve, interest maintenance reserve, and dividend reserve.

4. What is included in life insurer capital ratios? P/C insurer capital ratios?

---

17 See *Life Insurers Fact Books*, 1998 and 2003.

underwriting margin (NUM), which encompasses the main source of an insurer's revenues and expenses:

$$NUM = [\text{Premium Income} - \text{Policy Expenses}] / \text{Total Assets} \qquad [16.1]$$

Policy expenses include all benefit payments, additions to policy reserves, and operating expenses for life insurers and all loss expenses and operating expenses for P/L insurers. Policy expenses also include dividends to policyholders for mutual firms.

Sample Performance Analysis for a Life Insurance Company

Table 16.3 shows a financial analysis for trends in the Granite Life Insurance Company for 2004 and 2005. Just as in depository institution analysis, a DuPont analysis can be used, with the inclusion of NUM (versus net interest margin [NIM]) for a life insurer. Similar to depositories, life insurers have a small return on assets (ROA) but a high equity multiplier (EM), that is, high financial leverage, which produces a higher return on equity (ROE).

table **16.3** FINANCIAL PERFORMANCE ANALYSIS FOR GRANITE LIFE INSURANCE COMPANY

PANEL A: GRANITE LIFE INSURANCE COMPANY ASSETS & OBLIGATIONS, YEAR-END 2004 AND 2005 (IN MILS.)

Assets	2004	% Assets	2005	% Assets	Financial Ratios	2004	2005
Government Securities	$1,677	5.76%	$3,741	9.52%	Return on Equity	22.04%	13.27%
Corporate Securities					Return on Assets	1.53%	0.71%
Bonds	11,216	38.50%	13,836	35.20%	Net Underwr. Margin	−3.85%	−6.25%
Stock	1,294	4.44%	3,215	8.18%	Net Profit Margin	7.91%	3.19%
Real Estate Loans	10,989	37.72%	12,411	31.57%	Asset Utilization	0.193	0.221
Real Estate Investments	971	3.33%	1,678	4.27%	Equity Multiplier	14.43	18.84
Loans to Policyholders	1,322	4.54%	1,953	4.97%	Ave Yld Erng Assets	6.24%	7.94%
Other Assets	1,665	5.71%	2,475	6.30%			
Total Assets	$29,134	100.00%	$39,309	100.00%	Expenses to Assets		
					Benefits	10.60%	11.87%
Obligations & Net Worth					Add Policy Rsvs.	4.31%	5.37%
Policy Reserves	$26,622	91.38%	$33,534	85.31%	Op. Expense	2.41%	3.67%
Policy Dividend Obligations	595	2.04%	781	1.99%			
Other Obligations	1,898	6.51%	2,907	7.40%			
Total Obligations	27,115	93.07%	37,222	94.69%			
Total Net Worth (Surplus & Stock)	2,019	6.93%	2,087	5.31%			
Total Obligations & Net Worth	$29,134	100.00%	$39,309	100.00%			

PANEL B: GRANITE LIFE INSURANCE COMPANY INCOME & EXPENSES FOR 2004 AND 2005 (IN MILS.)

Revenues:	2004	% Revs.	2005	% Revs.	% Change
Premium Payments	$3,930	69.89%	$5,760	66.33%	
Net Investment Earnings & Other Income	1,693	30.11%	2,924	33.67%	
Total Revenues	$5,623	100.00%	$8,684	100.00%	54.44%
Expenses:					
Benefit Payments	$3,091	54.97%	$4,666	53.73%	
Additions to Policy Reserves	1,258	22.37%	2,109	24.29%	
Operating Expenses	703	12.50%	1,443	16.62%	
Total Expenses	5,052	89.85%	8,218	94.63%	62.67%
Net Operating Income	$541	9.62%	$466	5.37%	
Taxes	126	2.24%	189	2.18%	
Net Income	$445	7.91%	$277	3.19%	37.75%

Granite Life, for instance, has ROAs of 1.53 percent in 2004 and 0.71 percent in 2005. Its EM in 2004 is 14.43 (6.9 percent equity to assets). With a fall in equity to assets to 5.31 percent in 2005, the EM rises to 18.84. The higher EM has a positive effect on ROE, but with a much lower ROA in 2005, ROE falls from 22 percent in 2004 to 13.3 percent in 2005. The lower ROA is the result of cost efficiency problems. Although asset utilization rises in 2005 to 0.221 from 0.193, Granite's NPM falls from 7.91 percent in 2004 to 3.19 percent in 2005.

Because expenses rise 63 percent compared with revenues rising only 54 percent, net income falls by almost 38 percent. With premium expenses (benefit payments, additions to policy reserves, and operating expenses) much larger than premium revenues, Granite's NUM is −3.85 percent in 2004 and −6.25 percent in 2005, indicating net underwriting losses each year. Each expense item rises relative to assets in 2005. Benefit payments to assets rises from 10.6 percent to 11.87 percent, addition to policy reserves rise from 4.31 percent to 5.37 percent, and operating expenses rise from 2.41 percent to 3.67 percent. The average investment return (net investment revenues divided by earning assets) of 6.24 percent in 2004 and 7.94 percent in 2005 is responsible each year for Granite's having a profit.

Table 16.4 shows additional ratios often used by regulators and analysts. Other ratios include: (1) change in surplus, (2) change in premium payments, (3) commissions to premium payments, (4) real estate investments to total assets, (5) change in asset mix, and (6) change in product mix. Any decline in surplus or premiums alerts regulators to potential problems for an insurer. Commissions to premium payments is a cost efficiency measure. The other ratios represent signals of potential problems or strengths in terms of asset or product mix. Since real estate investments tend to be more risky than other types of assets, a large percentage of real estate investments signals greater risk. Granite has 37.7 percent of its assets in real estate investments in 2004 and 31.5 percent in 2005, which indicates a high proportion of more risky assets.

Sources of Financial Information

Financial information on life insurance firms can be found in *Best's Aggregates and Averages, Life-Health Edition,* and for P/L insurers, in *Best's Aggregates and Averages, Property-Liability Edition. Moody's Bank & Finance Manual* contains financial statements for large companies. *Best's* (Oldwick, NJ: A. M. Best Company) also contains ratings for insurance companies and publishes monthly *Best Reviews* (life/health and P/L editions) that discuss current issues. SNL Financial in Charlottesville, Virginia *(http://www.snl.com),* also publishes *The SNL Insurance Quarterly,* which contains year-end financials on all covered insurance companies as well as managerial and institutional ownership data.

Performance Evaluation of P/C Companies

In addition to NUM, P/C companies use other underwriting efficiency ratios, including:

$$\text{Loss Ratio} = \text{Loss Expenses} / \text{Total Premiums Earned} \qquad [16.2]$$

where Total Premiums Earned are premiums received and earned on insurance contracts without a claim being filed (total premiums written less unearned premiums), and Loss Expenses include losses and adjustment expenses for settling losses.

$$\text{Expense Ratio} = \text{Operating Expenses} / \text{Total Premiums Written} \qquad [16.3]$$

$$\text{Combined Ratio} = \text{Loss Ratio} + \text{Expense Ratio} \qquad [16.4]$$

$$\text{Operating Ratio} = \text{Combined Ratio (after dividends)} - \text{Investment Yield} \qquad [16.5]$$

$$\text{Overall Profitability} = 100\% - \text{Operating Ratio} \qquad [16.6]$$

where Investment Yield can be estimated as Investment Revenue / Earning Assets.[18]

The first two ratios reflect the two major expenses of P/L insurers: loss expenses and commissions and other operating expenses.

---

18 See Cornett and Saunders (1999, 2003); Saunders (1997); and Rejda (1995).

table **16.4** SELECTED INSURANCE REGULATORY INFORMATION SYSTEM RATIOS

PANEL A: ELEVEN IRIS SYSTEM RATIOS FOR EVALUATING THE PERFORMANCE OF LIFE AND P/L INSURERS

The National Association of Insurance Commissioners developed the following eleven IRIS System ratios for evaluating the performance of life and P/L insurers. These measures provide useful guidelines for industry analysts, and unusual figures are indicators of potential future problems.

1. **Premiums to Surplus** (Gross Premium to Surplus or Net Premium to Surplus)
2. **Change in Net Underwriting** (Change in Total Premiums Written / Previous Earned Premiums)
3. **Surplus Aid to Surplus** (Change in Surplus to Total Surplus)
4. **Two-year Overall Operating Ratio**
5. **Investment Yield**
6. **Change in Surplus**
7. **Liabilities to Liquid Assets**
8. **Agents' Balances to Surplus**
9. **One-year Reserve Development to Surplus**
10. **Two-year Reserve Development to Surplus**
11. **Estimated Current Reserve Deficiency to Surplus**

Source: Typical ratios used by the National Association of Insurance Commissioners (NAIC) to evaluate insurance firms. These are also listed on many insurance company Websites, such as the League of Minnesota Cities Insurance Trust's Website (LMCIT; http://www .osa.state.mn.us) with comparison to other companies. As noted on the LMCIT Website, regulators listed unusual values in 2002 for each of the ratios as (1) over 900 for the first ratio and over 300 for the second; (2) over +33 or under −33; (3) over 15; (4) over 100; (5) over 10 or under 4.5; (6) over 50 or under − 10; (7) over 105; (8) over 40; (9) over 20; (10) over 20; and (11) over 25. Averages and medians for the insurance industry in 2002 were listed as (1) for the first ratio 233 and 178; for the second 122 and 100; (2) 29 and 14; (3) 14 and 4; (4) 96 and 95; (5) 4.4 and 4.4; (6) 8.3 and 4; (7) 70 and 69; (8) 21 and 10; (9) 5 and 1; (10) −5 and −1; and (11) 13.3 and 2.

PANEL B: SUMMARY SAMPLE RATIO USED BY BEST'S TO EVALUATE P/L INSURERS PROFITABILITY, FINANCIAL LEVERAGE, LIQUIDITY, AND LOSS RESERVES PROFITABILITY

Combined Ratio after Policy Dividends: Sum Loss, Expense, and Dividend Ratio

Loss Ratio: Incurred Losses & Loss Adjustment Expenses to Net Premiums Earned

Expense Ratio: Underwriting Expenses (including commissions) to Net Premiums

Policyholder Dividend Ratio: Dividends to Policyholders to Net Premiums Earned

Operating Ratio: Combined Ratio − (Net Investment Income to Net Premiums Earned)

Pretax ROR (Return on Revenue): Pretax Operating Income to Net Premiums Earned

Yield on Invested Assets: Net Investment Income to Cash and Net Invested Assets

Change in PHS: % Change in Policyholder Surplus

Return PHS (ROE): (Net Income & Unrealized Capital Gains) to Average Policyholder Surplus

Leverage: Best's Capital Adequacy Relativity (BCAR): Company Capital Ratio / Peer Median Capital Ratio

NPW to PHS: Net Premiums Written to Policyholder Surplus

Net Liabilities to PHS: Net Liabilities to Policyholder Surplus

Liquidity: Overall Liquidity: Total Admitted Assets to Total Liabilities

Bonds to PHS: Noninvestment-Grade Bonds to Policyholder Surplus

Loss Reserve Tests: Loss and LAE Reserves to PHS: Reported Loss and Loss Adjustment Reserves to Policyholder Surplus

Source: Typical Ratios listed in Best's Insurance Reports—Property/Casualty.

Interpretation of the Loss Ratio

If the loss ratio is > 1 (> 100 percent), losses were greater than premiums earned. If the loss ratio is < 1 (< 100 percent), then premiums earned were greater than loss expenses. Often loss ratios are calculated individually for particular lines of business for a P/L. As Cornett and Saunders (1999) point out, loss ratios have risen on average for the industry over time. The average loss ratio was about 60 percent in 1951; 64 percent in 1961; 67.5 percent in 1971; 76.8 percent in 1981; 81.1 percent in 1991; 80 percent in 1996; and about 75.4 percent in the first nine months of 2003.[19]

Interpretation of the Expense Ratio

Expense ratios, in contrast to loss ratios, have fallen for the industry over time. The average expense ratio was about 34 percent in 1951; 32 percent in 1961; 27 percent in 1971; 27 percent in 1981; 26.4 percent in 1991; 26.2 percent in 1996; and 26.3 percent in the first nine months of 2003. P/L insurers have improved their efficiency in commission and other costs. Note that the premiums used in the denominators of the loss ratio and the expense ratio are different, so that losses incurred are related to premiums earned during the period, whereas operating expenses, most of which are agents' commissions, are related to premiums written during the same period.

Interpretation of the Combined Ratio

The combined ratio indicates the overall profitability in underwriting insurance for a P/L insurer or, if used for individual product lines, the profitability of a particular line of insurance. If the combined ratio is > 1 (> 100 percent), a P/L insurer has an underwriting loss with expenses greater than premium income. If the combined ratio is < 1 (< 100 percent), a P/L insurer has an underwriting profit. Trends in combined ratios or differences in combined ratios for different product lines can be evaluated. Also, a firm's combined ratio can be compared with similar firms writing similar lines of insurance. The combined ratio is also often calculated after dividends by subtracting dividends from premiums written. On average, P/L insurers have had underwriting losses in the last two decades. While the average combined ratio was 94.3 percent in 1951, in 1961 it was 96.5 percent; in 1971 it was 94.7 percent; in 1981 it was 104.1 percent; in 1991 it was 107.6 percent; and it continued to be greater than 100 percent during periods that encompassed hurricanes, catastrophic wildfires, and terrorist attacks in the United States, with a ratio of 105.9 percent in 1996 and a ratio of 116 percent in 2001. Performance improved in 2003, with the combined ratio falling to about 100.3 percent in the first nine months of 2003 and was expected to continue at this level in 2004. The Insurance Information Institute (I.I.I.) notes in its *Financial Services Fact Book, Financial Report for Property/Casualty Insurance Companies,* that for the first nine months of 2003 the improvement in the combined ratio resulted from both less terrorism and a much more disciplined approach to risk selection by insurers including better pricing of assumed risk. In the past, premiums for assumed risks were often underpriced, resulting in underwriting losses.[20]

Overall Profitability

Since P/C companies on average have had underwriting losses, as indicated by their combined ratios, that have been greater than 100 percent, their profitability has depended on generating revenue from their investment portfolios. The Operating Ratio is calculated as the Combined Ratio (after dividends) less the investment yield. The overall profitability ratio is 100 percent less the Operating Ratio, which provides a measure of a P/L insurer's overall profitability. The investment yield is usually calculated as net investment income divided by [the total of cash and net invested assets]. While in the 1980s investment yields were often very high, offsetting average industry underwriting losses, with low interest rates in the early 2000s, the average investment yields have been low, averaging about 4.4 percent in 2003, necessitating better risk management to produce a lower combined ratio to improve the Overall Profitability Ratio.[21]

---

19 See Cornett and Saunders (1999), 91–92.

20 Ibid and Financial Services Fact Book, 2003 (*http://financialservicefacts.org*), and other information provided on the Insurance Information Institute Website at *http://www.iii.org*.

21 Ibid.

Overall Performance in Recent Years

Although some insurers are mutual, the return on average net worth or equity (ROE) and return on assets are often used as a benchmark of overall profitability for insurers. As reported by the I.I.I. in 2002, the average industry ROEs have fallen in recent years; the average ROE for P/C insurers was about 11.6 percent in 1997, falling to 6 percent in 1999 to −1.2 percent in 2001—due to catastrophic losses from terrorist activities—and rising to 1 percent in 2002, with an estimated average ROE of 9.7 percent in 2003. For life/health insurers, the average net return on total assets fell from 8.08 percent in 1992 to 6.31 percent in 2001 to 5.38 percent at the end of 2002. Note with higher average ROAs and high equity multipliers, insurance companies can generate high ROEs. For stockholder-owned firms, given a wide range of equity multipliers, ROEs also ranged widely.[22]

Underwriting Cycles of P/C Insurers

Prior to the 1980s, research found the existence of underwriting cycles about every six years for the P/C business characterized by two subperiods known as a soft market and a hard market. In the soft portion of the cycle, premiums are lowered and insurance coverage is amply available. During the hard market, insurers raise premiums and some customers may have difficulty obtaining coverage. In a soft market, because premiums received are invested in financial assets, increases in the general level of interest rates may give insurers an incentive to write more policies to increase investment income and new firms to enter the market. Frequently, the desire to increase premium income to increase investment income results in price wars in which one company undercuts premiums charged by competitors. If rate wars continue long enough, premium income may be insufficient to cover underwriting expenses and policy claims during the year, resulting in a net underwriting loss. Actually, P/C insurers have had average net underwriting losses each year from 1979 to 2003. During the past three decades, the P/C industry compensated with high investment returns, leading to positive net incomes each year, with the exception of 2001, when the industry had its first full year net loss of −$6.9 billion. This contrasts with net income after taxes for the industry for the first half of 2003 of $14.496 billion. In the 1970s, the average combined ratio was 100.3; in the 1980s, 109.2; in the 1990s, 107.7; and in the 2000s, 111.00. The worst years for the industry were 1984 with a combined ratio of 118; 1985, 116.3; 1992, 115.7; and 2001, 115.7. In 2003 the combined ratio was estimated to be 101.4, and the Insurance Information Institute estimates a combined ratio of 100 in 2004, that is, a break-even point in net underwriting for the first time since 1978.[23]

Additional Performance Ratios

Table 16.4, Panel A shows some (of many) ratios that the NAIC and companies such as Best's Insurance consider for rating insurance companies. Many of these are similar to life insurer ratios, but others focus particularly on liquidity, which is more of a problem for P/L firms, especially liabilities/liquid assets. Changes in premium income and in surplus and total earned premiums / surplus indicate potential problems or improvements in premium income and surplus for companies. Net investment income / average invested assets provides the average yield on the insurer's investments.

Note on Financial Analysis for Insurance Companies

Many insurance companies are holding companies that offer both life and property/casualty insurance. Combined financial statements, such as those presented in *Best's* or *Moody's Bank & Finance Manual,* offer aggregate information, making it difficult to calculate separate loss and expense ratios, or do not distinguish between premiums earned and premiums written. Hence, the financial analyst must adjust

---

22 Ibid.

23 Ibid and Outreville (1999) points out similar P/L cycles in other countries. See Sean Mooney. "How Insurance Cycles Work." Insurance Review 15 (January 1990), 31–32. Cummins, Harrington, and Klein (1991) examine cycles and crises in P/L insurance markets, reviewing two possible explanations for market volatility: excessive price cutting by insurers and external pressures to industry capital.

to these limitations. Insurers also often buy insurance from other insurance companies known as reinsurers, who reinsure a portion of an insurer's potential losses. With a growing trend toward consolidation in the insurance industries, combined statements often reflect many different lines of business. There are other nuances and special accounts particular to different types of insurance companies, as well as complications with statutory versus GAAP accounting. With this caveat, the following section provides an illustration of an analysis for a P/L company. Panel B of Table 16.4 presents some of the ratios used by *Best's* for P/L insurers.

Sample Performance Analysis for a P/L Insurer

Table 16.5 provides information for Texas Farmers Insurance Company in Austin, Texas, for 1995 and 1996 from *Moody's Bank & Finance Manual.*

Moody's shows the premiums written for fire, allied lines, multiple peril for homeowners, multiple peril for commercial businesses, marine, medical malpractice, earthquake, other liabilities, and automobile liabilities. Thus, Texas Farmers underwrites a number of different product lines of liability insurance. Liability insurance lines are often problematic for P/L insurers since they have a so-called **long tail of liability,** whereby insurers are forced to pay millions of dollars for claims arising from injuries that occurred decades earlier. The majority of net premiums written for Texas Farmers Insurance Company comes from homeowners and auto insurance, which are liabilities that are more predictable and have less of a long tail problem.

A DuPont analysis shows that ROE rose from 3.44 percent in 1995 to 10.69 percent in 1996. The reason for the rise in ROE was a large rise in ROA, from 0.90 percent in 1995 to 3.5 percent in 1996. The EM fell with a rise in equity in 1996 (to 3.05 from 3.83) and thus did not contribute to the higher ROE. The higher ROA can be explained by both a higher asset utilization of 0.702 $\times$ in 1996 from 0.526 $\times$ in 1995 and a dramatically higher NPM of 4.99 percent versus 1.64 percent in 1995. AU rose as a result of both higher net premiums, which rose 16 percent in 1996, and a shrinkage of assets by about 10 percent.

Texas Farmer's NUM was negative in both years, which is typical of the P/L industry, but as the result of higher premiums earned in 1996, the negative NUM is much lower (-2.16 percent versus -4.98 percent). The operating expense ratio remained the same at 0.27, but the loss ratio fell to 0.76 in 1996 from 0.84 in 1995, resulting in a better combined ratio (1.03 versus 1.11 in 1995). Thus, Texas Farmers had a much lower net underwriting loss of 3 percent in 1996.

With a decline in investment assets, the average return on investment assets (excluding cash on hand and income due) rose to 7.26 percent in 1996 from 6.18 percent in 1995. In terms of investment mix, Texas Farmers reduced its cash on hand and short-term investments and increased its holdings of bonds, contributing to the higher average return on investments. With higher premiums earned relative to losses and other underwriting expenses and a higher average return on investments, Texas Farmers' performance improved significantly in 1996.

In terms of risk measures, the company's equity-to-asset ratio improved to 32.74 percent in 1996 from 26.13 percent in 1995. Liabilities to liquid assets, including cash and short-term investments, rose from 2.27 $\times$ in 1995 to 4.74 $\times$ in 1996. Similarly, the percentage of short-term investments to assets fell from 32 percent in 1995 to 14 percent in 1996. Thus, Texas Farmer's had greater liquidity risk in 1996.

Social and Economic Forces Affecting Insurers

Factors Affecting P/L Insurers

Litigation began increasing in the United States in the 1960s onward, and as product liability suits, malpractice suits, and other suits have escalated, juries have increased awards to plaintiffs, putting P/L insurers at great risk. To protect itself, the P/L industry often turns to reinsurers—insurance companies for insurance companies. Reinsurers agree, in exchange for a share of premium income, to assume responsibility for claims on policies written by other companies. Often insurance companies have a reinsurance subsidiary, or captive insurer, that provides reinsurance. The escalating costs of claims have required insurers to increase premium income, investment income, or both. These difficulties are compounded by the cost increases that occur during the downside of an underwriting cycle, a circumstance facing the industry by the mid-1980s. Adding to the challenge are increases in competition from other financial institutions, which further inhibit premium increases to compensate for losses.

table **16.5** PERFORMANCE ANALYSIS FOR TEXAS FARMERS INSURANCE COMPANY (P/L INSURER)

Net Premiums Written By Line of Business

	1996	% Total	1995	% Total
Fire	920	1.17%	946	1.39%
Allied Lines	783	1.00%	713	1.05%
Multiple Peril Homeowners	**14,553**	**18.52%**	**13,022**	**19.20%**
Multiple Peril Commercial	889	1.13%	696	1.03%
Marine	719	0.92%	662	0.98%
Medical Malpractice	dr10	−0.01%	dr163	−0.24%
Earthquake	1480	1.88%	926	1.37%
Other Liability	44	0.06%	33	0.05%
Auto Liability	**41,104**	**52.32%**	**39,730**	**58.58%**
Auto Physical Damage	18,078	23.01%	11,254	16.59%
Total	78,560	100.00%	67,819	100.00%

Cons. Income Statements	1996	% Revs.	1995	% Revs.
Premiums Earned	**76,272**	**89.79%**	**65,801**	**88.91%**
Losses incurred	51,427	60.54%	49,688	67.14%
Loss Expenses Incurred	6,808	8.01%	5,342	7.22%
Other Underwriting Expenses	20,653	24.31%	17,498	23.64%
Total Underwriting Deductions	**78,889**	**92.87%**	**72,527**	**98.00%**
Net Underwriting Gain	**−2,617**	**−3.08%**	**−6,726**	**−9.09%**
Net Investment Income Ernd.	7,957	9.37%	8,232	11.12%
Net real capital gains	595	0.70%	2	0.00%
Other Income Received	839	0.99%	866	1.17%
Finance/Service Charges	−721	−0.85%	−894	−1.21%
Adj. Net Investment Income	**8,670**	**10.21%**	**8,206**	**11.09%**
Net Income Before Dividends	**6,053**	**7.13%**	**1,480**	**2.00%**
Dividends to Policyholders	0	0.00%	0	0.00%
Net Income Before Taxes	6,053	7.13%	1,480	2.00%
Taxes	1,818	2.14%	263	0.36%
Net Income	**4,235**	**4.99%**	**1,217**	**1.64%**
Total Revenues	**84,942**	**100.00%**	**74,007**	**100.00%**
Net Investment Revenues	**8,670**	**10.21%**	**8,206**	**11.09%**
Premium Revenues	76,272	89.79%	65,801	88.91%

Financial Ratios

	1996	1995
Return on Equity	10.69%	3.44%
Return on Assets	3.50%	0.90%
Equity Multiplier	3.05	3.83
Net Profit Margin	4.99%	1.64%
Asset Utilization	0.702 ×	0.526 ×
Net Underwr. Margin	−2.16%	−4.98%
Loss Ratio	0.76 ×	0.84 ×
Expense Ratio	0.27 ×	0.27 ×
Combined Ratio	1.03 ×	1.11 ×
Ave Return Investmts	7.26%	6.18%
% Change Premiums	16%	
% Change in Assets	−10%	
Equity to Assets	32.74%	26.13%
Liabs./Liquid Assets	4.74 ×	2.27 ×
Short-term Investmts. to Assets	14.00%	32.00%

Consolidated Balance Sheet, as of Dec. 31 ($000)

Assets	1996	% Total	1995	% Total
Bonds	102,140	84.38%	88,883	65.83%
Cash	241	0.20%	940	0.70%
S.T. Inves.	**16,948**	**14.00%**	**43,025**	**31.87%**
Int. Due	1,371	1.13%	1,395	1.03%
Other	349	0.29%	772	0.57%
Total Assets	**121,050**	**100.00%**	**135,015**	**100.00%**
Liabilities				
Accrued Losses	28,371	23.44%	33,003	24.44%
Loss Adj. Expenses	10,444	8.63%	10,914	8.08%
Taxes, Licenses, Fees	968	0.80%	1,550	1.15%
Unearned Premiums	28,647	23.67%	26,715	19.79%
Other Liabilities	12,991	10.73%	27,547	20.40%
Total Liabilities	**81,421**	**67.26%**	**99,729**	**73.87%**
Equity Accounts	**39,629**	**32.74%**	**35,286**	**26.13%**
Total Liab. & Equity	**121,050**	**100.00%**	**135,015**	**100.00%**

Source: Moody's Bank & Finance Manual, *1997, p. 5937.*

In 1985, 1986, the 1990s, and the early 2000s, P/C companies and reinsurers responded to severe losses in key lines of insurance either by raising premiums or declining to sell some lines of insurance altogether. The industry also changed major features of some liability policies to protect itself against the so-called long tail of liability under which insurers were forced to pay millions of dollars for claims arising from injuries occurring decades earlier. This made liability insurance unaffordable for many

Concept Questions

1 How do you calculate the net underwriting margin (NUM), and what does it tell you?

2 Explain how to calculate the loss ratio, expense ratio, combined ratio, and overall profitability ratios and what they tell you about a P/C insurer's performance.

3 What have been recent trends in the combined ratio for P/C firms? Why was the combined ratio high in 2001 and lower in 2003? Why did ROEs for insurers fall in the early 2000s?

4 Why do underwriting cycles occur for P/C insurers? Why do you think P/C insurers have had net underwriting losses during 1979 to 2003 (i.e., does this reflect a long cycle of underwriting losses or normal behavior now for the industry)?

5 What is the long tail of liability for P/C insurers?

public school systems, charitable organizations, municipal governments, hospitals, and physicians in high-risk specialties, such as obstetrics, as well as small businesses in the early 2000s.[24]

Not surprisingly, customers and regulators were outraged, leading to major calls for reforms in the P/C industry and, in some instances, to outright customer revolt. Since the McCarran-Ferguson Act of 1945 permits federal regulation when (1) states fail to exercise their regulatory authority diligently, or (2) the industry itself engages in "boycott, coercion, or intimidation," the industry's refusal to insure some groups led to as yet unsuccessful attempts in the U.S. Congress to repeal or substantially modify McCarran-Ferguson to restore regulatory power to federal authorities and to bring the industry under antitrust rules. Currently, under McCarran-Ferguson, insurers are allowed to share information about losses so that actuaries can better estimate future costs. Industry opponents believe that the antitrust exemption simply makes it easy for insurers to collude to fix prices. Insurers argue that without access to shared data, small insurers could not survive because they could not afford to collect the necessary information on their own.

In 2004, at the time of this writing, Representative Michael G. Oxley had proposed new legislation for a federal insurance oversight committee and market versus state regulatory determined prices for insurance products. As noted in the opening quote, this legislation would end an absence of federal regulation for 150 years, allowing insurance firms to compete better with banks and other financial services firms by allowing greater efficiency including one-stop shopping and faster approval of new products. Some critics, however, argue that this change would lead to more lax regulation at the expense of customers. Currently, insurers operating on a national level must be licensed, undergo separate product approvals and separate market conduct examinations in all fifty states and territories, as well as meet fifty different sets of administrative and regulatory requirements. Under a regulatory efficiency and modernization reform initiative, state regulators and the NAIC have been trying to simplify and speed rate procedures and approvals in recent years as well, creating in 2001 the Coordinated Advertising Rate and Form Review Authority (CARFRA), a voluntary pilot program allowing regulators to set national product standards and create a single point of filing for designated products. However, CARFRA had difficulties eliminating differences among states. In 2002, NAIC members analyzed and developed options for an interstate compact where state regulators oversee uniform product standards and a single point for filing that was released for public comment, with legislation expected to be introduced in individual states in 2004 and 2005. Senator Ernest F. Hollings also introduced legislation in the summer of 2003 for an optional federal charter for insurers operating in multiple states, endorsed by the American Council of Life Insurers (ACLI) and the National Association of Insurance and Financial Advisors (NAIFA) by 2004, as well as large nationwide insurance companies.[25]

---

24 A financial analyst needs to be careful in examining underwriting cycles, since many large P/L insurers are mutually owned and report only on a statutory basis. Statutory profits are often lower than they would be if reported on a GAAP basis, which may exaggerate downturns in the cycle. See *Financial Services Fact Book, 2003* (http://financialservicefacts.org), and other information provided on the Insurance Information Institute Website at http://www.iii.org. See Marlys Harris. "Crisis in the Courts." *Insurance Review* 47 (April 1986), 52–57; and Thomas S. Healey. "Insurers under Siege." *Insurance Review* 47 (May 1986), 50–57. Also see various issues of *Property/Casualty Insurance Facts*. See "Now Even Insurers Have a Hard Time Getting Coverage." *Business Week* (December 2, 1985), 128–129; and David B. Hilder. "Uncollectable Reinsurance Hurts Firms." *The Wall Street Journal* (April 1, 1986), 6.

25 See Treaster. "New Momentum." C1, C8; and "Interstate Insurance Product Regulation Compact." NAIC Website (http:www.naic.org/compact/index.htm).

Factors Affecting P/C Insurers

In the past, different states have passed legislation initiated by consumer groups to limit the premiums that P/C insurers could charge. For example, California passed **Proposition 103 in 1988,** which included (1) a 20 percent rate cut in automobile insurance premiums for all drivers and an additional cut for "good" drivers; (2) permission for banks in California to sell insurance; (3) prohibition against insurers' charging premiums based on driver residence; (4) repeal of insurers' protection against state antitrust laws; and (5) popular election of the state's insurance commissioner. The California Supreme Court upheld Proposition 103, and its provisions took effect toward the end of 1989. Unfortunately, at times insurance companies have reacted by leaving these states, reducing availability of insurance to consumers. P/C insurers have also reacted by lobbying for changes in tort reform (negligence and legal liability) across the nation. Since 1986, dozens of states have enacted changes in their tort laws, some more sweeping than others. Insurers also promoted ways of reducing the cost of legal liability, including binding arbitration between plaintiff and defendant outside of court and a reduction of the percentage of damages a plaintiff's attorney may receive in a successful suit. P/C insurers also have made better public relations efforts, so consumers realize the costs involved and importance of insurance. They also have developed new coverage and purchasing techniques, including **risk retention** groups and **purchasing** groups that pool risk exposures reducing overall risks to insurers. Insurers have also offered a claims-made form of liability insurance to escape the long tail of liabilities.[26]

Premium Underpricing and Low Investment Returns to Cover Mounting Underwriting Losses

P/C insurers have been plagued with "chronic underpricing" in some lines of insurance, such as commercial lines and low investment returns with low interest rates in the late 1990s and early 2000s to cover mounting underwriting losses and slow premium growth. In addition, with what commercial consumers deemed as high premiums, companies have moved into self-insurance, where they create their own special separate insurance entity for self-insurance. Since the majority of P/C assets are bonds, even a small change in interest rates can reduce average investment yields. As noted by Robert Hartwig, Vice President and Chief Economist at the Insurance Information Institute, in 2002, investment income fell by about 2.8 percent and was at its lowest level since 1994. Many insurance firms faced the consequences of poor underwriting and underpricing of premiums from the 1990s and the early 2000s. P/C insurers and reinsurers also suffered stress in terms of hundreds of downgrades in ratings by major rating organizations in the early 2000s. The insolvency rate among P/C insurers rose to 1.33 percent in 2002 versus only 0.23 percent in 1999, and double the average ten-year rate of 0.72 percent.[27]

Catastrophes and Enron

Catastrophic losses in 2001 were also at a record $24.1 billion ($16.6 billion in 9/11 property and business interruption losses) and other losses including tropical storm Allison, which hit Texas with insurance losses of $2.5 billion and another $5 billion in losses throughout the year. In addition, as credit insurers and institutional investors, insurance companies lost billions of dollars with Enron's demise, and its debt became almost worthless to debtholders. Large insurers had guaranteed Enron's contracts with surety bonds and director and officer liability insurance.[28]

Factors Affecting Life Insurers

Life insurers, particularly in the health insurance arena, have faced adverse public opinion as well. To reduce costs, many health care insurers have resorted to health maintenance organizations (HMOs),

26 See Steven Waldman, Jennifer Foote, and Elisa Williams. "The Prop 103 'Prairie Fire.'" *Business Week* (May 15, 1989), 50–51; and "Proposition 103" and "Antitrust Issues" in *Property/Casualty Insurance Facts 1990*, 7–9. "Battle for the Cellar." *The Wall Street Journal* (August 28, 1988); and Peter Brimelow and Leslie Spencer. "The Plaintiff Attorneys' Great Honey Rush." *Forbes* (October 16, 1989), 197–203. As reported in the 1998 P/L Book, P/L companies had a 9.6 percent ROE compared to 16.5 percent for commercial banks, 18.5 percent for diversified financial firms, and 14 percent for Fortune 500 firms. Purchasing groups and risk retention groups were permitted by the Risk Retention Act of 1986. See Barbara Bowers. "A Year of Profits, Mergers and Regulation Tussles." *Best's Review, Life-Health Edition* (January, 1998), 36–41.

27 See *Financial Services Fact Book, 2003 (http://financialservicefacts.org)*, and other information provided on the Insurance Information Institute Website at *http://www.iii.org*; and *Life Insurers Fact Book, 2003*.

28 Ibid.

which limit services and the ability of the insured to choose their own doctors or hospitals, visit emergency rooms without permission, and see specialists. Although HMOs in many cases have been very effective, others have not, and consumers have reacted adversely to such restrictions. With the advent of the AIDS epidemic, which increased insurers' costs, some insurance companies began to require AIDS testing, along with tests for other illnesses, before insuring an individual. Many with such illnesses were left without the ability to be insured. Congress has consequently considered drastic reforms to the health insurance system and proposals that offer patients a bill of rights and choices in their medical provider. Although a national health care system was considered in the mid-1990s, legislation did not pass. Medical cost inflation has also increased costs for insurers, rising 4.6 percent in 2001. A tripling in the average jury award for medical malpractice cases from $1.1 million in 1994 to $3.5 million in 2000, as well as a rise in other jury awards also hurt profitability and almost resulted in a collapse in the medical malpractice insurance market in some states.[29]

Other trends include numerous intra-industry and interindustry mergers and convergence in products offered by other financial services firms, with many large insurers offering banking, mutual funds, security, pension investment, and other services. The best example of an interindustry merger is Travelers Group's purchase of two investment firms, Salomon Brothers and Smith Barney, as well as its merger with Citicorp in 1998 to form Citigroup. Later, however, in the early 2000s, the combined Citigroup became disenchanted with its P/C insurance operations, spinning off its Travelers' property/casualty insurance unit in 2002. In 2002, JPMorgan Chase introduced an annuity product, becoming one of the first bank holding companies to underwrite an insurance product since the passage of the Gramm-Leach-Bliley Act. Banks have also acquired insurance companies and insurance companies banks, although not as rapidly as expected. In 2002, for instance, Royal Bank of Canada acquired Assicurazioni Generali S.p.A.[30]

Other insurers are majority partners in joint ventures in which a bank and insurer together establish a third company in which they both have interests. While the bank becomes the majority partner in a **bancassurance** venture (the sale of insurance products through bank distribution channels), the insurer becomes the majority partner in an **assurbanking** operation (a system of taking bank products and selling them through the insurer's distribution channels), requiring less capital than an acquisition but necessitating revenue sharing. Alternatively, insurers have become minority partners, although there is risk of being bought out by the majority partner. Banks and insurers also may simply maintain distribution channels with each other without forming a separate firm, thus requiring less capital investment. In 2002, distribution channels for fixed rate annuities, reported by the I.I.I. *Financial Services Fact Book,* included 35 percent distribution through banks, representing a rise from 21 percent in 1995. For variable-rate annuities, however, only 9 percent were distributed through banks. Stockbrokers were the largest distributors of variable-rate annuities (41 percent) in 2002.

Other opportunities involve an insurer's furnishing outsourcing services to a new virtual bancassurer (similarly, a bank can provide services to a new virtual assurbank). With such an arrangement, the service provider generates additional revenue from an existing infrastructure but does not require affiliation. However, a virtual firm can in the future become a direct competitor of an established firm.[31]

Technological Changes in Insurer Distribution Systems

Insurance policies in the past have been distributed (or sold) through a **direct writer** system, involving an agent representing a single insurer, or through the independent agent system, involving an agent representing multiple insurers. An independent agent is responsible for running an agency and for the operating costs associate with it. Independent agencies are compensated through commissions, but direct writers may receive either commissions or salaries. With this system, customers become associated with the independent agency versus the insurance company. Direct writers have the advantage of support from the insurance company.

---

29 Ibid. Also see Barbara Bowers. "Banking on Insurance." *Best's Review, Life-Health Edition* (May 1998), 28–34.

30 See Note 27.

31 See Leslie Werstein Hann. "A Web of Changes"; Barbara Bowers. "The Long, Last Mile"; and "The Check Is in the E-mail." *Technology Supplement Best's Review* (November 1998), 11–26; and Bowers. "A Year of Profits," 36–41, and *Financial Services Fact Book, 2003* (http://financialservicefacts.org), and other information provided on the Insurance Information Institute Website at *http://www.iii.org.*

1 What recent proposals have been suggested to make insurance regulation more efficient by having federal or more uniform state regulations? What are the pros and cons for these proposals?

2 Consumers prefer lower premiums for P/C insurance, but P/C insurers at the same time have often underpriced insurance premiums. What are the arguments for and against higher insurance premiums?

3 What factors have increased P/C insurance underwriting losses in the past few decades? What have P/C insurers

done to try to reduce these losses and create a better public image?

4 What problems have life/health insurers faced in recent years?

5 What are ways insurers can enter the banking industry without actually purchasing a bank?

6 How has the distribution mechanism for insurance changed with technology?

Life insurers have also used the Internet to make life insurance sales, such as Zurich Kemper Life Insurance Company, which provides an instant quotation to an applicant and allows submission of an insurance policy application online. Similarly, a customer can buy a variable annuity from Lincoln Financial Direct directly over the Internet. However, sales of insurance on the Internet continue to remain a small percentage of total sales, with the majority of Internet sales for less complex, more commodity types of insurance such as auto, and some homeowner, term, and life products that need little explanation or risk analysis or tailoring. However, insurers do have a large Internet presence, with as early as 1998, 73 percent of insurance agencies with premiums of $25 million or more having such a presence. The Internet has also been used to increase agent productivity by large insurance firms, such as Chubb & Sons. The Tower Group reported that information technology (IT) spending increased for insurance firms, $19.5 billion by life insurers and $13 billion by P/C insurers in 2001 alone. Insurance companies in the health area, such as Kemper Insurance Company and Aetna U.S. Healthcare, have also made the filing of claims by customers, particularly doctors, more efficient using filing through the Internet, reducing transaction costs and increasing efficiency.[32]

U.S. Risk-Based Capital Requirements

NAIC developed a formula for risk-based capital (RBC) requirements for life/health companies in December 1992 and for P/L companies in December 1993. RBC requirements attempt to estimate the capital needed by a firm to safely absorb the losses to which it is subject. For P/L companies, four risk categories are given:

- Investment or asset risk
- Credit risk, such as reinsurance
- Off-balance-sheet risk, such as separate accounts
- Underwriting risk, such as the loss ratio and reserve adequacy

An RBC requirement is calculated for each category based on calculations of risk charges applying to potential risks for that category. These charges are weighted based on the importance of different types of risk and summed. Adjustments are then made for covariances to account for diversification to achieve the RBC requirement. Life insurance RBC is calculated in a similar fashion but with a heavier weight on asset risk because of the risk of asset values falling. In contrast, for P/C companies the risks of underestimating reserves and overestimating the profitability of incoming premiums are given heavier weights. Formulas shown in footnote 33 calculate a minimum capital or surplus amount that the insurer should maintain for adequate funding. If an insurer has a surplus below half of that amount, state insurance regulators are mandated to take over that company. Surplus fund balances are in addition to reserves that insurers have for actual and projected losses. Generally a threshold risk-based capital ratio of 100 percent is used, below which regulatory action will be triggered. Insurers also have rules of thumb for the proper surplus amount, such as 6-to-1 net leverage, 4-to-1 reserves to surplus, and 3-to-1 premium

---

32 Ibid.

to surplus ratios. In 2002, the American Council of Life Insurers reported that the average risk-based capital ratio for U.S. life insurers was 325 percent, with 89 percent of insurers (having 97 percent of industry assets) having risk-based capital ratios of 200 percent or more, well above the threshold. Only twenty-five life insurers had inadequate capital leading to regulatory action at year-end 2002.[33]

Regulatory Monitoring for Solvency

Regulators use early warning systems to monitor insurance companies for solvency risk. Some states have their own systems, but most use the system developed through NAIC, which prioritizes insurers according to their risk for greater analysis and onsite regulatory examinations. Insurers also receive a normal detailed financial examination every three to five years. NAIC's Insurance Regulatory System (IRIS), which has been used since the mid-1970s, involves eleven financial ratios shown in Panel A of Table 16.4, calculated for each insurer with reviews and analysis by an examiner team. A normal rate is established for each ratio based on historical data for failed versus nonfailed firms. Insurers are put into one of five categories for further analysis and/or actions. NAIC also developed a new solvency screening system for major insurers in the early 1990s known as FAST (Financial Analysis System Tracing) that has separate screening models for P/L, life, and health insurers and an expanded set of financial ratios with which each insurer is scored. FAST scores are used to prioritize how much regulatory scrutiny a major insurer needs; they are not available to the public.[34]

Private Insurer Solvency Ratings

Several agencies provide insurance company financial ratings based on subjective evaluations, including A.M. Best, Standard & Poor's, Moody's, and Duff and Phelps. Financial ratios, public information, news reports, private communications with managers, and visits with companies form the basis for these subjective evaluations. Best's gives ratings as Secure (A++ Superior, A+ Excellent, A−, B++ Very Good); Vulnerable (B, B− Adequate, C++, C+ Fair; C, C− Marginal); Very Vulnerable (D); Under Supervision (E); and in Liquidation (F).

Types of Life Insurance Policies and the Determination of Premiums

Life insurance products have changed over the years, as insurers have developed new products to compete with the investment products offered by other financial institutions. There are four main types of life insurance policies: (1) **Whole life insurance has a set fixed annual premium that is paid every year**

---

33 See Outreville (1999). For a more detailed discussion of RBC calculations for insurers, see Saunders (1997) and Cornett and Saunders (1999). For assets, securities are given higher RBC requirements based on their NAIC ratings. U.S. government bonds have 0 percent weights, the highest-rated securities (AAA to A+) have a 0.30 percent weighting; BBB, a 1 percent weighting; BB, a 4 percent weighting; B, a 9 percent weighting; CCC, a 20 percent weighting; and in near default, a 30 percent weighting. Residential mortgages have a 0.5 percent weighting, commercial mortgages a 3 percent weighting, common stocks a 30 percent weighting, and preferred stock a 2 percent weighting. Similar weightings with some variations are given for P/L investments. After calculating the dollar values for risk for different categories, which include for life insurers asset risk (C1), insurance risk (C2), interest rate risk (C3), and business risk (C4), RBC is calculated as:

$$RBC = [(C1 + C3)^2 + C2^2]^{1/2} + C4$$

The formula sums risks for the different categories and adjusts for correlations among risks. This is the minimum required capital that the life insurer must hold. The insurer is below the RBC requirement and would be subject to regulatory scrutiny if, when comparing total surplus and capital that the insurer holds to this measure by dividing RBC into the insurer's total surplus and capital, the comparison is below 1. For P/L insurers, risk types include R0, common stock and preferred stock investments in affiliates; R1, fixed income securities; R2, common and preferred stock securities; R3, reinsurance recoverables and other receivables for credit risk; R4, loss and loss adjustment expense reserves plus growth surcharges for underwriting risk; and R5, written premiums plus growth surcharges. For securities weights are similar, but somewhat different from those discussed for life insurers are used. RBC for P/L insurers is calculated as:

$$RBC = R0 + [R1^2 + R2^2 + R4^2 + R5^2]^{1/2}$$

Again, this ratio would be compared with the P/L insurer's total capital and surplus, similar to the example above, to determine whether capital was adequate. Also see *Life Insurers Fact Book, 2003*.

34 See Outreville (1999) and Harrington and Niehaus (1999) and *Best's Insurance Reports*. Best's ratings evaluate a company's financial strength, operating performance, and market profile by using quantitative and qualitative standards. Best's evaluation of financial strength includes capitalization, capital structure and holding company, quality and appropriateness of reinsurance program, adequacy of loss/policy reserves, quality and diversification of assets, and liquidity. Operating performance includes profitability, revenue composition, management experience, and objectives. Market profile factors include market risk, competitive market position, spread of risks, and event risk.

by a policyholder, with a known death benefit, the face amount of the policy. The beneficiary of the insured receives the full face amount regardless of the date of death. Premiums are set based on the average actuarial premium amount needed to cover claims for a policyholder's entire life, so excess premiums in earlier years above the actuarial need are invested at a fixed annual rate established at the time the policy is written (often states set a minimum yield). Policyholders build up cash values based on the earnings for excess premiums that can be cashed in, in lieu of maintaining full death protections, or against which low rate loans can be made; (2) **Term insurance,** in contrast, requires a lower yearly payment in earlier years based only on the actuarial premium amount needed, but which rises as needs rise as a person gets older, with no excess premium or accumulated cash value. Alternative policies offer constant premiums but decreasing coverage with age. Other options are also available, and term policies are frequently offered as group plans as part of employee benefit packages; (3) **Variable life** policies, first introduced in 1975, like whole life policies, require premiums over a policyholder's lifetime, but excess premiums earn variable rather than fixed rates of return based on the insurer's yield on assets of the policyholder's choice, passing investment risk and opportunity for higher returns to the policyholder. A minimum death benefit is specified in the policy, although there is no maximum. The actual payment to beneficiaries depends on yields earned on excess premiums; (4) **Universal life insurance** combines the death protection features of term insurance with the opportunity to earn market rates of return on excess premiums and to take advantage of tax-free investment accumulations, acting much more as a tax-deferred investment vehicle than an insurance vehicle, with lump sum premiums allowed as well as a series of payments and a minimum guaranteed return. Unlike whole or variable life policies, the face amount of guaranteed death protection in a universal life policy can be changed at the policyholder's option, including adjustments of death benefits, premium payments, and risk and return selections as their needs change. Investors also have the flexibility of investing excess premiums in different types of investments, such as mutual funds. Other products include annuities and guaranteed investment contracts that provide fixed cash flows and fixed investment returns, respectively, which are particularly helpful to individuals that are retired, who often put in lump sums at retirement in return for fixed cash flows each month with insurance annuity contracts. Insurers have also moved into the overall financial planning businesses, requiring very knowledgeable agents, often with security licenses and financial planning credentials, such as the Certified Financial Planner (CFP) credential to help customers with their investment and financial planning needs, as well as insurance needs.[35]

Illustration of How Premiums Are Set

Regardless of the policy, the insurer begins calculating the premium by examining a mortality table. Death rates per 1,000 are calculated conservatively, according to the number of insured men actually dying during the historical period examined, with an increase to allow for a margin of error. When setting premiums, an insurer uses actuarial estimates reflecting the most recent information available, including new causes of death, such as AIDS, or new treatments for formerly fatal diseases.[36]

Using an actuarial mortality table, suppose the rate of death for men before age 43 is a rate of 2.2 men per 1,000, or 0.0022 (an average probability of 0.22 percent). To set premiums, the insurer estimates the rate of return to be earned on premium payments made in advance of claims. Because most states require insurers to use conservative assumptions about the rate they will earn on invested premiums, this example assumes a rate of 4 percent and assumes that any claims paid will be paid at the end of the year. Hence, the premium on a $100,000, one-year term policy would be

$$\text{Present Value of Face Amount} \times \text{Probability of a Claim} = \text{Pure Premium} \qquad [16.7]$$
$$(\$100,000 \times 0.0022) / 1.04 = \$211.53$$

---

35 The tax-free status of universal life policies that serve more as investment vehicles than insurance vehicles has been under attack by Congress. Furthermore, sophisticated computer systems are needed to maintain accurate records on new flexible, tailor-made products. These expenses put further pressure on insurer earnings as their product mix changes.

36 Mortality tables, such as the Commissioners Standard Ordinary, are recommended as a basis for calculating required insurer reserves by NAIC. Death rates per 1,000 are calculated conservatively, according to the number of insured men or women actually dying during a period in a given population. Because mortality rates for men and women differ, life insurers use separate tables to calculate premiums for each sex. P/L companies also use separate premium schedules for men and women drivers because women have had better driving records. These practices have been challenged in courts as discriminating against both sexes. Most insurers, however, object vigorously to so-called unisex pricing, believing that premium and benefit differences between the sexes are justified. The issue has also been raised in Congress; see Dennon (1998). See *Life Insurers Fact Book,* 2003.

Suppose a man is 70 years old, and he wants to purchase one-year term insurance with a face value of $100,000. Given that the actuarial average for men this age is 25.8 deaths per 1,000, or 0.0258 (2.58 percent probability), the pure premium would be

$$(\$100,000 \times 0.0258) / 1.04 = \$2,480.77$$

Thus, term premiums rise significantly with age. Note that the low 4 percent discount rate assumed on the insurer's investment produces a higher premium versus if a higher discount rate is used. In the 1980s, for instance, life insurer returns were greater than 8 percent; however, insurers and state regulators justify the continued use of low rates in the interests of conservatism and the risk of claims not being met with lower premiums.[37]

For whole life policies, premiums are set based on the present value of the insurer's expected cash outflows over an individual's life adjusting for the probability that premium payments may not be made. Suppose that the whole life premium amount is $1,260.43 (based on actuarial estimates and coming up with an even premium for the individual's entire remaining life). For a 43-year-old individual who takes out a whole life policy, the excess premium of $1,260.43 less $211.53 equal to $1,048.90 will increase the cash value of the policy and will be invested as excess premiums for the policyholder. Cash value increases based on the assumed interest rate. Regardless of the insurer's actual investment earnings, nonparticipating whole life policyholders earn a fixed rate, and their beneficiaries receive a fixed death benefit. In contrast, participating policyholders may receive dividends in good years. This illustration shows the importance of both actuarial assumptions and investment assumptions often provided by state regulators on life insurance premium amounts.

Asset Management Considerations

Life Insurers

Because the assets of life insurers are mostly stocks and bonds, insurers need to carefully analyze the default and interest rate risk to which bond portfolios are exposed. In fact, because so many of the corporate bonds held by life insurers are privately placed, assessment of default risk is paramount. As noted in the opening paragraphs of this chapter, the financial problems of Executive Life, which was taken over by regulators in 1991, have been traced to the firm's investments in high-risk bonds. With greater liquidity needs caused by guaranteed investment contracts and other new investment products, insurers may have to sell assets before maturity, so they need to be well acquainted with interest rate theories and hedging techniques, as well as portfolio theory, discussed in investment courses. Immunization (protecting returns on fixed assets from interest rate swings) has become very important for insurers, particularly for insurers with substantial **separate accounts,** defined as groups of assets designated as backing for specific obligations. If an insurer manages pension fund obligations for an employer, separate accounts are often used to support these obligations. Also, reserves for variable and universal life policies are often backed by separate accounts. Like commercial banks, insurance firms have diversified into the pension and popular retirement annuity product management businesses.

Investment in real estate requires knowledge of real estate markets and finance. Earnings pressures have raised concerns both in and outside the industry as insurers have been tempted to invest in riskier than normal assets. Hence, risk management is very important. Other performance measures, such as economic value added (EVA) are sometimes used to evaluate publicly traded insurers, but some analysts question whether EVA can "accommodate" insurer's specialized capital needs.

---

37 Pure premiums are generally increased by a loading to cover operating expenses and profit for shareholders. Not every insurer would charge the pure premium plus the same loading. Individual insurance underwriters must decide what types of risks they are willing to bear. In some cases, if a company prefers to deal with one type of client (say, nonsmokers), it may undercharge them and overcharge smokers to make up the difference. As a result, policies with identical features may be priced differently, depending on the underwriter's risk preferences. For an example of the range of premiums on a given term policy, see Richard Morais. "Double Indemnity." *Forbes* 136 (November 18, 1985), 280. The present value of the expected outflow to the insurer is calculated as a lump sum, and the insurer calculates the probability of a customer surviving his premium at the beginning of each policy year. The weighted number of premium payments expected considering the probability of death and the impact of lost interest is divided into the expected cost of insuring the individual for life, resulting in an annual pure premium without considering operating costs.

P/C Insurers

P/C insurers are also increasingly using the immunization techniques to reduce interest rate and credit risk. Catastrophe futures hedge against large losses. Industry publications stress the importance of estimating a firm's anticipated cash outflows resulting from policy claims, many of which may not actually occur until months or even years after a policy is written. If estimates are carefully made, asset portfolios can be selected with cash inflows to match the anticipated series of outflows. Thus, insurers can attempt to immunize at least portions of the balance sheet. For hedging with futures positions, NAIC requires that gains and losses on futures be directly reflected in net worth rather than being amortized over time. Still, in an environment of rising rates, profitable hedges can protect insurers against the shrinkage of net worth caused by a decline in portfolio values, which also must be directly written off against net worth. Interest rate and risk management strategies are important for P/C firms.[38]

Concept Questions

1 What types of risk do risk-based capital requirements for insurance firms consider? Which types of risks are considered more for life insurers and for P/C insurers, respectively?

2 What type of regulatory monitoring is done for solvency by the NAIC? What is IRIS?

3 How are insurance premiums determined? Why are whole life premiums larger than term life premiums?

4 What are the advantages and disadvantages from a consumer perspective for whole life versus term life insurance?

5 What are some asset management considerations for life and P/C insurers, respectively?

Summary

Insurance companies are founded on probability estimation, better known to insurers as actuarial science. Premiums and reported obligations are based on estimates of the amount and timing of claims a firm will have to pay in the future. Successful financial management involves balancing premium income and investment income against benefits paid to policyholders. Life and P/C insurers have different financial characteristics that arise from the types of policies they write. They have structural characteristics in common, however, and all experienced earnings pressures in the past decade.

Life insurers have traditionally enjoyed predictable cash flows. Higher interest rates and changing consumer preferences, however, have forced insurers to develop alternative products, making premium income and obligations to policyholders subject to market conditions and policyholder preferences. Changes in operating conditions have made asset/liability management strategies increasingly important for life insurers.

P/C insurers have faced a similar need to adapt management strategies to changing market and economic conditions, although incentives for change are different. In recent years, the main influences on earnings of P/C insurers have been inflation, larger litigation awards, and consumer pressure for lower premiums. These factors, along with the traditional underwriting cycle, depressed underwriting income so strongly in the 1980s that even rapidly rising investment income could not protect earnings. As with life insurers, these operating changes require P/C insurers to adjust asset/liability management strategies.

38 See Lee McDonald. "Reading the Market." *Best's Review, Life-Health Edition* (June 1998), 73–74; Jeffrey B. Pantages. "Negating the Interest Rate Risk." *Best's Review, P/L Edition* (May 1984), 24–28, 120; Niehaus and Mann (1992); Charles P. Edmonds, John S. Jahera, Jr., and Terry Rose. "Hedging the Future." *Best's Review, Property-Casualty Edition* (September 1983), 30–32, 118; and Nye and Kolb (1986).

Questions

1. Compare and contrast the characteristics of insurance coverage offered by life and P/C insurers. Explain how these characteristics are reflected in the asset and liability choices of the two types of insurers.

2. In the opening quotations, recent problems of insurers are discussed. Explain some of the problems in terms of catastrophic losses and interest rate and liquidity problems. Why did many of these problems increase in the past two decades?

3. What are the two sources of insurance companies' revenues? Explain why investment income has become a more important source of revenues in recent years.

4. What types of securities do life insurers and P/C insurers, respectively, hold? Explain reasons for their differences in holdings. What changes have occurred in the security holdings of life insurers? Explain why these changes have occurred.

5. What is the majority of expenses for life insurers? For P/C insurers? How does this differ from depository institutions?

6. Explain what statutory accounting is. How does it differ from GAAP accounting?

7. How do the assets and liabilities of both life and P/C insurers differ from depository institutions? How do services offered and fund sources result in balance sheet differences? What are policy reserves? How are they calculated for life insurers?

8. Explain how the NUM differs from the NIM. How similar a role do the two ratios play in financial management decisions?

9. Explain what the loss ratio, expense ratio, combined ratio, and overall profitability ratios indicate in terms of the profitability of a P/C insurer. Why are P/C insurers very dependent on investment yields? What is the long tail of liability? How has it affected the financial performance of P/C insurers?

10. What are underwriting cycles, and why do P/C insurers have them?

11. Why do P/C insurers have problems raising insurance premiums? Give an example of attempts by consumers to limit premiums. How have P/C insurers reacted to consumer revolts and high court settlements for lawsuits?

12. What issues did life insurers face in the 1990s? What have insurers done to try to resolve these problems and to diversify? How has technology changed insurer distribution systems?

13. Discuss overall insurance operations and the importance of different areas, including product design and development, production and distribution, product management, administration, and finance and investment.

14. How do RBC requirements for insurers differ from those of depository institutions? How does NAIC monitor insurers for insolvency?

15. Explain the differences among whole life, term insurance, variable life, and universal insurance policies. How are premiums determined for whole life versus term insurance? Why have policyholders preferred term insurance? What implications does this have for the asset/liability management of insurers in terms of predictability of incoming premiums?

16. Briefly discuss recent asset management considerations for life and P/C insurers.

Problems

1. Perform a DuPont analysis and calculate the NUM, loss ratio, expense ratio, combined ratio, and overall profitability ratio for the Town and Country Mutual Automobile Insurance Company for the two years given in Table P16.1. Explain precisely why the ROE and ROA changed in 2005; be sure to include a review of the common size financial statements. What additional information would you like to know about Town and Country for your analysis?

2. Perform a DuPont financial analysis for the RLI Corporation, based on the data shown in Table P16.2, for 1997 to 1998. Explain why the company's ROA improved in 1997 and why it fell in 1998. Include an evaluation of the GAAP combined ratio and common size statements.

3. Evaluate the ratios from *Best's Insurance Reports: Property-Casualty Edition* for Gateway Insurance Company shown in Table P16.3. (Some ratios are particular to Best's and are defined in Table 16.4.) Do you agree with Best's rating of B++ for the company? Point out any strengths or weaknesses that you can find from the ratios given. What additional information would you like to have?

table P16.1   FINANCIAL INFORMATION FOR PERFORMANCE ANALYSIS FOR TOWN AND COUNTRY MUTUAL

Automobile Insurance Company Balance Sheets, Year-End 2004 and 2005 (in mils.)

Assets	2004	% Assets	2005	% Assets
U.S. Treasury Bonds	1,169	7.60%	1,106	6.63%
Municipal Bonds	2,779	18.07%	3,505	21.02%
Other Bonds	4,161	27.06%	4,554	27.32%
Total Bonds	$ 8,109	**52.74%**	$ 9,165	**54.98%**
Common & Preferred Stock	3,192	**20.76%**	3,260	**19.55%**
Mortgages & Other Loans	2,422	**15.75%**	2,501	**15.00%**
Other Assets	1,652	**10.74%**	1,745	**10.47%**
Total Assets	**$15,375**	100.00%	**$16,671**	100.00%
Liabilities & Net Worth				
Total Loss & Unearned Premium Reserves	7,185	46.73%	7,879	47.26%
Total Surplus (Net Worth)	8,190	**53.27%**	8,792	**52.74%**
Total Liabs. & Net Worth	**$15,375**	100.00%	**$16,671**	100.00%

Income Statements for 2004 and 2005 (mils.)

	2004	% Revs.	2005	% Revs.
Revenues				
Total Premiums Written	$ 8,011	96.31%	$ 8,975	94.24%
Less Unearned Premiums	(375)	−4.51%	(473)	−4.97%
Total Earned Premiums	$ 7,636	**91.80%**	$ 8,502	**89.27%**
Net Investment Earnings & Other Income	682	**8.20%**	1,022	**10.73%**
Total Revenues	$ 8,318	100.00%	$ 9,524	100.00%
Expenses				
Loss Expenses	$ 6,077	73.06%	$ 7,276	76.40%
Policyholder Dividends	136	1.64%	4	0.04%
Operating Expenses	1,355	16.29%	1,511	15.87%
Total Expenses	$ 7,568	**90.98%**	$ 8,791	**92.30%**
Underwriting Results				
Earned Premiums	$ 7,636	**91.80%**	$ 8,502	**89.27%**
Less: Loss Expenses	(6,077)	−73.06%	(7,276)	−76.40%
Operating Expenses	(1,355)	−16.29%	(1,511)	−15.87%
Statutory Underwriting Gain (Loss)	$ 204	**2.45%**	$ (285)	**23.00%**
Less Dividends to Policyholders	(136)	−1.64%	$0	0.00%
Net Underwriting Gain (Loss)	**$68**	0.81%	(289)	**−3.00%**

4. Using the CSO mortality table on page 596,
   a. What is the probability that a 30-year-old female policyholder will live to be 40?
   b. With a 6% investment rate, what is the pure premium on a $75,000, one-year term policy for a 40-year-old male?
   c. If the assumed rate of return on invested premiums were 9 percent, what would the pure premium be for the policy described in part b?

   d. If, instead, the male policyholder wished to take out a whole life policy with a face amount of $75,000, identify the additional steps needed to calculate the premium. Without doing any calculations, would the first year's premium on the whole life policy be higher or lower than the premium you calculated in part b? Explain.

5. a. Using an assumed rate of return of 8 percent, calculate the pure premium on a $1 million, one-year

table **P16.2** RLI CORPORATION (MULTILINE INSURER) YEAR-END 1997 & 1988

Assets (in thous.)	FISCAL YEAR END				Reported Financial Ratios	1997	1998
	1997	% Assets	1998	% Assets			
Cash & Investments	603,857	66.23%	677,293	66.88%	Return on Average Assets	3.43%	2.93%
Reinsurance Assets	211,386	23.18%	274,707	27.13%	Return on Average Equity	12.93%	10.08%
Deferred Policy Acq. Costs	21,985	2.41%	22,510	2.22%	Investment Yield	4.66%	4.03%
Other Assets	74,516	8.17%	38,175	3.77%	Operating Income to Revenues	23.95%	22.76%
Total Assets	911,744	100.00%	1,012,685	100.00%	**Underwriting Measures:**		
Liabilities & Equity					GAAP Combined Ratio	86.8	88.2
Policy Reserves	532,807	58.44%	557,546	55.06%	Statutory Combined Ratio	90.4	N/A
Debt	24,900	2.73%	39,644	3.91%			
Other Liabilities	87,482	9.60%	121,536	12.00%			
Total Liabilities	645,189	70.76%	718,726	70.97%	**Balance Sheet Ratios:**		
Total Common Equity	266,555	29.24%	293,959	29.03%	Policy Reserves to Equity %	2.00%	1.90%
Total Liabilities & Equity	911,744	100.00%	1,012,685	100.00%	Debt + Rdm. Prfd. to Equity	9.34	13.49
					Debt to Total Bk. Value Capital	8.54	11.88
Income Statement							
Revenues:							
Policy Revenues	141,884	83.28%	142,324	83.99%			
Net Investment Income	24,558	14.41%	23,937	14.13%			
Net Realized Gains	2,982	1.75%	1,853	1.09%			
Other Revenues	951	0.56%	1,337	0.79%			
Total Revenues	170,375	100.00%	169,451	100.00%			
Expenses:							
Policy Expenses	61,252	35.95%	64,728	38.20%			
Other Expenses	66,053	38.77%	64,722	38.20%			
Interest Expense	1,548	0.91%	2,280	1.35%			
Total Expenses	128,853	75.63%	131,730	77.74%			
Net Income Before Taxes	41,522	24.37%	37,721	22.26%			
Provision for Taxes	11,351	6.66%	9,482	5.60%			
After-Tax Net Income	30,171	17.71%	28,239	16.66%			

Source: SNL Insurance Quarterly, *SNL Securities, Charlottesville, Virginia, 1998.*

term policy for a 10-year-old girl. If you were the parent of this child, what factors might influence you to take out a life insurance policy on her? What type of policy would you prefer? Why?

b. With an assumed investment rate of 6%, calculate the premium on a $1 million, one-year term policy for a 70-year-old man. If you were 70 and had no life insurance, what type of policy would you choose? Why?

	MALE		FEMALE	
Age	Deaths per 1,000	Life Expectancy (Years)	Deaths per 1,000	Life Expectancy (Years)
10	0.2	66.9	0.2	71.0
20	1.0	57.2	0.5	61.3
30	1.1	47.8	0.7	51.6
40	1.7	38.3	1.3	42.0
50	3.8	29.2	3.1	32.7
60	9.9	20.6	8.0	24.1
70	25.8	13.3	17.8	16.4
80	70.1	7.5	43.9	9.9

Abstract from the CSO 2001 Table as Reported in the American Council of Life Insurers Annual Report 2002, 154–156.

table **P16.3** GATEWAY INSURANCE COMPANY, INSURANCE FROM BEST'S 1997 INSURANCE REPORTS, PROPERTY/CASUALTY

Current Rating: B++ (Very good) reflecting the company's conservative operating strategy, favorable liquidity position, and strong capital support from its parent company. Management has geographically diversified operations outside of the north-western/central region of the United States and additional licenses are being sought. Partially offsetting these positive factors is the company's fair return figures on its nonstandard auto and taxicab business, lack of surplus growth, and modest debt service requirements at the holding company level. Management has continued to implement more efficient loss control measures to improve its financial position and support additional growth. With the improvement in operating earnings along with the available capital support from its parent, Best views the company's rating as stable.

Key Financial Indicators

Period Ending	Direct Premiums Written	Net Premiums Written	Pretax Op Income	Net Income	Total Admitted Assets	Policy-holders' Surplus
1992	8,386	8,004	296	260	12,001	3,359
1993	8,675	8,370	129	246	13,438	4,143
1994	8,961	8,858	602	467	14,757	4,481
1995	12,651	12,563	−930	−563	18,746	6,546
1996	12,218	12,119	273	362	18,854	6,942

Profitability

	Loss Ratio	Expense Ratio	Combined Ratio	Industry Ave	Investmt. Yield %	Industry Ave	Pretax ROR %	Industry Ave	Leverage BCAR %	NPW to PHS	Industry Ave.	Liquidity Overall Liquidity
1992	70.5	32.0	102.5	103.0	5.60%	5.40%	3.70%	4.70%		2.4	2.1	138.90%
1993	75.5	30.9	106.4	96.8	5.00%	5.50%	1.50%	10.10%		2.0	2.2	144.60%
1994	62.0	34.3	96.3	97.0	4.80%	5.20%	7.50%	9.50%	96.10%	2.0	2.3	143.60%
1995	72.3	36.7	109.0	100.9	4.80%	5.60%	−8.30%	6.50%	83.50%	1.9	2.3	153.70%
1996	68.2	36.9	105.1	99.0	5.60%	5.50%	2.20%	7.65%	104.40%	1.7	2.3	158.30%
5-Year	69.8	34.6	104.4	99.2	5.20%	5.40%	0.80%	7.70%				

1996 Business Production & Profitability ($000)

Product Line	Premiums Direct	Written Net	% of Total NPW	Pure Loss Ratio	Loss & LAE Res.
Private Auto Liability	6,862	6,862	56.60%	64.00%	3,151
Commercial Auto Liab.	3,612	3,513	29.00%	39.10%	2,655
Auto Physical	1,744	1,744	14.40%	70.30%	154
All Other				−7.90%	41
Totals	12,218	12,119	100.0	57.9%	6,001

Major 1996 Direct Premium Writings by State ($000): Missouri $7,984 (65.3%); Louisiana $2,100 (17.2%); Indiana $921 (7.5%); Kansas $518 (4.2%) Tennessee $355 (2.9%); and three other jurisdictions, $340 (2.8%)

Business Review: *The overall business mix is 70 percent consumer and 30 percent commercial. The firm focuses on physical damage & liability coverage for nonstandard personal autos & smaller size taxicab fleets. About 90 percent of all business is produced by MidAmerican General Agency. Most volume is concentrated in Missouri. Licensed in twenty-two states, management is hoping to add six additional states in the future.*

Source: 1997 Best's Insurance Reports—Property-Casualty 1997, 1949.

Suggested Case Study

"Case 10: Rockhard Insurance." Darden School, University of Virginia: Richard D. Crawford and William W. Sihler. In *Financial Service Organizations: Cases in Strategic Management.* New York: HarperCollins College Publishers, 1994

(currently casebook is out of print, but also a Darden case). This case provides an opportunity for financial analysis and also covers strategic issues for a traditional insurer's decision whether or not to diversify into new activities, building on its strengths.

Selected References

Altman, Edward I., and Irwin T. Vanderhoof. *The Financial Dynamics of the Insurance Industry.* New York: Irwin Professional Publishing, 1995.

————. *The Strategic Dynamics of the Insurance Industry: Asset/Liability Management Issues.* New York: Irwin Professional Publishing, 1996.

American Council of Life Insurance. *Life Insurers Fact Books.* Washington, DC: American Council of Life Insurance, 1998, 2003.

Cornett, Marcia Millon, and Anthony Saunders. *Fundamentals of Financial Institutions Management.* New York: Irwin McGraw-Hill, 1999.

Crawford, Richard D., and William W. Sihler. *Financial Service Organizations: Cases in Strategic Management.* New York: HarperCollins, 1994.

Cummins, J. David, and Joan Lamm-Tennant. *Financial Management of Life Insurance Companies.* Boston: Kluwer Academic Publishers, 1993.

Cummins, J. David, Scott E. Harrington, and Robert W. Klein. "Cycles and Crisis in Property/Casualty Insurance: Causes and Implications for Public Policy." *Journal of Insurance Regulation* (Fall 1991), 50–93.

Dennon, A. R. "The Facts about Unisex Insurance." *Consumers' Research* 71 (February 1998), 25–27.

Harrington, Scott E., and Gregory R. Niehaus. *Risk Management and Insurance.* New York: Irwin McGraw-Hill, 1999.

Mehr, Robert I. *Fundamentals of Insurance.* Homewood, IL: Irwin, 1983.

Mehr, Robert I., and Sandra G. Gustavson. *Life Insurance: Theory and Practice.* Plano, TX: Business Publications, Inc., 1984.

Michelbacher, G. F., and N. R. Roos. *Multiple-Line Insurers: Their Nature and Operation.* New York: McGraw-Hill Book Co., 1970.

Niehaus, Greg, and Steven V. Mann. "The Trading of Underwriting Risk: An Analysis of Insurance Futures Contracts and Reinsurance." *Journal of Risk and Insurance* 59 (December 1992), 601–627.

Nye, David J., and Robert W. Kolb. "Inflation, Interest Rates, and Property-Liability Insurer Risk." *Journal of Risk and Insurance* 53 (March 1986), 144–154.

Outreville, J. François. *Theory and Practice of Insurance.* Boston: Kluwer Academic Publishers, 1998.

Property/Casualty Insurance Facts. New York: Insurance Information Institute, 1998, 2003.

Rejda, George E. *Principles of Risk Management and Insurance,* 5th ed. New York: HarperCollins College Publishers, 1995.

Saunders, Anthony. *Financial Institutions Management: A Modern Perspective,* 2nd ed. New York: Irwin, 1997.

Saunders, Anthony, and Marcia Million Cornett. *Financial Institution Management: A Risk Management Approach,* 3rd and 4th editions. Burr Ridge, IL: McGraw-Hill Higher Education, 1999, 2003.

Vaughan, Emmett J. *Fundamentals of Risk and Insurance.* New York: John Wiley & Sons, 1982.

COMPANY FINANCIAL MANAGEMENT ISSUES

1 A.M. Best Co. *(http://www.ambest.com)* was founded in 1899 with the purpose of performing "a constructive and objective role in the insurance industry towards the prevention and detection of insurer insolvency." This mission led to the development of Best's Ratings. Today, A.M. Best rates the financial strength of insurance companies and the security of holding company's debt and preferred stock. More than merely passing judgment on past performance, a Best's Rating gives an indication of how that company may be expected to perform in the future.

A Best's Rating is an independent third-party evaluation that subjects all insurers to the same rigorous criteria, providing a valuable benchmark for comparing insurers, regardless of their country of domicile. Such a benchmark is increasingly important to an international market that looks for a strong indication of stability in the face of widespread deregulation, mergers, acquisitions, and other dynamic factors.

A.M. Best assigns to insurance companies one of two types of rating opinions, a Best's Rating (A11 to F) or a Financial Performance Rating (9 to 1). For an explanation of Best's rating system, go to *http://www.ambest.com/ratings/guide.html*

2 Insurance company ratings from Standard & Poor's and Moody's are available through the Insurance News Network at *http://www.insure.com/ratings/index.html*

From this page, click on "Standard & Poor's Ratings" to get the rating by type of company (life/health, property/casualty, etc.). For example, to find all life insurance companies in the United States with a BB rating, fill out the online form as follows:

Type of insurance: **individual life**

Doing business in: **U.S. rankings**

Rated: **BB**

Sorted by: **Largest to smallest**

Then click "Go." The resulting table listing the BB-rated insurance firms also provides information on "What the ratings mean" and whether there is a credit watch on the firm. An insurer-rated "BB" has MARGINAL financial security characteristics. Positive attributes exist, but adverse business conditions could lead to insufficient ability to meet financial commitments.

OTHER USEFUL SITES FOR FINANCIAL INSTITUTION DATA:

American Risk and Insurance Association

http://www.aria.org/

American Council of Life Insurers

http://www.acli.org

ISO Website, premier source of information about risk and insurance

http://www.iso.com

Berkshire Hathaway Inc.

http://www.berkshirehathaway.com/

Insurance Industry Internet Network

http://www.iiin.com/

Insurance Information Institute

http://www.iii.org/

Progressive Insurance Online

http://www.progressive.com/

Wharton Risk Management and Decision Processes Center

http://grace.wharton.upenn.edu/risk/

Financial Services Fact Book

http://www.financialservicesfacts.org

International Insurance Facts

http://www.internationalinsurance.org

Disaster Insurance Information Office (DIIO)

http://www.disasterinformation.org

Insurance Scoring

http://www.insurancescoring.info

17 Investment Banks, Securities Firms, and Venture Capitalists

Management and Ethical Issues

"The only way to make investment banking more competitive would be to gouge eyes out."

ROBERT BALDWIN, Partner at Morgan Stanley, 1960s. Quote from Ron Chernow. The House of Morgan. *New York: Touchstone (Simon & Schuster), 1990, 587.*

"I am not a yesterday person. I don't really care about yesterday. If we did well yesterday, that is history. What I am worried about is how we are going to perform five years from now."

DAVID KOMANSKY, President and Chief Operating Officer—Merrill Lynch & Co., Inc. Quote from The New Financiers: Profiles of the Leaders Who Are Reshaping the Financial Services Industry, *ed. Charles B. Wendel. Chicago: Irwin Professional Publishing, 1996, 143.*

With the advent of the information age, the traditional methods that investment banks and securities firms had used to distribute securities changed. Online securities trading grew dramatically in the 1990s; Charles Schwab, an established discount brokerage firm, as well as new firms like E*Trade Group, Inc., and Ameritrade Holding Company, offered low-cost trading on the Internet. Other traditional full-service brokerage firms including Merrill Lynch, Citigroup Inc.'s Salomon Smith Barney, and Prudential Investments offered online research services to monitor and transfer accounts and to access pay-per-view research reports. By 1998, several traditional firms, such as Merrill Lynch, Morgan Stanley Dean Witter, and Prudential Securities, also began offering online trading services. Following the dot.com stock market crash in the early 2000s, however, many online investors decided that they preferred the advice of brokers. Hence, securities firms including Merrill Lynch and Charles Schwab, among others, now offer online advising as well, such as Schwab Advised Investing.[1]

Firms that do offer online trading are not always initially profitable. E*Trade, established in 1996 and now the third largest online broker, achieved 676,000 accounts in 1998. However, the firm lost $200,000 as a result of high advertising and other costs. It also faced a class action lawsuit by customers resulting from a three-day computer shutdown in February 1999. Similarly, Charles Schwab initially suffered a lower profit margin in the later 1990s as it switched customers from telephone and broker trades to cheaper Internet trades costing as little as $29.95 for up to 1,000 shares traded. Stock market prices for the securities industry including online brokerage firms can also be volatile, just as firms in the securities industry are. For instance, Yahoo! Finance reported a 52-week range for the price of E*Trade Group Inc (Etrade) (ET) from a

Learning Objectives

After completing this chapter, you will be able to:

1 Describe the structure of the securities industry, different types of firms, and profit cycles.
2 Understand the historical development and changes of securities firms and investment banks.
3 Discuss key areas of activity for securities firms and the change in importance of different areas over time.
4 Understand the financial statements of different types of securities firms and know how to do a financial analysis.
5 Describe the activities of securities firms and ways to hedge underwriter risk.
6 Understand the nature of venture capital and private equity firms.

$5.00 low to a $15.40 high. Similarly, Ameritrade had a 52-week high of $17.66 and low of $4.88 as of the end of April 2004. The volume of online trading is also high, with Ameritrade averaging about 212,000 trades a day, Charles Schwab 103,052, and E*Trade 103,052 in the first quarter of 2004. About 200 online brokerages operated in the United States in 2001, down to 110 in 2004, after the dot.com bust in the early 2000s. With the decline in the stock market after the dot.com bubble's crash beginning in April 2000, the securities industry had a pull-back with numerous layoffs. With the market's recovery in 2003, the security industry began to rebound, the typical cycle of this industry.[2]

In the long run, however, many online brokerage firms, such as Ameritrade Holding Corp., Charles Schwab, and E*Trade, are poised for success. E*Trade has pursued a promising business model as a "pipeline" for all sorts of products and services, including twenty-four-hour cross-currency trading, banking, and insurance, and in 1999, it received Securities and Exchange Commission (SEC) approval to sell its own brand of mutual funds. E*Trade even

1 Rebecca Buckman. "More Old-Line Brokers Test Waters Online." *The Wall Street Journal* (January 6, 1999), C1; Charles Gasparino and Randall Smith. "Internet Trades Put Merrill Bull on Horns of a Dilemma." *The Wall Street Journal* (February 12, 1999), C1; McNamee (1999); and Rebecca Buckman. "Wall Street Is Rocked by Merrill's Online Plans." *The Wall Street Journal* (June 2, 1999), C1, C27; also see Yahoo! Finance for lists and financial information on online brokerage firms and individual online and other securities firms (*http://finance.yahoo.com*); Hoover's Online (*http://www.hoovers.com*); Business.com (*http://www.business.com*); and individual rm Websites for E*Trade Financial (*https://us.etrade.com*) and other online brokerage firms..

2 Because of cost pressures some online broker fees rose in March 1999, including the online brokerage subsidiary of Fleet Financial Group, Suretrade; the discount brokerage unit of Lindner Funds; and the discount brokerage of Fidelity. See Rebecca Buckman. "Some Online Broker Fees Are Climbing." *The Wall Street Journal* (March 16, 1999), C21; Leah Nathans Spiro. "Will E*Trade Move Beyond E*Tragedy?" *Business Week* (February 22, 1999), 118; Rebecca Buckman. "E*Trade Hits Cyber-Bumps in Strategy." *The Wall Street Journal* (February 22, 1999), C1, C10; Joseph Kahn. "Schwab Lands Feet First on Net." *New York Times* (February 10, 1999); Steven Lipin, Rebecca Buckman, and Paul M. Sherer. "E*Trade to Announce Pact for Telebans." *The Wall Street Journal* (June 1, 1999), A3, A6; Rebecca Buckman. "Ex-Robertson Stephens Official, Others See Unveiling Online Investment Bank." *The Wall Street Journal* (January 12, 1999), C20; See Sean Davis. "On-Line Brokers Set to Report Profit Growth." *New York Times* (July 9, 1998), C15, C1; and Rebecca Buckman. "Schwab Clients Increase Activity in Online Trading." *The Wall Street Journal* (February 17, 1999), C13; and Joe Ruff, "Online Brokerage Ameritrade a Mainstay." *Associated Press*, April 28, 2004, reported on Yahoo! Finance (*http://biz.yahoo.com*).

opened offices providing a brick-and-mortar presence in major cities. As the chief executive of Ameritrade, Joe Moglia, noted in a recent Associated Press article, the focus of online brokerage firms changed from facilitators of cheap trades to helping customers to meet financial goals, with greater financial planning help by both online and off-line securities firms. It's also interesting to note that many online retail brokerages today, following the passage of the Gramm-Leach-Bliley Act of 1999, are subsidiaries of banks, insurance companies, and mutual fund companies as well. For instance, Hoover's Online notes the ten most viewed online retail brokerage companies on its site in early 2004 as JP Morgan Chase & Co., The Charles Schwab Corporation, FMR Corporation (Fidelity Mutual Fund Group), E*Trade Financial Corporation, The Toronto-Dominion Bank, Ameritrade Holding Corporation, Prudential, plc, T.D. Waterhouse Group, Inc, Harris Bankcorp, Inc., and Instinet Group Incorporated.[3]

In addition to online trading, the nature of investment banking is changing in the Internet age. In early February 1999, William Hambrecht, former chief executive officer and founder of Hambrecht & Quist, LLC, an innovative investment bank, announced the start-up of an Internet investment bank. This firm offers initial public offerings (IPOs) on the Internet in Dutch auctions, as opposed to setting the price of an IPO as investment bankers currently do. High bidders, rather than preferred investors (as is the common practice), are given shares. This process reduces the cost of underwriting issues for firms going public, including reducing current underpricing that occurs on average for issues. Under this system, firms are charged fees of 3 percent to 5 percent of the amount of money raised as opposed to the traditional 6 percent to 7 percent gross spread and fees collected by investment bankers. This provides just one example of the rapid adoption of new technology. With the initial public offering of Google, Inc. in the first half of 2004, traditional investment banking firms were also asked to sell Google's shares in an auction format, changing the rules for typical offerings. Google in its IPO of an estimated $2.7 billion shares asked that shares be sold through an auction method that had never been used before for such a large IPO, with the intention of putting more shares into the hands of individual investors and eliminating typical underpricing that often occurs after "hot" IPOs are issued.[4]

Securities firms have faced a number of challenges in recent years including a lack of consumer confidence in the industry following scandals involving conflicts of interest between research analysts and brokerage activities, with some research analysts pressured to tout the value of not-so-worthy securities offered by big customers of the brokerage firm division. Similarly, a number of securities firms were engaged in spinning activities where large corporate customers received sought-after shares in initial public offerings in exchange for other business given to the firm. The SEC prosecuted these firms, and they had to pay large settlements. Congress passed the Sarbanes-Oxley Act, providing greater separation between a securities firm's research and its securities activities. Also, self-regulatory organizations, the NASD and New York Stock Exchange, issued rulings and guidance governing behavior of research analysts, and the SEC proposed an Investment Advisor Code of Ethics in January 2004 (see *http://www.sec.gov/rules/proposed/ia-2209.htm*). The Security Information Association (SIA) also worked with regulators and Capitol Hill to develop legislation to address improper behavior on the part of mutual funds that led to scandals in late 2003 that included "late trading, market timing, inadequate disclosures, and incorrect sales charges."[5]

---

3 Ibid. Also see, Hoover's Online, Online Retail Brokerage Industry Fact Sheet (*http://www.hoovers.com*), and Websites for brokerage firms including Charles Schwab (*http://www.schwab.com*); E*Trade Financial (*https://us.etrade.com*); profiles of brokerage and investment banking and brokerage firms on Business.com (*http://www.business.com*); and Joe Ruff. "Online Brokerage Ameritrade a Mainstay." *Associated Press*, April 28, 2004, reported on Yahoo! Finance (*http://biz.yahoo.com*).

4 Under a traditional underwriting system, IPOs have on average been underpriced, with prices rising above the initial offering price on the date of the offering. Therefore, favored institutional investors, instead of the client firm, receive high returns. With the new Dutch auction process, underpricing should occur less often, and the client firm should get a more favorable price for shares. Lisa Bransten and Nick Wingfield. "New Company Aims to Shift IPO Playing Field." *The Wall Street Journal* (February 8, 1999), C1, C11; and Ruth Simon. "IPOs Over the Internet? Tread Carefully." *The Wall Street Journal* (February 24, 1999), C1. Also see Kevin J. Delaney and Robin Sidel, "Feeling Lucky Google IPO Aims to Change the Rules," *The Wall Street Journal*, April 30, 2004, A1, A10; and Alan Murray, "OpenIPO: In the Media," Washington Bureau Chief, CNBC, September 10, 2002 on the WRHambrecht+Co Website (*http://wrhambrecht.com*).

5 See *Securities Industry Trends* (1997, 1998, 2002), SIA Annual Report 2003, Key Issues and Year Review on the Securities Industry Association (SIA) Website (*http://www.sia.com*).

The securities industry rebounded in 2003 and 2004 after a significant stock market downturn from April 2000 through 2002 with a recession, sharp market adjustment, and the aftermath of the terrorist attacks on September 11, 2001. Despite a record "back to back" decline in the stock market's performance, with lower interest rates and intense cost cutting, the industry remained profitable, and as the stock market improved, profitability improved for the industry in 2003. With the passage of the Gramm-Leach-Bliley Act in 1999, which repealed portions of the Glass–Stegall Act of 1933, banks and securities firms and insurance firms have had some convergence (with Citigroup, for instance) among the top ten U.S. securities and investment companies by asset size.[6]

The securities industry is constantly evolving. This chapter discusses the structure of the investment banking industry, the financial statements of firms in this industry and how to analyze them, the key activities for these firms, and changes that have occurred and are occurring. The chapter also presents a brief overview of venture capital and private equity firms.

Structure of the Industry, Types of Firms, and Profit Cycles

The following sections present an overview of the structure of the investment banking and securities firm industry, a brief history of investment banking and key areas of activity, and a review of financial statements and a financial performance analysis.

Structure and Types of Firms

In the early 2000s, there were about 7,029 securities firms in the United States, which the Security Information Association (SIA) notes is 74 percent of the record number of 9,515 securities firms operating in the United States prior to the 1987 stock market crash. Over time there has been a good deal of consolidation. Four percent, or about 261 firms, account for 81 percent of industry assets and 70 percent of total revenues and capital. The top 25 firms account for approximately 79 percent of this. Employment in the securities and commodities industry peaked at 840,900 in March 2001, declining to a low of 793,700 in March 2003, and then rising after that time. The industry underwrote more than $2 trillion in securities in the United States each year from 2001 to 2003.[7]

The growth and size of the securities firm industry, however, is very cyclical, with rises during bull (upward) stock markets and declines during bear (downward) markets and periods of large trading losses. Frequently, layoffs occur during market downturns. For instance, in late September 1998, as the result of a "dearth of stock and bond deals" and huge trading losses, Wall Street securities firms posted their worst quarterly results since the fourth quarter of 1994, and some major firms, including Merrill Lynch and Salomon Smith Barney, considered layoffs. As noted by Dean Eberling, an analyst at Putnam, Lovell, de Guardiola, and Thornton, a New York investment banking boutique, "This [was] the wake-up call to remind people that . . . this business is cyclical." Similarly, with the stock market downturn in the second quarter of 2000 to 2002, the industry experienced a decline in revenues and profits and accompanying cutbacks and layoffs. In 2003, with a market upturn, securities firms began expanding and hiring again. There has also been a great deal of consolidation in the industry including 964 bank purchases of securities firms and 368 other securities firm mergers and acquisitions during 1997 to 2002, so 72.4 percent of mergers and acquisitions involved bank buyers.[8]

---

6 Ibid. Also see the *Financial Services Fact Book* (sponsored by Insurance Information Institute and Financial Services Information Institutes) at a link on *http://www.iii.org* or directly *(http://financialservicefacts.org/financial2/securities/overview/)*. Interestingly, some regulatory changes were thought to open the door to other abuses, such as the NASD prohibiting a securities firm from selling IPO shares to outside accounts in which any "restricted" individuals (employees or close relatives) had a beneficial interest by allowing the option of a brokerage firm to legally send "in-demand" IPO shares to a hedge fund or other investment account in which the banker can own as much as 10 percent, allowing the banker to participate in some gains from the shares. See Gregory Zuckerman. "NASD Opens Door to Profits for Brokers on IPOs." *The Wall Street Journal* (March 22, 2004), A1, A9.

7 Ibid.

8 Ibid; and Patrick McGeehan and Anita Raghavan. "Broker Profits Are Tumbling; Layoffs Mulled." *The Wall Street Journal* (September 22, 1998), A3.

Profit Cycles

The extent of the cyclical nature of securities firm profits is demonstrated in Figure 17.1, which shows changes in pretax profits and return on equity (ROE) for NYSE member securities firms during 1998 to 2003 that corresponded with the rise in the stock market at the same time. Pretax return on equity has been quite volatile over the last decade for the average securities firm with a high average pretax ROE of 29.1 percent in 1996 and a low in 1994 of 3.3 percent. During the last five years, the lowest average ROE was 8 percent in 2002 following a high of 26.5 percent in 2000. Earlier years also had highs and lows. With the stock market plunge in 1987, retail customers became wary of stocks, and fewer equity underwritings took place. With the recession, in 1990 securities firms had a 2.5 percent NPM and a 2.7 percent ROE. Similarly, in 1994, with a downturn in bond and stock underwriting by 31 percent from 1993, the average ROE fell. In 1995 and 1996, underwriting and brokerage activity picked up again during the bull market that continued until the peak of 2000, falling in 2001 and 2002, and then rising again with the stock market recovery to about 16 percent in 2003.[9]

Different Types of Firms

There are a number of different types of securities firms including the following typical classifications:

(1) National full-line firms offer both retail brokerage services and advice, along with corporate advisory and investment banking services and trading activities for customers and for the firm itself—principal transactions. Examples of full-line firms include Merrill Lynch and UBS. National full-line firms often receive the largest percentage of their revenues from brokerage commissions on securities sales as well as from the net interest spread (interest revenues from loans to customers less interest cost to borrow). Customers are loaned securities that are in the firm's name for short-selling and provided with margin credit. Firms have the advantage of using low-cost customer balances as well. National full-line firms also have a large number of employees with a national branch network.[10]

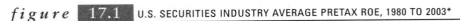

figure **17.1** U.S. SECURITIES INDUSTRY AVERAGE PRETAX ROE, 1980 TO 2003*

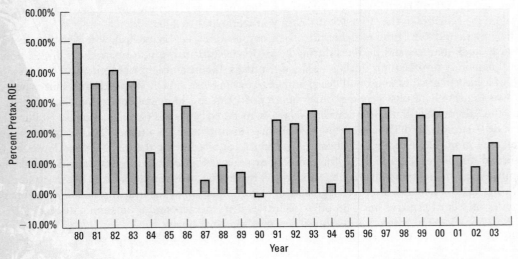

NYSE member firms doing a public business.
Source: *Created by the Authors from Pretax ROEs cited by the Securities Industry Association in the Insurance Information Institute's* Financial Services Fact Book, *2003.*

---

9 See Note 6.

10 See Saunders (1997); Crawford and Sihler (1994); Marshall and Ellis (1994); Bloch (1989); and Friend et al. (1967) and the Security Industry Association Annual Reports and Fact Books on its Website *(http://www.sia.com)*.

(2) Large investment banks usually focus on wholesale (corporate) underwriting and advisory services, underwriting and distributing common stock and corporate and municipal debt, arranging private placements, acting as advisors in mergers and acquisitions, and providing other corporate services. Examples are Goldman Sachs in New York and Credit Suisse First Boston in Boston. Note that this category is not mutually exclusive, since many full-service and New York investment banks are also large.

(3) Regional securities firms based in a particular region, such as A. G. Edwards, Inc., and Morgan Keegan, Inc., primarily provide brokerage service to clients in their region. These firms might also be involved in some regional investment banking activity, such as underwriting the stock or debt of select firms in their region and providing institutional investor and other services depending on the particular nature of the firm.

(4) New York City (NYC)-based investment banks, which include many large investment banks such as Goldman Sachs, Bear, Stearns, & Co., and Lehman Brothers, engage primarily in wholesale banking activities involving corporate underwriting and advisory services, and trading activities for both customers and principal transactions for the firm itself. Morgan Stanley would be included in this category; however, it recently became a full-service national firm with its acquisition of Dean Witter in 1997. NYC investment banks, generally as wholesale firms, receive a large percentage of their revenues from investment banking activities.

(5) Discounter firms trade for customers at low cost without offering investment advice, such as Quick & Reilly (subsidiary of FleetBoston, is part of Bank of America) and Charles Schwab. Many discount firms receive commission fee income from selling mutual funds for mutual fund companies as well. The majority of discount firm revenues come from commissions on trades for retail customers. As noted in the introduction, there are also pure online securities firms including E*Trade and Ameritrade that provide online trading services and advice, including financial planning advice.

These categories are not mutually exclusive and are in constant flux. For instance, Charles Schwab has become a full-service brokerage firm recently. Other categories may include securities firms that are subsidiaries of other financial institutions, such as Prudential Securities, the investment subsidiary of Prudential Insurance Company; Alex Brown, a subsidiary of Bankers Trust/Deutsche Bank; Quick and Reilly, a subsidiary of FleetBoston (now part of Bank of America) and Fidelity Brokerage, a subsidiary of the major mutual fund company Fidelity Investments. In the late 1990s many mutual funds began offering brokerage services. Also, there are securities firms that are private equity boutiques, such as Wasserstein and Perella, specializing in mergers and acquisitions, and merchant banking firms that take equity and debt interests in the firms that they advise for mergers and acquisitions and leveraged buyouts (taking a firm private with debt in the hopes of taking it public again when stock prices are high), such as Kohlberg, Kravis, and Roberts (KKR). Other categories include firms classified by the size of their typical underwriting corporate clients including large firms that take care of corporations greater than $1 billion, such as JPMorgan Chase, Goldman Sachs, Merrill Lynch, Citigroup, and Morgan Stanley; middle-market firms that take care of firms less than $1 billion including Raymond James Financial, MacDonald Investments, and UBS Financial Services, Inc., and small firms that take care of firms of $25 million or so, such as South Trust Corporation. Investment services firms are often ranked by the amount of underwriting they do in different areas and on their market capitalization. In early 2004, leaders in market capitalization included The Goldman Sachs Group Inc. ($47.4 billion), Nomura Holdings Inc. ($31.7 billion), Lehman Brothers Holdings Inc. ($20.7 billion), Charles Schwab Corp. ($14.3 billion), Franklin Resources Inc. ($13.8 billion), Bear Stearns Companies Inc. ($8.5 billion), T. Rowe Price Group Inc. ($6.5 billion), and Legg Mason Inc. ($6.2 billion).[11]

---

11 Fidelity's brokerage customers by March 1999 executed 71 percent of their stock trades online. See Vanessa O'Connell. "It's a Broker! It's a Banker! It's a Mutual-Fund Group!" *The Wall Street Journal* (February 19, 1998), C1, C27; Pui-Wing Tam. "Vanguard Group Flexes Its Brokerage Arm." *The Wall Street Journal* (October 13, 1998), C23; Anita Raghavan and Eleena De Lisser. "NationsBank, Montgomery Mine Client Ties." *The Wall Street Journal* (September 28, 1997), C1, C15; and Buckman. "Some Online Broker Fees Are Climbing," C1, C21. Also see the Careers in Finance Website, "Careers in Finance: Investment Banking: Top Firms" *(http://www.careers-in-finance.com/ibtop.htm)*, and also see Hoovers: The Business Information Authority Website *(http://www.hoovers.com;* search under investment banking). See Yahoo! Finance for a discussion of the investment services industry and list of market capitalization rankings *(http://biz.yahoo.com)*.

1 Why is the growth, size, and profitability of the securities industry cyclical?

2 How concentrated is the securities industry?

3 What are the major types of securities firms and their particular market niches?

4 What is the difference between a prestigious and non-prestigious firm?

5 What is a tombstone ad?

Prestigious and Nonprestigious Investment Banks

Investment banking firms also are often ranked as prestigious or nonprestigious based on their syndicate participation, as shown on advertisements for security issues, called tombstone ads because of the way they are laid out (see Figure 17.2). Lead underwriters in charge of an issue are listed first, followed by other underwriters based on their share of participation in the underwriting. Underwriters are selected for a syndicate based on their relationship with lead investment banks and their reputation in handling and selling an issue. Firms with continuous top rankings are deemed prestigious underwriters, such as Morgan Stanley Dean Witter, Merrill Lynch & Co., and Goldman Sachs. Prior to the 1970s, prestigious firms were predominantly prominent New York wholesale investment banks. In the 1970s, Merrill Lynch marked the entry of a full-service securities firm into the prestigious ranks, thus making them more competitive. A number of mergers occurred between wholesale and retail firms in the 1990s as well. For example, in 1997, Morgan Stanley, a wholesale firm, merged with Dean Witter, which has a large retail distribution chain. Online firms also began to be included in syndicates based on their ability to distribute securities to online customers, such as Schwab and E*Trade Securities, shown in the syndicate listing in the tombstone ad in Figure 17.2.[12]

A Historical Overview of Securities Firms

Table 17.1 provides a brief historical overview of securities firms, emphasizing securities firms in the United States. Trends over time are discussed in the following sections.[13]

The Sixteenth, Seventeenth, and Eighteenth Centuries: Merchant Banking and Large Family-Run Banking Houses

Because of religious dictums by the Catholic church at this time against lending for interest, banking and investment firms were generally operated by non-Catholics. However, Catholic restrictions gradually weakened over the sixteenth to eighteenth centuries. The prior restrictions resulted in the growth of a type of merchant banking in which investors take an equity interest in firms rather than debt. The problem with this type of banking is that only wealthy investors can afford this type of risk, where the investor only receives a return if an endeavor does very well. Hence, it limits lending and economic growth. However, economic prosperity and the need to finance government wartime activities in the late eighteenth century brought about the growth of major European family-run international banking houses, including the Rothschilds, Barings, and Warburgs.

---

12 See Hayes (1979); Hayes and Hubbard (1990); and Bloch (1989) for a more detailed discussion of prestigious versus nonprestigious investment bankers and syndicate rankings. Studies have shown greater IPO underpricing for nonprestigious investment bankers that take on riskier issues.

13 See Hayes and Hubbard (1990) and Chernow (1990) for excellent, detailed histories of the securities industry including the rise of the three major cities (London, New York, and Tokyo) as investment banking centers and the rise of different investment houses, including the House of Morgan (JPMorgan and Morgan Stanley). Also see Herbert R. Lottman. *The French Rothschilds: The Great Banking Dynasty Through Two Turbulent Centuries.* New York: Crown Publishers Inc., 1995. Ron Chernow's *The Warburgs* (1993) provides an excellent history of the Warburg Investment Banking family in Germany, whose house was taken over by the Nazis in World War II. The book describes the escape to the United States of some family members and their place in the history of investment banking in the United States and London during and following World War II.

figure **17.2** HYPOTHETICAL SAMPLE OF A TYPICAL TOMBSTONE AD WITH SYNDICATE LIST BY PARTICIPANTS

The announcement is neither an offer to sell nor a solicitation of an offer to buy any of these Securities.
The offer is made only be the Prospectus.

Number of Shares Offered

Name of Firm

Class of Common Stock

Price per Share

Copies of the Prospectus may be obtained in any State from only such
of the undersigned as may legally offer these Securities in
compliance with the securities laws of each state.

Number of Shares Offered by the Syndicate Below:

The portion of the offering is being offered (for example) in the United States and Canada by the undersigned.

Syndicate Member Names
Example: Some Prestigious Firms That Are Often Leaders of Syndicates

MORGAN STANLEY DEAN WITTER

MERRILL LYNCH & CO.

WARBURG DILLION READ, LLC

BEAR STEARNS & CO., INC.

HAMBRECHT & QUIST

Other retail and other securities firms that are included in the example syndicate that
may take a smaller share in a particular offering, to help sell the issue (usually put in
smaller type), such as the following as a hypothetical example:

A. G. EDWARDS & SONS, INC.   E*TRADE SECURITIES   CHARLES SCHWAB

SALOMON SMITH BARNEY   AMONG OTHERS.

Source: See typical tombstone Ads. A good example of a tombstone ad that includes prestigious, regional, and online firms is the tombstone ad for the offering for perotsystems shown in the New York Times, March 1, 1999, C14.

The Nineteenth Century: The Civil War, Financing Tycoons, and Railroad Expansion

In the nineteenth century, investment banking firms prospered as they financed the Industrial Revolution and much of the railroad expansion in Europe and the United States. In the United States, in addition to extensions of European investment houses, including J.P. Morgan, immigrants such as Joseph

table **17.1** HISTORICAL OVERVIEW OF SECURITIES FIRMS EMPHASIZING U.S. SECURITIES FIRMS

Time Period	Event
Prior to Renaissance	**Specialization in money-lending business by non-Catholics, since Catholics adhered to dictums against lending.**
Renaissance	Dictims weakened and in the 17th and 18th centuries economic prosperity leads to the growth of public securities, banking, and merchant banking.
Late 18th Century	**Growth of major European family-run international banking houses** (Rothschilds, Baring Brothers, Warburgs). Large European governments' needs to finance wartime activities brings rise of new merchant bankers.
19th Century	**Rise of London as financial capital;** large financings for Industrial Revolution; large railroad financings; emergence of large U.S. investment banks, such as J.P. Morgan.
	Immigrants start securities firms, such as Joseph Seligman and Goldman and Sachs; Jay Cooke & Co. uses **syndication process** to sell bonds to public during the Civil War.
	In the latter 1800s era of financing tycoons, such as J.P. Morgan and development of oligopolistic behavior by prestigious Wall Street firms.
20th Century 1914–1950s	**New York becomes major financial center** during World War I; U.S. securities firms assist in foreign and U.S. financings; during 1920s broader public interest in securities.
	Modernization of securities issue origination and distribution process with growth of telephone and telegraph;
	1929: Stock market crash followed by lawsuits and hearings against security firms;
	1933: Glass–Stegall breaks up banks and securities firms; poorly capitalized securities firms with severe underwriting losses remain; mergers and cutbacks during the Depression.
	WWII: Securities firms assist in government financings; anti–Wall Street sentiment ends; English merchant banks facilitate first postwar hostile takeovers.
1960s	**Dollar becomes principal currency of international trade.**
	With deficits in the United States, a stable international climate, the **1963 Interest Equalization tax** penalizing the sale of some foreign securities to American investors, and regulation Q preventing banks to offer market rates, banks and securities firms flock abroad, resulting in the development of the **Eurodollar and Eurobond market; and London is reestablished as a major financial market; First Eurobond issue for the Italian Autostrade in 1963. Greater trading activities; new breed of impersonal traders.**
	Greater number of investment banks with international subsidiaries; high inflation; more active management of investments by institutional investors; securities firms develop **services for institutional investors** including block trading; this made firms like Salomon Brothers with large trading operations prominent.
1970s	**Former hierarchy in underwriting of prestigious underwriters is challenged** by full-service securities firms such as Merrill Lynch. Securities firms introduce production-oriented compensation to attract traders that creates new rivalries and tensions; entry of new type of "gunslinger"; development of research services area to attract investors.
	Dollar becomes a floating currency;
	1972: Merrill Lynch receives first license to have a securities branch in Japan.
	Largest Japanese securities firms expand overseas; first yen-denominated bond (samurai bond) issued by non-Japanese issuer.
	May 1, 1975: Fixed brokerage commissions abolished, making commissions competitively based; a few discount brokerage firms spring up, and securities firms merge.
	High inflation leads to innovations to offer market rates, including cash management funds in 1977 by Merrill Lynch; other money and mutual funds followed.
1980s	**March 16, 1982:** Shelf Registration Rule (Rule 415) adopted by SEC, allowing corporations to register securities and issue them at any time over the next two years.
	SEC Rule 415 gives firms more flexibility to seek competitive bids for offerings, particularly debt offerings, which reduced underwriter gross spreads.
Mid-1980s	**Bull market; Go-Go Days; great merger and acquisition activity; innovation of junk bonds by Drexel Burnham Lambert;** leveraged buyouts; dramatic growth in underwriting; industry grows from 5,248 firms in 1980 to 9,515 in 1987; growth in **securitization.**
	1986: "Big Bang" in London removes fixed commissions and other reforms, including development of a new international Stock Exchange Automated System (SEAQ), allowing 24-hour off-exchange trading.

t a b l e   **17.1**   HISTORICAL OVERVIEW OF SECURITIES FIRMS EMPHASIZING U.S. SECURITIES FIRMS (CONTINUED)

Latter 1980s	**October 1987: Stock Market Crash** resulting in lower underwriting and a loss of confidence by investors in equity markets. Insider trading and other scandals contribute to poor perceptions of securities firms by the public.
	Profitability of securities industry declines with large drop in underwriting and brokerage commissions. Between 1987 and 1991, period of consolidation in the industry, mergers, and lay-offs. Number of firms declines by about 20 percent.
	Movement into venture capital, real estate venture, mortgage-backed securities, and principal investing.
1990s	**Greater competition from major commercial banks with Section 20 subsidiaries.**
	Recession; low profits; diversification into fixed-income security and derivatives trading; securitization to offset decline in underwriting.
	1992 on: Bull stock market and rise in profits but severe drop in underwriting and profits in 1994. Industry expands to about 8,000 firms. Mid and latter 1990s: **Acquisitions by large banks** and other financial institutions and mergers of wholesale and retail firms.
	Trading scandals by rogue traders caused large losses, such as the 1995 Barings scandal and collapse. 1992: European Economic Community harmonized regulations and allowed financial institutions to sell services throughout the EC. Lawsuits by customers and employees; greater oversight by SEC and exchanges. Innovations; growth of Internet services.
	Emergence of online brokerage firms and the first online investment bank.
Early 2000s	**Dot.com stock market correction;** spinning by investment bankers to favored clients; conflicts of interests between research analysts and underwriting and brokerage activities; mutual fund scandals; terrorist attacks affecting Wall Street firms; Gramm-Leach-Bliley Act of 1999 leads to more bank acquisitions of securities firms and convergence of different types of financial service activities; **Sarbanes-Oxley Act and SEC** regulations to prevent previous abuses; contraction of securities firms in 2000 to 2002; **recovery of securities firms in 2003.** Growth in private equity activities and venture capital to finance small businesses, and growth in hedge funds, funds for wealthy "accredited investors" necessitating less SEC scrutiny, as well as growth in structured financing activities and project financing.

Sources: Samuel L. Hayes, III, and Philip M. Hubbard. Investment Banking. Boston: Harvard Business School Press, 1990; Anthony Saunders. Financial Institutions Management: A Modern Perspective, 2nd ed. Burr Ridge, IL: Irwin, 1997; and Ron Chernow. The House of Morgan. New York: Touchstone (Simon & Schuster), 1990.

Seligman and Goldman and Sachs started securities firms from scratch. During the mid-1800s, Jay Cooke and Co. devised the first syndication process to sell Union debt as bonds across the country during the Civil War. This opened up the field to small investors.

In the United States, the late 1800s was an era of railroad and financing tycoons. By the 1870s, large U.S. investment banks were actively influencing client policies by serving on corporate boards and financing committees. Investment banks also were often directors on each other's boards (interlocking directorates), preventing new entrants into capital markets. A severe contraction in 1893 caused more than 15,000 commercial firms and more than 600 banks to fail. Investment banks such as J.P. Morgan created trusts out of reorganized companies, transferring the majority of companies' stocks in particular industries to "voting trusts," controlled by the investment banking firm involved. Thus, by 1900, the nation's railroads were consolidated into six huge systems controlled by Wall Street bankers. From 1898 to 1902, the United States experienced a wave of horizontal mergers; the number jumped from 69 in 1897 to more than 1,200 by 1899, providing large fees for investment banks and power as new trusts were created for different industries.

The Early to Mid Twentieth Century: Panics, World War I, and Wall Street Primacy, the Stock Market Crash of 1929, Modernization, and Anti–Wall Street Sentiment

In the early twentieth century, Wall Street suffered a panic in 1907, which led to clamor for bank reform and the emergence of the Federal Reserve System, along with later legislation breaking up the trusts. Hearings against the concentration of Wall Street bankers were held.

By 1914, New York investment banking firms were assisting in financing World War I. With economic prosperity in the United States and the dollar being the only remaining currency backed by gold, New York took over prominence from London as the world's financial capital. The growth of telephone and telegraph services helped to modernize the securities issue origination and distribution process and to attract greater public interest in stocks and bonds, and investment firms prospered in the 1920s. This prosperity ended with the stock market crash of 1929 and in reaction to anti-investment bank sentiment, which blamed bank failures on speculation by joint investment banks and commercial banks. This led to the passage of the Glass–Stegall Act of 1933, which forced commercial banks to divest their non-bank divisions. Poorly capitalized securities firms with severe underwriting losses remained, leading to mergers and cutbacks during the Great Depression. During World War II, investment banks helped in government financing, and by the mid-1950s, anti–Wall Street sentiment had diminished somewhat.

The 1960s: Globalization of Debt Securities and Institutionalization

The 1960s brought about greater internationalization of issues. Eurobond and Eurodollar markets emerged as a way to escape restrictions on the purchase of foreign securities under the 1963 Equalization Tax in the United States, and on paying market rates for deposits by banks under Regulation Q. In 1963, the first Eurobond issue was for the Italian Autostrade, an Italian state highway authority with British, German, Dutch, and Belgian investment firms participating. With the development of international bond markets, investment banks cultivated international subsidiaries. From the 1960s on, investment banking markets became more impersonal and competitive and less relationship-oriented with a new breed of impersonal traders. Retail firms increased their competitive power by consolidating. Institutional investors became more active portfolio managers, and investment banks responded by offering more services for these investors, including block trading (trading large blocks of securities), which made firms with large trading operations prominent.

The 1970s: More Competition, Changes in Culture, and Globalization

In the 1970s, the monopolistic underwriting ranks of prestigious wholesale underwriters eroded when Merrill Lynch, a full-service firm, entered the ranks as a major lead underwriter. Compensation became more production-oriented in the industry, particularly to attract star traders. The culture of many investment banks changed to more of a "gunslinger" mentality, creating new rivalries and tension. Investment banks developed new research services, particularly to attract institutional investors.

Globalization of investment banks continued; Japan opened up its securities markets to branches of foreign firms. In 1972, Merrill Lynch was the first foreign firm to receive a license for a branch in Japan. Soon other firms, such as Salomon Brothers, entered Japanese markets as well. Large Japanese firms also expanded overseas, and yen-denominated bonds (samurai bonds) were issued outside Japan by non-Japanese issuers. Brokerage fees became competitive as of May 1, 1975, often called May Day, when fixed brokerage commissions were abolished.

The 1980s: Shelf Registration, Casino Day Prosperity, and Innovations

In 1982, the Shelf Registration Rule (Rule 415) adopted by the SEC made corporate underwriting more competitive by allowing corporations to register securities and then issue them at any time over the next two years. This gave firms more flexibility to seek competitive bids, particularly for debt offerings, resulting in lower underwriter gross spread for these issues. The 1980s marked a period of "casino" or "go-go" days, characterized by a bull market, great merger and acquisition (M&A) activity, and junk bonds, an innovation by Drexel Burnham Lambert often used to finance leveraged buyouts. The securities industry grew dramatically from 5,248 to 9,515 firms in 1987. In London, fixed commissions were removed as well, and other reforms included the development of a domestic and international Stock Exchange Automated System (SEAQ) allowing twenty-four-hour off-exchange trading. London gained preeminence again as a major financial market.

The 1980s was also a decade of innovations. With greater competition, investment bankers developed new types of securities to win clients and generate fee income, introducing financial engineering. In 1982, Salomon Brothers created stripped zero-coupon issues from existing Treasury securities. In the uncertain interest rate environment of 1984, Merrill Lynch and Company and other investment bankers began giving investors puts on bonds, allowing investors to put securities back to issuers and receive par value, protecting investors against losses if interest rates rose. In late 1984, Salomon Brothers introduced securities backed by automobile loans (Certificates for Automobile Receivables, or CARs). Investment bankers led the development of mortgage-backed securities. And it was investment bankers who fueled the huge volume of leveraged buyouts with junk bonds and other innovative financing techniques. Securities firms also spurred growth in the interest rate swap market by matching suitable counterparties and sometimes even serving as counterparties themselves.

Investment bankers also developed other types of synthetic interest rate hedging instruments. Securities firms took advantage of great market volatility by developing new trading activities, such as program trading, whereby profits are made on differences in prices between stock market indexes and those on stock index futures by taking alternate positions in the two markets.[14]

The October 1987 Stock Market Crash and the Recession of the Early 1990s

The October 1987 stock market crash put an end to securities firms' growth over the decade. With a loss of public confidence reducing brokerage activity and underwriting activity, profits fell for securities firms dramatically until 1992, and the number of securities firms fell by 20 percent. Public scandals, such as insider trading by Michael Milken, the junk bond king at Drexel Burnham Lambert, resulted in jail sentences for investment bankers, and in the case of Drexel Burnham, the firm's failure. Congress passed the Insider Trading and Securities Fraud Enforcement Act in 1988, which revised the definition of insider trading, clarifying that it is "the purchase or sale of securities while in possession of 'material' information that is not available to the general public." The Act stiffened civil and criminal penalties as well.[15]

Restrictions on bank and thrift holdings of junk bonds also led to a downtrend in junk bond underwriting. Securities firms compensated for lower underwriting profits by taking on greater trading activity, particularly for fixed-income securities as interest rates fell in the 1990s. Larger investment banks also developed real estate and venture capital subsidiaries and engaged in securitization activities, greater principal trading, and mutual fund and investment management for wealthy clients.

The Bull Market of the 1990s, Harmonization of Regulations in Europe, Online Securities Firms, and Internet Day Trading

After 1992, a bull stock market caused underwriting and brokerage activity to rise; however, it dropped significantly in 1994. The industry expanded to about 8,000 firms. In the mid- and latter 1990s, acquisitions by large banks and other financial institutions and mergers of wholesale and retail firms occurred. Trading scandals by rogue traders resulted in large losses, such as the 1995 Barings trading scandal and collapse. A number of securities firms faced lawsuits for not revealing the extent of the risk involved in different investments, including Merrill Lynch concerning the Orange County derivative trading losses and Prudential Investments for losses to retail customers on real estate investment products.

In 1992, the European Economic Community harmonized regulations and allowed financial institutions to sell services through the EC. The advent of the Euro in January 1999 also brought about new investment opportunities in Europe for European and U.S. financial firms. With the rapid spread of the Internet, securities firms entered the information age: Online brokerage firms grew quickly and the first online investment bank debuted, as discussed at the beginning of the chapter.

Regulators became particularly concerned in the latter 1990s about the growing number of less sophisticated day traders on the Internet and the effect of these traders on the volatility of market

---

14 For further discussion of financial innovations and the securities industry, see Bloch (1989); Anthony Bianco. "The King of Wall Street." *Business Week* (December 9, 1985), 98–104; Norton (1987); Marshall and Ellis (1994); Stigum (1990); and Geisst (1995).

15 Anyone convicted of profiting from illegal insider trading can be required to pay up to three times the amount gained through the unlawful activity, and the maximum prison term for criminal penalties was increased to ten years. The SEC was given greater authority to pursue offenders and is now allowed to pay to obtain information about potential violations. The 1988 act also placed a responsibility on securities firms to strengthen written policies and procedures designed to prevent the misuse of privileged material information. A firm failing to do so may itself face civil penalties if employees are found guilty of insider trading. Renewed emphasis was placed on the securities industry's long-standing tradition of maintaining so-called Chinese Walls, an imaginary barrier between the investment banking activities of a securities firm and its brokerage and trading arm. Under the law, a firm may not profit on trades for its own inventory or that of its customers by using information obtained through investment bankers' privileged contacts with clients.

prices, which could reduce public confidence in financial markets. Day-trading firms, unlike online brokerage firms such as E*Trade, cater to individual investors who trade stocks full time over sophisticated computer systems at a firm's office instead of a home computer. However, in recent years day-trading firms have lured unsophisticated investors into the business by creating unrealistic expectations of becoming rich quickly. Often hefty upfront fees are charged before investors discover whether they have an aptitude as a trader. Consequently, many new day traders fail. In 1999, the number of U.S. day-trading firms fell from 3,000 in 1998 to 2,000, with many failures.[16]

Regulators and securities firms have also been concerned about a crush of trading in Internet stocks, which have been subject to wild price swings, unbelievably high valuations, and rapid trading from novice investors. NASDAQ considered authorizing trading halts for such stocks under certain circumstances. DLJ Direct, Schwab, Salomon Smith Barney, and Waterhouse Securities have also set limits on customers wishing to borrow funds to buy such stocks.[17]

The Early 2000s: Dot.com Market Crash, Terrorist Attacks, Breaches of Ethics, and Bank Mergers with Securities Firms

As noted earlier in the chapter, with the market decline, spinning activities by investment bankers giving initial public offering shares to better clients, mutual fund ethical breaches, and conflicts of interest between research and securities firm activities, the early 2000s marked a low in consumer confidence in securities firms. Hence, this period, as discussed earlier, was a period of recovery. It also was a period following the passage of the Gramm-Leach-Bliley Act of 1999 that led to hundreds of mergers of securities firms with banks, thereby leading to a greater convergence of different types of firms in the financial services industry. In reaction to the many ethical breaches, the Sarbanes-Oxley Act attempted to set up a framework separating research analysts from other underwriting and securities activities. The SEC, NYSE, and NASD also set up ethical codes to prevent abuses. Globalization of securities markets continued with the expansion of the European Union, privatization, and growing investment banking in China, India, and South Korea, among other countries. The liberalization and integration of security markets in many countries also led to growing foreign direct investment and merger and acquisition activities. The falling value of the dollar in the early 2000s also provided opportunities for cheaper acquisitions in the United States. UBS, for instance, a large Swiss commercial and investment bank, purchased Paine Webber, a large U.S. investment bank, among many other acquisitions. The following sections look in more detail at the key areas of activities for securities firms and provide an overview of their financial statements and financial analysis.

Overview of Key Areas of Activities for Securities Firms and Financial Statements

As suggested by the brief history of securities firms given in the previous section, they have diversified into many different activities and benefited from revenues from principal trading activities, for instance, in bear markets when commission and investment banking revenues are down. Key areas of activity for securities firms include the following:

1. **Investment banking underwriting fees and gross spread** (difference between the price paid for securities from a corporation and the offering price securities are sold for to the public) for debt and equity securities; private placements, management fees, M&A; restructuring, refinancing, advisory services, and so on.

2. **Principal transactions** involving trading and investments; for trading this involves making securities, foreign exchange, or commodity trades that are profitable for the firm; for investing it means managing an investment portfolio to reap returns for the firm itself. Principal transactions also include revenues from mortgage-backed securities, swaps, derivative securities, hedging strategies, and so on.

---

16 Rebecca Buckman. "Day-Trading Firms Facing Tougher Rivalry, Scrutiny." *The Wall Street Journal,* C1, C18; and Sana Siwolop. "Day Traders Place Risk, Reward Above Job Security." *Denver Post* (October 19, 1998), E1.

17 David Barboza. "N.A.S.D. Chief Cautions Firms about Internet Trading Risks." *New York Times* (February 10, 1999), C9; "On-Line Investors Who Chase Market's Every Blip." *New York Times* (October 1, 1998), D1; and Rebecca Buckman and Aaron Lucchetti. "Cooling It: Wall Street Firms Try to Keep Internet Mania from Ending Badly." *The Wall Street Journal* (February 24, 1999), A1, A10.

3. **Selling and dealing activities and trading for customers as an agent,** distributing securities and receiving commission income; making trades for customers in foreign exchange; commodities, bonds, or other instruments; and margin lending to customers.

4. **Investing activities as an agent**—managing mutual funds and pension funds or portfolios for wealthy investors; receiving fee income for this activity.

5. **Back office activities** including clearing and escrow services, research services, and advisory services, including M&A advice.

6. **Other types of activities,** such as merchant banking, in which the securities firm takes an equity financing position in a merger or leveraged buyout (for instance, venture capital and private equity subsidiary activities) and real estate subsidiary activities, including real estate investment trust and real estate partnerships, among others.

Investment banks have entered many other new areas as well, including offering banking-type services—such as small business, consumer, and mortgage loans—and small business consulting services. Recently, investment banks have also entered the reinsurance business. For instance, in 1998 Lehman Brothers Holdings invested $500 million to set up a Bermuda-based reinsurance subsidiary that will write policies to cover a variety of risks that corporations face, which will be packaged and sold as securities to investors. Investors get a share of both the premiums and any losses according to formulas in the securities.[18]

Sources of Revenue

Financial statements for securities firms differ according to the type of firm and the activities it engages in. Sources of revenues have changed dramatically over time, as shown in the following table:

Changing Revenue Sources

	1975	1996	2001
Commissions	49.9%	15.4%	13.77%
Principal Transactions	15.6	17.1	12.94
Underwriting Revenue	13.3	9.0	8.03
Margin Interest	7.8	5.8	6.60
Mutual Fund Sales	0.6	3.8	3.25
Commodities	3.0	1.3	2.51
All Other	9.9	47.6	52.9
Total Revenue	100.0%	100.0%	100.0%

For the securities industry as a whole, revenues have been spread over a larger variety of activities over the last two decades of the twentieth century. With the elimination of fixed commission brokerage fees, commission income as the primary source of revenues for firms fell from 49.9 percent in 1975 to 13.77 percent in 2001, with other activities providing 52.9 percent of revenues in 2001 compared with 9.9 percent in 1975. Other activities include M&A fees, private placements, market making, asset management, research, and other security related and unrelated (such as back office type) activities, and global investment management, with fee-based businesses increasing in importance. Fees for services to institutional investors also became a bigger source of revenue, with institutional investors holding more than 50 percent of equities. With globalization and people saving for retirement, investments in foreign securities and mutual funds rose, with mutual fund assets growing from $36 billion in 1974 to $3.5 trillion by 1996 to a peak of $6.98 trillion by 2001. U.S. securities industry global profits also rose dramatically, with estimated worldwide gross holding company revenue doubling from $223 billion in 1996 to a peak of $447 billion in 2000.[19]

---

18 Patrick McGeehan. "Investment Bankers Are Moving Fast to Offer Securities Backed by Pools of Insurance Policies." *The Wall Street Journal* (June 15, 1998), C4. Also see sources cited in Note 10.

19 See Securities Industry Association Annual Reports, Fact Books, and Key Issues (1998, 2002, 2003) *(http://www.sia.com).*

Concept Questions

1 How was economic growth hindered in the sixteenth to early eighteenth centuries by dictums against lending for interest? How did wealthy families provide equity financing?

2 What financing needs occurred in the nineteenth century, and how did this lead to the growth of investment banking in the United States?

3 Why was there anti–investment banker sentiment in the 1930s? What regulation did this lead to?

4 What led to globalization of securities markets in the 1960s? How did institutional investors change the services that investment bankers offered?

5 What is May Day in 1975, and how did it change the competition for securities brokers?

6 How did shelf registration affect securities firms' profits?

7 What regulations were imposed after the stock market crash of 1987?

8 What was the 1992 European Harmonization accord?

9 What events led to new regulations for securities firms in the early 2000s?

10 What are key areas of activities for securities firms, and how have they changed over time as percentage sources of revenues?

Examples of Financial Statements

Table 17.2 provides examples of typical financial statements for two different types of securities firms: Morgan Keegan, Inc., a regional securities broker/dealer, and Morgan Stanley Group, prior to its merger with Dean Witter, when it was predominantly a large New York investment banking firm.

Income Statement

Reviewing the income statements in Panel A of Table 17.2, note that Morgan Keegan received a large percentage of its revenues from commissions. In contrast, Morgan Stanley received a very low percentage of revenues from commissions at this time and a larger percentage of revenues from trading. Although Morgan Stanley has a larger percentage of revenues from interest revenue than Morgan Keegan, when netted out against interest expense, the interest spread is small relative to revenues, about 2.53 percent compared with 5.63 percent for Morgan Keegan in 1996, which is typical of retail versus wholesale securities firms.

Looking at expenses, the major expense (other than interest expense for Morgan Stanley, which nets out against interest revenues) is compensation. The industry is very labor intensive, and the labor environment is extremely sensitive to the state of the markets and the economy. For instance, in the bleak period of 1987 to 1990, the industry lost one in five of its employees and one of every five firms.[20]

Top managers in the industry receive large salaries, as do super-traders. For instance, in 1998, the class of partners receiving partnership in 1996 at Goldman Sachs earned about $6 million each, with more senior partners getting larger sums, and Goldman's senior executives earning up to $20 million. In addition, with Goldman going public in 1999, top managers would receive equity stakes worth more than $150 million each, and each junior partner would receive stakes worth more than $15 million. The danger with superstars is that they may leave the firm and take their customers with them. For example, in 1988 two M&A superstars at First Boston, Bruce Wasserstein and Joseph R. Perella, defected to start up their own M&A boutique, Wasserstein and Perella, taking a large number of corporate clients with them.[21]

Other expenses include fees for floor brokerage and clearance with exchanges and clearing corporations, communications, travel, promotion and business development, occupancy expense, and other operating expenses and taxes.

From Table 17.2, the pretax profit margin (income before taxes as a percentage of total revenue) for the regional securities brokerage firm, Morgan Keegan, is 18.30 percent, larger than that of the wholesale investment bank, Morgan Stanley, whose profit margin was 11.96 percent in 1996. Similar to

---

20 See Securities Industry Association Fact Book and Annual Report (1998).

21 See Crawford and Sihler (1994), Case 11: First Boston, Inc., p. 11.1.

table **17.2** EXAMPLES OF TYPICAL FINANCIAL STATEMENTS FOR SECURITIES FIRMS

PANEL A: TYPICAL INCOME STATEMENTS

Morgan Keegan, Inc., Regional Securities Broker/Dealer, incorporated 1984.

Focus: Retail Clients in Southeast U.S. and Institutional Investors Worldwide.

Incorporated in Tennessee

Consolidated Income Statement (Year-end July 31, in $ thous.)

Revenues	1996	% Revs.	1995	% Revs.	1994	% Revs.
Commissions	67,870	22.52%	46,162	20.24%	46,537	20.08%
Princ. Transactions	115,203	38.22%	87,110	38.19%	89,422	38.59%
Investments						
Investment Banking	50,301	16.69%	45,194	19.82%	55,832	24.09%
Interest Revenue & Dividends	49,923	16.56%	37,780	16.56%	24,894	10.74%
Asset Mgt. & Adm.						
Other Revenue	18,109	6.01%	11,826	5.19%	15,035	6.49%
Total Revenue	301,406	100.00%	228,072	100.00%	231,720	100.00%
Expenses						
Compensation	158,352	52.54%	120,795	52.96%	125,205	54.03%
Floor Brokerage & Clearance	4,397	1.46%	3,724	1.63%	3,875	1.67%
Communications, Travel, & Promotion & Bus. Dev., Prof. Servs.	7,336	2.43%	5,855	2.57%	5,721	2.47%
Occupancy & Equip.	11,812	3.92%	9,716	4.26%	8,320	3.59%
Interest Expense	32,930	10.93%	23,600	10.35%	14,393	6.21%
Other Taxes	7,006	2.32%	6,298	2.76%	4,972	2.15%
Other Oper. Expense	5,514	1.83%	3,774	1.65%	3,741	1.61%
Total Expenses	246,239	81.70%	189,724	83.19%	180,079	77.71%
Income before						
Income Taxes	55,167	18.30%	38,348	16.81%	51,641	22.29%
Income Tax Expense	21,300	7.07%	14,500	6.36%	19,800	8.54%
Net Income (NPM)	33,867	11.24%	23,848	10.46%	31,841	13.74%

Morgan Stanley Group, Inc., originally incorporated 1935.

Focus: Investment Banking and Trading; prior to merger with Dean Witter in 1997; Wall Street Investment Bank

Consolidated Income Statement (in $ mils.)

Revenues	1996	% Revs.	1995	% Revs.	1994	% Revs.
Commissions	613	4.66%	437	4.79%	449	4.79%
Princ. Transactions	2,296	17.47%	1,224	13.42%	1,243	13.26%
Trading	2,210	16.81%	1,122	12.30%	1,104	11.77%
Investments	86	0.65%	102	1.12%	139	1.48%
Investment Banking	1,944	14.79%	1,211	13.27%	919	9.80%
Interest Revenue & Dividends	7,701	58.59%	5,939	65.09%	6,406	68.32%
Asset Mgt.	582	4.43%	310	3.40%	350	3.73%
Other Revenue	8	0.06%	3	0.03%	9	0.10%
Total Revenue	13,144	100.00%	9,124	100.00%	9,376	100.00%
Expenses	**1996**	**% Revs.**	**1995**	**% Revs.**	**1994**	**% Revs.**
Compensation	2,863	21.78%	1,795	19.67%	1,733	18.48%
Floor Brokerage & Clearance	274	2.08%	211	2.31%	230	2.45%
Communications, Travel, & Promotion & Bus. Dev.	542	4.12%	349	3.83%	451	4.81%
Occupancy & Equip. Expenses	362	2.75%	276	3.02%	303	3.23%

table 17.2 EXAMPLES OF TYPICAL FINANCIAL STATEMENTS FOR SECURITIES FIRMS (CONTINUED)

Expenses	1996	% Revs.	1995	% Revs.	1994	% Revs.
Interest Expense	7,368	56.06%	5,501	60.29%	5,875	62.66%
Other Expense	163	1.24%	109	1.19%	190	2.03%
Total Expense	11,572	88.04%	8,241	90.32%	8,782	93.66%
Income before Tax	1,572	11.96%	883	9.68%	594	6.34%
Tax Expense	543	4.13%	283	3.10%	199	2.12%
Net Income (NPM)	1,029	7.83%	600	6.58%	395	4.21%

PANEL B: TYPICAL BALANCE SHEET OF SECURITIES FIRMS

Morgan Keegan, Inc., Regional Securities Broker/Dealer, incorporated 1984

Consolidated Balance Sheet as of July 31 (in $ thous.)

Assets	1996	% Assets	1995	% Assets
Cash	17,156	1.81%	22,287	2.53%
Segreg. Secs. at Mkt. Value	225,200	23.79%	226,000	25.62%
Deposits with Clearing Org.	7,655	0.81%	7,655	0.87%
Receivables from Broker/Dealers	16,978	1.79%	25,046	2.84%
Receivables from Customers	314,436	33.22%	260,707	29.55%
Securities Purchased Under Agreement to Resell	69,278	7.32%	91,861	10.41%
Securities Owned at Mkt. Value	229,278	24.22%	209,915	23.79%
Membership in Exchanges	719	0.08%	719	0.08%
Net Furniture & Equipment & Leasehold Improvements	18,492	1.95%	13,037	1.48%
Buildings & Equipment at Cost	19,908	2.10%	N/A	
Other Assets	27,548	2.91%	25,065	2.84%
Total Assets	946,648	100.00%	882,292	100.00%

Liabilities	1996	% Assets	1995	% Assets
Short-term Borrowings	31,400	3.32%	127,649	14.47%
Mortgage Note Payable	19,965	2.11%		
Commercial Paper	42,928	4.53%	7,468	0.85%
Payable to Brokers or Dealers & Clearing Organization	9,201	0.97%	5,387	0.61%
Payable to Customers	484,547	51.19%	438,518	49.70%
Customer Drafts Payable	14,456	1.53%	13,774	1.56%
Securities Sold under Agreement to Repurchase	54,826	5.79%	35,360	4.01%
Securities Sold, Not Yet Purchased at Market Value	62,972	6.65%	68,430	7.76%
Other Liabilities	57,345	6.06%	46,249	5.24%
Total Liabilities	777,640	82.15%	742,835	84.19%
Common Stock (par & surplus)	14,284	1.51%	13,317	1.51%
Retained Earnings	154,724	16.34%	126,140	14.30%
Total Equity	169,008	17.85%	139,457	15.81%
Total Liabilities & Equity	946,648	100.00%	882,292	100.00%

Morgan Stanley, Inc.

Consolidated Balance Sheet (in $ mils.)

Assets	1996	% Assets	1995	% Assets
Cash & Int.-bearing Equivalents	4,545	2.31%	2,471	1.72%
Cash & Secs. with Clearing Assn.	3,164	1.61%	1,339	0.93%
U.S. Gov. & Non-U.S. Gov. Secs.	30,552	15.55%	26,272	18.28%

table **17.2** EXAMPLES OF TYPICAL FINANCIAL STATEMENTS FOR SECURITIES FIRMS (CONTINUED)

Assets	1996	% Assets	1995	% Assets
Corp. Debt & Currency Swaps	19,473	9.91%	13,792	9.59%
Corporate Equities	12,622	6.43%	13,185	9.17%
Derivative Contracts	11,220	5.71%	8,043	5.60%
Physical Commodities	375	0.19%	410	0.29%
Secs. Borrowed or Purchased under Contract to Resell	100,137	50.97%	72,955	50.75%
Receivables from Customers	5,761	2.93%	3,413	2.37%
Other Receivables	7,486	3.81%	3,063	2.13%
Net Property & Equipment	1,301	0.66%	1,286	0.89%
Other Assets	3,305	1.68%	626	0.44%
Total Assets	196,446	100.00%	143,753	100.00%

Liabilities	1996	% Assets	1995	% Assets
Short-term Borrowing	20,461	10.42%	11,703	8.14%
U.S. & Non-U.S. Gov. & Agency Secs. Not Yet Purchased	16,709	8.51%	15,431	10.73%
Corp. Debt & Currency Swaps Sold	1,112	0.57%	1,076	0.75%
Corporate Equities Sold Not Yet Purchased	8,889	4.52%	3,585	2.49%
Derivative Contracts	9,982	5.08%	7,537	5.24%
Physical Commodities	476	0.24%	71	0.05%
Secs. Loaned or Sold under Repurchase Agreement	83,296	42.40%	60,738	42.25%
Securities Loaned	8,975	4.57%	9,340	6.50%
Accounts Payable	20,449	10.41%	15,792	10.99%
Interest & Dividends Payable	1,478	0.75%	1,019	0.71%
Other Liabilities & Accruals	2,718	1.38%	1,787	1.24%
Long-term Borrowings	14,498	7.38%	9,635	6.70%
Total Liabilities	189,043	96.23%	137,714	95.80%
Common & Preferred Stock	2,899	1.48%	2,224	1.55%
Retained Earnings	4,504	2.29%	3,815	2.65%
Total Equity	7,403	3.77%	6,039	4.20%
Total Liabilities & Equity	196,446	100.00%	143,753	100.00%

Source: Moody's Bank & Finance Manual, 1997.

wholesale money center banks, New York investment banks operate in competitive markets with smaller profit margins than smaller regional retail firms. For the securities industry as a whole, the average pretax profit margin was about 15.9 percent in 1996.

Typical ratios used to evaluate trends for securities firms based on the income statement include the following:[22]

- Commissions / revenues (%), which will be larger for retail firms
- Principal transactions / revenues (%)
- Investment banking / revenues (%)
- Revenues / expenses (%)
- Growth rate in revenues less growth rate in expenses

---

22 See SNL Securities (1994) and "Salomon Brothers' Strategic Review" in Hayes and Meerschwam (1992).

- Portfolio revenue / investments (%), that is, the average rate of return on the securities portfolio for the firm
- Revenue per employee
- Expenses per employee
- Compensation and benefits per employee
- Number of employees

Growth Rate in Expenses Relative to Growth Rate in Revenues over Time

Wholesale investment banking firms will typically have fewer employees and higher revenue, expense, compensation, and benefits per employee. Trends in these ratios, as well as trends in common size income statements, as shown in Table 17.2 for Morgan Keegan and Morgan Stanley, can reveal changes in sources of revenues and expenses and their relationships. A faster growth in expenses than revenues, for instance, can indicate a serious problem.

Analyzing the Trends in Net Income

Looking at the common size income statements for Morgan Keegan, the firm's net income (NPM) fell in 1995 from 13.74 percent to 10.46 percent in 1995 and then rose in 1996 to 11.24 percent. The fall in 1995 can be seen to be a result of a fall in total revenue by 3,648,000 (a fall of 1.57 percent) and a rise in total expenses by 9,645,000 (a rise of 5.36 percent), that is, expenses grew at a faster rate than revenues. Expenses to revenues increased from 77.71 percent to 83.19 percent. In particular, investment banking and other revenue declined, and travel and promotion and occupancy expenses particularly rose. In 1996 the NPM rose as total revenue rose 32 percent and total expenses rose less, by 29.8 percent. Expenses to revenues fell from 83.19 percent to 81.7 percent. Revenues from principal transactions, commissions, and other revenues rose particularly. The interest spread relative to total revenues was 4.53 percent in 1994, 6.21 percent in 1995, and 5.64 percent in 1996.

Morgan Stanley's NPM rose each year from 1994 to 1996. In 1995 total revenues fell with the growth rate in total revenues −2.69 percent, but the growth rate in expenses was lower, −6.16 percent. Trading income and investment banking increased as a percentage of revenues. For expenses, compensation increased as a percentage of expenses, with other items falling relative to revenues in 1995. The net interest spread relative to total revenues in 1995 was 4.80 percent compared with 5.66 percent in 1994. In 1996, the growth in revenues was 44 percent compared with 40.4 percent for expenses. Principal transactions rose as a percentage of revenues, particularly for trading, as did investment banking and asset management. Compensation, travel, promotion, business development, and other expenses rose as a percentage of revenues, and the net interest spread to revenues fell to 2.53 percent in 1996. However, overall, the expense-to-revenue ratio improved from 93.67 percent in 1994 to 90.32 percent in 1995 to 88.04 percent in 1996, resulting in the higher NPMs over time.

Balance Sheets

Panel B of Table 17.2 shows typical balance sheets for securities firms. The asset mix for each firm reflects the basic securities business. For trading and broker/dealer activities a large securities inventory is needed. Thus, a large percentage of assets are securities, including those that will be sold and those for the firm's investments. Other assets are predominantly receivables from customers and broker/dealers, with a relatively small percentage of fixed and other assets. As can be seen in Table 17.2, Panel B, Morgan Stanley, a large New York investment bank, is involved in many different activities holding derivative contracts, debt and currency swaps, and physical commodities as assets in addition to government and corporate bonds and equity.

Liabilities are primarily short-term; they include short-term borrowings and repurchase agreements and securities sold but not yet purchased, along with customer payables. Securities firms generally have very high financial leverage, particularly wholesale investment banks. Morgan Stanley, for instance, had a 3.77 percent equity-to-asset ratio in 1996, implying an equity multiplier of 26.53. In contrast, Morgan Keegan is much better capitalized with an equity-to-asset ratio of 17.85 percent, implying a much lower equity multiplier of 5.60. For securities firms, capital ratios are calculated using the market value of equity. Under the SEC's Rule C3–1 of 1975, the minimum equity-to-asset ratio for broker/dealers is 2 percent.[23]

Analyzing Trends in Asset and Liability Composition

Asset utilization (revenues / assets) for Morgan Keegan was 0.318 in 1996 compared with 0.259 in 1995. Whereas assets grew 7.29 percent, revenues grew 32.2 percent, hence, asset utilization improved. In terms of asset mix, there were few changes relative to total assets. Receivables from customers rose as a percentage of assets. Liability mix changed with a significant fall in short-term borrowings to assets and a rise in commercial paper to assets. Total liabilities to assets fell by almost 2 percent, as equity to assets rose by 2 percent.

For Morgan Stanley, asset utilization was 0.067 in 1995 compared with 0.063 in 1996. Assets grew by 36.7 percent and revenues grew by 44 percent, resulting in the slight rise in asset utilization. The asset composition relative to total assets remained relatively constant, with some small composition changes. Government and nongovernment securities to assets fell 3 percent, as did corporate equities, whereas cash-related assets, other receivables, and other assets rose. On the liability and equity side, the equity-to-asset ratio fell from 4.20 percent to 3.77 percent in 1996. Short-term borrowings to assets rose slightly, as did corporate equities sold, along with other minor changes in liabilities.

Overall DuPont Analysis

Similar to other financial institutions, a DuPont analysis can be used to provide an overall analysis of trends, as follows:

	MORGAN KEEGAN		MORGAN STANLEY	
	1996	1995	1996	1995
Return on Equity	20.04%	17.10%	13.90%	9.94%
Return on Assets	3.58%	2.70%	0.524%	0.417%
Equity Multiplier	5.60	6.33	26.53	23.81
Net Profit Margin	11.24%	10.46%	7.83%	6.58%
Asset Utilization	0.318	0.259	0.067	0.063

Note that because of rounding errors, DuPont-multiplied figures may be slightly different from actual return on assets (ROA) and ROE calculations. Using a DuPont analysis for Morgan Keegan, the firm's ROE improved as the result of a higher ROA and despite a lower equity multiplier. The higher ROA was the result of both a higher NPM and higher asset utilization.

Morgan Stanley's ROE improved as a result of both a higher ROA and a higher equity multiplier. The higher ROA was primarily due to a higher NPM and slightly higher asset utilization. Comparing the two firms, Morgan Keegan, the regional brokerage firm, has a much higher NPM and asset utilization and lower financial leverage than did Morgan Stanley, the New York investment banking firm.

Risk Management in Securities Firms

Trading Risk

As discussed in Chapter 2, in the 1990s, risk management had gained considerable importance for financial institutions and particularly for securities firms in the aftermath of huge losses by rogue traders in the late 1980s. One young trader in Singapore, Nick Lesson, accrued huge losses on Japanese

---

23 See Saunders (1997). As Saunders points out, the 2 percent represents a capital cushion for brokers/dealers sufficient to liquidate assets at market values and satisfy customer liabilities. Adjustments are made to book net worth by subtracting out fixed assets and other assets that cannot readily be converted to cash and securities that cannot be readily sold. Other adjustments are made to reflect profits and losses that are unrealized, subordinated liabilities, contractual commitments, deferred taxes, options, commodities and commodity futures, and certain collateralized liabilities. High equity multipliers or leverage ratios are typical for securities firms on Wall Street. For instance, in October 1998, the leverage ratio for Merrill Lynch was 31.9; for Morgan Stanley Dean Witter 33.7; for Lehman Brothers 35.2; for Donald, Lufkin & Jenrette 29; and for the PaineWebber Group 25. See Patrick McGeehan and Gregory Zuckerman. "High Leverage Isn't Unusual on Wall Street." *The Wall Street Journal* (October 13, 1998), C1, C19.

stock index futures, and a trader for Daiwa Bank, a leading Japanese investment bank, lost $1.1 billion through 30,000 unauthorized trades over eleven years as a senior manager in Daiwa's New York branch. Securities firms have attempted to develop better information on the risk exposure of traders using daily earnings at risk (DEAR) and value at risk (VAR) measures. They also have attempted to allocate greater capital and capital costs for potential losses associated with the risk of different activities using the risk-adjusted return on capital (RAROC) approach. Position limits for traders have also been devised, based on the market risk of traders' portfolios, and compensation methods now consider traders' returns, along with the additional risk that riskier trades impose on the firm. Higher market trading risk capital requirements were imposed for large international banks with subsidiaries engaging in trading activities, and the Basel Market Amendment in 1996, and the proposed Basel II Accord, has additional operational risk requirements.[24]

Underwriting Risks

In addition to trading risks, investment banking firms have considerable underwriting risk, the risk of adverse price movements immediately after the issue of new securities. Under a negotiated offering, investment bankers purchase securities at a given price and sell securities at a higher offering price to the public (i.e., a gross spread). To reduce selling risk, syndicates of securities firms are often formed (as noted in Figure 17.2) to take on a portion of the offering and reduce the underwriting and selling risk of the lead underwriter. To retain prestige associated with being a leading firm in syndicates, firms must maintain a high profile by managing a large volume of new offerings, putting them at greater risk.

Underwriters have had greater risk with **SEC 415 shelf registration** deals; they are often asked to provide bids for an offering, particularly debt offerings that may have to be offered in just a few days. With a shelf registration, the SEC gives prior approval for an issue and may take as little as two days to give final approval based on the final price and contract rate for the offering. Consequently, underwriters do not have time to market the bonds before making a bid. A **bought deal** is such an accepted bond transaction, often for Eurobonds, whereby an investment bank has not had time to develop a syndicate or access market interest before submitting a bid. Such a deal places an underwriter at considerable risk. A **kamikaze offer** is an offer by a prospective underwriter for a bought deal at such a low spread that other underwriters may decline to participate in a syndicate for it. With shelf offerings, gross spreads for bond issues have fallen dramatically. However, underwriters may feel compelled to participate in an offering to retain other types of business from corporations. Technological innovations have also allowed corporations to bypass securities firms. For instance, CapitaLink, a system innovation that allows blue chip corporations to issue bonds directly to institutional investors, became available in 1990. Such changes increase securities firms' operating risk.[25]

Hedging of Underwriting

One of the earliest and most widely publicized examples of hedging in the industry came in 1979, when Salomon Brothers underwrote an IBM bond issue. Just after the underwriting agreement was completed and the coupon rate was established, interest rates jumped sharply. The increase in market rates caused the bonds' market value to drop below Salomon's original estimates, wiping out expected profits. Industry observers assumed that Salomon had taken a big loss but soon learned that the deal had been hedged in the futures market, so the firm's losses were limited. (Hedging using futures basically entails taking a position on bonds in the futures market that will provide a gain to offset a loss on a spot position on bonds.) In an increasingly competitive securities market with narrower gross spreads and commission fees, hedges are commonplace. In 1986, the SEC recognized the importance of integrated asset/liability management in the industry by permitting lower capital requirements for securities firms whose corporate bond holdings were hedged, although the agency began placing pressure on securities firms to strengthen their capital positions.[26]

---

24 See Saunders (1997).

25 See Carey, et al. (1993); and Smith (1989), which provides excellent anecdotes of the author's experience as an investment banker doing deals in Europe and Japan.

26 "How Salomon Brothers Hedged the IBM Deal." *Business Week* (October 29, 1979), 50; and Cynthia S. Grisdella. "Capital Rules Eased for Securities Firms That Hedge Corporate Bond Holdings." *The Wall Street Journal* (November 5, 1986), 4.

Underwriters are allowed to use stabilization techniques during the first thirty days of a new stock issue, whereby they purchase or sell securities to stabilize the security's price. Often negotiated in an offering are **overallotment (greenshoe) options,** which allow a maximum of an additional 15 percent of the number of shares included in the basic offering. This allows the underwriter to sell to the public more shares than it must purchase under the underwriting agreement and to cover its "short position" to stabilize the price of an issue. In a falling market, the lead manager may attempt to use overallotments with syndicate participants as a way to encourage sales efforts.[27]

Venture Capital and Private Equity Firms

This section provides a short overview of venture capital (VC) and private equity firms. **Venture Capital firms** are organized as limited partnerships with managing partners and limited (passive) investors with the majority of investors institutional investors, including insurance companies and pension funds, corporations, endowments, foreign investors, and wealthy individuals, often known as "Angel" investors. VC firms are investment firms that provide seed capital to firms just starting, start-up capital to firms beginning to operate or manufacture a product, and later stage capital and temporary (bridge) financing. Many investment banks have VC firms as subsidiaries. VC firms' goal is to make a large return, averaging about 50 percent a year, for investors who are willing to take the risk of investing in relatively new companies. Returns required are higher depending on the risk and stage of the firm's growth. For instance, for firms just getting started (seed financing), an 80 percent return is required; 60 percent for a start-up actually beginning manufacturing; 50 percent for a first-stage firm making sales; 40 percent for a firm in a second major investment stage; 30 percent for a third-stage firm; and 25 percent for bridge financing. To make such an average return, VCs invest in a portfolio of firms with high growth potential, generally taking an equity interest. Since VCs invest in private firms, in order to make a return, they must "harvest" their investments by taking a firm public or selling it in the relatively short time frame of five to seven years. Normally, VC firms consider investments in excess of $2 million. Firms must give up a portion of control of the business, whereby the VC provides expertise and financial backing; VC firms prefer firms in such high-growth areas as biotech, software, media communications, and information technology. In 1997, of $12.2 billion invested, $2.6 billion was invested in software companies, $2.4 billion in communication companies, $0.6 billion in electronics, and $6.4 billion in other industries.[28]

Different types of venture capital firms include: (1) private VC firms, which are often subsidiaries of investment firms or other corporations or limited partnerships with general managing partners and institutional investors as limited partners or **angels,** wealthy individuals; (2) venture capital networks (VCNs), which provide anonymous matching; (3) small business investment corporations (SBICs), which are funded by $4 of low-cost government debt for every $1 of stockholder equity that provide capital often in the form of convertible debenture debt for small businesses capable of an annual cash flow that will allow SBICs to cover their commitments; and (4) minority enterprise small business investment companies (MESBICs), which provide debt and equity to small businesses that are at least 51 percent owned by socially or economically disadvantaged persons. Like SBICs, MESBICs receive low-cost government debt financing.[29]

Capital deals are designed by VC firms with commitment letters, investment agreements, loan covenants, rewards for performance, and penalties for failures. If goals are met, entrepreneurs reap financial rewards when the company goes public, is sold, or is refinanced. Through VC subsidiaries, investment banks can have access to promising firms to take public under initial public offerings (IPOs). A VC subsidiary's portfolio of firms may have a number of firms that fail, but with diversification

---

27 See Lipman (1994).

28 Matt Richtel. "Venture Capital Is Alive, and Plentiful." *New York Times* (April 6, 1998), C3; also see Bygrave and Timmons (1992).

29 Information on SBICs can be obtained from the National Association of Small Business Investment Companies, Suite 1101, 1156 15th St., N.W., Washington, D.C. 20005 and on MESBICs from the American Assn. of MESBICS, Suite 700, 915 15th St., N.W., Washington, D.C. 20005. With the Department of Labor's relaxed interpretation of the Employment Retirement Income Security Act's (ERISA) "prudent man" rule to allow diversification by investing in venture capital funds, pension funds were free to invest in funds, becoming the largest percentage of investors, providing about 40 percent of venture capital as limited partners during 1980 to 1994, with wealthy individuals providing 13 percent, and insurance companies, endowments, foreign investors, and corporations contributing about 12 percent each. See J. Chris Leach and Ronald W. Melicher. *Entrepreneurial Finance.* Mason, OH: Southwestern (Thomson), 2003.

large returns on stellar firms can result in an overall high return for the portfolio. Venture capital firms are in the business of harvesting companies, preferably within five years by generally either taking the firm public or selling it to another company. Hence, the valuation of a firm is very important, as is its potential to increase dramatically in value over time to generate an average annual return of 50 percent or more for the VC portfolio, although in the last decade the average VC portfolio return was 20 percent.[30]

Nonventure private equity firms are firms that invest in private firms with "buy-and-build" strategies by investing in, buying, and often combining different private firms with the goal to increase their value. Many nonventure private equity firms started out as leveraged buyout firms that provided debt and equity investments to help firms go private through leveraged buyouts (LBOs) or manager buyouts (MBOs). While private nonventure equity firms engaged in highly leveraged corporate breakups in the 1980s, in the 1990s they relied more on equity to make deals. The private equity market grew dramatically since 1991, raising record levels of capital during the 1990s. After the dot.com bust at the end of 2000 and the stock market downturn of the early 2000s, they had a decline, but performance improved as the market improved in 2003 and early 2004. Private equity firms have also been actively involved in global expansion. Strategies by private equity firms to maximize the value of firms that they acquire include "strengthening management, adding complementary companies, or rolling up companies and consolidated fragmented sectors."[31] Different private equity firms have different strategies and expertise in the type of firms they acquire for classic buy-and-build deals. Some prominent private equity firms include Kohlberg, Kravis & Roberts, Warburg Pincus, Apax Partners, Forstmann Little & Co, and Hicks, Muse, Tate & Furst Incorporated, among others. Often private equity firms specialize in different industries or regions or private investments in public equity.[32]

Ethical Considerations and SEC Proposed Code of Ethics in 2004

With the large number of scandals that occurred for security firms and mutual funds, the Security and Exchange Commission (SEC) proposed a new rule and related rule amendments under the Investment Advisers Act of 1940 that would require investment firms that advise funds to adopt ethics codes that would spell out the standards of conduct expected of advisory personnel, safeguard important nonpublic information concerning client transactions, and address conflicts of interest that may arise from personal trading by advisers. Employees would also have to have the adviser's approval before investing in an initial public offering or private placements. Advisers would be required to report personal security transactions, including transactions in any mutual fund managed by an adviser. The intent of codes of ethics would be to remind employees that they have positions of trust, requiring that employees act constantly with "the utmost integrity." Some ethical obligations would exceed those required by law, including the avoidance of even an appearance of conflict with clients. Codes of ethics under the proposal would also establish procedures that employees would be asked to follow to ensure that an adviser can determine whether the employee is in compliance with the principles of the firm. In addition, codes of ethics should lay out procedures to provide employees guidance and certainty concerning what activities are or are not permissible. Codes of ethics also protect the interests of clients and advisers and prevent fraud by demanding that advisory personnel are in performance of their duties "with complete propriety and do not take advantage of their position."[33] Firms are also encouraged to adopt broader codes covering additional matters. All employees would receive the code of ethics, including any amendments, and would acknowledge in writing receipts of copies. Any violations would be required to be reported to the adviser's chief compliance officer or other person designated in the code of ethics for any code violation. The SEC had asked for comments—including the costs and benefits from the proposed rules including establishing, maintaining, and enforcing codes of ethics for

---

30 See Lipman (1994). There are a number of excellent books on venture capital including William D. Bygrave, Michael Hay, and Jos B. Peeters. *The Venture Capital Handbook.* London: Financial Times Prentice Hall, 1999.

31 See J. B. Bird, "What is Private Equity Investment?". *Texas: The McCombs School of Business Magazine,* McCombs School of Business (Spring/Summer, 2001) (*http://www.mccombs.utexas.edu/news/magazine*).

32 See the Deloitte & Touche USA, LLP Website (*http://www.deloitte.com*) for a discussion of private equity investors and a private equity industry outlook. See also Steven Dresner (Editor) with E. Kurt Kim, *PIPES: A Guide to Private Investments in Public Equity,* New York: Bloomberg Press, 2003 and The PIPES Report, *http://www.pipesreport.com.*

33 See U.S. Securities and Exchange Commission, Proposed Rule: Investment Advisor Codes of Ethics, on the SEC Website (*http://www.sec.gov/rules/proposed/ia-2209.htm*).

supervised persons—before establishing this rule at the time of this writing. The SEC has also proposed having an independent chairman from the fund on the board of directors, which has been opposed by the mutual fund industry, since it would be operationally difficult.[34]

Before the SEC's vote in favor of the rule, SEC Chairman William Donaldson pointed out that "Advisers owe their clients more than mere honesty and good faith. What we are seeing leads me to believe that all too many advisers have been delivering much less." Examples of breach of fiduciary duty were numerous in 2003, and the SEC and states have imposed large fines for violations. Alliance Capital Management and Putnam, for instance, were required to pay $600 million and $110 million, respectively, for improper fund trading and breach of fiduciary duty. Other brokerage firms were fined for failure to disclose conflicts of interest including a $50 million civil fine by Morgan Stanley. The SEC also made a "sweep" inspection of brokerage firms selling mutual funds. They found that 14 of 15 of the firms inspected received revenue-sharing payments (in the form of commissions) for favoring particular mutual funds in Websites or promotional materials. The SEC also investigated other conflicts of interest including revenue arrangements where brokers were paid for putting certain mutual funds on their recommended broker purchase lists. Directors have also been accused of "negligent failure" in failing to monitor funds including cash flow and pricing of funds sold by firms. Critics have noted that the security industry often breeds a culture that promotes short-term performance over ethics. Security industry groups and firms have also developed their own codes of ethics to encourage employees to think about the ethical implications associated with their decisions and actions.[35]

Concept Questions

1. Explain the differences in the typical income statements and balance sheets for a regional securities firm versus a large Wall Street firm using Morgan Keegan and Morgan Stanley Group as examples.

2. What areas seem to be the drivers of profitability for the two respective firms?

3. How do securities firms attempt to reduce or manage their trading and underwriting risks?

4. What are the different types of venture capital and private equity firms? How do venture capital firms make profits for investors?

5. Why do you think there has been so much unethical behavior in the securities industry in recent years? What does the SEC's proposed investment adviser code of ethics mandate?

Summary

This chapter presents an overview of securities firms, which provide brokerage, trading, underwriting, merchant banking, and other financial services to wholesale and retail customers. Securities firms operate under unique regulatory guidelines in an increasingly competitive environment in which risk management is a necessary key to survival. The industry has been at the forefront of financial innovation in recent decades. With the techno-logical advances of the information age, the industry is undergoing continued restructuring, such as the development of online trading, selling securities on the Internet by electronic trading, and recently established online investment banks.

The securities industry has faced increased competition and great volatility in earnings. Narrowing profit margins for traditional lines of business provided an incentive for securities firms to seek fee income by serving M&A clients

---

34 See Robert Lordi and Jeffrey Salters. "Ethics: Marketing Investment Management Services: Surveys Suggest Ethics is Good Business." *AIMR Advocate,* Vol. 4, No. 5 (September/October 1999), 1–8 on the AIMR Website (*http://www.aimrpubs.org*); The Associated Press, "SEC Proposes Code for Investment Firms." AP article, January 14, 2004, on the MSNBC website (*http://msnbc.msn.com*); John Dobson, "Ethics and Professional Standards: Ethics in Finance II." *Financial Analysts Journal,* Vol. 53, No. 1 (January/February 1997), 15–25.

35 The Associated Press. "SEC Proposes Code for Investment Firms." MSNBC (January 14, 2004) on the MSNBC Website (*http://msnbc.msn.com/id/3958005/*).

and engaging in merchant banking activities, providing working capital and other services to small businesses, developing business in other countries, and engaging in greater trading activities. Securities firms have attempted to develop better risk management techniques to measure and to control for the risks associated with these activities. Some firms have become more diversified by becoming full-line service firms engaging in both retail and whole-sale activities, which entails meshing very different cultures.

Some of the problems the securities industry faces today were internally generated by the unethical and illegal insider trading activities of some industry participants. Congress responded to the growing number of violations by passing the Insider Trading Act of 1988, strengthening the regulatory authority of the SEC. The securities industry also has faced greater competition from commercial banks, who may pose even stronger challenges with the repeal of Glass–Stegall. Hundreds of mergers between securities firms and banks have occurred in recent years.

Questions

1. Rita and Jerry Kiefer are investors and would like to know what advantages and disadvantages online trading firms have compared to traditional brokerage firms. How have online firms changed their focus in recent years?

2. Smarty Jones and Iriane Welply are thinking of getting jobs in the securities industry. Explain to them why earnings in the securities industry are so cyclical. What factors affect securities firm profits? Where do brokerage firms' revenues and expenses chiefly come from? Where do investment banking firm revenues and profits come from? How do the different categories of securities firms differ in terms of sources of revenues and expenses?

3. Trish Ruppersburg is thinking of taking her firm public and would like to know the difference between a prestigious and non-prestigious investment bank. Explain these and other types of rankings for investment firms.

4. Margaret Ann and Edward Singleton are interested in the history of investment banking. Explain why investment banks were so important in the United States in the nineteenth century. How did trusts develop? In the twentieth century, why was there anti–Wall Street sentiment? What factors led to the development of the Eurobond market and the globalization of the industry? What changes led to greater competition in the 1970s and 1980s? How did the culture of securities firms change in the 1980s to early 2000s? Why do you think there are so many scandals today?

5. Bill and Diane Brennan would like you to give them some examples of innovations by securities firms. What factors encouraged these innovations? Look up articles in a recent *Wall Street Journal* and find an example of a recent innovation.

6. Andy, Ellie, Mary, and John McMurray are investors in the stock market and are concerned about stock market downturns. What happened with the 1987 stock market crash? What happened with the early 2000s dot.com stock market downturn? What internal corporate governance problems were associated with each market downturn? How did the Insider Trading and Securities Fraud Enforcement Act attempt to reduce fraud and insider trading? What does the SEC proposal for investment firms to establish codes of ethics entail? Do you think these codes will prevent self-interested versus fiduciary behavior by investment advisers? Explain why or why not.

7. Scott, Meredith, and Ann Singleton have been very interested in recent developments that have affected security firms. Answer the following questions for them. Why have there been so many security mergers in the past decade and recent mergers of security firms and banks and insurance firms? Why was the harmonization of regulations for the European Economic Community important in 1992? What is day trading? Why were regulators in the early 2000's concerned about day trading? Why did many day-trading firms fail in the early 2000s?

8. Alice Reich, Lee Shannon, and Jamie Roth ask you to find articles or news stories about a recent example of fraud by a securities firm or individual in the securities industry. Why is the securities industry prone to fraud? Why is ethical behavior particularly crucial for firms in the securities industry? Give some examples of recent lawsuits that different firms in the securities industry faced in the 1990s or early to mid-2000s. Can you suggest any solutions for reducing fraud?

9. Edward Tedjosaputro is interested in the different key areas of activities for securities firms. Explain these to Edward. Which areas have been more profitable in

recent years? Look in *The Wall Street Journal* at ads by securities firms. What are some new areas of activity that are advertised? How has the industry improved its profitability in recent years?

10. Susan Baillet and Herman Asarnow are very curious about the typical assets and liabilities that are on the balance sheet of a regional securities firm versus an investment bank. Explain these. Why do you think securities firms have such high financial leverage on average?

11. Manuel Knight and Joel Penick are concerned about the types of risks that securities firms and investment banks face. Explain some of the different types of risks that they have. How does their interest rate risk compare to that of depository institutions? Why is operational risk management particularly important for securities firms?

12. Rick Burns, Susan and Brad Jordan, and Austin Murphy would like to know how the Shelf Registration Rule SEC 415 makes underwriting issues, particularly bond issues, more competitive for investment bankers. Explain the rule and how it changed competition for issues by investment firms. What has been the effect on gross spreads for bonds? What is a bought deal? A kamikaze offering?

13. Hung Gay Fung would like you to answer the following questions. What is a venture capital firm? An angel investor? An SBIC? A MESBIC? A nonventure private equity firm? Why is harvesting so important for venture capital and nonventure equity firms? Who are the limited partners of these firms?

Problems

1. Renée Gash, the famous research analyst of Whole Lot of Bucks Analytics, has asked you to perform a financial analysis including a DuPont analysis for Charles Schwab, shown in Table P17.1. She asks that you include an analysis of asset and liability mix. Discuss the primary sources of revenues and expenses for a discount brokerage firm. How does this differ from a wholesale investment bank, like Morgan Stanley in 1996?

2. Nelson, Holly, and Alice Hilton, the super-analysts at Golden Boulder Securities Company, have asked you to perform a financial analysis including a DuPont analysis for Alex Brown, shown in Table P17.2, a regional investment banking firm prior to its merger with Bankers Trust. Include an analysis of any changes in asset and liability mix.

3. Stu Rosenstein and Scott Barnhart, investment managers of Big Country Securities, have asked you to perform a DuPont analysis for Legg Mason, as shown in Table P17.3, a regional brokerage and investment firm in Baltimore, Maryland. Include an analysis of changes in asset and liability mix and primary sources of revenues and expenses.

4. Look up Merrill Lynch or another publicly traded securities firm on the Internet. Click on "Investors Relations" and download its annual report. Perform a financial analysis to determine why its return on equity and assets either went up or down from the previous year. See if you can find the key drivers for its profitability from your analysis.

Suggested Case Studies

Darden School, University of Virginia (also in Richard D. Crawford and William W. Sihler, *Financial Service Organizations: Cases in Strategic Management,* New York: Harper-Collins College Publishers, 1994.)

1. **Case 11: First Boston, Inc.** Determining the Strategic Structure of a Major Investment Bank. Case analyzes differences in the performance of full-service firms versus wholesale investment banks and retail firms and some of the cultural problems within investment banking firms.

2. **Case 17: Winson Furniture Company, Inc.** Underwriting a public issue of common stock; gives students practice in valuation issues.

3. **Case 18: Dakota Menska, Inc.** Underwriting a public issue of debt. Information about changes in debt markets with the SEC's shelf registration process and the bond issuing process.

4. **Case 4: Jefferies Group, Inc.** Case involving a securities firm that deals with over-the-counter and off-the-board competition in trading stock and new technology.

Harvard Business School Cases

5. **Salomon Brothers' Strategic Review, 1987** (also in Hayes and Meerschwam, 1992). Strategic overview for Salomon Brothers at a time when it was facing financial problems.

table **P17.1** FINANCIAL STATEMENTS FOR CHARLES SCHWAB CORPORATION, 1995 & 1996

Business: Provide brokerage & related investment services to customers. Company's strategy is to attract and retain customers by focusing on retail brokerage, mutual funds, support services for independent investment managers, equity security market-making, online brokerage and 401(k) defined contribution plan. Competitive advantages include advertising and marketing programs that have created a national brand, a broad range of products and services, diverse delivery systems, and an ongoing investment in technology.

Consolidated Income Accounts, Years Ended Dec. 31 ($000)

	1996	% Revs.	1995	% Revs.
Revenues				
Commissions	954,129	51.55%	750,896	52.88%
Mutual Fund Service Fees	311,067	16.81%	218,784	15.41%
Interest Revenue	254,988	13.78%	210,897	14.85%
Principal Transactions	256,902	13.88%	191,392	13.48%
Other Revenues	73,836	3.99%	47,934	3.38%
Total Revenues	1,850,922	100.00%	1,419,903	100.00%
Expenses				
Compensation & Benefits	766,377	41.41%	594,105	41.84%
Communications	164,756	8.90%	128,554	9.05%
Occupancy & Equipment	130,494	7.05%	110,977	7.82%
Commissions, Clearance, & Floor Brokerage	80,674	4.36%	77,061	5.43%
Depreciation & Amortization	98,342	5.31%	68,793	4.84%
Advertising & Mktg. Developmt.	83,987	4.54%	52,772	3.72%
Professional Services	52,055	2.81%	41,304	2.91%
Other Expenses	80,174	4.33%	69,233	4.88%
Total Expenses Excluding Int.	1,456,859	78.71%	1,142,799	80.48%
Income before Taxes	394,063	21.29%	277,104	19.52%
Taxes on Income	160,260	8.66%	104,500	7.36%
Net Income	233,803	12.63%	172,604	12.16%

Consolidated Balance Sheet, as of December 31 ($000)

	1996	% Revs.	1995	% Revs.
Assets				
Cash & Equivalents	633,317	4.60%	454,996	4.31%
Cash & Investmts. Req'd to be Segregated	7,235,971	52.52%	5,426,619	51.43%
Receivables from Brokers, Dealers, & Clearing Orgs.	230,943	1.68%	141,916	1.34%
Receivables from Customers	5,012,815	36.38%	3,946,295	37.40%
Securities Owned at Market Value	127,866	0.93%	113,522	1.08%
Net Equipment & Property	315,376	2.29%	243,472	2.31%
Intangible Assets	68,922	0.50%	80,863	0.77%
Other Assets	153,558	1.11%	144,325	1.37%
Total Assets	13,778,768	100.00%	10,552,008	100.00%
Liabilities & Equity				
Drafts Payable	225,136	1.63%	212,961	2.02%
Payables to Brokers, Dealers, etc.	877,742	6.37%	581,226	5.51%
Payable to Customers	11,176,836	81.12%	8,551,996	81.05%
Accrued Exps. & Other	360,683	2.62%	326,785	3.10%
Borrowings	283,816	2.06%	246,146	2.33%
Total Liabilities	12,924,213	93.80%	9,919,114	94.00%
Equity	854,555	6.20%	632,894	6.00%
Total Liabilities & Equity	13,778,768	100.00%	10,552,008	100.00%

Source: Moody's Bank & Finance Manual, 1997

table **P17.2** FINANCIAL STATEMENTS FOR ALEX BROWN, INC., 1995 AND 1996 (PRIOR TO BANKERS TRUST MERGER)

Business: Major investment banking and securities brokerage firm located in Baltimore, Maryland

Income Statement

Revenues ($000)	1996	% Revs.	1995	% Revs.
Commissions	201,896	19.06%	173,471	21.43%
Investment Banking	414,891	39.16%	293,375	36.25%
Princ. Transactions	167,815	15.84%	139,383	17.22%
Int. & Dividends	142,307	13.43%	105,544	13.04%
Advisory & Other	132,512	12.51%	97,621	12.06%
Total Revenues	1,059,421	100.00%	809,394	100.00%

Expenses ($000)				
Comp. & Benefits	554,711	52.36%	432,880	53.48%
Communication Expense	38,388	3.62%	33,934	4.19%
Occupancy & Equip.	38,504	3.63%	39,758	4.91%
Interest Expense	50,668	4.78%	36,204	4.47%
Floor Brokerage, Exch. & Clearing Fees	20,755	1.96%	18,646	2.30%
Other Oper. Expenses	97,013	9.16%	89,797	11.09%
Total Oper. Exps.	800,039	75.52%	651,219	80.46%
Erngs. Before Income & Taxes	259,382	24.48%	158,175	19.54%
Income Taxes	105,237	9.93%	62,620	7.74%
Net Earnings	154,145	14.55%	95,555	11.81%

Balance Sheet

Assets ($000)	1996	% Assets	1995	% Assets
Cash & Equivalents	109,800	4.32%	62,103	4.32%
Customer Receivables	1,487,041	58.49%	1,277,869	58.49%
Rec. from Brokers Dealers & Clrg. Orgs.	368,099	14.48%	416,449	18.96%
Cur. State Inc. Tax	17,429	0.69%		0.00%
Other Receivables	59,097	2.32%	62,056	2.83%
Firm Trading Secs.	210,412	8.28%	110,564	5.03%
Sec. Purchased under Reale Agrmt.	15,510	0.61%	34,865	1.59%
Deferred Income Tax	46,433	1.83%	27,813	1.27%
Mmship. in Exchgs.	323	0.01%	323	0.01%
Net Off. & Equipment	48,079	1.89%	41,189	1.88%
Investment Secs.	56,889	2.24%	50,294	2.29%
Loans to Employees to Purch. Convertibles	54,454	2.14%	48,320	2.20%
Other Assets	69,009	2.71%	64,662	2.94%
Total Assets	2,542,575	100.00%	2,196,507	100.00%

Liabilities & Equity				
Bank Loans	29,900	1.18%	120,008	5.46%
Cash Mgt. Facil. Pay.	83,733	3.29%	70,338	3.20%
Customers, Incl. Free Credit Bals.	676,734	26.62%	506,993	23.08%
Brokers, Dealers, & Clrg. Orgs. Payable	495,947	19.51%	480,621	21.88%
Curr. Fed & State Inc. Tax Payable	1,840	0.07%	5,032	0.23%
Other Payables	378,981	14.91%	294,643	13.41%
Sec. Sold, Not Yet Purch. at Market	48,223	1.90%	54,276	2.47%
Secs. Sold under Repur. Agreement			2,460	0.11%
Senior Debt	183,315	7.21%	172,849	7.87%
Total Liabilities	1,898,673	74.68%	1,707,220	77.72%
Equity	643,902	25.32%	489,287	22.28%
Total Liabs. & Equity	2,542,575	100.00%	2,196,507	100.00%

Source: Moody's Bank & Finance Manual, 1996

table **P17.3** FINANCIAL STATEMENTS FOR LEGG MASON, 1997 AND 1996

Business: Holding company whose subsidiaries engage in securities brokerage and trading & investment management of individual & institutional accounts and company-sponsored mutual funds, investment banking for corporations & municipalities, commercial mortgage banking, and provision of other financial services.

Income Statement

Revenues ($000)	1997	% Revs.	1996	% Revs.
Commissions	189,980	29.70%	169,181	32.78%
Princ. Transactions	73,181	11.44%	65,870	12.76%
Investment Advisory & Related Fees	183,401	28.67%	144,790	28.06%
Investment Banking	77,062	12.05%	43,328	8.40%
Interest Revenue	84,076	13.14%	57,098	11.06%
Other Revenue	37,006	5.78%	35,776	6.93%
Total Revenues	639,706	100.00%	516,043	100.00%
Expenses				
Comp. & Benefits	362,876	56.73%	299,562	58.05%
Occu. & Equip. Rental	43,043	6.73%	36,403	7.05%
Communications	30,528	4.77%	28,081	5.44%
Floor Brokerage & Clearing Fees	5,912	0.92%	5,063	0.98%
Interest Expense	43,357	6.78%	26,177	5.07%
Other Expenses	58,788	9.19%	56,903	11.03%
Total Expenses	544,504	85.12%	452,189	87.63%
Earnings before Tax	95,202	14.88%	63,854	12.37%
Income Taxes	38,609	6.04%	25,987	5.04%
Net Earnings	56,593	8.85%	37,867	7.34%

Balance Sheet

Assets ($000)	1996	% Assets	1995	% Assets
Cash & Equivalents	150,976	8.04%	89,378	6.80%
Segregated Cash & Securities	442,305	23.54%	168,859	12.85%
Resale Agreements	132,801	7.07%	108,413	8.25%
Customer Receivbls.	527,456	28.07%	398,375	30.31%
Securities Borrowed	263,612	14.03%	196,569	14.95%
Secs. Owned at Market Value	78,862	4.20%	84,219	6.41%
Investment Secs.	66,983	3.56%	83,497	6.35%
Net. Prop. & Equipmt.	35,809	1.91%	33,339	2.54%
Intangible Assets	61,423	3.27%	67,370	5.13%
Other Assets	118,741	6.32%	84,481	6.43%
Total Assets	1,878,968	100.00%	1,314,500	100.00%

table **P17.3** FINANCIAL STATEMENTS FOR LEGG MASON, 1997 AND 1996 (CONTINUED)

Balance Sheet

Liabilities & Equity	1996	% Assets	1995	% Assets
Pay. to Customers	960,646	51.13%	564,698	42.96%
Pay. to Brks. & Dirs.	7,112	0.38%	3,854	0.29%
Securities Loaned	250,804	13.35%	170,829	13.00%
Short-term Borrowings	13,400	0.71%	6,800	0.52%
Secs. Sold, Not Yet Purch. at Mkt.	12,507	0.67%	10,693	0.81%
Accrued Compens.	58,893	22.28%	41,168	22.74%
Other Liabs.	57,396	3.05%	50,018	3.81%
Senior Notes	99,581	5.30%	99,534	7.57%
Subordinated Liabs.			68,000	
Total Liabilities	1,460,339	77.72%	1,015,594	77.26%
Common Stock	1,827	0.10%	1,538	0.12%
Additional Pd-in Cap.	192,817	10.26%	120,960	9.20%
Retained Earnings	223,752	11.91%	176,098	13.40%
Net Unrealized Appr. on Invest. Secs.	223	0.01%	310	0.02%
Total Equity	418,629	22.28%	298,906	22.74%
Total Liabs. & Equity	1,878,968	100.00%	1,314,500	100.00%

Source: Moody's Bank & Finance Manual, 1997

6. **Bankers Trust New York Corporation** (also in Hayes and Meerschwam, 1992). This case deals with cultural issues meshing a commercial bank with an investment bank culture.
7. **Morgan Stanley: The Tokyo Branch** (also in Hayes and Meerschwam, 1992). Morgan Stanley's attempt and cultural problems in setting up a branch office in Tokyo.
8. **CSFB and the International Capital Markets** (A) (also in Hayes and Meerschwam, 1992). History of Credit Suisse First Boston and strategic issues facing the firm, including a review of the Euromarkets and the firm's competitive environment.
9. **Alex Brown Incorporated,** Strategic Issues Facing a Regional Investment Banking Firm; also presents the trends in the industry.

Selected References

Arshadi, Nasser, and Gordon V. Karels. "Trends in Derivatives and the Management of Financial Risk." In *Modern Financial Intermediaries & Markets.* Upper Saddle River, NJ: Prentice Hall, 1997.

Bartlett, Sarah. *The Money Machine: How KKR Manufactured Power & Profits.* New York: Warner Books, 1991.

Bloch, Ernest. *Inside Investment Banking,* 2nd ed. Homewood, IL: Dow Jones-Irwin, 1989.

Brigham, Eugene F., Louis C. Gapenski, and Michael C. Ehrhardt. *Financial Management: Theory and Practice,* 9th ed. Fort Worth, TX: Dryden Press, Harcourt Brace College Publishers, 1999.

Bygrave, William D., and Jeffrey A. Timmons. *Venture Capital at the Crossroads.* Boston: Harvard Business School Press, 1992.

Carey, Mark S., et al. "Recent Developments in the Market for Privately Placed Debt." *Federal Reserve Bulletin* 79 (February 1993), 77–92.

Chernow, Ron. *The House of Morgan.* New York: Touchstone Books (Simon and Shuster, Inc.), 1990.

————. *The Warburgs.* New York: Vintage Press, 1993.

Crawford, Richard D., and William W. Sihler. *Financial Service Organizations: Cases in Strategic Management.* New York: Harper Collins College Publishers, 1994.

Endlich, Lisa. *Goldman Sachs: The Culture of Success.* New York: Knopf, 1999.

Geisst, Charles. *Investment Banking in the Financial System.* Englewood Cliffs, NJ: Prentice Hall, 1995.

Friend, Irwin, et. al. *Investment Banking and the New Issues Market.* Cleveland, OH: World Publishing Co., 1967.

Goldberg, Lawrence G., et al. "Economies of Scale and Scope in the Securities Industry." *Journal of Banking and Finance* (February 1991), 91–107.

Hayes, Samuel L., III. "The Transformation of Investment Banking." *Harvard Business Review* 57 (January/February 1979), 153–170.

Hayes, Samuel L., III, and Philip M. Hubbard. *Investment Banking: A Tale of Three Cities.* Boston: Harvard Business School Press, 1990.

Hayes, Samuel L., III. and David M. Meerschwam. *Managing Financial Institutions: Cases within the Financial Services Industry.* New York: The Dryden Press, 1992.

Kidwell, David S., et al. "SEC Rule 415: The Ultimate Competitive Bid." *Journal of Financial and Quantitative Analysis* 19 (June 1984), 183–196.

Langevoort, Donald C. *Securities Law Series: Insider Trading Legislation.* New York: Clark Boardman Co., 1988.

Lipman, Frederic D. *Going Public.* Rocklin, CA: Prima Publishing, 1994.

Marshall, John F., and M. E. Ellis. *Investment Banking and Brokerage.* Boulder, CO: Kolb Publishing Co., 1994.

McNamee, Mike. "Investor's Guide: How Do the Upstart Net Brokers Stack Up Against Traditional Firms Online?" *Business Week* (February 22, 1999), 120–124.

Norton, Robert E. "Upheaval Ahead on Wall Street." *Fortune* (September 14, 1987), 68–77.

Rogowski, Robert J., and Eric H. Sorenson. "Deregulation in Investment Banking: Shelf Registrations, Structure and Performance." *Financial Management* 14 (Spring 1985), 5–15.

Saunders, Anthony. *Financial Institutions Management: A Modern Perspective,* 2nd ed. Burr Ridge, IL: Irwin Press, 1997.

Securities Industry Association. *Securities Industries Trends.* New York, various issues.

Selby, Beth. "The Twilight of the Syndicate." *Institutional Investor* 19 (August 1985), 205–209.

Smith, Roy. *The Global Bankers.* New York: Truman Talley Books/Plume, 1989.

SNL Securities. *Industry Review: Broker/Dealers.* Charlottesville, VA: SNL Securities, 1994.

Sprio, Leah Nathans, and Edward C. Baig. "Who Needs a Broker?" *Business Week* (February 22, 1999), 113–118.

Stigum, Marcia. *The Money Market,* 3rd ed. Homewood, IL: Dow Jones-Irwin, 1990.

Walter, Ingo, and Roy C. Smith. "Investment Banking in Europe after 1992." In *Proceedings of a Conference on Bank Structure and Competition.* Chicago: Federal Reserve Bank of Chicago, 1989, 312–317.

internet *exercise*

1 Have concerns about a securities firm? The SEC has a large database of information on regulated securities firms. EDGAR, the Electronic Data Gathering, Analysis, and Retrieval system, performs automated collection, validation, indexing, acceptance, and forwarding of submissions by companies and others who are required by law to file forms with the U.S. SEC. Its primary purpose is to increase the efficiency and fairness of the securities market for the benefit of investors, corporations, and the economy by accelerating the receipt, acceptance, dissemination, and analysis of time-sensitive corporate information filed with the agency. The EDGAR database can be accessed from *http://www.sec.gov/edgar.shtml.*

To do a search, click on "Search for Company Filings." There are two kinds of basic searches: general and special purpose. The General Search includes Companies & Other Filers, Latest Filings, and Historical EDGAR Archives, where you can search with a keyword (search string of words) for a firm based on all the header information in all the filings in the database.

There are three Special-Purpose Searches: (1) EDGAR CIK (Central Index Key) Lookup (a unique identifier assigned by the SEC to all companies and people who file disclosure with the SEC); (2) Current Events Analysis of forms filed in the previous week; and (3) Mutual Fund Prospectuses.

2 There is no shortage of financial scandals, and you can find a guide with links to information sources at *http://www.ex.ac.uk/~RDavies/arian/scandals/.* The site includes links for classic financial scandals, political corruption, organized crime, money laundering, and links to regulatory and antifraud organizations that combat these scandals. There are also links to financial scandals in fiction.

The classic financial scandals link takes you to *http://www.ex.ac.uk/~RDavies/arian/scandals/ classic.html.* This guide contains lots of links to information on classic and other lesser-known financial scandals. Although most of the cases in these pages involve real or suspected criminal activity, a few are included simply because the scale of the incompetence or greed makes them scandalous: BCCI, Barings, Daiwa, Sumitomo, Credit Lyonnais, Bre-X, Lloyds, NASDAQ, Savings and Loan, and others.

3 Go to the Careers in Finance Website, *http://www.careers-in-finance.com,* and look up Investment Banking and Commercial Banking as a career. Write a brief summary of what you find including the different types of investment banks,

best resources for finding additional information, money management job options, and investment banking facts and advice. How does an investment banking career differ from that of a commercial banker? What are the differences in skills and culture that an investment banker has versus a commercial banker? Do you think this could cause conflicts with bank and securities firm mergers? Explain why or why not. Also, discuss the different trends in the two industries.

4 Go to the WR Hambrecht+Co Website *http:// wrhambrecht.com.* At the top of the page will be different tabs for brokerage accounts, auctions, private investing, WRH+Co Research, Market Data, and Market Strategy. Click the tap for Auctions. On the Auctions and Offering page (*http://wrhambrecht .com/ind/auctions/index.html*), on the left-hand side, under "OpenIPO," you'll see in the last row "Sample Auction (Flash demo). This will take you to a slide presentation that goes through a "Dutch Auction" or "Open IPOs" where shares are allocated based on the price that individual investors bid. The presentation allows you to make a sample bid as well, and shows you how shares would be allocated to individual investors according to their bids and the accepted bid for the auction.

USEFUL WEB LINKS

Securities Industry Association

http://www.sia.com

Financial Services Fact Book

http://financialservicefacts.org

Careers in Finance

http://www.careers-in-finance.com/

National Securities Clearing Corporation

http://www.nscc.com/

Moody's Investor's Services

http://www.moodys.com

National Association of Securities Dealers

http://www.nasd.com

International Securities Exchange: The First Electronic Securities Exchange in the U.S.

http://www.iseoptions.com

18 Mutual Fund and Pension Fund Management

"By virtually all accounts, the mutual fund industry is suffering through its most serious crisis of faith in more than six decades. . . . Fund company executives and portfolio managers have been accused of allowing favored clients to trade often and even after the market closed, at the expense of other customers. . . . Such a troubling series of events in an industry that had traded so successfully on a sterling reputation must have sent investors fleeing in droves, right? Not exactly, in fact, the mutual fund business is thriving."

PATRICK MCGEEHAN. *"A Scandal, But Business Booms."* New York Times *(Mutual Fund Report),* Sunday, January 11, 2004, 25.

"The Pension Benefit Guaranty Corporation's insurance program for pension plans sponsored by a single employer suffered a net loss of $7.6 billion in fiscal year 2003, according to the agency's annual report released today. As a result, the program's fiscal year-end deficit worsened to a record $11.2 billion, three times larger than any previously recorded deficit."

Press Releases: Pension Benefit Guaranty Corporation (PBGC) Website, *"PBGC Releases Fiscal Year 2003 Financial Results,"* Randy Clerihue, Director Communications and Public Affairs, January 15, 2004 (http://www.pbgc.gov/news/press_releases/2004)

A s noted in the first opening quote, during the last four months of 2003, some prominent mutual funds were involved in a number of scandals that received a great deal of publicity while being investigated by the New York Attorney's General Office and the U.S. Securities and Exchange Commission (SEC). Investigators scrutinized late-trading and market-timing activities (generally not allowed in fund prospectuses) by mutual funds, brokerage firms, hedge funds, and third parties involved in processing fund trades. This, in turn, led to a number of congressional bills proposed to eliminate abuses, as well as new rules proposed by the SEC and other industry groups that will be discussed in this chapter. At the time of this writing in 2004, Congress decided not to pass legislation and allow the SEC to enact rules to prevent future abuses instead.

Despite these scandals and a reported general loss of confidence by the public in the mutual fund and securities industries, financially, 2003 was a very good year for mutual funds and their shareholders. As of year-end 2003, the Investment Company Institute (ICI), the national association of the investment company industry, reported that industry assets rose by 16 percent (by more than $1 trillion) from 2002 to $7.4 trillion, and in late April 2004, the industry was reported to have a record $7.6 trillion in total assets. This rise in assets was primarily the result of a rise in performance for bond and stock markets at this time, as well as one of the largest net cash inflow in the previous three years as the economy and markets improved. In contrast, money market funds had their first average industry net cash outflow since 1988, with interest rates falling and investors seeking better opportunities or simply putting their deposits back into depository institution accounts.[1]

Corporate defined benefit pension plans had a very bad year in 2003. As noted in the second opening quote, the Pension Benefit Guaranty Insurance Corporation (PBGIC), the federal insurer of corporate defined benefit plans, suffered a net loss of $7.6 billion in fiscal year 2003. This net loss was particularly worrying since it increased the PBGC's deficit

Learning Objectives

After completing this chapter, you will be able to:

1 Understand the organizational structure of a mutual fund and its principal service providers and recent industry structure and mutual fund trends.

2 Describe different types of mutual funds and how open-end fund shares are priced.

3 Understand the costs of mutual fund ownership and recent controversies about these costs.

4 Explain techniques for measuring the performance and risk of mutual funds.

5 Discuss recent mutual fund scandals and new legislation to curb abuses.

6 Understand the different types of pension funds and management issues for defined benefit plans.

7 Understand the role of actuarial assumptions in determining whether defined benefit plans are adequately funded.

8 Describe recent pension fund problems and legislation for pension funds.

to a record $11.2 billion. In response to these problems Congress passed the Pension Funding Equity Act of 2004 to provide temporary relief to employers by allowing the use of a higher corporate bond interest rate as a discount rate to calculate the present value of their pension liabilities. Special industries having problems including the airlines, steel companies, and the Transportation Communication Union, were allowed to reduce pension plan contributions by 80 percent as well for 2004 and 2005 only.[2]

The managers of mutual funds and pension funds face just as many challenges as do those of depositories and insurance and securities firms. With the convergence of different types of financial services firms, banks, insurance firms, and securities firms may also provide mutual funds and manage pension funds. This chapter presents some of the challenges of managing mutual funds and pension funds, along with information about the mutual fund and pension fund industries. The following section begins by discussing the investment companies that manage mutual funds.

---

1 Brian Reid, Stephen Sevigny, and Bernhard Silli. "Mutual Fund and Economic Developments in 2003." *Investment Company Institute Perspective,* Investment Company Institute (ICI), Vol. 10, No. 1, 2004, 1–28 (on the ICI Website at *http://www.ici.org*); also see Kevin Drawbaugh, "US Congress Folds Tent on Mutual Fund Legislation," Reuters, April 20, 2004, as reported on Forbes.com (*http://www.forbes.com*).

2 Press Releases: Pension Benefit Guaranty Corporation (PBGC) Website. "PBGC Releases Fiscal Year 2003 Financial Results." Randy Clerihue, Director Communications and Public Affairs, January 15, 2004 *(http://www.pbgc.gov/news/press_releases/2004)*; also see "Pension Funding Relief Enacted; Immediate Impact on April 15th Deadline," CCH Tax Briefing Pension Funding Equity Act of 2004, April 13, 2004, 1–3.

Phenomenal Growth for Mutual Funds

Mutual funds are asset pools that are managed by professional investment managers for investors who are the shareholders of the funds. Mutual funds have grown phenomenally from only about 68 funds and 300,000 shareholder accounts in 1940 to a peak of about 8,256 funds and 250,981,045 shareholder accounts by the end of 2002. This accounts for 21 percent of the retirement market of the United States (about $2.1 trillion in retirement mutual fund assets). Figure 18.1, Panel A shows the phenomenal growth in net funds assets from a little over $1 trillion in 1990 to $7.536 trillion in early January 2004, representing 8,121 funds. Panel B shows the percentage of net mutual fund assets held by type of fund in January 2004 with 50 percent for stock funds, 23 percent for taxable money market funds, 12 percent for taxable bond funds, 6 percent for hybrid funds (a mix of different types of securities), 5 per-

figure **18.1** TRENDS IN NET ASSETS OF MUTUAL FUNDS, 1990 TO JANUARY 2004

PANEL A: NET ASSETS OF MUTUAL FUNDS, 1990 TO JANUARY 2004 (IN TRILLIONS)

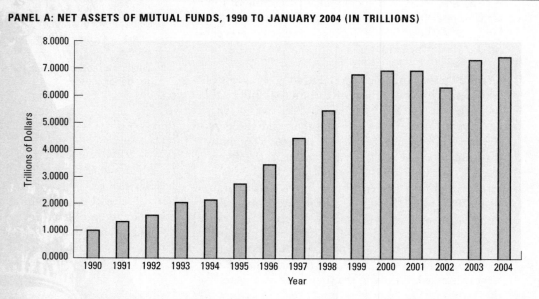

PANEL B: MUTUAL FUND TYPES AS A PERCENTAGE OF TOTAL ASSETS, JANUARY 2004

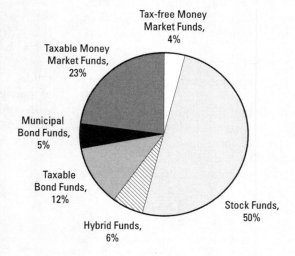

Source: *Panels A and B created by the Authors using yearly total net asset figures to calculate percentages. Total net asset figures by fund types come from "Trends in Mutual Fund Investing, January 2004," ICI Statistics and Research, Investment Company Institute Mutual Fund Connection, February 27, 2004, and the Mutual Fund Fact Book, 2002, on the ICI Website at http://www.ici.org.*

cent for municipal bond funds, and 4 percent for tax-free money market funds. Equity fund assets rose and taxable money market funds fell in terms of their 2002 percentages (respectively, 42 percent and 31 percent). The Investment Company Institute (ICI), the national association of the investment company industry, also reported that a little over 50 percent of households owned mutual funds and that mutual funds held more than 20 percent of total corporate equity in the United States.[3]

The Management Structure of Mutual Funds

Mutual funds include about 95 percent of professionally managed assets. The companies that manage the funds are generally privately or publicly owned, often by other companies, and are often subsidiaries of large financial services firms such as banks, securities firms, and insurance companies. Almost all mutual funds are externally managed, with operations conducted by investment companies and other affiliated organizations and independent contractors. This makes mutual funds unique, since, in some cases, many activities are outsourced to different companies, creating a complex network of companies as principal service providers. At least 40 percent of a fund's board of directors must be independent of its investment adviser or principal underwriter under a provision of the Investment Company Act of 1970. At the time of this writing, in April 2004, the SEC proposed increasing this mandate to 75 percent or at least a super-majority of directors and an independent chairman, with this proposal subject to public comment.[4]

Investment adviser affiliates manage funds and receive annual fees based on percentages of average net assets they control. They often provide administrative and accounting services, or an unaffiliated party does this work. Mutual funds usually distribute their shares through separate organizations designated as principal underwriters. The principal underwriters are regulated as brokers and dealers to continuously offer new shares to the public. Mutual funds are required by law to protect portfolio securities by placing them with custodians, usually qualified banks. Finally, transfer agents help mutual funds to conduct record-keeping and related functions and maintain customer service. Figure 18.2 shows the typical structure of a mutual fund. The key players in mutual fund areas follow:

1. **The board of directors.** The board of directors oversees the fund's activities, including approving contracts with management companies and other service providers. Directors are expected to exercise the care that a prudent person would take with his or her own business in overseeing and reviewing the performance of affiliates, including the investment adviser and the principal underwriter for the fund.

2. **The investment adviser/management company.** The investment adviser or management company manages the fund's portfolio according to the objectives and policies provided in a fund's prospectus. The investment adviser's job includes portfolio management and securities trading. Traders place portfolio orders with broker/dealers and try to obtain the most expedient and lowest-cost execution of these orders. Contracts with investment advisers specify compensation, generally in terms of an annual fee based on the percentage of the fund's average net assets. Advisers are subject to numerous legal restrictions, including those on any transactions between the adviser and the fund it advises. The investment adviser affiliate often provides administrative services overseeing operations and accounting services, but this can be done through an unaffiliated party.

3. **The distributor or principal underwriter.** Mutual funds usually distribute their shares through separate organizations designated as principal underwriters. The principal underwriters are regulated as brokers and dealers to continuously offer new shares to the public and are subject to National Association of Securities Dealers, Inc. (NASD) rules governing the sales practices of mutual funds.

---

3 Investment Company Institute, and also cited in the Insurance Information Institute (III) *Financial Services Fact Book,* at *http://financialservicefacts.org/financial2/securities/mutualfunds/.* Also see "Trends in Mutual Fund Investing, January 2004." ICI Statistics and Research, Investment Company Institute Mutual Fund Connection, February 27, 2004, on the ICI Website at *http://www.ici.org/new/trends_04_04.html,* or go to *http://www.ici.org* and click on "Latest Industry Statistics" to find the latest mutual fund trends. The ICC reported in January 2004 that of 8,121 total funds, there were 4,597 stock funds, 1,268 taxable bond funds, 778 municipal bond funds, 660 taxable money market funds, 506 hybrid funds, and 312 tax-free money market funds.

4 See Statement by the Investment Company Institute (ICI): "ICI Supports Efforts to Reinforce Fund Director Independence: Letter Endorses Many SEC Governance Initiatives, But Suggests Independent Chair Requirement Unlikely to Produce Desired Results," Washington, D.C., March 10, 2004 *(http://www.ici.org/statements/).*

figure **18.2** STRUCTURE OF A MUTUAL FUND'S MANAGEMENT

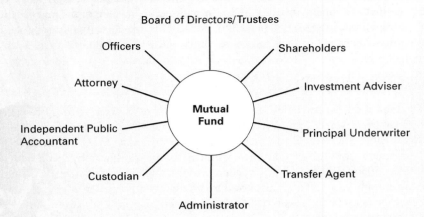

Source: 1998 Mutual Fund Fact Book, *38th ed. Washington, DC: The Investment Company Institute (ICI), 1998, p. 30 (figure also included in the* 2002 Mutual Fund Fact Book *on ICI's Website at* http://www.ici.org).

4. **The custodian.** By law mutual funds are required to place their securities with a custodian for protection. Almost all mutual funds use qualified bank custodians. Custodians are required to segregate mutual fund portfolio securities from other bank assets.

5. **The transfer agent.** A mutual fund employs a transfer agent to perform record-keeping and related functions, including maintaining record-keeping, calculating and disbursing dividends, and preparing and mailing shareholder account statements, tax information, and other notices. Some agents also prepare and mail statements confirming transactions and account balances and maintain customer service departments to respond to customer inquiries.

6. **Independent public accountants.** Independent public accountants are employed to certify the fund's financial statements.

Others involved in this nexus include traders for the investment fund managers, which may or may not be independent of the investment manager firm. Thus, the management of mutual funds not only includes portfolio management, but the careful management and timing of trades, meticulous record-keeping and correspondence, daily pricing, accounting, and custodial functions, along with intense customer service (often on a twenty-four-hour basis), marketing, and promotion. Different affiliate groups perform these functions. Many funds also commission brokers and dealers or agents at banks, insurance companies, and securities firms to help distribute and sell fund shares. Affiliates may be part of a single company or be a collection of different companies. Investment companies also have diverse ownership structures, as discussed in the following section.

Fidelity Investments provides an example of a typical ownership structure of a mutual fund. Fidelity Investments is owned by FMR Corporation, which owns several affiliates that provide services to each fund, subject to the approval of trustees and shareholders. For Fidelity's Magellan Fund, its investment adviser is Fidelity Management and Research, its distributor is Fidelity Distributors Company, its transfer agent is Fidelity Service Company, and its custodian and accounting service is Fidelity Custody Services. Hence, most of Fidelity's funds have contracts with the same agents and trustees, which often serve on the boards of many funds.[5]

Ownership Structure of Affiliates

Although mutual funds are owned by investors, the affiliated firms that run their operations can be mutually owned by shareholders, privately held, publicly owned, or subsidiaries of other companies. Many investment companies are subsidiaries of banks, insurance companies, and large securities firms. Other large corporations that may or may not engage in financial services own mutual funds. Many

---

5 Source: *Mutual Fund Fact Books,* 1998 to 2003. Washington, D.C.: The Investment Company Institute, available on the ICC Website *(http://www.ici.org).*

large funds, such as Vanguard and Fidelity, have their investment management operations centered on the East Coast, with affiliates in other areas. For instance, Fidelity has affiliates in Kentucky and Texas. Fidelity Investment Co. is privately owned by the Johnson family, as well as by the firm's top executives and mutual fund managers. It's interesting to note that Fidelity Investments Co. has held other types of companies as subsidiaries including a life insurance unit, and at times has owned a Boston coach car service, a newspaper company, as well as real estate interests. Fidelity's diversity of assets highlights the role of mutual funds as jacks-of-all-trades, offering wide varieties of financial services including servicing as a major discount brokerage firm, management and research, personal investments and brokerage, institutional retirement services, investment institutional services, wealth management services, securities execution and clearance, corporate systems and services, strategic investments including its life insurance unit, and Fidelity Capital, which invests in diverse businesses. Hence, in addition to mutual funds, Fidelity offers discount brokerage services, automated bill paying, insurance, annuities, debit cards, ATMs, check-writing services against fund balances, and even some Internet-based investing and home banking services.[6]

In terms of ownership structure, Vanguard is one of the few funds mutually owned by its fund investors, which allows the company to keep its expenses low. In 1998, a number of asset management firms that operated as partnerships took their firms public with initial public offerings (IPOs). These included Neuberger and Berman in New York with $56 billion in mutual funds and Federated Investors with $96 billion in assets under management at that time. This consideration was in response to high stock price multiples over earnings for other publicly traded investment companies, including T. Rowe Price Associates and Franklin Resources.[7] With the convergence of the financial services firm industry and the Gramm-Leach-Bliley (GLB) Act of 1999 allowing securities, insurance, and banking activities to be under the same umbrella, financial holding companies, bank holding companies, insurance companies, and securities firms all own mutual fund subsidiaries as well as separate mutual funds operated by separate investment companies, such as Fidelity Investments and the Vanguard Group.

Changes in the nature of the ownership structure of investment companies managing mutual funds from pure ownership by their investors to external stockholder ownership makes corporate governance issues for mutual funds more complicated. As noted by John C. Bogle, the founder and former CEO of Vanguard, mutual funds are "no-so-mutual" anymore. Hence, there may be conflicting goals for boards of directors of mutual funds in terms of who they are serving, the external stockholders or the fund's customers (the investors in the mutual fund). With the mutual fund scandals of the fall of 2003 and early 2004, discussed in Chapter 1, John Bogle points out that this change in the nature of mutual fund ownership to greater public ownership structure may have created a greater emphasis by boards of directors on maximizing external stockholder profits at the expense of a mutual fund's shareholder customers.[8]

Consolidation, Recent Decline in the Number of Mutual Funds, and Industry Concentration

Mutual funds experienced a large number of mergers in the 1990s. As reported in Pozen (1998), in 1996 alone, 96 acquisitions occurred involving over $530 billion in assets, and the Investment Company Institute (ICI) reported 270 mergers of mutual funds in 2002, with fund families combining funds in some cases where overlapping objectives existed. Other mergers have involved large funds trying to fill out their line of products. Still others involved institutional-oriented firms seeking a greater retail investor distribution. For instance, Morgan Stanley's merger with Dean Witter provided the firm with a broader line of retail mutual funds. Others have been associated with acquisitions of mutual fund companies by large banks, insurance firms, and securities firms, or diverse financial holding companies.

---

6 See James S. Hirsch and Robert McGough. "Fidelity Denies Rumors of Intention to Sell Firm." *The Wall Street Journal* (June 12, 1998), C1, C26. As noted in this article, unlike many other financial institution managers, Edward C. "Ned" Johnson, III, the CEO and chairman of the family-owned firm, believes that public shareholders' emphasis on short-term profits would undermine his philosophy of investing for long-term growth. Desiring to remain independent, Fidelity turned down purchase offers by Travelers and other companies. Fidelity went through a radical restructuring of its ownership in 1995, giving its top fifty executives and mutual fund managers a 51 percent voting stake and reducing the Johnson family's voting stock to 24.5 percent held by Ned Johnson and his daughter, who is also a fund manager. Also see Vanessa O'Connell. "It's a Broker! It's a Banker! It's a Mutual-Fund Group!" *The Wall Street Journal* (July 16, 1990), A1, A5.

7 See Jonathan Clements. "Money Machine: While Brokers Suffer, a Mutual Fund Firm Thrives in Stock Surge." *The Wall Street Journal* (July 16, 1990), A1, A5; Robert McGough. "Neuberger, After Half Century, Considers IPO." *The Wall Street Journal* (April 22, 1998), C1.

8 See John C. Bogle. "Not-So-Mutual Funds." *The Wall Street Journal* (November 14, 2003), A12.

While the number of mutual funds rose every year, with the entrance of new mutual funds in the booming stock market of the 1990s, the total number of mutual funds peaked in 2001 at 8,305 funds and then fell in 2002 to 8,244 and in 2003 to 8,126 funds. The decline in the number of funds reflected primarily a drop in stock funds with a bear market and the merger or liquidation of small stock funds, with a median size of $15 million. Industry assets are fairly concentrated, with the largest five mutual fund complexes holding 36 percent of total industry assets, the top ten, 48 percent, and the top 25, 72 percent.[9]

The Investment Company Institute (ICI) reported the top ten mutual fund companies in terms of net asset rankings as of May 2003 to include Fidelity Investments, Vanguard Group, Capital Research & Management, Merrill Lynch Investment Managers, Federated Investors, Morgan Stanley, Franklin Templeton Investments, Putnam Funds, Dreyfus Corporation, and Schwab Funds/U.S. Trust.[10]

International Diversification

In the late 1990s, many U.S. investment companies and securities firms managing mutual funds entered new markets in Asia and Europe, including Fidelity, Putnam Investments, and Merrill Lynch, where investors often did not commonly invest in mutual funds. A study of mutual fund name recognition in continental Europe found that European mutual funds had name recognition in their own regions but little recognition across borders, while other funds such as Fidelity Investments of the United States and Fleming Asset Management of Great Britain had greater name recognition across countries. On December 1, 1998, Japan, in the process of deregulating its financial markets, began permitting mutual fund managers, banks, and life insurers to sell mutual funds, a privilege previously reserved only for brokers. Roger Servison, a Fidelity managing director, predicted that Fidelity's assets under management in Japan could rise in the next decade to $100 billion, with $10 trillion in savings held by Japanese individuals and more than half in bank accounts paying interest of less than 0.5 percent. Fidelity and other securities including Morgan Stanley Dean Witter, Goldman Sachs, Merrill Lynch, and Citigroup have formed joint ventures with Japanese brokerage firms to sell their funds in Japan. This presented a challenge in educating individual investors on the benefits of diversification in a country where individual stock investments have been generally preferred.[11]

Concept Questions

1 Explain how mutual funds operate as a nexus of affiliates as shown in Figure 18.2. Who is in charge of the affiliates? What are the primary responsibilities of each type of affiliate?

2 John C. Bogle, the former CEO of Vanguard Group, has noted that mutual funds are not really mutual anymore. What form of ownership do most investment companies have? How can a stock ownership form lead to conflicts of interest between external stockholders and the shareholders of a mutual fund?

3 Why and how do investment companies diversify? Give an example.

4 How concentrated is the mutual fund industry? Who are the largest investment companies?

5 Why do you think mutual funds have been more popular in the United States than other countries?

9 Charles A. Jaffe. "Look for Fund Consolidation in '99." *The Denver Post* (January 4, 1999), 3C; Al Lewis. "Invesco Group Wants to Close or Merge 11 Mutual Funds." *The Rocky Mountain News* (March 25, 1999), B2; and Brian Reid, Stephen Sevigny, and Bernhard Silli. "Mutual Fund and Economic Developments in 2003." *Investment Company Institute Perspective*, Investment Company Institute (ICI), Vol. 10, No. 1, 2004, 1–28 (on the ICI Website at *http://www.ici.org*).

10 Ranks from the Investment Company Institute (ICI), at *http://www.ici.org*. Ranks are also cited in the Insurance Information Institute's *Financial Services Fact Book* at *http://financialservicesfacts.org/financial2/securities/mutualfunds/*.

11 Fund experts reported that in 1997 roughly 4 percent of Hong Kong households owned mutual funds, sliding to 2 percent in February 1998, as disappointed investors pulled out money from funds. See Ellen E. Schultz. "Mutual Funds Get Cold Shoulder in Asia." *The Wall Street Journal* (February 17, 1998), C25; Pui-Wing Tam. "New Funds Continue to Appear in Asia." *The Wall Street Journal* (March 25, 1998), C23; Bill Spindle. "Japan's Great Mutual-Fund Battle Begins." *The Wall Street Journal* (November 30, 1998), C25; Margaret Boitano. "Fund Companies' Overseas Ties Can Fray." *The Wall Street Journal* (March 3, 1999), C23; Robert Bonte-Friedheim. "Vanguard to Launch Funds in Europe." *The Wall Street Journal* (April 1, 1998), C27; Sara Callan. "European Funds Lack Broad Recognition." *The Wall Street Journal* (February 17, 1999), C23; and Robert Bonte-Friedheim. "European Funds Prepare Euro Strategies." *The Wall Street Journal* (April 22, 1998), C27.

Types of Mutual Funds

Investment companies are organized to permit investors to invest in a portfolio of assets. There are four broad groups or types of investment companies: open-end investment companies, closed-end investment companies, unit investment trusts, and exchange-traded funds (ETFs).

Open-End Mutual Funds

Open-end investment companies manage the most common type of mutual fund. As noted in Chapter 1, shareholders (investors) put money into funds that are portfolios of securities managed by the investment company. **Open-end funds** continuously offer new fund shares to the public (unless a fund becomes too large and is sometimes closed to new investors). By federal law, they are required to redeem (buy back) outstanding shares at any time upon a shareholder's (investor in the fund) request, at a price based on the current value of the fund's net assets (i.e., the fund's net asset value [NAV] or share price), which is linked to prices of the firm's underlying assets as follows:[12]

$$\text{NAV} = (\text{Mkt. Value in Dollars of Fund's Securities} - \text{Its Liabilities}) \, / \, \text{Number of Investor Shares Outstanding} \qquad [18.1]$$

A mutual fund's NAV is basically the price you can buy and sell the fund for, which is calculated at the end of the day on a daily basis. Here is an example of a mutual fund price quote for Fidelity's Puritan Fund listed by its Fund Family, Fidelity, in *The Wall Street Journal* on April 1, 2004 (p. C10):

Fidelity	NAV	Daily % Return	YTD % Return
Puritan	18.75	+0.1	+2.1

Here the NAV per share is $18.75 with a daily return of 0.1 percent from the previous day and a year-to-date return (YTD) of 2.1 percent. *The Wall Street Journal* and the *New York Times* also provide special mutual fund sections listing phone numbers for funds and more detailed tables on funds including: (1) **Type,** the investment type of the fund, with types listed at the top of each performance report based on the investment style of the fund; (2) **Rating (Rat.),** the performance rating for the past three years as calculated by Morningstar, Inc.; (3) **NAV;** (4) **Total % Return** for the total calendar quarter, the twelve-month and five-year returns including invested dividends; (5) **Exp. Ratio,** the percentage of fund assets paid for operating expenses and management fees and other fees; (6) **Turnover,** the rate at which the fund buys and sells assets (100 percent indicates a fund's trading over a year is equal to its assets); and (7) **Mgr. Yrs.,** the number of years the current manager has managed the fund. The performance for Vanguard's Equity Income Fund, for example, reported in the *New York Times* Mutual Funds Report on Sunday, April 4, 2004, is as follows:[13]

Total % Return

Vanguard	Type	Rat.	NPV	Qtr.	12-mo.	5-Yr.	Exp. Ratio	Turnover	Mgr. Yrs.
EqInc	LV	3/4	22.49	+1.3	+34.5	+3.7	0.45	55	4.3

Vanguard's Equity Income Fund (EqInc) is typed as a large value (LV) fund, a fund that seeks undervalued stock of large firms. Its Morningstar rating is 3 to 4 stars (5 stars is the highest rating and a rating of 1 is poor) for the past three years. The first rating of 3 is the fund's performance against a broad group of funds, and the second rating of 4 is the fund's performance against a narrower investment style group. The Morningstar ratings, to be discussed later in the chapter, are adjusted for risk and investment style. The quarterly return on the fund is 1.3 percent, annual return is 34.5 percent, and five-year return is 3.7 percent (reflecting down market years in the early 2000s). The fund has an expense ratio of 0.45 percent, which is very low, a low turnover of 55, and its fund manager has managed the fund for 4.3 years.

---

12 Information for this section comes from the 1998 and 2003 ICI *Mutual Fund Fact Books* on the ICI Website *(http://www.ici.org);* Fortune (1997); About Mutual Funds Website at *http://mutualfunds.about.com;* and Reid, Sevigny, and Silli. "Mutual Fund and Economic Developments in 2003," 1–27.

13 See *New York Times:* Sunday, Mutual Funds Report, April 4, 2004.

The Open-End Mutual Fund Pricing Process

As noted in the Investment Company Institute (ICI) *Mutual Fund Fact Book* for 2003, the mutual fund pricing process occurs at the end of each business day, generally at the close of the New York Stock Exchange at 4:00 p.m. Eastern Time (ET). The mutual fund obtains prices on the securities it holds from one or several pricing service companies, firms designated to collect prices on a wide variety of securities. If market prices for some securities are not readily available for other assets, they are priced at fair value determined "in good faith" by the fund. Fund accounting agents in turn validate internally the prices to ensure accuracy. Any income and expenses (including fees) is also accrued to the date of the share price calculation, and any change in the number of shares. If an event that is material is likely to affect the value of a security after the closure of the exchange but before the determination of the fund's share price, the fund may deem it necessary to determine a security's fair value "in light of that event." The majority of mutual funds release their prices daily to NASDAQ by 5:55 p.m. ET to have their prices posted in the next day's morning newspapers. Funds also post the prices on the Internet and often offer price information for customers through toll-free numbers.[14]

Returns on Open-End Mutual Funds

NAVs are not typically used as a fund performance measure, since NAVs drop when mutual funds distribute realized capital gains and dividend income each year. Funds are required by law to distribute at least 90 percent of dividends (dividend income plus any net short-term gains, after expenses that the fund paid) and capital gains (net gains from securities in a fund sold that were held more than one year) to investors. The most popular time for fund distributions is in late December, with **record dates,** the official date when a fund determines which shareholders will receive a distribution; the **X-date,** when the fund recognizes a drop in the NAV based on the amount it is going to distribute; and the **distribution date,** when the fund pays out the distribution. Hence, an investor needs to keep detailed records to be able to calculate the return on the mutual fund that includes the distributions that the investor has received. If the investor reinvests dividends and capital gains, the process of calculating the return on investment becomes more complex. The SEC adopted a rule to assist mutual fund investors by requiring that mutual funds disclose standardized after-tax returns for one-, five-, and ten-year periods based on distributions (yield) only and on distribution plus an assumed redemption of fund shares (total return). **Total return** is equal to the change in the value of the investment in a fund for a designated period, including the assumption that any dividends and capital gain distributions are reinvested, as a percentage of the investor's initial investment. **Yield,** in contrast, for a given period, is the income earned in terms of dividends and interest on a fund less any fund expenses for that period as a percentage of the maximum offering price per share on a specified date.[15]

Performance Reports for Open-End Mutual Funds

Measuring the performance of mutual funds is often controversial. Based on a fund's objectives and the risks that it takes, it may have higher or lower returns than general market benchmarks, such as the S&P 500; although the S&P 500 would be a good benchmark for a stock index fund. Morningstar, one of the most prominent independent analysis and rating firms of mutual funds, provides ratings of funds using benchmarks based on a fund's investment style (from one to five stars) that are widely touted by mutual fund companies in advertisements and their Websites. In 2004, Morningstar updated its two annual reference guides, *Morningstar Stocks 500*™ and *Morningstar Funds 500*™, to include corporate governance grades from A to F based on corporate governance practices including director independence, stock options, and executive compensation, among others, as well as strengths and weaknesses of the management team and the consistency of investment manager performance with its designated management style. Morningstar uses both general and narrow fund benchmarks based on investment style. Other benchmarks quoted daily in the financial press include the Dow Jones Industrial Average (DJIA), the Small Company Index Fund (by Vanguard, which tracks the Russell 2000), and indexes by

---

14 See references in Note 12.

15 Ibid.

another prominent global mutual fund research firm, Lipper, a Reuters Company, including the Lipper Index: Europe, the Lipper Index: Pacific, and the Lipper L-T Government Index for Bond Funds. Financial magazines publish annual mutual fund performance reports *(Forbes, Business Week, Money Magazine, Consumer Reports). Forbes,* for instance, gives rankings (from A1 to F), for both up and down markets and risk-adjusted performance measures, along with information on the transaction fees and annual wrap fees (annual fees on top of fund fees for advice, brokerage, and other services on the value of all assets, often 1 percent of assets or more). The American Association of Individual Investors' Quarterly Low-Load Mutual Fund Updates provides detailed information on funds including betas for funds, standard deviations of historical returns for different periods, and average returns during bear and bull markets. Yahoo! Finance *(http://finance.yahoo.com/)* and other online financial services also provide reports and charts on mutual funds on the Web.[16]

Open-End Fund Redemption and Liquidity Needs

Section 22(e) of the Investment Company Act of 1940 (1940 Act) requires that a mutual fund also must make payment of redemptions within seven days except when trading on the New York Stock Exchange is halted or when the Securities and Exchange Commission (SEC) issues an exemptive order to stop trading for a particular firm. Open-end funds often honor redemption requests at the end-of-the-day NAV and cut checks the next day. Since cash receipts from securities sales are often delayed for several days, open-end funds often require liquidity either by holding cash or short-term securities (cash equivalents) or by borrowing from a line of credit with a bank. Hence, open-end funds must have funds available or have borrowing sources to meet liquidity needs. In recent years, open-end funds have had fewer liquid assets, relying more on bank credit lines or other short-term borrowing for liquidity.[17]

Closed-End Funds and Unit Investment Trusts

Closed-end funds had combined assets of $213.97 billion at year-end 2003 for 586 closed-end funds. **Closed-end funds** issue a fixed number of shares that trade over the counter or on a stock exchange. Once funds are issued they are bought and sold in the public markets, and unlike open-end funds, shares are not redeemed by the fund. An investment company manages the fund according to the policies and objectives of the fund including stock, bond, or hybrid funds. Supply and demand determines share prices of closed-end funds, which can be above or below NAV. Closed-end fund shares often trade at a discount, below NAV, and have brokerage commissions attached, so they often offer less attractive net returns than open-end funds but can be traded more frequently. Many closed-end funds are bond, convertible bond, or preferred stock funds, allowing trading of a bond portfolio dedicated to a particular type of bond, such as Muni Bond Funds, High Yield Bond Funds, U.S. Government Bond Funds, or Investment Grade Bond Funds, among many others.[18]

Closed-end funds provide the NAV, along with the most recent market closing price from the exchange in which the securities are primarily traded. Here is an example of the price quotation for a closed-end fund from the *New York Times* Mutual Funds Report for Sunday, April 4, 2004 (p. 40):[19]

Quarterly % Return

Fund	Ticker	Ex.	NAV	Mkt Prc.	Prem./Disc.	NAV	Mkt.	Exp.	NAV Yld.	Mkt. Yld.
Salomon Bros. Fund	SBF	N	14.14	12.14	−14.1	+0.9	+1.1	0.6	+0.91	+1.06

The symbols are given in notes at the bottom of the price page in the newspaper. The fund quote is under General Equity Funds for the Salomon Brothers Fund, which has a ticker symbol of SBF listed on the NASDAQ (N) exchange. The NAV is 14.14, but the market price (Mkt. Prc.) that the fund is selling

---

16 See Morningstar Website press releases *(http://www.morningstar.com)* and Lipper's Website *(http://www.lipperweb.com).*

17 See Pozen (1998) and the 2003 and 1998 ICI *Mutual Fund Fact Books.*

18 See references in Notes 12 and 13.

19 Ibid.

for on the exchange is 12.14, with the fund selling at a discount (Disc.) of -14.1 percent on average. The quarterly return on the NAV is 0.9 percent, while the quarterly return based on the market price is 1.1 percent (assuming reinvestment of dividends). The percentage of fund assets paid for operating expenses (Exp.) in the latest fiscal year is 0.6 percent. The NAV yield (based on dividends paid to investors as a percentage of NAV) is 0.91 percent, while the Mkt. Yld. (as a percentage of market price) is 1.06 percent.

Unit investment companies often issue unit investment trusts (UITs) that offer interests in a fixed portfolio of securities that is held passively for an agreed-upon period of time, whereby assets are distributed among the shareholders. As of February 2004, unit investment trusts had total deposits of $1.13 billion. Real estate investment trusts (REITs) offer shares in real estate investments. Unit trusts may redeem shares at NAV but may only redeem shares in large blocks. Hence, closed-end funds and UITs do not have the liquidity concerns of open-end funds that agree to redeem shares at NAV upon request.[20]

Exchange-Traded Funds (ETFs)

Exchange-traded funds (ETFs) have become very popular in recent years, with assets of $159.53 billion in February of 2004. ETFs trade on the market like closed-end funds do. An investment company with ETFs has shares that are traded during the day on stock exchanges at prices determined by the market. ETF shares are purchased just like stocks from brokers. ETFs are similar to index mutual funds (passively managed mutual funds that contain stocks that mimic a stock index [such as the S&P 500]). ETFs are "securities certificates" that provide a legal right of ownership for a share of the basket of individual securities. ETFs have advantages such as their flexibility of being bought and sold throughout a trading day, that they can be bought on margin, and that traders can take a short position. They also have very low annual expenses. Disadvantages include commissions (like stocks) and bid/ask spreads, since ETFs generally must be bought and sold through a broker. Also, ETFs can potentially trade at above or below the net asset value of their underlying stocks. ETFs are targeted toward active trading, which most open-ended mutual funds discourage. As noted by Dustin Woodard in "What Are Exchange Traded Funds? (ETFs)"on the About Mutual Funds Website *(http://mutualfunds.about.com)*, ETFs have a considerable disadvantage for small investors because of commissions on trades which can eat up returns, especially compared to other passively held open-end stock index funds, such as the Vanguard S&P 500. Over the long run, studies have shown the S&P 500 to have higher returns on average than about 80 percent of funds that are actively managed.[21]

The Creation and Redemption of ETFs

As noted in an article in the Exchange Traded Fund (ETF) Center for Yahoo! Finance on "How ETFs Work," the process of creating an ETF can be complex for a fund manager, including submission of a detailed plan for approval by the SEC. Generally, only large investment company funds experienced in stock index funds have created ETFs (such as the Vanguard Group, Barclays Global Investors, or a stock exchange) since demand for new funds must be created through retail and institutional investors. Also, good relationships with pension funds with worldwide holdings are often necessary to borrow shares for the ETF. The process involves having a specialist put together the basket of stocks, a custodial bank to ensure that the stock basket is representative and to provide safekeeping for share certificates and distribution of ETF certificates to authorized participants. ETFs are passively managed, although sometimes a fund manager may have the authority to use derivatives to track an index. The Depository Trust Clearing Corporation keeps records of transactions, protecting against fraud. Like closed-end mutual funds, shares of ETFs can be freely traded on the market. When an ETF is redeemed, the fund purchases a large block of ETFs and relays it to the custodial bank that redeems it for the individual stock certificates, which are returned to the investors who lent the stocks or they are sold. Fund managers receive fees (often a small portion of the fund's annual assets) and parties fees or smaller asset amounts, often

---

20 Ibid.

21 Ibid and the About Mutual Funds Website *(http://mutualfunds.about.com)*.

paid from management fees. Arbitrage investors purchase ETFs to make profit on discrepancies between ETF prices and the value of its underlying securities. This arbitrage results in ETF prices closely tracking the value of their underlying stocks.[22]

Types of ETFs

ETFs come in different types and have interesting names, with many offered by stock exchanges. Prominent types include Diamonds Trust Series (**DIAMONDS**), which track the Dow Jones Industrial Average; Fixed Income Exchange Traded Securities (**FITRs**), which track various Treasury securities; Holding Company Depository Receipts (**HOLDRs**), which track narrow industry groups of about twenty stocks; **iShares**, a group of index shares ETFs by Barclays Global Investors; **QUBEs**, the NASDAQ-100 Tracking Index Stock (QQQ); **Spiders**, or **SPDRS**, Standard & Poors' Depository Receipts, which track a number of different S&P indexes; **StreetTracks**, issued by State Street Global Advisor, which track a variety of Dow Jones and Wilshire indexes among others; and **VIPERs**, Vanguard Index Participation Receipts, which track several Vanguard index funds. There are many other ETFs including **iShares Morningstar ETFs** (Barclays Global Investors under an agreement with Morningstar, Inc.) to track sixteen of Morningstar's style-based indexes.[23]

Hedge Funds (That Are Not Mutual Funds)

Hedge funds are another popular type of fund (for wealthy investors) that, as noted in a recent article by Dustin Woodard, are often mistaken for mutual funds. Instead, hedge funds are limited partnerships—private unregulated investment funds for wealthy, accredited investors (investors with net worth over $1 million and income greater than $200,000 or jointly greater than $300,000 in the previous past years, with similar expected income the following year). Accredited investors are required to have large minimum investments on average of $1 million and pay typically high fees, such as 1 to 2 percent of assets in addition to about 20 percent or so of profits. Hedge funds typically are not liquid and have strategies that go along with their name of hedging against market downturns, and often make use of derivatives, short selling, and high financial leverage. Hence, they are more risky than mutual funds and some have failed, such as Long-Term Capital Management in 1998. As unregulated funds, hedge funds are not subject to SEC monitoring and reporting. Thus, investors have less information on previous performance to consider. Morningstar in 2001 announced that it would create a global hedge fund and private partnership database to provide better information on hedge funds. Because of the recent growth in hedge funds with some appeals to smaller investors, the SEC has considered whether they should be subject to greater monitoring.[24]

Mutual Fund Families

As reported by Peter Fortune in a comprehensive article on mutual funds in the Federal Reserve Bank of Boston's *New England Economic Review*, the majority of funds in the United States are held by fund groups or families that allow for economies of scale and scope. Investment companies offer a variety of different types of equity, bond, hybrid (both equity and bonds), taxable money market funds, tax-exempt money market funds, among others, as well as annuities and other products. In 2003, the top twenty-five fund complexes held 72 percent of industry assets. Of these fund families, Fidelity has the largest family of funds, with more than 300 Fidelity mutual funds, total assets under management over $880 billion, and more than 19 million customers companywide. In addition to Fidelity, some of the most popular fund families include Vanguard, PBHG Funds, T. Rowe Price, Putnam, Kemper, Scudder Investments, American Century, and Janus Funds.[25]

---

22 Ibid.

23 Ibid.

24 Ibid and Note 16.

25 See Fortune (1997) and Note 12.

Marketing Techniques of Mutual Funds

Fund families use a combination of direct marketing and indirect marketing. With **direct marketing,** investors directly contact the fund through their Internet Websites, use toll-free phone numbers to make investments, or purchase funds through third parties, such as brokers, banks, and life insurance companies who receive a sales commission from the fund. Investment companies also manage pension fund and trust assets. Mutual fund family choices are often offered for investment selections in company 401(k) and other employee-defined contribution benefit plans, and are widely used for individual retirement accounts (IRAs). With **indirect marketing,** funds are sold through brokers at securities firms, banks, insurance, and other financial services firms that refer customers to an investment company's funds in return for fees and/or commissions. Despite the lower cost to the public of directly contacting a mutual fund family (i.e., no brokerage commission or advisory fees), many investors like to go through investment advisers to determine which funds to purchase. As noted in a July 2003 *ICI Perspective* article, distribution channels have changed dramatically and include: (1) the **direct channel;** (2) an **advice channel** offering financial advice and ongoing assistance from financial services firms including banks, insurance agencies, securities firms, and financial planning firms that are compensated by sales loads or asset-based fees; (3) a **retirement plan channel** offering employer-sponsored defined contribution plans purchased through payroll deductions for participants; (4) a **supermarket channel,** which includes discount brokers who offer different mutual funds from a large number of sponsors, often subject to no transaction charges or sales loads; and (5) an **institutional channel,** whereby endowments, foundations, businesses, financial institutions, and other institutional investors carry out transactions directly with mutual funds or through third parties to mutual funds. Studies show that in recent years the advice channel accounted for the largest share of mutual fund assets, 55 percent; then the retirement channel, 16 percent; followed by the institutional channel, 13 percent; the direct channel, 12 percent; and the supermarket channel, 5 percent. However, in a survey where individual investors ranked their primary source of mutual funds purchases, the retirement channel was the chief source (48 percent of those surveyed), followed by the adviser channel (37 percent), then the direct investment channel (10 percent), and finally the supermarket channel (five percent).[26]

Investment Manager Fund Strategies and Types of Equity (Often Called Discover) Funds

Equity fund managers specialize in different investment styles: (1) **value investing**—finding undervalued or overlooked (low price/earnings) large and mid-sized firm stocks, often paying dividends; (2) **growth strategies**—seeking long-term capital appreciation (rarely providing dividends) by investing in more risky, high growth stocks; (3) **income strategies**—seeking high dividend yield stocks; (4) **blend funds** combining growth and value stocks; (5) **specialty fund strategies by market value size**—such as companies based on market capitalization [i.e., **small-cap funds** (less than $1 million with high growth and low or no dividends); **mid-cap funds** (range of $1 billion to $9 billion); and **large-cap funds** (value greater than $9 billion)]; (6) **concentrated specialty funds**—investing in a single industry such as health care or Internet companies; (7) **international funds** investing outside of the United States; and (8) **index fund** (**passive investing strategies** investing in stocks mimicking a stock index, such as the S&P 500). In the late 1990s, index funds with a passive investment strategy, low turnover, and low fund expenses often surpassed the average return of managed funds, with better returns during downturns, although not as high returns in upturns. Different investment styles often fare better or worse depending on the state of the economy.[27]

Other classifications, such as those used by the ICI for equity funds, include: (1) **capital appreciation funds** seeking price appreciation as a key goal including **aggressive growth funds** investing in small, rapidly growing firms; **growth funds** that invest in well-established firms and **sector funds** that invest in firms in related fields; (2) **total return funds** seeking a combination of income and capital appreciation including **growth and income funds** investing in established companies and **income-equity** funds that invest in firms with consistent dividend payments, with income a priority; and (3) **world**

---

26 See Brian K. Reid and John D. Rea. "Mutual Fund Distribution Channels and Distribution Costs." *Investment Company Institute Perspective,* Investment Company Institute, Vol. 9, No. 3 (July 2003), 1–19, and the ICI *Mutual Fund Fact Book, 2003,* which can all be downloaded in PDF form from the ICI Website (http://www.ici.org).

1 What are open-end mutual funds? How is their net asset value (NAV) determined?

2 What are closed-end funds? Unit investment trusts? What advantages and disadvantages do they have compared to open-end funds?

3 How is an ETF created? What are different types of ETFs?

4 What are hedge funds? Why are they not mutual funds?

5 What are mutual fund families, and how are they marketed?

6 What are some different types of investment styles of mutual funds?

7 How is mutual fund performance measured?

equity funds that invest in stocks of foreign countries in emerging markets, global equity, international equity, or regional equity. **Hybrid funds,** investing in mixes of equities, fixed-income securities, and derivative instruments are also categorized as different types including: (1) **asset allocation funds** that invest in precise weightings in different classes of securities including equity, fixed-income securities, and money market instruments to seek high total returns including global asset allocation funds; and (2) **balanced funds** that maintain target percentages in different asset classes including equity and bonds with multi-objectives of preserving principal, providing income, and having long-term growth of both principal and income. **Bond funds** include funds for different durations and investment horizons including tax-free and taxable, while **money market funds** invest in high-grade money market securities with average maturities of ninety days or less, seeking a high level of income but preservation of capital in terms of maintaining a stable share price. Funds also focus on taxable and nontaxable securities. Some fund Websites, such as Vanguard *(http://www.vanguard.com)*, provide a short investor test to determine preferences for risk and return and time horizons and then recommend fund investment styles to meet these preferences.[28]

The Cost of Mutual Fund Ownership

Mutual fund shareholder fees must be disclosed in a standardized fee table at the front of a fund's prospectus. This fee table classifies fees and expenses so that shareholders can see what they will be paying for when purchasing fund shares and can compare these to the investing costs of other funds. Fees include two main categories: shareholder fees and annual fund operating expenses.[29]

Shareholder Fees

In addition to funds being classified as open-end, closed-end, or unit trust, mutual funds are also often classified as **no-load, low-load,** and **load funds.** Load funds are generally funds sold through brokers that have a front-load (upfront) sales charge or a back-end load, charged at the time of the fund's redemption. At times this back-end load is amortized so that it disappears if the fund is not redeemed for several years. The sales charge compensates the financial professional (broker) for this service. A **redemption fee** is paid to a fund to cover the costs (other than sales charges) associated with a redemption. An **exchange** fee may also be charged for a transfer of money from one fund to another fund within a fund family (often exchange fees may kick in after a certain number of free transfers). An **annual account maintenance fee** also is charged by funds to cover costs, such as providing service to customers with low-balance accounts.

---

27 See Note 12.

28 See Note 12 and Vanguard's Website *(http://www.vanguard.com)*.

29 See ICI's *Mutual Fund Fact Book, 2003,* on the ICI Website *(http://www.ici.org)* as well as articles on the Website on fees and expenses including: John D. Rea, Brian K. Reid, and Travis Lee. "Mutual Fund Costs, 1980–1998." *Investment Company Institute Perspective,* Vol. 5, No. 4 (September 1999), 1–11; and John D. Rea, Brian K. Reid, and Kimberlee W. Millar. "Operating Expense Ratios, Assets, and Economies of Scale in Equity Mutual Funds." *Investment Company Institute Perspective,* Vol. 5, No. 5 (December 1999), 1–15; also available at *http://www.ici.org* and About Mutual Funds Website at *http://mutualfunds.about.com.*

Annual Fund Operating Expenses

These fees are associated with the "normal costs" of fund operations and are expenses that are deducted from fund assets before earnings distributions to shareholders. They include: (1) a **management fee,** a fee to the fund's investment adviser for managing the fund portfolio and related services; (2) a **distribution (12b-1) fee** that may be deducted from fund assets as compensation to sales professionals for the provision of advice and ongoing services to mutual fund shareholders for fund marketing and advertising expenses; and (3) **other expenses** that include fees paid to a fund's transfer agent for providing fund shareholder services (i.e., toll-free phone numbers, computerized account services, Website services, record-keeping, printing, and mailing, among other expenses).

The SEC's approval of **Rule 12b-1** in 1980 allows continuing annual charges to cover the cost of sales commissions and other marketing expenses. This approval, in essence, made many previous no-load funds become, in effect, low-load funds. Investors are not directly charged for 12b-1 expenses, but the fee is deducted from fund assets before earnings are distributed. Funds that are direct marketed are more likely to be no-load or low-load funds. The American Association of Individual Investors publishes a *Quarterly Low-Load Mutual Fund Update* four times a year. The SEC limited 12b-1 fees to 1 percent annually, with a 0.25 percent maximum allowed for brokers, with the intention that fees be used for fund advertising to increase fund size and lower costs through economies of scale. However, in practice funds that are closed to new investors have continued to charge these fees to compensate brokers/dealers, and studies show that on average 63 percent of 12b-1 fees have been used to compensate brokers/dealers. Hence, 12b-1 fees have been controversial, being commonly used as a hidden brokerage fee load. The SEC mandates that fund companies clearly list fees in their prospectus, including 12b-1 fees and how they affect an investor's investment.[30]

Fund expenses are important for investors to monitor, because they can significantly lower net returns and result in negative net returns in down markets. The differences between total returns and net returns after fees and loads for major mutual funds can be significant. The twelve-month return as of July 31, 1998, for Fidelity Magellan, for instance, was 19 percent if unadjusted for fees and loads. With these adjustments, annual return of the Magellan Fund net annual return after expenses for this period is about 13.5 percent.[31]

In its most recent study, ICI research found that since 1980, the average cost of equity funds fell by 45 percent, of bond funds by 42 percent, and of money market funds by 38 percent using a total shareholder cost measure (including all major fees, expenses, and sales charges), with lower average costs for larger equity funds (greater than $5 billion), averaging 0.70 percent (70 basis points) versus an average 1.39 percent for smaller funds.[32] In recent years, funds have also increased their minimum investment requirement, with an estimated only 11 percent of funds requiring no minimum and 13 percent, a $500 or less minimum, and 37 percent requiring $501 to $1,000, although minimums are often lower for IRAs and reinvestments.[33]

Risk-Adjusted Performance Measures

The SEC has been particularly concerned about improving descriptions of risk and performance for mutual funds. In response to a request for comments on such improvements, the agency received 3,600 comment letters from investors. Katerina Simmons in the *New England Economic Review* of the Federal

---

30 The SEC's 12b-1 rule permits mutual funds to charge advertising and selling expenses, including sales commissions to brokers, as an annual operating cost against the fund's assets instead of assessing new purchasers. In 1988 the SEC began requiring all funds to provide a hypothetical example of the dollar fees that would be charged on a $1,000 investment earning a 5 percent return over periods of one, five, and ten years. Critics argued that the present value of fees should instead be used. See Fortune (1997) and Pozen (1998). Also see AAII's *The Individual Investor's Guide to Low-Load Mutual Funds* (1999). Also see Fortune (1997). Fidelity, for instance, distributes funds through direct market sales, as well as through brokers, insurance agents, and bank agents, who receive commissions for sales.

31 See Charles Gasparino. "Pain of Mutual-Fund Fees Is More Acute When the Market Is Going Down Than Up." *The Wall Street Journal* (August 25, 1998), C1. Also see John Markese. "How Much Are You Really Paying for Your Mutual Funds?" *AAII Journal* (February 1999), 2–5; and Jonathan Clements. "Selecting a Fund? Expenses Can Be Crucial." *The Wall Street Journal* (July 24, 1991), C1, C10.

32 See Note 28.

33 Ibid, and articles and information on different mutual fund topics by Dustin Woodard on the About Mutual Funds Website at *http://mutualfunds.about.com,* which also lists low minimum mutual funds.

Reserve Bank of Boston examines several of the most commonly used measures, including: (1) the standard deviation of returns; (2) value at risk; (3) the Sharpe ratio; (4) an M-square measure; and (5) the Morningstar return and risk measures, betas, and asset class measures.[34]

Standard Deviation of Returns

The monthly standard deviation of returns (r) is calculated as the square root of [the sum of the squared differences between each monthly return (Ri) from the average monthly return (mean R) divided by the number of observations]. Mutual fund analysts are usually interested in the standard deviation of excess returns over the risk-free rate or some appropriate benchmark index based on a fund's objective, known as its tracking error, which indicates its volatility over the average volatility of the market.

Value at Risk

As noted in Chapter 2, value at risk (VAR) is a popular risk measure, often used to measure a firm's trading risk, for derivatives and other securities. VAR provides an estimate of how much a firm's portfolio can decline with a given probability over a given time period, indicating the likely range of losses. If a 95 percent probability is selected, based on a normal distribution, 95 percent of all observations will occur within 1.96 standard deviations from the mean, with only 5 percent deviating from the mean, that is, 2.5 percent falling below the mean. For instance, if a fund has a mean monthly return of 2.00 percent and a standard deviation of 4.00 percent, its monthly VAR would be 2.00 percent − (1.96)(4.00) = −5.84 percent, or a 2.5 percent probability of losing no more than $58.40 a month for a $1,000 investment. Although VARs are based on historical volatilities, estimated volatilities and correlations can be used. Risk managers also can find a VAR for underperforming a fund's selected benchmark, known as a "relative" or "tracking" VAR.

Sharpe Ratio

To calculate the Sharpe ratio or index, a fund's average excess return over the risk-free rate or an appropriate benchmark is divided by the standard deviation of the fund's excess return. For instance, if the monthly mean excess return of a fund is 1.00 percent and the monthly standard deviation for this excess return is 4.00 percent, the monthly Sharpe ratio is 0.25. To annualize this ratio, the monthly Sharpe ratio can be multiplied by the square root of 12, or 3.46. Multiplying the monthly Sharpe ratio of 0.25 by 3.46, the annualized Sharpe ratio is 0.865. An alternative ratio often used is the Treynor index, which is a fund's average excess return divided by the beta of the fund portfolio. These ratios are measures of a fund's excess return adjusted for risk, providing a method to compare funds with different levels of risk. The Treynor ratio is based on the capital asset pricing model (CAPM), which assumes that investors can achieve any level of risk by investing in the fund with the highest ratio and reduce this risk by investing part of his or her portfolio in risk-free securities or leverage the investment (increasing its risk) by borrowing at the risk-free rate to purchase more of the portfolio. Institutional investors and academics have universally accepted this model, but, as Katerina Simmons notes, the general public and financial advisers often do not understand or use this model.

Modigliani or M-Square Measure

Modigliani and Modigliani (1997; M&M) proposed a different measure that they believed would be easier for investors to understand; often known as the M-square measure, it measures a fund's performance relative to the market in percentage terms defined as:

$$\text{M-Square} = \frac{\text{Fund's Average Excess Return}}{\text{STD of Fund's Excess Return}} \times \text{STD of Index Excess Return} \qquad [18.2]$$

34 The following sections on risk/return measures all come from Simmons (1998). For more detailed information on mutual fund performance and performance rankings, see Treynor (1965); Sharpe (1966, 1992, 1997); Shukla and Trzcinka (1992); Modigliani and Modigliani (1997); Financial Economists Roundtable (1996); Jensen (1968); French and Henderson (1985); Hendricks, Patel, and Zeckhauser (1993); and Lakonishok, Schleifer, and Vishny (1992).

M&M proposed using the standard deviation of the S&P 500 or some other broad-based market index for the second term. The M-square provides a measure equivalent to the return the fund would earn if its risk was the same as the market index. Similar to the Sharpe ratio, the higher the M-square, the higher is the fund's return for any level of risk. For example, if the S&P 500 index's excess return is 25 percent, the fund's average excess return is 15 percent, and the STD of the fund's excess return is 10 percent, the M-square measure is 15 percent / 10 percent $\times$ 25 percent = 37.5 percent. Investors could take on greater debt or financial leverage to increase the STD of the fund's excess return to achieve this 37.5 percent return.

Morningstar Ratings

Morningstar, Inc., publishes its own risk return measures, which are used for its star ratings that have become very popular. Morningstar divides mutual funds into four asset classes: domestic stock funds, international stock funds, taxable bond funds, and municipal bond funds. An excess return is calculated for each fund adjusting for sales loads and subtracting the ninety-day Treasury bill rate. This load-adjusted excess return is then divided by the average excess return for the fund's asset class as:

$$\text{Morningstar Return} = \frac{\text{Load Adjusted Fund Excess Return}}{\text{Average Excess Return for Asset Class}} \qquad [18.3]$$

A measure of downside risk is estimated by counting the number of months that a fund's excess return was negative, summing all negative returns, and dividing this sum by the total number of months over the measurement period. The same measure is calculated for the fund's asset class as a whole. The ratio of the two, Morningstar's risk measure, is as follows:

$$\text{Morningstar Risk} = \frac{\text{Fund's Average Underperformance}}{\text{Ave. Underperformance for Its Asset Class}} \qquad [18.4]$$

To rate funds, Morningstar subtracts the risk score in Equation 18.4 from the return score in Equation 18.3 and ranks funds by this raw rating within their asset class. Stars are then assigned as follows: The top 10 percent rankings receive five stars, the next 22.5 percent four stars, the middle 35 percent three stars, the next 22.5 percent two stars, and the lowest 10 percent one star. Overall rankings are calculated by combining stars that are calculated for three-, five-, and ten-year periods. Category ratings for each fund are also calculated for more narrowly defined fund categories; however, these ratings are not adjusted for sales load and are only calculated for a three-year period. Morningstar has sixteen style-based indexes that are used as benchmarks. Morningstar also has a U.S. Market Index to represent 97 percent of the U.S. market. Katerina Simmons performed a detailed study examining ranking based on these measures, which were highly correlated.[35]

Concept Questions

1 What is the difference among no-load, low-load, and load funds?

2 What are typical types of sales charges for load funds?

3 What are typical annual operating expenses for funds, and how are they deducted?

4 What is the SEC Rule 12b-1 and what are typical 12b-1 expenses for mutual funds? What controversy has occurred in the use by mutual funds of 12b-1 expenses?

5 What information do, respectively, the standard deviation of returns, tracking errors, value at risk, and tracking value at risk tell you about the risk of a mutual fund?

6 What type of information do Sharpe and Treynor ratios, M-square, and Morningstar ratings tell fund managers and fund investors about the risk and return profile for a mutual fund?

35 Ibid. Some analysts have criticized performance indexes for not reflecting particular mutual fund portfolio manager objectives; see Bogle (1994). For instance, value funds often had returns and risks that varied significantly from the market as a whole. Value funds performed very well in the 1980s but not as well as the market during the bull market of the 1990s. Bogle points out that by investing in value funds or a specialty fund, investors need to be aware that they are taking extra risk in accepting a lower level of diversification. Hence, the rewards of investing in such a fund that might rank in the top 10 percent of funds over a given period also implies the risk that they might perform in the bottom 10 percent of funds during a different period.

Mutual Fund Regulations

Mutual funds are subject to strict regulation and oversight by the SEC, which requires complete disclosures to investors in a written prospectus, including the fund's goals, fees, expenses, investment strategies, and risk, and information on purchasing and selling shares. The **Investment Act of 1933** mandates specific disclosures, and the **Securities Act of 1933** sets out antifraud rules covering the purchase and sale of fund shares. The **Investment Act of 1940** requires all funds to register with the SEC and to meet certain operating standards. Section 18 of the 1940 Act also limits the financial leverage of mutual funds with open-end funds not allowed to issue debt securities and only allowed bank loans up to 33 percent of a fund's total assets, as long as assets are greater than three times outstanding loans. In the 1990s, the SEC allowed funds to engage in other types of short-term borrowing (i.e., repurchase agreements, options, writing short futures positions, short sales, and lending securities for short-selling by broker/dealer clients) if approved by shareholders and directors to be put in the fund prospectus. Funds must hold securities (marked to market daily) in segregated accounts that are no less than equal to the value of the liabilities created.[36]

The 1940 Act (subchapter M) specifies the requirement for mutual funds to pass-through distributions of 90 percent of income and capital gains to shareholders to allow these not to be taxed under the Internal Revenue Code. Mutual funds also meet several tests: (1) The **Short 3's Test,** whereby no more than 30 percent of gross income can come from the sale of securities held for less than three months; and (2) **Diversification Tests,** whereby no more than 25 percent of assets can be held in securities of any one issuer for diversified funds, excluding government securities. Also, subject to limitations, at least 50 percent of assets must be invested in securities or cash-equivalents (cash or short-term securities).[37]

For **fund mergers,** the 1940 Act specifies that a change in control of an investment adviser terminates an advisory contract, so to renew a contract the acquirer must have the approval of the independent directors of the relevant funds. However, since an acquiring firm can dismiss directors, it could buy independent directors' approval. Congress in 1970 enacted special rules to ensure that such an acquisition did not impose an "unfair burden" on the involved mutual funds by requiring that a minimum of 75 percent of the fund directors be independent for at least three years following an acquisition.[38]

Mutual Fund Boom and New Regulations in the 1990s

The **National Securities Markets Improvement Act of 1996** transformed the regulatory structure for mutual funds by giving the SEC full regulatory oversight for securities with national versus local markets and also eliminated a previous 1940 Act provision that had prevented mutual funds from investing in shares of other mutual funds, now allowing shares to be issued in "funds of funds." Shares in unregistered private pools, such as hedge funds and venture capital funds, were allowed to be offered in an unlimited amount to "qualified shareholders" (investors with more than $5 million in assets and institutions with greater than $25 million in assets) or a trust established by a qualified investor.[39]

Streamlined Disclosure

With the boom in mutual funds in the 1990s, the SEC was concerned about unsophisticated investors not being aware of specific mutual fund risks. With this in mind, the **modernized Form N-1A,** which went into effect on June 1, 1998, mandated clearer prospectuses for mutual funds, using tables, bullet points, shorter sentences, and an active voice for presentation, leaving more technical information to a separate supplement, so average investors could understand the content. A statement of a fund's

---

36 See the ICI *Mutual Fund Fact Book, 2003 (http://www.ici.org)* and Fortune (1997) and Pozen (1998).

37 Ibid.

38 See Pozen (1998) and Charles A. Jaffe. "Look for Fund Consolidation in '99." *The Denver Post* (January 4, 999), 3C.

39 See Fortune (1997) and Pozen (1998).

objectives and a brief risk/return summary must be included at the start of each prospectus with a narrative risk summary, a bar chart showing annual return over one, five, and ten years contrasted with benchmark indexes, and the highest and lowest return in any one quarter, a table of performance figures, and a fee table. The SEC also cracked down and fined companies that advertised false performance and required that investor-paid fees be deducted from advertised performance data.[40]

The Mutual Fund Scandals in Late 2003 to Early 2004

In light of the Enron and WorldCom scandals that occurred in the early 2000s, passage of the Sarbanes-Oxley Act of 2002 put great emphasis on the role of corporate governance including enhancing independence and responsibilities of corporate directors. At that time there were also criticisms of the independence of mutual fund directors as well. Unfortunately, as noted in a recent article by Phillips (2003), at the same time as directors were criticized, the SEC placed greater reliance on the discipline imposed by directors in areas that could involve potential conflicts of interest. Later in the fall of 2003, mutual fund scandals occurred involving market timing and late trading in violation of statements in fund prospectuses, as well as misuse of 12b-1 fees for purposes other than advertising as the SEC intended.[41]

Market-Timing and Late-Trading Scandals

Since mutual fund NAVs are determined at 4:00 p.m. ET each day, orders to buy or sell funds are held until the end of the day when the closing NAV is determined, discouraging short-term trading. Although market timing is generally infeasible for domestic funds during normal trading hours, it provides an information advantage to more sophisticated investors who may be able to engage in market timing, particularly in the aftermarket. If a mutual fund has a policy against market timing, and it allows sophisticated investors to engage in market timing, it can be accused of violating its fiduciary duty to abide by its policies. Although "late trading" is not supposed to be allowed; often trades made by brokerage firms for 401(k) plans or by other large institutional investors take several hours to process and are allowed to go through despite the before 4:00 p.m. ET deadline. This allows institutional investors to trade on after-closing information, while still getting the "stale" closing NAV price versus a higher or lower NAV based on the new information for the following day. Millions of small mutual fund investors can be hurt by such after-market trades, since this large windfall (e.g., selling at today's higher NAV versus the true NAV the following day)—a gain for an elite investor—must be taken from fund assets, reducing the value of the pool of assets for other investors.[42]

Several U.S. mutual funds, investment banks, and hedge funds were prosecuted by the state and/or SEC for "market timing" and "illegal late trading." Funds involved included several mutual fund giants such as Putnam, Janus, Invesco, Strong Financial Corporation, as well as other smaller fund companies. Mutual funds and securities firm subsidiaries of large financial services firms were also involved including the brokerage firm of Prudential Securities and mutual funds of Bank One, Bank of America, and FleetBoston Financial Corporation. Allegations included secretly promoted arrangements allowing market timing by "favored institutional clients" in return for holding large accounts with the funds that generated fees to management or providing other benefits, such as advertising funds on Websites. In

40 See Pui-Wing Tam. "Mutual Fund Documents Are Simply Put." *The Wall Street Journal* (June 12, 1998), C1; and Edward Wyatt. "Big Changes Expected in the Sale of Mutual Funds." *New York Times* (March 7, 1998), B1.

41 See Richard M. Phillips. "Mutual Fund Independent Directors: A Model for Corporate America?" *Investment Company Institute Perspective*, Vol. 9, No. 4 (August 2003), 1–11 (also on the ICI Website at *http://www.ici.org*); and PowerPoint presentation on the Web, "Mutual Funds in Crisis: Issues for Plan Sponsors and Future Developments—Current and Proposed Changes," by Martha Hutzelman and Ice Miller (February 11, 2004), Ice Miller Legal and Business Advisors. Also see Karen Damato and Judith Burns. "Cleaning Up the Fund Industry." *The Journal Report Mutual Funds: A Quarterly Review, First Quarter 2004* (April 6, 2004), R1; and ICI Mutual Fund Connection: Key Issues at a Glance, "Restoring Investor Confidence: Late Trading and Market Timing Investigations," December 31, 2003 (on the ICI Website, under key issues, *http://www.ici.org*); and "Duties of Fiduciaries in Light of Recent Mutual Fund Scandals." Department of Labor Guidance, Statement of Ann L. Combs, Assistant Secretary, Employee Benefits Security Administration, U.S. Department of Labor (February 17, 2004), 1–2.

42 Ibid, and Joseph Kay. "U.S. Mutual Fund Industry Hit by Fraud Scandal." WSWS News and Analysis: North America (November 10, 2003), 1–6 *(http://www.wsws.org)*; and Press Release, Department of Law, Office of New York State Attorney General Eliot Spitzer, March 15, 2004, "Spitzer, S.E.C. Reach Largest Mutual Fund Settlement Ever" *(http://www.oag.state.ny.us/press/2004/mar/mar15c_04.html)*.

addition to being unfair to smaller investors, arrangements went against statements in prospectuses for funds that "did not permit short term or excessive trading."[43]

Bank of America and FleetBoston agreed to pay a $675 million settlement, in addition to setting new standards for the accountability of mutual fund directors and lowering investor fees by $160 million over the next five years. Other investment banking firms involved in other scandals settled for a total of $1.65 billion as of March 15, 2004, with funds going to a special fund to provide restitution to consumers. An SEC survey indicated that 10 percent of mutual funds may have allowed late trading and 30 percent of thirty-four major brokerage firms helped investors with market timing. Similarly, scandals occurred over misuse of 12b-1 fees for purposes other than advertising a fund and offering lower fees to "elite" investors. In response, CEOs and boards of directors were removed, and, in many cases, rebates given back to investors. Other private lawsuits by investors were also placed against companies accused of "widespread trading abuses."[44]

Proposed New Regulations in 2004 to Prevent Future Abuses

Scandals created a confidence crisis by investors in mutual funds and led to an overwhelming number of new proposals by the different parties in late 2003 and early 2004. However, in April of 2004, after much debate over whether Congress should legislate new laws to prevent abuses or leave this to the SEC, it was deemed unlikely that Congress would legislate reforms. The SEC proposed its own reforms with many aspects of bills proposed by Congress in late 2003 and 2004. To briefly summarize some of the legislation proposed, in late 2003, **H.R. 2420, Prevention of Abusive Mutual Fund Practices** proposed requiring funds to have a chief compliance officer, compliance policies and procedures, and that funds adopt a code of ethics (similar to the SEC's **Mandated Ethical Code for Investment Advisers** passed on May 26, 2004) as discussed in Chapter 17. The Assistant Secretary of the Department of Labor also published a statement emphasizing the role and duty of fiduciaries to select and monitor plan investments, determine if and to what extent improper trading is occurring, investigate the effect of abuses and any actions that should be taken on the plan's behalf, and restrict activities of participants engaging in market timing.[45] The U.S. Senate also introduced **S. 2059, the Mutual Fund Reform Act of 2004,** that included a mandated study of director compensation and independence, specification of fiduciary duties of directors and investment advisers, specification of independent accounting and auditing, internal compliance and control procedures to prevent fraud, cost consolidation and clarity, disclosure of broker compensation and portfolio turnover ratios, prohibition of revenue sharing and soft-dollar arrangements with brokerage houses, prevention of market timing, elimination of "stale prices" by applying and using fair value methods to determine NAV, and Internet investor education and ease of access to the SEC EDGAR database, among other provisions.[46]

SEC Commission Actions

In response to mandates by Congress and a public outcry, the SEC in January 2004 proposed a mandated code of ethics for fund advisers (discussed in Chapter 17), and on February 5, 2004 (with compliance due by October 5, 2004), a proposal requiring registered advisers and investment companies to

---

43 Ibid, and "Janus Nearing Settlement with Regulators." Associated Press announcement, Wednesday, March 24, 2004, 6:26 p.m. ET, on the Yahoo! Finance Website *(http://biz.yahoo.com)*.

44 Ibid, and Brian Witte, Associated Press Writer. "Mutual Fund Fraud Hearing to Begin in Maryland." April 2, 2004, 1:12 p.m. ET on the Yahoo! Finance Website *(http://biz.yahoo.com)*.

45 See CRS Report for Congress, "Mutual Fund Reform Bills: A Side-by-Side Comparison," by Mark Jickling, Specialist in Public Finance, Government and Finance Division, Congressional Research Service, The Library of Congress, Updated December 9, 2003, Order Code RL32157, as on the American Benefits Council Website *(http://www.americanbenefitscouncil.org)*; S. 2059, Mutual Fund Reform Act of 2004 (Introduced in Senate), 108th Congress, 2nd Session, February 10, 2004; American Benefits Council News Advisory, "Council Urges Senate Banking Panel to Take up Alternatives to SEC's 'Hard 4:00 p.m. Rule' for Mutual Fund Trades," March 2, 2004, PR-04/10, on the American Benefits Council Website *(http://www.americanbenefitscouncil.org/newsroom/pr04-10 .html)*; and Investment Company Institute Key Issues, "House Approves Legislation Affecting Mutual Funds," Washington D.C., February 26, 2004, on the ICI Website *(http://www.ici.org/issues)*. Also see Kevin Drawbaugh, "U.S. Congress Folds Tents on Mutual Fund Legislation," Reuters, April 20, 2004, reported on Forbes.com *(http://www.forbes.com)*, and Will Swarts, "SEC Wants to Own Mutual Fund Reform," TheStreet.com, April 28, 2004, 1-3 on the Street.com Website *(http://www.thestreet.com)*.

46 Ibid.

adopt compliance policies and procedures: (1) A fund must have a board-approved chief compliance officer to ensure that funds comply with SEC rules. (2) Procedures must be put in place and be annually reviewed by the board to ensure that funds comply with SEC rules covering portfolio management practices, trading practices, personal trading of the fund, accuracy of disclosures, the safeguard of client assets, record maintenance, marketing services, valuation and fair pricing, privacy of client records, a business continuity plan, oversight of the procedures of service providers, the use of a forward pricing method to process fund shares "to avoid late trading and market timing," and protection of nonpublic information to avoid insider trading. (3) The chief compliance officer will report to and have his or her compensation determined by the board. (4) The board's independent directors are also mandated to meet at least once a year with the chief compliance officer. (5) Copies of compliance policies must be maintained, and it is illegal to coerce or provide undue influence on the compliance officer.[47] The **SEC also proposed changes in regulations** including: (1) a hard trading close by 4:00 p.m. ET to get that day's price; and (2) greater corporate governance that encompasses the following areas: (i) 75 percent of board directors must be independent (prior requirement, 40 percent); (ii) the chairman of the board must be independent; (iii) a self-evaluation for the board must be performed at least annually; (iv) independent directors must have a separate meeting quarterly; (v) independent directors must be able to hire their own staff or outside experts; and (vi) the fund must keep copies of written materials used in considering and approving the fund's annual advisory contract, see the SEC Website (http://*www.sec.gov*, with updates). On May 26, 2004, the SEC approved required ethics codes for mutual funds and disclosure of discounts for large investors.[48]

State Regulators' Mutual Fund Protection Principles

In January 2004, state regulators in North Carolina, California, and New York also asked mutual funds that do business within their states [including mutual funds offered under state and public pension programs, 401(k), 403(b), and 457 plans] to abide by these principles, which include: (1) accurate billing that show shareholders in annual statements the actual charges that have been deducted from their accounts; (2) a reasonable management fee schedule, reasonable volume discount breakpoints, approval by independent directors of fees, and fees disclosed in a fund's prospectus; (3) a board of directors of whom at least 75 percent are independent, a chairman not affiliated with the fund in the past five years, separate meetings by independent directors with the chief compliance officer, and hiring by the board of its own staff or advisers; (4) disclosure of compensation of the portfolio manager or team and its basis in the prospectus and ownership of shares in a fund by the portfolio manager and trading during the past year and sale of funds; and (5) fund disclosures of holdings, trading costs, soft dollars, and professional staff.[49]

Current and Proposed Changes by the Mutual Fund Industry

In addition to Congress and regulators, the mutual fund industry also set up a number of self-regulatory changes and proposals including: (1) that portfolio managers be reviewed by the board of directors for replacement or removal decisions; (2) that the board should review and change as needed inter-

---

1 What does the Investment Act of 1940 require for all mutual funds?

2 What does the National Securities Markets Improvement Act of 1996 require?

3 What additional information is required in fund prospectuses under the modernized Form N-1A?

4 What was illegal about the market-timing and late-trading scandals of mutual funds in the early 2000s? How did this trading hurt millions of small investors?

5 Summarize the general legislative and SEC proposals to prevent future abuses of mutual funds. Which items do you think are most important to prevent future abuses?

---

47 See sources in Note 40 and summary of SEC proposals, "SEC Mutual Fund Initiatives," on SEC Website (http://www.sec.gov).

48 Ibid and Stephen Labaton, "SEC Backs Rules on Fund Ethics and Disclosure," *New York Times*, May 27, 2004, C1, C9

49 Ibid.

nal compliance procedures for funds; (3) that funds should increase their review of market timing and identify any plan participants engaged in this activity; (4) that settlements and discounted fees should be offered to shareholders as compensation for prior practices; and (5) that third-party administrators should potentially be given an earlier closing time, such as 2:00 p.m., with a hard close at 4:00 p.m., with a potential imposition of a 2 percent redemption fee for short-term trades, and increased record-keeping. In October 2003, the Investment Company Institute's Board of Governors adopted two additional governance best practices prohibiting close family members of employees in a fund from serving as independent directors and implementing auditing committee requirements in addition to the Institute's 1999 Advisory Group's Best Practices.[50]

Pension Fund and Mutual Fund Roles, and the Retirement Market

Average life expectancy at birth for Americans has increased from about 47.6 years in 1900 to about 77.2 years today; therefore, individuals have to plan more for retirement income. Because the U.S. social security system is currently underfunded, the majority of workers need to be enrolled in retirement plans other than social security, including profit-sharing plans.[51] Retirement savings come from federal, state and local, and private pension funds; and from personal savings plans, often with savings contributed to tax-qualified plans such as individual retirement accounts (IRAs) and annuities.

In contrast to private plans, which accumulate assets, federal plans, the largest of which is social security, have historically relied on a "pay-as-you-go" system whereby collections from those currently employed are used to pay retirement benefits, and assets under management are quite small in comparison with the number of workers covered. With a large number of Baby Boomers retiring in upcoming decades, and a large social security deficit, there has been much concern and debate on the adequacy of such a system. State and local retirement systems accumulate assets for retirement but differ in many ways from pension funds; they are regulated by different laws than the federal laws that govern private pension plans, so differ from state to state. The following sections focus on private pension plans and tax-deferred personal savings plans, focusing first on the growth in pension plans, ERISA, and types of plans.

Pension Growth and Types of Pension Plans

Following World War II, with firms competing for workers and support from labor unions, companies developed retirement benefits to attract workers, and in 1949, the Supreme Court ruled that pension benefits could be included in collective bargaining agreements, resulting in plans doubling by 1960. As pension plans grew, so did the possibility of sponsoring firms failing to meet their pension obligations, such as the 1964 failure of Studebaker, which left its employees with few or no pension benefits. Congress passed the Employee Retirement Income Security Act (ERISA) in 1974 to prevent fund insolvencies, ensuring that employers work toward **full funding,** the equality of pension assets and accrued liabilities.[52]

Retirement plans offered by firms are generally classified as either **defined benefit (DB)** or **defined contribution (DC)** plans. DB plans promise a specified benefit or income stream during retirement, giving the employer the responsibility for making adequate contributions based on the age of the plan participant, the level of benefits promised, and the plan's expected investment returns, and taking the

---

50 Ibid, and see Investment Company Institute Website *(http://www.ici.org)*, and ICI Statements and Publications Archive, "ICI Board Recommends Two New Governance Standards: Urges Universal Adoption of 17 Best Practices for Mutual Fund Directors," Washington, D.C., October 7, 2003 *(http://www.ici.org/statements/nr/2003/03_news_best_practices.html).*

51 See Steinberg and Dankner (1983) and *Life Insurance Fact Book,* 1998, 2003, Washington, D.C.: American Council of Life Insurance.

52 Besides ERISA, the Multiemployer Pension Plan Amendments Act of 1980 affects plans jointly sponsored by more than one employer. As noted in Chapter 3, ERISA set standards for 100 percent vesting of benefits for most employees after fifteen or fewer years of service; employees are entitled to vested benefits even if they leave the employer before retirement. ERISA also requires that fiduciaries make decisions for plans based on the prudent man rule, which requires a manager to make decisions with the same care and judgment that a prudent individual would use in handling personal investments. ERISA, however, did not place requirements on the level of benefits promised by an employer or on the dollar amount of employer contributions. Nor did ERISA require employers to establish pension plans. Rather, the intent is to protect employee interests once a plan has been established and benefits defined. Interpretations of ERISA's fiduciary requirements and the impact of ERISA are discussed in Cummins (1980), Pozen (1977), Ambachtsheer and Ezra (1998), and Logue and Rader (1998).

investment risk. A DB pension plan is fully funded if the present value of its assets equals the present value of its future pension obligations (pension liabilities) minus the present value of future contributions, known as its **funding target.** Since the total amount of the fund's liabilities are not known with certainty, the fund's liabilities are estimated using actuarial methods based on the actuarial assumptions including the retirement age of covered employees, their expected salaries at retirement, how long they will live after retirement, and the interest rate that will be earned on assets (used as the discount rate to find the present value of pension fund liabilities). Employer contributions are based on these calculations. A major question in the management and regulation of defined benefit plans is whether an employer's contribution to the fund is sufficient to meet future pension liabilities. ERISA established the **Pension Benefit Guaranty Corporation (PBGC)** to assure within limits the payment of up to 85 percent of vested benefits if a defined benefit pension fund fails. The PBGC is supported by annual premiums based on the number of participants covered. If a plan is terminated, the PBGC becomes the trustee, taking control of the fund's assets and using them to pay as large a portion of the basic vested benefits as possible. The sponsoring company of a terminated plan may be held liable for unfunded benefits based on a formula established by Congress in the Single Employer Pension Plan Amendment Act of 1986.[53]

With a DC plan, in contrast, the per-employee contributions made by the employer are specified, but the amount of retirement income generated is not defined or guaranteed. Contributions are passed on to employees who have choices to invest their funds in a choice of mutual funds, annuities, or other pension plan accounts. The employee is responsible for watching his/her retirement account. Hence, an employee's retirement income will depend on the fund's investment returns and the age and life expectancy of the plan's owner at retirement. Employees make the mutual fund choice and take on all of the investment risk. Often employers provide educational seminars for their employees to help them make the best choice. In addition to DB and DC plans, employer-sponsored retirement plans include **profit-sharing plans,** and **401(k), 403(b), 457,** and other similar plans. The 401(k) is a defined contribution employer-sponsored retirement savings program. Employers generally provide a choice of mutual funds in which employees may choose to invest. As of 2003 employees are allowed pretax contributions up to $12,000. The 403(b) plans under the U.S. Internal Revenue Code for employees of a public school system or qualified charitable organization allowed pretax contributions also up to $12,000. The 457 plans allow deferred compensation by employees of state and local governments and certain tax-exempt organizations.

ERISA also allowed individuals to set up their own **individual retirement accounts (IRAs)** if no private pension plans were available where an individual worked. As of 1982, the Economic Recovery Act of 1981 extended the eligibility for IRAs to persons covered by employer pension plans, with tax benefits associated with IRAs later limited under the Tax Reform Act of 1986. The Taxpayer's Relief Act of 1997 created the **Roth IRA,** which allows anyone to make a contribution regardless of whether they actively participate in a retirement plan. **Keogh or H.R. 10** plans allow self-employed individuals and proprietors of small businesses to set up individually defined contribution plans for themselves and their employees. The **Small Business Jobs Protection Act of 1996** also created simplified retirement plans: **SIMPLE-IRAs** and **401(k)** plans for businesses with 100 or fewer employees. About twenty years ago, most employer retirement plan contributions went to DB plans; today, however, the majority of contributions go to DC plans. As reported by the ICI in a recent article on mutual funds and the retirement market in 2002, at the end of 2002, federal and private defined benefit plans held 24 percent of U.S. total retirement market assets, while defined contribution plans held 21.5 percent, IRAs 23 percent, state and local government employee retirement funds 20 percent, and annuities 11.5 percent. Annuities provide a specific payment of money for a given fixed period, generally monthly, either fixed payments or with variable rate annuities, variable payments based on the return of underlying portfolio assets backing the annuity. A hybrid annuity is an equity index annuity that guarantees a minimum

---

53 In the late 1980s, similar to today, the PBGC was in poor financial condition with a deficit of almost $4 billion. After Congress raised insurance premiums, the deficit fell to about $1.5 billion by the end of 1987, when Congress again acted to assist the PBGC. In 1988 the premium structure was strengthened by another increase in the base rate, plus the ability to charge a risk-based premium related to a plan's unfunded vested benefit obligations. The PBGC also gained more hard-to-recover costs from firms terminating pension plans, even if the firms were in bankruptcy proceedings. For example, in 1990 the Supreme Court ruled that a firm could not transfer its existing pension liabilities to the PBGC, only to replace it with a new plan assuming future, not past, obligations. The PBGC has difficulties raising premiums for insurance, because profitable firms could discontinue their company-sponsored retirement plans to avoid the escalating cost of PBGC insurance, and riskier plans may not be able to pay higher risk-based premiums [see Abken (1992); Estrella and Hirtle (1988); Warshawsky (1988); Buynak (1987); Bodie (1985); and Munnell (1982)].

return, along with the opportunity to benefit from rises in the equity index. Annuity sales at the end of 2002 were about $13 billion. For fixed annuities the majority of sales are made by insurance agencies and banks, while the majority of variable annuities are sold by insurance agencies and securities firms.[54]

The Role of Mutual Funds in Managing Retirement Plan Assets

At year-end 2002, U.S. retirement market assets were about $10.2 trillion, and mutual funds maintained a 21 percent share of the market (about $2.1 trillion). Pension funds, insurance companies, banks, and securities firms held the remaining $8.1 trillion. The percentage held by mutual funds is a remarkable increase from only a 5 percent share in 1990 up to a peak of 22 percent in 1999. About 51 percent of mutual fund retirement assets are in employer-sponsored defined contribution plans [32 percent in 401(k) plans, 9.1 percent in 403(b) plans, and 8.3 percent in other retirement plans], and 49 percent of mutual fund retirement assets are in IRAs. In terms of total IRA assets held by financial institutions, mutual funds also held the largest share of 46 percent, followed by 34 percent for securities held in brokerage accounts, 11 percent held in bank and thrift deposits, and 5 percent by life insurance companies. Fifty-two percent of the mutual fund IRAs were held in equity funds, 17 percent in money market funds, 14 percent in bond funds, 9 percent in hybrid funds, and 8 percent in foreign equity funds. Mutual funds' share of the employer-sponsored pension market rose from 2 percent in 1990 to 13 percent at year-end 2002, accounting for $1.1 trillion of the about $7.9 trillion employer-sponsored pension market.[55]

Management Issues in Defined Benefit Plans

Although DC pension plans have dramatically increased in the United States (managed by mutual fund companies, insurance companies, commercial banks, and other institutions as chosen by individual employees based on opportunities offered by employers), about 24 percent of pension assets remain in DB plans, in which the firm agrees to provide a given retirement benefit to employees at retirement, and the firm takes on all the investment risk. Key issues for pension fund managers include (1) the proper pension contract between all plan stakeholders, (2) the measurement of performance after adjusting for risk and management costs, (3) active versus passive investing, (4) the optimal allocation for pension assets, (5) the use of smoothing techniques be used, and (6) the ownership of surplus pension assets. Although these issues can easily cover volumes, they are briefly discussed in the following sections.[56]

What Is the Pension Contract Between All Stakeholders?

As Ambachtsheer and Exra (1998; A&E) point out in an excellent book, *Pension Fund Excellence*,[57] pension managers need to determine whose goals they are maximizing in a DB plan. The employer is taking the investment risk, but higher returns on investments can help maximize the shareholder wealth of the firm, since lower firm contributions will be needed with higher investment income. In contrast, a pension manager may want to invest in safer securities that have lower returns, resulting in the need for higher contributions by employers, creating an agency problem. Investment returns on average contribute about 80 percent to pension wealth and contributions only about 20 percent for firms in North America, with variations during bear and bull markets; hence, investment returns determine not only wealth available for employees but also corporate profitability since lower contributions will be

54 See *Life Insurance Fact Books* (1998, 2003); *Mutual Fund Fact Books* (1998, 2003); Pozen (1998); "Mutual Funds and the U.S. Retirement Market in 2002," *Fundamentals: Investment Company Institute Research in Brief*, Vol. 12, No. 1 (June 2003), Washington, D.C.: Investment Company Institute *(http://www.ici .org)*; Insurance Information Institute, *Financial Service Facts (http://financialservicesfacts.org/financial2/asset/mutualfunds/)*; and PBGC Releases, Fiscal Year 2003 Financial Results, Pension Benefit Guaranty Corporation News, News Release, January 15, 2004 *(http://www.pbgc.gov/news/press_releases/2004/pr04_20.htm)*

55 Ibid.

56 Ambachtsheer and Ezra (1998) and Logue and Rader (1998) for an excellent and detailed discussion of these and other issues. This section summaries issues discussed in detail in these two sources.

57 See Ambachtsheer and Ezra (1998).

required if the firm's pension fund investment portfolio does well. As A&E observe, if fiduciaries consider stockholders as stakeholders, they should try to maximize returns for a pension fund, subject to risk and cost considerations.[58]

Pension Fund Performance Adjusting for Risk and Management Costs

A&E point out that the choice of an asset mix policy and the way in which such a policy is implemented depend on a number of different considerations, including the nature of the pension liabilities, risk tolerance of managers, the funded status of a pension plan, the prospects for long-term capital markets, and current perceptions for the standard asset mix of pension funds. They suggest using a risk-adjusted net value added (RANVA) approach to determine the performance of a fund which is equal to the gross annual return less the expected annual compound return for a passively managed (index fund) benchmark less the average extra cost of active management less the average risk penalty for active management risks. For instance, they note that in the early 1990s, ninety-eight pension funds in North America had a 10.7 percent gross return. When a RANVA was calculated (10.7 percent gross return less the 10.7 percent average return for a passive index fund less a 0.2 active management cost less a 2.3 percent risk premium), however, it was only on average −2.5 percent, suggesting that passive management (using an index fund) would have been better.[59]

Active or Passive Asset Allocation Management

As noted in the RANVA calculation, it might be better to invest in an index fund to avoid the higher costs and risks of active management. However, as A& E and Logue and Rader (L&R) in another excellent book, *Managing Pension Plans,* (1998) point out, sometimes boards of directors of pension funds might object to a passive index strategy that involves infrequent monitoring as a lack of duty. Also, choosing the right index includes estimating the costs of maintaining the fund and whether it has the proper risk/return mix for the pension fund and meets the fund's objectives.[60]

What Is the Optimal Allocation for Pension Assets?

L&R point out that pension funds have a broad choice of assets, from investing in indexes for different asset classes to investing in fixed income securities, preferred stock, common stock, or other assets. Other assets that a fund might invest in include emerging market stocks, limited partnerships with small firms, venture capital real estate, oil and gas, commodities, derivatives, managed futures, and market-neutral types of portfolios. The advantages of private equity market investments are higher potential returns, but fund managers must also consider the high costs in terms of greater risk from both a liquidity and default perspective. Funds may also receive greater total fund diversification with such private investments.[61]

Theoretical studies, including Sharpe (1976) and Harrison and Sharpe (1983), propose that DB pension plans, because they are partially insured by the PBGC, should take on more risky assets, holding the majority of their investments in stock. From the viewpoint of stockholders, because returns on stock are on average higher, if funds are invested in stock, the firm will not have to make as large a contribution to plans, maximizing shareholder value. Alternatively, theoretical arguments by Black and Dewhurst (1981) and Tepper (1981) contend that the firm should sell any equities held by the pension fund and take the money from the sale and buy risky bonds. The firm should then borrow from the fund and use the proceeds to buy stock for the firm's own account because stock is a tax-advantaged investment to the firm (70 percent of dividend income is excludable). In this way the firm achieves a type of tax arbitrage by using tax-deductible contributions to the pension fund in order to purchase a

---

58 Ibid.

59 Information in this section summaries a much more detailed discussion of RANVA by Ambachtsheer and Ezra (1998).

60 See sources in Note 55.

61 Ibid.

tax-advantaged investment for the firm.[62] From a more realistic standpoint, Logue and Rader point out that asset allocation generally should reflect a firm's financial condition and characteristics of a DB plan, with studies showing more profitable plans taking on a greater percentage of equity and more risky firms taking on a greater percentage of debt for plans. Similarly, studies show relatively new plans and DB plans to hold more equity in their portfolios. With bull markets and pressure for funds to perform, allocations for stock have increased in recent years. At the end of 2002, defined benefit pension plans had held 43 percent equity, 30 percent bonds, 12 percent other, 10 percent cash-type assets, and 5 percent mutual funds. In contrast, defined contribution plans held 39 percent equity, 22 percent mutual funds, 21 percent other, 11 percent bonds, and 7 percent cash-type assets.[63]

Other considerations involved in active asset management include investment style, management fees, derivatives, rebalancing, evaluation of money managers, and whether tactical asset allocation should be used. As noted in discussing mutual funds, different portfolio managers have different investment styles or expertise in some market sectors that entail more or less risk. For instance, an aggressive equity growth style entails greater risk than a balanced approach focusing on income and growth. Bond management styles for domestic or international bonds include true trading approaches, in which managers attempt to find under- or overvalued bonds, and structured bond portfolios, in which managers adjust a portfolio in response to expected changes in interest rates or other market conditions. Other investment styles pertain to special classes of assets, including leveraged buyout funds, real estate funds, commodities, venture capital, managed futures, and market-neutral strategies. As L&R point out, pension fund managers must determine which if any of these strategies are appropriate, particularly if funds are outsourced to other money managers.[64] Management fees are also a significant consideration with, as L&R note, active management fees for a pension fund averaging about 50 basis points whereas passive index fund fees for broad market index funds often average about 2 to 10 basis points and active index funds about 20 to 40 basis points. Mutual funds and other funds for managing employee pension plans have higher active equity fund expense ratios, averaging 100 basis points. Thus, pension managers need to monitor fees carefully as part of their due diligence.[65]

Pension funds' use of derivatives has been controversial since ERISA discourages the use of derivatives for speculation. Also, some huge investment losses have occurred for funds, including Orange County's fund, which used derivatives to make bets on interest rates. Policies must be put in place and implemented for how derivatives will be used for hedging or enhancing returns for risk management purposes and monitoring will be done of derivative exposures. Managers must also understand the payoff structures and risks entailed upon undertaking different derivative positions.[66] **Managed futures** are baskets of commodity and financial futures held by an institution not for hedging purposes but for investment purposes, generating their own return-risk contribution to a fund's performance. Managed futures attracted attention in 1991 when a conservative public fund, the Virginia Retirement System, first announced it was committing at least $100 million of assets to managed futures. The managed futures portion of a fund may consist of a wide variety of short and long positions in a wide variety of derivatives, without regard to the remaining composition of the fund's assets. Managed futures often have been found to have a negative correlation with other assets in a fund's pension plan, providing potential diversification without incurring the liquidity risk associated with other assets used for diversification, such as real estate. Critics point to the complexity of managed futures in multiple markets and to the additional costs, either in fees to hire new futures managers or in training existing

---

62 This overview of studies summarizes major points made by Logue and Rader (1998). Also see Ippolito (1985, 1986), Sharpe (1976, 1987, 1990, 1992); Harrison and Sharpe (1983); Black and Dewhurst (1981); and Tepper (1981).

63 These points come from Logue and Rader (1998). For a detailed discussion of previous studies, see their excellent book *Managing Pension Plans*. For statistics, see sources in Note 53. Pension funds have also been active in allocating a greater percentage of assets to real estate investments, although this has still been a small percentage of pension fund assets, about 2 percent. Critics have been concerned about fund managing entering areas where they have little expertise. The downturn in real estate in the late 1980s and early 1990s deterred some pension funds from further investing, although with an uptrend in real estate in the late 1990s, concerns have been expressed in the financial press again. See Richard D. Hylton. "How Real Estate Hit Pension Funds." *Fortune* (December 14, 1992), 123–131; Rosen (1982); Louargand (1992); and Bajtelsmit and Worzala (1995).

64 See Logue and Rader (1998) and Bogle (1994).

65 See Logue and Rader (1998). Also see "Institutional Investment Management: A Comparison of Portfolio Management Expenses of Mutual Funds and Defined Benefit Pension Plans," *Fundamentals Investment Company Institute Research in Brief*, Investment Company Institute, Vol. 12, No. 5 (November 2003) (also on the Web at *http://www.ici.org*).

66 Ibid.

managers. They also worry that the higher return on managed futures does not adequately compensate for the volatility in futures positions.[67]

Another important policy question for pension managers is when **asset rebalancing** should occur (such as when returns are outside a desired range by 5 or 10 percent), and whether rebalancing should occur once a year or over a shorter interval. Also, can futures or options be used to achieve rebalancing? The cost of rebalancing in terms of transaction costs and time and effort need to be weighed against the benefits.[68] Similarly, there are questions whether a fund should be outsourced, which includes considerations of the manager's benchmarked performance, investment style, and risks taken on. As Bogle (1994) points out, different categories of funds have different strategies and may perform differently in different markets. A value fund, for instance, which attempts to find undervalued stocks by focusing on stocks with above-average yields and below-average price-earnings ratios, should be judged against other value funds, rather than a market benchmark. A&E note that too many fiduciaries depend on ranking lists published in newspapers or industry journals to compare managers with completely different management styles and may invest in a particular substyle that happened to do well in one particular year. Finding the best benchmark can be problematic. When adjusting for risk, pension fund managers have used risk/return measures similar to those discussed for mutual funds, including the M-Square method and Sharpe and Treynor indexes.[69]

Some funds have used an active management strategy known as **tactical asset allocation,** in which money managers try to make timely movements among stocks, bonds, and cash based on complex quantitative models. These techniques were successful in shielding some funds from the 1987 crash but did not perform well during subsequent periods. In fact, comprehensive studies of pension fund performance indicate that high turnover and frequent reallocation of assets significantly hurt performance. Studies suggest that fund managers are better at selecting individual stocks than at timing the market, suggesting that tactical allocation might not be a successful strategy.[70]

Use of Smoothing Techniques

In contrast, some pension fund managers may want to use **smoothing techniques** to reduce the plan's risk, although at the expense of higher potential returns. One smoothing technique is to use guaranteed investment contracts (GICs), in which a pension fund contracts with a life insurer to earn a fixed rate of return over a specified period, in which a lump sum is invested in return for a fixed annuity return. Although GICs are designed to reduce uncertainty in pension fund earnings, they are not risk-free, since the guarantee is only as sound as the financial condition of the life insurer. Even when default risk on GICs is not high, interest rate risk can be a problem. If interest rates rise after a GIC contract is negotiated with an insurer, pension funds with a large volume of GIC investments are not able to profit from higher market yields.[71] Alternatively, **dedicated bond portfolios** are portions of bond portfolios that are designated to be immunized from changes in interest rates. The idea is to hold a portfolio of bonds whose present assets move exactly as the present value of the projected benefit obligation for the pension plan. To do this a fund sponsor matches the duration of the bonds to the holding period for the pension obligation. As L&R note, a dedicated portfolio technique works relatively well in immunizing a bond portfolio against interest rate risk, but if pension liabilities change, the fund could still be at risk and have insufficient returns to match pension liabilities. Also, the fund has the opportunity

---

67 See Stanley W. Angrist. "Virginia's Pension Plan Earmarks $100 Million for Futures Trading." *The Wall Street Journal* (April 26, 1991), C1, C5; "Futures Shock." *The Economist* (August 8, 1992), 69; Chicago Mercantile Exchange, "Roundtable for Pension Plan Sponsors on the Use of Managed Futures," 1991; and Chicago Board of Trade (1992).

68 See Logue and Rader (1998).

69 See Bogle (1994), Ambachtsheer and Ezra (1998), and Logue and Rader (1998).

70 See Robert A. G. Monks. "How to Earn More on $1 Trillion." *Fortune* (September 1985), 98–99; "The Forbes/TUCS Institutional Portfolio Report." *Forbes* (February 23, 1987), 156–157; and Lakonishok, Schleifer, and Vishny (1992). Also see Coggin, Fabozzi, and Rahman (1993); Berkowitz, Finney, and Logue (1988); James A. White. "Asset Allocators Long for Glory Days of 1987." *The Wall Street Journal* (May 16, 1989), C1, C23; and Gary Weiss. "Index Funds: Getting More Bonds for the Buck." *Business Week* (September 21, 1987), 104. Despite large support for indexing, surveys report that 89.9 percent of pension fund managers believe they can beat the market, regardless of evidence to the contrary. See "The Abiding Faith in Active Management." *Institutional Investor* 20 (May 1986), 97, 100.

71 See Robert L. Rose. "GICs: Popular, Safe—But Are They Smart?" *The Wall Street Journal* (March 5, 1986), 33; and Larry Light, et al. "Are You Really Insured?" *Business Week* (August 5, 1991), 42–48. Ambachtsheer and Ezra (1998, p. 189) report that for defined contribution plans in the late 1990s, the use of GICs as an investment choice by employees had fallen, with assets moving more into stocks and a balance asset mix.

cost of having been able to make higher returns without the immunization.[72] **Portfolio insurance or insured asset allocation** attempts to maintain a basic asset value for a portfolio. Above this basic asset value, the portfolio manager may take on additional risks, such as risky assets proportionately to this basic value cushion. For instance, if stock prices, with stock as a risky asset, are rising, additional stocks can be purchased. But, if stock prices are falling, consuming the cushion above the basic asset value, stocks should be sold to reduce this risk exposure. L&R point out that portfolio insurance was widely used by institutional investors in the mid-1980s, but during the October 1987 stock market crash, the trading strategies that it relied on could not be executed, reducing the effectiveness of this strategy, but in stable markets portfolio insurance can be useful. Hedging can also be done using derivative positions for a portion of the portfolio to offset a potential loss anticipated if rates or prices move the wrong way for securities in a fund's portfolio.[73]

Who Owns Pension Surplus Assets?

During the mid-1980s, the relationship between fund performance and corporate sponsors achieved a new dimension. As the economy strengthened and financial assets rose in value, a larger number of pension funds became overfunded, that is, the value of assets exceeded the estimated pension obligations, and the fund accumulated net worth, or a surplus of assets over liabilities. Some corporate executives took the position that any fund value in excess of the obligations to employees should accrue to the firm's shareholders in a more direct fashion than any considered thus far. By terminating an overfunded plan, the corporate sponsor could immediately capture the after-tax value of the excess assets. The terminated plan could be replaced by an identical plan or a defined contribution plan or by no plan at all with the purchase of annuities from an insurance company or other financial institution to fulfill the firm's previous obligations.

Firms with large plan surpluses became merger targets as well, whereby an acquirer would later terminate the plan of the acquired firm and use the recaptured surplus assets from the plan to finance the merge, such as when Carl Icahn and TWA acquired Ozark Airlines in 1986, where two of Ozark's pension plans were terminated, with a surplus recapture of $26 million.

In response to such abuses, Congress passed a bill to discourage surplus recaptures by charging an excise tax of 50 percent of the amount of the surplus that is withdrawn that reverts to the employer. Surpluses can also only be withdrawn if a plan is terminated. If an amount equal to a minimum of 20 percent of the reversion is first utilized to provide pro rata improvements to accrued benefits, or at least 25 percent of the terminated plan's excess is transferred to a replacement plan, the excise tax falls to 20 percent. These new regulations provided an impetus for corporate sponsors not to build up a surplus, such as reducing contributions if they are not needed.[74]

Pension Plan Underfunding and the Pension Funding Equity Act of 2004

The adequacy of contributions also depends on the actuarial assumptions, including the expected retirement age of covered employees and how long they live after retirement, and the discount rate used to find the present value of future liabilities. Similarly, it depends on the expected yield on the fund's assets over time. The net position of a defined benefit plan as over- or underfunded is equal to the present (market) value of its assets less the present value of its pension liabilities (future pension obligations). As noted earlier, actuarial assumptions are used to determine a fund's expected pension obligations. Like life insurance actuaries, pension actuaries are cautious, preferring to err by overestimating

---

72 See Logue and Rader (1998). See Chapter 16 for a detailed discussion of the use of duration for immunizing a dedicated bond portfolio.

73 See Logue and Rader (1998).

74 See Michael Tackett and Christopher Drew. "Pension Funds Become Bonanza for Companies." *Chicago Tribune* (December 4, 1989), Section 1, 1, 8; and Roger Thompson. "The Battle over Pension Surpluses." *Nation's Business* (August 1989), 66–67. Some state governments have raided their employees' pension funds, too, to balance operating budgets. See Alan Deutschman. "The Great Pension Robbery." *Fortune* (January 13, 1992), 76–78. See Logue and Rader (1998) for current rules and Ambachtsheer and Ezra (1998). Despite laws that discourage firms from terminating pension plans and taking pension assets, the issue of who is entitled to surplus pension assets remains controversial. See, for instance, Frances A. McMorris. "Sunbeam Unit Is Entitled to Surplus in Pension." *The Wall Street Journal* (April 5, 1999), B2.

future obligations rather than by underestimating them. When pension fund actuaries notify the corporate sponsor that a plan is overfunded, contributions may decrease, subsequently affecting pension fund management. This can cause problems and lead to underfunding later. For example, the stock market surge and falling interest rates between 1982 and 1986 increased the value of pension fund assets, resulting in some plans changing actuarial assumptions including an increase in the expected return assumption used as a discount rate to calculate pension liabilities, reducing the present value of liabilities. Accordingly, some corporations reduced contributions or terminated their pension plans to capture the excess assets, and later this came to haunt them as funds became seriously underfunded. In the early 2000s with low investment returns on assets with low interest rates on bonds and a fall in the stock market during 2001 to 2002, many DB pension plans became underfunded, creating a pension fund crisis continuing in 2004. Low interest rates in the early 2000s contributed to this underfunding, since a low investment rate (expected return assumption on investments) used to find the present value of pension obligations leads to large future pension obligations and, hence, more funds that must be set aside by employers for pension funds. In 2004, the required rate was linked to the thirty-year Treasury bond, which was at a very low level and, as noted in the opening quotations, on average defined benefit pension plans were severely underfunded. In 2004, Congress passed the Pension Funding Equity Act of 2004, which provided temporary relief for many pension plans by: (1) replacing for two years the thirty-year Treasury bond rate used to calculate employer's contributions to pension plans with a long-term corporate bond rate; (2) providing a temporary relief from corporation's having to pay deficit reduction contributions; and (3) bringing target relief to multiemployer plans. The relief was only for 2004 and 2005 to help firms recover from a temporary crisis until a long-term solution could be arranged. The bill also helps to keep the PBGC solvent.[75]

In addition, pension fund managers and officers of companies with DB pension plans faced increased liability for lawsuits under ERISA, in the wake of the huge losses for Enron's pension funds. Under the current provisions of ERISA, personal liability of fiduciaries cannot be contracted or delegated away even if the exposure to risk was not understood. Hence, litigation concerning employee benefits has become more common and fiduciary liability insurance may be necessary for those administering a pension plan against "breach of duty."[76]

The Pension Fund Crisis in 2004

The failures of Enron and WorldCom and their pension plans in the early 2000s resulted in huge pension losses for employees in these companies. Enron's pension plan was heavily invested in its own company stock. In July 2002, the Pension Security Act was put in place as part of the Sarbanes-Oxley corporate accountability law, which would help to prevent abuses when pension funds were invested in company stock. The act mandates that firms must give employees quarterly benefit statements including information about accounts, the value of their assets, their rights to diversify, and the importance of maintaining a diversified portfolio. Provisions also prevent company insiders from selling their own stock during blackout periods when employees aren't allowed to make changes in their 401(k) accounts and to require pension plan administrators to notify workers thirty days before the beginning of any blackout periods.[77]

In 2003 there was a rash of company and pension fund failures, and in 2003 and early 2004, significant underfunding of a large number of DB pension plans with a previous stock market downturn and

---

75 See Ezra and Ambachtsheer (1985); Light (1989); Warshawsky (1988); Neal Templin. "GM Says Pension Liabilities to Exceed Estimates and Will Hurt Balance Sheet." *The Wall Street Journal* (September 25, 1992), A2; and Susan Pulliam. "Hopeful Assumptions Let Firms Minimize Pension Contributions." *The Wall Street Journal* (September 2, 1993), A1, A6. For more detailed discussions of actuarial assumptions, see Ambachtsheer and Ezra (1998) and Logue and Rader (1998). See also "Pension Funding Equity Act of 2004, Special Report, CCH Tax Briefing," April 23, 2004, 1–3.

76 See Carrie Brodzinski. "Proposed Pension Reform Legislation—Expanding Liability? (Up Front)." *Risk and Insurance* (March 17, 2003); and House Education and the Workforce Committee Fact Sheet, John Boehner, Chairman on Pension Security *(http://edworkforce.house.gov/issues/108th/workforce/pension/summary.htm)*; and Summary of the "Pension and Retirement Security for U.S. Workers," H.R. 1000, Pension Security Act and H.R. 3108, Pension Funding Equity Act Summaries, Sponsor: Committee on Education and the Workforce, Chairman John A. Boehner (R-OH) on this site.

77 The 401(k) Pension Plan Protection Act in 1997, which took effect in 1999, forbids firms from requiring that employees invest more than 10 percent in their 401(k) assets in company stock. Voluntarily, however, employees may invest as much as they would like in their firm's stock. See cites in Note 75 and Kathy Kristof. "Reforms Too Late to Prevent Some Workers' 401(k) Losses." *The Denver Post* (April 5, 1999), 2C; and Susan Cornwell. "Veto Cloud Still Hangs Over U.S. Pension Bill-Senator." *Reuters*, Tuesday, March 30, 2004, 3:29 p.m. ET (reported on *http://biz.yahoo.com*); Mary Williams Walsh. "Agreement Is Reached on Pension Bill." *New York Times* (April 2, 2004), C1, C2; David Rogers. "House Passes Stopgap Pension Bill." *The Wall Street Journal* (April 5, 2004), A7; and David Rogers. "Negotiators Agree on Pension Bill to Aid Companies." *The Wall Street Journal* (April 2, 2004), A3, A4.

very low interest rate returns on investments with a fall in interest rates. In the United States, single-employer pension plans in early 2004 were underfunded by $350 billion and multiemployer plans by $100 billion. As noted in the chapter opening quote, the PBGC itself had a large deficit. At the end of 2002, the PBGC had a net deficit of −$3.48 billion for its combined programs with the PBGC insuring 43.9 million participants in 32,321 plans. Twenty-three plans received financial assistance of $5.0 million in 2002. In December of 2002 the PBGC announced that it would terminate the pension plans of two large steel companies—Bethlehem Steel and National Steel, with claims estimated at $3.9 billion and $1.3 billion, respectively, the largest and third largest claims that the PBGC had ever made. Hence, these terminations and total $5.2 billion in claims created a huge deficit for the PBGC, with 130,400 covered participants in these pension plans. The airline and steel industries were particularly vulnerable to poor economic conditions, creating the largest termination costs in the past for the PBGC, with the Pension Funding Relief Act, discussed earlier, enacted to relieve this crisis.[78]

Move to Hybrid Plans Including Cash-Balance Plans

As noted in the PBGC's annual report, the characteristics of plans that the PBGC insures changed significantly during the middle and late 1990s, with hundreds of traditional plans converting to what is often called "hybrid plans." These include newer cash-balance plans (CBPs) and other account-style programs, including pension-equity plans. **Hybrid plans** have elements of both defined benefit and defined contribution plans, with benefits often expressed in terms of an account balance similar to DC or 401(k) plans. However, contributions are made to the plan by the employer-sponsor, and the employer bears investment risk like defined benefit plans, but benefits accrue more in an employee's early working years versus later years. Mobile employees benefit from hybrid plans by being more likely to be allowed to take a lump-sum "portable" payment for their plans when they leave an employer. However, older employees who received retirement benefits based on their average salary prior to retirement may lose benefits. About 1,230 plans, or 4 percent of a total of 32,954 plans, were reported by the PBGC as hybrid, with a larger percentage for larger plans. Plans with 10,000 or more participants included 27 percent hybrid plans, resulting in more than 20 percent of PBGC-covered single employer participants in hybrid plans. With many hybrid plans converting from traditional DB plans, most of their retirees and some active participants continue to receive benefits based on the design of the original DB plan.[79]

Because older employees that have been with a plan a long time may be hurt by firms converting to hybrid plans, such plans have been controversial. Cash-benefit plans (CBPs) generally, as pointed out by A&E, have a defined benefit in terms of an agreement to a minimum rate of interest, such as the Treasury bill rate plus 1 percent on employees' retirement accounts. CBPs remain insured by the PBGC and subject to ERISA fund regulations. Benefits are generally paid out as lump sums, but an employer may provide other options such as a standard life annuity from the employer or the option to defer payments until they are needed. Like a DC, the employer contributes a minimum percentage of pay, such as 6 percent, into employees' retirement accounts, sometimes with an option to occasionally credit additional contributions and interest to the accounts. Employees receive regular account statements of benefits, and employees can take these accrued benefits with them if they leave the employer. Employers receive advantages in terms of greater simplicity in record-keeping, lower legal exposure, and lower education costs than DC plans, and may use CBPs to save costs, encourage early retirement, or bring benefits in line with those of a firm they are merging with, or to boost stock ownerships by tying the benefits of plans to company performance. Although employers still bear the investment risk of a plan, employees carry the risk of inflation and the risk of outliving the accrued benefits of their plans, similar to DC plans. Employee groups and unions have protested changes to CBPs, since CBPs may offer guaranteed returns that are not very competitive, producing inadequate income for a retiree. Critics also note that corporations have not given employees sufficient information on how conversions from traditional plans to cash plans may reduce an employee's pension benefits.[80]

---

78 See PBGC, *Pension Insurance Data Book*, 2002, Washington, D.C.: Pension Benefit Guaranty Corporation (available on the PBGC Website); Brodzinski, "Proposed Pension Reform Legislation," 1–2; and "Pension Funding Equity Act of 2004, Special Report, CCH Tax Briefing," April 23, 2004, 1–3.

79 See Note 77 and Ambachtsheer and Ezra (1998) and Logue and Rader (1998), which provide more detailed discussions of cash-balance plans; also see Paul Beckett. "Citigroup Makes Move to Change Pension Benefits." *The Wall Street Journal* (April 2, 1999), A4; and Ellen E. Schultz. "Your Pension May Be Changing; Go Figure How . . . If You Can." *The Wall Street Journal* (March 3, 1999), C1.

80 Ibid.

Concept Questions

1 What is ERISA, and what is its purpose?

2 What is the difference between a defined benefit and defined contribution plan? Which type of plan dominates today in the United States?

3 What are different types of defined contribution plans and individual retirement accounts?

4 What role do mutual funds play in managing retirement assets? Why has this role grown in recent years?

5 What decisions need to be made in managing defined benefit pension plans?

6 Why have defined benefit pension plans been recently underfunded?

7 What caused the pension crisis in 2004? What legislation was passed to help this situation?

8 Why have companies with defined benefit plans moved to hybrid plans in recent years? What are the advantages and disadvantages of cash-balance plans?

Summary

This chapter examines financial management issues for mutual funds and pension funds. In recent years with changing demographics and aging Baby Boomers, these financial institutions have had dramatic asset growth. U.S. mutual fund assets reached over $7.5 trillion in 2004. Mutual funds are managed by a number of different types of affiliate firms including an investment management company, a principal underwriter or distributor, a custodian, a transfer agent, and independent public accountants, all of which contribute to the efficient operations of a fund. Many funds operate as fund families offering hundreds of different types of mutual funds. Mutual funds have diversified into a wide variety of financial services in recent years including discount brokerage, automated bill paying services, insurance, annuities, check-writing services, and Internet investing services, among others. Mutual funds have also undergone great consolidation in the 1990s, similar to other financial institutions, to become more competitive. They have also diversified by offering their product outside the United States, including new markets for mutual funds in Asia and Europe.

With the tremendous growth in mutual funds, regulators have been concerned about mutual funds offering more streamlined disclosure to less sophisticated investors, and the SEC created a modernized simplified prospectus form that went into effect in June 1998. The SEC has also been concerned about the independence of mutual fund boards in protecting investors and reducing fund costs. Measuring the performance of mutual funds is often controversial, and

the chapter discusses alternative measures for mutual fund performance and risk. In the final quarter of 2003 and early 2004, a number of mutual fund scandals came to light, involving illegal after-market trading, market timing, and issues of soft money being passed on to brokers and favored institutional investors. In response to these scandals, funds engaging in unethical and illegal activities suffered large settlements with the SEC and state attorneys, and many passed on gains made on these activities back to investors. In addition, pension reform legislation and SEC rulings were proposed to prevent future abuses, emphasizing greater corporate governance by more independent directors.

Private pension funds are responsible for investing money to be used later to pay retirement benefits. ERISA established the fiduciary responsibilities of managers, funding standards, methods for guaranteeing benefits, and other important aspects of pension fund management. Most pension fund assets are invested in common stock and corporate bonds, and the funds' obligations are determined actuarially. The largest sources of pension funds are earnings on assets, followed by plan contributions. DC plans are those in which firms make defined contributions and employees are responsible for choosing among an array of investments, such as different mutual funds. Under a DC plan, the employee takes on all the investment risk. With DB plans the firm makes contributions and invests them in a pension fund, promising employees a given, defined benefit upon retirement. Hence, the firm takes on all the investment risk.

Management issues in DB plans include whether the firm wishes to maximize the wealth of shareholders as well as pension beneficiaries in terms of its investment policy. The firm's investment policy ultimately determines the risk and potential returns that the fund will make. By taking on greater risk, such as a larger percentage of equity investments, the firm has the potential to increase shareholder risk by reducing the necessary contributions to the plan that the firm has to make. Other issues include whether to pursue an active or passive management policy, and if an active policy is pursued, what the optimal allocation for pension assets is. The performance measurement of a pension portfolio needs to adjust for the risk of the plan and the management costs

that are incurred, which can be significant with active management strategies. Recently, hundreds of firms have converted to CBPs, which combine attributes of both DC and DB plans by making defined contributions to plan participants but guaranteeing a minimum return for these contributions. These plans have been controversial, however, because traditional plans may offer ultimately higher benefits to a participant at retirement. In 2004, the Pension Funding Equity Act of 2004 was also passed, with a large PBGC deficit at that time and significant underfunding by many corporate defined benefit contribution plans.

Questions

1. Charles Rammelkamp is interested in mutual funds. Discuss with Charles how mutual funds are managed as a group of affiliates using the affiliates in Figure 18.2 as an example. Also, discuss why mutual funds have grown so rapidly, their recent scandals, and new SEC proposals to limit these scandals.

2. Becky and Gene McCarthy are curious about different types of mutual funds. Explain the difference between an open-end mutual fund, a closed-end mutual fund, an exchange-traded fund (ETF), and a unit investment company. How do you calculate the NAV for an open-end mutual fund? How is the price determined for a closed-end mutual fund? Which of these funds has a larger liquidity management problem? Explain.

3. Carol Hamilton would like to know more about fund families and investment styles of funds. Explain what a fund family is, and what advantages a fund family has. Explain the difference between direct and indirect marketing strategies. Which strategy is more expensive? Why have 12b-1 funds become so controversial? How can a back-end load be used to discourage investors from holding a fund for only a short period of time? Why do funds have minimum investment requirements?

4. Rick Burns would like to know more about who regulates mutual funds. Briefly list the major provisions for mutual funds under the National Securities Market Improvement Act of 1996, the Investment Acts of 1933 and 1940, and the Securities Act of 1934. What tests must mutual funds meet under subchapter M of the Internal Revenue Code to be allowed pass-through taxation for dividends and capital gains? How did the SEC require mutual fund disclosure to be modernized in 1998?

5. Fred Negem would like to know more about the corporate governance of mutual funds. Why is the SEC concerned with the oversight of mutual fund boards? What

percentage of board members must be independent? How can independent board members be compromised by fund managers? Discuss the recent SEC proposals to provide better corporate governance and compliance by funds.

6. Beverly and Doug Walker would like to know the differences between the different risk-adjusted performance measures in the chapter. What are their advantages and disadvantages? Why are mutual fund managers concerned about being compared with broad market indexes versus being compared with funds with similar types of investment strategy objectives?

7. Amanda Crecy, Danny Divitowitz, and Murphy Cochran are considering jobs as portfolio managers for pension funds. Discuss the effects of ERISA on the fiduciary responsibility of pension fund managers. What is the difference between a DB and a DC plan? Which is partially insured by the PBGC? Why have corporations moved more to defined contribution plans? As an employee, which type of plan would you prefer?

8. Angus MacBride and Alfred Albion are curious about the role mutual funds have taken in the management of pension funds in recent years. Discuss mutual funds role in managing pension funds. Name at least two other types of financial institutions that manage large percentages of pension fund assets.

9. Mike and Kathy Nobles are curious about RANVA. Explain the RANVA approach to them for judging fund performance for risk and management costs, including the costs of active versus passive management of funds. If pension fund managers choose to invest in passive stock index funds, how might they be criticized by boards of directors?

10. Tommy and Teresa Tunbridge are pension managers considering the use of derivatives. Explain to them why pension funds' use of derivatives in the 1990s was

controversial. Explain what managed futures are. How does this differ from the use of futures for hedging (i.e., reducing the risk of a fund's portfolio)? Also, explain what tactical asset allocation is and what pension smoothing activities are. Give examples of different types of smoothing techniques.

11. Ken and Roberta Lyon are concerned about hybrid pension plans. Explain what a cash balance plan is. How does it benefit younger, mobile employees, but hurt older employees that have been with a firm for a long time with a firm with a conversion from a defined benefit plan.

12. Suree Bundittrakul and Kim Kita are curious about how a defined benefit pension plan determines whether it is over- or underfunded. Explain what the assets and liabilities of a defined benefit pension plan are. Also explain how the funding of a plan is determined and how actuarial assumptions are crucial in determining whether a DB plan has a surplus or a deficit. Under the Pension Funding Equity Act of 2004, how did Congress provide relief to DB funds by changing an actuarial assumption?

Problems

1. Colorado adventurers Dave and Liz Ingram are trying to decide which mutual fund to invest in: Vanguard's S&P 500 Index or a Van Kampen Aggressive Growth Fund. At this time, they find the following information on the two respective funds: The Van Kampen Aggressive Growth Fund A has a maximum sales charge of 5.75 percent, an annual expense percent of 1.44 percent, a NAV of $17.14, a first quarter return of 18.6 percent, and a one-year return of 39.9 percent with an A performance rating (new fund so no information on historical returns is available), and a minimum investment required of $500. The Vanguard 500 Index Fund has a minimum investment of $3,000, no sales charge, an annual expense of 0.19 percent, and a NAV of $118.90. The first quarter return was 5 percent. The index fund has A ratings for its one-, three-, and five-year returns with annual returns of 18.5 percent, 28 percent, and 26.2 percent and an eight-year average return of 19.4 percent.

   a. Assuming that the average annual return for each fund is the same as in the past, 39.9 percent for the Van Kampen Aggressive Growth Fund and 18.5 percent for the Vanguard Fund S&P 500 Index Fund, and Liz and Dave invest $10,000, what would be the net return on each fund after sales charges and annual expense charges at the end of one year?

   b. What other adjustments would Liz and Dave want to make if the Van Kampen Aggressive Growth Fund has greater risk than the Vanguard S&P Fund? Based on the discussion in the chapter, how could this be done?

2. Lenora Patterson, chief executive officer of a major mutual fund operating in Denver, Colorado, has asked Joe Maruffo, the super vice-president of research, to evaluate the performance of a potential mutual fund. The fund has a predicted monthly return of 3.0 percent with a monthly standard deviation of returns of 1.5 percent. At a 95 percent probability level, what would be

the fund's monthly VAR? If an investor invested $1,000, with a 2.5 percent probability, what is the likely maximum monthly loss for the investor?

3. For the same fund in Problem 2, Gail and Mike Welply, the Chief Executive Officers of International Funds, ask you to calculate the Sharpe ratio for monthly returns and an annualized Sharpe figure if the average monthly risk-free rate is 0.44 percent, and the monthly standard deviation for this excess return is 1.75. Alternatively, calculate the Treynor index if the average beta for the fund is 1.00. Explain what the Sharpe and Treynor ratios indicate and how they are used.

4. Using the same example in Problem 2, Sherry Lenert and Betsy Katz, two Texas mutual fund managers, ask you to use the standard deviation of the S&P 500 as an index for comparison as a benchmark. The average monthly return for the S&P 500 Index is expected to be 1.20 percent, the monthly standard deviation of the fund's excess return over the benchmark is 1.5 percent, and the standard deviation of the excess return for the S&P Index is 1.3 percent. What is the M-square (Modigliani) measure for the fund's performance? (Hint: You might want to annualize all figures before calculating this measure.) What does this measure tell you? How is Morningstar's ratings measure different from this measure?

5. The MassMutual Participation Investors Company is a closed-end diversified management investment company whose investment objective is to maximize total returns by providing a high level of current income. As reported in *Moody's Bank and Finance Manual, 1997*, the fund's investment adviser is Massachusetts Mutual Life Insurance Company, and MassMutual is paid a quarterly advisory and administrative services fee equal to 0.90 percent of the value of the Trust's net assets on an annual basis. At the end of 1996, the fund's percentage of different types of securities in its fund, income, and balance sheets were as shown in Table P18.1.

table **P18.1** INFORMATION FOR PROBLEM 5: MASSMUTUAL PARTICIPATION INVESTORS

Securities	Value	Value	% Total
Corporate Equity Restricted Securities	$ 72,985,477	72,985,477	71.17%
Convertible Bonds	2,297,838	2,297,838	2.24%
Bonds	16,040,232	16,040,232	15.64%
Warrants	60,250	60,250	0.06%
Common Stock	4,257,666	4,257,666	4.15%
Convertible Preferred Stock	1,994,917	1,994,917	1.95%
Commercial Paper	4,909,790	4,909,790	4.79%
Total Investments	$102,546,170	$102,546,170	100.00%

Source: The consolidated income statements and balance sheets for 1995 and 1996 are shown below.

Consolidated Income Statement, December 31 (in dollars)

	1996	% Revs 1995	% Revs
Interest Income	8,784,434	98.35%	8,088,960	97.90%
Dividend Income	147,618	1.65%	173,463	2.10%
Total Income	8,932,052	100.00%	8,262,423	100.00%
Management Fee	885,454	9.91%	822,845	9.96%
Trustees Fees	55,690	0.62%	50,625	0.61%
Transfer Agent Exps.	48,500	0.54%	90,187	1.09%
Custodian Fees			18,647	
Interest Expense	831,600	9.31%	378,840	4.59%
Reports to Shrhldrs.	26,513	0.30%	56,787	0.69%
Audit & Legal	42,935	0.48%	70,731	0.86%
Other Expenses	21,514	0.24%	32,075	0.39%
Total Expenses	1,912,206	21.41%	1,520,737	18.41%
Net Inv. Income	7,019,846	78.59%	6,741,686	81.59%
#Year-end Shares	9,216,665		9,216,665	
NinvIncome per Share	$0.78		$0.73	

Consolidated Balance Sheet (in dollars)

Assets	1996	% Revs	1995	% Revs
Corporate Restricted Securities (Fair Value)	81,145,818	69.82%	69,576,592	63.09%
Corporate Public Securities (Market Value)	24,650,903	21.21%	26,399,294	23.94%
Short-term Securities at Cost	4,909,790	4.22%	11,611,375	10.53%
Total Investments	110,706,511	95.25%	107,587,261	97.55%
Cash	4,414	0.00%	28,405	0.03%
Interest and Dividends Receivable	1,540,439	1.33%	1,804,874	1.64%
Receivable for Investments Sold	3,970,102	3.42%	866,010	0.79%
Total Assets	116,221,466	100.00%	110,286,550	100.00%

Liabilities	1996	%	1995	%
Dividends Payable	3,778,833	3.25%	1,751,358	1.59%
Payable for Investments Purchased	135,000	0.12%	500,000	0.45%
Management Fee Payable	218,596	0.19%	214,300	0.19%
Notes Payable	12,000,000	10.33%	12,000,000	10.88%
Interest Payable	170,940	0.15%	120,000	0.11%
Accrued Expenses	157,518	0.14%	160,000	0.15%
Accrued Taxes	2,606,720	2.24%	225,000	0.20%
Total Liabilities	19,067,607	16.41%	15,000,210	13.60%
Net Assets	97,153,859	83.59%	95,286,340	86.40%
Total Liabilities & Net Assets	116,221,466	100.00%	110,286,550	100.00%
Net Asset Value per Share	$10.54		$10.34	

Source: Moody's Bank & Finance Manual, 1997, p. 4348.

a. What are the largest components of revenues and expenses on MassMutual Participation Investors' income statement? What changes occurred in the expense composition in 1996 versus 1995? What was the return on total assets? What was the return on net assets? How much did revenues grow in 1996? How much did expenses grow in 1996? How much did net investment income grow?

b. Given the asset allocations for the securities portfolio, what type of fund is MassMutual Participation Investors? What type of liabilities does the fund have? How much did net assets grow in 1996? How much did total liabilities and net assets grow? Comment on any changes between 1995 and 1996.

6. T. Rowe Price, as noted on Yahoo! Finance *(http://finance.yahoo.com)*, has the following financial statements, presented in Table P18.2. An abbreviated profile from Reuters is also provided for T. Rowe Price Group, Inc. (TROW), which is a financial services holding company receiving the majority of its revenues and profits from its investment advisory services to individuals and institutional investors, with services of its subsidiaries T. Rowe Price Associates and T. Rowe Price International including mutual funds, brokerage services, college planning, banking services, and research. The company's largest mutual funds include Equity Income, Mid-Cap Growth, Prime Reserve, Blue Chip Growth, and International Stock (the Price funds). Do a financial performance analysis for T. Rowe, explaining trends between 2001 and 2002 and 2002 and 2003 using a DuPont Analysis including ROE, ROA, NPM, Asset Turnover, and the Equity Multiplier. Also, examine

profits more closely by looking at any percentage changes in expenses on the income statement and examining individual profit ratios including OPM and differences in growth rates for revenues and expenses. Also, explain what the cash flow statements tell you about how T. Rowe Price received and used cash to explain the change in cash each year.

7. Do the same analysis for Janus Capital Group, Inc. (JNS), looking up and printing out the financial statements (income, balance sheet, cash flow statement, and key statistics) on Yahoo! Finance *(http://finance.yahoo.com)*. Alternatively, do a similar analysis looking up the mutual fund company financial statements for the company that you're interested in on Yahoo! Finance. Note that if the company is privately traded, like Fidelity or Vanguard, you won't be able to find financial statements, but you can look up the performance of particular mutual funds.

Suggested Case Studies
Harvard Business School Publishing

T. Rowe Price: Managing Money Market Funds

Keller Fund's Option Investment Strategy: Effect of Using Options on a Fund's Profit Profile and the Pricing of Multiple Option Strategies

Fidelity Investments, Spartan Florida Municipal Fund: Decision on Buying Portfolio Insurance

JKJ Pension Fund: Issuing for a Pension Fund in Valuation and Real Estate Portfolio Management

Selected References

Abken, Peter J. "Corporate Pensions and Government Insurance." *Economic Review* (Federal Reserve Bank of Atlanta) 77 (March/April 1992), 1–16.

Ambachtsheer, Keith P., and D. Don Ezra. *Pension Fund Excellence: Creating Value for Stakeholders.* New York: John Wiley & Sons, 1998.

The American Association of Individual Investors. *The Individual Investor's Guide to Low-Load Mutual Funds,* 18th ed. Chicago: AAII, 1999.

American Council of Life Insurance. *Life Insurance Fact Book, 1998.* Washington, DC: ACLI, 1998.

Bajtelsmit, Vickie L., and Elaine M. Worzala. "Real Estate Allocation in Pension Fund Portfolios." *Journal of Real Estate Portfolio Management* 1, No. 1 (1995), 25–38.

Berkowitz, Stephen A., Louis D. Finney, and Dennis E. Logue. *The Investment Performance of Corporate Pension Plans.* New York: Quorum Books, 1988.

Bodie, Zvi, et al. "Corporation Pension Policy: An Empirical Investigation." *Financial Analysts Journal* 41 (September/October 1985), 10–16.

Bogle, John C. *Bogle on Mutual Funds.* New York: Irwin Professional Publishing Co., 1994.

Black, Fischer, and Moray P. Dewhurst. "A New Investment Strategy for Pension Funds." *Journal of Portfolio Management* 7, No. 4 (1981), 26–34.

Buynak, Thomas M. "Is the U.S. Pension-Insurance System Going Broke?" *Economic Commentary* (Federal Reserve Bank of Cleveland), January 15, 1987.

table **P18.2** ANNUAL FINANCIAL STATEMENTS FOR T. ROWE PRICE, 2001 TO 2003

T. Rowe Price Group Inc. (TROW) Income Statement (in thousands)

	December 2003	December 2002	December 2001
Total Revenue	$998,855	$925,829	$1,027,496
Cost of Revenue	382,957	359,913	384,943
Gross Profit	615,899	566,916	642,553
Operating Expenses			
Selling & Administrative	202,282	194,827	270,351
Other Expenses	45,289	50,578	28,921
Operating Income	368,328	320,511	343,281
Other Net Income/Expenses	476	(8,273)	0
Earnings Before Int. & Taxes	368,804	312,238	343,281
Interest Expense	3,288	2,634	12,692
Income Before Tax	365,516	309,604	330,589
Income Tax Expense	138,029	115,350	135,078
Minority Interest	0	0	357
Net Income	227,487	194,254	195,868

TROW Balance Sheet, Year-end, December 31 (in thousands)

Assets	2003	2002	2001
Current Assets			
Cash & Equivalents	236,533	111,418	79,741
Net Receivables	121,295	96,787	104,001
Total Current Assets	357,828	208,205	183,742
Long-Term Investments	273,245	216,080	154,208
Property & Equipment	201,094	215,590	241,825
Goodwill	665,692	665,692	665,692
Other Assets	48,718	64,866	67,648
Total Assets	1,546,577	1,370,433	1,313,115

Liabilities & Equity	2003	2002	2001
Accounts Payable	121,221	99,402	105,979
Other Current Liabilities	96,276	81,292	25,422
Total Current Liabilities	217,497	180,694	131,401
Long-term Debt	0	55,899	103,889
Total Liabilities	217,497	236,593	235,290
Common Stock	185,167	113,915	104,353
Retained Earnings	1,143,913	1,019,925	973,472
Total Stockholder Equity	1,329,080	1,133,840	1,077,825
Net Tangible Assets	$ 663,388	$ 468,148	$ 412,133

table **P18.2** ANNUAL FINANCIAL STATEMENTS FOR T. ROWE PRICE, 2001 TO 2003 (CONTINUED)

TROW Cash Flow Statement (in thousands) for December 31

	2003	2002	2001
Cash Flow from Operations			
Net Income	227,487	194,254	195,868
+ Depreciation	45,289	50,578	80,488
Adjustments to Net Income	0	0	(357)
Change in Other Op. Activities	24,179	24,466	14,355
Total Cash Flow from Op. Activities	296,955	269,298	290,354
Cash Flows Used in Investing			
Cash Expenditures	(31,742)	(26,047)	(41,375)
Investments	(27,123)	(70,732)	38,865
Other	5,206	1,808	(6,460)
Total Cash Flow from Investing	(53,659)	(94,971)	(8,970)
Cash from Financing Activities			
Dividends Paid	(83,672)	(78,701)	(73,838)
Sale/Purchase of Stock	7,206	(70,453)	(17,821)
Net Borrowings	(56,699)	6,504	(205,000)
Other Cash Flows from Financing	14,984	0	14,490
Total Cash Flows from Financing	(118,181)	(142,650)	(282,169)
Change in Cash	$ 125,115	$ 31,677	($785)

Note: Change in Cash = Cash Flow from Operations + Cash Flows Used in Investing + Cash Flows from Financing.
Source: TROW Public Annual Financial Statements listed on Yahoo! Finance Website as reported to SEC's public Website, Edgar Online (http://finance.yahoo.com).

Chicago Board of Trade. *Managed Futures: An Investment Opportunity for Institutional Investors.* Chicago: CBOT, 1992.

Coggin, T. Daniel, Frank J. Fabozzi, and Shafiqur Rahman. "The Investment Performance of U.S. Equity Fund Managers: An Empirical Investigation." *Journal of Finance* 48 (July 1993), 1039–1055.

Cummins, J. David, et al. "Effects of ERISA on the Investment Policies of Private Pension Plans: Survey Evidence." *Journal of Risk and Insurance* 47 (September 1980), 447–476.

Estrella, Arturo, and Beverly Hirtle. "Estimating the Funding Gap of the Pension Benefit Guaranty Corporation." *Quarterly Review* (Federal Reserve Bank of New York) (Autumn 1988), 45–59.

Ezra, D. Don, and Keith P. Ambachtsheer. "Pension Funds: Rich or Poor?" *Financial Analysis Journal* 41 (March/April 1985), 43–56.

Financial Economists Roundtable. "Statement on Risk Disclosure by Mutual Funds." September 18, 1996 *(http://www.stanford.edu/~wfsharpe/art/fer/fer96.htm).*

Fortune, Peter. "Mutual Funds, Part I: Reshaping the American Financial System." *New England Economic Review* (Federal Reserve Bank of Boston) (July/August 1997), 45–72.

French, Dan W., and Glenn V. Henderson, Jr. "How Well Does Performance Evaluation Perform?" *Journal of Portfolio Management* (Winter 1985), 15–18.

Harrison, J. Michael, and William F. Sharpe. "Optimal Funding and Asset Allocation Risks for Defined Benefit Pension Plans." In *Financial Aspects of the United States Pension System,* edited by Zvi Bodie and John B. Shoven. Chicago: University of Chicago Press, 1983, 91–103.

Hendricks, Darryll, Jayendu Patel, and Richard Zeckhauser. "Hot Hands in Mutual Funds: Short-Run Persistence of Relative Performance, 1974–1988." *Journal of Finance* 48 (March 1993), 93–130.

Ippolito, Richard A. "The Labor Contract and True Economic Pension Liabilities." *American Economic Review* 75, No. 6 (1985), 1031–1043.

———. *Pension, Economics and Public Policy.* Homewood, IL: Dow/Jones Irwin, 1986.

Jensen, Michael D. "The Performance of Mutual Funds in the Period 1945–1964." *Journal of Finance* 23 (May 1968), 389–416.

Laderman, Jeffrey M., and Geoffrey Smith. "The Power of Mutual Funds." *Business Week* (January 18, 1993), 62–68.

Lakonishok, Josef, Andrei Schleifer, and Robert Vishny. "The Structure and Performance of the Money Management Industry." *Brookings Papers on Economic Activity: Microeconomics.* Washington, DC: Brookings Institution, 1992.

Light, Larry. "The Power of Pension Funds." *Business Week* (November 6, 1989), 154–158.

Logue, Dennis E., and Jack S. Rader. *Managing Pension Plans: A Comprehensive Guide to Improving Plan Performance.* Boston: Harvard Business School Press, 1998.

Louargand, Marc A. "A Survey of Pension Fund Real Estate Portfolio Risk Management Practices." *Journal of Real Estate Research* 7 (Fall 1992), 361–374.

Modigliani, Franco, and Leah Modigliani. "Risk-Adjusted Performance." *Journal of Portfolio Management* 23 (Winter 1997), 45–54.

Munnell, Alice H. "Guaranteeing Private Pension Benefits: A Potentially Expensive Business." *New England Economic Review* (Federal Reserve Bank of Boston) (March/April 1982), 24–47.

Mutual Fund Fact Book, 38th ed. Washington, DC: Investment Company Institute, 1998, and various other issues.

Phillips, Richard M. "Mutual Fund Independent Directors: A Model for Corporate America?" *Investment Company Institute Perspective,* Investment Company Institute 9, No. 4 (August 2003), 1–12.

Pozen, Robert C. "The Prudent Person Rule and ERISA: A Legal Perspective." *Financial Analysts Journal* 33 (March/April 1977), 30–35.

———. *The Mutual Fund Business.* Cambridge, MA: The MIT Press, 1998.

Rosen, Kenneth T. "The Role of Pension Funds in Housing Finance." *Housing Finance Review* 1 (April 1982), 147–177.

Sharpe, William F. "Mutual Fund Performance." *Journal of Business Supplement on Security Prices* 39 (January 1966), 119–138.

———. "Corporate Pension Funding Policy." *Journal of Financial Economics* 4, No. 2 (1976), 183–193.

———. "Integrated Asset Allocation." *Financial Analysts Journal* 43, No. 5 (1987), 25–32.

———. "Asset Allocation." In *Managing Investment Portfolios: A Dynamic Process,* 2nd ed., edited by John L. Magin and Donald L. Tuttle. New York: Warren, Gorman, and Lamont, 1990, 7-1–7-70.

———. "Asset Allocation, Management Style and Performance Measurement." *Journal of Portfolio Management* 18, No. 2 (1992), 7–19.

———. "Morningstar Performance Measures." *(http://www.stanford.edu/~wfsharpe/art/stars/stars0.htm).*

Shukla, Ravi, and Charles Trzcinka. "Performance Measurement of Managed Portfolios." *Financial Markets, Institutions and Instruments* 1, No. 4 (1992).

Simmons, Katerina. "Risk-Adjusted Performance of Mutual Funds." *New England Economic Review* (Federal Reserve Bank of Boston) (September/October 1998), 33–48.

Steinberg, Richard M., and Harold Dankner. *Pensions: An ERISA Accounting and Management Guide.* New York: John Wiley & Sons, 1983.

Tepper, Irwin. "Taxation and Corporate Pension Policy." *Journal of Finance* 36, No. 1 (1981), 1–13.

Treynor, Jack L. "How to Rate Management of Investment Funds." *Harvard Business Review* (January/February 1965), 131–136.

Tufano, Peter, and Matthew Sevick. "Board Structure and Fee-Setting in the U.S. Mutual Fund Industry." *Journal of Financial Economics* 46 (1997), 321–355.

Warshawsky, Mark J. "Pension Plans: Funding, Assets, and Regulatory Environment." *Federal Reserve Bulletin* 74 (November 1988), 717–730.

Woerheide, Walt. "Investor Response to Suggested Criteria for the Selection of Mutual Funds." *Journal of Financial and Quantitative Analysis* 17 (March 1982), 129–137.

1 The Investment Company Institute Website *(http://www.ici.org/)* contains basic information about mutual funds in the United States. To find the latest figures on the size of the mutual fund industry, click on "Mutual Fund Statistics" or go to *http://www.ici.org/stats/mf/index.html,* which contains statistical releases, mutual fund developments, and a mutual fund fact book that can be downloaded in PDF form (requires Adobe Acrobat Reader). Click on "Trends in Mutual Fund Investing" to get the latest information on mutual fund trends for total assets, flows, and sales for open-end funds.

2 SEC Tool to Calculate Cost of Funds

In an effort to help investors better understand mutual fund expenses, the SEC provides a new online tool to calculate the costs of fund investing known as the Cost Calculator, which is available on the SEC's Website, *http://www.sec.gov.* The calculator lets investors evaluate and compare costs. The calculator provides a dollars-and-cents estimate of the cost of investing in a fund, which may be easier for many investors to grasp versus annual percentages or other comparisons. Investors using the calculator need to plug in actual costs, which are available in a fund's prospectus, and project the number of years they will hold the fund, as well as estimate the average annual return. An example for the calculator is the finding in the article by Richard Oppel cited below that a fund held for twenty-five years with an annual expense ratio of 0.70 percent will leave an investor with 16 percent more than a fund with a 1.3 percent expense ratio. Hence, the calculator demonstrates the impact of fees on fund net returns. See Judith Burns. "SEC Tool to Calculate Costs of Funds." *The Wall Street Journal* (April 7, 1999), C27; and Richard A. Oppel, Jr. "SEC Web Site Now Offers Mutual Fund Fees Calculator." *New York Times* (April 7, 1999), C10.

The SEC Mutual Fund Cost Calculator: A Tool for Comparing Mutual Funds can be found at *http://www.sec.gov/mfcc/mfcc-int.htm.* To use the online JavaScript version of the program, you will need a JavaScript-enabled browser such as Netscape Navigator™ 2.0 or higher or Microsoft® Internet Explorer 3.0 or higher. The SEC Cost Calculator estimates the cost of investing in a mutual fund based on information you provide. The results should be compared for several funds or different classes of a single fund. Before you begin, take out the prospectus or profile for the funds you want to evaluate. You will need to plug in information from the expense section of these documents. Here is the information you will need to supply:

(1) How many years do you plan to hold the fund?

(2) Enter the dollar value of your investment.

(3) What type of fund best describes what you want to analyze (e.g., money market, bond, stock)?

(4) Enter the annual rate of return you expect to receive.

(5) Enter the percentage sales charge on purchases for the amount of your investment.

(6) Enter the percentage deferred sales charge at the end of the period you plan to hold your fund.

(7) Does this fund convert from one share class to another by the end of the period you plan to hold your fund?

(8) Enter the percentage total annual operating expenses or expense ratio for this fund.

You will be given the total dollar cost of holding the fund and the value of the investment for the period that you plan to hold the fund.

3 Go to About Mutual Funds at *http://mutualfunds .about.com,* a useful Website that provides lots of good information and tutorials, history, and news items on mutual funds, with links to other helpful information as well. On the left-hand side of the home page under Subjects, click on "Test Your Mutual Fund Knowledge," and take the test and see how you do. You'll find lots of useful information about mutual funds and interesting articles about current topics as you explore this site. If you look up "Investment Professional Designations," you'll see a summary of different professional titles in the investment industry and the trade associations that give these credentials (or go to *http://mutualfunds .about.com/cs/tradeassociations/a/designations .htm*).

4 Go to the Vanguard Funds Website at *http://www .vanguard.com,* and click on the menu on the left-hand side for the Bogle Financial Markets Research Center or go directly to *http://www.vanguard .com/bogle_site/bogle_home.html.* This site provides lots of useful discussion and research on mutual funds by John C. Bogle, founder and former chairman of The Vanguard Group, who has written many excellent books on mutual funds, which are listed on the site. The Vanguard site *(http://www .vanguard.com)* also provides historical and performance information on its funds and the mutual fund industry. Similarly, the Fidelity Mutual Fund Website *(http://www.fidelity.com)* provides useful information about its funds and the industry and a profile test you can take to see what type of risk/return preferences you have and the type of funds you would be happier investing in, given these preferences. The Yahoo! Finance Website *(http://finance.yahoo.com)* provides lots of good information about mutual funds. Once you're on the home page, type in the symbol for a mutual fund or click "Symbol Lookup" to find its trading symbol and then type that symbol into the lookup box to find information on the fund. On the left-hand side of the home page, you can also click "Mutual Funds" to find information about mutual funds and ETFs, including top performers and other information.

5   Go to the American Association of Individual Investors (AAII) Website *(http://www.aaii.com/ mfunds/faqs/)* to find even more information on mutual funds. The AAII is a nonprofit education group helping small, individual investors, with lots of good educational publications and local chapters with speakers and events on investing, mutual funds, and other topics. You can find reports on funds by entering their trading symbols under "Tools" on the left-hand side of the Web page. The Education menu on the left-hand side of the Web page also has links to educational information on investing and mutual funds.

USEFUL SITES FOR PENSION FUND INFORMATION

Pension Benefit Guaranty Corporation (PBGC)

The PBGC Website provides information on defined benefit pension plans and a pension fund fact book, among other information.

http://www.pbgc.gov

The American Institute of Certified Public Accountants (AICPA)

The AICPA website contains information on defined contribution pension plans from an accounting perspective.

http://www.aicpa.org/ebpaqc/pens_defcon/about.htm

The ERISA Industry Committee (ERIC)

The ERISA Industry Committee provides information and breaking news on legislation affecting defined benefit pension plans.

http://www.eric.org

The U.S. Department of Labor (DOL)

The DOL Website provides information by topic including the Employee Retirement Income Security Act (ERISA) and other related topics.

http://www.dol.gov

The Brookings Institute and the National Bureau of Economic Research (NBER)

These research institutes often have research papers about pension funds and retirement. Some research information is free, and other papers can be ordered electronically for a cost.

http://www.brook.edu   and   *http://www.nber.org*

19 Managing Diversified Financial Services Firms

Corporate Governance and Merger and International Considerations

"Nonbanks are quite simply redefining the financial services industry. GE Capital may be the most prominent example of a large company that takes pride in managing itself as a small entrepreneurial firm."

CHARLES B. WENDEL, President, Financial Institutions Consulting, Inc. Quote from The New Financiers. *Chicago: Irwin Professional Publishing, 1996, 2–3.*

"Increased opportunities for diversification offer the prospect—though not the assurance—of lower overall volatility in earnings, but they also bring much more complicated management challenges in controlling conflicts, reputational risks, and operational risks. . . . These are formidable challenges even for the strongest management team. Trust and reputation are valuable competitive assets for financial institutions, and the desire to preserve those assets creates a powerful incentive for firms to manage conflicts and compliance with exceptional care."

TIMOTHY F. GEITHNER, President and Chief Executive Officer, Federal Reserve Bank of New York, "Change and Challenges Facing the U.S. Financial System," March 25, 2004 (Remarks before the New York Bankers Association's Annual Financial Services Forum), 1–6.[1]

I n the early 2000s, in the aftermath of the passage of the Gramm-Leach-Bliley (GLB) Act of 1999, more than 640 bank holding companies elected to become financial holding companies (FHCs), with many acquiring different types of firms to become diversified financial services firms. Hence, there has been a convergence in the financial services industry, with a wide variety of financial services offered under one umbrella. Many of these firms started out as finance companies for large nonfinancial firms, such as General Electric Capital, while others began with the merger of several finance, insurance, and investment companies over a decade, such as Travelers Group, which merged with Citicorp in 1998 to become Citigroup. It was the Travelers-Citicorp merger that led to the passage of GLB in 1999 and the new FHC designation.

Although more diversified financial firms appeared in the early 2000s after the passage of the GLB, several large financial and nonfinancial services firms experimented with diversification in the 1980s. Many, however, developed problems and later spun off financial subsidiaries in the early 1990s. Similarly, today, mega-financial services firms continue to face problems of how to meld cultures and manage a diverse group of firms. Some have decided to restructure or refocus by divesting or closing some subsidiaries that have not been profitable, such as FleetBoston's divestment of its Robertson Stephens investment bank subsidiary. In a surprise move in 2002, Citigroup (Citi) also divested part of its insurance operations, reducing some of its previous diversification.[2]

Regulators have been concerned about the challenges of corporate control and risk management for diversified financial companies. A number of large financial services firms have had corporate control problems in attempting to manage enormous and diverse operations. Citi, for instance, had a few of its financial advisers involved in helping to structure financing arrangements for Enron and Dynergy that hid debt from financial analysts, and also had a star telecommunications analyst involved in a conflict of interest scandal, whereby he suppressed negative information about telecommunica-

Learning Objectives

After completing this chapter, you will be able to:

1 Describe different types of finance companies and the nature of their operations.

2 Understand the structure of the finance company industry and recent trends and regulations.

3 Understand typical finance company financial statements and performance ratios.

4 Discuss reasons for their development and trends for diversified financial services firms.

5 Understand factors that have made some diversified financial services firms successful and others not successful.

6 Discuss how a RAROC approach can be used to evaluate business lines.

7 Understand some considerations for financial institution mergers.

8 Describe some international considerations for financial institutions.

tions industry problems to protect Citi's customers. The individuals and Citi faced prosecution by the SEC and very large fines and restitution, including fines of $400 million and restitution in a global settlement with regulators over misleading research. In reaction, Citi suffered a large stock price plunge in 2003 and early 2004, leading to pressure by pension fund investors, including the California Public Employees Retirement Funds (CALPERS), to make a change in Citi's management and improve corporate governance. With operations in more than 100 countries, Citi faces difficulties with corporate governance and other global financial management issues as well. For instance, Citi's international business units often have greater allegiance to their own local business units than to Citi headquarters in New York. With cultural, regulatory, and other country differences, management complexity increases. Citi went through considerable internal corporate governance reforms to ensure that unethical behavior will not continue. A recent article in *CFO Magazine* notes that some analysts suggest that these efforts may be quick attempts to remedy problems as "just in time" corporate governance, while others note that the changes represent a

---

1 See Federal Reserve Bank of New York's Website (News and Events, Speeches), at *http://www.ny.frb.org/newsevents/speeches.*

2 For an example of difficulties that mega-financial firms have had in blending cultures for diverse lines of business, see Crawford and Sihler (1994), Case 6: General Electric Financial Services, Inc. (casebook is out of print but should be available as a Darden Case). Also see Walters (2004) for a discussion of GEFS. For an updated listing of financial holding company elections, see "The Federal Reserve Board, Financial Holding Companies," on the Fed's Website: *http://www.federalreserve.gov/generalinfo/fhc/.*

valiant attempt, and the "true test of Citigroup's reforms" will be the "ability to remain scandal-free despite its staggering breadth of financial offerings and sprawling global operations."[3]

This concluding chapter discusses the nature, operations, and strategic considerations of finance companies and diversified financial services firms including the operations and trends for different types of finance companies, brief case histories of financial conglomerates, and their successes and failures, as well as some corporate control, merger, and international considerations.

Overview: Finance Companies and Diversified Financial Services Firms

Many of the largest financial services firms in the United States and in the world are or began as finance companies, such as GE Capital, which was ranked as the largest financial services company in the world by *Fortune Magazine* in 2002.[4] Finance companies make loans, but unlike banks, they finance their lending activities by issuing commercial paper or bonds or borrowing from other financial institutions, including banks. Finance companies also frequently do what is called subprime lending, granting loans to riskier customers who often would not qualify for bank loans. In the 1990s to early 2000s with consumers taking on high debt, analysts have been concerned about finance companies taking on too much risk. Finance companies generally charge higher rates than banks to compensate for the higher risk profile of their customers. There are several different types of finance companies including consumer, industrial loan companies, commercial and specialty, diversified, credit card banks, and GSEs, as discussed in the following section.

Types of Finance Companies

As noted in the chapter opening quotes, many finance companies (often referred to as nonbanks) are financial services firms that make loans but do not take deposits. Some are large and diversified, such as General Electric Financial Services, which includes as subsidiaries a diverse set of consumer (personal) and business finance firms. Others are smaller, specialized finance companies.

Consumer and Captive (Sales) Finance Companies

Consumer finances are twentieth-century creations, specializing in making consumer loans, including loans for automobiles and consumer retail goods, often as captive or sales company subsidiaries of large manufacturing or retail firms, to provide financing for these products. The first sales finance company was initiated in 1904 for a piano manufacturer. The piano finance company offered extended installment contracts to allow customers to purchase pianos that they otherwise could not afford. This idea was adopted quickly by other firms including car manufacturers, with more than 1,000 sales finance firms operating in the United States by 1922. Later, states put finance companies under usury laws, setting ceilings on loan rates that could be charged. Finance companies are now subject to state and federal laws governing the provision of credit, including usury statutes and truth-in-lending regulations. Captive sales companies remain popular for floor financing of retail dealers for their inventory from manufacturing firms, as well as for consumer financing. Well-known captive financing companies operating today include Sears Roebuck Acceptance Corporation, Toyota-Motor Credit, and Ford Credit

---

3 See "Citi's New Stance." *CFO Magazine* (November 1, 2003), 1–7, available at *http://www.CFO.com*.

4 See Insurance Information Website, *Financial Services Fact Book 2003*, for a listing of the largest financial services firms, available on its Website *(http://financial servicefacts.org)*. At the time of this writing, the list of the largest U.S. financial firms and financial services sections could be found on *http://financial servicefacts.org/financial2/today/leadingcos/*. The top twenty-five financial services firms by sector included seven banking firms (revenues of $283.2 billion), four diversified financial firms ($248.1 billion), ten insurance firms ($331.8 billion), and four security firms ($100.3 billion). Among these, two GSEs were included: Fannie Mae (ranked fourth) and Freddie Mac (ranked ninth).

Corporation, while other specialty finance companies remain independent. The top five U.S. consumer finance companies include subsidiaries of other large financial services firms as well, including Ford Motor Credit Company, Citigroup, Inc. (credit card subsidiary), MBNA Corporation, Household International, and SLM Corporation.[5]

Whether captive or independent, consumer finance companies make both unsecured and secured personal loans. Secured lending today includes residential mortgages, second mortgages (sometimes called *junior liens* to indicate their subordinate claim on mortgaged property), home equity loans (loans made against the equity ownership that has been built up as a home mortgage is paid off), and second mortgage loans, which offer higher yields than first mortgages to compensate for a subordinate claim on property if a loan defaults but have a lower rate than a personal cash loan, since secondary collateral is behind them. Loans for second mortgages tend to have cycles, becoming popular in high interest rate environments and expansion but becoming less popular in low interest rate environments and recessions, when defaults occur. With the passage of the Tax Reform Act of 1986, phasing out deductions paid on consumer loans, secondary mortgages and home equity lines of credit became popular, because their interest could be deducted. At the beginning of 2003, the Federal Reserve reported that of a total of $829.1 billion in U.S. home equity loans, finance companies held 16.3 percent of home equity loans (with banks holding 36.6 percent, thrifts 9.5 percent, credit unions 5.8 percent, and asset-backed security issuers 31.8 percent). Regulators have been concerned about the risk of home equity loans and subprime lending. In 2001, for instance, about 44 percent of the home equity loan market was subprime (borrower credit ratings of A− or lower). The top three subprime residential lenders in 2003 were Household Financial Services ($6.6 billion in subprime volume and 22.2 percent market share), Citi-Financial ($4.8 billion and 16 percent share), and New Century Financial ($4.7 billion and 15.8 percent share).[6]

Industrial Loan Companies and Their Limits under the Regulatory Relief Bill of 2004

Industrial loan companies (ILCs; sometimes called industrial banks) are an unusual type of nondepository finance company that nonfinancial (commercial) companies in recent years have taken over as a loophole to allow them to engage in banking activities (otherwise not allowed under Glass–Stegall). Walmart, for instance, in the early 2000s acquired a number of ILCs that community lenders were very concerned about since commercial companies are not allowed to own banks. ILCs were initially chartered in some states to provide credit for blue-collar workers by being allowed to engage in making nondepository credit and to offer certificates of deposit (often called certificates of investment) accounts and provide consumer cash loans secured by personal property, agricultural lending, and short-term inventory credit. ILCs generally are not allowed to provide credit cards, sales financing, consumer lending, real estate, international trade, and secondary market financing, with each state having its own particular regulations. Over time most states changed their regulations to disallow ILCs (except Utah, California, Colorado, Minnesota, and Nevada). Often ILCs have niches in real estate (if allowed by a state) or automobile loans and are not subject to other banking regulations as nonbanks. Congress, in response to regulatory concerns about commercial firm purchases of ILCs as well as the potential for money laundering and other criminal behavior by unregulated ILCs drafted legislation as part of the Financial Services Regulatory Relief Act of 2004 (H.R. 1375) to limit the freedom of ILCs, pending in the Senate at the time of this writing. Under this act, ILC branching for new charters would only be allowed for subsidiaries of financial firms that received 85 percent of their revenues from financial activities. In addition, both federal and state chartered depository institutions (banks, credit unions, and thrifts) would receive greater freedom in expanding across state lines. Credit unions would also receive easier eligibility to be FHLB members and be allowed to provide

---

5 Ibid and Selden (1981), 205–206.

6 Information for this section comes from James D. August, Michael R. Grupe, Charles Luckett, and Samuel M. Slowinski. "Survey of Finance Companies, 1996." *Federal Reserve Bulletin* 83 (July 1997), 543–556; and Dynan, Johnson, and Slowinski (January 2002). Surveys on finance companies are performed by the Fed every five years. Also see Dru Johnston Bergman. "Second Mortgages Build Image as First Class Investment." *Freddie Mac Reports* 3 (November 1985), 1–2.

check-clearing and wire transfer services. The act in addition proposes to allow interest to be paid on business demand deposit accounts.[7]

Commercial Finance Companies

Commercial finance companies make loans to businesses, provide equipment leasing, asset-based loans, and factoring (purchasing accounts receivables from businesses at a discount). In the past, commercial banks shunned asset-based lending (business loans collateralized by the borrowing firm's inventory or receivables). Commercial finance companies arose to fill this need, with the first commercial finance company, Mercantile Credit Company in Chicago, founded in 1905 by encyclopedia salesmen who could not get collateralized loans from banks based on their inventory and installment receivables as collateral. After 1954, states' widespread adoption of the Uniform Commercial Code clarified the rights of asset-based lenders and provided strong impetus for growth of commercial finance companies, which today offer both short-term and long-term asset-based loans and leasing.[8]

Commercial finance companies are also often captive companies of large manufacturing companies providing financing and leasing services for customers' purchases of machinery and equipment, such as John Deere Capital Corporation, Caterpillar Financial Services, and McDonnell Douglas Finance Company. Commercial finance companies also often sell participation in an asset-based loan to banks in exchange for cash. Proceeds from the loan are then divided between the finance company and the banks according to their relative shares in the participation. Although some loan participations are actually arranged by banks and then sold to finance companies, most require the finance company to remain active in tracking the performance of the assets pledged as collateral. Often, because bank lending rates are lower than finance company rates, the borrower is given a "blended" rate reflecting the relative shares of the two lenders. Commercial finance companies also are often subsidiaries of large financial services firms or "specialty" finance companies that specialize in particular types of lending, such as inventory lending, factoring (purchasing of accounting receivables for a large discount), leasing of aircraft, or financing or leasing particular types of equipment. The top five U.S. commercial finance companies cited in 2002 are GE Capital Corporation, General Motors Acceptance Corporation, CIT Group, Inc., Ford Motor Credit Company, and International Lease Finance Corporation.[9]

Diversified Finance Companies

Diversified finance companies make both consumer and business loans, and are often subsidiaries of financial holding companies or insurance companies such as the finance company subsidiaries of Citigroup and Transamerica Finance Corporation. The top five U.S. diversified consumer and commercial finance companies cited in 2002 include many of those listed previously as the top consumer and business finance companies: GE Capital Corporation, Ford Motor Credit Company, Household International, Inc., MBNA Corporation, and SLM Corporation.[10]

---

7 See Insurance Information Institute (III) *Financial Services Fact Book 2003*, also available on their Website at *http://financialservicefacts.org/financial2/banking/industrial/*. The III lists the top ten FDIC-Insured Industrial Banks in 2002 as Merrill Lynch Bank USA, American Express Centurion Bank, Fremont Investment & Loan, Morgan Stanley Bank, USAA Savings Bank, Mill Creek Bank, GE Capital Financial, Inc., Providian Bank, Imperial Capital Bank, and BMW Bank of North America, as provided by the FDIC and ranked by total assets. Other information comes from news and Web reports including Susan Cornwall. "U.S. House Votes to Curb New Industrial Banks' Reach." *Reuters*, March 18, 2004, as reported on the Forbes Website *(http://www.forbes.com/reuters/newswire/2004/03/18/rtr1304300.html)*; "House Passes Regulatory Relief Bill with Industrial Loan Company Compromise (BNA)," ACB News, Friday, March 19, 2004, on the American Community Bankers Website *(http://www.americascommunitybankers.com)*; and "H.R. 1375: Financial Services Regulatory Relief Act, Floor Situation and Summary," March 20, 2004, on the GOP.gov Committee Central-108th Website *(http://www.gop.gov/committeecentral)*. Also see Joe Hill Dispatch-Journal of Business, Finance and Economics, March 19, 2004, and April 15, 2004 *(http:// www.joehilldispatch.org)* for a summary of the ILC issues; Patti Murphy. The Takoma Group, "WalMart Settlement Could Reshape Bankcard Biz." Originally appearing, The Green Sheet, May 12, 2003, *(http://www.greensheet.com)* and on the Takoma Group Website, 2003 *(http://takomagroup.com/walmart_settlement_reshap.html)*.

8 For more information on historical trends in business lending by finance companies, see Harris (1979).

9 For more information on participations, see Logan and Dorgan (1984) and Dorgan (1984). Also see the III *Financial Services Fact Book* at *http://www.iii.org*.

10 See the III *Financial Services Fact Book* at *http://www.iii.org*. For a listing of the top firms for each type of finance company at the time of this writing, see *http://financialservicefacts.org/financial2/finance/top*. Information on the top firms is provided to III by SNL Financial, LC.

Credit Card Companies

Credit card companies are finance companies that issue credit cards to consumers and businesses. They make significant fee income from selling and securitizing credit card loans and continuing to earn fee income by servicing these loans. Examples of credit card companies include MBNA, AT&T Capital Corporation, American Express Credit Corporation, and Discover Bank. Many of these companies, such as MBNA, are extremely profitable in issuing specialty credit cards, purchasing consumer loans from financial institutions, and packaging and securitizing loans. These companies often operate internationally and have bank subsidiaries as well. MBNA, for instance, in 2004 discussed purchasing the British Internet bank and credit card issuer, Egg PLC, engaged in unsecured lending through credit card loans.[11]

In addition to major credit card companies, many consumer finance companies entered the credit card business as a supplement to personal cash loans. Most joined the national Visa and MasterCard networks. In late 1992, two of the largest finance companies entered the credit card markets with a different twist: General Electric (GE) and General Motors (GM) announced plans to offer MasterCards, and their new cards offered rebates on consumer products purchased from qualifying companies.[12]

Securitizations for Credit Cards and Other Loans

As the credit card receivables in the industry grew, firms had additional impetus to issue new securitized assets. Securitization of loans is an important development for finance companies, providing liquidity, lower cost financing, and fee income. The first automobile securitization occurred in February 1985, when Salomon Brothers bought $10 million in automobile loans from the Lloyd Anderson Group of finance companies. This transaction resulted in the first Certificates of Automobile Receivables (CARs). From this beginning, the market for asset-based securities has mushroomed. In 1991 alone, new issues reached over $50 billion. Credit card receivables, recreational and boat loans, home equity loans, leases, and small business loans have all been used to back newly issued securities. As noted in previous chapters, securitizations have had an enormous impact in the way financial services firms do business and have caused changes in the financial system, whereby a smaller percentage of loans are held on financial institution balance sheets, with more loans directly held by investors as asset-backed securities.[13]

Government-Sponsored Enterprises and Mortgage Banks

Often categorized as among the largest finance companies, government-sponsored enterprises (GSEs), discussed throughout the text, and other large mortgage banks originate loans and sell or securitize these loans, receiving a profit. They also often receive fee income for the servicing contract for these loans. In addition to purchasing and securitizing primary loans, secondary mortgages are also purchased. The Federal Home Loan Mortgage Association began purchasing selected types of secondary mortgages in 1981, and participation by other institutions has broadened substantially. Securities have been backed by home equity loans as well. Riskier loans can be brought to the market by obtaining sufficient credit enhancement from other institutions involved in the securitization process, giving the securities a higher credit rating.[14]

---

11 For excellent studies of credit card banks, see Robert C. Nash and Joseph F. Sinkey, Jr. "On Competition, Risk, and Hidden Assets in the Market for Bank Credit Cards." *Journal of Banking and Finance* 21 (January 1997), 89–112; and "Assessing the Riskiness and Profitability of Credit-Card Banks." *Journal of Financial Services Research* 7 (March 1993), 127–150. Also, see Anita Raghavan and Sara Callan, "MBNA Discusses Hatching Deal for British Internet Bank Egg," *The Wall Street Journal*, May 3, 2004, A3, A12; and the III *Financial Services Fact Book* at *http://www.iii.org*.

12 See Stephen Kleege. "Household Bank Still Virtually Unknown, But GM Card Issuer Has Insiders' Respect." *American Banker* (August 5, 1993), 15; Yvette Kantrow. "GE Offers Credit Card with Lure of Rebates." *American Banker* (September 3, 1992), 1, 10; Yvette Kantrow. "GM to Offer Credit Card Priced Lower than GE's." *American Banker* (September 9, 1992), 1, 14; and Leah Nathans Spiro. "More Cards in the Deck." *Business Week* (December 16, 1991), 100–104. Also see Aguilar (1990) and Jenster and Lindgren (1988).

13 See Cantor and Demsetz (1993); Caouette (1992); Olson (1986); and Shapiro (1985). Also see "Receivables Are Receivables." *Financial World* (March 6–19, 1985), 27; Suzanne Woolley. "You Can Securitize Virtually Everything." *Business Week* (July 20, 1992), 78–79; and "All the World's a Security." *The Economist* (August 29, 1992), 69.

14 See *Federal Reserve Bulletin* 85 (March 1998), A33.

GSEs include the Federal National Mortgage Corporation (Fannie Mae), Government National Mortgage Association (Ginnie Mae), Federal Home Loan Mortgage Corporation (Freddie Mac), and the Student Loan Marketing Association (Sallie Mae). In 2002, *Fortune Magazine* cited Fannie Mae as the ninth largest and Freddie Mac as the twenty-fourth largest financial services firms in the world.[15] Other prominent mortgage banks include Universal Lending and Countrywide Credit. Unlike banks, mortgage banks originate loans with the intent to sell or securitize them right away. By not keeping mortgages on their balance sheet, they avoid liquidity concerns and do not have to worry about funding gap problems as banks and thrifts do. However, mortgage banks still face the risk of interest rates falling between the time they purchase and sell mortgage loans, resulting in having to sell loans at a loss. Their profits are also subject to the cycles in home buying and the real estate markets. In the 1990s with lower interest rates making it less expensive for consumers to purchase homes, mortgage banking firms did quite well, with a large volume of new loans originated or refinanced through these firms. In the latter 1990s and early 2000s with falling rates, mortgage banks also earned significant fee income from loan refinancing. Large diversified financial services companies engage in considerable securitization activity, which provides liquidity, noninterest income, and a reduction in interest rate risk. GSEs (Fannie Mae and Freddie Mac) have been involved in some scandals regarding improper accounting of revenues with securitization and other activities. There have also been governmental concerns about the enormity of the GSEs' operations, which could result in severe repercussions and systemic risk for the home mortgage industry if either GSE suffers operational or financial difficulties. Other critics of the GSEs have been concerned about the government subsidy that they receive in terms of a lower cost of financing, due to the likelihood that they will be bailed out by the government, given the large scale of their operations, in the event of any financial crisis.[16]

Industry Structure and Trends

Like the banking industry, the finance company industry consists of very large firms that dominate the industry, along with hundreds of smaller firms. Also similar to the banking industry, securitization has taken over as a way to provide liquidity, noninterest income, and to remove the asset risk from a firm's balance sheet, placing that risk in the hands of millions of investors who hold mortgage-backed securities and thereby creating a change in the way financial services firms operate and a major change in the U.S. financial system.

Challenges with Greater Securitization Activities

This change in the financial services industry with greater securitization, globalization, and consolidation has created challenges for the U.S. financial system. Timothy Geithner, President and CEO of the Federal Reserve Bank of New York notes that the tremendous scale, concentration by large firms, securitization, and globalization of financial intermediation activities "creates new risks that must be managed," with shocks "transmitted more rapidly" and "diffused more broadly." This makes the financial system vulnerable to any "operational or financial disruption" by a single firm. With rapid securitization, he points out that only about 20 percent of overall credit market debt in the United States is now held on balance sheet by commercial banks, with investors holding shares in asset-backed securities individually or in mutual or pension funds, having risk placed in their hands. This increases the need for risk management for firms engaged in securitization activities.[17]

---

15 See the III *Financial Services Fact Book* at *http://www.iii.org.*

16 See Crawford and Sihler (1997); Edmund I. Andrews. "Fed Chief Warns of a Risk to Taxpayers: Fannie Mae and Freddie Mac Cannot Hedge Against Financial Crises." *New York Times* (February 25, 2004). C1, C4. Also see Federal Reserve Bank of Atlanta. "Emerging Competition and Risk-Taking Incentives at Fannie Mae and Freddie Mac." Working Paper 2004-4 (February 2004); and W. Scott Frame and Larry D Wall. "Fannie Mae's and Freddie Mac's Voluntary Initiatives: Lessons from Banking." *Economic Review* (Federal Reserve Bank of Atlanta) (First Quarter 2002), 45–59.

17 Timothy F. Geithner, President and Chief Executive Officer, Federal Reserve Bank of New York, Speech: "Change and Challenges Facing the U.S. Financial System," March 25, 2004, on the Federal Reserve Bank of New York Website at *http://www.ny.frb.org/newsevents/speeches/2004/gei040325.html.*

Industry Structure, Market Share, and Trends in the Number of Firms and Receivable Types

The structure of the finance company industry is quite concentrated. Although there are about 984 nondepository finance companies with assets over $1.12 trillion, the largest twenty firms hold a share of loans (typically called **receivables**) of about 69 percent.[18] The largest finance companies include predominantly captive finance companies such as General Electric Capital Corporation, General Electric Financial Services, and Ford Motor Credit Company, as well as GSEs including Fannie Mae, Freddie Mac, and Sallie Mae. For the twenty largest finance companies, loan (receivables) holdings totaled $639.9 billion.[19]

The number of finance companies fell by 20.5 percent to 984 in 2000 from 1,237 in 1996, with the largest decline of 25 percent in the smallest firm category of less than $10 million. The Fed reported an industry structure in 2000, with lots of small firms, but only a few very large firms holding the majority of assets. There were 11 firms in 2000 with assets of $20 billion or larger and 57 with assets of $1 billion to $19 billion in 2000. For smaller firms with assets less than $1 billion, 61 had assets between $200 to $999 million, and the remaining 855 firms had assets less than $200 million. In terms of types of loans (receivables) held, in 2002, 40.4 percent were consumer, 42.6 percent business, and 17 percent real estate. Consumer receivables and securitized assets have risen in recent years and to a small extent real estate receivables. The annual growth rate in assets for finance companies has been about 9 percent.[20]

Typical Funding Sources and Trends

Finance companies typically finance their receivables with bank loans, commercial paper, debt due to the parent (if a captive finance company), other types of debt, and equity. Similar to banks, finance companies have high financial leverage, with equity (common stock par value and surplus and undivided profits) averaging about 11.6 percent in 2000. Corporate bonds in recent years have been the most important funding source (about 38.4 percent of funding), followed by other sources of financing (22 percent), commercial paper financing (17.8 percent), debt due to parent company (7.6 percent of financing), and bank borrowing (2.6 percent). Since 1996, commercial paper has fallen as a source of financing, and debt due to parent and other debt as increased.[21]

Trends in Mergers and Acquisitions

Large, specialty finance companies were involved in a large number of mergers in the late 1990s and early 2000s. For instance, in the first three months of 1998, three huge mergers took place: Household International purchased Beneficial for $7.7 billion; Conseco acquired Green Tree Financial for $7.6 billion; and First Union acquired the Money Store for $2.1 billion. In anticipation of being future acquisition targets, other specialty finance firms' stock prices rose dramatically at that time. Similar to banks, finance companies are involved in a spread business, whereby they borrow and lend, making a profit on the spread. With new technology, the paperwork could be reduced, thereby increasing the efficiency of loan processing, reducing the cost to service loans, and allowing greater securitization activities. Hence, increasing size through mergers can reduce two firms' overall costs of funds and increase this spread, in addition to providing other synergies or economies of scale.

In addition to domestic mergers, in the early 2000s, large finance firms have merged internationally. HSBC Holdings, PLC, a large U.K. bank, acquired Household International, Inc., with a deal value of $14.861 billion. GE acquired the U.K. Structured Finance Operations of ABB, Ltd., with a deal value of $2.3 billion; Australian Guarantee Corp., Ltd., a specialty lender, with a deal value of $894.9 million; and Deutsche Financial Services Inventory Finance, a specialty lender, with a deal value of $450

---

18 See Dynan, Johnson, and Slowinski (January 2002).

19 See Dynan, Johnson, and Slowinski (January 2002) and the III *Financial Services Fact Book* at http://www.iii.org.

20 See Dynan, Johnson, and Slowinski (January 2002).

21 Ibid.

million. In 2002 alone there were 104 deals for specialty finance companies, with a deal value of $23.6 billion, the largest deal value of financial services industry mergers and acquisitions for that year, representing 40 percent of total deal value.[22]

Innovations

Finance companies have been reinventing themselves in recent decades, coming up with innovative products and strategies. Beneficial Finance Corporation, for instance, in the early 1990s, gave customers advances on expected tax refunds for $29, which Beneficial could collect quickly electronically, earning significant fee income from more than five million customers who took advantage of this service.[23] Other huge finance companies early on acquired nonbanks and became strong competitors in the credit card business. Others bought thrifts, to be able to offer financial alternatives to corporate customers. Finance companies like General Electric Capital Corporation, now the world's largest financial services firm, and MBNA, one of the largest credit card banks, also initiated and assumed a leadership role in new types of asset securitization.[24]

Trends in Profitability

Although many finance firms have been extremely profitable, such as GEFS and MBNA, on average the entire industry has had volatile average profits. At times, captive firms have been allowed to operate at a loss, acting more as sales firms to encourage consumer purchases of manufacturing or retail goods. Based on twenty-six publicly traded commercial finance firms, average ROEs fell, for instance, from 13.25 percent in 1998 to −4.76 percent in 1999 to −1.48 percent in 2000, rose to 2.03 percent in 2001, and fell to −5.14 percent in 2002. For twenty-nine publicly traded consumer finance firms, ROEs fell from 20.55 percent in 1998 to 11.24 percent in 1999, rose to 6.37 percent in 2000, plunged to −29.9 percent in 2001, but rose to 20.89 percent in 2002. Hence, average profitability has been incredibly volatile for publicly traded finance company firms.[25]

Concept Questions

1 Why would diversified financial services firms (i.e., financial conglomerates) be more likely to have corporate control problems that could result in financial scandals?

2 Define consumer and business finance companies, industrial loan companies (ILCs), credit card banks, and mortgage banks. Give examples of each. How are finance companies similar to and different from banks?

3 Why have regulators and community banks been concerned about the growth of ILCs? What provisions under the proposed Regulatory Relief Bill of 2004 would limit the growth of ILCs?

4 Why have regulators been concerned about the rapid growth of securitization activity and the rapid growth of Fannie Mae and Freddie Mac, in particular? How concentrated is the finance company industry?

5 What are the typical types of loans (receivables) held by finance companies? What are the typical liabilities (funding sources) of finance companies? What are recent trends in holdings and profitability?

6 What have been some problems with subprime lending?

---

22 See Insurance Information Institute Website, *Financial Services Fact Book 2003*, at *http://financialservicefacts.org*. At the time of this writing. the page for information on financial service mergers was provided at *http://financialservicefacts.org/financial2/today/consolidation/*. SNL Financial. LC, in Charlottesville, Virginia, provides information for the III Website and is a great source of financial and merger data for the financial services industry.

23 In 1998, many specialty finance companies had financial performance problems, yet high valuations, such as Beneficial, and were put up for sale. See Gregory Zuckerman. "Deals Boost Specialty Finance Firms." *The Wall Street Journal* (April 17, 1998), C1, C2; Steven Lipin and Jeff Bailey. "Beneficial Corp. Puts Itself on the Block as a Result of Pressure from Wall Street." *The Wall Street Journal* (February 17, 1998), 14; Laura M. Holson. "Beneficial May Put Itself Up for Sale." *New York Times* (February 17, 1998), C1; Richard Walters. "Money Store Acquired for $2.1 Billion." *The Rocky Mountain News* (March 5, 1998), B4; and Howard Rudnitsky. "Tax Play." *Forbes* (May 1, 1992), 48, 50.

24 See the Websites for General Electric, MBNA, and Countrywide Credit Financial *(http://about.countrywide.com)* for a history of many innovations by finance and credit card bank companies.

25 See Insurance Information Institute, *Financial Services Fact Book 2003 (http://www.iii.org)*. At the time of this writing, profitability ratios were found on *http://financialservicefacts.org/financial2/finance/profitability/*, with information provided to III by SNL Financial Services M&A DataSource, as cited on the III Website. For the Fed's Finance Company Survey 2000, see Dynan, Johnson, and Slowinski (January 2002).

Problems with Subprime Predatory Lending

State regulators, as well as banking regulators, the Federal Trade Commission (FTC), and legislators have been concerned in recent years about predatory lending by finance companies, including special subprime lending subsidiaries of large banks. Predatory lenders often target disadvantaged borrowers and charge excessive rates. While subprime lending is not necessarily a bad thing, if borrowers are charged higher rates than they could find elsewhere, not educated about the risks that they are undertaking, or are given high-cost loans that they do not have the financial capacity to repay, these practices constitute predatory lending. Such predatory lending often leads to abnormally high rates charged to borrowers and the bankruptcy of disadvantaged borrowers. Some states have passed anti-predatory lending laws, however, that have created unintended adverse effects by discouraging all subprime lending and making securitizers of loans reluctant to purchase loans in these states. For instance, Fannie Mae announced in 2002 that it would not purchase "high cost loans" in Georgia or New York, given the risk of new subprime lending laws in those states.[26] Experts in the mortgage banking industry have testified before the Congressional Financial Services Subcommittee calling for a Uniform National Standard of Laws to Combat Predatory Lending Practices, to create a uniform legal system for subprime lending to avoid the confusion of different state and local laws, particularly since 9 percent of all mortgage originations are subprime loans and the securitization of these loans has grown dramatically.[27]

Financial Analysis for Finance Companies

For non-publicly traded finance firms, little information is available on the income, expenses, and profitability of finance companies as a whole, because Fed surveys do not include income statement information. The American Financial Services Association (AFSA), a trade organization for finance companies, collected data from voluntarily reporting finance companies, but this database was discontinued after 1989. For large, publicly traded finance companies, information can be obtained by going to their Websites, clicking on menu choices similar to "investor relations," and then on "annual reports" or "financial" and downloading this information (often in a PDF form). A typical form for a finance company balance sheet and income statement and some specific financial ratios for finance firms are shown in Table 19.1. Many firms are subsidiaries of larger companies, but annual reports may provide financials by business specialty. The majority of finance company assets are typically gross receivables. Reserves are deducted to get net receivables including (1) a reserve for unearned income, and (2) a reserve for expected losses. Liabilities, as noted earlier, include bank loans, commercial paper, debt owed to parent, and other debt. Finance company income statements are similar to bank income statements, with the majority of income coming from their interest spreads and also fee income generated (noninterest revenue) and significant operating (noninterest expenses). Hence, financial analysis is similar to the analysis for depository firms, although other types of debts are the primarily liabilities instead. Special liquidity ratios reflect the ease with which the company's assets can be converted into cash. Because finance companies hold very few, if any, securities, cash relative to short-term debt and the percentage of maturing receivables help to estimate potential liquidity risk for a firm. The unused credit line to open market debt ratio indicates the company's unused credit lines that reflect future credit needs, often included in footnotes of annual reports.[28]

---

26 See "Economic Issues in Predatory Lending." OCC Working Paper, Comptroller of the Currency, Washington D.C. (Global Banking and Financial Analysis), July 30, 2003, 1–29 (no author given), OCC working papers available on the OCC Website. Also see "Predatory Lending." HUD Treasury Special Report, and "Unequal Burden in Atlanta: Income and Racial Disparities in Subprime Lending." U.S. Department of Housing and Urban Development, 451 7th Street SW, Washington, DC, 20410; Gregory Elliehausen and Michael Staten. "Regulation of Subprime Mortgage Products: An Analysis of North Carolina's Predatory Lending Law." Credit Research Center Working Paper # 66, November 2002; Christine Lachnicht. "Impact of Predatory Lending Laws on RMBS Securitizations." *Moody's Investors Service*, Structured Finance, Special Report, March 26, 2002, 1, 5.

27 See Testimony before the Financial Services Subcommittees calling for a Uniform National Standard of Laws to Combat Predatory Lending Practices by Teresa A. Bryce, Member of the Mortgage Bankers Association's (MBA) Board of Directors and Vice President and General Counsel of Nexstar Financial Corporation, Washington, D.C. (March 30, 2004) on the MBA Website: *http://www.mortgagebankers.org/news/2004/pr0330.html*.

28 See Dynan, Johnson, and Slowinski (January 2002) for typical balance sheets of finance companies, and the Insurance Information Institute, *Financial Services Fact Book*, on the III Website (*http://www.iii.org*), at the time of this writing at *http://financialservicefacts.org/financial2/finance/rec/* and *http://financialservicefacts.org/financial2/finance/assetsandliabilities/*. Also see Mark C. Kramer and Raymond M. Neihengen, Jr. "Analysis of Finance Company Ratios in 1991." *Journal of Commercial Lending* 75 (September 1992), 39–47. The *Journal of Commercial Lending* periodically has articles providing information on the finance company industry performance. Also see *Business Week*'s Corporate Scoreboard, which includes performance on diversified financial firms. Other sources of information for finance company ratios are Robert Morris Association, Moody's Financial Reports, ValueLine, the National Commercial Finance Association, and Dun and Bradstreet's Key Business Ratios.

table **19.1** TYPICAL FINANCE COMPANY FINANCIAL STATEMENTS AND FINANCIAL RATIOS

TYPICAL BALANCE SHEET FORMAT

Assets	Liabilities
Receivables (loans):	Bank Loans
Consumer	Commercial Paper
Business	Debt:
Real Estate	Owed to Parent
Less Reserves for Unearned Income	Debentures
Less Reserves for Losses	Other Debt
Net Receivables	Equity:
Other Assets	Common Stock
Total Assets	Retained Earnings
	Total Liabilities & Equity

TYPICAL INCOME STATEMENT	SPECIAL LIQUIDITY RATIOS FOR FINANCE COMPANIES
Interest Revenues	Maturing Receivables in 1 Year / Total Receivables
Interest Expenses	Unused Credit Lines / Open Market Debt
Interest Spread	Cash / Short-term Debt
Other Revenues	**Special Efficiency / Productivity Ratios**
Other Expenses	Operating Expenses / Average Net Receivables
Income Before Taxes & Extraordinary Items	Ave. Monthly Principal Collections / Ave. Net Monthly Receivables
Net Income	Annual Gross Finance Revenues / Average Net Receivables

Typically, finance company gross income includes interest and fee income on receivables (loans) and securitizations, as well as revenue from credit insurance payments and fees for other services. Operating expenses often range from 40 percent to 50 percent of expenses.

In a study titled "Finance Companies, Bank Competition, and Niche Markets," researchers Eli M. Remolona and Kurt C. Wulfekuhler of the Federal Reserve Bank of New York compared the performance of a sample of the nation's largest finance companies with all insured commercial banks. The finance company sample had a higher interest spread on average, despite a higher interest expense to assets, because of a larger proportion of higher yielding consumer loans in their portfolio that produced a higher average interest revenue to assets. Higher potential yields, however, also connote higher risk. During recessionary periods, finance companies have more bankruptcies and often have lower returns, while during economic expansion, their profitability improves.[29]

Finance Company Regulations

Finance companies are regulated almost entirely at the state level and are subject to all federal and state regulations on consumer, commercial, and mortgage credit, such as the Truth in Lending Act and Equal Credit Opportunity Act discussed in Chapter 13 under lending regulations, along with the Uniform Commercial Credit code. Most states require finance companies to demonstrate to authorities that a new branch office will provide "convenience and advantage" to customers. Finance companies are free from restrictions on interstate expansion, and, consequently, many of the largest finance companies have extensive nationwide branch networks. Recently, the cost of operating "brick and mortar" branches has risen, and finance companies have turned to less expensive ways, such as mail solicitations

---

29 See Remolona and Wulfekuhler (1992).

and credit cards to attract customers and deliver services. The result is a decline in the number of branches operated by finance companies.[30]

Like other consumer lenders, finance companies are affected by state usury laws, which restrict the interest rates lenders can charge on specific types of loans. One impact of these ceilings was to make less credit available to borrowers. For instance, one study of finance company lending found that the ratio of consumer installment loans to total loans held by finance companies declined from 50 percent to 39 percent from 1965 to 1974, a period characterized by increasing usury ceilings in most states. Also, some financial companies closed branches in states with low usury interest rate ceilings. With many state usury laws rewritten in the 1980s to permit higher ceilings, finance companies faced fewer problems in being able to offer rates sufficient to cover costs and potential high loan losses.[31]

Personal bankruptcy laws also have a significant effect on the profitability of consumer finance companies in terms of their ability to collect on loans that default. In the first year the 1978 Bankruptcy Reform Act went into effect, making it easier for consumers to declare bankruptcy while retaining many of their assets, loan losses at finance companies more than doubled, and accordingly operating expenses rose in 1980. In 1981, profits for the industry as a whole fell 20 percent. GE Credit, for example, estimated that by 1982, 3,085 consumer borrowers per month declared bankruptcy.[32] In response, finance companies have diversified away from unsecured consumer lending and moved into second mortgage lending for protection. In June 1984, a new federal bankruptcy law was passed after much lobbying by finance companies, making it more difficult for debtors to abuse their credit privileges by declaring bankruptcy. The new law encouraged the reentry of finance companies into the market for personal cash loans. Congress has continued to debate over whether new bankruptcy reform legislation is needed.[33]

The nation's largest finance companies are diversified finance companies with numerous financial services activities included in their financial statements, ranging from insurance activities, brokerage and other securities activities, activities related to thrifts, as well as finance company activities. The next section discusses the trend in diversification.

The Trend in Diversified Financial Firms

Financial services is a term encompassing all the deposit, credit, investment, insurance, and risk management operations discussed in this book. In the 1980s and continuing in the 1990s to the early 2000s, however, financial institutions have increasingly expanded their range of services, becoming financial service conglomerates. This trend increased with the GLB Act of 1999 and the creation of financial holding companies (FHCs). In preparation for the continuing emergence of financial conglomerates, in April 1998, the Basel Committee on Banking Supervision, the International Organization of Securities Commissions, and the International Association of Insurance Supervisors released documents prepared by the Joint Forum on Financial Conglomerates to address some of the most crucial supervisory issues that have arisen with the "blurring of distinctions" between different types of financial service firms including exchange of information among supervisors, assessing the capital adequacy of financial conglomerates, coordination among supervisors, and testing the fitness and propriety of managers, directors, and major shareholders.[34]

Citigroup is a good example of a combined financial conglomerate, with $1.3 trillion in assets, 275,000 employees in 100 countries, and operations with four major groups: (1) a global consumer group (55 percent of total income in 2003); (2) a global corporate and investment banking group

---

30 See Benston (1977).

31 Ibid.

32 See "A New Source of Mortgage Money." *Business Week* (March 23, 1981), 95; "Finance Companies Show the Strain." *Business Week* (March 22, 1982), 80–81; "The Allure of Second Mortgages." *Business Week* (March 16, 1981), 126; "Turning Back a Tide of Personal Bankruptcy." *Business Week* (June 14, 1982), 32; Johnson (1989); Staten (1989); Stephen Wermiel. "Court Clears Chapter 11 Use By Individuals." *The Wall Street Journal* (June 14, 1991), A2; and Stahl (1993).

33 In the second quarter of 1998, personal bankruptcies rose by 5.9 percent to 361,908 filings, up more than 20,000 from the first quarter. See Sougata Mukherjee. "Americans Flock to the Poor House: Bankruptcy Filings May Break Record." *Denver Business Journal* (August 27–31, 1998), 15-A.

34 See "International Group Addresses Supervision of Conglomerates." *Banking Policy Report* 18 (March 15, 1999), 2.

(31 percent); (3) a global investment management group (10 percent), and (4) Smith Barney, a private client services group (4 percent). Although financial conglomerates have not always performed well, Citi had excellent credit AA+ (Fitch) ratings and an ROE of 19.8 percent in 2003 and 18.6 percent in 2002. In its 2003 annual report, Citigroup notes that its highly diversified earnings base allows the company to "thrive in difficult market conditions."[35]

The following section discusses reasons for the development of financial conglomerates in the 1980s and in the 1990s. The experiences of several financial conglomerates are also discussed.

Reasons for the Development of Financial Conglomerates

The reasons for the emergence of both nonfinancial and financial conglomerates have often been debated throughout the 1990s and early 2000s. Reasons include the following:[36]

1. Firms can smooth their earnings by receiving interest and noninterest income from a variety of sources;

2. Smoother earnings allow firms to have greater debt capacity and a lower overall cost of funds;

3. Firms can achieve operating synergies including economies of scale and scope and more productive resource utilization;

4. Firms in maturing industries, such as the insurance or banking industries, can diversify for long-term survival and greater profitability and growth;

5. Managers can reduce unemployment risk by smoothing earnings or achieving greater ego satisfaction or compensation, if management compensation is related to growth; and

6. By applying management competencies, firms can improve the efficiency of inefficient firms in a related industry.

Other less theoretical but more practical considerations include ease of entry, substitutability of products, perceived profitability, and a significant decline in traditional net interest margins, spreading the cost of technology over many different services, and other synergies, necessitating a move into new areas that provide greater noninterest revenues and better returns for a company.

Ease of Entry

The cost of entering different aspects of the financial services industry can be low, because a major investment in capital may not be needed, particularly for a firm in the information or retailing business. For instance, in the 1980s and 1990s some nonfinancial firms, such as retailers already offering credit cards, found it particularly easy to expand their financial services. Nordstrom, a major retailing firm, set up banking services in 1998 for its consumer customers through a nonbank. Telecommunication and computer firms such as TCI and Microsoft similarly found it easy to set up joint ventures with banks to offer bill paying and mortgage shopping services. In 1999, three of the most popular banks for small businesses were major nonbank credit card issuers Mountain West Financial, American Express, and Advanta Corporation, which moved easily into the small firm financing area. Merrill Lynch and Boston Financial Network, a new Internet firm, also provide loans, credit lines, cash management, and other banking services for small firms. In 1999, Merrill Lynch hired 100 commercial bankers to work in regional offices around the country in cooperation with the firm's 14,000 brokers to provide counseling and loans to small businesses. By purchasing a cheap failed Florida savings and loan, Merrill Lynch can offer trust services in all states. Similarly, the Internet permits Boston Financial network, which has no branches for tellers, to act as a bank, brokerage firm, bookkeeping, and bill-paying service for small businesses anywhere through a single Website.[37]

---

35 See Citigroup Annual Report, 2003. Also, for a nice summary of the acquisitions that led to the Travelers and Citicorp mergers in 1998, see Joseph B. Treaster. "Financial Services Consolidate, But Regulation Is Still Fragmented." *New York Times* (January 2, 1998), D1, D5; and David Greising, Peter Galuszka, Kathleen Morris, Andrew Osterland, and Geoffrey Smith. "Are Megabanks—Once Unimaginable, Now Inevitable—Better?" *Business Week* (April 27, 1998), 33–36.

36 This summary comes from Lee and Cooperman (1989), 45. See Leonitades (1986).

37 See Joseph Kahn. "Banking on the Unbanks." *New York Times* (February 4, 1999), C1; and "Financial Services Coming to TV." *Rocky Mountain News* (March 25, 1998), 1B, 5B.

Substitutability of Products

Financial products have commodity-like characteristics. It is hard to tell one ear of corn from another, and one savings account is similar to another, as is one whole life policy to another. A single provider rarely can corner a market at the expense of competitors, and all firms offering a service have an equal opportunity to succeed—or fail. If one financial service provider does not provide a service efficiently or does not serve a particular market segment, another firm can move in. For example, in the preceding section, Boston Financial Network, which provides business loans and other financial services to firms over the Internet, started up because its chairman ran a small business for a while and could not get support from banks or brokerage firms. Similarly, Nordstrom has been able to provide cheaper consumer loans for its retail customers and check-cashing services.[38]

Perceived Profitability and Significant Decline in Traditional Profits

Many firms have entered new types of financial services businesses because they perceive it to be more profitable than their primary lines of business. An executive with JCPenney Company, a leading retailer with insurance and thrift subsidiaries, noted, "In general financial services are more profitable than retailing."[39] Sears also found entering the financial services arena to be profitable in the 1980s. Although many executives of financial services firms might quarrel with this thought, it has led several nonfinancial firms into the financial services business. As mentioned earlier, this pattern has continued with nonfinancial firms finding a loophole by purchasing ILCs in western states where they are allowed.

With a significant decline in traditional bank net interest margins, banks have also realized that they cannot depend on spread income for profits. As Arnold Danielson points out, financial services firms in the early to mid 1990s were much like the railroad industry in the early 1900s that were hampered by constraints from regulations and traditional iron rails not allowing them to keep pace with other forms of transportation. Similarly, traditional banks suffered declining spreads on traditional businesses, were stuck with "traditional delivery systems," were "hampered by regulatory constraints," and had reduced deposit-based financing needs. He also notes that with growth in noninterest revenues rising at a faster rate than the growth of overhead, banks with significant noninterest revenues were profitable. Similarly, insurance firms in the last two decades of the twentieth century faced slower profit growth in a maturing industry and the need to diversify into areas with more rapid growth, such as mutual funds and annuity products.[40]

Spreading Technology Costs over Diverse Products

With customers demanding new services and the need for financial services firms to take on new technology and the accompanying expenses, financial institutions need to gain economies of scale and scope by increasing their volume of customers and entering new product markets. Many financial service product lines involve informational and transactional services, which large financial service firms with new technology can provide, while reducing the cost of technology per unit with a large volume of customers and diverse products.

Synergy

A final motivation for diversified financial services is a belief that the earnings of a diversified firm will exceed those of two or more firms operating separately and/or reduce the volatility of the earnings of the two individual firms. As a reporter for *The Wall Street Journal* put it in an article on diversified financial services firms in the 1980s, "With each acquisition, the word 'synergy' was used to the point

---

38 Ibid.

39 Steve Weiner and Hank Gilman. "Debate Grows on Retailers' Bank Services." *The Wall Street Journal* (May 18, 1984).

40 See Danielson (1999), 15.

of exhaustion."[41] Without synergy, of course, firm growth through diversification will not be valued by shareholders, who can diversify their personal equity portfolios more cheaply and who recognize the high transaction costs incurred by diversifying corporations. Synergy has eluded some financial services firms and benefited others. In the preceding discussion, for instance, Merrill Lynch found synergies in offering loans and services to small businesses. Other firms, such as Sears, which attempted to offer a full range of financial services to its retail customers, did not find as much synergy in some cases, because customers did not necessarily wish to shop for clothes and goods and financial services at the same time, at least in the 1980s. A discussion of trends in financial service conglomerates and successful and less successful firms follows.

Trends in Financial Service Conglomerates

Conglomerate Waves

Leonitades (1986) describes the trends in conglomerations as waves, pointing out that for nonfinancial firms the first wave occurred from 1955 to 1968, when new conglomerates, fed by the expansion of the 1960s, "naively yet feverishly acquired firms in unrelated fields." Next followed a period of reevaluation from 1969 to 1976, in which time conglomerates were unprofitable during the recession of the mid-1970s. A third merger wave from 1977 to the early 1980s is associated with the emergence of professional managers, the entry of more conservative firms, and a corporate repositioning and restructuring of many mature conglomerates. This stage included the divesting of unrelated subsidiaries, resulting in more focused inter-industry strategic groups, in contrast to the random diversification of the past.[42]

Similarly, financial conglomerates have come in waves with the emergence of a number of financial conglomerates in the late 1970s to mid 1980s, although some early financial conglomerates, such as Sears, began diversifying as early as 1911. The early 1990s were characterized as a time when many financial conglomerates divested or spun off subsidiaries that they had acquired in the 1980s. The reasons for these spin-offs included problems blending cultures, the failure of the stock market to reflect the full value of individual businesses, and the need to refocus on a firm's central lines of business. In the 1990s, new financial conglomerates have emerged, such as Citigroup, Bank of America with its mergers with Nationsbank and FleetBoston, Deutsche Bank with its merger with Bankers Trust, and UBS with its merger with Paine Webber. Examples of successful and less successful financial conglomerates are discussed in the following section.[43]

Some Firms Are Successful, Others Are Not: Examples

Although many financial services firms have continued to be successful in their diversification activities, such as Citigroup, Prudential, and Merrill Lynch, at times these firms have navigated rocky roads attempting to manage and integrate diverse acquisitions. Similarly, other firms, such as Sears and General Electric Financial Services (GEFS), and Merrill Lynch again, have found it worthwhile to divest financial services firms in some areas. The experiences of Sears, GEFS, Merrill Lynch, and Prudential are briefly summarized in the following sections.

Sears

Sears entered the financial services business in 1911 by setting up a consumer finance subsidiary to provide credit to its customers. In 1931, Allstate was formed to market auto insurance to Sears customers, and in 1959, Sears formed a commercial real estate development and management firm. In the 1970s, Sears also purchased a mortgage company and a savings and loan. In 1981, Sears purchased a major real

---

41 See Hilder and Weiner (1985). In finance theory, a reduction of risk through diversification as a source of synergy is often not accepted, because stockholders can diversify their own portfolios. See Richard Booth. "Reducing Risk Doesn't Pay Off." *The Wall Street Journal* (March 15, 1999), A18, for a discussion of these arguments.

42 This summary comes from Lee and Cooperman (1989), 45. See Leonitades (1986).

43 Ibid.

estate brokerage firm, Coldwell Banker, and a major securities brokerage firm, Dean Witter Reynolds. Sears intended to provide full financial services within its retail stores, providing synergies in terms of cross-selling products with one-stop financial and retail shopping for its customers. Financial service revenues would also diversify the firm's profits, which was appealing because of stagnant retailing profits in the 1970s.

Unfortunately, by 1985, Sears found that its financial centers offering insurance, brokerage, and real estate services did not generate as much business and profit as expected. Dean Witter suffered large operating losses and the exit of talented brokers. Also, one-stop financial shopping failed to appeal to customers. Customers in the 1980s appeared to reject the idea of purchasing socks, mutual funds, and banking products in the same location, despite the fact that Dean Witter at the time had about 6,600 brokers on its payroll, making it the second largest securities firm, next to Merrill Lynch, in terms of number of brokers. When Dean Witter management cut costs, they were made somewhat indiscriminately, further hurting morale at Dean Witter. Despite the poor performance of Dean Witter, performance for Allstate and Coldwell Banker was good relative to the industry. In 1984, Sears earned 57 percent of its income from retailing, 42 percent from Allstate Insurance, 5 percent from Coldwell Banker Real Estate, and had losses at Dean Witter and its Sears World Trade Center building.[44]

Despite much criticism, Sears introduced the Discover Card in 1985; it was marketed nationally by 1986. Sears had the informational advantage of having names, addresses, and credit histories of more than sixty million customers with a Sears credit card, twenty-eight million of whom were active users, to target its new credit card to. It offered favorable terms of no fee for two years for its card, compared with higher fees offered by Visa, MasterCard, and American Express. Sears also offered rebates of up to 1 percent on a customer's annual credit balance. To get merchants to accept its card, Sears also undercut the fees competitors charged merchants to settle credit card transactions. With Discover, Sears hoped to be able to cross-sell products from Dean Witter and Sears Savings Bank by offering a Family Savings Account with the savings bank, which collected deposits by mail. Sears also offered tiered interest rates with larger deposits and individual retirement accounts to encourage customers to entrust their checks to the U.S. Postal Service.

To the surprise of analysts, Sears's Discover Card became quite a success, after initial losses in 1985 and 1986. By 1992, a healthy $239 million profit was earned, and Discover had more than forty million cardholders, making Sears the second largest credit card issuer (behind Visa) at that time. Sears also planned on synergies with its Coldwell Banker and Dean Witter divisions by having home mortgages financed by Sears, insured by private mortgage insurance, and packaged for resale by Dean Witter. However, when real estate and mortgage markets became troubled in the late 1980s and early 1990s, plans to be involved in more than 25 percent of all U.S. home sales and mortgages for those homes failed to materialize. Sears's core merchandising business continued to deteriorate during this period as well.[45]

By 1989 several of its large institutional shareholders, including the California Public Employees Retirement System (CALPERS), expressed great concern over Sears's performance. Sears's stock price fell significantly in 1990. Pressure from institutional investors continued, and in 1992, Sears's management announced a major restructuring, which involved selling Coldwell Banker, spinning off 20 percent of Dean Witter and 20 percent of Allstate, and refocusing on its core retail businesses, carried out in 1993. Later, other interests in Allstate were spun off as a tax-free dividend in 1994, and in 1997 Morgan Stanley purchased Dean Witter/Discover. Sears's stock price responded favorably to the spin-offs of its financial services firms. With considerable restructuring and a redefining of its retail business, Sears's stock price improved in the mid-1990s, although it faced some problems in 1998 and 1999, with a fall in retail profits. Sears continued to develop a credit card and financial services business, but it had large losses in the early 2000s, so it sold this business to Citigroup in 2003 for $21.4 billion. This acquisition enhanced Citigroup's card leadership position, giving it the largest managed receivables assets of $159.6 billion in 2003.[46]

---

44 See Martin, Kensinger, and Gillan (1996); Williams (1985); and Crawford and Sihler (1994), Discover Card, Case 5.

45 Ibid.

46 Ibid. Other sources on Sears include Haggerty (1984); Hilder and Weiner (1985); Williams (1985); Glynn (1985); Siconolfi (1991); Flynn, et al. (1992); Patterson and Schwadel (1992); Schwartz (1985); Key (1985); Greising (1989); Ellis (1986); Schmeitzer (1993); Roosevelt (1992); and Steinmetz (1993), and Citigroup's Annual Report, 2003.

In recent years, banks such as Wells Fargo have placed financial service kiosks in supermarkets with considerable success, suggesting that customers in the 1990s and beyond accept doing banking and purchasing mutual funds while shopping for dinner. This did not seem to be the case in the 1980s, when customers sent messages that they did not want one-stop financial shopping, preferring to shop around for financial services and products before making purchases. However, just as home banking was unsuccessful in the 1980s but became more successful in the 1990s for certain market segments, customer perceptions often change over time.

General Electric Financial Services, Inc. (GEFS)

General Electric Financial Services (GEFS) is an example of a very successful diversified financial services firm. As early as 1989, GEFS, a subsidiary of General Electric (GE) Company, was a global diversified financial services firm with $75 billion in assets and operations in more than seventeen different financial services businesses. In addition to serving as the captive finance company for GE to assist GE customers and other retail firms in financing purchases, it was active in other types of commercial finance activities, including leasing and equipment sales financing, and in accounts receivables financing. In 1998, GEFS purchased the First Factors Corporation, entering the U.S. factoring commercial finance business. GEFS also has considerable property and casualty and reinsurance subsidiaries.

In 1985, GEFS acquired Kidder Peabody to provide synergies in terms of diversification and to help GEFS with its financing and securitization of the loans that its finance subsidiaries made. In turn, GEFS provided a well-established customer base and financial strength for Kidder's investment banking business and future growth. Despite the potential synergies, the two firms had quite different cultures. GEFS had the more conservative, transaction-based culture of finance and insurance companies, whereas Kidder had the more deal-based, innovative, superstar, performance-based culture of an investment bank. Similarly, Kidder was involved in many activities, such as trading and deal making, that had large potential returns and losses, which could not be readily controlled or observed by GEFS.

In 1986, Kidder endured a scandal when one of its superstars was indicted in the Ivan Boesky insider-trading scandal, costing GEFS $25.3 million in fines to the SEC. With the 1987 stock market crash, Kidder also suffered losses. In response, GEFS exerted more cost controls over Kidder Peabody, including cutting more than 1,500 jobs, resulting in management battles between Kidder and GEFS. This ultimately led to the resignation of Kidder's chief executive officer and other senior managers. Investment banking profits continued to be low in the early 1990s, and trading income supplemented declines in underwriting income. In 1994, Kidder suffered huge trading losses by a rogue trader, resulting in the collapse of the firm. GE was forced to sell most of Kidder's assets to Paine Webber in 1994 for $670 million in exchange for stock. Ironically, GE eventually made a larger return on its original investment in Kidder, with a gain on its holdings of Paine Webber stock of $1.33 billion in 1998. GEFS's difficulties with its Kidder Peabody acquisition demonstrates some of the problems that diverse financial services firms have in controlling and managing an entirely different culture from the acquiring firm.[47]

GE continues to be a very successful diversified technology and financial services firm with $647.5 billion in assets, operating in 100 countries, and with more than 315,000 employees worldwide. Prior to 2002, GE Capital Services was a separate financial services conglomerate subsidiary with twenty-eight independent financial service businesses including GEFS. With the retirement of Jack Welch, falling valuation multiples for GE, and a concern for a lack of transparency in GE's financial operations, GE divided it financial activities into four separate businesses that were easier for investors to understand and easier to manage as a "corporate center": (1) GE Consumer Finance (about $70 billion in assets in 2002); (2) GE Commercial Finance ($180 billion); (3) GE Equipment Management ($25 billion); and (4) GE Insurance ($170 billion). As noted by Walter (2004), whether the breakup will make a difference in the previous "remarkable returns achieved by GE's financial businesses remains to be seen."[48]

---

47 See Crawford and Sihler (1994), Case 6: General Electric Financial Services, Inc. (out of print, but maybe available through Darden), for an excellent case on GEFS and the its history acquiring Kidder Peabody. Also see Anita Rahhavan and Patrick McGeehan. "GE Scores Big with Kidder 3 Years After." *The Wall Street Journal* (May 14, 1998), C21.

48 See Walter (2004) for a more detailed recent discussion of GE, and GE's annual report and a history of GE on the GE Website.

Merrill Lynch and Company

In the early 1970s. Merrill Lynch's (ML's) chairman, Donald Regan, announced a plan to transform ML into, as *Business Week* termed it, a "womb to tomb" financial services firm.[49] In 1977, ML diversified by initiating the first Cash Management Account (CMA), that is, a money market fund from which checks could be written, offered through its brokerage subsidiary. By the early 1990s, ML had a range of mutual funds with assets managed by its subsidiaries. In 1979, ML formed Merrill Lynch Realty, Inc., to acquire local real estate agencies, particularly in the rapidly growing Sun Belt. By the end of 1986, ML Realty had 500 residential real estate offices. By late 1986, however, ML officials realized that the synergy expected from adding real estate to its product offerings had not materialized. By 1989 ML sold all its remaining interests in ML Realty. ML introduced insurance to its range of services in the mid-1970s with the acquisition of Family Life Insurance Company and two additional insurance firms (with one sold in 1991). Merrill Lynch Life Insurance Company was founded in 1986 to develop life and annuity products to be marketed exclusively to ML clients.[50]

In 1985, ML unveiled the first of its retail "financial centers" in downtown Manhattan. The center was staffed with financial consultants (no longer called brokers) and onsite specialists in taxation, insurance, and other aspects of personal finance, with the objective of providing clients with a wide range of financial services that could be purchased from ML. Costs were reduced by consolidating offices in different areas, with 500 offices located throughout the world by the early 1990s. Personnel costs were reduced by hiring sales assistants to serve small account customers. In 1984, ML acquired the firm Becker Paribus to enhance its investment banking activities and became a major commercial paper dealer and among the largest underwriters of municipal and corporate bonds throughout the 1980s. ML also developed ties abroad to pursue its activities in Europe and Asia. ML is involved in international banking through Merrill Lynch International Banks, located in London, Geneva, Singapore, and other main financial centers.

In 1991 alone, assets in individual client accounts rose almost 20 percent and represented about 2.5 percent of total household financial assets in the United States. ML's retail services were also enhanced by two nonbanks, Merrill Lynch Bank and Trust in New Jersey and Merrill Lynch National Financial in Utah, which sell certificates of deposit (CDs), issue Visa cards, and offer consumer loans. Through Merrill Lynch Trust Company, personal trust services are offered throughout the United States. On the domestic front, ML launched efforts to attract commercial customers from its bank competitors. In the late 1980s, ML began an aggressive campaign to attract more small business borrowers. By 1992, ML had loaned more than $500 million to small businesses and was attracting their deposits to its working capital management accounts. In the later 1990s, with a surge in small businesses, ML provided a variety of consulting and banking services to small firms.[51]

Thus, ML's strengths include a major geographic presence with its worldwide offices, a huge retail customer base, cash management accounts with check-writing privileges, its own nonbanks, and international banking operations. Its investment banking strengths include strong relationships with wholesale corporate customers. ML's training programs, careful recruiting and training practices, and incentive compensation schemes have developed an effective and skilled workforce. Consequently, ML has had fewer cultural problems in its investment banking division and in integrating different types of firms. However, like Citigroup, ML has had more recent corporate control problems due to scandals with former investment bankers being prosecuted for contributing to the Enron scandal. In 2002, ML was prosecuted by the Attorney General of the State of New York for violations of conflict of interest by ML research analysts and the investment banking division, resulting in a $1.4 billion "global" settlement. ML also suffered a severe profit downturn along with the market downturn and dot.com bust in 2001. A new President, Stan O'Neal, took over in July 2001 and began major restructuring by cutting 22,000 employees and selling assets to reduce costs. In 2003 to the first quarter of 2004, Merrill achieved dramatic

49 See "How They Manage the New Financial Conglomerates." *Business Week* (December 20, 1982), 50.

50 See Merrill Lynch Annual Report, 1988, 37; Steve Swartz. "Merrill Lynch Real Estate Line Will Go Public." *The Wall Street Journal* (December 23, 1986), 2; and Merrill Lynch 1991 Annual Report, Form 10-K for information included In this section.

51 See Lynn W. Adams. "Merrill Lynch Beckoning Bank Customers." *American Banker* (September 9, 1992), 10; and Randall Smith and Michael Siconolfi. "Merrill Quietly Folds a Big Lending Operation." *The Wall Street Journal* (March 31, 1993), C1, C13. Also see Taub (1986); and Steve Swartz and Laurie P. Cohen. "Merrill Lynch Will Sell Units in Real Estate." *The Wall Street Journal* (September 30, 1986), 3–4.

profit improvement, with four quarters of more than $1 billion in profits, and $1.5 trillion in managed client assets.[52]

Prudential Insurance Company of America

Prudential Insurance Company of America (Pru), one of the nation's largest life insurers, has been operating since 1875. In 1981, Pru, a normally conservative insurer, sent shock waves through the financial community with its purchase of the Bache Group, Inc., the nation's sixth largest securities firm, after thirteen days of negotiations. Although Bache was in some turmoil, with complications in carrying out this acquisition, Pru's management was optimistic that Bache's problems were past and believed the acquisition was an ideal way to enter the brokerage, mutual fund, and underwriting business.[53]

Unfortunately, in the 1980s and early 1990s, the Bache acquisition (renamed Prudential Bache) failed to live up to the expectations of Pru's management, with a loss of $110 million in 1984, a huge loss in the 1987 stock market crash, and a loss of $50 million in 1989. Bache suffered from low productivity, with commissions and fees per employee nearly $15,000 less at Bache than at other leading brokers, and high salaries for new managers brought in to solve this problem. Undaunted, Pru's management decided to expand its securities business in 1989 by purchasing the brokerage segment of Thomson McKinnon (an additional 158 retail offices and 2,000 brokers). In March 1990, after most other brokerage firms had already let go employees, Pru announced layoffs. Pru also had to contribute parent capital to buoy up Bache. In 1991, Bache's CEO was replaced in the aftermath of class action lawsuits against securities brokers who were sued for not telling investors about the high risks of limited commercial real estate partnerships. Performance of the restructured and renamed Prudential Securities improved in 1992 but never achieved the desired synergies with cross-selling other Pru products. After a failed entry into investment banking (IB), IB activity was discontinued, and Prudential Securities was absorbed into the Prudential Asset Management Group offering a diverse set of investment operations and products including loan originations and private placement purchase and management services, serving more than 800 institutional clients. Pru also has a limited-service bank called Prudential Bank and Trust Company with services focused on individuals rather than business customers. Prudential Securities' performance improved with the bull market of the late 1990s. Pru did have some problems blending its insurance operations and securities operations, with large class action lawsuit settlements surrounding sales of insurance that consumers felt that they were being sold but didn't need and failure to notify customers of the risks of some investments, which hurt insurance sales with reactions by customers to lawsuits.[54]

In 1994, Pru sold several of its holdings to refocus on its core insurance businesses, but also benefiting from synergies in terms of its expertise in financial advisory, real estate, financial management, international insurance, and other asset management and corporate services, including a joint brokerage venture with Wachovia. Pru went public in 1998 to gain greater access to capital. Pru also diversified internationally, with its international insurance division operating in more than 30 countries. In 2004 Pru purchased Hyundai Investment and Securities and its subsidiary, Hyundai Investment Trust Management Co., Ltd., to become the largest foreign-owned asset management company in South Korea. Pru also entered the retirement plan management business, acquiring Cigna's retirement business in 2004. In April 2004 Pru's stock price rose significantly to $44.67 from $30.40 the previous year.

---

52 See Tully (1996), 269; also see Komansky (1996). These chapters from the book *The New Financiers* provide excellent insights from executives of Merrill Lynch. Also see on Merrill Lynch's Website *(http://www.ml.com)* and investor relations *(http://www.ir.ml.com)*, Merrill Lynch *2003 Factbook;* also see Reuters New York Report. "Merrill Lynch Does More for Less as Cuts Bear Fruit." (April 15, 2004), on the Star Online, BizWeek Business *(http://biz.thestar.com .mybizweek);* and Reuters New York Report. C. Bryson Hull. "Enron-Merrill Criminal Trial Date Moved Up." (April 15, 2004), on Yahoo! Finance, Financial News *(http://biz.yahoo.com)*. ML has also been very innovative with its resources on the Web *(http://www.newmlol.ml.com)* and direct trading on the Web at Merrill Lynch Direct *(http://www.mldirect.ml.com/)*.

53 See Carol J. Loomis. "The Fight for Financial Turf." *Fortune* 104 (December 28, 1981), 55.

54 See Moore (1983). The New York Stock Exchange fined Bache $400,000 for the incident, the largest fine ever for a member firm. See "New Bache Chief Pushes a Host of Changes, Including New Name, to Lift Firm's Image." *The Wall Street Journal* (October 29, 1982); Walter (2004),; Michael Siconolfi and William Power. "Prudential Securities Seeks New Identity But Seems to Be Revisiting '80s Pitfalls." *The Wall Street Journal* (January 28, 1992), C1, C14; Chuck Hawkins. "The Mess at Pru-Bache." *Business Week* (March 4, 1991), 66–72; Matthew Winkler and William Power. "Gap Between Rich and Poor Brokerage Firms Widen." *The Wall Street Journal* (January 24, 1990), C1, C17; Hilder and Weiner (1985); William Power. "Wall Street Wields Ax Again as Woes Deepen." *The Wall Street Journal* (January 29, 1990), C1, C17; and Michael Siconolfi. "Prudential-Bache Plans to Eliminate Hundreds of Jobs." *The Wall Street Journal* (March 29, 1990), A4.

As noted by Walter (2004), although a number of other insurance companies acquired investment banks in the 1990s, most of these were divested. Pru has stayed in the course in its diversification strategy.[55]

Managerial Implications of Diversified Financial Services Firms

The case histories for GEFS, Sears, ML, and Pru indicate that synergies in financial services may be easier to promise than achieve, at least in the 1980s. Managing diversified financial firms is challenging, especially when the business cultures of the combined firms are not compatible. All four of the firms profiled have had problems, often selling or spinning off many of their acquisitions in later years. Each suffered serious financial and managerial setbacks on the path to diversification. Effective integration and cross-selling of services has at times been elusive. Without such integration, synergy, which depends on a unified operating plan, may not be realized. And because diversification without synergy is not valued by shareholders, the equity markets often react positively to some announced divestitures, such as the sale of Dean Witter by Sears or Kidder Peabody by GE. Recently, a number of nonfinancial firms have had initial public offerings to spin off diverse segments as separate firms, being aware of a lack of transparency in conglomerate financial activities, creating a "conglomerate valuation discount." They did this based on the rationale that financial analysts are unable to determine the true value of a diversified firm, which results in a depression of their stock prices.[56]

The large size of a firm also does not always appear to be synonymous with efficiency, and larger firms may have more difficulty exerting control over different divisions, resulting in scandals for brokers, such as Pru and GE experienced. Without adequate risk management, the benefits of diversification in terms of smoothing earnings and reducing risk can be lost.

Likewise, the premise that customers prefer diversified financial services firms in terms of convenient, one-stop shopping can also be called to question. Sears in the 1980s learned that customers did not necessarily want to take care of all of their financial needs with one firm, preferring to shop around instead of placing their money with one institution. The atmosphere they prefer for financial service dealings may be more staunch and conservative than that of a retail establishment, although this preference may be changing, as the popularity of bank branches in grocery stores is growing.

Thus, institutional value may be created from careful identification of market opportunities; analysis of these opportunities, including assessments of risk and the expected impact on financial targets; and skillful execution, including the use of available risk-management tools. These principles hold regardless of the type, size, and location of the institution or its historical origins. In fact, financial deregulation has not changed the determinants of value at all; it has merely broadened the range of opportunities available to individual firms. Although diversified financial firms were not, as a whole, generally as successful as some other firms in the 1980s and to some extent for Pru and Merrill in the 1990s, some analysts think that market conditions are now right for diversified financial megaplayers, as exhibited by the 640 bank holding companies that have become or have applied to be financial holding companies (FHCs) under GLB, as discussed in the following section.

The Rationale for the Financial Megaplayers in the Twenty-First Century

Although financial conglomerates have not always been successful in the past, analysts such as Arnold Danielson (1999) and Mendonca and Wilson (1997) provide reasons for why diverse financial services

---

55 See Paulette Thomas. "Prudential Cleared to Buy Sick Thrift." *The Wall Street Journal* (August 8, 1989), A3; The Prudential 1991 Annual Report; Larry Light. "How Much Prudence Is Good for Prudential?" *Business Week* (July 13, 1992), 124–126; Melody Petersen. "Prudential's Leader Knows His Way Around in New Jersey." *New York Times* (February 13, 1998), C1, C3; Joseph B. Treaster. "Prudential Profit Falls 43 Percent on Life Insurance Problems." *New York Times* (March 3, 1998), C2; and Leslie Scism. "After the Fall: Prudential's Cleanup in Wake of Scandals Hurts Insurance Sales." *The Wall Street Journal* (November 17, 1997), A1, A6; Joseph B. Treaster. "A $12 Billion Carrot for Prudential Policyholders." *New York Times* (February 13, 1998), A1, C3; and Leslie Scism. "Prudential's Plan to Go Public Reflects Industry Trend: More Mutual Life Insurers Need to Seek Outside Capital to Stay Competitive." *The Wall Street Journal* (February 18, 1998), B4. Also see Prudential Financial's Website *(http://www.prudential.com)* for details on Prudential Financial Business Descriptions, Annual Reports, news releases, and other information; Yahoo! Finance for news and financial information *(http://finance.yahoo.com)*, using Prudential Financial's stock market symbol, PRU; and Hoover's Website for an overview and competitor listing *(http://www.hoovers.com)*.

56 Martin, Kensinger, and Gillan (1996) find evidence of positive wealth effects for Sears's stockholders in response to Sears's spin-off of Dean Witter. Also see Crawford and Sihler (1997), General Electric Financial Services, Inc., Case 6, for a discussion of this issue. Also see Ford (1982) and Anthony Bianco. "How a Financial Supermarket Was Born." *Business Week* (December 23, 1985), 10.

Concept Questions

1 What are some unusual financial ratios used in analyzing a finance company? How do interest spreads for finance companies compare to those of banks? Why do finance companies have more volatile returns?

2 What regulations are finance companies under?

3 What are some economic reasons for financial conglomerates? Why have conglomerate merger waves occurred?

4 How was Sears successful and unsuccessful in its entry into the financial services business? Why did Sears spin off its financial services firms?

5 Why has GEFS been so successful? What cultural problems did GEFS have with its acquisition of Kidder Peabody?

6 Why did Merrill Lynch want to become a diversified financial services firm? How did it implement this strategy, and what problems did ML encounter? How did ML try to avoid cultural problems? Did this strategy work?

7 How did Prudential Insurance Company implement its diversified financial services firm strategy? What problems did Pru face, and how did the firm restructure? Why do you think Pru kept on with this strategy despite setbacks?

firms may operate better in the twenty-first century including technology that makes it easier to manage large financial institutions operating across the world, improvements in efficiency, the ability to enter new markets and geographic regions with the passage of GLB, the opportunity of new fee-income products, a better cost-benefit balance for skilled players, greater knowledge and a reduction in the costs associated with consolidations, excess capital and profitability allowing institutions to afford the high costs of technology, the competitive advantage of large size, new delivery systems with computer/Internet banking, and a more beneficial effect of size and diversity in the information age. The evaluation of business line expansion is illustrated by Citigroup's use of a risk-adjusted return on capital approach (as discussed in Chapter 6) to make its acquisition and divestment decisions.[57]

Evaluating Business Lines Using RAROC: Citigroup's Approach

On March 29, 2004, Citigroup (Citi) presented a Webcast information section, "Citigroup Risk Capital and Capital Allocation," on the Investor Relations section of its Website *(http://www.citigroup.com/citigroup/fin/index.htm)* to explain its strategies for making its business entry and exit decisions based on a risk-adjusted return on capital (RAROC) approach. As noted in Citigroup's 2003 Annual Report, Citi's goal as a diversified financial services firm is to have "a highly diversified base of earnings that enables Citigroup to thrive in difficult market conditions." Using a value at risk (VAR) approach, Citi determines the amount of capital it needs to cover unexpected economic losses in both net income and the value of equity due to unusual events over a one-year period at a 99.97 percent confidence level (representing about a 3 in 10,000 risk of such an event). Implicitly, expected loss would be covered through business line profit margins. Risk capital necessary to cover losses, somewhat similar to the Basel II proposal but extending upon this, would include: (1) **credit risk** involving losses with a borrower or counterparty unable to repay its obligations, losses involving a downgrade (or migration) in a borrower's credit quality, and cross-border risks resulting from foreign government actions, such as exchange controls; (2) **market risk** from a loss in market value associated with trading positions, changes in "the cost to close accrual positions," and loss in capital as the result of a change in the value of investments; (3) **operational risk,** the Basel II definition of "loss resulting from inadequate or failed internal processes, people, systems or from external events"; (4) **insurance risk,** the risk of very high "pay-outs on insurance liabilities"; and (5) **cross-sector diversification,** the reduction in risk provided by diversification between business sectors.[58]

---

57 See Mendonca and Wilson (1997);.and Danielson (1999).

58 The information for this section is summarized from PowerPoint slides for the Webcast presentation by Citigroup provided on its Website, under Investor Presentations, "Citigroup Risk Capital Allocation Process," March 29, 2004, provided on the Citigroup Investor Relations Website at *http://www.citigroup.com/citigroup/fin/index.htm*, and the Citigroup 2003 annual report. This site can also be reached by going to the main Website *(http://www.citigroup.com)* and clicking on "Investor Relations." The Website provides detailed information on Citigroup's corporate governance and social responsibility practices, business-specific information, company information, and financial information, press releases, and Webcast information. Also see the Citigroup 2003 annual report on this site.

Using this VAR approach, Citigroup determines how much risk capital will be needed for different types of investments that Citi holds. The presentation gives an example. As of December 31, 2003, Citi based on this approach needed $51.9 billion in risk capital [55 percent for credit risk ($28.7 billion); 32 percent for market risk ($16.8 billion); 12 percent for operational risk ($6.1 billion); and 1 percent for insurance risk ($0.3 billion)]. Given cross-sector diversification for different business lines reducing the total risk for Citi, this amount would be reduced by $5.2 billion to total risk capital needed of $46.7 billion less than the regulatory capital held by Citi (i.e., for Tier 1 capital alone, $66.9 billion). Accordingly, using an "integrated risk-based capital management framework," the return on risk capital (income / risk capital) on current business lines or return on invested capital for new acquisitions (income adjusted for goodwill carrying costs divided by the additional economic risk capital held for a business line's risk) should cover Citi's average cost of equity capital (for Citi in early 2004, 10 to 12 percent).[59]

Citicorp uses this approach to compare the risk-adjusted return of business lines to Citi's cost of equity capital for different business lines to consider acquisition and divesture decisions. The strategic fit and growth opportunities of each line are also examined. Using this technique, for instance, in the early 2000s, Citi made acquisitions that had both high risk-adjusted returns on capital and high strategic fit/growth opportunities that included Home Depot Cards, Sears Cards, Forum Financial, WaMu Consumer Finance, and KorAm Bank. It also divested companies that had a low return on invested capital and low strategic fit and growth opportunities, including CitiCapital Fleet Leasing and Travelers Property and Casualty. In one case, Electronic Financial Services was divested, despite a high return on invested capital, because of a low strategic and growth opportunity fit within Citi. In each acquisition analysis, the return on invested capital [net income divided by (risk capital plus goodwill and intangibles)] is examined to measure the return on an acquisition's price and to examine the "multi-year performance metric for each acquisition." This method is used along with an assessment of the "strategic rationale" for each investment and any earnings dilution (earnings per share accretion requirements). In this way, acquisitions are carefully examined using a "disciplined measure of capital investment for acquisitions," with both growth and returns considered to "maximize long-term shareholder value." Returns on risk capital are also used for Citi's annual budget process and to examine the risk/return trade-off for investment decisions in terms of Citi's products, geographical positioning, and customer positioning. At the end of 2003, in its presentation, Citi noted that all of its product lines had higher returns on risk-based capital than Citi's cost of equity capital, except for some proprietary investments.[60]

Some Financial Services Firm Merger Considerations

This chapter and the text conclude with some merger and international considerations for financial services firms.

Regulatory and Market Structure Considerations for Acquisitions

Mergers and acquisitions for depository institutions in particular must meet regulatory and U.S. Department of Justice guidelines. The Federal Reserve approves mergers among bank holding companies (BHCs) and state member banks, the state for state-chartered banks, and the Comptroller of the Currency for nationally chartered banks. The Federal Reserve particularly looks at a BHC's Community Reinvestment Act (CRA) ratings, risk effects, potential efficiency gains, and the market concentration effects of the merger, among other factors. Often the Fed will demand certain divestments of branches or improvements in CRA activity before a merger will be allowed. The Fed also has a hearing period for community comments and public hearings before a merger's approval.

The Department of Justice (DOJ) also oversees decisions made by regulators that follow DOJ guidelines for whether acquisitions are acceptable based on the potential increase in concentration with a merger in an acquisition market [metropolitan statistical area (MSA), or non-MSA rural county] and the potential efficiency gains that could be achieved. In addition, for interstate mergers, as mentioned in Chapter 3, restrictions on the total concentration of deposits by a bank of financial holding company

---

59 Ibid.

60 Ibid.

within a state and for the nation as a whole cannot be surpassed. The basic measure of market concentration under merger guidelines is the Herfindahl-Hirschman Index (HHI), which is calculated as the sum of the square of the market share of each firm in the market. For market shares, the percentage of deposits held in the market is typically used to calculate market share measures. If only one bank operates in a market, its market share would be 100 percent, so its HHI would be the square of 100—the maximum HHI of 10,000—while the lowest HHI would be close to zero if a large number of banks had equal size market shares in a particular market. Under the Department of Justice merger guidelines, if a post-merger HHI is larger than 1,800, signifying a highly concentrated market, there will be antitrust concerns. Also, if, with a merger, the change in the HHI is greater than 100 (or possibly, given other factors, 50 to 100), the merger will likely be challenged. A moderately concentrated market is defined as an HHI of 1,000 to 1,800, and an HHI of less than 1,000 is deemed not concentrated (with a merger unlikely to be challenged). Rural markets where economic factors often only support one or two banks tend to be the most concentrated markets, while metropolitan statistical areas (MSAs) tend to be more competitive and less concentrated. A simple example for the calculation of the post-merger effect on a market's HHI would be if, in a market, Bank Leo had 30 percent market share, Bank Bear had 30 percent share, and Bank Alexie had 40 percent share. The HHI for the market is $30^2 + 30^2 + 40^2 = 3,400$. If Bank Alexie wants to acquire Bank Bear, the post-merger HHI would be $70^2 + 30^2 = 5,800$. The market was already highly concentrated ($> 1,800$), so the Fed and FTC would take a very close look at the merger. The change in HHI of 2,400 is greater than 100, and the HHI results in an even more highly concentrated market, so the merger will be challenged.[61]

Some critics consider this definition of bank markets that assumes that banks operate in individual metropolitan statistical areas or rural counties (versus across states or many states) to be very narrow, since many banks compete across states or nationally. Also controversial has been the notion that banks only compete against other banks in local markets, since finance companies, credit unions, and other financial services firms are competitors as well. Thrift deposits are typically used in calculating HHIs, but with the use of deposit market share (versus asset share, which is also controversial), only depository institutions are included. However, some studies have shown significant effects on deposit and loan market prices based on HHI concentration measures. Other studies show the potential entry of large banks may have positive competitive effects on market pricing, while others demonstrate that the issue is more complex and determined by the different sizes and types of banks that operate in different niches within a market. Figures 19.1 and 19.2 show, respectively, the large percentage of interstate deposits and the growing number of multistate bank and thrift organizations. Figure 19.1 indicates that for some states, the majority of deposits are held by interstate branches of out-of-state banks, such as Oregon (74.1 percent), Florida (70.2 percent), and Arizona (65 percent). The number of bank and thrift holding companies with operations in two or more states has also increased dramatically, as shown in Figure 19.2, to 539 in 2003.[62]

Brief Note about Pricing and Earnings Dilution with Financial Institution Mergers

Although generally a number of different pricing techniques are used for valuing mergers, often typical benchmark estimates are used based on pricing multiples including market value to book value (market/book) ratios and market price-to-earnings (price/earnings or P/E) and premium-to-assets or book value (comparing the per share price that is offered to the shareholders of the target bank to the book value of assets or of the book value of the common stock of the target) ratios. For example, if a target has earnings of $500,000 and the typical P/E ratio for similar targets is 3, a starting valuation point would be 3 × $500,000 = $1,500,000. Similarly, if a target had a book value of equity of $750,000, and the typical market-to-book ratio was 2, a starting valuation using this method would be 2 × $750,000 = $1,500,000. The premium percentage that is paid over book value could be calculated as

---

61 See U.S. Department of Justice Merger Guidelines *(http://www.usdoj.gov)*. Also see Saunders and Cornett (2000, 2004); FDIC Summary of Deposits, Market Share MSA Selection, which provides new MSA Definitions for Consolidate Metropolitan Statistical Areas (CMSAs), and Metropolitan Statistical Areas (MSAs) at *(http://www2.fdic.gov/sod)*.

62 See Lawrence J. Radecki. "The Expanding Geographic Reach of Retail Banking Markets." Federal Reserve Bank of New York Policy Review 4 (June 1998), 15-34; and Allen N. Berger, "The Profit-structure Relationship in Banking-Tests of Market-power and Efficient-structure Hypotheses," Journal of Money, Credit, and Banking 27 (2), May 1995, pp. 404–431. Also see recent Federal Reserve Board Research papers on this issue on that Website *(www.federalreserve.gov)*.

figure **19.1**   INTERSTATE BRANCH DEPOSITS AS A PERCENT OF TOTAL DEPOSITS FOR FDIC-INSURED INSTITUTIONS, JUNE 30, 2003

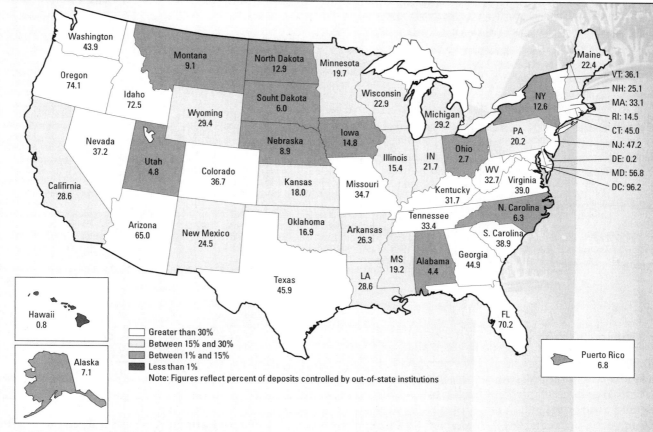

Washington 43.9
Oregon 74.1
Montana 9.1
North Dakota 12.9
Minnesota 19.7
Maine 22.4
VT: 36.1
NH: 25.1
MA: 33.1
RI: 14.5
CT: 45.0
NJ: 47.2
DE: 0.2
MD: 56.8
DC: 96.2
Idaho 72.5
Souht Dakota 6.0
Wisconsin 22.9
NY 12.6
Wyoming 29.4
Michigan 29.2
PA 20.2
Nevada 37.2
Iowa 14.8
Nebraska 8.9
Illinois 15.4
IN 21.7
Ohio 2.7
WV 32.7
Virginia 39.0
Utah 4.8
Colorado 36.7
Kansas 18.0
Missouri 34.7
Kentucky 31.7
Califirnia 28.6
N. Carolina 6.3
Arizona 65.0
New Mexico 24.5
Oklahoma 16.9
Arkansas 26.3
Tennessee 33.4
S. Carolina 38.9
MS 19.2
Alabama 4.4
Georgia 44.9
Texas 45.9
LA 28.6
FL 70.2

Hawaii 0.8
Alaska 7.1

Greater than 30%
Between 15% and 30%
Between 1% and 15%
Less than 1%
Note: Figures reflect percent of deposits controlled by out-of-state institutions

Puerto Rico 6.8

Note: Figures reflect percent of deposits controlled by out-of-state institutions.

Source: *FDIC Summary of Deposits (SOD), charts and graphs from selected FDIC SOD data on the FDIC Summary of Deposits Website* (http://www2.fdic.gov/sod/index.asp).

(market price / book value) − 1. In this case, with a market value of $1,500,000 and a book value of $750,000, this premium would be (1,500 / 750) − 1, which equals 1, or a 100 percent premium. The larger the premium paid, the more difficult it will be for the acquirer to earn a return on the investment to justify the purchase price and the risk involved with the acquisition. In addition to these approaches, often present value valuation approaches are used based on the present value of future cash flow of an acquired firm and the additional cash flows that will be generated for the combined firm, as noted in firm security analysis and valuation courses. Discounts (haircuts) are also given for private firms that lack liquidity.[63]

The average merger premium, however, tends to follow trends. During periods when targets are in great demand, merger premiums can be quite high, such as from 1994 to 1997 for banks, when massive consolidation occurred with the advent of interstate branching, compared with the low multiples in the early 1990s when banks suffered low profits. Average premiums, price-to-earnings ratios, and average price-to-book value also vary by regions. During 1996 to 2000, the average premium to assets for bank acquisitions was 13.2 percent (20.2 national P/E and 224 percent national average price-to-

63   See Koch (1995) and Koch and MacDonald (2000) for a more detailed discussion of bank merger premiums and earnings dilution. The average acquisition premium for bank/thrifts changes with the supply and demand for targets, as well as market conditions. In the 1970s and 1980s, with a seller's market, acquired banks had large premiums. From 1992 to 1993, the market was more of a buyer's market, with premiums declining since many of the best deals were taken. After 1994, premiums rose again with greater demand for targets. For instance, in 1997, bank stocks sold for about twelve times their earnings, which was much less than the eighteen times its earnings that the average bank target was getting. See Saul Hansell. "Merger-Hungry Banks Find the Pickings Slim." *New York Times* (January 2, 1997), C22.

figure **19.2** NUMBER OF MULTISTATE ORGANIZATIONS* AND THEIR SHARE OF ASSETS AND DEPOSITS HELD BY COM-
MERCIAL BANKS AND SAVINGS INSTITUTIONS, JUNE 30, 1989 TO 2003

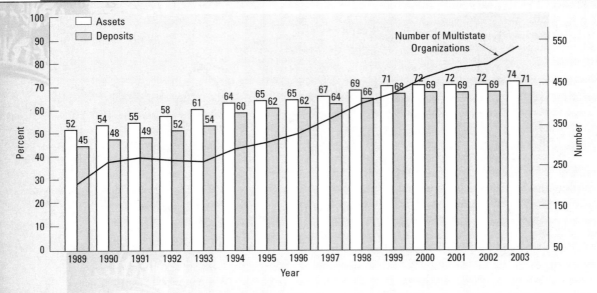

*Multistate organizations are bank holding companies and independent depository institutions with offices in two or more states.
Source: FDIC Summary of Deposits (SOD), charts and graphs from selected FDIC SOD data on the FDIC Summary of Deposits Website
(http://www2.fdic.gov/sod/index.asp).

book value) compared to a 10.1 percent average premium to assets (15.4 P/E and 222 percent price-to-book value) for many regional western states, with a wide range across states (for instance, Utah's average was about 17 percent compared to 6.4 percent for Nebraska). Prior to FASB's removal of pooling accounting, acquisitions associated with pooling accounting also had a higher price-to-earnings and price-to-book ratio than those with purchased accounting in the late 1990s.[64]

If a stock swap is used, whereby the target's shareholders receive shares in the acquiring firm as payment, the exchange ratio is calculated as the market price per share of the target firm / market price per share of the acquirer. For instance, in the previous example, if the market price for the target was $1,500,000 and the target had 100,000 shares, its market price per share would be $15. If the share price for the acquirer was also $15, then the exchange ratio would be 1 share of the acquirer for 1 share of the target. Financial institutions depend on investment bankers specializing in financial institution acquisitions for different regions to help find buyers/sellers of financial institutions and negotiate mergers. Often a frequent group of acquirers are on the lookout for good investments in a region. Prominent investment firms with the top ten financial institution M&A rankings by number of deals in 2000 include Keefe, Bruyette & Woods, Inc.; Sandler O'Neil and Partners, LP; McDonald Investments/The Wallach Company/Trident; RP Financial LC; Hoefer & Arnett, Inc.; Alex Sheshunoff & Co.; Austin Associates, Inc.; McConnell Budd & Downes, Inc.; Hovde Financial, LLC; Merrill Lynch & Co.; The Findley Group; and Baxtor, Fentriss, & Co. Many of these firms are in New York City, while others specialize in regions outside of New York, including McDonald Investments/Wallach Company/Trident group, which is one of the largest investment banking firms serving financial institutions outside New York City. TWC and McDonald Investments, for instance, managed or comanaged more than eighty-five financings for financial institutions, raising an aggregate of $6.3 billion from 1992 to 2000, focusing on public and private transactions in the range of $10 to $200 million, having six equity research

64 *Sources:* Ibid, MacDonald Investments/The Wallach Company Investment Bankers, and Hooke (1999).

analysts follow more than sixty financial services companies, and actively trading over 250 stocks of financial institutions, as well as public underwritings and private placements for financial institutions including equity securities and fixed-income securities.[65]

For diversified financial firms, price multiples used for valuations are often calculated by taking a weighted average of price multiples for a firm's different businesses. For instance, if a firm received 50 percent of its earnings from insurance, 25 percent from securities activities, 25 percent from finance company operations, and the respective market-to-book ratios for the three different industries were hypothetically 1.10, 1.46, and 1.30, the weighted average market-to-book ratio would be $(0.50)1.10 + (0.25)1.46 + (0.25)1.30 = 1.24$, so 1.24 could be used as the weighted average market-to-book ratio for the diversified firm. Other adjustments might be made based on the liquidity (marketability of the firm's equity), and an analysis of the firm's different risks compared to those of the acquirer.[66]

Many financial institutions calculate expected earnings dilution measures as well. Earnings per share (EPS) dilution is calculated as follows:

$$\text{EPS Dilution} = [(\text{EPS of Acquirer} - \text{Expected EPS with Consolidation})] / (\text{EPS of Acquirer})$$

For example, if the acquirer has an expected EPS of $10 and the expected EPS with the consolidation is $8, then the earnings dilution expected is as follows:

$$\text{EPS Dilution} = (\$10 - \$8) / \$10 = -0.20, \text{ or } -20\% \text{ Earnings Dilution}$$

As a rule of thumb, EPS dilution should not be greater than 5 percent to get a reasonable return on an acquisition.[67]

Purchase Accounting Required for Mergers

In April 1999, the Financial Accounting Standards Board (FASB) ruled that companies in the future would no longer be allowed to use the favorable "pooling of interests" accounting method, which was mandated by June 30, 2001. Under purchase accounting, the acquirer is treated as having purchased the assets and assumed the liabilities of the acquired firm, which are subsequently written up or down relative to their fair market value. Any difference between the purchase price and the net assets that are acquired is then allocated to goodwill. With pooled accounting, instead the combined assets of merged firms would be consolidated using book value, which avoids the creation and goodwill and earnings dilution. "However, as noted by FASB with the rule change, purchase accounting makes it easier to evaluate transactions and therefore makes it easier for investors to analyze mergers by being able to see what is being bought."[68]

Qualitative Considerations in Financial Institution Acquisition

As noted by Jeffrey C. Hooke (1999) in *Security Analysis on Wall Street: A Comprehensive Guide to Today's Valuation Methods,* in addition to different valuation techniques used to begin negotiations for an acquisition, qualitative factors are very important. In Chapter 20, "Financial Industry Stocks," he

---

65 Ibid.

66 See Crawford and Sihler (1994), Primerica Corporation, Case 12, (currently out of print, but case may be available through Darden) for an illustration of using a weighted average price/earnings ratio to value a diversified financial firm.

67 See McCoy, Frieder, and Hedges (1994) and Koch (1995). Some studies find the average workout time for mergers in 1986 to 1990 to eliminate earnings dilution to be quite long, often greater than twenty years based on a 10 percent growth rate in net income, suggesting overpayment. The average workout time for Bank One was about ten years. High expected growth rates in earnings for the consolidated firm are needed to prevent such dilution. At times banks are willing to pay large premiums to gain access to strategic options.

68 Under the pooling method (which previously was allowed), when two companies merge, they simply add their balance sheets together line by line, making it difficult for investors to see the premium paid for assets acquired. With purchase accounting, the acquired company is treated as an investment asset with any premium paid over a target's value shown as goodwill, which must be expensed (amortized) over several years. See Todd N. Lebor. "Goodwill's Real Value: Revising the Purchase Method." The Motley Fool, *http://www.fool.com*, April 5, 2001, 1–3; Highlight Investment Group, Market Trader Glossary, "Purchase Accounting," "Pooling of Interests," "Merger," "Acquirer" *(http://www.trading-glossary.com)*; Craig Schneider. "Why Wachovia Is Banking on Purchase Accounting." *http://www.cfo.com*, April 17, 2001, 1–2; and "FASB Rules Out Pooling of Interests." AICPA Website announcement, July 1999 *(http://www.aicpa.org).*

notes that firms in the financial industry have special considerations since they are highly leveraged, subject to regulatory environment influences, and are involved in activities that have "uncertain future obligations," such as whether an insurance company or derivative security underwriting will have to pay off a claim. Hence, he points out that there are many nonprice competitive elements to consider for different types of financial institution acquisitions, including, for instance, "reputation," "service efficiency," "convenience," "personal relationships," "credit-worthiness," "specialized expertise," "distribution and trading ability for corporate accounts," "claims of above-average performance potential," and "marketing abilities." Similarly, the business model followed by an institution and whether this model provides superior returns for given risk involves superstars that will or will not stay after the acquisition; the operational controls for assembly-type operations, such as check-clearing or back office operations; and "the investment decision-making culture," among other qualitative factors that need to be considered. As Jeffrey Hooke notes, different types of financial institutions have typical acquisition valuation comparisons. Bank analysts typically emphasize P/E and price/book multiples versus EBIT or EBITDA multiples. Because bank loans rarely have a market value greater than their book value, market-to-price book ratios are closely examined, with only in rare cases a market-to-book value breaking above 2 times. He also notes that too high a price/book ratio is often thought of as a "danger signal" even for a growth-oriented bank. Finance companies, in contrast, look more at P/E ratios and projected earnings growth to justify valuations. Potential acquirers for depository institutions will carefully review the asset quality of loans and the asset composition. Other factors that affect premiums paid include the percentage of core deposits (cheap financing) that an institution has and the potential for growth, asset quality, population growth, and per capita income, factors that make a region a promising, lucrative area to enter. Off-balance-sheet items, profit efficiency, historical and expected future performance, and risk management are among other factors to be considered.[69]

As noted by Koch and MacDonald (2000), acquirers have to be careful to avoid complications that can occur with the blending of different operations and technology, the potential loss of key employees and customers with a merger, and to ensure that the best aspects of the culture of an acquired bank are kept. For banks, as pointed out by Walter (2004), financial firms often want to gain economies of scale with successful IT integration, and such an integration depends on good arrangements between the top management cultures of the merged firms, including setting up plans to create a joint culture and avoid culture clashes that could seriously affect the positive benefits of such an integration. As noted in a recent *AFP Exchange* article, a careful plan needs to be made for post-acquisition integration. An integrated plan should cover actions that need to be completed in the first days of the acquisition including communications to employees and customers and long-term steps based on the key actions that will determine synergies and revenue growth with the acquisitions. As the article notes, "Often significant value is lost as a result of poor management and people decisions after an acquisition."[70]

The number and value of announced mergers and acquisitions for different types of financial institutions shows the changing nature of demand for different types of firms. The percentages for different types of firms for the entire 1999 to 2002 period are shown in Figure 19.3. The total deal value was $989.4 billion for 4,987 deals. In terms of total deal value, 52.4 percent were depository institution acquisitions, 22.5 percent insurance, 14 percent specialty finance firms, and 11 percent securities firms. However, in terms of total deals, 33.9 percent were insurance, 32.7 percent depository institution, 17.2 percent securities firms, and 16.2 percent specialty finance. The number of deals peaked in 1998 at 1,294, falling to 1,112 in 1999, 949 in 2000, 858 in 2001, and 774 in 2002, tending to follow movements in the stock market. The number of bank and thrift mergers declined from a peak of 725 in 1997 to 275 in 2003. With the economy and stock market improving, some large deals surfaced including Bank of America's acquisition proposal for FleetBoston, and JPMorgan Chase's acquisition proposal for Banc One, to take place in 2004.[71]

---

69 See Hooke (1999), Chapter 20, "Financial Industry Stocks," 359–400.

70 See Koch and MacDonald (2000); Walter (2004); and Ian Cookson, Corporate Finance Director, Grant Thornton, LLP. "Growing Pain: Tips to Consider Before You Acquire." *AFP Exchange* (March/April 2004), 64–65.

71 See Insurance Information Institute, *Financial Services Fact Book* (http://www.iii.org). At the time of this writing, the number and value of announced mergers by sector in 2002 was presented at *http://financialservicefacts.org/financial2/today/consolidation/*, as provided to III by SNL Financial, LC.

figure **19.3** MERGERS AND ACQUISITION PERCENTAGES BY FINANCIAL INSTITUTION TYPE FOR $989.4 BILLION IN TOTAL DEAL VALUE, 1999 TO 2002

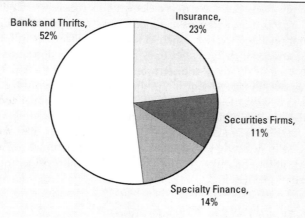

Source: Created by Authors, based on information provided on the Insurance Information Institute (III) Website, Financial Services Fact Book (http://financialservicefacts.org/financial2/today/consolidation/), *as cited by SNL Financial, LC.*

Much research has been conducted on investor reactions to merger announcements and on the post-merger performance of mergers. Generally, studies have been disappointing from the perspective of finding negative announcement (wealth) effects for acquirers, but positive announcement effects for targets, suggesting to some extent that acquirers are overpaying for acquisitions. Similarly, post-merger studies have not found evidence of improved cost efficiency in performance for firms following mergers; however, recent studies suggest that revenue efficiencies that result in net profit efficiencies may occur.[72]

Concept Questions

1 What motivations do analysts give for new economic reasons for large, diversified mega-financial services firms in the twenty-first century?

2 How does Citgroup use RAROC to determine whether acquisitions should be made and business lines divested?

3 What is a Herfindahl-Hirschman Index (HHI), and how do regulators use it to determine the market concentration effects of a merger? What HHI changes in a market would trigger a regulatory challenge to a merger?

4 What are some common pricing benchmarks for financial institution mergers? Why do merger premiums follow trends? What is the exchange ratio? Who are some prominent investment firms specializing in bank mergers?

5 How is EPS earnings dilution calculated? Why would earnings dilution likely occur with a merger?

6 Why does FASB mandate purchase accounting for mergers?

7 What qualitative and managerial factors need to be considered for financial institution acquisitions?

8 What are some recent trends in financial service acquisition deals? Why do you think deals fell off after 1999?

---

72 See Allen N. Berger, William C. Hunter, and Stephen G. Timme. "Efficiency of Financial Institutions: International Survey and Directions for Future Research." *European Journal of Operational Research* 98, April 1997, 175–212 for an excellent survey of efficiency studies. Also, see Akhavein, J. D., A. N. Berger, and D. B. Humphrey. "The Effects of Megamergers on Efficiency and Prices: Evidence from a Bank Profit Function." *Review of Industrial Organization* 12 (February 1997), 95–139. Most cost efficiency studies have not found evidence of greater cost efficiency following mergers, but studies examining profit efficiency do find benefits in profit efficiency, generating from the revenue side.

Considerations for International Business Lines

With international acquisitions there are many elements to consider including cultural differences, country risk, translation and transaction risk, and economic risks (discussed in Chapter 2). There are also a number of operational and tax risks, such as taxes on the transfer of funds from one subsidiary to another across countries, which often becomes a problem when country regulations view these transfers as taxable income or dividend transfers. Similarly, there is the risk of expropriation or currency controls that restrict the movement of funds from and to a country from one subsidiary to another. For banks, particularly, there are also many different operational and accounting differences that are complex. Gaining access to international markets is difficult and usually requires special facilities for lending. Also, lenders bear added regulatory burdens because of separate provisions applying to international loans. Although a detailed examination of international considerations is beyond the scope of this text, the chapter ends with mention of some special considerations for financial institutions involved in international lending.

Special Bank International Lending Considerations

For depository institutions desiring to enter international markets, loan participations with another bank are often the easiest route to begin such operations, in which another bank takes the lead in lending, and the bank participates in a large international loan. However, just as in the domestic markets, loan participations expose banks to significant risks, so even nonlead banks must proceed carefully and perform conscientious credit analysis. Banks have been allowed since 1981 to establish **international banking facilities (IBFs)** that are located in the United States but serve international customers exclusively. Another alternative for originating international loans is through **Edge Act subsidiaries,** branches of the parent institution serving international customers. Unlike IBFs, Edge Act offices operate as full-service branches and are subject to regulation. International banks also have **shell branches,** which are offices overseas that permit banks to participate in the Eurocurrency markets in terms of Eurodollar liabilities or issuing foreign loans. Such offshore offices often operate in places such as the Bahamas where operations can be free of local taxes. In addition, full-service foreign branches are used to conduct wholesale banking activities, often utilizing deposits that are purchased from a network of international banks, often called interbank markets. Bank holding companies under the **Bank Export Services Act of 1982** are also allowed to invest and participate and lend to export trading companies, with banks often handling transportation and shipping documents, field warehousing, and insurance coverage. Also, since banks are not allowed to take title to trade items, they can do so indirectly through export/import companies.[73]

In response to large international loan exposure and losses for large money center banks in the United States in the 1980s, Congress passed the **International Lending Supervision Act (ILSA)** in 1983 to try to control the magnitude of future problems. The act established special examination procedures for international loan portfolios, granted power to supervisory agencies to set minimum capital guidelines to ensure adequate support in the case of loan losses, and required a special allocation to loan loss reserves by institutions engaged in foreign lending. A final deterrent to excessive international exposure came in the form of a requirement that income from loan loss origination fees be amortized over the life of the loan rather than be recognized as income in the year negotiated, generally diluting the importance of those fees to bank earnings. Federal banking regulators also carefully monitor the financial position of foreign governments that borrow heavily from U.S. banks, and they have at times issued special directives for reporting interest income and reserves for loans to specific countries deemed

---

73 See George H. Hempel, Donald G. Simonson, and Alan B. Coleman. *Bank Management: Text and Cases,* 4th ed. New York: John Wiley & Sons, 1994; Charles F. Maxwell. *Financial Markets and Institutions: The Global View.* New York: West Publishing Company, 1992; Walker F. Todd. "Developing Country Lending and Current Banking Conditions." *Economic Review* (Federal Reserve Bank of Cleveland) 24 (Quarter 2 1988), 27–36; Koch (1995); and Saunders and Cornett (2000, 2004). Also see "Statement of Robert J. Herrmann, Senior Deputy Comptroller for Bank Supervision Policy, before the House Subcommittee on International Development, Finance, Trade, and Monetary Policy of the Committee on Banking, Finance, and Urban Affairs." *Quarterly Journal* 8 (September 1989), 47–53; John Meehan, David Woodruff, and Chuck Hawkins. "For Most Banks, There Was Nowhere to Hide." *Business Week* (April 2, 1990), 94–95; and Duca and McLaughlin (1990).

highly risky. As noted in Chapter 6, the Bank of International Settlements (BIS) also sets standards for large international banks, including capital requirements, as noted under Basel I and the proposed Basel II.[74]

Risk Management Considerations for International Loans

As noted in the Citicorp example, geographically diversified financial services firms often use risk-adjusted return on capital (RAROC) models to examine diversification effects for business lines in different geographic as well as product areas. Bank managers are also engaging in a more realistic risk assessment of LDC (less-developed-country) loans. Also, new techniques for managing LDC debt exposure have developed including secondary markets for these loans, securitization of international debt as bonds (such as Brady Bonds, mentioned in Chapter 2, which were created under the 1989 Brady Plan to remove debt from U.S. bank balance sheets), and debt for equity swaps, in which a lender converts a debt contract to an equity investment in the debtor nation, and the restructuring of existing debt agreements to ease cash flow burdens on LDCs. Salomon Brothers (Citigroup) and other investment banks post benchmark bond prices for different countries. The risk premium on these bonds provides an indication of a particular country's default risk, and by being able to buy and sell these bonds, financial institutions can have more diversified loan portfolios. Financial institution managers have also developed better measures of country risk.

In evaluating the risk of entering a country, as noted in Chapter 2, country or **sovereign risk** needs to be carefully examined. Uncertainty can arise from many sources, such as social unrest, dependence on one export, which can lead to unrest if prices for that product fall, civil or international wars, economic decline, changes in political ideology, terrorism, cultural attitudes toward indebtedness, among other sources of uncertainty specific to international lending that can affect a borrower's timely repayment. The ILSA requires special procedures for rating the country risk of a bank's international loan portfolio. These ratings are based on ex post assessments that reflect the repayment record of a borrower once a loan has been granted. Finding reliable signals for ex ante risk is difficult, because it depends on a country's future economic and political stability. Measuring that with any degree of confidence is difficult, yet necessary if the institution expects to earn a rate of return sufficient to compensate for the additional risk. Moody's and S&P assign Sovereign Ratings for bonds in different countries. Country risk ratings by rating agencies, as well as country risk ratings (such as rating providing by *Euromoney* and the *Institutional Investor*) are often based on economic and political riskfactors, as well as surveys of loan officers at multinational banks.

One prominent ratio in risk indexes is a country's **debt service ratio** (the interest plus amortization on a country's debt divided by its exports). If this ratio is high, a country will have greater difficulty repaying its debt and a higher probability of default or rescheduling. In addition, although exchange rate and country risk need to be managed and can increase the variability of an institution's earnings, international loans do provide an avenue for diversification. Financial institutions often try to diversify their operations to reduce their overall portfolio risk. As noted in Citi's 2003 annual report by region, diversification of income internationally includes 64 percent in North America, 10 percent in Asia, 4 percent in Japan, 8 percent in Mexico, 10 percent in EMEA (Europe), and 4 percent in Latin America. Hence, the impact on returns and income for Citi for each region can be quantified, along with correlations that reduce the overall risk of Citi's product and geographic portfolio. Hedging foreign exchange risk and understanding economic forces to avoid surprises in the country and exchange rate risk as discussed in earlier chapters are also important management issues. In addition, financial institutions with international operations and customers need to be careful to monitor for suspicious activity and money laundering under the Bank Secrecy Act and USA Patriot Act. For instance, the Riggs National Corporation, a Washington D.C. based bank became involved in wide-ranging federal investigations for possible money laundering and terrorist financing problems as a result of not being vigilant in its monitoring of international customers. Consequently, in late April 2004, Riggs planned to sell or exit most of its embassy and international banking operations. Financial institutions have also used

---

74 Ibid and Saunders and Cornett (2003) and Koch and MacDonald (2000).

credit derivatives as a tool for managing sovereign risk, and there also have been innovations for international securitizations.[75]

Regulation of Foreign Banks in the United States

Under the **International Banking Act (IBA) of 1978,** any non-U.S. bank operating in the United States must purchase deposit insurance and choose a home state and operate under its laws. In response to some countries' criticisms of IBA, the Fed in 1981 authorized domestic and foreign banks to establish **international banking facilities (IBFs)** to conduct business solely with international customers. Unlike Edge Act corporations, IBFs are not subject to reserve requirements, nor does deposit insurance protect their account balances. IBFs were made relatively easy to establish, not needing separate physical facilities, but requiring separate bookkeeping entities, making IBFs very popular. FDICIA includes the **Foreign Bank Supervision Enhancement Act** (FBSEA) of 1991 with additional restrictions for foreign banks in reaction to the scandal surrounding the Bank of Credit and Commerce International (BCCI), in which thousands of small depositors worldwide lost nearly $20 billion as the result of fraud and mismanagement. The law directs the Fed to tighten regulations on foreign banks operating in the United States and requires Fed approval of the establishment of all new branches or agencies of foreign banks. Also, in determining whether foreign banks can enter the United States, the Fed must evaluate home country supervisors' procedures for monitoring and controlling the institutions' worldwide operations, including relationships between banks and nonbank affiliates (comprehensive consolidate supervision). The extent to which the home country supervisor enforces safety and soundness regulations on all the bank's activities is also an important consideration. Under FBSEA all banks accepting domestic retail deposits under $100,000 must purchase deposit insurance. Finally, the Fed analyzes secrecy laws from the home countries of foreign financial institutions. Such secrecy laws may prohibit institutions from providing the Fed with complete financial information. If Fed officials believe that foreign laws interfere substantially with adequate disclosure in the United States, regulators may deny entry to a foreign institution. In recent years with a fall in the value of the U.S. dollar making U.S. acquisitions cheaper to foreign investors, a number of U.S. financial institutions have been acquired by firms from non-U.S. companies. For instance in 2002, HSBC Holdings, PLC, in the United Kingdom acquired Household International, Inc., a specialty finance company, for a deal value of $14.861 billion, and Deutsche Bank AG in Germany took over RoPro U.S. Holdings, Inc., a large investment adviser for a deal value of $490 million.[76]

Concept Questions

1 What are some justifications for diversifying internationally?

2 What are different ways of diversifying internationally without establishing separate international bank subsidiaries?

3 What did the International Lending Supervision Act (ILSA) do to try to reduce the magnitude of international lending problems for U.S. banks?

4 What are some risk considerations with international lending?

5 What are sovereign risk ratios? What does a country's debt service ratio indicate to lenders?

6 What restrictions do foreign banks operating in the United States have under IBA of 1978 and FBSEA of 1991?

---

75 See Saunders and Cornett (2000, 2003) for a detailed discussion of different country risk indexes; and Richard Cantor and Frank Packer. "Sovereign Credit Ratings." Federal Reserve Bank of New York, *Current Issues in Economics and Finance,* Vol. 1, No. 3 (June 1995), 1–5. Also see Timothy L. O'Brien, "Riggs Plans to Jettison Most Units Overseas," *The New York Times,* April 30, 2004, C3. For discussions of hedging international risk with derivatives and innovations in international securitization, see Laurent L. Jacque and Paul M. Vaaler, editors, *Financial Innovations and the Welfare of Nations.* Boston: Kluwer Academic Publishers, 2001.

76 See Insurance Information Institute, *Financial Services Fact Book* (http://www.iii.org). See Deirdre Fanning. "Set Us Free." *Forbes* (February 23, 1987), 94–96; Betty Buttrill White. "Foreign Banking in the United States: A Regulatory and Supervisory Perspective." *Quarterly Review* (Federal Reserve Bank of New York) 7 (Summer 1982), 48–58; K. Alec Chrystal. "International Banking Facilities." *Review* (Federal Reserve Bank of St. Louis) 66 (April 1984), 5–11; James V. Houpt. "International Trends for U.S. Banks and Banking Markets." *Federal Reserve Bulletin* 74 (May 1988), 289–290; Board of Governors of the Federal Reserve System, 78th Annual Report, Washington, DC: Federal Reserve System, 1991, 211; Ann E. Misback. "The Foreign Bank Supervision Enhancement Act of 1991." *Federal Reserve Bulletin* 79 (January 1993), 1–10; and James R. Kraus. "Foreign Banks Face Hurdles." *American Banker* (April 19, 1993), 2A.

Summary

This chapter discusses finance companies and diversified financial services firms. Finance companies are diverse financial institutions grouped together under one industry classification. They share an emphasis on consumer and business lending, and they differ from depositories because they lack deposits as a source of funds. The industry was historically grouped into consumer and commercial finance companies, along with special function firms, but these distinctions are now blurred. Many firms that started out as finance companies are now diversified financial services firms, such as Citigroup, American Express, and GEFS. Other diversified financial firms began as banks or as securities firms or insurance firms, such as Merrill Lynch and Prudential Insurance Company.

Finance companies make loans like banks but finance these loans through borrowings rather than deposits. Finance companies also take on a more risky group of borrowers than banks, and asset management includes managing this greater default risk. Finance companies have increasingly moved into securitization of all types of loans, which increases their managerial flexibility and competitiveness with banks and other financial institutions.

The chapter also discusses the economic rationale for diversified financial firms and provides case histories of four. These firms faced difficulties developing synergies to create value for stockholders. Similarly, analysts often fail to identify the value of diversified divisions, resulting in depressed stock prices for these firms. As a consequence, many of the firms that diversified in the 1980s have divested many of their acquisitions to improve their stock prices and refocus on core businesses. Trying to integrate diverse cultures also created management problems for these firms. In the information age of the 1990s, with more liberal regulations, changes in delivery systems, and greater opportunities to create synergies, diversified financial institutions may have greater opportunities to create synergies and value than they had in the past. Some analysts point out that it may be essential for financial institutions to become megaplayers to have the economic backing to provide innovative services through technology, to create national brands to compete, and to provide low-cost, high-quality products to consumers.

The valuation of acquisitions is complex, but often price/earnings or market-to-book multiples are used based on the price paid for similar acquisitions. For diversified targets, weighted average of price/earnings multiples are often used based on the percentage of earnings of each of the target's businesses. The premium paid over book value is equal to the market price divided by the target firm's book value minus 1. The higher this premium, the more difficult it will be to generate returns to cover the cost and risk of the acquisition. Earnings dilution measures are also often estimated as the expected earnings of an acquirer less the expected earnings of the consolidated firm as a percentage of the expected earnings of the acquirer. As a rule of thumb, if the earnings dilution is greater than 5 percent, an acquirer should be wary. The greater the earnings dilution and the higher the market-to-book premium, the longer it will take to reap benefits from the acquisition.

Questions

1. Leo Tucker is thinking about investing in finance companies. Describe the different types of finance companies for Leo, how they are different from depository institutions in terms of the types of loans they make and their sources of financing. Also, explain why finance companies hold more capital than depository institutions, and compare the default, liquidity, and interest rate risk of finance companies to depository institutions. Also, discuss differences in regulation for finance companies.

2. Yih Pin Tang is curious about recent trends affecting finance companies. Explain to her about trends in industrial loan companies, mortgage banks, subprime lending, and securitization. Also, discuss recent regulations in these areas.

3. Dave Cather and Glenn Wolfe are curious about the effects of some regulations on the operations of finance companies. What was the past impact of state usury laws, special state laws on subprime lending, and more lenient bankruptcy laws in the past on finance company operations. Give an example of how laws may help but also hurt consumers (i.e., good effects and unintended bad effects).

4. Sharon Curran and Skip and Skye Wescott are curious about how the financial analysis of finance companies differs from depository institutions. Explain how it is similar and discuss some different ratios that are used.

What sources of industry performance information are available for finance companies?

5. Alison and Sam Asarnow would like you to explain some of the theoretical and practical reasons for the development of financial conglomerates discussed in the chapter. Which explanations do you agree with most? Why did conglomerate waves occur in the 1970s to 1980s, as suggested by Leonitades (1986)? What are the reasons financial conglomerates are popular today?

6. Susie and Sean Rudman would like you to compare and contrast the diversification strategies used by GEFS, Sears, Prudential, and Merrill Lynch. Explain the similarities and differences in their responses to problems that occurred and how they implemented their diversification strategies. Which firms seemed more successful in their diversification?

7. Trish, Hugh, and Max Ruppersburg would like to know how valuations of bank mergers are done. Briefly discuss how targets can be valued using P/E or market-to-book value ratios. How is the percentage premium paid calculated? What is earnings dilution, and how is it calculated? Why is an estimation of expected earnings dilution so important?

8. Beverly and Doug Walker are curious how large diversified firms decide whether or not to make acquisitions and divestments. Explain how Citigroup uses risk-adjusted return on capital to evaluate its product lines and international diversification. What do you think about this approach? What other subjective considerations need to be made in acquisitions decisions?

9. Cindy Sutfin is curious how regulators determine the competitive effects of a merger. Explain to Cindy how the Herfindahl-Hirschman Indexes are used to measure market concentration and what levels of concentration would be challenged. Do you agree with the use of local market measures? Explain why or why not.

10. Hung Gay Fung asks you to discuss the regulations that U.S. banks must meet to engage in international lending. Also, discuss the regulations that non-U.S. banks must abide by to operate in the United States. How is sovereign risk measured?

11. Jeff, Lori, Alison, and David Cooperman would like to know more about the corporate governance problems of large international diversified firms. What extra difficulties in corporate governance do these firms have? Give examples of recent scandals for large diversified firms. How can corporate governance be improved to reduce the risk of such scandals?

Problems

1. As a financial analyst for Euphoria Securities, Phil and Roz Lerner ask you to do a DuPont financial analysis for the trends in the mortgage banking firm shown in Table P19.1. Look at changes in the firm's balance sheet to explain why profits improved in the latest year. Discuss differences in this mortgage bank's balance sheet and income statement compared to commercial banks. How do these differences reflect differences in the operations of a finance company compared to a bank?

2. Ann and Al Fox of Fox Famous Funds ask you to do a trend financial analysis for the Travelers Group's consolidated financial statements shown in Table P19.2. Explain precisely why the ROE went down in 1997. From what sources does the Travelers Group get most of its revenues? Where do most of its expenses come from? Does Travelers appear to benefit from its diversification?

3. Rae Blumberg, Ellen Blumberg, and Sharon Gold of Blumberg Boca Securities ask you to do a trend financial analysis for Ford Motor Credit shown in Table P19.3. Explain reasons for changes in Ford Motor Credit's performance in 1996 and 1997. How does your analysis differ from the analysis for depository information? What additional information would you like to have?

4. MegaBank is thinking about acquiring Beta Bank. Mergers with similar banks have had a market-to-book ratio of 2.0. If Beta Bank has a book value of equity of $2 million, what would be its value based on this market-to-book ratio? What would be the premium that MegaBank would pay if it paid this amount? If consolidated EPS is expected to be $10 and Megabank's expected earnings is $9, what would be the earnings dilution with the merger?

5. Steven Lerner, Michelle, Joshua, John, and Mathew Learn, and Ed Smith live in or near New York City and are interested in learning about Citigroup and its corporate governance policies. Look up Citigroup on the Internet through a search engine like Google (*http://www.google.com*) and see what you can find out about Citigroup's corporate governance policies. What efforts has Citigroup made to improve these policies?

6. Look up Countrywide Financial Corporation on the Web (*http://about.countrywide.com*) and read about the company's history and innovations and changes that have been made. Also, look under investor relations and

table **P19.1** FINANCIAL STATEMENTS FOR COUNTRYWIDE CREDIT INDUSTRIES, INC.

BALANCE SHEET ASSETS (THOUSANDS)

	1997	% Assets	1996	% Assets
Cash	18,269	0.23%	16,444	0.19%
Receivables for Mtg. Loans				
Mtg. Loans Held for Sale	2,579,972	31.89%	4,740,087	54.75%
Finance Receivables, Net				
Other Receivables	1,451,979	17.95%	912,613	10.54%
Net Prop. Equipment, etc.	190,104	2.35%	140,963	1.63%
Capitalized Servicing fees rc.				
Mortgage Servicing Rights	3,023,826	37.38%	2,323,665	26.84%
Other Assets	825,142	10.20%	523,881	6.05%
Total Assets	**8,089,292**	100.00%	**8,657,653**	100.00%
Liabilities & Equity				
Notes Payable	4,713,324	58.27%	6,097,518	70.43%
Drafts Pay with Mfg. Closings	221,757	2.74%	238,020	2.75%
Accounts Payable & Accurals	607,037	7.50%	505,148	5.83%
Thrift Investment Accts.				
Deferred Income Taxes	635,643	7.86%	497,212	5.74%
Convertible Sub. Debentures				
Total Liabilities	6,177,761	76.37%	7,337,898	84.76%
Equity	1,911,531	23.63%	1,319,755	15.24%
Total Liabilities & Equity	**8,089,292**	100.00%	**8,657,653**	100.00%

Source: Moody's Bank & Finance Manual, *1997.*
Business: Mortgage Banking Business; Originates, Purchases, Sells & Services Mortgage Loans

CONSOLIDATED INCOME STATEMENT (THOUSANDS)

	1997	% Revs.	1996	% Revs.
Loan Origination Fees	193,079	17.36%	199,724	23.20%
Gain on Sale of Loans, Net of Commt. Fees	247,450	22.24%	92,341	10.73%
Loan Production Revenue	440,529	39.60%	292,065	33.93%
Interest Earned	350,263	31.49%	308,449	35.84%
Interest Charges	(316,205)	−28.42%	(281,573)	−32.71%
Net Interest Income	33,558	3.02%	26,876	3.12%
Total Servicing Income	773,715	69.55%	620,835	72.13%
Loan Amortization, Net of Serv. Hedge Gain	(101,380)	−9.11%	(342,811)	−39.83%
Servicing Hedge Gain (Loss)	(125,306)	−11.26%	200,135	23.25%
Loan Admin. Income, Net	547,029	49.17%	478,159	55.55%
Commissions, Fees & Other Income	91,346	8.21%	63,642	7.39%
Total Revenues	**1,112,462**	100.00%	**860,742**	100.00%
Expenses				
Salaries and Related Expenses	286,884	25.79%	229,668	26.68%
Occupancy & Other Office Expenses	129,877	11.67%	106,298	12.35%
Guarantee Fees	159,360	14.32%	121,197	14.08%
Marketing Expenses	34,255	3.08%	27,115	3.15%
Other Operating Expenses	80,188	7.21%	50,264	5.84%
Total Expenses	690,564	62.08%	534,542	62.10%
Earnings Before Income Tax	421,898	37.92%	326,200	37.90%
Provision for Income Tax	164,540	14.79%	130,480	15.16%
Net Earnings	**257,358**	**23.13%**	**195,720**	**22.74%**

table P19.2 CONSOLIDATED FINANCIAL STATEMENTS FOR TRAVELERS GROUP FROM ANNUAL REPORT 1997

BALANCE SHEET (MILLIONS)

Assets	1997	% Assets	1996	% Assets
Cash & Equiv.	4,033	1.04%	3,260	0.94%
Investments	61,834	16.00%	56,509	16.33%
Repurchase Agreements	109,734	28.39%	97,985	28.32%
Brokerage Receivables	15,627	4.04%	11,592	3.35%
Trading Securities	139,732	36.15%	126,573	36.59%
Net Consumer Receivables	10,816	2.80%	7,885	2.28%
Reinsurance Recoverables	9,579	2.48%	10,234	2.96%
Value of Insurance in Force and Deferred Policy Acq. Costs	2,812	0.73%	2,563	0.74%
Cost of Acqd Businesses in Excess of Net Assets	3,446	0.89%	3,060	0.88%
Separate & Variable Accounts	11,319	2.93%	9,023	2.61%
Other Receivables	5,733	1.48%	4,869	1.41%
Other Assets	11,890	3.08%	12,395	3.58%
Total Assets	386,555	100.00%	345,948	100.00%
Liabilities				
Investment Banking & Brokerage Borrowing	11,464	2.97%	10,020	2.90%
Short-term Borrowings	3,979	1.03%	1,557	0.45%
Long-term Debt	28,352	7.33%	24,696	7.14%
Repurchase Agreements	120,921	31.28%	103,572	29.94%
Brokerage Payables	12,763	3.30%	10,019	2.90%
Trading Secs. Not Yet Purchased	96,166	24.88%	92,141	26.63%
Contract Holder Funds	14,848	3.84%	13,621	3.94%
Insurance Policy & Claims Reserves	43,782	11.33%	43,944	12.70%
Separate & Variable Accounts	11,309	2.93%	8,949	2.59%
Accounts Payable & Other	19,418	5.02%	16,693	4.83%
Total Liabilities	363,002	**93.91%**	325,212	**94.01%**
Preferred Stock	2,660	0.69%	2,194	0.63%
Stockholders Equity	20,893	**5.40%**	17,942	**5.19%**
Total Liabilities & Equity	386,555	100.00%	345,948	100.00%

download the financial section of its annual report. Do a financial trend performance and risk analysis for Countrywide's most recent two years.

7. Just as in Problem 6, do a financial performance and risk analysis for another finance company or diversified finance company that you are interested in, such as Prudential *(http://www.prudential.com)*, Merrill Lynch, or Citigroup. Discuss other interesting information about the firms that you find on their Websites. Often, such as on Citigroup's Website, you'll find interesting Web tuto-

rials for different aspects on the firm and its strategies and investor educational information.

Suggested Case Studies

Harvard Business School (Case 9–292–089): MNC Financial: The Credit Card Business

This case provides an excellent overview of the credit card business, the credit card securitization process, and Mary-

table **P19.2** CONSOLIDATED FINANCIAL STATEMENTS FOR TRAVELERS GROUP FROM ANNUAL REPORT 1997 (CONTINUED)

CONSOLIDATED INCOME STATEMENT (MILLIONS)

Revenues	1997	% Revs.	1996	% Revs.
Insurance Premiums	8,995	23.92%	7,633	23.55%
Commissions and Fees	5,119	13.61%	4,637	14.31%
Interest and Dividends	16,214	43.11%	13,286	40.99%
Principal Transactions	2,504	6.66%	3,027	9.34%
Asset Management & Administration Fees	1,715	4.56%	1,390	4.29%
Finance Related Interest & Other Charges	1,404	3.73%	1,163	3.59%
Other Income	1,658	4.41%	1,278	3.94%
Total Revenues	**37,609**	100.00%	**32,414**	100.00%
Expenses				
Policyholder Benefits & Claims	7,714	20.51%	7,366	22.72%
Noninsurance Compensation & Benefits	6,345	16.87%	5,804	17.91%
Insurance Underwriting, Acquisition, & Operating Expenses	3,236	8.60%	3,013	9.30%
Interest Expense	11,443	30.43%	8,927	27.54%
Provision for Consumer	277	0.74%	260	0.80%
Finance Credit Losses				
Other Operating Expenses	3,582	9.52%	2,481	7.65%
Total Expenses	**32,597**	**86.67%**	**27,851**	**85.92%**
Gain (Loss) on Sale of Subs. & Affiliates			445	
Income Before Income Taxes & Minority Interest	5,012	13.33%	5,008	15.45%
Provision for Income Taxes	1,696	4.51%	1,679	5.18%
Minority Interest, Net of Income Taxes	212	0.56%	47	0.14%
Income from Continuing Operations	3,104	8.25%	3,282	10.13%
Income from Discontinued Operations			−334	
Net Income	**3,104**	**8.25%**	**2,948**	**9.09%**

land National Bank's initial public offering for MBNA, a specialized credit card bank. Also see **HBR Case, Chase/Chemical Bank Merger** for an overview of considerations and analysis for the merger between Chase and Chemical Bank in New York.

Darden School, University of Virginia

1. Primerica Corporation, Case 12 in Crawford and Sihler (1994), now out of print, but should be available through Darden. This case provides an excellent understanding of the development of a diversified financial services firm,

the predecessor of Travelers Group. It also goes through the valuation process for such a firm and strategic considerations.

2. General Electric Financial Services, Inc. (GEFS), Case 6 in Crawford and Sihler (1994). This case looks at GEFS as a diversified financial services firm and its problems integrating Kidder Peabody into its corporate culture.

3. Discover Card, Case 5 in Crawford and Sihler (1994). This case looks at Sears's financial service businesses and its strategy in introducing its Discover Card to enter the consumer finance business.

table P19.3 FINANCIAL STATEMENTS FOR FORD MOTOR CREDIT CORPORATION

BALANCE SHEET (MILLIONS)

Assets	1997	% Assets	1996	% Assets
Cash	2,716.0	2.23%	1,478.1	1.33%
Security Investments	1,324.8	1.09%	1,914.3	1.72%
Net Finance Receivables	80,848.0	66.43%	76,376.7	68.65%
Notes Rec. from Affiliates	30,645.2	25.18%	25,680.2	23.08%
Net Operating Leases	1,133.0	0.93%	672.9	0.60%
Property, Plant, & Equipment	44.4	0.04%	1,730.5	1.56%
Other Assets	4,985.0	4.10%	3,405.2	3.06%
Total Assets	121,696.4	100.00%	111,257.9	100.00%
Liabilities				
Accounts Payable	5,677.8	4.67%	3,683.5	3.31%
Income Tax Payable	0.0	0.00%	0.0	0.00%
Subordinated Notes	325.0	0.27%	325.0	0.29%
Long-term Debt	0.0	0.00%	0.0	0.00%
Deferred Income Tax	4,260.4	3.50%	3,109.8	2.80%
Other Liabs. & Defd. Income	2,929.9	2.41%	2,340.2	2.10%
Total Liabilities	**110,892.4**	**91.12%**	**101,313.8**	**91.06%**
Minority Interest	**1,313.8**	**1.08%**	**988.9**	**0.89%**
Total Stockholders Equity	**9,205.7**	**7.56%**	**8,670.7**	**7.79%**
Total Liabs. & Equity	121,696.4	100.00%	111,257.9	100.00%

Note: With rounding, sum of percentages may be less 100 percent.
Source: Moody's Bank & Finance Manual, 1997, 3366–3367.

CONSOLIDATED INCOME STATEMENT (MILLIONS)

Revenues	1997	% Revs.	1996	% Revs.
Operating Leases	8,223.6	49.50%	7,300.8	48.68%
Retail Receivables	5,000.7	30.10%	4,522.7	30.16%
Wholesale Receivables	1,645.8	9.91%	1,875.2	12.50%
Diversified Receivables	84.0	0.51%	152.2	1.01%
Other Receivables	393.5	2.37%	354.9	2.37%
Total Financing Revenues	**15,347.6**	**92.37%**	**14,205.8**	**94.72%**
Insurance Premiums Earned	225.7	1.36%	0.0	0.00%
Investment & Other Income	1,041.4	6.27%	791.4	5.28%
Total Revenues	16,614.7	100.00%	14,997.2	100.00%
Expenses				
Interest Expense	6,224.2	37.46%	5,998.3	40.00%
Depreciation	5,537.6	33.33%	5,235.1	34.91%
Operating Expense	1,467.4	8.83%	1,211.0	8.07%
Provision for Losses	993.3	5.98%	480.4	3.20%
Other Insurance Claims	207.3	1.25%	0.0	0.00%
Total Expenses	**14,429.8**	**86.85%**	**12,924.8**	**86.18%**
Equity in Income of Affiliates	55.3	0.33%	255.4	1.70%
Income Before Income Taxes	**2,240.2**	**13.48%**	**2,327.8**	**15.52%**
Provision for Income Taxes	731.6	4.40%	682.9	4.55%
Income Before Minority Interests	**1,508.6**	**9.08%**	**1,644.9**	**10.97%**
Minority Interests	68	0.41%	65.5	0.44%
Net Income	**1,440.6**	**8.67%**	**1,579.4**	**10.53%**

Selected References

Aguilar, Linda. "Still Toe-to-Toe: Banks and Nonbanks at the End of the '80s." *Economic Perspectives* (Federal Reserve Bank of Chicago) 14 (January/February 1990), 12–23.

Benston, George J. "Rating Ceiling Implications of the Cost Structure of Consumer Finance Companies." *Journal of Finance* 21 (September 1977), 1169–1194.

Cantor, Richard, and Rebecca Demsetz. "Securitization, Loan Sales, and the Credit Slowdown." *Quarterly Review* (Federal Reserve Bank of New York) (Summer 1993), 27–38.

Caouette, John B. "Securitization: What's Next?" In *Proceedings of a Conference on Bank Structure and Competition.* Chicago: Federal Reserve Bank of Chicago, 1992.

Crawford, Richard D., and William W. Sihler. *Financial Service Organizations: Cases in Strategic Management.* New York: HarperCollins Publishers, 1994.

Danielson, Arnold G. "Getting Ready for the 21st Century: A Look at Recent Banking Trends." *Banking Policy Report* 18 (March 15, 1999), 1, 13–20.

Dorgan, Richard J. "Banks Keen to Make Asset-Based Loans." *NCFA Journal* 40 (September 1984), 5–14.

Duca, John V. and Mary M. McLaughlin. "Developments Affecting the Profitability of Commercial Banks," *Federal Reserve Bulletin* 76 (July 1990): 477–499.

Durkin, Thomas A., and Gregory E. Elliehausen. "The Cost Structure of the Consumer Finance Industry." *Journal of Financial Services Research* 13 (February 1998), 71–86.

Dynan, Karen E., Kathleen W. Johnson, and Samuel M. Slowinski. "Survey of Finance Companies, 2000." *Federal Reserve Bulletin* (January 2002), 1–13.

Ellis, James E. "Sears' Discover Card Finds Its Way." *Business Week* (September 15, 1986), 166–167.

Ford, William F. "Banking's New Competition: Myths and Realities." *Economic Review* (Federal Reserve Bank of Atlanta) 67 (January/February 1982), 4–11.

Flynn, Julia, et al. "Small but Wiser." *Business Week* (October 12, 1992), 28–29.

Glynn, Lenny. "The Dismantling of Dean Witter." *Institutional Investor* 19 (August 1985), 80–92.

Greising, David. "The Discover Card Is No Longer a Joker." *Business Week* (October 9, 1989), 138.

Haggerty, Alfred G. "Financial Centers a Big Success for Sears." *National Underwriter* (November 23, 1984), 56.

Harris, Maury. "Finance Companies as Business Lenders." *Quarterly Review* (Federal Reserve Bank of New York) 4 (Summer 1979), 35–39.

Hilder, David B., and Steve Weiner. "Big Brokerage Houses Are Problem Children for Their New Parents." *The Wall Street Journal* (September 13, 1985), 1.

Hooke, Jeffrey C. *Security Analysis on Wall Street: A Comprehensive Guide to Today's Valuation Methods.* New York: John Wiley Frontiers in Finance, 1999.

Jenster, Per V., and John H. Lindgren, Jr. "The New Game in Retail Auto Financing." *Journal of Retail Banking* 10 (Winter 1988), 39–45.

Johnson, Robert W. "The Consumer Banking Problem: Causes and Cures." *Journal of Retail Banking* 11 (Winter 1989), 39–45.

Key, Janet. "New Card Chief Focus for Sears." *Chicago Tribune* (October 3, 1985), Section 3, 1, 6.

Koch, Timothy W. *Bank Management,* 3rd ed. Fort Worth, TX: Dryden Press, 1995.

Koch, Timothy W., and S. Scott MacDonald. *Bank Management,* 4th ed. Fort Worth, TX: Dryden Press (South-Western Thomson Publishing), 2000.

Komansky, David H. "Inheriting the Mantle." In *The New Financiers,* ed. by Charles B. Wendel. Chicago: Irwin Professional Publishing Co., 1996, 133–151.

Lee, Winson B., and Elizabeth S. Cooperman. "Conglomerates in the 1980s: A Performance Appraisal." *Financial Management* (Spring 1989), 45–54.

Leonitades, M. *Managing the Unmanageable: Strategies for Success Within the Conglomerate.* Reading, MA: Addison Wesley Publishing Co., Inc., 1986.

Logan, John, and Richard J. Dorgan. "Asset-Based Lending: You're Doing It, But Are You Doing It Right?" *Journal of Commercial Bank Lending* 67 (June 1984), 9–16.

Martin, John D., John W. Kensinger, and Stuart L. Gillan. "Value Creation and Corporate Diversification: The Case of Sears, Roebuck & Co." Working Paper, University of Texas, August 6, 1996.

McCoy, John, Larry A. Frieder, and Robert B. Hedges, Jr. *Bottomline Banking: Meeting the Challenges for Survival and Success.* Chicago: Probus Publishing Co., 1994.

Mendonca, Lenny, and Greg Wilson. "Financial Megaplayers' Time Is Here." *The Wall Street Journal* (September 29, 1997), A22.

Moore, Thomas. "Ball Takes Bache and Runs With It." *Fortune* (January 24, 1983), 97–100.

Olson, Wayne. "Securitization Comes to Other Assets." *Savings Institutions* 107 (May 1986), 81–85.

Patterson, Gregory A., and Francine Schwadel. "Sears Suddenly Undoes Years of Diversifying Beyond Retailing Field." *The Wall Street Journal* (September 30, 1992), A1, A6.

Remolona, Eli M., and Kurt C. Wulfekuhler. "Finance Companies, Bank Competition, and Niche Markets." *Quarterly Review* (Federal Reserve Bank of New York) (Summer 1992), 25–38.

Roosevelt, Phil. "Sears to Pull Out of Banking." *American Banker* (September 30, 1992), 1, 7.

Saunders, Anthony, and Marcia Million Cornett. *Financial Institutions Management: A Risk Management Approach,* 3rd and 4th editions. Burr Ridge, IL: McGraw-Hill Irwin, 2000, 2003.

Schmeitzer, John. "3.9 Billion Loss Sears' Worst Ever." *Chicago Tribune* (February 10, 1993), Section 3, 1, 3.

Schwartz, David M. "When Home Sweet Home Was Just a Mailbox Away." *Smithsonian* 16 (November 1985), 91–100.

Selden, Richard T. "Consumer-Oriented Intermediaries." In *Financial Institutions and Markets,* 2nd ed. Ed. by Murray Polakoff and Thomas A. Durkin. Boston: Houghton Mifflin, 1981, 202–215.

Sellers, Patricia. "Why Bigger Is Badder at Sears." *Fortune* (December 5, 1988), 79–84.

Shapiro, Harvey D. "Securitizing Corporate Assets." *Institutional Investor* 19 (December 1985).

Siconolfi, Michael. "Dean Witter Proves an Asset to Sears, Confounding Pundits." *The Wall Street Journal* (March 15, 1991), A1.

SNL Securities. *Industry Review—Finance Companies.* Charlottesville, VA: SNL Securities Corporation, 1996.

Stahl, David. "The Rising Tide of Bankruptcy." *Savings and Community Banker* 2 (May 1993), 14–20.

Staten, Michael. "Statistics: Bankruptcy Watch." *Journal of Retail Banking* 11 (Winter 1989), 65–69.

Steinmetz, Greg. "Sears' Allstate Unit Expects to Raise More than $2 Billion in Initial Offering." *The Wall Street Journal* (March 19, 1993), A3.

Taub, Stephen. "Sizing Up the Brokers." *Financial World* (January 8–21, 1986), 1–4.

Tully, Daniel P. "Reflections on Transforming a Company." In *The New Financiers,* ed. by Charles B. Wendel. Chicago: Irwin Professional Publishing Co., 1996, 259–282.

Walter, Ingo. *Mergers and Acquisitions in Banking and Finance; What Works, What Fails, and Why.* New York: Oxford University Press, 2004.

Wendel, Charles B. *The New Financiers.* Chicago: Irwin Professional Publishing Co., 1996.

Williams, Monci Jo. "Sears Roebuck's Struggling Financial Empire." *Fortune* (October 14, 1985), 40–43.

internet exercise

1 HHI Calculation Exercise

(a) Go to the FDIC Summary of Deposit Website at *http://www2.fdic.gov/sod/ index.asp.* [Alternatively, you can go to the FDIC Website *(http://www.fdic.gov)* and find the Summary of Deposit page from the Quick Links by User menu by clicking on **"Analysts,"** then click on **"Summary of Deposits."**]

(b) On the Summary of Deposits page, click on **"Market Share and Bank Holding Company."** You'll come to a **Market Share Selection page;** click on **"Metropolitan Statistical Area (MSA)."** (Note you can also get a market summary by state if you select State instead.)

(c) You'll come to the **Market Share MSA Selection page,** where you can select any city you'd like and get the summary of deposits for that city ordered by market share (or you can have it ordered by BHC/Institution name). For this exercise, use the down tab and move down the list of cities to Denver, CO. Then click **"Continue."**

(d) After a brief delay, a **Market Share Report for Denver, Colorado,** will appear, listing all the banks and savings institutions in the Metropolitan Statistical Area (MSA) of Denver, Colorado, ordered by total deposits held in Denver. The report will also give the deposits held by each bank outside of the Denver market and, in the last column, the market share for each bank. At the very bottom of the report will be the total deposits for the Denver, Colorado, MSA.

(e) Using the Market Share Report and the market share given for each bank in the Denver MSA in the right-hand column, calculate the HHI for Denver (i.e., square each market share given for each bank and sum them). Explain what this tells you about the concentration of the Denver market.

(f) Note that often, as a shorthand for an HHI, the three-firm (five-firm) concentration index is calculated for just the largest three (five) banks in a market. At the time of this writing (April 2004), the three largest depository institutions included Wells Fargo with 20 percent market share, U.S. Bank National Association with 15 percent share, and World Savings Bank, FSB (Federal Savings Bank, a very large California thrift) with 8.2 percent share. Thus, the three-firm concentration ratio would be 43.20 percent. So all three holding companies that control 43.2 percent of the market share for deposits in Denver are out-of-state, with large deposits outside of the Denver market, a growing trend with interstate banking.

(g) Go back to *http://www2.fdic.gov/sod,* and on the Market Share Selection page, select state and do a market share state selection for Colorado and calculate the HHI for the state. You can also do this for your home city and state, or for any FDIC-defined geographic region, to examine the banks and their share of deposits.

2   Information on a wide range of topics in securitization can be found at *http://www.asset-backed .com/*. A library of papers on securitization can be found at *http://www.the-financier.com/finance/ library.htm#four2.*

The papers are catalogued by subject: corporate finance, risk management, project finance, securitization, public finance, emerging markets, and banking.

USEFUL LINKS

Federal Reserve Bulletin: Articles on financial institutions, including a survey of finance companies every four years

http://www.federalreserve.gov/pubs/bulletin/default.htm

Federal Reserve Board Website: Information on financial holding companies including a list of companies that have effectively elected to be FHCs

http://www.federalreserve.gov/

FDIC Banking Review: Articles on financial institutions and trends including mergers

http://www.fdic.gov/bank/analytical/banking/index.html

Mortgage Bankers Association (MBA) Website: Articles, speeches, and news for the mortgage banking industry provided by the MBA, the national association representing the real estate finance industry in Washington, D.C.

http://www.mortgagebankers.org

American Financial Services Association

http://www.americanfinsvcs.org/

The Conference on Consumer Finance Law

http://www.theccfl.com/

Name Index

Subject Index

A

ABS. *See* Asset-backed securities (ABS)
"Access to America Initiative," for credit unions, 194
Accounting
  GAAP and, 83
  for insurers, 575
  investment, 522
  issues at financial institutions, 25
  market value, 215
  for mergers, 697
  for mutual funds, 636
  for quasi-GSEs, 26–27
  RAP and, 83
  rules for, 390–391
Accreting swap, 431
Accrual bonds, 529
ACH services. *See* Automated clearinghouses (ACHs)
Acquisitions
  of finance companies, 679–680
  by financial institution type, 699
  international, 700–702
  of mutual intern, 637–638
  number and value of, 698
  operational risk and, 49
  qualitative considerations in, 697–699
  regulation, market structure, and, 70, 693–694
Adjustable-rate mortgages (ARMs), 81, 476
Adjustable-rate preferred stock, 557
Advanced Internal Ratings-Based (A-IRB)
    approach, 44, 230, 231
Advanced Measurement Approach (AMA), 50, 230,
    231
Advance Notice of Proposed Rulemaking (ANPR)
    Guidelines, 231
Advertising
  by depository institutions, 546
  for deposits, 550
Aetna U.S. Healthcare, 589
Affiliates, of mutual funds, 636–638
Affiliation, among banks, securities firms, and
    insurance companies, 98
Affordable Housing Program (AHP), 543
After-hours trading, mutual fund abuses of, 76
Agency costs, 28
Agency relationships, with government, 30
Agency theory, 28–29
Agents, 28
Aggregate measures, of money supply, 112, 113
Aggregate money supply, lender of last resort
    and, 111
Aggressive growth funds, 644
Agricultural loans, 473
AI. *See* Artificial intelligence (AI) systems
A-IRB approach. *See* Advanced Internal Ratings-
    Based (A-IRB) approach
Alex Brown, Inc., 15, 53, 605, 627
Allied Irish Banks, 50
Alternative Mortgage Transaction Act (1982), 84
AMA. *See* Advanced Measurement Approach (AMA)
Amendments
  to BHC Act (1970), 63
  to national banking laws, 83
  to National Credit Union Act (1970), 63

American Association of Individual Investors,
    Quarterly Low-Load Mutual Fund Updates of,
    641, 646
American Council of Life Insurers (ACLI), 586, 590
American Express Membership Banking, 255
American Financial Services Association (AFSA), 681
American options, 417
American Stock Exchange, 421
Ameritrade Holding Corp., 601
AMEX Market Value Index, 408
Amortizing swaps, 431
Angels, 621
Annual account maintenance fee, 645
Annual mutual fund operating expenses, 646
Annual yields, calculating, 285–286
Annuities, 547, 654–655
Antithesis, in regulatory dialectic, 79, 80
Arbitrage, 330
  index, 414–416
ARMs. *See* Adjustable rate mortgage loans (ARMs)
Artificial intelligence (AI) systems, 503–504
Asia. *See also* specific countries
  exchange rates and, 119
  financial crisis in, 5, 8, 52, 269
Asset(s). *See also* Duration; Duration gap
  average yield on, 46
  of banks, 137–138, 194–206, 199
  capital allocation and, 235–236
  of credit unions, 192, 194–206
  of FDIC-insured banks, 134, 135, 136
  of Fed, 107–109
  financial, 8–9, 19
  of financial institutions, 17
  fixed rate, 11
  held in trading accounts, 138
  interest revenue and expense to, 46, 47
  of life and property/casualty insurers, 576
  liquid and illiquid, 512–513
  of mutual funds, 634
  noncurrent, 40
  rate-sensitive, 45, 47
  ratio of core and noncore deposits to, 49
  ratio of short-term securities to, 48–49
  real, 8, 9
  regulation of insurers', 74
  risk-based, 224–228, 227
  in savings institutions, 200
  of thrifts, 194–206
  trends for securities firms, 619
  yield on, 152
Asset allocation
  active or passive management, 656
  funds, 645
Asset-backed commercial paper, 249–250
Asset-backed securities (ABS), 15, 245–246
Asset-based lending, 457
Asset/liability management, 80, 351–355, 446, 447,
    514. *See also* Asset management; Liability
    management
  futures in, 392–393
  liquidity reserves, securities portfolio, and,
    506–539
  monetary policy and, 115–118
  objectives of, 30–31
Asset/liability mix analysis, for Wells Fargo, 161
Asset management, by insurers, 592–593

Asset management firms, public offerings by, 637
Asset rebalancing, 658
Assets to assets, 47
Asset swaps, 429, 431
Asset utilization (AU) ratios, 148
Asset valuation reserve (AVR), 578
Assignment, 251
Assurbanking operation, 588
Astoria Financial Corporation, 182
Asymmetric information, 21
ATM, 546
  cards, 253–254
  Internet networks and, 258
  payments system and, 258–260
AU. *See* Asset utilization (AU) ratios
Auctions, T-bill, 286–287
Aussie (index of Australian stocks), 407
Automated clearinghouses (ACHs), 257, 546
  services of, 23, 50
  transfers by, 256
Automobile loans, securitizing, 246, 247, 248, 677
Available for sale, investment securities as, 137
Average cost of funding assets, 46
Average total assets, 151

B

Baby Boomers, social security and, 14
Background, of company, 464
Balanced funds, 645
Balance sheet, 152–153, 465
  for depository institutions (2003), 194
  FDIC-insured, 136–140
  of Federal Reserve System, 109
  for finance company, 682
  immunized, 358–359
  industry differences and, 16–17
  of insurance companies, 576–578, 596
  for manufacturing firm and bank, 9–10
  for Morgan Keegan, 616–617
  negative bank, 45
  positive bank, 46
  for securities firms, 618–619
  trends in composition of (1950-2003), 135
Bancassurance, 588
Banc One, 43, 372, 430, 698
Banc One Capital Markets Report, 246, 252
Bank Boston Corporation, 3
Bank capital, 218–219. *See also* Capital
Bank Conservation Act, amendments to, 87
Bank discount yield, 285
Banker's acceptance, 140, 289–290
Bankers Trust, 15, 53, 370
Bank European, 52
Bank Export Services Act (1982), 700
Bank for International Settlements (BIS), 119,
    220–221
Bank holding companies (BHCs), 92–99, 181
  capital targets of, 218
Bank Holding Company (BHC) Act (1956), 63, 84,
    95, 97
Bank holding company subsidiaries, 60
Banking Act (1933). *See* Glass–Steagall Act (1933)
Banking Act (1935), 62, 111, 114

N